This book is dedicated to my beloved wife Marcella, who has travelled with me on the journeys related in this book and through life.

THE YEAR
CHINA
DISCOVERED
THE
WORLD

GAVIN MENZIES

BANTAM BOOKS

LONDON • NEW YORK • TORONTO • SYDNEY • AUCKLAND

1421
A BANTAM BOOK: 0 553 81522 9

Originally published in Great Britain by Bantam Press,
a division of Transworld Publishers

PRINTING HISTORY
Bantam Press edition published 2002
Bantam edition published 2003

10

Set in 11/13.5pt Granjon by
Falcon Oast Graphic Art Ltd.

Bantam Books are published by Transworld Publishers,
61–63 Uxbridge Road, London W5 5SA,
a division of The Random House Group Ltd,
in Australia by Random House Australia (Pty) Ltd,
20 Alfred Street, Milsons Point, Sydney, NSW 2061, Australia,
in New Zealand by Random House New Zealand Ltd,
18 Poland Road, Glenfield, Auckland 10, New Zealand
and in South Africa by Random House (Pty) Ltd,
Endulini, 5a Jubilee Road, Parktown 2193, South Africa.

Printed and bound in Great Britain by
Cox & Wyman Ltd, Reading, Berkshire.

Papers used by Transworld Publishers are natural, recyclable products made from
wood grown in sustainable forests. The manufacturing processes conform to the
environmental regulations of the country of origin.

Gavin Menzies (Royal Navy Submarine Commanding Officer, retired) was born in 1937 in China, where he spent the first two years of his life. He joined the Royal Navy in 1953 and served in submarines from 1959 to 1970. As a junior officer he sailed the world in the wake of Columbus, Dias, Cabral and Vasco da Gama. When in command of HMS *Rorqual* (1968–1970), he sailed the routes pioneered by Magellan and Captain Cook. Since leaving the Royal Navy, he has returned to China and the Far East many times, and in the course of researching *1421* he has visited 120 countries, over 900 museums and libraries and every major sea port of the late Middle Ages. Gavin Menzies is married with two daughters and lives in North London.

For more information visit Gavin Menzies website:
www.1421.tv

CONTENTS

LIST OF MAPS AND DIAGRAMS

LIST OF PLATES

Ming Emperor Ch'êng-tsu (Zhu Di), anonymous painting on silk, Ming period. National Palace Museum, Taipei.

The Gate of Heavenly Purity, the Forbidden City, Beijing, early 15th century. *Werner Forman Archive*; the Hall of Harvest Prayer, the Temple of Heaven, early 15th century. *Getty Images/Image Bank*; the Great Wall near Beijing. *Getty Images/Telegraph Colour Library*; general view of the Forbidden City from Coal Hill Park, *Getty Images/Tony Stone*.

Taoist ceramic shrine from Longquan, Zhejiang province, 1406. British Museum; quilin, the Spirit Way. *Jane Taylor/Sonia Halliday Photographs*; military dignitary, the Spirit Way, Ming tombs, near Beijing. *Jane Taylor/ Sonia Halliday Photographs*; civil dignitary, the Spirit Way. *Christine Pemberton/Hutchison Picture Library*; kneeling elephant, the Spirit Way. *Jane Taylor/Sonia Halliday Photographs*.

Blue and white porcelain dish with melon decoration, Ming, Yongle (Zhu Di) period (1403–24), Jingdezhen, Jiangxi province. British Museum; blue and white porcelain flask with lychee decoration, Ming, Yongle (Zhu Di) period (1403–24), Jingdezhen, Jiangxi province. British Museum; jade recumbent dog, 14th or 15th century. Royal Ontario Museum, Toronto; mallet-shaped lacquer vase, probably early 15th century. *Christie's Images*; woven silk textile with climbing boys motif, 13th to 15th century. *The Textile Gallery, London*.

The Tribute Giraffe with Attendant by Shen Tu (1357–1434), ink and water-colour on silk. Philadelphia Museum of Art. Given by John T. Dorrance.

Fra Mauro's map, 1459, Biblioteca Nazionale Marciana, Venice. *Foto Toso*.

Kangnido map by Ch'uan Chin and Li Hui. 1402. Ryukoku University Library; the Cape of Good Hope on a stormy day. © *Nik Wheeler/Corbis*.

Galle stele. *Dominic Sansoni*; straits of Malacca, Malaysia. *Chris Caldicott*; Chinese fishing nets at Cochin, Kerala, India. *Ancient Art & Architecture Collection*; coast of Zanzibar. *Chris Caldicott*; the fort at Kilwa, Tanzania. *Werner Forman Archive*; pillar tomb at Kunduchi, Tanzania. *Werner Forman Archive*.

The Piri Reis map, 1513. Topkapi Museum, Istanbul.

View of the South Orkney Islands, Antarctica. *John Noble/Wilderness Photographic Library*; a tabular iceberg, South Ocean, Antarctica. *John Noble/Wilderness Photographic Library*.

Fourteenth-century blue and white porcelain bowl with a phoenix and a quilin cavorting between lotus scrolls, recovered from the Pandanan wreck, Palawan, Philippines. Courtesy of the National Museum of the Philippines.

The Jean Rotz map, 1542. British Library, Department of Maps.

Lacquer chest by Dámaso Ayala Jiménez, 1997, from the collection of Fomento Cultural Banamex, A.C.; *Rosa laevigata*. © *Dr Koonlin Tan*; bronze cannon; Chinese bronze mirror; coin of Zhu Di (1403–24); two Central American grinding stones. All recovered from the Pandanan wreck, Palawan, Philippines. Courtesy of the National Museum of the Philippines.

The Waldseemüller map, 1507. *Library of Congress, Washington, D.C.*

The Pizzigano chart, 1424. James Ford Bell Library, University of Minnesota, Minneapolis.

Guadeloupe: La Souffrière, Basse Terre, and Les Saintes from the sea. *Both courtesy Gérard Lafleur*.

The Vinland map. Beinecke Rare Book and Manuscript Library, New Haven; diver above the Bimini Road. *Lynne Sladky/Associated Press*; underwater view of the Bimini Road. *Wade Pemberton*; pyramid, Guímar, Tenerife, Canary Islands. *Courtesy Casa Chacona Museum*.

Cantino world chart, 1502. Biblioteca Estense, Modena.

Sixteenth-century engraved view of Calicut. *Ancient Art & Architecture Collection*; detail of a 14th-century Catalan atlas, Bibliothèque Nationale, Paris; Christopher Columbus by Ridolfo Ghirlandaio (1483–1561), Museo Navale di Pegli, Genoa. *Photo Scala*; Vasco da Gama, from a Portuguese manuscript, c. 1558, the Pierpont Morgan Library, New York. *Photo Pierpont Morgan Library/Art Resource/Scala*; contemporary anonymous portrait of Ferdinand Magellan. *Photo Scala*; *Captain James Cook, Sir Joseph Banks, Lord Sandwich and two others* by John Hamilton Mortimer, c. 1771, National Library of Australia, Canberra. © *Bridgeman Art Library*; *A View of the 'Endeavour's' Watering Place in the Bay of Good Success*, 1769, British Library. © *Bridgeman Art Library*.

Henry the Navigator, from *The Monument to the Discoveries*, Belèm, Lisbon. © *Dave G. Houser/Corbis*

The line illustrations appearing on the opening pages of the chapters are taken from *The Illustrated Record of Strange Countries (I Yü Thu Chih)*, c. 1420, and are reproduced by courtesy of the Cambridge University Library.

Sources of other line illustrations are as follows: 120: Bridgeman Art Library; 168: from *Science and Civilisation in China*, Joseph Needham, 1971, Cambridge University Press; 245: from *Nova typis transacta navigatio* by Honorius Philoponus, 1621; 286: The Newport Historical Society (P2278); 323: Mark Horton/Debbie Fulford, from *Shanga, the archaeology of a Muslim trading community on the coast of East Africa* by Mark Horton, 1996, British Institute in East Africa; 360: Heritage-Images/© the British Library; 389: the British Library, Department of Manuscripts.

The illustration on page 25, the maps on pages 22 and 23 were drawn by Neil Gower; the remaining maps were compiled by Jerry Fowler and Julia Lloyd.

CHINESE NOMENCLATURE

MOST NAMES ARE RENDERED IN PINYIN, WHICH IS NOW standard in China – for example, Mao Zedong is the modern spelling, not Mao Tse-tung. For simplicity, however, I have retained the older form of romanization known as Wade-Giles for names that have long been familiar to Western readers. The *Wu Pei Chi*, for instance, is more readily recognized than the *Wu Bei Zhi*. I have also kept the more established spellings of Cantonese place names, writing of Hong Kong and Canton rather than Xianggang and Guangdong. Inscriptions on navigational charts have been left in the older form, as have academic texts in the bibliography.

ACKNOWLEDGEMENTS

A BRIEF OUTLINE OF SOME OF THE MORE IMPORTANT MAPS, documents and other pieces of evidence I have used to form the conclusions presented in this book has been included in the Appendices, and the primary and secondary sources I have used are cited in the Bibliography. However, this is a book for the general reader, not the academic; three-quarters of the evidence has had to be omitted for lack of space. For that reason much of the detail of my proofs and calculations and a large amount of other supporting material have been placed on the internet at www.1421.tv. In addition, I am happy to answer any specific queries and to make my research notes available to any bona fide researcher. Contact should be made in writing, via my publisher in the first instance.

Although my name appears on the cover, this book is a collective endeavour and would not have been possible without the dedicated efforts of many more people than I can possibly name in the limited space available. My sincere thanks to all those who have helped me with advice, guidance and support, and to those who have been inadvertently omitted my sincere apologies – corrections will follow in the next edition.

I am indebted first to those in the Royal Navy who educated me in seamanship, cartography and astro-navigation. The discoveries on which the book is based could never have come about without that knowledge. I visited over nine hundred museums in the course of my researches, but must single out the wonderful collections of the British Museum, the Shaanxi Historical Museum in Xian, China, and Lima's Museum of History. I am also grateful to the Biblioteca Marciana and the Museo Correr in Venice; Barcelona's Museu Marítim; the Fornsals Museum, Visby, on the island of

Gottland; the National Maritime Museum, Greenwich; the Smithsonian Institution; the James Cook Museum in northern Australia; the Waikato Museum of Art and History, Auckland, New Zealand; the Tillamook County Pioneer Museum, Oregon; the Natural History Museum of North California; the Zihuantanejo Museum, Michoacán, Mexico; the National Museum of Australia; and the Warrnambool Art Gallery.

In England, my sincere thanks go to the British Library, particularly the staff of the Map Library and Humanities I, with its matchless collection and superb service. The School of Oriental and African Studies, the School of Slavonic Studies, and the School of Islamic Studies of the University of London; the Royal Asiatic Society; the Public Record Office; the Hakluyt Society; the Science Museum and the Natural History Museum; the Bodleian Library, Oxford; the Cambridge University Library and the Eastern Art Library, Oxford, have also been very helpful.

All the distinguished experts I asked to read and comment on my draft have generously given of their time. I am grateful for their help but must stress that responsibility for the opinions expressed in this book and for any errors and omissions rests with me alone. First and foremost, my thanks go to Professor Carol Urness, curator of the James Ford Bell Library at the University of Minnesota, Minneapolis; and also to Dr Joseph McDermott, Faculty of Oriental Studies, University of Cambridge; Professor John E. Wills Jr, Professor of History at the University of Southern California; Professor G. R. Hawting, Professor of Medieval and Islamic History at the School of Oriental and African Studies, London; Dr Konrad Hirschler; John Julius Norwich; Dr Taylor Terlecki of the Faculty of Medieval and Modern Languages and Literature, University of Oxford; Dr Ilenya Schiavon of the Venice State Archive; Dr Marjorie Grice-Hutchinson; Professor Sir John Elliott, Regius Professor of Modern History, University of Oxford; and Admiral Sir John Woodward GBE KCB.

Among other individuals, I must mention Dr Linda Clark at the History of Parliament Offices; Professor Mike Baillie of the Palaeoecology Centre of the School of Archaeology and Palaeoecology, Queen's University, Belfast; Dr Robert Massey of the Royal Observatory, Greenwich; Ms Helen Stafford and Professor Philip Woodworth of the Proudman Oceanographic Laboratory, Birkenhead; Bob Headland of the Scott Polar Research Institute, Cambridge; Shane Winser of the Royal Geographical Society (with the Institute of British Geographers); Brian Thynne of the Caird Library of the National Maritime Museum, Greenwich; Dr Piero Falchetta, librarian of the Biblioteca Marciana, Venice; Chris Stringer of London's Natural History Museum; Professor Bryan Sykes, Professor of Human Genetics at the University of Oxford; Vice-Admiral Sir Ian McIntosh KBE CB DSO DSC; Dr Fernanda Allen; and Ron Hughes.

My thanks also go to Dr Johan de Zoete, curator of the Museum Enschede, Haarlem; Dr Muhammad Waley, curator of the Persian and Turkish Collection at the British Museum; Stuart Stirling; Professor Timothy Laughton, Department of Art History, University of Essex; Professor Sue Povey, a human geneticist at the Department of Biology, University College, London; the late Dr Josie Hicks; Professor Christie G. Turner II, Regent's Professor of Anthropology, Arizona State University; Professor John Oliver, Department of Astronomy, University of Florida; Marshall Payn; Alan Stimson, formerly Keeper of Navigation, Royal Observatory, Greenwich; and Dr K. Tan.

Professor João Camilo dos Santos of the Portuguese Embassy, London; the curator of the Torre do Tombo in Lisbon; Daphne Horne, curator of the Gympie Historical Society Museum, Queensland; Brett Green; Vanessa Collingridge; Michael Fitzgerald, curator of the Tepapa Museum, Tongarewa; Catherine Mercer, librarian at the Waikato Museum; Robin J. Watt; and Professor Roderich Ptak of Munich University have all been very helpful to me too, and my thanks must also go to Steven Hallett of Xanadu Productions; Professor Yingsheng Liu, Nanjing; Dr Eusebio Dizon, Director of Underwater Research, Museum of Manila, Philippines; Madam Wenlan Peng, formerly Head of

English Language Broadcasting for Central China Television; Captain Richard Channon; Commander Mike Tuohy; Christine Handte, the captain of the sailing junk *RV Heraclitus*; the curator of the Macao Maritime Museum; Dr Wang Tao of the School of Oriental and African Studies; Miss Viviana Wong; Professor Kenneth Hsu; Dr John Furry; David Stewart and the Reed and St Louis families; Robert Metcalf; Commodore Bill Swinley, former Chief of the Bahamas Armed Forces; Monsieur Gérard Lafleur; David Borden; Kirsten and Professor Paul Seaver; Professor George Maul, Florida Institute of Technology; Professor Maude Phipps; and Dr K.K. Tan.

I am indebted to the following Chinese experts. For reconstructing junks of Zheng He's fleet, Rear Admiral and Professor Zheng Ming, Professor Yuan-Ou (president of the Chinese Marine History Researchers Association) and Associate Professor Kong Ling-Ren; for ancient Chinese maps, Professor Zhu Jianqu; for Ming foreign policy as it related to Zheng He's expeditions, Professors Shi Ping, Chen Xiansi, Zhu Yafei, Chao Zhong Chang, Chen Qimao and Vice-Admiral Liu Ta Tsai; for Sino-African relations, Professor Zheng Yi-Jun; for Sino-Sri Lankan relations, Dr Tao Jingyi; for Sino-Malaccan relations, Professor Liao Dake; for Sino-Thai relations, Professor Li Dao Gang; for Sino-Indian relations, Professors Zhu Wei and Cheng Bei Bei; for Nanjing's garrison, Professor Xu Yuhu; for provisioning Zheng He's fleet and the role of Taicang, Shouping Huang (director of the Zheng He Memorial Hall of Liu He), Huiming Cheng (secretary of the Taicang Municipal Committee of the Communist Party) and Yao Ming Sun (vice-secretary); for Zheng He's treatment of foreign envoys, Professors Yang Zhao, Yang Suming, Yang Hong Wei and Zhou Zhiya; for the aims of Zheng He's voyages, Professors Chen Xiansi, Du Xiujuan and Yan Xiamei; for Chinese colonies in south-east Asia, Professors Su Haitao, Zhaojijun Duxiujuan, Luo Mi, Zhengyong Tao and Liu Kun; for the Chinese 'Discovery of America', Professors Zhu Jianqiu, Luo Zong Zhen and Liu Manchum; for medical support for Zheng He's fleet, Professor

Gong Jinhan; and for astronavigation, Professor Zhang Guo Ying.

After the American edition was published in January 2003, the following (in no particular order) very kindly provided new evidence: Adela Lee, Professor Fayuan Gao, Admiral Zheng Ming, Lt Lee Juntao, Katherine Zhou, Al Cornett, Albert Yuen, Fran Chunge, Ma Yinghui, Alice Mong, Alphonse Vinh, Elizabeth Flower Miller, Bob Hassell, Brett Green, Bruce Tickell Taylor, Dr Edgardo Caceres, Joel Fressa, Anthony Moya, A. Armstrong, Duncan Craig, Bruno and Chiara Condi, Dr Catherine Skinner, David and Cedric Bell, J. D. Van Horn, Edwin Davey, E. O. Jeago, Charlie and Dottie Marshner, Charlotte Rees, Chung Chee Kit, Greg Jefferies, Bill Ward, Vaughan Cullen, David Crockett, David Borden, Ger Nijman, David Sims, Larry D. Clark, Commodore Bill Swinley, Charles Huegy, Guy Dru Drury, Hector Williams, B. Morelan, Ken Holmes, Howard Smith, Jerry Warsing, Jim Mullins, Shaun Griffin, Paul Yia, Romeo Hristov, Joan Butcher, John Braine Hartnell, Barbara and John McEwan, R. V. Remsen, A. D. Palmer, Steve Haynes, Steve Elkins, John Robinson, Dr John Marr, Kerson Huang, Jake Smothers, Thad Daly, Margo Donovan, Key Sun, Linden Chubin, Mark Zhang, Ms Fan, Mike Armstrong, Jean Elder, Martin Tai, Mary Doerflein, Tony Brooks, R. Wertz, Meg Stocker, Dean Dey, Miranda Mraekts, Scott McClean, Gary Jennings, Michael Osinski, Ambassador Nicolas Platt, Paolo Costa, Peter Robinson, Howard Smith, Sandy Lydon, Durdock Riley, R. Dick Reed, Rene Kollmyer, Professor Bryan Sykes, William Goggins, Richard F. Chauvet, Robert A. Hefner III, Katrina Van Tassel, Gerald Thompson, Robin J. Watt, Philip Mulholland, Greg Autry, Rodney Gordon, Bernard Chang, Holly Midgley, Professor Gary Tee, Roger L. Olesen, Sun Shuyun, Jonathan F. Ormes, Christopher Spedding, Professor Gabriel Novick and colleagues, T. Lang, Dr Gregory Chambers, Dr Winston Peters, Tan Ta Sen, Dr Wang Tao, Dr Shong, L.A.R. Clark, Brent Kennedy, Jack Pizzey, Judge William Hupy, Bruce Trinque, Marti Brodel, William McVicar, D. D. Jevans, Baxter Smith, B. S. Cullins, Professor Yao Jide, Professor Yingsheng Liu, Ken Welch,

W. Feickert, Dutch Meteorological Institute KNMR, Delft Technical University, C. G. Hunt, F. Hochstetter, E. Alan Aubin, Bill Ward, Norm Fuller, A. D. Fletcher, E. N. R. Fletcher, John Grubber, Jeff McCabe, Terry Glavin, Paul Wagner, G. Berteig, Dom Mollick, Ken Holmes, Susan Crockford, Steve Hayes, Jim Tanner, John Ting, F. Lizuka, Dr Theodore Bainbridge, Barbara Vibert, R. Wertz, R. Banzo, B. Remsen, Clay Ranger, Mrazert, Dr Annabel Arends, Zerallos Palmer, Craig Hill Handy, Dr Felipe Vilchis and colleagues, Valary Porter, Glenn R. Whitley, Xiao-Qing Li, Armando Rozari, Stevie Tan, Tan Ing Soon, Regina Faresin, H. C. Hartman, Willard S. Bacon, Richard Zimmerman, National Park Service (United States Department of the Interior), Edwin H. Spencer, Ralph McGeeham, Alan McGillivray III, Peter Sommer, Anthony Fletcher, Tom Bender, Patrick Donohue, Jo Ann Alkamraikhi, Greg Coelho, T. Michael Stanley, Capt. Roddy Innes, Mathias Hartmann, Robert Gariup, Frank Wells, Professor Liu Kan, Professor Quin, David Knight, Rodney Gordon, Professor Edward Bryant, Drs Greg and Laura Little, Michael Ferrero, Cheuk Kwan, Siew Hong Wong, Francis Pickett, An Ping, Ric Baez, Frank Fitch, William Vigil, Alan Moks, J. Peter Thurmond, Heindri Bailey, Lynda Nutter, David Borden, Rewi Kemp, Professor John Oliver, Enrique Garcia Barthe, Charles N. Rudkin, Lindsay Peet, John Weyrich, Tony Abramson, Brian Darcey, Ian McDonald, Aytac Tekin, Steven Lutz, Anthony Fletcher, Greg Jeffer, Annette Brown, Jessica Hanson-Hall, Lindsey Sayvin, Philip Hahl, Vanessa Collingridge, Merle O'Doherty, John and Erica Parker, Darril Fosty, T. Michael Stanley, Dom Kropfer, Robert Chase, Kurt Cox, Tom Felion, Lanton Roberts, Andy Asp, Susie Brumfitt, Andrew D. Basiago, P. J. Evans, Raphael Banzo, Bob Ward, Sydney Stout, Philip Bramble, Bob Shipp, Dom Raab, Orlando J. Martinez, Carlos Quirino, Celia Heil, Jack Andrews, Ciro Matuck, Joy Mertz, Ray Howgego, Adam Dunn, Don Hughes, David Sims, Jim Jackson, Alan Armstrong, Ronald Monroe, Ginni MacRobert, Jack Nixon, Lennart Siltberg, Roy Sandor, Shizhang Ling, Errol Kirk, Steve Mumme, Nico Boon,

Professor David Price, Robert N. Heath, Dr M. E. Phipps, Dr K. K. Tan, Tin Lam and colleagues at Netism Solutions, Dr Alan Leibowitz, B. S. McElney, Perry Debell and Dr John S. Marr.

I must also express my gratitude to Voyages Jules Verne, which provides wonderful tours with extremely knowledgeable guides; Anthony Simonds-Gooding; Wendi and Mike Watson and their team; Steven Williams and Sophie Ransom of Midas Public Relations; Jack Pizzey; Pearson Broadband and Paladin Invision and their teams. I'm also grateful to Dr Joseph McDermott, Elizabeth Hay, Dr Hubert Lal, Dr Taylor Terlecki, Dr Marjorie Grice-Hutchinson, Ian Hudson, Amy Crocker, my wife Marcella Menzies and our elder daughter, Vanessa Gilodi-Johnson, all of whom have provided translations from a variety of foreign languages.

Luigi Bonomi of Sheil Land Associates has been a wonderful literary agent, and at my publishers, Transworld, my heartfelt thanks go to Larry Finlay, Sally Gaminara, publishing director of Bantam Press, Simon Thorogood, Deborah Adams, Julia Lloyd, Alison Martin, Rebecca Winfield, Helen Edwards, Sheila Lee, Neil Hanson, Garry Prior, John Blake, Ed Christie and their teams. I'm also grateful to Gillian Bromley, Daniel Balado, Elizabeth Dobson, Joanne Hill and Sarah Ereira for their work on the text.

Finally, my appreciation to those who have stood by me and the book for fourteen long years. My special thanks to Frank Hopkins, an old friend and an Oxford history scholar, and to Laura Tatham – no writer could have had a more skilful, loyal and dedicated assistant. Last of all, Marcella, my wife, has provided enduring love and support and the finances to pay for my researches. I and this book owe everything to her.

Gavin Menzies
London
May 2003

The countries beyond the horizon and at the ends of the earth have all become subjects and to the most western of the western or the most northern of the northern countries, however far away they may be.

– part of an inscription on a memorial stone erected by Admiral Zheng He at Ch'ang Lo on the banks of the Yangtze estuary in 1431

Voyages of the Treasur

settlements where Chinese people live today

INTRODUCTION

OVER TEN YEARS AGO I STUMBLED UPON AN INCREDIBLE discovery, a clue hidden in an ancient map which, though it did not lead to buried treasure, suggested that the history of the world as it has been known and handed down for centuries would have to be radically revised.

I was pursuing an interest that had become a consuming passion for me: medieval history, and in particular the maps and charts of early explorers. I loved to examine these old charts, tracing contours, coastlines, the shifting shapes of shoals and sandbars, the menace of rocks and reefs. I followed the ebb and flow of tides, the pull of unseen currents and the track of prevailing winds, peeling back the layers of meaning contained within the charts.

The wintry plains of Minnesota started me on my research. It was not necessarily the first place you would think of to discover a document with such profound implications, but the James Ford Bell Library at the University of Minnesota has a remarkable collection of early maps and charts, and one in particular had attracted my attention. It had been in the collection of Sir Thomas Phillips, a wealthy British collector born in the late eighteenth century, but its existence had remained virtually unknown until the collection was rediscovered half a century ago.

The chart was dated 1424 and signed by a Venetian cartographer by the name of Zuane Pizzigano. It showed Europe and parts of Africa, and as I compared it with a modern map, I realized that the cartographer had drawn the coastlines of Europe accurately. It was an extraordinary cartographic achievement for that era, but not one of earth-shattering significance in itself. However, my eye was then drawn to the most curious feature of the map. The cartographer had also drawn a group of four islands far out in the western Atlantic. The names he gave them – Satanazes, Antilia, Saya and Ymana – did not correspond to any modern place-names and there are no large islands in the area where he had positioned them. That could have been a simple error in calculating longitude, for Europeans did not master that difficult art until well into the eighteenth century, but my first, troubling thought was that the islands were imaginary and had existed only in the mind of the man who drew the chart.

I looked again. The two biggest islands were painted in bold colours, Antilia in dark blue, Satanazes in pillar-box red. The rest of the chart was uncoloured, and it seemed certain that Pizzigano wished to emphasize that these were important, recently discovered islands. All the names marked on the chart appeared to be in medieval Portuguese. Antilia – *anti* 'on the opposite side of' and *ilha* 'island' – meant an island on the opposite side of the Atlantic to Portugal; other than that, there was nothing in the name to help me identify it. Satanazes, 'Satan's or Devil's Island', was a very distinctive name. A greater number of towns were marked on the largest island, Antilia, indicating that it was better known. Satanazes had only five names, and featured the enigmatic words *con* and *ymana*.

My interest was now thoroughly aroused. What were these islands? Did they really exist? The date of the map, its provenance and authenticity were unimpeachable, yet if it was genuine, it marked lands in places where, according to the accepted history, no Europeans had ventured for another seven decades. After several months of examining charts and documents in map rooms and archives, I became convinced that Antilia and Satanazes were actually the Caribbean islands of Puerto Rico and Guadeloupe. There were far too many points of similarity between them for it to be a coincidence, but that meant that somebody had accurately surveyed the islands some seventy years before Columbus reached the Caribbean. This seemed an incredible revelation – Columbus had not discovered the New World, yet his voyage had always been regarded as an absolutely defining moment. It marked the point when, led by the

Portuguese, Europeans had begun to embark on the great voyages of discovery, the long, restless expansion over the face of the globe that was to characterize the next five hundred years.

I needed further evidence to support my discovery and I sought the help of an expert in medieval Portuguese, Professor João Camilo dos Santos, who was then at the Portuguese Embassy in London. He examined the Pizzigano chart and corrected my translation of *con/ymana* to 'volcano erupts there'. The words had been placed in the southern part of Satanazes, just where there are three volcanoes on Guadeloupe today. Did they erupt before 1424? In high excitement I rang the Smithsonian Institution in Washington DC. The volcanoes had erupted twice between 1400 and 1440 but had otherwise been dormant during the previous hundred years and the succeeding two and a half centuries. Moreover, there were no other volcanic eruptions in the Caribbean at that time. I felt I was home and dry; I believed I had found solid evidence that someone had reached the Caribbean and established a secret colony there sixty-eight years before Columbus.

Professor Camilo dos Santos gave me an introduction to the curator of the State Archives in the Torre do Tombo in Lisbon, and on a beautiful early autumn afternoon I began further research there, hoping for corroboration of my hunch about Portuguese landings in the Caribbean. To my astonishment, I came across something entirely different: far from the Portuguese having discovered those Caribbean islands, they were completely unknown to them at the time Pizzigano was drawing his chart. They were, however, shown on another, slightly later chart – drawn by some other, unknown cartographer – that had not come into Portuguese hands until 1428. In addition, I found a command issued by the Portuguese prince Henry the Navigator to his sea-captains in 1431, ordering them to go and find the islands of Antilia shown on the 1428 chart; had the Portuguese discovered them, Henry's edict would scarcely have been necessary. But if the Portuguese had not discovered and surveyed Antilia and Satanazes, who on earth had? Who had provided Pizzigano and the other cartographers with their information?

I began more research, tracing the rise and fall of medieval civilizations that had long since crumbled into dust. In turn, I eliminated virtually every navy in the world that could feasibly have undertaken such an ambitious voyage in the early decades of the fifteenth century. Venice, the oldest and most powerful naval power in Europe, was in disarray. The old Doge was ill, his powers waning, and his successor was waiting in the wings, determined that Venice should abandon its maritime tradition and become a land power. Northern European powers barely had the ships to cross the English Channel, let alone explore new worlds. The Egyptian rulers were mired in civil wars – there were no fewer than five sultans in 1421 alone. The Islamic world was also disintegrating: the Portuguese had invaded its North African heartlands and the once-mighty Asian empire of the Mongol emperor Tamerlane was in pieces.

Who else could have explored the Caribbean? I decided to see if there were other charts like the 1424 map, showing continents that had been surveyed before the European voyages of discovery. The deeper I dug, the more bombshells I uncovered. I was astonished to find that Patagonia and the Andes had been mapped a century before the first European sighted them, and Antarctica had been accurately drawn some four centuries before Europeans reached the continent. The east coast of Africa was shown on another chart, with longitudes that were perfectly correct – something Europeans did not manage to achieve for another three centuries. Australia appeared on another map, three centuries before Cook, and other charts showed the Caribbean, Greenland, the Arctic and the Pacific and Atlantic coasts of both North and South America long before Europeans arrived.

To have drawn maps of the entire world with such accuracy, these explorers, whoever they were, must have circumnavigated the globe. They must have been skilled in astro-navigation and must have found a method of determining longitude to draw maps with negligible longitude errors. To cover the enormous distances involved, they must have been able to sail the oceans for months at a time and that would have meant desalinating sea-water. As I was later to discover, they also prospected and mined for metals, and they were skilled horticulturalists, transplanting animals and plants right across the globe. In short, they had changed the face of the medieval world. I seemed to be looking at a series of the most incredible journeys in the history of mankind, but one that had been completely expunged from human memory, the majority of records destroyed, the achievements ignored and finally forgotten.

These revelations were both astounding and horrifying. If I was to pursue them I would be challenging some of the most basic assumptions about the history of the exploration of the world. Every schoolchild knows the names of the great European explorers and navigators whose exploits have resounded down the ages. Bartolomeu Dias (c. 1450–1500) left Portugal in 1487 and became the first man to round the Cape of Good Hope, the southern tip of Africa. He was driven to the south of the Cape by a storm and when he found no land he turned north, rounding the Cape and making landfall on the east coast of Africa. Vasco da Gama (c. 1469–1525) followed in Dias's wake ten years later. He sailed up the east coast of Africa and crossed the Indian Ocean to India, opening up the first sea route for the spice trade. On 12 October 1492, Christopher Columbus (1451–1506) sighted land in the modern Bahamas. He has gone down in history as the first European to glimpse the New World, though Columbus himself never appreciated this, believing that he had actually reached Asia. He made three further voyages, discovering many of the Caribbean islands and the mainland of

Central America. Ferdinand Magellan (c. 1480–1521) followed Columbus and is credited with the discovery of the strait between the Atlantic and the Pacific that bears his name to this day. His ship continued west to complete the first circumnavigation of the world, though Magellan did not survive to see the expedition's triumphant return to Spain, having been killed in the Philippines on 27 April 1521.

All these men owed a huge debt to the great figure of Henry the Navigator (1394–1460), the Portuguese prince whose base in south-west Portugal became an academy for explorers, cartographers, shipwrights and instrument makers. There, the design of European ships was revolutionized, navigational instruments and techniques developed and improved, and impetus given to the great voyages of exploration and colonization.

As I ended my researches in the Torre do Tombo, a mood of utter confusion engulfed me. I spent a misty evening sitting in a bar on Lisbon's waterfront, looking out at Henry the Navigator's statue. His enigmatic smile was one I now understood. We both shared a secret: he had followed others to the New World. The more I brooded, the more intrigued I became. Who were these master mariners who had discovered and charted these new lands and oceans without leaving any trace of having done so, other than these enigmatic maps?

The identity of the master hand was revealed in a curious way. The coasts of Patagonia, the Andes mountains, the Antarctic mainland and the South Shetland Islands had all been drawn with remarkable accuracy on one chart. The distances covered, from Ecuador in the north to the Antarctic peninsula in the south, were immense; a huge fleet must have been required. There was only one nation at that time with the material resources, the scientific knowledge, the ships and the seafaring experience to mount such an epic voyage of discovery. That nation was China, but the thought of searching for incontestable proof that a Chinese fleet had explored the world long before the Europeans filled me with dread. An attempt to uncover the details of any event from nearly six centuries ago would have been daunting enough, but this one was made even more difficult by one massive, perhaps insurmountable, obstacle. In the mid-fifteenth century almost every Chinese map and document of the period was deliberately destroyed by officials of the Chinese court, following an abrupt reversal of its foreign policy. Far from embracing the outside world, after these momentous discoveries China turned in on itself. Anything commemorating its expansionist past was expunged from the record.

If I was to piece together the remarkable story of the Chinese voyages of discovery, I would have to look elsewhere for proof, but I feared almost to begin. It seemed arrogance bordering on hubris to believe that a retired submarine captain could reveal a story many great minds had failed to unearth, but though I was a mere amateur compared to the distinguished academics in the field, I started with one crucial advantage. In 1953, when I joined the Royal Navy at the age of fifteen, Britain was still a world power with great fleets and bases to support them strung right across the globe. During my seventeen years in the Navy I sailed the world in the wake of the great European explorers. Between 1968 and 1970, for example, I was in command of HMS *Rorqual* and took her from China to Australasia, the Pacific and the Americas.

The coasts, cliffs and mountains early explorers had viewed from their quarterdecks were those I saw through a submarine periscope, with roughly the same perspective. I quickly learned that what is seen from sea level is not necessarily what is actually there. In those days satellite navigation was unknown; we had to find our way by the stars. I saw the same stars those great European explorers had seen and calculated my position by measuring the height and direction of the sun, just as they had attempted to do. The mariner's guiding stars in the southern hemisphere are Canopus and the Southern Cross. These stars played a vital role in the extraordinary story I was to uncover, and without the experience of astro-navigation I had gained in the Navy, this book would never have been written and the discoveries I made might have remained unrecognized for many more years.

A layman, no matter how distinguished in other fields, looks at a map or a chart and sees only a series of outlines that may or may not be the misshapen representations of familiar lands. An experienced navigator looking at the same map can deduce far more: where the cartographer who had first charted it had sailed, in what direction, how fast or slow, how near to or far from the land he had been, the state of his knowledge of latitude and longitude, even whether it was night or day. Given sufficient knowledge of the lands and oceans depicted on the chart, a navigator can also explain why what the chart shows as islands could be mountain peaks, why what was then an extensive body of land might now be shoals, reefs and islands, and hence why some lands might have been depicted with curiously distended forms.

I had seen the maps, dating from the fifteenth and early sixteenth centuries, that show parts of the world then unknown to European explorers. There are inaccuracies – some of the lands depicted are unrecognizable, or misshapen, or in locations where no land exists – and because the picture they offer of the world contradicts the accepted history of exploration they have long been dismissed as fables, forgeries or, at best, puzzling anomalies. But I found myself returning to those early maps and charts again and again, and as I studied them and evaluated them, a new picture of the medieval world began to emerge.

My research confirmed that several Chinese fleets had indeed made voyages of exploration in the early years of the fifteenth century. The last and greatest of them all – four fleets combining in one vast armada – set sail in early 1421. The last surviving ships returned to China in the summer and autumn of 1423. There was no extant record of where they had voyaged in the intervening years, but the maps showed that they had not merely rounded the Cape of Good Hope and traversed the Atlantic to chart the islands I had seen on the Pizzigano map of 1424, they had then gone on to explore Antarctica and the Arctic, North and South America, and had crossed the Pacific to Australia. They had solved the problems of calculating latitude and longitude and had mapped the earth and the heavens with equal accuracy.

I was educated by a Chinese *amah* for the first five years of my life – I remember to this day my sorrow at our parting – and I had made a number of visits to China over the years, but despite my interest in that great country, my knowledge of its history was by no means deep. Before I could follow the incredible course of these Chinese voyages of discovery, I would first have to immerse myself in the unfamiliar world of medieval China. That was a voyage of discovery in itself, and my ignorance of those remarkable people was shared, I suspect, by many in the West. The more I learned, the more I was awe-struck by the glory of that ancient, learned and incredibly sophisticated civilization. Their science and technology and their knowledge of the world around them were so far in advance of our own in that era that it was to be three, four and in some cases five centuries before European know-how matched that of the medieval Chinese.

Having learned something of that great civilization, I spent years travelling the globe on the track of the Chinese voyages of exploration. I researched in archives, museums and libraries, visited ancient monuments, castles, palaces and the major sea-ports of the late Middle Ages, explored rocky headlands, coral reefs, lonely beaches and remote islands. Everywhere I went I discovered more and more evidence to support the thesis. It turned out that a tiny handful of Chinese documents and sailing directions had escaped the wholesale destruction of records, and there were several first-person accounts: two by Chinese historians, another by a European merchant, and others by the first European explorers to follow in the Chinese wake, who discovered evidence and artefacts left by their predecessors.

There was also a wealth of physical evidence: Chinese porcelain, silk, votive offerings, artefacts, carved stones left by the Chinese admirals as monuments to their achievements, the wrecks of Chinese junks on the coasts of Africa, America, Australia and New Zealand, and the flora and fauna transplanted far from their places of origin and thriving when the first Europeans appeared. Everything I found was confirmation of the accuracy of the maps that had first captured my imagination. The remarkable information that those maps contain is, and always has been, there for all to see, but it has eluded many eminent historians of China, not for want of any diligence on their part but simply because of their lack of knowledge of astronavigation and the world's oceans. If I have found information that escaped them, it is only because I knew how to interpret the extraordinary maps and charts that reveal the course and the extent of the voyages of the great Chinese fleets between 1421 and 1423.

Columbus, da Gama, Magellan and Cook were later to make the same 'discoveries' but they all knew they were following in the footsteps of others, for they were carrying copies of the Chinese maps with them when they set off on their own journeys into the 'unknown'. To misuse a famous quotation: if they could see further than others, it was because they were standing on the shoulders of giants.

I

Imperial China

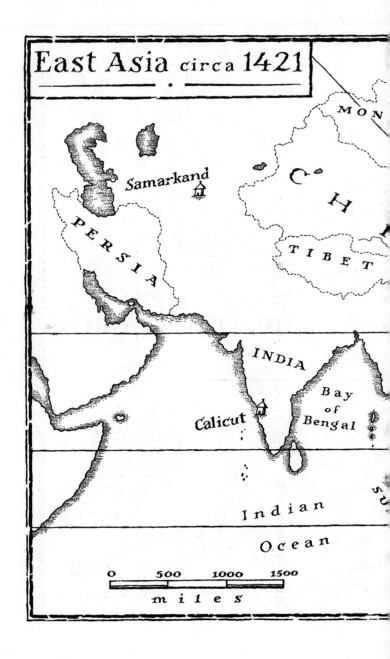

East Asia *circa* 1421

MON

C° H
TIBET

Samarkand

PERSIA

INDIA

Bay
of
Bengal

Calicut

SU

Indian

Ocean

0   500   1000   1500

m i l e s

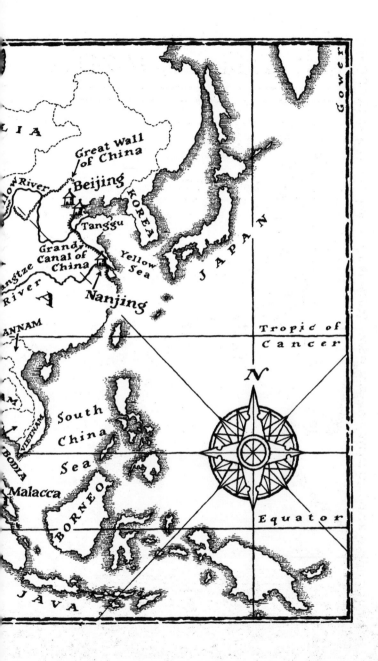

1

THE

EMPEROR'S

GRAND

PLAN

ON 2 FEBRUARY 1421, CHINA DWARFED EVERY NATION ON earth. On that Chinese New Year's Day, kings and envoys from the length and breadth of Asia, Arabia, Africa and the Indian Ocean assembled amid the splendours of Beijing to pay homage to the Emperor Zhu Di, the Son of Heaven. A fleet of leviathan ships, navigating the oceans with pinpoint accuracy, had brought the rulers and their envoys to pay tribute to the emperor and bear witness to the inauguration of his majestic and mysterious walled capital, the Forbidden City. No fewer than twenty-eight heads of state were present, but the Holy Roman Emperor, the Emperor of Byzantium, the Doge of Venice and the kings of England, France, Castille and Portugal were not among them. They had not been invited, for such backward states, lacking trade goods or any worthwhile scientific knowledge, ranked low on the Chinese emperor's scale of priorities.

Zhu Di was the fourth son of Zhu Yuanzhang, who had risen to become the first Ming emperor despite his lowly birth as the son of a hired labourer from one of the poorest parts of China.[1] In 1352, eight years before Zhu Di's birth, a terrible flood had struck parts of China. The Yellow River had burst its banks, submerging vast areas of farmland, washing away villages and leaving famine and disease in its wake. The country was still in the throes of a terrible epidemic. The Mongols had ruled China since its conquest in 1279 by the great Kublai Khan, grandson of the greatest warlord of them all, Genghis Khan. But in 1352, plagued by famine and disease and desperately poor as a result of the depredations of their Mongol overlords, the peasants around Guangzhou on the Pearl River delta rose in revolt. Zhu Yuanzhang joined the rebels and rapidly emerged as their leader, rallying soldiers and farmers to his cause. During the next three years the revolt spread throughout China. Over decades of peace, the once ferocious Mongol warriors, the scourge of all Asia, had grown idle and complacent. Riven by internal dissension, they proved no match for the army raised by Zhu Di's father. In 1356, his forces captured Nanjing and cut off corn supplies to the Mongols' northern capital, Ta-tu (Beijing).

Zhu Di was eight years old when his father's army entered Ta-tu itself, in 1368. The last Mongol Emperor of China, Toghon Temur, fled the country, retreating north to the steppe, the Mongol heartland. Zhu Yuanzhang pronounced a new dynasty, the Ming, and proclaimed himself the first emperor, taking the dynastic title Hong Wu.[2] Zhu Di joined the Chinese cavalry and proved himself a brave and skilful officer. At the age of twenty-one he was sent to join the campaign against the Mongol forces still occupying the mountainous south-western province of Yunnan, bordering modern Tibet and Laos, and in 1382 he was ordered to destroy Kunming, to the south of the Cloud Mountains, the remaining Mongol stronghold in the province. After the city was taken, the Chinese butchered the adult defenders and castrated those prisoners who had not reached puberty. Thousands of young Mongol boys had their penises and testicles severed. Many perished of shock and disease; the surviving eunuchs were conscripted into the imperial armies or kept as servants or retainers.

Eunuchs served as 'palace menials, harem watch dogs and spies'[3] for rulers throughout the ancient world, in Rome, Greece, North Africa and much of Asia, and they had played an important role throughout Chinese history.[4] Surprisingly, they were intensely loyal to the emperors who had authorized their mutilation. There had been eunuchs at the imperial court since at least the eighth century BC and as many as seventy thousand were employed in and around the capital. Only sexless males were permitted to act as personal servants to the emperor and to guard the women of his family and the quarters occupied by his concubines in the 'Great Within', inside the palace doors. Emperors retained thousands of concubines both as a symbol of their power and to ensure a number of male heirs at a time of high infant mortality; guaranteeing the continuity of the dynasty and the worship of ancestors was a vital part of Chinese cultural rites. Non-eunuchs, even relatives of the emperor and his consorts, were barred from the vicinity of the women's quarters on pain of death. The absence of potent males ensured that any children born to the concubines had been sired by the emperor alone.

Eunuchs also helped to preserve the aura of sanctity and secrecy that surrounded the imperial throne. While the gods granted a 'Mandate of Heaven' to legitimize the emperor's rule, they could rescind it if he proved guilty of human failings, mis-government or misconduct. It was forbidden to look upon the emperor: even senior officials kept their eyes downcast in the imperial presence, and when he passed through the streets, screens were erected to shield him from public gaze. Only the 'effeminate, cringing eunuchs', slavishly dependent upon the emperor for their very lives, were considered cowed enough to be silent witnesses to his private foibles and weaknesses.[5]

Ma He, one of the boys castrated at Kunming, was billeted in the household of Zhu Di, where his name was changed to Zheng He. Many of the Mongols whom Zhu Di and his father expelled had adopted the Muslim faith. Zheng He was a devout Muslim besides being a formidable soldier, and he became Zhu Di's closest adviser. He was a powerful figure, towering above Zhu Di; some accounts say he was over two metres tall and weighed over a hundred kilograms, with 'a stride like a tiger's'.[6] When Zhu Di was elevated to Prince of Yen – a region centred on Beijing – and given the new and more important responsibility of guarding China's northern provinces, Zheng He went with him. Zhu Di based himself in the former Mongol capital, Ta-tu, and renamed it Beijing. By 1387, after over thirty years of fighting, the last vestiges of Mongol rule had been purged from China. Zhu Di's father, the ageing and increasingly paranoid Emperor Hong

Wu, systematically purged his military command, eliminating anyone who might offer even the most remote challenge to his authority. Many senior commanders committed suicide rather than bring dishonour and disgrace to their families and their ancestors by being dismissed or executed, but nonetheless, tens of thousands of civil and military officers were put to the sword.

After the death of his first-born son, Hong Wu had chosen his grandson, Zhu Yunwen – Zhu Di's nephew – to succeed him. He distrusted Zhu Di, wrongly believing he was a Mongol. Hong Wu had married a princess but had not been told she was already pregnant (with Zhu Di). When the old emperor died six years later in 1398, Zhu Yunwen duly continued his policy of eliminating potential rivals. In the summer of the following year, assassins were sent north to kill Zhu Di. To escape execution, he abandoned his fine house and for several months became a vagrant on the streets of Beijing, sleeping in gutters at night and wandering the streets by day. He feigned madness, growing filthy and unkempt, unrecognizable as a prince of the imperial line, and the execution squad passed by this apparently harmless vagrant. Then Zhu Di turned on his pursuers. Aided by his loyal eunuch bodyguard, headed by Zheng He, Zhu Di gathered his forces in secret to strike against his would-be killers. He assembled eight hundred men in a park in Beijing, having previously filled it with honking geese to muffle the clanking of their armour and weapons. Taken by surprise, the assassins were themselves butchered. The victorious Zhu Di at once began to raise and train an army.

When he received the news of his men's failure, Zhu Yunwen immediately despatched an army of half a million men to crush Zhu Di, but the seasons were turning, and his troops were sent north from Nanjing wearing only their summer uniforms and straw sandals. Many men froze as the pitiless winter advanced. Zhu Di's army was on manoeuvres outside Beijing when the demoralized troops of Zhu Yunwen began their advance on the city. They were routed in a battle in which even the women of Beijing took part, hurling pots down on their attackers from the city walls.

In 1402, Zhu Di marched south to Nanjing at the head of a great army. The imperial capital was a divided city. The mandarins, the educated elite in Nanjing, loathed the court eunuchs. Their antipathy was deep-seated and almost as old as imperial China itself. As his personal attendants, the eunuchs had the emperor's ear; like the courtiers of European rulers, they grew wealthy through their imperial connections. But while the eunuchs held sway in the 'Great Within', mandarins alone were entitled to hold office in the 'Great Without' beyond the palace walls.

Men became mandarins and holders of exalted official positions only after years of intensive study and examinations based exclusively upon the teaching of Confucius (551–479 BC),

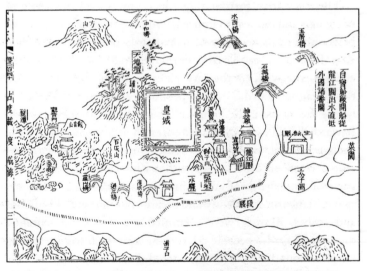

A plan of imperial Nanjing from the *Wu Pei Chi* (*Wu Bei Zhi*). This seventeenth-century treatise on armaments drew on illustrations from earlier manuals; the shipyards are on the right across the bridge.

the 'Great Sage' who had expressed his own disapproval of eunuchs holding positions of power. Eunuchs received no Confucian education and relied solely upon the emperor for advancement. Mandarins were steeped in Confucian ethics and a code of moral values intended to maintain order and hierarchy in society by eliminating the opportunity for people to disturb the *tao* (interaction of natural forces). It determined everyone's life, their rank, their rites and the position allocated to them in the social hierarchy. The Confucian definition of good government required that 'a prince be a prince . . . the subject a subject, the father a father, the son a son'.[7] Orderly, well-mannered continuity was at the heart of Confucianism and of mandarin government, and the mandarins saw rural farmers, not foreigners or merchants, as the backbone of society. The farmers represented stability, whereas merchants and foreigners continually upset the *tao*.

The mandarins surrounding Zhu Yunwen had succeeded in marginalizing the court eunuchs, stripping them of much of the power and influence they had previously possessed, and when Zhu Di's army appeared before the walls of Nanjing, the eunuchs threw open the city gates to them. Zhu Di seized the Dragon Throne[8] and pronounced himself emperor, taking the dynastic title Yong Le. Zhu Yunwen was never found. It was believed he had escaped, dressed as a monk. Zheng He remained at the new emperor's side, one of a group of eunuchs who formed an inner circle within Zhu Di's staff. They had personal knowledge of and gained influence in affairs of state, saw the emperor frequently and became familiar with his moods and wishes. As they were permitted to enter the concubines' quarters, they also became conversant with the intrigues among the two thousand women sequestered there.

The eunuchs were once more a political force. In recognition of his service to the emperor, the most powerful figure of all was the Grand Eunuch, Zheng He. He had earned the nickname San

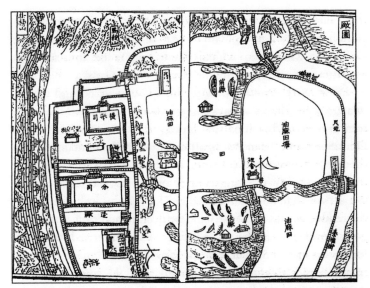

A plan of the Longjiang shipyards from the *Lung Chiang Chhang Chih*, a history of the yards at the time of Zheng He, published in 1553. The administrative offices are on the left, the slipways and docks on the right.

Bao, 'Three Treasures', which referred to the three *raisons d'être* of a Buddhist: Buddha, doctrine and meditation. Zheng He had placed his severed penis in a temple. The casket containing his *pao* – 'manhood treasures' – would accompany him to the next world, where once again he could become a whole man. But in this earthly life, he was sworn to serve and do the bidding of his patron and ruler, the third Ming emperor, Zhu Di.

Within twelve months, despite never having been to sea, Zheng He had been appointed Commander-in-Chief of one of the largest fleets ever built. One of Zhu Di's first orders had been to double the size of the Longjiang shipyards, near Nanjing. Already the principal shipyards in China, they were now vastly expanded, covering several square miles on the banks of the Yangtze beyond the eastern gate of Nanjing. Seven vast dry-docks were built, connected by a series of locks to the river, and each one could be subdivided to permit three ships to be built simultaneously. They remain there to this day.[9] Zhu Di's aim was to create what even Kublai Khan had failed to achieve: a maritime empire spanning the oceans.

Prior to the ninth century, ships voyaging beyond coastal waters were almost always foreign-owned, but from the ninth century onwards China developed its own ocean-going fleet. The Song and Yuan (Mongol) dynasties had maintained large fleets, sent emissaries overseas and built a substantial foreign trade, gradually wresting control of the spice trade from the Arabs who had once dominated it. Zhu Di now embarked on an incredible expansion of the Chinese fleet. In addition to the warships and the merchant fleet he had inherited, Zhu Di commissioned 1,681 new ships, among them many gigantic nine-masted 'treasure ships', named after the huge value and quantity of goods they could carry in their vast holds. Tens of thousands of carpenters, sailmakers and shipwrights from the southern provinces around the shipyards were put to work to build them. In addition to 250 treasure ships, the fleet contained more than 3,500 other vessels. There were 1,350 patrol ships and the same number of combat vessels based at guard stations or island bases, 400 larger warships and another 400 freighters for transporting grain, water and horses for the fleet. The emperor's ships were to sail the oceans of the world and chart them, impressing and intimidating foreign rulers, bringing the entire world into China's 'tribute system'. Rulers paid tribute to China in return for trading privileges and protection against their enemies, but China always gave its trading partners a greater value of goods – silks and porcelain at discounted prices, often funded by soft loans – than was received from them. They were thus in perpetual debt to China. These ships were also tasked with hunting down the fugitive Zhu Yunwen: 'There are some who say he is abroad. The emperor ordered Zheng He to seek out traces of him.'[10] All should know who was the rightful occupant of the Dragon Throne: the Emperor on Horseback, Son of Heaven – Zhu Di.

As soon as he had claimed the imperial throne, Zhu Di decided to relocate the capital to his former stronghold of Beijing. The ageing Tamerlane, the last of the great nomadic leaders, had decided to seize his last and greatest prize of all, China, and Zhu Di resolved to meet the threat head on. Tamerlane (the anglicized form of the Persian Timur-i-Lang, or 'Timur the Lame', a nickname he received as a result of arrow wounds sustained in battle) had proved a worthy successor to his forebears Genghis Khan and Kublai Khan. 'He loved bold and valiant soldiers, by whose aid he opened the locks of terror, tore men to pieces like lions and overturned mountains.'[11] From his capital Samarkand, straddling the Silk Road, the great trading route through central Asia, Tamerlane had waged relentless campaigns across Asia, conquering northern India, Persia and Syria, and defeating the Ottomans at Ankara in 1402. Now his gaze had turned eastwards, his aim to destroy the Chinese armies, overthrow Zhu Di and restore China to Mongol rule.

To counter this potent threat, the new emperor took with him to Beijing his court, guarded by a million-strong army, but his vision for the new imperial capital encompassed far more than its being a defensive stronghold to thwart Tamerlane. Kublai Khan had built Ta-tu to a traditional Chinese design and diverted rivers to encircle the city. Zhu Di incorporated the basic elements of Kublai Khan's capital, but he demolished the royal enclosure and replaced it with a classic imperial complex, the Forbidden City, with far more perfect proportions than its former design. The walled capital surrounding it was to be built on an awesome scale: fifteen hundred times the area of walled London at that time and housing fifty times the population.

Yet building the world's greatest city to dazzle his people and intimidate his enemies and all the rulers of the world was only one part of Zhu Di's master plan. He would also repair the Great

Wall, built by the first Chinese emperor, Qin Shi Huangdi, during the Qin dynasty (221–206 BC). Qin Shi Huangdi had united the warring provinces of China and was the first man to rule the entire country. The wall was erected at ruinous expense to protect China's northern frontiers from attack, but over the following 1,600 years it had been allowed to crumble into disrepair. Zhu Di began a programme of rebuilding and strengthening, adding watchtowers and turrets along the wall's existing 5,000 kilometres and extending it by a further 1,400. It ran from the Pacific as far west as the Heavenly Mountains in central Asia.

Still Zhu Di's aims were higher. He despatched expeditions to China's eastern neighbours and along the Silk Road across central Asia to recreate the trading empire China had possessed in the golden age of the Tang dynasty over five centuries earlier. All this in addition to his fleet-expansion programme.

Zhu Di intended to achieve all these stupendous goals within two decades. Running through all his policies was his determination that the Chinese should once again believe in themselves and their illustrious history. The Mongols had been expelled, China was Chinese again. Zhu Di was always concerned by the fact that he was not his father's designated heir, and he constantly sought to demonstrate that the gods had bestowed legitimacy on his ascent to the Dragon Throne. Hence the first buildings he commissioned were those of the great ceremonial complex, the Temple of Heaven, at the centre of the new city. It was to be not only the stage for the annual ceremonies the emperor, the Son of Heaven, was required to perform, but the very heart of the new Chinese empire. A new observatory, in turn, would be at the epicentre of Beijing. Zhu Di took a personal interest in astronomy, and in the means by which he could build on the wonderful legacy he had inherited in this field. Chinese astronomers had well over two thousand years' experience of recording events in the night sky. They had noted the appearance of a new star in 1300 BC, had charted every arrival of Halley's comet since 240 BC, and by 1054 were describing the remnants of the supernova explosion known as the Crab Nebula, with its rapidly spinning neutron star, or pulsar, at its centre.

During eighty-nine years of rule over China, the Mongol emperors had neglected this priceless inheritance; in the first year of his reign, Zhu Di restored the nightly practice of recording the stars. His astronomers charted no fewer than 1,400 of them as they traversed the sky, and they were able to predict both solar and lunar eclipses with considerable accuracy. Zhu Di also set up a committee of distinguished astronomers to 'compare and correct the drawings of the guiding stars'[12] and eventually persuaded the Shogun of Japan, the King of Korea, and Prince Ulugh Begh, grandson of Tamerlane, to do the same. The emperor's interest in astronomy was practical, not theoretical. He was determined that his astronomers should perfect new methods of using these guiding stars, enabling his admirals to navigate accurately at sea and correctly locate the new territories they would find on their journeys of discovery. His aim was to ensure that Beijing's great observatory was the reference point from which the entire world would be explored and charted, and all new discoveries located – in short, the centre of the known universe.

The relocation of the capital from Nanjing to Beijing was by far the most complex and far-reaching project undertaken during the Ming dynasty. The move started in 1404, when ten thousand households were forcibly moved north to increase Beijing's population. A vast army of workers was also required to accomplish Zhu Di's vision and hundreds of thousands of Chinese labourers were force-marched to the north; some 335 army divisions were re-deployed to guard them, even though the threat from Tamerlane's Mongol hordes had quickly evaporated. The great warlord had left Samarkand at the head of a vast army in January 1405, his aim to march eastwards through the mountains, set up encampments near the Chinese border, and await the first sign of the approach of spring before striking deep into China, catching the emperor's forces unprepared. Sick and old, Tamerlane was too weak to march and was carried in a litter – a couch carried by bearers – but even so, the privations of the journey over such bleak terrain in the depths of winter were too much for him. He died on 18 February without even sighting the Chinese frontier. His army broke up into rival factions and dispersed.

Zhu Di's plans for Beijing remained unaltered by the news of Tamerlane's death, but feeding the first construction workers soon began to prove difficult. The growing season in the north was short; millet could be grown, but not rice, and wheat and barley produced poor yields. There was nowhere near enough grain to feed the tidal waves of workers continuing to arrive. Zhu Di delegated his third son, Zhu Gaozhi, to assume military command of Beijing, and tax rebates were granted to anyone who could grow grain around the city. When this measure failed to produce enough to feed the growing armies of workmen, the emperor decided that the Grand Canal must be repaired and enlarged to carry shipments of grain northwards.

Begun in 486 BC under the Wu dynasty, the canal was one of the wonders of the ancient world. From AD 584 onwards it was extended and the individual sections linked together to form a system stretching for 1,800 kilometres – to this day the longest man-made waterway in the world. However, it was built at a horrific human cost: it is estimated that half of the six million labour force perished at their work. The financial stresses and domestic upheavals caused by the building of the canal were also one of the principal causes of the rapid collapse of the short-lived Sui dynasty (AD 589–618).

The Grand Canal was the main artery of commerce between north and south China, but its capacity was no longer equal to the demands being placed upon it. The work to enlarge it was

An early Ming grain freighter from the *Thien Kung Kai Wu*
(*Tian Gong Kai Wu*), 'The Exploitation of the Works of Nature', 1637.

carried out in two stages. In 1411, dredging and reconstruction
of the northern section began to clear 130 miles of channel, and
thirty-six new locks were built, for Beijing was over a hundred
feet higher than the Yellow River. Three hundred thousand
labourers were employed on the task. The southern section from
the Yellow River to the Yangtze was opened in 1415. The completed canal stretched from Beijing in the north to Hangzhou on
the coast, south of Shanghai. Grain was transported in close to
ten thousand flat-bottomed barges, and shipments rose from 2.8
million piculs (approximately 170 million kilograms) in 1416 to
five million (300 million kilograms) by the following year.

The insatiable demand for grain to feed the workforce in
Beijing led to shortages and famine elsewhere in China, and the
timber required for Zhu Di's great schemes stripped the forests
of hardwood. Quite apart from the timber needed to build the
Forbidden City, each treasure ship in the emperor's huge fleet
consumed the wood of three hundred acres of prime teak forest.

The imperial navy was supported by a new fleet of auxiliary store ships, and hundreds of smaller merchant ships were also built to trade between Chinese, Indian and African ports. Yet more hardwood was used in the construction of the thousands of grain barges plying the Grand Canal. Hundreds of thousands, if not millions, of acres of forest were felled. Annam (the northern part of modern Vietnam) and Vietnam were also denuded of trees, sparking off the first of a series of uprisings against Chinese rule.

Zhu Di also faced domestic problems. The scale and cost of his grandiose schemes provoked increasingly ferocious opposition from the mandarins, and even an emperor could not undertake a massive project like the building of the Forbidden City without their co-operation. The mandarins were responsible for raising the tax revenues to fund Zhu Di's projects, and, as with officials of any court in any country, there were a thousand ways for them to delay or hinder schemes they did not favour. Zhu Di continued to pursue his dreams with a customary mixture of guile and ruthlessness, even going so far as to exploit the arrival of a 'qilin' – in reality a common giraffe obtained by Admiral Zheng He on one of the epic expeditions that began in 1405, when his fleet visited East Africa – to bamboozle and out-manoeuvre his opponents.

The qilin was an important animal in Chinese mythology, said to have the body of a musk deer, the tail of an ox, the forehead of a wolf, the hoofs of a horse, and a fleshy horn like a unicorn. In legend, a qilin had appeared before a young woman, Yen Tschen-tsaii, in the sixth century BC. It dropped a piece of jade into her hand on which was engraved a message: she would bear a son, 'a king without a throne'.[13] The son she bore was Confucius, whose philosophy of system and order was to dominate Chinese thought for over two millennia.

The 'qilin' was presented to Zhu Di by Zheng He on 16 November 1416. Proclaiming its arrival as a sign of heavenly approval for his rule, Zhu Di immediately convened a council to confirm once and for all the merits of transferring the capital from Nanjing to Beijing. The court poet wrote a eulogy to the emperor and, astounded by the appearance of the celestial animal, the mandarins duly obliged him.

The whole of China was now mobilized to achieve the completion of the imperial design. Gangs were sent to fell yet more teak in the forests of the Chinese provinces of Jiangxi, Shanxi and Sichuan, and in Annam and Vietnam. Kilns were built to manufacture enormous quantities of bricks. A workforce of artisans, soldiers and labourers was recruited from all over the Chinese empire. In all, one million men were employed directly on constructing the Forbidden City, three and a half million indirectly. A further one million soldiers stood guard over them.

Once barges could carry food along the Grand Canal to this multitude of workmen, the rate of progress on the Forbidden City accelerated. Improvements were made to the moats, walls and bridges of the former Ta-tu and a start was made on the emperor's residence, the western palace in the Forbidden City. In March 1417, the emperor left Nanjing for the last time, and by the end of that year most of the palace buildings had been completed. In 1420, sections of the southern city wall that had fallen into disrepair under the Mongols were restored, and later that year the Temple of Heaven was completed. Sufficient buildings had also been erected to enable the court permanently to move north, and on Chinese New Year's Day, 2 February 1421, the magnificent new capital was inaugurated. To emphasize the importance of the occasion, the envoys of all visiting heads of state were required to bow and kow-tow – prostrate themselves and press their foreheads to the ground – at Zhu Di's feet. China's absolute dominance was further highlighted by the humiliation imposed on two of the most powerful men in the world: the son and grandson of the mighty Tamerlane. Their first attempt at kow-towing before Zhu Di was deemed unsatisfactory and one of Zhu Di's eunuchs, Haji Maulana, made them repeat it. Their second attempt was also inadequate. Only after their third prostration at his feet did the emperor pronounce himself satisfied.

This array of foreign heads of state kow-towing before the emperor was the culmination of fifteen years' assiduous diplomacy. Chinese foreign policy was quite different from that of the Europeans who followed them to the Indian Ocean many years later. The Chinese preferred to pursue their aims by trade, influence and bribery rather than by open conflict and direct colonization. Zhu Di's policy was to despatch huge armadas every few years throughout the known world, bearing gifts and trade goods; the massive treasure ships carrying a huge array of guns and a travelling army of soldiers were also a potent reminder of his imperial might: China alone had the necessary firepower to protect friendly countries from invasion and quash insurrections against their rulers. The treasure ships returned to China with all manner of exotic items: 'dragon saliva [ambergris], incense and golden amber' and 'lions, gold spotted leopards and camel-birds [ostriches] which are six or seven feet tall' from Africa; gold cloth from Calicut in south-west India, studded with pearls and precious stones; elephants, parrots, sandalwood, peacocks, hardwood, incense, tin and cardamom from Siam (modern Thailand).

Those rulers who accepted the emperor's overlordship were rewarded with titles, protection and trade missions. In south-east Asia, Malacca was rewarded for its loyalty by being promoted as a trading port at the expense of Java and Sumatra; the emperor even personally composed a poem for the Malaccan sultan, and can be said to have been the founder of Malaysia. The subservient Siamese were also extended trading privileges to the detriment of the truculent Cambodians. Korea was especially important to China: Zhu Di lost no time in despatching an envoy to the King of Korea, Yi Pang-Won, granting him an honorary

Chinese title. The Koreans needed Chinese medicine, books and astronomical instruments, and in return they agreed to set up an observatory to co-operate with Zhu Di in charting the world. They traded leopards, seals, gold, silver and horses – one thousand of them in 1403, ten thousand the next year. Despite some reluctance, they also found it expedient to comply with Chinese requests to fill Zhu Di's harem with virgins. Many Korean ships were to join the Chinese fleets when they left to sail the world.

As soon as he had expelled the last Mongols from China in 1382, Zhu Di had despatched his eunuch Isiha to the perennially troublesome region of Manchuria in the far north-east, and in 1413 the Jurchen people of Manchuria responded by sending a prestigious mission to Beijing, where its members were showered with titles, gifts and trading rights. Japan was also assiduously courted. The third Ashikaga Shogun Yoshimitsu was a Sinophile; he lost no time in kow-towing as 'your subject, the King of Japan'.[14] His reward was a string of special ports opened to promote trade with Japan, at Ningbo, Quanzhou and Guangdong (Canton). Like Korea, Japan also set up an observatory to aid Zhu Di's astronomical research, and Japanese ships also joined the globetrotting Chinese convoys.

Having pacified Manchuria and brought Korea and Japan into the Chinese tribute system, Zhu Di next turned his attention to Tibet. Another court eunuch, Hau-Xian, led a mission to court the famous holy man the Karmapa, leader of one of the four sects of Tibetan Buddhism, and bring him to China. When he arrived, a procession of Buddhist monks met him outside the city and Zhu Di bestowed upon him the title 'Divine Son of India Below the Sky and Upon the Earth, Inventor of the Alphabet, Incarnated Buddha, Maintainer of the Kingdom's Prosperity, Source of Rhetoric'. The emperor then presented the Karmapa with a square black hat bearing a diamond-studded emblem. It has been worn by successive incarnations of the Karmapa ever since.

Joining China's tribute system also gave rulers and their envoys the opportunity to visit the capital of the oldest and finest civilization in the world. The traditional imperial capital of Nanjing had received dignitaries from around the world, and now the new capital of Beijing began to welcome the latest arrivals. Although the emperor's main concern was to awe all countries into becoming tribute-bearing states, great efforts were also made to learn about their history, geography, manners and customs. Beijing was to be not only the world's greatest city but its intellectual capital, with encyclopedias and libraries covering every subject known to man. In December 1404, Zhu Di had appointed two long-time advisers, Yao Guang Xiao and Lui Chi'ih, assisted by 2,180 scholars, to take charge of a project, the Yong-le-Dadian, to preserve all known literature and knowledge. It was the largest scholarly enterprise ever undertaken. The result, a massive encyclopedia of four thousand volumes containing some fifty million characters, was completed just before the Forbidden City was inaugurated.

In parallel with this great endeavour, Zhu Di ordered the opinions of 120 philosophers and sages of the Song dynasty to be collated and stored in the Forbidden City together with the complete commentaries of thinkers from the eleventh to the thirteenth centuries. In addition to this wealth of academic knowledge, hundreds of printed novels could be bought from Beijing market stalls. There was nothing remotely comparable anywhere in the world. Printing was unknown in Europe – Gutenberg did not complete his printed Bible for another thirty years – and though Europe was on the eve of the Renaissance that was to transform its culture and scientific knowledge, it lagged far behind China. The library of Henry V (1387–1422) comprised six handwritten books, three of which were on loan to him from a nunnery, and the Florentine Francesco Datini, the wealthiest European merchant of the same era, possessed twelve books, eight of which were on religious subjects.

The voyage to the intellectual paradise of Beijing also offered foreign potentates and envoys many earthly delights. Carried in sumptuous comfort aboard the leviathan ships, they consumed the finest foods and wines, and pleasured themselves with the concubines whose only role was to please these foreign dignitaries. The formal inauguration of the Forbidden City was followed by a sumptuous banquet. Its scale and opulence emphasized China's position at the summit of the civilized world. In comparison, Europe was backward, crude and barbaric. Henry V's marriage to Catherine of Valois took place in London just three weeks after the inauguration of the Forbidden City. Twenty-six thousand guests were entertained in Beijing, where they ate a ten-course banquet served on dishes of the finest porcelain; a mere six hundred guests attended Henry's nuptials and they were served stockfish (salted cod) on rounds of stale bread that acted as plates. Catherine de Valois wore neither knickers nor stockings at her wedding; Zhu Di's favourite concubine was clad in the finest silks and her jewellery included cornelians from Persia, rubies from Sri Lanka, Indian diamonds and jade from Kotan (in Chinese Turkestan). Her perfume contained ambergris from the Pacific, myrrh from Arabia and sandalwood from the Spice Islands. China's army numbered one million men, armed with guns; Henry V could put five thousand men in the field, armed only with longbows, swords and pikes. The fleet that would carry Zhu Di's guests home numbered over a hundred ships with a complement of thirty thousand men; when Henry went to war against France in June of that year, he ferried his army across the Channel in four fishing boats, carrying a hundred men on each crossing and sailing only in daylight hours.

For a further month after the inauguration of the Forbidden City, the rulers and envoys in Beijing were provided with lavish imperial hospitality – the finest foods and wines, the most splendid entertainments and the most beautiful concubines, skilled in the arts of love. Finally, on 3 March 1421, a great ceremony was mounted to commemorate the departure of the envoys for their native lands. A vast honour guard was assembled: 'First came commanders of ten thousands, next commanders of thousands, all numbering about one hundred thousand men ... Behind them stood troops in serried ranks, two hundred thousand strong ... The whole body ... stood so silent it seemed there was not a breathing soul there.'[15] At noon precisely, cymbals clashed, elephants lowered their trunks, and clouds of smoke wafted from incense-holders in the shape of tortoises and cranes. The emperor appeared, striding through the smoke to present the departing ambassadors with their farewell gifts – crates of blue and white porcelain, rolls of silk, bundles of cotton cloth and bamboo cases of jade. His great fleets stood ready to carry them back to Hormuz, Aden, La'Sa and Dhofar in Arabia; to Mogadishu, Brava, Malindi and Mombasa in Africa; to Sri Lanka, Calicut, Cochin and Cambay in India; to Japan, Vietnam, Java, Sumatra, Malacca and Borneo in south-east Asia, and elsewhere.

Admiral Zheng He, dressed in his formal uniform – a long red robe and a tall black hat – presented the emperor with his compliments and reported that an armada comprising four of the emperor's great fleets was ready to set sail; the fifth, commanded by Grand Eunuch Yang Qing, had put to sea the previous month. The return of the envoys to their homelands was only the first part of this armada's overall mission. It was then to 'proceed all the way to the end of the earth to collect tribute from the barbarians beyond the seas ... to attract all under heaven to be civilised in Confucian harmony'.[16] Zheng He's reward for his lifelong, devoted service to his emperor had been the command of five[17] previous treasure fleets tasked with promoting Chinese trade and influence in Asia, India, Africa and the Middle East. Now he was to lead one of the largest armadas the world had ever seen. Zhu Di had also rewarded other eunuchs for their part in helping him to liberate China. Many of the army commanders in the war against the Mongols were now admirals and captains of his treasure fleets. Zheng He had become a master of delegation. By the fourth voyage fleets were sailing separately. On this great sixth voyage loyal eunuchs would command separate fleets. Zheng He would lead them to the Indian Ocean then return home confident that they would handle their fleets as he had taught them.

The envoys' parting gifts were packed into their carriages, the emperor made a short speech, and then, after kow-towing one last time, the envoys embarked and the procession moved off. Servants ran behind the carriages as they rumbled down to the Grand Canal a mile to the east of the city. There, a fleet of barges decked with silk awnings awaited them. Teams of horses, ten to twelve for each barge, stood on the banks, bamboo poles tied to their harnesses. When the envoys were aboard, whips cracked and the sturdy animals began to drag the barges on their slow journey down to the coast.

Two days and thirty-six locks later, they arrived at Tanggu (near the modern city of Tianjin) on the Yellow Sea. The sight that greeted the envoys at Tanggu was one that must have lingered long in their minds. More than one hundred huge junks rode at anchor, towering above the watchers on the quayside – the ships were taller by far than the thatched houses lining the bay. Surrounding them was a fleet of smaller merchant ships. Each capital ship was about 480 feet in length (444 *chi*, the standard Chinese unit of measurement, equivalent to about 12.5 inches or 32 centimetres) and 180 feet across – big enough to swallow fifty fishing boats. On the prow, glaring serpents' eyes served to frighten away evil spirits. Pennants streamed from the tips of a forest of a thousand masts; below them great sails of red silk, light but immensely strong, were furled on each ship's nine masts. 'When their sails are spread, they are like great clouds in the sky.'[18]

The armada was composed very much like a Second World War convoy. At the centre were the great leviathan flagships, surrounded by a host of merchant junks, most 90 feet long and 30 feet wide. Around the perimeters were squadrons of fast, manoeuvrable warships. As the voyage progressed, trading ships of several other nations, especially Japan, Korea, Burma, Vietnam and India, joined the convoy, taking advantage of the protection afforded by the warships and the opportunities offered as the magnificent armada, almost a trading country in its own right, swept over the oceans. By the time it reached Calicut, it comprised more than eight hundred vessels whose combined population exceeded that of any city between China and India. Each treasure ship had sixteen internal watertight compartments, any two of which could be flooded without sinking the ship. Some internal compartments could also be partially flooded to act as tanks for the trained sea-otters used in fishing, or for use by divers entering and leaving the sea. The otters, held on long cords, were employed to herd shoals of fish into nets, a method still practised in parts of China, Malaysia and Bengal today. The admiral's sea cabin was above the stern of his flagship. Below were sixty staterooms for foreign ambassadors, envoys and their entourages. Their concubines were housed in adjacent cabins and most had balconies overlooking the sea. Chinese ambassadors, one for each country to be visited, were housed in less grand but nonetheless spacious apartments. Each ambassador had ten assistants as *chefs de protocol* and a further fifty-two eunuchs served as secretaries. The crewmen's quarters were on the lower decks.

In 1407, Zheng He had established a language school in Nanjing, the Ssu-i-Quan (Si Yi Guan), to train interpreters, and sixteen of its finest graduates travelled with the fleets, enabling the admirals to communicate with rulers from India to Africa in Arabic, Persian, Swahili, Hindi, Tamil and many other languages. Zhu Di and Zheng He also actively sought out foreign navigators and cartographers; the diaries of one of them, an Indonesian by the name of Master Bentun, have survived. Religious tolerance was one of Zhu Di's great virtues, and the junks also habitually carried Islamic, Hindu and Buddhist savants to provide advice and guidance. Buddhism, with its teachings of universal compassion and tolerance, had been the religion of the majority of the Chinese people for centuries. Buddhism in no way conflicted with Confucianism, which could be said to be a code of civic values rather than a religion. On this sixth and final voyage of the treasure fleets which would last until 1423, the Buddhist monk Sheng Hui and the religious leaders Ha San and Pu He Ri were aboard.[19] After the inauguration of the Forbidden City and the dedication of the awesome encyclopedia the Yong-le-Dadian, thousands of scholars found themselves without an obvious role. It would have been natural for Zhu Di to send them overseas on the great voyages of exploration. Through interpreters, Chinese mathematicians, astronomers, navigators, engineers and architects would have been able to converse with and learn from their counterparts throughout the Indian Ocean. Once the ambassadors and their entourages had disembarked, the vast ships with their labyrinths of cabins would have been well suited to use as laboratories for scientific experiments. Metallurgists could prospect for minerals in the countries the Chinese visited, physicians could search out new healing plants, medicines and treatments that might help to combat plagues and epidemics, and botanists could propagate valuable food plants. Chinese agricultural scientists and farmers had millennia of experience of developing and propagating hybrids.

The native Chinese flora is perhaps the richest in the world: 'In wealth of its endemic species and in the extent of the genus and species potential of its cultivated plants, China is conspicuous among other centres of origin of plant forms. Moreover the species are usually represented by enormous numbers of botanical varieties and hereditary forms.'[20] In Europe, a long

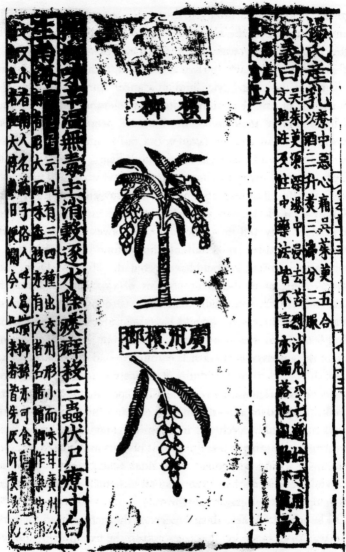

The betel-nut tree from the *Chêng Lei Pên Tshao* (*Cheng Lei Ben Cao*),
'Classified Pharmaceutical Natural History', 1468. Above is the whole palm,
below the fruit. The description to the left of the drawings states that it grows
in the South Seas.

period of economic and agricultural decline followed the fall of the Roman Empire. The plant forms known to the Western world from Theophrastus to the German fathers of botany show that European knowledge had slumped, but there was no corresponding 'dark age' in Chinese scientific history. Botanical knowledge, and the number of plant species recorded by the Chinese, grew steadily as the centuries passed. The contrast between the voyages of discovery of the Chinese and those of the Europeans cannot be overestimated. The only interest of the Spanish and Portuguese was in gathering sustenance, gold and spices, while warding off attacks from the natives. The great Chinese fleets undertook scientific expeditions the Europeans could not even begin to equal in scale or scope until Captain Cook set sail three and a half centuries later.

As the admirals and envoys embarked, and the armada was readied for sea, the water around the great ships was still black with smaller craft shuttling from ship to shore. For days the port had been in turmoil as cartloads of vegetables and dried fish and hundreds of tons of water were hauled aboard to provision this armada of thirty thousand men for their voyage. Even at this late hour, barges were still bringing final supplies of fresh water and rice. The great armada's ships could remain at sea for over three months and cover at least 4,500 miles without making landfall to replenish food or water, for separate grain ships and water tankers sailed with them. The grain ships also carried an array of flora the Chinese intended to plant in foreign lands, some as further benefits of the tribute system and others to provide food for the Chinese colonies that would be created in new lands. Dogs were also taken aboard as pets, others to be bred for food and to hunt rats, and there were coops of Asiatic chickens as valuable presents for foreign dignitaries. The larger ships even kept sties of Chinese pigs. Separate horse-ships carried the mounts for the cavalry.

The staggering size of the individual ships, not to mention the armada itself, can best be understood by comparison with other navies of the same era. In 1421, the next most powerful fleet afloat was that of Venice. The Venetians possessed around three hundred galleys – fast, light, thin-skinned ships built with soft-wood planking, rowed by oarsmen and only suitable for island-hopping in the calm of a Mediterranean summer. The biggest Venetian galleys were some 150 feet long and 20 feet wide and carried at best 50 tons of cargo. In comparison, Zhu Di's treasure ships were ocean-going monsters built of teak. The rudder of one of these great ships stood 36 feet high – almost as long as the whole of the flagship the *Niña* in which Columbus was later to set sail for the New World. Each treasure ship could carry more than two thousand tons of cargo and reach Malacca in five weeks, Hormuz in the Persian Gulf in twelve. They were capable of sailing the wildest oceans of the world, in voyages lasting years at a time. That so many ships were lost on the Chinese voyages of discovery testifies not to any lack of strength in their construction but rather to the perilous, uncharted waters they explored and the hurricanes and tsunami they encountered along rocky coasts and razor-sharp coral reefs to the ice-strewn oceans of the far north and far south. Venetian galleys were protected by archers; Chinese ships were armed with gunpowder weapons, brass and iron cannon, mortars, flaming arrows and exploding shells that sprayed excrement over their adversaries. In every single respect – construction, cargo capacity, damage control, armament, range, communications, the ability to navigate in the trackless ocean and to repair and maintain their ships at sea for months on end – the Chinese were centuries ahead of Europe. Admiral Zheng He would have had no difficulty in destroying any fleet that crossed his path. A battle between this Chinese armada and the other navies of the world combined would have resembled one between a pack of sharks and a shoal of sprats.

By the end of the middle watch – four in the morning – the

last provisions had been lashed down and the armada weighed anchor. A prayer was said to Ma Tsu, Taoist goddess of the sea, and then, as their red silk sails slowly filled, the ships, resembling great houses, gathered way before the winds of the north-east monsoon. As they sailed out across the Yellow Sea, the last flickering lights of Tanggu faded into the darkness while the sailors clustered at the rails, straining for a last sight of their homeland. In the long months they would spend travelling the oceans, their only remaining links to the land would be memories, keepsakes and the scented roses many brought with them, growing them in pots and even sharing their water rations with them. The majority of those seamen at the rails would never see China again. Many would die, many others would be shipwrecked or left behind to set up colonies on foreign shores. Those who eventually returned after two and a half years at sea would find their country convulsed and transformed beyond all recognition.

2

A

THUNDERBOLT

STRIKES

O N THE NIGHT OF 9 MAY 1421, TWO MONTHS AFTER
Zheng He's armada had set sail, a violent storm broke
over the Forbidden City.

On this night by chance a conflagration started . . . lightning struck
the top of the palace that had been newly constructed by the
Emperor. The fire that started in that building enveloped it in such
a manner that it seemed as if 100,000 torches provided with oil and
wicks had been lit up therein . . . so much so that the whole city
was set ablaze with the light of that conflagration and the fire
spreading . . . it burnt down the Ladies' Apartments behind the
Hall of Audience . . . about 250 quarters were consumed to ashes,
burning a large number of men and women. It continued burning
like that until it was day and in spite of all efforts, the fire could
not be brought under control until it was afternoon prayer time.[1]

Balls of fire appeared to travel down the Imperial Way itself,
along the very axis of the Forbidden City, destroying what we
now call the Hall of Great Harmony, the Hall of Central
Harmony and the Hall of Preserving Harmony – the magnificent palaces where Zhu Di had received leaders of the world
three months earlier. The emperor's throne was burned to
cinders. 'In his anguish he repaired to the temple and prayed
with great importunity, saying, "The God of Heaven is angry
with me, and, therefore, has burnt my palace; although I have
done no evil act. I have neither offended my father, nor mother,
nor have I acted tyrannically." '[2]

The shock killed the emperor's favourite concubine. Zhu Di
was so distraught that he was unable to make proper arrangements for her burial in the imperial mausoleum.

He fell ill owing to his anguish and on account of this it could not
be ascertained as to in what manner the dead personage was
buried . . . The private horses of the deceased lady were let loose to

graze freely . . . on the mountain where the sepulchre was situated. They had also posted about that sepulchre a number of maidens and eunuchs . . . leaving for them provisions to last five years so that after that period when their food got exhausted, they might likewise die there.[3]

Chinese emperors believed they ruled with the mandate of heaven. The manner in which the lightning struck and the severity of the fire that followed could hardly have been more ominous for Zhu Di. An event of this terrible nature could only signal the gods' demand for a change of emperor. Zhu Di temporarily handed power to his son, Zhu Gaozhi. 'The illness of the Emperor having increased, his son used to come and sit in the audience hall.'[4] Struggling to comprehend the nature of the calamity that had befallen him, the emperor then issued an edict to his people:

> My heart is full of trepidation, I do not know how to handle it. It seems that there has been some laxness in the rituals of honouring heaven and serving the spirits. Perhaps there has been some trans-gression of the ancestral law or some perversion of government affairs. Perhaps mean men hold rank while good men flee and hide themselves, and the good and evil are not distinguished. Perhaps punishments and jailings have been excessive and unjustly applied to the innocent, and the straight and the crooked not discriminated . . . Is this what brought about [the fire]? Harshness to the people below and above, going against heaven. I cannot find the reason in my con-fusion . . . If our actions have in fact been improper, you should lay these out one by one, hiding nothing, so that we may try to reform ourselves and regain the favour of heaven.[5]

The edict unleashed a predictable storm of criticism from the mandarins. Most of it was targeted on Zhu Di's grandiose plans and projects, notably the Forbidden City that the gods had destroyed. Vast areas had been denuded of trees to build the enormous halls, tens of thousands of artisans had laboured for years on the fabulous rooms, huge sums had been invested in marble and jade, the Grand Canal had been rebuilt using a million teaspoons to ferry grain, and the treasury drained to such an extent that peasants had even been reduced to eating grass. And all this toil, suffering and sacrifice had led only to a carpet of ashes and cinders. The fires also coincided with a terrible epidemic of some unknown disease that had been raging in the south for two years. More than 174,000 people had died in the province of Fujian alone and their bodies lay rotting in the fields, for there was no-one to bury them. The epidemic seemed yet another sign of the gods' anger.

The mandarin Minister of Revenue, Xia Yuanji, who had managed to find the funds for the Forbidden City and for Zheng He's great armada, bravely stepped forward to accept personal responsibility for the catastrophe, but to no avail. Frantic efforts were made to pacify the people. Twenty-six high-ranking mandarin court officials were sent on 'calming and soothing' missions[6] and, in an attempt to save his throne, Zhu Di issued a series of ill-conceived decrees. A halt was placed on future voyages of the treasure fleets and foreign travel was prohibited.

Zhu Di had been plagued by other indignities and misfortunes. He had suffered a series of strokes during the previous four years and was being treated with an elixir containing arsenic and mercury that was probably poisoning him. Shortly before the great fire, he had also been thrown from his charger, Tamerlane's former steed and a present from one of the Mongol conqueror's sons, King Shah Rukh of Persia. Zhu Di was so furious that he was determined to put Shah Rukh's ambassador to death.

Thereafter the Qazi, coming forward, said to the ambassadors: 'Dismount and when the Emperor arrives prostrate yourselves on the ground!' They did so.

When the Emperor came near he asked them to mount again. The ambassadors mounted and proceeded along with him. The Emperor began to make complaint saying to Shadi Khwaja: 'I mounted for chase one of the horses which you brought me, and it being extremely old and feeble fell down throwing me off. Ever since that day my hand is giving me pain and has become black and blue. It is only by applying gold a good deal that the pain has abated a little.'[7]

A mandarin replied on behalf of the Persians:

The ambassadors are in no way to blame, for if their sovereign had sent good horses or bad as presents, those persons had no choice in the matter . . . Moreover, even if your Majesty has the envoys cut in pieces it shall make no difference to their sovereign. On the other hand . . . the whole world would say that the Emperor of China had acted contrary to all convention by imprisoning the envoys.[8]

Slurs on Zhu Di's manhood were even more humiliating. He had fathered no children after 1404, and had probably been impotent since the Empress Xiu's death in 1407. Two imperial concubines had been found trying to assuage their sexual frustration by attempting intercourse with one of the eunuchs who guarded them. In the subsequent witch hunt, 2,800 concubines and eunuchs were alleged to have been involved in treasonable activity; Zhu Di personally executed many of them, but before they died a number of Korean concubines flung insults at him, taunting him for his impotence: 'You have lost your yang power and that is why your concubines resorted to a relationship with a young eunuch.'[9]

Apparently abandoned by heaven, the humiliated, ill and distraught old emperor also faced mounting political problems. The construction of the Forbidden City, the Grand Canal, the fleet of treasure ships and the repair of hundreds of miles of the Great Wall had placed enormous strains on China's economy, and the felling of the vast hardwood forests had provoked rebellions in Annam and Vietnam. The first rebellion, in 1407, was led by Le Qui Ly, a former minister of the Vietnamese court who usurped the throne and introduced reforms that won him wide support. Taxation was simplified, ports were opened to foreigners and trade boomed. Restrictions were placed on the acquisition of land by the wealthy at the expense of peasants, a system of health care was introduced, and the army and civil service were reorganized; ability was henceforth to be the key word. His ultimate aim was to end his country's subjugation by China. Vietnam would no longer be a colony, but a proud and united sovereign nation. Zhu Di had sent an army southwards to crush the rebellion, depose Le Qui Ly and begin the systematic obliteration of Vietnamese national identity. Native literature was burnt and works of art destroyed. Chinese classics became required reading in schools and Chinese dress and hairstyle were imposed on Vietnamese women. Local religious rites were outlawed and private fortunes confiscated, while the pillage of the forests continued.

Another uprising began in 1418, this time led by an aristocratic landowner, Le L'oi, the founder of the dynasty that was to rule Vietnam for 360 years. Although twice defeated by the Chinese armies, each time he managed to escape to the jungle and continue the war. Despite a massive commitment of combat troops, the Chinese could neither find Le L'oi nor suppress his guerrilla army.

Insurrection spread throughout Annam and Vietnam; the entire coastal region south of the Red River delta (near modern Hanoi) was in revolt. Enormous numbers of Chinese troops were now tied down in the jungle at vast cost to the treasury and Chinese pride. The rebellion was a serious political and military problem, but it was one that a fit, powerful emperor such as Zhu Di in his prime would have solved with ruthless efficiency.

Weighed down by his domestic troubles, he failed to suppress the revolt; Le L'oi then inflicted on the Chinese armies the first serious defeat the Ming dynasty had ever experienced. It was another shattering blow to the morale of the Chinese and their emperor, and though Le L'oi did not secure his country's formal independence until 1428, Zhu Di had effectively abandoned Vietnam by July 1421.

The demoralized old emperor had also lost control of his cabinet, and of China itself. There had always been an inherent contradiction at the heart of Zhu Di's government: it was effectively two separate administrations – a mandarin cabinet in charge of finance, economics, home affairs and law and order, and the eunuchs, who led the armed forces and executed Zhu Di's foreign policy. At the peak of his powers, Zhu Di had tolerated his mandarin critics, allowing them to influence his favourite son and successor, Zhu Gaozhi. Deep down the mandarins loathed Zhu Di's grandiose plans, his foreign policy, and the bleak northern location of the Forbidden City. They seized the opportunity offered by his illness and waning powers and looked to the crown prince, Zhu Gaozhi, to reverse his father's policies.

A diplomatic crisis accelerated the disintegration of Zhu Di's government. Sensing the emperor's weakness after the fire in the Forbidden City, the Mongol leader Arughtai refused to pay the tribute demanded by China. Zhu Di saw a heaven-sent opportunity to reassert his authority; the emperor himself would lead an army to bring Arughtai to heel. As a young man, Zhu Di had relied on the speed of his cavalry to outwit and outmanoeuvre the Mongol army. Now, he and his eunuch generals assembled an enormous, ponderous force of almost a million men and 340,000 horses and mules and plodded northwards into the steppe. Some 177,500 carts were needed just to transport the grain to feed this vast army. The mandarin Minister of Revenue, Xia Yuanji, the financial genius who had raised the funds for the Forbidden City, for widening the Grand Canal, for the fleet of grain barges and for Zheng He's armada, baldly stated he could not find the money for this latest imperial adventure. The Minister of Justice, Wu Zhong, also objected. Zhu Di had both ministers arrested. Fang Bin, Minister of War, then committed suicide. By the end of that terrible year, Zhu Di had lost his most able, loyal and long-serving ministers and his cabinet had disintegrated.

As his ministers had feared, Zhu Di's expedition was a fiasco. Arughtai simply disappeared into the vastness of the steppe. On 12 August 1424, while still pursuing Arughtai, Zhu Di, a broken man, died at the age of sixty-four. Some of the army's pots and pans were melted down to make a coffin to carry him back to the burnt remains of the Forbidden City in Beijing, where his body lay in state for one hundred days.

Zhu Di's funeral had the same epic quality as his life. The procession was led by the old emperor's honour guard. Ten thousand soldiers and officials surrounded the cortège as it slowly zigzagged on its two-day march to the magnificent imperial mausoleum at Chang Ling in the foothills north-west of Beijing. There, in hazy autumn sunshine, they marched down an avenue lined with stone animals to lay the emperor's body in his magnificent tomb. Animals were sacrificed to his ancestral gods and then his cloak of imperial yellow and military decorations were laid beside him. Sixteen concubines were buried alive with Zhu Di. The complex was sealed as the cries of the doomed women marked the end of the mortal life of one of the greatest visionaries and gamblers in history.

On 7 September 1424, Zhu Di's son, Zhu Gaozhi, ascended the throne. That very day he issued an edict:

> All voyages of the treasure ships are to be stopped. All ships moored at Taicang [a Yangtze port] are ordered back to Nanjing and all goods on the ships are to be turned over to the Department

of Internal Affairs and stored. If there are any foreign envoys wishing to return home, they will be provided with a small escort. Those officials who are currently abroad on business are ordered back to the capital immediately ... and all those who have been called to go on future voyages are ordered back to their homes.

The building and repair of all treasure ships is to be stopped immediately. Harvesting *tieli mu* [hardwood for shipbuilding] is to be conducted in the same way as it was in the time of the Hongwu Emperor [Zhu Di's father]. [Additional harvesting] is to be stopped. All official procurement for expeditions abroad (with the exception of items already delivered at official depots), the making of copper coins, buying of musk, raw copper and raw silk must also be stopped ... All those employed in purchasing should return to the capital.[10]

Zhu Gaozhi also ordered the immediate release of those senior officials who had been imprisoned by his father, including the former finance minister, the mandarin Xia Yuanji. Xia took immediate steps to control inflation, forbidding the mining of gold and silver and stabilizing the amount of non-paper currency in circulation (paper money had been invented by the Chinese in AD 806, centuries before it came into use in Europe). Such was the value of pepper that it had been used as a means of payment by the Chinese. Now, all the pepper in the imperial warehouses was given away, the purchase of all luxury goods banned, the budget deficit slashed and all expenditure on the treasure fleets curtailed. China's territory produced all goods in abundance, so why buy useless trifles from abroad?[11]

The young emperor, fat, studious and religious, had shown no interest in military affairs and had hardly ever accompanied his father on his military expeditions, preferring to remain surrounded by his mandarin advisers. His priorities were in strict accordance with their Confucian values; 'Relieving people's poverty ought to be handled as though one were rescuing them from fire or saving them from drowning. One cannot hesitate.'[12] He saw no need to listen to the eunuchs who, in aiding and abetting his father's expansionary schemes, had brought China to the brink of disaster.

As two of the battered treasure fleets limped home in October 1423 after two and a half years at sea. Zheng He's men had no idea of the dramatic events unfolding at home and must have been expecting a heroes' welcome. Their voyages had been a remarkable success. They had reached countless unknown lands and immeasurably furthered their knowledge of navigation, but instead of plaudits, the returning admirals were spurned by those who now ruled China. Only Zheng He was spared from humiliation; perhaps his prestige was too great to strip him of his rank. The old admiral was pensioned off as an imperial harbour master in Nanjing, but was allowed to keep his sumptuous palace there and to continue building his mosque.

Zhu Gaozhi died in 1425 after only a year as emperor, and was succeeded by his son, Zhu Zhanji, who intensified his father's policies. Social harmony returned, but China had reverted to rule by traditional rural gentry. As long as the irrigation systems were maintained, the farmers were well fed and famine averted, there was little requirement for economic or political change, or the exercise of China's inventive genius. The country's institutions remained as if preserved in amber. Merchants wielded little political power, bankers and soldiers virtually none, and revenue from foreign trade dropped to less than 1 per cent of government income. Zhu Zhanji did allow Admiral Zheng He his swansong – one final voyage to Mecca – but with Zhu Zhanji's death in 1435, complete xenophobia set in. All voyages of the treasure fleets were halted and the first of a stream of imperial edicts banned overseas trade and travel. Any merchant attempting to engage in foreign trade was to be tried as a pirate and executed. For a time, even learning a foreign language or teaching Chinese to foreigners was prohibited.

The embargo on overseas trade was rigidly maintained throughout the next hundred years, and the Qing dynasty that succeeded the last of the Ming emperors in 1644 went even further. To prevent any foreign trade or contact, a strip of land along the southern coast 700 miles long and 30 miles wide was devastated and burnt, and the population moved inland. Not only were the shipyards put out of commission, the plans for building the great treasure ships and the accounts of Zheng He's voyages were deliberately destroyed. The mandarin Liu Daxia, a senior official at the Ministry of War, seized the records from the archives. He declared that 'the expeditions of San Bao (Zheng He) to the Western ocean wasted myriads of money and grain, and moreover the people who met their deaths may be counted in the myriads'. The goods the fleets had brought home – 'betel, bamboo staves, grape-wine, pomegranates and ostrich eggs and such like things' – were useless, and all the records of these expeditions – 'deceitful exaggerations of bizarre things far removed from the testimony of people's eyes and ears' – should therefore be burned. Liu then blandly reported to the Minister of War that the logs and records of Zheng He's expeditions had been 'lost'.[13] Not only was the priceless legacy of the greatest maritime expeditions of all time gone for ever, foreign lands were to be banished from the minds of the Chinese people. Only piracy and smuggling would be left to connect the fallen colossus with the outside world. The colonies established in Africa, Australia, New Zealand and North and South America were abandoned and left to their fate.

By late 1421, China's history was set for centuries to come. The legacy of Zhu Di, Zheng He and their great treasure fleets would be all but obliterated. What oceans they had sailed, what lands they had seen, what discoveries they had made, what settlements they had created were no longer of interest to the Chinese hierarchy. The ships that had made those voyages were left to rot and were never replaced. The logs and records

were destroyed and the memory of them expunged so completely over the succeeding decades that they might never have
existed. As China turned its back on its glorious maritime and
scientific heritage and retreated into a long, self-imposed
isolation from the outside world, other nations took up the torch.
But all their explorers, colonizers and discoverers voyaged in the
long shadows cast by Zhu Di's fleets.

3

THE

FLEETS

SET

SAIL

U NAWARE OF THE UPHEAVAL THAT WAS ABOUT TO OVER-
take China, the great armada sailed majestically south
across the Yellow Sea, beginning a journey that would
take them to the ends of the earth. Early on the first morning of
the voyage, 5 March 1421, the helmsmen kept the Pole Star,
Polaris, dead astern while the navigators measured the star's
altitude with their sextants. After taking their first readings, the
navigators held their course due south for exactly twenty-four
hours, then took another measurement of Polaris. By sailing due
south, at the end of their first day at sea not only were they able
to determine their change in latitude – their distance south of the
North Pole – but could also adjust their compasses for magnetic
variation, measure their speed and the distance covered, and
calibrate their logs.

The methods of navigation employed by Zhu Di's admirals
are revealed by one of the few documents of the era to have
survived, the *Wu Pei Chi*. These Chinese sailing instructions,
essentially a manual of the arts of seamanship and naval warfare,
somehow escaped the purges of the mandarins.[1] There were
instructions, inscribed on a long, thin strip of paper, for each regular voyage they made, giving detailed directions including star
positions, latitudes, bearings and the physical description of
islands, prominent headlands, bays and inlets that would be
clearly visible along the route. By studying these sailing
directions, it is possible to deduce not only the course the Chinese
had steered but the accuracy of their navigation and their ability
to set a course by the stars. It is an invaluable document.

The Pole Star was of great importance to the Chinese, both
symbolically and for navigation. It was the fundamental basis of
Chinese astronomy, for the celestial pole was regarded as the
heavenly equivalent of the position of the emperor on earth. As
mandarins, courtiers and servants circled around the emperor, so
the other stars rotated around the Pole Star; as the clothes of the
servants and their proximity to the emperor signified their

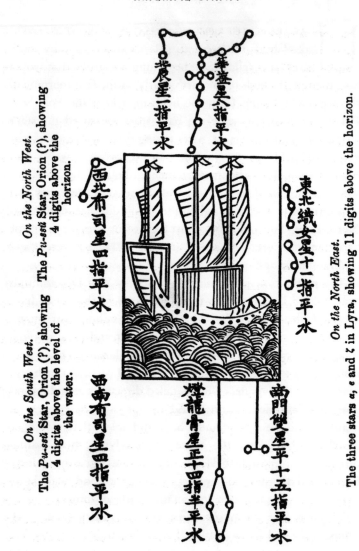

紫辰星一指平水

華蓋星八指平水

西北布司星四指平水

東北織女星十一指平水

西南布司星四指平水

燈籠骨星正十四指半平水

南門雙星平十五指半平水

On the North West.
The *Pu-ssŭ* Star, Orion (?), showing 4 digits above the horizon.

On the North East.
The three stars α, ε and ζ in Lyra, showing 11 digits above the horizon.

On the South West.
The *Pu-ssŭ* Star, Orion (?), showing 4 digits above the level of the water.

On the South.

Navigational diagram used by Zheng He for the Sri Lanka–Sumatra run and reproduced in the *Wu Pei Chi*, 1628.

importance, so did the brightness, colour and positioning of the stars that were 'tied' to the Pole Star. 'There is high Confucian authority. The master says, "He who exercises government by means of his virtue may be compared to the Pole Star which keeps its place while all the stars turn around it." '[2]

Western methods of astronomy embodied the principles first enunciated by Greek astronomers such as Aristotle and Ptolemy, basing latitude on the equator. In Chinese astronomy, latitude was determined not by the distance north of the equator but by the distance from the North Pole, which was determined by the altitude of the Pole Star, Polaris. A bright and easily identifiable star, Polaris sits directly above the North Pole, billions of miles out in space. When viewed from the North Pole it is directly above the observer at 90° altitude or 90° latitude; at the equator it sits on the horizon at 0° altitude or 0° latitude. Measuring its height above the horizon (altitude) enables the navigator to calculate his latitude. Moreover, since Polaris is due north it enables magnetic variation – the difference between due north and the magnetic north of a compass – to be determined and adjustments made.

By 1421, the Chinese had well over six centuries' experience of ocean navigation, basing their calculations on both the Pole Star and the stars circling the pole at high altitudes which never rise and never set. In effect, once the Chinese had determined the absolute position of Polaris in the celestial sphere, they 'tied' other stars in the northern hemisphere to it. When viewing one star or constellation, they knew exactly where the others were in relation to it, even when they had not yet risen in the night sky. They were thus in a position to know a star's exact location, even when invisible below the horizon, by observing the meridian passage – the highest point of their track across the night sky viewed from any particular point – of the circumpolar stars to which it was 'tied'. However, the Chinese had not yet mastered using the sun to obtain latitude,[3] something the Portuguese first achieved in 1474 and which enabled them to measure latitude in the southern as well as the northern hemisphere. The Chinese could not determine their latitude south of the equator, where Polaris was invisible. It was a problem that had to be solved. A star or stars in the southern hemisphere that could fulfil the function of Polaris in the northern had to be identified before Zhu Di's dream of charting the whole world could be realized.

By the seventh century, the Chinese could accurately determine the course to steer, for they had discovered the compass. They knew that the magnetic properties of lodestone could be transferred by induction to iron, and that this magnetized iron could be floated on oil, allowing it to swivel freely, one end pointing always to the earth's magnetic south. In 1421 the Chinese could steer to within two degrees of their chosen course using reliable magnetic compasses. They could also measure the distance travelled using hour-glasses of sand. A day was divided into ten parts, each hour-glass equalling 2.4 hours, the length of one watch for the seamen on duty.

The calculation of longitude, however, remained a problem they had not fully resolved at the start of this sixth voyage. Changes in longitude depend on four things: the course steered, the speed of the ship, the time that has elapsed and the distance north or south of the equator. By recording the number of watches, the speed through the water and the compass course, the navigator could estimate his change in longitude. But there was one great disadvantage to the Chinese method of navigation: if the body of water over which the ship was sailing was itself moving – for example, when a current was moving with or against the ship – the mariner had no way of measuring his change of longitude. This could only be achieved by measuring absolute time, something Europeans were not to achieve for another three and a half centuries, when John Harrison finally perfected a clock that could keep precise time at sea. At the start of the sixth voyage, this defect caused huge errors in Chinese calculations of longitude. Polaris navigation enabled them to calculate latitude and make landfalls north of the equator with astonishing accuracy, but a method of calculating longitude with anything approaching the same accuracy was not perfected until near the end of their voyages.

With centuries of experience in building ships to sail storm-tossed oceans, the Chinese marine engineers had evolved a robust frame built in sections. Each section was contained by watertight bulkheads at either end, resembling the internal partitions of a bamboo, and the watertight sections were bolted together with brass pins weighing several kilograms. Three layers of hardwood were nailed to a teak frame, then the planks were caulked (made waterproof) with coir (coconut fibre) and sealed with a mixture of boiled tung oil and lime. This hard, waterproof lacquer had been used to seal Chinese ocean-going ships since the seventh century, but so much tung oil was required to build Zheng He's treasure fleets that acres of land along the Yangtze banks were acquired to plant orchards of tung trees.

Marine engineers at the Longjiang shipyards designed their ships to survive the fiercest storms on the open ocean. Reinforced bows enabled the vessel to smash through the waves, and at either side of the bow were channels leading to internal compartments. As the square bow pitched in heavy seas, water was funnelled in; as the bow surfaced above the waves, the water drained out, modifying the pitching motion. A teak keel bound together by iron hoops ran the length of the ship, and specially cut, large rectangular stones – or composite stone and mud balls – were packed around it for ballast. Additional keels that could be raised and lowered were fitted at either side for more stability. In a storm, semi-submersible sea anchors could also be thrown overboard to reduce rolling. Even in the roughest weather and sea conditions, pitching and rolling were greatly reduced by these ingenious modifications.

The giant ships could survive typhoons and the sectional construction reduced the risk of sinking through a collision with a reef or an iceberg. They were designed to remain afloat even if two compartments were flooded after being punctured by coral or ice. To increase cargo capacity, the hulls of the junks were very wide compared with their length and they were flat-bottomed. Their sails were balanced lugs, four-sided sails hanging from a yardarm set at an oblique angle – the characteristic sail of China. They were stiffened by a series of bamboo battens, so the design was extremely efficient when sailing before the wind. It also allowed the sails to be reefed, or lowered, quickly in an emergency.

The most reliable ships in the world in the fourteenth and early fifteenth century, and by far the biggest, were these Chinese junks. Ibn Battuta, the Moroccan traveller and writer who journeyed through Asia in the fourteenth century, wrote that the trade of the whole world between the Malabar coast of India and China was carried in Chinese ships. Centuries later, in 1848, a junk built to the designs of that era was sailed from China via New York to London by a party of British naval officers. They sailed before the wind all the way and the junk handled beautifully. But magnificent though these ships were, they had been designed to operate primarily between China and Africa, sailing before the monsoon winds (which changed direction twice yearly), as they had for centuries. Although a lug-sail is also quite efficient when sailing into the wind, the combination of the hull shape and sail design meant that the Chinese monsters were crab-like and inefficient when attempting to do so. They had to wear rather than tack, and for all practical purposes were constrained to sail before the wind – a severe limitation when outside the monsoon belt of the Indian Ocean and South China Sea. It was to be one of the crucial clues when it came to tracking the course of the Chinese fleets during the great voyages of 1421 to 1423.

The eunuch captains and admirals of these great treasure ships were men of awesome ability but, like the European explorers who followed them, they often drew their crews from the lowest levels of society. Most were criminals, sent to sea in lieu of imprisonment or internal exile, and in some respects life as a crewman was far better than a prison sentence. They were provided with a uniform – a knee-length white robe – food and wine, and were well cared for when at sea. The admiral's staff included 180 medical officers, and every ship and company of soldiers had a medical officer for every 150 men. There was a varied and plentiful diet on the treasure ships, but the perils of voyaging through uncharted waters meant that life expectancy was short: only one in ten returned from the great voyages of exploration and discovery. But those who had survived the earlier voyages of the treasure fleets had been well rewarded. They were often freed and given endowments or pensions.

Like all sailors, the Chinese were superstitious. Each of Zheng He's ships had a small cabin dedicated to Ma Tsu, the mariners' deity, and prayers were said to her every evening before supper. When the crew went ashore in foreign lands, they carried round bronze mirrors to ward off evil spirits; on the reverse was the eight-spoked Taoist wheel.

The elite of the crew were the navigators and 'compass-men', operating from an enclosed small bridge and living and dining separately from the rest of the men. The junks also carried artisans and craftsmen of every description, capable of performing any task. Caulkers, sailmakers, anchor- and pump-repairers, scaffolders, carpenters and tung oil painters would keep the ships in good repair on their long voyage into the distant oceans. Their work in the Forbidden City complete, stone-carvers and stone masons were also embarked to leave permanent legacies of the fleets' voyages across the world. There was even a historian, Ma Huan, to document the voyage. His diaries, *The Overall Survey of the Ocean Shores*, were published in 1433, after Zheng He's final voyage.

The staple foods – soya beans, wheat, millet and rice – were carried in separate grain ships, enabling a fleet to stay at sea for several months without replenishing supplies, but if the grain ships sank, the whole fleet was in desperate trouble. Soya beans, grown in tubs all year round, were used in several ways. Soaked in water, they sprouted 'yellow curls' from the green bean. The sprouting process increased the content of ascorbic acid, riboflavin and nicotinic acid, the basis of vitamin C, and protected the crew from the deficiency disease scurvy. The Chinese knew well the dangers of scurvy and the remedies to prevent it. Enough citrus fruit – limes, lemons, oranges, pomelos and coconuts – was taken aboard to give every man protection against the disease for three months. Pomelos – a grapefruit-like fruit, also known as a shaddock – had been particularly valued ever since the Warring States period from the fifth to second centuries BC. 'The candid and ingenious prince should know . . . the State of Chu must necessarily gain wealth from its groves of orange and pomelo trees.'[4]

Some of the rice was brown, not polished, and the husks contained vitamin B1. As a result, beri-beri – a disease causing degeneration of the nervous system – was rare among the crew. Fresh vegetables mainly comprised cabbages, turnips and bamboo shoots. When they ran out, the sprouting soya beans were particularly valuable. Soya beans also produced 'milk'. When boiled, it became curd, or tofu, rich in vitamin D, while fermentation of soya produced soy sauce. Tofu and vegetables were flavoured with a sauce made from fermented fish, soy, dried herbs and spices, or glutamate made by chewing wheat flour. The grains were chewed, spat out into a container and left to ferment. The method is still used in South America today. Noodles, pasta and dumplings were also made from wheat flour. Sugar cane was used to sweeten dried fruit and was also chewed raw by the crew.

Fruits and vegetables were preserved in ingenious ways. Fruit was dried or caramelized, pears, bamboo shoots and grapes were buried in sand, and vegetables were salted, pickled and marinated in vinegar and sugar.[5] Meat was limited, for the most part comprising Chinese pigs, dogs bred for the purpose and frogs kept in tubs. Chickens were kept for divination and were never eaten on board, but fresh, salted, dried and fermented fish were plentiful. They were caught by the trained otters, working in pairs to herd shoals into the nets, and by an array of hooks and nets. The crew drank green oolong and red tea, carried in both leaf and cake form, and rice wine (*jiu*) was hugely popular. 'In the sixth month [August] we gather wild plums and berries; in the seventh we boil marrows and beans; in the eighth we dry the dates; in the tenth we take the rice to make with it the spring wine so that we may be granted long life.'[6]

Wine was also distilled into liqueurs, brandy and vinegar. The junks required huge quantities of fresh water for crew and horses and replenished their tanks whenever an opportunity arose, but they also knew how to distil it from sea-water, using paraffin wax or seal blubber for fuel. Their capacity to desalinate sea-water and the fresh vegetables they carried gave them the ability to cross the broadest oceans. The overall diet was infinitely more varied and nutritious than that provided for Magellan the best part of a century later – 'We ate only old biscuits turned to powder, all full of worms and stinking of the urine the rats had made on it.'[7] On the junks, rats were hunted by the sailors' little ship-dogs. Arsenic was used to kill bugs and insects and to promote the growth of plants.

The concubines for the treasure fleets were recruited from the floating brothels of Canton.[8] They belonged to an ethnic group called the 'Tanka', descendants of people who had emigrated from the remote interior of China to the coast to engage in pearl fishing. They spoke a peculiar dialect and differed from Chinese women by refusing to have their feet bound. They were prohibited from going ashore at any ports of call and from marrying

Chinese men. They attended the sumptuous banquets aboard the treasure ships and were taught how to hold their drink; they consumed huge amounts. They were well educated and, as well as satisfying the sexual demands of the ambassadors and envoys, were expected to play cards and chess, to act in plays and to sing and dance. Most of them were Buddhists, a creed they adopted because of its teaching of universal love, compassion and equality of all beings, man and woman, emperor or prostitute.

Concubines were not viewed with contempt because of their profession; they were regarded as a long-established, legitimate and necessary part of society. Indeed, sex was viewed as a sanctified act. 'Of all the ten thousand things created by heaven, man is the most precious. Of all things that make man prosper, none can be compared to sexual intercourse. It is modelled after heaven.'[9] All men were free to have concubines, and 'class or fortune mean nothing in the selection as the only standard of preference is physical beauty'.[10] The Chinese invariably invited rulers back to Beijing, and foreign envoys could dwell in heaven from the time they left their home country until they returned, often a year or more later. Little wonder that they accepted invitations to Beijing with such alacrity.

Sex aids and aphrodisiacs were available to concubines and their guests. The most popular aphrodisiac was a pair of red lizards caught while copulating and drowned alive in a jar of wine. The wine was left for a year before being sold. There were also 'the genitals of a lewd animal, the beaver, with the drug so obtained to anoint the penis', and 'bald chicken potion'[11] was very popular. The name derived from a prefect of Shu who started drinking the elixir when he was seventy. His wife was so exhausted by his subsequent virility that 'she could neither sit nor lie down', and insisted that her husband throw the potion away. A cockerel then ate it, jumped on a hen and 'continued copulating several days without interruption, pecking the hen's head until it was completely bald'.[12]

The 'classic' concubine's bed was decorated with symbolic fruit. Bedspreads were embroidered with patterns of blossoming plum branches – the plum denoted sexual pleasure and fulfilment. The peach represented women's genitalia, and pomegranates represented the vulva. When envoys boarded treasure ships they frequently gave pomegranates as gifts. By day, concubines wore pantaloons, wide trousers; they usually made love wearing the *mo xiong*, a red brassière and silk stockings. Envoys and concubines were expected to wash their private parts before and after intercourse. A male contraceptive, a condom called *yin jia*, was available, and agar-agar jelly acted as a lubricant and mild disinfectant; venereal disease in the era of the treasure ships was rare, though it was to spread like wildfire in the late Ming period.

For the courtesan, the voyages offered an opportunity to attain the ultimate aim: to be freed to join a man who loved her. An envoy would request that a particular favoured concubine be disembarked with him at his home port, and she would remain with him as the fleet sailed on. Aboard she was respected and protected. If she failed to attain her dream and became too old to attract men, she was given the job of instructing the younger women in dancing and singing. By the time the foreign envoys left the treasure ships, some of the courtesans would undoubtedly have been pregnant. What happened to their children will become an interesting part of our story as more and more DNA analysis results come in. The concubines also assumed other duties – cooking, weaving and sewing silk, making hemp ropes and looking after the tubs of beans and coops of chickens. The eunuchs clearly had no use for the concubines and crewmen would have been executed for even approaching their quarters.

As the armada continued south on the first stage of the great voyage, the power to drive its huge ships was provided by the massive energy of the monsoon winds. Monsoons had always determined sailing patterns from China through the Indian Ocean to India and Africa. Ports such as Malacca (modern Melaka in Malaysia) developed where goods could be stored between the monsoons, the south-west in July and the north-east starting in January. Chinese ships took advantage of the north-east monsoon to sail before the wind to India, returning home on the next monsoon. The south-west monsoon reaches India in July, several weeks before it breaks over the coast of China. Ships from India sailing before the north-east monsoon winds arrived in Malacca before the junks from China had even set sail, and had unloaded and sailed for home by the time the junks arrived in Malacca.

According to Ma Huan, Zheng He's fleet arrived in Malacca six weeks after leaving Beijing. First established by the Chinese as a port where spices from the Moluccas – the Spice Islands (the modern Maluku Islands of Indonesia) – could be collected, Malacca soon expanded into a distribution centre for Chinese porcelain and Indian textiles, and grew to become one of the principal hubs of Indian Ocean trade. Halfway between India and China and 120 miles up the west coast of Malaysia from modern Singapore, Malacca lies on a strait through which sailing vessels must pass and has a sheltered location protected from storms by a ring of islands. There were rich tin mines in the surrounding area, a freshwater river bisected the town and the abundant water and teak from the surrounding forests made Malacca an ideal port. The trade in spices remained of paramount importance, offering merchants and traders the chance to amass vast fortunes. The attempt to exploit and control this vastly lucrative spice trade was later to be one of the principal engines driving the European voyages of discovery.

The Chinese set up a series of trading ports such as Malacca and Calicut on the south-west coast of India throughout southeast Asia and around the Indian Ocean. They were used as forward bases by Zheng He's fleets, providing fresh provisions,

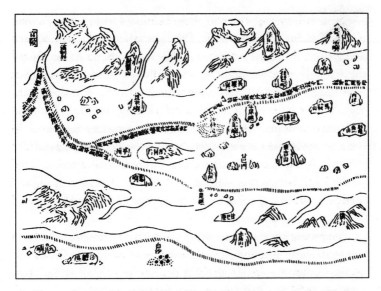

Chart of the Straits of Malacca from the Mao Kun map in the *Wu Pei Chi*. Malacca is in the top left-hand corner and Sumatra runs along the bottom.

water and wood all the way from China to East Africa. They were an essential prerequisite for Zhu Di's plan to bring the entire world into China's tribute system. In 1421, trade throughout the Indian Ocean was dominated by the Chinese and Arabs from Egypt and the Gulf States; relations between them were friendly. Like the rest of the known world, the Arabs craved Chinese porcelain and silk, and Chinese junks were almost always welcomed in Arab ports.

A report came from Mecca, the honoured, that a number of junks had come from China to the sea ports of India and two of them had anchored in the port of Aden, but their goods, chinaware, silk, musk and the like, were not disposed of there because of the disorders of the State of Yemen ... The Sultan wrote to them to let them come to Jeddah and to show them honour.[13]

Chinese and Arabs met in equal numbers at the great Indian port of Calicut. Hormuz in the Persian Gulf and Malindi, Kilwa and Zanzibar in East Africa were Arab ports used extensively by the Chinese, but Malacca was virtually a Chinese colony and epitomized the Chinese forward base.

> Formerly this place [Malacca] was not designated a 'country' ... There was no king of the country; it was controlled only by a chief. This territory was subordinate to the jurisdiction of Hsien Lo [Thailand]; it paid an annual tribute of forty Liang of gold [approx. 48 troy ounces]; if it were not [to pay] then Hsien Lo would send men to attack it.
>
> In the seventh year of the Yung Lo [1409] the Emperor ordered the principal envoy the grand eunuch Cheng Ho [Zheng He] and others to assume command and to take the imperial edicts and to bestow upon the chief two strong seals, a hat, a girdle and a robe ... Thereafter Hsien Lo did not dare to invade it (Ma Huan, 1424).[14]

In effect, this was the birth of Malaysia.

The diaries of Ma Huan also give a vivid picture of south-east Asia – the crocodiles that inhabit the mangrove swamps, rubber being tapped, the tin mines and coconut plantations.

> The coconut has ten different uses. The young tree has a syrup, very sweet and good to drink; it can be made into wine by fermentation. The old coconut has flesh, from which they express oil, and make sugar, and make a food stuff for eating. From the fibre which envelops the outside they make ropes for shipbuilding. The shell of the coconut makes bowls and cups; it is also good for burning to ash for the delicate operation of inlaying gold or silver. The trees are good for building houses, and the leaves are good for roofing houses.[15]

Ma Huan also described the procedures followed by the Chinese fleets when in port:

> When Malacca is visited by Chinese merchant vessels, [the inhabitants] erect a barrier [for the collection of duties]. There are four gates in the city wall, each furnished with watch and drum towers. At night men with hand bells patrol the precincts. Inside the walls, a second small enclosure of palisades has been built where godowns [warehouses] have been constructed for the storage of specie and provisions. When the government ships [Zheng He's fleet] were returning homewards, they visited this place in order both to repair their vessels and to load local products. Here they waited for a favourable wind from the south and in the middle of the fifth month [June] they put to sea on their return voyage.[16]

As well as trade, the Chinese were also greatly intrigued by the erotic Thai and Malaccan women. 'The mental capacity of the wives far exceeds that of their husbands. Should it happen that one of their wives is on terms of great intimacy with one of our countrymen, and allows him to feast and carouse with her, her husband looks calmly on and is not angry, but simply remarks: "My wife is beautiful and the Chinaman is delighted with her."'[17] Malaccan men went to considerable lengths to give pleasure to their women. Chinese-made tin or hollow gold beads assisted them, a custom still practised in some parts of south-east Asia today.

> When a man has attained his twentieth year, they take the skin which surrounds the penis (*membrum virile*), and with a fine knife shaped like an onion they open it up and insert a dozen tin beads inside the skin . . . [The beads] look like a cluster of grapes. The King and the great chiefs or the rich people use hollow beads of gold in which is placed a grain of sand. After these have been

inserted, when they walk there is a tinkling sound which is considered beautiful. Men who have no beads inserted [in the manner described] are people of the lower class.[18]

All manner of peoples visited Malacca – Thais, Bengalis, Gujaratis, Parsees, Arabs and many others conversed in eighty-four languages – and all returned home with Chinese goods. Boats that brought spices from the Spice Islands of Ternate and Tidore in the Moluccas returned with Chinese porcelain. Arab dhows sailed north-west for India, the Gulf, Egypt and Venice laden with silk, supplemented with batiks and tin from Malacca and Java. After the Chinese junks had unloaded their silk and porcelain, they refilled their holds with spice, Indian gems and Venetian glass.

> [The Chinese] go about the country, scales in hand, buying up all the pepper they find, and after weighing a small amount so that they can judge approximately the quantity, they offer the payment for it in a lump sum, depending on the need for money of those who are selling it, and in this way they amass such a quantity they can fill the ships from China when they arrive, selling fifty thousand caixas' [a Portuguese trading currency] worth, which has cost them no more than twelve thousand.[19]

Throughout the archipelago and the whole of south-east Asia, trade was focused on Malacca and dominated by the Chinese. China consumed a hundred times more spice than distant Europe, and the Chinese merchants not only controlled commodity and currency markets but property prices too, even amusement and gambling. For ten months on end there was a Chinese fair where merchants gambled. 'As their merchandise is sold, they occupy less room and rent fewer houses. As sales fall, the gaming increases'.[20] Malacca was used as a forward base on each of Admiral Zheng He's voyages, and the importance he attached to the port is demonstrated by the temple he established there. It still stands in the road that bears his name, a few yards east of the Malacca River. According to legend, his flagship was once holed on a reef but its triple hull and watertight compartments enabled him to reach Malacca without sinking.

Zheng He's expeditions had become progressively more adventurous. His first, between 1405 and 1407, had sailed in sixty-two treasure ships manned by 27,800 men. En route for Malacca, they visited Cambodia and Java, then sailed on the next south-west monsoon for Sri Lanka and Calicut on the west coast of India. An incident on this voyage cemented a belief among the sailors that Zheng He's fleet was under divine protection. In the midst of a storm so ferocious that the sailors were praying to Ma Tsu to save them from death, a 'divine light' – presumably St Elmo's Fire, a luminous electrical discharge sometimes seen during a storm at sea – appeared at the tips of the masts of Zheng He's flagship. 'As soon as this miraculous light appeared, the danger was appeased.'[21]

By the time of the third expedition, 1409 to 1411, Zheng He had established a settled programme. The fleet used Malacca as its forward base and there divided into squadrons that sailed on independently to separate destinations. The next great fleet set sail from China in 1413. One squadron departed from Malacca for Bengal, the Maldives and Africa; another sailed for the Arabian Sea and up the Persian Gulf to Hormuz. The fleets of the following expedition, 1417 to 1419, visited every major trading port in Africa, Arabia, India and Asia, then brought back the rulers and ambassadors travelling to Beijing for the inauguration of the Forbidden City. They were to spend almost two years enjoying the lavish hospitality of the emperor before the inauguration of his capital. Now, another fleet led by Admiral Yang Qing had been sent on ahead of the main armada. After returning rulers and ambassadors to the Gulf states, his daunting task was to solve the problem of determining longitude.

The rest of Zheng He's armada was embarked on the greatest voyage of them all. After provisioning in Malacca, they sailed northwards for five days before anchoring off Semudera (modern Sumatra) at the entrance to the Indian Ocean. There, the admiral divided his armada into four fleets. Each carried an army equipped with gunpowder weapons. Three of these great fleets were placed under the command of Grand Eunuch Hong Bao, Eunuch Zhou Man and Admiral Zhou Wen.[22] The fourth, by far the smallest fleet, remained under Zheng He's direct command. He was the emperor's right-hand man and could not be spared for the entire duration of the voyage. He would return envoys to south-east Asia and then sail for home, arriving in November 1421.

We know from an account by the widely travelled Portuguese poet Camões (1524–1580) that by the time the Chinese fleets reached Calicut so many foreign merchant ships had joined the convoy that it comprised over eight hundred sail. Assuming that Zheng He would have taken only a handful of ships with him for a brief and relatively easy passage home, it is safe to estimate that each of the remaining Chinese fleets numbered nearly two hundred ships – the largest armada the world had ever known. Zheng He delegated powers of life and death to his admirals, and command was further delegated within each fleet: two brigadiers and ninety-three captains commanded regiments, and 104 lieutenants and 103 sub-lieutenants reported to them. The first task of the fleets was to return the rulers, ambassadors and envoys to their home ports in India, Arabia and East Africa. They were then to rendezvous off the southern coast of Africa and set sail into uncharted waters to fulfil Zhu Di's vision. They knew exactly what was expected of them. They would proceed all the way to the end of the earth to collect tribute from the barbarians beyond the seas or they would die in the attempt.

II

The Guiding Stars

4

ROUNDING

THE

CAPE

IN ORDER TO TRACE THE STORY TO THIS POINT, I HAD HAD TO learn the history of medieval China almost from scratch; my previous knowledge of Chinese history and culture had been modest at best. However, as I began to trace the voyages of the great treasure fleets in the 'missing years' from 1421 to 1423, I was entering familiar territory, making use of knowledge and skills I had acquired over many years' experience as a navigator and commanding officer on the high seas. During that sixth voyage, the fleets of Hong Bao, Zhou Man, Zhou Wen and Yang Qing sailed the oceans for as many as five years, but the mandarin official at the Ministry of War, Liu Daxia, had ordered the destruction of all written records and there was virtually no evidence to show where they had sailed or what discoveries they had made. But where before I had been plodding in the footsteps of academics and historians far more knowledgeable and gifted than myself, I could now use my skills to decipher the fragmentary evidence offered by ancient maps and charts, and those few documents and artefacts to have survived.

Two of these artefacts were carved stones. Old, virtually ignored by the new regime in China and perhaps fearing that he might never return, Admiral Zheng He erected two carved stones in palaces of the Celestial Spouse, a Taoist goddess, before he set sail on his final voyage in late 1431. The first was in Chiang-su, Fujian province, and the second at Liu-Chia-Chang. Only rediscovered in 1930, the stones commemorate the crowning achievements of his life, the great voyages of the treasure fleets. Their inscriptions are the key to unlocking the riddle of the sixth voyage.

Inscription at Chiang-su

From the time when we, Cheng Ho [Zheng He] and his companions at the beginning of the Yung Lo Period [or Yong Le – Zhu Di, 1403], received the imperial commission as envoys to the barbarians, up until now seven voyages have taken place and each time we have commanded several tens of thousands of government soldiers and more than a hundred oceangoing vessels. Starting from T'ai Ts'ang and taking the sea, we have by way of the countries of Chan-Ch'eng (Champa), Hsien-Lo (Siam), Kua-Wa (Java), K'o Chih (Cochin) and Ku-Li (Calicut) reached Hu-Lu-Mo-Ssu [Hormuz, in the Gulf] and other countries of the western regions, more than three thousand countries in all.[2]

Inscription at Liu-Chia-Chang

We have traversed more than 100,000 *li* of immense water spaces and have beheld in the ocean huge waves like mountains rising sky-high [tsunami], and we have set eyes on barbarian regions far away, hidden in a blue transparency of light vapours, while our sails, loftily unfurled like clouds, day and night continued their course, rapid like that of a star, traversing those savage waves.[3]

The original English translation of Zheng He's Chiang-su inscription had been made by that great scholar of medieval China J.J.L. Duyvendak in the 1930s. In his article 'The True Dates of the Chinese Maritime Expeditions in the Early Fifteenth Century', the translation of a key phrase in the inscription was given as 'three thousand countries'. He and later scholars[4] thought that such a claim was so wildly implausible that the stone mason who carved the inscription must have made a mistake. On these grounds, the translation was amended to read 'thirty countries'. This was then repeated by subsequent writers and historians, and it was only when I consulted Duyvendak's text that I realized the original translation could have been correct; there was no logical reason why the mason who carved the inscription should have made such a gross error. But could such an extraordinary claim really be true? Had Zheng He's fleets reached three thousand countries? If so, the history of the exploration of the globe would have to be rewritten.

In attempting to reconstruct the voyages the fleets had made,

I first had to put myself into the shoes of the Chinese admirals. There was no better way of doing that than by sailing in their wake, as I had done as a young officer in the British Royal Navy aboard HMS *Newfoundland*. Our captain was a very brave and distinguished submariner, now Vice-Admiral Sir Arthur Hezlet KBE CB DSO and bar DSC. *Newfoundland* left Singapore in February 1959, passed through the Malacca Straits into the Indian Ocean and then turned westwards for Africa. We visited the Seychelles in the Indian Ocean before continuing west, making landfall on the East African coast at Mombasa. From there we went on to call at Zanzibar and Dar es Salaam before arriving at Lourenço Marques. We then sailed on down the east coast of Africa, visiting East London and Port Elizabeth before rounding the Cape, calling in at Cape Town, and sailing up the west coast round the 'bulge' of Africa to Sierra Leone, through the Cape Verde Islands and back home to England.

That journey gave me an invaluable insight into the winds, currents and navigational problems the Chinese admirals had encountered. Without that experience I could never have followed the elusive trail of evidence across the globe that revealed the incredible journeys made by the great Chinese treasure fleets. If I was able to state with confidence the course a Chinese fleet had taken, it was because the surviving maps and charts and my own knowledge of the winds, currents and sea conditions they faced told me the route as surely as if there had been a written record of it.

After parting company with Zheng He, the three Chinese fleets sailed for Calicut, the capital of Kerala in southern India and by far the most important port in the Indian Ocean. The Chinese had been trading with Calicut since the Tang dynasty (AD 618–907). It was not only an important Chinese forward base but a great trading port, holding a huge stockpile of Indian cotton and textiles (calico), and the foremost centre for the trade in pepper. Its rulers, the Zamorins – Hindu kings – had built up an extensive network of trading relations throughout the Indian Ocean, East Africa and south-east Asia. Nearly all the celebrated travellers and explorers of the Middle Ages, such as Marco Polo (1254–1324), Ibn Battuta (1304–1368) and Abdul Razak (active 1349–1387), travelled to Calicut. In Zhu Di's reign, the Chinese explicitly recognized Calicut, which they called Ku-Li, as the leading emporium of the Indian Ocean, describing it as 'the most important harbour in the western ocean' and 'the meeting port of all foreign merchants'.[5] Chinese sailing directions for the Indian Ocean specified distances to and from Calicut and gave courses to steer between Calicut, Malacca, northern India, the Gulf and Africa. For their part, Calicut's rulers venerated China; between 1405 and 1419 they sent a series of diplomatic missions to Nanjing and Beijing, and a delegation attended the inauguration of the Forbidden City and presented Zhu Di with valuable horses.

The official historian Ma Huan described the Chinese voyage from China via Malacca to Calicut in great detail: no fewer than nine pages of his account were devoted to the city. He gave an enthralling account of life in a medieval Indian city through Chinese eyes, noting the religious practices of the Zamorin king in contrast to those of his Muslim subjects, and bringing to life the habits of the people, their festivals, music and dancing, clothing and food: 'The King of the country and the people of the country all refrain from eating the flesh of the ox. The great chiefs are Muslim people, they all refrain from eating the flesh of the pig.'[6] Ma Huan went on to describe local crime and punishment, in particular how the guilt or innocence of a person was determined in a 'trial by ordeal' in which the accused's fingers were held in boiling ghee, or clarified butter, before being wrapped in cotton. He also detailed the way in which goods from the treasure fleets were sold, and the form of contract used:

If a treasure ship goes there, it is left entirely to the two men to superintend the buying and selling: the King sends a Chief and a Chei-Ti [a port customs official] to examine the account books in the official bureau; a broker comes and joins them [and] a high officer who commands the ships discusses the choice of a certain date for fixing prices. When the day arrives, they first of all take the silk embroideries and the open-work silks ... when the price has been fixed, they write out an agreement ...

The Chief and the Chei-Ti with his excellency the Eunuch all join hands together and the broker then says: 'In such and such a moon on such and such a day, we have all joined hands and sealed our agreement with a hand clasp. Whether [the price] be dear or cheap, we will never repudiate or change it.'[7]

By an extraordinary coincidence, at the very time the treasure fleets were in the city in 1421, a young Venetian, Niccolò da Conti (c. 1395–1469), also arrived. A well-connected trader, da Conti had left Venice in 1414 for Alexandria. The Islamic rulers in Egypt, the Mamluk sultans from the steppes of Asia, did not then permit Christians to travel south of Cairo for they were determined that the Indian Ocean should remain an Islamic lake. While in Egypt, da Conti had learned Arabic, married a Muslim woman and converted to Islam. Now travelling as a Muslim merchant, he journeyed to the Euphrates delta (in modern Iraq) and on to India, arriving by late 1420. He made for Calicut, because at the time it was a centre for Nestorian Christians – a cult of followers of St Thomas, also known as 'The Holy Apostolic Catholic Assyrian Church of the East', that had thrived in Syria in the sixth century and still exists in parts of western Asia – who were allowed to worship there by the tolerant Zamorins.

Years later, as penance for da Conti's renunciation of Christianity, Pope Eugenius IV made him relate the story of his journeys to the papal secretary Poggio Bracciolini, who had them published.[8] Da Conti described Calicut as 'eight miles in circumference, a noble emporium for all India, abounding in pepper, lac [a kind of insect gum used in making lacquer] and ginger'. There can be no doubt that da Conti was in Calicut when the Chinese fleets passed through, nor that he had at the very least boarded a junk, for he later described them in conversation with his friend, the Castilian Pedro Tafur: 'Ships [junks] like great houses and not fashioned at all like ours. They have ten or twelve sails and great cisterns of water within ... the lower part is constructed with triple planks. But some ships are built in compartments, so that should one part be shattered, the other part remaining entire, they may accomplish the voyage.'[9] The description could only refer to warships of Zheng He's fleet; Chinese merchantmen did not have that type of construction, or that number of sails. I felt certain that da Conti also met Ma Huan in Calicut, for he described scenes almost identical to those Ma Huan recounted, as I discovered when comparing their two accounts. It was as if two different witnesses were describing the same things: the land surrounding Calicut, the trial by ordeal,

Chart of the Arabian Sea from the Mao Kun map in the *Wu Pei Chi*. At the top is the west coast of India and at the bottom the coast of Arabia.

capons and partridges kept in coops, the price and quality of ginger and pepper. Only in writing about sex did their emphases differ: da Conti described how women's orgasms were heightened by the beads inserted in boys' penises; the more fastidious Ma Huan mentioned only the tinkling noise the beads made.

Having travelled through India and the Far East on many occasions over several decades, I can vouchsafe for the accuracy of da Conti's descriptions – durians (a luscious but curious fruit) smelling of cheese in Malaysia, the musk of civet cats on the Malabar coast, the sweet smell of the scent used by Goanese women. He describes African ostriches and hippopotami, the rubies of Sri Lanka, Hindu women practising suttee (self-immolation on their husbands' funeral pyres), vegetarian Brahmins (the priestly caste of Hindu India), the dusty smell of cinnamon. Da Conti's descriptions of his subsequent travels in Chinese junks were to prove a vital link in solving the riddle of where the Chinese fleets had gone in the 'lost' years, for, as Ma Huan's account makes clear, with his role as official chronicler

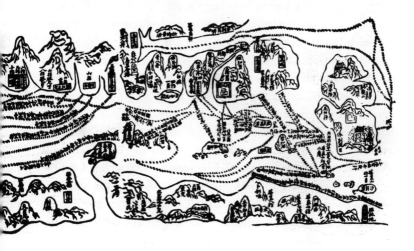

apparently over, he left the treasure fleets at Calicut. His departure meant that one useful source of information had dried up, and I had to look for other sources to replace him. The importance of da Conti to the story of the Chinese voyages became increasingly clear. Someone must have brought back copies of maps showing the discoveries made by the Chinese fleets, for how else could this information have reached Europe and become incorporated in the charts that were later to guide the Portuguese explorers? If it turned out that da Conti had also conversed with the Chinese on their return journey, he would be a prime candidate. Those charts were now proving equally vital to me as I endeavoured to trace the routes the Chinese fleets had followed.

The first task of the Chinese admirals after leaving Calicut was to return ambassadors to the coastal states of East Africa. Their passage plan was marked on the Chinese Mao Kun chart compiled after the sixth voyage. The Mao Kun forms part of the much larger *Wu Pei Chi*. That part of the Mao Kun that has survived – no-one knows how large it originally was – is in strip form, 21 feet long and plastered with hundreds of names of ports and prominent coastal features, and the courses to steer and distances between them. It is 'believed to have been compiled in about 1422 from a mass of information brought back by Zheng He's fleet or collected for their use'.[10] Only a part of it has been translated to date, and as I write, scholars of medieval Chinese are working on the remainder. The translations of the Mao Kun and the *Wu Pei Chi*, and other documents of the period, will almost certainly produce further evidence of the great Chinese voyages. The quest to find further records was formally inaugurated at a conference in Nanjing on 18 October 2002.[11]

The treasure fleets sailed from Calicut on the tail end of the north-east monsoon into the Indian Ocean, altering course to the south-west to make landings in Africa to return the ambassadors to their home ports – the route we followed over

The voyage to Sofala.

half a millennium later in HMS *Newfoundland*. It would have been uneconomical for all the fleets to have gone to each African state, so they would almost certainly have divided, with one returning ambassadors to Mogadishu (in modern Somalia) in the north, another to Zanzibar in the middle of the east coast, and a third to Kilwa (in modern Tanzania) further south. After all the ambassadors had been returned to their home countries, the Mao Kun indicates that the fleets rendezvoused off Sofala (near Maputo in modern Mozambique).

Finding the rendezvous must have posed a major problem, for during a voyage from India to southern Africa, Polaris, the Chinese guiding star, would have sunk closer and closer to the horizon and become invisible at 3°40′N, north of Mogadishu in Somalia. Until they found another guiding star in the southern hemisphere to fulfil the same purpose as Polaris in the north, they were sailing into the unknown. They could use the Southern Cross for direction, for they knew that its leading stars, Crucis Alpha and Crucis Gamma, pointed to the South Pole, but as yet they had no star they could use to determine latitude. To locate one, they would have to sail far into the icy waters of the deep south. This was to be one of the most important aims of the expedition.

Allowing for sailing a hundred nautical miles (115 statute miles) in a day (the average speed recorded in the surviving records of Chinese voyages in the Indian Ocean) and for remaining a maximum of one week in each port to re-provision (it usually took two to four days), all three fleets had probably completed the return of the envoys and ambassadors to their home ports by July 1421. By the time they had arrived at the rendezvous off Sofala, the admirals had already sailed some ten thousand miles since leaving China four months earlier. Some would not return for five years, but they did leave signposts of where they had sailed. The Chinese were rightly proud of their great voyages, and whenever they landed they usually carved stones in commemoration, like those erected by Zheng He in China. There are other similar stones near Cochin and Calicut in India, and near Galle in Sri Lanka. Some of the masons and stone-carvers who had worked on the Forbidden City had been brought with the fleets for precisely this purpose. The discovery of such stones was to prove one of the crucial links in the chain of evidence I was assembling. From the inscriptions on the carved stone erected by Zheng He in the Palace of the Celestial Spouse at Liu-Chia-Chang, I knew they had sailed forty thousand miles on their sixth voyage – almost twice around the globe.[12] The *Wu Pei Chi* and the Mao Kun covered only the Chinese routes across the Indian and Southern Oceans. Without Chinese records to help me, how could I find out how far they had sailed, what new oceans they had traversed and what new lands they had discovered?

My first recourse was to turn to the other great seafarers of the fifteenth century, the Arabs. My initial instinct has always been to look first for evidence in maps. The British Library holds copies of the great collection of early Arab maps assembled by Prince Youssuf Kamal, a wealthy Egyptian. These maps showed that the Arabs had certainly visited the east coast of Africa, and made regular voyages from the Gulf to collect slaves. However, dependent upon the prevailing winds, they had not ventured beyond the monsoon belt that spans the Indian Ocean but stops short of southern Africa. They set off from the Gulf on the north-east monsoon, sailed down to Zanzibar or sometimes further south to Kilwa and Sofala, then returned on the next south-west monsoon to the Gulf, laden with their tragic cargoes of slaves. I could not trace a single Arab chart that accurately depicted the east coast of Africa south of Sofala.

I knew of, but at that stage had never seen, a planisphere – a map of the world – showing the Indian Ocean and southern Africa. It was drawn in 1459 by Fra Mauro, a cartographer based on the island of San Michele in the Venetian Lagoon but working for Dom Pedro of Portugal, Henry the Navigator's brother and another leading light in the first wave of European journeys of exploration, who was then compiling a map of the world. I wondered if Fra Mauro's map, now held by the Biblioteca Nazionale Marciana, could throw some light on the Chinese voyages.

When I flew to Venice, the curator, Dr Piero Falchetta, took me into his office and proudly showed me Fra Mauro's map, a grandiose undertaking: the first map of the entire world to be drawn since the days of the Roman Empire. It was to be the first, vital clue to the course taken by the Chinese fleets. Dr Falchetta pointed out that Fra Mauro had correctly drawn the Cape of Good Hope (which he had called Cap de Diab) with its easily identifiable triangular shape, and had done so thirty years before Bartolomeu Dias rounded the Cape. That this was no mistake was emphasized by Fra Mauro himself, for he had appended notes stating that a ship or junk had rounded the Cape:

> Around the year 1420, a ship or junk [coming] from India on a non-stop crossing of the Indian Ocean past 'the Isles of Men and Women' was driven beyond Cap de Diab [Cape of Good Hope] and through the Isole Verde and obscured islands [or darkness] towards the west and south-west for 40 days, found nothing but sea and sky. In their estimation, they ran for 2,000 miles and fortune deserted them. They made their return to the said Cap de Diab in 70 days.[13]

Near the note, Fra Mauro had drawn a picture of a Chinese junk. It had the highly unusual broad, square bow, like a modern tank landing-craft, typical of Zheng He's junks, and was shown much bigger than his depiction of European caravels. Another inscription, placed in the middle of the Indian Ocean, read: 'The ships or junks that navigate these seas carry four masts or more, some of which can be raised or lowered, and have 40 to 60 cabins for the merchants.'[14] A further note described the huge eggs the crew found when replenishing at Cap de Diab and the giant size of the birds that laid them. That description could only have applied to ostriches.

Fra Mauro's planisphere of 1459 showed the Cape of Good Hope correctly drawn, had an accurate depiction of Zheng He's junks and described birds unique to southern Africa several decades before the first Europeans, Dias and da Gama, got to the Cape. The immediate and obvious question was, how did Fra

Mauro get his information? How did he know the shape of a junk, and that the Cape was triangular? I found a partial answer in another fifteenth-century document describing the Portuguese conquest of Guinea: 'Fra Mauro has himself spoken with "a trustworthy person" who said that he had sailed from India past Sofala to Garbin, a place located in the middle of the west coast of Africa.'[15] There was no other clue to help identify the location of Garbin; the name does not correspond to that of any modern place. It is a bastardized version of the Arabic Al Gharb, meaning 'a place in the West'. The identity of the 'trustworthy person' would vitally affect the provenance and credibility of the notes on Fra Mauro's planisphere.

I was convinced that the person could only have been Niccolò da Conti. He was in Calicut when the Chinese junks berthed to offload passengers and cargo and take on supplies on their way across the Indian Ocean. The notes on Fra Mauro's map alluding to the voyage of the junk refer to 'the Isles of Men and Women', a peculiar name also used by da Conti in the account related to the papal secretary Poggio Bracciolini. Da Conti (c. 1395–1469) was a contemporary of Fra Mauro (c. 1385–1459), both came from Venice, and both were engaged in exploration or documenting exploration. Fra Mauro was working for the Portuguese government, and as well as publishing da Conti's stories, Poggio Bracciolini was also the intermediary between the Pope, Fra Mauro and the Portuguese government. There are no records of other Venetian merchants in India at the time, let alone in Calicut, when the Chinese passed through. It would be extraordinary if Fra Mauro's 'trustworthy person' were not da Conti.[16]

This was the crucial link in the chain connecting the maps drawn by the Chinese cartographers during the great voyages of exploration by the treasure fleets to the later Portuguese discoveries based on the mysterious maps they were soon to obtain. Chinese knowledge and Chinese maps passed from da Conti to Fra Mauro, and from him to Dom Pedro of Portugal and Prince

Henry the Navigator. The Papal Secretary, Poggio Bracciolini, was, as we shall see, a key intermediary.

If Fra Mauro's description did come courtesy of da Conti's travels aboard a Chinese junk, it came from a reliable and accurate eyewitness, as I had already discovered. In those circumstances it seemed sensible to examine Fra Mauro/da Conti's claim that a ship or junk had indeed rounded the Cape of Good Hope and then sailed into the South Atlantic. If so, it was a towering achievement, for Pedro Álvares Cabral (1467–1520) and Bartolomeu Dias (c. 1450–1500), the first Europeans to round the Cape and venture into the Indian Ocean, did not do so until 1488. To have drawn the Cape so accurately Fra Mauro must have had a copy of a chart showing the exact shape and location of the southern tip of Africa. Da Conti could have brought him such a map, obtained during his voyages aboard the Chinese fleet.

As I know from my own naval career, rounding the Cape remains an emotional experience for sailors today. As the clouds peel off the strange flat mountain tops of the fabled Cape, another ocean and another world – the exotic East – beckons. To the Chinese in 1421, coming from the opposite direction, it must have seemed that at last they had reached the brink of the unknown – not even the great admirals of the Tang dynasty had sailed this far. As they saw the lengthening waves and deepening troughs, they must have prayed that their ships would prove equal to the colossal challenges the vast and stormy Atlantic Ocean would surely bring.

I now had to discover where the mysterious ship described by Fra Mauro had sailed after rounding the Cape, and look for further independent evidence that it was a junk of one of the Chinese fleets. I started from the treasure fleets' last recorded position, shown on the Mao Kun chart of 1422 as off Sofala, sailing southwards at 6.25 knots, a good speed explained by the Aghulas current that sweeps southwards along the east coast of

South Africa down to the tip. At that speed, the Chinese would have rounded the Cape of Good Hope in approximately three weeks, by August 1421.

As they have for millennia, winds and currents in the South Atlantic circle anti-clockwise in a huge oval loop from the Cape of Good Hope in the south to the 'bulge' of Africa in the north. At the Cape, the mariner meets the Benguela current that carries him due north up the west coast of Africa. After some three thousand miles, the current starts to hook first to the north-west, then westwards to South America. Off the coast of South America the current continues its anti-clockwise movement, running southwards off Brazil and Patagonia down the east coast as far as Cape Horn before sweeping to the east, back to South Africa. If a sailing ship, carrying sufficient supplies and robust enough to withstand the 'Roaring Forties' – powerful winds that circle the globe for hundreds of miles north and south of the latitude that gives them their name – were to hoist its sails off South Africa and sail before the wind and current, then several months later, having crossed thousands of miles of ocean in this great anti-clockwise loop, it would return more or less to where it started. An illustration of this is provided by the epic voyage of a very brave and distinguished submarine captain, now Vice-Admiral Sir Ian McIntosh KBE CB DSO DSC, once captain of the submarine squadron in which I served. He wrote to me:

In March 1941 I was a Sub Lieutenant in a merchant ship taking passage to Alexandria. She was sunk by gun-fire by an armed commerce raider some 500 to 600 miles west of Freetown at about 08°N 30°W. The 28-foot standard wooden lifeboat, 'authorised' capacity 56, finally had 82 souls on board.

Even when I had repaired the shrapnel holes in the hull and the boat was reasonably dry I could not get her to sail closer than 5 or 6 points to the wind, a brisk NE Trade. This would never have

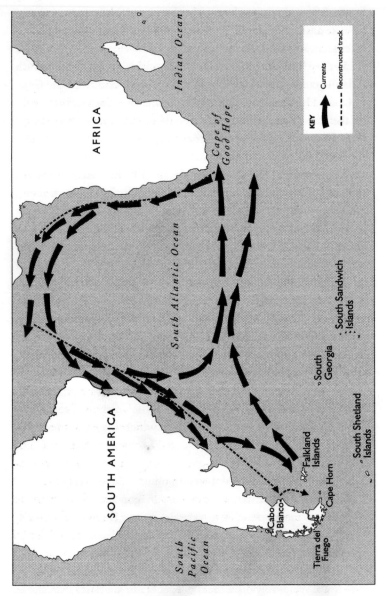

The circulatory winds and currents in the South Atlantic Ocean.

allowed us to reach Africa, and to run before the wind to Brazil some 1,600 miles distant by the route chosen seemed preferable.

The plan was to steer due west until reaching 33° West then alter course to SW. This made full use of the NE Trades and gave us only a few days of shifting winds (and some most welcome rain) in the Doldrums before picking up light SE Trade winds. We made the [South American] coast on the 22nd day, ran NW along the coast looking for a suitable landing, which we found on the afternoon of the 23rd day.

I had estimated a maximum of 28 days for rationing purposes knowing that the equatorial currents were helping us but I had no idea at our latitude and time of the year whether they were a quarter knot or more than 1 knot, so I disregarded it in my noon DR [Dead Reckoning] positions.[17]

It is entirely feasible that the treasure fleets did reach the Cape of Good Hope where they would have been swept by the wind and current around the Cape and up the west coast of Africa to the 'Garbin' described by Fra Mauro. What I now urgently needed was independent evidence that this had happened. I pondered this question for months. Then I had a stroke of luck. John E. Wills Jr, Professor of History at the University of Southern California, and Dr Joseph McDermott, Professor of Chinese at Cambridge University, England, suggested to me that although the charts and records of the treasure fleets in China had been destroyed, there might be copies in Japan, for Japanese scholars were particularly interested in the early Ming era.

Subsequent research revealed that Ryukoku University in Kyoto held a copy of a Chinese/Korean chart known colloquially as the Kangnido. The Korean ambassador had presented Zhu Di with this extraordinary world map in 1403 after his inauguration as emperor. The original map, however, has been lost, and the Ryukoku version of the Kangnido was extensively modified after 1420. It is nearly square and strikingly large, measuring 1.7

by 1.6 metres. Painted on silk, it remains in excellent condition, its colours little faded by the passing centuries. It is 'nicely organized and well worth admiration. One can indeed know the world without going out of the door.'[18]

The Kangnido gave a grandiose panoramic view of the world as seen in the early fifteenth century, and was compiled from many different sources. Names for Europe were in Persian Arabic, central Asia came from the Mongols, China and southeast Asia from old Chinese maps. Europe was covered in names as far north as Germany (named Alumangia). Spain was depicted, as were the straits of Gibraltar leading into the Mediterranean and the North African coast with the Atlas mountains. Europe, Africa, Asia, Korea and China were in their correct positions relative to one another, though Korea, perhaps for reasons connected with national pride and its traditional rivalry with Japan, was shown vastly larger than it should be and Japan much smaller. Nonetheless, it was an extraordinary piece of mapmaking.

For the moment, the part of the Kangnido that interested me most was Africa. So accurately does the Kangnido depict the coasts of East, South and West Africa that there cannot be a shred of doubt that it was charted by someone who had sailed round the Cape. Europeans did not reach South Africa for another sixty years; Arab navigators on the west coast never sailed south of Agadir in modern Morocco, eight thousand kilometres away, and the Mongols never reached Africa at all. The accuracy of the Kangnido told me that Mauro/da Conti's description made absolute sense. A Chinese navigator could indeed have reached 'Garbin' and then drawn the Kangnido. Still I had no precise location for Garbin save that, from the shape of the coastline shown on the Kangnido, it appeared to be near the Bay of Biafra, off western Nigeria. It was a problem I would have to address later. For now, I felt justified in assuming that the 'junk' referred to by Fra Mauro and drawn on his planisphere was from

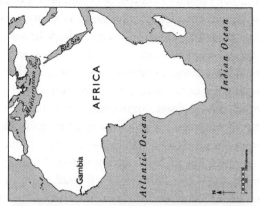

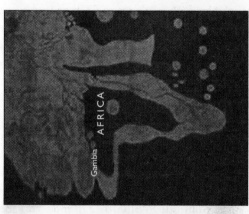

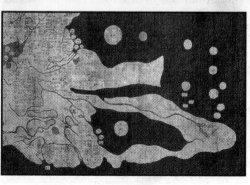

(i) The Kangnido map showing Africa.

(ii) The Kangnido map corrected for longitude.

(iii) Modern Africa.

the treasure fleets, for Chinese merchant ships did not sail beyond Kilwa in East Africa. The Kangnido was much less accurate when it came to the 'bulge' of Africa north of the Bay of Biafra, so I next turned my attention to that part of the voyage. If they had managed to survey the coast of southern Africa with such accuracy, why was the bulge of West Africa not shown on the Kangnido chart?

By the time the Chinese fleets reached the Bay of Biafra, they had sailed some three thousand miles north from the Cape. I assumed that they rounded the Cape on their outward journey some time in August. At their average speed of 4.8 knots it would have taken about twenty days to sail from the Cape to 'Garbin'. They would have reached it in late August or early September 1421, the end of summer and towards the end of the rainy season. As I well know from my own time at sea in the South Atlantic, there is an extraordinary natural phenomenon in this part of Africa. Starting in the Bay of Biafra, the south equatorial current runs first to the north past São Tomé e Príncipe Island (where the bulge starts) then hooks westwards to flow due west along the south coast of the bulge, past Nigeria, Ghana and the Ivory and Gold Coasts until it peters out a thousand miles out into the Atlantic around 21°W. This massive body of cold water flows westwards with considerable speed the whole year round; a minor change occurs in summer when it extends further north to reach 5°N, a similar latitude to Monrovia in modern Liberia.

This current would have had two important implications for the Chinese: they would have been carried due west for some 1,800 miles, but they would not have known that this had happened. At this stage of their voyage the Chinese could only measure longitude by estimating their speed through the water, and if the great body of water was itself moving, either against them or with them, there was no way that they could determine their position with any accuracy, any more than a man walking up an escalator can judge the distance he has travelled by the number of paces he has taken. With mounting excitement, I realized that the charts drawn after they had entered the south equatorial current had to be adjusted to take account of this discrepancy, and the land they showed moved by up to 1,800 miles further to the west. I went back to my copy of the Kangnido and adjusted the land north of the Bay of Biafra to allow for this longitudinal error. The result was startling: the familiar outline of Africa became immediately recognizable. It appeared that the Chinese had been carried by the wind and current to the 'bulge' of Africa forty years before the first Europeans set eyes on it.

The south equatorial current gave them a 'free ride' westwards until the current petered out a thousand miles into the Atlantic. By then, they were in the south-east trade belt and being blown towards the coast of Senegal. In the wet season, running from April to October, the Sénégal current off this coast of West Africa reverses its normal direction and runs northwards along the coast at a rate of 0.6 to 1 knot. Yet again the junks would have had a free ride, this time to the north for around five hundred miles until the current itself petered out off Dakar, the modern capital of Senegal. By then they were in the belt of the north-east trade winds, blowing them south-west to the Cape Verde Islands. These lonely islands, then unknown to Europeans, were to play a vital part in unravelling the mystery of the Chinese voyages.

I checked and rechecked my calculations. By late September the junks that left the Cape of Good Hope in August would have found themselves approaching the Cape Verde Islands from the north-east. The design of the ships and the prevailing winds and currents would have prevented these flat-bottomed, broad-beamed monsters from sailing south at any point. It was now clear that Fra Mauro's account was entirely possible and that the Cape Verde Islands could have been the 'Isole Verde' reached by the ship or junk from India, forty days after leaving the Cape of Good Hope; they even had the same name. At 4.8 knots, the speed the treasure fleets averaged over all six great voyages, this would have taken

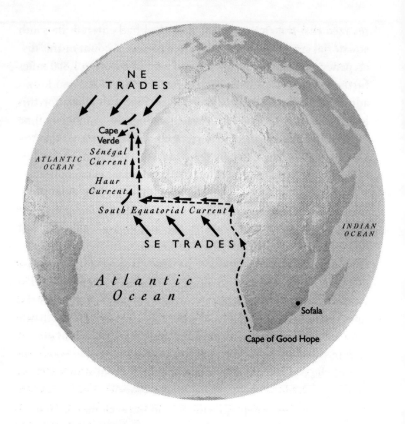

The journey to the Cape Verde Islands.

forty days. Vasco da Gama took thirty-three days to make the same passage in the closing years of the century.

To have been called the 'Isole Verde', the islands Niccolò da Conti described to Fra Mauro must have been strikingly green. I knew the Cape Verde Islands well, having sailed through them in HMS *Newfoundland*. They are divided into two groups, and the windward (*balaventos*) are significantly wetter than the leeward (*sotaventos*). Of the windward islands, the biggest, highest, wettest and greenest is Santo Antão. It is an island of savage grandeur, awesome and eye-catching from the sea, particularly to a mariner seeking fresh water. The Chinese admirals would have been approaching from the north-east on the trade winds, and from that direction they would have sighted Santo Antão first. On the north coast of Santo Antão, clearly visible from miles out as you approach from the north-east, there is a dramatic volcano. Streams pour down its sides and rush through lush valleys to the sea around what is now the small settlement of Janela. That strip of coast would have been an obvious and immediate place for the Chinese fleets to anchor and obtain water. If the Chinese had indeed landed there, I was confident that a legacy of their visit should exist.

The Cape Verde Islands were uninhabited when the first European, Cà da Mosto (1432–88), a Venetian explorer in the service of Henry the Navigator, arrived in 1456, so I could not expect to find goods that the Chinese had traded for food, such as the blue and white plates that were their currency on the south-east coast of Africa. On the Cape Verde Islands the Chinese could have obtained any amount of food and water for nothing. The seas teemed with swordfish, sole, shark, octopus, crayfish and tiny sweet mussels, the island was lush with fruit, and flocks of tame birds could be picked up by hand, for they had never learned to be wary of humans, as Cà da Mosto's crew found to their joy thirty-five years later. Nonetheless, there should have been other mementoes. A carved stone similar to the one erected by Zheng He on the estuary of the Yangtze stands at Galle, near Dondra Head in southern Sri Lanka. Inscribed in Chinese, Tamil and Persian, it extols the virtues of Hinduism (the local religion), Buddhism (Emperor Zhu Di's faith) and Islam (the religion of most Indian rulers in the early fifteenth century). There are other similar stones near Cochin and Calicut. I wondered if a carved stone might have been erected here.

The Chinese were always careful to respect local sensibilities;

the language school in Nanjing, the Ssu-i-Quan, was, after all, set up by Zheng He specifically to train interpreters, and the fleets on this sixth voyage carried interpreters fluent in seventeen different Indian and African languages. It was highly probable that they had also left a stone on one of the Cape Verde Islands, carved with inscriptions in a language they thought people from the surrounding areas would understand. Such stones were always sited in prominent places where they would readily be discovered by others – what would be the point of erecting a monument to your achievements and then hiding it where it would never be found? If such a stone existed, the first Europeans should have found it when they reached Santo Antão thirty-five years later.

I referred to the journals describing Antonio da Noli, Cà da Mosto and Diego Alfonso's first voyages to the islands, and discovered that they had indeed found a large, free-standing stone near the coast at Janela. The stone still stands there today, in a dramatic setting framed by encircling mountains, beside the Ribeira de Penedo. Until a century ago, a clear, rushing stream tumbled down the side of the volcano, but now the stream has dried up and the stone is surrounded by agave plants. The stone, called locally Pedra do Letreiro (Stone of Letters), is of red sandstone, some three metres high and covered with inscriptions from top to bottom. The later carvings are in medieval Portuguese, commemorating the death of a mariner, Antonio of Fez, but underneath them I could see more calligraphy, unfortunately obscured by moss and lichen. The stone was so badly weatherworn and defaced by recent graffiti that it was very difficult to decipher the underlying calligraphy. A series of experts had tried – first a Frenchman, M. Chevalier, in 1934, then several learned Portuguese and Cape Verde historians over the past twenty years. They could tell me what the calligraphy was not – it was not Arabic, Judaic, Berber, Tifnaq, Aramaic, Phoenician, Latin, or any other European language – but they could not tell me what it was.

After receiving the necessary approval from the Cape Verde authorities, some of the lichen was removed. This revealed two pieces of calligraphy. I hoped that, helped by computer enhancement, I would at least be able to determine the language, but the calligraphy was quite extraordinary, unlike anything I had ever seen in my travels anywhere in the world. It appeared to have two characteristics: whorls like interlocking ram's horns, and a number of concentric circles.

My first thought was that it could be medieval Chinese, either the Zhu Qi Shan script or 'Flowinghand'. I sent photographs to experts at the Forest of Steles in Xian, China. Once the Temple of Confucius, it is now a museum and library holding a huge collection of steles, or engraved stone tablets, a timeless memorial to the Chinese written language. It was neither script. Could it be Tamil, similar to the writing on the stone the Chinese erected in southern Sri Lanka? It does resemble Tamil, but not closely enough. Nor is it Swahili, the lingua franca of the east coast of Africa. I then wondered if it could be another Indian language, perhaps one of the thirteen shown on today's high-denomination Indian banknotes. Could the Bank of India help? I faxed them a photo of a small section of one of the pieces of calligraphy.

'It looks like Malayalam,' they replied.

It was a language I had never even heard of. I faxed again.

'Where was this language spoken?'

'It was the language of Kerala.'

'Was it in use in the fifteenth century?'

'Yes, it had been in common use since the ninth century.'

Once I'd put down the phone, I punched the air in my excitement. In 1421, Kerala's capital was Calicut, the great port of India from which the Chinese had sailed. Once again, Fra Mauro and Niccolò da Conti seem to have been correct: a ship or junk from India appeared to have reached the Cape Verde Islands before the Portuguese arrived.

I next trawled through the learned experts' research[19] to see whether they had come across another, similar stone while they were attempting to decipher the writing at Janela. They had, but not in the Cape Verde Islands. The other stone was sited at the Matadi Falls in the Congo. My first impression was that this was a wild goose chase. Why should a ship voyaging from India have visited a waterfall in Africa? But closer examination revealed the Matadi Falls to be at the upper navigable limit of the Congo River, where a mariner may anchor in beautiful surroundings and obtain clean, fresh water. A succession of ships had done just that down the centuries, from the Portuguese in 1485 to the Chinese today. The river pours over a series of cataracts before reaching the falls. The carved stone stands sentinel above a dark pool near the foot of the falls, where in days gone by fishermen would sit motionless while prostitutes patrolled the banks awaiting the arrival of the crews of foreign ships sailing upstream to water and gather provisions.

I had to retrace my route back to the coast of Africa to investigate this discovery. Like its Janela counterpart, the Matadi Falls stone has calligraphy beneath medieval Portuguese. The Portuguese writing once again commemorated a deceased comrade, here the navigator Álvares. There is less underlying material than at Janela, but experts confirmed that it was the same calligraphy, that once again it looked like Malayalam. Its identity appeared to have been solved, although the concentric circles remained a mystery. It was likely that the Chinese had come here on their journey up the African coast. Not only is the Matadi Falls an ideal place for watering, it is 'in the middle of the west coast of Africa', and fits the description of 'Garbin' given by Fra Mauro. It is a busy port today.

Once again, Fra Mauro and da Conti appeared to have been vindicated: a ship sailing from India 'around the year 1420' seems to have reached Garbin. This does not, of course, guarantee that the ship was Chinese rather than Indian, but Indian ships were sailing with the Chinese fleets. It appeared the Chinese had reached there. The simple and obvious explanation was that the calligraphy carved on the 'Garbin' and Janela stones was inscribed by stonemasons travelling with the Chinese fleet, just as they had carved inscriptions in foreign languages at Dondra Head, Cochin and Calicut.

Despite the wholesale destruction of Chinese records carried out in the fifteenth century, I now had a trail of evidence of the treasure fleets' movements from departure from Tanggu to arrival in the Cape Verde Islands in September 1421. Ma Huan had described the voyage from China via Malacca to Calicut, and the Mao Kun chart of 1422 had then put the armada off Sofala in south-eastern Africa. My evidence for it having rounded the Cape of Good Hope and sailed north up the west coast of Africa was provided by the Kangnido map in Japan, and corroborated by Mauro/da Conti's descriptions. Their accounts, together with the inscribed stones, also showed that 'Garbin' in the middle of the west coast of Africa was the Matadi Falls, and that 'Isole Verde' was Santo Antão in the Cape Verde Islands. The Chinese were sailing before the wind and current all the way. It was precisely the route a ship sailing from India would have been obliged to follow, and at the Chinese average speed of 4.8 knots the latter part of the voyage would have lasted the forty days Fra Mauro had stated.

The great Chinese armada had already voyaged far into the distant and uncharted oceans, but I now had to discover where they had sailed next. The account by Mauro/da Conti described a seventy-day voyage after leaving the Cape Verde Islands, through *le oscuritade*, which can be translated as 'the obscured islands' or 'darkness'. My task was now to identify them. My first line of approach was to search for independent evidence of the next part of the Chinese voyage, for example in another chart that might throw some light on the location of these 'obscured islands'. In that era, Venice was the cartographic capital of Europe. If such a map existed, Venice was the most likely source.

During my researches in Venice I was told of a description by the Portuguese historian Antonio Galvão (died 1557) of a world map the Portuguese dauphin, Dom Pedro, Henry the Navigator's brother, had brought back with him from Venice in 1428 (my italics):

> In the yeere 1428, it is written that Dom Peter, the King of Portugal's eldest sonne, was a great traveller. He went into England, France, Almaine [Germany] and from thence into the Holy Land, and to other places; and came home by Italie, taking Rome and Venice in his way: from whence he brought *a map of the world, which had all the parts of the world and earth described. The Streight of Magelan was called in it the dragon's taile: the Cape of Boa Esperança, the forefront of Afrike* and so foorth of other places: by which Map Dom Henry the King's third sonne was much helped and furthered in his Discouveries.[20]

Here was an unequivocal assertion that by 1428 both the Cape of Good Hope (Boa Esperança) and 'the Streight of Magelan' (separating Argentina from Tierra del Fuego) had been charted on a map. It was an extraordinary claim. How could the Strait of Magellan have appeared on a map – for simplicity, I shall call it the 1428 World Map – nearly a century before Ferdinand Magellan discovered it? To emphasize that this was no mistake, Galvão continued:

> It was tolde me by Francis de Sousa Tavares that in the yeere 1528, Dom Fernando, the King's sonne and heire did show him a map which was found in the studie of the Alcobaza [a renowned Cistercian monastery traditionally used as a library by Portuguese kings] which had beene made 120 yeeres before which map did set forth all the navigation of the East Indies with the Cape of Boa Esperança according as our later maps have described it; whereby it appeareth that in ancient time there was as much or more discovered than now there is.[21]

This 1428 World Map was of huge importance to the
Portuguese government, for in December 1421 the overland
route to China and the Spice Islands – the great Silk Road running from China right across central Asia to the Middle East –
had been blocked when the Ottomans surrounded Byzantium.
In that same climactic month, on 6 December, the Mamluk
Sultan Barsbey seized power in Egypt and nationalized the spice
trade. The effect of the two events was to ruin the merchants
who had controlled the spice trade, seal Egypt's borders to international trade and sever the sea route through the Bosphorus to
the western end of the Silk Road. With the canal linking the Red
Sea and the Nile (completed in the tenth century) collapsing and
unusable, all land and sea routes to the East were now closed to
Christians. A new ocean route to the East had to be found.

I knew from Antonio Galvão's description that the 1428
World Map showed the 'East Indies' (the Indian Ocean and
what is now Indonesia) and revealed the ocean routes to the
Spice Islands (Ternate and Tidore in eastern Indonesia), Asia
and China round the Cape of Good Hope and through the Strait
of Magellan. The information it contained was of incalculable
commercial value and it was kept for decades under lock and
key in the Portuguese treasury in Lisbon. However, the secret
eventually leaked out and others became determined to get their
hands on this vital map, even though the penalty for stealing it
was death.[22] Certainly, Christopher Columbus was in possession
of a copy in 1492 (see chapter 18).

The 1428 World Map has long been lost, but the information
contained on some sections of it has survived, the most important
of which is the section showing South America. A Spanish seaman who had sailed to the Americas with Columbus kept that
portion of the map together with some notes Columbus had
written about it. In 1501, the Ottomans captured the ship in
which the seaman was serving; he still had the map in his
possession. Neither the seaman nor any other who sailed with

Columbus could have been the originator of this map because Columbus never sailed south of the equator. The information can only have come from the 1428 map.

Appreciating the extraordinary value of this captured document, the Ottoman Admiral Piri Reis incorporated it into a map known from that day to this as the Piri Reis map of 1513. This beautiful map can be seen today in the Topkapi Serai Museum high above the Bosphorus in Istanbul. It was based on several different maps, pieced together by the admiral from a number of different sources, and parts of it are unreliable, but the south-western portion based on the map taken from Columbus's seaman is very accurate. The trail I had begun to follow the day I visited the Torre do Tombo in Lisbon and read Antonio Galvão's description of a mysterious map that had come into Portuguese hands in 1428 had now led me to another chart that would prove one of the most valuable keys to unlocking the secrets of the Chinese voyages.

In recreating the Chinese route I remained certain of one thing: because of the hull shape of the Chinese junks, they would have had to sail before the wind. Their route after leaving the Cape Verde Islands was not hard to establish for there, as Admiral McIntosh described so many centuries later, the wind blows relentlessly westwards, towards South America. Moreover, at the Cape Verde Islands 'the north equatorial and south equatorial current converge, forming a broad belt of current setting west. Average rates reach two knots.'[23] The converged currents separate near the Caribbean: the northern part sweeps through the Caribbean to New England where it becomes the Gulf Stream; the southern part turns south-west towards South America.

My study of the old maps and charts, together with the evidence from wrecks and artefacts found around South America and in the Caribbean (to be examined more fully later), led me to conclude that the Chinese fleets had separated with the current. Admiral Zhou Wen sailed north-west through the Caribbean towards North America, while Admirals Hong Bao and Zhou Man took the south-west branch of the equatorial current towards South America. It must have been an emotional parting as the great ships began to drift apart, gathering speed as the wind filled their sails. They were sailing into hazardous, uncharted waters and the admirals and their men would have been well aware that they might never set eyes on their companions again.

The evidence of the Piri Reis map and of the winds and currents seemed conclusive; the Chinese fleet must have sailed in this direction from the Cape Verde islands. Perhaps I would find the answer to the mystery of the 'obscured islands' somewhere off the coast of the Americas. I would return later to track the northward voyage of Zhou Wen's fleet, but for the moment I had to follow the course of Zhou Man and Hong Bao on their south-west track towards the 'New World'.

THE

NEW

WORLD

THE FLEETS OF HONG BAO AND ZHOU MAN WOULD HAVE sighted the coast of what is now Brazil approximately three weeks after leaving the Cape Verde Islands. What a moment that must have been, a sprawling, unknown land filling the horizon before them, the air full of unfamiliar scents and the calls of strange birds. They may well have wondered if this was the land of Fusang, described by their forebears almost a thousand years earlier.

During the Northern and Southern dynasties in the first year of the 'Everlasting Origin' Emperor, AD 499, a Buddhist priest named Hoei-Shin ('Universal Compassion') returned from a land twenty thousand *li* (eight thousand nautical miles) east of China. He named this continent Fusang after the trees that grew there. The Fusang tree bore fruit like a red pear, and had edible shoots and bark the inhabitants used for clothing and paper. Coupled with his statement that the country had no iron, Hoei-Shin's description suggests that the Fusang was the maguey tree that grows only in Central and South America. It bears red fruit and is also used in the other ways he described. Iron is found in almost every part of the world except for Central America, just as Hoei-Shin indicated. Whether or not Hoei-Shin reached the Americas, the Chinese certainly believed he had, for his report was regularly entered in the yearbooks or annals (official histories) of the Chinese Empire. From there it passed not only to historians but also to poets and writers, and down the centuries innumerable tales were told of Hoei-Shin's exploits and adventures in the land of Fusang.

Fusang is about twenty thousand Chinese miles [eight thousand nautical miles] in an easterly direction from Tahan, and east of the Middle Kingdoms [China]. Many fusang trees grow there, whose leaves resemble the *Dryanda cordifolia*; the sprouts, on the contrary, resemble those of the bamboo tree, and are eaten by the inhabitants of the land. The fruit is like a pear in form but is red. From the

bark they prepare a sort of linen which they use for clothing ...
The houses are built of wooden beams; fortified and walled places
are there unknown ... They have written characters in this land
[which the Olmecs did have] and prepare paper from the bark of
the Fusang [which the Olmecs did from the maguey tree, which
indeed has red fruit like pears].[1]

Zheng He and his admirals certainly knew these tales when
they set sail, as did the Chinese seamen crowding at the rail for a
sight of this new land. Was it a land of no iron? Did it have the
famous Fusang trees? No doubt they were nervous, perhaps
even frightened, but they must also have been immensely
curious. Their landfall must have been around the Orinoco
delta, for the Piri Reis map shows that they had surveyed that
small part of the coast with great accuracy. My search for the
obscured islands Fra Mauro/da Conti had described during the
junk's seventy-day voyage after leaving the Cape Verde Islands
could now begin in earnest.

Just before the book went to print I was informed that a considerable amount of research had been carried out into the DNA
of American Indian peoples of the Amazon and the Orinoco and
the diseases that they carried which were otherwise unique to
China and South East Asia. Briefly, it concerns a skin disease of
the Indians of the Mato Grosso of Brazil; hookworms occurring
in the Lengua Indians of Paraguay; roundworm in Peru and
Mexico; ancylostoma duodenale in Mexico; and Chinese DNA in
the Indian peoples of the Amazon, Brazil and Venezuela. It is
conclusive proof of Chinese sea voyages to the Americas before
Columbus. For the moment, however, I had to continue with the
charts.

After making landfall near the Orinoco, where they would
have replenished their water and taken on fresh food, they
would then have set sail once more for the south. The
winds would have carried them past the Amazon delta down

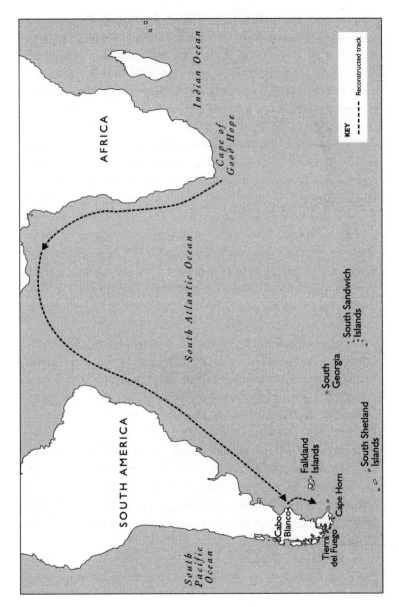

The journey to Tierra del Fuego.

the east coast of Brazil to Cabo Blanco in southern Argentina. I had found an inscription on the southern part of the Piri Reis map stating: 'It is related by the Portuguese Infidel [Columbus] that in this place, night and day are, at their shortest period, of two hours duration, and at their longest phase of 22 hours.'[2] For the winter daylight to have lasted only two hours, the man who originally drew the chart and made that note must have been in the deep south at a latitude of about 60°S, well to the south of the southern tip of Tierra del Fuego. The map also shows what appears to be ice connecting the tip of South America to Antarctica.

I was able to use the inscription on the Piri Reis map and the position of the ice shown on it to fix the southern tip of South America to approximately 55°S, the northern limit of drift ice. Establishing the latitude of Tierra del Fuego allowed me to make a closer examination of the southern part of the Piri Reis and compare it with a modern chart. This revealed at once that the original cartographer had drawn the east coast of Patagonia with great accuracy. The prominent features of the coastline – headlands, bays, rivers, estuaries and ports – tally from Cabo Blanco in the north to the entrance of the Strait of Magellan in the south. The cartographer of the Piri Reis also drew a number of animals on the land.

It is a bleak, desolate, windswept region, as Darwin recalled: 'Without habitations, without water, without trees, without mountains, they support merely a few dwarf plants . . . The plains of Patagonia are boundless, for the area is scarcely passable, and hence unknown.'[3] Columbus could not possibly have been the original cartographer; he never got south of the equator. His knowledge of the region, including his description of the islands in the South Atlantic being in darkness – obscured – for twenty-two hours each day, can only have come from the inscriptions on another chart he had copied.

The first European, Magellan, did not set sail for Patagonia

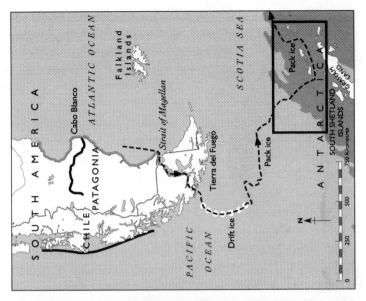

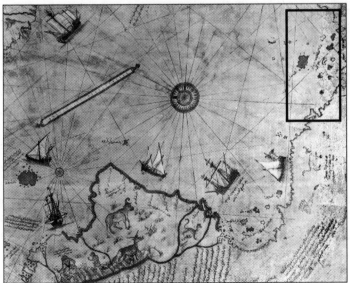

The Piri Reis map compared to modern Patagonia, showing
the Strait of Magellan.

until years after the Piri Reis was drawn. So who originally provided the information to enable Patagonia to be drawn on the Piri Reis, and how did he obtain it? Knowing I was looking at Patagonia, a desperate place but nonetheless one that supports animal life, I began to examine the five creatures depicted on the map.

The first, a deer with prominent horns, was superimposed on an area that has now been designated a national park, the Parque Nacional Perito Moreno. This animal is clearly a huemil, an Andean deer, with the head and antlers accurately depicted. There are still huge herds of these deer where the animal is shown on the Piri Reis. The next creature was placed in what is now the Monumento Natural Bosques Petrificados, 150 kilometres south of modern Caleta Olivia. I have spent some time photographing animals in the Andes and instantly recognized the creature as a guanaco. Guanacos are members of the camel family. They have curious, floppy ears which are bent forwards when they are excited or anxious. Andean people decorate guanacos' ears with red tassels in the same way we would plait a horse's mane. From a side view, the bent ears resemble forward-pointing horns. Clearly, the cartographer who copied the original chart mistook the bent ears for horns. Large herds of guanaco are found in the Monumento Natural Bosques Petrificados, just where they are shown on the Piri Reis, and, like the huemils, guanacos are unique to South America. The third animal, a mountain lion, was placed in what is now the Parque Nacional Monte León where, as the name indicates, mountain lions are common. All three animals were shown exactly where I have seen them in Patagonia and were drawn before Europeans arrived.

There is also a drawing of a naked bearded man. At first glance, he appears to have his head in the middle of his body, but on closer examination it seems perfectly possible that he had been drawn in a crouching position, allowing his thick beard to cover his genitals. I surmised that the Turkish cartographer who copied the captured Portuguese chart onto the Piri Reis was almost certainly a Muslim. Muslims are very conservative about exposing their bodies; if the cartographer had indeed been of that faith, he would not have been comfortable depicting naked men. When Magellan arrived in Patagonia long after the original map was drawn, he was surprised to find that despite the cold weather the people did indeed go about naked, keeping themselves warm with fires, even when they were travelling in boats. As a result, he named the land 'Tierra del Fuego' – the land of fire.[4]

That left one last creature to identify, a beast that appeared to have come from fable: a dog-headed man. There were two notes describing the creature: 'In this place there are . . . wild beasts of this shape',[5] and 'These wild beasts attain a length of seven spans . . . between their eyes there is a distance of only one span [the distance between the outspread tips of the thumb and the little finger]. Yet it is said they are harmless souls.'[6] The Piri Reis map had depicted the other Patagonian animals with remarkable accuracy and placed them precisely where they are found today. I could therefore expect the monster, if it ever really existed, to have lived in the south of the Santa Cruz province of Argentina or in the north part of the Chilean province of Magallanes. Did such monsters ever walk the earth there? London's Natural History Museum could offer no help in identifying the creature, so I contacted natural history museums within a two-hundred-mile radius of where the monster was shown and described on the Piri Reis.

My first call, to the Museo de Fauna, Rio Verde in Magellanes province, Chile, was answered in the negative, with barely suppressed mirth. The fourth call, to the nearby Museo de Sitio in Puerto Natales, was much more fruitful.

'I'm looking for a monster twice the size of a human. Were there ever any creatures like that in your area?'

'Yes.'

'Does your museum exhibit one?'

'Yes.'

'What is its name?'

'The mylodon.'

The mylodon is a creature of which I had been wholly ignorant until then, but London's Natural History Museum now provided a wealth of information about it. The monster was a giant sloth weighing around two hundred kilograms, unique to South America. In 1834, Darwin found a skeleton on a beach at Bahía Blanca in Patagonia near to where the creature is shown on the Piri Reis map; from the oil still present in the remnants of attached flesh, he concluded that the creature's demise was 'recent'. He sent the bones to Dr Richard Owen at the Royal College of Surgeons in London, who reconstructed the skeleton. It resembled a giant man with a dog's head, rearing on its

A nineteenth-century engraving of the skeleton of a mylodon.

haunches and using its legs and tail as a tripod while it knocked down small trees. It would strip the branches bare of fruit before lumbering off to demolish the next tree. The animal was said to reach three metres, sometimes even more, in height and slept for most of the time. The native people of Patagonia harnessed these 'harmless souls'[7] in caves during the winter, taking them out to graze in summer; their meat apparently tasted like bland mutton.

Later I was to find a Chinese book published in 1430 entitled *The Illustrated Record of Strange Countries*. As its title implies, this book records the strange animals the Chinese found on their travels. A dog-headed creature very similar to that drawn on the Piri Reis map is shown, with a note – the only part of the document that has yet been translated – stating that it was found after travelling for two years west of China.

The Chinese must have looked upon such alien creatures with wonder, and at once would have begun efforts to capture some specimens. When encountering strange and exotic animals, it was their custom to take them back to China to present to the emperor for his zoo.[8] A stream of quilins (giraffes) had returned with Zheng He's captains to astound and delight Zhu Di, and I believe that a number of mylodons were also taken aboard the Chinese junks, two of which did reach China.[9] I could imagine the Chinese seamen luring these lumbering, dog-headed creatures out of their caves and onto the giant ships, accompanied by tons of leaves for them to eat.

The Piri Reis map was so accurate both in its depictions of physical features and its descriptions of animals unique to South America that it could only be charting Patagonia. For that reason, I was also certain that the mountains drawn on the western side were the Andes. These mountains, running northwards up the Pacific coast, are not visible from the Atlantic; they are hundreds of miles away from the east coast. The original cartographer must have sailed that Pacific coast long before the first

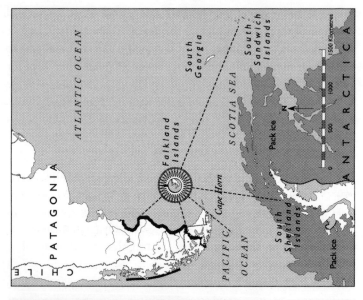

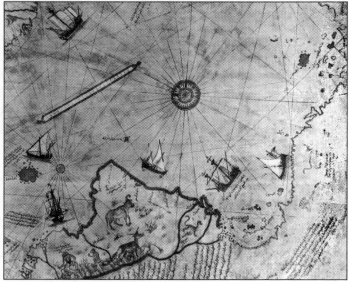

The Falkland Islands on the Piri Reis, compared to a modern map.

Europeans reached South America or the Pacific, and the fleet that carried him can only have passed through the Strait of Magellan or braved the blizzards, incessant gales and mountainous seas of Cape Horn.

Knowing the size of Patagonia, I could accurately determine the scale of the Piri Reis map and fix the latitudes of the land and islands shown on it. Cabo Blanco is at 47°20'S, so the islands shown at the bottom of the Piri Reis must be at 68°43'S – exactly the latitude of the South Shetland Islands. I now knew that the original cartographer had been aboard a ship that had discovered the Antarctic continent and the South Shetland Islands four centuries before the first Europeans reached them. As I was later to discover, these obscure, almost uninhabited islands were of vital importance to the Chinese.

It must have taken thousands of man-hours for the skilled surveyors and navigators to chart such a large area of land and ocean, stretching thousands of miles from Antarctica in the south to the Peruvian Andes in the north. To cover such vast distances, the charting must have been co-ordinated, involving the use of different fleets. Before Europeans reached the South Atlantic, the only nation capable of putting such fleets to sea was China, and the only plausible opportunity was provided by the Chinese treasure fleets during the 'missing' two years of the great voyage of 1421–3. Although I was convinced I was right, I had not yet found any first-hand evidence of a Chinese visit to South America. The clearest evidence would come from the surviving wreck of a treasure ship full of early Ming porcelain. Such wrecks were to play a vital part in establishing the presence of the Chinese treasure fleets elsewhere in the world, but finding such a wreck on the coasts of South America is likely to be a lengthy task. The seas are buffeted by incessant storms and strong tides break up and sweep away wreckage and spilled cargoes. The search is in hand, but it is unlikely to yield short-term results.

Meanwhile, I needed an interim solution. For example, did the first Europeans to reach South America find plants or animals unique to China when they landed there, or were plants unique to the Americas seen in China when the first Europeans arrived there? If so, had the Chinese junks carried them home with them? Fortunately, a number of distinguished scholars have worked on this problem for many years.[10] I was led to their work as a result of waking at cockcrow on my first morning during a visit to Peru. I had lived in Malaysia and remembered well how the morning call of Asiatic hens – 'kik-kiri-kee' – was markedly different from the 'cock-a-doodle-do' of their European counterparts. As I lay in bed, I recognized the familiar 'kik-kiri-kee' and began to wonder how Asiatic rather than European hens had come to be in Peru.

The domesticated Asiatic cock and hen originated several thousand years ago in the jungles of south-east Asia, in South China, Annam, Vietnam, Cambodia and Malaysia. The strain remains quite distinct from the European hen. When Magellan arrived off Rio (as it is now called), he 'picked up a great store of chickens ... for one fish hook or a knife, they gave me six chickens, fearing even so that they were cheating me'.[11] But the chickens Magellan and the Spanish conquistadors found in South America had virtually nothing in common with European 'dunghill fowl'. They were of four principal, wholly different types. The Malay class were tall and thin – the cocks were able to peck food off a dinner table. They had thin heads, more like a turkey's than a chicken's, with a bare throat and a bare strip running down the breast. The Chinese class had stocky, heavy bodies, fluffy feathers, short wings and feathered legs. The cocks had modest tail feathers and very small, short, blunt spurs. They were poor flyers and notably tame. To this day, the silky-feathered melanotic chicken ('melanotic' denotes the black feathers, skin, flesh and bones of this strange bird) is found throughout Latin America; I have seen them in Amazonian villages. The fourth type of hen was the Asian frizzle fowl, with feathers that curve back towards the body instead of lying flat. Again, there was nothing remotely resembling this bird in the Mediterranean world of 1500, when frizzle fowl were found all over South America. Perhaps the most striking difference was that the Asiatic hens laid blue-shelled eggs whereas those of European hens were white or cream. Blue eggs are still found all the way from Chile to Mexico.

There were two other significant differences. If the Europeans had brought chickens, then the European name would have been adopted by the Indians of South America. This did not happen. The Arawak of northern South America called melanotic chickens *karaka*; the Indian name is *karaknath*. In north-west Mexico, chicken was *tori*; in Japanese it is *nihuatori*, meaning 'yard bird'. The Inca emperors, who were just embarking on a period of imperial expansion in 1421, frequently wore feathers and adopted the names of birds. In their Quechua language, chicken was *hualpa*, and the name Yupánqui (c. 1438–1493) was adopted; Atahualpa was the formal name of the emperor overthrown by Francisco Pizarro. The Incas therefore had a word for chicken at least forty years before the arrival of the conquistadors.

The Chinese practices of divination using eggs or dripping chicken blood on bark paper before burning the paper, and the belief that a melanotic chicken protects the household from evil spirits, were also found in South America. Like the Chinese, the Amerindians used them for sacrifice, divination and healing the sick.

Asiatic chickens were found the length of both the Atlantic and Pacific coasts of the Americas as far north as Rhode Island. These birds cannot fly and must have been brought by ship. The only non-European ships that could travel such vast distances were Chinese. The spread of Asiatic chickens prior to the European conquest closely correlates with the lands shown on

The frizzle fowl from Aldrovandi's *Ornithologia*, 1604.

the Piri Reis map – the Amazon and Orinoco deltas in Venezuela, Brazil, Patagonia, Chile and Peru. Even today, in areas of South America where there has been minimal Spanish (or other European) influence, one still finds chickens which lay pale blue eggs and possess other Asiatic characteristics unknown in European birds.[12] The conclusion is inescapable: Chinese fleets must have brought chickens to South America.

Since the Asiatic chickens are very different from the Mediterranean chickens and most of the traits that reappear in the flocks of the Amerindians are found in Asia, the obvious conclusion would be that the Amerind chickens were first introduced [to South America] from Asia and not from the Mediterranean ...[13]

When one considers the total data available on the chicken in America, a conclusion for a Spanish or Portuguese first introduction of chickens into America is simply counter to all the evidence. The Mediterraneans, as late as 1600, did not have, and did not even know of, the galaxy of chickens present in Amerind hands ... If a scholarly and scientific approach to the subject is taken, an approach that pays attention to the data instead of the clichés of the past, then the only possible conclusion is that chickens were introduced from across the Pacific, probably repeatedly, long before the Mediterranean discoveries of America.[14]

The second line of evidence came from maize, a very unusual plant that originated in the Americas and was unknown in China before Zheng He's voyages. Just as chickens cannot fly, maize is incapable of self-propagation. Wherever it is found, it has been propagated by man. There is considerable evidence that maize was carried to Asia before Columbus landed in America in 1492.[15] For example, within his description of the expedition landing at Limasava in the Philippines in 1520, Antonio Pigafetta, Magellan's diarist, noted this: 'The islanders invited the General [Magellan] into their boats in which were their merchandise, viz. cloves, cinnamon, ginger, pepper, nutmegs and maize.'[16] There is no possibility that Pigafetta had misidentified the plant. In his notes in the original Italian, maize is translated as *miglio* against which Pigafetta had written the Caribbean word, *maíz*. He knew what maize looked like – it had 'ears like Indian corn and is shelled off and called *lada*' – and not only had he spent months with Magellan in South America on his way to Limasava but several seamen aboard had also served with Columbus in the Caribbean.[17] Chinese records state that Zheng He's admirals brought back 'extraordinarily large ears of grain'.[18] The Chinese were used to rice with ears the size of barley. The only 'extraordinarily large' ears compared to rice were those of maize. There is a wealth of further evidence, for the Portuguese also found maize in Indonesia, the Philippines and China, and *metates* – utensils for grinding maize unique to

South America – were found in the hold of a junk, built in 1414, that was recently discovered on the sea-bed at Pandanan in the south-west Philippines where it had sunk in about 1423.

There was now not a scintilla of doubt in my mind that the Chinese fleet had been in South America in 1421 and had surveyed the lands shown on the Piri Reis map a century before Magellan. But they were sailing on this epic voyage to bring the entire world into the Chinese tribute system. Why should they have taken such inordinate trouble to chart this part of in-hospitable Patagonia, a land of driving snow and bitter cold occupied only by unsophisticated, naked people with nothing to trade and with little natural wealth save for burberries and fish?

Could the Piri Reis map provide a further clue? At first it seemed only to deepen the mystery, for it showed a series of 'spokes' extending from the Patagonian coast and intersecting in a hub – the centre of a compass-rose – in the wastes of the South Atlantic. These spokes are what navigators call 'portolan lines', used in portolan navigation, also known as triangulation. Comparing the Piri Reis with a modern map, I identified the prominent points on the Patagonian coast from where each portolan line was drawn. The cartographers must have been aboard seven ships that set sail from Puntas Guzmán and Mercedes on the northern coast, Cabos Curioso and San Francisco in the centre and Punta Norte, Cabos Buen Tempo and Espíritu Santo in the south.

Knowing the scale of the Piri Reis map, I could now readily identify the true location of the centre of the compass-rose. The portolan lines intersected in King George's Bay in the West Falkland Islands. At the absolute centre of the compass-rose is Mount Adams (2,917 feet), the most conspicuous mountain in the Falklands. Was either Zhou Man or Hong Bao a secret mountaineer at heart? Is that why the ships were ordered to steer towards a mountain peak? For weeks I was baffled by this conundrum, then suddenly the answer came to me. The Chinese needed a star in the southern hemisphere to replace Polaris in the northern, and in the event they selected two: Canopus for latitude and the Southern Cross for navigation.[19]

Canopus, a yellow-white, super giant star, sits in space three hundred light years from Earth towards the South Pole and pumps out more than a thousand times the power of the sun. The combination of its power and distance makes it the second brightest star in the sky, nearly as bright as Venus, and instantly identifiable because of the colour of its light. Like the Southern Cross, Canopus is in the far south but not directly above the South Pole. To use Canopus for latitude, the Chinese had to determine its precise position by sailing to a point directly underneath the star. The Southern Cross points to the South Pole but, unlike Polaris, it is not directly above the Pole. To be able to use the Southern Cross for accurate navigation, the Chinese also had to locate its position in the sky – its height and longitude. Once again, the only way to calculate the precise position of the Southern Cross was to sail to a position directly beneath it.

The Chinese had been attempting to locate the positions of both the Southern Cross and Canopus for centuries:

> In the eighth month of the twelfth year of the Khai-Yuan period [in the eighth century AD] [an expedition was sent to the] south seas to observe Lao Jen [Canopus] at high altitudes and all the stars still further south [Southern Cross] which, though large, brilliant and numerous, had never in former times been named and charted. They were all observed to about 20° from the south [Celestial] Pole [viz. 70°S]. This is the region that the astronomers of old considered was always hidden and invisible below the horizon.[20]

Only when Canopus and the Southern Cross had been located could new lands in the southern hemisphere be accurately placed on charts. When they reached Mount Adams in the West Falklands the Chinese cartographers were nearly underneath

Canopus. They were taking such pains to fix their position so that they could calculate their precise latitude: 52°40′ South. By cross-referencing Canopus to Polaris they could establish Canopus's height and then use that star to obtain their latitude anywhere in the southern oceans, just as they used Polaris in the northern hemisphere. Given the importance of this location to them, I would expect the Chinese to have erected a carved stone near Mount Adams, and I have asked the governor of the Falklands for his help in organizing a search for it.

Once the latitude of Canopus had been discovered, the fleets of Zhou Man and Hong Bao could have returned independently to China, sailing westwards across the Pacific and eastwards across the southern oceans, along the same line of latitude, directly under Canopus. By doing so, all ships would be conducting surveys from the same latitude. I also came to the conclusion that it would have been logical to survey the world at latitudes where the position of other stars could be precisely determined, for example at 3°40′N, where Polaris disappeared below the horizon. It also seemed logical to expect that other latitudes of particular significance to the Chinese, for example that of their capital city Beijing at 39°53′N, might also have served the same function. As will be seen, my hunches were to prove correct.

The first Chinese 'anchor point' was the Falkland Islands, selected because they are not only underneath Canopus but also almost exactly half the world away (179°) from Beijing. At this stage, although the Chinese could not measure longitude they knew the earth was a sphere. Moreover, by using Polaris they could determine the semi-circumference of that sphere (180° × 60 nautical miles) and thus approximate when they were half the world away from Beijing (days sailed multiplied by average speed). If a fleet sailed westwards from this anchor position in the Falklands and found another island south of Australia at 52°40′ South, the cartographers could chart that continent by triangulation as precisely as they had charted Patagonia. Similarly, a fleet sailing eastwards and finding another island south of Africa at 52°40' South could chart the Indian Ocean.

I pondered how I could track the onward movements of the Chinese fleets from this anchor position. I already knew the dates on which the fleets under Zhou Man and Hong Bao had eventually returned to China and the number of ambassadors each one had brought with them. I soon realized that by using the charts and maps, and noting the locations from which the ambassadors had been collected, I could make a rational deduction about the course each fleet had followed in the intervening period. It was another significant link in the chain of evidence leading me in the wake of the treasure fleets.

Whereas the fleet under the senior admiral, Yang Qing, had remained in the Indian Ocean throughout the duration of the voyage, and returned to China in September 1422 with seventeen envoys from states in East Africa and India, Zhou Man and Hong Bao did not reach China until the autumn of 1423. Zhou Man brought no ambassadors and Hong Bao only one, from Calicut. From that, I deduced that Admiral Zhou Man's fleet had sailed westwards to chart the Pacific and returned via the Spice Islands. Admiral Hong Bao's fleet had sailed southwards for Antarctica to measure the Southern Cross and then made its way home eastwards via the southern oceans, Malacca and Calicut. I began the search for traces of their voyages, first of all by tracking Hong Bao across the southern oceans.

III

The Voyage of
Hong Bao

6

VOYAGE

TO

ANTARCTICA

AND

AUSTRALIA

ADMIRAL HONG BAO'S DESIGNATED TASK WAS TO chart the world eastwards from the fixed reference point established at the Falkland Islands – 52°40′S – but by now the rice in his container ships must have been running low and the bean shoots growing in tubs would all have been eaten. Before setting sail eastwards into the unknown waters of the southern oceans, he had to take on fresh supplies of food.

The Falklands offered cabbage, wild celery, penguins, geese and fish, but little other meat and no fruit at all. The only mammal ever discovered on the Falkland Islands was the warrah, an indigenous fox, described by Charles Darwin: 'There is no other instance in any part of the world of so small a mass of broken land, distant from a continent, possessing so large an aboriginal quadruped [the warrah] peculiar to itself . . . Within a very few years after these islands shall have become regularly settled, in all probability this fox will be classed with the dodo, as an animal which has perished from the face of the earth.'[1]

There is something curious about this creature which, as Darwin predicted, was wiped out in the Falklands by the 1870s. Darwin and other naturalists remarked on the warrah's extraordinary tameness. The British biologist Juliet Clutton-Brock has analysed the animal's physical characteristics from specimens in the Natural History Museum in London and concluded that, like the aboriginal dingo, the warrah had once been domesticated. It was a cross between the South American fox and a feral dog brought across the sea to the Falklands before the Europeans arrived. The most plausible explanation of its origins is that the Chinese left some of their dogs on the Falklands (they bred them on the junks for food) which then interbred with the local foxes. A request has been made to the Natural History Museum in London for DNA samples from the now-extinct warrah so that they can be compared to the DNA of Chinese food dogs. Results will be posted on the website.

If the Falklands offered a very limited food supply, Patagonia, three hundred nautical miles to the west, resembled an enormous larder, as later explorers were to find to their delight. Enough fish to feed the whole fleet could be netted in a morning; mussels the size of crabs littered the shallow pools. Guanaco, huemil and hares as large as dogs were almost tame; only snarling mountain lions stood between the sailors and limitless meat. Burberries and wild apples rich in vitamin C were also plentiful. Perhaps taking advantage of one of the periods of calm weather frequently found in an Antarctic summer, Admiral Hong Bao returned due west from the Falkland Islands to Patagonia to replenish his supplies. Still underneath Canopus at 52°40'S, he would have found what appeared to be a safe anchorage in a large bay just south of Cape Virgines. Unknown to him, the bay was the entrance to a strait leading to the Pacific. As he entered the bay, a ferocious current running at up to six knots would have dragged his fleet south-westwards through the strait like water down a plughole.

By the next morning the fleet had been sucked halfway through the strait. At last out of the current, they found themselves off the Brunswick Peninsula (the southernmost tip of the South American mainland), clearly identifiable on the Piri Reis map. By now the fleet was south of Canopus, and Hong Bao would have wished to sail north to get underneath his reference point once again, the latitude from which he was to chart the world to the east. The strait becomes narrower and narrower leading into the Canal Geronimo – less than a mile wide and far too narrow for his huge ships to manoeuvre, their turning circle being nearly a mile. As a result, the fleet was forced to reverse its course, and hence the cartographers drew the Canal Geronimo as a river, just as it must have appeared to them.

Back off the Brunswick Peninsula, the fleet took the Canal Magdalena south-westwards for the Pacific, entering the ocean near Isla Aguirre, a small, uninhabited island but one of the few out of the hundreds lining the coast to have been named, even today. The 'Strait of Magellan' had been discovered and charted by a complete accident: the latitude of the entrance to the strait is also the latitude of Canopus, the Chinese guiding star in the southern hemisphere. But although the Chinese had discovered the strait by chance, that does not diminish their astonishing achievement in piloting their enormous, square-sailed junks through such a narrow strait in the fierce gales and sudden violent snow squalls common in that region, which reduce visibility to a few yards. Magellan would not have known of this strait had the Chinese not charted it. Europeans thus owe a huge debt to the Chinese for pioneering the link between the Atlantic and Pacific Oceans, and opening up the sea route to the Spice Islands.

Not without reason was the remote, inhospitable land on either side of the dreaded strait named 'the uttermost part of the earth' by the earliest European explorers. Despite the near-endless snowstorms, often driven horizontally across the land by the force of the wind, Tierra del Fuego has an enthralling grandeur. I have seen glaciers tumble vertically into the ocean, and ice-bound mountain peaks glistening like diamonds against the pale skies. Today, as for centuries past, navigators dread the violent currents that seem to start and finish without warning or apparent cause, and the westerly gales that spring from nowhere and whip the seas into a boiling cauldron within minutes. Until the nineteenth century, its howling gales and bleak terrain discouraged settlement, leaving the Yahgan natives who inhabited this grim terrain to live in peace, huddling around the fires that led Magellan to name the region Tierra del Fuego. The Yahgan seemed to Darwin 'among the most abject and miserable creatures I ever saw, the difference between them and Europeans being greater than that between wild and domestic animals'.[2]

The discovery that the Chinese had made the first ever voyage through this daunting region was a tremendous moment for me.

I wondered if Hong Bao had also realized its remarkable importance and significance. I returned to the British Library to see if the diaries of the Portuguese explorer Ferdinand Magellan and Antonio Pigafetta, who sailed with Magellan's fleet, could offer any further verification of this ground-breaking voyage of a century before.

Magellan renounced his own country and set sail on his great voyage of circumnavigation on 20 September 1519 under the colours of Spain. He had a fleet of five ships and a crew of 265 men. Only one ship and eighteen men survived to complete the circumnavigation. Magellan himself was fatally wounded in the Philippines on 27 April 1521 after becoming involved in a dispute between two warring tribes. Pigafetta had this to say about the critical point in their journey:

> After going and setting course to the fifty-second degree towards the said Antarctic Pole on the festival of the Eleven Thousand Virgins (19th October), we found by a miracle a Strait [near what] we called the Cape of the Eleven Thousand Virgins [today Cape Virgines]. Which Strait is in length 110 leagues which are 440 miles and in width somewhat less than half a league.[3]

The fact that they were 'setting course to the fifty-second degree' indicates that Magellan knew that at 52°S he would find the strait that was later to bear his name, linking the Atlantic with the Pacific. His fleet reached the dark and forbidding region on 19 October 1520. By that stage, Magellan and his crew were in a wretched state. Howling gales battered the ships and blizzards obscured both the passage ahead and the rocky islands surrounding them. He had problems finding an anchorage, many of his sailors were dying from scurvy, and he had succeeded in quelling a mutiny only by the brutal expedient of hanging, drawing and quartering the leaders. Now mutiny was again in the air.

'This Strait was a circular place surrounded by mountains . . . and to most of those in the ships it seemed there was no way out from it to enter the said Pacific sea.'[4] Magellan could not persuade his men that it was safe to go onward through the strait, so he ordered his critics to put their reasons in writing for either continuing or returning to Spain. He read their opinions aloud, then, taking a sacred oath on St James whose insignia he wore upon his cloak, he solemnly swore to his men that 'there was another Strait which led out [to the Pacific] saying that he knew it well and had seen it in a marine chart of the King of Portugal, which a great pilot and sailor named Martin of Bohemia [Martin Behain] had made'.[5]

Magellan was telling the truth, though not the whole truth. The existence of the strait leading from the Atlantic to the Pacific was well known both to the King of Spain and Magellan before he set sail. He took with him on the voyage a marine chart that showed the strait and the Pacific Ocean beyond it. The contract he had signed with the king specified the aims of the voyage – to sail westwards for the Spice Islands – and the share of the profits each was to enjoy. Magellan wanted knowledge of the strait to be restricted to himself alone to prevent others from following in his wake and claiming their own share of the riches that awaited him, but the King of Spain was in no position to grant his request, for the Portuguese held the master chart.

Magellan's words, and his ruthless and inspired leadership, persuaded his men to continue, and they completed the passage of the strait that ever afterwards bore his name rather than that of the first man to do so, Hong Bao. In his description of the ships clearing the strait and entering the Pacific, Pigafetta made a vitally significant comment: 'When we had left that Strait, if we had sailed always westwards, we should have gone without finding any island other than the Cape of the Eleven Thousand Virgins . . . in 52 degrees of latitude exactly towards the Antarctic Pole.'[6] Pigafetta's statement contained information that could only have been obtained by someone who had either sailed the world at that latitude or seen a chart showing the Pacific empty of land at 52°S. Magellan turned to the north towards the equator when leaving the strait and so could not have discovered for himself that there was no land at that latitude. He must therefore have seen a chart. Magellan knew that he was not the first to sail through the strait, nor the first to cross the Pacific. Indeed, the first Spanish ships to pass through the strait found wrecked Chinese junks off the coast of Chile.

Once again, Fra Mauro had been correct: a ship from India had rounded the Cape of Good Hope and sailed to the 'obscured islands'. The riddle of the Piri Reis map had also been solved. Patagonia and the 'Strait of Magellan' were indeed drawn long before Magellan set sail, but not by a civilization predating the Pharaohs, as one authority has suggested,[7] nor by aliens from outer space, as another, rather less academic writer argued,[8] but by a great Chinese treasure fleet during the 'missing years' of 1421–3.

After passing through the strait, Admiral Hong Bao took his fleet southwards, sailing to the west of the islands of Tierra del Fuego. The cartography of the Piri Reis map clearly shows the route the fleet took: while Patagonia is very accurately charted, the low eastern islands of Tierra del Fuego are not recorded at all, indicating that the Chinese had sailed down the mountainous west coast.

I compared the Piri Reis map with a modern satellite photograph and immediately identified the bays and small islands surrounding the Chinese passage to the south. Further down the coast, Cook Bay is accurately positioned, suggesting that Admiral Hong Bao had anchored there. From this anchorage, he would have seen the magnificent snow-capped mountains of the Cordillera Darwin towering in an arc to the east of him. They appear on the map as separate islands, for from that distance the cartographer could have seen only their snow-capped peaks. I magnified the Piri Reis map to the same scale as a modern chart[9] and found that all eleven 'islands' shown on the Piri Reis south of Patagonia coincide with mountain peaks on the islands that collectively form western Tierra del Fuego. My detailed workings will appear on the website.

The Chinese had already established the position of Canopus in the sky, the nearest and brightest equivalent in the southern hemisphere to Polaris in the northern, but to fix its position relative to the South Pole they had to establish the precise position of the pole itself. Only then would they be able to navigate and chart lands as accurately as they did in the northern hemisphere. Since they already knew from their observations of the night sky that the two leading stars of the Southern Cross, Crucis Gamma and Crucis Alpha, were aligned with the pole, they believed that they only had to sail in the same direction to reach the pole.

The polar regions can be a terrible place for a mariner. In summer there are periods of flat calm, clear skies and limpid blue seas speckled with ice floes, but when the weather breaks massive waves crash over the bows and the wind screams through the sails, driving squalls and flurries of snow and ice that sting the skin like needles. For weeks in midwinter there is unbroken black darkness; even when the sun does begin to re-appear it is no more than a brief, dim disc on the northern horizon. Often cloud and freezing mist cloak every outline, leaving the seamen on watch straining their eyes into the murk for the first warning sign of drifting ice floes or a towering iceberg in their track.

However, the prospect of sailing into these frozen regions would have held few terrors for the Chinese, who had eight centuries' experience of navigating in northern polar latitudes behind them and a thousand-year tradition of navigating in ice: the nearest port to Beijing, Tanggu, is ice-bound for three months each year. I found the first anecdotal evidence that the Chinese had indeed attempted to set sail for the South Pole after leaving Cook Bay in an account[10] of the travels of a young nobleman from Bologna, Ludovico de Varthema, in 1506. Ludovico de Varthema was sailing between Borneo and Java where he was told a strange tale. His companions, two Chinese Christians and an East Indian navigator, told him sailors from the other (Chinese) side of Java had sailed by the Southern Cross to regions where it was very cold and the days were only four hours long.[11] How could they have known without sailing there?

The Piri Reis map provided further evidence that they had sailed south. Ice is shown running due south of the Strait of Magellan, and to have drawn it the Chinese must have been sailing alongside it. They were heading due south, making straight for the South Pole. The two leading stars of the Southern Cross were overhead,[12] pointing in the direction they had to sail. Some two hundred miles south of Tierra del Fuego,[13] they met the first drift ice, which had begun to curve to the east, drawn as a C-shaped arc on the Piri Reis map. They attempted to continue southwards around the ice but were unable to do so and were obliged to alter course, first to the east and then to the south-east, all the time trying to find a way to continue towards the pole. After sailing another two hundred miles south,[14] they met pack ice that continued all the way down to the Antarctic peninsula. The ice depicted on the Piri Reis map corresponds with the normal maximum limits of drift and pack ice in midsummer.[15]

Admiral Hong Bao was now approaching the Antarctic Circle. At this latitude strange things happen. At the South Pole itself, longitude has no meaning. It becomes a dot; there are no directions other than north. In midsummer (December), the sun is always in the north and it is light all day; in winter, it is permanently dark. The navigational difficulties are exacerbated by magnetic anomalies caused by the South Magnetic Pole, far

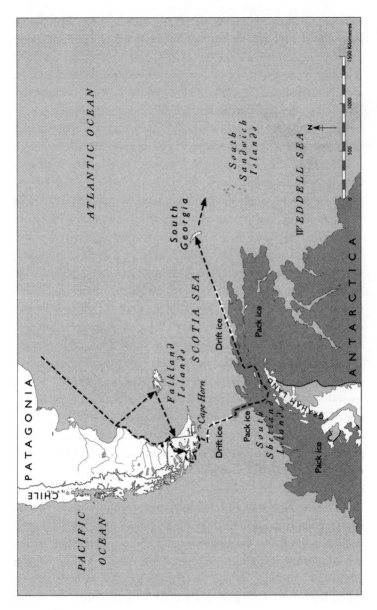

The journey to Antarctica.

removed from the true South Pole. This would have played havoc with the Chinese magnetic compasses; the only navigational aids they could then rely on were bearings obtained from the constellation of the leading stars of the Southern Cross and the latitude of Canopus, both of which become circumpolar – never rising and setting and visible in the sky at all times – below 68°S. The intensity of its light and the clarity of the Antarctic air often make Canopus visible in daylight.

The Piri Reis map shows Graham Land, the northern-extremity of the Antarctic peninsula, largely ice-free, confirming that the expedition reached the Antarctic in January 1422. The C-shape of the drift ice shown stretching from Cape Horn indicates that they had first met a current flowing from the east. Further south, where the current had more or less disappeared, the chart shows the pack ice stretching east–west before once again curving in a shallower curve to the south-east as it met another, weaker current. The uniform shape of these curves of ice showed that the Chinese were favoured with good weather and sailing into the circumpolar current before a light breeze, insufficient to break up the ice. I estimated that they would have made an average speed of approximately three knots. At that rate the voyage from Cape Horn to the Antarctic peninsula would have taken approximately fourteen days.

A group of islands was shown on the Piri Reis map where none exists in reality. In shape they resembled the South Shetland Islands, and I wondered if they were indeed what the map was depicting. The Chinese could measure latitude precisely from Canopus, but they could not yet determine longitude with similar accuracy, and once again, I had to adjust the longitudinal positions of the islands recorded on the Piri Reis map to allow for the movement of the water in which the Chinese fleet was sailing, just as I had for the Kangnido map of Africa. Allowing for an average current of two-thirds of a knot against them during their passage south, the islands shown on the Piri

Reis map would be in fact four hundred miles further west than they were charted – precisely the position of the South Shetlands.

I knew from the Piri Reis map that the Chinese must have approached Antarctica from the north-west, skirting the edge of the ice, and would have made landfall on the south-western edge of the South Shetland Islands. Three of the islands are charted very accurately: Snow Island in the west, horseshoe-shaped Deception Island in the south, and four mountains on Livingstone Island in the north. A note near Deception Island also states: 'Here it is hot'. At first sight this appears a curious comment to make about a snowbound island in the Antarctic, but Deception Island is volcanic and active. Modern cruise ships anchor in the lagoon to allow tourists to bathe in the hot volcanic waters of Benjamin Cove.

Apart from Deception Island, the South Shetlands are an un-inhabited wilderness of frost-shattered rock, glaciers and ice-fields, without so much as a blade of grass to be seen. As I knew from my own time in submarines sailing in polar regions, the cold can be so severe that metal objects stick to your fingers. To avoid tearing the flesh, you need to warm the fingers. The only way of doing so is usually to urinate on them, but if you attempt to do this while exposed to the Antarctic winds, you risk a very painful frostbite. The Chinese would have huddled below decks, trying to keep warm among their horses, pigs and dogs, returning to the upper deck for as short a time as possible. Their rice supplies would have had to be carefully covered and in-sulated to prevent the intense cold causing permanent damage to the grains, and the flooded sections of the holds where they kept their supplies of fish and their trained otters would have had to be emptied to prevent the water expanding as it froze, and forc-ing apart the seams of the hull. Furthermore, in these terrible conditions, surveying this part of the islands so precisely would have taken some considerable time. Why had the Chinese bothered to do so? I began to wonder if they really had gone

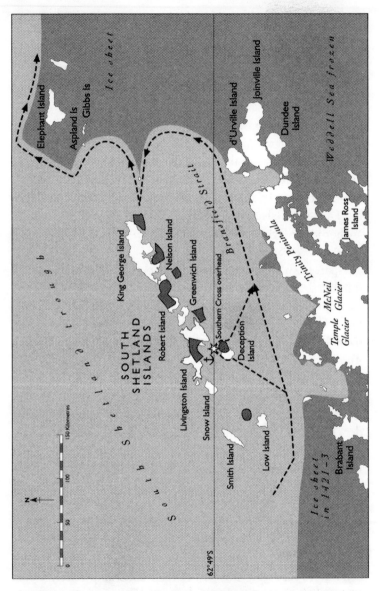

Locating the Southern Cross. The darker shaded portion is what is shown on the Piri Reis; the light areas are what is shown on modern Admiralty charts.

there. Then the answer that I should have seen at once suddenly came to me. They had chosen to sail to the Antarctic in order to get underneath Crucis Alpha, the leading star of the Southern Cross.

I could only shake my head in wonder at the skill and sophistication of these Chinese mariners of so many centuries ago. The Chinese astronomers' determination of the positions of Canopus and the Southern Cross in the sky was a pivotal moment in the history of man's knowledge of the globe. Because they knew the circumference of the earth, they could now calculate the true position of the South Pole. By observing the difference between the true bearing shown by the Southern Cross and that shown by their magnetic compasses, they could determine the position of the Magnetic South Pole and therefore make the necessary corrections to their compasses. In 1421–3, the stars of the Southern Cross and Canopus could be observed as far as 28°N – the latitude of the Canary Islands – where Polaris was also clearly visible.[16] A cross-reference to check latitudes could be obtained by comparing the latitudes derived from Canopus and Polaris. The *Wu Pei Chi* confirms that this was indeed a practice of Chinese navigators, whereas the Portuguese did not adopt this method of calculating latitude for another fifty years.

The Chinese could now steer a completely accurate course in the southern as well as the northern hemisphere and determine exact latitudes. Only the problem of longitude remained to be solved. Once true latitudes in the southern hemisphere could be calculated, Chinese charts could be drawn in a readily comprehensible form – not as a table or as a long strip of sailing directions such as the *Wu Pei Chi*, but as a recognizable geometric depiction. A note appended to the Piri Reis map confirms this change: '[This map was] drawn . . . from about twenty charts and mappae mundi . . . which shows the countries of Sint, Hint, and Cin [China] geometrically drawn . . . By reducing all these maps to one scale, this final form was arrived at.'[17]

To have found a way of accurately charting the whole world in a recognizable form must have been an incredibly exciting, triumphant moment for the Chinese astronomers, navigators and cartographers, just as it was for the Europeans when they made the same discoveries in 1473. The Chinese fleets could now go on to survey the world, using the latitude of Canopus as a baseline. They had accomplished one of the prime tasks their emperor had set them. They could now brave the biting cold of the air to enjoy a hot bath in the lagoon inside Deception Island, gather up penguins for food and cut off blocks of ice for fresh water. This would have been the moment to enjoy a cask of rice wine and feast on some of the pigs, before setting sail once again to explore the Antarctic mainland further south.

As the junks sailed through the strait separating the South Shetlands from the Antarctic peninsula, the islands would still have been visible thirty-five miles away to the north-west, with the mainland twenty miles to the south. At that range they would have seen only mountains, but they located them, with just a very small error. Their charting of mainland Antarctica was equally accurate. I was able to identify sixty-three prominent features of the Antarctic mainland on the Piri Reis map. My detailed working drawings will appear on the website. Only one thing seemed out of place – a strange serpent shown resting on the ice of Elephant Island. But the leopard seal resembles a serpent as it slithers across the ice, and, like serpents, leopard seals have fangs. East of Elephant Island, the Weddell Sea was shown as solid ice, and it is indeed ice-bound throughout the year. It is remarkably accurate cartography.

There was no longer the slightest shred of doubt in my mind. There was no need to summon ancient Egyptians or space aliens to explain how the Piri Reis map could have depicted Antarctica with such accuracy four hundred years before the first Europeans arrived there. The information came from surveyors aboard Admiral Hong Bao's fleet in 1422, who had been charting the precise position of the Southern Cross.

The Piri Reis map also showed another, smaller compass-rose south-east of the Falklands and north-east of the South Shetlands. The centre of this secondary rose corresponds to Bird Island, the north-west island of South Georgia. As its name implies, Bird Island is populated by millions of sea-birds using it as a launching platform for feeding forays into the plankton- and fish-rich Antarctic Ocean. It is a tiny island, two miles long and nowhere more than half a mile wide, fringed by sheer one-thousand-foot cliffs on its north side but with sandy beaches to the south.

The compass-rose showed that Bird Island was used as a pivotal point by the Chinese cartographers. Having established the course and distances the fleet had sailed from the South Shetlands and the Falklands to Bird Island, they could reduce longitude errors by cross-referencing the three. I applied the same scale as I had worked out for measuring Patagonia and discovered that the distance shown on the Piri Reis map from Deception Island in the Antarctic to Bird Island was correct. The only mistake was that both the South Shetlands and South Georgia were shown further east than they should be. Once again, the circumpolar current accounted for the longitudinal error.

After he had reached and charted Bird Island, Admiral Hong Bao would have had no choice but to continue eastwards, sailing beneath Canopus, for around these latitudes, as the name implies, the Roaring Forties would have driven his ships before the wind to the east. These are winds to test the courage of the bravest sailor. They howl over towering seas, great walls of green water capped with foam, hurling spume through the air. Seamen would have worked frozen and soaked to the skin and shouted themselves hoarse in a vain attempt to be heard amid the shriek-ing of the wind through the rigging, the creaks and groans of timbers as the hull flexed and twisted in a swell like none other on earth, and the roar and hiss of waves breaking over the bows and foaming away through the scuppers. The prow would have dragged itself free of one giant wave only to bury itself immediately in the next. There would have been little respite for the men below decks, their clothes permanently sodden and the pitching and heaving of the ship so severe that sleep would have been all but impossible.

Driven eastwards by the relentless winds, Admiral Hong Bao would not have anchored until he next found land along 52°40′S, enabling him to conduct another detailed cartographic survey, just as he had in South America. But travelling eastwards at this latitude there is no substantial landmass, only a few scattered islands. At last, after a voyage of some five thousand miles across the southern oceans, all the time with the brilliant yellow-white Canopus directly above him, the increasing numbers of sea-birds – albatross, terns, skua and petrels – would have alerted him to the fact that land was nearby, and at last his look-outs would have spotted the volcanic Mawson's Peak on Heard Island silhouetted above a group of smaller islands just fifteen miles to the south. Now he could begin a survey to establish another 'anchor' position for his cartographers.

Heard Island would have seemed a far from inviting prospect to Hong Bao and his men. It is heavily glaciated and much of the coastline is covered by ice cliffs. There are a few isolated patches of tussock grass, moss and lichen, but 80 per cent of the island is permanently ice-bound. However, a group of somewhat less forbidding islands, the Kerguelens – named after the Frenchman Le Comte Yves de Kerguelen-Tremarec, who is credited with discovering them on 12 February 1772 – lies three hundred miles to the north. The driving winds in that region mean that the Kerguelens can most readily be approached by square-rigged ships from the west – from South America, precisely the direction from which Hong Bao's fleet was sailing.

I found some independent evidence[18] that Hong Bao's fleet

had reached the islands: the *Dictionary of Ming Biography* records, 'Some of the ships reached as far as a place called Ha-buer which may be identified as Kerguelen Island in the Antarctic Ocean.'[19] The island of Ha-bu-er is also shown on the Chinese Mao Kun chart, part of the *Wu Pei Chi*, compiled around 1422,[20] alongside a note stating that 'storms prevented the fleet sailing further south'. Hong Bao had found more new lands.

Dominated by the six-thousand-foot Mount Ross, the main island of Kerguelen is sufficiently barren to have been described as 'Desolation Island' by Captain Cook. Rain, sleet or snow falls on three hundred days a year and 30 per cent of the island is permanently ice-covered, but the coasts are rich in penguins and elephant seals, and Kerguelen cabbages, very valuable plants for seamen, grow among the tussock grass and moss. A relative of our own cabbage, Kerguelen cabbages are rich in vitamin C and were much harvested and eaten by whalers and sealers in the following centuries to prevent scurvy. Hong Bao's crew would almost certainly have been suffering from scurvy after their marathon voyage across the southern oceans and would have gathered as many cabbages as possible, but Kerguelen's sour and barren soil did not support anywhere near enough of the plants to feed the thousands of men carried by the fleet. The search for fresh supplies would now have been becoming urgent.

The revelation that the Chinese had discovered Ha-bu-er/Kerguelen Island filled me with excitement, for after leaving the island Hong Bao's ships could have sailed in only one direction. As the Mao Kun says, the Roaring Forties would have prevented them from sailing further south, and they would also have stopped them from going north or retracing their route westwards. Instead, the Chinese junks would have been propelled eastwards before mountainous waves along a sea-corridor that led straight to the south-west coast of Australia. I had no doubt that Hong Bao must have reached Australia, so I returned to the British Library to search for a chart of the continent that had been

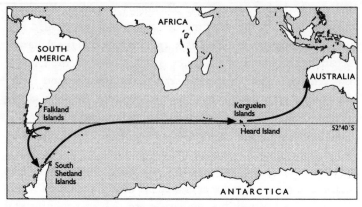

Hong Bao's journey to Australia.

surveyed and drawn before the first Europeans discovered it.

Australia is not depicted on the Piri Reis map, but it is shown on another very early chart, held by the British Library. It was drawn by Jean Rotz, appointed 'Hydrographer to the King' by Henry VIII of England, and was included in the *Boke of Idrography* Rotz presented to the king in 1542, two centuries before Captain Cook 'discovered' Australia. Rotz came from the Dieppe School of Cartography, celebrated throughout Europe for the clarity and accuracy of the maps and charts they produced. He was the leading mapmaker of his day, renowned for the meticulousness with which he depicted new lands. He never invented or fudged; what is shown on his charts is exactly what he had seen on older charts.

It is commonly accepted[21] that Rotz, and indeed the other Dieppe cartographers of his day, copied much older Portuguese charts. The styles of the Piri Reis and Jean Rotz charts are very similar, and both use Portuguese names to describe the newly discovered lands. The Rotz chart shows Malaysia, Cambodia, Vietnam and China all the way up to modern Hong Kong, and the whole coast is extremely well charted. The Persian Gulf,

India and south-east Asia are also instantly recognizable. The original chart can only have been drawn by someone with intimate knowledge of the coastlines of the Indian Ocean, China and Indochina. That at once ruled out the Portuguese, for although the Rotz chart was made after Magellan's circum-navigation of the world, neither Magellan nor the Portuguese explorers who followed him spent long enough on the Chinese coast to chart it with such compelling accuracy. Their target was the Spice Islands; they were making for the Moluccas far further south. If the original cartographer was not Portuguese, he in turn must have copied an earlier original.

Despite his accurate depiction of the coasts of China, Asia, India and Africa, many historians have failed to identify a vast new landmass Rotz showed south of the equator. It consists of two islands, 'Little Java' south of Sumatra and 'Greater Java', a huge continent stretching away from near the equator towards the South Pole. At its northern end, this continent has a pro-truding spit resembling Cape York, the northernmost tip of Australia. The north-east part of this southern continent also resembles the north-east Australian coast, but the land shown on the Rotz chart stretches far further to the south-east than Australia actually does.

The theories of Ptolemy – the astronomer, mathematician and geographer who lived in Alexandria in Egypt c. AD 87–150 – had been rediscovered in the late Middle Ages. Ptolemy's belief in the symmetry of the stars and the planets had led him to advance a theory in his book *Geographia* that a substantial southern land-mass must exist to 'balance' the continents of Europe and Asia in the northern hemisphere. My first assumption was that when drawing the land in the far south the original cartographer of the Rotz chart had based it not on observation but on Ptolemy's fore-cast, but this did not square with Rotz's reputation for precision. For the moment I had to set that puzzle aside and concentrate my attention on the south-west coast of 'Greater Java', which was depicted with considerably more accuracy. The shape of the coast accords with Hong Bao's fleet having made a landfall near modern Bunbury, a hundred miles to the south of Perth in Western Australia. The prevailing wind and current would then have driven them up the coast to an anchor point in the estuary of the Swan River that separates modern Perth and Fremantle, shown as a deep indentation on the Rotz chart.

The Kerguelen cabbages they had collected would have been of only modest help in staving off scurvy among the crew of the fleet, but in south-west Australia they would have found plentiful supplies of vitamin C in the berries that abound in the area. Blue fairy penguins and manna crabs were also there for the taking, the quokkas (small wallabies) were slow, timid and easy prey, and the jarrah, marri and karri trees would have provided plenty of hardwood for repairing their junks. Although the Rotz chart also shows the eastern and northern coasts of the Australian continent with great fidelity, the west coast is drawn no further south than Bunbury, where it ends abruptly. The most plausible reason for this curtailment of the survey, I would argue, is that the junk despatched by Admiral Hong Bao to chart the south coast of Australia foundered off Warrnambool in modern Victoria, south-east Australia, where a wreck was indeed discovered 166 years ago that could well have been a ship from Hong Bao's fleet.

In 1836, three men hunting seals sailed into the muddy Hopkins River and continued westwards down the small estuaries and lagoons of that coast. Where the Merri River joins the sea, they came across the wreck of a very old ship known from that day to this as the 'Mahogany Ship' because of the timber used in its construction. Seven years later, Captain Mills, a local harbour master, inspected the wreck on behalf of the government. He was astonished at the hardness of the wood; when he tried to cut a piece, his knife was useless, 'like glancing off iron'.[22] European ships were not then built of mahogany – the contemporary name used for any of a variety of reddish-brown hardwood trees – for there were no such trees in Europe, but Chinese ships were built of teak, a reddish-brown hardwood from the forests of Annam. Captain Mills was also baffled by the ship's origins: 'She struck me as a vessel of a model altogether unfamiliar and at variance in some respects with the rules of shipbuilding as far as we know them ... As regards to the nationality of the wreck, I do not profess to be a judge ... I should say the wreck in question is connected with neither [Spanish or Portuguese] build.'[23]

Twenty years later, an Australian woman, Mrs Manifold, examined the wreck, one of a further twenty-five people to record their impressions of it. She was impressed by the internal bulkheads, 'stout and strong'.[24] I am confident that this is probably a missing ship from Hong Bao's fleet.[25] The Aboriginal Yangery tribe, who then lived on the mainland close to the wreck-site of the ship, have a legend that 'yellow men' long ago settled among them.[26] Since then many observers have commented on the distinctive colour and facial characteristics of Aborigines who come from this small area of southern Australia. Pending carbon-dating of the material to establish the date of the wreck, at the very least it is arguable that sailors aboard the ship detached by Admiral Hong Bao to chart the south Australian coast were shipwrecked, and that some of the men and their concubines managed to reach the shore and settled among the Aborigines. Professor Wei Chuh-Hsien (Wei Chu Xian) goes further, believing that the men wrecked at Warrnambool rode on horseback up the valleys of the Murray, Darling and Murrambidgee Rivers to what is now Cooktown, leaving traces of their journey along the route.[27] Professor Wei's theory seems to be corroborated by Toscanelli's map of 1474 which shows the rivers explored by the Chinese cavalry.

By March 1423, the Chinese fleets had been at sea for two years and had sailed the nethermost reaches of the oceans. Admirals Hong Bao and Zhou Man had accomplished the major part of their mission – locating Canopus and the Southern Cross and going on to chart the southern hemisphere – but one aspect of the voyage had not gone according to plan. After leaving the Indian Ocean, the admirals had expected to greet foreign potentates and present them with fine silks and porcelains, bringing their countries into China's tribute system. Yet the people they had met along the route were unused to trade and appeared to have no kings. The Bantu in South Africa, Aborigines in Australia and naked men in Patagonia had no use for silk or porcelain, and places such as the Antarctic and Cape Verde Islands were un-inhabited. Life in the lands the Chinese had discovered was far more primitive than they had expected, and as a consequence the holds of their surviving ships must still have been full of their 'treasure' of porcelain and silks. But as he set sail from the west coast of Australia, Hong Bao would have known that he still had the opportunity to trade his goods before making for home, for the Spice Islands and the great trading port of Malacca were well within his reach.

The Rotz chart depicts western Australia, Sumatra, the Malay Peninsula, Indochina and the west coast of Borneo with considerable accuracy. This suggests that, having sailed north-westwards from Perth, the remainder of the fleet under Hong Bao circumnavigated Sumatra, berthed at Malacca, one of the prime trading ports in the Indian Ocean, and then returned home through the South China Sea, sailing along the west coast of Borneo – the east coast is not charted – and to the west of the Philippines before eventually arriving home on 22 October 1423.

Admiral Hong Bao's fleet had been the first voyagers ever to sail through the Strait of Magellan. They had discovered the Antarctic continent and reached southern Australia over two centuries before Abel Tasman (1603–c. 1659), who discovered the island of Tasmania that bears his name. Taken in isolation,

Hong Bao's voyage would have been more than worthy of modern commemoration. He had made one of the epic journeys in the history of mankind's exploration of the planet and his name deserves to be remembered and celebrated. But that was not the end of the Chinese achievements. As Hong Bao prepared to return home in triumph, another Chinese fleet under Admiral Zhou Man was also sailing along southern latitudes making for Australia from the opposite direction, crossing the Pacific a century before Magellan.

IV

The Voyage of
Zhou Man

AUSTRALIA

THE DESIGNATED TASK OF ZHOU MAN WAS TO SURVEY THE world west of South America; like Admiral Hong Bao, who had sailed eastwards, Zhou Man would have needed 'anchor' reference points at 52°40'S as he crossed the oceans beneath Canopus. But as his fleet entered the Pacific, the square-rigged junks would have met the cold Humboldt current and been swept northwards up the coast of what is now Chile. Magellan, Carteret, Bougainville and countless other explorers following in the wake of the Chinese had the same experience. The depiction of the Andes on the Piri Reis map[1] gives clear evidence that this had also happened to Zhou Man's fleet, but I did not yet know how far north the Chinese had travelled and whether they had reached Peru or met the Incas, one of the great civilizations of pre-Columbian South America.

For once, there was a helpful Chinese document that had escaped destruction by the mandarins. Dr Wang Tao of the School of Oriental and African Studies in London told me of a novel about Zheng He's voyages written in 1597, the *Hsi-Yang-Chi* (*Xi Yang Ji*). It became hugely popular in China after its publication, but is now so rare that the copy held by the library of the School of Oriental and African Studies is the only one in the world. Although it was written the best part of two centuries after the voyages it describes, and most of the book is taken up with fanciful adventures, the author did the modern researcher a valuable service by giving a detailed list of the tributes offered to the Chinese fleet by the barbarians they encountered on their voyages. The descriptions differ from the lists of goods given by Ma Huan (who never sailed beyond the Indian Ocean), suggesting that the author must have drawn on a different, now vanished source, but the detail and oddity of the list makes a convincing impression:

One pair of whale's eyes, commonly called bright-eyed pearls.
Two bream whiskers. These are lustrous and may be used for

hairpins or ear-ornaments. The price is very high.

One pair of camels that go to a thousand *li* [four hundred miles – possibly a reference to the distance the animals could travel without water].

Four boxes of dragon's saliva [ambergris].

Eight boxes of frankincense.

Four pairs of landscape porcelain bowls. In these is a landscape; by pouring water into the bowl, the mountains become blue and the water green.

Four pairs of porcelain bowls with representations of men and things: by pouring water into them there is gradually a picture of men saluting each other.

Four pairs of porcelain bowls with flowers and plants. In these are flowers and plants. By pouring water into them, they appear to move and wave.

Four pairs of porcelain bowls with feathers. In these are feathers, and by pouring water into them, they appear to fly.[2]

Clearly, these bowls greatly impressed the Chinese, who had prided themselves on making the world's finest and thinnest porcelain. These bowls must have been even finer. They became translucent when filled with water, allowing scenes painted on the undersides to be seen through the porcelain. It was beyond the capacity of any Indian, African or Islamic states of that or any earlier era to produce ceramics of such quality, and Europeans did not discover the technology to produce fine porcelain until the early eighteenth century. The only porcelain of that thinness at the time came from Cholula (in modern Mexico); the Aztec emperor Montezuma II (1480–1520) was eating off Cholula ware when the Spanish conquistadors encountered him. It was literally eggshell-thin, extremely expensive and much sought after, and was exported from Cholula to the Pacific coast and South America.

At the time of the Chinese voyages, Cholula was in its prime, producing huge quantities of this renowned porcelain and building pyramids more colossal than those of Egypt. Assuming that 'the pair of camels' were llamas (camelids), then everything in the tribute list, including the ambergris (from small whales called cachalots), could have been found in northern Peru. Asiatic hens were found there when the Spanish first landed, and at the very least it is arguable that they could have been left by Zhou Man's fleet after an exchange of gifts with the bird-loving Incas. I was later to find overwhelming evidence of pre-Columbian voyages between China and the Americas in Mexico, Guatemala, Colombia, Ecuador and Peru, as will be discussed later.

I returned to the task of tracing the course taken by Zhou Man. After leaving Peru, his fleet would first have been carried by the equatorial current as far north as Ecuador, where the current turns due west and carries mariners across the Pacific, the route along which explorer after explorer was swept in later centuries. Don Luis Arias, a Spanish envoy to South America in the sixteenth century, sent a memorandum to his king describing a South American legend of a Pacific crossing from Chile before the European voyages of discovery, carried out by 'light coloured or white skinned people . . . who wore white woven garments'.[3]

The course followed by the fleet would have taken it through the Tuamotu archipelago, four thousand miles west of South America. In 1606, Pedro Fernandez de Quirós (1565–1615), a Portuguese explorer working for the Spanish Crown, landed at Hao Atoll in the Tuamotu archipelago.[4] There he encountered an old lady wearing a gold ring set with an emerald. He offered trade goods for it but she greeted his offer with disdain – it was far too valuable. Neither gold nor emeralds are found within thousands of miles of the Tuamotu archipelago, but it is well documented that such rings were exported during the early Ming dynasty and given as presents by Zhu Di's ambassadors. Stepped pyramids were also found along this south-western route and in Australia, and the first Europeans to reach Fiji found that someone had been mining copper before them – something the locals did not do. Polynesians could have carried artefacts across the Pacific in their canoes, but that does not explain the Chinese hens and artefacts found in the Americas or the sheer volume of goods carried from the Americas to the Pacific. I would suggest that the only logical explanation is that they were carried by the junks of a Chinese treasure fleet and the ships of the traders that accompanied them.

When those legendary voyagers reached the mid-Pacific off Samoa, they found that the south equatorial current split there, just as it does today. The northern part carries on towards the Carolines, New Guinea and the Philippines; the southern part sweeps south-west towards Australia.

There is substantial evidence that Zhou Man's fleet separated at this point. The northern squadron built observation platforms at Kiribati in the Carolines, and another five in New Guinea. They were stepped pyramids with truncated tops like those in China. Rose-pink beads, made by rubbing a spiny oyster against cowrie shells, exactly similar in size and design to those found in the rivers of Mitla in Central America were found in the Caroline Islands last century, together with a fragment of obsidian and a piece of iron resembling a spearhead – all items foreign to the islands. Chinese hens were found in Peru by the first European explorers; maize, indigenous to the Americas, was found by the first Europeans to reach the Philippines; *metates* – tools used to grind maize – were in the holds of the junk found on the sea-bed in the Philippines in 1993, which was believed to have sunk about 1423. All of this is consistent with the Chinese sailing with the wind up the west coast of South America (shown on the Piri Reis map) and then across the Pacific.

The southern squadron swept on to chart Norfolk Island and, still carried westward by the current, made a landfall on the east coast of Australia just north of where Sydney is sited today. The

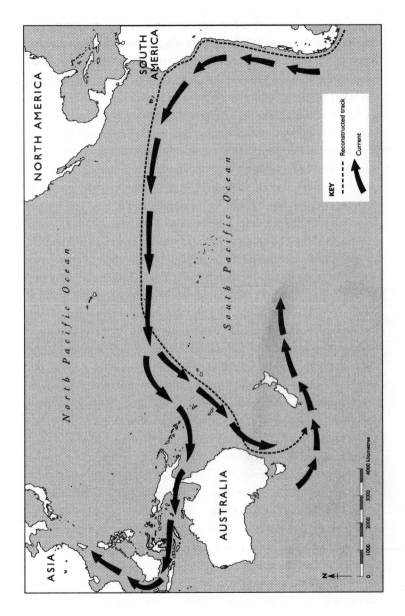

Zhou Man's journey to Australia.

great voyage across the Pacific had covered more than seven thousand miles and taken around three months. The current turns to the south when it meets the Australian coast, and Zhou Man's fleet would have been carried with it towards the latitude of Canopus, their reference point.

Admiral Hong Bao's voyage to Australia has been described in chapter 6. Admiral Zhou Man knew of Australia's existence before he landed there, for since Sui dynasty times (AD 589–618) the Chinese had known of a great landmass peopled by men who threw boomerangs, one hundred days' sailing south of Asia.[5] In the *Shan-Hai Jing* ('Classic of Mountains and Seas'), Chinese historians of that era described an animal with the head of a deer that hopped on its hind legs and had a second head in the middle of its body – the baby in the pouch. By the time Marco Polo reached China in the thirteenth century, Chinese charts were showing two Javas – the island we know today as Java and 'Greater Java', the source of the trepangs, or sea slugs, the Chinese ate with such relish. They remained a lucrative catch for fishing vessels and are still a highly prized delicacy in China. After his visit to China, Marco Polo called Greater Java 'the largest island in the world', and even before his time there were kangaroos in the imperial zoo in Beijing. Kangaroos, of course, are unique to Australia. Further evidence of the Chinese voyages to Australia could be seen at Taiwan University: a map on porcelain dated to 1447 showed the coastline of New Guinea, the east coast of Australia as far south as Victoria, and the north-east coast of Tasmania. Unfortunately, at the time of writing it appears this map has been lost.

It seemed probable that cartographers aboard Zhou Man's fleet had surveyed these lands and provided the information for the charts, but since the records of his voyage were destroyed after he returned to China in 1423 I had to look abroad to find corroborative evidence of his landfall in Australia. My analysis started from the assumption that this great southern continent was already well known to the Chinese, but was surveyed in more detail during their 1421–3 voyage. If so, I expected the cartography to be of a very high standard, with the latitudes and the alignment of the land correct, but possibly with substantial errors in longitude.

The great landmass shown on the Jean Rotz chart (pp. 151-2) could be Australia, but with some longitudinal errors and some distortion of the land in the south-east of the continent. I began my investigation by examining the eastern coast of the continent from just south of Byron Bay in New South Wales down to Flinders Island off the south-eastern tip of Australia. A close examination of this part of the Rotz chart in comparison to a modern map showed that it depicted eastern Australia to a great degree of accuracy from Nelson Bay[6] down to the southern tip of Tasmania.[7] I could readily identify Port Stephens, Broken Bay and Botany Bay with their correct latitudes.

If Zhou Man's fleet had reached south-east Australia after crossing the Pacific, there should be evidence of that landfall in the area depicted with most precision on the Rotz chart. As soon as I started a search of the coastline south of Newcastle, I found a mine of information. In the 1840s, a ruined fortress was found by Benjamin Boyd, one of the earliest European settlers, at Bittangabee Bay near Eden in the far south of New South Wales. He noted a large, fully mature old tree with its roots growing under the stones of the complex. Bittangabee's substantial ruins comprise a square platform surrounded by large rocks that had once formed a sturdy, defensive perimeter wall. Foundations and parts of the walls of a blockhouse formed by large stones bound with mortar lie inside the perimeter wall. It must have taken a large labour force to bring the stones to the site and then dress and erect them. There is no evidence anywhere in Australia of Aborigines constructing such fortifications, and the age of the tree and the position of its roots show that construction can only have been carried out long before the British first arrived. More stone buildings erected before Europeans reached Australia can be found south of Sydney; a group of twenty, like a small village, are set beside the coast, and there are well-built paths leading from a reservoir to a fifteen-metre stone wharf beside the sea. Similar stone dwellings are found at Newcastle.

Further indications that visitors had landed in Australia were found in ancient Aboriginal rock carvings depicting a foreign ship similar to a junk on the Hawkesbury River north of Sydney. There are similar carvings further up the coast at Cape York, Gympie, and in Arnhem Land. This does not, of course, guarantee that the foreigners were Chinese – they might have arrived on an unknown Portuguese voyage – but rock carvings near the Hawkesbury River show people wearing long robes, which narrows the choice to Asian or Chinese people. Furthermore, an Aboriginal tradition from the Tweed River area tells of strange visitors attempting to mine metals in the Mount Warning area, south-west of Brisbane, many generations before the British did so.

The most compelling evidence for the date of these foreign

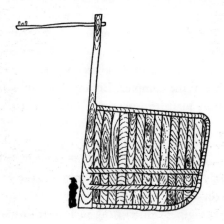

Reconstruction of the rudder of a treasure ship with a figure to the left for scale.

visits came from shipwrecks, especially one found near Byron Bay in northern New South Wales. Two wooden pegs were unearthed, provisionally carbon-dated to the mid-fifteenth century but with a potential error of plus or minus fifty years. Before sand-mining destroyed the wreck, local people had described part of the hull and three masts protruding from the sand. In 1965, sand-miners unearthed a huge wooden rudder from this site; some said it was 40 feet (12.2 metres) high. If this description was even remotely accurate, it eliminates the possibility of an unknown Portuguese or Dutch voyage, for their caravels weren't much bigger than that rudder. It can only have come from an enormous ship several hundred feet long – the rudders of treasure ships were 36 feet high. The wreckage of another ancient ship was found at Wollongong on the coast south of Sydney, and two more were found in swampland near Perth. An ancient Chinese stone head depicting a goddess has also been found at Ulladulla,[8] south of Wollongong, and a

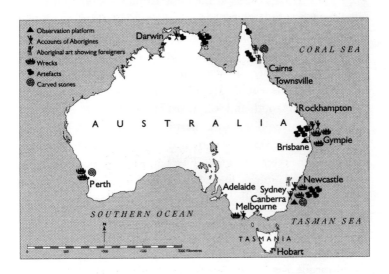

Evidence of the visit of the Chinese treasure fleet to Australia.

similar votive offering was unearthed on the Nepean River.

The 'mahogany ship' at Warrnambool, the similarities of the three wrecks at Perth and Wollongong, the age of the wooden pin and the size of the huge rudder in Byron Bay point to a Chinese origin. Only the Chinese built ships that could house a rudder the size of that found in Byron Bay, and only they could afford to lose so many ships in one area. The addition of the findings from the wrecks to the Aboriginal legends and carvings depicting foreigners in robes arriving by ship, the groups of stone buildings and the votive offerings produces powerful if not yet conclusive evidence that a large Chinese fleet visited south-east Australia in the fifteenth century.

South of Bittangabee Bay, the original cartographer of the Rotz chart drew the southern curved part of Tasmania, but the chart also shows what appears to be a great landmass running first eastwards then southwards. This has always baffled professional cartographers, but when I compared the Jean Rotz and Piri Reis charts at the same latitude I saw at once that what appears to be land south of Tasmania is in fact ice. It is drawn in identical fashion to the ice shown on the Piri Reis map, and the line drawn on the Rotz chart corresponds to the northern limit of pack ice to the south of Tasmania in midwinter (June) in 1421–3.

At a stroke this would have solved the mystery of the apparent landmass to the south and south-east of Australia were it not for two rivers shown on the Rotz chart flowing eastwards out of the ice. These two 'rivers' are shown well south of New Zealand; there are none there, of course. There appeared to be nothing but ocean at those latitudes, but when I examined a large-scale map I discovered two small islands of which I had previously been ignorant, Auckland Island and Campbell Island, at a similar latitude to Tierra del Fuego. Both have identical long thin bays lying east–west, precisely as drawn on the Rotz chart, and at the same latitude.

The two islands were shown at the edge of the normal limit of

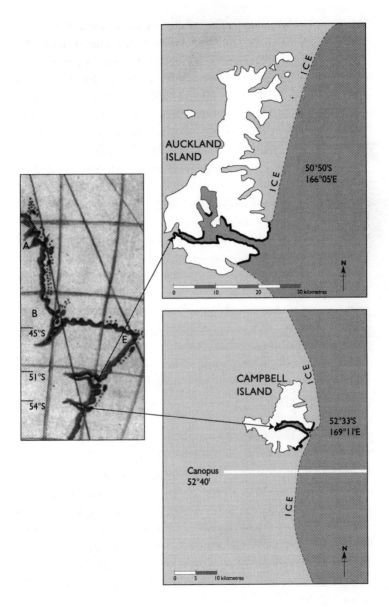

Auckland and Campbell Islands, as shown on the Jean Rotz map.

the pack ice that links them in midwinter. This explains the apparent anomaly on the Rotz chart. The Chinese could not possibly have known that they were islands rather than part of an ice-bound landmass because continuous ice lay between them and stretched away north to Tasmania; once again, they had drawn precisely what they saw. They were sailing to Campbell Island to fix the position of Canopus – 52°40'S, precisely the latitude of the southernmost tip of the island. They had their reference position, and they could now start a detailed survey of this part of the world.

I found further indications that Zhou Man's fleet had reached Campbell Island in the accounts of the early Europeans who explored the island, discovered by Frederick Hasseburg, the captain of a sealing ship, in 1810. In Camp Cove, they found the wreck of an old wooden ship and a tree stunted by the endless winds, but recognizable as a mature Norfolk Island pine, a tree unique to Norfolk Island. It was the Chinese custom to collect saplings, seeds and pine-cones on their voyages, planting them as shrines at places where they made landfall and burying votive offerings in the roots. The Norfolk Island pine on Campbell Island could well have been brought there by one of Zhou Man's junks.

The fleet had now surveyed and charted eastern Australia from Nelson Bay down to Campbell Island in the far south, but they were faced with real difficulties when it came to setting course back to Australia. Unknown to them, the Antarctic drift current was pushing them to the east, towards the South Island of New Zealand. I have many happy memories of that beautiful land after taking my submarine there at Christmas in 1969. The South Island is a place of rugged grandeur, spectacular mountains and crystalline lakes, a land where the Antarctic winds scour the skies clean. However, the Tasman Sea is a nightmare for navigators. The skies are frequently clouded and the currents are irregular. They can reverse their direction without warning.

The Chinese would have had to claw their way back against the current; as they did so, at least two of the great treasure ships were lost. The wreck of an old wooden ship was found two centuries ago at Dusky Sound in Fjordland at the south-west tip of New Zealand's South Island. It was said to be very old and of Chinese build and 'to have been there before Cook', according to the local people.[9] A Sydney packet visited Dusky Sound in 1831 and two sailors from the crew 'saw a strange animal perching at the edge of the bush and nibbling the foliage. It stood on its hind legs, the lower part of its body curving to a thick pointed tail, and when they took note of the height it reached against the trees allowing a metre and a half for the tail, they estimated it stood nearly nine metres in height. The men were to windward of the animal and were able to watch it feeding for some time before it spotted them. They watched it pull down a heavy branch with comparative ease, turn it over and tilt it up to reach the leaves it wanted.'[10] The animal described corresponds in size, posture and eating habits with the mylodons the Chinese could have taken aboard in Patagonia. Perhaps a pair escaped from the wreck, survived and bred in similar conditions to their home territory in Patagonia – the latitudes are the same. Sea-otters, which are not indigenous to New Zealand but, of course, were kept in the Chinese junks to herd fish, have been seen swimming in the fjords of South Island.

Further north, on the west coast of the North Island of New Zealand, the deck and sides of part of a large and very old ship were exposed in 1875 after a violent storm. The wreck was found near the mouth of the Torei Palma River at Whaingaroa; it is known as the Ruapuke Ship after the beach of that name. The wreck was said to have diagonal planking, and its internal bulk-heads were bolted together by large brass pins, each weighing 6.3 kilograms. There has, though, been some dispute about the wood from which the wreck was built. Those who originally found it said that it was teak, but in May 2002 pieces of European oak were found in the area, leading certain experts to conclude that a European ship was wrecked there.

However, a huge stone carved in what local experts say is Tamil calligraphy stands at the point where the river empties into a little harbour. In shape, size and location this stone corresponds with those set up by the Chinese mariners in the Yangtze estuary, at Dondra Head, at Cochin on the Malabar coast of India, at Janela in the Cape Verde Islands and by the Matadi Falls in the Congo delta. In addition to the calligraphy, the Ruapuke stone has the same patterns of concentric circles as the stone at Janela. I had already found a number of carved stones at sites visited by the Chinese fleets, so my next step was an obvious one. Sure enough, a search on the internet soon revealed several more on the route from the Cape Verde Islands down to Patagonia, at Santa Catarina, Coral Island, Campeche and Arrorado Island on the east coast of South America. Each is also sited beside a watering place and overlooks the sea, and the concentric circles inscribed on them match those at Ruapuke. But this could still have been a coincidence; after all, pyramids were built in Central and South America as well as in Egypt. The proof would be more conclusive if I could find similar carved stones in China. Another long search produced three more, at Wong Chuk Ha, Chang Zhou and Po Ti in Hong Kong. Again, these stones had similar markings to the ones I had already found. I now believed that the concentric circles were a 'signature' agreed upon before the armada set sail, denoting where each fleet had landed and watered.

Perhaps the most controversial piece of evidence unearthed in New Zealand is the celebrated bell found near the wreck on Ruapuke beach, named the 'Colenso Bell' after Bishop Colenso who discovered it being used as a kettle by the Maoris. It looks like a smaller version of Zheng He's bell cast after the sixth voyage, and the lip of the bell is inscribed in Tamil calligraphy similar to that carved on the stone near the wreck. It has been

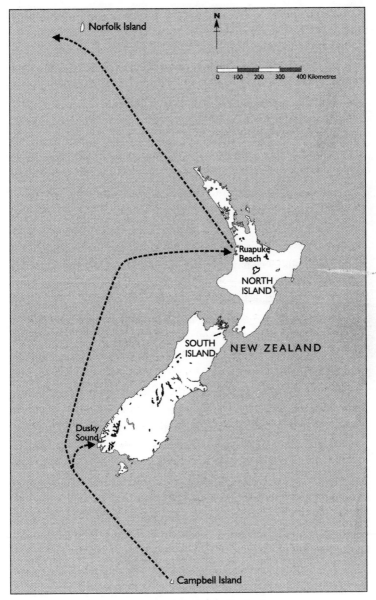

The journey around New Zealand.

translated as 'Bell of the ship Mohaideen Baksh'. The inscription suggests that the owner was a Muslim Tamil, probably from one of the well-known ship-owning families based on the port of Naga Pattinam on the eastern coast of Tamil Nadu in south-east India.[11] This is evidence of an Indian not a Chinese ship, but, as the Pandanan wreck found in the Philippines (see chapter 10) demonstrates, it was common for local ship-owners to sail with Zheng He's fleets for they not only provided protection from pirates, they also afforded valuable opportunities to trade. It seems most unlikely that a Tamil ship would have travelled from India to South America and then to New Zealand on its own.

Within a mile of the Ruapuke wreck is a large fallen tree. When it was blown over in a gale, a duck, beautifully carved in dark green serpentine, was revealed nestling among its roots. The duck could well have been a Chinese votive offering. A similar offering, a lion, was found in East Africa, and others have been found in Queensland and the Northern Territory of Australia. This type of shrine is typical of, and unique to, the culture of southern China. Although they are clear evidence of Chinese visits to Australia, I accept that on their own the votive offerings are not proof of a landing by a treasure fleet; they could have been carried by Chinese merchants. However, the collective evidence – the ship, the votive offering, the bell, the stone and the carving – leads me to the conclusion that the ship at Ruapuke was almost certainly the wreck of a Tamil junk attached to the Chinese fleet.

The final piece of evidence is another votive offering found on the banks of a tributary of the Waikato River some thirty miles north of the Ruapuke wreck. The find was made in the late 1800s by Elsdon Best, the distinguished historian and then curator of the Dominion Museum in Hamilton. The small oriental figurine was

found under singular and interesting circumstances at Mauku near Auckland. The lands around the place of discovery have been uninhabited since the arrival of Europeans until twenty years ago, and since then merely occupied by farm employees; nor have these lands ever been ploughed. In pre-European times, however, natives occupied the place, as shown by the remains of old settlements ... The figurine is undoubtedly Oriental in design and workmanship ... having the grotesque aspect so common in Oriental designs, some form of turban-like head dress is depicted, also a loose cloak or wide-sleeved garment ... Altogether, this snub-nosed Tartar-looking figure represents an interesting discovery when the conditions of that discovery are noted.[12]

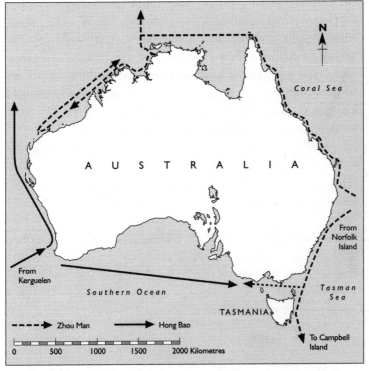

The routes of Hong Bao and Zhou Man around Australia.

The Chinese fleets were losing ships with almost every land-fall, a rate of attrition that continued throughout their voyages across the world, for of the 107 treasure ships that left China in 1421, a mere handful survived to return home in 1423. As the mandarins complained, 'Myriads were lost.' Those huge losses increase the likelihood that the wrecks at Ruapuke and else-where on the Chinese route were ships from the treasure fleets.

If the ship at Ruapuke is a wrecked treasure ship, then tales of the shipwrecked crew must exist in local legends, just as they do in Central America and southern Australia near wreck-sites. When I investigated, I found that Maoris living near Ruapuke had just such a legend.[13] The strangers who settled among them were called 'Patupaiarehe', or pale-skinned, almost supernatural people. Another meaning of the word is 'fairies'. They wore white woven garments and also differed from the Maoris in having no tattoos and by carrying their children in their arms. Some married Maori women. I believe this local legend is true, and that the first non-Maori settlers in New Zealand were not Europeans, but Chinese. Subsequent DNA analysis (see post-script) has only strengthened my belief.

THE

BARRIER

REEF

AND THE

SPICE

ISLANDS

ONCE BACK IN THE TASMAN SEA, ZHOU MAN'S SURVIVING ships entered a counter-clockwise, circular current that at last propelled them back to the Australian coast. The shape of the south-east Australian coast, coupled with the location of Campbell Island on the Jean Rotz chart and the wrecks in the south-west and north-west of New Zealand, are all consistent with the junks being swept before the winds and currents from the Australian coast down to Campbell Island and then in a loop with the wind back to New Zealand. Continuing before the wind would have caused them to make their second landfall on the Australian coast just north of Brisbane. Assuming an average speed of 4.8 knots, reduced to 3.8 by the current and storms, the journey down to Campbell Island and back again would have taken at least ten weeks.

The coast around Brisbane is shown on the Rotz chart with incredible precision, and that chart was not the only one of Australia to be drawn by cartographers of the Dieppe School, all of them drawn centuries before Europeans reached Australia. The Dauphin chart of 1536 and those of Desliens (1551) and Desceliers (1553) gave an almost identical depiction of the continent. Two decades ago, one of the Dieppe maps was exhibited. Visitors were stunned: 'Look at Brisbane. Look, there's Stradbroke Island, Moreton Island, the Pine River, the Heads and Fraser Island. There's the lagoon at Surfers' Paradise.'[1] The accuracy with which the eastern Australia coast had been drawn left me equally dumbstruck. To have surveyed it with such precision, the Chinese fleet must have spent some time on the east coast of Australia in what is now New South Wales and Queensland, and one obvious reason for that is the mineral wealth of the region.

Perhaps the most commercially valuable scientists carried by the great treasure fleets were mining engineers. At that time, China and India together accounted for almost half the world's entire wealth[2] and Indian engineers led the world in mining technology. They had opened up gold and iron fields in East Africa, stimulating a flow of raw materials eastwards across the Indian Ocean. Indian engineers and metallurgists sailed with the treasure fleets, but China also had centuries of experience in geology, mineral extraction and processing. As is claimed in Chinese records of a much earlier period,[3] the treasure fleets would have mined ores and carried gemstones and refined metals back to China in their holds, but the Chinese would also have set up longer-term settlements to exploit the mineral riches they discovered on their voyages.

Chinese scientists had classified minerals into groups by the first century AD.[4] Those early Chinese scientists could distinguish between different chlorides, sulphides and nitrates, and knew how to exploit them. They used mercuric sulphide (cinnabar) for red inks and paints; steatite was added to paper as a filler; and skins were first dried with saltpetre (potassium nitrate), then treated with ammonium chloride, and finally dyed with ferrous sulphate.

They were equally skilled in geological prospecting, capable of detecting minerals and metals by magnetic surveys or by measuring shock waves caused by explosive detonations, even by the lie of the land. They also knew that the ores and minerals they sought were often geologically linked with others. Greenstones always occurred in the neighbourhood of copper ores. They even had a rhyme for such associations: 'When there is cinnabar above, gold will be found below; when there is magnetite above, copper and gold will be found below.'[5] Similarly, iron was associated with haematite on the surface, and both sulphur and iron pyrites signified alum. Chinese chemists had also deduced that certain plants thrived on particular minerals, to the extent that they changed colour and taste when growing near them. Cybule onions signified silver; shallots, gold; ginger, copper and tin. Western scientists did not establish until the eighteenth century what the Chinese had known for centuries, that some plants can indeed signal the presence of gold and other metals.[6]

The Rotz chart of Australia and the wealth of wrecks and Chinese artefacts found in and around that country show that, by luck or design, the great Chinese fleets had discovered the location of some of the most varied and rich mineral seams in the world. They had done so accompanied by horse-ships. The Chinese took inordinate care in the selection of their horses. Their favourites were the famous 'blood ponies' of Tajikistan, so named because they supposedly sweated blood (the red markings on the skin were actually caused by a skin parasite). Blood ponies were bred in the high, rolling valleys of China's Tian Shan – 'Heavenly Mountains' – where they galloped through the walnut forests that cloak the slopes. They were incredibly swift, but also hardy and strong enough to make their way through dense snow and survive the worst weather. Zhu Di imported millions during his reign, placing such a strain on the imperial treasury that a special 'Tea for Horses' bureau was established to barter tea for the animals, thus avoiding further payments in silver.

Thousands of horses for the Chinese cavalry were carried on the horse-ships accompanying the treasure fleets. They were fed on mashed boiled rice, necessitating three gallons of water per horse per day. There is evidence that the Chinese took them ashore. Horses were then unknown in Australia, but they are beautifully depicted in drawings on the Vallard chart of the Dieppe School, although not, it must be said, on the Rotz chart. There was good pasturage for them around Sydney, from where an easy trail led up the Nepean and Hawkesbury valleys into the interior. A huge range of minerals including gold, silver, gemstones, coal and iron can be found within two hundred kilometres of Sydney. Further up the coast at Newcastle, also clearly identifiable on the Rotz chart, there was an equally spectacular array of riches. Within a week's ride from the coast were diamonds, sapphires and a wealth of other minerals.

Like their modern counterparts, the Chinese and Indian geologists with Zhou Man's fleet must have felt they had arrived in a mineral paradise. Many of Australia's minerals were of direct use to the fleet. Combining copper and zinc gave them brass; saltpetre mixed with sulphur and charcoal made gunpowder. Arsenic was a poison and insect repellent, yet also accelerated the growth of silkworms. White paint made of lead and copper prevented wood decay along the hull line. Kaolin was available for ceramics, while oxides of cobalt, copper and lead served for colours and glazes. Alum was particularly useful for making hides supple, for making drinking water potable and for its astringent properties. Asbestos has been used for fire protection since the sixth century BC: 'When King Mu of the Zhou dynasty made an expedition to the western people ... fireproof cloth was cleaned by being thrown into a fire ... when taken out and shaken it became as white as snow.'[7] Local Aboriginal legends mention foreign people coming to these parts and mining materials while 'dressed in stone clothes'.[8]

There is further evidence in the accounts of Franciscan missionaries to China in the sixteenth century, who spoke of Chinese expeditions to Australia recorded on copper scrolls (dating from the sixth century onwards) together with maps of the continent.[9] These early Chinese records, which have since disappeared, described voyages carried out by gigantic fleets of massive junks (sixty to a hundred ships), each carrying several hundred men, with the aim of gathering minerals.

The wrecks on the coast and the stone buildings ashore, Aboriginal rock carvings and paintings depicting foreigners in their long robes, and the carved votive offerings are all signs of a Chinese presence in the mining areas of New South Wales. A beautiful carved stone head of the goddess MaTsu, the protector of mariners at sea, was recovered from the beach front at Milton, New South Wales, in 1983. It is now in the Kedumba Nature Museum in Katoomba. Each of Zheng He's ships had a small cabin dedicated to her. However, the most direct and persuasive evidence of the Chinese visits to Australia comes from Gympie, a mining area further up the coast, two hours' drive north of Brisbane. In 1422, a creek connected Gympie to Tin Can Bay and the Pacific; according to ancient Aboriginal tradition, a race of 'culture heroes' sailed up this creek and into Gympie's harbour in ships 'shaped like birds'. They later returned to their ships carrying rocks.[10]

While ashore, these mysterious people built truncated pyramids, one of which was discovered by a local researcher, Rex Gilroy, in 1975 and subsequently photographed. Now sadly vandalized, the pyramid was built of granite blocks and stood a hundred feet high, with the stepped construction typical of the other pyramids I had seen in South America and right across the Pacific. Mr Gilroy describes local people uncovering pre-European opencut copper, tin and gold mines, and he personally found an ancient pipe similar to those used to pour mercury to separate gold from ore. Half a mile from the Gympie pyramid, near an ancient opencast gold mine, were hearths that contained nodules of melted metal. Until 1920, Gympie remained Queensland's largest and richest goldfield. Many other artefacts have been found in the area. Two beautifully carved votive offerings are of particular interest: one is of the Hindu god Ganesh, the elephant god, carved in beige granite; the other is of Hanuman, the Hindu monkey god, this time made of conglomerate ironstone. Ganesh and Hanuman are two of the most important deities of Hindu worshippers in southern India, whence the fleet sailed and where they embarked Hindu priests, mining engineers and geologists.

Two equally fascinating carved animals can still be seen in the Gold Museum at Gympie today. The 'Gympie ape', dug up in 1966, is a monster with a head much larger than a human's. Its snout has been broken off, but a photograph of the second animal (it has now disappeared) shows the snout, nose and mouth[11] of a beast closely resembling a mylodon. Whether through intent or happenstance, animals were collected and carried from one continent to another – giraffes, ostriches and rhinoceros from Africa to China, Asiatic chickens to South America, Chinese ship dogs left in South America and on islands across the Pacific to New Zealand, kangaroos from Australia to China and otters from China to New Zealand. A number of mylodons might well have been captured and taken aboard the Chinese ships in Patagonia; one pair might have escaped in New Zealand and another pair landed in China. Perhaps Chinese sculptors wished to immortalize these strange creatures before the memory of them faded. A century later the arrival of exotic species brought back from the New World was to create a similar sensation in the courts of Europe.

The purpose of the Gympie pyramid has baffled Australian observers, but its size, height and shape are typical of Ming dynasty observation platforms, and it would have been wholly logical for the Chinese to build observatories to determine precisely the location of the phenomenal riches they had discovered, so that future fleets could return to the same place.

When Zhou Man's fleet resumed its voyage, it sailed north up the Great Barrier Reef, again shown with amazing accuracy on the Rotz chart. The reef itself and the islands inside and out-side it have the correct latitudes and can be clearly identified for more than a thousand miles. However, when they returned to Australia after their voyage to Campbell Island to locate Canopus, their calculations of longitude (as shown on the Rotz map) are twenty degrees in error. Why should they have believed they were 1,800 miles further west than they really were? The answer, of course, was that they had been in the Antarctic drift current during their ten weeks in the southern oceans. The body of water in which they had sailed was itself moving eastwards, and Admiral Zhou Man as yet had no means of measuring longitude accurately.

I realized that the coastline of Australia on the Rotz chart north of where Zhou Man's fleet returned had to be adjusted to the east by 1,800 miles. As soon as I did this, the result was electrifying. Australia was laid out before me. The cartographer had done a remarkable job and had made only one mistake – longitude, which he had had no means of measuring. He had drawn the eastern Australian coast and the Great Barrier Reef with phenomenal accuracy 247 years before Captain Cook was to do so. When I further corrected the southern coast of New South Wales and Tasmania by removing the ice, I had an instantly identifiable map of Australia.

Cook was awestruck by the size and shape of the Great Barrier Reef, a type of structure 'scarcely known in Europe. It is a wall of coral rock rising almost perpendicular out of the unfathomable Ocean.'[12] For a mariner, any voyage near razor-sharp coral reefs is a nerve-racking prospect, particularly at night or in low visibility when the only warning is the noise of breaking surf. If your ship hits coral, it punctures the hull and it is difficult to get off the reef without tearing the vessel to bits. I knew the dangers only too well from my own experience of taking my submarine HMS *Rorqual* inside the Barrier Reef, and that was with accurate charts at my disposal. A voyage through uncharted reefs is a constant waking nightmare. At night one sees not a single light ashore, by day nothing but an unbroken belt of grey-green jungle, as if man had never penetrated this beautiful but forbidding region. The Barrier Reef stretches for more than 1,500 miles from Hickson Bay, south of Brisbane, up to Cape York in the north. Captain Cook narrowly escaped death after striking it, and like me, he had a chart to help him. It is inconceivable that Zhou Man's fleet could have made the passage through those uncharted waters without suffering severe damage or loss of ships. To have got through it at all was an incredible feat.

The Rotz chart shows the Great Barrier Reef, the islands between the reef and the coast, and yet more islands in the ocean beyond the reef. In many places, once inside the reef it is not possible to leave it. I remember very well how my submarine was hemmed in by the reef, and the relief I felt as I escaped from the straitjacket where the reef ends off Brisbane. The wealth of detail on the Rotz chart indicates that several Chinese ships must have been charting the coast, reef and islands. They would have been more or less in line abreast as they sailed north, some inside the reef and others in the ocean outside it. I estimate that there must have been at least six, probably ten or more ships to have gathered such a mass of information.

The Barrier Reef itself, the coastline and the islands both inside and outside are particularly accurately charted around what is now Cooktown, indicating that the Chinese had spent some time surveying there. Captain Cook later used some of the maps of the Dieppe School to get to Cooktown, where he beached his ship, HMS *Endeavour*, after it hit a reef that was also shown on the earlier charts. The detail and precision of this part of the Rotz chart suggests that the Chinese might well have been forced to make a similar halt for repairs.

The Barrier Reef ends abruptly north of the Cape York Peninsula. The nightmare was over, and those Chinese junks that had survived the hazardous passage – and there must have been several casualties – could at last set course to the north-west for China. What an incredible sense of relief the eunuch captains and navigators of the surviving Chinese ships must have felt as they rounded the northern tip of Australia and sailed on past Cape York and the islands to the west. Here, the junks entered the Torres Strait, separating Australia from New Guinea, where the current flows from the east, sweeping the mariner westwards across the Gulf of Carpentaria. The Gulf is shown on the Rotz chart narrower than it should be; once again, the Chinese underestimated their change in longitude as the body of water in which they were sailing moved westwards across northern Australia.[13] (After publication of the hardback, it was pointed out to me that Zheng He's charts show the Barrier Reef and northern Australia.)

In the folio of charts he presented to Henry VIII of England, Jean Rotz included another map of this part of Australia drawn in greater detail and to a much larger scale. He drew the island of Lesser Java – the Chinese knew it as Little Java – separated from Greater Java by a narrow channel, though some of his contemporaries in the Dieppe School showed it as a river. It was a simple matter to determine who was right. I compared it with a modern map at the same latitude and saw at once that the channel Rotz had drawn was the Victoria River in the west and the Roper River in the east. Lesser Java on the Rotz chart is Arnhem Land, part of the mainland of Australia. The shape of north-east Australia was now instantly recognizable.

A number of descriptions in medieval Portuguese were written on Rotz's more detailed chart. The names are easy to translate and all of them correspond to what is found there today. *Canal de Sonda* – 'narrow sea ford' in medieval Portuguese – is marked where the long, narrow Apsley Strait bisects Melville and Bathurst Islands. *Aguada dillim* – 'waterway leading to inland sea' – corresponds to the Dundas Strait that does indeed lead into the Van Diemen Gulf. *Agarsim* – translated as 'yes indeed water is here' – is inscribed beside the Yellow Water Billabong in the Kakadu National Park, designated by the United Nations as 'wet lands of international importance'. *Nungrania* means 'no farmland' – there is none there – and *lingrania* means 'lime trees', which still grow there today. The Gove Peninsula, the eastern tip of Arnhem Land, is *finjava*, or 'the end of Java'. Only one inscription had me baffled – *chumbão*, or 'lead'.

The west coast of Arnhem Land is drawn with great fidelity. Rotz showed the main coastal features at their correct latitudes right up to 10°S, beyond the northern tip of Australia, and drew a mass of fishing stakes straddling Trepang Bay – as its name implies, the centre of sea-slug fishing. The first Chinese map of Australia was drawn by fishermen centuries before Europeans reached the continent, and Chinese boats still fish this part of the coast today for the much-prized trepang. All this remarkably precise information predates the arrival of the first Europeans by over two centuries. The chart also shows details of the interior – the Finniss River wending westwards, and trees recognizable as eucalyptus and blackwood pines, both common in Arnhem Land. A tall rock is also depicted on the chart by what is now the Nourlangie Anbanbang Billabong in the Kakadu National Park. The original cartographer must have seen the rock to have drawn it so accurately.

As I studied the modern map of Arnhem Land, I realized I had found the answer to the mystery of the word *chumbāo*. Lead is still mined in substantial quantities at the huge Jabiru Ranger Mines. It is the natural derivative of uranium 235 as it breaks down through the process of nuclear decay. Uranium is, of course, highly radioactive, and lethal to touch or ingest. The Jabiru Ranger Mines contain one of the world's largest deposits of uranium 235. Not realizing the danger they were placing themselves in, the Chinese must have been digging uranium out of the ground alongside the lead ore they sought. This may help to account for the appalling loss of life among Zhou Man's fleet, for only a tenth of the original nine thousand men remained alive when it finally reached home in October 1423.

To discover the lead, the Chinese had to penetrate well into the interior of the country. At that time, as now, Aborigines had made Arnhem Land their spiritual home. They were skilful artists, painting beautiful frescoes in caves, and I hoped to find evidence of the Chinese visit depicted in their cave art. George Grey, later the governor of South Australia, led an expedition to Arnhem Land in 1838. When they entered a group of caves twenty miles upstream from where the Glenelg River pours into Colliers Bay, they saw a group of paintings prominent among which was 'the figure of a man, 10ft 6in in height, clothed from the chin downwards in a red garment which reached to his wrists and ankles'.[14] Captain Grey's description accords with the picture drawn by the native Mexican tribes at Jucutácato (see chapter 10) of the Chinese arriving in their red robes reaching to their ankles. Grey's find also accords with Aboriginal lore, which records that long before the Europeans a honey-coloured people settled north-east Arnhem Land. The men wore long robes and the women pantaloons. They went far inland for freshwater prawns, sandalwood and tortoiseshell, grew rice and lived in stone houses, unlike the Aborigines whose dwellings were of wood. The women wove silk dyed with local herbs.

Adze anchors with the curved fluke (the piece that holds the anchor in the mud) set at right angles to the stock of the anchor – a Chinese design – have been discovered on the coastline of north-east Arnhem Land, and substantial quantities of broken Chinese ceramics dating from the Han dynasty (202 BC–AD 220) to the early Ming (1368–1644) have been found at Port Bradshaw on the eastern shore of the Gulf of Carpentaria and on the nearby mainland, just where the currents and the reefs would make it likely that wrecks would be found.

Even with horses, the Chinese would have needed several months to carry out the detailed survey of the coast and interior lands depicted on the Rotz chart. For this they would have needed a base in a protected anchorage with fresh water. I expected to locate it on the most accurately charted part of the coast. The Beagle Gulf off the north-west part of Arnhem Land is very well drawn, and Darwin, at the south-western end of the gulf, has a splendidly protected anchorage. Today, a hotel, the Banyan View Lodge, stands on Doctor's Gully, shaded by a magnificent banyan tree. The stream running through Doctor's Gully is now paved over, but in those days fresh water would have been available from it. The lodge is a popular haunt of backpackers drinking lager, oblivious of the history that surrounds them.

Late in the nineteenth century, a figure of a Taoist immortal, Shu Lao, was found buried beneath that banyan tree. It is now in the Chinese collection of the Technological Museum in Sydney. Although very valuable, it had been deliberately wedged deep down in the roots. Dated by one expert as early Ming (late fourteenth century),[15] the figure sits upon a deer and in its right hand carries a peach, the symbol of longevity. It is made from very fine pinite and is beautifully carved and polished. Shu Lao is one of the Triad of Gods of long life in the Taoist pantheon; unlike Buddhism and Confucianism, Taoism is a religion peculiar to China and was never disseminated overseas.

Moreover, the banyan is foreign to Australia and must have been imported. This one was already several hundred years old when the statue was discovered over a century ago. In southern China and Burma, shrines were often built in cavities between the spreading roots of large trees such as banyans which are holy trees to Theravada Buddhists. The shrine at Darwin was almost certainly built by a Chinese centuries ago, and in structure and location it resembles the one at Ruapuke in New Zealand. It is theoretically possible that the shrines were created by the crews of Chinese boats fishing for trepang, but the possibility is very small indeed. No fishing boat would carry such a valuable statue – it would be worth a lifetime's wages to the crew; it is far more likely that it belonged to a wealthy Chinese captain or admiral from a great ship. By far the most plausible explanation is that Zhou Man's fleet used Darwin as its base and created a shrine in which the figure was placed in thanks for having survived a long voyage.

I am strongly inclined to believe that the Venetian Niccolò da Conti was telling the truth when he informed the Papal Secretary, Poggio Bracciolini, that he had landed in Greater Java on a Chinese junk and had spent nine months there with his wife. Perhaps she was one of the women in pantaloons.

When Europeans eventually arrived, they were not sailing blindly into a great unknown. The Dauphin chart, one of the other charts from the Dieppe School and almost identical to the Rotz chart, came into the possession of Edmund Harley, Earl of Oxford and First Lord of the Admiralty, in the mid-eighteenth century and became known as the Harleian. It was later acquired by Joseph Banks, the young scientist who sailed in the *Endeavour* with Captain Cook. At the time Captain Cook sailed, the British government therefore had access to both the Harleian and Rotz charts, since the latter was at that stage owned by the Admiralty. Cook's orders from the Admiralty were to search down to 40°S – the latitude of South Australia shown on both charts – where they 'had good reason'[16] to suppose the southern continent existed. They certainly did – they already had two charts showing such a continent at 40°S.

As they left Australia, like Hong Bao's fleet before them Zhou Man's ships were still laden with porcelain and silk, but the fabled Spice Islands lay between Australia and home, and spice was then an extremely valuable commodity in China. Even when the fleet had been reduced to a few ships, their holds could still carry thousands of tons of ceramics, and by sailing for the Spice Islands Zhou Man would at last have an opportunity to exchange them for goods of real value, such as nutmeg, pepper and cloves.

If the Rotz chart was based on an earlier map drawn by cartographers aboard Zhou Man's fleet, it should show the Spice Islands. It does. The importance of Ambon, then the collecting centre for the two Spice Islands of Ternate and Tidore – so tiny one can walk around them in a couple of days – is emphasized by its being coloured red. In the Middle Ages, Ternate and Tidore were the hub of the spice trade, far and away the most productive islands. They were legendary, and had been fought over for centuries, for virtually all spices could be obtained there in huge quantities. To this day, the distinctive scent of cloves is detectable far out at sea, long before the islands themselves are sighted.

Further north, at a latitude of 10°N, the Rotz chart shows the channel between the Philippine islands of Mindanao in the south and Leyte in the north, but Rotz drew only the south coast of Leyte, leading to the obvious conclusion that the cartographer was in a ship passing down the middle of the channel. Using a similar common-sense approach, I could determine the angle from which the Spice Islands and the other islands between Australia and the Philippines were drawn, and hence deduce the route taken by Zhou Man's fleet through the islands. Along the way, now sailing in calm and sunny seas, Zhou Man would have had many opportunities not only to obtain spices but to barter his porcelain for batiks, artefacts, fresh water, fruit and meat.

There would once have been plentiful examples of the silks and porcelain Zhou Man's fleet had exchanged for spices and supplies, but would any traces remain today? How could I find such evidence after an interval of nearly six hundred years? I wondered if Magellan had also sailed this way on his circumnavigation of the world. If so, his account might throw some light on the question. When I went to the British Library and consulted a copy of the detailed map of Magellan's route produced after his death, I was staggered to discover that his course from the Pacific through the Philippines and down to the Spice Islands, a distance of well over a thousand miles, was identical but in the opposite direction to the track of Zhou Man's fleet I had just reconstructed. It was as if the two were using the same passage drawn on the same chart. The chances of this being a coincidence are microscopic. I surmise that Magellan's chart showed Zhou Man's route.

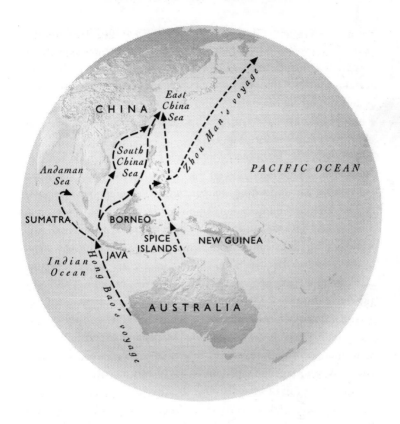

Hong Bao's journey home and Zhou Man's journey through the Spice Islands.

As well as Pigafetta's description of Magellan's voyage, I found that the British Library also held an account by the Genoese pilot who sailed with Magellan. He described Magellan's landfall in the Philippines and how he found a strait leading from the Pacific to the Spice Islands – the same strait between Mindanao and Leyte shown on the Rotz chart. Magellan passed through this strait and anchored at the first island, Limasava, where the king greeted him. Pigafetta described the king and queen wearing Chinese silk and eating off Chinese porcelain that had been buried for fifty years to increase its value. Their houses had silk curtains and porcelain ornaments, and their trading currency was Chinese coins with square centres. The same story was repeated on island after island visited by Magellan's ships en route to the Spice Islands. Zhou Man must have emptied his holds of porcelain as he went along, a century before Magellan.

Pigafetta also recounted Magellan's meeting with the King of Limasava. Magellan showed him *'the marine chart* and the compass of his ship *telling him how he had found the Strait to come hither* and how many moons [months] he had spent in coming; also, *he had not seen any land*, in which the King marvelled' (my italics). Magellan showed the king a chart depicting the strait and the empty Pacific. There was also a letter from Sebastian Alvarez, the King of Spain's factor (a merchant buying and selling on commission), to his king: 'From Cape Frío until the Islands of the Moloccas throughout this navigation there are no lands laid down in the maps they [Magellan's expedition] carry with them.'[17] Taken together, these accounts can mean only one thing. When Magellan sailed, he had with him a chart that not only showed the Strait of Magellan but also the Pacific at 52° South and an empty ocean from there to the Spice Islands on the equator. Someone must have sailed through the Strait of Magellan and across the Pacific before Magellan to make that chart. Who else but the Chinese, 'the yellow men wearing long robes'?[18]

Fortunately, the evidence from Magellan's visit to the Philippines was further confirmation of a Chinese voyage between 1421 and 1423. Chinese porcelain, silk and coinage of Zhu Di's reign, seen by Magellan in the Philippines, might have been the result of Chinese trade before Zhou Man's voyage, but Magellan noted substantial quantities on island after island. Clearly, huge amounts must have been exchanged, and that in turn must have resulted in Zhou Man taking aboard a vast quantity of traded goods, principally the greatly valued pepper. If so, that pepper would appear in the records of the Chinese stockpiles of the spice soon after he returned to China in October 1423.

I searched among copies of the few Chinese records that exist and found that my deductions were absolutely correct. By 1424 there were such massive stocks of pepper in the imperial warehouses that on his accession that year Emperor Zhu Gaozhi ordered much of it to be given away: 'To each banner bearer, housekeeper, soldier and guardsman one catty [half a kilo] of pepper ... to each first degree literary graduate and licentiate, district police chief, prison warder, astronomer and physician, one catty ... to each resident of the city and the environs of Beijing, each Buddhist or Taoist priest, artisan, musician, professional cook ... one catty.'[19] The population of Beijing in 1423 certainly exceeded one million and the soldiers of the imperial army and their dependants accounted for another six hundred thousand people. The weight of pepper distributed is likely to have been more than 1,500 tons. When Magellan's ship returned home, he had less than twenty-six tons of usable pepper aboard. It was sold at ten thousand times the price he had paid for it in the Spice Islands, sufficient to generate a profit for the entire voyage. Contrary to the claims of the Chinese mandarins, the voyages of the treasure ships brought substantial tangible rewards, for the pepper added to Chinese stockpiles late in 1423 was of colossal value on the international market.

Pigafetta's account of Magellan's voyage yielded still more evidence that Zhou Man's fleet had sailed from the Americas to the Spice Islands and the Philippines. Pigafetta described maize growing in the Philippines and Magellan's crew loading it. Maize is not only unique to the Americas but a crop that can only be propagated by man. Furthermore, some of the surviving Chinese records state that Zheng He's fleets brought back maize from their voyages. Not only had junks brought porcelain, silk and currency from China and carried pepper back there, they had also brought maize from South America to the Philippines.[20]

THE
FIRST
COLONY
IN THE
AMERICAS

ALTHOUGH HE WAS NOW LITTLE MORE THAN A thousand miles from the Chinese mainland, Zhou Man's remarkable voyage was still far from over. I next had to track his fleet as it sailed onwards from the Philippines to reach the coast of yet another new land. After leaving the Spice Islands with his rich cargo, the most direct route home for his fleet would have been to continue north, sailing west of Mindoro in the Philippines. From there, the prevailing summer wind would have blown him north towards China. Yet the manner in which the islands were drawn on the Rotz chart suggests that Zhou Man had chosen to alter course to the east, passing south of Leyte and re-entering the Pacific.[1] Assuming that he had left Darwin at the beginning of the south-west monsoon, in late April, he would have entered the Pacific by early June. I knew that Zhou Man had arrived in Nanjing on 8 October 1423, carrying no foreign envoys. What had he been doing and where had he sailed in the four months he had been in the Pacific?

The north Pacific is a vast circulatory system, with winds constantly blowing in a clockwise oval direction. In June, the prevailing wind off Leyte is to the north. As Admiral Zhou Man's fleet entered the Pacific, the Kuroshio or Japanese current would also have carried them northwards before starting a clockwise sweep towards the coast of North America. In fact, had Zhou Man simply unfurled his sails off Leyte, the winds and currents would have carried him to the Pacific coast of modern Canada. The California current would then have taken over, sweeping the fleet southwards down the western seaboard of the United States to Panama. From there, the north equatorial current would carry a square-rigged ship back across the Pacific towards the Philippines. The whole round trip, before the wind and current all the way, would have been about sixteen thousand nautical miles. At an average of 4.8 knots, the voyage would have taken some four months, matching the date of Zhou Man's return to Nanjing in October. My surmise, for reasons which will become apparent later, was that squadrons of ships from the main fleet were detached to establish colonies along the Pacific coast from California down to Ecuador.

I began the search for corroboration that Zhou Man's fleet had indeed reached the Pacific coast of North America. The first European to explore that coast was Hernando de Alarcón in 1540. Having sought fame and fortune in New Spain, he left Acapulco on 9 May of that year in command of a fleet supporting the conquistador Coronado's expedition to New Mexico. Alarcón first charted the peninsula of Baja California, and then California itself. I knew that he was the first European to chart it, for neither Columbus nor any of the other early explorers reached any part of the west coast of North America, so any map of the Pacific coast predating Alarcón's voyage would be powerful evidence that he was not the first to reach it.

Such evidence does exist in the form of the Waldseemüller world map, published in 1507, the first to chart latitude and longitude with precision. Originally owned by Johannes Schöner (1477–1547), a Nuremberg astronomer and geographer, it had long been thought lost and was only rediscovered in 1901 in the castle of Wolfegg in southern Germany. It remained there in relative obscurity until 2001, when in a blaze of publicity the US Library of Congress acquired it from Prince Johannes Waldburg-Wolfegg for ten million dollars. The man who drew the map, Martin Waldseemüller (c. 1470–1518), was German-born and one of the foremost cosmographers – combining the study of geography and astronomy – of his era. The globe and wall maps he made in 1507 are the first ever to call the continent 'America'; for some unknown reason this was not included on the 1516 map. The 1516 map, *Carta Marina – A Portuguese Navigational Seachart of the Known Earth and Oceans*, was 'the first and only printed version of the world charts previously known only to Spanish and Portuguese explorers and their patrons'.[2] The east coast of North America is clearly charted, with several place names.

The Caribbean and Florida, shown on the Waldseemüller map, were also depicted on two earlier charts, the Cantino (1502) in the Biblioteca Estense, Modena, Italy – a map which would play a significant role in my researches elsewhere in the world (see chapter 11) – and the Caverio map (1505) in the James Ford Bell Library at the University of Minnesota, Minneapolis. They too showed lands drawn before the first Europeans had reached them, but those maps cannot have been the original source of the Waldseemüller. The Great Bahama Bank is drawn identically on all three maps, but the Caverio map shows the Yucatán Peninsula in Mexico, which was not depicted on the earlier Cantino. Hence the Caverio cannot have been a copy of the Cantino, any more than the Waldseemüller is a copy of them, for the latest of the three, the Waldseemüller, shows the Pacific coast of North America and the Cantino and Caverio do not. All three maps have different original features, and all must have been copied from an even earlier map.

The Pacific coast of America is strikingly drawn on the Waldseemüller chart and the latitudes correspond to those of Vancouver Island in Canada right down to Ecuador in the south. This is completely consistent with a cartographer aboard a ship sailing down the Pacific coast, but not charting the coast in great detail. Oregon is clearly identifiable, and several very old wrecks have been discovered there on the beach at Neahkahnie. One was of teak with a pulley for hoisting sails made of calophyllum, a wood unique to south-east Asia. The wood has yet to be carbon-dated, but if it proves to be from the early fifteenth century it will provide strong circumstantial evidence that one of Zhou Man's junks was wrecked off Neahkahnie Beach. Some examiners of the wreckage there claim to have found paraffin wax, which was used by Zheng He's fleet to desalinate sea-water for the horses.

Even without finds from wrecked junks, the Pacific coasts of Central and South America are full of evidence of Chinese voyages. The Asiatic chickens found from Chile to California were described in chapter 5, and many other flora and fauna were carried across the globe by the Chinese fleets. On my first visit to California many years ago, I remember coming across a bank of beautiful camellia roses (*Rosa laevigata*). It was a still summer's evening and their lovely fragrance filled the air around me. In 1803, European settlers found a beautiful fragrant rose growing wild; they named it the Cherokee Rose. Yet it was indigenous to south-east China and had been illustrated in a twelfth-century Chinese pharmacopoeia. 'When and by what means it reached America is one of the unsolved problems of plant introductions,'[3] but it was a common practice for sailors aboard Zheng He's junks to keep pots of roses, their scent an enduring reminder of home. The Chinese also took plants and seeds home with them. Amaranth, a native North American grain with a high protein content, was brought from America to Asia in the early fifteenth century, as of course was maize – brought to the Philippines and seen there by Magellan. Coconuts, native to the South Pacific, were found by the first Europeans on the Pacific coasts of Costa Rica, Panama and Ecuador and on Cocos Island west of Costa Rica. The carriers of grain from the Americas to Asia, of roses and chickens from China to the Americas, and coconuts from the South Pacific to Ecuador can only have been the Chinese.

San Francisco and Los Angeles are clearly depicted at the correct latitudes on the Waldseemüller chart, and I was certain that Zhou Man must have sailed down that coast. Crossing such an enormous expanse of ocean after two years at sea must have left some of his junks in bad condition and in urgent need of repair. Even the best-built ships could not remain at sea for such long periods without suffering at least some damage from storms and the pounding of the waves. At the very least they would have required running repairs and careening – scraping the barnacles from their hulls – and the most badly damaged might well have

From 1406 to 1420 Zhu Di presided over the building of the Forbidden City with the Imperial Palace (*below* and *bottom*) as its centre. The Temple of Heaven was its place of ritual; it encompasses the Hall of Prayer for Good Harvests (*opposite left*) where the emperor came to pray at the new year. When the capital moved north, the renovation of the Great Wall (*opposite right*) became a priority.

The third Ming emperor, Zhu Di, under whom exploration flourished.

The Ming court in life and death: the emperor sits ensconced at the bottom level of a Taoist shrine (*above*) between a civil and a military adviser and flanked by two guardian figures.

The Spirit Way leading to the Ming tombs in Beijing is lined by stone warriors (*above left*) and high officials, here a Grand Secretary (*above right*), as well as powerful beasts – exotic elephants (*below*) and the mythical quilin (*opposite, below*).

The treasure ships took with them not only the much-prized blue and white porcelain (*above* and *top*), but also jade (*middle*), lacquer (*right*) and luxurious silk textiles (*opposite*).

A giraffe, with its attendant, sent from Africa
to the Ming imperial court as tribute.

been cannibalized to repair the others. If so, the remains of these wrecked ships should have been found off the coast of California, just as other wrecks had been in Australia and other parts of the globe.

My enquiries into strange wrecks on the coast of California drew a blank, but I did discover that museums there held substantial quantities of Ming blue and white ceramics. The accepted wisdom is that these items were brought to California in the holds of Spanish galleons, but a number of medieval Chinese anchors have been found off the California coast, and these are unlikely to have been brought by Spanish ships. I began to question seriously the provenance of the Ming porcelain; had it really been brought by the Spanish? Medieval Chinese porcelain can be dated by its cobalt content: the greater the amount of iron in the cobalt, the deeper blue the glaze. The dark cobalt of the Mongol era came from Persia, also ruled by the Mongols, but Zhu Di's father sealed the Chinese borders after he drove out the Mongols in 1368 and Persian cobalt was no longer available. However, Zhu Di reopened the frontiers and restored trade along the Silk Road through Asia allowing Persian cobalt to be imported once more. The period when Chinese pale blue porcelain was produced and used in Ming China is thus limited, and the colour of the porcelain held by Californian museums would indicate whether or not it was made during this period in China's history.

I was certain that a great treasure fleet had discovered the Pacific coasts of North and South America, but my researches failed to uncover conclusive evidence such as the wreck of a Chinese junk. In the hope that others might have found traces I had missed, I decided to 'go public' on the issue in a lecture at the Royal Geographical Society in London in March 2002. It was broadcast around the world; within forty-eight hours reports began to come in from California, drawing my attention to the wreck of a medieval Chinese junk buried under a sandbank in the Sacramento River off the north-east corner of San Francisco Bay. My first reaction was to discount the reports – the site was more than a hundred miles from open sea and the discovery seemed too good to be true – but over the next few days more e-mails describing the same junk continued to arrive. As soon as I had carried out some preliminary research, I discovered that the prevailing north-easterly winds on this coast could have blown a junk straight across the bay and into the Sacramento River. Six centuries ago the river was broader and deeper than today, for deforestation and mining have caused the water level to fall. It was indeed possible, if not probable, that a junk entering San Francisco Bay would have been driven by the winds into the Sacramento River. The tide would also have carried the ship upstream as far as Sacramento.

Dr John Furry of the Natural History Museum of Northern California first became aware of the junk twenty years ago when he read an account of the strange armour that once had been found in its hold (the wreck was then evidently less deeply buried in sand and silt than it is now). The armour was of an unusual metal (native Americans did not know how to forge metal) and curiously silver-grey in colour. It was shown to a local expert who is said to have identified it as of medieval Chinese origin. Dr Furry's attempts to pursue the story met a brick wall – the expert had died in the intervening years, and the armour had been lent to a local school and was now lost – but he was sufficiently intrigued to begin investigating the wreck-site.

The site was covered with a 40-foot layer of the accumulated sand and silt of centuries, so Dr Furry began by taking magnetometer readings of the area. These showed a strong magnetic anomaly outlining a buried object 85 feet long and 30 feet wide, very similar in size and shape to the trading junks that accompanied Zheng He's fleets. Core samples were then extracted from the site. The fragments of wood brought up were carbon-dated to 1410, indicating that the junk was built in that

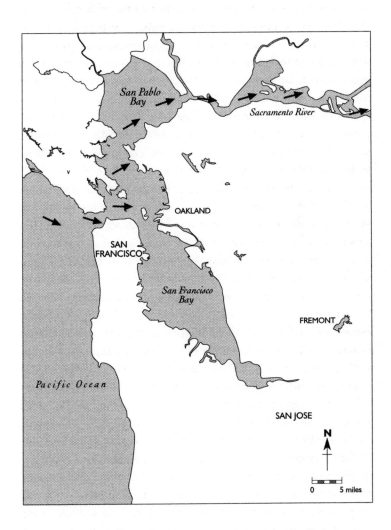

The San Francisco Bay area, showing the winds blowing into
the Sacramento River.

year, 'a period that included a maritime highpoint for the ancient Chinese',[4] as local newspapers laconically reported.

The evidence from the carbon-dating encouraged Dr Furry to drill again with more sophisticated equipment. This yielded much larger samples including further pieces of wood and a compacted 80lb mass of millions of black seeds. He sent fragments of the wood and the seeds to China for analysis, and according to Dr Furry, the Chinese Academy of Forestry have provisionally identified the wood as Keteleria, a conifer native to south-east China but not to North America. In the Middle Ages, the Chinese cultivated Keteleria for ship-building. Dr Furry also told me that Dr Zhang Wenxu, a former professor at the Chinese Agricultural University in Beijing and the leading Chinese expert on ancient seeds, had provisionally identified four different types of seeds in the black mass brought up from the wreck-site. Three were native to both China and North America, but the other was found only in China. Most interesting of all, however, was Dr Furry's further discovery of rice grains and the body of a beetle among the material raised. Rice, indigenous to Africa and China, was unknown in the Americas in the fifteenth century. Further analysis of the rice and the beetle is being carried out as I write, but to date no written reports on the analysis of the wood or the seeds have been received from China.

I now had little doubt that the site contained the wreck of a Chinese junk; it was exactly the evidence I had been looking for. It seemed highly improbable that the crew would have drowned when the junk grounded on the sandbank in the Sacramento River. It was far more likely that they had come ashore onto the lush, fertile lands of the valley. Their first task would have been to rescue as much rice as possible from the holds of the ship. Much would have been needed to meet their short-term food requirements, but they would also have set some aside as seed and planted it in a suitable location – the floodplain of the Sacramento River.

It has long been claimed that rice was introduced to West Africa by Europeans and then to the Americas by the Spanish, but Professor Judith A. Carney of the University of California has argued that this thesis is fundamentally flawed. It is widely accepted that the Chinese made a major contribution to developing agriculture in the rich soils of California, particularly the cultivation of rice in the swamplands of the lower Sacramento. By the 1870s, 75 per cent of the farm labourers in California were of Chinese origin. 'The Chinese actually taught the American farmer how to plant, cultivate and harvest.'[5] But were these Chinese working in the fields and plantations of the Sacramento Valley all part of the great nineteenth-century waves of immigration into the United States, or could some have been descendants of settlers left on the banks of the Sacramento by Zhou Man in 1423? I found a clue to this mystery in an unlikely source.

In 1874, Stephen Powers, an official inspector appointed by the government of California who had spent years collecting data on the languages of the tribes of California, published an article claiming that he had found linguistic evidence of a Chinese colony on the Russian River in California, some seventy miles north-west of the Sacramento junk.[6] Powers also claimed that diseases brought by European settlers had decimated this Chinese colony as well as the other Indian people of California, '[the] remittent fever which desolated the Sacramento valleys in 1833 and reduced these great plains from a condition of remarkable populousness to one of almost utter silence and solitude ... there was scarcely a human being left alive'.[7] Powers' report was badly received by his government employers, and although he courteously and bravely attempted to maintain his position, his official report, published in 1877, is a watered-down version of his claims. Nonetheless, it makes for fascinating reading.

Quite apart from his claim of a Chinese colony based on linguistic evidence, Powers described Chinese settlers as having intermarried with local Indians over centuries. Their descendants were paler than the people of the coast, and, unlike other Indian tribes, the older generation had magnificent beards while the women 'are as proud of their black hair as the Chinese'. Rather than skins, women wore 'a single garment in the shape of a wool sack, sleeveless and gathered at the neck, more or less white once'. They were 'simple, friendly, peaceable and inoffensive'. After death, 'they generally desire like the Chinese to be buried in the ancestral soil of their tribe'. Again like the Chinese, but unlike other hunter-gatherer tribes of North America, the peoples around the Sacramento and Russian Rivers were sedentary: 'at least four fifths of their diet was derived from the vegetable kingdom ... They knew the qualities of all herbs, shrubs, leaves, having a command of a much greater catalogue of [botanical] names than nine tenths of Americans.' Their ancestors' legacy could also be seen in pottery beautifully formed in classic Chinese shapes, whereas the '[modern] Indian merely picks up a boulder of trap [a dark, igneous rock] or greenstone and beats out a hollow leaving the outside rough'. The ancestors of the Sacramento and Russian River tribes also used 'long, heavy knives of obsidian or jasper' their descendants, Powers found, no longer knew how to make. And while the ancestors had fashioned elegant tobacco pipes from serpentine, their descendants made use of simple wooden ones. They had also 'developed a Chinese inventiveness'[8] in devising methods of snaring wildfowl using decoy ducks – a Chinese custom, but one not found among the Indians. Like the Chinese, they ate snails, slugs, lizards and snakes, and built large middens of clam shells. (For DNA corroboration, see Synopsis of Evidence.)

On the eastern side of San Francisco Bay, some seventy miles south of the site of the Sacramento junk, there is a small, stone-built village with low walls. In 1904, Dr John Fryer, Professor of Oriental Languages at University College, Berkeley, California, stated, 'This is undoubtedly the work of Mongolians ... The

Chinese would naturally wall themselves in, as they do in all their towns in China."[9] This accords with Powers' succinct description of Chinese people who had created a colony and then intermarried with native Americans.

It certainly seems that Zhou Man's fleet left a settlement in California. Were they the first to cultivate rice in the Americas? And was the wealth of blue and white Ming porcelain found in California really brought by Spanish galleons, as conventional wisdom has it, or was it carried in the holds of the junks of Zhou Man's fleet? The investigation is ongoing, the definitive conclusion yet to be written; meanwhile, I had to press on with my own research, tracking the fleet as it set sail once more from San Francisco Bay.

After emerging from the bay, Zhou Man's fleet would have been carried southwards by the wind and current to Mexico. The Waldseemüller map shows the coast with reasonable accuracy, charted just as one would expect from a ship passing by, but there is a gap at the latitude of the Gulf of Tehuantepec in Guatemala, as if the Pacific and Atlantic Oceans met there, which of course is not the case. This is consistent with the Chinese having sailed into the Gulf, but finding it too shallow to proceed, turning back and then drawing what they could see from the entrance: water stretching away for miles in front of them, marking an apparent opening between North and South America.

I made the assumption that they had sailed beyond the isthmus of Panama, clearly shown on the Waldseemüller, and then been driven back across the Pacific towards China by the winds and current, as one would expect with a square-rigged sailing ship. But on their way down that coast they would have been swept across the Gulf of California and could have made a landfall on the Mexican coast somewhere near Manzanillo in the modern province of Colima. Here a spectacular volcano, the Colima, some 12,700 feet high and clearly visible for miles out to sea, would have attracted them.

I decided to make a search for another wreck between Manzanillo and Acapulco, a stretch of coastline only around three hundred miles long and again clearly shown on the Waldseemüller map. I started my search with the accounts of the first Spaniards to reach that coast in the 1520s, Fra Bernardino de Sahagún[10] and Bernal Diaz del Castillo,[11] both of whom described the exotic Mayan civilization, still surviving in 1421 but in decline when they arrived. Many of the things de Sahagún and del Castillo described – chickens, lacquer boxes, dye-stuffs, metalwork and jewellery – seemed to have the imprint of China all over them.

As in California, when they arrived in Mexico the conquistadors found Asiatic chickens quite different from the European fowl they had left behind. The Mayan names for the birds, *Kek* or *Ki*, were identical to those used by the Chinese; like the Chinese but unlike the Europeans, Mexicans used chickens for ceremonial purposes such as divination. These were such remarkable similarities that for these reasons alone I felt a visit to that small strip of the Mexican coast was justified.

Before departing, I also investigated whether plants originating in China grew in New Mexico or western Mexico. The Chinese Rose did, but that could have been propagated southwards from California. Other than the rose, I found no plants growing in Mexico that had originated in China, but I did find the opposite; plants indigenous to Central America had found their way across the world before the European voyages of discovery.[12] Sweet potatoes, tomatoes and papayas were found in Easter Island, sweet potatoes in Hawaii, and maize in China and the Philippines. Maize could have come from South or North America, but the other plants had come from a much narrower area, from what we now call Mexico, Guatemala and Nicaragua.

The Mayan civilization the Chinese would have encountered was almost as old as their own. The Maya's predecessors were the Olmecs, the earliest civilization in Central America and possibly the whole of the Americas, whose capital was at La Venta on the Atlantic coast of Mexico. By 1200 BC, the Olmec people had constructed two large artificial plateaux at La Venta and San Lorenzo on which they built religious cities nearly as old as Babylon. These great mounds stretching for miles were the centre of a settlement system that integrated Olmec villages and hamlets into one social, political and economic unit straddling what we now know as southern Mexico.

They set up extensive trade networks with the peoples to the south, importing obsidian, basalt, greenstone and iron ore, and exporting pottery, jaguar pelts, coca and wonderfully expressive sculpture. Examples can be seen to this day in Parque La Venta: mischievous stone monkeys hang from trees; stone dolphins, so lively that one can almost see the water splashing off their bodies, leap between ponds; a man crawls out of the entrance of a tomb carved out of basalt; a distraught mother cradles her dead child in her arms. It is fabulous sculpture, the work of a truly amazing people. But around 300 BC, the Olmecs vanished for reasons that remain unclear. They were followed by the Maya, who created a trading empire spanning Central America. The Mayan epoch was already coming to an end by 1421 and civil war had broken out in Yucatan, but the Chinese would have found a very old and very distinguished civilization.

I saw traces of that great Mayan civilization everywhere as I took a bus from the Atlantic to the Pacific coast of Mexico. The Atlantic coast is littered with mooring posts, each of which seems to have its own sentinel pelican, watching over a sea teeming with fish. Then come mile upon mile of marshes, with flocks of ducks and skeins of geese crossing the sky. Ibises and storks stand motionless in pools and lagoons. This is Mayan country, with a system of agriculture unchanged for centuries. *Milpas* – cultivated fields – sprawl across the jungle, the result of the slash and burn system. In the dry season, around Christmas, farmers cut trees with their machetes. From March until May there is little rain and the heat becomes oppressive, an ideal time for burning dried wood, leaving a cleared area for cultivation covered with a nutrient-rich bed of ashes.

The first rains come at the end of May, preceded by silent lightning. Now farmers take long thick staffs and poke small holes into the wet earth into which they drop kernels of maize, beans and squash seeds. This marvellous trio has provided the healthy diet on which the peoples of the Americas – Olmec, Maya, Toltec, Inca and Aztec – have sustained themselves for millennia. As the corn grows, the beans wind around the stems and the squashes spread across the ground. By July, the sun is blistering but there is abundant rainfall, and in September it is time for harvest. The Chinese would have found such rich agriculture spread right across the land together with a sophisti- cated irrigation system and raised fields supporting a far higher density of population than is found in the Mexican countryside today. It rivalled their own.

Beehives are scattered along the fringes of the forest; honey was important to the Maya for sugar, as a basis for wheat- fermented alcohol and as a cash crop enabling the farmers to buy shoes and the cotton cloth their wives embroidered in traditional patterns. To this day, their children wear smocks exquisitely embroidered in vivid colours identifying family and village, very similar to those painted in the frescoes of long ago. The traditional *Na* houses peep out of the rainforest, unchanged for millennia. The foundations, an oval platform of rocks, are bound together by limestone cement. Horizontal beams are lashed to the uprights with rope made from fibres of the agave plant. Smaller bamboos complete the framework and the roofs are of dried fan palms. This traditional construction is still used in hotels and resorts throughout southern Mexico and Guatemala. The Maya still sleep in hammocks, and their everyday greeting remains 'Have a hammock.'

The jungle of Central America provides a rich and varied

diet; man only needs to hunt, fish and gather fruit for two or three days each month, and in the sultry heat he needs few clothes. Building materials, vegetables, medicines, coca, coffee, edible birds and animals of all descriptions surround him. The jungle is never silent; night is punctuated by cries, whistles, screams, muffled roars and croaks. In this rich jungle environment, the Maya built glorious stone cities. Nothing I have seen on this fabulous planet, not even Machu Picchu or the Acropolis, has equalled the Mayan city of Palenque in Chiapas, Mexico, rising out of the white mist of a perfect summer's day. The city was built by the Maya in their glorious golden age (c. AD 325–925) and lay hidden under its cloak of jungle for a thousand years. Constructed on a series of adjacent hills overlooking the plains, it spreads over three and a half square miles. Each hill group comprises a cluster of buildings – pyramids, temples and palaces. Within each group, white stone palaces surround an enchanting central plaza with a backdrop of verdant, bottle-green jungle. The buildings have been superbly positioned to accentuate the natural features of hill and valley, while a placid river wends through the middle of the site. When the Chinese met the people of Mexico it is highly probable that they would have been shown Palenque, the finest Mayan city.

At the time, Palenque would have appeared to the Chinese as the work of a people whose talent equalled their own. It is the complete Mayan city, suddenly abandoned with its treasures intact. Here there is everything the archaeologist or historian could wish for: the fabulous tomb of a 'pharaoh of the jungle', filled with treasures; palaces of kings and priests covered in hieroglyphics telling the story of the site; observatories, temples, ball courts and, perhaps most important of all, the houses of ordinary people. Every aspect of art is here, from masks, statues, jewellery and ceramics to the humble pots and pans, fishing hooks and spears used by ordinary folk to hunt game.

The extraordinary white pyramid of King Pakal dominates

the site. The Cuban scholar Alberto Ruz Lhuillier spent years digging down a secret stairway into the chamber at the very bottom. In 1952 his team wrenched aside a huge stone and entered a darkened vault.

> Out of the dim shadows emerged a vision from a fairytale, a fantastic ethereal sight from another world. It seemed a huge magic grotto, carved out of ice, the walls sparkling and glistening like snow crystals ... the impression, in fact, was that of an abandoned chapel. Across the walls marched stucco figures in low relief. Then my eyes sought the floor. This was almost entirely filled with the great carved stone slab, in perfect condition ... Ours were the first eyes that gazed upon it for more than a thousand years.

In feverish excitement, Alberto Ruz Lhuillier and his team jacked up the huge lid and peered inside.

> My first impression was that of a mosaic of green, red and white. Then it resolved itself into details – green jade ornaments, red painted teeth and bones, and a fragment of the mask. I was gazing at the death face of him for whom all this stupendous work – the crypt, the sculpture, the stairway, the great pyramid with its crowning temple – had been built ... This, then, was a sarcophagus, the first ever found in a Mayan pyramid.[13]

The most spectacular of the exotic treasures that accompanied Pakal to the next life was his burial mask of jade, with shell eyes and obsidian irises. It must be one of the finest works of art ever made by man, of incalculable value. The dead king's wrist, neck, fingers and ears were adorned with exquisitely carved jade jewellery. Here were objects to rival or even eclipse the finest products of the Chinese or Japanese craftsmen. The beautifully proportioned pyramid with its simple, smoothly faced stone, the hidden stairway, the interior crypt and the superb mask and jewellery are the work of a people of immense architectural, engineering and artistic talent.

A walk downriver from Pakal's pyramid brought me to a museum filled with Mayan decorative art, mostly symbolic plants and animals – jaguars, serpents with fangs and claws, birds with their feathers and scales, so lifelike they appear to leap out of the display cases. It is an astounding cornucopia of artistic treasure. At last, after years of sailing the storm-tossed oceans, the Chinese had met a civilization nearly as old and as fine as their own. They had found jade jewellery as exquisite as theirs, and Cholula ware even thinner than the best Chinese porcelain, Jingdezhen from Jiangxi province. At long last, they could exchange their silks and blue and white ceramics for wonderful works of art.

COLONIES

IN

CENTRAL

AMERICA

IFOUND SOME OF THE STRONGEST SIGNS OF CHINESE influence when I arrived in Uruapan in the mountains of western Mexico. It lies approximately two hundred miles upriver from the Pacific, with the river and the sea to the south and the mountains to the north. The town owes its name to the Spanish monk Fra Juan de San Miguel who was so impressed by the lush vegetation when he arrived in 1533 that he christened the area Uruapan – 'eternal spring'. To this day, it is renowned for its avocados and fruit, and for the beautiful lacquer boxes and trays that delight tourists.

Lacquer, known in Mexico as *maque* and in China as *Ch'i-ch'i*, is a highly unusual, complex and time-consuming method of decoration. The lacquer tree occurs in a wild state in China, regarded as the original birthplace of lacquer, and is also culti-vated in plantations. The Chinese recognized the protective qualities of seshime, the resin extracted from the branches of the lacquer tree, at least three thousand years ago. They introduced it throughout south-east Asia; the Chinese and Japanese lacquer-ing processes are essentially the same. The oldest known Chinese examples date from the Shang dynasties (c. 1523–1028 BC) when the Middle Kingdoms began using lacquer on household utensils, furniture and art objects, and to preserve historical objects carved on bamboo. To their astonishment, the first Europeans to reach southern California and Mexico found that the process of lacquer decoration was flourishing in the states of Chiapas, Guerrero, Michoacán and as far north as Sinaloa on the Gulf of California.[1] Uruapan is considered to be the centre of the *maque* art, but how could the people of Pacific Mexico have come to know of it? Was it developed independently, or did the Chinese introduce it?

Lacquer's unique characteristic is its need for a moist and temperate atmosphere in order to dry. Warm dampness converts the sap into a dense mass that hardens as enamel. Density and drying vary with temperature, thickness and humidity. Perfect conditions are found in the moist, warm Pacific winds of Uruapan. Before applying lacquer in the traditional way, the surface of a box or other object is prepared by filling all the cracks with a mixture of rice flour and seshime. The correct consistency is achieved by mixing it with rice paste, or, in the case of Mexico, with volcanic ash. The box is then sanded down and the first of between ten and a hundred coats of lacquer applied with a very fine brush made of human hair. Each layer has to be completely dry, sanded and polished before the next is applied. Polishing was an art in itself, using a whetstone and deer-horn powder applied with a soft cloth; sixty or seventy coats were common.

This process is virtually identical in China and Mexico, with Chinese technology being adapted to the climate and materials found in Mexico. Preparation of the surface is identical: cracks are filled with a mixture called *nimacarta*, the object is sanded until completely smooth, and as many coats of *nimacarta* as necessary are applied, each one dried, sanded and polished with a whetstone.

Although the process is the same, the ingredients in Mexico do vary. The *maque* is a semi-liquid paste formed using a mixture of animal and vegetable oils and natural refined clays. The principal animal ingredient is grease extracted from the *aje* insects (*Coccus lacca*) bred by the local people around Uruapan. The insects are gathered during the rainy season and dropped alive into boiling water until their bodies release a hard, waxy substance that floats to the surface. When the water cools, the substance is collected, washed and reheated to remove any water. It cools like slabs of butter. The second ingredient, *chia* vegetable oil, serves to thin the *aje* mixture. The oil is extracted from the seeds of the sage plant, a native of Mexico. *Chia* oil has a high glycerine content that quickly absorbs oxygen from the air, forming a hard elastic surface when dried. The third ingredient, finely ground dolomite called *teputzuta*, a mineral clay, gives body to the *maque* mixture.

The decorative techniques and colours used in Mexico and China are also remarkably similar, with spectacular reds incised into a deep black background. In both countries, the traditional colour is black obtained from the fine powder of burnt animal bones or burnt corncobs. Decorative *maque* techniques used in today's states of southern Mexico are the same as in China and Japan. The design is carved using the point of a sharp cactus needle inserted in a turkey quill. The soft plume of the feather is used to brush off the excess clay, or *maque*, as it is carved off. The fine incised lines are then filled with contrasting colours, one colour at a time, with plenty of drying, scouring and polishing after each application. The end result, the wonderful decorated plate or box, is so similar in Uruapan and China that it is almost impossible for those who are not experts to differentiate between them.

Theoretically, if very implausibly, this elaborate and time-consuming process could have evolved simultaneously in China and Mexico, countries thousands of miles apart, but lacquering is not the only congruity when it comes to the artwork of western Mexico and China. Both also have extraordinarily similar and highly unusual methods of obtaining the dyes used in their artwork. Madder red, indigo blue, scarlet and shellfish purple are obscure dye-stuffs producing brilliant colours but requiring complex procedures to extract and fix them. Again, I would argue, too large a coincidence to be probable.

Madder is a red dye derived in China from the roots of shrubs of the Rubiacea family. The dye is prepared by digging up, drying, cleaning and pulverizing the roots, then soaking the mash overnight and steeping it for a short time at about 150° Celsius. The fabric is first mordanted, or fixed, with an aluminium sulphate before being boiled in the dye bath. It is then rinsed in water mixed with wood ash. In Mexico, the roots come from relatives of the Rubiacea – R. *relbunium* and R. *nitidum*, small, sub-tropical shrubs found as far south as Argentina. The New

World mordant includes aluminium, oxalic acid and tannin.

The brilliant blue indigo, used for millennia throughout south-east Asia, is the oldest of all the natural dye-stuffs and requires the most complicated technology. The plant must be very carefully cultivated. The fresh cut leaves, whole or ground, have to be steeped in hot water for nine to fourteen hours, during which time the leaves ferment and produce the most unpleasant smell. The resultant liquid is clear, but yarn or cloth soaked in it turns a vivid blue upon oxidization with the air. The process used for dyeing in pre-Columbian Central America was almost identical, save that ash and lime were employed as solubility enhancers.

Vermilion dyes, obtained from tiny insects scraped off oak leaves, were extensively used in south-east Asia. The insects were drowned in a vinegar bath, giving them a reddish brown colour, and when crushed they yielded a dye that was dissolved in alcohol and then fixed with alum or urine. The other red dye that occurred throughout south-east Asia was lac (laccaic acid), obtained from wild or domesticated curmese or lac insects parasitic on various trees. The twigs were broken off, dried in the sun and dropped into a hot soda solution from which the liquid was evaporated and the residue made into cakes. Both Ma Huan and Niccolò da Conti described them on sale in Calicut.[2]

The New World equivalent made use of another scaled insect, the cochineal, parasitic on cactus plants. The insect envelops itself in a cottony white film, and when crushed produces a spectacular scarlet colour ten times richer than the curmes and lac of Asia. After the Spanish invaded Mesoamerica, they exported cochineal to the Middle East and Asia. As in China, cochineal's colour was associated with royalty. True Mexican cochineal had reached southern Asia before Columbus set sail.[3]

The final dye was royal (tyrian) purple obtained from marine snails. This was the most celebrated of all colours used in the Old World. It was so expensive that only the wealthy could afford it, and purple robes became synonymous with high rank. The rulers of Byzantium were brought up in purple rooms and clothed in purple robes. In the New World, shellfish purple was produced from the region of Michoacán – the province surrounding Uruapan – and as far afield as Ecuador, and was very widely used on the Pacific coast. As early as 1898, this method of extracting shellfish purple was considered a possible indicator of pre-Columbian transoceanic trade.

> ... in many areas where the step of applying these substances as colorants might have occurred, it didn't, and sophisticated application of them to fiber is so involved that it seems remarkable that it developed at all, not to say multiple times ... thus when we find several of these dye stuffs, together with use of mordants, shared by distant regions, we must consider the possibility of historical contact, and rather intimate, repeated contact at that – especially in light of a host of other shared, and often arbitrary, traits.[4]

It is inconceivable that these dyeing processes could have been accidental, independent discoveries; 'a common source of the two civilisations must therefore be assumed'.[5]

But the links between Mexico and China do not end with natural dyes, lacquerwork, hens and plants. Lake Pátzcuaro, upriver from Uruapan, is surrounded by mountains rich in copper ore. To this day, lakeside towns such as San Christobal sell beautiful copper artefacts to swarms of tourists, and the museums are filled with treasures from the past. In Michoacán, as in China, metals were separated after they had been mined, stored in different warehouses and catalogued according to the quality and type of the metal and whether it was to be used for religious offerings or as tributes.

The *Florentine Codex* – Fra Bernardino de Sahagún's great book,[6] completed in 1569, describing pre-Hispanic civilizations in Mexico – illustrates the processing of the metals by blowing oxygen through them to separate impurities, an advanced process not used in pre-Columbian North America. The metals used by the Michoacáns were copper, gold, silver and metal alloys. They were particularly adept at casting bells, which took up nearly 60 per cent of the metals fabricated. The resonance of a bell is determined by the type of metal alloy used; just as in Asia, the proportions were carefully measured to give the correct resonance. Metal bells using these same alloys were important symbols in the Buddhist religion, and visitors to Thailand, Burma, China and India are still charmed by the sweet notes of such bells through the day, as I know from dreamy afternoons spent in monasteries in Burma and Tibet.

Metal *hachuelas* – burial offerings in the shape of a crescent moon – are also found in abundance in Mexican tombs. *Hachuelas* were often placed in the mouth of the deceased, just as jade marbles were placed in the mouth of the dead in China. The curved, moon-shaped form was an important universal symbol of Lamaist Buddhism. Emperor Zhu Di made significant efforts to encourage Lamaism in China by inviting the Tibetan Karmapa to visit him and bestowing honours upon him. Moon-shaped ceremonial knives were used symbolically to sever the attachment with life, and can be found in Buddhist temples and tombs throughout Tibet and China to this day. While the eunuch captains were Muslims, the crews of Zheng He's fleet were almost all Buddhist, attracted by Buddha's teaching of universal compassion to all sentient creatures.

Mirrors also had an important place in the cultures of both Central America and China. In China, a mirror was believed to assist the transition of the soul to other planes, to the abodes of the spirits of gods and the souls of the ancestors. Most Chinese bronze mirrors were round, embodying the Taoist concept of the circle as a universal space. In China and Japan, the reverse side of a mirror was inscribed with symbols of animals and flowers, and with religious reliefs. It became a tradition to carry a symbolically decorated, round, bronze mirror as protection from evil spirits. In Michoacán, round metal discs called *rodelas* were used in ceremonies and rituals. Like bells, they were produced in large numbers from gold, silver, copper and alloys, and were decorated on the reverse side with symbols of nature and the universe.

As a result of this research, I was certain that the Chinese had been to Uruapan, had traded hens there, and that they must have stayed for months or possibly years to impart their knowledge of lacquerwork and dye technology to the Mexicans. My tentative conclusion – that squadrons or individual ships had been detached as the fleet passed down the coast in order to set up colonies – seemed more and more plausible. There was corroboration of that in the oral history of the Nayarit, to the north-west of Guadalajara – tales of a pre-Columbian ship from Asia that arrived on the Mexican coast and was cordially received by the chief of the Coras, a prominent Nayarit people. I began to search through the museum collections. It was a long haul with little to show for it at first. Then I came across the *lienzo de Jucutácato* (the linen of Jucutácato), a painting discovered in the nineteenth century in the village of that name.

The *lienzo* comprises around thirty-five squares, thirty of which are about the same size, and each square tells a little story. The first scene shows men disembarking from a ship. Running ahead of them is a dog with a distinctive tail curved in a bow over its back. In shape, size and gait, especially its peculiar tail, it resembles the Chinese shar-pei, a hunting dog originally from Guangzhou, and much prized by poor Cantonese for its extreme devotion to its keeper and his family.[7] At least one of the men is on horseback, a creature the local people would have found very strange and worthy of note; there were none in the Americas prior to the Spanish conquest. The leader emerging from the bows is dressed in a red tunic (the same garment Zheng He is wearing on the statue recently found buried in the Fujian Palace – see postscript) and he holds a round mirror. The mirror clearly had symbolic importance for it is repeated no fewer than fourteen times in the other pictures. In some of them the reverse side of the mirror is shown 'marked with eight divisions'; this 'wheel of doctrine' relates to a major event in the life of the Buddha, particularly his preaching and enlightenment. The mirror being carried by the red-robed leader is entirely consistent with a Buddhist religious leader coming ashore to meet local people.

In the centre of the picture, a leader sits while local people lay trays of minerals on the ground at his feet – to my mind an obvious reference to their selling copper to the Chinese. At the bottom is a tree with rays of light emanating from it. It may symbolize the tree of enlightenment under which the Buddha sat. Finally, there are several drawings of a large bird with a drooping tail trailing on the ground. In size and posture, the bird resembles the Asiatic Malay chicken. Taken as a whole, the picture is wholly consistent with Chinese disembarking on horseback and on foot from a great ship, striding ashore with their mirrors to ward off evil spirits, assisted by the tree of enlightenment and the wheel of doctrine. The local people brought them minerals and perhaps in return the Chinese bequeathed their chickens, lacquerwork, dye-stuff and mineral technology.

According to the historian Nicolás León,[8] the first person to have the *lienzo* analysed and copied, it was painted with black vegetable ink on a coarsely woven cloth and dates to long before the Spaniards arrived in Mexico. He states that it was altered in the sixteenth century by the Spaniards who added buildings and words in an attempt to explain it. These alterations were made with a different type of ink and at a later date.

Was it plausible that the Chinese had reached Jucutácato, even though it lies inland from the coast? The village stands some ten kilometres south of Uruapan where the Cupatitzio River ceases to be navigable. The Cupatitzio empties into a large lake some forty kilometres further south, which in turn is connected to the sea by the Balsas River. Just as at Sacramento, it is entirely possible that a junk could have reached Jucutácato from the sea, to obtain minerals and plants in return for trade goods and technology.

If the Chinese had made such a visit to trade and teach the Maya the secrets of lacquer technology, evidence of their stay should still exist. Professor Needham, one of the great experts on Ming China, visited Mexico in 1947 and described his experiences. 'I was deeply impressed during my stay with the palpable similarities between many features of high Central American civilisations and those of East and Southwest Asia,'[9] he wrote, then listed more than thirty cultural parallels. In addition to the metallurgy described earlier, he cited Mayan drums resembling those found in China, tripod pottery, games, computing devices, jade used to demonstrate a panoply of complex beliefs, music (more than half the types of Mayan musical instruments are also found in Burma and Laos), Chinese carrying poles and Chinese neck-rest pillows. With respect to the great professor, I would go even further. From the Pacific coast of Mexico down to central Peru one can be forgiven for thinking one is in China, so similar is the atmosphere, so familiar the bustle, so reminiscent the 'kik-kiri-kee' of the hens in the morning, so alike the people.

To my mind, direct evidence of an early Chinese presence is littered right across the Mayan landscape. Pre-Columbian Chinese bronze figures were found in Peru, and Nazca figurines of the sun god have on their base a Chinese figure for heaven. The museum at Teotihuacan, then an important city, has Chinese medallions, and Chinese jade necklace decorations were found at Chiapa de Corzo in the modern state of Chiapas. Don Ramón Mena, then director of the National Museum of Mexico, described one medallion as 'centuries old ... carried to America when the Chinese came to this continent'.[10] In the celebrated

Cueva Pintada caves on the Mexican peninsula of Baja California, there are paintings of men pierced with arrows and a depiction of the Crab Nebula supernova of 1054 recorded by the Chinese (see chapter 1). In the debris at the foot of the paintings, charred wood has been found and carbon-dated to between 1352 and 1512.

Further evidence of a Chinese stay in Mayan lands comes from Guatemala. The distinguished biologists Carl Johannessen and M. Fogg describe the divination and witchcraft practised by the local people using black-fleshed melanotic chickens.[11] They make a compelling case that not only were the chickens brought from China, but the Chinese must have spent a long time indoctrinating the different groups of people.

Seemingly incontrovertible proof of Chinese colonies in Central America also comes from the foothills of the mountains west of the Gulf of Venezuela, an area clearly shown on the Waldseemüller chart. I have seen these mountains from far out to sea, their snow-capped peaks silhouetted against the setting sun – an unforgettable sight. Some of the native tribes living in this remote area have traces of Chinese genes in their blood.

In 1962, Dr Tulio Arends and Dr M.L. Gallengo of the Instituto Venezolano de Investigaciones Científicas, Caracas, reported the findings of their electrophoretic study of the distribution of transferrin phenotypes (the study of the migration of suspended particles in particular protein macro-molecules under the influence of an electric field) in linguistic and ethnological groups of the mature population of the American continent. They identified transferrins (proteins transporting iron in blood) in the Irapa, Paraujano and Macoita people who inhabited the foothills of the Sierra de Perija ($9°$ to $11°N$; $72°40'$ to $73°30'W$). These tribes were primitive populations on the verge of extinction. In 58 per cent of these people, the scientists found a slow-moving transferrin indistinguishable from one which to date has been found only in Chinese natives of the province of

Kwantung in south-east China.[12] As the report says, 'this finding is additional evidence for the existence of a racial link between South American Indians and Chinese'. A goodly proportion of the crews of Zhou Man's and Hong Bao's fleets would have been born in Kwantung, for then, as now, its ports were among the busiest in China, thronged with boats and the seamen who sailed them. It appears that some of the Kwantung sailors aboard Zhou Man's ships interbred with Venezuelan women.

There is also linguistic evidence of Chinese visits to South America. A sailing ship is *chamban* in Colombia, *sampan* in China; a raft, *balsa* in South America and *palso* in China; a log raft, *jangada* in Brazil, *ziangada* in Tamil. Until the late nineteenth century, villagers in a mountain village of Peru spoke Chinese.[13] A mountain of evidence – wrecks, blood groups, architecture, painting, customs, linguistics, clothes, technology, artefacts, dye-stuffs, plants and animals transferred between China and South America – points to a pervasive Chinese influence the length of the Pacific coast of Central and South America, and inland. So broad and deep is the influence that one may almost call the continent of that era 'Chinese America'.

There is one further incontrovertible proof that the Chinese reached Mexico. When I commanded HMS *Rorqual*, I took her through the South China Sea and Philippine Islands to Subic Bay. There were many legends about Chinese junks lying on the sea-bed with their treasures intact. I searched for them with my sonar, but alas without success. Then I discovered that on 9 June 1993 a pearl fisher diving off Coral Bay in south-west Pandanan, a small island to the south-west of the Philippines (and marked on the Rotz chart), had found the wreck of a Chinese junk. The wreck was encrusted with barnacles, but much of the hull – of teak – remained intact. Under the supervision of Dr Eusebio Dizon, the head of the underwater archaeology section of the National Museum of the Philippines, the wreck was excavated in the spring of 1995 and 4,722 artefacts brought to the surface.

They provide a vivid illustration of trade between China, south-east Asia and the Americas.

The wood of the hull has been carbon-dated to 1410 – very similar to the date of the wood found at Sacramento, the site of a possible junk. Both are of the same length and beam, approximately 97 feet by 26 feet, and both apparently carried iron woks in their holds – those at Pandanan have been photographed on the sea-bed and those at Sacramento were located by 3D magnetometer readings. Both junks carried exotic as well as ordinary commercial goods. The Pandanan junk had millions of tiny glass beads the size of those used by the Chinese as a sex aid, a practice noticed by both Ma Huan and Niccolò da Conti in south-east Asia (see chapter 3), and extant in the Philippines today. The (unconfirmed) Sacramento junk carried millions of tiny black seeds, some of which have been provisionally analysed as those of a poppy unique to south-east China. If this analysis is confirmed, it is possible the Chinese were trading in drugs. The Pandanan junk also carried *metates* – pestles for grinding maize – which were then unique to South America, and what appears to be Cholula ware, the eggshell-thin ceramics made in Mexico. The junk had been trading throughout south-east Asia before she sank, for the hold contained porcelain from eight separate countries, including superb ceramics from Vietnam and blue and white Chinese porcelain from the celebrated kilns at Jingdezhen. Complementing these beautiful pieces were ordinary household goods such as clay cooking pots and stoneware storage jars for rice, beans and seeds. There were also three bronze gongs from Dongson (Vietnam) and a peculiar bronze scale balance that may have been the compensating mechanism for a Chinese water clock.

Of the 4,722 items brought up, about a thousand currently remain to be identified. When they have been, it should be possible to reconstruct the junk's route. On the evidence already available, it appears to have returned from Central America with the north equatorial current (the route sailed by Zhou Man's fleet) and been wrecked off Pandanan, perhaps in a sudden squall. This would put the date of its demise at about early September 1423, towards the end of the south-west monsoon, a time when there are unpredictable squalls.

Uncovering the evidence of these early-fifteenth-century Chinese voyages of discovery had been immensely stimulating and exciting, but the implications of what I was learning were now beginning to dawn on me. There seemed to be a mass of powerful evidence that the Chinese had not only traded with the Americas but set up colonies from California to Peru (indeed, recent DNA analysis shows conclusively that local peoples in Mexico, Panama, Colombia, Venezuela and Peru share Chinese DNA). They had also explored the world long before the Europeans and appeared to have been well on the way to setting up colonies in East Africa and Australia and across the Pacific as well as in America. If all this was true, history would need to be radically revised, but it seemed extremely presumptuous for a retired Royal Navy submarine captain to be the one initiating this process. Although I was confident in the veracity of the evidence I had assembled, the thought of the potential responses in academic circles was causing me nightmares. I decided it was imperative to find corroborative evidence from the academic world, for, generous though they had been in helping me so far, I could well imagine the reaction of some distinguished professors of history to a radical reinterpretation of the subject they had devoted their lives to studying and teaching.

Although all the Chinese records had allegedly been destroyed, I felt sure that somewhere something like the *Wu Pei Chi* and Ma Huan's diaries must have been missed; the mandarins could not have been so thorough that they had obliterated every description, every letter, every mention of what had been found during the voyages. Surely another private memoir or account must have survived somewhere.

My first approach was to the Zheng He Museum in Nanjing. The museum is situated in the centre of the city in what used to be the private park encircling Zheng He's palace and has been built in early Ming style, surrounded by bamboo groves and carpets of green grass dotted with flowers. The principal exhibit is entitled 'Historical Relics and Material Exhibitions of Zheng He's Expeditions'. The most interesting and important relic is the 36-foot-high rudder post. By the standards of conventional ship engineering, a vessel carrying such a gigantic rudder must have been around four hundred feet long. The only other artefacts of interest I found in the museum were Zheng He's bell, resembling a larger version of that found at Ruapuke Beach, and the highly unusual claw-shaped anchors like those found in Australia.

These findings, though interesting, were inconclusive. I then wrote to professors in the Chinese or Asian Studies departments of the universities of California, world-renowned for their research into medieval China, to the relevant professors at Oxford and Cambridge and to the librarians of the great libraries of England, America and Australia to enquire if their collections included books of the early Ming era unknown to the outside world.

After a wealth of friendly but negative replies, I at last struck lucky. Professor Charles Aylmer, the librarian of the East Asian Collection at Cambridge University in England, informed me of a unique book, *I Yü Thu Chih* – 'The Illustrated Record of Strange Countries' – a compilation of the people and places known to the Chinese in 1430. The book's cover page is missing so the author is not known for certain, but it is believed to have been written by the Ming prince Ning Xian Wang (Zhu Quan) and printed within a year or so of 1430. It formed part of the magnificent collection donated to the University of Cambridge in the late nineteenth century by Professor Wade, who had spent most of his life in China and was the first professor of Chinese at

Cambridge. The Cambridge copy is the only one in existence, anywhere in the world. It has never been translated and only one photocopy has ever been taken, by the Chinese Embassy in London. Professor Aylmer and other learned sinologists are absolutely convinced of the provenance and authenticity of the book.

I hurried to Cambridge. Although the book itself is in very poor shape, Professor Aylmer had arranged for it to be photographed onto a microfiche which showed all ninety-eight pages with remarkable clarity. There are some eight thousand characters in medieval Chinese and 132 illustrations drawn by different artists. Some are quite brilliant, catching the atmosphere with a few strokes of the brush. There are plants, animals and people from practically every continent in the world. It is a most concise and powerful illustration of Chinese knowledge of the world and its creatures in 1430 – hence the title of the book. The Chinese incorporated only what they found strange, and there are therefore very few scenes of China itself. Instead, the illustrations showcase all the principal religions on earth: Muslims in long robes praying to Mecca; the Hindu trinity of Lord Brahma, the creator and supreme being with his four arms, Lord Vishnu, the maintainer and preserver of the universe, and Lord Shiva, its destroyer; there is Ganesh, the elephant god, and a wonderfully lively picture of monkeys dancing around Hanuman, the Indian monkey god; Buddha is depicted in contemplation under the holy tree and praying towards the holy mountain. The artist has drawn Sikhs in their turbans and Venetians in their distinctive hats, long boots and flowing cloaks, but most vivid of all are the animals: a well-fed zebra with its fat, rounded belly; African elephants and lions; Indian peacocks and tigers, all drawn with masterful economy of line. There are pictures of the deer of south-east Asia and the steppe, and the hunters who pursued them with their different weapons – the double-ended bow of the Mongols and the western Asian longbow. There are also drawings of creatures unique to the Americas: llamas, an armadillo plodding across the ground in search of ants, a jaguar with its slack belly, men chewing coca, the naked men of Patagonia, and the dog-headed mylodon, 'which is found two years and nine months' journey west of China'.[14]

Two things particularly surprised me. The first was the emphasis placed on people from the far north. There were Eskimos in their fur-lined hoods carrying harpoons, and a wonderful Cossack dancer. At that time, Moscow was the leading principality of Russia but had not yet started to expand eastwards across Asia. The Chinese could conceivably have seen Eskimos in the Aleutian Islands, but not Cossacks. There are no records in that era of any Chinese expeditions overland into Muscovy, but recently undertaken analysis shows that fishermen in northern Norway have Korean DNA, and Aleuts have Chinese DNA. It appears that Korean and Chinese ships did indeed sail along the coast of northern Siberia.

The second curious aspect was how little space was devoted to Australia; I could only assume that was because by 1430 it was no longer considered a 'strange country'. By the fifteenth century there had been many descriptions of fleets of junks, each carrying hundreds of people on voyages from China to Australia. In one, the north coast of 'the great south land of Chui Hiao' was described as lying thirty thousand *li* – approximately twelve thousand miles – from China and being in the south temperate zone, where seasons are opposed to those in the northern hemisphere.[15] It was inhabited by a race of small (just one metre tall) black people identified by the Australian anthropologist Norman B. Tyndale as Aborigines from the mountains above Cairns in north Queensland.[16]

In March 2002, the talk I gave at the Royal Geographical Society in London was broadcast live to Australia. The television station Channel 9 then invited me to take part in a live interview in which a number of distinguished Australian professors participated. The fact that Zheng He's fleet had reached Australia came as no surprise to them, and I was subsequently referred to several books that made the same claim. If my theory seemed to be broadly accepted in Australia, did this hold true in China? Dr Wang Tao of the School of Oriental and African Studies, University of London, kindly offered to introduce me to the widow of Professor Wei of Nanjing. Professor Wei's life work was a study of Zheng He's voyages, in particular his fleet's discovery of the Americas. He was about to publish a book entitled *The Chinese Discovery of America* when, sadly, he died. Professor Wei's work is widely known in the academic community in China, though it is yet to be translated into English (or published in China). The revelations in my book caused no particular surprise there either.

I began to wonder why American and European historians had managed to persuade the world for so long that Columbus had discovered America and Cook Australia. Were they ignorant of the Chinese voyages to the Americas before Columbus? I decided to find out. To my amazement, I discovered that there were more than a thousand books providing overwhelming evidence of pre-Columbian Chinese journeys to the Americas. This literature has even been summarized in a two-volume bibliography.[17] As Professor George F. Carter, an expert on hens in the Americas and author of several fascinating books on the subject of early Chinese voyages, remarked, 'Sinologists and Asiatic art historians are normally struck by the overwhelming, all-pervasive evidence of Chinese influence in Amerindian civilization. Seemingly the Americanists are not aware of the Chinese literature suggesting not only discovery but colonization of America.'[18] Professor Carter's phrasing is a masterpiece of tact. Perhaps, as he suggests, those academics are not aware of the evidence; perhaps they have chosen to ignore it, presumably because it contradicts the accepted wisdom on which

1 Neahkahnie Bay – wooden pulley
2 Sacramento junk – plus Chinese speaking peoples and location of a Chinese village
3 Los Angeles – Chinese anchor
4 Cave art – depicting foreigners arriving
5 Michoacán artefacts – lacquers, dye-stuffs, both with Chinese influence
6 Asiatic chickens
7 Gulf of Fonseca
8 Venezuelan Indians with Chinese DNA
9 Peruvian village with Chinese-speaking people
10 Peruvian bronzes with Chinese inscriptions
11 Ecuador – Chinese anchor and fish hooks

Evidence of the visit of the Chinese treasure fleet to the Americas.

not a few careers have been based. Academics with rather more open minds will look again.

The thesis that the Chinese explored virtually the whole world between 1421 and 1423 might be a radical departure from convention when it comes to the dates of the discovery of these 'new worlds' and the identity of those who first explored and charted them, but I was confident that there was solid evidence to support it. My training in astro-navigation had also enabled me to find further proofs that no academic, unless he were an astronomer, could have reached. No matter what heavy artillery was brought to bear, I was confident the thesis could withstand it. Reassured, I turned the spotlight onto Admiral Zhou Wen and his fleet.

V

The Voyage of Zhou Wen

SATAN'S

ISLAND

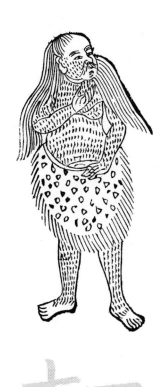

IN OCTOBER 1421, WHEN THE FLEETS OF HONG BAO AND ZHOU Man had sailed south-west from the entrance to the Caribbean towards the coast of South America, they had left the fleet of Admiral Zhou Wen taking a course to the north-west following the northern branch of the equatorial current. I already knew that this fleet must have later reached the Azores, at the latitude of Beijing, for the islands appear on the Kangnido map, drawn before the first Europeans discovered those islands. My task was now to find where Zhou Wen had sailed between those two landfalls.

When Admiral Zhou Wen reached the Cape Verde Islands he had already sailed across a substantial part of the globe and must have known that the mysterious land of Fusang lay to the west of him. By the time of the great cartographer Chu Ssu Pen (1273–1337), the Chinese had made an accurate estimate of the distance from the Pacific to the Atlantic, but how far to the west Zhou Wen thought Fusang lay would depend on how far he considered he had already sailed. The Kangnido shows that, because of the effects of the ocean currents, the Chinese fleets had underestimated their voyage across the 'bulge' of Africa by a couple of thousand miles. As he lay at anchor at Santo Antão in the Cape Verde Islands, Zhou Wen might well have assumed that Fusang lay four thousand rather than two thousand miles to the west of him, but that was still well within his range, without the need for fresh provisions or water en route.

North of the equator, the Atlantic is a vast oval-shaped wind and current system rotating clockwise day in, day out, throughout the year. British Admiralty sailing directions advise mariners on how to make use of these winds and currents: 'From Madeira the best track is to pass just west of, but in sight of, the Cape Verde Archipelago . . . from Cape Verde steer a direct course [for the Caribbean] . . . thereafter . . . the north equatorial current and south equatorial current converge, forming a broad band of current setting west. Average rates reach 2 knots.'[1] From the

Cape Verde Islands they carry the mariner due west to the Caribbean, then north-west towards Florida and north up the American seaboard before taking him clockwise to the east, where the current becomes the Gulf Stream carrying the mariner across the Atlantic to the Azores, a thousand miles west of Portugal. It then hooks southwards, back once again to the Cape Verde Islands. The commander of a ship with sufficient provisions can hoist sail off the Cape Verde Islands and sit back and do nothing. Provided he is not capsized by a storm, a common occurrence in the North Atlantic, he will eventually end up more or less where he started.

The westerly current from the Cape Verde Islands reaches its strongest flow when approaching the Caribbean at the latitude of the island of Dominica. As a result, explorer after explorer down the centuries – Columbus on his second voyage, the Spanish explorers Rodrigo de Bastida and Juan de la Cosa in the early years of the sixteenth century, the French and English fleets during the Napoleonic Wars – has entered the Caribbean through the passage between Dominica and Guadeloupe. I would put the likelihood as high as 80 per cent that if, having replenished with fruit and fresh water, the Chinese had sailed from the Cape Verde Islands in October they would have been entering the Caribbean by early November.

The track of the junks of Admiral Zhou Wen's fleet through the Caribbean should logically have been the same as that of Columbus, for the winds and tides have remained unaltered from that day to this. Whatever the Chinese discovered should have been rediscovered by Columbus seventy years later. By examining Columbus's diaries of his second voyage, I should be able to reconstruct the most likely track. If the Chinese had found any islands or land on their voyage across the North Atlantic, I could expect those discoveries to be recorded on charts drawn after they returned to China in 1423. Just as I had done for South America and Australia, I now began to search for a

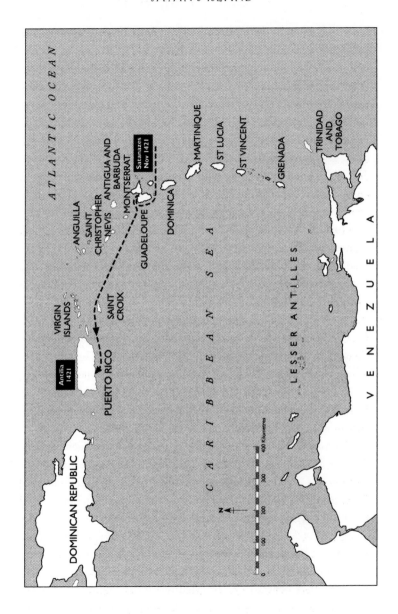

Zhou Wen's journey through the Caribbean.

chart that, like the Piri Reis and Jean Rotz maps, appeared to depict lands Europeans had yet to discover.

In that era, Venice, the base of Fra Mauro, the Venetian cartographer working for the Portuguese government, led the West in mapmaking. As I expected, Venetian and Catalan charts (Catalonia was then part of the Kingdom of Aragon; the Catalans were redoubtable seafarers) drawn before 1423 disclosed nothing new in the western Atlantic, but a chart dated 1424 and signed by the Venetian cartographer Zuane Pizzigano was an entirely different matter. The Pizzigano chart was rediscovered some seventy years ago and in the early 1950s it was sold to the James Ford Bell Library at the University of Minnesota. Its authenticity and provenance have never been questioned and several books have been written about it by distinguished historians.

[The 1424 chart] is a document of capital importance to the history of geography. From the historical point of view, it is undoubtedly one of the most, if not the most, precious jewel yielded by the disclosure of the almost unknown treasures contained in the unique collection of early manuscripts assembled by Sir Thomas Phillips during the first three-quarters of the nineteenth century. The great importance of this chart lies in the fact that it is the first to represent a group of four islands in the western Atlantic, called Saya, Satanazes, Antilia and Ymana ... there are many and good reasons for concluding that the Antilia group of four islands shown for the first time in the 1424 chart should be regarded as the earliest cartographic representation of any American lands.[2]

This was high praise indeed. I made a close study of the chart (see Introduction). It is markedly different from its contemporaries. It is not centred on the Mediterranean, as earlier charts were, but looks westwards across the Atlantic, where two large islands, Antilia and Satanazes, hitherto unknown to Europeans, are depicted. Two smaller islands are also shown: Saya, a parabolic island to the south of Satanazes, and the box-shaped island of Ymana to the north of Antilia.

Other accounts of the era put the islands '700 large leagues'[3] west of the Canaries, which would put them near the Bahamas, but no large islands are located there. Were the islands imaginary? Other chartmakers clearly believed they were genuine, for the group was subsequently represented on at least nineteen fifteenth-century maps and two globes, all of them drawn before Columbus set sail (see chapter 17). But as time went by, successive cartographers relocated the islands further and further to the south-west, until they ended up in the Netherlands Antilles.

The Portuguese names on the chart had made me presume that they were the original cartographers, but the names on the Piri Reis and the Jean Rotz charts were also in Portuguese and they could not possibly have been the discoverers of the Antarctic, Patagonia or Australia. Portuguese records in the Torre do Tombo, the National Archives of Portugal in Lisbon, state unequivocally that Henry the Navigator sent caravels to discover Antilia after he had received a similar but slightly later chart (the 1428 World Map discussed in chapter 4).[4] Moreover, in 1424 the Portuguese simply did not have the capacity to survey the islands with such accuracy – for the cartography of Antilia was amazingly good. I concluded that it could only have been the Chinese. However, I needed further proof that this was the case, and I found once again that the best way of tackling this puzzle was to put myself in the cartographers' shoes. When in submarines, we used to spend time in the Barents Sea photographing military installations. Part of our training was in periscope photography and the obscure art of constructing charts from near sea level. At the time I was work-ing from about the same height as the cartographers of the Pizzigano chart, standing on the deck of a medieval ship.

As Zhou Wen's ships approached the Caribbean, they would have had warning some two days out that they would shortly sight land. Clouds, winds, weather and sea-bird types would all change, and finally, a few hours before the islands became visible, the crew would have begun to detect the soft, subtle smell of wet foliage. Because Columbus sailed through the Dominica Passage on a Sunday, he named the island to the south Dominica, the Spanish name for that day of the week; that to the north was named Marie-Galante after his flagship. He first landed at Marie-Galante but found little and pushed on northwards with the current, landing the next day at an island he named Guadeloupe in memory of his visit to a monastery of that name in Extremadura in Spain. Had they known, the monks might have raised objections to his choice of name, for the inhabitants of the island were Carib cannibals. Dr Chanca, a chronicler of Columbus's second voyage, recorded his men striding through the soft sand into the coconut groves where they found 'houses, about 30, built with logs or poles interwoven with branches and huge reeds and thatched ... with palm ... square and cottage like ... For dishes [they use] calabashes [a gourd] ... and, oh horrors!, human skulls for drinking vessels.'[5] Only women were left in the villages; the native men had fled to the hills in terror at the sight of the sails of Columbus's fleet.

The stench of bodies horrified Columbus's men. 'Limbs of human bodies hung up in houses as if curing for provisions; the head of a youth so recently severed from the body that the blood was yet dripping from it, and parts of his body were roasting before the fire, along with savoury flesh of geese and parrots.'[6] The natives used arrow-heads made from human bones, and

in their attacks upon the neighbouring islands, these people capture as many of the women as they can, especially those who are young and beautiful, and keep them as concubines ... they eat the children which they bear to them ... Such of their male enemies as they can take alive they bring to their houses to make a feast of them, and those who are killed they devour at once. They say that man's flesh is so good, that there is nothing like it in the world . . . in one of the houses we found the neck of a man undergoing the process of cooking in a pot. When they take any boys prisoners, they dismember [castrate] them and make use of them until they grow up to manhood, and then when they wish to make a feast they kill and eat them, for they say that the flesh of boys and women is good to eat. Three of these boys came fleeing to us, thus mutilated.[7]

Another contemporary writer noted that it was 'their custom to dismember the male children and young slaves, whom they capture and fatten like capons'.[8]

To fifteenth-century eyes, the cannibalism Columbus encountered could easily have been seen as the work of the devil. Could that be the explanation of the name Satanazes – Satan's

Cannibalism in the Caribbean: a fanciful seventeenth-century reconstruction of Columbus's encounter with the Caribs

Island? Was this what the Chinese had found, and was Guadeloupe the Satanazes shown on the Pizzigano chart? If so, like Columbus seventy years later, the Chinese would have approached the island from the south-east on the prevailing wind and current.

I turned my attention to the island of Saya lying to the south-east of Satanazes on the Pizzigano chart. I could vividly picture the scene as the Chinese approached because I spent some time in the Caribbean in command of the submarine HMS *Rorqual* and had visited and photographed many of the islands. In many cases the mountains appear black, surrounded by green jungle. Heavy rainstorms occur without warning, blotting out the islands. Frequently, birds take flight just before the rains arrive, circling in flocks, shrieking with foreboding.

As soon as I consulted a modern map, I saw that Saya on the Pizzigano map corresponded to Les Saintes. It is approximately the same shape and lies in the same position relative to Guadeloupe as Saya to Satanazes. I assumed that Saya was indeed Les Saintes, Satanazes was Guadeloupe and, based on my calculations of their course and speed, that the Chinese had arrived off the islands in November 1421. Given the maximum height of Les Saintes (about a thousand feet) and the height of eye of a seaman on the deck of a Chinese junk, I estimated that they would have seen the island from twenty-five miles away, while still in the Dominica Passage. From that position they should also have seen the plateau island of Marie-Galante ten miles north of them and the mountainous Dominica ten miles to the south, yet neither was recorded on the chart. I made the obvious deduction that they had passed through the passage in darkness with no moon. When I checked the records, I discovered that the new moon occurred on 25 November 1421, so I took it that they had probably approached Les Saintes from the south-east around dawn, possibly on 26 November 1421.

Les Saintes is composed of two large islands, Terre de Basse

Chinese supremacy in the Indian Ocean: the Galle stele (*above left*), inscribed in four languages, testifies to Zheng He's attempts at diplomacy with the diverse inhabitants of Sri Lanka. By the time Zheng He set sail, the Chinese had well-established routes along the Malabar coast (*below*), where Chinese fishing nets are still used (*above*), and across the ocean to East African trading forts such as Kilwa (*opposite, below*), where Ming porcelain is incorporated into the mosque, just as in these pillar-tombs further up the coast at Kunduchi (*opposite, inset*).

A detail of Africa and Asia from the Kangnido world map of 1402 (*opposite*) by Ch'uan Chin and Li Hui, the most advanced of its day. The Cape of Good Hope is delineated with extraordinary accuracy.

Europe and Africa from Fra Mauro's planisphere of 1459: south is at the top. The surface is a glittering pattern of text and schematic walled medieval towns, but the map itself is informed by real geography, the result of up-to-date knowledge gleaned from contemporary explorers.

The Piri Reis map of 1513, oriented with north to the left, so that South America is at the bottom of the page and Africa and Europe at the top.

The inhospitable shores of Antarctica (*above*): it is easy to see how giant icebergs (*below*) could be mistaken for islands.

and Terre de Haut, and three smaller ones, La Coche and Grand Ilet in the south, and Ilet a Cabrit in the north. The big islands are much higher than the smaller ones and, approached from the south-east, the lower Grand Ilet and La Coche would merge with the taller islands in the background and appear to form a single block of land. The south coast would appear as a single parabolic island, just as it is drawn on the Pizzigano chart. Knowing the height from which they had surveyed it – the deck level of a treasure ship – I could now make an estimate to within two miles of the location from where Saya was charted.

What else would the Chinese have seen from this position? Just what Columbus saw from the same spot seven decades later: 'Dawn reveals a most romantic landscape. A volcanic peak rises to an immense height, and cataracts pouring down its sides appear like water falling out of heaven ... Flights of brightly coloured noisy parrots and other brilliant tropical birds are winging their way from one island to another and the wind of the land is laden with sweet odours.'[9] The 'volcanic peak' is La Souffrière on Guadeloupe, eighteen miles to the north-west. La Souffrière is well inland, its peak frequently shrouded by clouds and heavy rain, and seven rivers pour down its eastern side, the most spectacular among them the 120-metre Karukera Falls. The Chinese junks would have been at sea for at least three weeks, and I am sure the chance to take on water would not have been spurned. They would have altered course for the cataracts.

I turned to the words *con* and *ymana* marked on Satanazes on the Pizzigano chart. My first attempt to solve the riddle of these names was to recruit an expert at crosswords, who came up with *con* as a shell, conical mountain or volcano – interesting, but not much help. Then Professor João Camilo dos Santos, an expert in medieval Portuguese attached to the Portuguese Embassy in London, translated these words for me as 'a volcano' (*con*) 'erupts there' (*ymana*). The description was highly significant. Transposing the location of these words on the Pizzigano chart onto the corresponding modern map placed them directly above the volcanoes of La Souffrière, La Citerne and L'Echelle. Had these volcanoes erupted in 1421? The Smithsonian Institution confirmed there were two eruptions of the three volcanoes between 1400 and 1440; the dates, calculated by radio carbon-dating, cannot be determined more precisely.[10] There were no further eruptions from these volcanoes for another 250 years, and no eruptions of other volcanoes in the Caribbean during the whole of the fifteenth century.[11] Since the Pizzigano chart can only have recorded an eruption of the volcanoes on southern Guadeloupe, I had first-hand evidence that a cartographer had been in the Caribbean no later than 1424, sixty-eight years before Columbus.

There are some anomalies in the map, but they are easily explicable when one retraces the route the ships must have taken. As the Chinese junks headed for the waterfalls on Guadeloupe, they would have had to sail closer and closer to Les Saintes, for all the time the current was pushing them westwards. As they passed the north-east tip of Les Saintes, the cartographer drew Baie du Marigot from half a mile away with the morning sun behind him. Because this bay was so close and so well lit, its size was somewhat exaggerated on the Pizzigano chart. As the junks neared land, the cartographer drew two further bays on the north coast of Saya. The third, Passe du Pain du Sucre, was drawn from a distance of seven miles, much further away than the first drawing, and it was now nearly noon (assuming their speed through the water was 4.8 knots) so the sun was in the cartographer's eyes. The combination of the position of the sun and the greater distance resulted in the third bay being drawn smaller than it should have been. To check that my conclusions were accurate, I showed the chart and my navigational workings to a fellow of the Royal Geographical Society, like myself a professional navigator. He was also convinced that Saya is Les Saintes; it is drawn precisely as it would have been

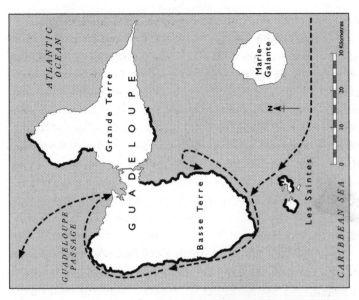

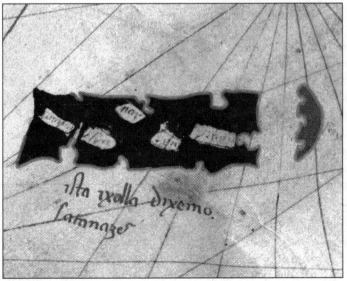

Guadeloupe shown on the Pizzigano map, compared with a modern map.

seen from sea level when approaching from the south-east.

Having calculated the time of day at which the cartographer drew Les Saintes, I was able to estimate with some certainty that by noon the junks had landed in the Baie de Grande Anse on southern Guadeloupe. I could imagine them replenishing their fresh water supplies against a backdrop of white, purple and blue hibiscus and orchids ('the wind of the land is laden with sweet odours'). Cassava, peppers and yuccas were there for the taking. The sea is a kaleidoscope of fish, crabs bask on exposed coral and crayfish are abundant. I could visualize the mariners gambolling in the surf before they feasted, washed their clothes and stocked their ships with fruit. How delightful it must have been to swim in the warm water after being at sea for nearly a month. It used to be my practice when in command of HMS *Rorqual* to anchor off an inhabited bay and send the sailors ashore in the inflatable dinghies we carried. It always proved a popular excursion – a swim in the sea, followed by rum toddies and roast lobster.

In the eastern Caribbean, an offshore breeze usually springs up as the land cools in the early evening. The Chinese had landed on an exposed Atlantic shore and would have had to find a sheltered anchorage for the night. Two hours' sailing up the east coast would have brought them to a secluded anchorage between two coral islands in the southern part of Baie de Sainte Marie. My assumption was that the Chinese had landed, watered and anchored at precisely the same spot Columbus found seventy years later, and the French and English fleets centuries after that. At first sight that may seem an incredible proposition: why should ships of so many different nations over several centuries all end up at the same spot on a remote Caribbean island thousands of miles from home? They did so because they were all subject to the same natural forces.

The clockwise movement of current and winds drew Zhou Wen's fleet from the Cape Verde Islands to a latitude of 18°N, where the equatorial currents converged to sweep them towards the Dominica Passage. As they entered the Caribbean, they were greeted by the magnificent volcano of La Souffrière in Guadeloupe with its cataracts of 'water falling out of heaven'. After watering on the Atlantic shore they needed to find shelter for the night; their anchorage was the nearest sheltered bay to the waterfalls. What they did not know was that this seeming paradise was 'Satan's Island' – Satanazes – populated by cannibalistic Carib tribesmen. Guadeloupe was the Caribs' principal lair in the Caribbean, and they were skilful hunters of men, even when swimming. I spent a day in the British Library poring over Columbus's journal of his second voyage, which includes a description of a Carib attack on his fleet: 'These Caribs can fight about as well in water as in their canoe . . . the Spaniard dies in consequence.' After a Spanish sailor was killed, Columbus retaliated, and one of the Caribs had his belly slit open. His intestines were floating on the sea but, according to the Spanish accounts, the wounded Carib pushed them back inside his stomach with one hand while still firing arrows with the other.[12]

On that gruesome note, I decided to end my researches for the day, but as I was making my way home that evening, it occurred to me that if the Chinese had landed on the island, they must have been attacked by the Caribs, just as Columbus was. Might there be some record or legacy of that landing? When I went back to the British Library to look again at the account of Columbus's second voyage, I made another extraordinary discovery as I read the following passage:

In one house they find what seems to be an iron pot . . . but here is a curiosity amongst savages – the stern post of a vessel. This must have drifted across the ocean from some civilized country. Perhaps, it is a part of the wreck of the *Santa María*. Now all stand aghast at the sight of a pile of human bones – probably the remains of many an unnatural repast.[13]

Iron is not found on the Caribbean islands, nor indeed in Central America. The islanders used hollowed-out tree trunks for their boats, and they did not build them with stern posts, a sophisticated design. Stern posts had been in use in China since the first century AD; they did not reach Europe until the fourteenth century. Columbus's *Santa María* was wrecked off the north coast of Haiti, far away to the north-west of Guadeloupe, and the Gulf Stream would have carried flotsam from that wreck in precisely the opposite direction, north-west towards New England. I strongly suspected that the stern post came from a junk and the iron pot was one brought by the Chinese.

The Chinese would have put to sea to escape the Caribs, just as Columbus's fleet did. When safe in open water, three miles offshore, they would have rounded the southern tip of Guadeloupe and sailed before the wind up the west coast where they charted the headland of Vieux Habitants, the Bay of Anse de la Barque and the Bay of Deshaies. By the next evening they would have been sailing into the bay now known as Le Grand cul de sac Marin, and from there the cartographer drew what he could see of Grande Terre, the eastern island of Guadeloupe. It is a low-lying island, rising from fifty metres near the shore to no more than a hundred metres further inland. By this stage it would have been after dusk and Grande Terre would have appeared as no more than a hazy blur. The cartographer probably saw little of it, and never properly charted it. The Chinese then set sail once more before the wind and current, heading north-westwards across the Caribbean, probably making for 39°53′N, the latitude of modern Atlantic City, New Jersey, but also of Beijing, and another obvious reference point for the Chinese fleets to have chosen.

The cartographer had charted Les Saintes as he saw it from sea level, and placed it in the correct position relative to the western island of Guadeloupe, Basse Terre. He had accurately charted the east, south and west coasts of Basse Terre and Le

Grand cul de sac Marin, placing the bays and rivers in their correct position, and had described the volcano La Souffrière and its sisters erupting. The chances of finding another island with erupting volcanoes, coupled with the same-shaped islands in the south and the bay in the north, are nil; there cannot be the slightest doubt that Satanazes is Guadeloupe (Basse Terre) and Saya is Les Saintes. Knowing Basse Terre's true size, I could adjust Satanazes' size to true, and as the Pizzigano chart gave Antilia's size and orientation in relation to Satanazes, I could also calculate the true size and orientation of Antilia. The Pizzigano chart also showed the relative positions of and distance between Satanazes and Antilia. To find Antilia, all I had to do was look for an island 135 kilometres long by 50 kilometres wide, aligned east–west, and lying some six hundred kilometres west-north-west of Guadeloupe, once again in the track of the prevailing current and wind.

I turned to a modern map to see if I could find a match for Antilia. The map revealed that Puerto Rico was in the correct position, had the true alignment and size, and lay directly on the route along which the wind and current would have swept the junks after they left Basse Terre. I compared the shape of Antilia on the Pizzigano chart with Puerto Rico. It was a very good match. I remember this still as a tremendous breakthrough. Overwhelmed by the importance of what I had discovered, I wandered off into the night in search of a celebratory drink.

I returned to the British Library early the next morning worried that tiredness and elation might have caused me to misread the evidence, but a comparison of a large-scale modern-day map of Puerto Rico with Antilia on the Pizzigano chart at once removed any residual uncertainties. There are striking similarities, particularly the overall shape and the bays of Guayanilla, San Juan and Mayaguez. Save for the south-east tip, Antilia and its harbours fitted Puerto Rico like a glove. The standard of the cartography was astounding, way

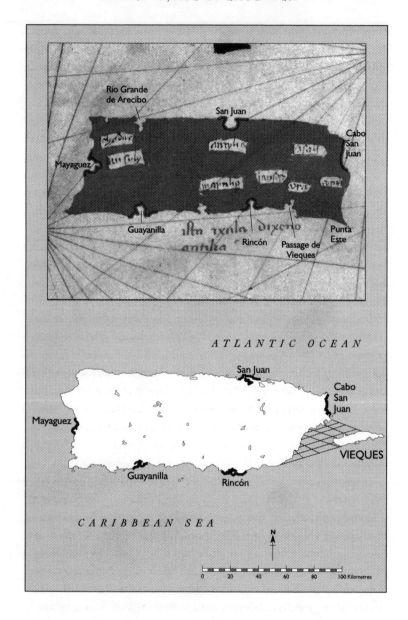

Puerto Rico shown on the Pizzigano map, compared with a modern map.

beyond what the Portuguese could have achieved in 1424.

But the exaggerated south-east tip is easily explained. After leaving Guadeloupe, the winds and currents would have driven the Chinese to the north-west – the same track Columbus later followed – to a point sixty miles east of Puerto Rico. There, they would have sighted the menacing, anvil-shaped volcano El Yunque near the east coast and turned towards it for water. As they had done many times when surveying other islands during their voyages, the Chinese squadron would have been split in two, one sailing north and one south of Puerto Rico to chart both coasts simultaneously. Had they sighted the volcano in the evening, and if they were travelling at their average rate of 4.8 knots, they would have passed south of Vieques Island during the night. In the darkness they could not have seen that Vieques is a separate island, and accordingly drew it as part of the mainland of Antilia.[14] The Pizzigano chart is also inscribed with the word *ura* – hurricane – near the east coast of Puerto Rico, a clear indication that Zhou Wen's fleet had been battered by a hurricane as it sailed away from the island. It would have been prudent of him to run before the storm on as few sails as possible so as to find anchor in a sheltered bay. This is consistent with the astonishingly precise cartography of the harbours on Puerto Rico's south, west and north coasts, drawn before Columbus had even been born.

The storm-damaged Chinese fleet had completed its survey of Puerto Rico, and I could imagine the junks unfurling their great sails at the tail end of the hurricane and setting sail for the north from Puerto Rico towards the latitude of Beijing. If that theory was correct, there should have been evidence of their voyage at that latitude. I was confident that the Chinese had sailed to the North Atlantic, for the stone erected by Zheng He at Liu-Chia-Chang in south China after this epic sixth voyage states 'the countries beyond the horizon and at the ends of the earth have all become subjects and the most western of the western or the

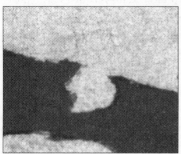

Bay of San Juan
18°28′N 66°07′W

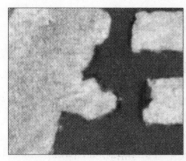

Mayaguez
18°12′N 67°11′W

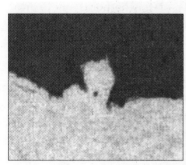

Guayanilla
18°00′N 66°46′W

The bays and inlets of Puerto Rico, depicted with extraordinary precision on the Pizzigano map.

most northern of the northern countries, however far away they may be'.[15] From a Chinese perspective, the most northern of the northern countries and the most western of the western could only be referring to the Atlantic coasts of North America, but as ever, my problem was that the mandarins had destroyed all records of the treasure fleets. Once again, I had to look for clues in maps and charts of the northern hemisphere drawn before the first Europeans reached the Americas. I had to find a counterpart to the Pizzigano chart.

A world map popularly known as the Cantino came to my rescue. I had unearthed this extraordinary chart in the Biblioteca Estense in Modena, Italy, during my investigation into Zhou Man's visit to the Americas. It was drawn by an anonymous Portuguese cartographer and surreptitiously obtained by Alberto Cantino, the agent of the Duke Ercole d'Este of Ferrara. The Cantino's provenance and credibility have never been questioned, and there is firm evidence for dating its acquisition to October 1502. The Chinese fleet had to sail before the wind and current; after leaving Puerto Rico, it would have been blown north-west towards Hispaniola and Cuba, and then through the Caribbean to the coast of Florida. The Cantino indeed reflects this, for it shows Hispaniola, Cuba and many other islands in the Caribbean and off Florida, but though it portrays the coast of Africa and the Indian Ocean and its archipelagos of islands with extraordinary accuracy, at first glance its depiction of the Caribbean appears woefully inadequate. Many of the islands seem to bear little relation to their present sizes and shapes, and I was baffled as to why it was so much in error.

I struggled to make sense of this for some considerable time; then, all at once, the answer came to me. Sea levels in 1421 were lower than they are today. Global warming has caused the south polar ice to melt, causing sea levels to rise slowly but inexorably. The best estimate of the Proudman Oceanic Laboratory of Birkenhead in England is that they have risen over the past centuries by about one to two millimetres a year. Other reputable oceanographers put the rise a little higher, at an average of four millimetres a year. In the almost six centuries since 1421 it is safe to say that sea levels have risen between just under four and just under eight feet. For simplicity, I assumed that the overall rise had been one fathom, or six feet, roughly the midpoint of the range of estimates.

The British Admiralty charts of the Caribbean[16] enabled me to visualize a completely new picture of the region. In 1421, vast areas that today are submerged would have been either above water or with rocks and reefs showing as breaking water and shoals. The banks and reefs of the Great Bahama Bank, stretching south of Andros Island towards Cuba, would in 1421 have been above water down to the latitude of the Tropic of Cancer, and the numerous sand ridges today marked as 'almost uncovered' on the modern chart[17] would also have been above water. To the Chinese cartographers, everything from Cayo Guajava in the middle of Cuba's north coast as far as the latitude of Miami would have appeared as one large low-lying island, an extension of Cuba.

The prevailing wind and current would have driven the fleet along the north-east coast of Cuba, then due north to the east of Andros, up towards Grand Bahama. (Andros Island is a favourite submarine haunt, for there is a deep-water trench well to the east of the coast along which thousands of tons of nuclear submarine can hurtle at forty miles an hour in order to test its silence at depth and speed. Afterwards we would surface and relax under the palms on Andros beach, drinking Bacardi and Coke.) If the Chinese fleet had made the passage at night, they would never have seen any openings to the west and could only have drawn what appears on the Cantino. When I adjusted the modern chart to show everything to a depth of one fathom, many of the shallow lagoons between the Caribbean islands became dry land, and when I superimposed these adjustments onto the Cantino it was clear the Caribbean had been drawn with incredible accuracy, just as it would have appeared to mariners sailing through it on a following wind six centuries ago. Once again, it was extraordinarily good cartography.

The question I now had to face head on was whether this mapping could have been carried out by Columbus, who had reached the Caribbean in 1492, ten years before the Cantino was acquired. A number of learned professors have slightly different interpretations on the location of his first landfall in the Caribbean, varying between Samana Cay and Cat Island, and on where he first landed on the coast of Cuba. Columbus was a poor cartographer. On his first voyage his calculations of latitude were twenty degrees out – he believed he was somewhere in Nova Scotia – and his longitude was a thousand miles in error. Even if Columbus had a secret, and rather better, cartographer aboard who could have accurately drawn the Caribbean islands shown on the Cantino during all four of Columbus's voyages, that still left hundreds of thousands of square miles of ocean and islands shown on the Cantino that neither Columbus nor any other European explorer reached until twenty years after the chart was drawn. I concluded that the chart could not have been the product of any voyage by Columbus.

Could it have been drawn by an unknown Portuguese or Spanish expedition? One has to look at the overall picture of the lands covered by the Piri Reis and the Cantino together. By 1501, when the source chart was obtained from Columbus's sailor, the maker of the Piri Reis map could accurately depict South America and Antarctica. By the next year, 1502, the Cantino was showing Africa, the Indian Ocean and the Caribbean. To achieve the remarkable precision and wealth of detail of the Cantino and Piri Reis charts would have required at least thirty ships just to survey the Indian Ocean, let alone South America, Antarctica and Africa. Neither Portugal nor Spain could have sent so many huge fleets simultaneously to different quarters of the world.

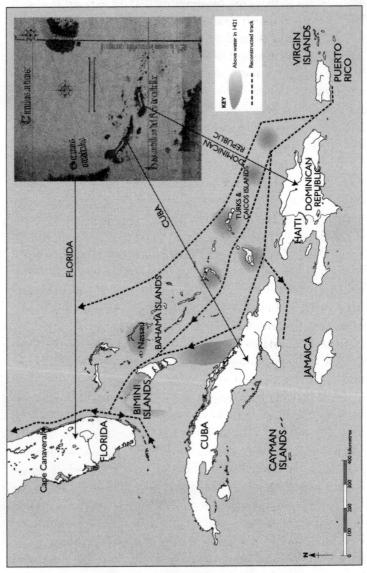

The Cantino map showing the Caribbean and Florida, compared
with a modern map.

Only China had the ships, the resources and the expertise to have done so. Cartographers aboard the Chinese treasure fleets had to be the originators of these remarkable charts.

By looking at the Caribbean islands charted on the Cantino, I could reconstruct the passage of the cartographers who had drawn them. To chart the islands, they had to see both coasts, and sailing always before the wind and current, square-rigged sailing ships had no opportunity of turning back for a second pass. To survey both coasts of an island required at least two ships, one either side of it. The way the charts are drawn, coupled with the prevailing winds and currents, leads me to believe that at least five squadrons of ships would have been needed to chart the Caribbean. By my best estimate, at least ten to twenty ships would have had to sail through the Caribbean to collect this mass of information in one pass. Assuming they were within sight of one another, working for ten hours a day, and travelling at an average speed of 4.8 knots, they would have charted fifteen thousand square miles per day and could have obtained the information in four to six weeks.

Many of the islands are very low-lying, and to survey them with the accuracy shown the junks must have been within ten miles of each one, exposing themselves to horrific risks. To cross the Great Bahama Bank from Cuba to the east of Andros Island and inside the Berry Islands (all shown on the Cantino), the ships must have passed, frequently and at night, what the British Admiralty charts call 'numerous sand ridges almost uncovered', and 'numerous rocky heads'. In one small stretch of forty nautical miles,[18] there are literally hundreds of rocks and reefs capable of ripping wooden hulls apart. That short distance must have been achieved at a terrible cost. I cannot conceive how they could have made that passage without losing ships. By the time the junks had crossed the Great Bahama Bank and reached the Berry Islands they would surely have been in desperate trouble, the internal compartments of many ships flooded. The calm, moonlit seas might well have been echoing with the cries of dying seamen.

It was a sombre thought, but it also highlighted the fact that I was closing on my quarry. The charts told me exactly where to look. I had to search for traces of the wrecks of treasure ships within a few miles of the Berry Islands in the Florida Strait.

THE
TREASURE
FLEET
RUNS
AGROUND

A S YOU PASS FROM SHALLOW WATER INTO THE DEEPER waters of the open ocean, the pattern and length of the waves change and they have a different colour and smell. It is a phenomenon familiar to all blue-water sailors, and as his fleet passed the Berry Islands, Admiral Zhou Wen would have known at once that his fleet had entered deep water – the Northwest Providence Channel leading into the Florida Strait. I made the assumption that several of his junks had been damaged in crossing the reefs, and he would have had to find somewhere to beach his fleet before it sank in deep water. The search for a suitable island would have been a matter of desperate urgency, for many of the junks must have been in a critical condition, unable to survive in the open ocean.

My detailed research of the area surrounding the Berry Islands now began in earnest. Large-scale British Admiralty charts[1] and Coffman's treasure atlas[2] show wrecks strewn along the Chinese track. These wrecks have been classified by Coffman as Spanish galleons, later ships and earlier, unidentified ones. I focused my attention on the latter class of wrecks, and compared them with the Admiralty chart. It was a dramatic moment, for eight unidentified wrecks were disclosed within six hours' or forty miles' sailing from the point where the Chinese would have entered the Florida Strait. Four wrecks[3] are shown on the Little Bahama reef and the Florida coast; another four[4] are due south. When I examined a large-scale chart, it revealed that the track of these four southern wrecks was pointing towards a group of small islands, North and South Bimini, Gun and Ocean Cay, fifteen miles away. The position of the wrecks was consistent with four junks making a desperate but doomed bid to reach the islands; the last wreck is within a mile of North Bimini. All are in shallow water; if the sharks did not get them first, the crew could have swum ashore. I felt sure that there should be evidence of other wrecks – ships that had managed to struggle to land – on Bimini itself.

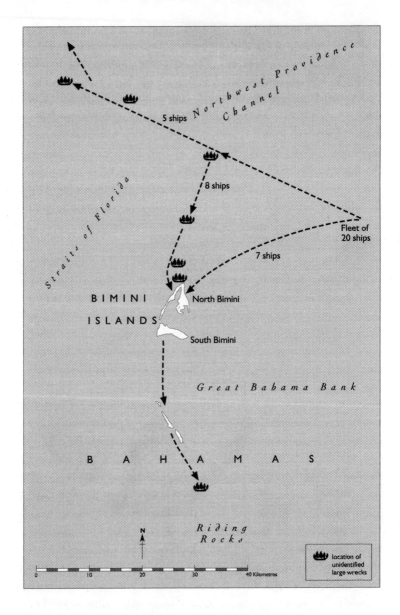

Locations of unidentified wrecks on the route to Bimini.

Before I flew there to begin a detailed search of the island, it seemed sensible to see if the first European to reach Bimini had found anything, such as wrecks or porcelain, left behind by the Chinese. The first European on Bimini was Juan Ponce de León (c. 1460–1521), a Spanish conquistador and governor of Puerto Rico from 1510 to 1511. On 23 February 1512, he was given a commission by the King of Spain:

<u>The King</u>

To the officials of the island of Española upon the agreement which they have made with Juan Ponce de León upon that and the said island of Biminy which he has to go to discover.[5]

The king's eagerness to locate the mystical island of Bimini was based on the legend that its waters conferred perpetual youth on those who drank them: 'There is an island about three hundred and twenty-five leagues from Española in which there is a continual spring of running water of such marvellous virtue that, the water thereof being drunk, perhaps with some diet, maketh old men young again . . . bathing in it, or in the fountain, old men were turned into youths.'[6] This legend was widespread before Columbus set sail. The waters have subsequently been identified as a foul-smelling sulphurous spring on the east side of North Bimini island. It can be reached via a shallow creek infested with caymans – members of the alligator family. Few kings could have resisted the allure of immortality, however remote the possibility, and such a discovery would have been of incalculable commercial value. There was not a rich man living who would not have exchanged the greater part of his wealth for the promise of eternal youth, as is the case to this day.

The bays to the north and south of Bimini are clearly marked on the Cantino chart, drawn twelve years before Ponce de León set sail. Someone must have been there before him, not only to draw the island that appears on the Cantino but to convey descriptions of its magical spring. Bimini is only a few feet high and can be circumnavigated in a day. It was uninhabited for centuries save for wreckers, who based themselves there for salvage during the hurricane seasons. In the twentieth century, Ernest Hemingway took a liking to the island and drank the night away in local bars while writing *The Old Man and the Sea*. Today, thousands of trippers come by seaplane and yacht from Florida to see Hemingway's haunts, oblivious of the history that surrounds them.

In September 1968, Dr J. Manson Valentine, a zoologist and underwater archaeologist, was swimming off North Bimini. He was in ten feet of water about a thousand yards from the shore when he spotted hundreds of flat rocks, eight to ten feet square, arranged in regular patterns. His discovery, named the 'Bimini Road', comprises two parallel lines of stones on the sand dunes of Bimini Bay running south-west towards the deep ocean. The western section starts at an angle of 160° to the beach and curves round to run directly to the shore. The curved part, some 330 feet long, is composed of large, well-laid stones. The straight, shoreward section is 1,200 feet long by 200 feet wide and has a trench in the middle where there are no slabs. (The website has further details.)

In 1974, an American scientist, Dr David Zink, led an expedition (the first of nine) to survey these mysterious stones. He produced overwhelming evidence that the road was man-made. Small stones are placed underneath large ones, apparently to make the sea-bed level, and the larger of the two structures contains arrow-shaped 'pointers' that can only have been man-made. Parts of the road contain stones cut to the same size and laid in rows, and some small square stones have tongued and grooved joints. They have been submerged over a long span of time, for the edges of some have become rounded by wave action, giving them something of the appearance of huge loaves of bread. Some of them were not of Caribbean origin. The road is clearly visible from the air through the azure water. It runs straight as a die down into the depths, a broad band of beige stone. After Dr Zink's expeditions, Jacques Cousteau surveyed the 'road' in detail for a television programme,[7] and *National Geographic* has published several features. The 'road' has been surveyed by a number of different experts, and there is almost universal agreement that the structure is man-made.

Dr Zink later reached the bizarre conclusion that the stones of the Bimini road were part of the fallen pillars of a sacred temple built about 28,000 BC by a long-lost civilization, the Atlanteans, who employed aliens from the star cluster Pleiades to build a megalithic temple complex similar to Stonehenge.[8] Although I disagree with the strange conclusions Dr Zink reached, they do not detract from the value of his basic observations, measurements and surveys, which were meticulous.

As Admiral Zhou Wen's fleet made for Bimini, many of his ships must have been holed below the waterline, with one or more flooded compartments. The captains of the crippled junks desperately needed to beach them before they sank so that they could carry out repairs to the hulls and pump out the sea-water before it reached the rice that was their principal food supply. The standard practice with crippled ships, established over centuries and used extensively during the Second World War, is for damaged ones to be lashed alongside seaworthy ones to keep them afloat and offer all possible assistance. It is likely that some flooded horse and grain ships were tied to capital ships limping towards the shore. One can imagine the relief of the seamen and concubines as they saw the sandy spit of land fringed by palm trees.

As soon as they saw North Bimini, the ships' captains would have made straight for it. Since the water levels in 1421 were approximately one fathom lower than today, and the junks drew an average of two fathoms (twelve feet), depending on the cargo or ballast they were carrying, I calculated that the junks would have grounded where today there is eighteen feet of water – the depth of the seaward end of the Bimini Road. The inverted 'J' section at that end is in the exact position a junk rounding the Great Bahama Bank and then turning directly towards North Bimini would have beached.

This supposition enabled me to look at the Bimini Road with fresh eyes. As I studied it, I hit upon a possible solution to the mystery of the road's purpose. Could the road have been a slip-way made of smooth stone to prevent further damage to the hulls of ships being beached and refloated? The curved section of the road could have acted as a turntable. When one of the treasure ships beached, its keel and rudder would have prevented it from being dragged sideways to the shore. The great ship's stern would have had to be swivelled to face the beach before it could be hauled ashore backwards. When I drew a treasure ship and a grain ship on the same scale as the road, and then rotated their sterns, the treasure ship ended up on the larger stretch of road and the grain ship on the smaller. Both roads had grooves for the ships' keels and rudders, enabling them to be dragged stern first to the beach.

Obtaining stones and rocks of the required size for the Bimini slipway would have been a simple exercise. The junks would have contained thousands of tons of stone ballast. Zhou Wen's fleet carried gunpowder that could be used to blow up rocks, and Chinese stone masons were aboard the ships. They had built thousands of miles of Great Wall between 1403 and 1421 using a wide variety of percussion hammers, drills, awls, saws and sledgehammers. Assuming, for reasons I shall explain later, that fifteen treasure ships had reached Bimini, about six thousand sailors and concubines would have been available as labourers. At first sight, laying the stones on the sea-bed appears problematic, but the Chinese also had more than six centuries' experience of building coffer-dams, watertight enclosures pumped dry using 'Archimedes' screw-pumps to permit work

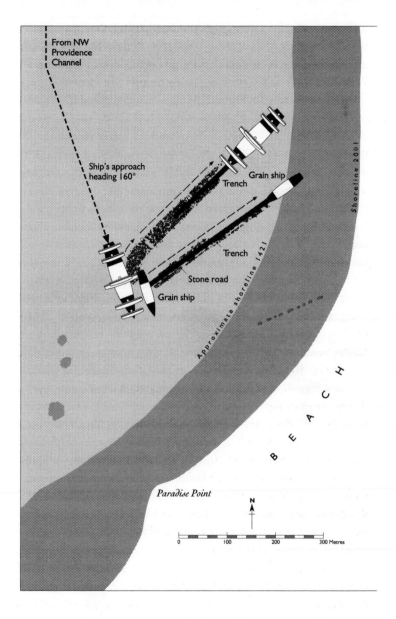

The junks' approach to Bimini and the Bimini Road.

below the waterline. By the early Ming period they even had diving equipment with breathing tubes and face masks.[9] Laying stonework under water was a problem they were well equipped to overcome.

When the slipway had been completed, each huge ship would have had to be hauled ashore in turn, keeping the rudder and keel in the groove. Again, this appears to be a tremendous engineering challenge, but although the treasure ships displaced thousands of tons, Chinese engineers had developed a wide variety of capstans using wire or hemp ropes in order to haul ships. The capstans had geared ratchet-wheels and differential drives, and were designed to be powered by men or horses. The Chinese would have expected their square-rigged junks with shallow draughts and flat bottoms to run aground occasionally, and it is probable that the crew's training included practising hauling flooded ships ashore for repairs. It was reasonable to suppose that the necessary equipment would have been aboard each ship to enable them to do so.

There remained several unsolved puzzles that did not yet fit my scenario. Many of the big rectangular stones were not made from rock found at Bimini. The bedrock there was softer, and laid in a far more disordered pattern than the 'imported' slabs.[10] The 'cement' which appeared to bond the sections also differed. Dr Zink found one sample to be dominated by aragonite crystals, another by spalling calcite, implying that adjacent stones had different physical properties and hence had been formed in different locations. But why would it be necessary to transport huge stones and those square 'building blocks' to Bimini when there was plenty of usable rock there – unless they were part of the ballast carried by the Chinese junks?

Dr Zink sent a sample to the Brookhaven National Laboratory on Long Island. As it had never been fired in a kiln, they were unable to carbon-date the blocks but the head chemist, Dr Edward V. Sayre, confirmed that some of the smaller square blocks were made with a sandstone-limestone mixture and suggested that they 'might have been created by an ancient technique of mass production'. Moreover, each 'building block' was tongued and grooved to slot into its neighbour, and although they had square sides, they tapered in thickness. There appeared to be no need for the tongue and groove on the sea-bed, for the stones were not joined together with them. The solution could be that the building blocks were tongued and grooved so that they could be joined together around ballast in the bottom of a junk, preventing the large stones from moving in a heavy sea and damaging the hull.

A junk's beam was very wide in comparison to its length, and because it was flat-bottomed, substantial ballast was required. The displacement of the capital ships was around 3,400 tons; according to standard nautical engineering I would expect each of them to have carried between five and six hundred tons of ballast – around thirty tons in each of the eighteen watertight compartments. The slipway is composed of a mixture of local rock, building blocks and large 'imported' stones. Some 450 of the latter are still in place on the slipway, but in recent years dredgers have removed part of it to build a seawall in Miami. I calculated that originally there were about six hundred stones on the slipway, each weighing about ten tons, the equivalent of the ballast carried by a dozen junks.

I could now reconstruct a plausible scenario for what had happened. A junk hit the shore, its hull fractured, and some stones or building blocks spilled out onto the sea-bed – the first part of the 'road'. To increase buoyancy, other large stones might have been lowered through the ruptured hulls using long stones as 'straps' beneath them, held by ropes at either end. The 'support' stones on the sea-bed might have been the straps left when the stone reached the sea-bed.

Although the 'imported' large stones[11] are commonplace (save in the Caribbean) throughout the world, they are found in the

Yangtze area and could have been mined and cut to size in the Ming quarries in the eastern suburbs of Nanjing, where the treasure ships were built. The building blocks on the sea-bed are one *chi* (thirty-two centimetres) square, and the sandstone-limestone mixture used to make them was widely available in the Yangtze area.

Once the junks had been hauled onto the beach, the sea-water could be pumped out and the urgent task of drying the rice stores could begin. The Chinese crewmen would have been able to supplement their basic diet with the abundant conches, turtles and gamefish around Bimini. Water could be obtained from the celebrated spring, the bubbling pool of sulphurous water later described to Ponce de León as a fountain of life. But however skilful the Chinese carpenters, some junks would have been damaged beyond repair. They would have been cannibalized, their holds emptied of stores, their hull planking used for the repair of potentially seaworthy junks and for firewood. The remainder of the hulls would have been left as giant wooden skeletons on the beach beyond the slipway. If this had happened, some evidence might remain.

In 1989, Raymond E. Leigh, a land surveyor attached to Dr Zink's expedition, flew across North Bimini and took measurements with infra-red equipment of the north-eastern end of the island, opposite the place where the slipway comes ashore. He discovered four rectangular sand mounds, the largest 500 feet long and 300 feet wide. Their size and shape suggest that they may be the sand-covered hulls of treasure ships, and they are just where I would expect to find the skeletons of junks swept ashore by a hurricane. Another mound was found by Dr Zink on the beach near the slipway. As Chinese warships, the remains of the junks may technically still be the property of the Chinese government. Negotiations are in hand between the Bahamian authorities and myself to resolve the issue of ownership of any artefacts that may be found. When these protracted negotiations are complete, archaeologists may be allowed to excavate the mounds. Their contents may yield detailed knowledge of Zhou Wen's fleet, and perhaps some of the treasure it carried. It could be a priceless discovery in every sense: each junk could carry two thousand tons of cargo, and a single early Ming plate was recently auctioned for £89,500.[12]

I concluded that four junks had sunk just short of North Bimini, another five had been abandoned on East Bimini and the remainder had been repaired and refloated. The lost ships would have carried several thousand sailors and concubines, and Bimini could probably not have supported more than a hundred. A large number would have been taken aboard the surviving junks, but it is inconceivable that room could have been found to carry all of them back to China. Some must have been left on Bimini, others put ashore wherever conditions seemed to offer better hope of survival. As Admiral Zhou Wen's shrunken fleet continued its voyage, its upper decks crowded with crew and passengers from the abandoned junks, many others must have been left to their fate, as happened to sailors from Columbus's ships seventy years later: one of his ships and crew were left behind on Hispaniola. Once the available food on Bimini was exhausted, the abandoned Chinese would have had to attempt the crossing to Cuba, the nearest large island, some 180 miles to the south, or to Florida. Had they managed to do so, some of their descendants should have been alive when Columbus arrived.

In the summer of 1494, on Columbus' second voyage, he anchored his ships off Cuba near a beautiful palm grove to get fresh water and wood.

As the landing party cut wood and filled their water casks, an archer strayed into the forest in search of game, only to return a few minutes later to relate a baffling and frightening experience ... He had come across a band of about thirty well-armed Indians

... three white men were in the company of the natives.

The white men, who wore white tunics which reached to their knees, immediately spotted the intruder ... one of them stepped towards the hunter and started to speak.[13]

The hunter then fled. Upon hearing his story, Columbus despatched another party who failed to find the men. White men with 'white tunics which reached to their knees' is the description local people in Mexico (Jucutácato) and Australia (Arnhem Land) gave to the strangers landing on their shores. Not without reason did Columbus conclude that the men were people of Mangon (China) and that he had reached the shores of Asia.[14]

In isolation, the description of the men in white tunics who greeted Columbus's men could be taken with a pinch of salt, but explorer after explorer in continent after continent reported the same story, all along the Chinese track I had reconstructed from the charts published before the first Europeans reached those continents. In South America, the Spanish envoy, Don Luis Arias, recounted tales in the sixteenth century of light-coloured people who wore white woven garments and crossed the Pacific after leaving what is now Chile. Father Monclaro, a Jesuit priest who accompanied a Portuguese expedition to East Africa in 1569, described the inhabitants of Pate whose claim to be descendants of shipwrecked Chinese sailors was reinforced by their story of the giraffe, the 'quilin' presented to Emperor Zhu Di. Indian sailors reported a Chinese expedition to Antarctica following the Southern Cross constellation. In southern Australia, the Yangery tribe, living beside the wreck of a 'mahogany' ship, claimed that 'yellow men' had settled among them; and in northern Australia the Aborigines said that a honey-coloured people, the men wearing long robes and the women pantaloons, had settled in north-east Arnhem Land. The Maoris made a similar claim, and the French explorer

Bougainville reported meeting Chinese people in the Pacific in 1769. It is scarcely credible that all these accounts are imaginary or fabricated.

The Bimini Road has, of course, excited great controversy and interest. All sorts of exotic ideas and theories have been put forward; mine is but the latest. I fully accept that it requires some leaps of the imagination that are not, as yet, backed up by hard evidence. Only when the Bahamian authorities grant permission for the archaeological excavation of the sand mounds on the beach will we be able to determine whether or not my theory is correct. For the time being, frustrating though it was, I had to leave the mounds undisturbed and depart from Bimini, following in the wake of Admiral Zhou Wen as he assembled the remnants of his fleet and sailed northwards.

SETTLEMENT

IN

NORTH

AMERICA

十三

IN SOLVING THE IMMEDIATE PROBLEM OF HIS DAMAGED AND destroyed ships, Admiral Zhou Wen had fallen foul of another. Some of his ships were again seaworthy and some of the rice had been salvaged, but he now had to make provision for the crews and concubines from the wrecks that had been left on the beach at Bimini. There would have been several thousand additional sailors and several hundred concubines to be accommodated and fed from a much-reduced food supply. The rulers of many Arabian, African and Indian states had been served by the concubines. Many must have been pregnant when the fleet left India, and some would already have given birth. The only way to cope with the chronic overcrowding in the surviving junks would have been to create settlements ashore where some of the crewmen, concubines and their children at least had a chance of survival. A later voyage would have to return for them.

If such Chinese settlements had been made in North America – and the results of recent tests on the Moskoke people of southeastern United States show that they do have Chinese DNA – my problem, as ever, was to locate the physical evidence. Along the Florida coast marked on the Cantino map, the cartographer drew the Florida Keys, Port Sewall, Cape Canaveral and the Savannah estuary. I know Cape Canaveral well. I was operations officer on HMS *Resolution* when we fired Britain's first Polaris missile there in February 1968. It splashed down 2,800 miles away off South America, just fifteen feet shy of the target buoy – the splash as the warhead hit the water temporarily blinded the reading apparatus. As we surfaced back in Florida, we found sea snakes nestling in the conning tower, attracted by the submarine's warmth. The cape itself is a bleak place, renowned for its manatees, the strange sea mammals that gave birth to the legend of the mermaids. Both Cape Canaveral and St Augustine are littered with wrecks, some of them ancient and unidentified, but the fierce current has carried away the timbers to such an extent that identification is very difficult. Nonetheless, the attempt is in hand.

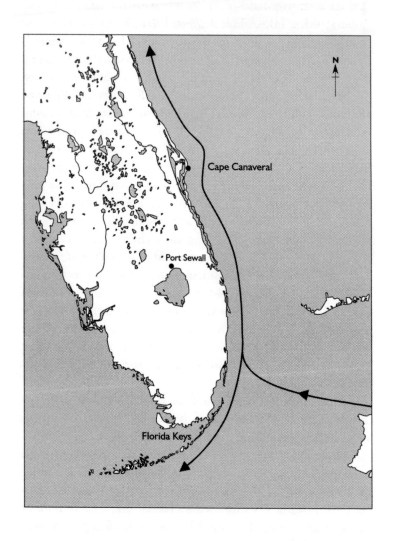

Zhou Wen's journey up the east coast of Florida.

The Cantino ends abruptly at the estuary of the Savannah River, at Point Tybee. This suggested that, having reached this point, the junks had then been carried away from land towards the north-east, exactly the direction in which the prevailing winds and the Gulf Stream run there. These would have carried the junks up to Cape Hatteras in North Carolina. Off Cape Hatteras, the Gulf Stream divides in two, one branch flowing north-east towards the Azores. Those islands appear on the Kangnido, drawn before the first Portuguese reached the islands, and I was certain that the Chinese had reached them. The other, westerly branch of the current off Cape Hatteras flows at first due north, then slowly rotates to the north-east past Philadelphia. At latitude 40°N, the current flows inshore towards Long Island, Rhode Island and Cape Cod.

Once again, this part of the coast is littered with unidentified wrecks, many of them ancient, and a sensible point to begin a detailed search for traces of the Chinese was at the latitude of Beijing – 39°53'N. On the course the junks were taking, they would have reached this point off the coast of modern New Jersey. I have taken my submarine up that coast and can confirm that a huge volume of water flows north-east and the wind and current push ships directly towards Cape Cod. I began the search around Narragansett Bay and Buzzards Bay, and on the Cape Cod peninsula, making sure first of all to consult the accounts of the first Europeans to reach this part of the coast.

The renowned Venetian explorer Giovanni de Verrazzano (c. 1480–c. 1527) arrived there in 1524, twenty-two years after the Cantino was produced. Francis I of France had retained him to explore the North American coast with the aim of finding a seaway to the Pacific and the Spice Islands – 'the happy shores of Cathay'.[1] Verrazzano's voyage was carried out at the same time as the Spanish sent Magellan around South America and the Portuguese despatched a series of expeditions around the Cape of Good Hope. All three countries were in a race to find the most

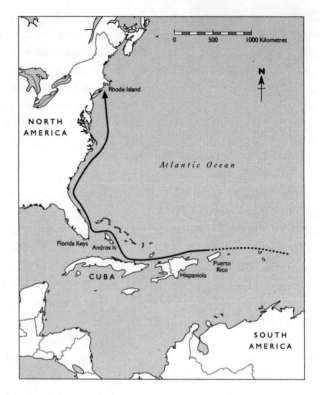

The journey to Rhode Island.

cost-effective and secure means of reaching the Spice Islands of Ternate and Tidore now that the overland route to the East, the Silk Road, had been severed.

In 1524, Verrazzano with his small squadron sailed northwards up the coast from Virginia to the eastern tip of Nova Scotia, describing the pleasant land and its savage people as he went. When at the parallel of Rome, '41 degrees and 2 terstices north', he entered a large bay, corresponding with Narragansett Bay off Rhode Island, where he spent fifteen days. The local people were:

the colour of brass, some of them incline more to whiteness: others are of yellow colour, of comely visage, with long and black hair, which they are very careful to trim and deck up; they are black and quick eyed, and of sweet and pleasant countenance . . .

The women are of the like conformity and beauty; very handsome and well favoured, of pleasant countenance and comely to behold; they are as well-mannered and continent as any woman, and of good education . . . [women] use other kinds of dressing themselves like unto the women of Egypt and Syria; these are of the elder sort: and when they are married, they wear divers toys [jewellery] according to the usage of the people of the East, as well men as women.[2]

This is a very significant passage. Verrazzano was comparing elegant people with brass-coloured skin to the much darker and more uncouth people he had met further south. He referred twice to the women's connection with the East and their clothes – dresses rather than the furs and animal skins worn by the people he had encountered previously. Most important of all, Verrazzano was not describing local women married to foreigners, but women resembling those from the East who had somehow ended up in North America. Clearly they were from a different civilization and were not natives of North America, nor of Europe.

Verrazzano's description suggests that the younger girls were not following their grandmothers' traditions; the original customs they had brought were dying out, indicating that they had been there a few generations. The description would indeed have fitted Syrian or Egyptian women just as much as it would Chinese. All of these women would have worn long dresses and jewellery and had their black hair decked up, but Egyptian and Syrian seafarers never reached the Atlantic; in any case, their women were not taken on long voyages. The description would fit the descendants of the Chinese concubines pregnant by

Middle Eastern rulers and ambassadors. It could have been they who greeted Verrazzano.

There is another clue in Verrazzano's account of leaving Narragansett Bay: 'In the midst of this entrance [to the harbour] there is a rock of stone produced by nature apt to build any castle or fortress there, for the keeping of the haven . . . which we call La Petra Viva [the living rock].'[3] Verrazzano's description fits the rock on which the Round Tower still stands, in a park in Newport, Rhode Island, on a promontory overlooking the harbour. The tower is a mystery; visitors muse over whether or not it was built by strange people who arrived before Columbus. To me it is a curiosity, quite unlike any other colonial building in America, placed in isolation, in a commanding position but not a fortress, and out of the wind, so unlikely to be a mill. Historians have furiously debated its origins. One school claims it was a sixteenth-century flour mill, another that it served as a lighthouse and was built around the end of the fourteenth century. Both theories could be correct; an earlier building could have been modified to serve as a flour repository, if not a mill. Historians in the flour-mill camp rely for their evidence on the first Rhode Island governor, Benedict Arnold, a prosperous merchant whose will referred to 'my stone builte tower'.

A detailed survey of the tower by the respected Danish Committee for Research on Norse Activities in North America AD 1000–1500 took place in the early 1990s. The publication in 1992 of the results of investigations and analyses seemed to confirm the flour-mill thesis. The report, prepared by Johannes Hertz of the National Museum in Copenhagen, concluded that Arnold was the builder in 1667, but an American architect, Suzanne O. Carlson, who has made a meticulous examination of the tower, recently challenged these findings.[4] She argued that closer study of the report revealed the tower could not have been built by Arnold at that date, and she cited four specific pieces of scientific evidence in support of her argument.

The Rhode Island Tower.

Firstly, she contended that every seventeenth-century colonial structure in New England was built using English measurements – yards, feet and inches – yet not a single dimension of the Newport Round Tower conforms. Secondly, she claimed that the seventeenth-century trench surrounding the tower, which the flour-mill camp says supports their argument, could only have been built to stabilize an earlier building. Thirdly, she argued that the Danish committee's carbon-dating was based on a new and experimental technique that measured the carbon 14 in carbon dioxide bubbles in the mortar. The actual range of dates measured was between 1410 and 1970, and while the Danish committee attributed it to the late 1600s, the analysis could equally well apply to any date after 1409. Lastly, the tower was built using an unusual type of mortar made from crushed shells, rather than the standard lime mortar habitually used by colonial builders.

However, the details of the tower's construction do not reveal its purpose, which has been described as follows:

> The first storey of the tower served as a lighthouse. The larger windows of the first storey were so placed in relation to the fireplace that the light from the fire at night seen through the south window would be a guide to a ship approaching the entrance to Narragansett Bay ... fireplace light through the two-foot opening of the west window would guide a ship to the harbour landing at the bottom of Tower Hill ... The ingenious builder of the tower had obviously had considerable experience ... in designing lighthouses.[5]

The Norse were present in Greenland from the end of the tenth to the early fifteenth century. Greenland had no wood, so each summer they set sail to Vinland – North America – to gather wood, returning each autumn. At first sight the narrow windows and rounded arches of the Rhode Island tower appeared Romanesque, and my initial reaction was that it was a lighthouse built by the Norsemen. It could have been; they had penetrated nearly as far south as Newport. However, the Norse had little experience of lighthouse design and are not known to have built one overseas; and in my view the design and position of the windows closely resembled those on the Song dynasty (960–1279) lighthouse that guided Chinese and Arab trading fleets into the port of Zaiton (Quanzhou) in Fujian province in southern China. A number of the crewmen aboard the Chinese fleet would certainly have known Zaiton and its lighthouse, for at the time of the Chinese treasure fleets Zaiton was probably the largest commercial port in the world. Marco Polo described it as 'a great resort of ships and merchandise ... for one spice ship that goes to Alexandria or elsewhere to pick up pepper for export to Christendom, Zaiton is visited by a hundred. For you must know that it is one of the two ports in the world with the biggest flow of merchandise.'[6]

The Zaiton lighthouse is twice the size of the Newport Round Tower and is five storeys high rather than three, but the windows are notably similar, as is the design of the central fireplace. Like Zaiton, too, the tower at Newport was once covered in smooth plaster. There are several other striking resemblances. The Rhode Island tower is a grey shell of stones rising above arches that span eight columns set on an octagonal base, just as at Zaiton. The masonry consists of stones of various shapes held together by a powerful and long-lasting mortar; neither the stones at Newport nor those at Zaiton have moved since the wall was built. Furthermore, the dimensions of the tower show that it conforms to the standard Chinese units of measurement used in the fifteenth century: the external diameter is 2 *chang* 40 *chi* and the internal 1 *chang* 80 *chi* (1 *chang* = 10.167 feet; 1 *chi* = 32 centimetres).

Professor William Penhallow, Professor of Physics and Astronomy at the University of Rhode Island, offered an alternative explanation for the purpose of the Round Tower. He made a study of astronomical alignments and discovered that the seemingly random openings and asymmetrical, splayed window-jambs framed specific astronomical events, notably lunar eclipses and the rising and setting of the sun at its solstices and equinox.[7] This accords precisely with the design of Ming observatories and observation platforms. The length of the sun's shadow at solstice and equinox at any particular latitude gives the precise time, and viewing a lunar eclipse gave the Chinese the opportunity to observe the leading star on the zenith and so determine the longitude of the Newport Round Tower when they returned to Beijing,[8] just as they did with observation platforms around the world.

The tower could thus have served two vital purposes. It could have been used to determine the exact location of the settlement set up by the Chinese crewmen and concubines left behind, so that they could be found and rescued on a subsequent voyage of the treasure fleets. It could also have been a lighthouse to guide the rescuers safely into Narragansett Bay. Although now obscured by encroaching woods, the tower was sited in a prominent position and was once a distinctive landmark clearly visible from the sea. Like the Zaiton lighthouse, it was angled so that the light burning from its fire could warn of danger through one set of windows, but also act as a guide through another set to bring mariners to a safe anchorage.

An analysis of the mortar used in the Newport Round Tower would settle the matter once and for all, for Chinese mortar had a very distinctive property – it contained gypsum as a hardening and rice as a bonding agent. It can also be dated; from analysis of the mortar on the Great Wall, it has been possible to determine the different rice and gypsum contents used in the Tang and Ming eras, and therefore when each section of the wall was built. I have asked the authorities at Newport for permission to arrange an analysis, but this has been denied. The first duty of the authorities is of course to preserve the fabric of the monuments in their care, not to make them available for experiments, but I hope they can be persuaded to change their minds. It would then be possible not only to determine the nature of the mortar but also to date it, and early Ming is particularly easy to date.

There is a substantial body of evidence that the Chinese landed at Newport. They had reached Bimini and later the Azores, and a detailed cartographic survey of the coast of Florida had been carried out before the first European reached North America. The route from Bimini to New England and then the Azores is precisely the one a square-rigged sailing ship would have followed, before the wind and current all the way. And the first Europeans to reach New England described – there exist six separate accounts – civilized white- or bronze-skinned women living around Newport who wore clothes of the East and dressed their hair in buns, as Chinese women did.

In view of all this evidence, it is more likely that the tower was erected by the Chinese, who had centuries of experience of lighthouse and observatory building, than by Norsemen, who had virtually no experience of either. The Newport Round Tower faces south, the direction from which the Chinese would have arrived, sailing with wind and current. It would have been useless to Norsemen approaching from Greenland to the north, sailing against the prevailing winds and currents.

I contend that the people Verrazzano met at what is now Newport, Rhode Island, can only have been Chinese men and women, the descendants of sailors and concubines from Zhou Wen's great fleet. Knowing the longitude of the tower, the junks of the next treasure fleet would have been able to sail directly to Newport, and it would have been natural for those stranded there to have built a lighthouse to guide their rescuers safely into harbour, protecting them from the tragedy that had overtaken Zhou Wen's fleet in the Caribbean. If my surmise was correct that Zhou Wen had several thousand men and concubines to land around Narragansett Bay, a substantial amount of evidence should remain in the countryside surrounding the Newport tower. I would expect at least to find stones similar to those the Chinese erected elsewhere on their journey.

I began my search on the internet to see if there were any carved stones in eastern Massachusetts. My search produced immediate and dramatic results. Thirty miles upriver from the tower is the celebrated Dighton Rock. It is a free-standing, easily identifiable rock of a distinctive reddish-brown colour with an exposed face measuring approximately five feet high by eleven feet wide. It stands on the banks of the Taunton River and is covered with ancient carvings, on top of which is a Portuguese cross and graffiti. In that respect, Dighton Rock strongly resembles examples in the Cape Verde Islands and at the Matadi Falls. I felt that another link in the ever-lengthening chain of evidence had fallen into place.

Dighton Rock would have been the logical place for any explorer of the Taunton River to stop to leave a mark. It is the largest rock in the bay on the south side of what is now Perry Point, the northernmost point any large vessel can reach along the Taunton River. Above Perry Point, the river narrows to under two hundred feet and the depth falls to a few feet. It is the reason why the Taunton Yacht Club is located there rather than further north.

The rock was first drawn in 1680 by a local clergyman, Mr Danforth, who also related the legend associated with the rock that had passed into the folklore of the local Indians: 'Then there came a wooden house (and men of another country in it) swimming up the River Asooner [as the River Taunton was then called] who fought the Indians with some mighty success.'9 The Chinese themselves described their junks as 'wooden houses', as did other observers such as Niccolò da Conti and Pedro Tafur, a Spanish traveller to whom da Conti related his story (see chapter 4). In 1421, the sea level was some six feet lower than today, and the rock, now covered at high water, would have been above the waterline in all but the highest spring tide. It was certainly respected and deemed old by local native Americans:

> This monument was esteemed by the oldest Indians not only very antique but a work of a different nature from any of theirs ... some reckon the figures here to be hieroglyphicall [sic] the first figure representing a ship without masts, and a mere wrack [wreck] cast upon the shoals. The second representing an head of land, possibly a cape with a peninsula. Hence a gulf.10

This description accords with the dreadful experiences a few weeks earlier of Zhou Wen's fleet.

After Mr Danforth's drawing of 1680, at least six more were made before 1830. I have received accounts of an artist and another clergyman who visited Dighton Rock after Mr Danforth; they met Mongolian people there and stated that the carving on the rock was Mongolian. However, it was the practice of local boatmen to take tourists to the rock and scrub off the algae to reveal the hieroglyphics underneath, and as time went by fewer and fewer of the hieroglyphics remained legible and the drawings grew more and more extravagant and fanciful, bearing little relation to Mr Danforth's sketch. Whatever message the stone carried can no longer be read, and sadly all I or anyone else can conclude is that the rock was carved in a non-European language by foreign mariners sailing upriver in a ship like a house, that the inscription described a shipwreck and that the Portuguese later found the rock and inscribed a cross upon it.

I next searched the work of local historians for further evidence. Narragansett Bay is open to the North Atlantic and experiences brutal winter weather. Snowstorms lash the coast, and the native Americans who inhabited this bleak region, even the wild animals, sought refuge inland, away from the worst of the weather. It would have been natural for the Chinese also to seek shelter up one of the arms of the bay, and the Taunton River was the most obvious route. It was the native Americans' highway to the interior, and it would have been logical for the Chinese to sail upriver to the highest navigable point, beside Dighton Rock, to escape the sudden squalls that might have caused the ships to drag their anchors and run aground.

In the 1950s, just before a housing development started at Perry Point, a cluster of very old stone buildings was found. They were all the same size, arranged in a cruciform pattern and held together by mortar. Hops and wild rice, not indigenous to the area, grew nearby. No-one at the time thought the matter sufficiently important to attempt to stop the housing development or to arrange an extensive excavation.[11] Could this have been a settlement established by the Chinese? Sadly we will never know as all traces of these buildings have been destroyed.

Professor Delabarre, a distinguished North American historian,[12] contended that there were noticeable differences in physiology and colouration between the 'pure blood Wampanoag Indians' living near Dighton Rock and adjacent tribes in Massachusetts. Based upon this, he postulated that while exploring what is now Narragansett Bay, the ship of the Portuguese explorer Miguel Cortreal was wrecked in 1510.[13] He and his crew were accepted by the Wampanoag and inter-married within the tribe. Professor Delabarre's theory could, of course, also apply to the bronze-skinned people Verrazzano met. The Wampanoag later proved hospitable to the first pilgrims, contrary to experiences elsewhere: male pilgrims were frequently killed by other tribes and women and possessions taken. One can speculate that the Wampanoag might earlier have been fairly treated by shipwrecked Chinese.

I began to search for more corroborative evidence such as other carved stones, without any great hope of finding any. After discovering the Cape Verde stone, I had spent considerable time searching for inscribed rocks around each Chinese landfall and had very rarely found more than one, at most two, in any one area. To my amazement, I discovered no fewer than twelve curious stones in one small area of eastern Massachusetts.[14] The size, position and aspect of these rocks was strikingly similar to those I located on the Cape Verde Islands, at the Matadi Falls on the Congo River and at Ruapuke beach in New Zealand. Many were propped up with round stones at one corner in precisely the same way as the Cape Verde stone. Someone must have pushed the rocks into this odd position, recalling the description given by the Aborigines of foreign visitors to Australia 'pushing the rocks in long lines'.

I decided to plot these stones on a map of eastern Massachusetts and immediately saw that they were either beside the Taunton River in the south, the Merrimack River in the north or around Massachusetts Bay. What appears highly likely is that the people who hauled the huge stones into position had sailed upriver, one 'great house' sailing up the Taunton River, another up the Merrimack.

One of these stones, the 'Shutesbury', appears to have carved upon it a figure of a seated Buddha in the classic position, 'contemplating ageing'. If the carving could be dated to the pre-Columbus period this would be highly significant but unfortunately the museums I have approached so far have been unable to give a final opinion of the date. Curiously, at North Salem, a hundred miles south of Shutesbury, there is an instantly recognizable carving of a horse – pre-Columbus. If the people who raised the stones had used horses the likelihood would be that they came with horse-ships, for the rocks were found in place by the first European settlers and horses died out in North America round 10,000 BC. At this stage all one can say is that it is possible the huge stones were hauled into position by people using horses. The investigations continue and the results will be posted on the 1421 website.

It could be argued that the similarities of site, size, shape and method of support among the twelve large stones found in eastern Massachusetts and those in the Cape Verde Islands, at the Matadi Falls and at Ruapuke beach are coincidental, and that the inscriptions on the Dighton Rock represented shipwrecked mariners other than the Chinese, but I was sure the Chinese fleet had reached the Caribbean, and later the Azores. In between these two landfalls, the winds and currents would have taken them to exactly the place where the rocks have been found. The most plausible explanation is that the rocks were erected by the Chinese and that the women Verrazzano met were the descendants of Chinese concubines. I suggest that the first settlers of North America came not with Columbus nor any other European pioneer, but in the junks of Admiral Zhou

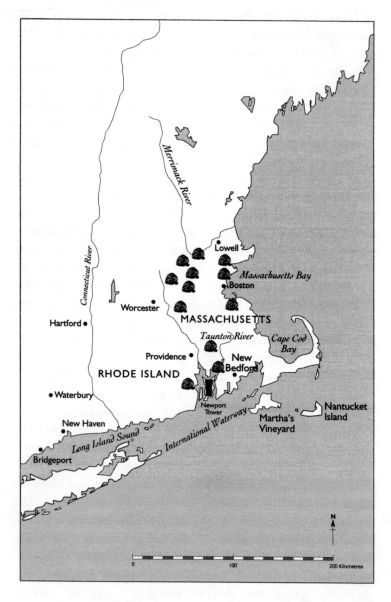

The locations of standing stones in Massachusetts.

Wen's fleet, landing around Christmas 1421, and there is now ample DNA evidence to back up this assertion. Perhaps New England should now be renamed New China.

After establishing the settlements, the junks would have set sail. How desolate the crew and concubines left ashore must have felt, watching the great red sails unfurl and fill with wind, carrying the junks away. Those lining the beach would have strained their eyes until the ships were no larger than specks on the horizon, and as they turned away at last, their hearts must have been full of foreboding. No doubt promises were made that the next great treasure fleet would return for them, bringing fresh supplies and more people and carrying those who so wished back to their homeland. As the years passed, amid the daily struggle to survive – building shelters, catching fish, tilling the soil and foraging inland for food – they must have paused often to cast their eyes out to sea, raking the horizon for the first smudge of red that might signal the arrival of a rescue fleet. But as the years went by, hope must have faded, as must talk of their homeland, constant in the conversation of the old but dimming to a half-remembered tale and then forgotten altogether by succeeding generations. Not one single Chinese ship ever returned to collect them.

EXPEDITION

TO THE

NORTH

POLE

ADMIRAL ZHOU WEN'S ALREADY DEPLETED FLEET WAS to be further reduced in strength on the next stage of its epic voyage, for the surviving medieval maps suggest that as the Chinese fleet crossed the icy waters of the North Atlantic, it was divided into two squadrons. One set sail even further to the north; the other carried on eastwards and, swept before the winds and currents, it would have been approaching the Azores from the north-west within a month of leaving New England. The Azores chain stretches four hundred miles from north-west to south-east, and the first island the Chinese would have sighted approaching from the Americas is the most north-westerly of the Azores, the small but dramatic island of Corvo on the same latitude as Beijing.

Like Santo Antão in the Cape Verde Islands and Guadeloupe, Corvo is dominated by a huge volcano, the long-extinct Caldeirão, usually capped by a large white cloud. Streams tumble down the sides of the volcano, visible from miles out into the Atlantic. Only five miles long, the island looks verdant green, rising above a sea of the deepest blue, but the living is hard, for there is only a narrow strip of fertile land on the south shore around what is now the capital, Vila Nova, between the foothills of the volcano and the sea. All the houses huddle together as if begrudging even a single lost yard of the precious soil.

Here I began to look for a lighthouse, or a carved stone like the ones I had already located along the routes the Chinese had sailed. If it existed, it would have been placed in a prominent site and would have been noted by the Portuguese when they first discovered the island. The earliest account of the Portuguese arrival in the 1430s has this to say:

On the summit of a mountain on an island they call The Raven [Corvo] . . . a statue of a man seated upon a horse; his head is uncovered and he is bald; his left hand rests upon his horse, his right hand points towards the west. The statue is set firmly upon a stone base carved out of rock. At the bottom are inscriptions in a writing which we could not understand.

This statement is significant on several counts. The people who carved the horse and the writing were clearly not European, and the horseman is not only hatless but bald. Some of the terra-cotta army guarding the Emperor Quin's tomb were depicted with shaven heads covered by a close-fitting stocking, like a tight hairnet. They do, indeed, look bare-headed and bald. The Corvo horseman is pointing to the west, to New England, the direction from which the Chinese would have arrived. The Azores are easy for a junk to reach from the Americas, but very difficult to

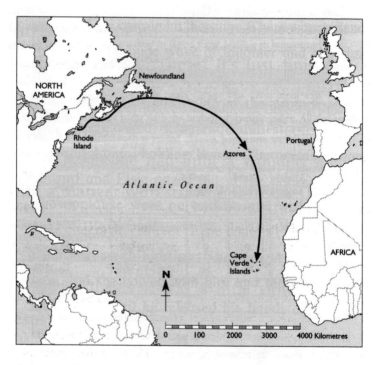

The voyage to the Azores and Cape Verde Islands.

reach from Portugal because from there ships would be sailing into the wind. That is why the Portuguese discovered them long after the Canaries and the Cape Verde Islands, despite the Azores being nearer to Portugal.

For me, the final confirmation that the Corvo horseman was indeed a Chinese statue, perhaps even of 'The Emperor on Horseback' Zhu Di, is that the Azores appear on the Chinese/Korean Kangnido chart, produced before the Portuguese discovered the islands. They had never appeared on any Arab maps, not even those of the famous historians Al Idrisi (1099–1166) and Ibn Khaldun (1332–1406). If the Azores were not discovered by the Chinese, who could have discovered the islands before the Portuguese, and why should they have informed the cartographer in distant China?

Surprisingly, corroborative evidence that the Chinese may have inhabited the Azores comes from Christopher Columbus, who reported a local story of non-European bodies washed onto the beach at Flores, some twenty miles south of Corvo. This report came before Columbus set sail for the Americas and Ferdinand Columbus indicates that his father believed these bodies, together with 'artistically carved pieces of wood', were evidence of contact between Cathay and the West.[2]

While one squadron of Admiral Zhou Wen's fleet set sail for home from the Azores via the Indian Ocean, the early maps show that the other squadron had taken a different route. South of the Grand Banks off Newfoundland,[3] the Gulf Stream separates. While the main body flows clockwise, carrying ships to the Azores and then via the Canaries to the Cape Verde Islands, a second, smaller part of the stream, the Irminger current, carries on to the east. Due south of Iceland, it veers counter-clockwise, first to the north, then the north-west and then north again, carrying a ship into the Davis Strait separating Greenland from northern Canada. There it becomes the West Greenland current, which flows up the west coast of

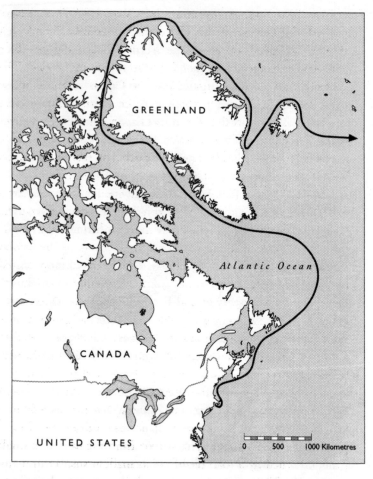

The journey around Greenland.

Greenland, circles around the north coast and then comes back down the east coast as the East Greenland current, leading back into the Atlantic. Any ship circumnavigating Greenland in this way would never have to sail into an opposing wind or current at any stage.

I was faced with two questions: why would the Chinese have wanted to circumnavigate such a barren, frozen land, and even if they had good reason to do so, was it actually possible? The answer to the first was easier to find than the second. The symbolic and practical significance of Polaris to the Chinese made fixing the absolute position of the North Pole of great importance. Not without reason had the emperor ordered them to reach 'the most northern of the northern . . . countries', and to explore the nethermost parts of the earth – as their compatriots were doing in the far south, locating the South Pole.

I found the first circumstantial evidence that their thrilling gamble might have succeeded in two charts. The first was the Cantino, the remarkable medieval map that had already led me to so many discoveries about the Chinese voyages. The second chart was far more controversial: the Vinland map, dated to between 1420 and 1440. The Vinland map shows Newfoundland, Labrador and the whole of Greenland with great accuracy and in considerable detail. If it is genuine, it is proof that someone – perhaps the Chinese – had penetrated to within 250 miles of the North Pole four centuries before the first recorded European exploration of the High Arctic.

By using information from the Vinland map, I knew I would be opening a Pandora's box of controversy. The map's credibility has been attacked on many grounds. Its extraordinary provenance – it first appeared in 1965 from the back of a small Fiat car owned by a map-dealer – has made it suspect in many expert eyes. There is no shortage of historians who believe its cartography just too good to be true; Greenland is so accurately drawn that it simply must be a modern fake. Walter McCrone of McCrone Associates, a respected Chicago firm expert in chemical analysis, claimed in 1972 that the ink's composition, in particular its anatase content (a form of titanium that first appeared in inks in the 1920s) made impossible the purported date of the map's creation. However, in 1992, Dr Thomas Cahill

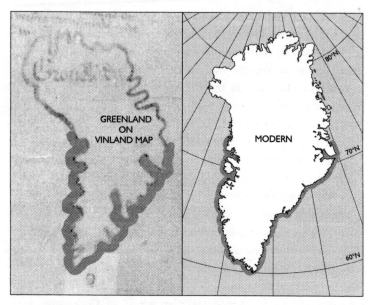

Greenland shown on the Vinland map, compared to a modern map.

of UC Davis found anatase in a variety of medieval manuscripts, reopening the question of the Vinland map's authenticity.

The other grounds for attacking the map's credibility are that the Norsemen who first settled Greenland had no cartographic knowledge, only an oral tradition that substituted for map making, and the map could not conceivably have been drawn from an oral description. Furthermore, it was believed that Greenland could not have been circumnavigated, and that the names on the Vinland map supposedly placed there by Claudius Clavius, an eminent Danish cartographer who is believed to have drawn the map in about 1424, are fairytale names; surely the Norsemen would have told him what they had called places in the north. However, if the original cartographers had been Chinese, Clavius would probably not have been able to translate the names marked on the chart, which might explain why he felt the need to invent them. The ink remains the one controversial issue that has not yet been resolved. Several books have been written about it. No less an authority than the then Keeper of Maps of the British Library, Mr R.A. Skelton, considers it genuine; in this he has been supported by several learned professors corroborating Dr Cahill's discovery that anatase was in fact contained in some medieval inks, particularly those used in Alpine monasteries early in the fifteenth century.

Those claiming the Vinland map is a forgery have not remotely satisfied the burden of proof, and it is my belief that it is genuine and that the original cartographers who produced the information on which it was based were aboard several Chinese junks, at least one of which circumnavigated Greenland on a quest to reach the North Pole. To justify that belief, I had to answer the question of whether Greenland really could have been circumnavigated. It is completely impossible today, even in a nuclear-powered icebreaker, for the seas surrounding the far north are frozen solid all year round. However, there is direct evidence that conditions in the early fifteenth century were markedly different from those ruling today.

Contemporary accounts of the wedding of Sigrid Bjornsdottir in 1408, preserved in the state archives in Oslo, paint a very different picture of the land we know as Greenland. Sigrid was a widow; her father and sisters had died and she had inherited the family land, becoming the wealthiest landowner in Greenland. She possessed substantial flocks of sheep and cattle that fed on lush Greenland pastures, a scene quite un-recognizable from today's barren, ice-bound land. The church in which Sigrid was married still stands in bleak and splendid isolation above the dark fjord. We can imagine her that September Sunday as the service ended, hurrying from the church into the dark warmth of her house to begin her wedding celebrations.

Excavations of the floors of the houses in which she, her

family and her retainers and servants lived show that the climate in Greenland was far warmer before the onset of a miniature Ice Age in the 1430s. The evidence is supplied by a change in the type of flies found during the excavations. Those that inhabit warm houses disappeared and were replaced by flies that can live in cold, empty houses off the rotting flesh of the dead. Evidence of an abrupt change in climate came from the skeleton of an elkhound whose throat had been slit – perhaps a last meal for the dying inhabitants. A valuable hunting dog would only have been slaughtered like this in the most dire circumstances, for without it a family's chances of killing enough game to survive the winter would be drastically reduced. I am now in receipt of expert corroberative evidence that the summers of 1422 to 1428 were exceptionally warm (see postscript).

I found further corroboration that Greenland can periodically be navigated in the accounts of Captain George Nares's voyage to the Arctic in 1875–6.[4] One of his ships reached 83°20′ North, just nineteen miles from the northern tip of Greenland. An officer, Lieutenant Lockwood, marched the nineteen miles to the northernmost tip, Lockwood Island, later named after him. And this at a time when the climate was much colder than in 1422.

It is safe to conclude, therefore, that Greenland was circum-navigable in 1421–2, for the climate of Greenland was far warmer than it is today. In 1421 it would have been a country of green pastures where cattle grazed in the open from Pentecost (fifty days after Easter) to Cross Sunday (the second Sunday in September). The rivers were full of salmon, the coasts rich in walrus.

Additional corroboration that the Chinese did reach Greenland comes from a most curious letter written in 1448 by Pope Nicholas V to the bishops of Skalholt and Holar in Iceland, setting out the background to his desire to appoint a new bishop to Greenland: '[Thirty years ago,] the barbarians came from the nearby coast of the heathens, and attacked the inhabitants of Greenland most cruelly and so devastated the mother country and the holy buildings with fire and sword that there remained no more than nine parish churches ... The pitiable inhabitants of both sexes they carried away ... the greater number have since returned from captivity to their own houses.'[5] The Pope referred to 'barbarians' who came from 'the nearby coast of the heathens'. In other letters, he referred to the Inuit tribes of the Canadian Arctic as 'the heathen', so 'the nearby coast' can reasonably be assumed to refer to the Canadian Arctic. Addressing a Christian audience, the Pope distinguished between heathens and barbarians – they were not interchangeable terms. He cannot be referring to Norsemen – Greenland was a Norse colony – nor to any other Christian invader; they might have been heretics in the Pope's eyes, but they would not have been barbarians. In those days, as is commonly accepted, barbarians were people who invaded Europe from the East; the Pope was almost certainly referring to a Mongolian or Chinese invader of Greenland. The Pope would not have been referring to North American Indians as the barbarians, for these people had no 'swords' or 'fire' with which to fight. They used bows and arrows. I believe the only rational view to take is that this letter is describing a Chinese fleet arriving from North America and attacking the local people, perhaps with cannon (Hvalsey, Sigrid Bjornsdottir's home town and the main settlement of Greenland, was within cannon range from the sea). They took them away in their great ships then returned them. But why the Chinese should have acted in this uncharacteristic way is inexplicable. Perhaps they were attacked first.

Assuming that the Chinese did indeed reach the settlement at Hvalsey – and DNA analysis has again shown that the native people around Hvalsey possess Chinese DNA – the Vinland map should show where they had most accurately surveyed the coast, and therefore the sites where further direct evidence of settlements, wrecks and artefacts might be found. Peter Schlederman and Farley Mowat, two well-known authors and explorers, have carried out years of painstaking research in the High Arctic at the extraordinary villages of stone houses centred on the Bache Peninsula of Ellesmere Island, to the west of Greenland on the west shore of the Kane Basin, and made some remarkable discoveries.[6]

The colony on the Bache Peninsula is of particular interest. There are about twenty-five houses and a similar number of beacons on the peninsula, and some of the houses are immense – nearly 150 feet (45 metres) long and over 5 metres wide. The houses are so large and the stonework so well constructed that it is unlikely they were built by Inuit peoples. They have other notable characteristics too. Stone beacons resembling small light-houses were built alongside the houses, and there is one very curious omission: none of the houses has a roof. The Norse settlers of Greenland almost invariably roofed their houses with sod, but there is not a trace of such roofing on any of the houses on the Bache Peninsula. That there are no roofs at all is astounding. The buildings are large enough to have accommodated as many as three thousand people, but without a roof over their heads they would have been lucky to survive a single Arctic night. The ruined walls of the buildings can be seen today. Outside the houses, row upon row of hearths had been constructed, 142 in all, each separated from its neighbour by a stone wall. This multiple arrangement of outdoor hearths is again quite unique; nothing like it has ever been identified among pre-historic sites in the Canadian Arctic.

In trying to solve the mystery of these curious buildings, my first clue came from the local geography. The settlement at Ellesmere Island was built on a spit near a large polynya – a stretch of open water, a curious phenomenon found all the way to the North Pole. As I can vouch from navigating submarines under the ice in this part of the world, polynyas remain ice-free in both summer and winter. The reason for this is still not fully understood, but because they are permanently free of ice, they are extraordinarily attractive not only to submariners in search of fresh air but as breathing-holes for mammals. There, mammals can also seek their prey. The polynya off the Bache Peninsula is particularly rich in fish and attracts large numbers of walrus. Walrus were very greatly valued in the Middle Ages for their meat, their magnificent ivory tusks and their hides, which could be boiled to make blubber oil for heating and lighting and distilled to make pitch to seal the hulls of ships. That the villagers on the Bache Peninsula in the High Arctic were there for the walrus is confirmed by the superb artefacts of exquisite workmanship that have been found nearby, such as fish hooks made from walrus ivory.

Ellesmere Island also has another very valuable commodity: copper. Evidence of ancient mining and processing of copper has recently come to light on nearby Devon Island;[7] of course, the Chinese were adept at surveying for, mining and refining metals. Coal originating from Newport, Rhode Island, has also been found in Greenland. Someone must have carried it there.

All of this was reasonably logical, but it begged the question of why the Chinese, with their magnificent ships, should have bothered to build stone houses at all. Why not simply anchor off the polynya to hunt the walrus and prospect for copper? But if one or more of the great ships had been holed by ice and forced to beach, they would then have found themselves on land with thousands of tons of teak near a rich fishing ground that would keep them alive if only they could withstand the cold. In such circumstances they would probably have done what Shackleton was to do centuries later: they built houses of the local material – stone – and roofed them using the timbers of their ships. By my calculations, one three-thousand-ton junk could have roofed all twenty-five houses of the settlement on the Bache peninsula.

I next turned to the stone hearths. If they had been designed for cooking, they would have been inside the houses: sited outside, they must have been built for industrial purposes. The sheer number of them – 142 in total – supports this thesis. One explanation would be that the hearths were used to boil blubber, both to make pitch for sealing the wooden roofs of the houses and to provide heating and lighting oil for winter. They could also have been used for desalinating sea-water or melting snow for drinking water, but so many hearths would scarcely have been required for these purposes. I believe that the Chinese were also smelting copper.

Part of the Chinese fleet must have remained at the settlement for some time, but at least one ship must have gone on to circum-navigate Greenland because the northern and eastern coasts of Greenland appear on the Vinland map. The south-western and south-eastern coasts are very accurately drawn with correct latitudes, but the north-west coast has a substantial 'bulge' in the area from Cape York through the Kane Basin to Petermann Fjord and Peary Land. To work out how this might have happened, I studied modern ice maps of the region[8] and con-cluded that the bulge shown on the Vinland map is in fact ice protruding into the sea from the huge glaciers of Mylius Erichsen's Land and Kronprins Christian's Land. Superimposing the shape of the glaciers onto a modern map of Greenland reconciles the disparity on the Vinland map.

Excepting this one error, the coastline is well drawn. Once again, it is a staggering cartographic achievement. The cumulative evidence – the Chinese reaching the Caribbean, the currents and winds that could have carried them from there around Greenland, the Pope's letter and the stone village – is suggestive of a Chinese attempt to reach the North Pole. By reaching Greenland they failed only by four hundred nautical miles ... or did they? The most exquisite artefacts – snow geese, polar bears, seals and walruses of sumptuous workmanship carved from walrus ivory – have been found in the High Arctic even further north than Greenland, within 250 miles of the North Pole. They were designed by artists of genius. Could the Inuit have made them, or were they the art of a civilization almost as old as time?

After setting sail from Greenland, the currents and prevailing winds would have driven the Chinese fleet on towards Iceland. Confirmation that this was feasible came from Christopher Columbus: 'In the month of February 1477, I sailed 100 leagues [approximately 470 nautical miles] beyond the island of Tile [Iceland], whose southern part is in latitude 73 degrees north . . . and at the time when I was there, the sea was not frozen, but there were vast tides, so great that they rose and fell as much as 26 braccia [about 50 feet] twice a day.'[9] Professor Mike Baillie of Queen's University, Belfast, a world expert on dendrochronology – the analysis of tree rings to establish dates – has shown that 1477 was indeed an unusually warm year, hence Columbus's claim is perfectly acceptable. Such a voyage would have taken him to the coast of Greenland. Then came the bombshell. Columbus summarized his voyage in his own handwriting in the margins of his copy of Pope Pius II's book *History of Remarkable Things that Happened in my Time*. He wrote: 'Men have come hither [to Iceland] from Cathay in the Orient.'[10]

I now had separate testimony from a pope and from Columbus that the Chinese had reached Greenland and Iceland, documentary evidence corroborated by the Vinland map of c. 1424 that shows the south coast of Greenland with stunning precision. In addition, the great expert on Ming China, Professor Needham, says that there exist more than twenty separate Chinese claims that they actually reached the North Pole.[11]

When they rounded Greenland's North Cape, the Chinese would have been just 180 miles south of the North Pole, for its position in 1422, as determined by Polaris at 90° altitude (*Wu Pei Chi*), was well to the south of where it is today. To reach the pole, the Chinese had only to travel a further 180 miles to the north – less than two days' sailing. Could the Arctic waters have been ice-free over those last 180 miles? A current (2000) temperature chart for the Arctic in July shows a tongue of relatively warm water off the North Cape of Greenland – perhaps the last feeble remnant of a branch of the Gulf Stream – extending northwards beyond the North Cape towards the North Pole. It is entirely possible that the Chinese claims are true, that they had indeed reached the North Pole five centuries before Europeans did. Having been in a submarine on patrol near the North Pole using a series of polynyas, I can only marvel at the Chinese achievement. They could now eat the last of the dogs and drain the remaining bottles of rice wine in celebration before at last setting sail for their homeland.

Their route home from these far northern latitudes may solve yet another mystery, for the Waldseemüller map, published in 1507, shows the north coast of Siberia from the White Sea in the west to the Chukchi Peninsula and the Bering Strait in the east. The whole coast, with its rivers and islands, is clearly identifiable. If not the Chinese, who could have surveyed that enormous coastline? How was this chart drawn, showing lands that were not 'officially' discovered by Europeans for another three centuries, unless the Chinese had also travelled there? The first Russian surveys of Siberia did not take place for another two centuries, and the first Russian map did not appear until the nineteenth century.

The only logical explanation, and the DNA evidence backs it up, is that it was surveyed by Zhou Wen's fleet as it made its way back to China through the Bering Strait. As discussed previously, *The Illustrated Record of Strange Countries* features drawings of Cossack dancers and Eskimos hunting. The Eskimos could have been those of the Aleutian Islands, known to the Chinese, but the drawings of Cossacks cannot be explained in this way. There are no records of any Chinese visits to Muscovy in the first half of the fifteenth century. How could the drawings have been made without a visit to the Arctic?

Another Chinese admiral, Zhou Wen, had now completed an

epic voyage of discovery, equalling if not surpassing the extraordinary voyages of Hong Bao and Zhou Man. Yang Qing had also been at sea with a great fleet in the missing years of 1421 to 1423, and I now turned my attention to him. He may not have travelled as far as the others, remaining for the most part in waters already familiar to the Chinese, but his achievements during the voyage he made lose nothing in comparison to the successes of the other great admirals.

VI

The Voyage of
Yang Qing

SOLVING

THE

RIDDLE

W HILE HIS PEERS HAD BEEN LOCATING CANOPUS AND the Southern Cross, penetrating the polar regions and discovering new lands and continents across the globe, Grand Eunuch Yang Qing's fleet, having left Beijing a month before the rest, spent the entire voyage in the waters of the Indian Ocean. Nowhere was more familiar to Chinese seamen, for trade with the states of the Indian Ocean, particularly the vastly lucrative spice trade, was the source of much of the Chinese national wealth. Trade was carried on not just with the Spice Islands, the countries of south-east Asia, India and the Arab states of the Gulf, but with ports and states the length of the East African seaboard.

By the early fifteenth century, Arab ports along that coast traded directly with China, exporting gold, ivory and rhino horn. Rulers of East African states habitually travelled aboard the junks of Zheng He's fleets to the Forbidden City. Many were returned to their home states as the fleets made their outward voyages in 1421, and more were collected and taken to China by two of the fleets limping homeward at the end of their remarkable voyages: Yang Qing himself returned from the Indian Ocean in September 1422 bearing the envoys of seventeen states from the East African and Indian coasts, and Hong Bao sailed home in October 1423 with the ambassador of Calicut. Once again, the emperor's foreign policy had succeeded brilliantly. The Indian Ocean had become a Chinese lake.

As most of the Chinese records had been destroyed, I had as usual to look elsewhere for evidence of the route Yang Qing's fleet had taken around the Indian Ocean. I found it in a familiar source: the Cantino map of 1502. My belief that it was based on information obtained from the Chinese voyages of 1421–3 arose from Portuguese historian Antonio Galvão's comment about a map (the 1428 World Map) that 'set forth all the navigation of the East Indies, with the Cape of Boa Esperança' (see chapter 4).[1] In those days, the 'East Indies' meant India, the Indian Ocean,

Malaysia and Indonesia. It was an unequivocal declaration that the Cape of Good Hope, the Indian Ocean and the East had been set out on a map drawn early in the fifteenth century. Further corroboration that the Portuguese had a map showing the Cape of Good Hope before Dias or da Gama set sail came from the instructions of King João II of Portugal to the explorer Pêro da Covilha (c. 1450–c. 1520) in May 1487, when he sent him on a voyage to search for a sea route to India:

> He recommended him very much to enquire whether beyond the Cape of Good Hope it was possible to navigate to India . . . Then the King sent two of his trustworthy men who could speak Arabic well and were experienced travellers, Pero de Covilha, a knight of his household, and Alfonso de Paiva . . . [the future] King Dom Manuel gave them a chart (*Carta de Marear*) taken from the Map of the World [1428 chart] . . . all these showed as well as they could how they would have set about going and finding the countries the spices came from [the Moluccas].[2]

Significantly, Dias had not 'discovered' the Cape of Good Hope in May 1487, when these instructions were issued.

By the fifteenth century, the Chinese had hundreds of years' experience of navigating the Indian Ocean and the east coast of Africa; they had been visiting Africa since the time of the Tang dynasty (AD 618–907). The chronicles of Ma Huan and Fei Xin, who sailed on five voyages prior to 1421, the detailed sailing directions in the *Wu Pei Chi*, listing the courses to reach East Africa, and the accounts of medieval travellers recording the wealth of early Ming blue and white porcelain in merchants' palaces along the East African coast as far south as Sofala, all show the extent of Chinese trade and influence.

When serving in HMS *Newfoundland*, I travelled thousands of miles along the East African coast from Kenya to South Africa. In 1958 it was largely unspoilt, lined by the remains of old

Arab and Portuguese slave towns and the occasional musty British club, the last remnants of empire. One incident remains vivid in my memory. People on safari in Africa in those days carried guns, not cameras, as their essential equipment. We decided to go on a crocodile shoot in the estuary of the Limpopo, and duly borrowed the ship's motor boat, several rifles and a crate of rum. We arrived in the glassy, greasy estuary under a leaden sky, a scene Kipling would have recognized. There were no crocodiles but plenty of hippos with their ugly snouts and big ears showing above the muddy water. This was sport! We soon discovered two things: hippos' hides are tough (the bullets bounced off) and hippos do not enjoy being peppered with shot. One charged us; I can see the boat now, flying through the air upside down, its propellers whirring away as it passed overhead. Both we and the hippo retired bruised but otherwise undamaged. From then on I found my entertainment in more environmentally sensitive ways, by exploring some of the old Arab and Portuguese trading and slaving towns along the coast.

When the Portuguese first arrived in East Africa, they found that the kings and queens of Zanzibar and Pemba (in modern Tanzania)[3] were dressed in fine Chinese silk and lived in stone houses decorated with Chinese porcelain. Further evidence of the Chinese presence in the Indian Ocean comes from the Lamu archipelago or Bajun Islands, five hundred miles north-east of Zanzibar, off the northern coast of modern Kenya. The Bajun capital, Pate, was habitually used by Zheng He's fleets, and when the Portuguese arrived they found 'Bajuni', honey-skinned people with fine features. A Jesuit priest, Father Monclaro, wrote in 1569: '[They produced] very rich silk cloths, from which the Portuguese derive great profit in other Moorish cities where they are not to be had, because they are only manufactured on Pate, and are sent to the others from that place.'[4] Craftsmen from Pate also specialized in lacquerwork, another craft unknown to medieval Africa, and wove baskets using the same technique as in southern China.

An Italian anthropologist, Signor N. Puccioni, made an expedition to the Juba River in Africa in 1935 and concluded that the Bajuni at Pate were of 'a physical type absolutely different from other people in the region. The skin is rather light, in some lightly olive, and in the men you can spot flowing beards, and the women part their hair in the middle and then braid it into two side braids.'[5] One of the clans on the island, the Washanga, claimed that their forebears were Chinese sailors wrecked off the island, and their folklore relates that the King of Malindi, the most powerful local potentate, presented two giraffes to the Emperor of China.[6] This indeed happened in 1416.

Pate has changed little since the fifteenth century, save that for a while after the 1960s the island became a haunt of hippies. The people are Islamic, the men still wear the full-length white robes known as *Khanzus* with *Kofia* caps, and the women are shrouded in black capes known as *Bui Bui*. Dhows still ply the coast, their design unaltered for centuries – a triangular lateen sail and a broad, roughly planed hull sturdy enough to beach on the rocky shores. Most have coconut matting tied to their sides and a wooden 'eye' painted on their bow. Those of the Lamu archipelago are distinctive through having perpendicular bows. Dhows are remarkably fast and particularly good at tacking into the wind. Because of the stinking fish bait they carry, dhows can frequently be smelt before they are seen. I used to surface my submarine alongside to load up with flying fish, which made a very welcome variation from the standard Navy diet.

The remains of the former Arab trading town of Shanga, supposedly named after Shanghai, lie at the eastern edge of Pate Island. Today, the town is almost deserted save for mangrove pole cutters. Two centuries ago, large quantities of Chinese ceramics of the Song (960–1280) to early Ming (1368–1430) era were found there, together with the statuette of a Song lion,

A bronze Song lion statuette found off the Kenya coast.

buried as a votive offering. Even the name for these settlers, Bajuni, may be of Chinese origin: *bjun* is Chinese patois for 'long-robed'. Native people on the East African coast wore loin cloths. Long, silken robes would have been striking and unusual enough for the name to be bestowed upon the settlers.

The Chinese were already sailing those waters and they certainly had the capacity in terms of both ships and scientific knowledge to make an accurate survey of the Indian Ocean. They could measure time accurately, plot the course of the stars in the heavens, and determine accurate latitudes in both hemispheres. But could they also determine longitude? East Africa on the Cantino bears an astonishing likeness to a modern chart; the latitudes of inlets, bays and rivers are correct from the Cape of Good Hope in the south to Djibouti at the mouth of the Red Sea in the north, a straight-line distance of seven thousand kilometres. Even more startling, the longitudes on the Cantino are correct to within thirty nautical miles – a mere thirty seconds of time. How had the cartographers achieved this incredible feat?

To date there is no connection between the Chinese and the calculation of longitude. All we can say is that an accurate calculation of longitude had been achieved before 1502 when the Cantino arrived in Italy.

Finding longitude without clocks has a long history. The key is to mark the precise moment when a heavenly event occurs, one which may be seen simultaneously across the globe. One of the oldest and best-tried methods was by observing lunar eclipses and elapsed time. Ptolemy in his *Geographia* in the first century AD records Hipparchos (c. 190–120 BC) advocating this method and giving an example of its use in 330 BC. However, Hipparchos does not explain how local time was to be found, a problem because the sun must be below the horizon during a lunar eclipse.[7] It is quite possible that a few Europeans knew of Hipparchos' method by 1415, when Ptolemy's *Geographia* was brought to Venice by two Byzantines escaping the Ottomans, who were by then threatening Byzantium. The Arabs certainly knew of Hipparchos' theory.

The observatories the Chinese built and the written records they kept show that they measured the passage of time by the length of the sun's shadow. The most famous observatory, the Zhou Gong Tower fifty miles south-east of Luoyang, still stands. Built seven centuries ago, it is a truncated pyramid with stairways leading from ground level to a 25-foot-square platform. A small building in the centre of the platform houses a thin vertical rod for observation of the stars on the local meridian, and a clepsydra, a large water clock. A gnomon – a 40-foot metal measuring pole – was set in a bed of stones extending for 120 feet to the north of the tower, between two parallel troughs of water. The stones were laid perfectly flat, parallel with the water surface. The Chinese measured the sun's noon shadow cast by the gnomon on to the stones. At the equinox on the equator, the sun rises due east and sets due west. At midday it is directly above the observer and casts no shadow at all. The longest shadows are cast at sunrise and sunset, and the length of the shadows between those points determines the precise time at that particular location.

CLAVDII PTHOLOMEI ALEX
ANDRINI COSMOGRAPHIA

CHOR

ZEPHIR

UNIVERSALIS   COSMOGRAPHIA   SECVNDVM PTHOLOMEI TRA   DITIONEM

Chinese influence abroad: a contemporary lacquer chest produced in Mexico (*opposite, main image*); the Cherokee rose (*opposite, inset*) originating in China and found in North America.

Artefacts recovered from the Pandanan wreck, including a bronze ceremonial saluting cannon (*top*), a bronze mirror (*above left*), a coin of Zhu Di's reign (*centre right*) and grinding stones from Central America (*above and right*).

The Jean Rotz world map, 1542.

A magnificent Ming porcelain bowl, decorated with a phoenix and a quilin, recovered from the Pandanan wreck.

The Waldseemüller map of 1507
(reproduction coloured in the style of the period).

The Pizzigano chart of 1424 and an enlarged detail of Antilia/Puerto Rico. The rectangular, blue island above is Satanazes/Guadeloupe.

As far back as AD 721, the Chinese had realized that the length of the sun's shadow varies not only with the time of day but with the day of the year and the latitude of the observation points. Using a smaller, standard 8-foot gnomon, they made simultaneous measurements of the lengths of shadows during the summer and winter solstices at several different locations from the latitude of modern Hue in Vietnam due north to Beijing. They calculated that the shadow lengths varied by just over 3.56 inches for every 400 miles of latitude, allowing them to make corrections for their position anywhere on earth on one particular day.

However, the shadow length also varied day by day throughout the year. In one remarkable measurement they calculated that the length of the shadow was 12.3695 feet at the summer solstice and 76.7400 feet at the winter solstice. By extrapolating from the two experiments described above, the Chinese were able to make corrections for each day of the year as well as for different latitudes on the earth's surface. Furthermore, by the length of the noon shadow they could establish which day of the year it was. At this time, Europeans' only means of measuring time was hour-glasses, which could not give them either the date or any more than a rough estimate of time on any particular day.

A third adjustment was necessary to correct for the irregular motion of the earth around the sun, occasioned by the eccentricity of the earth's orbit and the difference between the equator and the ecliptic (the great circle of the celestial sphere representing the sun's apparent path through the sky during a year). This causes differences between absolute time and the apparent time obtained from the sun which reach a maximum positive difference of 14 minutes 30 seconds in February and a maximum negative difference of 16 minutes 30 seconds in November. The Chinese determined this with such accuracy that 'observations made from 1277 to 1280 are valuable for their great precision and prove incontestably the diminution of the obliquity of the ecliptic and the eccentricity of the earth's orbit between then and now'.[8] In layman's language, the earth's orbit around the sun has changed in the past seven centuries.

The Chinese replicated the Zhou Gong Tower first in Nanjing and then in Beijing after the capital was moved there. Zheng He's treasure fleets went on to build similar observatories around the world. Each was equipped with instruments for amplifying the sun's shadow and measuring its length, recognizing stars in the sky, determining the exact positions of the sun and moon at eclipses, and observing Polaris.[9] The stone tower at Rhode Island (see chapter 13) may prove to be one such example. Each observation platform thus had everything needed to measure latitude and longitude.

The Chinese had long known that the taller the gnomon and the longer the shadow it cast, the more accurate the measurement of time. However, as it grew longer, the shadow also became fainter and more attenuated. In the early Ming era, the Chinese devised a 'camera obscura' by cutting a tiny hole in the roof of the observation chamber. This resulted in a sharper shadow that was intensified through a type of magnifying glass. The long shadow could then be measured to an accuracy of one hundredth of an inch.

The outstanding precision of this Chinese measurement of time is illustrated by their calculation of the length of lunation – the interval between new moons – which they estimated at 29.530591 days.[10] This figure would produce an error of less than one second in a month. Using these methods, measurements of time could only be taken when the sun was above the horizon. Measurements after dark were made using clepsydras (water clocks) that were calibrated in daylight against a gnomon.[11] With their gnomons and clepsydras, the Chinese were able to determine the passage of time, day by day, minute by minute and second by second, both day and night. They could also forecast and make use of the full lunar eclipses that take place somewhere across the globe roughly every six months.

Solar and lunar eclipses occur when the sun, moon and earth are in line with one another and when the moon's orbit around the earth is in the same plane as the earth's orbit around the sun. In a solar eclipse, the moon's shadow blots out the sun over a small portion of the earth and it becomes night for a very short period. The spot of darkness, the umbra, travels across the earth as the moon rotates around the earth, and the earth itself rotates. Observers in different locations see the solar eclipse at different times. In a lunar eclipse, the earth is between sun and moon, and because the earth is so much bigger than the moon, its shadow obscures the moon. The great difference for astronomical observations is that the event may be seen simultaneously by observers across half the earth, whereas in a solar eclipse the event occurs only above a very small part of the earth at any one time. The ability to time a lunar eclipse with absolute precision and the fact that the same event could be seen simultaneously from different parts of the globe were to prove the vital steps in Chinese attempts to find a method of calculating longitude.

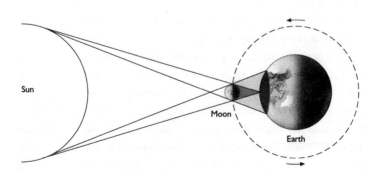

Solar eclipse

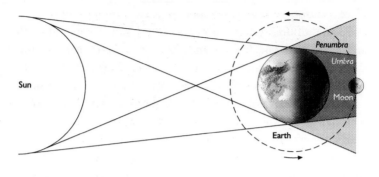

Lunar eclipse

The keys to using a lunar eclipse to determine longitude are, first, that the event is seen across half the world simultaneously, and secondly, while the eclipse is taking place, the earth's rotation makes the stars appear to move across the sky. There are four distinguishable events during an eclipse: U1 – first contact, when the moon enters the dark umbral shadow; U2 – second contact, when the moon has just fully entered the umbra and is totally covered; U3 – third contact, when the moon first starts to emerge; and U4 – fourth contact, when the moon has just fully emerged. The Chinese concentrated on U3 and used it as the basis of their calculations.

After landing in an unknown territory, Chinese navigators and astronomers would have been instructed to observe the lunar eclipse, wait until the moment when the third event (U3) occurred, then determine what star was just crossing the local meridian in the night sky. The local meridian was the imaginary longitudinal line, starting on the horizon directly north of the observer, passing over his head and ending at the horizon due south of him. The known star crossing that line at the time of the third event of the eclipse was the key sighting for the observers in the new territory, and for those back in Beijing.

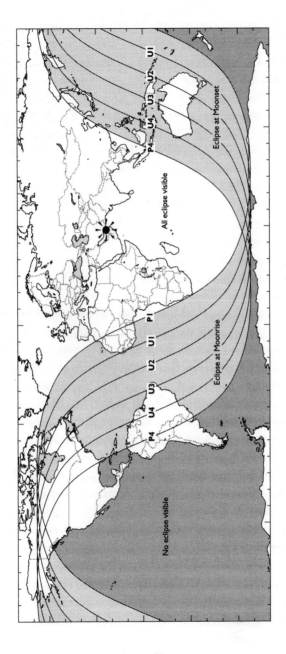

The progression of a lunar eclipse across the Earth's surface.

When the astronomer returned from his voyage, he and his colleagues in Beijing compared their data. Using their time-keeping device, calibrated from the gnomon, they timed the interval between the transits of the star observed in the new territory at the time of the eclipse and the star seen by the astronomers in Beijing at the same moment. The earth rotates 360° in twenty-four hours. If the elapsed time between the two transits was six hours, a quarter of the time it takes the earth to rotate, the difference in longitude between Beijing and the new territory would be a quarter of the total longitude around the world – 90°, one quarter of 360°. Errors could be reduced by timing each of the four events of the eclipse, U1, U2, U3 and U4, then averaging the results. By observing the same event at different locations around the globe and fixing the exact time at which this event took place, the Chinese could then compare their results. By determining the differences in the time when the event took place, as observed from the separate locations, they could then calculate the difference in longitude.

Professor John Oliver, Professor of Astronomy at the University of Florida, put the theory to the test by observing the lunar eclipse of 16 and 17 July 2000. He set up teams of observers across the Pacific from Tahiti to Malacca, near Singapore, choosing the same sites as the Chinese observation platforms (Appendix 4). The average longitudinal errors produced by this method were minuscule: 1.1 degrees in Tahiti, 0.1 degree in New Zealand, 0.1 degree in Melbourne and zero degrees in Singapore. This has startling implications. In Professor Oliver's experiments, there was a six-mile longitudinal error between Singapore and New Zealand, and none between New Zealand and Australia. In all, longitude was calculated across one-third of the world's surface, a distance of some eight thousand miles, with a maximum error anywhere of just sixty-six miles. And Professor Oliver's observers were amateurs; with more training and experience, the errors could have been reduced even further. Using their observation platforms at the same sites, the Chinese would have determined longitude just as accurately as Professor Oliver's team, maybe more so. The brilliance of the method is that, unlike calculations for latitude, neither a sextant nor a clock is required.

Having accurately determined the longitude of Malacca near Singapore, for example, the Chinese fleets could then use Malacca as a base to repeat the process using the observation platforms and gnomons on their other bases around the Indian Ocean: Semudera (Sumatra), the Andamans, Dondra Head (Sri Lanka), Cochin and Calicut on the Malabar coast of India, Malindi and Zanzibar in East Africa, and the Seychelle and Maldive archipelagos, all of which appear on the *Wu Pei Chi*. If a sufficiently large fleet was deployed, there is no reason why longitudes across the whole of the Indian Ocean should not have been established in a single lunar eclipse. Men would have been despatched to different locations in readiness to take readings of the lunar eclipse, all on the same night. They could then return to base to compare measurements.

One can imagine the ships of the great fleet dispersing across the Indian Ocean to take their measurements, the eunuch captains anxious to arrive in good time, the sailors doubtless far more interested in meeting the local women, renowned for their beauty and sexual appetite. They welcomed sailors with open arms, as Marco Polo noted: 'They are all black-skinned and go stark naked, both males and females, except for gay loin cloths: they regard no form of lechery or sensual indulgence as sin. Their marriage customs are such that a man may wed his cousin german or his father's widow or his brother's. And these customs prevail throughout the Indies.'[12] However, the crews would have had to postpone their pleasures until the business of the fleet had been completed and the lunar eclipse timed. The results of this Chinese expertise can be seen in the Cantino map of 1502, where the coast of East Africa is depicted with such accuracy that it appears to have been drawn with the aid of satellite navigation. Who else but the Chinese could have drawn this astounding chart two centuries before Europeans had clocks, and four centuries before they knew how to separate the South Pole from the magnetic pole? Was there even the remotest possibility that it could have been an earlier, unknown Portuguese voyage?

The Portuguese had no accurate method of calculating longitude; in 1541, thirty-nine years after the Cantino was drawn, a Portuguese attempt to determine the longitude of Mexico City by the measurement of a solar eclipse put it nearly 1,500 miles too far to the west. Yet the Cantino had longitudes correct to within thirty miles along thousands of miles of coastline. The reason was that the Portuguese were using solar eclipses, the Chinese lunar eclipses. The Portuguese did not have enough ships to determine longitude by trigonometry.

Three expeditions to the Indian Ocean had returned to Portugal before the Cantino was made. Vasco da Gama visited Sofala, Kilwa and Mombasa in 1498–9. At Malindi, he took an Arab pilot who guided him directly to Calicut, therefore he could not have charted the coast north of Malindi. Pedro Álvares Cabral's second expedition set off in 1499 and returned in June 1501. Early in the voyage, his fleet was hit by a terrible storm and four ships were lost. One, commanded by Diego Dias, sailed along the east coast of Madagascar, and from there to Mogadishu. His ship was severely damaged and he lost many men. On his voyage home, Dias stood well out to sea, and the only part of the East African coast he could have charted was between Mogadishu and Berbera. Cabral's broken fleet limped from Sofala to Kilwa, then to Malindi.

Thus none of the three fleets that arrived back in Lisbon before the Cantino was drawn had spent long enough on the East African coast to make such an accurate cartographic survey, and none could have charted the entire coast. Moreover, the Cantino covers about nine million square miles of ocean. It would have taken forty ships at least two years to carry out such a vast survey, an undertaking far beyond Portugal's resources at the time. Indeed, it took sixty years for the Portuguese to survey Africa's west coast. To expect a few battered caravels to have done the same on the east coast while simultaneously charting nine million square miles of ocean and six island archipelagos in the few months they were in the Indian Ocean before 1502 is as realistic as expecting a lone surveyor to map a continent with nothing more than a measuring stick and a horse and cart.

Having ruled out the Portuguese, I wondered if Arab navigators could have been the original cartographers. I made an exhaustive examination of the wonderful collection assembled by the wealthy and dedicated map collector Prince Youssuf Kamal, copies of which are in the Map Library of the British Library, but found not one detailed Arabic chart of the east coast of Africa in that whole monumental collection. The best Arabic medieval maps, such as those of Al Idrisi, bear no comparison in detail or accuracy to the Cantino of 1502.

Admiral Yang Qing journeyed much less far than the other Chinese admirals, yet the task he had been set was as vital and as demanding as those of Hong Bao, Zhou Man and Zhou Wen, and his success matches their towering achievements, for by the end of that voyage his men had perfected a method of determining longitude over three centuries before John Harrison's invention of the chronometer.

Though the Western world is largely silent on the origin of these extraordinary world maps, now correct both for latitude and longitude, the inscription on the stone erected by Zheng He in commemoration of his voyages shows where the credit is due: 'And now as a result of the voyages the distances and courses between the distant lands may be calculated.' It was another towering achievement by the Chinese fleets, one that should have burned like a beacon in the annals of global history. Instead, it was to be snuffed out and forgotten, along with the discovery of the Americas, Australia, Antarctica and the Arctic; Europeans would claim the glory that should have belonged to the great Chinese admirals and their fleets. The Portuguese were to lead this European wave of exploration and colonization. They more than any other nation benefited from the hard-won Chinese knowledge of the oceans and new lands that lay beyond them.

VII

Portugal Inherits the Crown

16

WHERE

THE

EARTH

ENDS

IN JUNE 1421, AT THE SAME TIME AS THE CHINESE FLEET WAS rounding the Cape of Good Hope to head north for the Cape Verde Islands, far out in the Atlantic a little caravel – a small Portuguese sailing ship – lay at anchor in a wooded bay of the uninhabited island of Madeira. The great wave of European expansion and colonization that was to spread across the globe and, for better or worse, change the lives and destinies of billions of people had begun, in the most unobtrusive manner. This first small, hesitant step was taken by the Portuguese on their own initiative, but within three years news of the great Chinese discoveries and charts showing those far-flung lands and seas would be filtering into Portugal. No longer would they be sailing into the unknown.

On that June day in 1421, the Portuguese explorer João Gonçalves Zarco and his family must have felt they had arrived in paradise. A kaleidoscope of fish circled the caravel – black espadas, blue tunny, silver-striped mackerel, red bream and grey mullet – and sea lions were Zarco's only competitors for this bounty of nature. Streams of crystal water tumbled into a small lagoon, rich in langoustines and snails. The air was heavy with the sweet smell of jasmine and alive with the songs of birds that had never learned to fear man. Beyond the vivid banks of orchids, azaleas, begonias and jacarandas lining the Madeiran shore stretched mile upon mile of fennel interspersed with clumps of passion fruit.[1]

The same streams, the Ribeira de Santa Luzia and the Ribeira de São João, still tumble into the Atlantic, but in place of the lush fields of green fennel are now the quiet streets of Madeira's capital, Funchal. The statue of its founder dominates the Avenida Zarco. The Santa Catarina chapel, erected by Zarco's wife, stands on another street named after him, and next to it is the statue of Prince Henry the Navigator, the man who had made the expedition possible.

The colonization of Madeira, begun on that June day in 1421, was a pivotal moment in the history of European exploration. Zarco, a knight in the service of Prince Henry, discovered the island by accident. In December 1418, Zarco and Tristão Vaz Teixeira ('Vaz'), another Portuguese knight who had loyally served Prince Henry, had been ordered to explore the African coast down to Guinea, two thousand miles south of Portugal, but their ship was blown off course and driven before the wind to Porto Santo, an island sixty kilometres north-east of Madeira[2] then populated by crying seabirds and *câmara de lobos* (sea lions). One sunset, while on the island, Zarco spied a smudge on the horizon in the direction of the setting sun. They set off a week later and took formal possession of the new land in the name of the King of Portugal, of Prince Henry and the Order of Christ, naming the mountainous, densely forested island 'Ilha da Madeira', the Island of Wood. They returned almost immediately to Portugal where Zarco, Vaz and their companions were received with acclaim. Zarco was knighted and given the title Count of Câmara de Lobos.

Prince Henry warmly endorsed Zarco's plan to colonize the islands and financed two further expeditions, providing Zarco with ships and stores. The island was to be divided in two, with Vaz governor of the northern half and Zarco of the southern. Another of Zarco's shipmates, Bartolomeu Perestrello, was sent to establish a colony on the neighbouring island of Porto Santo. It was an ill-starred choice. Perestrello's children had a pet rabbit, a doe. It gave birth to a litter during the voyage to Porto Santo, and when the colonizers settled on the island the rabbits multiplied so fast without natural predators to control their numbers that the island was soon reduced to a desert.

In contrast, the colonization of Madeira was an enormous success and vividly demonstrated the benefits of overseas exploration. Prince Henry pioneered the introduction of grape vines and sugar cane from Crete, which flourished in the warm, damp climate. The famous Madeira wines made from the grapes were exported throughout Europe, and sugar cane production showed equally spectacular profits. Entrepreneurs flocked to Prince Henry's court to participate in future bonanzas, and Portuguese explorers set sail on ever more adventurous voyages, in the vanguard of an expansion that was to see European nations dominate the world for another five hundred years.

Henry was the third son of King John I of Portugal and his wife, Queen Philippa, daughter of England's John of Gaunt. With English help, John had led an uprising in 1383 and replaced the old Portuguese nobility with a new landed aristocracy, the House of Avis, loyal only to himself. John proved a cautious and pragmatic king, negotiating a defensive treaty with England and exploiting that arrangement to make an uneasy truce with Castile. The existing treaty between the separate Spanish kingdoms of Castile and Aragon left the whole peninsula at peace. John's foreign policy was equally cautious, and he was particularly careful not to antagonize Castile by interfering in its sphere of influence abroad.

It was an era of massive Christian confidence throughout the peninsula. After six centuries, the Moors had finally been driven out of the Algarve, their last stronghold in Portugal. King Sancho I of Portugal had invaded the Algarve in 1189, and by 1249 the whole region, once the westernmost province of the majestic Arab caliphate of Cordoba, was in royal hands, allowing the capital to be moved south from Coimbra to Lisbon. With the *Reconquista* complete, Portugal's soldiers, like their counterparts in Aragon, had nowhere to go but overseas.

John and Philippa were devout Christians, but their court was one of the most enlightened in Europe, a centre for men of scholarship and ability regardless of religion. China remained years ahead of Europe in terms of science, technology and, arguably, culture, but fifteenth-century Portugal was beginning to flower and would quickly grow into the principal European centre for voyages of discovery and exploration. It was an age of rapid change, and his parents ensured that young Prince Henry received an appropriate education. In 1415, just out of his teens, he was entrusted with the command of the Portuguese attack on Ceuta, an important Arab port on the north coast of Africa over-looking the Strait of Gibraltar. Plans were well advanced when Queen Philippa fell gravely ill. As she lay dying, she gave a sword to Henry with the words, 'I give you, Henry, this ... sword. It is as strong as you are. To you I commend all the lords, knights, squires and those of noble blood.'³ She also insisted that Henry proceed with the attack on Ceuta rather than remain at her bedside.

In past centuries, the Moors had launched three invasions of Spain using troops drawn from Senegal to Arabia, and Islamic rulers still controlled a vast empire. Even for someone as daring and resolute as Henry, an attack on Islam's heartland was a colossal gamble, the first European invasion of Africa since that of the Emperor Justinian eight hundred years earlier. Henry's army was drawn from all over Europe, the Christian forces uniting under the banner of a new crusader prince. The attack on Ceuta was preceded by all manner of ruses to disguise the real plan; Portugal even declared war on Holland as a distraction to mislead the Moors. When the assault on Ceuta began, Henry handled his forces so skilfully that the battle was quickly over.

The capture of Ceuta was the first European victory over the Moors in their own territories, an event of great moral and psychological significance. A despatch rider was sent post haste with news of the victory to the Holy Roman Emperor Sigismund and the royal houses of Europe. Henry's success brought him invitations to take up all manner of commands – from the Pope to head the papal armies, and from Henry V of England to lead a crusade against the infidels – but he declined all offers, preferring to act as his father's representative in Ceuta, from where he set about building a Portuguese empire based on the wealth of the gold trade that stemmed from the capture of the city.

The Mediterranean world cried out for gold; Arab camel caravans plodded across the Sahara from Mali through Marrakesh, Fez and Meknes – glorious, immensely prosperous cities – to Ceuta. Capturing Ceuta had given Henry's army a secure harbour on African soil, and the opportunity to intercept bullion shipments and strike at the wealth of the fabled Moroccan cities, in the process depriving the Arabs of the money to lubricate their trading routes. Henry had a stranglehold on one of Islam's prime sources of wealth.

Arabs had enriched Portugal and Spain in many ways, and were skilled at exploiting the trading opportunities presented by their far-flung empire. They brought Syrian engineers to irrigate Portugal's Algarve and improve rice cultivation, and developed the corn lands of the Alentejo, where they also introduced cotton and sugar cane. 'Persian' carpets were woven in Bera and Caleena, Chinese methods of paper manufacture were copied in Játiva, and 'Moroccan' leather and textiles were made in Cordoba where there were thirteen thousand leather workers and weavers. Islamic ships carried the finished products from the Tagus estuary in Portugal to Cairo and North Africa.

At the time of the attack on Ceuta, Portugal was still a medieval land, riddled with superstition. Books described the incredible wealth of lands beyond the seas, the extraordinary challenges that awaited explorers and the strange people and monsters lying in wait to attack them. On the way to India there was 'a sea so hot that it boils like water over a fire, and it is all green; and in that sea serpents breed bigger than crocodiles, having wings wherewith they fly, and so venomous that all people run from them in fear ... because [the serpent] grew in the boiling sea, no fire can burn it ... in that sea is a whirlpool, so terrible that men fear to venture'.[4] India was a land 'of wild beasts that are in the wilderness, blue dragons, serpents and other ravening beasts that eat all they can get. There are many elephants, all white; some are blue and of other colours, quite

Sea monsters from Sebastian Münster's Cosmographia, 1546.

numberless; there are also many unicorns and lions and other hideous beasts.'[5] In those far-off lands, men had heads in the middle of their chests, their eyes were in their shoulders; 'They have two small holes, all round, instead of eyes, and their mouth is flat also without lips.' Women hid snakes in their vaginas 'which stung the husbands on their penises'.[6] By taking Ceuta, Prince Henry and his countrymen had the opportunity to learn the true facts. In his four years in the city, Henry became familiar with the blinding African sun, the bite of sand in the air when the wind comes off the desert, the hot dusty streets, the soft smell of cloves and the extraordinary clarity of desert nights.

Ceuta was also an important port, attracting a cosmopolitan population, and a home to fine Islamic universities. The Arabs revered scholarship and had carefully stored the masterpieces of Greece and Rome, including the geographical works of Ptolemy. They did not subscribe to myths and superstitions about the world around them. They had been trading from the Atlantic to the Pacific for centuries. The Arab geographer Al Barouwi had charted North and East Africa from the Atlantic to Zanzibar by 1315, and in 1327 another famous Arab traveller, Al Dimisqui, had described the real world of the East peopled by ordinary beings and reached by sea voyages across natural oceans. Although the Arabs had not drawn accurate maps of Africa or the Indian Ocean, they did know the relative positions of Africa,

India, China and the Far East as early as 1340, when Hama Allah Moustawfi Qazami drew his mappa mundi based on the work of Ptolemy. The Arabs described the sea route to India in 1342 and produced an encyclopedia of Asia in 1391, giving detailed descriptions of the major towns, cities and mosques.

It must have been a life-changing moment for Prince Henry to learn that Arabs had traded over the whole known world for centuries. He had only to follow in the wake of Arab dhows to discover those same exotic lands. The whole world lay at his feet if he could build an ocean-going fleet, and to do that he had to return to Portugal. By Christmas 1419 he had chosen Sagres in south-west Portugal as his permanent base. There Henry the Navigator built a *forteleza* (fortress) and founded a chapel, a hospital, and the school of navigation that earned him his name and changed the course of world history. A painting in Lisbon's Maritime Museum depicts Henry's court at Sagres, peopled by Catalan sea captains, Jewish cartographers, Arab astronomers, Portuguese knights, men-at-arms, sailmakers, priests, ship-wrights, physicians, sailors and court retainers, all of whom lived, prayed, ate and worked together.

There are some parts of the ocean where a mariner knows his position by the smell of the sea. The Grand Banks off Newfoundland is one, the Straits of Malacca another, but most potent of all is the scent of pines off Sagres on a warm summer's night, a smell that for me always brings back memories of voyages to the East, for after Sagres one alters course to the south-east for the Mediterranean and the lands beyond. Even today, Sagres is daunting. It stands some two hundred feet above the Atlantic, jutting out into the ocean, looking out over Cape St Vincent, passing ships no more than a distant blur on the horizon. Below, long rolling breakers smash into the cliffs, their dull boom a constant background to the haunting cries of sea-birds. In winter and spring the promontory is lashed by rain; at many other times it is veiled in spray and sea-mist. The lush vegetation of the mainland gives way to stony scrub; neither flowers nor trees grow. A great grey wall, its stones hewn from the cliffs, guards the entrance, and through a dark oak door one can glimpse a row of austere houses and the simple chapel of St Catherine.

To the Portuguese, Sagres was the end of the world, 'where the earth ends and sea begins'.[7] Closer inspection reveals that the promontory was an inspired choice as a base. Each winter and spring, the prevailing north-west wind sucks vast quantities of water out of the Atlantic and dumps it onto the mountains of the Sierra Monchique; despite the torrid summer heat – it is further south than most of Spain – the area is sub-tropical in character. A day on horseback takes the rider into foothills where lush, verdant forests are interspersed with cork and oak trees, and white almonds, oleanders, hibiscus, lilies and geraniums thrive on the heat and moisture. Groves of orange and lemon trees, laden with fruit, grow among dark pine forests. Cabbages are planted beneath date palms, and vines are cultivated on trellises among the heather. The edge of the continental shelf is only a few miles offshore from Sagres where the ocean falls steeply to two thousand fathoms, over two miles deep. The seas teem with fish; over a hundred species have been found around Cape St Vincent. Fleets of small boats bring in heavy catches of cod, anchovies and sardines for drying and salting. The cliffs afford shelter, the small harbours safe mooring against the prevailing northerly storms.

Here, in the south-west Algarve, Henry the Navigator had access to everything necessary to build, fit out and provision a fleet – limitless supplies of soft pine for ribs, resinous pine for planking, oak for rudders and keels, gum for caulking, wool and hides to clothe the crews, bamboo and reeds for their beds and baskets. Provisions for a two-month voyage – salt fish, rice, wheat, olives, dates, oranges, lemons and almonds – were in abundant supply. Sailors also need alcohol; as in Henry's day, the

A Portuguese caravel in full lateen rigging.

full, fruity and strong Alentejo wine, made from Periquita grapes, is still fermented in large earthenware jars cast from the heavy red soil.

When Henry arrived at Sagres, Catalan cogs – small cargo vessels – were evolving into good ocean-going ships, but they were still square-rigged. From his experiences at Ceuta, Henry knew that Arab dhows bound for the eastern Mediterranean spent much of their voyage in light, variable winds, and had to be able to sail into the wind. Square-rigged ships, sailing always before the wind, often had no rudder. Dhows had rudders, and the Arabs had refined the lateen (triangular) sail so that two men, hoisting it on a simple block and tackle, could control a large area of canvas. Henry incorporated a stern rudder into the design of his new sailing ship, the caravel, a cross between a Catalan cog and an Arab dhow – the design lives on in the modern ketch – but of all the improvements Henry introduced, none surpasses his brilliant adaptation of the Arabic lateen sail. The later caravels had lateen sails on mizzen and main masts and a square sail on the foremast, and could be converted at sea to be either square- or lateen-rigged. A mariner could sail south-wards from Portugal square-rigged before the prevailing wind, then convert to lateen sails to return north into the wind. Although tiny in comparison to Chinese junks, caravels were much more nimble and manoeuvrable.

Henry's next problem was to enable his captains to measure their position on the earth's surface. Determining the correct position of new discoveries and then finding the way home depended upon knowing latitude and steering the correct course, and that in turn depended upon the compass. Arabs had used compasses for centuries, after obtaining the device from the Chinese with whom they regularly swapped nautical know-ledge. However, the Chinese knowledge of navigation, astronomy and the means by which latitude and longitude could be calculated, perfected on the last great voyage of the treasure fleets from 1421 to 1423, remained theirs alone. Europeans were still floundering in their wake decades, and in the case of longitude centuries, later.

Henry was a dedicated mathematician, and by the late 1460s, just after Henry's death, his astronomers, assisted by Arabs, had solved the problem of latitude. Arabs had an old civilization and they, too, were dedicated mathematicians. In Henry's era they were far better educated than Europeans and were used to sail-ing the Mediterranean and Indian Oceans out of sight of land. To this day, many stars in the sky – Betelgeuse, Aldebaran, Mikah – have Arab names, and British Admiralty charts credit Arab navigators in the use of names such as Ras Nungwi and Ras Al Khaimah. Arab navigators knew that the altitude of the meridian passage of the sun – its maximum height in the sky at noon each day – could be measured by lining up the sun with the

A European determining latitude, from Pedro de Medina's *Regimiento de Navigación*, 1563.

horizon. Either wooden or brass instruments would do; one of the simplest and best was designed by Gil Eannes, one of Henry's captains, in the 1460s.

The sun's maximum height varies day by day throughout the year, and the difference between this daily height and the height at its lowest point in midwinter was named the declination of the sun. The Arabs had discovered that the sun's declination, when subtracted from its height at midday, gave the latitude of a place in the northern hemisphere.[8] In 1473, Regiomontanus, the Viennese astronomer who had attended Henry's court, produced a set of 'ephemerides tables' giving day-by-day declinations of the sun. A captain in the distant oceans now merely had to measure with a quadrant – a rudimentary type of sextant – the altitude of the sun at its meridian passage, then consult the tables to find the sun's declination for that day. By subtracting declination from altitude the mariner knew how many degrees south (and hence how many miles) he was from home. With a caravel and a quadrant, sailing back to Sagres was relatively simple. The mariner sailed due north, following the Pole Star by night and setting a course opposite to the sun's noon position by day, until he reached the latitude of Sagres, whereupon he altered course to the east, keeping to that same latitude until he could see Cape St Vincent or smell the scent of pines in the air.

By 1420 Henry had designed and built an ocean-going caravel that could remain at sea for weeks at a time and could return home. He knew from the Arabs that the medieval fables of monsters and boiling seas were nonsense, and that the oceans of the world could be crossed to discover new worlds. The last piece of the jigsaw was the production of accurate charts to enable his captains to reach the East. In 1416, Prince (Dom) Pedro, Henry's elder brother, 'seized with the desire to gain enlightenment by travel through the principal countries of Europe and Western Asia',[9] had set off on an odyssey to garner every possible piece of information about the world beyond the Mediterranean. King John had invested a substantial sum in Florentine bonds to cover his son's travelling expenses, and the King of Spain had provided him with a retinue of servants, translators and scholars. He travelled through Spain, Palestine, the Holy Land, the Ottoman Empire – 'the Grand Sultan of Babylon' – Rome, the Holy Roman Empire, Hungary, Denmark, England and Venice, and 'at the end of twelve years' travel Dom Pedro returned in 1428 to Portugal'.[10]

He had departed the year after Ceuta was taken, a time when the Portuguese were lionized throughout Christian Europe. All had shared in the excitement of Prince Henry's daring gamble to form a bridgehead in Africa, the heartland of Islam, and now Dom Pedro was treated as a conquering hero at whose feet Europe lay. He could go where he wanted, ask what questions he wished and receive all the knowledge his hosts possessed. In England, he had been created a Knight of the Garter; the Doge had personally entertained him in Venice; the King of Spain had showered him with gold; and Emperor Sigismund had given him valuable land in the March of Treviso, a fertile province a few miles north of Venice that had served as his base from 1421 to 1425.[11]

In many ways, Dom Pedro was the ideal complement to his younger brother. Henry was a practical man of action, Pedro a dreamer and a visionary of immense charm who was appalled by European conflicts and fired his hosts with his ideal of uniting Christians in Africa, India and Cathay (China) by voyages of discovery. His twelve-year odyssey was a brilliant success, and he returned to Portugal in 1428 with 'a map of the world, which had all the parts of the world and earth described'.[12] This seemingly incredible map showed the 'Streight of Magelan' and the Cape of Good Hope sixty years before Dias and nearly a hundred years before Magellan set sail (see p. 107). Until it appeared, most European maps of the world had Jerusalem at their centre, their edges patrolled by wild beasts. This new knowledge of the world, hard-won by the Chinese during their great voyages of exploration, was to become the driving force behind the European voyages of discovery.

Dom Pedro, like Henry, had been well educated in an enlightened court, and tutored by Venetian scholars. When the princes were young, the Council of Pisa (1409) had been convened, primarily in an attempt to end the thirty-year 'Great Schism' between the rival popes established in Rome and Avignon. It failed in its aim – the attempt to depose the rivals and install a new pope merely led to there being three popes instead of two – but Portugal sent a major mission to that council, and Dom Pedro and Prince Henry took great interest in its other deliberations. They could not have failed as a result to become acquainted with a revolutionary work, Ptolemy's *Geographia*, long forgotten in Europe but now translated into Latin. It was brought to that council and delivered to the newest pope, Alexander V.

The rediscovery of the *Geographia* created a sensation in

Europe, for it maintained that the earth was not flat, but a sphere – something the Chinese already knew – and set out the principles of latitude and longitude by which man could determine his own position and that of new discoveries on that sphere. More than anything else, the reintroduction of Ptolemy into the mainstream of European political life revolutionized cartography and exploration. But brilliant as the *Geographia* was, it contained no maps, only explanations of how to use information to make them. This deficiency was rectified when the Byzantine cartographers Lappacino and Bonnisegni fled the Turks encircling Byzantium, to settle in Venice in 1415. They brought with them a number of maps based upon Ptolemy's *Geographia* showing Africa and India in their correct positions. At the latest, Dom Pedro would have known of these maps by 1428, when he paid his state visit to Venice, though almost certainly he knew of them by 1424, when Niccolò da Conti returned from his travels.

There are two versions of how da Conti returned to what we now call Italy. One school contends that he had returned from the East by 1424, but he had come in fear of his life, in disguise and under the *nom de guerre* 'Bartholomew of Florence' because he was a renegade who had converted to Islam at a time of intense religious persecution and wished to avoid being burned like John Huss, the Czech protestant reformer who had been executed for heresy only nine years earlier.[13] The other school claims that Dom Pedro instructed a famed Franciscan friar, Alberto de Sarteano, to bring da Conti back from Cairo, where he was in hiding, on the promise of absolution.[14] Fra Sarteano succeeded, escorting da Conti to Florence, and Dom Pedro then immediately summoned his envoy to Portugal for a complete debrief of his voyage with the Chinese fleet.

Dom Pedro's principal aim in this was to link Portugal with isolated Christian communities in the East supposedly founded by the apostle Saint Thomas, to encircle Islam and to find a new way to Cathay – a route urgently needed, for while Dom Pedro was travelling, the borders of Egypt were sealed by the Mamluk sultans who ruled the country. By the end of 1421, the Ottomans, who were already in possession of Asia Minor, had surrounded Byzantium and taken control of the terminus of the Silk Road across Asia. An impenetrable barrier had been erected across the eastern Mediterranean and the Near East.

Dom Pedro achieved a magnificent intelligence coup by retaining Fra Mauro and Poggio Bracciolini, the Papal Secretary, and by debriefing the 'renegade', Niccolò da Conti. By doing so he obtained the knowledge that da Conti ('Bartholomew of Florence') had acquired in twenty years' sailing the world – from India to the Cape Verde and Falkland Islands, to Australia and China. Dom Pedro now knew that Cathay and the Spice Islands could be reached by sailing westwards.[15]

The cartographer Paolo Toscanelli (1397–1482) made the same claim after meeting da Conti and extracting every scrap of usable information from him. He later relayed the material in a letter to Christopher Columbus:

> I notice your splendid and lofty desire to sail to the regions of the East [China] by those of the West as is shown by the chart which I send you, which would be better shown in the shape of a round sphere . . . not only is the said voyage possible, but it is sure and certain, and of honour and countless gain . . .
>
> I have had most fully the good and true information . . . of other merchants who have long trafficked in those parts, men of great authority.[16]

Toscanelli sent a map to Columbus showing the westwards route across the Atlantic via Antilia. He also passed on da Conti's information to Behain of Bohemia[17] (1459–1507), who was working for the Portuguese government. Behain then showed the strait leading from the Atlantic to the Pacific on both the globe he produced in 1492 and on his maps, and Magellan acknowledged that he had seen them in Portugal before he set sail.[18] A number of other accounts describe Magellan examining Toscanelli's charts in the Portuguese treasury. One can only imagine the extraordinary impact these charts, based on the Chinese voyages of 1421 to 1423, must have had on the Europeans, for they traced the boundaries of vast, unknown oceans and of lands such as South America and the Antarctic whose very existence had previously been clouded and uncertain.

Toscanelli's letter to Columbus and the statements of Magellan and his diarist Pigafetta are further evidence that, long before Magellan set sail, the Portuguese knew that the quickest way to China lay westwards through the strait later named after Magellan but first navigated and charted by the Chinese. The information came from Niccolò da Conti, 'the merchant who travelled in those parts'.[19]

With the reappearance of Niccolò da Conti, I felt I had almost come full circle. It had been in every sense a long and extraordinary journey since I had first seen a mention of his name and his presence in Calicut at the time Zheng He's treasure fleet passed through the port. It had led me to every corner of the globe, and everywhere I had found traces of the Chinese voyages da Conti had described. Now it was clear that the Portuguese and Spanish had read and heard the same accounts and been inspired to make their own voyages of discovery.

Having learned of the existence of new lands beyond the seas from da Conti in 1424, Dom Pedro carried back to Portugal in 1428 a map of the world showing 'all the parts of the world and earth'[20] – Africa, the Caribbean (Antilia), North and South America, the Arctic and Antarctic, India, Australia and China. The information it contained was hugely valuable, and for over a century afterwards the Portuguese went to considerable trouble to prevent any knowledge of it from reaching competing European powers.

Coupled with Henry's improvements to navigation and ship design, the world map revolutionized European exploration for all time. Henry knew that if he could fund his expeditions, Portugal could dominate the world. He needed substantial capital, for there was a large retinue to feed and house, a hospital to maintain, a chapel to be endowed and caravels to be built and fitted out for voyages that might last for months.

The Pope had appointed Prince Henry Grand Master of the Order of Christ in 1420, and its Red Cross motif adorned the sails of his caravels. Funded by tax revenues, the order's principal duties were to defend Portugal and to lead crusades against the infidel. Both Niccolò da Conti and Marco Polo had described a series of Christian states extending all across India.[21] Dom Pedro and Prince Henry now had the knowledge that would enable Portuguese seafarers to reach those Christian communities, and the Order of Christ could fulfil its destiny by linking them.

The order, then, was Henry's prime source of funds, but even its substantial wealth would have been swiftly exhausted without a return on the capital invested in those voyages of discovery. The return was to come first through the colonization of Madeira, an uninhabited island with fertile soil, abundant rainfall and plentiful sunshine. As we have already seen, by June 1421 João Gonçalves Zarco had claimed the island for Portugal and begun the work of planting crops that were to yield huge profits for Portuguese investors and drive the search for new territories to explore, exploit and colonize.

Colonization was carried out methodically, and the governors of Madeira were required to produce monthly reports of progress. Although vast areas of virgin forest were devastated by fires soon after settlers began to arrive, it proved to be a blessing in disguise. By clearing the forest and enriching the soil with potash, the fires merely speeded the growth of an island economy based on the planting of grape vines and sugar cane, and ever larger quantities of sugar and Madeira wine were produced and exported.

The island provided a vivid illustration of the commercial gains to be won from successful exploration, and as increasing numbers of Portuguese entrepreneurs beat a path to Henry's court, financing voyages of exploration became easier. In the earlier years the strain of fund-raising had taken a heavy toll on the resources of the Order of Christ and on Henry's stamina, but after colonizing Madeira he was financially secure. Portugal could now begin to look further across the oceans to the west. If one small island could yield such wealth, what untold riches might be made from new colonies beyond the seas? Those lands were not unknown to Prince Henry and his sea-captains, for they had the Chinese charts to lead and guide them.

COLONIZING

THE

NEW

WORLD

THE PORTUGUESE LOST LITTLE TIME IN EXTENDING THEIR search for new territories in which colonies could be established westwards across the Atlantic: 'As early as 1431 we see Prince Henry the Navigator send Gonzalo Velho Cabral in search of the islands marked on the map which Dom Pedro, the son of King João I, had brought from Italy in 1428.'[1]

As they voyaged further and further, Prince Henry's caravels must have quickly discovered Antilia – Puerto Rico – and established a colony there. Andrea Bianco's 1436 chart describes the Sargasso Sea with the Portuguese name for seaweed, *mar de baga* – powerful evidence that they had reached the Caribbean, for the Sargasso Sea, a mass of floating seaweed, is unique in the world. It could only have been described by someone who had sailed there; and because of the circular wind and current systems, it can only be easily reached from Europe after passing through the Caribbean. The Portuguese could not have been the creators of the first map showing these lands, for of course it predates their voyages. I could only wonder if those first Portuguese settlers had found traces of the Chinese voyages – a carved stone, fragments of porcelain, utensils or artefacts, or a once neat but long overgrown plantation of rice. Would they have paused to wonder at them, or merely shrugged their shoulders, dismissed them as native curiosities and turned their minds from high-flown thoughts to the gritty reality of winning a living from the soil?

Unlike Guadeloupe, Puerto Rico was populated by peaceable people. If the Portuguese did settle here in 1431, some ten years after the Chinese visit, their descendants should have survived to greet Columbus or later explorers. Columbus's first visit to Puerto Rico in 1493, during his second voyage to the New World, was a fleeting one. He was in a hurry to reach the Spanish garrison of La Navidad and the gold mines in Hispaniola, the next island to the west, and visited a single port in Puerto Rico, remaining only a few days. Nonetheless, Columbus found the port to be a civilized one:

King Ferdinand sending Columbus to the New World. From Giuliano Dati's
verse rendition of Columbus's first letter to the King of Spain published
in 1493.

The fleet moved on past Saint Ursula and her eleven thousand
virgins [the Virgin Islands] till it reached Porto Rico which was the
home of most of the captives taking refuge with the Spaniards
[refugees taken aboard at Guadeloupe]. On the west end they
found a fine harbour abounding in fish. Here was a native village
with a public square, a main road, a terrace – all in all quite an
artistic home-like place.[2]

As I dug deeper into Columbus's records, I found another
story: 'A storm driven ship landed at the Isle of the Seven Cities
[Antilia] in the time of the Infante D Henriques [Henry the
Navigator].' The crew were welcomed by the inhabitants,
invited in good Portuguese to attend divine service and urged to
remain until their ruler showed up.[3] Prince Henry, of course,

had died long before Columbus set sail. The story was corroborated by the sixteenth-century Portuguese historian Antonio Galvão:

> So in this year, also 1447, it happened that there came to Portugal a ship through the streight of Gibraltar, and being taken with a great tempest, was forced to run westward more willingly than the men would [wish], and at last they fell upon an island which had seven cities, and the people spake the Portuguese tongue, and they demanded if the Moors did yet trouble Spain . . . The boatswain of the ship brought home a little of the sand, and sold it unto a gold-smith of Lisbon, out of which they had a good quantity of gold.
>
> Dom Pedro understanding this, being then governor of the realm, caused all the things thus brought home, and made known, to be recorded in the House of Justice.
>
> There be some that think that those islands whereupon the Portugals were thus driven were the Antiles or New Spain, alleging good reasons for their opinion.[4]

It was compelling evidence that the Portuguese did settle Antilia in 1431, and were still there in 1447. The Portuguese regent, Dom Pedro, certainly knew of the island; it had appeared on the 1428 map he had personally brought back to Portugal. I was sure that records of what those visiting caravels found must have existed. It would be absurd to imagine that they had travelled for weeks across the oceans, come across an island of Portuguese-speaking people, then sailed on without making a record of the island and their compatriots' way of life. It was also likely that some of the people who had landed in Puerto Rico in 1431 would have wished to return home by 1447. Some of them were doubtless yearning for their homeland, longing to hear once more the sad, lilting *fado*, and hoping to pass their twilight years in their native land. Those people who did return after the 1447 voyage would also have given the necessary information to the cartographers to correct the earlier chart.

Zuane Pizzigano, author of the 1424 map showing Antilia, never produced another chart and history does not record his fate – I assumed that he had died by the 1440s – but I returned yet again to the Map Room of the British Library and examined the first charts drawn after 1447. These proved a remarkable source of information. A series of charts followed one another in quick succession between 1448 and 1489.[5] In all, I looked at seven pre-Columbian charts, containing seventy-three names and describing features on Antilia and Satanazes. I would have expected these later charts to be updated with further information, but in fact the map drawn in 1463 by Grazioso Benincasa had the same number of cities as the Pizzigano chart. The only change was that all seven cities shown on the earlier chart had been renamed on the later one. The drawing of the island was identical, save for the addition of one more bay on the north coast of Antilia and a more accurate depiction of the south-west and east coasts. I could not understand why the cartographer had renamed all the cities. The mystery deepened with another chart, from 1476, which yielded yet another set of names. Why had they kept changing the names of the cities?

I was convinced that the names must be in medieval Portuguese because the caravels despatched by Prince Henry would hardly have been manned by mercenaries, so I turned to a dictionary for a translation. With the exception of Antilia, not a single name on the later charts appeared to be in medieval Portuguese. They were incomprehensible.[6] If the islands were indeed populated, why did the seven cities not have Portuguese rather than fairytale names?

I asked the owners of the Pizzigano chart for help. The Royal Geographical Society in London had a copy of a pamphlet[7] by Professor Carol Urness, the custodian of the chart, describing the efforts of historians over the last fifty years to solve the question of the identity of the islands. It appeared from the pamphlet that the experts were baffled, and it seemed presumptuous of me to expect to succeed where they had failed. I decided to abandon my quest and leave the mystery for others. I headed home from the Royal Geographical Society thoroughly despondent after being frustrated at this last hurdle, unable to get corroborative evidence that the Portuguese had settled in Puerto Rico after the Chinese had discovered the island but before Columbus set sail.

In times of trouble, my habit is to pray to the Virgin and eat bacon sandwiches. Having done so, a thought occurred to me. Sagres, the home base of the caravels, is only a day's sailing from Sanlúcar de Barrameda on the estuary of the Guadalquivir. In 1431, it was a major Castilian port. Had there been any Castilians aboard those caravels, and if so, could the writing be in medieval Castilian? I hurried back to the British Library. I found a Castilian dictionary in six volumes, but only A–D was available. That scarcely mattered, because six of the seven names on Grazioso Benincasa's 1463 chart began with the letter 'A'. Not one appeared in this massive medieval dictionary; the names were not Castilian. Were they from Aragon, then? The people of Aragon spoke Catalan, but once again, not one name appeared in the dictionary of medieval Catalan. I made a final, desperate search in the Basque and Latin dictionaries, to no avail. I was beaten.

I left the reading room and paced around the courtyard outside the library, cudgelling my brains without success. I then went back to the reading room to put away the dictionaries. There were seven of them strewn across my desk. As I closed the medieval *Dizionario Etimologico* my eye was caught by a section on the code employed in medieval times. Y meant 'there is' or 'and'; *a* meant 'towards'; *j* emphasized the letter before or after it; and *an* before a word meant *particular negativa*, 'the opposite of'. To describe black, they would write *anblanco* (the opposite of white). Was this the key I was looking for?

I went back to the charts. Six of the names began with *an*, 'the opposite of'. Instead of looking for *ansollj* in the dictionary, I should have been looking for its opposite, *sollj* – and *sollj* meant 'sun'. Feverishly, I worked through the medieval Catalan, Castilian and Portuguese dictionaries, cross-referencing with modern dictionaries. There were now ten of them scattered across the desk. One of the names was indeed Catalan, a few were Castilian, but the great majority were medieval Portuguese. I began to compile an alphabetical list. Sixty-three of the seventy-three names were in medieval Portuguese, four of the remaining ten were Castilian, one was Catalan and five were unaccounted for. I expected the last five to be medieval Venetian – Pizzigano came from Venice – but surprisingly, only one was. Three were in the Veneto language of Treviso. One name, *anthib*, had me beaten.

I checked the names against a modern map of Puerto Rico and within half an hour I had found the solution: the names were not of the seven cities but descriptions of natural and man-made features, and the descriptions on the 1448–89 charts put it beyond argument that Antilia was Puerto Rico. Mountains, rainforests, harbours, rivers and salt-pans were described on Antilia exactly where they are found on Puerto Rico. There were no discrepancies between the charts: the later ones merely amplified the former. Some Castilian names were used on later charts, but they still described the same place. Only two islands in the whole world fit these descriptions: Puerto Rico and Guadeloupe.

Con is marked on the south-east part of the island of Antilia/Puerto Rico – the conical mountain of Pico del Este. To the north, the cartographer has placed *ansollj*, 'no sun', corresponding precisely to the El Yunque rainforest, deluged with 240 inches of rain a year. Similar tropical downpours – *choue, chouedue, cyodue* – are shown at the western end of the island at the end of the Cordillera Central. This area has an annual rainfall of a hundred inches, still prodigious by European standards. The draughtsman described marshes (*ensa*) around present-day

Mayaguez, the waterlogged estuary of the Grande Rio de Añasco, but one of the most interesting descriptions was *antuub* or *an tuub*, literally 'without drainage tubes', placed on the north coast to the east of Arecibo. Today, the area remains a vast mosquito-ridden swamp called Cienaga Tiburones. The name Tiburones is Castilian, *tiberon*, or 'drainage', in turn deriving from the Portuguese *tubaro*. Brilliant red and green Puerto Rican parrots, *ansaros*, are denoted in the south-west – presumably the Portuguese wore the feathers of these exotic birds in the same way Columbus's sailors later did. The forest of Boquerón where the cartographer drew these parrots remains a bird watcher's paradise today. The lack of arable and fertile land is vividly caught in the descriptions of the cartographers (Puerto Rico to this day has less than 5 per cent arable land): *ansessel*, 'no grass', appears four times, supplemented by *an suolo*, 'no arable land'. Redeeming features are found on the narrow coastal plains.

The translation that caused me most difficulty was *asal*. My dictionary[8] said that the word is derived from the Latin *acinus*, meaning 'berry, especially grape, also any berry or the seeds in a berry', but *asal* is placed on the chart on a mountain slope behind Ponce. Winters in Puerto Rico are too hot for grapes – they need very cold winters to thrive – but *asal* was written above modern-day Yauco, the 'coffee capital' of Puerto Rico, so I wondered if the Portuguese were describing coffee beans. This theory provoked a vigorous debate among the historians advising me. Some pointed out that coffee was indigenous to East Africa and was introduced to the Caribbean by the Spanish, so it could not have been marked on charts made before the Spanish landed. But further research[9] revealed that at least nineteen strains of coffee were found in the Caribbean before the Spanish arrived. It grew on mountain slopes, usually between three and four and a half thousand feet, in temperate climates within the tropics where there is no wind but plenty of morning sun. These conditions are found on the southern slopes of the Cordillera Central behind Ponce, just where *asal* is marked on the charts of Antilia. Could the Chinese have introduced coffee when they arrived in late 1421?

The second translation that provoked a heated debate was *cua cusa* – pumpkin – shown on the coastal plain in the east near Naguabo. Had pumpkins and squashes really grown there? It transpired that they still do. On a visit to Puerto Rico while researching this book, I took photographs of twenty varieties piled in heaps beside the road: long yellow, champion market, hackensack, manu, rocky ford and white Japan musk squashes; yellow, crookneck, orange, white, delicate and golden scalloped melons; and an assortment of cucumbers, gherkins and egg-plants.[10] They grow in such variety and profusion and to such a size because of the sunshine, volcanic soil and moderate rainfall particular to the eastern coastal strip of Puerto Rico.

The really fascinating aspect of the translations of these names is that they were shown on charts published before Columbus set sail and they describe plants foreign to Puerto Rico. Coffee was then native to Africa, cucumbers to India, mangoes to south-east Asia. Columbus also found coconuts, native to the Pacific. Not only had someone reached the Caribbean before Columbus and drawn Puerto Rico with incredible accuracy, they had also brought plants there from all over the world. It seems to me that only the great Chinese fleet commanded by Admiral Zhou Wen could have achieved these things.

Marolio was another interesting name, on a chart drawn by Albino Canepa in the 1480s. It was placed in the same position as *marnlio* on the Pizzigano chart; I assumed that the lower edge of the *o* had become erased. *Marolio* is medieval Portuguese for 'plants of the Annonaceae family' – star fruit, sweet and sour sops, pawpaws and custard apples. On both charts the car-tographer had placed the description just north of modern Ponce in the middle of the south coast. This area remains the centre of the tropical fruit industry of Puerto Rico, rejoicing in plantations of star fruit, sour sops and papaya. Their juice is exported all over the Americas and forms the basis for the rum punches tourists continue to enjoy. These fruits were indigenous to south-east Asia and South America. Once again, I concluded that the Chinese had introduced them to Puerto Rico in 1421.

The cartographers depicted Satanazes (Guadeloupe) in an entirely different light to Puerto Rico. They changed the name from Satan's or Devil's Island to Saluagio (Island of Savages) in later charts.[11] Those later charts of Guadeloupe merely amplified what could be seen from the sea – a second volcano (*con*), Mont Carmichael at 1,414 metres, with a plateau (*silla*) between it and La Souffrière. The waterfalls flowing down the east side of La Souffrière (Karukeka and Trois Rivières) had the soubriquets *duchal* and *tubo de agua* – 'showers from heaven'. Villages and cultivated fields (*aralia y sya*) are shown on the low land on the west coast of Grande Terre, just where Columbus described them as he sailed past years later. Satanazes is clearly a horrible place, summarized by Albino Canepa as *nar i sua*, 'nothing but sweltering heat', but the description of the island of Saya (Les Saintes), 'any number of tropical birds', was apt, for the island is still renowned for its kingfishers, hummingbirds and bananaquits – little flying jewels flitting across the turquoise sea that separates the islands.

The most unusual name Zuane Pizzigano had written on Antilia (in the south-east, covering Vieques Island) was *ura*, placed next to *con* on later charts. *Uracano* is Venetian for 'violent explosion', 'eruption' or 'tempest'. By 1421, the volcanoes on the south-east coast of Puerto Rico had long been extinct, and earthquakes were and are more prevalent on the west of the island, near Mayaguez, but hurricanes invariably approach from the east and roar north-westwards from Vieques Island to San Juan. I was sure that this was what the Chinese cartographer had seen when the junks arrived in November, during the hurricane season that runs from June to the end of November.

All these names, coupled with the physical similarity between the islands on the Pizzigano chart (and others) and what is actually there, put it beyond argument that Antilia is Puerto Rico, Satanazes is Guadeloupe and Saya is Les Saintes. Although it is possible to quibble over the nuances of a few of the medieval Catalan or Castilian translations, continued debate about the identity of the Antilia group of islands is pointless. These names and maps are unequivocal proof that the islands were continuously settled by the Portuguese from before 1447 until 1492, the time of Columbus's first voyage. The plants foreign to Puerto Rico were brought there before Columbus set sail. To my mind, this is proof that the Chinese discovered Puerto Rico.

Although the depiction of the islands was accurate, their location and orientation was not. They were shown in the Atlantic rather than in the Caribbean, more than two thousand miles away from their correct position. The error was gradually corrected by succeeding cartographers. By 1448, the islands were 1,500 miles west of the Canaries (750 miles in error), and by 1474 they had again shifted westwards, just 500 miles in error. The mistake is easily explicable. In 1431, Henry's captains did not have good astrolabes (sextants), nor did they understand declination. Portuguese navigators did not know how to use Polaris until 1451; only after 1473, using declination tables, could they finally determine latitude with accuracy (Toscanelli's 1474 chart places Antilia at the correct latitude). Longitude remained a problem. Columbus put the Americas a thousand miles out for longitude, as well as twenty degrees for latitude. When he returned from his first voyage, he did not know where he had gone, what he had found or where it was. He thought he had reached China.

In the fifteenth century, the Portuguese navigated by compass and measured their speed through the water by throwing logs off the bow. They positioned the islands by dead reckoning, calculating their position by speed through the water multiplied by the number of days travelled. But they did not realize that the great mass of water over which they were sailing was itself moving, taking them away from their dead-reckoning position. Like Columbus, the Portuguese did not know where they had gone. When I made adjustments to allow for the movement of water during their ten-week voyage from Madeira to Guadeloupe,[12] I found that the Portuguese had placed the islands in their correct dead-reckoning position and orientation.

I felt that there were two further questions about the Pizzigano chart still to be answered. The first concerned the size of the islands. In the earlier charts, Antilia was depicted as bigger than Puerto Rico, and Satanazes was also shown larger than Guadeloupe; a mistake caused, I believe, by transposing not only the wrong position of the islands but their scale from the earlier (Chinese) map onto a European one. The other outstanding question was when and where the Pizzigano chart had been made. It seems likely that he was working under the direction of Dom Pedro, whose cartographers were searching for information about new lands in order to create a world map for Prince Henry. I knew that the Holy Roman Emperor had given Dom Pedro substantial estates in the Veneto at Treviso, fifteen miles north of Venice, and this became the Portuguese delegation's base. It struck me that the Portuguese cartographers probably met Niccolò da Conti there in 1424. He, of course, had spent years aboard a junk of the Chinese treasure fleet, the original discoverers of Antilia. The chart was almost certainly made in Treviso, since the majority of the 'non-Portuguese' names on the chart were in the dialect of Veneto rather than Venice. Pizzigano may have been a monk at the great Dominican sanctuary of San Niccolò at Treviso.

The Pizzigano chart depicted Puerto Rico so accurately that whoever collated the information must have been a master of his craft; in that era, that meant the original cartographer can only have been Chinese. The importance of the chart and those that followed is twofold: not only do they provide evidence that the Chinese discovered the Americas seventy years before Columbus, they also show that Puerto Rico had become a permanent Portuguese settlement before 1447. The names on the subsequent charts continually hone the descriptions of the islands long before Columbus reached them. The positions of the islands were also continually corrected, and the charts from 1463 and 1470 contain a wealth of additional information about Antilia, including further bays on the north-west and east coasts, and the slightly exaggerated south-west tip was redrawn with greater accuracy. The island of Ymana, to the north of Puerto Rico, was also better drawn on later charts, its name changed to Rosellia. As European navigators discovered declination and the measurement of latitude, and improved their sextants and their measurement of time, the positions of the islands on the charts were moved to the south-west.[13]

Identifying Antilia and Satanazes enabled me to pinpoint the other 'islands' surrounding them on the medieval charts. Andrea Bianco's chart of 1448, for example, includes the north-east coast of Brazil, and Cristobal Soligo's 1489 chart[14] shows a further seven 'islands' – the tip of Hispaniola in the west, Trinidad, the Virgin Islands, St Vincent, St Lucia, Barbados and the north coast of Venezuela in the south – all before Columbus had even set sail.

I returned to the chart of Puerto Rico and began to search for the probable site of the first settlement. Both the Portuguese and the Chinese must have approached from the south-east on the prevailing winds. The southern and western coasts of Antilia were more accurately drawn on the Pizzigano chart than the northern or eastern coasts, so I concentrated the search there.

The Pizzigano chart has *cyodue*, 'incessant rain', to the west, *ansuly*, 'lack of fertile land', in the south-west and *ura*, 'hurricane', to the east; none of these sounded a particularly inviting place to settle. On the other hand, *marolio*, 'luscious tropical fruit', is shown just north of Ponce, and Ponce Bay was drawn with striking accuracy on all the charts, showing a prominent headland, La Guancha, to the east of the bay. For centuries, this headland has provided sheltered anchorage from the easterly winds. The sea abounds in fish and, located as it is in the rain shadow of the mountains, Ponce has by far the best climate in Puerto Rico. When I flew there to take a look on the ground, I could see the purple clouds of an afternoon thunderstorm breaking on the central Cordillera to the north, leaving the town dry. Not without reason was Ponce named 'the pearl of the south'. It is likely the Portuguese made their first settlement here; this is where they would have greeted newcomers on the 1447 voyage and invited them to attend divine service.

The river leading from the harbour into the old town still retains the name Rio Portugués. The brilliant-white cathedral of Our Lady of Guadeloupe stands on its banks, and as I sat in the main square of Ponce one evening, sipping bitter black Puerto Rican coffee at the end of another day spent combing the island for evidence of the Chinese voyages and the early Portuguese colonists, I watched people pouring into the cathedral to attend evening mass. Some men had red hair, the women fine chiselled faces, sharper features and paler skins than in the north. In their looks, their way of life, their *fado* songs and their *ferrapeira* dances, the people of Ponce to this day resemble their Portuguese ancestors from the Algarve. Will the bones of their brave forefathers who set sail from Sagres long ago to found this, the first European colony in the New World, one day be found beneath the cathedral of Our Lady of Guadeloupe?

The Portuguese had taken their first steps into the New World that the Chinese had discovered, but despite the evidence offered by copies of the charts drawn by the Chinese, one obstacle – as much psychological as physical – remained to be overcome before the Portuguese empire could spread across the globe. The fear of the unknown still dominated the minds of ordinary Portuguese seamen, and a lifetime of myth, legend and superstition could not be erased overnight. Magellan was still struggling to overcome the fears of his crewmen in the early years of the sixteenth century as he tried to coax them through the strait that was to bear his name.

In the summer of 1432, with Madeira, the Azores (discovered by La Salle) and Puerto Rico already colonized, Prince Henry called Gil Eannes, a skilled seaman and loyal retainer, to his court at Sagres. Eannes had been despatched on a mission the previous year to the Canary Islands. Now Henry insisted that, come what may, he must round Cape Bojador on the coast of modern Western Sahara, to the south of Morocco. The cape featured in many lurid seamen's myths about the unknown world. It was a place where vast cataracts crashed into the sea, fierce currents dragged ships to their doom and even the sea-water itself had been turned into 'red slime'.

Eannes followed Prince Henry's commands with understandable caution, standing well out to sea so as to approach the dreaded Cape Bojador from the south and thus avoid the legendary waterfall off the cape, but he found no serpents or giant sea monsters as he made his first landfall a few miles beyond the cape. The land appeared uninhabited; there were even a few flowers on the beach. Eannes plucked a bouquet for Prince Henry: 'My Lord, I thought that I ought to bring some token of the land since I was on it. I gathered these herbs which I here present to your gaze, which we in this country call Roses of Saint Mary.'[15] Returning northwards to Bojador itself, Eannes found the 'eternally rushing water' was but vast shoals of grey mullet, the 'waterfalls tumbling off the earth' were cliffs, rising sheer from the sea, and the 'sea baked into red slime' was water discoloured by the red Sahara sand.

Eannes's achievement in rounding Cape Bojador completely

Guadeloupe. Les Saintes, approached from the south-east
(*below*), would look like one island curving to the north-west.
La Souffrière (*above*) on Basse Terre is not far to the north.

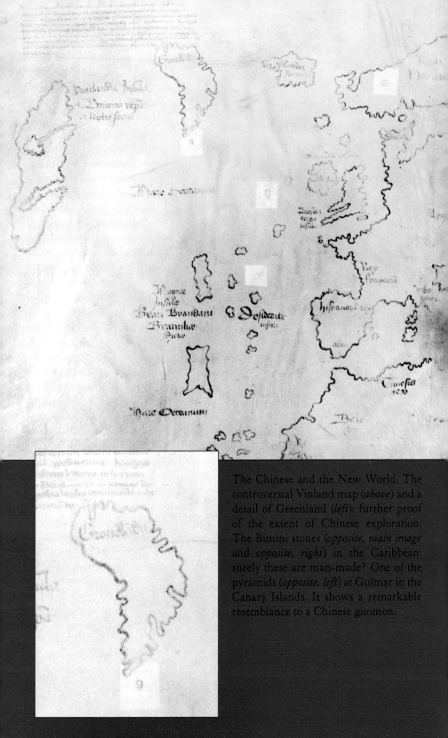

The Chinese and the New World. The controversial Vinland map (*above*) and a detail of Greenland (*left*): further proof of the extent of Chinese exploration. The Bimini stones (*opposite, main image* and *opposite, right*) in the Caribbean: surely these are man-made? One of the pyramids (*opposite, left*) at Guímar in the Canary Islands. It shows a remarkable resemblance to a Chinese gnomon.

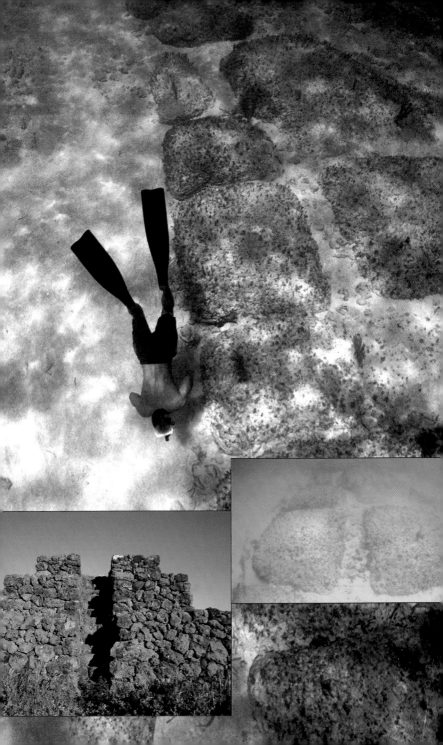

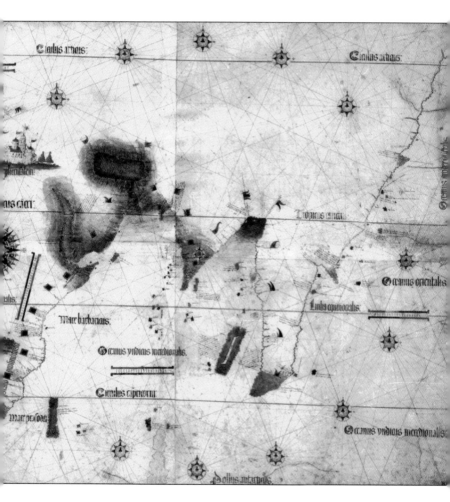

The influential Cantino world chart of 1502.

European exploration: in the fourteenth century Marco Polo with his father and uncle (*below*); in the fifteenth (*opposite, centre, left to right*) Christopher Columbus; Vasco da Gama and Ferdinand Magellan. By the sixteenth century trade with ports such as Calicut was thriving (*above*), but the level of scientific inquiry did not reach Chinese proportions until the advent of Captain James Cook and Joseph Banks (*opposite, bottom left*), who stopped off for water in Tierra del Fuego en route for Tahiti in 1769 (*opposite, bottom right*).

Prince Henry the Navigator looking westwards from the prow of the monument at Belèm to four hundred years of Portuguese exploration.

changed European man's attitude to seafaring. At a stroke, he had shattered centuries of legend and superstition. If a ship could safely round Cape Bojador, man could sail anywhere. There was no need for irrational fears about falling off the edge of the earth. With the Chinese charts to guide them, there was nowhere the Portuguese sea-captains would not venture, once they had persuaded their men to follow where they led; exploring the limits of the world became merely a matter of time.

ON THE

SHOULDERS

OF

GIANTS

B Y 1460, THE YEAR HENRY THE NAVIGATOR DIED, PUERTO RICO was well known and Portuguese exploration of the three groups of islands in the Atlantic – the Azores, the Canaries and the Cape Verde Islands – was complete. The islands were stocked with animals and became bases for explorers making their way between North and South America and Africa. By a fortunate coincidence, all lay in the track of the circulatory wind systems; the Canaries and Cape Verde Islands on the way out to the Americas and the Azores on the way back. Gradually, Europeans reached the lands the Chinese admirals had discovered.

In parallel with his systematic and continual improvements to ocean navigation, Henry the Navigator had relentlessly pushed his captains further and further across the seas. By the time Portuguese ships set sail for the Cape of Good Hope, the measurement of latitude in the northern hemisphere was as accurate as the Chinese calculations had been years earlier.

Bartolomeu Dias (c. 1450–1500) led the way. In 1482, he was captain of one of the ships exploring the Gold Coast and Africa past the 'bulge', and in 1487 he was appointed to the command of a small squadron of three ships that was to attempt to round the southern tip of Africa. Neither Dias nor his masters knew how far south the Cape really stretched – the charting of West Africa by the Chinese fleet had been carried out before they had mastered the calculation of latitude in the southern hemisphere – but they had no doubts that it could be rounded. Dom Pedro's map of 1428 had showed the Cape's triangular shape, and before Dias set sail the Portuguese king gave his emissary, Pêro da Covilha, a map of the world (*Carta de Marear*) showing that the Cape could be rounded to reach India. When Dias duly reached the Cape, he

came in sight of that Great and Famous Cape *concealed for so many centuries*, which when it was seen made known not only itself but also another new world of countries. Bartolomeu Dias, and those of his company, because of the perils and storms they had endured in doubling it, called it the Stormy Cape, but on their return to the Kingdom, the King Dom João gave it another illustrious name, calling it the Cape of Good Hope [my italics].[1]

Dias was followed by Vasco da Gama (c. 1469–1525) who was ordered to continue round the Cape to India and the source of spice. Da Gama was provided with charts showing the Cape, and precise declination tables:

Tables showing the declination of the sun were provided by the Astronomer Royal, Abraham Zacuto Ben Samuel. These ... had been translated from Hebrew into Latin the previous year and printed at Leira under the title *Almanach Perpetuum Celestium Motuum Cujus Radix Est 1473*. Other books, maps and charts were supplied ... amongst these documents almost certainly ... [were] the log and charts of Dias.[2]

After rounding the Cape, da Gama proceeded up the east coast of Africa, finding the famous ports of Sofala, Kilwa, Zanzibar, Mombasa and Malindi, developed by Chinese and Indian fleets over the centuries when the Indian Ocean trade was by far the most busy and lucrative in the world. By the late 1400s the Chinese had closed their trading routes with the outside world; nonetheless, the Portuguese explorers found evidence of the earlier Chinese visits in the mass of blue and white porcelain decorating many houses the length of East Africa. When da Gama returned from his second voyage, he knew the way to Malacca and the Spice Islands in the East. The world's spice trade was now within Portugal's grasp. Anyone who opposed them was mown down with grapeshot. In effect, da Gama stole the trade the Indians and Chinese had spent centuries developing. Skilful though he was, like Dias before him, da Gama discovered nothing new.

In parallel with da Gama's pursuit of the spice trade in the East, King João of Portugal had sent Pedro Álvares Cabral (1467–1520) to South America, to the lands shown on the 1428 World Map. In 1500, King João's successor, Manuel I, ordered Cabral to take possession of the western parts of the Indies. Like Dias and da Gama, Cabral used the Canaries and then the Cape Verde Islands as his bases before making landfall on the South American coast. At this time, a cluster of explorers reached South America within a year of one another: Vespucci, Pinzón and De Lepe in 1499, and Mendoza the next year. The first three made landfall on the Amazon delta, then sailed north-westwards.

This north-east coast of Brazil, discovered by the Chinese treasure fleets of Zhou Man and Hong Bao, had appeared on many maps drawn before any of those European explorers set sail. Andrea Bianco's map of 1448 referred to *Ixola Otinticha Xe Longa a Ponente 1500 mia* – 'a genuine island is 1,500 miles west of here [West Africa]' – and Master João de Barros, on the 1500 expedition to the Brazilian coast, confirmed that the land had appeared on earlier maps: 'The lands might the King see represented on the Mappa Mundi which Pêro daz Bisagudo had.'[3] Bisagudo was a nickname given to the famous explorer Pero da Cunha who had been sent with a Portuguese map of the world to colonize what is now Ghana in Africa. De Barros said the only real difference between what Cabral's expedition saw in 1500 and what appeared on Bisagudo's earlier 'Mappa Mundi' was that he, de Barros, could now certify Brazil was inhabited. Christopher Columbus also confirmed that Brazil was known to the Portuguese before any of their expeditions set sail for South America. He noted in his diaries that he wished to proceed further south of Trinidad 'to see what was the meaning of King John of Portugal who said there was terra firma to the south'.[4]

So, Andrea Bianco, Columbus and de Barros all state that a map of Brazil existed before the first European expedition sailed in 1500. The only possible sources of the information on that map, the 1428 World Map, were the cartographers with the Chinese fleets of 1421–3. The port of San Luis is instantly recognizable on the Piri Reis map (derived from the 1428 map) and the latitudes of the Orinoco and Amazon deltas are precisely correct. In addition, there is no shortage of other, permanent traces of the Chinese visit to South America: Asiatic chickens were found in the Orinoco delta by the first European explorers, and Venezuelan Indians and other native peoples have blood groups that are otherwise unique to south-west China.

With the Cape of Good Hope rounded and South America discovered, the exploration of the rest of the world quickly followed. Ferdinand Magellan (c. 1480–1521) was orphaned when he was ten years old and became a page at the Portuguese court, where he was trained in navigation. He was sent to East Africa in 1505, and for the next seven years saw service in the Indian Ocean. He took part in the expedition to establish a Portuguese colony in India, and in 1511 he played a significant part in the conquest of Zheng He's former forward base, Malacca. He returned home in 1512 and sailed with the Portuguese expedition to Morocco, where he was severely wounded. After a disagreement with his commander, he left the army without permission. As a result he was disgraced and was refused a pension.

In disgust, he moved to Spain and in 1518 was appointed captain general of a fleet to explore a westward route to the Spice Islands, across the Pacific. He sailed from the Guadalquivir estuary the next year with five ships and 241 men. Magellan knew of the strait that bears his name before he set sail, for it was shown on a map in the King of Portugal's treasury that Magellan inspected and took with him.[5] On reaching the Spice Islands, Magellan showed the chart to the local king.[6] It depicted a way through the Strait of Magellan and across the Pacific; 'From Cape Frio until the Islands of the Maluccas throughout this navigation there are no lands laid down in the maps they [Magellan's expedition] carry with them.'[7]

Magellan never claimed to be the first man to have circumnavigated the world; nevertheless, his was still an amazing feat. He was in a tiny ship, a toy compared to the Chinese leviathans, and, unlike the Chinese, the Portuguese had very little experience of long transoceanic voyages and were unaware that certain foods could prevent scurvy. Magellan, Dias, da Gama and Cabral were very skilful navigators and seamen, they were also brave and resolute men with awesome qualities of leadership, but not one of them actually discovered 'new lands'. When they set sail, each one of them had a chart showing where he was going. All their 'discoveries' had been made nearly a century earlier by the Chinese.

Nor did Christopher Columbus 'discover' the Americas. Far from setting sail full of fear that his fleet might fall off the edge of the world, he knew where he was going, as can be seen in excerpts from his logs when he was still in mid-Atlantic:

Wednesday September 19th [1492]
The Admiral did not wish to be delayed by beating to the windward in order to make sure whether there was land in that direction, but he was certain that to the north and to the south there were some islands, as in truth there were ... [he said] 'and there is time enough, for, God willing, on the return voyage, all will be seen'. These are his words.

Wednesday October 24th
[describing how to reach Antilia] I should steer west-south-west to go there ... and in the spheres which I have seen and in the drawings of mappae mundi it is in this region.

Wednesday November 14th
And he says that he believes that these islands are those without

number which in the mappae mundi are placed at the end of the east.[8]

It is clear from these three entries that Columbus had seen spheres and mappae mundi showing islands in the Atlantic, and that these lay, in Columbus's opinion, to the north and south of his position on 19 September 1492. Puerto Rico (Antilia) appears on the 1424 Pizzigano chart, the coast of New England on the Cantino, Brazil on Andrea Bianco's map of 1448 and many West Indian islands on Cristobal Soligo's chart of 1489 – all drawn before Columbus reached them.

In 1479, Columbus had married Doña Felipa Perestrello, the daughter of the governor of Porto Santo, the small island near Madeira settled by the Portuguese. His forthcoming marriage gave him sufficient confidence to correspond with the celebrated scientist Toscanelli, who replied at once: 'I have received thy letters with the things that thou didst send me and with them I received a great favour. I notice thy splendid and lofty desire to sail to the regions of the east by those of the west [i.e. reach China by sailing westwards], as is shown by the chart which I send you.'[9] The 'chart' that accompanied Toscanelli's letter to Columbus has been lost, but it can be reconstructed using another letter from Toscanelli to the King of Portugal, enclosing a chart of the Atlantic: 'But from the Island of Antilia known to you to the far famed island of Cipangu there are ten spaces . . . so there is not a great space to be traversed over unknown waters.'[10]

Antilia was indeed very well known to the Portuguese. They had settled there in 1431, and were still there when Columbus set sail in 1492, but his knowledge of the Americas went far further. By his own evidence he knew of the 'Strait of Magellan' in the south and the coast of north-east Brazil.[11] He had seen mappae mundi and spheres showing the Atlantic. He also knew well that China and the Spice Islands could be reached by sailing east-wards round the Cape of Good Hope, for Christopher and his brother Bartholomew were both present when Dias reported to the king that he had rounded the Cape at that latitude.[12] Columbus was hell bent on gaining fame and glory by sailing westwards for China and the Spice Islands.

Columbus certainly saw the 1428 master chart of the world. This is corroborated in a number of ways: in notes on the 1513 Piri Reis map which credit Columbus with knowing that there were only two hours of daylight in the far south; in Columbus's letter to the King of Portugal in which he writes about lands in South America, a letter written before the Portuguese explorers had set sail for that continent; and in his notes inscribed on the inside flap of his own copy of Marco Polo's book about his voyage from China to India by sea. In short, Columbus knew that China could be reached by sailing westabout (Toscanelli's letter) or by sailing eastabout. He must have known from the 1428 World Map that the eastabout voyage was the shorter.

In these circumstances, it must have been horrifying for Columbus to realize that the Portuguese were well on their way to rounding the Cape of Good Hope and sailing into the Indian Ocean, whence they could sail with the monsoon winds to China. The Portuguese advances down the African coast must have been a matter of grave concern to him. By 1485, Dias had reached the African coast as far as 13°S. At that stage, not only did Columbus know of the route westwards, but he had sailed to Iceland (in 1477), which country he was told Chinese people had visited.

In 1485, Christopher Columbus left Portugal, where he had been on and off since his marriage. During that time he may well have sailed to Antilia on a secret voyage funded by the Pope, as Señor Ruggero Marino has stated. Marino bases his assumption largely on the inscription on the tomb of Pope Innocent VIII, who died in July 1492, i.e. before Columbus set out on his first 'voyage to the Bahamas'. On the Pope's tomb were the words 'novi orbis suo aevo inventi gloria' – 'the glory of the new world having been found with his gold'.

Bartholomew Columbus remained in Portugal as a member of the team improving the Portuguese maps as and when new evidence came in from the voyages of discovery. In 1487–8, Dias pushed on further down the African coast and reached what we call the Cape of Good Hope. In 1473, the Portuguese had discovered how to calculate latitude from the sun's declination, so Dias was able to put the latitude of the Cape of Good Hope at 34°22′ South. Both Bartholomew and Christopher knew this correct latitude (see p. 430).

Columbus's plans for a voyage westwards were now in desperate trouble, for the Portuguese were on the verge of opening up the route to India round the Cape of Good Hope. Unless he acted quickly, his chances of glory were over. At this time, the Catholic monarchs Ferdinand and Isabella had begun their assault on the last Moorish enclave in Spain, south of the Sierra Nevada mountains around Granada. Columbus had no chance of extracting funds from the Portuguese, who were concentrating on the easterly route to China, and knew that his only chance lay with the Catholic monarchs who did not have the 1428 chart and thus did not know that the shorter route lay eastabout. It was therefore in Columbus's interests to persuade Ferdinand and Isabella that the quickest route to China lay westwards. This, in my submission, is the motive for the forgery and theft Christopher and Bartholomew Columbus now perpetrated.

Their timing was extraordinarily fortunate, for in 1492 Granada had fallen and the Catholic monarchs wished to extend the pursuit of the Moors overseas. Columbus's plan to sail westabout for China would fall on receptive ears if he could persuade Ferdinand and Isabella that his plan was realistic and that it offered the chance of reaching the Spice Islands before the Portuguese.

In 1963, Alexander O. Vietor, the map curator at Yale University, reported a gift by an anonymous donor 'in the form of a magnificent painted world map signed by Henricus

Martellus approximately six feet by four feet [180 × 120 cm]'. Vietor went on:

> It is painted in what seems to be tempera over a base of paper in sheets of different sizes, the whole backed up with a large framed canvas, much in the manner of a painting . . . It has graduations of latitude and of longitude in the margins, the first instance of longitudes being shown on the map . . . on this map Cipango is placed 90 degrees from the Canaries.[13]

Mr Vietor subsequently corresponded on the matter with Professor Arthur Davies, who at the time held the Reardon Smith Chair of Geography at the University of Exeter (1948–71). Vietor also provided Professor Davies with infrared photographs of the map for close study. This map, which I shall call the 'Yale Martellus', is four times the size of another map Martellus published in 1489. The experts, principally Davies and Vietor, are unanimous that the Yale Martellus was the original and the 1489 Martellus a copy at one-quarter the scale. Ashleigh Skelton has also concluded that the Yale map is genuine, its author Martellus. My belief is that both maps, although genuine, contain forgeries, and the forger was Bartholomew Columbus.

The 1489 Martellus map extends from the Canaries to the east coast of China. Although no meridians or longitude scales are given, estimates based on the measurement of the map show that the distance from Lisbon to the east coast of China eastabout is not less than 230° and probably 240°. Westabout, the coast of China is shown approximately 130° west of Lisbon. This is a colossal exaggeration of the distance eastabout. The Catalan atlas of 1376 had the distance from Portugal to China eastabout at approximately 116°; the Genoese map of 1457 approximately 136°; and the Fra Mauro of 1459 about 120°. The true measurement is 141° from the Canaries to Shanghai, so the 1489 Martellus exaggerates the distance to China from Portugal eastabout by nearly 100°. The Columbus brothers of course knew the true distance eastwards from Lisbon to China because the Portuguese had the 1428 World Map.

The 1489 Martellus map could not have been completed before that year, for it featured complete details of the discoveries of Bartolomeu Dias's voyage of 1487 – when he doubled the Cape of Good Hope and reached the Indian Ocean. He returned to Portugal in December 1488. Within a year, then, full details of this trip, including Dias's rich nomenclature, had appeared on the map Martellus made in Italy, this despite strenuous efforts on the part of the King of Portugal to keep the map secret. The penalty for stealing maps was death. The Portuguese government's policy had been shattered in one fell swoop by someone in a unique position to know all the details.

The second forgery, on both Martellus maps, is that a huge dogleg of fictitious land has been appended to the Malayan peninsula from the equator south to 29° South, thereafter being widened to reach China. So enormous and wide was this peninsula that it seemed to render impossible any voyage between China and India. In short, anyone who had got into the Indian Ocean could not continue to the east. To a third party, such as the Catholic monarchs, who did not have the 1428 map, it showed that eastabout China could not be reached by rounding the Cape of Good Hope.

The third forgery is that Martellus's two maps extend southwards to the latitude of the Cape of Good Hope, which Dias had fixed at 34°22' South, to 45° South. That Bartholomew Columbus was responsible for this addition is beyond doubt, for it was made in his own hand. In the volume of *Imago Mundi* found among the possessions of Christopher Columbus after his death are numerous notes written in the margins or below the printed matter. Number 23 has been identified by Professor Davies, who has spent a lifetime analysing the characteristics of the Columbus brothers' scripts, as being the handwriting of Bartholomew. It reads:

Note in the year '88 in the month of December arrived in Lisbon Bartholomew Diaz [sic], captain of three caravelles which the most serene king of Portugal had sent to try out the land in Guinea. He reported to the same most serene king that he had sailed beyond Yan 600 leagues, namely 450 to the south and 250 to the north, up a promontory which he calls Capa de Buon Esperanza [Cape of Good Hope] which we believe to be in Abyssinia. He says that in this place he found by the astrolabe that he was 45 degrees below the equator and that this place is 3,100 leagues distant from Lisbon. He has described this voyage and plotted it league by league on a marine chart in order to place it under the eyes of the most serene king himself. I was present in all of this.[14]

Bartholomew Columbus's claim that Dias had put the Cape of Good Hope at 45° South was blatantly untrue. No-one in Lisbon at the time bar the Columbus brothers knew of this 45° assertion, for Bartholomew made it after he had left Portugal.

To date, no link has been shown between the Columbus brothers and Martellus; it could have been that Martellus was the forger. The link, however, can be deduced in two ways. The first is that Martellus's map contains information only the Portuguese knew (Martellus was Italian), moreover information guarded upon pain of death which had been acquired only months earlier. Someone with access to top-secret Portuguese maps must have provided the information to Martellus. That points the finger at Bartholomew Columbus, or others who were part of that trusted mapmaking circle, which includes Behain of Bohemia, for example.

The direct link between Bartholomew Columbus and the Martellus map, however, comes from the construction of the Yale Martellus. The sheets of paper on which the Yale map is drawn are of different sizes, which excludes the possibility that they were printed map sheets, for they would then have had to be the same size to fit within the map portfolio. In private letters between Alexander Vietor and Professor Davies, Vietor stated that an X-ray examination had revealed no evidence of printing on the paper sheets and that everything on the Yale map was hand-drawn, lettered and coloured. In short, it came from a tracing. The tracings have been identified by Professor Davies as being in the hand of Bartholomew Columbus. In making this devastating assertion, Professor Davies wrote:

When Columbus left Lisbon in 1485 for Spain, Bartholomew, with his highly trained skills as a cartographer in the Genoese style, stayed on in the map workshop of King John II. He was engaged in building up a large map of the world based on Donnus Nicolaus and on the Portuguese charts. It was, like all important maps at that time, drawn on sheets of parchment which could be joined together almost invisibly, and mounted on linen. This large map, 180cm by 120cm, formed a standard Portuguese world map, continually added to by new discoveries, including those of Cão and Dias. By the beginning of 1489, Columbus faced poverty and failure in Spain: his pension had been ended in 1488 and he no longer had free board and lodging from Medina Seli or the Marquess de Moya. Bartholomew prepared to join him in Spain and help his projects. They needed money, and in particular the vital and continued support of the Bank of St George in Genoa. They got both. Money could be obtained from the sale of maps kept secret in Portugal. Before leaving Lisbon, Bartholomew copied maps of convenient size. The large standard world map he had to copy in some secrecy and, because of its size, he needed eleven sheets of paper, cheaper, thinner and quieter than parchment. These sheets of the Yale Martellus were tracings in the hand of Bartholomew. Early in 1489 he left Lisbon. He went first to Seville to help his brother and there altered the Yale map by substituting another sheet of paper which showed Africa to 45° South rather than its true latitude of 34° 22′ South. The Martellus map was rather like a picture with a picture frame. The frame ends at 41°S. To get the addition into the picture, it has to burst through the frame down to 45°S.[15]

A second lead comes from a legend shown on the east coast of Africa which reads 'Ultima navigatio Portuga A.D., 1489'. On the face of it, seeing the Martellus map extending down to 45°S, this inscription would appear to assert that Dias had proceeded north along the east coast of South Africa to beyond Natal. This he did not do on that voyage. The legend is shown between 33° and 34°S, which exactly accords with where Dias got to – the Rio de Infante, the Great Fish River at 34°S. It appears to be north of Natal only because Africa is shown as extending to 45°S. When Bartholomew altered the prototype map to 45°S, he was unable to remove the legend.

The three forgeries combined appeared to all but rule out the possibility of reaching China eastabout from Portugal. The purpose of the Martellus maps clearly was not to influence the Portuguese, who knew the true situation for they had the 1428 World Map; it was to influence the Catholic sovereigns who were completely in the dark. At that time, one degree of latitude was thought to be fifty nautical miles (ninety kilometres), according to Toscanelli's letter. To reach India round Africa, according to the forged Martellus maps, would involve sailing from 39°N to 45°S, and then north to India, another 45° + 15° – all told, the voyage to India would be some fifteen thousand miles. Moreover, and perhaps this was the decisive factor, ships would have had to sail below 45° South in order to round Africa through seas Dias had already described as the roughest he had encountered anywhere in the world.

In several ways, the forged Martellus maps depicted a monumental eastward journey, whereas by sailing westwards for Antilia to China, Spanish ships could pass through the Strait of Magellan and beat the Portuguese to it. This is the reason, I submit, why the Portuguese concentrated on the eastern route to

China and the Spanish tried to reach the same destination via South America. Bartholomew Columbus stole the intellectual property of the Portuguese government. He then forged a chart he and Christopher knew was bogus, and both of them used that chart to extract money and backing under false pretences from the Bank of Genoa and the Catholic monarchs of Spain. Columbus's true legacy to posterity is not the discovery of the Americas, but of the circulatory wind systems of the Atlantic he so brilliantly analysed and exploited on his later voyages. Knowledge of these wind and current patterns proved invaluable in the preparation and execution of the voyages that led to the colonization of the Americas in the following centuries.

Finally, to that brilliant seaman, Captain James Cook, 'the ablest and most renowned navigator this or any country hath ever produced. He possessed all the qualities necessary for his profession and great undertakings.'[16] Cook made the first of his three great voyages in 1768, sailing to the Pacific to observe the transit of Venus. He then continued across the Pacific and 'discovered' New Zealand, finding it a suitable country for settlement 'should this ever be thought an object worthy of the attention of Englishmen'. He explored Australia's east coast, claimed the whole country in the name of the king, and sailed for home via New Guinea and the Cape.

On his second voyage, in 1772, 'to complete the discovery of the southern hemisphere', Cook put in at New Zealand and landed animals and planted vegetables to provide food supplies for future explorers and settlers. He then sailed south to the edge of the Antarctic continent. Cook's mission on his third voyage to the Pacific was to find a northern passage from the Pacific to the Atlantic. He again visited New Zealand and Australia, then sailed for North America, exploring the coast from Oregon northwards. He entered the Bering Strait, could find no ice-free route through and began the journey home. He was killed in Hawaii on 14 February 1779 after a dispute with the natives.

Cook was a great man, and the greatest navigator of all time, but he discovered neither New Zealand nor Australia. More than two centuries before he embarked on his voyages, a cluster of maps from the Dieppe School showed Australia with remarkable clarity. The Jean Rotz map was in the possession of the British government when Cook set sail, and Joseph Banks, who sailed with Cook, had acquired another of the finest, the Harleian (Dauphin), showing Australia with the same precision as the Rotz map. The Desliens and Desceliers charts from the Dieppe School were also known to the Admiralty. The Endeavour Reef, on which Cook later ran aground, is clearly shown on these earlier maps, together with what later became known as Cooktown Harbour. When Cook had extricated himself from the reef, he sailed directly for Cooktown. 'This harbour will do excellently for our purposes, although it is not as large as I had been told.'[17]

When Cook returned, claiming to have discovered Australia, the head of the Map Department at the British Admiralty, Commander Dalrymple, wrote a furious protest. Captain James Cook had enormous courage, determination and integrity, but he had not discovered the continent. The Admiralty had maps showing Australia drawn 250 years earlier.

Brave and determined though they were, Columbus, Dias, da Gama, Magellan, Cook and the rest of the European explorers set sail with maps showing the way to their destinations. They owed everything to the first explorers, the Chinese on their epic voyages of 1421–3. How lucky Europe was, and how unfortunate China, that fire had ravaged the Forbidden City on 9 May 1421. Europeans had now rediscovered almost the entire world, known at first hand until then only by the Chinese and Niccolò da Conti. The charts, ships and systems of ocean navigation used by the great European explorers owed much to Henry the Navigator and his brother, Dom Pedro, but more

Cook's ship, the *Endeavour*, sketched by Sydney Parkinson in June 1770.

to the Chinese emperor, Zhu Di, and his brave and skilful eunuch admirals, Zheng He, Zhou Man, Hong Bao, Zhou Wen and Yang Qing.

The revelation that Vasco da Gama was not the first to sail to India round the Cape of Good Hope, that Christopher Columbus did not discover America, that Magellan was not the first to circumnavigate the world, and that Australia was surveyed three centuries before Captain Cook and Antarctica four centuries before the first European attempt may come as a disappointment, even a shock, to the champions of those brave and skilful explorers, but the Kangnido, Pizzigano, Piri Reis, Jean Rotz, Cantino and Waldseemüller charts are indisputably genuine. They contain information that can only have come from cartographers aboard the pioneering Chinese fleets. Niccolò da Conti was aboard the junks that reached Australia from India; Dom Pedro obtained this information from da Conti himself, and had it incorporated in the map that showed the whole world. Toscanelli persuaded Columbus that China could be reached by sailing west, and Magellan spoke no less than the truth when he told his near mutinous crew that he had seen the 'Strait of Magellan' on a map in the Portuguese treasury before he set sail. Truth, after all, is stranger than fiction.

And what epitaph is there at Sagres to commemorate the lifetime of sacrifice and achievement of Prince Henry the Navigator, the man who began this wave of European exploration that was to conquer the world? Nothing but a run-down sundial where the weeds grow among the stones. Zheng He's tomb on Bull's Head Hill in the west of Jiangsu province is also neglected and weed-choked. These great men must have their reward in heaven.

EPILOGUE:

THE

CHINESE

LEGACY

T HE LEGACY OF THOSE GOLDEN YEARS WHEN CHINA'S power and influence extended from Japan to Africa and beyond to encompass the whole world remains. Chinese Buddhist architecture graces the Asian skyline from Malacca to Kobe. Chinese silk of the Ming dynasty is found from Africa to Japan, glorious blue and white ceramics from Australia to Manchuria, and graves in many places across the globe bear witness to Chinese jade jewellery of that era. Even the most blasé traveller to south-east Asia must be struck by the pervasiveness of China's legacy. From Sumatra to Timor to Japan, communities are still united by trade, religion and a written language inherited from China. For four thousand kilometres west to east and an equal distance from north to south, China's imperial footprint remains, the imprint of a colossus.

The depth of Chinese culture is as awesome as its width. Three thousand years ago the Chinese had mastered bronze moulding and casting with simple yet stunning designs. By the Qin dynasty (221–206 BC), pottery was being cast as sublime as anything our planet has seen, epitomized by the graceful horses and fluid soldiers of Emperor Qin's terracotta army. By the Tang dynasty (AD 618–907), at a time when our European ancestors were clothed in rags, rich Chinese were dining off gold plates adorned with phoenixes and dragons and drinking their wine from silver chalices engraved with dancing horses. Fruit was displayed in white jade bowls. Merchants' wives, sheathed in fine embroidered silk, wore subtle Persian scents. Exquisite jade and gold jewellery adorned their ears, throats and wrists.

The Chinese had millennia of experience and expertise in every sphere of human activity. By 305 BC conservation of land and rotation of crops had been the subject of letters to the emperor. Zhu Di's huge ships and incredible expeditions were the culmination of eight hundred years of voyages of discovery – Song dynasty (960–1279) ships had reached Australia. Chinese trade with India was six hundred years old when Admiral

Zheng He set sail, and even his vast fleet was dwarfed by that of Kublai Khan two centuries earlier. Chinese science and technology were centuries ahead of the rest of the world, their military and civil engineering know-how epitomized by the Great Wall. The stability and protection that wall provided ensured that, of all the great civilizations of antiquity, China alone survived. Its most striking national symbol is a monument to the history, resilience and enduring power of China and its people.

Although much evidence of the Chinese voyages of discovery has been lost or destroyed over the centuries, one very tangible kind is visible everywhere today: the plants and animals the Chinese fleets carried with them to new lands, and those they brought back to China and south-east Asia. China's greatest contribution to civilization may well be the cultivation and propagation of plants.

For centuries it was believed that the global propagation of the world's plants began after Columbus 'discovered' the Americas in 1492, and accelerated when the British founded their great maritime empire after the Battle of Trafalgar. In fact, although the Victorians were certainly great plant collectors, almost all of the important agricultural plants had been spread across the world before Columbus set sail on his first voyage. Europeans not only had charts showing them the way to the New World, they found the most important crops already flourishing when they arrived there. No fewer than twenty-seven important cash crops are known to have been brought to the islands of Hawaii from India, Asia, Indonesia, the Americas and even Africa. The sweet potato, sugar cane, bamboo, coconut palm, arrowroot, yam, banana, turmeric, ginger, kava, breadfruit, mulberry, bottle gourd, hibiscus and candlenut tree were all growing in Hawaii when the first Europeans arrived; none of them is indigenous to the islands.

This pattern was repeated throughout Polynesia and halfway

across the world to Easter Island. There the first Europeans found totora reeds from Lake Titicaca, tomatoes, wild pineapples and sweet potatoes from South America, tobacco from Central and North America, gourds from Africa, papayas from Central America, yams from south-east Asia and coconuts from the South Pacific. The first Europeans to reach the Caribbean also found coconuts; Magellan loaded maize in the Philippines that had originated in Central America; California was graced with Chinese roses; South America had Asiatic chickens. No fewer than ninety-four genera of plants were found to be common only to South America and Australasia;[1] another seventy-four genera, including 108 distinct species, are common only to tropical West Africa and tropical America.

It has been argued that this mass of plants could have been propagated naturally, by seeds carried by ocean current and wind, or by birds. Coconuts will float, and in theory they could have found their own way from the South Pacific across the Indian Ocean, the South Atlantic and the North Atlantic to end up in the Caribbean. Some certainly did float from island to island, and some seeds and spores were undoubtedly carried on the wind, but to suggest that all plants were propagated in this way is preposterous. The argument collapses with maize and sweet potatoes; they do not float, and sweet potatoes are far too heavy for birds to carry from country to country. In the last three decades, a number of distinguished botanists have carried out research into the places of origin of cultivated plants. Improved understanding of the classification of plants has radically altered views on their wild relatives and hence place of origin. An example is the coconut, which early European explorers found on Atlantic and Pacific coasts of Central America.

The coconut (*Cocos nucifera*) was once thought to have originated in the New World because this is where the other species of *Cocos* occurred. Now, however, *Cocos* is treated as a monotypic genus whose closest living relative is African. This, together with the fossil records of the coconut and its variability and range of uses in south-east Asia, suggests that the coconut originated in the western Pacific and spread west to east, not east to west, across the ocean.[2]

An analysis of the plants common to Africa and South America and of those common to South America and Australasia discloses that they were all carried in the direction of the prevailing winds and currents – in short, by ships crewed by men. No Polynesian ships are known to have left the Pacific to enter the South Atlantic ocean, and propagation predates the European voyages of discovery. Only one nation could have transported this array of plants and animals around the globe. The Chinese ships certainly carried plants and seeds and they not only circumnavigated the world but did so in precisely the direction propagation has been found to have occurred, from China through south-east Asia to India, thence to Africa, from there across the South Atlantic to South America, and finally on to Australasia.

Rice was by far the most important Chinese crop, perhaps the most diverse and adaptable crop on our planet. The Chinese developed varieties that could flourish on dry mountain slopes, while others needed to be submerged. Some species took months to ripen, others only two. Some were sensitive to temperature, others to sunlight. Some crossbred species became so tolerant of salt that they could be used to reclaim marshes along the sea shores. Rice is an ideal food crop – it tastes good and, flavoured with soy products, has high nutritious value. It stores well, and is easy and economical to cook. Until the twentieth century, rice produced seven times as many calories per hectare of land as any other grain,[3] and China was the most efficient agricultural country in the world.

The entire way of life of over a billion people revolves around rice, the ideal crop for sustaining the dense populations of Asia, where it has even higher status than bread in Western societies. In China, a man who has lost his job has 'broken his rice bowl'. Marriages and business deals are sealed over cups of sake – rice wine. In the West, we throw confetti as a symbol of rice, to bring good luck at weddings. When Japanese children look at the night sky, rather than the man in the moon, they see a rabbit making rice cakes.

In the Ming era, China exported rice to the Pacific, principally through Makassar (Selat in modern Indonesia). Rice ships accompanied the treasure fleets, and rice was found in the hold of the Sacramento junk.[4] But the Chinese were also importers of plants, and they showed their inventive genius by utilizing the crops they found in distant lands. The south-east Asian climatic zone, stretching from China to Indonesia, was an important source of crop plants. A case can be made that the domestication of such crucial crops as millet, rice and yams originated in this zone. Later introductions to China included sugar cane, bananas, ginger and some species of citrus fruits, and cotton was imported from India, but perhaps the most spectacular example was the maize brought back by Zheng He's fleets from the Americas.

After rice, maize is the world's most prolific crop; compared to wheat, at least three times as much can be harvested from the same area. Furthermore, it can grow in arid deserts or in humid jungles, at sea level or up to 12,000 feet (3,600 metres). Maize originated in Central America, yet it was loaded in the Philippines by Magellan, the first European to reach there, and surviving Chinese records tell of 'extraordinarily large ears of grain' being carried back by Zheng He's fleets to China. Maize was ideal for China's mountain dwellers for it had deep roots, preventing the plant being washed away by heavy rain, and cultivation on the mountain slopes minimized the danger of frost damage. To the Miao people of southern China, the introduction of maize with its extremely high yield was an enormous benefit. Today, maize, the third most important crop in the world, has spread across Asia and is the staple food in many African countries.

The third group of foods carried by the Chinese were taros, yams and sweet potatoes. Sweet potatoes (*Ipomoea batatas*) thrive in the hot, moist climate of South America where they originated, and they have subsequently become an important root crop in warm, sub-tropical countries. By the time Captain Cook arrived in New Zealand, sweet potatoes had become the principal food of the Maori. Their name for them, *kumara*, is almost identical to the name *kumar* still used in the Lima region of coastal Peru. True yams (the *Dioscorea* species) originated in Africa and south-east Asia, yet they were growing in Hawaii when the first Europeans landed there. Taros originated in south-east Asia but had also reached Hawaii before the Europeans. They are members of the Arum family (*Aracheae*) and, like potatoes, are rich in starch. Taros are widely cultivated throughout the Pacific from Tahiti in the south – taro ponds greet the visitor leaving Tahiti's airport – to Hawaii in the north.

It can be said that rice, maize, sweet potatoes, taros and yams, originating in entirely different parts of the world, provided the essential food for those living in the tropics and sub-tropics. Their transportation was of incalculable benefit to mankind, for man now had the capacity to grow and harvest crops in almost every soil and climatic condition.

Apart from its role as the world's leading producer and exporter of silk, China also led the way in other fabrics. First used in the Indus valley several millennia ago, cotton is probably the world's most important cash crop, accounting for 5 per cent of the world's agricultural output. Scientists and scholars were initially baffled by the chromosomal structure of South American cotton, but after a series of painstaking experiments experts have now agreed that one parent of American cotton undoubtedly came from Asia. The wild American cotton the first Europeans found in the Americas had one gene that came from India. Cotton had been brought from India to Canton, where it was cultivated by the eighth century. It was widely grown during the Mongol Yuan dynasty that preceded the Ming, and Ming fleets carried huge amounts of cotton on their voyages.[5] The King of Cochin was rightly grateful to Emperor Zhu Di: 'How fortunate we are that the teachings of the sages of China have benefited us. For several years now, we have had abundant harvests in our country and our people have had houses to live in, have had the bounty of the sea to eat their fill of, and enough fabrics for clothes.'[6]

Coconut is far and away the most important nut crop in the world. Its native home was in the islands of Indonesia, yet coconuts were found by the first Europeans when they arrived in the Caribbean and on the Pacific coast of Central America, and there are now about 3.5 million hectares of coconut plantations in the Philippines, India, Indonesia, Sri Lanka and the Caribbean. Coconuts grow within the tropics, yet can withstand slight frost. Besides providing delicious meat and coconut milk, oil extracted from the dried white meat has been used for centuries for cooking and frying and in the manufacture of soaps, cosmetics and lubricants. After extracting the oil, dried copra cake can be ground to a meal high in protein, used for cattle and chicken feed. The trunk provides roof beams, and the fibres of the husk (coir) can be used to make ropes. Ming fleets traded coir extensively.

Bananas originated in south-east Asia, but were also found in Hawaii by the early European explorers and have subsequently spread to India, Africa and tropical America. Along with grapes, oranges and apples, bananas are the world's most important fruit crop; their cousins, starchy plantains, are eaten as a vegetable throughout the tropics. Pineapples originated on the hot, steamy Atlantic coast of South America, yet Columbus noted pineapples on his second voyage to the West Indies in 1493. The evidence of the great voyages by the Chinese treasure fleets is literally growing all around us today.

At the start of my long journey in the tracks of the great fifteenth-century Chinese explorers, I had learned of a monument, a carved stone erected by Zheng He overlooking a bay in the Yangtze estuary in China, and read the inscription incised on its surface. It was almost the only surviving physical evidence on the whole Chinese mainland of that epic sixth voyage of the treasure fleets. Little else had survived the purges of the mandarins. Translated, it read:

> The emperor ... has ordered us [Zheng He] and others [Zhou Man, Hong Bao, Zhou Wen and Yang Qing] at the head of several tens of thousands of officers and imperial troops to journey in more than a hundred ships ... to treat distant people with kindness ... We have gone to the western regions ... altogether more than three thousand countries large and small. We have traversed more than a hundred thousand *li* [forty thousand nautical miles] of immense water spaces.

I had puzzled over this inscription as I began the voyage of discovery that was to consume me for years. Now at the conclusion of my journey, I returned, believing that I had found the evidence to overturn the long-accepted history of the Western world. I had found a wealth of evidence that the Chinese fleets commanded by Admirals Zheng He, Yang Qing, Zhou Man, Hong Bao and Zhou Wen on that epic sixth expedition had surveyed every continent in the world. They had sailed through sixty-two island archipelagos comprising more than seventeen thousand islands and charted tens of thousands of miles of coastline. Admiral Zheng He's claim to have visited three thousand countries large and small appeared to be true. The Chinese fleets had voyaged across the Indian Ocean to East Africa, around the Cape of Good Hope to the Cape Verde Islands, through the Caribbean to North America and the Arctic, down to Cape Horn, the Antarctic, Australia, New Zealand and across the Pacific. Throughout the entire hundred thousand *li*, only in the Antarctic would the treasure ships have had to sail into the wind or an opposing current.

Before that great voyage of 1421 to 1423, Zhu Di had already brought all of south-east Asia, including Manchuria, Korea and Japan, into China's tribute system. The eastern end of the Silk Road had been reopened from China as far as Persia (modern Iran). Central Asia was in thrall to China, and the Indian Ocean was dominated by Chinese shipping. The treasure fleets of 1421 to 1423 added to this already vast trading empire. They created permanent colonies along the Pacific coast of North and South America, from California to Peru. Settlements were also initiated in Australia and New Zealand and throughout the Indian Ocean as far as East Africa. Supply bases were established right across the Pacific to link first the Americas with China, and then Australia and New Zealand with China. Vast distances were covered: there were bases from Easter Island to Pitcairn Island, through the Marquesas and the Tuamotu Archipelago, at Tahiti, Sarai in Western Samoa, Tonga, San Christobal in the Solomons, Nan Madol, Yap and Tobi in the Carolines, and Saipan in the Marianas. The remains of stone barracks, quays, houses, reservoirs and observation platforms may be seen on many of these islands to this day. Zheng He's great fleets and their supply trains were to link all these settlements and supply bases.

My claims about the Chinese voyages in the 'missing years' from 1421 to 1423 rest on the authenticity of the Kangnido, Piri Reis, Jean Rotz, Cantino, Waldseemüller and Pizzigano charts. No-one has ever questioned their veracity. The Vinland map has been questioned in the past, but as I have demonstrated (see chapter 14 and postscript), I believe it passes the authenticity test. The Piri Reis, Jean Rotz and Cantino charts depict the whole of the southern hemisphere, covering tens of millions of square miles of ocean, thousands of islands, and tens of thousands of miles of coastline from the Antarctic to the equator. The lands they show can only have been surveyed by fleets that had sailed the southern hemisphere before the European voyages of discovery, and those fleets can only have been Chinese.

There is also a wealth of physical evidence for these great Chinese voyages. The Pandanan junk in the Philippines vividly demonstrates the extent of Chinese trade with the states of the Indian Ocean, the Americas and south-east Asia. Ming porcelain has been found down the East African coast, in the Persian Gulf and Australia, Ming silk as far north as Cairo. The wrecks of treasure ships lie off New Zealand and southern Australia, and there is also a wealth of other evidence of a Chinese presence in those countries. Carved stones were erected across the Indian Ocean, in the Cape Verde Islands, New Zealand and South America. Chinese chickens were carried to South America, maize brought from the Americas to China. Votive offerings have been found in the Lamu archipelago, at Darwin and on Ruapuke beach in New Zealand.

It is the spread, depth and variety of the evidence that makes the great Chinese voyages of 1421–3 so credible. One mahogany wreck in Australia may be explained away as an Indian merchantman blown far off course, but several wrecks, accompanied by Chinese votive offerings, ceramics and adze anchors, tell an entirely different story, one corroborated by Aboriginal folklore and cave paintings and clearly recognizable charts of the Barrier Reef drawn hundreds of years before the first Europeans reached Australia. The Chinese porcelain dating from the Ming era found throughout the Indian Ocean might have come from the cargoes of shipwrecked Portuguese caravels, but again, the evidence does not exist in isolation. There are the accounts of

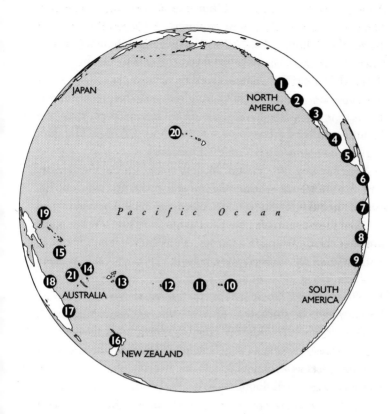

1 Sacramento	8 North Peru	15 Caroline Islands
2 Los Angeles	9 South Peru	16 New Zealand – Waikato River
3 Baja California	10 Easter Island	17 New South Wales
4 Mexico – Michoacán	11 Pitcairn Island	18 Gympie
5 Guatemala	12 Tahiti	19 Micronesia
6 Colombia	13 Kiribati	20 Hawaiian Islands
7 Ecuador	14 Samoa	21 Norfolk Island

Chinese bases across the Pacific Ocean.

yellow-skinned people, the Chinese votive offerings, and silk found by the first Portuguese explorers. There is also a detailed chart of millions of square miles of ocean that was drawn before the Portuguese could have surveyed the Indian Ocean in such detail. The only explanations to date of how Antarctica could have appeared on a chart four hundred years before Europeans reached those parts have come from the pens of Erik von Daniken (aliens from outer space) and Charles Hapgood (Egyptian civilization before the Pharaohs).

Magellan saw the 'Strait of Magellan' and the Pacific depicted on a chart before he set sail; that can only mean that someone had passed through the strait and crossed the Pacific before he did, and had drawn animals native to Patagonia before any European knew of them. That the 'someone' was Chinese is confirmed by the pictures of animals (published 1430) and the Chinese artefacts along the route they followed, and the continents shown on the Chinese charts that have survived. That the Chinese had the ships, the expertise, the funds and the time to make such an extraordinary circumnavigation of the world is beyond question, just as it is beyond doubt that no-one else in that era could have done it.

These claims will doubtless be greeted with astonishment, yet if one takes a dispassionate view, there is nothing illogical about them. The Chinese enjoyed a far older and richer maritime tradition than the Europeans. When Zhu Di's fleets set sail in 1421, they had at least six centuries of ocean exploration and astro-navigation behind them; when Dias and Magellan set sail, the Portuguese had no means of accurately navigating south of the equator. Zheng He's fleets of treasure ships with their attendant supply ships were the products of a massive ship-building programme made possible by the economic strength of China; the tiny caravels of Cabral, Dias and Magellan would have looked like dinghies alongside the Chinese craft. Until the French built the *Dauphin Royale* – later renamed *L'Oriente* when

Napoleon came to power – almost four centuries later, no wooden ship had ever approached the size of the giant treasure ships that epitomized Chinese naval supremacy and domination of the oceans. Even the European warships at Trafalgar could barely match the Chinese junks in size, range or firepower. Nelson's fleet of, at best, thirty ships carrying eighteen thousand men would have been dwarfed by Zheng He's armada of more than a hundred ships carrying twenty-eight thousand men. His treasure ships were twice the length and three times the beam of HMS *Victory*. They had far better damage control and logistical support, and could remain at sea far longer, for months on end if necessary.

The Chinese fleets had charted the world, they could determine longitude by means of lunar eclipses, and by comparing charts they were able to resolve any remaining longitudinal differences and complete the first map of the world as we know it today. But that knowledge was bought at a terrible cost. Only four of Hong Bao's ships and just one of Zhou Man's returned to China – a loss of at least fifty ships in those two fleets alone. The human toll was equally high: a mere nine hundred of the nine thousand men in Zhou Man's fleet were still with their admiral come October 1423. Up to three-quarters of the fleets' original complement must have died or been abandoned in the scattered settlements around the globe.

Twenty-four wrecks have already been located around the world; many more, carrying thousands of tons of treasure, remain to be found. The oceans will inevitably release more and more evidence as time goes by. The costs in both human and financial terms remain unparalleled – even the mightiest empire the world had ever seen was unable to sustain them – but the tasks Zhu Di had set his admirals had been achieved. It was a towering achievement, unequalled in the annals of mankind.

Zhu Di's master plan to discover and chart the entire world, and bring it into Confucian harmony through trade and foreign policy, could have succeeded, for the whole world now lay at China's feet – or so it must have seemed to his admirals when the handful of surviving ships of the treasure fleets limped home during the autumn of 1423, only to find that China, and the world, had changed for ever. Zhu Di was dying, a broken man, and the mandarins were dismantling the apparatus of the world-wide empire he had so nearly created. There would be no more tribute system, no more great scientific experiments, no more epic voyages of trade and discovery. China was entering its long night of isolation from the outside world. The eunuch admirals were dismissed, their ships broken up or left to rot at their moorings, the maps and charts and thousands of precious documents recording their exploits destroyed. Zhu Di's great achievements were disowned, ignored and, in time, forgotten.

One of the fascinating 'what ifs' of history is what would have happened had lightning not struck the Forbidden City on 9 May 1421, had fire not roared down the Imperial Way and turned the emperor's palaces and throne to cinders. Would the emperor's favourite concubine have survived? Would the emperor have kept his nerve? Would he have ordered Admiral Zheng He's squadrons to continue their voyages? Would they have carried on establishing permanent colonies in Africa, the Americas and Australia? Would New York now be called New Beijing? Would Sydney have an 'English' rather than a 'Chinese' quarter? Would Buddhism rather than Christianity have become the religion of the New World?

Instead of the cultured Chinese, instructed to 'treat distant people with kindness', it was the cruel, almost barbaric Christians who were the colonizers. Francisco Pizarro gained Peru from the Incas by massacring five thousand Indians in cold blood. Today he would be considered a war criminal.

In effect the Portuguese used Chinese cartography to show them the way to the East. Then they stole the spice trade, which the Indians and Chinese had spent centuries building. Anyone who might stop them was mown down. When da Gama reached Calicut he told his men to parade Indian prisoners, then to hack off their hands, ears and noses. All the amputated pieces were piled up in a small boat. The historian Gaspar Correa describes da Gama's next move:

> When all the Indians had been thus executed [*sic*], he ordered their feet to be tied together, as they had no hands with which to untie them: and in order that they should not untie them with their teeth, he ordered them to strike upon their teeth with staves, and they knocked them down their throats . . .[7]

Then a Brahmin was sent from Calicut to plead for peace. The 'brave' da Gama had his lips and ears cut off and the ears of a dog sewn on instead.

It seems certain that a further voyage by Zheng He's fleets would have included the one section of the globe they had not yet reached and charted – Europe. The upheavals in Beijing ended any possibility of that, but who can say what the subsequent history of the world would have been had the Chinese treasure ships appeared over the European horizon in the 1420s? One thing seems certain: had the emperors who followed Zhu Di not retreated into xenophobia and isolation, China, not Europe, would have become the mistress of the world.

The Forbidden City still stands as a monument to the vision of the great Zhu Di, but what more fitting epitaph could there be to the 'Emperor on Horseback' than the valiant horseman mounted on the tip of Corvo's volcano in the Azores, high above the Atlantic rollers crashing onto the cliffs far below? He pointed dramatically to the west, towards Fusang, the Americas, the land his brave and skilful mariners had discovered. As China began to draw in on itself, abandoning Zhu Di's great ambitions, others, notably the Portuguese and Spanish, began to fill the vacuum they had left. For centuries they have basked in the glory that rightfully belonged to others; it is now time, at last, for us to redress the balance of history and give credit where it is due.

To assert the primacy of the Chinese exploration of the New World and of Australia is not to denigrate the achievements and memories of Dias, Columbus, Magellan and Cook. The exploits of these brave and skilful men will never be forgotten, but it is now time to honour other men who have been allowed to languish in obscurity for too long. These remarkable Chinese admirals rounded the Cape of Good Hope sixty-six years before Dias, passed through the Strait of Magellan ninety-eight years before Magellan, surveyed Australia three centuries before Captain Cook, Antarctica and the Arctic four centuries before the first Europeans, and America seventy years before Columbus. The great admirals Zheng He, Hong Bao, Zhou Man, Zhou Wen and Yang Qing deserve to be remembered and celebrated too, for they were the first, the bravest and most daring of all. Those who followed them, no matter how great their achievements, were sailing in their wake.

POSTSCRIPT

B Y GREAT GOOD LUCK, THE TALK I GAVE AT THE ROYAL
Geographical Society in London in March 2002 was broadcast around the world, and a subsequent article in the *Daily Telegraph* was also published in seventy-four other newspapers and magazines. As a result, new evidence began to pour in from all over the world, all of which had to be evaluated and checked for accuracy by experts in each different field. The text was continually expanded and rewritten to incorporate this new material, but eventually a line had to be drawn for publication. However, emails, faxes and letters about exciting new discoveries have continued to arrive almost every day, and as the book goes to press, this postscript allows me a final opportunity to summarize the very latest evidence available.

Perhaps the most striking recent discovery has been the wreck of a very old and large ship or junk found near Fraser Island, off Queensland in Australia. It was unearthed as a result of research by a local historian, Brett Green, followed by a sonar search of the sands of the eastern part of the island. On 5 October 2002, during the period of the lowest tides of the year, a private firm of salvage experts deployed huge sand pumps over the area where metal traces had been detected by the sonar scan. They unearthed three cast-iron cannon in a remarkable state of preservation, as well as the huge wooden ribs of the wreck. The provisional analysis was that the wreck was around six hundred years old and the cannon of hitherto unknown origin. However, on 8 November, before the cannon or other artefacts could be raised from the sea-bed, the local authorities reclassified the area as a heritage site. Only government-appointed archaeologists are now allowed to continue investigations there, and I await their findings with great interest. The wreck is almost certainly of Portuguese or Chinese origin, and in either case it should provide definitive proof that Captain Cook was not the first to discover the eastern coast of Australia.

The great majority of the other new evidence I have received relates to the Pacific and Atlantic coasts of North and South America. I have been notified of countless new discoveries from Vancouver Island in the north to Chile in the south, and the evidence takes many different forms. Dr Annabel Arends and her colleagues are continuing the pioneering work begun by her father, Dr Tulio Arends, and Dr Gallengo into the DNA (transferrins) of the Indians of northern Brazil, Venezuela, Surinam and Guyana, proving that these transferrins are otherwise unique to natives of Kwantung province in China. Diseases previously unknown in South America but common in southeast Asia – hookworm, roundworm, lice and nits – were also found among the indigenous population of Mexico, where Chinese methods of extracting dyes from roots, insects, tubers and leaves were commonplace, as were complex, time-consuming and highly individualistic methods of lacquer technology.

In addition to that discussed in the book, there is other evidence that a wide variety of animals and birds were carried to and from the Americas in pre-Columbian times. Wild pigs (*babiroussa*) were brought from Sulawesi in Indonesia to British Columbia; horses – extinct in the Americas by around 10,000 BC – were found by the first Europeans in Peru; the almost flightless fulvous (tawny) tree duck is found only in pockets in India and on the Caribbean coast of South America; turkeys – a type of large Central American pheasant – reached Turkey via the Silk Road before Columbus set sail; and camels indigenous to the Mahgreb area of Morocco and the Canary Islands were found in South America by the first European explorers.

Plants provide still more evidence: the Europeans found fields of rice – a crop foreign to the Americas – in Mexico and Brazil; cotton with chromosomes otherwise unique to North America were found in the Cape Verde Islands by the first Europeans to arrive there, long before Columbus set sail; and coconuts brought from the South Pacific grew in Puerto Rico and right across the isthmus of Darién to the Pacific coast, sugar cane in plantations besides the Amazon and Orinoco Rivers, and bananas beside tributaries of the Amazon, where there were also Chinese root crops. Tobacco, sweet potatoes and maize from the same area were exported to south-east Asia and the Pacific. All of these animals and plants confirm that there were seaborne voyages to and from the Americas prior to Columbus.

Linguistics provide further evidence. The people of the Eten and Monsefu villages in the Lambayeque province of Peru can understand Chinese but not each other's patois, despite living only three miles apart. Stephen Powers, a nineteenth-century inspector employed by the government of California to survey the native population, found linguistic evidence of a Chinese-speaking colony in the state,[1] and research among the Othomis people of Mexico also suggests a Chinese connection.

In Mexico, a Nayarit legend tells of 'ships like houses' arriving off the coast. At the nearby beach of Playa la Ropa, on the seaward end of the Rio Balsas, is a Chinese wreck that even now disgorges Chinese cloth after storms at sea. There are also many other Chinese artefacts: a statue unearthed at Huehuetla, a vase at Azcapotzalco, ceramic horses on the coast, lions and horses on medallions at Palenque, amulets and earplugs found at Teotihuacan (Mexico City) and numerous carvings of horses on the Yucatán peninsula and at Teotihuacan.

There is strong evidence of a Chinese presence in the old Mexican capital at Teotihuacan, and another beside the River Balsas leading from Uruapan to the coast. A further search for records of finds, focused in Teotihuacan, produced Chinese jade earplugs, jade medallions and, most fascinating of all, a tomb at the base of the Pyramid of the Sun which housed a Mongolian or Chinese body of an important person, for the tomb bore a small statue that was clearly a portrait of the buried individual[2] and the body itself was adorned with jade jewellery.[3] Professor William Niven 'found slabs at Teotihuacan containing Chinese characters that were easily read by the secretary of the Chinese legation, as well as a tomb and statue said to be "wholly Chinese" in design. The "Mongol-type" skeleton in the tomb was said to have borne a necklace of green jade,[4] which was unknown in Mexico. The new information – presented in the synopsis that follows – together with the material I have already assembled, produces an overwhelming impression of a widespread and long-standing Chinese presence in the New World that was later 'discovered' by Columbus and other European explorers.

Emboldened by the new evidence of Chinese colonies in Mexico, I next turned my attention to Queen Charlotte Island, off British Columbia in Canada. The Waldseemüller map clearly depicts the island, and the Kurashio current off the coast of north-west Canada could have carried Zhou Man's junks there. If they did make landfall, there should be evidence of the Chinese presence. Like the Waldseemüller chart, another map of Queen Charlotte Island, called 'colonia dei Chinesi' by its Venetian cartographer Antonio Zatta, was published before Vancouver or Cook 'discovered' the island. The Squamish Indians there have more than forty words in common with Chinese, including *tsil* (wet), also *tsil* in Chinese; *chi* (wood), which is *chin* in Chinese; and *tsu* (grandmother), which is *etsu* in Chinese.

Grant Keddie, curator of archaeology at the Royal British Columbia Museum in Victoria, has analysed the evidence that the Native American cultures of the north Pacific coast may have been influenced by contact with ancient Chinese culture.[5] Thousands of Chinese coins have been found in the area, but Keddie considers that most were probably brought by later Chinese traders, and none provides direct evidence of pre-Columbian voyages by the Chinese. However, the discovery of a Taoist talisman and a Chinese stone lamp were far more significant. The talisman may be identified 'with Shou Lau',[6] whose talismans I have seen in many locations around the world.

In 1747, a boy from Attu in the Aleutians spoke of a legend in which 'men dressed in long, many-coloured silk and cotton clothing came to the island in small ships with one sail, their heads were shaved to the crown and the hair on the back was plaited into tresses'.[7] Scholars have been discussing the parallels between the culture of ancient China and the advanced societies of the New World ever since the Dutch jurist and politician Hugo Grotius (1583–1645) wrote of the accounts of Spaniards who observed 'Asiatic' shipwrecks on the Pacific coast of Mexico.[8] The Portuguese sailor Antonio Galvão was told about early Chinese voyages to the New World when he visited China in 1555, and he noted that 'the people of China were sometimes lords of the most parts of Syria and sailed ordinarily the coast which seemeth to reach unto seventy degrees towards the north'[9] – the latitude of Baffin Island in Canada and the north coasts of Alaska and Siberia.

The advance royalties from my book enabled me to set up a small team of researchers who could read medieval Spanish and Portuguese, including Brazilian Portuguese. I put them to work on the first-hand accounts of the early Spanish and Portuguese explorers to the New World, many of which had never before been translated. I decided to concentrate on areas where the accumulation of evidence of Chinese influence was strongest: California, around San Francisco; the Mississippi River west of Kansas City; Florida; Mexico between the Pacific coast and Mexico City; the Caribbean coast of Venezuela, Colombia and Guyana; the Amazon, particularly around Santarém, where the Tapajos River branches south from the main Amazon stream; and the far south of Brazil near Cuiabá, where the Paraná River of Paraguay and the São Francisco branch of the Amazon both rise.

At first sight it appeared unlikely that the Chinese would have voyaged so far inland – nearly three thousand miles in the case of the Amazon – but there was compelling evidence in a series of charts clearly showing the course of North and South American rivers before Europeans had reached and 'discovered' them. Just as the Toscanelli chart (1474) shows the Murray, Darling, Cooper, Diamantina and Flinders Rivers of Australia, so the Martellus map (1489) depicts the Magdalena in Colombia, the Orinoco in Venezuela, the Amazon and its tributary the São Francisco, the Paraná and Paraguay Rivers in Paraguay, the Colorado and Negro in Argentina, and the Chubut in Patagonia. The Magdalena River also appears on the Cantino (1502), as does the Cavra branch of the Orinoco, while the Waldseemüller (1507) shows nearly a thousand miles of the Mississippi as well as the Brazos, Alabama, Roanoke, Delaware and Hudson Rivers of North America.

The rivers of Colombia and Venezuela are also linked to the Chinese voyages by the DNA (transferrins) of the people who lived beside them. Surinam, Guyana and the Orinoco delta also have a similar 'Chinese' connection; as in parts of China, the native tribes of the Mato Grosso in Brazil have an absence of Duffy blood groups (a system of classifying blood used in tracing and predicting the spread of certain sorts of malaria). There are also skin diseases in the flood plains of the São Francisco and Xingu Rivers and the Mato Grosso of southern Brazil that can only have been transmitted by seaborne voyages from south-east Asia.

Ancient stone carvings from the floodplains of the Mississippi and Missouri Rivers also yield fascinating evidence. There are clear depictions of horses in the Oklahoma Panhandle; near Springfield, Colorado; in Hickling Springs, Colorado; and in Le Flore County on the borders of Arkansas and Oklahoma. Somebody must have brought horses to the area, for how else could the unknown artists have drawn them? There are also many petroglyphs of ships, most in the same areas: Picture Canyon, Colorado, near the Oklahoma border; Le Flore County, Oklahoma; the Oklahoma Panhandle; Baca County, Colorado; and beside the Arkansas River in Colorado. In total there are more than fifty carvings of ships and forty of horses, strongly suggesting that the horses were brought by ship.

These findings prompted me to devote some effort to researching the diaries of the first European explorers to reach the Mississippi and its tributaries, especially the Missouri. In 1540, Francisco Vasquez de Coronado (c.1510–54), the Spanish governor of an important Mexican province, led an enormous expedition through what is now the American West, searching for the fabled 'seven cities of Cibola', first described to an earlier Spanish conquistador, Cabeza de Vaca, on his expedition from Florida to the Pacific coast of Mexico in 1528–36. These lost cities were supposedly built on land rich in gold somewhere on the alluvial plains between the Mississippi and the Rio Grande. The historian Pedro de Castaneda recorded Coronado searching first for the lost city of Quivira, which he believed to be 'not far from the great bend in the Arkansas River whose course they had followed from the neighbourhood of [Dodge City]'.[10] Coronado described encounters with Indian hunters, and then an entirely different people:

> These people, since they are few, and their manners, government and habits so different from all the nations [peoples] that have been seen and discovered in these western regions, must come from that part of Greater India, the coast of which lies to the West of this country [i.e. China], crossing the mountain chains and following down the river, settling in what seemed to be the best place. The settlements and people already named were all that were seen 70 leagues wide and 130 long in the settled country along the river Tiguex [Missouri] ... Silver metals were found in many of their villages, which they use for glazing and painting their earthenware. [11]

Even more fascinating, 'vessels were found of which the sterns were gilded, and Pedro Menendez, in Acosta, speaks of the wrecks of Chinese vessels seen upon the coast. It is also an unquestionable fact that foreign merchants clothed in silk formerly came among the Catualcans. All of these accounts, added to those which we have adduced, became so many proofs that the Chinese traded at the north of California, near the county of Quivira.'[12]

The story is the same further east. Acosta, the great sixteenth-century historian, described meeting Chinese people in Mexico, and wrote of

> the Strait which some hold to be in Florida . . . Even as Magellan found out this strait from the south [the Straits of Magellan], so some have pretended to discover another strait, which they say is in the north, and suppose it to be in Florida . . . Pedro Menendez, the Adelantado, a man very expert at sea, affirmeth for certaine that there is a strait and that the king had commanded him to discover it, wherein he showed a great desire; he propounded his reasons to prove his opinion, saying that they have seene some remainders of shippes in the North Sea [Atlantic] like unto those which the Chinois use, which had become impossible if there were no passage from one sea into another.[13]

The Caribbean, too, and the areas bordering it, are full of legacies of Chinese voyages, but the evidence strewn along the banks of the Amazon is perhaps the most compelling of all. The earliest maps of these regions show that seafarers had travelled far down the Amazon towards Cuiabá, and when I began research into the Tapajos tributary that joins the Amazon by the modern town of Santarém, I learned that a mass of jade and other Asian artefacts had been found there. Senhor João Barbosa Rodrigues, a Brazilian botanist and anthropologist, argued that the jade amulets he named Muyrakyta had come from China.[14] The written opinions of several professors supported his contention that at least some of the jade found by the first Europeans in Central and South America was 'unquestionably Chinese' in origin, and a jade duck found in a hoard near Santarém was strikingly similar to a duck found in New Zealand. I now had evidence of jade talismans the length of Central and South America. Some of this may eventually prove to be Guatemalan, but the bulk of it is undoubtedly of Chinese origin. Moreover, much of the jade, especially that found in Brazil and Venezuela, was discovered in the places where the native people have DNA or intestinal afflictions otherwise unique to China and south-east Asia. As this book goes to press, it appears that yet another hoard of jade has been unearthed at Maracay in Venezuela.

The jade artefacts were found where today there is only jungle, but I was certain that the Chinese would only have traded these exquisite pieces if they stood to gain something of real value in return. I returned to the diaries of the first Europeans to sail down the Amazon to Peru, notably the conquistador Francisco de Orellana (1511–46), second in command of Pizarro's 1542 expedition to the east of the Andes; the Portuguese explorer Gabriel Soares de Sousa (1558); and the Spanish friar Gaspar de Carvajal (1539–96). Carvajal's accounts are particularly riveting. At the confluence of the Amazon and the Tapajos, he discovered 'a vast city' of splendid buildings, filled with beautiful, multicoloured ceramics of very fine quality.

There may now be much more recent confirmation of his discovery. On 7 September 2002, Dr Denise Gomes of São Paulo University described a lost city amid a 'green hell entirely peopled by Indians'[15] in the jungle near Santarém, but was it built by the indigenous people or by the Chinese eunuch admirals as the range of Chinese artefacts discovered there might suggest? The nephrite amulets are similar in origin, form, colour, density and chemical composition to Chinese jade amulets, as are items found in Nicaragua and Costa Rica. All are 'unquestionably Chinese jade'.[16] Terracotta amulets have also been found inscribed with the Chinese yin-yang symbol, and terracotta urns were found near Santarém. They were painted in the traditional symbolic colours of Asia – red, yellow, black and white. Why were these four 'Chinese' mineral colours used, given the local availability of vegetable dyes? The mountain range near the site of the Muyrakyta find is named Serra da Chinella; *chinella* means 'sandal/slipper' in Brazilian Portuguese, an item of Chinese origin and possibly an early variation of the Portuguese word for the Chinese, *chinês*.

These finds, together with mortuary customs, folklore very similar to that of China, and the divination processes using chickens and chicken blood on paper, all signify indoctrination over an extended period. The substantial evidence of a Chinese presence, coupled with the vast wealth that could have been extracted from the Brazilian diamond mines and the silver mines of the Chapada Range, make it quite conceivable that the Chinese set up a network of trading posts and settlements along the Amazon and its tributaries. Several expeditions have been mounted in search of these lost cities, yet the majority of explorers have returned empty-handed, or indeed – like Colonel Percy Fawcett, who set off into the jungle in search of fabled riches but disappeared soon afterwards – never returned at all.

Over the years of researching and writing this book, I have been struck again and again by the truth and accuracy of the descriptions recorded by the early explorers. Far from being fanciful or bizarre exaggerations, almost everything I have investigated as a result of reading their accounts has turned out to be true. For example, the 'Island of the Seven Cities' was Antilia, and the Portuguese did travel to and from it long before Columbus. Hence, there seems good reason to believe that many of the early European accounts of lost cities in North and South America will also turn out to be correct. Friar Gaspar de Carvajal recorded these impressions as he travelled down the Amazon in the 1540s:

We saw emptying into the river another very powerful and wider river on the right; so wide was it that at the place where it emptied in it formed three islands . . . At this junction there were numerous and very large settlements and very fruitful country and very fruitful land . . . There was a great deal of porcelain ware of various makes, both jars and pitchers, very large with a capacity of more than 25 arrovas [100 gallons] and other small pieces such as plates and bowls and candelabra of this porcelain of the best that has ever been seen for that of Malaga is not its equal for it is all glazed and embellished with all colours so bright that they astonish, and more than this, the drawings and paintings which they make on them are so accurately worked out . . . and the Indians have told us that as much as there was porcelain in this house, so much there was back in the country in gold and silver . . . From this village there went out many roads and fine highways inland . . . Cristobal Maldonado . . . and some other companions started to follow them and had not gone half a league when the roads became more like royal highways and wider . . . Countries very rich in silver . . . and plentifully supplied with all kinds of fruit, pineapples, pears, plums and custard apples.[17]

After studying the rest of Friar Carvajal's account, I was certain that the 'very powerful and wider river on the right' was the Tapajos and the three islands were those in the stream to the north of Santarém. The mention of large royal highways is very important, for today this area is jungle. The people who created the highways that astonished the Spanish must have had substantial surplus capacity and engineering skill. The excavation of the lost city reported by Dr Gomes will be of great interest.

The Tapajos River splits into several tributaries further south, the southernmost of which rises in the Chapada Range in the Mato Grosso, north-east of Cuíaba.[18] This small area is also where the Paraná rises – a mighty river that runs first west and then south-east to empty into the estuary of the River Plate.

When the Portuguese reached this area a century after Friar Carvajal, they found a way of sailing with the wind from the coast against the current all the way up to Cuíaba. It is entirely possible that the Chinese had also done so: the first Europeans saw rice growing beside the Paraná, and the skin diseases of south-east Asia are endemic among the native population. There are substantial silver mines around the headwaters of these rivers. The Chapada Range is a far healthier environment than the marshy plains below and therefore would have been a sensible place to build a city. A map of lost cities of the Americas[19] states that this is where Colonel Fawcett vanished in 1925 while searching for the legendary lost city of Moribeca.

In 1743, a native of Minas Gerais made a search for Moribeca with a party of a few Portuguese, Indians and Negro slaves. After a fruitless ten-year search, they were scouting for food one day when the pursuit of a deer led them through a deep crevice in a precipice. Gaining the summit, they 'stood dumb at the view spread before them'.

In the immediate foreground lay extensive plains brilliantly green, with patches here and there of silver water, changing to yellowish brown and dull greens as they drew near the foothills. On this was a sight that made the adventurers gasp and hastily draw back behind the crest line. For at a distance of some three or four miles and so clear that buildings could be distinctly made out, was a huge city . . .

The overwhelming dignity of the design, the awesome silence and mystery of an old abandoned city possessed them, rough men as they were. High above the crown of the central arch and deeply engraved into the weathered stone were characters of some sort. They knew enough to realize this was no familiar script. The arches were in a good state of preservation; the very few huge blocks had fallen from the summit, and portions had slipped somewhere out of plumb. Passing through the archway they found themselves in a wide street, littered with fallen masonry and broken pillars. They gazed in amazement. There was not a sign of human occupation. It was all incredibly old, and yet for its age amazingly perfect. Here were two storeyed houses on either side all built up of carefully squared blocks carved in elaborate time-worn designs. In many cases roofs had fallen in, in others great stone slabs still covered the dark interiors, and he who had the temerity to enter the windowless chambers through the vaulted doorways and to raise his voice, fled at the echoes hurled at him by the vaulted ceilings and solid walls . . .

Dumb with amazement, the party, huddled together like a flock of scared sheep, passed down the street into a vast square or plaza . . . In the centre of the plaza, dominating its surroundings in sublime majesty, was a gigantic black stone column set upon a plinth of the same rock, and upon it the statue of a man, one hand on his hip, the other arm extended with the index finger pointing to the north . . . Magnificent in design, perfect in preservation. In each corner of the plaza had been great obelisks in black stone covered with carvings . . . The whole of the right-hand side of the plaza was occupied by a building so magnificent in its design as to have been obviously a palace, its square columns intact with walls and roof partly demolished. A vast entrance hall was approached by a broad flight of steps, much of which was displaced. The interior of this hall was rich in exquisite carving, and still showed signs of a brilliance of colouring comparable with some of the finest relics of Egypt . . .

On the far side of the plaza the city was open to a river some thirty yards or so in width . . . evidently there had been a highly decorative terrace to this river, and most of it had been swallowed up or lay beneath the waters . . . About a quarter of a mile outside the city and standing by itself was a palatial building with a front of 250 paces approached by a broad flight of steps of many coloured stones. It was heavily columned all round, and the noble portico opened up upon a vast hall, with mural decorations and gorgeous colouring that still remained more or less intact. From this hall opened fifteen smaller chambers, in each of which was the carved head of a serpent; from his opened jaws poured a small stream of water . . .

The leader decided to follow the river down on the chance of striking some civilized settlement . . . Soon after the departure of this party he found to the east of the fall unmistakable signs of mining. The shafts whose depths he had no means of plumbing excited his curiosity. On the surface of the ground were specimens of silver ore of great richness, presumably brought up from the shafts, encouraging him to believe he had really discovered the lost mines of Moribeca.[20]

It is hoped that a fresh expedition will be mounted to find the lost city of Moribeca, following in the footsteps of Colonel Fawcett. We have enough clues of where to look!

A third lost city, Quivira, another of the fabled 'seven cities of Cibola', was reputedly located in the area of modern Wichita. Coronado's expedition set out from Compostela on the Pacific coast and marched northwards along the Gulf of California to what is now Sonora. Near Zuni, he turned eastwards towards what is now Albuquerque, and then made his way north-east from there to the Missouri. The land between the Rocky Mountains and the Missouri he named Tiguex, and there he encountered Chinese people. Coronado sent exploratory parties in all directions, one of which, under the command of Garcia Lopez de Cardeno, discovered the Grand Canyon of Colorado. In the spring of 1541, Coronado's main party reached what is now Wichita, but though they found 'ships with gilded sterns' there, they did not discover the lost city of Quivira that they were seeking. Is that the end of the matter? I certainly do not think so. There are far too many carvings of foreign ships and horses in western Oklahoma filled with a wealth of ancient writing and related petroglyphs.

Further up the Mississippi, in Wisconsin and Michigan, native American lore cites 'ancient maritime foreigners who came to mine the "red rock"', and Rock Lake, Wisconsin, holds in its depths a possible clue to these 'ancient foreigners'. It is an area rich in copper, perhaps the 'red rock' of native lore. By AD 900 copper had become the coin of the Mayan realm. Mayan miners and astronomers knew of copper deposits in northern Michigan and sent expeditions to establish control of the area. They built a large settlement at 'Aztalan', which became the centre of copper trading for several centuries, but in about 1300, copper deposits were found in Mexico itself and Aztalan was apparently abandoned.

For five centuries, including the period of the great Chinese voyages of exploration, its history went unrecorded, but between 1830 and 1840 early settlers in the Rock Lake area saw strange protrusions sticking out of the water, described by the natives as the 'rock tepees of the ancient foreigners'. Within twenty years, the sawmill dams built by the settlers led to a rise in the water level of Rock Lake and the structures were completely submerged. But after a prolonged drought in the autumn of 1900, two local residents out duck-shooting saw mysterious structures under the water. Dozens of local people converged on the lake, and several young boys dived down and touched the flat-topped pyramids, one of which was described as 'a long tent-shaped structure' approximately eight hundred feet in length. However, the very next day the drought broke, the water became murky and no more sightings were made.

In the 1980s, a team led by local journalist and author Frank Joseph began sonar sweeps of the lake and photographed the underwater structures,[21] and between 2000 and 2002 the Rock Lake Research Society carried out further sonar scans, attempting to fix the location of the structures using ground positioning systems. A diver recorded his impressions:

I would say the first one is about eight feet high, twelve to fifteen feet wide, and more than a hundred feet long. The second is ten to twenty feet south of the first and about the same width, with a steeper slant to the sides, and is shorter in length. They look to be the same height and exactly north and south on a compass alignment ... The area of rocks looks like a tent-shaped pyramid, collapsed ... It is like a pile of rubble, large stones on the bottom and smaller ones on top ... Some kind of plaster had been used on the sides. Slabs of fragments of cement or plaster, or at least something man-made, were on top of the large one.[22]

Local historians developed a theory that these truncated pyramids of 'Aztalan' were used as observation points to record the movements of the sun and planets.

The Louisiana Mounds Society refers to remains of horses in Wisconsin,[23] and a horse's skull was found with other Indian artefacts in a burial mound in Wisconsin, long before Columbus' era. A vertebrate palaeontologist pronounced the bones to be 'those of a horse and not petrified'.[24] In addition, recent test results have shown that the Sioux and Cree Ojibwa people native to the region have 'Chinese' DNA (please refer to *Synopsis of Evidence*).

Taken together, all this evidence makes it at least arguable that the Chinese came to mine copper at Aztalan. There is certainly enough cause to mount further explorations near there. Truth, after all, as I have found many times earlier in the course of my researches, really is far stranger than fiction.

When I began my research years ago, all I had was a blank sheet of paper. As I write this in the late autumn of 2002, my book is soon to be published in the USA, Canada, Australia, New Zealand, South Africa, China, Spain, Portugal, Italy, Poland, Finland, Holland, Scandinavia, West Germany, Japan and a host of other countries. Television rights have also been sold worldwide. A potential worldwide audience and readership of millions have the opportunity to join in the quest for further evidence of those great Chinese voyages of the early fifteenth century. A 1421 website (www.1421.tv) has been established, and I welcome all contributions and help, especially in the search for those fabled lost cities. The great adventure has only just begun.

In the hectic months since I wrote this postscript for the American edition of *1421*, a stream of invaluable evidence has poured into our website from 127 countries around the world. We now have very persuasive information, not least from DNA evidence, of where the Chinese fleets created settlements in the New World.

In October 2002, my wife Marcella, four researchers and I set off for Nanjing, some two hundred miles up the Yangtze, the great river that enters the Yellow Sea near Shanghai. Every two years, the Association of Zheng He Studies holds a conference in Nanjing to which leading scholars of Zheng He are invited – about a hundred of them attended this one. Professor Yingsheng Liu of Nanjing University very kindly invited me to give the keynote address; afterwards, many learned professors who had spent their lives researching Zheng He were kind enough to share with me the fruits of their lifetime's labours. Thus we returned home with an almost priceless cache of published and unpublished works about the great admiral and his voyages. I had dreaded this conference, fearing there might be some bombshell that would destroy my theory. However, it was not to be. Not only did the Nanjing conference enable me to have my book vetted by the world's leading experts on Zheng He, it also gave me confidence in my overall argument. Indeed, the majority considered my central thesis to be essentially correct.

At the end of the conference, the leader of Taicang's Communist Party kindly invited me to stay in their sumptuous guest apartments. Taicang was the port which provisioned the treasure ships after they had sailed downriver from the shipyards at Nanjing. When I arrived, I found the committee, all twelve of them, standing on the step of the banqueting hall, each holding a large glass of water buffalo milk. The reason soon became apparent: local custom has it that during a banquet each person may propose one toast to the guest and a second to their particular friend – that meant twenty-four glasses of Mao Tai. That wonderful stuff was still coursing through my veins the following morning as we staggered around Taicang's old harbour and into the temple dedicated to the Goddess of the Sea. This temple also serves as Admiral Chou Wen's family mausoleum. Recently discovered family records confirm that he spent twelve years at sea with Admiral Zheng He. It appears Chou Wen was the one vice-admiral who was not a eunuch, for he had a wife and children.

In December, Marcella and I returned to Yunnan in southwest China to honour the invitation of Professor Yao Jide and Professor Fayuan Gao to the Kunming Conference on Zheng He studies. This, too, is held biannually, and the emphasis is on Zheng He's life, for Yunnan is where he was born. Once again, nearly a hundred distinguished professors attended the conference, their field of research China's relations with overseas countries. Once again they very kindly offered me the keynote speech on the first day. Professor Bi Quanzhong followed me. His speech was enthralling.

Some years ago, while researching into the prefecture of Fujian province, he had come across accounts of a Brazilian delegation that had landed in the Fujian province after leaving Brazil some ten years earlier, in 1501. They had found their way from Brazil to China by means of a map and had brought very valuable tribute in the form of six wooden boxes of emeralds. Their letters of credential were embossed in gold, so it was a very important delegation. Professor Bi Quanzhong realized that in 1501 Europeans had not yet reached Brazil and China and therefore could not have provided the maps on which the Brazilian delegation relied. Moreover, China was sealed in 1431; this led the professor to the conclusion that the Brazilian delegation must have used a map drawn by the Chinese before that date. He began to research Zheng He's voyages but found, as I had done, that the records had been destroyed. He therefore decided to pursue research into the accounts of private individuals to see if there were any who had sailed with Zheng He. He found two separate accounts: the first told him that the Chinese fleets had reached Brazil, the second that they had reached North America.

The professor decided to write a book in which he would claim that the Chinese had discovered the Americas before Europeans, and he was in negotiations with his publisher when he heard of the talk I gave at the Royal Geographical Society in March 2002. He therefore decided to postpone the publication of his book until he had read mine; I understand his will be published shortly. Professor Bi Quanzhong's evidence, much more succinctly and elegantly presented than mine, stunned the Kunming Conference, for here was a wholly independent Chinese expert who had come to exactly the same conclusions as I had!

Another bombshell followed. Admiral Zheng Ming, former comptroller of the Chinese Navy, described an airport-runway-extension excavation in Fujian during which workmen had come across an underground palace. In the palace were statues of Zheng He and his vice-admirals shown planning the voyage – the first recorded description of Zheng He, faithfully depicting his immense height and his red uniform. This in itself was of great importance, for it enabled me to compare the Fujian statues with the descriptions, drawings and paintings I had found around the world – not least in terms of the colour and shape of the admiral's robes and his strange cap. However, even more exciting was that standing next to Zheng He, and closer to him than his vice-admirals, was a small European with a bulbous nose and large ears. In his hand he clutched a bundle of documents or maps. He looked like the Venetian drawn in the *Illustrated Record of Strange Countries*. Obviously this European was of considerable importance to Admiral Zheng He – here, I realized, was Niccolò da Conti!

Admiral Zheng Ming's talk, following on from mine and Professor Bi Quanzhong's, electrified the conference, which split into three groups to discuss the evidence. At the end of three days the conference unanimously voted to adopt my evidence. There was barely a voice against the motion.

On the last day of the conference, we visited Zheng He's family estate on the banks of a beautiful lake near the Burmese border. There, surrounded by pine trees and in the shadow of the statue of the great man, the proceedings were brought to a close. I was immensely honoured to be granted the keys – that is, the freedom – of the city of Kunming and to be elected a visiting professor of Yunnan University. The university has a great reputation, not least for its genetic studies into minority Chinese peoples. They kindly agreed to make available their resources to carry out DNA analysis of the peoples in the New World among whom, I believe, the Chinese settled on their great voyage. This was a significant breakthrough.

Now that my central thesis was accepted, many Chinese historians cast their eyes once again over official Chinese histories. Many separate accounts were found claiming that not only had Zheng He's fleets been away for more than four years (not two and a half, as I stated) but that his fleets had reached North and South America and Australia. No longer were Professor Bi Quanzhong and I lone voices; we were suddenly in the majority. (Please refer to the Synopsis of Evidence for details of official records recently found or retranslated.)

It also transpired that I may have been too conservative in my estimate of the size of the Chinese fleets. Professor Robert Finlay called my attention to the accounts of Vasco da Gama arriving in

Calicut to be told of a fleet of eight hundred ships having visited the port some eighty years earlier; the fleet had been joined by junks from the Ryuku Islands (Japan) and by Korean, Burmese and Indian ships. That would explain not only the wealth of evidence left around the world but the traces of the Japanese language and 'Chinese' DNA found among the Zuni peoples of Pacific America. It also explains the Korean DNA that regularly turns up in the blood of Norwegian fishermen – in my book I contend that one squadron had sailed past the north coast of Norway, along the coast of Siberia and through the Bering Straits.

I was also delighted to have independent evidence for the authenticity of the Vinland Map and the capacity of the Chinese to circumnavigate Greenland in 1422. I knew that bringing the Vinland Map into the book would unleash a storm, as indeed it did. The nitpickers had a field day, for they claimed a mini ice age had started in the fourteenth century, Greenland could not have been circumnavigated, the Vinland Map could not have been drawn and thus my book was clearly rubbish from beginning to end. Late in 2002, the age of the parchment of the Vinland Map was dated by D. J. Donahue, J. S. Olin and G. Harbottle, and the results were published in *Radiocarbon* (vol. 44). The radiocarbon age of the map's parchment, as determined by accelerator mass spectrometry with a 95 per cent confidence level, is AD 1411–1468. Even more devastating for the 'forgery' school, an ink transfer was found hidden under the end papers of the binding. It related to the appointment of the notary Bartholomaeus Poignare to the Council of Basle on 16 September 1435. The Delft Technical University in the Netherlands has carried out a study into Arctic sea ice and concluded that 'Five consecutive extremely warm winters could lead to the complete melting of the ice in the Arctic Sea.' The Dutch Meteorological Institute KNMI, in collaboration with the European Union, found that the 1420, 1422 and 1428 summers in northern Europe were extremely dry and hot. This backed up my evidence of the strontium 90 levels in Greenland's glaciers between 1400 and 1450, of the thickness of tooth enamel on skeletons in graves in Greenland, and of the absence of certain houseflies in Greenland's dwellings. In short, not only was the Vinland map genuine, Greenland could indeed have been circumnavigated in 1422.

Our travels, delightful as they were, ensured that we missed the traditional parties leading up to Christmas with the result that I set off for the launch of the American edition of this book on 4 January 2003 with a reasonably clear head and healthy liver. Shortly before leaving for America I had received a summary of a review which, it was said, would skewer my arguments. Arriving gravely concerned in a blizzard in New York, I hastily scanned the *New York Times*. Its review was, in my opinion, pretty awful, but the public ignored it for the book went from 2,834th in the *New York Times* list to the third-placed bestseller in a week, and it stayed a bestseller until April.

By this stage we had our website, www.1421.tv, up and running with a team to handle the torrent of new evidence (we'd received 16,000 emails since the book was published in the UK in the autumn of 2002). Every day while I was in America, I emailed my team in London a summary of the phone calls and emails I had received, and they in turn emailed me a synopsis of everything they had received. The stream of evidence became a river, then a flood. It became clear after a few days that thousands of people agreed with my theories.

As more time went by, I became less defensive and started to ask people what they thought. For example, I asked Bostonians whether they had ever had their blood analysed to see if they had Chinese forebears (this, incidentally, produced several who had Chinese teeth, or the Chinese 'purple spot' on their buttocks, and a score of them went off to have their DNA tested). In California, I asked how many of the audience had collected

Chinese artefacts from the seashore. This triggered dozens of emails: people had found Ming brass plates, ceramics, stones incised with Chinese writings and Chinese jade. They knew of local legends describing Chinese people landing in California; they knew of a Chinese wreck off Santa Catalina; they knew of Chinese trees, plants and bushes; they knew of Chinese colonies that had existed in California until the last century; they knew of Native Americans in California who understood Chinese; they knew that early European explorers had found Chinese people, and that Jesuit and Franciscan missionaries found those same people a century later toiling away in California's rice fields. Hardly anyone doubted that the Chinese had arrived in California before Europeans. With this new evidence we could pinpoint the locations of Chinese colonies down the Pacific coast of North America: in Queen Charlotte Islands, British Columbia; in Washington State; in Oregon near Neahkahnie Beach; in California between the Sacramento and Russian Rivers; in Mexico on the Yucatán peninsula.

The next step was obvious – to read and, if necessary, translate the original diaries of the Europeans who first arrived in those places. Did they find Chinese people? The full results are on the website, but in short in almost every place where I claim the Chinese settled, the first Europeans met Chinese people. To me, this was once again incredible. How had 'professional' historians managed to ignore Coronado's accounts of finding Chinese junks with gilded sterns? How could they explain away Columbus's secret records describing his meeting with Chinese miners in 'bird' ships, or the accounts of José de Acosta, Antonio Galvão, Giovanni de Verrazzano, Pedro de Castaneda, González de Mendoza, Father Antonio de la Calancha, Carlos Prince, Cabrillo, Bartolomeo Ferrello, Pedro Menendez de Aviles and Father Louis Sales OP, all of whom found Chinese people or Chinese junks when they first arrived in the Americas? How could they not have tackled the fact that all the great European explorers – da Gama, Columbus, Magellan, Dias, Cabral – set sail with maps showing them their destination.

The final piece of the jigsaw was DNA evidence. In the places where the first European explorers met Chinese people, did the indigenous Native American people have Chinese DNA?

I was not prepared for how immediate and powerful the DNA evidence would be. When my researcher Antonia Bowen-Jones handed me a copy of Professor Novick and colleague's report in *Human Biology* (vol. 70) entitled 'Polymorphic Alu Insertions and the Asian Origin of Native American Populations', I nearly fainted. *Alu* sequences are, the authors state, 'exceptional genetic markers'. The report summarises:

> The results corroborate the Asian origin of Native American populations but do not support the multiple-wave hypothesis supposedly responsible for the tripartite Eskaleut, Nadene and Amerind linguistic groups. Instead, these populations exhibit three major identifiable clusters reflecting geographic distribution. Close similarity between the Chinese and Native Americans suggests recent gene flow from Asia.

Figure 1 of that report shows the geographic distribution of the people tested – it was as if my map showing where the Chinese had settled had been transcribed by Professor Novick and his colleagues. (This, of course, could not have been the case, for their research had been carried out years before my book was written and I did not read their report until five months after my book was published.) Figure 2 shows the 'maximum likelihood tree' – that is, how close Native American peoples' DNA is to Chinese DNA, and how much that DNA has been diluted over the years. It can be seen that the phylogenetic link between the Buctzozt Maya (Yucatán peninsula) and the Chinese is so close that these people could be more accurately classified as Chinese. In short, 22 of the 24 Native American populations whose DNA was analysed are from areas where I contend the Chinese fleet settled: far down the Amazon River; on the banks of the Paraná and Paraguay tributaries; in California; in Tiguex (Colorado/Arizona); on the Yucatán peninsula; in Peru; on the Venezuela/Colombian borders; and even at Hvalsey in south Greenland, where the Pope described the local people being carried off by barbarians before being brought home. Professor Novick's report will be placed on my website once his permission is obtained.

Figure 2 also shows that the DNA of the Aleut people of Alaska is virtually identical to that found in Hvalsey, yet these places are thousands of miles apart. If the people of Greenland had started their journey in the Aleutians, then marched eastward to Greenland, the people of North America between those two areas should have similar DNA – but they don't. Similarly, the DNA of the Maya people of Yucatán is far closer to the Chinese, Aleuts and Greenlanders than to that of the native populations who lived around them. All the Native American peoples with DNA described in the Novick report as having close similarity with Chinese DNA can be reached by sea. This also applies to the Amazon and Paraguay River peoples, and to the Sioux and Cree Ojibwa, reached via the Mississippi. The inescapable conclusion is that Chinese DNA was brought by sea, and the only recent sea voyage carried out by very large numbers of Chinese – sufficient to create the twenty-four settlements cited in Professor Novick's report – was that of Admiral Zheng He. In my submission, Carlos Prince was correct all those centuries ago. He researched Chinese records that claimed 'Chinese ... with Tartairs, Japanese and Koreans ... crossed the maritime stretch ... into the Kingdom of Quivira [Arkansas], Mexico, Panama, Peru and other eastern countries of the Indies ...' long before Europeans reached the Americas. The synopsis (and my website) details more supporting evidence, such as the existence of American populations with genetic markers for hookworm and roundworm, which cannot survive Arctic crossings on account of the cold.

I believe the evidence to be near incontrovertible, and more evidence continues to pour in. The talk I gave at the Royal Geographical Society in March 2002 created such interest and produced so much new evidence that by the time the UK book went to print that summer it had trebled in size. In the months since then, people who had been chary of giving me explosive evidence came forward in large numbers. As a result, I now feel free to throw off the constraining shackles of caution and go much further than I've gone so far – starting in North America with the research of Jerry Warsing.

Several years ago, long before my book was published, Jerry came to the conclusion that a huge Chinese fleet under the command of Admiral Zheng He encountered a severe storm off South Africa and was blown north-westwards to the Atlantic coast of North America. His evidence, which has taken years to assemble, is wide-ranging and fascinating. Jerry believes up to two hundred ships were wrecked on the coast between Florida and Newport, Virginia; separated by the storm, they landed in small numbers at different places. Because of the close similarity between the Ming dynasty spoken language and the language of earlier Chinese who had come across the Bering Straits, they were able to understand the local people and assimilate. One of these groups was the Oceanye Ho, who landed near Norfolk, Virginia. Oceanye Ho has since been corrupted to Shawnee. Another group, the Ming Ho, landed 150 miles further south, near Southport, North Carolina. A third group, the Wyo Ming, marched inland and settled in a rugged mountainous area of the Appalachians. A fourth, the Lyco Ming, trekked from the coast to a county in Pennsylvania adjacent to Wyoming country.

Jerry's first line of evidence is Machado-Joseph disease, which is prevalent among these peoples. It is 'accepted' that

Machado-Joseph disease spread via Portuguese sea routes in the mid to late fifteenth century. However, the disease appeared in the Yunnan province of China (Zheng He's birthplace) before the Portuguese reached China. It was also found in Arnhem Land and the Yemen, which were not visited on early Portuguese voyages. Every place the disease has been found is a location where the Chinese fleet visited. It is at the least arguable that the Chinese brought Machado-Joseph disease to the eastern seaboard of North America, and to the Azores, where the Portuguese contracted it.

Jerry's second line of evidence comes from the accounts of captured Shawnee prisoners at the battle of Fallen Timbers (1794), who protested they were not Native Americans (as reported by Captain John Smith in his *Notes taken while Prisoner of Powhatan*). The third line of evidence is Chinese plants and trees found by the first European settlers. His fourth is Virginia's array of ancient stone buildings – Native American peoples did not build in stone. My evidence is the DNA of the local (Moskoke) people mentioned earlier; Pedro Menendez de Aviles' accounts of finding Chinese junks wrecked off the coast when he arrived; and Giovanni de Verrazzano's report to the King of France that he found Chinese people in what is now New York. Finally, an old Chinese junk was discovered by George Washington's friends when they started draining the Great Dismal Swamp – further evidence that the Chinese landed on the eastern seaboard before Europeans arrived. The theory can be further validated by DNA tests on the Ming Ho people, and Jerry is attempting to obtain their co-operation for this.

We now get progressively more controversial. In the first part of this postscript, published in the American edition of *1421*, I wrote, 'the wreck of a very old, large ship or junk [was] found near Fraser Island, off Queensland in Australia', and continued, 'however, on 8 November 2002, before the cannon or other artefacts could be raised from the sea-bed, the local authorities reclassified the area as a "heritage" site. Only government-appointed archaeologists are now allowed to continue investigations there . . .'

As may be expected my book raised a furore in Australia. Those who wished to maintain the fairy tales that the Dutch or Captain Cook first discovered Australia leapt on the retraction Greg Jeffreys, leader of the excavation team, was forced to make about the Fraser Island junk. He accepted the local authority's claim that in fact it was an Italian liner, the *Marloo*, which sank there last century, and that the cannon found by Jeffreys' team are in fact the stanchions of the *Marloo*'s lifeboats. But why classify the wreck of an Italian liner as a National Heritage site? I have seen photographs of the same wreck taken in 1919 and again in 1972; the earlier ones clearly show wooden ribs that had washed away by October 2002, when Jeffreys' team excavated again. All three sets of photos were taken exactly where John Green vividly described the Chinese junk rising out of the sea on 28 February 1862. In addition, I have received photos of a Ming wine cooler excavated from the site and Chinese teak wood (the *Marloo* was built of steel), which is currently being dated. It is a great pity that those dedicated to the memory of Captain Cook, the finest navigator of all time, should wish to deny the public the opportunity of having the Fraser Island wreck excavated.

The same goes for southern Australia, where my claim that the Warrnambool wreck was a Chinese junk created hysteria among 'professional' Australian historians. Since my book was published, a huge amount of new evidence has poured in about Zhou Man's fleet reaching southern Australia from the Antarctic, but only a short synopsis can be given here. What happened was that Zhou Man lost one junk in Storm Bay, Tasmania, and a second on King Island in the Bass Strait; the third made it to Warrnambool, where it was wrecked. The survivors clambered ashore with their horses and set up a farm, connected to the sea near Warrnambool, where they smoked eels and elvers exported by horseback up the Glenlenty, Murray, Darling and Murrambidgee Rivers – hence the depiction of Australia's rivers on Toscanelli's chart of 1474 and Vallard's 1536 map of Australia, and of Chinese people on horseback in Aboriginal paintings.

We now up the ante once again, this time in Peru. My claim that Peru was de facto a Chinese colony was greeted with incredulity, not least the fact that nearly a hundred villages to this day have Chinese names. Not one of the detractors took up my offer to visit us to inspect our large-scale maps of the Ancash province to see the Chinese names for themselves. No-one has any explanation of Father Antonio de la Calancha's description of Chinese cavalry; neither could anyone explain the mass of Chinese artefacts, plants and animals found by the first Europeans to reach Peru. Now we have the DNA of the Incas from two sources: the Novick report, and the analysis of the body of the ice maiden 'Juanita' carried out in Japan. Inca DNA is so close to Chinese (Novick et al) that one can reasonably argue that some of them were Chinese.

And last of all comes the biggest controversy. New Zealand historians have been the most apoplectic of all about my book. Anything that challenges Maori legend is to be resisted at all costs! Accepted New Zealand history has it that the foreign animals and plants found by the first Europeans were brought by the Maoris in their open canoes – that is, horses, pigs, dogs, rats and an array of plants from South America, North America, Asia and the Pacific. According to New Zealand historians, the Maoris traded all over the world.

A number of critics have emailed me about the size of the tankers required by Zheng He's fleets to provide water for horses, arguing that the limiting factor on the number of horses was the number of water tankers; it would have been impossible to desalinate anywhere near enough water to satisfy more than a handful of horses as each needs about three gallons a day. Now, apply this to the Maori scenario, travelling from Tahiti to New Zealand in open canoes. They must have brought at least two horses to breed as one pregnant mare would not produce a line. I have taken my submarine from New Zealand to Tahiti; the seas are short and choppy most of the year which makes for a difficult journey which would probably have taken at least six weeks. Horses drink more in exposed conditions of high humidity such as spray in an open boat, so the consumption is likely to have been at least five gallons a day per horse, which for a six-week journey amounts to 420 gallons or around a ton of water per animal. Then, of course, the animals would have needed hay, and that's not to mention food and water for the boats' crews. I submit that it would have been impossible for Maoris to bring horses to New Zealand. The wild Kaimanawa ponies on North Island must therefore have been brought by others, either Europeans or Chinese. DNA tests are in hand for the Kaimanawa, the Pasos of Peru, the Assateague of the islands off Virginia and the Kiger mustangs of North America. I believe their common ancestor will turn out to be the blood horses of Tajikistan which were the mounts of the Chinese cavalry. Emperor Zhu Di imported millions to China during his reign.

When the first Europeans arrived in New Zealand they came across an array of plants foreign to the island. The most common was *Chenopodium album*, introduced from North America, where it has been used by native peoples to make cakes since time immemorial. Captain Cook discovered it in 1769. The second is marsh cress, *Rorippa palustris*, identified by the French expedition of 1826–9 aboard *L'Astrobole*. Again, this was used by the Navajo – who have Chinese DNA, and whose elders to this day understand Chinese – as a ritual eyewash. Others include maize, which originated in Peru; scented grass from Colombia; taro from China (Captain Cook); yams from the Pacific (Captain Cook); and, most celebrated of all, the kumara, the sweet potato, from South America (where it is called kumar), which, as

Captain Cook rightly said, was a vitall\
Maori people.

Someone, either Maoris, Polynesians,
Indians or Chinese, must have brought the\
Zealand. The carriers clearly were not Europea\
the plants there. Thor Heyerdahl, to my mind on\
explorers of all time, argued that it was Incas w   sailed
from Peru to Tahiti then onwards. Regrettably, DNA has shown
that his hypothesis is incorrect; if it were true, Inca DNA should
be found on the Pacific islands. An investigative team of
Cambridge archaeologists and geneticists led by Matt Hurles
published their findings in the *American Journal of Human
Genetics*: only on one island around Tahiti, Rapa, did they find
the distinctive DNA of native South Americans, and these Rapa
genes had come from the crew of a Peruvian ship that stopped
off at the island in 1862 to kidnap slaves.

Could it have been Maoris or Polynesians who travelled to
South America and returned with the plants? This possibility
has been examined by Professor Bryan Sykes and his team at
Oxford University and written up in Bryan's wonderful book
The Seven Daughters of Eve. 'If we found DNA matches [of
Polynesians] in Chile or Peru, or even in coastal North America,'
he wrote, 'then Heyerdahl was right. If we found them in south-
east Asia, he was wrong.' Later, he concluded: 'I had to be sure
that 247, the defining variant of Polynesian mitochondrial DNA,
was not abundant in the Americas. No-one had ever seen it. Not
even once. Heyerdahl was wrong.'

So that, in my view, leaves only the Chinese as the possible
carriers to Australia (seventy-four species) and New Zealand
(eight species) of those South American plants found by the first
Europeans. If it was the Chinese, their DNA should be found on
both sides of the Pacific, in the Incas and the Maoris. We know
that's true for the Incas, but does Chinese DNA turn up in the
Maoris?

, a short digression. The Maoris were not the first to settle New Zealand. Carbon dating of rat bones found in Hawkes Bay on the east coast of North Island shows them to be at least two thousand years old. The oldest Maori settlement dates back to AD 800. Dr Richard Holdaway, a Christchurch palaeontologist, says the rats must have arrived with human voyagers – in short, humans must have arrived 800 years before the Maoris. As Dr Rau Kirikiri, a leading Maori academic, reflected, 'this could lead Maoris to question their own history'.

Back to Maori DNA. For the past fifty years debate has raged over where the Maori came from. Some say China (Taiwan), others Indonesia. Events have recently taken a startling turn. Adele White, for the ABC television programme *Catalyst* (broadcast on 27 March 2003), used mitochondrial (female line) DNA to trace Maori origins back as far as mainland Asia. But where in mainland Asia? The answer came from a surprising quarter – by looking at the gene for alcohol. Adele's supervisor, Dr Geoff Chambers, found a match between one of the variant genes for alcohol with people from Taiwan, so it seemed the original homeland of the Maori people was Taiwan. Or was it? When Dr Chambers' team studied the Y (male) chromosome, they found a different story. While the females came from China, most of the men came from Melanesia.

What might have happened is that a small number of Melanesians settled in New Zealand about two thousand years ago; it was they who brought the rats whose bones have been carbon dated. Zhou Man's fleet arrived from the Antarctic (Campbell Island) in 1422/23. They landed in substantial numbers in South Island and some ships were wrecked on North Island (Ruapuke Beach). The fleets carried Chinese Tanka concubines. The Melanesians murdered the Chinese men and took the concubines as their wives. If this was the case, evidence of the Chinese visit to South Island should be there. Thanks to Cedric Bell, to whom I am indebted, that evidence has been found. We have carbon dating of wood, mortar, stone and slag as evidence that the Chinese lived on South Island and mined her minerals for five centuries before Captain Cook 'discovered' New Zealand.

I am, now more than ever, convinced that accepted history has been turned upside down, not only in New Zealand and Australia but in North and South America, across the Pacific and in the Arctic and Antarctic. The great bulk of the new evidence that has enabled me to make such startling claims has come from readers of my book. It is you, not historians or academics, who have rewritten history.

Gavin Menzies
London, May 2003

APPENDIX 1

CHINESE

CIRCUMNAVIGATION

OF THE WORLD 1421−3:

SYNOPSIS OF EVIDENCE

As well as consulting the historians mentioned in the Acknowledgements, in October, November and December 2002 the author visited Nanjing, Shanghai, Taicang, Kunming and Beijing and presented one hundred copies of his book to professors and historians at the following institutions, together with his latest synopses of evidence translated into Chinese: Chinese Academy of Sciences, Chinese Academy of Social Sciences, National Museum of Chinese History, History Institute of Chinese Academy of Social Sciences, Chinese Society on Ming Dynasty History, Ming Division of the History Institute of China, Chinese Society of Histories of China's Foreign Relations, Chinese Institute for Marine Affairs, C.S. Name Consultancy Group, CMHIA Ocean Association, CSO Military Oceanography Committee, Association of Studies of Ming Dynasty, Overseas Chinese Affairs Office of the State Council of the People's Republic of China, History and Natural Science and Technology Institute of Chinese Academy of Sciences, Geographical Studies Institute, Beijing Academy of Social Sciences, Ministry of Transport Research Institute, Yunnan University (Kunming), Peking University (Beijing), Nanjing University, Chinese Society for Historians of China's Foreign Relations, Chinese American Oceanic and Atmospheric Association, Shanghai Society for International Relations, Shanghai Centre for Strategic and International Societies, Zheng He Memorial Hall of Liu He (Taicang), Chinese Marine History Researchers Association, Zheng He Research Association, Navy Command College of the People's Republic of China, National Cheng Kung University, Zheng He family archives, Taicang Museum, Zheng He's Museum (Mausoleum) in Nanjing, Zheng He's Museum (birthplace) in Kunming, Cheng He Navigation Research Foundation, Jiantong University (Shanghai), and the China Institute for Ethnic Chinese History Studies. The evidence has been carefully considered by more than two hundred experts. Of these, approximately 85 per cent accept the author's argument that Chinese fleets discovered the New World before Europeans. Details of the issues over which about 15 per cent disagree will be provided to any researcher who requests them.

Part I: European explorers did not discover the New World

Part II: Only the Chinese had the capacity to chart the world at that time

Part III: Evidence of the voyages of Zheng He's fleets
- Key to the discoveries: the determination of latitude and longitude
- Chinese maps, star charts and records that escaped destruction
- Chinese or Asiatic peoples found by the first European explorers
- Local peoples' descriptions of Chinese or Asiatic peoples who settled among them before Europeans arrived
- Linguistics and languages common to New World and China
- Accounts of contemporary and other historians
- Shipwrecks
- Chinese porcelain/ceramics found in wake of Zheng He's fleets
- Pre-Columbian Chinese jade found in wake of Zheng He's fleets
- Artefacts, gems and votive offerings found in wake of Zheng He's fleets
- Stone buildings or artefacts found in wake of Zheng He's fleets
- Mining operations found by Europeans when they reached the New World
- Advanced technologies found by first Europeans
- Plants indigenous to one continent found on another by early European explorers
- Animals indigenous to one continent found on another by early European explorers
- Art exported by Zheng He's fleets
- Customs and games exported from China to the New World, as found by European explorers
- Armour
- Links with the years 1421–3
- Chinese already in the Americas when the first Europeans arrived: bibliographical evidence

Part IV: Evidence of Zheng He's fleets' visits to specific places
- Indian Ocean
- East Africa
- The Atlantic and the Cape Verde Islands

- The Caribbean
- Florida (including 'Florida' as defined in 17th century)
- The Carolinas/Virginia
- New England, Massachusetts and Boston/New York
- Upper Mississippi
- British Columbia (Queen Charlotte and Vancouver Islands) and Washington State
- Arizona, New Mexico, Texas, Oklahoma, Arkansas, Colorado and Oregon
- California
- The Azores
- Mexico
- Panama and Venezuela
- Peru
- Brazil (1421–5)
- Patagonia and Straits of Magellan
- Greenland to North Pole, across Arctic to Bering Straits
- Antarctica
- The Pacific
- New Zealand
- Australia
- The Spice Islands, Indonesia and the Philippines

Part V: Genetic fingerprints left by Zheng He's fleets – the DNA evidence

- The Navajo
- The Mazatec people of Mexico (Olmec culture)
- Campeche and Buctzozt Maya
- Waunana and Ngobe peoples of Panama
- Inca peoples
- Indian peoples of Venezuela and Colombia: Irapa, Paraujano and Macoita
- Surui people of Amazonia and Solimões/Rio Negro Junction
- Quechua (Bolivia/Mato Grosso borders) and Toba (NW Argentina, Salado River) peoples
- Haida and Aleut peoples
- Moskoke people of SE USA and NW Florida

- Ming Ho and Melungeon peoples
- Sioux and Cree Ojibwa peoples of America and Canada
- Maidu, Yuki, Pima and Wintun peoples of California
- Maori people of New Zealand, North Island
- Gunditjmara Aborigines of Victoria, South Australia

Part 1: European explorers did not discover the New World

1. Evidence provided at the Royal Geographical Society 15 March 2002 (which included charts, medieval documents and the evidence of Dr Eusebio Dizon – circulated separately).

2. The whole world was charted by 1423, before European voyages of discovery started.

THEORY

- Four huge Chinese fleets circumnavigated the world between March 1421 and October 1423. The fleets comprised more than 800 vessels. These fleets charted the world.

- Sailors and concubines from those great fleets settled in Malaysia, India, Africa, North and South America, Australia, New Zealand and on islands across the Pacific.

- The first European explorers had maps showing where they were going before they set sail. They met Chinese settlers when they arrived in the New World.

- China, not Europe, discovered and settled the New World. European 'discoveries' relied on China leading the way.

(i) The whole world was charted by 1428 – by whom?

- Portuguese claim they had a chart of the whole world by then. They do not claim to have created that chart.

- Pizzigano, Fra Mauro, Piri Reis, Cantino, Caverio, Waldseemüller and Jean Rotz charts show whole world charted before Europeans set sail.

- European explorers referred to earlier maps made before they set sail – contemporary accounts of Columbus, Dias, Cabral, da Gama and Magellan's voyages are the evidence.

(ii) Continents shown on maps before European explorers set sail for that particular region:

   (a) North America – shown on Waldseemüller, Cantino and Caverio charts

   (b) Caribbean – Pizzigano, Cantino, Caverio and Waldseemüller

   (c) South America – Piri Reis, Cantino and Waldseemüller

(d)   Africa, India and East – Cantino, Jean Rotz, Fra Mauro, Waldseemüller and Kangnido

(e)   Antarctica – Piri Reis and Francesco Roselli

(f)   Arctic and Siberia – Waldseemüller (1507)

(g)   Australia – Jean Rotz, Desliens, Vallard, Desceliers

(h)   China and Far East – Jean Rotz

(i)   Canada (Vancouver and Queen Charlotte Islands) – Zatta

(j)   Straits of Magellan – Waldseemüller (Small Globes)

(k)   South Africa – Fra Mauro, Kangnido and Da Ming Yi Tu

(iii)   The great rivers of the world were shown on the key charts long before Europeans set sail

(a)   The Martellus Maps (1489), Gallez, P. and Davis, H.
South America:
Colombia – Magdalena
Venezuela – Orinoco (Meta)
Brazil – Amazon, São Francisco
Paraguay – Paraguay, Paraná
Argentina – Colorado, Negro, Chubut (Patagonia)

(b)   Cantino (1502)
South America:
Colombia – Magdalena
Venezuela – Apure, Orinoco (Cavra)

(c)   Waldseemüller (1507)
Siberia: Ob, Yenisei, Kotuy, Olenek, Lena, Yana, Indigirka and Kolyma
North America: Mississippi, Brazos, Alabama, Roanoke, Delaware, Hudson

(d)   Toscanelli (1474)
Australia: Murray, Darling, Cooper, Diamantina, Flinders

(iv)   Straits of Magellan/Patagonia

'Dragon's Tail' (1428 chart) and its giants described on anon. (Durand 1440) and Walsperger (1448), and shown on Waldseemüller globe.

(v)   Correlations between charts of the world before Europeans set sail and the 1428 master chart of the world

(a) Waldseemüller (1507), Cantino (1502) and Caverio (1505). These three draw the Great Bahamas Bank identically and as it would have appeared in 1421 with water levels one fathom lower than today. However, the earlier charts have features which do not appear on later ones, viz. Waldseemüller shows Pacific coast of America, the later ones do not; the (earlier) Cantino shows Florida, the later Caverio does not. The three charts must therefore be based on an earlier original.

(b) Anon. (Durand 1440) and Walsperger (1448). Both refer to Tierra del Fuego as the 'Dragon's Tail', the name given by the 1428 master. Both refer in identical terms to the Giants of Patagonia, hence must have a common source.

(c) Desliens, Desceliers, Vallard and Jean Rotz all show Australia with great similarity – but each has original features, e.g. Vallard has horses. All must have been based on an earlier original that was subsequently lost.

(d) Waldseemüller and Martellus (1489). Both show the Cape of Good Hope at 45°S and the same 'dogleg', 'India Meridionales', in the east. The Waldseemüller shows South America, the Martellus does not. Both must have been based on an earlier original.

(e) Piri Reis and Pizzigano are linked by Columbus's description (note on Piri Reis) of Antilia (on Pizzigano).

(f) Anon. (Durand 1440), Walsperger (1448) and Piri Reis 1513 (1501) are linked by descriptions of the giants of Tierra del Fuego and of Columbus' description of two hours' daylight (Piri Reis).

(g) Waldseemüller (1507), Cantino (1502) and Piri Reis 1513 (1501) are linked by their drawings of Arecibo (Venezuela).

These maps between them chart the entire world. They must, because of the links, have been based on an earlier original which must have been made before 1440 (Durand) and after 1423 (Pizzigano).

(vi) Links connecting the charts with the Chinese

The charts described below were published before Europeans reached that particular part of the world.

(a) Jean Rotz: depiction of China, Australia and Hong Kong; **link** – kangaroos in Chinese emperor's zoo

(b) Martellus (1489): the Orinoco and Amazon Rivers; **link** – Chinese DNA is found among American Indian peoples there, pre-Columbus (Arends and Gallengo)

(c) Piri Reis (1501): **link** – animals unique to Patagonia are shown and are also to be seen in *The Chinese Illustrated Record of Strange Countries* (1430). Description of the mylodon in Chinese records.

(d) Anon. (Durand 1440), Walsperger (1448) and 1428 chart: **link** – description of the giants found in Patagonia and described in *The Chinese Illustrated Record of Strange Countries* (1430). The name 'Dragon's Tail' is found in the three charts, denoting Tierra del Fuego.

(e) Cantino: **link** – longitude of East Africa almost perfect (± 30 miles). The Chinese alone could determine longitude at that time.

(f) Cantino, Waldseemüller and Caverio: Arecibo; **link** – Venezuelan tribes have Chinese DNA (Arends and Gallengo)

(vii) Chinese cartography and transmission of maps to the West

(a) The author contends Europeans could 'translate' Chinese maps into ones understandable to Europeans. Australia appeared on Father Ricci's map (1589) and on Hessel Gerrit's chart (1618 – Seville) (M. Righton); the Pacific from Vancouver to 'the Straits of Magellan' appeared on the Waldseemüller (1507) before Balboa 'discovered' the Pacific; the Amazon appeared on the Piri Reis (1513 [1501]) before Orellana 'discovered' the river.

(b) The author contends the Chinese had the best cartographers in the world prior to the Renaissance – witness: Chang Heng (AD 78–139), flat surface grid system (Bob Butcher's evidence); Phei Hsiu (224–71), grid system; Phei Chu (605), classic grid map; Chia Tan (730–805), map of empire; cartographer unknown (940), cylindrical projection (precursor of Mercator); cartographer unknown (1137), Yu Chi Thu stone map; cartographer unknown (1155), first

Chinese printed map (predates European by two centuries);
Chu Ssu Pen (1273–1337), map of China, Asia, Africa (with
triangular shape) and Europe; Li Tse-Min and Ching-Chun
(1328–92) expand on Chu Ssu Pen.

(c) Star charts – *Wu Pei Chi* and Gan D. E. (Jupiter's moons
c. 200 BC)

(viii) China sends her maps to the West

The author contends it was Chinese policy to send her maps to the
West – otherwise how could countries reach China to pay tribute?
Evidence:

(a) Brazilian delegation setting sail for China in 1501/02 with
map showing route (Professor Bi Quanzhong, evidence to
Kunming Conference, 10 December 2002)

(b) Chinese emperor's order to send maps to West which resulted
in Liu Daxia destroying all available records of Zheng He's
voyage (Professor Bi Quanzhong, evidence, 10 December
2002)

(ix) Niccolò da Conti as the intermediary between the Chinese and
Europeans

The author relies upon the evidence given in his book and that
recently found in the Fujian Palace (Admiral Zheng Ming's evidence
to Kunming Conference, 10 December 2002). In the Fujian Palace,
uncovered during runway-extension works at Fujian International
airport, are statues of Zheng He and his admirals. Standing next to
Zheng He, and closer to him than his admirals, is a European
medieval merchant, as evidenced by his clothes and hat. The merchant carries documents/maps. The most likely explanation is that
this statue is of Niccolò da Conti, who describes his passage from
Calicut to China via Australia and who was in Calicut when the
Chinese fleets arrived in 1421. His statue resembles the drawing in
The Illustrated Record of Strange Countries (1430).

(x) The Portuguese claim

Antonio Galvão's description of the world map which the Portuguese

Dauphin Dom Pedro brought back with him from Venice in 1428: 'Dom Peter, the King of Portugal's eldest sonne, was a great traveller . . . came home by Italie, taking Rome and Venice in his way from where he brought a map of the world which had all the parts of the world and earth described. The Strait of Magellan was called in it "the dragon's taile": the Cape of Bona Sperancia, the forefront of Afrike and so forth.'

Galvão again: 'It was told me by Francis de Sousa Tavares that in the year 1528 Don Fernando the King's eldest son showed him a map found in the study of the Alcobaza that had been made 120 years before which map set forth all the navigation of the East Indies, with the Cape of Bona Sperancia as our later maps have described it; whereby it appeareth that in ancient times that was as much or more discovered than there is now.'

So who drew the 1428 chart? It is the author's claim that Dom Pedro debriefed Niccolò da Conti in Florence in 1424. Da Conti had sailed with the Chinese fleet from India to Australia and China (*Travels of Niccolò da Conti*).

3. Europeans set sail with accurate maps showing their destination.

Accounts of first European explorers to reach land it is claimed they discovered:

- Columbus's 'discovery' of the Americas.
  Letter from Toscanelli to Columbus: 'I notice your splendid and lofty desire to sail to the regions of the East by those of the West [i.e. to sail to China westabout] . . . as is shown by the chart which I send you . . .' [chart is excerpt of Portuguese 1428 chart of world showing Antilia].
  Letter from Toscanelli to the King of Portugal: '[before Christopher Columbus set sail] . . . from the island of Antilia known to you [Antilia is Puerto Rico, discovered by the Chinese in 1421] . . . to Cepangu [China].'
  Columbus's log, Wednesday, 24 October 1492 (when in west Atlantic): 'I should steer west-south-west to go there [to reach Antilia] . . . and in the sphere which I have seen and in the drawings and mappae mundi it is in this region.' Thus, according to Columbus, Caribbean islands appeared on Portuguese

maps of the world ('mappae mundi') before Columbus set sail.

- Cabral expedition to South America.

  João de Barros, arriving on the first expedition to South America, writes to King Manuel of Portugal: 'The lands might the king see represented on the Mappa Mundi whom Pero daz Bisagudo has.' De Barros continues that the only difference between the Brazil the Portuguese have discovered in 1500 and the Brazil shown on Bisagudo [da Cunha] was whether or not Brazil was inhabited. Thus, Brazil had appeared on a Portuguese map before the first European expedition set forth.

- Dias and da Gama rounding the Cape of Good Hope.

  Dias' chronicler describing their approach to Cape of Good Hope: 'They came in sight of that Great and Famous Cape concealed for so many centuries . . .' This is the Cape drawn on Fra Mauro's planisphere of 1459 (Fra Mauro was working for the Portuguese government when making his planisphere). Thus, southern Africa appeared on Fra Mauro's map, prepared for the Portuguese, before the first European expedition reached the Cape.

- Magellan, 'first circumnavigation of the world'.

  On entering the 'Straits of Magellan', Magellan faced a mutiny, but he managed to quell it. 'The Captain General said there was another Strait which led out [to the Pacific], saying he knew it well and had seen it in a marine chart of the King of Portugal . . . Later, Magellan, having crossed the Pacific, met the King of Limasarra.' Note from Magellan's chronicler: 'And he [Magellan] shows him the marine chart . . . telling him how he had found the Strait to come hither.' Thus, according to Magellan's official chronicler, the so-called Straits of Magellan appeared on a Portuguese chart before Magellan set sail, as did the Pacific.

- Cook's 'discovery' of Australia and New Zealand.

  The 'Dauphin' map (1536) showing Australia was owned by the First Lord of the British Admiralty Edward Harley. Dr Joseph Banks, who travelled with Captain Cook, bought it. Since Henry VIII's day the British government had owned the Jean Rotz chart, which also showed Australia. Thus, Australia was known to the Admiralty from two sources before Captain Cook set sail.

Part II: Only the Chinese had the capacity to chart the world at that time

1. CHINESE RECORDS

(i)   Orders to sail

    (a)   13 January 1421, to Yang Qing, sending him to 'Hormuz and other places' to present all foreign rulers with gifts (Shih – Erh – Yüeh Ch'u Shih Jih) – Professor Ptak

    (b)   3 March 1421, to Zheng He, to 'take the envoys' (KC ch.17 p.1117; MC ch.10 p.99; MS ch.7 p.100; MTC ch.17 p.743) – Professor Ptak

    (c)   10 November 1421, to Zheng He (now that Hong Bao is entrusted to return envoys . . .)

(ii)   Dates of return

    (a)   8 October 1423, Zhou Man with 93 men (YLSL ch.26 p.2401). Chan Cheng vol. I, p.165 – Professor Duyvendak, Dates, p. 385.

    (b)   24 October 1423. Envoys of 16 countries, a total of 1,200 people, arrive with tribute (YLSL p.2403; KC ch.17, p.1205; TWL ch.36 p.69; MS ch.7 p.102 and ch.326 p.8440; KTTC ch.30 p.516) – Professor Ptak

    (c)   1425 – by then part of Zheng He's fleet has still not returned – Professor Zhu Jianqui (paper 24, Nanjing Conference, October 2002). Ming Record Xiang Chen Ming (Zhu Jian Qiu – Navy Ocean Research Institute, 28 November 2002)

    (d)   One squadron lagged behind. Not back ZD23 (1426) – Director of Studies Ming History, Chinese Academy Social Sciences.

Author contends that the Chinese fleet could have circumnavigated the whole world four times between 1421 and 1426.

2. CHINESE KNOWLEDGE OF THE WORLD IN 1421

(i)   Four major expeditions had been conducted by Zheng He, the first in 1405. Fleets had acted independently in voyages to Pacific, Indian Ocean, the Persian Gulf and Africa (Ma Huan).

(ii) Japan, Korea and central Asia had been known for centuries (Ma Huan).

(iii) Chinese had known of North and South Poles since 3rd century BC (Zhuangzi) and that the earth was round (para 9(b))

(iv) Australia had been known since AD 316 (para 9)

(v) Americas known since 6th century AD. Fu Sang, the accounts of the monk Huei Sen, were entered in Chinese official records (Annals).

(vi) Three Chinese path-breaking books summarising knowledge of world (Martin Tai evidence): *Knowledge of South China and Beyond (Lingwai Daida)* by Qhou Qu Fei, 1178; *Records of Foreign Peoples (Zhu Fan Zhi)* by Zhao Ru Kua, 1225; *Records of Overseas Countries and Peoples (Daoyi Zhilue)* by Wang Da Yuan, 1349.

(vii) The Yuan traveller of the world – Wang Da Yuan – *Barbarians of the Isles* (includes Australia). T'oung Pao vol.16, 1915 (Martin Tai).

(viii) Chinese knowledge of Australia – Melchior Thevenot, *Relations*, 1663 (M. Righton)

(ix) British missionary to Beijing – map of Australia (Martin Tai)

(x) Father Ricci's 1589 map of Australia

(xi) Dong Fan Shue of Western Han dynasty reached North Pole in 132 BC (*Beijing Morning News*, 9 February 2003 – report of historian Ju de Yuan)

(xii) Trade with Spain: Zhao Ru Kua's (1170–1228) Zhu Fan Zhi (description of various barbarians) has chapter on 'Muranbi Kingdom' = Al Murabitum (Kingdom of Spain) – Rock Hill (Martin Tai).

Author submits that by 1421 China knew of the whole world.

3. CHINESE CLAIMS AS TO WHERE ZHENG HE'S FLEETS SAILED

(i) Worldwide – Zheng He's evidence

    (a) To '3,000 countries' large and small (Duyvendak's first translation). A voyage of 40,000 *li* (100,000 miles) recorded on

stone memorials erected by Zheng He at Liu Shia Chang
(31°07′N, 121°35′E) and Ch'ang Su (26°08′N, 119°35′E).

(b   Further carved stone tablets at Malacca, Dondra Head
(Ceylon), Calicut and the Malabar coast of India.

(c)   Master Bentou (Zheng He's navigator) diaries (evidence of
Kerson Huang), 1403–30.

(ii)   Australia

   (a)   Zheng He's passage chart which shows coral reef from NE
Australian coast – Zhao Zhi Hua 1990 (Zhu Jian Qiu,
November 2002) (Martin Tai translation).

   (b)   Professor Wei Chu Hsieh, *The Chinese Discovery of Australia*.

   (c)   Professor Liu Manchum, paper 26, Nanjing Conference
(October 2002) – 'Beira' or 'Sunla' is Australia.

   (d)   Ma Huan (Martin Tai evidence, 26 February 2003), Wang Da
Huan/Barbarians of the Isles. T'oung Pao vol.16, 1915,
Ropose = Australia, Marani = Darwin.

   (e)   Records of kangaroos in Chinese emperor's zoo.

   (f)   Chinese knowledge of Australia – Melchior Thevenot,
Relations, 1663 (M. Righton).

   (g)   The *Wu Pei Chi* shows Australia (Sun Shuyun translation).

(iii   Reaching America

   (a)   Professor Liu Manchum (paper 26, Nanjing Conference,
October 2002). Fleet reached 'extremely far Beira'
[= America].

   (b)   Professor Bi Quanzhong's evidence to Kunming Conference
(December 2002). Fleet reached Brazil – Brazil delegation to
China.

   (c)   The sailor Zayan's claim to have sailed to America with
Zheng He's fleet (Professor Bi Quanzhong's evidence).

   (d)   Chinese pictorial record, *The Illustrated Record of Strange
Countries* (I Yü Thu Chih), published 1430, which shows ani-
mals unique to South America, e.g. armadillos – Professor
Wade's collection.

   (e)   Chinese pictorial record of herbs and plants known to China
(published 1511) which includes plants unique to the

Americas (e.g. peanuts) – Zhong Guo Ben Cao Quanshan (Key Sun's evidence).

(f)   *The Notebook of Wilderness* by Ming dynasty writer Zu Yun Ming about the official delegation to China from Balazi = Brazil. Brazilians left in 1500 with Chinese map showing route (Martin Tai translation).

(g)   The *Ming Shi* history of the Ming Empire and *The General Registry of Sea Countries* by Shen Mao Shang which names Balazi (Brazil) as a place visited (Zhu Jian Qiu, *Navy Ocean Survey* – 28 November 2002) (Martin Tai translation).

The author submits that official Chinese records do claim Zheng He's fleets reached Australia, America and Brazil. Their reinterpretation follows Professor Bi Quanzhong's evidence to the Nanjing Conference. The author also contends that not only did the Chinese know of the whole world before 1421, the fleets were away for five years, long enough to circumnavigate the world four times, and they had the experience, expertise and ships to explore the globe.

Part III: Evidence of the voyages of Zheng He's fleets

Key to the discoveries: the determination of latitude and longitude

- The extraordinary precision of the southern portion of the Piri Reis map showing Patagonia's coast, the Falklands, South Shetlands and South Sandwich Islands. Not only is the coast perfectly drawn but animals unique to South America – huemils, guanacos and the mylodon – appear. (They also appear in the I Yü Thu Chih – i.e. they were known to the Chinese before Europeans got to South America.)

- The Piri Reis was drawn 400 years before Europeans reached Antarctica. It shows the Andes as far north as Ecuador. The precision of the Piri Reis coupled with the extent of the coastline from the equator to the Antarctic can only mean the cartography was carried out by people who could determine latitude even in the Antarctic with dozens of ships surveying simultaneously. This was achieved long before European explorers set sail for South America.

- Who but the Chinese with six centuries of experience of ocean navigation could have reached the Antarctic? Chinese records claim their fleets reached both North Pole (30 claims) and South Pole (5 claims) (Professor Wei).

- Do Chinese navigational and star charts provide the answer? The most notable is the *Wu Pei Chi*. The problem is the *Wu Pei Chi* has been amended over the years and not all the amendments were dated. Chinese sailing instructions (*Wu Pei Chi*) give the course to steer between Dondra Head (Ceylon) and Sumatra. By a very fortunate coincidence, this course is due east. The current latitude of their track is 06°N. However, Chinese navigators were advised to keep Polaris 1 *chih* above the horizon; this means there is a difference of 3°40′ between the position of Polaris in *Wu Pei Chi* and its position today. Using the Microsoft *Starry Night* computer program (which enables the position of the stars in the night sky to be determined every night for the past two millennia) enables us to date the *Wu Pei Chi* to 1420–30 (Polaris's apparent position changes one degree every 175 years due to the earth's precession.) Knowing the *Wu Pei Chi* date, we can compare the stars on it with the *Starry Night* program. We can also establish that near the 'compass rose' position shown on the Piri Reis (SW Falklands), Canopus is at 90° elevation. The reason the cartographers took such inordinate trouble surveying the coast of Patagonia is that they established the declination and right ascension of Canopus when it was above them. Chinese records reveal that the need to 'fix' the position of Canopus and the Southern Cross constellation had long preoccupied Chinese astronomers. Conference in Nanjing, October 2002, emphasised this preoccupation with Canopus; Kunming Conference (December 2002) emphasised the Chinese standard operating procedure of sailing directly beneath (90° altitude) selected stars. Knowing the position of Canopus, latitude in the southern hemisphere can be determined by cross- referencing Canopus with Polaris in the northern hemisphere.

- These measurements gave the Chinese the capacity to chart the whole world, but where would they have been likely to do so? At 52°40′S, the declination of Canopus, all ships could keep the star right overhead, all thus surveying from the same base line.

Evidence of the Chinese voyage is indeed found all the way across the world at 52°40′S, in Patagonia, Kerguelen and Campbell Island (which appears precisely drawn on the Jean Rotz). (Evidence of this method of sailing given by Chinese professors at Kunming Conference, December 2002.) At which other latitudes would it have been sensible to survey? Where Canopus disappeared below the horizon at 38°30′N (evidence is found at this latitude around the world) and at 3°20′N where Polaris disappeared below the horizon in 1421 (evidence of the Chinese voyage also found here).

For the determination of longitude, see Appendix 2.

Observation platforms used by the Chinese 1421–2

South America to Australia

Marquesas (Temoe)	134°29′W	23°22′S
Society Islands (Tahiti)	149°00′W	17°50′S
Bora Bora	151°00′W	17°30′S
W. Samoa (Savai)	172°42′W	13°30′S
Tonga Tabu	175°04′W	19°43′S
Gympie (Australia)	152°42′E	26°12′S
Gosford (NSW)	151°13′E	33°26′S
New Zealand (Komowin Hill)	175°52′E	38°59′S

South America to Indonesia

Temoe	134°28′W	23°22′S
Tahiti	149°00′W	17°50′S
Malden (Kirimati)	157°43′E	01°55′N
Solomons (San Cristobal)	161°51′E	10°26′S
Carolines (Nan Madol)	158°21′E	06°51′N
Mariannas (Saipan)	145°45′E	15°09′N
Carolines (Yap)	138°09′E	09°31′N
New Guinea	140°00′E	05°00′S
Nanjing	118°45′E	32°06′N
Beijing	116°25′E	39°55′N

Areas of the world surveyed: fleets required
- Indian Ocean (Cantino): nine million square miles and thousands of islands. Assuming ships 15 miles apart, sailing at 4.8 knots and surveying for 10 hours a day, then 30 ships would have had to be at sea for 18 months.
- South America and Antarctic (Piri Reis): approximately 6 million square miles – about 20 ships required over an 18-month period.
- North America and North Atlantic (Cantino): approximately 12 million square miles – about 40 ships.
- Far East (Rotz): no fewer than 20 ships over an 18-month period.
- Australasia (Rotz): no fewer than 20 ships over an 18-month period.
- Rivers of the world (Waldseemüller): thousands of miles of the Orinoco, Amazon and Mississippi and hundreds of miles of rivers in Siberia, Australia and Pacific America are depicted on European charts before voyages of discovery. No fewer than 130 ships over 18 months would be required.

The Chinese fleet
'In its heyday, about +1420, the Ming navy probably outclassed that of any other Asian nation at any time in history, and would have been more than a match for that of any contemporary European state or even a combination of them. Under the Yung-Lo emperor it consisted of some 3,800 ships in all: 1,350 patrol vessels and 1,350 combat ships attached to guard stations (*wei* and *so*) or island bases (chai), a main fleet of 400 large warships stationed at Hsin-chiang-khou near Nanking, and 400 grain-transport freighters. In addition there were more than 250 long-distance "treasure ships" or galleons (*pao chuan*), the average complement of which grew from 450 men in +1403 to over 690 in 1431, and certainly overstepped 1,000 in the largest vessels. A further 3,000 merchantmen were always ready as auxiliaries, and a host of small craft did duty as despatch-boats and police launches. But the peak of the development which had started in 1130 came in 1433, and after the great reversal of policy the navy declined much more rapidly than it had grown, so that by the middle of the 16th century almost nothing was left of its former grandeur.' (Needham, vol.3, p.484)

'More than eight hundred sail of large and small ships had come to India from the ports of Malacca and China and the Lequeos [Ryuku Islands], with people of many nations, and all laden with merchandise of great value which they brought for sale ... they were so numerous that they filled the country and settled as dwellers in all of the towns of the sea coast.' (Chaudhuri, p.154; evidence provided by Professor Robert Finlay of Arkansas University)

In parallel with Zheng He's development of his fleet went that of overseas bases. By 1421, the Chinese had bases around the Indian Ocean and down the east African coast to Sofala. They already had an extensive network across Indonesia and the South China Sea. Since 1405 there had been five voyages becoming progressively more adventurous as the years went by. During the fourth voyage the Chinese had separated their fleets and sailed far down the east African coast: 'Chinese ... with Tartairs, Japanese and Koreans ... crossed the Maritime Stretch ... into the Kingdoms of Quivira populating Mexico, Peru and other eastern countries of the Indies [America].' (Carlos Prince)

The author contends that the whole world had been charted before Europeans set sail, and that only the Chinese could have done so.

1. Chinese maps, star charts and records that escaped destruction

Title and approx. date of amendments	Subject/relevance
Wu Pei Chi, c.1422 (only a small part translated)	Chinese accept this contains information brought by Zheng He. It gives courses to steer between China and Africa and between other continents, and shows Australia.
Mao Kun, c.1422	Kerguelen, Indian Ocean and Islands. East African coast.
Kangnido (1402–73)	Asia, East, South and West Africa including Atlantic, Azores.
Star Chart (Mao Kun) c.1422	Polaris compared with Southern Cross and Alpha Centauri.

Matteo Ricci (c.1588) globe	Australia (drawn when Fra Ricci was in China)
Xi Yang Fang No Zhi by Gong Zhen, navigator on Zheng He's seventh voyage (Tai-Peng Wang)	*Description of Barbarian Countries of the West*.
Taiwan Porcelain Map (1447) painted by Chinese	Australian east coast down to Tasmania. See also accounts of missionary to Beijing and Chinese fisherman's charts (Martin Tai evidence).
Da Ming Hun Yu Ti	South Africa (Map of the Great Amalgamated Ming Empire)

These charts describe the whole world save for the Americas. The following list of extant records is taken from *Chinese Discovery of Australia* by Professor Wei Ju Xian.

(i)   Australia
  (a)   Confucius: *Spring and Autumn Annals* (481 BC) recorded solar eclipses in Australia on 17 April 592 and 11 August 553.
  (b)   *Classics of Mountains and Seas* (338 BC) describes boomerangs, black millet and kangaroos.
  (c)   *Atlas of Foreign Countries* (AD 265–316) describes small black natives of northern Australia.

(ii)   North Pole
  (a)   Zhuangzi (3rd century BC): 'It takes six months including flying and resting time for seagulls to fly 90,000 *li* from North to South Pole.' (Old Chinese *li* = half a kilometre.) Zhuangzi also mentions going round the earth from east to west, as does Xun Zi (40 years after Zhuangzi).
  (b)   Ancient Chinese books: 'Distance North Pole to South Pole is more than 80,000 *li*.'
  (c)   Qi-xie (643 BC): 'If a person of Yan State [Hebei province] goes north and a person of Yue State [Zhejian, South China] goes south they will meet each other at the very end of their journey.'
  (d)   Lienzi (3rd century BC): 'South of Africa sun cannot be seen

for 50 consecutive days.'
(e) *Illustrated Record of Strange Countries* (published 1430) describes North Pole: Eskimos, coldness, sunshine, polar lights, sea elephants and seals.

2. Chinese or Asiatic peoples found by the first European explorers

(i) Far East and Indian Ocean: Chinese found throughout Indian Ocean to China. Chinese graveyards remain today in Malacca, Indonesia and Philippines (Sulu).

(ii) Africa: Pate – Father Monclavo.

(iii) Atlantic: Azores – bodies from Corvo (Columbus). (Azores/Machado-Joseph disease there.)

(iv) Greenland: 'People from Cathay have visited here' (Columbus). (Greenland peoples have Chinese DNA.)

(v) South America
Brazil: Cabral – 'Men with pale skins'; Orellana – Apara, meets 'white men' (B. McEwen). (Chinese DNA in Amazonian Indians.)
Peru: Chinese-speaking (understanding) villages (Eten and Monsefu) Ludovico de Varthema (voyages to Antarctica). (Chinese DNA in Incas.)
Chile: S Arias (Pacific crossing); Hugo Grotius – Chinese junks found off Chile
Venezuela: Vespucci 'brownish yellow' – Maracaibo (B. McEwen). (Chinese DNA.)

(vi) Mesoamerica and Caribbean
California: Stephen Powers, Chinese colony between Sacramento and Russian Rivers. Antonio Galvão (1555) – 'Chinese ruled over locations in Central and South America'. Grotius – Asiatic shipwrecks on Pacific coast. (Chinese DNA.)
Mexico: Acosta and Vasquez de Coronado's expedition met Chinese. (Mazatecs – Chinese DNA.) Gregorio Garcia – 'Chinese coming to populate Mexico' (before European voyages). Hernán Cortes – Montezuma recounting grandfather (light-coloured people from East returning).
Lower California to Kansas City (Tiguex): Coronado expedition – Coronado, Mafeo and Frois – Chinese ships, Chinese

merchants had come to Quatulco and Panuco all dressed in silk (Loayza). (Chinese DNA in Navajo/Zuni.)

Cuba: Columbus' expedition (men in white robes, Washington Irvine); Columbus' secret report (met Chinese); Columbus met Muslims (Dr Shou).

(vii) North America/Florida

Rhode Island: Verrazzano – 'Chinese' people (Hakluyt, vol. III, 1910, p.350).

Florida: Pedro Menendez de Aviles – Chinese junks. (Chinese DNA in Moskoke.) Plus Powhatan's account to Captain John Smith; Virginia – Jerry Warsing; Alexander von Wuthenau, *Unexpected Faces in Ancient America*, shows Chinese (B. McEwan). (Sioux, Cree Ojibwa – Chinese DNA.)

(viii) Pacific

Bougainville, Wallace – found Chinese people on many islands

Bodies of Chinese in Indonesia

Saavedra – Micronesia

(ix) Australasia: Cook was not the first – men preceded Cook in 'ships like clouds'; descriptions of local people. (Maori – Chinese DNA.)

3. Local peoples' descriptions of Chinese or Asiatic peoples who settled among them before Europeans arrived

(i) Far East and Indian Ocean: too numerous to include. Widespread intermarriages between Chinese men and local women.

(ii) Africa: Pate – story of giraffe presented in 1416 to Chinese emperor

(iii) North America and Atlantic coast

Rhode Island: 'great ship-like house firing cannon sailing upriver'; carvings of foreign ship and shipwreck (Chelmsford and Dighton Rocks); Pope's letter to Bishop of Greenland; Chinese naval party landed and murdered (Frank Fitch); Cherokees murdered foreign miners near Minay Sotor River (Scott McLean); barbarians' ship attacking local people.

Florida: (as defined in 17th century) Natchez people – 'Ancestors came from East by sea' (Pratz).

Mississippi and tributaries: numerous (more than 100) carvings of foreign ships and horses (extinct in Americas by c.10,000 BC); Powhatan's account to Captain John Smith.

(iv) North America and Pacific coast
Canada: Huron Indians – 'very far to the West, epicureans without beards came to trade their wool' (Loayza)
Haida: 'people sailing from west' (Marius Barbeau) (R. Hassell)
California: 'ships like great houses' off coast; Cherokees slaughter strangers with yellow countenances (S. McLean).

(v) Mexico: Nayarit legends of Asian ships (Mazatecs – Chinese DNA); Lienzo of Jucutácato – foreign visitors arriving on horseback; Cueva Pintada – foreigners being shot at; Yucatán – six carvings of horses and possibly elephants (Campeche Maya – Chinese DNA); legend of wrecked Chinese junk (Joel Fressa); Indian pueblos – Chinese warriors (A. Moya); Montezuma – ancestors came by sea from East in company with a mighty lord (Ranking pp.257–326).

(vi) South America
Peru: pre-Columbian pictures of Chinese cavalry at Trujillo (Friar Antonio de la Calancha) and at Ayacucho (G. Squier); 'Giants came by sea to settle amongst them' (Garcilaso de la Vega/Pedro Cieza de Leon).
Brazil: paintings of foreign horses (Confins cave).
Patagonia: anonymous (1440) and Durand (1448) maps describing giants of Patagonia; yellow-skinned people crossed Pacific before Europeans (S. Arias); Afghanistan legend (Z. Pradya) – Indian ships accompanied Chinese to South America prior to European voyages; Guarani – ancestors crossed ocean from a far land to settle in Amazon (M. Garcia).

(vii Pacific
Fiji: Yasawa Islands – 'yellow men visited us'.
Hawaii/Oahu: Menehune legends (A. Armstrong) – are Menehune Chinese?

(viii) Australia
Arnhem Land: paintings of men on horseback (Vallard); 'honey-coloured people' settle, 'women in pantaloons, men in long robes'; painting of robed strangers (Governor Grey); painting of man being thrown from horse (Glenelg River); drawings of

trees, fauna and flora (Rotz); visits of Chinese junks.

Gympie: men in stone garments attempt to mine Mount Warning area; 'culture heroes' sail into Gympie harbour and take away rocks; Dhamuri people – foreigners land to build pyramids (J. Green).

Fraser Island – small boats leave big ship (J. Green 1862)

Sydney/Newcastle, carvings: Hawkesbury River, strange visitors in long robes; foreign ship and funeral of foreign visitors; Byron Bay, massacre of foreign sailors

Warrnambool: Yangerry tribe – yellow people from shipwreck settled among them and created farms

Glenelty River: carving of foreign sailors.

(ix) New Zealand

North Island: two large ships preceded Captain Cook (Maori accounts); light-coloured people settled among Maoris and begat children; Tamil calligraphy.

South Island: large ship wrecked; Tamil calligraphy.

4. Linguistics and languages common to New World and China

(i) Chinese spoken

California: Chinese-speaking colony on Russian River (Powers)

Mexico: Othomis people

Canada, British Columbia: 'Colonia dei Chinesi' (Zatta)

Peru: Eten and Monsefu villages (Lambaeque Province) three miles apart understood Chinese (19th century) but did not understand each other's patois.

(ii) Chinese names

In northern Peru, mainly in the Ancash province, there are 95 geographical names which are Chinese words and have no significance in Quechua, Aymara or any of the other dialects of northern Peru (examples follow). There are also 130 geographical names in Peru which correspond to names in China. The very name 'Peru' means 'white mist' in Chinese – the white mist which cloaks the coast many days each year. The name given to Chile (Ch-Li) was pre-Spanish (= 'dependent territory' in Chinese).

Peruvian Name	Chinese Translation
Cha-Wan (La Pampa)	Land prepared for sowing
Chancan (Tarma)	To harden metals
Chamtan (San Gregorio)	Covered in sand
Chaolan (Margos)	Ready for combustion (viz. coal-mine)
Chulin (Caras)	Forest
(Har) (Bongara)	Red (i.e. red earth)
Hu-Pa (Huasta)	Leguminous plant
Colan	Difficult passage
Chanchan (area between Moche and Viru Rivers)	Canton
Laychi (Ochros)	Small fruit
Lahan (Huancay)	Clamour (viz. waterfall)
Linche (Chincha)	Snake
Mongtan (Cochabamba)	Big stream
Payhan (Trujillo)	Damaging drought
Hon Kon (Moche River)	Red hole

(iii) Linguistics

East Africa: *bajun* (local name for boat people)

Australia: *bajun* (SW Australia), and Japanese (Lynda Nutter) simulants

China (Hokkien): *joon* (boat which persists southwards to Amoy in Taiwan, and the ports of Bangkok, Penang and Singapore) (Dr Tan Koolin evidence)

Peru: (Loayza) at least 37 words other than the village names given above, including *quipu* (knotted string) – China *qipu*, Hawaii kiipúu, Marquesas KaulaKipu'u (Duncan Craig)

New Zealand: *kumara* (sweet potato); Peru – *kumar*

Mesoamerica: *kik* (chicken); India – *kikh* (chicken)

South America: *sampan* (boat), China – *sampan*; *balsa* (raft), China – *balsa*

Pacific America: Zuni language and Japanese (Nancy Yaw Davis)

British Columbia (Squamish Indians): *tsil* (wet), *chi* (wood), *tsu* (grandmother); China – *tsil* (wet), *chin* (wood), *etsu* (grandmother), and another 37 words.

North America (Virginia): Ming Ho people (J Warsing), Wyo Ming

county, Lyco Ming people, Ho down, ho cakes
Tiguex: 'Huri Shan'
Mexico: Pi k'w; Saka (Henriette Mertz – *Pale Ink*). Towns are strung out from central Arizona to Yucatán – viz. Huetamo, Huichol, Huizontla, Huepac, Huitzo, Huila, Huitepec, etc., to Zacapa. The cultures these towns possess have no linguistic affinity for one another. In none of the cultures is there a meaning for any one of the three base words.
Chiapas: Tse-Tsai; tso tsil (R. Banzo)
Guatemala: Lord of Guatama? (H. Mertz and J.D. van Horn)

Turkeys and maize originated in America and reached Europe from two directions: from China then the Silk Road to Turkey (here the words are *granoturco* (maize) and *turco* (turkey) – the names in Italy and England); and brought back by Spaniards (the word in France for turkey is *dindon* – de l'Inde).

The fulvous tree duck is a poor flyer found in Brazil but which originally came from India (Bengal): *irere* (Brazil and Guyana), *sarere* (Burma), *sarara* (India).

American Indian names that are Chinese (Martin Tai): on his arrival, Columbus met Indians = Yin Dian (people from Yin [China]); Pizarro, Inca = Yinca (people who live in Yin); Vancouver, Inuit = Yin Uit (people originating in Yin).

5. Accounts of contemporary and other historians

Author	Title/Description	Date Written (Published)
Chen Cheng (Chinese)	*Diary of Travel in the Western Regions*. Chinese emperor's overtures to Persia and description of reopening trade to Mediterranean.	1405–14 (1414)
Ma Huan (Chinese)	*Ying Yai Shenlan*: the overall survey of the ocean shores. Chinese fleet in south-east Asia and Indian Ocean.	1416–31 (1435)

Fei Xin (Chinese)	*Marvellous Visions from the Star Raft.* Chinese fleet reaching Africa and then Timor (east Indonesia), 300 miles from Australia.	1405–31
Ibn Tagri Birdi (Egyptian)	*Nujum* (A History of Egypt). Chinese fleet reaching Red Sea and Jeddah.	1431
Ghiyash D Din Naqqash (dictated to Hafez Abru) (Persian)	*Subdatu-T'Tawarikh* (Cream of Chronicles). Inauguration of the Forbidden City, 2 February 1421, delegates arriving and returning.	1419–22 (1424)
Niccolò da Conti (Venetian)	*The Travels of Niccolò da Conti.* Claims to have travelled to Australia. Describes Chinese fleet passing through Indian Ocean and his passage to Australia and China. Corroborated by statue in Fujian Palace.	c.1420–4 (1434)
Fra Mauro (Venetian)	Planisphere notes. Describe Chinese junk sailing across Indian Ocean non-stop (about end of 1420), rounding Cape of Good Hope to Cape Verde Islands and 'obscured islands'.	c.1420 (1459)
Ibn Battuta (Moroccan)	*The Travels of Ibn Battuta* describes huge Chinese ships in Indian Ocean.	
Acosta (Spanish Jesuit)	Chinese ships – Florida Chinese people – Mexico	
Coronado (Castilian)	Chinese people, Mexico (Tiguex); ships with golden sterns (Mississippi, Missouri)	
Hugo Grotius (Dutch)	*Bibliotheca Cuirosa*, 'Asiatic shipwrecks on Pacific coast of Mexico'. Wrecks of Chinese junks seen by first Spanish to reach Chile.	.
Father Luis Sales OP	*Observations on California* – Chinese colony – Santa Barbara.	1772–90 1772–90 (translated and re-edited by Charles N. Rudkin, L.A. 1956)

Antonio Galvão (quoted by Richard Hakluyt) (Spanish)	*A Selection of Curious Rare and Early Voyages.* 'Chinese ruled over locations in Central and South America'.	1555
Zatta (Italian)	Describes Queen Charlotte Island as 'Colonia dei Chinesi'.	
Juan Gonzales de Mendoza (Castilian)	*The Historie of the Great and Mighty Kingdom of China and the Situation Thereof.*	
da Gama (Portuguese)	*Journal of the First Voyage of Vasco da Gama*, p.131. As quoted by Professor Robert Finlay in *Terrae Incognitae*, vol. XXIII. Chinese fleet (c.1421) was of 800 vessels.	
John Brereton	Diary of Bartholomew Grisnold's 1602 voyage: at Buzzards Bay he found Indian people wearing armour, as did Martin Pring at Cape Cod the following year.	
Christopher Columbus (Genoese)	Christopher Columbus' secret report	Describes meeting Chinese (Martin Tai)
Gonzalo Ximenez de Quesada	Travelled from River Magdalena to Attiphare near Bogotà. Meets Muyscas, Guanes, Myuzoes, Calimas in cotton, entirely different from other tribes.	1537
Clavigero, Abbé, Don Francisco Saverio	*History of Mexico* (2 vols)	London 1787
Garcilaso de le Vega	*Histoire de la Conquête de la Floride* (trans. P. Richelet)	London 1731 (translation)
Vega	*Commentarios Reales del Origen de los Incas, Reyes del Peru* (describes Chinese in Peru and Chile)	1609 Madrid
Barton, Benjamin	*New Views of the Origin of the Tribes and Nations of America* (8 vols)	1797 Philadelphia

Carver, J.	*Travels in the Interior of North America* (8 vols)	London 1779
Chappe d'Anteroche	*Voyage to California*	London 1778
Jefferson, T.	*Notes on the State of Virginia*	Philadelphia 1794
Humboldt, A. de	*Researches concerning the Ancient Americas*	London 1814
Venegas, M. (Jesuit)	*History of California*	London 1759
Ulloa, Don Antonio	*Voyage to South America*	Dublin 1758
Terry	*Voyages to the East Indies*	London 1665
Cochrane, Captain C. S.	*Journal in Colombia* (2 vols)	
Molina	*History of Chile* (see Ranking – renamed)	1726
Du Pratz	*Unexpected Faces in Ancient America*	
Von Wuthenau, Alexander	(p.210 and fig.75c); *The Art of Terracotta Pottery in Central and South America*. Numerous Chinese people in North and South America before Columbus.	
Kotztbue	*First Voyage* (Darwin, p.456)	
Padre Kino	*The Padre on Horseback*	1542–1606

6. Shipwrecks

(i) Large shipwrecks with 'Chinese' characteristics found in the wake of the Chinese fleets by European explorers

	Location	Details	Year	Contacts
1	China, Nanjing dry dock No. 6	The giant rudder (42 ft high) was found here, also much very old teak – with which local people make furniture. Dock is huge: 500m × 80m. Flooded 1431 until today.		Mayor of Nanjing, Professor Yinsheng Liu o Admiral Zheng Ming.
2	Philippines, North	All contents brought from seabed under direction of		Dr Eusebio Dizon's information. Junk from

Pandanan Island (S tip, Palowan Island)	Dr Eusebio Dizon – an amazing haul of more than 4,700 pieces giving a graphic view of trade in the Pacific and Indian Ocean in 1421 – including Zhu Di's coins.	Zheng He's fleet 30m ×8m. Second junk discovered off Pandanan 1995 with 3,000 pieces. *The Pearl Road*.
3	Philippines, Santa Cruz	Off Santa Cruz (N. Philippines). More than 11,500 pieces of 15th-century Chinese porcelain of the finest quality and of incredible value have been recovered in perfect condition.

Off Santa Cruz section continued column: Frank Goddio's information. In 32m water – discovered 2001, in v. good condition – 5m × 5.8m. Goods packed perfectly. For info: Iris Weissen, +49(40) 22658 323.

4	Singapore Straits, Bakau	23m, wrecked early 15th century, Chinese construction, hull of hard pine *Pinus sylvesteris* group, iron nails, chu-nam caulking, flat bottom, Zhu Di (1403–24) coins, bronze guns, bronze mirrors and handles, cast stones, iron pots, grindstones kendis, numerous copper artefacts, sounding weight – fascinating for comparison with Jucutácato shroud and Sacramento.
5	Thailand, Longquan	Wrecked 1390–1420 in 63m of water, 30m × 8m. Wreck largely intact with largest ever cargo of Ming porcelain – possibly 100,000 pieces including Celadon. Tin sounding weights (compare with Fraser Island). Obviously of colossal value but deep and difficult. Wreck should yield

		hugely important details of Chinese junk design. No-one is attempting to raise it.	
6	Vietnam, Hoi An (off Da Nang)	Sunk late 1400/early 1500. Stuffed with Ming porcelain which is now being auctioned.	D.F. Sedwick information.
7	Vietnam, Phu Quoc		
8	Fiji, Nanuku Passage 14°15′S, 178°10′W	Vivid description of Chinese landing and being murdered by Fijians (French missionaries' accounts of c. 1550) after they had intermarried. Chinese tomb on Alofi. 1875	Captain Wilson's *Mariners' Mirror* 1924, reporting earlier French missionaries and Cornelius Schouten in Eindracht 1616.
9	Japan	Wrecks of Genghis Khan's fleet which invaded Japan 1281. Amazing finds – watertight compartments, mortars, fragmentation bombs, etc.	*Archaeology*, Feb 03. Edwin Davey information.
10	Malaysia, Turiang	Chinese junk sailing to Borneo. Cargo Chinese, Vietnamese, Thai ceramics, iron ore, fish. Wood: temperate wood joined by iron nails.	Report in *Turiang*, Malaysian branch, Royal Asiatic Society.
11	Warrnambool (South Australia)	Double planking. Brass bolt. c.1880 Now lost because junk appears to have drifted. c. 1880	King Edward Island 150 nautical miles away. Desliens world map depicts coastline – drawn two centuries before Captain Cook.
12	King Edward Island	Double planking; brass pins c.1980 (5/8 inch). Among sand dunes near sea, Elephant River.	E.O. Jeago information. Warrnambool

	(South Australia) 39°49′S, 144° 67′E		150 nautical miles away. Desliens world map depicts coastline.
13	Tasmania, Storm Bay	Disgorges Hong Wu coins after storms	
14	Australia, King Sound	Discovered by Allan Robinson on sea bed. Local legends say yellow people settled among them. Linguistic similarities Aborigines with Japanese.	DNA has been carried out on certain Aborigines but Australian government will not allow release.
15	Blackwood River, South Australia	Junk '1km east of Blackwood River'. River enters sea at Augusta close to Cape Leeuwin. Unknown graves in Julien Bay. Aborigines pale colour. Aboriginal legends of visiting ship.	*Legend of Sam Chalwell*. Jim Mullins' information, organising over-flying in April 03.
16	East Australia, Fraser Island	John Green (1862) saw a Chinese junk rise out of the sea following a great storm. Numerous local legends collected by J. Green report foreign ship landing small boats to mine minerals. Photos 1919, 1972, 2002.	B. Green information from J. Green account. B. Green found wine cooler. 1972 photos of cannon. Gympie pyramid nearby.
17	East Australia, Stradbrooke Island swamp	Accessible on foot; 4WD can get within 200 metres. Need chopper for precise location. Should be easy to spot from small aircraft. Cost Aus $350 approx.	Local report (via Greg Jeffer) wreck in swamp called Golden Dragon – a Chinese junk. Three other wrecks nearby to predate Cook.

18	East Australia, Indian Head, Fraser Island	Wreck near shore, approachable by Zodiac, not deeply buried, visible at low spring tides (Greg J.).	Greg Jeffer's and Bill Ward information. Bill Ward has found ancient lead weight (*Oceania*, vol. 34).
19	New Zealand, Ruapuke Beach (1890 sighting)	Nearby Colenso Bell (Tamil) carved stone (Tamil), carved jade duck (Chinese), Mauku figurine (Chinese), Komowin (stepped pyramid – ?Chinese). Local legends. Teak built, triple hull, willow pattern plate.	Vaughan Cullen information. The wreck is offshore, has shifted position and is lost. Latest finds by David Sims (rivet, teak wood).
20	New Zealand, south coast, Dusky Sound	The wreck disappeared many years ago. It was classified as a Chinese junk by local people.	Robyn Gossett information. *New Zealand Mysteries*.
21	America, east coast, Bimini – 'shark mounds'	Six mounds in swamp on E. Bimini, second Bimini road found Anguilla, Cay Sal, stone reservoir Andros. Florida – Menendez reports junks. Chinese landing party massacred – Frank Fitch.	Bill Swinley has most info on second Bimini Road. 'Bruce' information. Andros Reservoir C. Huegy.
22	America, east coast, Great Dismal Swamp	To west of Norfolk, VA. Sarah Jackson's story of discovery of 'an ancient Chinese sailing ship uncovered when the swamp was first drained by George Washington and his friends'. Bartlett Doty investigating.	Larry D. Clark information (01/03) from *Merrill Reading Skill Text Series 1977*, Bell & Howell, ISBN 0-675-06757.

23	America, west coast, Vancouver Island, Schooner Cove/ Lovekin Rock	Wreck is approx 130 × 30 × 27ft – longer than Cook's *Endeavour* or Vancouver's *Discovery*. Many Chinese artefacts found nearby. (Lake River Potters, Chinese vases, etc). Wreck of teak (?), carrying rice (?).	Hector Williams and Bob Hassell's information; HW to London 04/03 with Park Canada file on wreck. Exact location known. Magnetometer surveys bronze fastenings.
24	America, west coast, Vancouver Island 'Asian Ucluelet'	'Asian Pot Wreck' 15 nautical miles off mouth of Juan de Fuca Strait hauled up Asian pot. Numerous articles of Japanese/ Korean/Chinese origin on Vancouver Island.	In c.1400 mysterious colony of potters settled in valley between Vancouver Lake and Columbus River (Robert Hassell's information) and disappeared c. 1700.
25	America, west coast, Vancouver Island (Clatsop Beach)	Point Adams, mouth of Columbia River. Swan, J. G., *The Northwest Coast*, 1857.	
26	America, west coast, Oregon, near Neahkahnie Beach	Ming porcelain found on Netarts sand spit. Pulley made of SE Asian hard-wood dated c. 1410. Cabrillo's map of California (c. 1543) shows wrecked Chinese junks.	Cabrillo – Goetzman & Williams of Oklahoma Pub 1992, *Atlas of N. American Exploration*.

27	South America, west coast, Chile	Grotius p. 68, first Spanish to round Horn, found junks near Taroja (22°S)	Ranking Supplement p.35.
28	America, west coast, California, Drake's Bay	Considerable amount of Chinese porcelain found here. Drake reported to have 'chased a junk'. Cabrillo's map shows junk.	Drake and Cermeno in California: 16th-century Chinese ceramics – Navigator's Guild, 1965,1968, 1972.
29	America, west coast, Sacramento	Pearson investigating. Core drilling April 03. Electromagnetic survey completed 02/03. Wood carbon dated c. 1410 (Beta Analytic Lab, Miami, Florida). Chinese brass plate found buried Susanville.	Dr John Furry and Mr David Stewart information. Approx 30m × 8m (as Report by Pro Conyers, Oct 2002
30	America/ Mexico, west coast, Bahia de	Wreck disgorges Chinese (Nanking) cloth after storms, hence name 'Playa la Ropa'. Exact location unknown.	Ming porcelain in local museum. Local legends – Joel Fressa infor-mation
31	America, west coast	Grimes and Knights landing. Appears to be very old ship/junk full of seeds, accessible at low water. Kathleen Pickard nearest to site.	Mary Doerflein information. Mary lives near Seattle, Washington.)
32	Americas, Caribbean	Guadeloupe – wreck found by Columbus.	
33	Americas, Mississippi, Caribbean	Coronado's junks with gilded sterns: 'Three shippes on the sea coast which bore Alcatarzes or pelicans of gold and silver in their prows.'	See *Haykluyt's Voyages* under Vasquez de Coronado

34	Caribbean	Columbus secret report. *The Origin of Dragon and Phoenix Culture*, 1988 – Wang da Yiu, song Bao Zhong, Chinese mirrors in 'Bird boats'.	Historian Fang Zhong Pu.
35	Peru	Wrecks of Chinese Ships	Ranking J., *Conquest of Peru*, London 1827
36	Chile	Grotius, p. 68	Ranking J., *Conquest of Peru*, London 1827
37	California	Santa Catalina Island (Channel Island)	

The following are wrecks identified by magnetic anomaly survey. Permission is being requested from the relevant authorities to carry out corroborative testing using different types of equipment.

No.	Type/Codename	Lat/Long	Barracks Harboured Yes/No Barracks – Ref. Para 19(x)
38	Rorqual	AB°38′28″ T°38′53″	Yes. Boulge (para 10 (xi))
39	Rorqual	AB°50′50″ M°57′45″	Yes. Boulge (para 10 (xi)) Otley Orwell
40	Rorqual	AB°50′50″ M°57′45″	Yes. Orford, Orwell
41	Rorqual	AB°51′20″ M°02′30″	Yes, Orford, Bairdsey
42	Alcide	AB°50′30″ M°03′30″	Yes. Otley, Orwell
43	X Craft	AB°44′48″ M°05′45″	No. Nacton
44	Rorqual	AB°44′44″ M°05′51″	Yes. Nacton
45	Resolution	AB°44′47″ M°05′48″	No. Nacton

46	Alcide	AB°44′48″ M°05′45″	Yes. Nacton
47	Seraph	AB°44′48″ M°05′45″	Yes. Nacton
48	Rorqual	AY°27′50″ S°45′30″	Yes. Loxfield, Iken
49	Rorqual	AY°27′50″ S°45′30″	Yes. Loxfield
50	Rorqual	AY°28′29″ S°45′07″	Yes. Loxfield
51	Rorqual	AY°28′40″ S°44′33″	Yes. Loxfield
52	Rorqual	AY°28′41″ S°44′24″	Yes. Loxfield
53	Rorqual	AY°28′44″ S°44′15″	No. Loxfield
54	Rorqual	AY°28′47″ S°43′48″	Unfinished Loxfield
55	Rorqual	AY°28′47″ S°43′48″	Yes. Loxfield
56	Rorqual	AY°28′49″ S°43′27″	No. Loxfield
57	Resolution	AY°28′51″ S°43′00″	No. Loxfield
58	Seraph	AY°33′33″ S°27′40″	Yes. Trimley
59	Seraph	AY°33′34″ S°27′40″	Yes. Trimley
60	X Craft	AY°33′34″ S°28′20″	Yes. Trimley
61	X Craft	AY°33′43″ S°28′20″	Yes. Trimley
62	Rorqual	AY°33′37″ S°29′30″	No. Trimley
63	Rorqual	AY°33′37″ S°29′20″	No. Trimley
64	Rorqual	AY°33′40″ S°28′03″	Yes. Trimley

65	Resolution	AY°33′44″ S°28′03″	Ballast blocks alongside Trimley Bows on to beach
66	Resolution	AY°33′42″ S°27′55″	Ballast blocks alongside Trimley Broached
67	Vanguard	AY°33′46″ S°28′00″	Ballast blocks alongside Trimley Bows on to beach.
68	Seraph	AY°37′00″ S°22′15″	No. Trimley?(four-mile walk)
69	Seraph	AY°37′00″ S°22′15″	No. Trimley
70	X Craft	AY°37′00″ S°22′15″	No. Trimley?
71	Rorqual	AY°39′50″ S°06′00″	Yes. Trimley? (six-mile walk)
72	Rorqual	AY°39′50″ S°06′00″	Yes. Trimley (seven-mile walk)
73	Rorqual	AY°39′50″ S°39′50″	No. Trimley (seven-mile walk)
74	Rorqual	AY°45′16″ V°38′51″	Yes. Holbrook
75	Resolution	AY°20′45″ S°49′34″	No barracks, but there should be. A mystery – all crew lost?
76 lost?	Resolution	AY°20′45″ V°49′34″	No. A mystery. All crew
77 lost?	Vanguard	AY°20′44″ V°49′34″	No. A mystery. All crew

(i) 'Chinese' anchors and fishing gear

   (a) Indian Ocean/Far East/Pacific: Chinese 'butterfly' fishing
        nets throughout.

(b) California: stone anchors in San Pedro Bay, Redondo Beach, Palos Verdes, central Los Angeles (under subway); Santa Barbara – fish hooks. (Barnacles dated pre-Columbian radiometric dating. Professor Lin Xiao Han of Beijing.)

(c) Ecuador: fish hooks and labrets.

(d) Australia, Arnhem Land and Gulf of Carpenteria: anchors, fish hooks.

(e) Mexico: Rio Balsas – butterfly fishing nets; Yucatán (Chinese? anchor used for worship).

7. Chinese porcelain/ceramics found in wake of Zheng He's fleets

(i) Indian Ocean and East Africa: early Ming porcelain found by first European explorers in palaces of rulers the length of the east African coast from Djibouti to Sofala and inland as far as Zimbabwe (Philip Snow/Martin Tai evidence); Mauritius – Celadon

(ii) North America, Pacific coast
Oregon: the Netarts sand spit (Site 35-Ti) – including some of Zhu Di's reign
California: dates to be confirmed
Canada, Vancouver Island (BC): Chinese clay vase (B. Morelan); Chinese storage jars from seabed (Tofino) (Hector Williams)
Washington State: (Ken Holmes and Sean Griffin); Lake River Potters – Washington coast (R Hassell)

(iii) Central and South America
Mexico, Zihuantanejo
Peru: Ica, Chan Chan, Miraflores – Tai chih symbols
Amazonia: (Paul Yih and Beloit University, Wisconsin)

(iv) Australia: Bradshaw, Elecho Island, Yirrkalla, Winchelsea Island, Cape York, Gympie, Tasmania.

(v) Pacific: Magellan's descriptions of rulers dressed in silk, eating off Ming porcelain from Leyte to Spice Islands.

8. Pre-Columbian Chinese jade found in wake of Zheng He's fleets

(i) Amazon/Tapajos River juncture (Barbosa Rodrigues): Trombetas River; Lago Sapakua; Lago de Faro; Serra da

Chinella (Hill of Chinese); unnamed island; Ilha Jacinta; Costa do Parvo; Villa de Faro; Rio Yamunda; Cujumu

(ii) Elsewhere in Brazil (Barbosa Rodrigues): Amargosa (BA); Campanas (SP); Pivi (MG); Pinheiros (RJ); Olinda (PE); Obidos (AM); São Francisco River

(iii) Argentina: (Barbosa Rodrigues and Palmatory)

(iv) Colombia: (Barbosa Rodrigues and Palmatory)

(v)   Panama: (Barbosa Rodrigues and Palmatory)

(vi) Costa Rica: (A131; P2698)

(vii) Guatemala (border El Salvador): figurines (BN139)

(viii) Mexico: Teotihuacan; Isthmus of Tehuantepec; Chiapas de Corzo; La Venta (L273; K094; M342C; L240; W154; P269B)

(ix) Nicaragua (A131; P269B)

(x)   North America: Georgia (Nacooche Mound); Michigan Mound (P269B)

(xi) Cuba: (Barbosa Rodrigues and Palmatory)

(xii) Virgin Islands: (Barbosa Rodrigues and Palmatory)

(xiii) Canada, British Columbia: (C405; H070); Shu Lao Buddha lamp

(xiv) Australia: Darwin – Shu Lao; NSW – Ganesh, Hanuman; Queensland – Buddha; Gympie – orange-coloured jade belt buckle, carved monkey/bear/animal and blue jade necklace (Brett Green)

(xv) New Zealand: Ruapuke Beach – korotangi duck; Mauku – Mongol warrior

(xvi) Pacific/Polynesia: to follow

(xvii) Galapagos: (Barbosa Rodrigues and Palmatory)

(xviii) Peru: mummy – Mongolian features with jade necklace (Lima Museum) (Loayza)

9. Artefacts, gems and votive offerings found in wake of Zheng He's fleets

(i)   Far East and Indian Ocean: all over the area, too numerous to mention

(ii) Africa: Pate – bronze lion

(iii) Atlantic and Caribbean: Azores – Corvo statue of rider on horseback; Bimini – marble head

(iv) Meso and Central America
      Mexico: lacquer boxes, Roman bust (Joluca), dyestuffs,

Jucutácato shroud, copper ornaments, Chinese vases (Azacapotazlo and Hue Hutitlan); little Chinaman (Teotihuacan), terracotta figurines of SE Asian people (Niven); Chinese bronzes (Romeo Hristov); Chinese totems (I. B. Remsen).

(v) North America (Pacific coast)

Washington: ceramic artefacts, Lake River (Terry Glavin, *The Last Great Sea*)

British Columbia: carved totem faces (Wu Han), 'Chinese' lamp, votive offerings, Shu Lao, sackfuls of Chinese coins, Buddhist statuette, Korean burial urn (R. Hassell)

California: early Ming brass plate (A. D. Palmer), Avalon Harbour treasure box (Steve Haynes), stone with Chinese writing (Steve Elkins)

Arizona, Grand Canyon: statuettes of Buddha (Jake Smothers)

Colorado, Granby Dam: 'guardian' statue with Chinese inscriptions (Thad Daly)

(vi) South America

Peru: bronzes with Chinese inscriptions (Trujillo), pottery with Chinese inscriptions (Nasca), figurines with Chinese inscriptions, e.g. Tai-chi, silver idol with Chinese inscriptions (Trujillo) and clay figurines.

Brazil, Surui: gems (Paul Yih)

(vii) Australia

NSW: onyx scarab, Shao Lin's head, stone heads

Queensland: Hanuman, Ganesh, onyx scarab

Arnhem Land: figurine of Shu Lao

(viii) Pacific

Hua Atoll (Tuomotu Archipelago): emerald ring

Hawaii: helmet and iron weapons (there is no iron in Hawaii)

(ix) New Zealand: two lions (Brett Green)

10. Stone buildings or artefacts found in wake of Zheng He's fleets

(i) Observation platforms and observatories

(a) Australia (5): Penrith; west of Blue Mountains; Gympie; central NSW coast; Atherton

(b) North Atlantic: Newport round tower (mortar contains gypsum, foreign to area); Canaries

(c) Arctic – Kane basin

(d) Pacific – Tuomotu (Tahiti); Marquesas; Society Islands; Carolines – Lele, Ponape, Nan Madol, Yap, Tobi; Marianas – Saipan; Gilberts –Kiribati; Solomons – San Cristobal; Mala; New Guinea (5); Malden Island; Magnetic Island; Samoa (Jenny Gore evidence)

(e) North America: Casa Grande (Grand Canyon) (J. Andrews)

Note: An analysis of the mortar of as many of these platforms as possible will be conducted; results will be posted on the website.

(ii) Carved stones recording voyage
China – Liu Shia Chang (Fukien province); Lingshan Mountain (Quanzhow); Malaya – Malacca; Thailand; Ceylon – Dondra Head; India – Guli, Calicut, Cochin; Africa – Matadi Falls (Congo); Cape Verde Islands (Janela); South America – Santa Catarina; New Zealand – Ruapuke Beach and South Island; North America – Dighton Rock and McCook Point (B. Trinque); American Pacific coast – 'Sacramento stone'?

(iii) Stone markers to denote position
North America (South Peabody, Royaston, Barre, Shutesbury, Chelmsford, Upton, Concord, Waltham, Carlisle, Acton, Lynn, Cohasset, Newport, California), Newfoundland, Labrador, Kane Basin, Outer Hebrides?, Patagonia – S Julien (Darwin), British Columbia coast, Queen Charlotte Island (Margo Donovan evidence).

iv) Miscellaneous stone dwellings
North America: Narraganset Beach, ruins of village
High Arctic: Newfoundland, Labrador, Kane Basin
Australia: Newcastle, Sydney
California: east of San Francisco Bay (Chinese village)
Azores: Corvo (on beach)
Peru: the great wall of Chimu (compare with Vietnam) – 40 miles long near Chan-Chan; Quinoa subterranean palace

(Geographical Review, vol. XXIII, 1932)
Mexico: Teotihuacan, inscribed rocks (Professor Niven)
Vietnam: great wall of Vietnam (evidence Ms Fran, Kunming Conference, 2002)
British Columbia/Washington State: submerged village
Mississippi (44°10´N 93°W), circular fortress (to house 5,000 men)

(v) The Newport Round Tower – astronomical alignments
Carbon dating of tower now puts earliest date as 1410. Professor William S. Penhallow, Professor Emeritus of Physics, University of Rhode Island, has concluded the tower is a cylinder with arches sitting on eight pillars whose windows are cut so as to enable astronomical sightings (in 3D) of the sun, moon, Polaris and Dubhe (Ursa Major) at spring equinox and winter solstice. Everything required to determine longitude by an eclipse of the moon is found in the alignment of the windows. A structure north-east of the tower has been located (gnomon line?) and is being investigated. The author has requested an analysis of the mortar of the tower to see whether it contains rice flour, an ingredient used by the Chinese to add strength to mortar. Results will be posted on website.

(vi) Stone dams and fishponds
   Hawaii: (M Armstrong) Menehune (Oahu)
   Virginia: (J Warsing) Wyoming County – forts, dams
   New Zealand (South Island): (Fletcher)
   Westport, Mass.: (Jean Elder)
   Fiji, Alof islet: (Fortune) – mariner's mirror (14°15´S 178°10´W)

(vii) Carved stone artwork
   Easter Island: Chinese lion's head (Kerson Huang)
   Honan: Chinese lion head (T. Brooks)
   Bali: Chinese lion head
   Yucatán: Mayan gargoyles – serpents (Alan Moks); carvings on temple wall in Chinese (R. Wertz); Phaspa writing (R. Wertz); elephants; Chinese heron
   Copan: Chinese heron (Dean Dey); lion's head (Dean Dey);

Chinese man with moustache (Mrazekts)
Guatemala, La Democracia: carved Chinese stones (C. Skinner)
Massachusetts: carved Buddha (Shutesbury)
California: sculpture (C. Marschner); carved stone with Chinese writing (Steve Elkins)

(viii) Slipways
Bimini North Island, Bahamas): hull ballast and slipway, walls (Andros); Bimini Road (B. Swinley)
Anguilla, Bahamas: (Bruce, Andros) harbour (Charles Huegy)

(ix) Factories/wells
Malacca (Ta Tan Sen)

(x) Barrack blocks

Note: standard block = 40 × 30 metres

	Codename	Position (Code)	No. of blocks
1	Burgh	AX°09′29″ D°47′29″	3
2	Boulge	AB°38′28″ J°38′53″	4
3	Debach		
4	Otley	AB°50′30″ J°57′45″	3
5	Orford	AB°52′05″ M°00′25″	3
6	Snape	AB°52′05″ M°00′25″	3
7	Tunstall	AB°52′05″ M°00′25″	3
8	Bawdsey	AB°51′20″ M°02′30″	4
9 &10	Orwell	AB°50′30″ M°03′30″	6
11	Shotley	AB°48′40″ M°59′15″	3?

12	Naoton	AB°44′48″ M°05′45″	1 + 9?
13	Hoo	AB°48′06″ T°59′01″	24
14	Iken	AY°23′26″ S°14′34″	Not yet surveyed
15	Laxfield	AY°28′29″ S°45′07″	3 (cannibals)
16	Bauton	AY°28′51″ S°43′27″	Not yet surveyed
17	Butley	AY°33′31″ S°27′30″	3
18	Blyth	AY°33′43″ S°28′20″	3
19	Trimley	AY°33′40″ S°29′03″	200 (2 × Seraph; 2 × Craft' 3 × Rorqual; 2 × Resolution; 1 × Vanguard, wrecked nearby)
20	Harwich	AY°39′50″ S°06′00″	Not surveyed yet
21	Holbrook	AR°51′30″ S°31′14″	8
22	Clopton	AR°45′16″ V°38′51″	3
23	Kersey	AR°48′53″ V°41′25″	Not surveyed
24	Eye	AR°20′56″ V°49′34″	3 (a mystery – there should be a lot more)
25	Hoxne	AA°29′10″ V°57′59″	2

If each barrack block housed 64 people and 293 located, then at least 18,752 sailors and/or concubines survived – see Shipwrecks 38 to 77. But there are no barracks for wrecks 75 to 77 comprising two Resolution and one Vanguard class – another 3,000 people, viz. at least 22,000 men sailed with this fleet.

11. Mining operations found by Europeans when they reached the New World

(i)   Australia: gold (Gympie); lead, uranium (Arnhem Land)
       (J. Green)
(ii)   Fiji: copper (Lasawa)
(iii) Arctic: smelted bronze, iron, copper (Devon Island and Bathurst
       Island)
(iv)   North America: coal (Newport Island to Greenland); St Peter's
       River (Minay Sotor); Cherokee country east coast (Scott McLean),
       Chinese miners
(v)   Mexico: copper and gold
(vi)   Canada: jadeite (British Columbia)
(vii) New Zealand: antimony, iron and gold (Cedric Bell)

12. Advanced technologies found by first Europeans

(i)   Mexico: extraction of dyestuffs from insects, roots, leaves, barks,
       identical to Chinese processes; lacquer and boxes using compli-
       cated technology identical to Chinese methods; mirror
       manufacture very similar to Lamaist designs; copper technology
       similar to Chinese Aztec papermaking; metal working (Gary
       Jennings, Howard Smith)
(ii)   South America: Inca cotton; Inca roads using cement – road
       systems more extensive than those of Rome

13. Plants indigenous to one continent found on another by early European explorers

(i)   From China to:
•   Australia – lotuses and papyrus
•   North America – rice, poppy seeds, keteleria, roses (*R.
       Laevigata*), hibiscus (*Rosa sinensis*) (Dr Tan Koolin); Monterey
       pines (California) (Bruce Tickell Taylor/Sandy Lydon)
•   Pacific islands – mulberries, hibiscus (*Rosa sinensis*)
•   Amazon (Goyaz)– rice (Paraguayan Chaco (C229))
•   Mexico – rice, hibiscus (*Rosa sinensis* – Mexican national flower)
       (Secret Journal)
•   Malaysia – *Rosa sinensis* (Malaysian national flower)
•   Brazil – oats (Svetlana)

- USA, Virginia – mulberry trees, honeywort, *Paulownia tomentosae* trees (Pallowaddies), 'Yellow Delicious' apples (J. Warsing)

From Tropical Asia to:
- Pacific Islands – taro, yam, banana, turmeric, bottle gourds
- Amazon – bananas
- New Zealand – taro, yam (Captain Cook)

From Malaysia to:
- Pacific Islands – arrowroot (*pia*)
- China – rubber (*damar*), pepper (Ma Huan)

From India to:
- China – cotton
- North Pacific islands – sugar cane, wild ginger
- North and Central America – cotton (via China)
- North Africa and Cape Verde Islands – cotton (from China and America)
- Marquesas (and across the world) – 26 chromosome cotton
- Pacific islands – cotton
- Brazil – sugar cane

From Africa to:
- Central Pacific – bottle gourds
- Puerto Rico – coffee
- Brazil – root crops

From South America to:
- China – maize
- South-east Asia – maize
- New Zealand – kumera
- Pacific islands – yams, sweet potato
- Australia – separate list of 74 items
- Philippines – potatoes, maize (and metates)
- South America – rice, bananas, sugar cane, coconuts, root crops

From South Pacific to:
- North Pacific (Hawaii) – bamboo, coconuts, kava, candlenut

tree, hibiscus
- Central America (Pacific coast) – coconuts
- Brazil – coconuts
- Puerto Rico – coconuts

From Norfolk Island to:
- Campbell Island – Norfolk pines

From Indonesia to:
- China – spice

From Spice Islands to:
- China – pepper

From North America to:
- China – maize, amaranth
- New Zealand – *Chenopodium album* (Durdock Riley, Dave Bell), discovered by Cook, 1769; marsh cress (Navajo cosmetic)

From Mexico to:
- Philippines – tobacco, sweet potatoes, maize seen by Magellan (first European); possibly pineapple, arrowroot, peanut, lima and yam beans, balimbing, cassava, chico, papaya, zapute, tomato and squash (Magellan does not record seeing these)
- India and SE Africa - cochineal

To South America (Amazonia):
- Rice
- Bananas
- Sugar cane
- Coconuts
- Root crops

(ii) Found in Hawaii by early European explorers
- from Tropical America – sweet potatoes
- from India – wild ginger
- from Pacific islands – bamboo, breadfruit, candlenut trees, hibiscus, kava

- from Tropical Asia – taro, ti plants, yam (five-leafed), banana, turmeric
- from Malayan Archipelago – arrowroot
- from east Asia – paper, mulberry

(iii) Found on Easter Island before early European explorers
- from South America – totora reeds (originally from Egypt), tomato, tobacco, sweet potato, 26 chromosome cotton.
- South Pacific – coconuts
- SE Asia – yam
- Mesoamerica – papaya

(iv) Found in New Zealand by early European explorers
- from South America – kumara
- from Colombia – 'scented grass'
- from Asia – dove's foot geranium
- from China – taro
- from North America – *Chenopodium album* and marsh cress

(v) Tobacco: pre-Columbian dispersion
From America to:
- India (A176)
- Australia, Indonesia, New Guinea, Melanesia (F027)
- Africa (before 1525) (J058B)
- New Guinea (L194)

(vi) Californian trees
San Diego County Park: markings on trees cut by Chinese explorers (Esther Daniels)

(vii) Shell mounds on uninhabited islands which the Chinese passed
- Caribbean (Bimini)
- Pacific: Kuriles, Aleutians, Kamchatka, Chuchoi
- New Zealand (Cedric and Dave Bell)

14. Animals indigenous to one continent found on another by early European explorers

(i)   Asiatic chickens in South America. The chickens found by the Spanish and Portuguese arriving in South America were entirely different from those they had left at home. Amerind chickens laid blue-shelled eggs, had Asiatic names and were not used for food – rather for religious practices. They had different combs, feathers, spurs, sizes, shapes, legs, necks and heads and names – Malayan, Melanotic silkies, frizzle fowls and Cochin Chinese. As late as 1600 Mediterranean peoples did not have and did not know of the galaxy of Asiatic chickens found in the Americas. Asiatic chickens cannot fly; someone took them to the Americas before Europeans got there. (See Acosta for South America, Coronado for Tiguex.) (Evidence from William Goggins.)

(ii)   Horses. Venezuela; Peru (Acosta); North America (bones and skulls); Mississippi drainage area and Canada; Brazil (Confins cave); pictures/carvings of horses in Australia; Mexico (Jucutácato shroud); Yucatán and South America (Trujillo and Ayacucho); Panama (Columbus); Tierra del Fuego (Sarmiento) (Evidence from Gerald Thompson, Katrina Van Tassell); Fraser Island (Australia), Carolines (Assateague ponies), Peruvian Pasos, Kaimanawa wild horses (New Zealand)).

(iii   Chinese ship's dogs. Mexico (Acosta), South America, Peru, South Africa, SE Asia, Pacific (further details to be provided); Falklands; Tahiti (Captain Cook); New Zealand (Captain Cook) (Crozet 1771) (Gossett p.158); Santo Domingo (Acosta); Wooldogs – Washington State and British Columbia; Kuri dog to New Zealand? (Evidence from Elizabeth Miller, Philip Mulholland, Greg Autry, Bernard Chang.)

(iv)   Otters found in New Zealand, South Island (Gossett p.151)

(v)   Giraffes and zebras from Africa, kangaroos from Australia to Chinese emperor's zoo

(vi)   Mylodons? Dusky Sound (Gossett, p.148) Vancouver Island?, Gympie?, China?

(vii)   Camels to Peru (Acosta)

(viii)   Pigs from Sulawesi/Java to British Columbia (*babiroussa*);
         Asiatic or Chinese pigs (*tatu*) to Brazil (São Paulo and Minas
         Gerais – Pirapenga), Mexico (*cuino*) and New Zealand (*kune
         kune*)

(ix)   Fulvous tree duck from Bengal to Madagascar, Brazil and
         Venezuela

(x)   Australian dingo to Carolina (wild dog)?

(xi)   Hippopotamus from Africa to China (Beijing Museum –
         'Western Han c.208 BC')

(xii)   Water buffalo to South America

(xiii)   Elephants from Africa to Yucatán, Chile, Peru and Ecuador,
         and (note: authority/junks built to accommodate them – Terry
         1665, p.137) from Africa/India to:

   (a)   Mexico: Mexico City (Clavigero 1 p.84, Vega ii p.394);
         Culican (lat 23°30′), ambassador despatched to Montezuma
         (Ranking Supplement)

   (b)   Colombia: Bogotá (Ranking, p.23); Choco near Granada
         (Ranking, p.396 and Captain Cochran's Journal ii, p.390)

   (c)   Mississippi/Missouri: Mr Stanley captured and taken by
         elephant over mountains west of Missouri (Ranking, p.401);
         elephant bones 36°30′N 83°00′W and 32°50′N 80°10′W

   (d)   Chile: Tarija (22°S – Ranking Supplement)

   (e)   Elephants on Chinese ships – Polly Midgley

15. Art exported by Zheng He's fleets

From China to:

- New Zealand and Pacific coast NW Canada: 'The Protruding
  Tongue' and related motifs (Mino Baders 1966 in *Wiener
  Beithraege zur Kultur Geschichte und Lingvistik*, vol.15, Vienna)
- The Inuits: masks – Henry Collins, many articles
- Easter Island and the Maya (Copan): carved stone lions (Brooks)
  – Copan (Dean Dey), Easter Island (Kerson Huang) and Bali
- The Peoples of the Andes – Music: inland from the Peruvian
  coast Chinese pentatonic scales (C D E G A) prevail, as does a
  large quarter higher on the piano (FX_X GX_X AX $_X$ CX_X DX_X).
  Indian peoples of North and Central America do not deploy the
  Chinese scales. Thus either Chinese music scales somehow

'leapfrogged' North and Central America or were brought by sea to Peru (Ger Nijman).

- Vancouver Island and Wuhan – Totem Poles: totem poles are identical
- Central America: carved stonework – Chichen Itza, Copan
- South America: pottery styles – South American puma ware/Chinese tiger ware (Professor Gary Tee)
- The Americas: clothes styles – see Alexander von Wuthenau, *Unexpected Faces in Ancient America*, in which pre-Columbian peoples are depicted with their distinctive clothes and hats living among Indian peoples.
- Washington Potters (R. Hassel evidence)
- Peru, British Columbia (Wampandaa) and Hawaii (Marquesas): *quipus* (Carver p.362)

From Burma to:
- Sioux: the Burmese swastika sign on Sioux and Ladoga peoples; tilted stone of Kyaiktiyo to Massachusetts, USA

16. Customs and games exported from China to the New World, as found by European explorers

(i) To Mexico and Central America:
- Complicated rain-making ceremonies, identical in every detail
- Jade, with its complex panoply of beliefs
- Music – more than 50 per cent of Central American music instruments occur in Burmese hinterland
- Neck-rest pillows and Chinese carrying poles
- Identical children's fairy stories – 'Rabbit in the Moon'
- Papermaking and dye extraction
- Copper processing
- Divination rituals using chickens
- Tao/tie in Mayan artwork (Karin)
- Lakota tribe – 'swastika' symbol/Tibetan peace and harmony (R. Chauvet)

(ii)   To California (between Russian and Sacramento Rivers)
(Stephen Powers' report):
- Chinese-speaking
- Farmers and hunters
- Language
- Gambling
- Theatrical performances
- Women's dresses and hairstyles
- Snaring wildfowl with decoys
- Burying in ancestral soil
- Men with beards
- Sophisticated pottery
- Elegant carved jasper knives
- Methods of irrigation
- Stone villages

(iii) To South America:
Peru
- Roads using gypsum cement
- Cotton manufacture
- Games (Patolli)
- Quipus
- Computing devices
- Tripod pottery
- Divination rituals using chickens
- Jade rituals
- Musical jade gongs
- Inheritance traditions
- Mortuary customs
- Sacrificial customs
- Observation and cataloguing of lunar cycles and equinoxes
- Castration of criminals

Brazil
- Divination rituals using chickens
- Jade, with its complex panoply of beliefs
- Bearded men (*karayaba*)

(iv)   To British Columbia (NW Canada)
- Chinese secret societies
- Song similarities
- Chinese origin of Indian names
- Similarities with potlatch ceremonies
- Wampum (compare with quipus in Peru and China) (Ranking)

17. Armour

(i)   New Zealand: Pitu peninsula (Dave Bell), 'Spanish helmet'
       (Robin Watt

(ii)   North America: copper breastplates (Kotze Bue); Mississippi;
       Sacramento (Dr John Furry); Buzzards Bay (Bartholomew
       Griswold, 1602); Cape Cod (Martin Prinz, 1603)

18. Links with the years 1421–3

A number of historians, while accepting the author's contention that
China reached the New World before Europeans, contend that they
did so in sporadic voyages over centuries. The author relies on the
scale of the voyages as well as detailed evidence linking settlements to
the 1421–3 voyage. The author contends that at least 10,000 people
settled in Peru, at least 25,000 in Australasia, and at least 5,000 in
Mexico.

Scale

(i)   Evidence of da Gama's voyage is that '800 sail' preceded him
       to Calicut 80 years earlier (viz. 1421–2, before China was
       sealed in 1431), and that the population of the fleet was
       greater than any city between China and India – virtually a
       small nation on the move (Professor Finlay, *Terrae Incognitae,*
       vol.xxiii)

(ii)   The whole world was charted by 1428. This massive under-
       taking across tens of millions of square miles of ocean would
       have required at least 120 ships working for 18 months.
       Several hundred ships would be required to transport 50,000
       people.

(iii) Evidence has been provided of Chinese settlements in
       Australia and New Zealand, the length and breadth of the

Indian Ocean, across the Pacific and the lengths of the Pacific and Atlantic coasts of North and South America. Again, this would have involved hundreds of ships.

(iv) Nearly a hundred villages in Peru have Chinese names – around 10,000 people must have settled

(v) 'The treasure hunt' – at least 2,500 people in Australasia.

Detailed evidence

(i) Eruption of Soufriere, La Citerne and L'Echelle volcanoes on Pizzigano chart, twice between 1400 and 1440 (1424 chart)

(ii) Wrecks with gilded sterns: Chinese junks in Mississippi near Quivira (Coronado 1550) and in Caribbean (Mafeo) and north Atlantic (Menendez); gilt does not last, so junks wrecked relatively recently

(iii) Chinese people not intermarried seen in California, Mexico, Texas and Florida by Coronado, Acosta, Menendez and Mafeo (1550s)

(iv) Ming porcelain dated either by cobalt or by Zhu Di's stamp – 1403 to 1421 – found in Americas, Africa, Australia

(v) Hull wood of junks carbon dated: Pandanan 1410, Nanjing 1406, Sacramento 1410, Turiang early 15th century, Bakau c.1410, Santa Cruz (Philippines) 15th century, Byron's Bay (Australia) 1410 – and some of these contain evidence of voyages to America

(vi) Jade figurine at Darwin dated by shape of Canopus head to early Ming, between 1008 and 1523 (Professor Wei's evidence)

(vii) Zheng He states '3,000 countries large and small' visited; Liu Shia Chang, Chian Su (unveiled 1431) – Duyvendak first translation

(viii) Pope's letter, 1448, about Chinese/Asians in Greenland 'about 30 years ago', viz. c.1421/2; Chinese DNA in Greenland people of Hvalsey

(ix) Columbus's records (1477), '70 years before, people from Cathay in Orient' (Greenland)

(x) Fra Mauro's map, 'about the year 1420', ship or junk from India

(xi) Zhu Di coins (1403–24) found in wrecks dated by hull wood, for example Pandanan

(xii)   Chinese star charts (*Wu Pei Chi*) dated by precession of Polaris to 1420 ± 20 years

(xiii)   Mao Kun map, Chinese dated 1422, shows Australia (Sun Shuyun)

(xiv)   Chinese records give dates fleet set sail, dates returned, and ambassadors brought – Ming Shi (MS); Ming Shi W (MSL); Hsi Yang Fan Kuo Chih (HYFKC); Kio Ch'veh; Hsu Chiao Min Tung; Chien (MTC), Ming Chih (MC), all early Ming; see Part II of this synopsis.

(xv)   *Illustrated Record of Strange Countries* published 1430 featuring animals from across the world

(xvi)   Chinese official records (Qing) listing countries visited by Zheng He's fleet includes America and Australia

(xvii)   Newport Round Tower mortar (post 1409)

(xviii) Bimini hull ballast (after last 600 years) (evidence of Admiral Zheng Ming)

(xix)   Dating of Pizzigano, Piri Reis, Jean Rotz, Waldseemüller, Cantino charts, and Vinland map (2002 radiocarbon dating); Portuguese master chart of world dated 1428; Brazilian chart showing route to China (1501)

19. Chinese already in the Americas when the first Europeans arrived: bibliographical evidence

Giovanni di Verrazzano (1480–1524)	Met Chinese near (modern) New York; met Asiatic people near Rhode Island	Verrazzano's letter to Fancis I of France. Hakluyt's *Collection of the Early Voyages and Discoveries of the English Nation*, London 1810, pp. 358 et seq.
Francis Vasquez de Coronado (1510–1554)	Met people 'so different from all the nations that [we] have seen . . . must have come from that part of Greater India the coast of which lies to the west of this country' (viz. China)	Coronado was despatched by Viceroy Antonio de Mendoza in April 1541 to seek Quivira beyond the Arkansas River.
Pedro de Castaneda	Official chronicler to Coronado's expedition,	*The Journey of Coronado*, trans. George Parker

(1544)	reported the journey and peoples above described	Winship, Dover Publications New York 1933, at pp.58 et seq.
Antonio Galvão (c.1563)	*The Apostle of the Moluccas* reports pre-Columbian voyages from China to America and Chinese settlements in America	*An Excellent Treatise of Antonio Galvão*, Hakluyt, London 1812 (British Library 209 h.z.)
José de Acosta (1540–1600)	Spanish Jesuit missionary who describes the people, animals, birds, plants and flowers found by the first Europeans in Americas	*Historia Natural y Moral de Las Indias*, pub. Salamanca 1588–90 by Society of Jesus. Chinese in Mexico (272), horses (273), dogs (274), hens (284), coconuts (253), etc.
Juan Gonzalez de Mendoza (1588)	Chinese voyages to the New World before Europeans	*The Historie of the Great and Mighty Kingdom of China …* trans. Robert Parke 1588, pub. Hakluyt Society 1853–4, London
Gregorio Garcia	Chinese coming to populate Mexico (before Europeans) in *El Reino de Anian*	
Hugo Grotius (1583–1645)	Report of Asiatic shipwrecks (pre-Columbus) on the Pacific coast of Mexico	*Bibliotheca Curiosa*, pub. Hakluyt Society, London 1884
Father Antonio de la Calancha (1638) F. de Guignes (1761)	Describes Chinese graves and pictures of Chinese horsemen in Peru, pre-Columbus Collates earlier accounts of pre-Columbian Chinese people and ships in Americas – Coronado's 'gilded sterns' *at* Quivira, Chinese merchants in Quatulco and among Catualcans	*Crónica Moralizadora*, Barcelona 1638, Book II, p.486 et seq. *Recherches sur les Navigations des Chinois du Côte de l'Amerique et sur Quelques Peuples Situées a l'Extrémité Orientale de l'Asie*, Paris 1761
Antonio Zatta (1775)	Published map showing Queen Charlotte Islands (British Columbia) which	Queen Charlotte Islands described as 'Colonia dei Chinesi'. Published Venice

	preceded Captain Cook or Vancouver's 'discovery' of that island	1775. (British Library (Maps) c. 26.6.14)
Stephen Powers (1877)	Describes Chinese colony in California between Russian and Sacramento Rivers	*Anthropological Journal of Canada*, vol.14, no.1, 1976; and 'Tribes of California' in *Contributing to North American Ethnology*, Washington 1877, vols 1–3
Loayza, F.	A summary of the discoveries made by the first Europeans to the Americas who found Chinese people, villages, bodies, relics and Chinese animals, plants, birds, etc. (trans. Ian Hudson)	*Chinos Ilegaron antes que Colon*, pub. D. Miranda, Lima 1948; Chinese in Peru (p.42); Chinese in Mexico (p.67); Chinese bodies
Carlos Prince	Biographer of Pedro Menendez de Aviles the Adelantado,who found pre-Columbian junks in the North Sea	'Chinese . . . with Tartairs, Japanese and Koreans . . . crossed the maritime stretch . . . into the Kingdom of Quivira, populating Mexico, Panama, Peru and other eastern countries of the Indies'
Professor William Niven	Found the body of an important Chinese navigator buried with pomp (pre-Columbian)	'Mélanges et Nouvelles Americanistes', *Journal de la Société de Americanistes de Paris*, vol.X, p.303 et seq.
Christopher Columbus	Met Chinese when he arrived in Cuba, and reported Chinese visitors to Greenland before 1477 and Chinese bodies in Azores before 1492	Biography in 1421
Christopher Columbus	Secret report (Madrid)	Chinese miners in 'bird ship' (Martin Tai)
Cabrillo	Chinese junk seen by Bartolomeo Ferrello in 1543	Cabrillo's map of California shows 'Nave de Cataio' in *Atlas 9 of American Civilisation*, University of Oklahoma Press 1992

Pedro Menendez de Aviles	Chinese junks in north Atlantic off Florida coast	
Jodicus Hondius (1606)	Chinese junk in Pacific	Robert Hassell's evidence
Alexander von Wuthenau		*Unexpected Faces in Ancient America*; many Chinese faces in pre-Columbian America
Father Luis Sales OP	Chinese colony from Santa Barbara to San Francisco	*Observations on California* 1772–90, republished 1956 Los Angeles
Gonzales Ximenez de Quesada	Muyscas, Guanes, Calimas of Colombia entirely different from local Indian people	
Garcilaso de La Vega	Chinese in Peru and Chile before Europeans	*Commentarios Reales del Origin de los Incas, Reis del Peru*

Part IV: Evidence of Zheng He's fleets' visits to specific places

1. Indian Ocean
(i) Ma Huan
(ii) Fei Xin
(iii) Vasco da Gama – 'fleet of 800 ships reached Calicut 80 years earlier'
(iv) Malacca – graveyards, factory, well (Ta Tan Sen), Zheng He's temple (Mark Zhong)

2. East Africa
(i) Substantial early blue and white Ming the length of East African coast (Philip Snow)
(ii) Pate Island (evidence in book)
(iii) Fleet visited city of Zimbabwe (Martin Tai evidence) and Ming blue and white finds
(iv) Mao Kun/*Wu Pei Chi* (1422) show Chinese fleet proceeding south off East African coast
(v) Fei Xin
(vi) Needham

3. The Atlantic and the Cape Verde Islands

(i)   Cape of Good Hope and West Africa appear on charts drawn
       before Europeans reached Cape (Fra Mauro 1459, Mao Kun
       c.1402, Da Ming Yi Tu 1389)
(ii)   Fra Mauro drew Chinese junks accurately
(iii) Fra Mauro's story of ship or junks from India rounding Cape
(iv)   26 chromosome American cotton, originally from North
       America then to Africa and Cape Verde Islands, found by first
       Europeans in Cape Verde
(v)   the carved (Malayalam) stone on Cape Verde Islands at Santo
       Antão (Janela)
(vi)   the similar carved stone at Matadi Falls

4. The Caribbean

(i)   The Caribbean appears on the Cantino, Caverio and
       Waldseemüller maps published before Europeans arrived there
(ii)   Vasquez de Coronado met Chinese people in Tiguex and
       found Chinese junks with gilded sterns
(iii) João de Acosta found coconuts in Puerto Rico (originated SE
       Asia) and dogs (originated China) in San Domingo.
(iv)   The Moskoke tribe in south-east USA and the Campeche
       Maya and Buctzozt Maya of the Yucatán have Chinese (post
       Bering Straits flooding) DNA
(v)   Chinese carvings at Maya sites in Yucatán
(vi)   Carvings of horses and elephants at Maya sites in Yucatán
(vii) Chinese anchor, Yucatán
(viii) Chinese jade and ceramics, Yucatán
(ix)   Horses in Panama (Columbus) (Barbara McEwen)
(x)   Chinese miners in bird boats (Columbus) (Martin Tai)
(xi)   Possible Chinese ceramic shards, Indian Quay (Ken Welch)
(xii) Bimini Road (Bill Swinley)
(xiii) Anguilla road (Bruce) (Third Bimini Road)
(xiv) Andros reservoir (Charles Huegy)
(xv)   Chinese ship's dogs (B. Chang)
(xvi) Columbus, and people who call themselves Indian = Yin Dian
       (people from Yin) (Martin Tai)
(xvii) Elephants from Africa to Yucatán and Colombia (Ranking)
(xviii) Wreck at Guadeloupe (Columbus)

5. Florida (including 'Florida' as defined in 17th century)

(i) Moskoke tribe have Chinese DNA, inherited after Bering land-bridge flooded (Novick et al)

(ii) Pedro Menendez de Aviles (first European) found wrecks of Chinese junks off Florida coast

(iii) Columbus' secret report describes Chinese mining operations

(iv) Florida appears on Cantino chart published before Europeans reached Florida

(v) Chinese jade in Indian burial mounds (Barbosa Rodrigues)

(vi) Chinese themselves claim Zheng He's fleet reached North America (Zayan) (Professor Bi Quanzhong)

(vii) Cotton plants exported from North America to Africa before Columbus (thence to Cape Verde Islands)

(viii) Columbus, and people who call themselves Indian = Yin Dian (people from Yin) (Martin Tai)

(ix) Nayarit legends, 'ancestors came by sea from the east' (Dr Pratzii 123)

(x) Columbus describes horses (Barbara McEwan) and meeting Muslims (Dr Shong)

(xi) Columbus saw great ship (Jerry Warsing)

(xii) Second 'Bimini Road' at Palar Beach (W. Feickert)

6. The Carolinas Virginia

(i) Chinese junk found by early settlers buried in Great Dismal Swamp (L. A. R. Clark)

(ii) Linguistics (Ming Ho, Lyco Ming, Wyo Ming), customs and Machado-Joseph disease (Jerry Warsing)

(iii) Early European settlers met Chinese miners on the Minay Sotor – later murdered by Cherokees (Scott McLean)

(iv) The Cherokee rose – a Chinese flower found by first Europeans

(v) Maize exported from North America pre-Columbus found by da Gama in South Africa and by Magellan in Philippines

(vi) Chinese landing party ambushed and murdered (Frank Fitch)

(vii) Chinese hens

(viii) Assateague wild horses

(ix) Mulberry trees, honeywort root and *Paulownia tomentosae* (or Pallowaddie) trees from China and 'Yellow Delicious' apples (Warsing)

(x)   Turkeys reached Europe before Columbus set sail (Professor Wu)

(xi)   Melungeons are Chinese (J. Warsing, Brent Kennedy)

7. New England, Massachusetts and Boston/New York

(i)   Sioux tribe have Chinese DNA (post Bering Straits flooding)

(ii)   Dighton Rock carvings/writings/local Indian legends (giant foreign ship like a house sailing upriver firing cannon); Dighton Rock writing Mongolian (Humboldt, vol.i p.15, and Ranking, pp.419, 562); similar stones at McCook Point and Niantic Bay (B. Trinque)

(iii)   Newport Round Tower/Chinese observatory

(iv)   Rhode Island Reds – a Chinese chicken – found by first Europeans (Jack Pizzey)

(v)   Professor de la Barre's evidence – local people have Asian characteristics

(vi)   The Salem horse carving

(vii)   'Buddhist' stones of New England

(viii) Massachusetts, buried soldier in armour

(ix)   Giovanni di Verrazzano met Asian people quite different from local Indians; he described some as Chinese

(x)   Area appears on Vinland map (1440) – genuine (see Radiocarbon, vol. 44, no.1, 2002, and postscript) – and on the Waldseemüller map (1507)

(xi)   Navajo, Chamorro and Flathead tribes have unique retrovirus gene (Natural Academy of Sciences, 1997)

(xii) Elephants from Africa (Ranking)

(xiii) Rice found by early explorers

(xiv) Pedro Menendez de Aviles found Chinese junks wrecked in North Atlantic – wind would have carried surviving junks to Rhode Island

(xv) People around Newport different from other Indian tribes (Professor de la Barre)

(xvi) 'Stone village' (pre-Columbian) near Dighton Rock

(xvii) Shutesbury Stone – 'Buddha contemplating the truth of ageing' (Theravada Buddhism)

(xviii) Carving of a pre-Columbian horse 100 miles west of the Shutesbury Stone at N. Salem

(xix)   Tilted stones, similar in posture to the holy (Theravada Buddhism) boulder at Kyaiktiyo in Burma.

(xx)   Teeth of Narragansetts (Wydants) have 'Chinese characteristics' (Katrina van Tassel) (similar story Marty Brodell)

(xxi)   Machado-Joseph disease (Warsing)

(xxii)   Bishop Berkeley's accounts of Mongolian peoples living around Dighton Rock (Ranking, Smibert).

(xxiii)   Skeleton and brass objects found at Permaquid near Portland, Maine (www.frpd.org/historicalskeleton)

(xxiv)   Stone graveyard/Westport River (Jean Elder)

The author submits that only one explanation is consistent with Verrazzano's sightings – the Shutesbury Stone, the carved horse's head and the balanced rocks at Savoy, Upton, Prospect Park, South Peabody, Royalston, Barr, Cape Ann, Athol (and six more), the rice and the Chinese chickens – and that is that Chinese junks manned in part by Theravada Buddhists sailed up the Connecticut and Taunton Rivers and created the settlements Verrazzano came across. This explanation accords with Professor de la Barre's and Bishop Berkeley's evidence.

8. Upper Mississippi

(i)   The Upper Mississippi appears on charts drawn before Europeans arrived there, e.g. Waldseemüller (1507)

(ii)   Native carvings of foreign ships and horses found near tributaries of the Mississippi

(iii)   Chinese jade found in tombs near the Mississippi (Georgia – Nacooche Mound; Michigan Mound, p.269B)

(iv)   Coronado report of junks with gilded sterns found near estuary of Mississippi

(v)   Chinese DNA found among Sioux and Cree Ojibwa peoples of Upper Mississippi

(vi)   Horse remains found near Lake Superior

(vii)   Elephant remains at 32°50′N, 80°10′W

(viii)   Carvings of monkeys and elephants

(ix)   Buried stone observation platforms at Rock Lake

(x)   Stone fortresses at 44°10′N, 93°00′W

(xi)   Turkeys exported from North America to Europe (via Silk

Road) before Columbus set sail

(xii) Chinese hens found by first Europeans in North America

(xiii) Amaranth exported to China before Europeans reached North America

(xiv) Cherokees murder foreign miners near St Peter's River – Minay Sotor (Scott McLean)

(xv) 26 chromosome cotton from North America to Africa

(xvi) *Chenopodium album* and marsh cress to New Zealand

(xvii) Mustangs?

9. British Columbia (Queen Charlotte and Vancouver Islands) and Washington State

(i) Queen Charlotte and Vancouver Islands appear on the Waldseemüller and Zatta maps drawn before Europeans arrived in British Columbia; on Zatta's map, Queen Charlotte Island is called 'Colonia dei Chinesi'

(ii) Hugo Grotius (1624), reporting Galvão: 'The people of China ... sailed ordinarily the coast, which seems to reach unto 70 degrees towards the north', viz. as far north as the Bering Straits

(iii) Squamish Indian accounts of visits of Chinese traders before Europeans (Robert Hassell)

(iv) Tens of thousands of Chinese copper coins found either buried or attached as ornaments to Native American and Chinese objects on Vancouver Island, dated pre-Columbus

(v) Chinese talisman and lamp, dated pre-Columbus (Vancouver Island)

(vi) Bronze figurine of Garuda – pre-European arrival (John Grubber)

(vii) *Babiroussa* – wild pigs of Sulawesi – found buried in chieftain's grave (Vancouver Island)

(viii) Squamish Indians have identical words to Chinese, more than 37 examples, e.g. *tsil* (wet) and *chin* (wood)

(ix) Recent (post Bering Straits flooding) Chinese DNA in Queen Charlotte Islands people (Professor Bryan Sykes, *Seven Daughters of Eve*)

(x) Chinese storage jars, Tofino (Hector Williams)

(xi) Chinese clay vase, Vancouver Island (B. Morelan)

(xii)   Totem poles identical to Wuhan (Geoff McCabe)

(xiii)   Washington Potters – Lake River (Terry Glavin, *The Last Great Sea*)

(xiv)   Lovekin Rock wreck (R. Hassell)

(xv)   Long Beach wreck (R. Hassell)

(xvi)   Haida myths – people sailing from west towards sunrise before Europeans (Paul Wagner)

(xvii)   Queen Charlotte Islands – small deer (G. Berteig)

(xviii) Chinese coins on coast (G. Berteig)

(xix)   Ancient Chinese bronzes (John Grubber); ancient Asian ceramics (Hector Williams); Jodicus Hondius map (Chinese junk) (Robert Hassell)

(xx)   Washington State Pacific coast, Ozette Lake site – Chinese artefacts (Don Mollick)

(xxi)   Point Adams – wreck (Clatsop Beach) (Ed Mitchell); Asian pot wreck (H. Williams)

(xxii)   Neahkahnie Beach – wreck (Cabrillo)

(xxiii) Washington State dig – Ming porcelain (Ken Holmes, Sean Griffin, Terry Glavin)

(xxiv)   Wool dogs (E. Miller and Susan Crockford)

(xxv)   Inuit = Yin Uit (people from Yin) (Martin Tai)

(xxvi)   Aleut people have Chinese DNA

(xxvii) Haida and Aleut people have same language

(xxviii) Lakotas resemble Chinese – clothes/swastikas (Richard Chauvet)

10. Arizona, New Mexico, Texas, Oklahoma, Arkansas, Colorado and Oregon

(i)   The area appears on the Cantino (1502) and Waldseemüller (1507) charts, drawn before Europeans arrived there

(ii)   Antonio Galvão (1555) reports Chinese claims to be 'lords' of Mexico

(iii)   Coronado found Chinese people in Tiguex (near Albuquerque)

(iv)   Coronado's expedition found ships with gilded sterns (Mafeo and Frois corroborate); treasure ships had large gilded carvings of an eagle on their sterns

(v)   Chinese merchants reported in ports of Quatulco and Panuco (Gregorio Garcia)

(vi)   Acosta met Chinese

(vii)   Asiatic shipwrecks on Mexican Pacific coast (Hugo Grotius)

(viii)   Chinese jade buried in Nacooche Mound, Michigan Mound

(ix)   Pictures of horses (foreign to Americas prior to Columbus) and foreign ships carved by Indian peoples (more than 100), dated pre-Columbus

(x)   Hibiscus (*Rosa sinensis*) and Chinese roses found by first Europeans (Secret Journal) (Dr Tan Koolin)

(xi)   Chinese ship's dogs (Acosta)

(xii)   Maize (Mexican corn) found by first Europeans to reach China

(xiii)   Chinese chickens found by Coronado (Topira)

(xiv)   The Navajo and Zuni tribes have Chinese DNA (post Bering Straits flooding) (Novick et al)

(xv)   Maize found by da Gama – Cape of Good Hope

(xvi)   Statuettes of Buddha, Grand Canyon; Buddhist ceremonial dishes of solid silver (J. Smothers)

(xvii)   Names of towns (Henriette Merz)

(xviii) Granby Dam, Colorado – statuette (Thad Daly)

(xix)   Navajo people understood Chinese last century (John Ting)

(xx)   Zuni people understand Japanese (Jim Tanner, Nancy Yaw Davis, Barbara Vibbert)

(xxi)   Cabrillo/Bartholomeu Ferreiro, *Nave de Cataio* – ship of China wrecked at Oregon

11. California

(i)   California is accurately depicted on the Waldseemüller map (1507), drawn before the first Europeans arrived

(ii)   Antonio Galvão (1555) reports Chinese claims to be 'lords' of the Pacific coast of America

(iii)   Major Powers describes a Chinese colony between the Russian and Sacramento Rivers

(iv)   Professor Fryer describes Chinese as the builders of the stone walls on the eastern side of San Francisco Bay (Clayton Roberts, Andy Asp)

(v)   Wreck of junk at Sacramento (Dr John Furry): hull wood dated to 1410; magnetometer reading showing iron in hull;

seeds in hull; rice in hold (supposedly brought to the Americas by Europeans)

(vi)   Diseases of Native American peoples otherwise found in China and SE Asia – hookworm, roundworm; Chinese DNA in Navajo and Zuni peoples (Novick et al)

(vii)   Chinese chickens, which cannot fly or swim, found by first Europeans (Acosta)

(viii) Chinese anchors – Palos Verdes, San Pedro Bay, Redondo Beach (barnacles dated pre-Columbian) (Elliot Stiles, Michael Bleidistel)

(ix)   Chinese roses and hibiscus (*Rosa sinensis*) found by first Europeans (Dr Tan Koolin)

(x)   Chinese porcelain

(xi)   Chinese jade (Bill McVicar)

(xii)   Turkeys and maize exported to China before Columbus set sail

(xiii) Drake chased a Chinese junk

(xiv)   Gregorio Garcia, *El Reino de Anian* – Chinese came to Pacific coast before Europeans

(xv)   Avalon Harbour – treasure box (Steve Hayes)

(xvi)   Chinese carved stone (Steve Elkins) – raised ink characters

(xvii) Founder of LA was Chinese (Sylia)

(xviii) San Francisco Chinese can trace ancestry to before Europeans (R. Ohlsen)

(xix)   Chinese stone sculpture (C. Marschner)

(xx)   Early Ming bronze plate buried at Susanville (A. D. Palmer)

(xxi)   Monterey Pines indigenous to China (Bruce Tickell Taylor, Sandy Lydon)

(xxii) Father Luis Sales OP finds Chinese colony at Santa Barbara, 1772–90

(xxiii) Navajo elders understand Chinese (Jim Tanner and John Ting)

(xxiv) Zuni understand Japanese (Jim Tanner and Nancy Yaw Davis)

(xxv)   Similarities between Zuni and Jomon of Japan (F. Lizuka)

(xxvi) 'Dragon' ships before Columbus (Theodore Bainbridge)

(xxvii) Santa Catalina Island – wrecked junk

12. The Azores

(i)   Sorensen & Raish B 003 007, C 116 383, F 112 B, G 066B (big storm – ancient street appears on Corvo), 071, L 364 B, R 017 074 B, S 155

(ii)   Islands appear on Kangnido – published before Europeans arrived there

(iii)   First Portuguese found a statue of mounted horsemen 'with writing we could not understand'

(iv)   Columbus reported Chinese bodies washed ashore at Flores

(v)   After great storm of 1870 stone village was exposed on Corvo

(vi)   Azores lies on the route from America with wind and current – Chinese had been in America

(vii)   Machado-Joseph disease is prevalent among Flores natives; author believes this disease originated in China.

(viii) In 1421 there was 0° magnetic variation on the summit of Corvo – important to medieval navigators; this is where the statue was found

13. Mexico

(i)   Mexico appears on Waldseemüller chart (1507) before Europeans set sail

(ii)   Chinese body in tomb at Teotihuacan (NE of Mexico City) (Professor Niven)

(iii)   Chinese people described by Europeans – Coronado, Acosta, Galvão

(iv)   Jucutácato shroud depicting arrival of horsemen and Chinese ship's dogs

(v)   Chinese wreck – Playa La Ropa (Bahia de Zihuatanejo) and on coast (Acosta)

(vi)   Chinese figurine beside body in tomb at Teotihuacan

(vii)   Chinese chickens (Acosta)

(viii) Chinese roses and hibiscus (*Rosa sinensis*) (Dr Tan Koolin)

(ix)   Chinese lacquer technology

(x)   Chinese jade medallions and ear plugs – Teotihuacan

(xi)   Diseases otherwise unique to Far East – roundworm, hookworm, lice and nits

(xii)   Pictures of horses (unknown in Americas prior to Columbus) in Mayapan, Chichen Itza and Teotihuacan

(xiii)   Nayarit legends: 'ships like houses' visited them before Europeans

(xiv)   Chinese rice found by first Europeans

(xv)   Chinese paper-making technology

(xvi)   Mexican plants taken to China and Far East – maize, papaya, tobacco – before European voyages

(xvii)   Chinese butterfly fishing nets – Rio Balsas

(xviii)   Chinese statue – Teotitlan

(xix)   Chinese vase – Azacapotzaco

(xx)   Chinese dyestuff technology practised by local people

(xxi)   Chinese ship's dogs (Acosta and B. Chang)

(xxii)   Chinese merchants visited port of Quatulco before Europeans (Loayza)

(xxiii)   Export of tobacco, sweet potatoes, maize to Philippines (Magellan/Pigafetta); tortora reeds, tomatoes, sweet potatoes to Easter Island; and sweet potato to Hawaii

(xxiv)   The Campeche Maya and Buctzozt Maya have Chinese DNA (post Bering Straits flooding)

(xxv)   The Othmis tribe closely resemble the Chinese

(xxvi)   Zecharia Sitchin's website – extraordinary similarity between late Mayan/Chinese art

(xxvii)   Chinese musical instruments – more than 50 per cent of Central American instruments occur in Burma (Needham)

(xxviii)   Neck-rest pillows and Chinese carrying pots (Needham)

(xxix)   Identical fairy stories – 'Rabbit in the Moon' (Needham)

(xxx)   Chinese artefacts – Isthmus of Tehuantepec, Chiapas do Corzo, La Venta (L27, K094, M342C, L240, W269)

(xxxi)   Chinese bronzes (R. Hristov) (Ming – Mixtec Tomb, Oaxaca)

(xxxii)   Stone carvings in Chichen Itza almost identical to Beijing – snake head fountains/drainage spouts (Zecharia Sitchin)

(xxxiii)   Toy elephant, Jalapa

(xxxiv)   Mayan glyphs on west wall of temple are Chinese; Mongolian script on same wall – Phaspa (R. Wertz)

(xxxv)   Certain tribes worked in metal pre-Europeans (Gary Jennings, Howard Smith)

(xxxvi)   New Mexico – Indian Pueblos – legend of Chinese warriors (A. Moya)

(xxxvii)   Linguistics – Chiapas Tse-Tsal, Tso Tsil (R. Banzo) (xxxviii)Legend of wrecked Chinese junk (Joel Fressa)

(xxxix) 'Chinese totem figurines' of west Mexico (I. B. Remsen, Clay Ranger)

(xl) Copan (Honduras) Chinese man with moustache (Mrazerts)

(xli) Montezuma – Aztec ancestors came from east by sea in company of a great lord (Ranking)

(xlii) First Spaniards found rulers wearing silk (Ranking; Cortez to Charles V)

(xliii) First Spaniards found Mongol script written on paper (Ranking – Staenburg 325)

(xliv) Alexander von Wuthenau – 'pre-Columbian statues of Chinese', Tlapacoya, Guerro, La Venta (fig.77 and p.210)

(xlv) Similarity between late Mayan/Chinese art/Tao Taio (Karin and Alan Moks)

(xlvi) Guatemala/La Democracia Chinese carved stones (Catherine Skinner)

(xlvii) Copan Maya/Chinese art (Heron) (Dean Dey)

(xlviii) Chinese pigs (*cuino*)

14. Panama and Venezuela

(i) Venezuela shown on maps before Europeans set sail – Cantino (1502), Waldseemüller (1507); Orinoco shown on Martellus (1489)

(ii) DNA of Indian people shows transferrins otherwise unique to Kwantung, SW China (Arends and Gallengo); DNA of Indian peoples of Surinam, Guyana and northern Brazil shows similar 'Chinese' connection (Arends and colleagues – M443)

(iii) Chinese chickens found the length of Peru; Peruvian emperors use the Chinese name for chickens, *atahualpa*

(iv) Coconuts, native to south Pacific, found by first Europeans (Acosta), and bananas (Maldonado's expedition)

(v) *Illustrated Record of Strange Countries* (published China, 1430) shows armadillos, unique to South America

(vi) *Sampan* (boat), *balsa* (raft) – identical words in Chinese

(vii) Chinese claim to have ruled over 'locations in Central and South America' – Antonio Galvão, quoted by Richard Hakluyt

(viii) Chinese jade – Panama and Costa Rica (Barbosa Rodrigues and Palmatory)

(ix)   Rice, cotton from India and Chinese ship's dogs found by first Europeans

(x)   Papayas (unique to Central America) found by first Europeans on Easter Island

(xi)   The Waunaba and Ngoye people have Chinese DNA (post Bering Straits flooding)

(xii)   Horses in Panama (Columbus) (B. McEwan)

(xiii)   Columbus's secret report – Chinese miners in bird boats (Martin Tai)

15. Peru

(i)   Waldseemüller (1507) and Piri Reis (1513) show Peru before Europeans arrived there

(ii)   Pictures of Chinese horsemen at Trujillo (Friar Antonio de la Calancha) and Ayacucho (G. Squier); lances and swords are similar to early Ming in the National History Museum, Beijing

(iii)   Names of 95 villages are Chinese and have no significance in Quechua or Aymara (Loayza) – listed earlier

(iv)   Villages of Eten and Monsefu (three miles apart) understand Chinese but not each other's patois

(v)   'Great wall of Chimu', 40 miles long, in shape and size resembling Great Wall of China, and great wall of Vietnam (built by Zheng He)

(vi)   Pottery decorated with Chinese calligraphy – Las Trancas, Nazca and Ica (Pablo Patron), and Cajamarca (Zerallos Palmer)

(vii)   Mummy with Chinese inscriptions (Loayza, Cultural College Lima)

(viii)   Tomb with Chinese statues, Chan Chan (Gustavo de la Torre)

(ix)   Linguistic similarities, and folklore and divination practices identical to Chinese

(x)   Roundworm found in local people, otherwise found in SE Asia

(xi)   Sweet potatoes exported from South America found by first Europeans in New Zealand and across Pacific

(xii)   74 separate plants exported from South America to Australia found by first Europeans

(xiii)   Chinese jade

(xiv)   Inca cotton technology – crib of Chinese methods

(xv)   Horses and Chinese ship's dogs seen by first Europeans (Acosta)

(xvi)   Chinese book *Illustrated Record of Strange Countries* (1430) shows animals unique to South America

(xvii)   Inca cement/road building

(xviii)   The Paez, Guambiano, Ingano, Guayabero and Inca peoples have Chinese DNA (post Bering Straits flooding) (Novick et al)

(xix)   The name Inca = Yinca (people from Yin) (Martin Tai)

(xx)   Legend of local people: 'Giants came by sea to settle amongst them' (Garcilaso de la Vega and Pedro Cieza de Leon)

(xxi)   Elephants to Peru and Chile (Ranking); elephants seen, wild, by Captain Cochrane

(xxii)   First Spaniards in Chile found wrecked Chinese junks (Grotius)

(xxiii)   Elephant bones at Tarija, 22°S

(xxiv)   Chile was named before Spanish arrived (Molina): Chi-le = 'dependent colony' in Chinese

16. Brazil (1421–5)

The author contends that a cultured and wealthy civilisation existed in 1421 at the confluence of the Amazon and Tapajos Rivers (near modern Santarem) and at the confluence of the Negro and Solimões Rivers in the region of Iranduba (near Manaus) where today there is nothing but jungle. This civilisation sent a delegation to China in 1502 with six boxes of emeralds as tribute. They reached China by means of a map left by the Chinese on the 1421–5 voyage (Professor Bi Quanzhong evidence).

(i)   Maps

    (a)   Brazil is shown on maps published before Columbus set sail (1492) and before Brazil was 'discovered' by Cabral (1500), viz. 1428 master chart of world, 1448 Andrea Bianco, and

1489 Martellus showing the rivers Magdalena, Amazon–São Francisco, Paraguay, Panama, Colorado, Negro and Chubut.

(b) The Treaty of Tordesillas (1474) only makes sense if the Portuguese already knew of Brazil by then.

(c) Report by João de Barros to King of Portugal; Columbus – he should steer south 'to enquire of the meaning of the King of Portugal who says land is there'.

(ii) DNA

(a) Indian peoples living west of Arecibo have Chinese DNA (Arends and Gallengo)

(b) Indian peoples of Guyana, Surinam and Venezuela have a similar Chinese connection (Dr Annabel Arends)

(c) The Karitiana and Surui peoples of Amazonia have Chinese DNA (post Bering Straits flooding) (Novick et al)

(d) The Quechua and Toba peoples of the Mato Grosso have Chinese DNA (post Bering Straits flooding) (Novick et al)

(e) Absence of Duffy blood groups in Indians of Mato Grosso

(f) Hookworm among Lengua, and roundworm (Fonseca)

(g) Tokelau in Amazonian people (Fonseca)

(iii) What the first Europeans found

(a) Cabral: 'men with pale skins'

(b) Franciso de Orellana, as reported by Friar Antonio de Carvajal: rice fields (Chinese), bananas (originated in Pacific islands) and coconuts (originated in south Pacific)

(c) Maldonado: sugar cane (India)

(d) José de Acosta: chickens – Frizzle fowl (China), Black Melanotic (China/SE Asia), Asian jungle fowl (SE Asia), Langerian gourds (SE Asia) – and Chinese ship's dogs (B. Chang)

(e) Marajoara – pre-Columbian culture where people, tall or pale-skinned, made fine ceramics (Martin Tai evidence); water buffalo found there

(f) Chinese pigs (*canastrinho*) in São Paulo and Minas Gerais

(g) Horses – remains found in Confins cave

(h) Fulvous tree duck (from Bengal)

   (i)   Chinese jade (pre-Columbus), near Amazon/Tapajos River juncture (Barbosa Rodrigues), at Trombetas River, Lago Sapakua, Lago de Faro, Ilha Jacinta, Costa do Parvo, Villa de Faro, Rio Yamunda, Cojmuru

(iv) Linguistics
- (a) *Sampan* = boat in Brazil and China
- (b) *Balsa* = raft in Brazil and China
- (c) Chickens = *kik* (Venezuela), *kikh* (India)
- (d) Sweet potato = *kumar* (Peru), *kumara* (Pacific)
- (e) Fulvous tree duck (which fly with difficulty) = *irere* (Brazil), *irere* (Guyana), *Sarere* (Burma), *Sarari* (India)

(v)   Local legends
Guarani legend – their ancestors crossed a great and wide ocean to settle in Amazonia (M. Garcia)

(vi) Chinese claims to have discovered Brazil before Cabral
- (a) Professor Liu Manchum: 'extremely far Beira' refers to Brazil
- (b) Professor Zhu Jianqui: Zheng He's fleet still at sea in 1425
- (c) Professor Bi Quanzhong: Brazilian delegation left for China in 1501 with map showing way (*Notebook of Wilderness* – Ming dynasty writer Zu Yun Ming, delegation from Balazi = Brazil)
- (d) *Illustrated Record of Strange Countries* (1430) shows armadillo (unique to South America)
- (e) *The Complete Herb Book of China* (1530) shows herbs unique to South America – Zhong Guo Ben Cao Quan Shu
- (f) The Karayaba tribe have Chinese features, skin and hands
- (g) Ceramics – Amazonia (Paul Yih and Beloit University Wisconsin)

17. Patagonia and Straits of Magellan
- (i)   The name 'Chile' is Chinese for 'dependent territory', and was in use before the Spanish arrived (Molina)
- (ii)   The first Spanish to round the Horn found wrecked junks (Grotius) at Taroja (22°S)
- (iii) Molina – ancestors of Chileans

(iv)   Chilean *palican* (a ball game) is the same as *Chowgar* (Molina 1)

(v)   Chilean chess, *Comican* (Molina ii 125)

(vi)   Custom of covering chicken heads (Molina ii 25) 1726

(vii)   Chileans treat smallpox with milk, similar to Chinese (Molina ii 321)

(viii)   Chilean knowledge of iron metallurgy (Molina ii 22)

(ix)   Lassos – same as in China (Molina ii 26)

(x)   *Qipus* – as in China (Molina ii 26), and in Marquesas and Hawaii

(xi)   Characteristics of Chilean tribes (Molina)

(xii)   Names of tribes of Chile (Molina): Arvacans – from Arracan (Burma); Promancians – from Prome (on borders of Arracan); Poy-yus – from Po Yeon in Cochin, China; Chuotes from Che Li; Cunches from Cunchi, Szechuan; Pi-Cunches – Northern Condis (Pi = North); Mappuchinians (Mapa in Chinese)

(xiii)   Chinese inscribed stones between Mendoza and La Punta (lats 33°–34°S) and near Diamond River (Ranking)

(xiv)   Legends of giants coming ashore on coast – Garcilaso de la Vega and Pedro Cieza de Leon

(xv)   *Illustrated Record of Strange Countries* (1430) shows armadillo (unique to South America)

(xvi)   The Karayaba tribe have Chinese features, skin and hands

(xvii)   Horses on Tierra del Fuego (Sarmiento)

(xviii)   Rabbits on Tierra del Fuego (Magellan)

(xix)   Chinese DNA (post Bering Straits flooding) of the Toba Indian people of Patagonia

(xx)   Hookworm/roundworm afflictions of the Lengua people of the Mato Grosso

(xxi)   Piri Reis map shows Patagonia before Europeans arrived, with pictures of guanacos and pumas

(xxii)   The mylodon (alive in 19th century – Darwin) shown in *Illustrated Record of Strange Countries* and on Piri Reis

(xxiii)   First Europeans found rice in Mato Grosso

18. Greenland to North Pole, across Arctic to Bering Straits

(i)   Greenland appears on Vinland Map (c.1440) published before Europeans 'discovered' the island; map is genuine

(2002 radiocarbon dating)

(ii) Pope's letter describes barbarian ship destroying local people by fire and taking them captive c.1418

(iii) Columbus reports Chinese people had preceded him to Greenland

(iv) Greenland native people (of Hvalsey) have Chinese DNA (post Bering Straits flooding)

(v) Inuit people = Yin Uit (people from Yin) (Martin Tai)

(vi) Greenland was habitable for Europeans in 1420 (Sigrid Bjorndottir)

(vii) In 1421, climate was warmer than today, evidenced by horse flies; enamel on teeth in graves in Hvalsey; strontium levels in core ice samples taken from Greenland's glaciers

(viii) Due to the earth's precession, the North Pole as determined by Polaris at 90° elevation was approx. 200nm nearer to Greenland than it is today

(ix) Chinese claim to have reached North Pole (Professor Wei's evidence) which is corroborated by Ju de Yuan's account of the explorer Dong Fang Shuo (Martin Tai)

(x) Chinese circumpolar star charts, which could only have been drawn by people who had seen the stars at a latitude north of 73°N

(xi) In 1870s, a British expedition got to within 19 miles of the latitude of the northern cape of Greenland – by then climate far colder than in 1421

(xii) The 'mini Ice Age' started in 1432 (Buisman – Dutch Meteorological Institute KNMI and European Union) (G. E. R. Nijman evidence)

(xiii) 1420, 1422 and 1428 summers were extremely dry and hot, and the Arctic north of Siberia was clear of ice in summers of 1422 and 1428 (Buisman)

(xiv) 'Five consecutive warm winters could lead to the complete melting of the ice in the Arctic Sea' (Delft Technical University NL)

(xv) Siberia appears on Waldseemüller map (1507) drawn two centuries before Europeans 'discovered' Siberian coast

(xvi) *The Illustrated Record of Strange Countries* (1430) describes Eskimos

(xvii)   D. D. Jevans evidence – Latin MS – *Barbarians on the Coast*
(xviii) Korean DNA in north Norwegian and Hebridean fishermen (Professor Bryan Sykes)
(xix)   Stone cairns
(xx)   Innu are Chinese (Baxter Smith)

19. Antarctica

(i)   Falkland Islands dog 'the Warrah' (Charles Darwin); recent DNA investigation
(ii)   'Lt Kendall's foreign seaman's body' deep frozen on Deception Island (*Geographical Journal* 1830 pp.65, 66)
(iii)   Piri Reis map shows Antarctica well before Europeans arrived
(iv)   Chinese claims to have reached South Pole (Professor Wei)
(v)   Diego Hominems' map showing Antarctica a decade before Magellan set sail
(vi)   Ludovico de Varthema's story of Chinese people setting sail for South Pole by following Southern Cross

20. The Pacific

Note: No Polynesian DNA has been found in South American people (Professor Bryan Sykes); no Inca DNA has been found in Pacific people (Cambridge Study).

Southern route

(i)   Senõr Arias' story of Asian people setting sail across Pacific from South America.
(ii)   Easter Island: Chinese carved lion (Kerson Huang); array of plants from across the world found by first Europeans; quadrangular observation platform (John Robinson)
(iii)   Pitcairn: quadrangular stepped observation platform; carved rocks showing star alignments; skeleton with pearl shell from Tuamotu archipelago
(iv)   Temoe: raised stepped stone observation platform; cotton – wild form of cultivated *Gossypium amphidiploid* species H.
(v)   Tuamotu – Bora Bora: stone platforms
(vi)   Raia Tea: raised stone platform
(vii)   Tahiti: ziggurat stone observation platform (Marae of Mahaiatea); cotton – as for Temoe

(viii)   Society Islands – Tuahaia: round stepped stone observation platform; tokelau disease

(ix)   Samoa – Savai: tiered observation platforms; tokelau disease

(x)   Tonga – Tabu: ziggurat observation platforms and stone archway; tokelau disease; 'Chinese' people (Craig Hill Handy)

(xi)   Fiji: cotton – as for Tahiti and Temoe; tokelau disease

(xii)   New Caledonia, Magnetic Island: stone pyramid observation platform

(xiii)   Cape York (Australia): cotton, as for Revilagigedo Islands, Marquesas (Temoe), Tahiti, Fiji

The author contends that the people who built the stepped pyramids (see table on p. 572) also brought cotton from the Americas, where no Polynesian DNA has been found. They also brought tokelau disease from Malaysia and China (Fonseca).

Northern route

(i)   Revilagigedo Archipelago: cotton – wild form of cultivated *Gossypium amphidiploid* species H.

(ii)   Hawaii: stone fishponds; Menehune aqueduct; Menehune lizards; plants foreign to Hawaii found by first Europeans; stone platforms (Necker) remarkably similar to those of Marquesas

(iii)   Kiribati (Gilberts)/Malden: stepped stone observation platforms; tokelau disease (Fonseca)

(iv)   Micronesia: cotton, as in Revilagigedo Archipelago

(v)   Marshalls/Marianas: cotton, as in Revilagigedo Archipelago; tokelau disease; stepped stone observation platforms

(vi)   Solomons – Mala, Ulawa and San Cristobal: stone observation platforms; tokelau disease

(vii)   Carolines – Pohn Pei, Nan Madol and Tobi: Nan Madol, stone canals, observation platforms and fishponds; Tobi, stone observation platforms; Yao, stone wharves; Lele, canals, stepped stone observation platforms, shell money from North America

(viii)   New Guinea: tokelau disease

Note: For information on cotton, see *Man Across the Sea* (ed. Carol

Riley, ch.22); for information on stone platforms, see *Geographical Journal* XIII (1899).

Stepped Pyramid Sizes

Place/ Lat/ Long	Discoverer/ Description	Length/ Width (feet)	Height (feet)	Remarks
*Tahiti (Marae) 149°W, 175°S	Capt Cook (McDuff)	259 × 85	c. 45 stepped pyramid	Drawn by Domany de Rienzi
*Savai'I Pulenei		200 × 160	Approx. 37	Squarely oriented with compass directions. Platform 40m with connecting walkway.
Tonga Tabu 175°4′W, 19°14′S	Local artists painted it			Ziggurat pyramid
Malden (Line Islands)	Drawn by Dr Macmillan Brown & K. P. Emory			'Great temple pyramids', 'early Chinese navigators'
San Cristobal (Solomons)		60 × 40	20	Mound with shaft
*Pohn Pei		185 × 115	Approx. 40	Stepped pyramids
*Gympie, Australia		100 high, terraces 4	Terraces 100	
*Kaimanaw B. a Wall (New Zealand)	Brailsford, D. H. Childress (May 1946)	Blocks, stones approx 1.5 × 1		Axes facing north-east; possible step pyramid structure
Canaries				Compare with Korean

(Guimar)

28°N, 16°S

King Jiang Jung Toms
(base 31.6m). More than
1,000 blocks

21. New Zealand

(i) New Zealand appears on maps published two centuries before
Captain Cook 'discovered' the islands, viz. Jean Rotz, where the
bays of Auckland Island and Campbell Island are drawn with
correct latitudes
(ii) Captain Cook accepts he was not the first to Australasia
(iii) Kumera and cassava were found by first Europeans – the plants
originate in South America, and no Polynesian DNA has ever
been found in peoples of South America (Professor Bryan
Sykes), thus some non-Polynesian people must have charted the
islands and brought kumera (Inca people's DNA is absent from
Pacific)

North Island

(i) The Ruapuke wreck, associated with: the 'Colenso' bell with its
Tamil inscription naming the ship's owner; the rivet; the jade
korotangi – Chinese (F. Hochstetter and V. S. Cullen); inscribed
writing on two stones nearby; Tamil plaque on ship (V.S.
Cullen); willow-pattern ceramics in ship (E. Allen Aubin); teak
wood from wreck (T. B. Hill); copper and iron bolts (Phillips &
Liddell); triple hull
(ii) Mauku steatite figure
(iii) Stone wall at Lake Taupo (Kaimanawa) – a Chinese observation
platform
(iv) Maori claims that foreigners settled among them and begat
children; Maori mitochondrial DNA shows a 'Chinese'
connection

South Island

(i) Campbell Island – tree from Norfolk Island
(ii) Dusky Sound 'Chinese' wreck coupled with local history (Robyn
Gossett)
(iii) *Chenopodium album* discovered by Cook, 1769 (indigenous to
China and North America) (Dave Bell)

(iv) Marsh cress (Navajo Indian cosmetic) discovered by French, 1828 (Dave Bell)

(v) Scented grass from Colombia (Dave Bell)

(vi) Taro from China

(vii) Chinese pigs – *kune kune*

(viii) Kaimanawa wild horses (from Tajikistan?)

New evidence for Zhou Man fleet wreck on south coast

(i) The tsunami off New Zealand can be dated to 1422 (Professor Bryant); Chinese plates have been discovered on cliff tops in South Australia among tsunami debris; meeting waves as high as mountains, as described by Zheng He

(ii) A meteorite impact in position 50°S 175°E (Lamont Doherty Observatory USA) could have triggered the tsunami; it hit the sea approximately 100km east of Zhou Man's track

(iii) Classification of wood near wreck (Dave Bell) from Pitcairn

(iv) Maori history, extinction of the moa in North Island and the economic consequences (Dave Bell).

(v) Fernandez 1569 expedition to New Zealand, met 'Chinese' people wearing white woven garments

(vi) Dating of mortar (1676–1764) and wood (1360–1380) from South Island (Rafter Radiocarbon Laboratory)

(vii) Chinese junk and Chinese Hottentots of south-west Africa (J. Parkinson); flightless duck found in Amazon, Falklands and Campbell Islands; Pitcairn (wood to New Zealand); Niue Island (Chinese linguistics)

(viii) Megalithic history of New Zealand – people lived there before Maoris (Dave Bell)

(ix) The New Zealand wild pig – Chinese DNA (Antonia Bowen-Jones & Dave Bell)

(x) Maori axes (Perry Debell)

(xi) Preliminary discussion on DNA with Professor Susan Povey

Possible scenario

- March 1421, fleets sailed; July, Cape of Good Hope; junks wrecked Namibia, crew got ashore (Chinese Hottentots)

- October, Amazon; November, Falklands – left flightless ducks, dogs, horses, DNA, diseases

- December to May 1422, crossed Pacific leaving trail of evidence
- June 1422, landfall SE Australia; sail for Campbell Island (52°40′S, Canopus); leave wreck, Norfolk Islands pine, flightless ducks
- August/September, set sail for home; at 50°S 160°E meet tsunami generated by large meteorite, which hit ocean and penetrated the seabed at 50°S 175°E; junks hurled north-west to South Australia and north-north-west to New Zealand's South Island
- Survivors on South Island live peacefully among Melanesians building barracks, reservoirs, fishponds, pig sties, stables; visited by Fernandez' small fleet in 1569; moa nearing extinction on North Island by 1660s; food scarce; Maoris invade South Island; Chinese build forts (mortar dating) but are eventually wiped out; some are eaten by Maoris, who also take the Chinese women, resulting in 'modern' Maori mitochondrial DNA being Chinese and male (Y chromosome) Melanesian

22. Australia
(i) Maps
   (a) Australia appears on European maps of the Dieppe school published well before Europeans reached Australia, viz. Desliens, Vallard (showing horses), Desceliers, Jean Rotz (1540s)
   (b) Australia appears on Jesuit maps drawn when in China, based on Chinese maps, viz. Father Ricci (1589) and Taiwan porcelain map (1447) showing east coast to Tasmania
   (c) Zheng He's passage chart shows Barrier Reef (Martin Tai)
   (d) Australia shown on *Wu Pei Chi* (Sun Shuyun)

(ii) Chinese claims (Professor Wei)
   (a) Confucius, *Spring and Autumn Annals* (481 BC), recording solar eclipses in Australia
   (b) *Classics of Mountains and Seas* (338 BC) describes kangaroos, quiong-giong, boomerangs and black millet (South Australia)
   (c) *Shizi* (338 BC) reports kangaroos in China
   (d) *Atlas of Foreign Countries* (AD 265–316) describes small black pygmies (North Australia), Jiaojiao people; plants grow leaves in winter, shed them in summer

(e) 11th- and 12th-century Franciscan missionaries' evidence describes voyages by huge fleets of junks (60 to 100) sailing for Australia to mine minerals

(iii) Accounts of local people

(a) Arnhem Land: paintings of men on horseback (Vallard); 'honey-coloured people settle amongst us'; 'women in pantaloons, men in long robes'; cave painting (Governor Grey) of Chinese – compare with Zheng He's statue in Fujian Palace; painting of man being thrown from horse (Glenelg River); drawings of trees, fauna and flora (Rotz) which are found in Arnhem Land, together with written descriptions

(b) Cape York/Gympie (John Green's evidence 1862): Fraser Island, 'small boats leave big ship'; 'culture heroes sail into Gympie harbour and take away rocks'; Dhamuri people – 'foreigners land to build pyramids'

(c) South Australia: Warrnambool, Yanguy tribe – yellow people from shipwreck settle amongst them and create eel farms; Glenelty River – drawings of foreign sailors

(iv) Linguistics

Bajuni – boat people in Australia (Arnhem Land); in Chinese (Hokkien), joon = boat.

(v) Shipwrecks with 'Chinese' characteristics

(a) South coast: Warrnambool, mahogany ships (1980 Symposium and Avis Quarrey's evidence); King Island (Bass Strait); Tasmania (Storm Bay)

(b) West coast: Blackwood River estuary, 34°19′S, 115°11′E (*Legend of Sam Chalwell*); Perth, King Sound (evidence of Jim Mullins/Norm Fuller)

(c) East coast: Byron Bay – remains 40ft rudder; Woolongong (dated 1410)

(d) Queensland: Fraser Island (J. Green account 1862); 1919 and 1972 photos of cannon (compare with Nanjing photos); North Stradbrooke Island, 18-mile swamp (27°30′S, 153°27′E approx. position); wrecks of Indian Head (Bill Ward); ancient lead weight with Loisels pumice dated 1410–1630 (Bill Ward)

    (e)   Arnhem Land and Gulf of Carpentaria: anchors, fish hooks

(vi)   Chinese porcelain/ceramics/coins/bronzes
    (a)   Bradshaw, Elecho Island, Yirrkalla, Winchelsea Island, Cape York, Gympie, Tasmania
    (b)   Chinese wine cooler, Fraser's Island
    (c)   Palmer River goldfields – Chinese coins

(vii) 'Chinese' jade artefacts
    (a)   Darwin: Chu Lao (Professor Wei and Professor Needham's evidence)
    (b)   NSW: Ganesh and Hanuman statuettes
    (c)   Queensland: Buddha
    (d)   Gympie (Brett Green): orange-coloured jade carvings of bear/monkey plus belt buckle; necklace of jade on silk cord

(viii) Observation platforms
West of Blue Mountains; Penrith; Gympie; Atherton; central NSW coast; Blaxlands Flat, Nymboida, NSW – stone cairns (A. D. Fletcher); Copmanhurst stone cairns (E. N. R. Fletcher)

(ix)   Ancient mining operations found by first Europeans
    (a)   Gympie: gold, silver, copper, quartz crystals, pure white ceramic clay, limestone, antimony (Brett Green)
    (b)   Arnhem Land: lead, uranium

(x)   Metalwork
Gympie/Fraser Island: bronze Chinese wine cooler (Brett Green)

(xi)   Plants and animals foreign to Australia
    (a)   From China: lotus and papyrus; from South America: 74 plant species
    (b)   Brumby horses from Fraser Island (originally from Tajikistan?)
    (c)   Ma Huan (= Australia, Darwin and Marani) (Martin Tai)
    (d)   Father Ricci's map (1589)
    (e)   Hessel Gerrit's chart (1618) (M. Righton)

23. The Spice Islands, Indonesia and the Philippines

(i)   Fei Xin's poems – Chinese fleet reached Sulu

(ii)   Zheng He Research Institute director Nin Dian Nian, published
        article, 'Zheng He reached Philippines'

(iii)   The Pandanan junk: hull wood dated 1440; Zhu Di (1403–24)
        coins aboard and Zhu Di blue and white porcelain; Dr Dizon's
        evidence at Royal Geographical Society, 15 March 2002; in hold
        were metates from South America

(iv)   Chinese sailor's grave at Sulu

(v)   Tokelau (Fonseca)

(vi)   Diaries of Master Bentou (Zheng He's navigator) (Kerson
        Huang)

Part V: Genetic fingerprints left by Zheng He's fleets – the DNA evidence

The following is the author's draft. It will be radically revised when experts' views have been received.

We know from an accumulation of different strands of evidence (not least from the reports of the first Europeans to reach the New World) where the Chinese settled. It has been relatively easy to obtain DNA results from local peoples who live in these areas today. To date, the principal report relied upon is that of Professor Novick and his colleagues (Corina C. Novick, Juan Yunis, Emilio Yunis, Pamela Antunez de Mayolo, W. Douglas Scheer, Prescott L. Deininger, Mark Stoneking, Daniel S. York, Mark A. Batzer and Rene J. Herrera), 'Polymorphic Alu Insertions and the Asian Origin of Native American Populations'. After studying twenty-four peoples of North and South America in locations in which Zheng He's fleets settled, Professor Novick found that 'close similarity between the Chinese and native Americans suggests recent gene flow from Asia'. This leaves a few gaps, i.e. places where the Chinese settled not covered by Professor Novick's report, but again, it has been relatively easy to fill in these gaps with other DNA reports by distinguished geneticists, reports which also show close similarity between the Chinese and native people in all the areas in which the author claims the Chinese settled.

The author wishes to date as accurately as possible the 'recent gene flow' described by Professor Novick et al. It seems dating by mutation rate is far too controversial to say with any certainty that 'recent' means settlements arising from the 1421–3 voyages. Other methods must be found. It seems to the author that this can be achieved in stages: to show the DNA came as a result of seaborne voyages post Bering Straits flooding; to determine which seaborne voyage; and to adduce the corroborative evidence – i.e. wrecked junks containing coins of Zhu Di's era but no later.

1. Seaborne voyages

Certain diseases or afflictions cannot survive in the extremely cold conditions of a frozen Bering Straits crossing, e.g. hookworm and roundworm, where the eggs need moisture and warmth to propagate. Linking hookworm and roundworm diseases found in the Indian people of the Mato Grosso area of Brazil with peoples who have 'recent' Chinese DNA (Novick et al) is thus evidence that the 'recent' DNA was brought by sea post Bering Straits thawing. The author thinks (but needs advice on this) that the following may provide corroborative evidence of seaborne DNA.

(i)   Hookworm/roundworm/A Duodenale Necator (Dr Olympio Fonseca)

(ii)   Machado-Joseph disease (Jerry Warsing). This disease appears to have originated in the Yunnan province of SW China and spread along the sea routes of Zheng He's fleets, viz. India, the Carolines (USA), the Azores, Brazil, San Francisco, Yemen and NW Australia.

(iii)   Tokelau (Dr Olympio Fonseca). This highly distinctive infection was found in 1928 among native Indian people of the Mato Grosso area of Brazil. These people had lived isolated from Europeans for centuries. This endemic parasitic disease has such a unique appearance that ancient narrators and naturalists referred to it even if they were not medical experts. The centre of tokelau's sphere of affliction is the Malayan peninsula. It is found on the southern coast of China in the Honnan province and the coasts and hinterland of Indochina (Cambodia, Thailand, Annam, Vietnam) to the

Yunnan province of China, Burma and Bangladesh. It is prevalent across the Pacific: Formosa, Marianas, Moluccas, Gilbert and Marshall groups, New Caledonia, Fiji, Samoa and Tonga groups, Tokelau islands, Society and Celebes groups, Solomons and Loyalty Islands, Sumatra and New Guinea – all places visited by Chinese fleets. It is the author's contention that the Chinese also sailed down the Amazon to the Mato Grosso.

(iv)   Hanta virus (Dr Alan Leibowitz). Carried by rats and found among Indian peoples of the Rio Grande (west Texas and Mexico). The Zuni and Navajo peoples in the upper reaches of the Rio Grande have 'recent' Chinese DNA (Novick et al).

(v)   Smallpox (Jonathan F. Ormes and Chris Spedding). The Native American population was decimated by smallpox before most of them had ever seen a European. How was it brought to the Americas?

(vi)   *Paragorimus westermani* – lung fluke (Dr John S. Marr). As with hookworm, roundworm, Machado-Joseph disease and tokelau, this is common in China and South America.

(vii)   Herpes? (Sorenson and Raish S479, F119 & 120)

(viii) Polio? (Sorenson and Raish S479, F119 & 120)

(ix)   Pertussi? (Sorenson and Raish S479, F119 & 120)

(x)   Hepatitis B? (Dr John S. Marr)

(xi)   Pierre Noire (Sorenson and Raish L014, F119 & 120)

(xii)   Typhus Murin (Sorenson and Raish L014, F119 & 120)

(xiii) *Tinea imbicata* (Sorenson and Raish L014, F119 & 120)

(xiv)   Lice and nits/tick-borne diseases (Sorenson and Raish S479, F119 & 120)

2. To determine which seaborne voyage

Professor Novick et al report: 'The results corroborate the Asian origin of native American populations but do not support the multiple-wave migration hypothesis supposedly responsible for the tripartite Eskaleut, Nadene and Amerind linguistic groups.' The multiple-wave hypothesis refers to the waves across the Bering Straits. Table 1 of Professor Novick's report shows the geographical distribution of the twenty-four studied Native American peoples; Figure 2 is a maximum likelihood tree showing (inter alia) the closeness of the studied peoples' DNA to Chinese and to one another. Comparing the two reveals that Greenland natives, Alaska natives, Inca, Buctzozt Maya and Campeche Maya are all closer to Chinese DNA than to the DNA of the Indian peoples who surround them.

(i) The Greenland natives and Alaska natives are 3,000 miles apart. If the 'Chinese' DNA was brought across the Bering Straits to Alaska by people who then marched across northern Canada to Greenland, one would expect the DNA of intervening peoples initially to resemble Alaskan DNA then gradually mutate. This is not the case. For the Greenland and Alaska natives' DNA to be so strikingly similar, the implication must be that these peoples received 'recent gene flow from Asia' at about the same time. Alaska is on the Pacific coast, Greenland in the Atlantic. The only way the Greenland and Alaska people could have received the gene flow at about the same time is by ship, moreover by ships which sailed in the Pacific and the Atlantic. Because of the prevailing winds and tides these simultaneous voyages must have been conducted by different fleets.

(ii) The Greenland and Alaska natives and the Maya of the Yucatán Peninsula are thousands of miles apart.
Had the 'recent gene flow' from Asia been across the Bering Straits, one would expect intervening peoples between Alaska and the Yucatán to have DNA which gradually mutates from Alaska until Yucatán, and this gradual mutation should be reflected in intervening peoples. This is not the case. Buctzozt Maya DNA is so close to Chinese that the Buctzozt could almost be called Chinese. Mayan DNA is far closer to Alaskan DNA than it is to the Indian people who live along the route from Alaska to Yucatán (viz. Navajo). The Maya on the Atlantic coast and the Alaskans on the Pacific coast must have received their 'recent gene flow from Asia' at about the same time. Again, multiple fleets would be required.

(iii) The same argument can be applied to the Incas of Pacific South America, whose DNA is closer to the Chinese and Maya of the

Atlantic coast and to the Aleuts of Alaska than it is to other Indian peoples of South America. In addition, Professor Novick reports that the 'close similarity between the Chinese and native Americans' covers people far distant from one another: Atlantic – High Arctic; Pacific – High Arctic;   Amazonia – thousands of miles upriver; and Patagonia/Bolivia – again, thousands of miles upriver.

To reach these places thousands of miles apart in different hemispheres at about the same time, not only would different fleets be required, but huge fleets: the Atlantic fleet sailing to Greenland, the Yucatán, the Caribbean, the Amazon and Patagonia; the Pacific fleet from Alaska right down the coast to South America. The author contends that the only huge fleets which sailed to North and South America were those under the command of Admiral Zheng He, and that there is a wealth of supporting evidence summarised in this synopsis that Admiral Zheng He's fleets visited each place where Professor Novick's team has found DNA evidence of 'recent gene flow from Asia'.

3. Chinese settlers from Zheng He's voyages – DNA evidence
(i)   The Navajo
   (a)   Principal DNA report relied upon: Novick et al
   (b)   Précis of the report's findings: close similarity between the Chinese and Native Americans suggests recent gene flow from Asia
   (c)   Corroboration or supporting DNA reports
      • Professor Bryan Sykes, *Seven Daughters of Eve*, p.282
      • Study (1997) by US National Academy of Sciences – Navajo possess unique type of retrovirus gene JCV found only in China and Japan
   (d)   Corroboration or supporting reports into ailments or diseases that suggest Chinese arrived by sea
      • 'Amerindian mitochondrial DNAs have rare Asian mutations at high frequencies suggesting they derived from four primary maternal lineages', Schurr et al (see 'papers referred to' at end)
   (e)   Did the first Europeans to reach the area in which the

Navajo people live find Chinese already there?

- Yes. Francis Vasquez de Coronado (1510–1554) found Chinese people in Tiguex, home of the Navajo. He also found junks with gilded sterns.

(f) Other evidence showing links with China

- The Navajo elders could, 70 years ago, converse in Chinese with missionaries from SW China. Many visitors to www.1421.tv have commented on the striking physical similarities between the Navajo and the Chinese.

- Local legends telling of pre-Columbian visitors from the West. Certain linguistics. Accounts of European historians (Acosta, Grotius). Wrecks of probable junks – Sacramento and Coronado/Mafeo and Frois accounts. Europeans found Chinese plants (Cherokee rose, hibiscus (*Rosa sinensis*), rice, 26 chromosome cotton); Europeans found Chinese animals – hens (Melanotic silkie, Frizzle fowl), Chinese ship's dogs (Acosta), carvings of horses. 'Tiguex' (name of Navajo) appeared on European maps before Europeans arrived there (Cantino 1502, Waldseemüller 1507). Antonio Galvão reports Chinese claims to be 'Lords of Mexico' pre-European voyages. Garcia reports Chinese merchants in ports of Quatulco and Panuco. Asiatic shipwrecks on coast (Hugo Grotius). Foreign ships carved by Indian people of Tiguex. Statuettes of Buddha – Grand Canyon, Granby Dam, Colorado.

(g) See Synopsis of Evidence on www.1421.tv, paras 3, 6, 7, 8(a), 15, 16 and Annex XVIII

(ii) The Mazatec people of Mexico (Olmec culture)

(a) Principal DNA report relied upon: *H.L.A. Genes and the Origins of the Amerindians*, Dr Felipe Vilchis

(b) Précis of the report's findings: 'The results of the phylogenetic analysis reported here support the idea that the autochthonous pueblos based in Meso-America and South America had common ancestors, with as many coming with the migratory wave from the north as those that took the transpacific route.' Allelic distribution among the Mazatecs showed a garotypic pattern that was very similar to that found among Asian peoples.

(c)   Corroboration or supporting DNA reports: A. Arnaiz-Villena, J. Granados

(d)   Corroboration or supporting reports into ailments or diseases that suggest Chinese arrived by sea
    • Hookworm and roundworm
    • Greenbeak, J. H. et al, *The Settlement of the Americas*
    • Vilchis et al, *Clin Genet*, 1997

(e)   Did the first Europeans to reach the area in which the Mazatec people live find Chinese already there?
    • Yes – Acosta (people); Coronado (people and junks); Galvão (junks); Gregorio Garcia (people)

(f)   Other evidence showing links with China
    • Pre-Columbian Chinese presence in Mexico – Chinese who came by sea – is overwhelming

(g)   See Synopsis of Evidence on www.1421.tv, paras 1 to 21 incl., Annexes XIX, XXVI and XXVII

(iii)   Campeche and Buctzozt Maya

(a)   Principal DNA report relied upon: Novick et al

(b)   Précis of the report's findings: close similarity between the Chinese and Native Americans suggests recent gene flow from Asia

(c)   Corroboration or supporting DNA reports
    • 'Amerindian mitochondrial DNAs have rare Asian mutations at high frequencies . . .', Schurr et al. Investigated Maya, Ticuna (South America) and Pima (North America).

(d)   Corroboration or supporting reports into ailments or diseases that suggest Chinese arrived by sea
    • The astonishing finding by Novick et al that Mayan DNA is closer to Chinese DNA than Mayan DNA is to North, Central or South American DNA
    • Hookworm/roundworm diseases endemic to SE Asia and China

(e)   Did the first Europeans to reach the area in which the Campeche and Buctzozt peoples live find Chinese already there?
    • Yes, Columbus (secret report)

(f)   Other evidence showing links with China
    • Late Mayan art at Chichen Itza and Copan is Chinese art.
    Yucatán appears on world maps, viz. Cantino, Caverio,
    before Europeans arrived there. Jucutácato shroud shows
    foreign visitors on horseback, and dogs. Chinese figurines
    at Teotihuacan. Chinese body entombed, Teotihuacan.
    Chinese chickens, roses, hibiscus, rice, ship's dogs found by
    first Europeans. Chinese lacquer technology used by Maya.
    Chinese jade medallions and earplugs. Chinese dyestuff
    technology used by Maya. Close physical similarity between
    Othomi, Maya and Chinese. Mayan glyphs in temples inter-
    spersed with Chinese and Phaspa (eunuch secret language).
(g)   See Synopsis of Evidence on www.1421.tv, paras 2–4, 6–11,
    14–20, Annex XIX

(iv)   Waunana and Ngobe peoples of Panama
(a)   Principal DNA report relied upon: Novick et al
(b)   Précis of the report's findings: close similarity between the
    Chinese and Native Americans suggests recent gene flow
    from Asia
(c)   Corroboration or supporting DNA reports
    • *Peoples of Venezuela, Surinam and Guyana*, Dr Annabel
    Arends
    • *Peoples of Venezuela*, Arends and Gallengo
(d)   Corroboration or supporting reports into ailments or diseases
    that suggest Chinese arrived by sea
    • Hookworm/roundworm
(e)   Did the first Europeans to reach the area in which the
    Waunana and Ngobe peoples live find Chinese already
    there?
    • Yes, Columbus (secret report)
(f)   Other evidence showing links with China
    • Chinese claims to have ruled over 'locations in Central and
    South America' before Europeans arrived (Antonio
    Galvão). Substantial evidence of Chinese settlements in
    Panama pre-Columbus.
(g)   See Synopsis of Evidence on www.1421.tv, paras 2, 3, 7–11,
    20, Annexes XX, XXV, XXVI, XXVII

(v)   Inca peoples
   (a)   Principal DNA report relied upon: Novick et al
   (b)   Précis of the report's findings: close similarity between the Chinese and Native Americans suggests recent gene flow from Asia
   (c)   Corroboration or supporting DNA reports
      • DNA of 'Juanita' the ice maiden (Kyoto University) shows she has 'Taiwanese' DNA
   (d)   Corroboration or supporting reports into ailments or diseases that suggest Chinese arrived by sea
      • Hookworm/roundworm
   (e)   Did the first Europeans to reach the area in which the Inca people live find Chinese already there?
      • Yes, dead ones, and wrecked junks on Chilean coast (Grotius)
      • Garcilaso de la Vega (Chinese in Peru and Chile)
   (f)   Other evidence showing links with China
      • 'Peru' is a Chinese name; villagers of Eten and Monsefu understood Chinese until a century ago; nearly 100 Peruvian villages have Chinese names to this day. First (British) colonists saw wild elephants (Ecuador/Colombia border) brought by Chinese. Friar Antonio de la Calancha found pictures of Chinese cavalry. Chinese body found entombed at Trujillo (Calancha/Loayza). Peru shown on maps before Europeans arrived there – Waldseemüller 1507, Martellus 1489. Chinese chickens found the length of Peru. Coconuts and bananas (indigenous to SE Asia) found by first Europeans; 74 other plants carried to Australasia, etc. 'Great wall of Chimu' built by Chinese. Inca pottery with Chinese calligraphy. Folklore identical to Chinese, as are divination ceremonies.
   (g)   See Synopsis of Evidence on www.1421.tv, paras 2–19 incl., Annex XXI

(vi)   Indian peoples of Venezuela and Colombia: Irapa, Paraujano and Macoita
   (a)   Principal DNA report relied upon: *Transferrins in Venezuelan Indians: High Frequency of a Slow-Moving Variant*, Drs

Arends and Gallengo

(b) Précis of the report's findings: in 50 per cent of the Yupa Indians of Venezuela there is a slow-moving transferrin electrophonetically indistinguishable from Tf Dchi which to date has only been found in Chinese. This finding is additional evidence for the existence of a racial link between South American Indians and Chinese.

(c) Corroboration or supporting DNA Reports
  • Parker and Bearn
  • Novick et al report into Kobi, Chimilia and Wayuu peoples of Venezuela/Colombia

(d) Corroboration or supporting reports into ailments or diseases that suggest Chinese arrived by sea
  • Hookworm/roundworm
  • 'Amerindian mitrochondrial DNAs have rare Asian mutations at high frequencies', Schurr et al
  • the work of Dr Annabel Arends

(e) Did the first Europeans to reach the area in which the Irapa, Paraujano and Macoita peoples live find Chinese already there?
  • Yes, Gonzalo Ximenez de Quesoa (Muyscas, Guanes and Calima peoples)

(f) Other evidence showing links with China
  • The combination of the work of Arends and Gallengo, Professor Novick and Parker and Bearn seems to make an overwhelming case that a Chinese colony existed in the foothills west of Maracaibo
  • Venezuela shown on maps before Europeans arrived there – Cantino (1502), Martellus (1484), Waldseemüller (1507). Chinese chickens and coconuts found by first Europeans. *Illustrated Record of Strange Countries* published 1430 in China shows South American animals. Antonio Galvão cites Chinese claims to have ruled South America before Europeans. Chinese jade in Costa Rica/Panama. 26 chromosome cotton in Revilagigedo Islands. Columbus found Chinese people and horses in Panama; Chinese ship's dogs also found.

(g) See Synopsis of Evidence on www.1421.tv, paras 4, 5, 10,

15–17, 20, Annex XX

(vii) Surui people of Amazonia and Solimões/Rio Negro Junction

(a) Principal DNA report relied upon: Novick et al

(b) Précis of the report's findings: close similarity between the Chinese and Native Americans suggests recent gene flow from Asia

(c) Corroboration or supporting DNA reports: none yet

(d) Corroboration or supporting reports into ailments or diseases that suggest Chinese arrived by sea
- Tokelau/chimbere found in Amazonian people – tokelau a disease of SE Asia (Fonseca)
- Hepatitis B prevalent
- Hookworm/roundworm prevalent
- Absence of Duffy blood groups
- Lung fluke (*Paragorimus westermani*)

(e) Did the first Europeans to reach the area in which the Surui people live find Chinese already there?
- Yes, Friar Gaspar de Carvajal – 'men with pale skins'

(f) Other evidence showing links with China
- Diseases common to SE Asia but not to Americas found in Amazonian people who had been isolated from European contact for centuries; tokelau, hepatitis B and hookworm/roundworm could not have been carried over Bering Straits on account of the cold. The site of Hatahara recently discovered at junction of Negro and Solimões Rivers indicates very old settlement. Brazilian delegation reached China before Europeans reached Brazil and China (Professor Bi Quanzhong). Brazil shown on maps before Columbus set sail and before Europeans arrived there – 1436 Andrea Bianco. First Europeans (Orellana/Carvajal) found rice fields, banana and coconut plantations, frizzle fowl, black Melanotic, Asian jungle fowl, water buffalo – all indigenous to China/SE Asia; subsequent finds of pre-European Chinese animals and artefacts: fulvous tree duck, jade at Amazon/Tapajos and Solimões/Rio Negro junctions, Lago Sapakua, Lago de Faro.

(g) See Synopsis of Evidence on www.1421.tv, paras 1–7, 10,

15–17, Annex X

(viii) Quechua (Bolivia/Mato Grosso borders) and Toba (NW
Argentina, Salado River) peoples

   (a) Principal DNA report relied upon: Novick et al

   (b) Précis of the report's findings: close similarity between the
Chinese and Native Americans suggests recent gene flow
from Asia

   (c) Corroboration or supporting DNA reports: none yet

   (d) Corroboration or supporting reports into ailments or diseases
that suggest Chinese arrived by sea

       • Tokelau, hepatitis B and hookworm/roundworm

   (e) Did the first Europeans to reach the area in which the
Quechua and Toba peoples live find Chinese already there?

       • Not as far as we know, but we have not yet studied the
reports of the Jesuits, a project we hope to undertake
shortly

   (f) Other evidence showing links with China

       • Rice fields found by the first Europeans to reach the
Paraguay and Panama Rivers. Chinese junks found
wrecked by the first Spaniards to round the Horn.
Drawings on the Piri Reis (and in *The Illustrated Record of
Strange Countries* published in China in 1430) show animals
of Patagonia drawn long before Europeans arrived there.

   (g) See Synopsis of Evidence on www.1421.tv, paras 1, 4, 5, 8,
15–17, 20A, Annexes XXII, XXVI, XXVII

(ix) Haida and Aleut peoples

   (a) Principal DNA report relied upon: Novick et al

   (b) Précis of the report's findings: close similarity between the
Chinese and Native Americans suggests recent gene flow
from Asia

   (c) Corroboration or supporting DNA reports

       • The astonishing similarity between Alaska (Aleut) and
Chinese DNA – closer to each other than North American
DNA is to Aleut

       • Professor Bryan Sykes, 'Chinese DNA in Vancouver Island
people'

(d) Corroboration or supporting reports into ailments or diseases that suggest Chinese arrived by sea: none yet

(e) Did the first Europeans to reach the area in which the Haida and Aleut peoples live find Chinese already there?
- Yes, Zatta (pre-Vancouver and pre-Cook) described Queen Charlotte Islands as 'Colonia dei Chinesi'

(f) Other evidence showing links with China
- Haida lore states their ancestors came from the Aleut Islands, which they did, because the Aleut and Haida languages are one. Hugo Grotius – Chinese sail to 70°N. Jodicus Hondius map shows junk. Overwhelming evidence of pre-Columbian presence of Chinese people on Vancouver and Queen Charlotte Islands, the home of the Haida.

(g) See Synopsis of Evidence on www.1421.tv, paras 2–4, 6–9, 11–13, 19–20, Annexes XVI, XXVI and XXVII

(x) Moskoke people of SE USA and NW Florida

(a) Principal DNA report relied upon: Novick et al

(b) Précis of the report's findings: close similarity between the Chinese and Native Americans suggests recent gene flow from Asia (note: the Moskoke are the furthest away from the Chinese on the 'tree' – further DNA evidence for Florida people is advisable)

(c) Corroboration or supporting DNA reports: none yet

(d) Corroboration or supporting reports into ailments or diseases that suggest Chinese arrived by sea
- Machado-Joseph disease prevalent among Melungeon people to the north of Moskoke

(e) Did the first Europeans to reach the area in which the Moskoke people live find Chinese already there?
- Yes, Pedro Menendez de Aviles found Chinese junks wrecked off Florida

(f) Other evidence showing links with China
- Wrecked junks in Caribbean, off Florida coast and in Great Dismal Swamp (Virginia) found by first Europeans. Chinese people met by Giovanni de Verrazzano off what is now New York. Overwhelming evidence of pre-

Columbian visits to the Caribbean and up the east coast of
North America.
(g) See Synopsis of Evidence on www.1421.tv, Annexes IV, V,
XXIV, XXVI and XXVII

(xi) Ming Ho and Melungeon peoples
(a) Principal DNA report relied upon: none yet
(b) Précis of the report's findings: N/A
(c) Corroboration or supporting DNA reports: none yet
(d) Corroboration or supporting reports into ailments or diseases
that suggest Chinese arrived by sea
• Machado-Joseph disease is prevalent among the
Melungeons (Jerry Warsing)
(e) Did the first Europeans to reach the area in which the Ming
Ho and Melungeon peoples live find Chinese already there?
• Yes – Captain John Smith's accounts (Jerry Warsing, *Battle
of the Fallen Timbers*)
(f) Other evidence showing links with China
• Wrecked Chinese junks found by first Europeans (Pedro
Menendez de Aviles) downwind from Virginia, off Florida
and upwind, Great Dismal Swamp. Chinese people found
on Atlantic coast of North America (Giovanni di
Verrazzano). Many readers have commented on the
'Chinese' appearance of the Melungeons.
(g) See Synopsis of Evidence on www.1421.tv, paras 1–20,
Annexes V, VI, XXIV, XXVI and XXVII

(xii) Sioux and Cree Ojibwa peoples of America and Canada
(a) Principal DNA report relied upon: Novick et al
(b) Précis of the report's findings: close similarity between the
Chinese and Native Americans suggests recent gene flow
from Asia
(c) Corroboration or supporting DNA reports
• A 1997 study published by the National Academy of
Sciences appears to support the fact that the New World's
first migrants came from Asia. Researchers studied Native
Americans from the Navajo, Chamorro and Flathead tribes
(Montana) and determined that all three groups possess a

unique type of retrovirus gene JCV found only in China and Japan.

(d)   Corroboration or supporting reports into ailments or diseases that suggest Chinese arrived by sea: none yet

(e)   Did the first Europeans to reach the area in which the Sioux and Cree Ojibwa peoples live find Chinese already there? Not known.

(f)   Other evidence showing links with China
  • Substantial evidence that foreign visitors came by ship with horses and sailed up the Mississippi. Horse remains (pre-Columbus) have been found near Thunder Bay, Lake Superior. Rock Lake, Wisconsin, contains flat-topped stepped pyramids under its waters. Elephant bones have been found, and a round stone fortress.

(g)   See Synopsis of Evidence on www.1421.tv, paras 12 and 16, Annex VIII

(xiii) Maidu, Yuki, Pima and Wintun peoples of California

(a)   Principal DNA report relied upon: (Schurr et al on the Pima)

(b)   Précis of the report's findings: N/A

(c)   Corroboration or supporting DNA reports: none yet

(d)   Corroboration or supporting reports into ailments or diseases which suggest Chinese arrived by sea: none yet

(e)   Did the first Europeans to reach the area in which the Maidu, Yuki, Pima and Wintun peoples live find Chinese already there?
  • Yes – Cabrillo/Ferrello found wrecked Chinese junks off the north California/Oregon coast

(f)   Other evidence showing links with China
  • After Cabrillo and Ferrello's sightings, a stream of European explorers found Chinese people or colonies existing in California. There is overwhelming evidence of a Chinese settlement in California before Europeans arrived. Stephen Powers found a Chinese-speaking colony between the Russian and Sacramento Rivers; Father Luis Sales found one between San Francisco and Santa Barbara. All manner of pre-Columbian Chinese plants, trees, animals, porcelain, jade, stones, bronzes. Gregorio Garcia and

Antonio Galvão describe pre-European Chinese settlements in California. Professor Fryer reports Chinese walls.

(g) See Synopsis of Evidence on www.1421.tv, paras 2, 3, 6–12, 15–16, 18, Annexes XVII, XXV and XXVI

(xiv) Maori people of New Zealand, North Island

(a) Principal DNA report relied upon: not known; reported on ABC programme *Catalyst*, 27 March 2003, author Dr Gregory Chambers

(b) Précis of the report's findings: (as reported by David Knight 7.4.03) mitochondrial DNA shows female line is entirely Asian while Y chromosome DNA shows males came from Papua New Guinea

(c) Corroboration or supporting DNA reports: none yet

(d) Corroboration or supporting reports into ailments or diseases which suggest Chinese arrived by sea: none yet

(e) Did the first Europeans to reach the area in which the Maori people live find Chinese already there?
   • Captain Cook's diaries do not say Chinese, but they do say Maoris had met earlier seafarers in New Zealand

(f) Other evidence showing links with China
   • Plants and animals foreign to New Zealand were already there when the first Europeans arrived. The Ruapuke wreck and its associated Chinese artefacts. Campbell and Auckland Islands are shown on the Jean Rotz chart two centuries before Cook arrived.

(g) See Synopsis of Evidence on www.1421.tv

(xv) Gunditjmara Aborigines of Victoria, South Australia

(a) Principal DNA report relied upon: 'Evolution of Modern Humans' by Joanna Mountain in *Philosophical Transactions of the Royal Society of London* 337 (1992) 159–165

(b) Précis of the report's findings: this is a very generalised report and weak evidence of recent Chinese voyages

(c) Corroboration or supporting DNA reports: it is believed there are reports which the Australian government does not wish to have published

(d) Corroboration or supporting reports into ailments or diseases which suggest Chinese arrived by sea: none that are known, save for Machado-Joseph disease among the Aborigines of Arnhem Land

(e) Did the first Europeans to reach the area in which the Gunditjmara people live find Chinese already there? Not known.

(f) Other evidence showing links with China
   • The Gunditjmara people claim their ancestors came from overseas and instituted eel farming in Australia. Wrecked junks at Warrnambool and King Island. Maps of Australia drawn centuries before Europeans arrived there, e.g. Toscanelli (1474), which shows the internal river systems of Australia.

(g) See Synopsis of Evidence on www.1421.tv

Papers referred to

Araújo, Adauto José Goncalves de, 'Contribuição ao Estudo de Helmintos encontrados em Material Arqueológico do Brasil' (parasites common to Asia and South America)

Arnaiz-Villena, A., Vargas-Alarón Granados, J. et al, 'HCA Genes in Mexican Mazatecans, the peopling of the Americas, and the uniqueness of Amerindians', Tissue Antigero 2000

Biocca, Ettore, 'Hookworms and the Origin of American Indians', *L'Anthropologie* 55/5

Bruce-Chwatt, L. J., 'Paleogenesis and paleo-epidemiology of primate malaria', *Bulletin, World Health Organisation* 32: pp.363–87 (malaria in pre-Columbian America)

Cambridge Study (Incas to Polynesia) – see postscript

Darling, S. T., 'Hookworms, Ancylostoria and Necator in Pre-Columbian America', *Parasitology*, 12/3

Fonseca, Olympio da, 'Parasitismo e Migrações da Parasitologia', 'Contribuiçóés das origens do Hominem Americano' (para 15 in *The Americans re Human Migration*), Estudos da Préhistoria Geral e Brasileira, São Paolo, 1970

Laming-Emperaire, Annette, 'Le Problème de Origines Américains: théories, hypotheses, documents', Editions de la Maison des Sciences de l'Homme, Presses Universitaires de Lille, Lille 1980 (summary of diseases shared between Old World and pre-Columbian Indians)

Morael, Virginia, 'Research News: Confusion in Earliest America', *Science*, no.248 (genetic diversity of American Indians)

Needham, J., 'The mountain of evidence of pre-Columbian contact with the Americas before Columbus', *Science and Civilisation in China*, vol.4, p.540

New Zealand Study (Maori DNA) – see postscript (Dr Gregory Chambers)

Nicolle, Charles, 'Un argument medical en faveur de l'opinion de Paul Rivet sur l'origine océanienne du certain tribus indiennes du Nouveau Monde', *Journal de la société des Américanistes de Paris 24* (typhus of Mexico and Guatemala differs from Eurasian)

Novick, Gabriel E., Corina C. Novick, Juan Yunis, Emilio Yunis, Pamela Antunez de Mayolo, W. Douglas Scheer, Prescott L. Deininger, Mark Stoneking, Daniel S. York, Mark A. Batzer and Rene J. Herrera, 'Polymorphic Alu Insertions and the Asian Origin of Native American Populations', *Human Biology*, vol.70, no.1, p.23, copyright 1998 Wayne State University Press, Detroit, Michigan.

Sandison, A. T., 'Diseases in antiquity: a survey of the diseases, injuries and surgery of early populations', in *Parasitic Diseases*, C. T. Thomas, Springhurst, Illinois, 1967

Schurr, T. G., Ballinger, S. W., Gan Y-Y et al, 'Amerindian mitrochondrial DNAs have rare Asian mutations at high frequencies', *American Journal of Human Genetics*, 46, 1990, 613–23

Soper, T., 'The report of a nearly pure Ancylostoma duodenale infestation in native South American Indians and a discussion of ethnological signatures', *American Journal of Hygiene*, 1927

Sykes, Bryan, *The Seven Daughters of Eve*, Bantam Press, 2000, pp.101–6 and 282–95

Vilchis, F., Zúñiga, J., Granados, J. et al, 'Análisis del polimorfismo V89L de Sa esteroide reductasa en un groupo étnicamente preservado', *Genética y Biomedicina Molecular 200*, Resumen C., Monterrey, NL (Mexico)

NOTE: for a full bibliography for 1421, please refer to the website www.1421.tv

APPENDIX 2

THE DETERMINATION
OF LONGITUDE BY
THE CHINESE IN THE
EARLY FIFTEENTH
CENTURY

Authors: Professor John Oliver, co-chairman and Professor of the Department of Astronomy, University of Florida (JO)

Mr Marshall Payn (MP)

Gavin Menzies, author of *1421 – The Year China Discovered the World* (GM)

This paper is set out as follows:

Introduction (GM)

GM contends that during its sixth voyage (1421–3), the Chinese fleet perfected a method of determining longitude. This is illustrated by the longitude of the East African coast being accurately charted by the Chinese, then later shown on the Cantino map (1502) some three centuries before John Harrison invented the chronometer. Longitude on the East African coast between Cape Town and Djibouti, a distance of seven thousand nautical miles, is correct to within twenty nautical miles (twenty seconds of time). Detailed reasons for concluding that the Chinese were the original surveyors whose work was used to create the Cantino can be found in chapter 6 of this book.

Chinese astronomical knowledge in 1421 (GM)

By the time of their sixth voyage Zheng He's fleets had inherited expertise gained from six centuries of charting the stars in the night sky and had predicted and noted the return of Halley's comet on every pass since the second century BC. They were aware that the earth was a globe and had divided it into 365 and a quarter degrees (the number of days in the year) of latitude and longitude. Longitude was determined by the position on the globe east or west of Beijing; latitude was determined not from the equator but from Polaris in the north and the mid-point of the circumpolar stars in the south. The end result was the same as achieved later by Europeans. Following the voyage of Grand Eunuch Hong Bao to the Antarctic in early 1422, the Chinese knew the correct position of the South Pole. They were thus able to eliminate magnetic variation and to calculate latitude in the southern hemisphere as they did with Polaris in the north. In the early Ming era, Beijing's astronomers charted no fewer than 1,400 stars each night as they traversed the sky, a practice Emperor Zhu Di had reinstated. The Chinese were able to predict both solar and lunar eclipses with considerable accuracy.

The Chinese determination of elapsed time (GM)

An essential requirement for determining longitude was a precise measurement of elapsed time. The Chinese measured the passage of time by the sun's shadow.

The most famous existing observatory is the Zhou Gong Tower, built seven centuries ago. It is a truncated pyramid measuring twenty-five feet square at the top. Stairways lead from ground level to the platform on the top, upon which stands a three-roomed building with a good view to the north of a forty-foot gnomon, or vertical pole. The observatory, too, has a thin vertical rod for observation of meridian transits, and one of the rooms is equipped with a clepsydra, or large water clock.

Lying on the ground to the north of the tower and extending for 120 feet is the device for measuring the sun's shadow. To ensure this device was level, two parallel troughs of water extended along its length, enabling its stones to be laid precisely parallel with the water.

The gnomon itself extended forty feet into the sky. This enabled the sun's shadow thrown by the pole to be measured. As an illustration, at the equinox on the equator the sun rises in the east and sets in the west. At midday it is exactly above the observer and hence casts no shadow – it is a dot. The longest shadows are cast at sunrise and sunset. The length of the shadow will tell the time on that particular day at that particular place.

Back in ad 721, the Chinese realized that the length of the sun's shadow varied not only according to the time of day but for every day of the year, and depended on the observer's latitude. They conducted an experiment between latitudes 17°209N and 40°N. Along this meridian line, thousands of miles long, they measured simultaneously the length of shadows at the summer and winter solstices using a standard eight-foot gnomon. This showed that shadow lengths varied just over 3.56 inches for each four hundred miles of latitude. They could thus make corrections for their position.

They also appreciated that the length of shadow varied with the seasons. In one celebrated measurement, it was 12.3695 feet at the summer solstice and 76.7400 feet at the winter. This enabled them to make corrections for each day of the year as well as for different positions on the earth's surface.

The final adjustment was to correct the irregular motion of the earth around the sun occasioned by the eccentricity of the earth's orbit and the difference between the equator and the ecliptic – this is known as 'The Equation of Time'. It causes differences between absolute and solar time, reaching a maximum positive difference of fourteen minutes and thirty seconds in February and a maximum negative difference of sixteen minutes and thirty seconds in November. So accurately did the Chinese determine this equation of time that the great mathematician Laplace wrote: 'The [Chinese] observations made from 1277 to 1280 are valuable on account of their great precision and prove incontestably the diminution of the obliquity of the ecliptic and the eccentricity of the earth's orbit between then and now' (Needham, 1954, vol. 3, p. 398). This outstanding precision is illustrated by their estimate of the length of lunation at 29.530591 days – an error of less than one second in a month.

Chinese observatories (GM)

The Chinese replicated the Zhou Gong Tower, first in Nanjing, then, when the capital was moved north in 1421, in Beijing. Later, as noted in chapters 4 and 8, they built observatories around the world. We know what equipment was in the observatories from an inventory listed in *History of the Yuan Dynasty* (1276–9) (Needham, 1954, vol. 3, p. 369). Here are the principal pieces of equipment:

Hun thien hsiang – celestial globe (Ricci's first instrument)
Yang i – hemispherical sundial
Kao piao – lofty gnomon, forty feet, as at Yang Cheng
Li yun i – theodolite
Cheng li – verification instrument to determine exact positions of sun and moon near eclipse
Ching-fu – shadow amplifier
Jih yueh shi yi – instrument for observation of solar and lunar eclipses
Hsing kuei – star dial
Ting shih – time-determining instrument
Hou chi – pole-observing instrument

Chiu piao hsuan – plumb lines
Chengi – rectifying instrument

As may be seen, the list has instruments for recognizing stars in the sky (celestial globe); for measuring the length of the sun's shadow (lofty gnomon); for determining exact positions of the sun and moon at eclipses (cheng li); for amplifying the sun's shadow (ching-fu); for observing lunar eclipses (jih yueh shi yi); and for observing the Pole Star (hou chi).

Some of the instruments need explanation. The Chinese had long known that the longer the sun's shadow (i.e. the bigger the gnomon), the more accurate the measurement of time. However, the longer the shadow got, the more attenuated and fainter it became. In the early Ming era they devised a 'camera obscura', a hole in the top of the roof of the observation chamber which resulted in a sharper shadow. They intensified this with a type of magnifying glass. The upshot was that a long shadow could now be measured to within one-hundredth of an inch.

The measurements of time so far described would only work when the sun was out. Measuring time in darkness was accomplished using various types of water clock – clepsydras – which themselves were calibrated by day against the gnomons. There were several types of clepsydra; one of the best known was a steelyard type (chheng lou) which had compensating mechanisms to take account of both air pressure in the atmosphere and the height of water in the clock itself. One of these was found in the Pandanan junk wreck. We can see and marvel at the ingenuity of these astonishing devices for the poly-vascular type is illustrated and explained in the Chinese encyclopedia printed in 1478 (*Shi Lin Guang Ji*) now in the Cambridge University Library. We can summarize by saying that by the end of the voyage of 1421–3 the Chinese had the ability to measure time from their observation platforms which by then straddled the globe.

Eclipses (GM)

Eclipses of the earth's moon and the sun, that is solar and lunar eclipses, occur when the sun, moon and earth are in line with one another and when the moon's orbit around the earth is in the same plane as the earth's orbit around the sun. When these planes differ the result is a new or full moon rather than an eclipse.

Solar eclipse

In an eclipse of the sun, the line-up is like this:

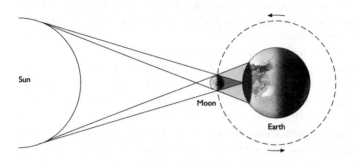

The moon's shadow blots out the sun over a small portion of the earth. It becomes night for a very short period. The spot of darkness, the umbra, travels across the earth as the moon rotates around the earth, and the earth itself rotates. Thus, observers in different locations see the solar eclipse at different times.

Lunar eclipse

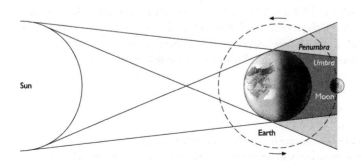

In a lunar eclipse, the earth is between sun and moon. Because the earth is so much bigger than the moon, the earth's shadow blots out the moon. The great difference, insofar as astronomical observations are concerned, is that in a lunar eclipse the event may be seen simultaneously by observers across half the earth, whereas in a solar eclipse the event occurs only above a small piece of earth at any one time.

The key to using a lunar eclipse to determine longitude is (i) that the event is seen across the world simultaneously; and (ii) while the event is seen, the earth is rotating, which has the effect that the heavens appear to rotate in the opposite direction to the earth.

Passage of events during a lunar eclipse (JO and MP)

There are four distinguishable events during an eclipse: U1 – first contact, when the moon enters the dark umbral shadow; U2 – second contact, when the moon has just fully entered the umbra (totally covered); U3 – third contact, when the moon first starts to emerge; and U4 – fourth contact, when the moon has just fully emerged. These events can be observed across almost 180 degrees of longitude (east to west).

Longitude determined by elapsed time during a lunar eclipse (JO and MP)

With their gnomons and water clocks, the Chinese were able to determine the passage of time, minute by minute, throughout the day and night. They could also forecast when a full lunar eclipse would occur – about every six months somewhere across the globe. The instruction to the navigators and astronomers was as follows: 'After landing in unknown territory, when the next total eclipse begins, wait until the third event [U3] occurs and the last bit of darkness disappears. Just when the first sliver of light appears as the moon starts to come out of its eclipse [U3], both the observer in the new territories and the astronomer in Beijing look into the night sky and determine which major star is transiting the local meridian.' The local meridian is an imaginary line on the celestial sphere which starts at the celestial pole north of the observer, extends directly over the observer's head (the observer's zenith), and ends at the celestial pole south of the observer. Along this imaginary line, the observer selects a known star crossing the line. This is both observers' key sighting at this point.

When the astronomer in the newly discovered territories has returned to Beijing, he and the astronomer at Beijing's observatory compare notes. The one who has returned from abroad relates that at event U3, star alpha was transiting his local meridian. The Beijing observer relates that at that U3 moment, star beta was transiting his local meridian, both well-known stars. They now get out their time-keeping device. This has been calibrated from the gnomons. They wait until star alpha crosses the zenith and then start counting with their time-measuring device until star beta crosses their zenith. The time elapsed between star alpha and star beta crossing the zenith is the distance the earth has rotated between the two observers – the one in Beijing, the other in the newly discovered lands. The earth rotates 360 degrees every twenty-four hours. Thus, if we assume that the time elapsed between the transit of star alpha and star beta was exactly six hours (i.e. a quarter of the time it takes the earth to rotate), then the difference in longitude between Beijing and the new territory is also a quarter of the total longitude around the world, i.e. one-quarter of 360 degrees, or 90 degrees.

Note by GM: Refinements can be introduced by conducting this procedure four times at U1, U2, U3 and U4 and then applying the averages to reduce errors.

Proof of the theory (JO and MP)

We decided to test our theory by observing the lunar eclipse of 16 and 17 July 2000. We positioned our team across the Pacific from Tahiti to Singapore. By a happy coincidence, we chose the same positions on which the Chinese had erected observation platforms.

Where	Long	Obs?	Observations				Local Sidereal Time				Uobs-LST				Error	
			U1	U2	U3	U4	LST1	LST2	LST3	LST4	U1	U2	U3	U4	Ave	rms
Papeele, Tahiti	-149°	yes		339°	0.8°			341.2°	08.0°			-2.2°	-0.0°		-1.1°	±1.5
Singapore	103.8°	yes		235°		276°		234.0°		277.1°		-1.0°		-1.1°	0.0°	±1.5
near Melbourne, Australia	145°	yes	258°	275°	301°		258.4°	274.7°	301.5°		-0.4°	0.3°	-0.5°		-0.2°	±0.5
Tekapo, New Zealand	170.5°	yes	284°	301°	329°	343°	284.4°	300.7°	327.5°	343.8°	-0.4°	0.3°	1.5°	-0.8°	0.1°	±1.0
Nelson, New Zealand	173.1°	yes	285°	305°	330°	345°	287.0°	303.3°	330.1°	346.4°	-2.0°	1.7°	-0.1°	-1.4°	-0.5°	±1.6

Table 1: Observations of the 16/17 July 2000 lunar eclipse. As can be seen, the error of a single observation was typically ±1.5° or better. Since one degree is the equivalent of four minutes of time, this error is the equivalent of about six minutes of time. The error of the combination of two observations would be better by √2 and would thus be about ±1°.

The observations list the celestial longitude measured from the vernal equinox of whatever star was transiting the local meridian – that is, the straight line passing from north over the observer's head to south. The celestial longitude is measured along the equator of a star map. Thus, 339° (Tahiti) measures the position of a rotating cylindrical star map. The time elapsed between U2 and U3 enabled that cylindrical star map to rotate for 339° past 360° to 8° – about two hours. Average errors were: Tahiti 1.1 degrees, New Zealand 0.1 degree, Melbourne 0.1 degree, Singapore zero degrees. Our observers were amateurs; with more training and experience than we could provide the errors could be reduced.

Practical implementation (GM)

The result has startling implications, for longitude has been calculated from Tahiti in the east with sixty-six nautical miles' error to Singapore in the west with no longitudinal error. There is six nautical miles' longitudinal error between Singapore and New Zealand, none between New Zealand and Australia. Longitude has been calculated across nearly one-third of the world correct to within sixty-six miles.

The Chinese could have determined longitude just as accurately as Professor Oliver's team did. The brilliance of this method is that, unlike calculations for latitude, no sextant is required. Neither is a clock; the only instrument needed is one to accurately determine elapsed time, a role fulfilled by the gnomon.

Having accurately determined the longitude of Malacca (Singapore), the Chinese fleets could now use observation platforms and gnomons on their bases around the Indian Ocean – at Semudera (Sumatra), the Andamans, Dondra Head (Ceylon/Sri Lanka), Calicut on the Malabar coast of India, Zanzibar in East Africa, the Seychelles and Maldive archipelagos – all of which appear on the *Wu Pei Chi* charts which credit Zheng He with providing the information. There is no reason why longitudes across the whole Indian Ocean should not have been determined in one eclipse, provided a sufficiently large fleet was deployed. This, I think, happened with the results seen in the Cantino, where the coast of East Africa appears as if drawn with the aid of satellite navigation.

The brilliance of Zheng He's astro-navigation arises both from its simplicity and because each part contributes towards a composite whole greater than its parts.

Establishing the right ascension and declination of Canopus and of Crucis Alpha and Beta (Southern Cross) had enabled them to be cross-referenced to Polaris (see *Wu Pei Chi* chart for passage between Dondra Head and Sumatra). Measuring Polaris's altitude as they sailed north would have enabled Chinese navigators to calculate half the circumference of the earth. Sailing due north between the equator and 40°N was 2,400 nautical miles (10,000 *li*); thus, continuing to the North Pole would be a further 50° or 12,500 *li;* thus, the earth's circumference must be 100,000 *li*. Because they knew the position of Canopus and the Southern Cross, they could use the size of the earth to determine the true position of the South Pole (the centre of the cirumpolar stars – Canopus becomes circumpolar below 68°S). Hence, they could determine the position of the South Magnetic Pole so as to establish true south and north.

The Chinese now had everything needed to accurately chart the world – latitude, longitude, size, direction. They went on to chart every continent with great accuracy. The fruits of their labours reached Europe via Niccolò da Conti and enabled Europeans to set sail on their voyages of discovery with maps based on Chinese cartography.

OBSERVATION PLATFORMS USED BY THE CHINESE 1421–3

Pacific, east to west

Marquesas	140°W	9°30'S
Tahiti	149°W	17°50'S
Society Islands (Bora Bora)	151°W	17°30'S
Kiribati (Gilberts, Phoenix) Islands	160°4'W	0°24'N
Ruapuke beach	174°47'E	37°56'S
Nan Madol	158°21'E	6°51'N
Gympie (New South Wales)	152°42'E	26°12'S
Gosford (central NSW)	151°13'E	33°26'S
New Guinea	143°38'E	3°35'S
Yap Island	138°9'E	9°31'N
Nanjing	118°45'E	32°6'N
Beijing	116°25'E	39°55'N

Indian Ocean

Malacca	102°15'E	2°11'N
Semudera (Bandar Aceh)	95°19'E	5°32'N
Nicobars (Polo Milo)	93°42'E	7°27'N
Andamans (Lapatte)	92°47'E	9°22'N
Ceylon/Sri Lanka (Dondra Head)	80°13'E	6°02'N
Calicut	75°49'E	11°16'N
Maldives (Male)	73°30'E	4°7'N
Seychelles	55°29'E	4°36'N
Madagascar (Mahajanga)	46°14'E	15°45'S
Zanzibar	39°11'E	6°11'N
Sofala	39°44'E	20°9'S

NOTES

Chapter 1: The Emperor's Grand Plan

1   Anlui province on the north bank of the Yangtze in eastern central China.

2   Chinese emperors were known not by their personal name but by their title, and, after death, a 'temple name', such as 'Sincere Emperor', reflecting the course of their life.

3   Mary M. Anderson, *Hidden Power: The Palace Eunuchs of Imperial China*, Prometheus, Buffalo, New York, 1990, pp. 15–18, 307–11.

4   R.H. Van Gulik, *Sexual Life in Ancient China*, Leiden, 1961, p. 256.

5   Anderson, op. cit.

6   Dorothy and Thomas Hoobler, *Images across the Ages: Chinese Portraits*, Raintree, Austin, Texas, 1993.

7   Confucius, as quoted by F. Braudel in *A History of Civilisations*, trs. R. Mayne, Penguin, Harmondsworth, 1994, p. 178.

8   The dragon was credited with miraculous powers and was used as a metaphor for people of great virtue and talent. Almost all the items and artefacts closely connected with the emperor – his throne, his robes, his bed, etc. – were prefixed with 'dragon' or 'phoenix', the phoenix being another mystical creature with extraordinary powers.

9   In early 2002 the Chinese government announced ambitious plans to restore the dry-docks and build a full-size replica of one of Zheng He's junks.

10 Ming Tong Jian, *Comprehensive Mirror of Ming History*, 1873, Ch. 14, quoted in Louise Levathes, *When China Ruled the Seas*, Simon & Schuster, 1994, pp. 73–4.

11 Ahmad ibn Arabshah, *Miracles of Destiny in Timur's History*, 1636.

12 *Shun Feng Hsiang Seng* ('Fair Winds for Escort'), anon., c. 1430, Bodleian Library.

13 Miles Menander Dawson, *The Wisdom of Confucius*, Boston, Mass., 1932, pp. 57–8.

14 Quoted by Edmund L. Dreyer in *Early Ming China: A Political History 1355–1435*, Stanford University Press, Calif., p. 204.

15 Hafiz Abru, *A Persian Embassy in China*, 1421, trs. K.M. Maitra, Lahore, 1934, p. 55.

16 Emperor Zhu Di's instructions to Zheng He, paraphrased from the two stone steles of 1431.

17 The number of voyages made by the treasure fleets is, and will continue to be, a matter of dispute. The inscriptions on commemorative stones erected by Zheng He before his final voyage claim that his fleets had, until then, made seven. Most authorities classify his fourth and fifth

voyages as one. I have adhered to this classification; the voyages beginning in 1421 were therefore the sixth.

18 Hoobler, op. cit.

19 L. Carrington Goodrich (ed.), *The Dictionary of Ming Biography*, Columbia UP, New York, 1976, p. 1365.

20 N.I. Vavilov, 'The Origin, Variation, Immunity and Breeding of Cultivated Plants', trs. K.S. Chester, *Chronica Botanica*, Vol. 13, Waltham, Mass., 1949–50; and J. Needham, *Science and Civilisation in China*, Vol. VI, Pt 2, sec. 41, p. 428.

Chapter 2: A Thunderbolt Strikes

1 Hafiz Abru, *A Persian Embassy to China*, 1421, trs. K.M. Maitra, Lahore, 1934, pp. 113–15.

2 Ibid., p. 115.

3 Ibid., pp. 115–17.

4 Ibid., p. 117

5 Shang Chuan, *Yongle Huang Di*, Beijing, 1989, pp. 214–15, citing the Cochin tablet 'Taizong Shi Lu', ch. 236.

6 S.W. Mote and Denis Twitchett (eds), *The Cambridge History of China*, Vol. 7, *The Ming Dynasty*, Cambridge UP, Cambridge, 1988, p. 292.

7 Abru, op. cit., p. 108.

8 Quoted in Louise Levathes, *When China Ruled the Seas*, Oxford UP, Oxford, 1994, p. 157.

9 Ellen F. Soullière, *Palace Women in the Ming Dynasty*, Princeton University doctoral thesis, 1987, quoted in Levathes, op. cit., p. 226.

10 Levathes, op. cit., pp. 163 and 164.

11 P.B. Ebrey, *The Cambridge Illustrated History of China*, Cambridge UP, Cambridge, 1996, p. 278.

12 Quoted in L. Carrington Goodrich (ed.), *The Dictionary of Ming Biography*, Columbia UP, New York, 1976, p. 338.

13 See J. Needham, *Science and Civilisation in China*, Vol. 4, Pt 3, Cambridge UP, Cambridge, 1954, p. 525; and J.J.L. Duyvendak, *China's Discovery of Africa*, Probsthain, 1949, p. 27, and 'The True Dates of the Chinese Maritime Expeditions in the Early Fifteenth Century', *T'oung Pao*, XXXIV, pp. 395–8.

Chapter 3: The Fleets Set Sail

1   The originals are in Beijing, but the British Library holds copies.
2   J. Needham, *Science and Civilisation in China*, Vol. 3, sec. 20, Cambridge UP, Cambridge, 1954, p. 230.
3   Ibid., Vol. 4, Pt 3, pp. 565ff.
4   Ibid., Vol. 6, Pt 1, pp. 365ff.
5   Ibid., Vol. 6, Pt 5, pp. 19ff.
6   Ibid.
7   Antonio Pigafetta, *Magellan's Voyage*, trs. R.A. Skelton, Yale UP, New Haven, Conn., 1969, p. 56.
8   R.H. Van Gulik, *Sexual Life in Ancient China*, Leiden, 1961, pp. 308ff.
9   Ibid., p. 125.
10   Ibid., p. 265.
11   Ibid., p. 133.
12   Ibid.
13   Ibn Taghri-Birdi, *A History of Egypt, 1382–1469 AD,* Berkeley, California, 1954.
14   Ma Huan, *The Overall Survey of the Ocean Shores*, Beijing, 1433, trs. J.V.G. Mills, Cambridge UP (for Hakluyt Society), 1970, p. 108.
15   Ibid., p. 143.
16   Ma Huan, op. cit., trs. Paul Wheatley in *The Golden Khersonese*, University of Malaya Press, Kuala Lumpur, 1961, p. 143.
17   Ma Huan, op. cit., trs. Mills, p. 104.
18   Ibid. A slightly different translation is quoted by Richard Hall in *Empires of the Monsoon*. HarperCollins, 1996, p 89.
19   F. Braudel, *The Wheels of Commerce*, trs. Siân Reynolds, Fontana, 1985, p. 130.
20   Ibid., p. 131.
21   Zheng He, quoted in Dorothy and Thomas Hoobler, *Images across the Ages: Chinese Portraits*, Raintree, Austin, Texas, 1993.
22   The identity of the admiral in command of the third fleet is not known with absolute certainty, but after corresponding with Professor Roderich Ptak of the University of Munich I believe Chou Wen to be the most probable leader.

Chapter 4: Rounding the Cape

1   See ch. 3, n. 22.
2   Stone inscription in the Palace of the Celestial Spouse at Chiang-su,

dated 1431, trs. J.J.L. Duyvendak, 'The True Dates of the Chinese Maritime Expeditions in the Early Fifteenth Century', *T'oung Pao*, XXXIV, p. 347.

3   Stone inscription in the Palace of the Celestial Spouse at Liu-Chia-Chang, dated 1431, trs. J.J.L. Duyvendak, *China's Discovery of Africa*, Probsthain, 1949, p. 29.

4   Professor Needham, Richard Hall and Louise Levathes.

5   Richard Hall, *Empires of the Monsoon*, HarperCollins, 1996, p. 550, has splendid illustrations.

6   Ma Huan, *The Overall Survey of the Ocean Shores*, Beijing, 1433, trs. J.V.G. Mills, Cambridge UP (for Hakluyt Society), 1970, p. 138. It can be seen that Muslim people are ruling Hindus.

7   Ibid., pp. 140 and 141.

8   Poggio Bracciolini, *The Travels of Niccolò da Conti*, 1434, partial translation in R.H. Major (ed.), *India in the Fifteenth Century*, Hakluyt Society, 1857.

9   *The Travels of Niccolò da Conti*, quoted in Hall, op. cit., p. 124.

10   J.H. Parry, *The Discovery of the Sea*, Elek, 1979, p. 45.

11   See postscript for details of this and a further conference in Kunming.

12   100,000 *li* equals 40,000 nautical miles. The circumference of the globe is 21,600 nautical miles.

13   As translated by J. Needham in *Science and Civilisation in China*, Vol. 4, Pt 3, Cambridge UP, Cambridge, 1954, p. 572.

14   Ibid.

15   Quoted by Eannes de Zuzara, *The Chronicle of the Discovery and Conquest of Guinea*, trs. C.R. Beazley, Hakluyt Society, 1896–9.

16   Hall, op. cit., pp. 124–6. See postscript for an important update on the status of da Conti.

17   Vice-Admiral Sir Ian McIntosh, letter to the author, 2001.

18   Chuan Chin, one of the Koreans who organized the publication of the Kangnido.

19   The work of M. Chevalier and his colleagues.

20   Antonio Galvão, *Tratado Dos Diversos e Desayados Caminhos*, Lisbon, 1563. The translation I have used is that of Richard Hakluyt, 1601, pp. 23–4, quoted by F.M. Rogers in *The Travels of the Infante Dom Pedro*, Harvard UP, Cambridge, Mass., 1961, p. 48.

21   Ibid.

22   H. Harisse, *The Discovery of North America*, 1892, p. 272.

23   [British] Admiralty, *Ocean Passages of the World*, third edn, 1973.

NOTES

Chapter 5: The New World

1   Bibliography in J. Needham, *Science and Civilisation in China*, Vol. 4, Pt 3, sec. 29, Cambridge UP, Cambridge, 1954, p. 542.
2   Note VII on the Piri Reis map, translated by G.C. McIntosh in *The Piri Reis Map of 1513*, University of Georgia Press, Athens, Georgia, 2000, p. 46.
3   Charles R. Darwin, *Journal of Researches into the Geology and Natural History of the Various Countries Visited by HMS Beagle, 1832–36*, Henry Colburn, 1839, pp. 54 and 124.
4   Antonio Pigafetta, *Magellan's Voyage*, trs. R.A. Skelton, Yale UP, New Haven, Conn., 1934, p. 54.
5   Note XXIII, in McIntosh, op. cit., p. 44.
6   Note XXIV, ibid.
7   Ibid.
8   Ma Huan, *The Overall Survey of the Ocean Shores*, Beijing, 1433, trs. J.V.G. Mills, Cambridge UP (for Hakluyt Society), 1970, p. 155.
9   See chapter 9.
10 A detailed and extensive bibliography of plants and animals brought to the Americas before the European voyages of exploration is contained in J.L. Sorenson and M.H. Raish, *Pre-Columbian Contact with the Americas across the Oceans: An Annotated Bibliography*, Provo Research Press, 1990.
11 Ferdinand Magellan, 13 December 1519, in *The First Voyage round the World by Magellan*, translated from the Accounts of Pigafetta by Lord Stanley of Alderley, Hakluyt Society, 1874, and Antonio Pigafetta, *Primer Viage Alrededor del Mundo*, Leoncio Cabrero Fernandez, Madrid, 1985.
12 J. de Acosta, '*Historia Natural y Moral de las Indias*', No. 34, Cronic., Venice, 1596. Acosta used linguistic evidence to demonstrate the spread of pre-Columbian chickens in South America.
13 George F. Carter, 'The Chicken in America', in Donald Y. Gilmore and Linda S. McElroy (eds), *Across before Columbus?*, NEARA Publications, Edgecomb, Maine, 1998, p. 154.
14 Ibid., p. 158.
15 M.D.W. Jeffreys, 'Pre-Columbian Maize in Asia', in Carroll Riley et al. (eds), *Men across the Sea*, University of Texas Press, 1971, pp. 382ff.
16 Maize: Antonio Pigafetta, *Primo Viaggio intorno al Mondo*, MS version of c. 1524 translated in E.H. Blair and J.A. Robertson, *The Philippine Islands 1493–1893*, 1906, Vols 33 and 34, pp. 154, 164, 182 and 186; M.D.W. Jeffreys, 'Who Introduced Maize into Southern Africa?', *South Africa Journal of Science*, Vol. 63, Johannesburg, 1963, pp. 23–40; A. de

Candolle, *Origin of Cultivated Plants*, 1967, p. 355. See also ch. 8, n. 20, and ch. 5, n. 18.

17 Ibid.
18 J.J.L. Duyvendak, *China's Discovery of Africa*, Probsthain, 1949, p. 32.
19 *Wu Pei Chi* and the *Shun Feng Hsiang Seng*, Beijing.
20 Chiu Thang Shu, quoted in J. Needham, *Science and Civilisation in China*, Vol. 4, sec. 20, Cambridge UP, Cambridge, 1954, p. 274.

Chapter 6: Voyage to Antarctica and Australia

1 Charles R. Darwin, *Journal of Researches into the Geology and Natural History of the Various Countries Visited by HMS Beagle, 1832–36*, 1839.
2 Ibid.
3 Antonio Pigafetta, *Magellan's Voyage*, trs. R.A. Skelton, Folio Society, 1975, p. 49.
4 Ibid.
5 Ibid., p. 50.
6 Ibid., p. 57.
7 Professor C.H. Hapgood, *Maps of the Ancient Sea Kings*, Chilton Books, New York, 1966, pp. 193ff.
8 Erich von Daniken, *Chariots of the Gods*, trans. M. Heron, Souvenir, 1969, p. 20.
9 British Admiralty Chart 554.
10 Ludovico Varthema, *Travels of L. de Varthema* (1510), trs. J.W. Jones, Hakluyt Society, 1863, p. 249. 'He told us that on the other side of the said island [Java] . . . there are some other races who navigate by the said four or five stars opposite to ours [the Southern Cross] and moreover . . . beyond the said island the day does not last more than four hours, and that it was colder than in any other part of the world.'
11 Ibid.
12 Longitude 70°W.
13 Latitude 60°S.
14 Latitude 64°S.
15 The Scott Polar Research Institute of Cambridge has kindly provided ice charts for the Antarctic.
16 As may be verified with the Microsoft computer program *Starry Night*.
17 See Note VI on the Piri Reis map, translated by G.C. McIntosh in *The Piri Reis Map of 1513*, University of Georgia Press, Athens, Georgia, 2000, pp. 16 and 17.

18 L. Carrington Goodrich (ed.), *The Dictionary of Ming Biography*, Columbia UP, New York, 1976, p. 1365.

19 Ibid., p. 199.

20 Zvi Dor-Ner, *Columbus and the Age of Discovery*, Grafton, 1992, p. 10, and Richard Hall, *Empires of the Monsoon*, HarperCollins, 1996, p. 92.

21 Vanessa Collingridge, *Captain Cook, Obsession and Betrayal in the New World*, Ebury, 2002.

22 K.G. McIntyre, *The Secret Discovery of Australia*, Souvenir, Melbourne, 1977, p. 268.

23 Ibid., p. 269.

24 Ibid., pp. 271ff.

25 See postscript for an update.

26 Ibid., p. 289.

27 Professor Wei Chuh-Hsien, *The Chinese Discovery of Australia*, Hong Kong, 1961.

Chapter 7: Australia

1 The southern portion of the map was based on a chart found on the person of a Spanish seaman captured by the Ottomans in 1501.

2 *Hsi-Yang-Chi*, quoted by J.J.L. Duyvendak in 'Desultory Notes on the *Hsi-Yang-Chi*', *T'oung Pao*, XLII, 1953, pp. 20ff.

3 Don Luis Arias, letter to the King of Spain, quoted in A.W. Miller, *The Straits of Magellan*, Portsmouth, 1884, p. 7.

4 F. Fernández-Armesto (ed.), *Times Atlas of World Exploration*, Times, 1991, p. 167.

5 Lin Dao, *Sui Shu* (official history of the Sui dynasty), AD 636, ch. 82.

6 32°40′S; 152°11′E.

7 43°42′S; 146°32′E.

8 Rex Gilroy, *Pyramids in the Pacific*, Gympie, Australia, 1999.

9 Robyn Gossett, *New Zealand Mysteries*, Auckland, 1996, p. 31.

10 Gilroy, op. cit.; Brett J. Green, *The Gympie Pyramid Story*, Gympie, Australia, 2000, and Gossett, op. cit., p. 148.

11 B. Hilder, 'The Story of the Tamil Bell', in *Journal of the Polynesian Society*, Vol. 84, 1975.

12 Elsdon Best, 'Note on a Curious Steatite Figurine Found at Mauku, Auckland', in *NZ Journal of Science and Technology*, Vol. II, 1919, p. 77.

13 Gossett, op. cit.

Chapter 8: The Barrier Reef and the Spice Islands

1   K.G. McIntyre, *The Secret Discovery of Australia*, Souvenir, 1977, and
    'Early European Exploration of Australia', unpublished paper, p. 11.

2   China 29%, India 16% – Angus Maddison, *Class Structure and Economic
    Growth in India and Pakistan since the Moghuls*, Allen & Unwin, 1971.

3   Those records seen by Fr Ricci and early Jesuit missionaries to China:
    Chui Hiao ('Atlas of Foreign Countries') and sixth-century scrolls telling
    of voyages of massive junks to Australia, and *The Classics of Shan Hai
    Jing*. Rex Gilroy, *Pyramids in the Pacific*, Gympie, Australia, 1999.

4   Saltpetre, copper, carbonates, haematites, quartz, amethyst, alum and
    cinnabar formed the first; the second comprised sulphur, mercury,
    feldspar, copper sulphate, magnetite, azurite and realgar; and the third
    group included stalagmites, iron, iron oxides, lead carbonate, lead
    tetroxide, tin, agate and fuller's earth. J. Needham, *Science and
    Civilisation in China*, Vol. 3, sec. 25, Cambridge UP, Cambridge, 1954,
    p. 643.

5   Ibid., pp. 653ff.

6   Warren, Delavault, Hawksworth and others. Ibid., p. 678.

7   Ibid., pp. 653ff.

8   For this information I am indebted to Brett Green, whose family
    recorded the Aboriginal songs and folklore of this coast. See Brett J.
    Green, *The Gympie Pyramid Story*, Gympie, Australia, 1998, and Gilroy,
    op. cit.

9   Needham, op. cit.

10 Gilroy, op. cit., and Green, op. cit.

11 Green, op. cit.

12 A. Grenfell Pike (ed.), *The Explorations of Captain James Cook in the
    Pacific*, Limited Editions Club, New York, 1957, p. 77.

13 Other cartographers of the Dieppe School depicted the Gulf differently:
    Desliens showed it narrower than it should be while Desceliers depicted
    it close to its actual size, suggesting that the Dieppe cartographers were
    using more than one Portuguese chart – a note on the Piri Reis map
    referred to four Portuguese mappae mundi.

14 Governor Grey, quoted in McIntyre, *Secret Discovery*, p. 79.

15 The date of this figurine has recently been disputed. Professor
    Needham, in *Science and Civilisation in China*, Vol. 4, Pt 3, p. 537 and at
    Fig. 991, states, 'The statuette is in style Ming or early Ching, quite
    reasonably contemporary with Cheng Ho.' He writes at p. 537, 'Wei
    Chu-Hsien (4), p. 99, concurs.' (This reference is to *The Chinese
    Discovery of Australia*, Hong Kong, 1960). Professor Needham further

cites H. Doré, *Recherches sur les superstitions en Chine*, Vol. XI, p. 966, and P.M. Worsley, 'Early Asian Contacts with Australia', in *Past and Present*, No. 7, 1955. The current curator of the Technological Museum in Sydney, where the statuette is housed, states, 'The Museum's preferred dating of this object is the early nineteenth century.'

16   Admiralty sailing instructions, Cook, op. cit.

17   Cdr A.W. Miller, RN, *The Straits of Magellan*, Griffin, Portsmouth, 1884, p. 7.

18   Don Luis Arias, letter to the King of Spain, quoted, ibid.

19   John Merson, *Roads to Xanadu*, Weidenfeld and Nicolson, 1989, p. 75.

20   On maize found in the Philippines: M.D.W. Jeffreys, 'Pre-Columbian Maize in Asia', in Carroll Riley et al. (eds), *Men across the Sea*, University of Texas Press, 1971, pp. 382ff.; E.L. Sturtevant, 'Notes on Edible Plants', New York State Department of Agriculture 27th Annual Report, 1919, p. 616 ('In 1521 maize was found by Magellan at the island of Limasava'); H.W. Krueger, 'Peoples of the Philippines', Smithsonian Institution War Background Studies No. 4, Washington DC, 1942, p. 23 (Pigafetta observing maize cultivation on Limasava); W. Richardson, *General Collection of Voyages and Discoveries Made by the Portuguese and Spaniards during the 15th and 16th Centuries*, 1789, p. 496 ('The islanders invited the General into their boats in which were their merchandise viz cloves . . . and maize'; C.O. Saver, 'Maize into Europe', in *Accounts 34th Int. Cong. Amer.*, Vienna, 1960, pp. 777–88 (Pigafetta's 'miglio' translated as maize); Antonio Pigafetta, *Primo Viaggio intorno al Mondo*, MS version of c. 1524 translated in E.H. Blair and J.A. Robertson, *The Philippine Islands 1493–1893*, 1906, pp. 164 and 182 (cakes of 'riso e miglio' on island of Zubu (Cebu)); Pigafetta, op. cit., p. 154 ('ears like Indian corn . . . shelled off like lada'); J.J.L. Duyvendak, *China's Discovery of Africa*, Probsthain, 1949, p. 32.

Chapter 9: The First Colony in the Americas

1   11°N.

2   Peter Whitfield, *New Found Lands: Maps in the History of Exploration*, British Library, 1998, pp. 54–5.

3   Article by Dr Tan Koonlin in *The Rose* (journal of the American Rose Society), Vol. 92, Pt 4; R.E. Shepherd, *History of the Rose*, Macmillan, New York, 1954; E. Wilson, *Plant Hunting*, Vol. 2, Stratford, Boston, Mass., 1927.

4   *Sacramento Bee*, 26 January 2001, and *Enterprise Record of Chico*, 23 January 2001.

5   Carey McWilliams, *Factories in the Field*, University of California Press, Berkeley, 2000, pp. 68–80.

6   Stephen Powers, 'Aborigines of California: An Indo-Chinese Study' in *Atlantic*, Vol. 33, 1874, and Stephen Powers, *Contributions to North American Ethnology*, Vol. 3, Department of the Interior, Washington DC, 1877.

7   Powers, *Ethnology*, p. 417.

8   All ibid., introduction and pp. 146–434.

9   Referring to California's East Bay walls in John Fryer, *Ancients in America*.

10 Fra Bernardino de Sahagún, *The Florentine Codex: General History of the Things of New Spain 1325–1550*, School of American Research, Santa Fe, 11 vols, 1950–69.

11 Bernardino Diaz del Castillo, *The Conquest of New Spain*, New York, 1956.

12 Barbara Pickersgill, 'Origin and Evolution of Cultivated Plants in the New World', *Nature*, 268 (18), pp. 591–4.

13 Alberto Ruz Lhuillier, 'The Mystery of the Temple of the Inscriptions', *Archaeology*, Vol. 6, No. 1, 1953, as quoted by Charles Gallenkamp in *Maya: The Riddle and Rediscovery of a Lost Civilisation*, Penguin, Harmondsworth, 1987, pp. 93–104.

Chapter 10: Colonies in Central America

1   Lacquering is described by Fra Bernadino de Sahagún in *The Florentine Codex: General History of the Affairs of New Spain 1325–1550*, trs. A.J.O. Anderson and C.E. Dibble, Salt Lake City, 1970.

2   Ma Huan, *The Overall Survey of the Ocean Shores*, trs. J.V.G. Mills, Cambridge UP (for Hakluyt Society), Cambridge, 1970.

3   H. Mertz, *Gods from the Far East: How the Chinese Discovered America*, New York, 1972, pp. 72–3.

4   Stephen C. Jett, 'Dyestuffs and Possible Early Contacts between South Western Asia and Nuclear America', in *Across before Columbus?*, NEARA Publications, Edgecomb, Maine, 1998, pp. 141ff.

5   Ibid., p. 146.

6   De Sahagún, op. cit.

7   An attempt is being made to compare DNA of Michoacán dogs with that of shar-peis. The results will be posted on the website.

8   Nicolás León, 'Studies in the Archaeology of Michoacán: The Lienzo of Jucutácato', in *Smithsonian Institution Annual Report*, Washington DC, 1889.

9   J. Needham, *Science and Civilisation in China*, Vol. 4, Pt. 3, Cambridge UP, Cambridge, 1954, pp. 540–3.

10   The Peruvian historian Pablo Padron, 'Un Huaco con Caracteres Chinos', Sociedad Geográfica de Lima, Vol. 23, pp. 24–5.

11   Carl Johannessen and M. Fogg, 'Melanotic Chicken Use and Chinese Traits in Guatemala', in *Revista de Historia de América*, Vol. 93, 1962, p. 75.

12   W.C. Parker and A.G. Bearn, *Annals of Human Genetics* 25, 1961 (227).

13   Padron, op. cit.

14   This is the only part of the *I Yü Thu Chih* to have been translated – by Viviana Wong, to whom I am most grateful.

15   In the *Atlas of Foreign Countries*, anon., AD 265–316, China.

16   K.G. McIntyre, *The Secret Discovery of Australia*, Souvenir, Melbourne, 1977.

17   J.L. Sorenson and M.H. Raish, *Pre-Columbian Contact with the Americas across the Oceans: An Annotated Bibliography*, Provo Research Press, 1990.

18   George F. Carter, 'Fusang: Chinese Contact with America', in *Anthropological Journal of Canada*, 14, No. 1, 1976.

Chapter 11: Satan's Island

1   [British] Admiralty, *Ocean Passages of the World*, third edn, 1973.

2   Armando Cortesão, *The Nautical Chart of 1424*, University of Coimbra, Portugal, 1954, pp. 105 and 110.

3   Bartolomeu las Casas, *Historia de las Indias*, Lisbon, 1552.

4   Antonio Galvão, *Tratado Dos Diversos e Desayados Caminhos*, Lisbon, 1563, and Cortesão, op. cit., p. 73.

5   Dr Chanca, quoted in J.H. Longille, *Christopher Columbus*, Inscribers, Washington DC, 1903, p. 184.

6   Chanca, ibid., p. 187.

7   Ibid., p. 184.

8   Syllacius, quoted, ibid., pp. 184ff.

9   Chanca, quoted, ibid., pp. 181 and 182.

10   See the website for more detailed information.

11   Letters between Smithsonian Institution, Washington DC, and author, 6 and 7 July 2002.

12   Syllacius, quoted in Longille, op. cit., pp. 184ff.

13   Ibid., p. 185.

14   This is explained in more detail on the website.

15   Inscription translated by J.J.L. Duyvendak, *China's Discovery of Africa*, Probsthain, 1949, p. 28.

16 4403, 3912 and 2710 (see the website for more detailed information).
17 3912.
18 77°30′W between 23°10′ and 23°50′N.

Chapter 12: The Treasure Fleet Runs Aground

1 2710, 3810 and 3912.
2 F.L. Coffman, *Atlas of Treasure Maps*, New York, 1957.
3 26, 61, 63 and 64 in Coffman's numbering system.
4 27, 28, 29 and 30 in Coffman's numbering system.
5 Peter Martyr, quoted in E.W. Lawson, *The Discovery of Florida and Its Discoverer Juan Ponce de León*, 1946, p. 8.
6 Martyr, quoted, ibid., p. 11.
7 *The Undersea World of Jacques Cousteau* and the TV series *In Search Of . . . Atlantis*, narrated by Leonard Nimoy, Channel 4 (UK) and National Geographical Channel (USA).
8 Dr David Zink's discoveries are featured in two books, *The Ancient Stones Speak*, Dutton, 1979, and *The Stones of Atlantis*, W.H. Allen, 1978.
9 J. Needham, *Science and Civilisation in China*, Vol. 4, Pt 3, Cambridge UP, Cambridge, 1954, p. 669.
10 This was confirmed by the Old Dominion University of Virginia, to which Dr Zink sent samples.
11 Alemanide, rhaotide and celtide.
12 At Christie's.
13 Washington Irving, *Life and Voyages of Christopher Columbus*, quoted in Loren Coleman, *Mysterious America*, Faber, 1983, p. 218.
14 Ferdinand Columbus, *La Historia della Vita di Cristoforo Columbus*, Milan, 1930.

Chapter 13: Settlement in North America

1 Francis I, King of France, to Verrazzano, quoted in D.B. Quinn (ed.), *North American Discovery*, Harper & Row, 1971.
2 The account of Verrazzano's voyage is given in his letter of 8 July 1524 to Francis I, quoted, ibid., p. 65.
3 Ibid.
4 Suzanne O. Carlson's finds were published in an article on the internet on 4 March 2002: www.neara.org/carlson/atlantic.html.
5 Professor F.J. Pohl, *Atlantic Crossings before Columbus*, W.W. Norton, New York, 1961, pp. 185ff.

6 Marco Polo, *The Travels of Marco Polo*, trs. R. Latham, Penguin, Harmondsworth, 1958, p. 237.

7 William S. Penhallow, 'Astronomical Alignments in the Newport Tower', in *Across before Columbus?*, NEARA Publications, Edgecombe, Maine, 1998, pp. 85ff.

8 This is explained more fully in chapter 15.

9 E.R. Snow, *Tales of the Atlantic Coast*, Redman, 1962, p. 19.

10 Ibid., pp. 26ff.

11 David Borden, of Marblehead, Massachusetts, and his friend Fred Chester, who grew up near the Dighton Rock State Park, gave me this information.

12 Borden to author.

13 Borden to author.

14 A full list, together with a photograph, is shown on the website.

Chapter 14: Expedition to the North Pole

1 Manuel Faria de Souza, *Epítome de las Historias Portuguesas*, Madrid, 1638 (my translation of his Medieval Castilian).

2 Rebecca Catz, 'Spain and Portugal and the Navigators', unpublished paper presented 25 September 1990, Washington DC.

3 About 51°40′W.

4 Quoted in Farley Mowat, *The Farfarers: Before the Norse*, Seal Books, Toronto, 1998, p. 176.

5 Pope Nicholas V, quoted ibid., p. 308.

6 Peter Schlederman, *Voices in Stone*, Calgary, Canada, 1996, and Mowat, op. cit. Although my conclusions differ from those drawn by Peter Schlederman and Farley Mowat, I rely heavily on their research, without which this chapter could not have been written.

7 Schlederman, op. cit., p. 127.

8 Canadian Government maps of the Canadian Arctic (Hydrographic and Map Service of Canada, Map X1734); *Eskimo Maps of the Canadian Eastern Arctic* by John Spink and D.W. Moodie (1972); the *Sea Ice Atlas of Arctic Canada*, published by the Ottawa Department of Energy, Mines and Resources, 1982, and the map of Greenland drawn by the Geo Daetisk Institut of Copenhagen, 2000.

9 Ferdinand Columbus, *La Historia della Vita di Cristoforo Columbus*, Milan, 1930, quoting a now lost memorandum by his father, seeking to prove that the Arctic was habitable.

10 Catz, translation of Columbus's note in a copy of Pope Pius II, *History of Remarkable Things that Happened in My Time*, in op. cit.

11   J. Needham, *Science and Civilisation in China*, Cambridge UP, Cambridge, 1954.

Chapter 15: Solving the Riddle

1   Antonio Galvão, *The Discoveries of the World*, Hakluyt Society, 1862, p. 369.
2   The Portuguese historian Castaneda.
3   Eric Axelson (ed.), *Dias and His Successors*, Saayman & Weber, Cape Town, 1988, p. 66.
4   The Jesuit Father Monclaro, 1569, quoted in Louise Levathes, *When China Ruled the Seas*, Simon & Schuster, 1994, p. 198.
5   N. Puccioni, *Giuba e OltreGiuba* ('The River Juba and Beyond'), Florence, 1937, p. 110.
6   Levathes, op. cit., p. 199.
7   H.D. Howse, *Greenwich Time and the Discovery of Longitude*, National Maritime Museum, Greenwich, 1980, p. 2.
8   J. Needham, citing *History of the Yan Dynasty*, in *Science and Civilisation in China*, Vol. 3, Pt 2, sec. 20, Cambridge UP, Cambridge, 1954, p. 398, and La Place calculations, p. 299.
9   Ibid., p. 369.
10   Ibid., p. 392.
11   Those wishing to marvel at the ingenuity of these astonishing devices will find an illustration of the polyvascular type in a Chinese encyclopedia, the *Shi Lin Kuang Chi* of 1478, held by Cambridge University Library, England.
12   Marco Polo, *The Travels of Marco Polo*, trs. R. Latham, Penguin, Harmondsworth, 1958, p. 288.

Chapter 16: Where the Earth Ends

1   Francisco Alcaforado, report of proceedings to Prince Henry the Navigator.
2   Gomes Eannes de Zuzara, *The Chronicle of the Discovery and Conquest of Guinea*, trs. C.R. Beazley, Hakluyt Society, 1896–9.
3   E.D.S. Bradford, *Southward the Caravels*, Hutchinson, 1961, p. 8.
4   Vasco Lobeira, *Amadis de Gaul*, ed. and trs. R. Southey, 1872.
5   Malcolm Letts (ed. and trans.), *Mandeville's Travels*, Hakluyt Society, 1953, p. 116 (Egerton text), p. 321 (Paris text). Mandeville was an English squire with a vivid imagination that allowed him to describe far-off

lands without visiting them.

6   Ibid.

7   Camões, *Os Luciades* ('The Luciads'), Lisbon, 1572.

8   This is a simplified explanation; there are refinements to take into account the earth's tilt and curvature.

9   Quoted in F.M. Rogers, *The Travels of the Infante Dom Pedro of Portugal*, Harvard UP, Cambridge, Mass., 1961.

10 Ibid.

11 I have used the chronology of Oliveira Martins, but the precise details of Dom Pedro's itinerary are disputed by different historians. The confusion arises because many countries used different calendars, and because Dom Pedro made not one but many journeys between 1416 and 1428. It is most probable that he left Portugal again in 1419 to visit the Emperor Sigismund and served the Emperor in the wars against the Ottomans. He then settled in Treviso and visited Venice in the summer of 1421, as soon as another war, between the Emperor and Venice, was over. He then went to Egypt in 1424, returning via England (1426) and Venice again (1428) to Portugal.

12 Antonio Galvão, *The Discoveries of the World*, Hakluyt Society, 1862. See p. 107.

13 For the connection between Niccolò da Conti and 'Bartholomew the Florentine', see F.M. Rogers, op. cit., pp. 42 and 264; Gustavo Uzielli, *La Vita e i Tempi di Paolo dal Pozzo Toscanelli*, Rome, 1894, and W. Sensburg, *Poggio Bracciolini und Niccolò da Conti*, Vienna, 1906. For the connection between Toscanelli and 'Bartholomew the Florentine', see Gustavo Uzielli, *Paolo dal Pozzo Toscanelli: Iniziatore della Scoperta d'America*, Florence, 1892; Sidney Welch, *Europe's Discovery of South Africa*; Arnold J. Pomerans, *The Great Age of Discovery*, New York, 1958, p. 18, and P. Kermann, *Zeigt Mir Adams Testament*. For the connection between Toscanelli and Dom Pedro, see Uzielli, *Toscanelli: Iniziatore*, p. 76. For the connection between 'Bartholomew the Florentine' and Martin Behaim, see F.M. Rogers, *The Quest for Eastern Christians*, University of Minnesota Press, 1962, pp. 42 and 95.

14 For Niccolò da Conti, see: (i) G. Uzielli, *La Vita e i Tempi di Paolo dal Pozzo Toscanelli*, Rome, 1894, pp. 10, 11, 63, 90, 122, 141, 154–75, 189–92, 228, 246, 386, 566–7; (ii) 'The Travels of Niccolò da Conti', partial translation in R.H. Major (ed.), *India in the Fifteenth Century*, Hakluyt Society, 1857; (iii) W. Heyd, *Histoire*, Vol. 1, 1885, pp. 378, 380; (iv) V. Bellemo, *Nicolo da Conti*, 1882, pp. 331–47; C. Desimoni, *Pero Tafur*, 1882, pp. 331–47; (vi) F. Kunstman, *Afrika vor den Entdeckungen der Portugiesen*, Aufrosten der Academie, Munich, 1853.
For 'Bartholomew the Florentine', see: (i) Uzielli, *La Vita e i Tempi*, pp. 63, 165–6; (ii) T. de Mura, *M. Behaim*, Treutel et Wurz, Strasbourg, 1802, pp. 33–5; (iii) p. Amat (ed.), *Studi Bibliografichi in Italia*, Pt 1, Ed.

2, Rome, 1882, p. 123.

For Pope Eugenius IV (Gabriele Condulmaro), see Uzielli, *La Vita e i Tempi*, p. 166: 'Gabriele Condulmaro poteva essere a Venezia nel 1424, ma non era ancora Papa, essendo stato assunto alla tiara soltanto nel 1431.'

For Bartholomew of Florence's journey, see Uzielli, *La Vita e i Tempi*, p. 63: 'Ecco ciò che ne dice maestro Bartolomeo Florentino che tornò dalle Indie nel 1424 e che accompagnò a Venezia il Papa Eugenio IV, e al quale raffontò ciò aveva veduto e osservato in un soggiorno di ventiquattro anni in oriente.'

15 See n. 13.
16 Paolo Toscanelli, letter to Columbus, in H. Vignaud, *Toscanelli and Columbus*, Sands, 1902, pp. 322 and 323.
17 Also known as 'Behaim' and 'Martin of Bohemia'. See note 13.
18 Antonio Pigafetta, *Magellan's Voyage*, trs. R.A. Skelton, New Haven, Conn., 1969, pp. 58ff.
19 See ns 13 and 14.
20 See ns 13 and 14, and p. 107.
21 See n. 13.

Chapter 17: Colonizing the New World

1 Antonio Galvão, *Tratado Dos Diversos e Desayados Caminhos*, Lisbon, 1563, and Antonio Cordeyro, *Historia Insulana*, Lisbon, 1717, quoted in H. Harrisse, *The Discovery of North America*, 1892, p. 51.
2 J.H. Longille, *Christopher Columbus*, Inscribers, Washington DC, 1903, p. 191.
3 Extract from Columbus's notebook, quoted in Bartolomeu las Casas, *Historia de las Indias*, Lisbon, 1552.
4 Galvão, op. cit., p. 370.
5 Those of Andrea Bianco in 1448; Grazioso Benincasa in 1463, 1470 and 1482; Andrea Benincasa in 1476, and Albino Canepa in 1480 and 1489.
6 Cf. Armando Cortesão, *The Nautical Chart of 1424*, Coimbra, 1954, p. 106.
7 Carol Urness, *Portolan Charts*, James Ford Bell Library, University of Minnesota, 1999.
8 Published by the Lisbon Academy of Sciences.
9 For coffee in Puerto Rico before European voyages, see D. Maclellan, 'Coffee Varieties in Puerto Rico', *Puerto Rico Agriculture Station Bulletin No. 30*, Mayaguez, Puerto Rico, 1924; P.C. Stanley, *The Rubiaceae of Central America*, Chicago, 1930 (Field Museum of Natural History, Botanical Series Vol. 7, no. 1); E.C. Hill, *Coffee Planting*, Higginbotham, Madias, 1877, pp. 1–3 and 17–19; E.R. Thurber, *Coffee from Plantation to*

Cup, American Grocer Publishing Association, New York, 1881, intro. and pp. 4–5.

10   Produce photographed at Mayaguez Agricultural Station.

11   Albino Canepa: the domain of *saluagio viúadi (nom vulgar des alguns brasilieros)*, the common name for people coming from Brazil, the Caribs.

12   Using the average flows described in the Admiralty's *Ocean Passages of the World* and the relevant Admiralty pilots.

13   To date I have only studied the catalogue of Prince Youssuf Kamal to see how many corrections or additions were made to Antilia. This discloses fourteen before Columbus set sail: by the Beccarios (1435 and 1436), Andrea Bianco (1436 and 1448), Parreto (1455), the Benincasas (1463, 1470, 1476 and 1482), Toscanelli (1474), the Canepas (1480 and 1489), Jaime Bertram (1482) and Christofal Soligo (1489).

14   Prince Youssuf Kamal, *Monumenta Cartographica Africae et Aegypti*, 16 vols, Cairo, 1926–51. This catalogue lists an enormously valuable collection of surviving charts and maps showing European and Chinese exploration of West Africa.

15   Quoted in E.D.S. Bradford, *Southward the Caravels*, Hutchinson, 1961, p. 107.

Chapter 18: On the Shoulders of Giants

1   João de Barros, letter to the future King Manuel of Portugal, quoted in Eric Axelson, *Dias and His Successors*, Cape Town, 1988, p. 3.

2   K.G. Jayne, *Vasco da Gama and His Successors 1460–1580*, Methuen, 1970, p. 36.

3   João de Barros, letter to the King of Portugal, 1 May 1500, quoted in Jaime Batalha Reis, *Estudios Géográficos y Históricos*, Ministry of Colonial Affairs, Lisbon, 1941, p. 286.

4   S.E. Morison, *Portuguese Voyages to America in the Fifteenth Century*, Harvard UP, Cambridge, Mass., 1940, p. 131.

5   See chs 5 and 6, where these matters are considered in detail.

6   As above, and ch. 8.

7   Sebastian Alvarez, the King of Castile's factor, quoted in Cdr A.W. Miller, RN, *The Straits of Magellan*, Griffin, Portsmouth, 1884, p. 7.

8   *The Journal of Columbus*, trs. Cecil Jane, revised and annotated by L.A. Vigneras, Anthony Blond and Orion Press, 1960, pp. 12, 43 and 62.

9   H. Vignaud, *Toscanelli and Columbus*, Sands, 1902, p. 323.

10   Toscanelli, letter to the King of Spain, 1474, quoted in J.H. Parry, *The Discovery of South America*, Elek, 1979, p. 48.

11   Note VII on the Piri Reis map, translated by G.C. McIntosh in *The Piri Reis Map of 1513*, University of Georgia Press, Athens, Georgia, 2000, p. 46.

NOTES

12 Arthur Davies, 'Behain, Marcellus and Columbus', *Geographical Journal*, Vol. 143, p. 454.

13 A.O. Vietor, 'A Pre-Columbian Map of the World circa 1489', *Imago Mundi* xvii, 1963.

14 Davies, op. cit., p. 458.

15 Davies, op. cit.

16 Lord Palliser, Captain Cook's commander.

17 K.G. McIntyre, *Early European Exploration of Australia*, unpublished paper, p. 12.

Epilogue: The Chinese Legacy

1 Barbara Pickersgill, 'Origin and Evolution of Cultivated Plants in the New World', *Nature* 268 (18), pp. 591–4.

2 R.A. Whitehead, *Evolution of Crop Plants*, Longman, 1996, pp. 221–5.

3 F. Braudel, *A History of Civilisations*, trs. R. Mayne, Penguin, 1994, pp. 158–9.

4 Judith A. Carney, Professor of Geography at the University of California, Los Angeles, has written a fascinating book, *Black Rice: The African Origins of Rice Cultivation in the Americas* (Harvard UP, Cambridge, Mass., 2001), which tells the story of the true origins of rice in the Americas and argues that the standard belief that Europeans introduced rice to West Africa and then brought the knowledge of its cultivation to the Americas is a fundamental fallacy.

5 Roderich Ptak, 'China and Calicut in the Early Ming Period: Envoys and Tribute Emissaries', in *Journal of the Royal Asiatic Society*, 1989, St 447, and private letters between Professor Ptak and the author.

6 Cochin tablet, 'Taizong Shi Lu', ch. 183, quoted in Louise Levathes, *When China Ruled the Seas*, Oxford UP, Oxford, 1996, p. 145.

7 Gaspar Correa, *The Three Voyages of Vasco da Gama*, trs. H.E.J. Stanley from *Lendas da India*, 1869.

Postscript

1 See Chapter 9.

2 Leon Poutrin, 'L'origine Chinois de Anciennes Civilisations de Mexico et du Peru', in *Journal de la Société des Américanistes de Paris*, 1913.

3 Francisco A. Loayza, *Chins Ilegaron antes que Colon: Tesis arqueológica, transcendental, sustenada por 150 de los más famosos autores, antiguos y modernos*, Lima, Peru, 1948, pp. 44–45.

4 *Journal de la Société des Américanistes de Paris* 10 (1913), p. 303.

5 Grant Keddie, 'Contributions to Human History', *Royal British*

Columbian Museum Publication, No. 3, 19 March 1990, Victoria, B.C., Canada.

6 Letter from Professor Hummel (an expert on medieval Chinese art), 29 August 1927, quoted in Keddie, op. cit.

7 Professor Hummel, op. cit.

8 Hugo Grotius, *On the Law of War and Peace*, London, 1884, p. 18.

9 Lee Eldridge Huddleston, *Origins of American Indians*, University of Texas Press, Austin, 1967, p. 27.

10 Pedro de Castaneda, *The Journey of Coronado, 1540–42*, trs. George Parker Winship, Dover Publications, New York, 1933.

11 de Castaneda, op. cit.

12 M. De Guignes, *Memoires*, Paris, 1761, p. 31.

13 Jose de Acosta, *Historia natural y moral de las Indias*, Seville, 1590, p. 140.

14 João Barbosa Rodrigues, *Estudo da origen Asiatica da civilizção Amazónica*, Manaus, Brazil, 1889.

15 'Nouvelles Découvertes sur les Société Complexes d'Amazonie,' *Le Monde*, Paris, 7 September 2002.

16 At the semiannual meeting of the American Antiquarian Society Proceedings, 28 April 1886, F.W. Putnam exhibited specimens of jade from old and new worlds and appended a letter from the chemical laboratory of Harvard University, stating that the three Central American specimens of jade it had tested were 'unquestionably Chinese jade'.

17 Gaspar de Carvajal, *The Discovery of the Amazon*, 1542.

18 In about 16° 01'S, 52° 20'N.

19 Harold T. Wilkins, *Secret Cities of Old South America*, New York, 1952.

20 *Blackmore's Magazine*, January 1933, quoted in Colonel Percy Fawcett, *Lost Trails, Lost Cities*, New York, 1953.

21 See Frank Joseph, *The Lost Pyramids of Rock Lake: Wisconsin's Sunken Civilization*, Galde Press, Lakeville, Minn., 1992.

22 John Shulak of Lake Mill, quoted in Janesville, Wis. *Gazette*, 7 June 1989.

23 Newsletters of the Louisiana Mounds Society, January–March 1990.

24 Laurence I. Lambe, quoted in T. L. Tanton in *Geological Survey of Canada Memoir* 167, Ottawa, 1931.

INDEX

HUMAN INSTINCT
How our primeval impulses shape our modern lives
By Robert Winston

From caveman to modern man. . .

What drives a happily married man to fantasize about pretty, slim,
young women seen on a tube train? Why does a seriously injured
mountaineer battle against impossible weather conditions to spend
three days crawling down to the safety of base camp? How is it that
thousands of people spend their week entirely focused on whether
their team will win their next crucial match? What stimulates that
urge to press the pedal as hard as possible at traffic lights to make the
fastest getaway? And how is it that so many people still hold religious
views when the notion of an all-powerful being is irrational? All of
these impulses are driven by our human instincts – sexual drive,
survival, competition, aggression and our search for knowledge.

Few people have a problem with the idea that humans are descended
from the apes. But while people believe that our general shape and
structure are derived from other creatures, few consider, let alone accept,
the psychological implications. Man not only looks, moves and breathes
like an ape, he also thinks like one. It is back in our primeval past that
we find the first clues to the understanding of our human instincts.

But how well do instincts equip us for the twenty-first century? Do
they help or hinder us as we deal with large anonymous cities and the
fracturing of communal life, low-level stress and the battle of the
sexes? In this erudite and fascinating book, Robert Winston takes us
on a journey deep into the human mind in search of the answers to
these questions and many more. Along the way he takes a very
personal look at the relationship between science and religion and
explores those instincts that make us human.

'Wide-ranging and thoroughly entertaining'
New Scientist

A Bantam Paperback

0 553 81492 3

THE DRAGON SYNDICATES
by Martin Booth

'The most wide-ranging and spectacular study yet . . . explosive stuff'
Literary Review

According to UN sources, the Triads pose the greatest potential
criminal threat the world has ever known.

Over the last three centuries, wherever the Chinese have emigrated,
they have taken their outlawed secret brotherhoods. Bound by archaic
oaths, the Triads demand absolute loyalty, exacting brutal retribution
from transgressors and opponents alike. Few have ever infiltrated
their ranks; fewer still have survived to tell the tale.

Now internationally recognised Oriental expert and bestselling author
Martin Booth tells the full, incredible story of the Triads – from their
beginnings over two thousand years ago to the unrivalled criminal
empire they operate today. Here he explains their rituals and
mythologies, identifies the key figures and, perhaps most disturbingly
of all, reveals how the Triads' interests have extended beyond the
more 'traditional' realms of extortion, narcotics, prostitution and
money laundering to include hi-tech computer crime, arms dealing,
blackmail and politics. Today, their insidious influence transcends
national and international boundaries to encompass the globe.

A Bantam Paperback

0 553 50590 4

FATAL PASSAGE
by Ken McGoogan

The true story of the remarkable John Rae – Arctic traveller and
Hudson's Bay Company doctor – *Fatal Passage* is a tale of imperial
ambition and high adventure. Rae solved the two great Arctic
mysteries: the fate of the doomed Franklin expedition and the
location of the last navigable link in the Northwest Passage.

But Rae was to be denied the recognition he so richly deserved. On
returning to London, he faced a campaign of denial and vilification
led by two of the most powerful people in Victorian England: Lady
Jane Franklin, the widow of the lost Sir John, and Charles Dickens,
the most influential writer of the age. A remarkable story of courage
and determination, *Fatal Passage* is Ken McGoogan's passionate
redemption of Rae's rightful place in history. In this richly
documented and illustrated work, McGoogan captures the essence of
one man's indomitable spirit.

'In Ken McGoogan's artful telling, John Rae emerges from the
shadows to take his place among the most intriguing of the 19th
century Arctic explorers. This is delightful reading'
Andrea Barrett, author of *The Voyage of the Narwhal*

'An overdue book that makes an important contribution to Arctic
exploration history and yet remains compulsively readable for the
non-specialist'
Quill & Quire

A Bantam Paperback

0 553 81493 1

THE LAST MISSION
The Secret History of the Second World War's Final Battle
By Jim Smith and Malcolm McConnell

14 August 1945. As Japan's Emperor Hirohito recorded his message
of surrender, rebel troops commanded by elite officers from the War
Ministry burst into the imperial palace. Their intention was to stage a
coup, destroy the recording and issue forged orders for Japan to
continue the war. Had they succeeded there would have been massive
kamikaze attacks on allied forces, possibly provoking America to drop
a third atomic bomb. . .

But on that fateful night, in the skies approaching Tokyo, a stream of
B-29B 'Superfortress' bombers were heading towards Japan's last
functioning oil refinery. Fearing that they could be carrying another
atom bomb, Japanese air defences ordered a total blackout of the city
and the imperial palace. In the hours of chaos that followed, the rebels
were foiled and soldiers loyal to the emperor wrested back control. At
midday on 15 August 1945, the imperial message of surrender was
broadcast. The war was finally over.

The result of more than twenty years research by Jim Smith, who
took part in that final air raid, *The Last Mission* is a gripping work of
speculative investigation into one of the least known yet profoundly
significant episodes of the Second World War.

'Skillfully weaving personal and archival history, *The Last Mission*
gives us a haunting glimpse of just how close we came to the brink of
waging a final desperate war on Japanese soil'
Hampton Sides, author of *Ghost Soldiers*

'Fascinating . . . a breathtaking blend of memoir, investigative
research and imagination'
Iris Chang, author of *The Rape of Nanking*

A Bantam Paperback

0 553 81610 1

A SELECTED LIST OF NON-FICTION TITLES
AVAILABLE FROM CORGI, BANTAM AND BLACK SWAN

'Exhaustively researched . . . an intriguing and highly
persuasive thesis, told with passion and energy'
Evening Standard

On 8 March 1421, the largest fleet the world had ever seen set sail
from China. The ships, some nearly five hundred feet long, were
under the command of Emperor Zhu Di's loyal eunuch admirals.
Their orders were 'to proceed all the way to the end of the earth'.

The voyage would last for two years and by the time the fleet
returned, China was beginning its long, self-imposed isolation from
the world it had so recently embraced. And so the great ships were
left to rot, and the records of their journey destroyed. And with them,
the knowledge that the Chinese had circumnavigated the globe a
century before Magellan, reached America seventy years before
Columbus, and Australia three hundred and fifty years before Cook.

The result of fifteen years research, *1421* is Gavin Menzies'
enthralling account of this remarkable journey, of his discoveries
and the persuasive evidence to support them: ancient maps,
precise navigational knowledge, astronomy, surviving accounts
of Chinese explorers and later European navigators as well
as the traces the fleet left behind.

Revised and updated with new material – including evidence
of an entire Chinese fleet wrecked on New Zealand's
South Island – for this paperback edition, *1421* is a brilliant,
epoch-making work of historical detection that radically
alters our understanding of world exploration and
rewrites history itself.

'Menzies has come up with something entirely new…
it is a startling claim'
Guardian

ISBN 0-553-81522-9

UK £8.99
CAN $25.00

9 780553 815221

PENGUIN BOOKS

DARWIN

'Desmond and Moore have pr_____ _____ _e *force* which, like a good novel, invites the rea____ _____ from one chapter to the next. Pick it up and _____ ___ _, by the racy writing, the memorable turns o_ ____ ____ _storical insights and the sheer bravado of their ___ ___ William Bynum in the *New Scientist*

'Their app____ ___ _liantly successful. *Darwin* is a rich, entertaining an_ ___ _ays convincing portrait' – Stephen Young in the *Guardian*

'A sprawling tome which combines scholarship with compulsive readability and goes right to the heart of the mystery of why Darwin hesitated so long before publishing his theory of evolution' – John Naughton in the *Observer*

'The author of *The Origin of Species* deserves a major biography and *Darwin* fully matches the man' – David Owen in *The Sunday Times*

'Certainly the most ambitious biography of Darwin yet seen ... The conflict between his intellectual daring and his need to live a life of intense respectability is the strange and terrible thing about Darwin, and it is rightly at the centre of this book' – Fiona McCarthy in *The Times*

'An exhilarating biography and a social history of much of the nineteenth century. A full, fat work setting one of our indisputable men of genius in the fullest context' – Melvyn Bragg in *The Sunday Times*

ABOUT THE AUTHORS

Adrian Desmond's acclaimed study of the pre-Darwinian generation, *The Politics of Evolution*, was published in 1989. Described as 'intellectual dynamite, and certainly one of the most important books in the history of science published during the past decade' (*The Times Literary Supplement*), it received the Pfizer Award from the American History of Science Society in 1991. His other books are the international bestseller *The Hot-Blooded Dinosaurs*, *The Ape's Reflexion* and *Archetypes and Ancestors*. He studied at London University and at Harvard, has higher degrees in palaeontology and history of science and a Ph.D. for his work on Victorian evolution. He is an honorary research fellow in the Biology Department at University College London.

James Moore has made a twenty-year study of Darwin's life, and his *Post-Darwinian Controversies* detailed Protestant responses to evolution. He has edited a source book, *Religion in Victorian Britain*, and a series of essays, *History, Humanity and Evolution*. He teaches the history of science at the Open University and has degrees in science, divinity and history and a Ph.D. from Manchester University. In 1992–3 he is Visiting Associate Professor in the history of science at Harvard University.

DARWIN

ADRIAN DESMOND
AND
JAMES MOORE

PENGUIN BOOKS

PENGUIN BOOKS

Published by the Penguin Group
Penguin Books Ltd, 27 Wrights Lane, London W8 5TZ, England
Penguin Books USA Inc., 375 Hudson Street, New York, New York 10014, USA
Penguin Books Australia Ltd, Ringwood, Victoria, Australia
Penguin Books Canada Ltd, 10 Alcorn Avenue, Toronto, Ontario, Canada M4V 3B2
Penguin Books (NZ) Ltd, 182–190 Wairau Road, Auckland 10, New Zealand

Penguin Books Ltd, Registered Offices: Harmondsworth, Middlesex, England

First published by Michael Joseph 1991
Published in Penguin Books 1992
1 3 5 7 9 10 8 6 4 2

Contents

Contents

Illustrations

Acknowledgements

WE ARE ESPECIALLY grateful to friends and colleagues who interrupted busy lives to help us meet our deadlines: to Fred Burkhardt, Nellie Flexner, Elisabeth Leedham-Green, David Kohn, Mike Petty, Jim and Anne Secord, and Steven Shapin for reading draft chapters; to Alison Winter for listening to extracts; to John Thackray, Jim Secord, and David Stanbury for providing information; to Fiona Erskine, Marsha Richmond, and Godfrey Waller for supplying manuscript material (and the late Dov Ospovat for a transcription of Darwin's notes on his 1856 meeting with Huxley, Hooker, and Wollaston); to Richard Milner for sharing his unpublished research on Darwin and Wallace; to Stephen Pocock, Anne Secord, and the Darwin letters project team at Cambridge University Library for supplying advance proofs of volumes of the Darwin correspondence; to Peter Gautrey and Simon Schaffer for assisting with transcriptions and a translation; to Jane Clark, Tony Coulson, Kirsteen Mitcalfe, Solene Morris, and Mike Petty for supplying illustrations; and to the Revd Geoffrey Evans for a tour of Shrewsbury and the High Street Unitarian Church.

Personal debts can never be adequately acknowledged. John and Ellen Greene gave unstinting support in more ways than one; their detailed commentary on the manuscript was a labour of love. Ralph Colp, Jr, was a constant inspiration and resource for his insight into the details of Darwin's private life; we thank him heartily for sharing Darwin's health diary, reading our chapters, and discussing them on a transatlantic phone. Nick Furbank and Dick Aulie also perused our pages and gave expert advice.

Gordon Moore and Robert Tollemache kept half the project going when all else seemed to fail. Similar timely help came from Simon

Acknowledgements

Schaffer and Anita Herle, Alison Winter, Iwan Morus, and Nigel Leask. Gill Knott and Marcus offered escapes to Ilkley and other regions, while Chris and Barrie Vincent at the White Hart kept a snuggery nearer home. Jessica Drader and Harry Flexner Desmond will now see more of their dads. We thank them most of all, for their patience and love.

We would like to thank George Pember Darwin who graciously consented to our publishing extracts of Darwin's letters and manuscripts. We are indebted to the Syndics of Cambridge University Library for allowing us to quote from unpublished material held in the Darwin Archive and in other collections. And we express our gratitude to the Syndics of Cambridge University Press, whose magnificent *Correspondence of Charles Darwin* provides such a rich source of material.

For allowing us to study, and in instances quote from, manuscript material, we also wish to thank the following institutions and individuals: American Philosophical Society Library; Avon County library, Bath Central library for the Leonard Jenyns correspondence; British Museum (Natural History) for the Richard Owen papers; British Library, Department of Manuscripts; Charles Darwin Museum, Down House, by courtesy of the Royal College of Surgeons of England; Christ's College Library, Cambridge, for the Darwin-Fox letters; County of Hereford and Worcester Record Office; Dr Williams's Library, London; Edinburgh University Library; Ernst-Haeckel Haus, Friedrich-Schiller-Universität, Jena; General Register Office, London; Harvard University Library for the University Archives; Imperial College of Science and Technology, London, for the Huxley Papers, Ramsay Papers, and College Archives; R. G. Jenyns, Bottisham Hall, Bottisham, Cambridgeshire, for the Leonard Jenyns papers; Keele University Library for the Wedgwood-Mosley Collection by courtesy of the Wedgwood Museum Trustees, Barlaston, Stoke-on-Trent, Staffordshire; Kent County Archives Office for the Downe parish papers; Public Record Office, Kew and Quality Court, London; Royal Botanic Gardens, Kew; Royal Institution, London, for the Tyndall Papers; University College London Library for the Brougham Papers and Society for the Diffusion of Useful Knowledge correspondence; University of British Columbia Library, Vancouver; Wellcome Institute for the History of Medicine Library, London; and the Zoological Society of London Library.

What a book a Devil's Chaplain might write on the clumsy, wasteful, blundering low & horridly cruel works of nature!

Charles Darwin in 1856, about to start the *Origin of Species*

A Devil's Chaplain?

It is 1839. England is tumbling towards anarchy, with countrywide unrest and riots. The gutter presses are fizzing, fire-bombs flying. The shout on the streets is for revolution. Red evolutionists – visionaries who see life marching inexorably upward, powered from below – denounce the props of an old static society: priestly privilege, wage exploitation, and the workhouses. A million socialists are castigating marriage, capitalism, and the fat, corrupt Established Church. Radical Christians join them, hymn-singing Dissenters who condemn the 'fornicating' Church as a 'harlot,' in bed with the State.

Even science must be purged: for the gutter atheists, material atoms are all that exist, and like the 'social atoms' – people – they are self-organizing. Spirits and souls are a delusion, part of the gentry's cruel deceit to subjugate working people. The science of life – biology – lies ruined, prostituted, turned into a Creationist citadel by the clergy. Britain now stands teetering on the brink of collapse – or so it seems to the gentry, who close ranks to protect their privileges.

At this moment, how could an ambitious thirty-year-old gentleman open a secret notebook and, with a devil-may-care sweep, suggest that headless hermaphrodite molluscs were the ancestors of mankind? A squire's son, moreover, Cambridge-trained and once destined for the cloth. A man whose whole family hated the 'fierce & licentious' radical hooligans.

The gentleman was Charles Darwin: well heeled, imperturbably Whig, a privately financed world traveller who had spent five years aboard HMS *Beagle* as a dining companion to the aristocratic captain. He had a private fortune in prospect and a reputation as an up-and-coming geologist. He also had an enduring wish to escape 'abominable murky' London, to live in a rustic parish like his clerical friends, so vilified by the mob.

Clergymen from molluscs! How had he arrived at such damning beliefs?

And this was not the worst part. He embraced a terrifying materialism. Only months before he had concluded in his covert notebooks that the human mind, morality, and even belief in God were artefacts of the brain: 'love of the deity [is the] effect of organization, oh you Materialist!' he upbraided himself. Working through the implications gave him migraines, left him writhing on his sick bed, fearing persecution. Wasn't it treachery? Didn't it threaten the last scientific safeguards of the old social order? Weren't these incendiary beliefs perfect weapons for the loutish hordes, already at the gates? He peered into the future. The 'whole fabric totters & falls,' he prophesied of the unreformed Creationist cosmos.

Tormented, he finally fled London's 'dirt, noise vice & misery' to lead a clergyman's life in rural Kent. He sought sanctuary, emulating the man most 'respectable and happy,' the country curate. Idyllic and isolated it might have been, living in an old parsonage, but a third of his working life was spent doubled up, trembling, vomiting, and dowsing himself in icy water. He sat on his theory of evolution for twenty years, scarcely mooting his innermost thoughts about 'monkey-men' and apes evolving morality, castigating himself as a 'Devil's Chaplain.' Even in 1859 he had to be prodded into publishing the *Origin of Species*, and then he let it go with barely a hint about human origins.

The full enigma of Darwin's life has never been grasped. Indeed, previous biographies have been curiously bloodless affairs.[1] They have broken little new ground and made no contact with the inflammatory issues and events of his day.

Our *Darwin* sets out to be different – to pose the awkward questions, to probe interests and motivations, to portray the scientific expert as a product of his time; to depict a man grappling with immensities in a society undergoing reform.

When Darwin did come out of his closet and bare his soul to a friend, he used a telling expression. He said it was 'like confessing a murder.' Nothing captures better the idea of evolution as a social crime in early Victorian Britain. Anglicans damned it as false, foul, French, atheistic, materialistic, and immoral. It was dangerous knowledge, and tempting. Darwin had known this for years, hence his ruminations were confined to secret notebooks. He cut himself off, ducked parties and declined engagements; he even installed a mirror outside his study window to spy on visitors as they came up his drive. Day after day, week after week, his stomach plagued him, and for years after reaching his rural retreat he refused to sleep anywhere else, unless it was a safe house, a close relative's home. This was a worried man.

How then did such a wealthy Whig gentleman break the impasse and make evolution acceptable? How did he present it as underpinning middle-class values? Did he ever resolve the antitheses? – failed ordinand and pillar of the parish, reformer of nature and friend of the unreformed clergy, upright citizen who wrote of 'monkey-men.' Understand Darwin's scientific status, his social obligations, his Dissenting heritage, the political context, and the contradictions start to resolve themselves.

In building this new picture of Darwin, we have exploited a spate of new material. Darwin was a hoarder; he destroyed precious little. Notebooks, old manuscripts, torn-out pages, annotated offprints, and letters were all salted away. Gradually these sources have been tapped by a generation of transcribers.[2] But only in the last few years has the trickle of published material turned into a torrent.

Since 1985 alone a staggering amount has come out, capped by the meticulously edited *Correspondence of Charles Darwin* (which has reached volume seven by 1991). The Victorian *Life and Letters*, censored, shorn, and stitched, is covered in dusty cobwebs. It served a purpose a century ago in securing Darwin's immortality. But today's needs are different. We want to know about his personality, his business acumen, his domestic life, and his science. We want to understand how his theories and strategies were embedded in a reforming Whig society.

A second injection for the so-called 'Darwin Industry' came with the definitive 750-page transcription of *Charles Darwin's Notebooks* in 1987. Painstaking research by an international team, hacking through the intractable jungle of Darwin's illegible and cryptic script, has revealed unimaginable treasures. We now know more about the piecemeal, day-by-day development of Darwin's evolutionary views than about any other scientific theory in history. But then we need to; no other has been so shattering.

We also have a *Calendar* (1985) of the fourteen thousand known letters to and from him. At a stroke the biographer is faced by a fivefold increase in correspondence. The harvest is enormously rich. It gives insights into how he sealed and severed friendships, cajoled and equivocated, courted champions, dispensed patronage, and winkled out scientific tidbits. It opens up a new world, showing us his social circle – his neighbours, house-guests, extended family, and colleagues.[3]

In the last few years, too, historians have revolutionized our understanding of Darwin's dogged, jogging path to the theory of natural selection – the central plank of biology today. The path was riddled with dead-ends and littered with half truths. We see his persistence, like a terrier shaking a rat, teasing at the evolutionary mechanism from every side, trying for any new angle. We can trace the political roots of his key ideas, following his reading on population, the poor laws, and charity.[4] But we cannot stop at mere reading of books. We have to see him as part of an active Whig circle, in an age when the Whig government was building the workhouses and the poor were burning them down. Appreciate Darwin's attitude to the workhouse culture, and his science acquires a deeper political meaning.

So far this wider context has been largely ignored. The textual analysts and historians of disembodied ideas – of intellectual ghosts – have carried the day. Social historians have consistently failed to follow up, to re-locate Darwin in his age.[5] As a result we have lost sight of the larger world that made Darwin's evolution possible.

Any new biography must take account of the recent upheaval in the history of science, and its new emphasis on the cultural conditioning of knowledge. Gone is the day when Darwin could be depicted as a seer, a genius out of time. Ours is a defiantly social portrait. We make contact with the public events and institutions of Victorian England, with reform bills, poor law riots, learned societies, industrial innovation, radical medicine, Church debates – and, not least, with the new views of creation among reforming naturalists, and the old practices of museum keepers. We see Darwin on the streets, sitting in with apes at the zoo, picking up pigeon lore in gin palaces, conniving with his heterodox dining circle, living a squire's life, investing in factories, worrying about religion and confronting death. Viewed in this light, his fears and foibles become intelligible and his evolutionary achievements make sense.[6]

Irony and ambiguity shrouded Darwin as no other eminent Victorian. He hunted with the clergy and ran with the radical hounds; he was a paternalist full of *noblesse oblige*, sensitive, mollycoddled, cut off from wage-labour and competition, who unleashed a bloody struggle for existence; a hard-core scientist addicted to quackery, who strapped 'electric chains' to his stomach and settled for weeks at fashionable hydropathic spas; a man of clockwork routine, his days alike as 'two peas,' who infused natural history with contingency and chance.

What of Darwin's own latter-day prejudices? He thought blacks inferior but was sickened by slavery; he subordinated women but was totally dependent on his redoubtable wife. How did his views on sex, race, and empire reflect the late-Victorian ethos? Was he still remaking the world in the image of his times in the *Descent of Man* (1871)? Did he see society, like nature, progress by culling its unfit members? 'Social Darwinism' is often taken to be something extraneous, an ugly concretion added to the pure Darwinian corpus after the event, tarnishing Darwin's image. But his notebooks make plain that competition, free trade, imperialism, racial extermination, and sexual inequality were written into the equation from the start – 'Darwinism' was always intended to explain human society.

And how did grave Victorians observe the observer? – this man who, Ruskin rudely noted, felt 'a deep and tender interest about the brightly coloured hinder half of certain monkeys.' The butt of jokes, yes. The godsend to cartoonists, of course. Yet his science became a pillar of late-Victorian liberalism. How else to explain the earl and two dukes, representing Gladstone's government, acting as pallbearers in his Westminster Abbey funeral? How, indeed, to explain the body ending up there at all? Or *The Times*'s comment that 'the Abbey needed it more than it needed the Abbey'?

Beetle-browed, scowling physiognomy: everyone knows the image – it is one of the totems of the twentieth century. To some he was the founder of a new biology, to one outraged Welshman just 'an old Ape with a hairy face.' But for everyone his gentleness was overwhelming. Leslie Stephen felt that there was 'something almost pathetic in his simplicity and friendliness.'[7] Darwin is arguably the best known scientist in history. More than any modern thinker – even Freud or Marx – this affable old-world naturalist from the minor Shropshire gentry has transformed the way we see ourselves on the planet.

The time is ripe for a richer portrait of a troubled man at a turning point of history.

1809–1831

1

Catching a Falling Christian

CHARLES DARWIN'S grandfather Erasmus had a lacerating wit and a loathing of meddling gods. Scurrility and whimsy wrapped themselves up in his rotund frame, and no one was spared. He could roast a goose-brained king, or kick the crutch from a friend's faith. 'A featherbed to catch a falling Christian' he called the Unitarian beliefs of Charles's other grandfather, the pottery patriarch Josiah Wedgwood.[1]

Josiah had dropped so much supernatural paraphernalia that he had lost sight of the Christian heights. Fall any further and he would land with an atheistic bump. Josiah's was Christianity stripped naked: the Trinity had been discarded, along with Jesus's divinity.

The featherbed had broken Josiah's fall; but there was no such soft landing for Erasmus. 'Horrid wretches' like him had already crashed resoundingly to earth.[2] What need of Christianity when men can sup 'the milk of science'? Did not the priestess of Nature explain all things? – even Creation itself?

> Nurs'd by warm sun-beams in primeval caves
> Organic Life began beneath the waves . . .
> Hence without parent by spontaneous birth
> Rise the first specks of animated earth.[3]

There spoke Erasmus, a hard-headed freethinker, like so many in the sun-lit years of the Enlightenment. He adored in the Temple of Nature; for him Reason was divine, and Progress its prophet. The two grandfathers agreed on much, but on religion they parted company, bequeathing a mixture of freethought and radical Christianity to their grandchildren.

*

5

Charles Darwin mused on this twin inheritance in 1879 as he put the finishing touches to a sketch of old Erasmus's life. He had just turned seventy himself and felt as though he were already communing 'with the dead.' It was time to take stock of his life. How much of Erasmus's make-up had he inherited, and how much was he passing on? There was Josiah's blood in him too, and his wife Emma was a Wedgwood. So what future for their offspring if traits run in families?⁴ Which grandfather would they take after?

Dr Erasmus Darwin was a giant, a brilliant *bon viveur* whose shadow stretched across the generations. Blasted by smallpox, crippled and corpulent, he was a renowned physician with a fatal attraction for women. He sired a dozen children by a pair of wives and two more by a governess. He prescribed sex for hypochondria and composed lush erotic verse. With his close friend Josiah Wedgwood, he helped to foment England's industrial revolution in the eighteenth century. He rhapsodized about England's great inventors – Matthew Boulton and James Watt – dreamt up mechanical marvels of his own, and maintained a deep commitment to evolution.⁵

Charles caught glimpses of himself here. Erasmus admitted the natural ascent of life and the kinship of all creatures; he 'abhorred slavery,' 'admired philanthropy,' and 'insisted on humanity to the lower animals.' He believed in a distant Deity – a 'Potent-power, all-great, all-good' - and prayed, 'Teach me, Creation, teach me how / T'adore the vast Unknown.' Yet 'he was unorthodox,' and for this he was 'grossly calumniated.' No sooner had he died in 1802 than he was attacked for doubting the Bible. A story was even started that he had called for Jesus on his deathbed. 'Such was the state of Christian feeling in this country at the beginning of the present century,' Charles wryly closed; 'we may at least hope that nothing of the kind now prevails.'

He sent the biography in proof to his daughter Henrietta. She had long hovered at his elbow, an able critic, fussy about the family reputation – the in-house editor to touch up his lack-lustre prose. She was her mother's watchdog, eight years married but still wedded to Emma's welfare. They saw eye-to-eye on most things, and Henrietta had a nose for trouble. She sniffed through the proofs. Unitarianism a 'featherbed' – old Josiah and her mother 'falling Christians'! Was this how Emma was to be portrayed for her Wedgwood faith? And as for advertising Erasmus's debauchery, let alone his religious infidelity! It was permissible a hundred years ago, perhaps, but unbecoming a Darwin now. Alluding to his foibles was sheer folly; it could cost the family dear. The proofs needed pruning, not polishing.

Wielding a bright red pencil, Henrietta pitched in. The sex was cut back. Too much talk of illegitimacy, too much 'wine, women, [and] warmth.' A quotation from Erasmus with 'damned' in it was lopped, and his lines about the 'vast Unknown' sounded awfully agnostic. The paragraph on his unorthodoxy was plucked altogether. It reflected ill on Christianity and was too obviously written by the 'calumniated' author of the *Origin of Species*. The deathbed story had to go. Henrietta slashed scarlet down the page, marking the spots where her father should cut and chop.

She returned the proofs, and her father resigned himself to the changes. The biography now contained more than family history; it held hard evidence of heredity. The assertions and deletions spoke for the two sides of the family. Henrietta was like her mother and old Josiah after all. A hundred years of Unitarian piety had marked the Wedgwood mind.[6] The censor had her way. The world could wait another century to read about the family forces that had shaped Charles's destiny.

These forces were generated in the age of iron and steam. The blasts of Coalbrookdale and the wheeze and snort of Boulton engines echoed across the English Midlands in the mid-eighteenth century. New money was to be made, new families were on the rise. These calliper-carrying industrialists had faith in a progressive nature, a democracy of intellect, and technological salvation. They were marginal men, but on the make; *arrivistes*-merchants, standing outside the old, complacent squirearchy.

Typical was Charles's maternal grandfather, Josiah Wedgwood, who built his pottery business at Burslem, near Stoke-on-Trent. From the 1760s, he was one of the technocrats inside Birmingham's élite industrial circle, the 'Lunar Society' – so called because its members, the 'Lunaticks,' met on moonlit nights, when they could see to stumble home afterwards. Birmingham was the centre of the new industrial culture. The Lunar mechanics introduced new technology, a chemical industry, and a factory mentality. Boulton and Watt were turning out steam engines, and employing a thousand men at their Soho works in Birmingham. Here they sold 'what all the world desires to have – POWER.' Other Lunar craftsmen specialized in clocks and precision instruments. Wedgwood perfected factory organization on the Soho model. In his ceramics sheds he regimented the workforce and created a division of labour, making 'such *machines* of the Men as cannot err.' His factory's name, 'Etruria' (after the Etruscan painting techniques on his ceramics), was coined

7

by his 'favorite Asculapius,' the physician to the group, Charles's paternal grandfather Erasmus Darwin.

Erasmus was a poetic, inventive physician, a mechanic himself who tinkered with 'the animal machine.' His lucrative practice was in the town of Lichfield, fifteen miles north of Birmingham. Lichfield's other literary son, Dr Johnson, defended the locals as 'the most sober, decent people in England, the genteelest in proportion to their wealth.' He could not say the same of Erasmus; their mutual loathing was apparent, and the stammering Darwin dodged Dr Johnson's stiletto wit and 'stentor lungs.' Erasmus's diagnostic skills were extraordinary and in demand far outside Lichfield's sober circle. He designed a carriage that could steer at speed without overturning and travelled 10,000 miles a year to minister to the new Midlands élite. He was a polymathic 'Lunatick,' a doctor suffering from an 'Infection of Steam Enginry,' a poet with an eye to industry. He designed a horizontal windmill for grinding pigments at Wedgwood's works, and even a speaking-machine 'capable of pronouncing the Lord's Prayer, the Creed and Ten Commandments in the Vulgar Tongue,' for which Boulton promised to pay £1000.[7]

Not that these men of 'mechanical Fame' put much store in orthodoxy. Most were self-made Dissenters, outsiders in a world where political and educational opportunities were reserved for members of the Anglican Church. They belonged to a chapel counter-culture, thriving in the growing industrial towns. Erasmus's freethinking apart, their intellectual avant-garde were Unitarians, like Josiah.[8] When Joseph Priestley came to Birmingham in 1780 to serve as minister of the New Meeting House, the Lunar Society acquired a powerful ally in the leading Unitarian philosopher, chemist, and theologian of the day.

Priestley studied airs and gases, and arguably discovered oxygen (and ammonia, carbon monoxide, sulphur dioxide . . . the list goes on). His researches intrigued Erasmus, who soon had people breathing '6 gallons of pure oxygene a day' from balloon-like bladders to cure their lung diseases. Wedgwood thought Priestley a genius. Josiah supplied the minister with lab-ware, subsidized his experiments, and followed up with industrial trials. Priestley's works provided clues about clays and colours, which Josiah used to improve the pottery's output. The Wedgwood firm even honoured their preacher by casting a medallion with his bust in bas-relief.[9]

Priestley's theology was probably even more influential, for it shaped the outlook of three generations of intermarried Darwins and Wedgwoods. He aimed to restore Christianity to its pristine purity

8

and make it a religion of universal happiness in this life and the next. Anglicans found this dangerous, with God ordaining happiness for everyone impartially, without regard for rank or ritual. It was damnable too. For Priestley immortal souls do not exist any more than immaterial 'spirits' in chemistry. Nor were miracles and mysteries like the Trinity and the Incarnation part of his Christianity. God's benevolence is expressed in a wholly material world, where the laws of nature hold sway and everything has a physical cause. Human flesh is resurrected in the next life, as Jesus's was, according to some unknown physical law.

This was a robust, hopeful faith, reflecting the self-confidence of the new industrial élite. As in some self-correcting engine, pleasure and pain operate almost mechanically on people to improve them. Those who abide by Christian principles will live this life happily. In the next, any remaining defective parts will be repaired, and everyone will be restored to a perfect existence. Wedgwood remained Priestley's disciple and appointed a Unitarian minister to teach in his school at Etruria. Erasmus's young son Robert (Charles's father) was educated here, as were the 'Wedgwoodikins' – as Erasmus called them – Jos Jr and Susannah (Charles's mother).

Not all Unitarians went so far as to deny a soul. On the other hand freethinkers like Erasmus went much further, discarding the Bible and Jesus as well – and claiming that 'no particular providence is necessary to roll this Planet round the Sun.'[10] But all shared an optimistic egalitarianism in the long eighteenth-century summer before the French Revolution of 1789.

Erasmus's wife drank gin and died inebriate, leaving him with five children. A decade's philandering followed, and then, at forty-nine, Erasmus found himself fat, lame, and in love – to which end he dedicated his devastating pen:

> Ah, who unmoved that radiant brow descrys,
> Sweet pouting lips, and blue voluptuous eyes?

This was to a beautiful married patient, herself unconventional and the illegitimate daughter of an earl. When her rich husband died in 1780, the widowed Erasmus married her, moved in, and shifted his operations to her country mansion outside Derby. They pooled their eight offspring, who lived amid the trappings of wealth (Erasmus commanded ten guineas a day – four months' wages for a farm hand). Included among the growing brood were his two bastards and her late husband's one. Such open profligacy was a sign that a fashionable libertinism affected the best families. But then polite society seemed to be cemented by its adulteries and ménages, and Dr Johnson advised sensible wives to turn a blind eye to philandering husbands.[11] This wasn't what Priestley meant by the pleasure-and-pain principle, but sin and sex were peeling apart, and Erasmus prescribed the latter to cure the guilt of the former.

In 1783 his son Robert made room for the first of seven more babies when he left for Edinburgh University. Robert was reluctant to take up medicine at first, and Edinburgh had melancholy associations. His eldest brother, Charles, had died delirious and paralysed as a student there five years earlier, having infected his finger dissecting a child's brain. But after the death, Erasmus's medical hopes had transferred to Robert, and the Doctor had to be obeyed.

Erasmus himself was not above pulling strings. Robert switched to the University of Leiden and received his MD in only two years, for a thesis partly written by Erasmus, or based on his work. Erasmus settled his twenty-year-old son into a practice in the quaint old market town of Shrewsbury. It was an ideal spot, the resort of Shropshire's leading families who came for the 'balls, suppers,' and 'oyster-feasts.' It was only a day's journey from Birmingham and Etruria, yet far enough from the family home to ensure his independence. Erasmus's contacts brought Robert a steady stream of patients, while the Lunaticks inducted him into London's élite scientific club, the Royal Society, in the hope that it would give him a philosophical bent. Robert not only had his father's money; he had his shrewdness and sympathy, and an uncanny ability to win patients' confidence. Business was brisk, and the Darwin name acted as a beacon.[12]

The hysterical aftermath to the French Revolution threatened to dim that beacon. Erasmus was a democrat, who cheered the 'success of the French against a confederacy of kings' – indeed, who thought 'a goose may govern a kingdom' as well as any 'idiot . . . in his royal senses.' In Britain a period of unprecedented repression set in: radical Dissenters were attacked for believing in the '*wrongs* of Providence, and *rights* of Man.' The Lunaticks' republicanism was ridiculed, their egalitarian religion denounced. Erasmus had put out feelers for the post of Poet Laureate, but what chance now? The Lord Chamberlain seemed curiously indisposed to offer a royal reward to this supporter of the American and French Revolutions – this poet of love and machines who spreads 'the happy contagion of Liberty.'

Erasmus was versifying about the new French liberties and finishing his medico-evolutionary book *Zoonomia* when Priestley fell into the 'sacrilegious hands of the savages of Birmingham.' His chapel and house were gutted by a mob crying 'No philosophers – Church and King for ever.' The riots of 1791 spelled the end of the Lunar Society. Priestley was offered asylum at Etruria but eventually fled to America. Darwin's erotic botany was denounced as titillating trash; his 'atheism' lambasted as the sort of demoralizing philosophy which had spawned the Terror. This backlash finally put an end to the fashionable libertinism of Erasmus's day. It ushered in a period of respectability and evangelical rectitude, which was to mark the younger generations of Darwin-Wedgwoods.

Wedgwood was now in bad health. He saw his second son Tom – a keen chemical (and opium) experimenter – suffer a nervous breakdown. With England and France at war in 1793, he withdrew from the business and made out his will. He placed the factory in the hands of his eldest son, Jos II, now married to a squire's daughter, Bessy Allen.[13]

Marriage for the Darwins, like everything else, was managed by old Erasmus. For Robert he picked that Etruscan beauty of the Lunar circle, Josiah's daughter Susannah. She had been in and out of the Darwins' Derby house since childhood, and had given Erasmus music lessons. Clever and capable, she was her father's favourite. Josiah and Erasmus reached an understanding that Robert would marry her when his means permitted. In the event they wed in April 1796, a year after Josiah's death. Robert was now established, and Susannah's £25,000 inheritance was an acceptable addition to the family fortune.[14]

Robert bought land on the edge of Shrewsbury, on a steep 100-foot bank along the Severn, and built a plain but imposing red-brick residence, The Mount. With five bays adorning the two-and-a-half storeys, and ample lower wings, it emphasized the young doctor's stature. He was a man of substance, in every way: tall, six feet two inches, with a steadily increasing girth. Their first child was a girl, Marianne; two more daughters followed, Caroline in 1800 and Susan in 1803, the year after Erasmus's peaceful death. Then came their first son. Susannah delivered him on 29 December 1804, five years to the day after Robert's elder brother, a rich solicitor with a bank of debts, had drowned himself in the River Derwent.[15] They named the baby after him and his late grandfather – Erasmus.

The second generation Wedgwoods were – like the Darwins – aspiring gentry. Jos was Sheriff of Dorset, and dashed around 'like Royalty,' in a velvet-curtained carriage drawn by four white horses. In the war economy the pottery business had slumped; Jos moved back to Staffordshire to take charge of the firm and, unhappy as a manufacturer, sought a second home in the country, a weekend bolt-hole away from the business grind. Robert Darwin loaned him £30,000 to buy a thousand-acre estate near the Staffordshire village of Maer, an hour's ride from Etruria and thirty miles from Shrewsbury. The manor had a large Elizabethan house, Maer Hall, set in extensive gardens (designed by Capability Brown) on a hill overlooking a lake, and surrounded by woods full of game. Here Jos and Bessy came to live in 1807 with their six children. On 2 May 1808, when Bessy was forty-four, their last baby, Emma, was born. Jos's social elevation was reflected in his choice of schools. He sent the two oldest boys to Eton.[16]

Susannah Darwin was long-suffering as the Doctor's wife, amanuensis, and receptionist. He might have been sympathetic to patients, but he had a brusqueness at home that sat incongruously with his 'high squeaky voice.' Even trifles riled him, and sometimes Susannah caught the brunt of his temper. Since her difficult second pregnancy, her 'old life and spirits' had waned, and she aged quickly. 'Everybody seems young but me,' she once sighed to Jos at The Mount.[17]

Another baby was delivered on 12 February 1809, in her forty-fourth year. They called him Charles Robert Darwin, after the medical men in the family – his father Robert and dead uncle Charles – in the hope of a bright career. Respectable gentry themselves now, ensconced in the imposing Mount, they had the baby baptized at the new St Chad's Anglican Church on 17 November. It was becoming for the Doctor, and prudent. The country was still at war with France and a conspiratorial underground suspected; now was no time to wave the family's liberal flag. Old Erasmus had been pilloried by government-inspired propaganda for his pro-French poetry. The name of Darwin was already associated with subversive atheism.[18] Dr Robert was himself a closet freethinker, so it paid to tread carefully in these conservative years.

But Susannah stood quietly by her heritage. She took the children on Sundays to the Unitarian chapel. Set back from the High Street, it stood on the site of Shrewsbury's first meeting house for Dissenters, which had been razed by an Anglican mob a century before. George Case had been invited to preach here by Susannah and the town's Unitarian leaders, and to augment his pay he ran a day school at his house in Claremont Hill.[19]

Charles's education began at home, with his sister Caroline, in her early teens, taking charge. He competed for her affection with

Catherine, fifteen months younger, and Susannah's last child. Charles was boisterous and mischievous, and one of his earliest memories was of trying to break the windows in a room where he had been locked as a punishment. He was an attention-seeker; he wanted praise, and was often made to feel guilty for it. For her part Caroline was inexperienced and at times heavy-handed, and Charles came to dread facing her, wondering 'What will she blame me for now?'

To be let alone was liberating under Caroline's zealous regime. With the others so much older, Charles learned to amuse himself around The Mount. The Doctor had a splendid library, and a flair for fashionable natural history. The greenhouse, just off the morning-room, was an exotic indoor jungle. His mother kept fancy pigeons, famed for their 'beauty, variety, and tameness,' and the gardens contained fruit trees and rare shrubs. Beyond the north terrace, down a steep wooded incline, was the river. Here Charles sat fishing for hours. He used worms for bait, killing them first in salt water – as his sisters instructed – to spare them the ordeal of being spitted.

He was an inveterate collector and hoarder – shells, postal franks, birds' eggs, and minerals. They were trophies, piled up for praise. He craved it so much – he even started imagining that people admired him, only to feel guilty about it. But then he was guilty anyway. He was stealing to gain attention: at night he made off with the Doctor's peaches and plums, then hid the fruit so that he could 'discover' and report the cache the next day. Or sometimes his booty became a bribe. He offered apples to older boys if they would first marvel at how quickly he could run. Innocent mischief, but it helped him to stand out in a house full of older sisters. 'Inventing deliberate falsehoods' became a regular method of seeking the spotlight.[20]

Susannah sent him to Mr Case's school shortly after his eighth birthday in 1817. Each morning he walked over from The Mount, across the Welsh Bridge and up through narrow winding streets to the three-storey manse overlooking St Chad's churchyard. Many of the boys were older. Charles, reserved and rather chunky, shrank from their ritual wrestling matches and hurried home in the afternoon, dodging the dogs in Barker Street. He would still do anything at school 'for the pure pleasure of exciting attention & surprise,' and his cultivated 'lies . . . gave [him] pleasure, like a tragedy.' He told tall tales about natural history, reported strange birds, and boasted of being able to change the colour of flowers. Once he invented an elaborate story designed to show how fond he was of telling the truth. It was a boy's way of manipulating the world.[21]

The shock of Susannah's death in July was traumatic for the family. Its impact on Charles, difficult to assess, was certainly profound. She suffered appallingly with a tumour, and in the last days only Marianne and Caroline – who helped with the nursing – were allowed to see her. On the 15th, when the end came, Charles and the others were sent for. The Doctor showed them the body on the bed, dressed in a black velvet gown. Caroline comforted Charles, and they cried together. But after the funeral on the 20th the children's feelings were bottled up. The older ones could not even mention their mother's name.

When Charles returned to Case's school, his grief manifested itself in peculiar ways. One month after his mother's burial, he watched, transfixed, out of the classroom window, as a horse was led to an open grave in the churchyard. The saddle was empty, with a man's boots and carbine hanging at the side. So soon after his mother's interment, the effect overwhelmed him. The military cortège assembled and the clergyman read the service as the coffin was lowered. Then a cavalryman from the 15th Hussars stepped out, in full regimental attire, and raised his rifle. As the shots echoed across the Severn valley, pent-up emotion surged through the eight-year-old's body. Though in later life he could barely remember his mother, or her death – indeed he would have 'no particularly happy or unhappy recollections of this time' – he never forgot this scene. He remembered the dead soldier.[22]

The Mount became a teenage matriarchy, with Marianne heading up the household, Caroline acting as Catherine's minder, and Susan becoming her father's aide. The triumvirate was not to be trifled with. The sisters were a moral force, the inheritors of Susannah's piety. Charles and brother Erasmus submitted to their discipline, knowing that they could still escape to school.

When the Doctor arrived from his rounds, there was no escape for anyone. His portly presence, like some immense gravitational field, made life whirl about him. It was a vertiginous experience, and nobody felt at ease. With patients he was renowned for gentleness, and his advice always reassured. At home these qualities became less apparent after Susannah's death. His tenderness could still inspire love, but his tactlessness made the children fearful; he grew fastidious and opinionated, overwhelming them with his prodigious memory and his power to read minds, which 'seemed almost supernatural.' He interrogated and pontificated by turns; to be summoned was like being hauled before the Most High – except for the tiny falsetto voice. It was a subtle reminder that this overfed hulk was a mere mortal.[23]

Visitors noted the tension. After Maer's 'careless freedom and absence of restraint,' the young Wedgwoods found The Mount claustrophobic. Everyone had to conform to the Doctor's 'orderly and correct' standards. He was harder on the boys, whose untidiness repulsed him, but the girls suffered too. Elizabeth and Charlotte, in their twenties, were best friends with the Darwin sisters. Bessy Wedgwood had lived in 'nervous dread' of her own table-thumping father, and had brought up her daughters to view men as 'dangerous creatures who must be humoured.' Certainly the precept applied to The Mount. The girls laughed while the Doctor was away, always aware of the sea-change that was in store. 'Sunday we dined at half-past one, drest afterwards, and sat about 3 hours expecting the tide to come in about dark,' Elizabeth reported gloomily on one visit; 'and rather stiff and awful the evening was.'[24]

Overawed, the Darwin boys formed a close alliance. In September 1818, Charles joined thirteen-year-old Eras as a boarder at Shrewsbury School: a minor public school, across the river, opposite the castle ruins. The buildings were centuries old, dating back to Edward VI, with facilities to match – dark, damp dormitories and frigid baths. The brothers endured the hardships, knowing that home comforts were only a sprint away. Although, faced with the Doctor and mothering sisters, they may even have preferred the regime of the Revd Samuel Butler.

Butler had been headmaster for twenty years. Locally, his status rivalled Dr Darwin's; nationally his school was becoming known as a seat of excellence. The reputation had been hard won, for pampered squires' sons were not easy to restrain; one, caught drunk, pulled a knife on him; another carried a loaded pistol; and a whole gang terrorized local farmers, killing their pigs. The Revd Butler cracked the whip, or when appropriate, allowed the boys to settle their differences honourably in fist-fights.[25] He enforced hard-working habits, convinced that disciplined young men were Anglican society's first need.

The classics provided the core curriculum. The ability to read, write, and dissect dead languages was the mark of a gentleman. The more he knew about ancient cultures, the better able he was to command his own. Such was the theory. The practice Charles loathed. Latin and Greek numbed him. Education at Shrewsbury consisted of rote learning and recitation, with verse-making as a creative outlet. On the whole his lessons were 'carefully prepared & correctly said,' but only as a result of hand-me-down schoolboy tricks. He and his friends compiled a 'grand collection of old verses' that could be patched together to meet any contingency of poem writing. True, he enjoyed some of the odes of Horace, when he could recall them, but, like his other lines, most left him within a week. Byron's poetry was more memorable, and Shakespeare's historical plays. Propped up in a window seat, set in the school's thick walls, he pored over them by the hour.[26]

Classmates remembered Charles being 'old for his age,' both 'in manner and in mind.' The Mount had left its solemn mark on him; he was keen to please yet anxious to avoid pain, and reticence masked his frustration. Craving acceptance, he swallowed his anger (as he was always to do) and took after his frail and studious elder brother. Neither liked sports. While Eras burrowed into books and pottered with plants, Charles amassed his collections and went on 'long solitary walks.' Stirred by the Revd C. C. Clarke's *Wonders of the World*, he fantasized about more distant trips, day-dreaming of tropical islands and South American landscapes. It was all a refuge from the stultifying grown-ups.[27]

The ten-year-old was a handful for his mothering sisters. When, in July 1819, they took him to the Welsh coast for three weeks, he was quarrelsome and morose; he 'swore like a trooper' and took off alone, walking the beach, watching the sea-birds, entering another world. There was the excitement of new insects – large mottled sap-suckers and splendid moths. Another collection was started, but then a sister dictated that 'it was not right to kill insects' for this purpose – dead ones would have to do. A year later, freed from his female chaperones, he rode a short distance into Wales with Erasmus. By twelve, he and Eras were galloping all the way to Bangor with their Wedgwood cousins Frank and Hensleigh. Over the Welsh mountains they rode; past rugged peaks with their sombre scenes of primal desolation.

No longer so withdrawn, he was beginning to share his interests. At school he became keen to 'gratify his fellows.' He brought plants for the boys' garden and struggled to explain how his mother used to name them from their blossoms. He looked up to the older boys, Eras's friends, and one, the tall John Price, looked down on him 'in every sense.' Darwin brought 'Old Price' a shell one day to see if he could identify it. A 'dog periwinkle' of course, Price snapped, which left Charles wide-eyed with wonder.[28] Learning names was essential when every genteel drawing-room had its cabinet of curios, and Charles's training began in the playground.

*

The five years between the brothers shrank once Charles reached his teens. Erasmus led the way as always, pulling Charles fast up behind him. Bored with the classical curriculum, Eras took an explosive interest in chemistry, and in 1822 he co-opted Charles as his assistant. A 'Lab' was fitted out in the garden shed, after the Doctor banished them and their noxious gases from the house.

It was an expensive hobby, fit for gentlemen dilettantes in an industrial age. Probably the boys picked it up from the practical Wedgwoods, who understood kiln chemistry and kept recipe books of experiments. Eras and Charles set up a fund for apparatus and fuelled it from the family purse (the 'cow' to be 'milked,' as they called it). Fifty pounds or so – over a year's wage for a servant – went a long way.[29] They bought test tubes from a glass-blower, fetched stop-cocks from London, and equipped benches full of crucibles, retorts, evaporating dishes, and burners. But there was scarcely time to enjoy being together. Eras was seventeen and leaving school, intending to follow the family tradition in medicine. As the experiments began, the Doctor considered the educational choices.

Eras could go to Scotland to receive a liberal, science-based training, perhaps to Edinburgh University, as he himself had. Or he could purchase an expensive apprenticeship for the boy at one of the best London hospitals; £500 would buy him a top spot in the profession.

Or Eras could proceed to Oxford or Cambridge, the only two English universities. If, that is, he did not mind subscribing to the Thirty-nine Articles of the Anglican faith; and the Darwins did not – two generations of wealth had left them cloaked in Anglican respectability. These were Church universities, and members had to toe the doctrinal line. Here Eras would receive an upstanding rather than an outstanding education, starting – as in Shrewsbury School – with a grounding in classics. It was designed to keep the physician on a social par with his gentrified patients. Here the future gentry, doctors, and clergy were to be united – they would close ranks against the vulgar classes and protect the 'precious birthright of an *English gentleman*.' Oxford and Cambridge moulded 'the morals, manners, yea, the whole formation' of a gentleman physician, allying rank and wealth with professional honour.[30]

Cambridge it was, and Eras went up to Christ's College in October 1822. Thereafter father received notes from his 'spendpenny son,' with essential termly bills attached – debts to be cleared, thirteen guineas owed to the wine merchant, '& I shall be much obliged to the D^r if he will pay it.' Charles's letters were chock-full of chemical tidbits. Sights and smells were quintessential, and Eras described the mineralogy professor, John Stevens Henslow, incinerating arsenic with a blowpipe to release a gastronomic garlic odour. He reported back on students who 'got perfectly tipsy with ... laughing gas' (something first tried by the Wedgwoods' friend Coleridge twenty years earlier). 'One man said he felt just as if he could fly, & when he was drinking the gas, he began to jump, & twiddle his fingers, & make a kind half laughing & screaming noise.'

'The lab will look very insignificant after all the grand things I see here,' Eras confessed. The boys had money to burn, or rather corrode, and obtained their silver by dissolving up sixpences. It was pure indulgence and burnt a hole in both pockets. Charles planned to visit Eras at Christ's during the summer holidays of 1823, to marvel at the strutting 'Noblemen & such.' Eras, dissipated and broke from his amusements, told him to 'bring up a good supply of money, for by that time I shall not have so much as a brass farthing to buy some broth with when you come starving off ye coach.' During term-time, Charles scurried home at weekends, eager to exchange the classics for Parkes's *Chemical Catechism* or Brande's *Manual of Chemistry*. Inevitably, word spread at school about his smelly shed, and 'Gas' became his nickname. Revd Butler got wind of it too. He embarrassed Charles in front of the boys by calling him a 'poco curante' (a trifler), which sounded dreadful. Classics, not chemistry, moulded the character.[31]

It was a fad, but 'Gas' Darwin enjoyed the hours out in the shed alone, and he always had fond memories of his chemical self-education. By fifteen, he took up a more characteristic pursuit for a son of the Shropshire gentry. He was old enough to carry a gun and hunting became his passion. Blasting at birds was a 'most holy cause,' and since quail were more edible than insects his sisters did not cavil. He felt powerful, armed and tramping through the field. Making gas was nothing to massacring his first snipe, although the thrill was just as physical. It left him trembling so violently that he could barely reload.

Permission was needed to hunt, but the Doctor was hand in glove with the local squires, and Charles had no lack of bushes to beat. The best hunting was at Maer, where the easy-going Wedgwoods turned the shoots into parties, a respite from the autocratic atmosphere of The Mount. Uncle Jos joined in, and there were always cousins Jos III, Harry, Frank, and Hensleigh. They were all in their twenties, and Hensleigh was Eras's age and had been at Cambridge with him. He was the scholar of the family and reminded Uncle Jos of his precocious brother Tom, who had died at thirty-four, a burnt-out opium addict. Charles also took after Tom, who had been similarly obsessed with chemistry; Uncle Jos doted on him and Hensleigh alike. And lanky Charles, unprepossessing but full of promise, was bracing company for his girls.[32]

The four Wedgwood daughters were easy-going. They wore spectacles and came in pairs. Of the older ones, Charlotte was considered eligible, but Elizabeth was dwarfish, with severe spinal curvature. The others, Fanny and Emma, had been inseparable since childhood and were known as the 'Doveleys,' the family pets. Fanny was short, plain, and tidy, Emma quite the opposite. She had thick brown hair, grey eyes, a high forehead, and was as charming as she was chaotic, as messy as a boy. 'Little Miss Slip-Slop,' they called her. The pair had already studied abroad and spent a year at a London school, while at home the older sisters were in charge of their lessons. Emma helped Elizabeth with the village Sunday school and even wrote simple moral tales to aid the instruction. The school was held in the Maer Hall laundry; here the girls gave sixty children their only formal training in the three Rs – reading, writing, and religion.

Religion was a serious matter for the Wedgwoods, but since the 1790s the family had become more conformist. Like so many second- and third-generation Unitarians, cosseted in wealth, secure in business, they were adopting Anglican respectability. Jos was the parish patron, lining up his nephew to take charge as vicar. It made sense for Emma to stay on the safe side and be confirmed as an Anglican. Certainly her mother was for the respectability, or at least for covering her options. It was 'better to conform to the ceremonies' of the Church, she said, 'for one can never be quite sure that in omitting them we are not liable to sin.'

So Emma was duly confirmed at St Peter's Church, Maer. The ceremony took place on 17 September 1824. The partridge season had opened, and a fortnight later Charles drove over with Susan and Catherine to celebrate the rite. Besides the shooting, there was an impromptu family performance of *The Merry Wives of Windsor*, an apt choice for Charles with his Shakespearean tastes, and for the girls. They had 'wicked times,' it was reported: '1st Oct. Revels; 2nd, Revels; 4th, Revels . . . 6th Oct., quiet evening!'[33] One wonders who played Falstaff . . .

No such revels occurred at Shrewsbury. The Doctor was becoming more censorious, and Charles a trial. He was not shining at Dr Butler's school, the whole family knew it. He seemed too ordinary for a Darwin, perhaps even deficient. The spectres of his self-destructive uncles, Tom and Erasmus, hovered about The Mount. And with Eras away, he had become too fond of the gun. Determined to shake Charles to his senses, the Doctor reacted like one of the boys' experiments. Towards the end of the school year he exploded: 'You care for nothing but shooting, dogs, and rat-catching, and you will be a disgrace to yourself and all your family'![34]

The Doctor had a strong purgative, something to cleanse him of this partridge affliction. He took Charles out of school in June 1825, two years early. Give him a career, a direction – the rigours of medicine would do the trick. Charles was to follow in his brother's and father's footsteps to professional respectability.

2

The Northern Athens

WITH A MEDICAL CAREER in mind the sixteen-year-old, qualified only by a squire's confidence and the family's good name, spent the summer of 1825 practising on the sick poor of Shropshire. Sometimes he accompanied the Doctor, administering the medicines. He relished his father's approval and enjoyed the apprenticeship. Within weeks he had a dozen patients of his own – 'chiefly women and children in Shrewsbury.' He recorded symptoms and his father made up the prescriptions. All in all, the Doctor saw distinct prospects in his bedside manner.[1]

The reports from Erasmus at Christ's were less encouraging. Charles heard how his brother was given the filthy jobs, preparing the corpses for dissection and cleaning up the limbs afterwards. Eras was inured to the blood and stench of the anatomy theatre, but he felt Charles becoming queasy even as he talked of his menial work on the cadavers: 'I dont fancy it w^ld. have suited your stomack especially before breakfast.'

Erasmus thought it 'ten thousand pities if you do not come to Cambridge.' But to no avail. The Doctor had decided on Edinburgh University for Charles, the 'Northern Athens.' It was more the family tradition. He would be a third-generation Darwin to study medicine here, following his father and grandfather. Family ties with the Edinburgh academics went back a long way. The professor of natural philosophy, John Leslie, 'an enormous mass of flesh and an extremely agreeable man,' had even once tutored the Wedgwood sons at Maer.[2] As a result Charles would leave home with letters that would place him at the best intellectual dinner tables.

Then there were the medical considerations. Edinburgh was better equipped, better staffed, and offered better hospital facilities than the cloistered English universities. It turned out not only better-educated MDs than Oxford and Cambridge, but vastly more of them.[3] Edinburgh had long been a haven for wealthy Dissenters, barred from Oxford and Cambridge by the Thirty-nine Articles. Here they studied a wide array of medical and scientific subjects, including botany, chemistry, and natural history. The students were also exposed to the latest Continental thought, particularly in the thriving extramural schools clustered around the university. Many graduates went to Paris after their final year and returned full of the latest French notions. They kept Edinburgh students briefed on the best, the most heterodox, and the most innovative new sciences, as Charles was to find out.

Fortunately, Erasmus could do his external hospital study at Edinburgh, so plans were laid for him to accompany Charles, to cast a protective coat over his brother's shoulders. Eras came home from Cambridge in July and the two began planning. They would anatomize, collect fossils, and continue their chemical entertainments. Erasmus could not wait. 'It will be very pleasant our being together, we shall be as cozy as possible, & I almost think that when you have arrived at the dignity of a "Varsity" man, that I shall leave of[f] licking you.'

Charles and Eras arrived at Edinburgh late in October. They checked in to the Star Hotel in Princes Street, overlooking the ravine that bisects the city, and began hunting for digs. There was no lack of choice with all the lodging houses packed claustrophobically around the university. But most rooms were dark, dank 'little holes.' They found the exception. At 11 Lothian Street the landlady, Mrs Mackay, specialized in students. She was 'a nice clean old body, and exceedingly civil & attentive.' (A generation of doctors and naturalists had their first taste of Edinburgh hospitality from Mrs Mackay.) It was convenient, the university stood at the end of the street, a few minutes' walk away. She gave the lads two light and airy bedrooms and a sitting-room four flights up for twenty-six shillings a week. They settled in and began to explore.

They walked all over town, lost in admiration. The ravine was astonishing, the city seemed perched on a precipice: 'indeed Bridge Street is the most extraordinary thing I ever saw,' Charles wrote home, 'and when we first looked over the side we could hardly believe our eyes, when, instead of a fine river we saw a stream of people.' They took in everything: the Old Town with its gothic skyline, the business centre, and the bustling university area, teeming with students. 'Auld Reekie' lived up to its name here, with overcrowded tenements and crime. Then there was the classical New Town, now favoured by the merchants and professionals. The boys paced the broad cobbled streets, up and down winding flights of steps, admiring the imposing stone buildings. At the Parliament House they could see the clubbing Tory barristers 'showing their feathers at their more-employed and laborious Whigs, as a race soon to be exterminated.'[4] The sons of Dr Darwin, Whigs to a tee, appreciated this fine piece of political miscalculation.

Scotch fare had to be tried: fried oysters, stewed herrings, cods' heads stuffed with oatmeal. And shopping in the new market, with its narrow stalls crammed with fresh vegetables. Then it was off to see Weber's *Der Freischütz* or some other terpsichorean delight at the Theatre-Royal by night.

On Sundays they sampled the churches. Edinburgh was the religious capital of Scotland and soot-stained steeples littered the hilly landscape. The mighty edifices were the backbone of the Establishment, their stern preachers appointed by noble patrons and the Crown. This was the Church of Scotland: wealthy, dogmatic, and self-assured. The Kirk's legislative body, the General Assembly, met in Edinburgh amid much pomp. Everyone turned out – Charles and Eras included – to see the black-robed delegates convening to debate the moral health of the nation. The boys' first service, though, came as a bit of a surprise; instead of a two-hour 'soul-cutting discourse,' they were agreeably released after a moderate twenty-minute sermon.

The city was cosmopolitan. One would pass a German physician here, a French nobleman there. The American John James Audubon, dressed like a backwoodsman, was in town in 1826 to sign up subscribers for his *Birds of America*. Rosy-faced women trundled along, leather straps of their baskets over foreheads; their bearded menfolk rude and unkempt. It was a city of wonderful sights and fearful sciences: of socialists experimenting with cooperative living, and phrenological shopkeepers eyeing their customers' heads; of professors debating the earth's origin, and anatomists debunking the creation of life. Visitors could only marvel at the metropolis, basking in the 'brazenfrontedness of her own self-idolatry.'[5]

There were plenty of social contacts for the grandsons of Erasmus Darwin to make. They looked up friends of their father's and dined with professors. Charles kept Susan apprised of the 'Gaieties:'

> We also have been very dissipated. – We dined at D^r. Hawley's
> on Saturday, & had a very pleasant party, after which we
> went to the Theatre . . . D^r. Hawley has procured some
> information about my Fathers questions, & I will write it
> shortly to him. Next Friday we are going to the old D^r.
> Duncan [an octogenarian, but still joint-professor of the
> Theory of Physic], & I hope it will be a pleasanter party than
> the last; which [was] a very specimen of stupidity . . . I have
> been most shockingly idle, actually reading two novels at once.
> [A] good scolding would do me a vast deal of good, & I hope
> you will send one of your most severe one's.

This party-going was diplomatic; the Duncans had long known the Darwins. Charles's uncle and namesake – who died after the dissecting accident – lay interred in Duncan's family vault. The old doctor inevitably had a paternal attitude towards the latest Charles in his class.[6]

Elegant Whig doors were opened to the boys. Perhaps no longer boys: a mocking indignance that the Doctor should *still* be calling Charles one showed his changing persona. Relatives gave him a letter of introduction to the Whig leading-light Leonard Horner, geologist, educationalist, and soon to be Warden of the new London University. Horner took Charles off to the Royal Society of Edinburgh, where they saw Sir Walter Scott, Audubon's 'celestial being,' though a sad one after his shocking bankruptcy. Still, greatness told, and Charles viewed 'the whole scene with some awe and reverence.'[7]

All his life Charles had been cosseted in a world of wealthy Whiggism. Now it was his *entrée* into liberal Edinburgh. He never had to find his political feet. The whole family was committed to the Whigs' manifesto of extended suffrage, open competition, religious emancipation (allowing Dissenters, Jews, and Catholics to hold office), and the abolition of slavery. The Church-and-King Tories governed in 1825, as they had for the best part of fifty years, and Whigs like the Darwin-Wedgwoods detested their opponents' corrupt hold on power. But the family's dyed-in-the-wool Whiggism did not preclude a certain devilment on Charles's part. He delighted in telling Susan that he was taking the scandalous Tory rag *John Bull*. It was pure political titillation: he revelled in its outrageous xenophobic extremism, its scandal-and-scare format. Eras went one better. Not for him *John Bull*; he switched to *The Age* because it was 'ten times the more scurrilous of the two.' 'Do you approve?' he asked Charles impishly.

The girls did not. Charles's good-natured rebellion against his mothering sisters was one thing; posting them his copies of *John Bull* was another. Tory gutter journalism got pretty near the knuckle, no more so than on the subject of slavery, which for the Darwin-Wedgwoods was sacrosanct. Reading this lurid rag, Catherine was appalled that it should make slaves out to be happy and content. Susan wondered why he was not reading a reforming daily: 'I shall be better pleased when I hear you are studying "The Morning Chronicle",' she scolded him.[8]

Then there was student life. This was the usual brew of heavy work and high spirits, and as always the older generation worried. To the devout Scottish mind the students were notorious. Drunkenness and brawling were common. And the teachers who spread scare stories did not help, warning apocalyptically that long hours stretched over corpses were driving these young souls into bars and brothels. Even the theatre was suspect; some thought it sure to arouse the passions already awakened by anatomy. For many, medical schools were no better than charnel houses dealing in stolen flesh, corrupting young minds. Wasn't it true that those who dissected flesh and bone lost their faith in a residual soul? Some teachers hardly set the best example. In London it was nothing to find one dictating notes in his local gin palace or indoctrinating students with political propaganda. London was bad enough; there, students were to riot in the new university. But Erasmus believed that the Scottish students were worse.[9]

Of course things were never as bad as the press made out. Newspapers thrived on public outrage; there was money in drunken students playing high jinks. Prurient readers wanted to be shocked. True, the Darwins' chemical experiments turned into a jape as they got tipsy on laughing gas, and they indulged in the craze for Syrian snuff. But their gambling was hardly new; hot toddies merely kept out the cold, and theatre-going was innocent enough to be the mainstay of letters home.

Actually the boys were diligent at the start. Erasmus had wanted to get to Edinburgh early so 'we can both read like horses.' After they had settled in, this is what they did. They were voracious bookworms, taking more volumes out of the library that first term than anybody else in the university. Other texts Charles bought. Money was no problem, with the Doctor there to pick up the tab, and Charles could always send home for a ten-pound note to tide him over.[10] Anyway, if things became desperate he could sell his insects to buy a botany book, as Erasmus was to do.

The medical school enrolled nine hundred pupils in Charles's year, more than a quarter of them from England. It still offered the best medical education in Britain, although no one was blind to its decline since the halcyon days of the Enlightenment. And most recognized the cause: the Tory Town Council (rather than the university) appointed two thirds of the professors, often from its list of party loyalists, and always with the Kirk's approval. This political influence led to bickering and hardly the best set of teachers.

Some professors even inherited their chairs, treating them as family property. Charles was appalled by the crusty professor of anatomy, Alexander Monro III. He held his father's and grandfather's seat, and it showed. 'Unimpassioned indifference' was how one student described his manner, and his classes later degenerated into riots. Like so many anatomy lecturers fresh from the dissecting theatre, he was bloody and begrimed. 'I dislike him & his Lectures so much that I cannot speak with decency about them,' said Charles, moved to anger. 'He is so dirty in person & actions.'[11]

Monro's soporific talks forced many students over the road to hear Robert Knox's scintillating Continental lectures. The foppish Knox taught in one of the competing private schools in Surgeons' Square. His lectures were not all they came to hear. The flamboyant, one-eyed, gold-vested Knox savaged the city's clergy and elders, to the undoubted delight of his listeners. His slashing satires on religion made him the scourge of the Kirk. But the student response was rapturous. His stiletto wit only served to make Monro appear more of a drudge, and Knox's class numbers shot up. Between 1826 and 1828 – when he was caught unwittingly accepting Burke and Hare's murder victims for dissection – he taught more students than all the other private lecturers put together.[12]

Erasmus enrolled with Knox's chief rival, John Lizars, on the other side of Surgeons' Square. He was 'charming' and certainly more respectable. Charles enrolled with no private teacher. He found surgery stomach-churning, and one can see why. In 1826 Audubon met Knox, 'dressed in an overgown and with bloody fingers,' and was escorted around his dissecting theatre. It was a moment of indescribable horror. The severed limbs and dissected torsos left him gasping. 'The sights were extremely disagreeable, many of them shocking beyond all I ever thought could be. I was glad to leave this charnel house and breathe again the salubrious atmosphere of the streets.' Charles felt the same.[13] Monro had put him off human anatomy for life. As a consequence he was never taught dissection techniques properly, something he was later to regret.

It was not only Monro whom he disliked. Charles complained to Caroline in January 1826 about 'a long stupid lecture from Duncan' on medicines. Dr Andrew Duncan *secundus* was a fellow professor with his father and, in Charles's view, 'so very learned that his wisdom has left no room for his sense.' The lecture could not 'be translated into any word expressive enough of its stupidity.' Unmerited criticism perhaps, for Duncan, well travelled, *au fait* with the best French thought, was reckoned 'a man of most versatile genius.' (He was also the man who isolated the quinine-relative cinchonin from Peruvian bark.) The problem was young Charles. He was simply not ready for the drudgery of medical learning. He persevered on frosty mornings, listening to Duncan's descriptions of medicinal plants; indeed – having paid his half-a-crown experiment money – 'tasting and smelling them' from a smorgasbord spread out at the front of the class. But in the end he just could not reconcile himself to clambering out of bed to spend 'a whole, cold, breakfastless hour on the properties of rhubarb!'[14]

Charles's disenchantment was accelerated by his clinical studies. He walked the wards of the Royal Infirmary, next to the College, but what he saw distressed him. He shared his father's horror of bleeding, but, unlike the Doctor, he never persevered to overcome his squeamishness. His two visits to operating theatres turned his stomach, reinforcing his morbid fear of human blood. Here the cutting was gory and swift; in the days of heroic surgery, before anaesthetic, speed was of the essence to reduce the trauma in the strapped, screaming patient. Dirty hands clasped dirty saws, hacking and cutting quickly, the blood running into buckets of sawdust. The students jostled all around in the tense, steamy atmosphere, straining for a view. During a particularly bad operation on a child, Charles finally fled the room, unable to watch, and determined never again to enter an operating theatre.[15] The vision remained to haunt him for life.

About the only lectures to escape his epithet 'dull' were Professor Thomas Hope's on chemistry. But then Tommy Hope's 'chemical drama' was unabashed entertainment. It was all done 'with great *eclat*,' and as a result it attracted the largest class in the university. (Charles was one of 503 students that year.) Living solely off his fees, Hope had dropped all research and perfected his chemical amusements, using large-scale apparatus visible to everybody. He even started a popular course, which ladies could attend, even if they had to slip in through a back door. This became the talk of the town. 'The Doctor is in absolute extacy [sic] with his audience of veils and feathers,' quipped a commentator. 'I wish some of his experiments would blow him up. Each female student would get a bit of him.' Charles thought differently. He dined with Hope and wrote home, 'I like both him & his lectures *very* much.'[16] As with all the boys, it seems, 'Gas' Darwin, himself a chemical dilettante, relished the distraction from the grim realities of the sickbed. It was about the only saving grace of his first year at Edinburgh.

There were, of course, diversions. He walked along the coastline with Eras, picking up cuttlefish, sea-mice, and sea-slugs. And for a game-shooting squire's son, needing to display trophies, he found other digressions.

'I am going to learn to stuff birds, from a blackamoor,' he informed his sisters. The 'blackamoor' in question was a freed black slave, John Edmonstone, whom the eccentric Catholic 'Squire' and traveller Charles Waterton had brought back from Guiana in South America. John (the 'Edmonstone' was adopted from his master) had been taught taxidermy by the Squire, one of the best stuffers in the country. John had taken lodgings at 37 Lothian Street and set up shop in the Edinburgh Museum, passing on his skill to the students. The lessons were cheap; 'he only charges one guinea, for an hour every day for two months,' Charles reported. His tutor was 'very pleasant and intelligent,' and he frequently sat with him.[17] John, who had travelled with the eccentric Waterton, found a willing listener for his daily stories of the Tropics. Charles learned the tricks of the stuffing trade. More, he heard at first hand of a slave's life and the luxuriance of the South American rain-forest.

This daily escape to torrid places was a far cry from the reality of frosty Edinburgh. It was icy cold and he was miserable. Romantic talk of forests he revelled in; getting up for Duncan's dreary lectures he resented. Susan tried to cheer him up, writing in March: 'For this next month devote y[ou]rself to wisdom & you will be much happier.' But he could see no wisdom in medicine. It probably did not help to receive a stream of girlish gossip on the jollities at home, or tales of the flirtations at Shrewsbury's spring balls.

Caroline, concerned as usual about the hereafter, tried a different message. She exhorted him to read the Bible in order to learn 'what is necessary to feel & do to go to heaven after you die.' 'I suppose,' she added, wanting a stronger commitment, 'you do not feel ready yet to take the sacrament.' A suppliant Charles responded: 'What part of the Bible do you like best? I like the Gospels. Do you know which of them is generally reckoned the best?' They agreed on the Gospel of John, and Caroline lamented, 'I often regret myself that when I was younger & fuller of pursuits & high spirits I was not more religious – but it is difficult to be so habitually.'

Charles began to reflect on a life he had taken for granted. He was starting to appreciate the devotion Susan and Caroline had shown him after his mother's death. Their letters now sparked an emotional response as he tried to put his thoughts into words. 'It makes me feel how very ungrateful I have been to you for all the kindness and trouble you took for me when I was a child,' he conceded to Caroline. 'Indeed I often cannot help wondering at my own blind Ungratefulness.'

His half-heartedness at medical school was apparent to the Doctor. He scolded Charles in March for the desultory manner in which he picked and chose lectures, telling him bluntly: 'If you do not discontinue your present indulgent way, your course of study will be utterly useless.'[18] And he warned him against cutting lectures and coming home early.

Charles finally escaped Edinburgh at the end of term. The summer was infinitely more pleasant, hiking through the Welsh hills with a Shrewsbury School friend. A copy of the Revd Gilbert White's classic *Natural History of Selborne* taught him to treat birds less like moving targets; and he began to observe their habits and habitats, scrawling his observations in a pocket diary. He relived the enchantment of his childhood rambles by the Welsh coast, and wondered to himself 'why every gentleman did not become an ornithologist.' Not that he was entirely converted to such placid avocations. When the season opened on 1 September, he made a good effort at reducing Maer's bird population, and his diary switched from notes on behaviour to a body count – fifty-five partridges, three hares, and a rabbit in the first week.[19]

He did not relish returning to Edinburgh by himself. During the first year Erasmus and Charles had explored and studied together. They were inseparable, whether reading, lecture-going, or sampling the dissipations of Edinburgh nightlife. But Erasmus had finished his year and now enrolled at a London anatomy school, leaving Charles to his own devices.

Pressured by his father, Charles kept reading. He browsed through his grandfather's medical *magnum opus* on the laws of life and health, the *Zoonomia*. The Doctor doted on it, praising the book for its insights into inheritable disease; although the tome dwelt on much more, the connection of mind and body, and the perpetual transformation of life.[20] Charles read sympathetically and was full of admiration – for what he wasn't sure, perhaps because it was written by his grandfather. But it left his view of medicine unchanged.

3

Sea-Mats & Seditious Science

CHARLES WAS BACK IN Edinburgh in November 1826. Away from home and alone, he began drifting, unsure of the future. Hints that his father would leave him comfortably off dampened any remaining determination to make a go of medicine. The professors had seen it all before. Losing their well-to-do students when they came into money was a perennial problem in an age of occupational gentlemen.[1]

The disenchantment showed; he did not even bother to join the library this year. His interest had plainly petered out. With little commitment and a lot of time, he threw himself into the student societies, and here he found excitement in the unlikeliest place.

In these bustling societies the lawyers and doctors-to-be sharpened their wits by debating contemporary topics. The gatherings provided camaraderie, and the debates were often raucous. The Plinian Society's meetings could be electric, while some topics bordered on the indictable. The Plinian had been founded in 1823 by Robert Jameson, the shy, wild-haired Regius Professor of Natural History.[2] Every Tuesday, all types, from sixteen-year-olds to long-standing graduates, streamed into one of the basement rooms to hear the talks. When Darwin joined in 1826 it had been penetrated by radical students – fiery, freethinking democrats who demanded that science be based on physical causes, not supernatural forces. They were challenged by the religiously orthodox, and for many listeners, like Darwin, the ensuing clashes provided that *frisson* missing from mainstream lectures.

Darwin was actually proposed for the Plinian by the militant William Browne (one of its five Presidents – the Plinian was a very democratic affair). Browne was a brilliant 21-year-old demagogue

31

who graduated in 1826 with an interest in madness. He was deeply involved in radical science and anti-clerical politics. He had no time for souls and saints. Radicals like him were intent on reforming a Church-dominated society. The Established Churches of Scotland and England ruled all aspects of life, monopolizing political offices, regulating hospital, university, and legal posts, prescribing the rites surrounding birth, marriage and death, restricting civil liberties, and suppressing other religious groups. They were hated by the radical democrats for their corrupt power, and Browne himself despised 'Priestcraft.' Moreover, he had a unique way of lampooning it. He studied the inmates of Montrose Lunatic Asylum to prove that the fanatics canonized by the Church across the centuries had been madmen. They had over-developed organs of 'Veneration' in the brain. A more enlightened nineteenth century would have locked them away as insane.[3]

The very day Darwin petitioned to join, on 21 November 1826, he heard Browne announce his intention of refuting Charles Bell's pious *Anatomy and Physiology of Expression* (a book, by the self-proclaimed 'captain of anatomists,' that Darwin himself was to target in later years). Bell claimed that the Creator had endowed the human face with unique muscles that allowed man to express his unique emotions, which reflected his unique moral nature. Browne scorned such anatomical chauvinism and, seeing no essential difference between men and animals, issued a flat denial.

The following week Darwin was elected with William Greg, a student his own age. Greg was just as heretical as Browne. He immediately offered to give a talk proving that 'the lower animals possess every faculty & propensity of the human mind.' The son of a mill owner, a Manchester cotton king, Greg had been educated in a Unitarian school. Here he had learned to see nature purely in terms of physical forces. (Unitarians had no truck with orthodox Creationist science, the sort taught in Anglican schools: species were not miraculously created, nor did man stand outside nature.) His masters had even proclaimed the human mind subject to physical law – an idea that Anglicans abhorred, knowing that morality was God's gift, not nature's. Greg read his paper on the animal and human mind.[4] Darwin, with his heritage of Wedgwood Unitarianism, heard it, and probably without surprise. The illicit excitement of these meetings was enormous. Established Church doctrines were being impugned, dissident sciences championed. It must have affected the impressionable seventeen-year-old. He was quick to take an active part. On 5 December, the day Browne tore Bell's book apart, Darwin was elected to the Council.

Darwin's new-found friends were not only involved in politics. Browne and Greg were fierce phrenologists intent on proselytizing the students. Phrenology was a fashionable anti-establishment science among Edinburgh's traders, pressing for more political power. Its advocates argued that each faculty of thought – Love, Morality, Veneration, or whatever – was located in its own 'organ' of the brain, and the size of each organ was reflected in the shape of the head. This is what made phrenology popular. There was no art or mystery. Anyone could look at the bumps on a person's head and see their gifts. Self-help appealed to the mandarins of new wealth confronted by the hauteur of the old; knowing one's true talents made a mockery of patronage and the old-boy network.[5]

Of course, the meetings were not all high-brow heresy and student radicalism; they flew high and low, moving from the cuckoo's habits to the classification of animals, from instinct to the existence of sea-serpents. Many talks concerned local sightings – of whales, algal blooms, and rare plants – which left great scope for audience participation. The young Darwin stood to add his bit on cuckoos and classification, and, all in all, seems to have found the Society a great boon.

He went scouring the Firth of Forth shoreline with his Plinian friends and accompanying the trawlers dredging the ocean bottom. Sometimes they ventured further afield: along the coast of Fifeshire, where they sheltered from storms in the Inchkeith lighthouse, or to the Isle of May out in the estuary.[6] Always, however, Darwin was looking for washed-up sea creatures, especially sponges or stalked, feathery sea-pens and their relatives.

Others shared his fascination. The studious John Coldstream was two years older than Darwin, and equally absorbed by the local corals, sponges, and sea-pens, which he collected and shared. Coldstream had joined the Plinian on its foundation, and he was another of the Presidents who put Darwin up for election. But he was a different cut from Browne and Greg. As a boy in nearby Leith, Coldstream had been intensely evangelical – an earnest Bible-believing proselytizer. He maintained that Britain should be saved through Christian moral regeneration, not Browne's irreligious politics. Coldstream had written for the local Bible Society, and even at Edinburgh Darwin found him 'prim, formal, highly religious and most kind-hearted.'[7]

Of all Darwin's Edinburgh mentors, one stood out: a tall, satirical, sponge expert, Robert Edmond Grant. He became closer to Charles and did more to influence him than anyone else in this period.

Grant was a native of the city, born in fashionable Argyle Square. He was sixteen years older and a doctor of twelve years' standing. But he had forsaken medical practice to study marine life, living on a legacy after his father's death (although the money was running out). He was another Plinian stalwart, and a sad, cynical, and fascinating figure. There was no more passionate Francophile, nor one so committed to a radical overhaul of science and society. Theirs was a decisive meeting. Darwin was coming under the wing of an uncompromising evolutionist.

Nothing was sacred for Grant. As a freethinker, he saw no spiritual power behind nature's throne. The origin and evolution of life were due simply to physical and chemical forces, all obeying natural laws. Like his French heroes, the maligned Jean-Baptiste Lamarck and Etienne Geoffroy St Hilaire – evolutionists both – he believed that a new imaginative vision was needed. But evolution was almost universally condemned by Church and scientific authorities. It was castigated as morally degenerate and subversive. Were men to see themselves as brutes, they would act accordingly. God was the arch-paternalist, working through patrician priests; His beneficence flowed from His Church into society. If nature and culture were *self*-evolving, if the clergy could not point to miraculously created species as a sign of His power operating from above, the Church's legitimacy was undermined. The logic was stark – even if it was rarely spelled out. The day people accepted that nature and society evolved unaided, the Church would crash, the moral fabric of society would be torn apart, and civilized man would return to savagery.

The few evolutionists kept their heads down. They were usually inspired by the revolutionary French, and were often radical democrats wanting to open up society. For them the power for change came from below, in both nature and politics. (Hence their democratic ideals – power came from the people, it was not delegated downwards from wealthy paternalists.) Grant's praise for old Lamarck in France was unbounded. Lamarck was still alive, a blind octogenarian in Paris. In his day he had been an exceptional biologist (he coined the word) – the Kepler of Biology, as a contemporary called him. The professor of 'insects and worms' at the Natural History Museum in Paris, he had revolutionized study of the lower invertebrates. Even the British Museum's collection of shells was arranged according to Lamarck's principles. Yet there was another side to Lamarck's science – his evolution – which met with a hysterical reaction. Execrable, most called it. The Old Etonian keeper rearranging the Museum's shells spat venom at the Frenchman for his evolutionary ideals. He seethed at the 'abominable trash vomited forth by Lamarck and his disciples,' damning these naturalists 'who have rashly, and almost blasphemously, imputed a period of comparative imbecility to Omnipotence.'[8]

So godless evolutionary talk was anathema in conservative Britain. The libertarian freedoms of the eighteenth century were gone, crushed underfoot in the reaction to the French Revolution. In the long Tory-dominated years after the Napoleonic Wars, pedantic specialization and description were safer occupations for a savant. The time was past for blasphemous babblings about a self-evolving nature.

But Grant was no blinkered patriot, and he was never one to kow-tow. A quiet intransigence dominated his career. His cavalier attitude to convention verged on the self-destructive. He continually touched a raw nerve, not only in his scientific views and sham-hating radicalism, but in his lifestyle (tittle-tattle had him a homosexual, though no one is sure).

In a jingoistic age, he was a man of deep European learning. He had travelled widely and was well known in Paris. Like Lamarck, Grant worked on the sponges, fascinated because they were so little understood. The very simplicity of these primitive sea animals, he believed, would enable us to understand their tissues more easily, and thereby to solve some of the knottier problems of the complex higher animals, including man. Grant rejected the wisdom of the Oxford and Cambridge clergy – that the fossil record, with its progression of extinct animals and plants, testified to a series of divine Creations. Rather, the evolution of men and monkeys could be put down to environmental and climatic causes. The naturalist's job was to expose these causes. This irreverent probing of Creation put him out of step with the safe taxonomic preoccupations south of the border.

This was Darwin's walking companion. And a good walking companion, too. Grant had already crossed the Alps seven times on foot, visiting the universities in France, Germany, Italy, and Switzerland. They marched out towards the coast together, umbrellas in hand, rapt in conversation, an inquisitive Darwin learning the questions to ask. Grant was a marvellous raconteur, and their talk would take in exotic sponges, the life in some Hungarian hamlet, or the soprano at the Theatre-Royal. Leaving Edinburgh, they could look back on the city, 'rising in gradual amphitheatre, most sublimely backed by mountainous clouds.'[9] On to Leith, with its iron jetty and new harbour full of Dutch vessels and herring fishermen. They would greet the returning oyster boats. Grant was fascinated by a strange fleshy creature that colonized oyster shells, and which he interpreted as an evolutionary half-way house between sponges and polyps. Darwin struck up friendships with the trawler crews himself and began accompanying them out to sea, examining the catch as it was dredged up.

Through the winter and spring of 1827 he got to know Grant well. Darwin found him stiff and starchy at first, not surprisingly, for Grant was always formally dressed in tail coat and choker. Beneath the exterior, though, he was kind, enthusiastic, and funny, with a lashing wit that left nothing sacrosanct. Not even the Scriptures; and a succession of students, Darwin undoubtedly one, listened guiltily to Grant's jokes about Providence. Grant's austere crust concealed an even greater enthusiasm for microscopic life. Others called it a 'burning zeal' for his precious polyps – and he attacked the subject, like so much else, with selfless energy. He would tell his students of the

> eight or ten hours of a sleety day in February which he had spent, cold and hungry, wading in the shallows of the Firth of Forth . . . 'I had nothing to eat or drink, I was wet through, my hands were half-frozen, and I was chilled to the marrow; but, gentlemen, I was amply rewarded: I became the happy possessor of no less than three of these beautiful little creatures, these Dorises [sea-slugs],' and he held up a phial containing three hardly visible little bladder-like animals.[10]

The sacrifice was obviously lost on some students, but not Darwin. He was quickly infected by Grant's enthusiasm for sea-slugs and their like. What he learned from Grant in these months was to shape his own initial approach to evolution ten years later.

Grant took a house on the rocky shore at Prestonpans, ten miles from Edinburgh. Here he spent the chilly winter months scouring the tidal pools for cast-up sponges and stalked sea-pens. The bay, though on the cold, choppy North Sea, had one of the richest marine environments, and he was able to catch and keep alive hundreds of sponges, sea-mats, sea-pens, and dead-men's fingers. He bred them all from eggs, spending weeks poring over the tiny frail organisms, each sea-mat and sea-pen a colony of tiny tentacled polyps. The result was a string of twenty papers in the Edinburgh journals in 1826 and 1827, during Darwin's stay, mostly on sponges, eggs, and larvae. It won him a European reputation. Even the French – world leaders in these matters – admitted the importance of his sponge papers, and in a show of magnanimity had them translated. Darwin's unofficial tutor was now a world expert on marine invertebrates.

Grant pointed out what to look for, and Darwin filled a notebook in March and April 1827 with observations on the larvae of molluscs and sea-mats, and the stalked sea-pens. He was fascinated. These creatures were very primitive; arguments even flared over whether sponges were animals or plants. With Darwin's help, Grant was showing that they lay close to the root of the animal kingdom, and he believed that they held clues to the common foundations of all life. His talks on the sea-mat *Flustra*, a primitive moss-like animal comprising a colony of tentacle-waving polyps, were illustrated by huge blown-up drawings, making their microscopic structure easier to understand.[11] Darwin, drinking it all in, began to make original observations himself, and the first of these was announced at another of the student bodies – the Wernerian Natural History Society.

The Wernerian was a longer-established society, which met fortnightly in Professor Jameson's room in the university museum. To the newcomer the setting was stark indeed, just two tables, a fireplace, and rows of benches; no adornments, no warmth, nothing but a stuffed swordfish or such on the table. But the thronged meetings gave it instant life: Kirk ministers would discuss Noah's Flood, tyros brought their sea-slugs and octopuses, senior students reported on the marsupials shipped from the new Australian settlements. Here Grant – a council member who had given fifteen talks since 1825 – exhibited live sponges and unravelled their structure. He had shown that the larvae of many sponges and polyps could swim using their surface cilia. Late in 1826 Grant began bringing Darwin to meetings (only MDs could join, the students came as guests). As an old man Darwin could still remember seeing Audubon, with his black flowing locks, exhibit a drawing of a buzzard at the Society and describe his ingenious method of wiring up dead birds for painting. Grant also blew Darwin's trumpet; on 24 March 1827 he announced that Darwin had unravelled the mystery of the black peppercorn-like bodies found inside oyster shells, and thought by fishermen to be seaweed spores. They were the eggs of a skate leech. Grant published an account of the parasite, and congratulated his 'zealous young friend Mr Charles Darwin' for his discovery.[12]

Darwin was now treading in Grant's footsteps. He too observed waving hair-like cilia on the larvae of another species of *Flustra* brought up by the dredge boats. He checked the Paris authorities to see if anyone else had noticed them. Grant, a fluent French speaker and friend of the savants, pushed him deeper into the writings of

Lamarck and his colleagues. French was a bother for Darwin. Susan had insisted he keep up the language. 'I hope,' she badgered him, 'you are reading something more interesting than the *Baroness & Countess*' silly letters' and that 'you like French better than you did.' In truth it remained a chore, but at least Lamarck could not be dismissed as so much French fripperie. Darwin also got hold of Lamarck's *System of Invertebrate Animals* and found the classification charts easier to translate. No, the French had not spotted the cilia. Darwin saw his observation help to confirm Grant's belief that the larvae of all these marine animals were free-swimming.[13]

This was what he said three days later at the Plinian Society, during an eventful meeting on 27 March. He stood to announce his modest discoveries, that the sea-mat's larvae could swim, and that the black specks in old oyster shells were leech eggs. It was his first public presentation, and he proudly responded when asked to lay his specimens before the Society. Grant followed up with an authoritative talk on the strange, amorphous sea-mat.

But what happened next eclipsed all innocent talk of polyps. Browne, the fiery radical, gave such an inflammatory harangue on matter and mind that it sparked a raging debate. He provoked the students by arguing that mind and consciousness are not spiritual entities, separate from the body; they are simple spin-offs from brain activity.[14] Such a notion raised dreadful questions, the sort that terrorized the Kirk's élite: if life was not a supernatural gift, if the mind was not some incorporeal entity, what became of the soul? With no soul, no after-life, no punishment or reward, where was the deterrent against immorality? What would stop the downtrodden masses from rising up to redress their grievances? All Darwin's new-found friends entered the fray.

Someone was so incensed that he struck Browne's proposition from the Minutes. Whoever it was even went back to the previous week's announcement of Browne's paper to cross that out too. Heresy, censorship: the younger students were agog. It was Darwin's first exposure to militant freethought – and to the storm it whipped up.

The reaction was typical. Conservatives across the country were aghast at this sort of godless philosophy. An ageing Coleridge damned it as subversive. He saw it undermine religious authority and encourage political upheaval. The staunch *Quarterly Review* wanted it legally suppressed: such wretched views would 'impair the welfare of society ... break down the best and holiest sanctions of moral obligation, and ... give a free rein to the worst passions of the human heart.' In an undemocratic age, with Church and State striving to keep order, the reaction was shrill. Nor was it surprising: the Cato Street conspiracy, a plan to assassinate the Cabinet in 1820 and proclaim a democracy, was still fresh in the authorities' minds.

Vigilant teachers feared that the young bud would be blighted by these poisonous ideas. The future headmaster of Rugby School, Thomas Arnold, knew it to be true; he believed the rumours of medical students degenerating into 'materialist atheists of the greatest personal profligacy.'[15] Here was the teenage Darwin, mixing with just such people. He was watching debates that touched on the most sensitive issues of the day.

Darwin's tiny polyps were important beyond their own sake. They were a central plank in Grant's evolutionary research. Grant rejected the conventional explanation: that animals were Creatively 'designed,' each unique and perfect for its niche. This did not explain why a bird's wing, a man's hand, and a bear's paw have identical bones. Grant believed that the same organs in different animals were homologous; the livers of, say, fish, frogs, and fowl were built of the same parts and conformed to a common blueprint. There was an underlying plan.

The notion that vertebrates displayed a 'unity of plan' was much in vogue in Paris in the early 1820s. But Grant, like his friend Geoffroy (a professor at the Paris Muséum), took it to radical extremes. He argued that *all* animals, from people to polyps, shared similar organs, which differed only in their complexity. This was not immediately apparent; jellyfish did not seem to have nervous systems, nor sponges hearts. Hence his excitement at one Wernerian meeting, when he announced that he had identified the pancreas in molluscs – and he exhibited a pinned-out *Doris* to prove the point.[16] He had found the homology of a mammal's organ in the sea-slugs.

The pay-off was this: with all animals structurally related, they could be threaded into a chain. And this is what gave the lowly beings at the base a fundamental importance. Their tissues were simpler versions of those in man. They could be used to explain human organs – to reveal their primitive origin and primal function.

Grant was even more controversial in giving the animals in this threaded sequence a real blood line. Walking with Darwin, he sang Lamarck's praises. At first Darwin was surprised – after all, the prevailing view was that each species had been directly created. But Grant's provocative ideas were well known. In his talks he had presented the sponge as the 'parent' of higher animals. Nor was he alone; free rein was given to speculation in the Edinburgh Museum. Even dry-as-dust Jameson penned an anonymous paper in 1826 praising 'Mr Lamarck' for explaining how the higher animals had 'evolved' from the 'simplest worms.' (This was the first use of the word 'evolved' in a modern sense.) Grant assumed that, as the primal earth cooled, changing conditions drove life towards higher, hotter-blooded forms. A progressive sequence of fossils stood as proof. He explained it as they strode along, and Darwin listened in 'silent astonishment.'[17]

Grant probably also mentioned his love of old Erasmus's *Zoonomia*. He had cited the book in his doctoral thesis, and admitted that it opened his 'mind to some of "the laws of organic life".' Now, here he was, walking with Erasmus's grandson; the opportunity was surely not lost. With Charles equally fond of the *Zoonomia*, their talk must have turned to those 'perpetual transformations' of nature which had so delighted its author.[18]

Grant went beyond Lamarck on one point: he traced the plant and animal kingdoms back to the simplest algae and polyps and accepted that they were related – that they had a common evolutionary starting point. The similar eggs of these primitive plants and animals were, he believed, analogous to the 'monads,' or elementary living particles. They gave a glimpse of life's basic building blocks. Since these monads could also emerge spontaneously from non-living matter, they held the key to the ultimate laws of life. Here, where the kingdoms converged, was the most fertile ground for the philosophical naturalist.

However unwittingly, Darwin was involved in research that was designed to reveal nature's innermost secrets. He had been offered a Lamarckian solution to one of the most profound problems of biology. Later he was to rejoin the path that Grant had started him on; for the present, he gave no hint that he appreciated its direction. But his teachers had shown him that naturalists *could* attempt to lift 'the veil that hangs over the origin and progress of the organic world.'[19] The trouble was that those tearing aside the veil, men like Knox and Grant, were so savagely anti-Christian. If Darwin knew that transmutation was not forbidden, he could see that it was far from respectable.

Others in Scotland were reinforcing the point, inexorably connecting politics and science. A timber merchant, Patrick Matthew, announced that inherited privilege ran counter to nature's law of progress through competition. An aristocracy was debilitating, it bucked evolution. If society did not change, he warned, Nature would 'avenge' herself; she would plunge the British race into decrepitude, push it into a bywater of history. Commercial struggle in a meritocracy, and that alone, could make the political leaders – degenerate aristocrats had no place in an evolving world.[20] It was a rationale for unfettered capitalism, and Darwin was to take this science to its logical extreme.

But in 1827 it was subversive science. It was what evangelicals had in view when they declared that evolutionists 'become turbulent subjects and bad men.' The false philosophy turns them into flaming democrats and Church-haters. They trust in lowly matter instead of Mind. Without a restraining faith in the soul, they lose their moral moorings and seek political redress in this world rather than the next. And innocent young lives run the risk of being devastated, swept along by the radical tide.

Just how devastated was shown by Coldstream. The Plinian debates on mind and matter threw him into a crisis. Nagging doubts crippled him throughout the 1826-27 session. Shortly after the 27 March meeting he graduated and went to Paris to gain hospital experience, but almost immediately he suffered a mental breakdown. The doctor reported that, although the young man was of 'blameless life,' he was still 'more or less in the dark on the vital question of religion, and was troubled with doubts arising from certain Materialist views.'[21]

But Darwin took all the heretical talk in his stride. Perhaps, coming from a line of freethinking males and Unitarians, he considered it passé. But he did learn one lesson: that passions were aroused by this alternative science. He also saw that it was the firebrands who were exploiting it, subversives intent on undermining Church authority and shifting power to the merchants.

Darwin's Plinian friends spent much of their time in the museum run by Robert Jameson. They probably advised Darwin to sit Jameson's natural history course, which he did. Jameson was famous as a 'Neptunian' geologist: he taught that the rock strata had been precipitated from a universal ocean. Darwin had already heard an opposite view from Professor Hope. Hope told *his* students that the granites had crystallized from a white-hot molten mass. The question – were the rocks solidified crust or muddy sediment – was of long standing. Too long, in fact; it had run its course elsewhere. But Hope and Jameson prolonged the set-piece debate in Edinburgh, to the delight of the students, whose fees provided the inducement. 'It would be a misfortune if we all had the same way of thinking,'

Jameson admitted. 'Dr. Hope is decidedly opposed to me, and I am opposed to Dr. Hope, and between us we make the subject interesting.'

Not enough for Darwin, evidently. He liked Hope, liked his style, and took his side, seeing geology in terms of the chemistry of cooling rock. Charles, the chemical dabbler, appreciated this sort of geology and the way it drove what his grandfather called the 'Earth-machine.'[22] Jameson on the other hand bored him. The Regius Professor, seen by some as one of the academic immortals, was dismissed with a yawn.

And yet Jameson's course was immensely popular, and Darwin learned from it. It was popular almost in spite of Jameson, who had all the flair of a master reading a roll call. *Geology* was what the audience came to hear. The subject was in vogue; it was practical and popular with the town's tradesmen, and in Darwin's year 200 attended, from students to city silversmiths and surveyors. The course was as comprehensively assorted as the audience. There was something for the jewellers and farmers as well as the students: mineralogy and meteorology, geology and natural history. Perhaps a little more if one looked; given Jameson's Lamarckian paper, one wonders what Charles made of his closing lectures on the 'Origin of the Species of Animals.'

Jameson met his students three times a week for practicals in the museum. Here he described exhibits, especially the minerals; and Darwin assiduously studied these, scribbling notes in his textbook and checking specimens against those in his own 'Cabinet.' He also learned the sequence of the rock strata, from the Scottish Old Red Sandstone to the Downs Chalk, and how to 'read' them like the pages of a book.[23]

The field trips too were popular, because many of the students were training to become surveyors and civil engineers. Jameson showed them rocks *in situ*, and Darwin heard him on the Salisbury Crags just outside town, ridiculing his rivals. For Jameson these trips were a crucial part of his course. Many of his auditors were young East India Company men, budding military surgeons and engineers. The Army Board recommended his class because it taught recruits leaving for the colonies how to keep records of the flora and fauna. It was designed to prepare the empire's doctor-wallahs for their travels.[24]

There were benefits from attending Jameson's class. His students were given free access to the magnificent museum. Here Darwin spent untold hours browsing, bird-stuffing, and taking notes. The museum was the 'city's pride and the country's boast.' Jameson had built it up, moving the exhibits into extensive new premises in 1820. The collection grew rapidly as ex-students sent exotic species from the colonies, the more so as their packages came in duty free by special concession. By now, too, His Majesty's surveying ships deposited half their natural treasures here (the rest went to the British Museum). As a result still more rooms had to be fitted out in 1826. In Darwin's day it was the fourth largest museum of its kind in Europe. But it was very much Jameson's preserve, and he ran it in a despotic manner. He hid skulls from phrenologists and kept rocks out of the hands of his rivals, causing one of Darwin's friends to dub him the 'absolute Dictator.'[25] Still, there is no denying that Darwin found himself in a rich environment, and he made good use of it.

The image of Darwin dissecting, stuffing, annotating, observing, taking sides, making discoveries, and enthralled by debates shows that his second year was no sterile period. His intellectual training had begun. Britain's best invertebrate zoologist had taught him to study minute detail while asking the larger questions. Darwin had become a geological observer, of the rocks as much as of the rocky debates. Even the medical lectures were formative in unexpected ways. Duncan's, however else they failed, promoted the Swiss botanist Augustin de Candolle's 'natural system' of classification.[26] This was Darwin's introduction to de Candolle, whose emphasis on the 'war' among competing species was to prove useful in later years. Even now, he was challenged to understand why plants and animals are classified the way they are.

Still more burning issues engulfed him: mind and matter, a disquieting Lamarckism, censorship, and authority. These were the issues that inflamed passions, and they revealed science as something more than accurate observation. It was a complex piece of political negotiation.

Of course, he was young, and much of it passed over his head. Moreover, he was actually here to study medicine, which he loathed. He was no nearer finding his professional feet. His mind was just not on a career. His homesickness increased as he thought of the shooting season. He asked Caroline, staying with the Wedgwoods, whether the gamekeeper 'was still Lord paramount' at Maer, and he wanted 'to know how many head of game have been killed.' 'He and Erasmus are quite troublesome in being so fond of letters from home,' Elizabeth Wedgwood confided. His misery with medicine was all too apparent, and in April 1827 he left for good – without a degree.

It was a decisive parting; most of his friends now went their separate ways. Grant accepted the chair of zoology at the new 'godless college,' London University. Browne went off to revolutionary Paris. Coldstream, recovering from his breakdown, at last found 'joy and peace in believing' and set up the Edinburgh Medical Mission Society. And Greg was called away to manage one of his father's mills.[27]

These reforming sons, flexing their professional muscles, had shown Darwin the meaning of intellectual dissidence. Nowhere was the tension between natural and supernatural explanations, capitalism and privilege, more apparent than in these Edinburgh debates. The struggle to redefine man as a material being, and nature as a secular, competitive market place, was a move against the old Kirk authority. For a moment, Darwin had glimpsed the social side to science. Perhaps, even, a new world in the making.

4

Anglican Orders

CHARLES DID NOT GO straight home to Shrewsbury. With spring in the air, he sniffed sweet freedom and set out from Edinburgh to explore. He travelled around Scotland, then on to Belfast and Dublin. In May 1827 he went to see sister Caroline in London. This was his first glimpse of the capital. Cousin Harry Wedgwood, a fresh-faced barrister at the Temple, met him and played the jaded city-dweller to his visiting innocent. Charles enjoyed himself, whatever his reservations about this 'horrid smoky wilderness.'[1] The two of them represented the clans at Dr Henry Holland's 'family' dinner, where their host, a fashionable society physician and distant relative, shocked Charles by calling whales cold-blooded, and everybody else by eating off his knife.

In town Charles plotted an excursion to Paris, his first (and only) trip across the Channel. The Doctor tipped off Jos Wedgwood: 'He has a lark in plan, which is, if you allow him, to join you & cross the sea, that he may have been in France, then return back again.' Uncle Jos was just leaving for Geneva, to fetch his younger daughters Fanny and Emma, who had been staying with their Aunt Jessie – Madame de Sismondi – for eight months. Caroline was to accompany him ('and how agreeable a companion she is'); Charles could travel safely in her company. Permission was granted, and he survived the rainy crossing, just. Even 'though not quite well' he managed to tuck into a hearty dinner of roast beef on board. At Paris the party divided, leaving Charles to fend for himself. With Browne and Coldstream in Paris, perhaps they showed him the *arrondissements* and scientific landmarks – the Natural History Muséum and the Jardin des Plantes. Anyway, a few weeks later Charles was rejoined by Uncle Jos and the girls, Emma looking lovely though 'a little bronzed,' and Fanny only 'one degree nearer prettiness' than before.[2] The trip was over too soon, and by July they were all safely back in England.

He took up where he left off the previous summer, hobnobbing with the Shropshire squires and planning the autumn shoot. His few friends were spread far and wide, but then it was nothing for the gentry to ride a dozen miles to visit one another's homes. Many were old family friends, like the Owens of Woodhouse, a morning's canter from Shrewsbury. William Mostyn Owen, formerly of the Royal Dragoons, was a 'peppery and despotic squire of the old school,' but he had daughters. Sarah and Fanny Owen had been close to the Darwin sisters since childhood, when they took singing lessons together at The Mount. Here was sport of a more genteel sort. Charles had heard at Edinburgh of how 'agreeable' they were, 'full of fun and nonsense.' 'They are very much admired,' Catherine baited him, 'and get plenty of partners at the Balls,' but 'Fanny . . . has quite the preference to Sarah . . . there is something so very engaging and delightful about her.' Neither of the girls, however, was in love with anything but France, and Charles, fresh from Paris, had stories to tell.[3]

The hunting season opened on 1 September. Squire Owen had a magnificent wooded estate, teeming with game, and Charles's own love was shooting. He paid so many visits to Woodhouse in the next few months that the girls began to see him as a 'shootable' too – eligible and personable, a catch. At times it was difficult to tell who was chasing whom. Sarah at twenty-three was slightly disadvantaged, being five years older than Charles. She also suffered by comparison with her precocious sister. Fanny, just turned twenty, was a natural charmer, dark-eyed and petite, with a rollicking spirit. She endured painting lessons for her father's sake, but preferred to play at billiards with the boys and to ride with the hunt. This sent her hot blood racing – and Charles noticed. He took her in tow and together they galloped off into the forest. Fanny would not hear of standing by while he enjoyed the action, a 'housemaid' to his 'postillion' as she put it in her quaint, coded language. She insisted on shooting too, and he helped her point the gun. The kick was fierce and left her slim shoulder black and blue, as she proved. But she did not wince. She was dreaming about the future, and bigger game.

All grand flirtation, of course – and maybe more. Charles, teased and tantalized by this raven-haired beauty, was infatuated. But he knew that he would have to make something of himself before he could ask the daunting Squire Owen for her hand. He thought of his own uncertain future as he travelled on to Maer, his usual hunting ground. On arrival he found Sir James Mackintosh in residence. The venerable Whig MP, Uncle Jos's brother-in-law, was licking his wounds after failing to get into Canning's Cabinet, and working hard at his *History of England*. Here was a success story for Charles to savour: a man made eminent after scraping through medical studies at Edinburgh only to change his career. Sir James was now the doyen of British political commentators and an expert on economics. He talked Darwin's ear off – about history, moral philosophy, and public affairs. The encounter made a lasting impression on them both. Darwin was awe-struck that anyone so famous should talk shop with him. And even Sir James confided afterwards, 'There is something in that young man that interests me.'⁴ A rare compliment, for the only other male inhabitant of Maer Hall he seems to have found agreeable was Charles's cousin Hensleigh Wedgwood, who had taken a shine to one of his daughters.

When it came to a career, Darwin now had little choice. While he was swanning about the country, carefree, his life was being mapped out. The Doctor, disappointed about Edinburgh and his son's disdain for medicine, now laid down the law with his usual heavy-handedness. No more misspent money, no more wasted time: if Charles reckoned he could fall back on his father's wealth, he had better think again. He would have to give an account of himself in a profession before he could have the security of the family purse. The only question was, if not medicine, which? The Darwins had produced lawyers and military men, true, but Charles lacked the self-discipline required of their ranks. There was, however, a safety-net to stop second sons becoming wastrels: the Church of England.

Dr Darwin, a confirmed freethinker, was sensible and shrewd. He had only to look around him, recall the vicarages he had visited, ponder the country parsons he entertained at home. One did not have to be a believer to see that an aimless son with a penchant for field sports would fit in nicely. Was the Church not a haven for dullards and dawdlers, the last resort of spendthrifts? What calling but the highest for those whose sense of calling was nil? And in what other profession were the risks of failure so low and the rewards so high?⁵

The Anglican Church, fat, complacent, and corrupt, lived luxuriously on its tithes and endowments, as it had for a century. Desirable parishes were routinely auctioned to the highest bidder. A fine rural 'living' with a commodious rectory, a few acres to rent or farm, and perhaps a tithe barn to hold the local levy worth hundreds of pounds a year, could easily be bought as an investment by a gentleman of Dr Darwin's means and held for his son. It was inducement enough for a young man to subscribe to almost any creed. When Charles was duly educated and ordained, he would simply step into the job. He would be set up for life. Among the gentry he knew so well, he would enjoy social prominence, a steady income, and eventually a handsome legacy.[6] He could even resume the hunting and hobnobbing that, at the moment, were jeopardizing his career.

There were family precedents besides. Both the Doctor's uncle and his half-brother had been Nottinghamshire rectors, and a couple of years earlier Uncle Jos had installed his own nephew as vicar of Maer.[7] Even now a Darwin cousin, William Darwin Fox, was preparing for the Church at Christ's College, Cambridge. That settled the matter. Charles would keep faith with one family tradition if not another. Send the boy to study with Fox, who would set him an example. Let him be educated for three years as a gentleman, take the Bachelor of Arts degree, and spend another year, if he liked, attending theology lectures to prepare for ordination. He could marry afterwards while apprenticed as a curate, and then be presented to a rural benefice not far from Shrewsbury – the perfect resting-place for a wayward second son.

It sounded like a *fait accompli*, but Charles wanted to think it over. Being a country parson would suit him to a tee, and not just the recreational aspects. It would buy him the time to follow in Grant's footsteps; in a rural parish he could devote himself to the tiniest members of creation. There was, needless to say, the small matter of his faith. He had a niggling doubt about what he actually believed. Edinburgh, after all, had exposed him to every conceivable type of unorthodoxy. But he had learned from his sisters to take religion seriously. And his own father, though not renowned for piety, counselled rectitude in all things, intellectual and moral alike – as did Uncle Jos, whom everyone respected as 'the very type of an upright man.' Anyway, a spell with divinity books would salve his conscience. So between the hunting and flirting, Charles ploughed through Bishop Pearson's elderly *Exposition of the Creed* and a few other turgid tomes.

One was by an up-and-coming Anglican apologist, the Revd John Bird Sumner. His *Evidences of Christianity* had been published only three years before, and its reasoning was overwhelming. Charles pitched into the book with pen poised, following Sumner step by step. This was the best defence of the faith he had ever come across. It stretched into one long argument, and the logic-chopping, massing of evidence, and weighing of probabilities all made sceptics look silly. Deftly, Sumner reduced their unbelief to a dilemma and impaled them on its horns: if Christianity be untrue, then 'either Jesus did not exist, or he actually lived, but was not the Son of God, hence an imposter.' The supposition of non-existence was 'evidently absurd,' Charles jotted, therefore sceptics must hold that Jesus 'deceived himself.' But the Gospels made this highly 'improbable.' They revealed a man whose miracles convinced unbelievers; we have 'no right to deny' the possibility of such events, Charles noted. And Jesus's religion remained 'wonderfully suitable . . . to our ideas of happiness in this & the next world.' Thus scepticism was undermined, Christianity proved. There was 'no other way except by [Jesus's] divinity,' Darwin concluded, 'of explaining the series of evidence & probability.'[8]

Charles found nothing objectionable in Sumner and the other books – nothing he could not say he believed – and in October, accordingly, he was accepted as a 'pensioner' to Christ's College, a full fee-paying undergraduate. Even so, he did not go up to the university that term – Michaelmas in Cambridge. Having examined his conscience, he had some hard swotting to do first.

Cambridge was a long way from Edinburgh. Intellectually it was much closer to Shrewsbury School. The classical learning that the Revd Butler drilled into young heads was *de rigueur* at the great Anglican seminary; yet much of it had gone right through Charles's, and he could scarcely remember the Greek alphabet, let alone parse a verb. The Doctor paid for a private tutor, and soon Charles was puzzling out the optative and wrestling with crasis. It was onerous work, and boring. Twice again he escaped to Woodhouse, but there was only game to stalk, the Owen girls having gone on holiday to Brighton. He dragged himself back to the books. By Christmas he was translating bits of Homer and the New Testament. Erasmus returned from London for the festivities and was revising too. After months at the Great Windmill Street Anatomy School, he was ready to qualify in medicine at Cambridge. So early in the new year, 1828, the brothers set off together once more.[9] Eras would sit the Bachelor of Medicine exam and reward himself with a grand tour of the Continent. But Charles faced four years' further study before taking his reward – a country parish.

The spires of Cambridge stuck out of the flat fenland like stalagmites, encrustments of feudal privilege built up over six centuries. This was low country, God's country. Fourteen parishes, seventeen colleges, sixteen thousand inhabitants – all crammed into little more than a square mile along the banks of the River Cam. The land was rich, like its owners, and the river flushed the soil down among the colleges where the drains spewed out, and the open sewer swilled northwards past Ely Cathedral to empty into the sea. This was a commercial artery, and Cambridge was the furthest navigable point inland. Bargees heaved and cursed their twenty-ton cargoes – coal and corn, oil and butter – dragging them upstream through the sediment and stench, along the 'backs' of the colleges to the Mill Pool, where the line to unload often stretched boisterously beneath the sacred precincts. Collegians objected to the racket, and their own imprecations only added to the din. A half-mile away in the town centre lay the market-place. Supplied by wagon from the Pool and surrounding farms, it offered provisions of all sorts. Prices were high, as they were in the shops and lodging houses packed together in the narrow streets that honeycombed the neighbourhood. The two thousand resident collegians had an appetite to match their collective wealth. And unlike the gownsmen of Edinburgh, they dominated the town.

All were Anglicans of course. They subscribed to the Thirty-nine Articles and accepted Christianity – according to the Church of England – as part and parcel of the law of the land. Cambridge and environs, if not a society of Christians, was at least regarded as a Christian society. Belief and conduct went together like high pheasant and vintage port. The fabric was held together by God himself through his personal agents, the clergy. Virtually all the college heads and most of the professors and Fellows had taken holy orders. About half the undergraduates, like Darwin, were destined for the Church. Many could look forward to a comfortable living with public responsibilities to match. The colleges held the patronage of a third of the parishes in Cambridgeshire, and almost half of the county's magistrates were parish priests. With agrarian disturbances on the rise, as impoverished farm workers fought for fair wages, the university was a cornerstone of law and order.[10]

In the town its influence was greater still. The mayor was obliged to maintain the privileges of the university, which were extensive and resented. Traders could be visited by the university Taxors, who monitored the market and fixed the price of bread. Publicans, landlords, and others with establishments used by undergraduates had licences from the university Vice-Chancellor, and these could be withdrawn if the Proctors reported any irregularities. The Proctors and their 'bulldogs,' burly college servants who backed them up, were the university's own police force. They shared duties with the local constabulary. They maintained 'public morals' – sexual proprieties – and regulated the behaviour of ex-students in town for three years after graduation. The Proctors' powers extended a mile beyond the town in all directions, and included the right to enter any suspect house and apprehend anyone they deemed in breach of regulations.[11]

These regulations were complex, archaic, and generally ignored. Few had read them and fewer worried about them. The situation was ripe for selective enforcement, and the Proctors were not above making examples of students. To stay on the right side of the law, Darwin learned a simpler set of rules from Eras: keep the college curfew, no fisticuffs or duelling, remain sober in public, *never* be seen with girls, and always, always wear a cap and gown.

Nothing was more likely to land an undergraduate in trouble than being out-of-gown. It was practically an admission that he was up to mischief. Why else would anyone wish to appear incognito? The cap and gown told who you were. Gownsmen could be spotted at once among the townsmen, who outnumbered them three to one. And the quality of the gown, its embellishments, and the cap announced your place in the university hierarchy. A Doctor of Divinity looked different from a Doctor of Civil Law; a graduate could be distinguished from an undergraduate. Even an undergraduate's social class was revealed in his dress.[12]

But while every student could be identified, the Proctors wore the same dress as the other Masters of Arts who milled about the town: plain black gowns with full-length, square-cut sleeves. Such camouflage had advantages, Erasmus warned his brother; it made proctorizing more like spying than policing. Anonymity was the privilege of those who enforced the law. And like spies, the Proctors were few in number – just a Senior Proctor, a Junior, and a couple of Proproctors to help them. To be really effective they needed extra eyes and ears, so they relied on tip-offs from students and staff. Once informed, they swung into action. Offenders were arrested, tried, and sentenced by the university's own court, presided over by the Vice-Chancellor.

The Vice-Chancellor had autocratic powers. He was almost invariably a senior clergyman, and sometimes a chaplain-in-ordinary to the King. He sat as solitary judge over town and gown alike. Justice was summary: townspeople could be fined, imprisoned, or 'discommuned' – banned from associating with collegians – which often meant economic ruin. But the nearest to imprisonment a collegian ever came was short-term confinement to college. Even severer penalties left him at large: banishment from town for a number of terms, or – at worst – expulsion from the university.[13]

Still, the pall of repression that hung over Cambridge was punctured from time to time by resentful outbursts. The Darwins reached town just as the reverberations of the latest incident were being felt. On the pretext of celebrating the failure of the Gunpowder Plot – Guy Fawkes's legendary attempt to blow up Parliament in 1605 – a crowd had taken to the streets on 5 November and tried to blow up the police and Proctors by hurling fireworks. At first gownsmen led the way, only to be swamped by locals. The Proctors waded in and arrested the troublemakers. A few students were reprimanded, but seven townsmen were hauled before the Vice-Chancellor and given gaol terms ranging from a month to a year.

The felons were thrown into the Town Gaol in St Andrew's Street, and were being held there the day Darwin reported to Christ's College, two minutes up the road. Next door to the gaol was the university's own penitentiary, the so-called Spinning House, which was even more notorious among the collegians. It was 'chiefly used for the confinement of such lewd women as the Proctors apprehend,' Darwin heard with astonishment, and could accommodate ten of them in squalid nine-by-seven-foot cells. The town-crier had been known to drop in and 'discipline the ladies of pleasure with his whip,' for which he received a fee of one shilling each. It was paid by the Vice-Chancellor, who was also the women's judge and jury. He held court in the Spinning House as often as required, with only the Proctors giving evidence. Convictions were inevitable; sentences could last up to several months, with worse treatment for reoffenders, including a spell on Castle Hill in the County Gaol.[14]

Charles found Christ's College full at the beginning of the new term – Lent (lasting until Easter). So he took lodgings over Bacon the tobacconist's in Sidney Street, a main thoroughfare leading straight up from St Andrew's Street towards the Cam and Castle Hill. Here he was in the thick of things, with the market-place a block away, Holy Trinity Church next door, and his college just across the road. Eras had briefed him well on the local lore and mores.[15] The authorities were despots all right, but he had little to fear so long as he kept in good company. Charles, for his part, could see his social options from the first day he donned cap and gown to explore the town.

On every street corner, in every pub, he saw examples of how young gents went about studying for the BA. The bookshops even sold a ribald guide that caricatured the two approaches: the 'varmint method' and the 'reading method.' The varmint was a man who cut lectures, skipped college chapel (thereby incurring fines), gave late-night feasts, smoked cigars, drove a coach, drank copiously, gambled compulsively, and proved 'a rum one at Barnwell,' home of the 'Cyprian tribes' (the riverside district a mile or so behind Christ's College noted for its young women). He cared only for field sports when sober, caught 'Barnwell ague' one drunken night, got picked up by the Proctors, and was threatened with 'rustication' (banishment). Only in his last term did he realize that he had to *read* for his degree, which he somehow managed to scrape through by 'cramming' for the exam.

The 'reading man' was a model of diligence. He attended lectures, never missed chapel, shunned parties, kept curfew, read twelve hours a day, seldom drank or smoked, never gambled, strove for academic honours and walked off with all the prizes. Though not the cleverest student, he would become a college tutor, then a Fellow, even a leader in the university – and all through his 'desperate perseverance in study.'[16]

Walking around, Charles could see that varmints tended to be well-heeled and upper-class. He could not afford the high life, even if so inclined, though he was a dab hand at having fun. He would happily mix with the reading men instead. Besides, he was under Doctor's orders to behave himself. Then there was his oath of matriculation. This was administered on the cold marble pavement of the Senate House, with the freshmen swearing in groups. Charles marched up one morning in January 1828, stood in a line before the Senior Proctor, and repeated after him in crisp ecclesiastical Latin that he would observe all the statutes and customs, remain unfalteringly attached to the university, and defend it under all circumstances, '*ita me Deus adjuvet et sancta Dei Evangelia*' – 'so help me God and his holy Gospels.'[17]

The Senior Proctor was the Revd Adam Sedgwick, whom Charles would come to know well in future years. Sedgwick had come up the hard way, a poor Yorkshire vicar's son who entered Trinity College as a sizar, took holy orders and gave up marriage to obtain a college Fellowship, became Woodwardian Professor of Geology at the age of thirty-three, and now, ten years later, was head of the vice squad and campus police. It showed what a reading man could achieve. Sedgwick, however, was no plodder, like other reverend professors. He was an established scholar – a Vice-President of the Geological Society of London – and passionately devoted to research on the

most ancient and little-known stratified rocks. At the moment he was
describing the magnesian limestone of northern England, or would
have been but for his pressing proctorial duties. They called for the
same fine eye, the same attention to detail as geological fieldwork. As
Charles settled in that winter Sedgwick honed his skills razor-sharp
on the lower strata of society, scouring the streets of Cambridge
rather than the dales of Yorkshire. He was left 'hardly a spare hour'
for weeks on end.[18]

Sedgwick penetrated the Cambridge underworld: layer upon layer
of laxity, just beneath the surface, with suggestive outcrops
everywhere. In the all-male collegiate community who could miss
them? Old bachelors and young bucks alike knew where to take their
pleasure. The geological Proctor's job was to study the terrain
minutely, map it and make it his own. He knew from personal
experience that temptation was rife (siring 'bastards' was all too
common among students, as court cases showed). His object was to
eradicate the cause, flush out those infernal females. The blasted girls
flocked to town from across East Anglia and Lincolnshire, endless
Janes and Sarahs and Elizas and Mary Anns. They were young,
usually in their teens, labourers' daughters and sisters, or sad orphans.
All of them were hungry, especially the pregnant ones and the
mothers. There were rich pickings in Cambridge: tables to be cleared,
laundry to be done, young sirs eager to spend. The temptation was
irresistible, though a girl might be forced to live out along 'Maid's
Causeway,' past the 'Garden of Eden,' as far as the gas works in
Barnwell.

If she dared. No wandering woman was safe with the Revd
Sedgwick on the prowl. In the market-place, along the Cam, on the
Barnwell footpath that led from the rear of Darwin's college, he was
ready to arrest her and swear in court that she had been 'streetwalk-
ing.' This January alone Sedgwick committed fifteen girls to the
Spinning House, seven of them in one day. It was the more necessary
at the start of term. Innocent freshmen like Charles had to be
protected, lest they be ruined and the moral fabric of society with
them. The ploy seemed to work. For the rest of the year Sedgwick's
busy schedule was interrupted by less than two committals a week.[19]

Charles could tell. He wrote to Sarah Owen that he had not set
eyes on a girl since leaving home. 'What *can* you mean,' she retorted
incredulously; 'have the Doctors, Proctors, Deans &c &c &c neither
Wives or Daughters!! or are the Cambridge shootables thought too
dangereux to be seen by them? pray satisfy my curiosity.' She had
missed the point, unfamiliar with the game laws in Cambridge. Here

the shootables were never in season; the hunters were always too *dangereuse*. But then Charles himself hardly needed protection; his first thoughts were all of Fanny. She seemed to be slipping away.

Fanny had been shocked to hear from Sarah that he was 'to become a *DD* instead of an *MD*.' You 'never let *me* into the secret,' she protested from Brighton. Charles could feel the chill in her letter. With seaside balls and nightly parties and real shootables galore, she would forget their autumn trysts. The romance was as good as over, even if she flaunted her eligibility – 'the Housemaid . . . is a year *older*,' she reminded him, and ordered 'Burn this'! He wrote back with a heavy heart, supposing that his would be the letter burned. Fanny played for time, and then offered a lame excuse. The gossiping old dears would be aghast at their exchanges – couldn't he just hear them? 'Dear me Ma'am would you believe it Miss "*Fanny Owen corresponds with a young man Ma'am at the University*".' Why, the very thought of such chit-chat 'worked upon my *heated fancy* to such a degree that *after mature deliberation* I thought it best to *remain silent* and if the Postillion should be in a *fury* at *my ingratitude* to explain it all away when we shall meet once more at the Forest.'

Cold comfort this, in the dead of winter, with Easter vacation two months away. Anything could happen before he looked into those dark eyes again. Still, his hopes rekindled, Charles answered warmly. But once more Fanny was coy, sitting on his 'long effusion' until just before term ended. Then off went another of her sparkling newsy notes, with talk of rectory parties and intrigues at the Assizes. In between she beckoned beguilingly: 'I have not yet learn't to play at *Billiards* . . . I have not been riding *near so much* as I *wish* . . . [P]ray tell me . . . when you expect to come home.' She assumed that 'my d^r. Postillion' would soon be paying his 'faithfull Housemaid' a long visit at Woodhouse. But 'for *Heaven's* sake burn this,' she insisted again, fantasizing about the stir her note would make if this time it fell 'into the hands of any of the *young men*.'

The reply came as spring broke. Woodhouse was in flower, the Assizes had begun, and the sisters were planning a trip to Wrexham Fair to shop and gad about – when, that is, Fanny was fully recovered. For she had taken to the upstairs bedrooms – '*Paradise Row*' in her secret coded notes – and had lain sick for days. Charles would be spending the vacation in Cambridge. If only he 'could *chaunce to come by*,' even '*out of the shooting Season*,' he might accompany them to the Fair.[20] But no, it was impossible. Fanny was devastated.

*

That first term above Bacon's shop had been a social whirl. Cambridge, for all its strictness, could be exhilarating. Young men confined at close quarters for months on end made fast friendships and shared new horizons. By Easter 1828 Charles's priorities had changed. Fanny, for all her flirtation, was not so much forgotten as demoted. Nor was it entirely her own fault.

College routine was absorbing enough, with compulsory tutorials and daily chapel. But it was the endless extra-mural activities that made Cambridge unique. Everywhere freshmen like Charles were discovering common interests and combining to indulge them. With their other lusts held in check, they expected meat and drink in pleasurable excess. Dining clubs proliferated and provided their gratification, although the loutish element needed only a bottle. Outdoor sports divided up similarly: there were popular pastimes for reading men and reckless diversions for the varmints. Shooting, steeplechasing, and carriage racing took place far away from town, where they were frowned on. But cricket was all the rage, and rowing on the Cam had just received official sanction with the formation of the University Boat Club (making the cruder water combats between gownsmen and bargees redundant). And, with so much loose money around, betting was ubiquitous; everything had odds, from batsmen bowled out to bottles drunk. Serious gamblers met regularly, playing 'Van John' (Blackjack) until the small hours, or having a flutter on the horses at Newmarket.

Leisure time was not just for games. Everyone joined conversation clubs where the hottest topics were thrashed out in smoke-filled rooms. The Union Debating Society, favoured by aspiring barristers and politicians, was open to anyone who subscribed one gold sovereign a year. It met on Tuesday evenings in the 'low, ill-ventilated, ill-lit, cavernous, tavernous gallery, at the back of the Red Lion Inn' in Petty Cury, a stone's throw from Darwin's digs. Other clubs provided for more genial discussion. The most exclusive, and reputedly most brilliant, was 'The Apostles,' whose twelve members included young Alfred Tennyson. (Erasmus had been a member briefly in 1823.) They gathered on Saturday evenings to wrangle over everything from fornication and the division of labour to the fraught question of whether mankind had 'descended from one stock.' No curriculum dared embrace such issues, and the Apostles, missionaries of romantic enlightenment, condemned the whole unreformed Cambridge system. Tennyson himself, in some bitter undergraduate lines, stigmatized

> . . . your Halls, your ancient Colleges,
> Your portals statued with old kings and queens,
> Your gardens, myriad-volumed libraries,
> Wax-lighted chapels, and rich carven screens,
> Your doctors, and your proctors, and your deans,

for hypocrisy and humbug, for reducing Christianity to rote learning, and for failing to meet the moral and intellectual needs of the rising generation.[21]

The Apostles had no monopoly on religious seriousness. The 'Sims,' as their detractors called them, were a pious clique who pestered students like Darwin continually. They followed the Revd Charles Simeon, the evangelical vicar of Holy Trinity Church, who had spent the best part of fifty years convincing the university that saving lost souls did not conflict with its traditions. Simeon held forth to capacity congregations, within earshot of Darwin's bedroom. 'His action is absurd in the extreme,' reported a curious freshman that year. 'He brandishes his spectacles when he talks of the terrible, and smirks and smiles when he offers consolation.' It was unctuousness rather than eloquence that brought Simeon his following, and on Friday evenings he welcomed the Sims to his rooms in King's College, 'smiling and bowing with the accomplished manners of a courtier.' Tea was served, with the young ordinands seated at their master's feet. Many were destined for the livings that the wealthy Simeon and his friends bought as a means of spreading their evangelical message.[22]

Charles was headed for the Church but unconcerned about his soul; the Sims failed to recruit him. Nor did he fall in with the literary set, or the cricketing and boating fraternity. That spring – Easter term – he read Shakespeare with his old friend Jonathan Cameron from Shrewsbury and took in the Fitzwilliam Museum with another schoolmate, Charles Whitley, who showed him the fine engravings. He acquired a taste for music, though he was tone-deaf, and went with Whitley's cousin, John Herbert, to King's College chapel, where he was ecstatic about the anthems.[23] But his real passion, his one serious sport, was the pursuit of beetles. Even chasing Fanny took second place.

He was in good company, with a beetle craze sweeping the nation. City dwellers, shut off from nature by the ugly industrial sprawl, were filling their cabinets with remnants of a lost Arcadia. Their bible was a beautifully written four-volume handbook, *An Introduction to*

Entomology, by the Suffolk rector William Kirby and a Hull business-man, William Spence. The craze spread to pastoral Cambridge too, indeed flourished there. The neighbouring fens teemed with rare species, and the colleges were crawling with trainee clergymen, taught to treasure the infinite diversity of God's creation.[24] And if ever there were an infinity of insects, it was shiny beetles. Many students were bitten by the bug, as species after species turned up new. Beetling was a field sport as much as any other, and one of the chief competitors was William Darwin Fox.

Cousin Fox belonged to the Derbyshire branch of the family – he was Charles's great-uncle's grandson, to be precise. A country gentle-man, like so many student pensioners, he had grown up at Osmaston Hall near Derby, surrounded by hunting parsons and wild life, which he adored. After three years at Cambridge – he had been at Christ's with Erasmus and was the same age – he was well groomed for a rural parish. He had mastered the fens, knew all the authorities on local flora and fauna, and perfected the art of netting beetles. Fox was a storehouse of facts about natural history, as Charles discovered the day they met. When Fox strode up, with his dog 'little Fan' trotting dutifully behind, Charles took to him instantly. Here was someone to look up to – a respectable Grant and Erasmus all in one, a companion and role-model. Soon Charles was sporting a dog of his own, a pint-sized bitch he called Sappho, who followed him around town and slept in his bed at night.[25]

The cousins and their dogs were inseparable during Easter term. They explored along the Cam, rooted through Jesus Ditch, and ransacked Midsummer Common in the quest for beetles. Sometimes Fox's friend Albert Way joined them. Charles clung to Fox's every word. Now was his chance to shine. He already had a head start, having conquered the most esoteric aspects of invertebrate anatomy in Edinburgh. Fox and his friends could be bettered, Charles felt sure, if only he listened attentively and helped himself to their lore. Beetling in Cambridge had become just as competitive as cricket or rowing – but with one difference. It was no team sport. A painstaking observer could win the student accolades. Charles, such a disappoint-ment to his father, became obsessed with the idea.

Nothing was spared in the trophy hunt. He bought a sweeping net and learned how to trap tiny jumping and flying insects. Sheaves of cardboard were festooned with beetles, each pinned in its proper place. He also hired a local to collect the debris from the bottom of barges that brought reeds from the fens, which he sifted through, hunting down his prey. It was not a simple slaughter, for some beetles had unexpected defences. One day, on stripping bark from a dead tree, he pinned down two rare types, one in each hand. Suddenly he saw a third, a new species, too good to lose. His action was that of a trained egg-collector. He popped the right-hand one in his mouth. Unfortunately it was a bombardier beetle, which promptly lived up to its name by squirting a noxious boiling fluid into his throat, momentarily stunning him. He spat the beetle out, losing it on the ground, and in the confusion dropped the others too.[26]

Charles had been well prepared for the ups and downs of small-game hunting on his annual outings at Woodhouse and Maer. Indeed, the chase, the mounting for display, and the ritual bragging among the beetle brotherhood were like the shoot, on a smaller scale. But there was another, technical side. The insects had to be identified, which meant scrutinizing their structure and habits. Manuals had to be consulted and their descriptions compared – Stephens's *Illustrations of British Entomology*, Samouelle's *Entomologist's Useful Compendium*, and the trusty Kirby and Spence. As in Edinburgh, Charles ran into problems of classification, and again he turned to the world leader on invertebrates, Lamarck. Proudly he informed Fox that he had identified a most 'valuable insect' in his collection: it was a rough-bodied, black beetle with red antennae, which the books gave as *Melasis flabellicornis*. With rising excitement, he exclaimed, 'the description & habits in Samouelle & Lamarck *perfectly* agree.'[27] He had caught a German species. At last he was in the running, with a beetle so rare in England that it had been seen only twice before, and never around Cambridge.

When really stuck for a name, Charles had experts he could call on. There was more to the academic side of beetling than books. While other gownsmen drank themselves into a stupor on Friday nights or sipped tea with the Revd Simeon, Fox took Darwin to the home of the Revd John Stevens Henslow for claret and convivial discussions on natural history. Henslow, only thirty-two, had taught Erasmus mineralogy, and Charles knew of his reputation for scientific omnicompetence. Now in his third year as professor of botany, Henslow made his soirées a hive of activity for budding naturalists, a club for young ordinands like Charles whose main interests lay outside the classical curriculum. Occasionally other reverend professors attended – great guns like Sedgwick, or the polymathic William Whewell, the new professor of mineralogy.[28] Clerical tutors such as George Peacock or country parsons such as Leonard Jenyns, Henslow's brother-in-law, would also drop in to mingle with the undergraduates.

No raucous Plinian Society this, torn by infidel ideas, but it was still a thrill to hear the dons 'conversing on all sorts of subjects, with the most varied and brilliant powers.'[29] They could answer Charles's queries, and some, like Jenyns, collected beetles themselves. By term's end Darwin was fired up for natural history as never before. He knew he had found his niche. The Doctor had been right, the Church was the place to be.

5

Paradise & Punishment

HOME FROM CAMBRIDGE for the summer, he kicked his heels, 'dying by inches from not having any body to talk to about insects.' He mooched around, intoning 'I do wish Fox was here.' The beetles had deserted him too, and even his collecting slackened off. A long list of captures from Fox and Way sent a 'pang of jealousy' shooting through him. It was not unlike the chill feeling when he worried about his girlfriend Fanny and her other flames. He fretted, fearing that she was with someone else. There was nothing for it but to find out. Who knew, maybe she had forgiven his absence at Easter? And if not, he might still turn up some beetles in Squire Owen's forest. Anything was better than idling around Shrewsbury with clucking sisters and Erasmus away. So towards the end of June 1828 he trotted off. Yes, Fanny was waiting for him; the 'dutiful Housemaid' was still there, delighted to see her 'd^r. Postillion.' Nothing had changed.

Or almost nothing; they were a year older, and growing up fast. Charles was tall, nearly six feet, and rather 'thick set,' though hardly overweight. He had a new 'varsity' poise about him, yet he was still his 'placid, unpretending, & amiable' self. Not by any stretch handsome, but Fanny found him fun – in fact, he gave her an illicit thrill. She was definitely a young woman now, coming of age and filling out. Charles thought her 'the prettiest, plumpest, Charming personage that Shropshire posseses [sic],' and it showed. He took her hunting again, for beetles. It was strawberry season and Woodhouse was full of beds. Perfect stalking ground: they got down on hands and knees, then lower still, and before long they were stretched out 'full length' beside each other, 'grazing' the luscious fruit, behaving like beasts.[1]

It was almost too much of a good thing, and Charles had to tear himself away. He had an appointment with Cambridge friends at Barmouth on the Welsh coast. Here they planned to read for three months with private tutors. Reading parties were a jolly junket, an excuse for undergraduates to dress as they pleased, stay out late, and let off steam without fear of the Proctors. Charles's own subject was maths, but he wanted to combine both worlds and looked on it as an 'Entomo-Mathematical expedition,' although he hoped 'by the blessings of Providence' that '*the science*' (insects) would not 'drive out of my poor noddle the Mathematics.' It was a tacit admission that his maths was suffering. After two terms of tutoring, he was still baffled by the basics of algebra. The binomial theorem was beyond him, and he could see no reason in irrational numbers.[2] The time should have been used in catching up.

Instead, insects got the upper hand. By the end of July he had all but given up maths. 'I stick fast in the mud at the bottom & there I shall remain in statu quo,' he admitted to Fox, struggling to stay afloat himself while revising for his BA exam. In truth, there were too many diversions along the Cardigan Bay shore. He could not have kept his mind on algebraic abstractions had he wanted to. Most days were spent boating in the estuary, or walking the hills, or flyfishing in nearby lakes. His constant companions were two other hopeful ordinands, Thomas Butler, the son of his old Shrewsbury headmaster, and his musical friend John Herbert, who had taken him to King's College chapel. Both were older, but for the first time Charles was the leader, and he savoured the experience. Climbing 3000 feet to the top of Cader Idris, eight miles away, he perched on a precipice and nonchalantly shot the passing birds, while the others waited below to retrieve the corpses for stuffing. Herbert had the alcohol for killing insects, and Darwin netted untold numbers of beetles and butterflies, showing his friends the tricks of the trade.[3] Dealing with nature, he felt more at ease, more in control.

Beetling was the 'Business,' though Fox left him feeling that he had a lot to learn. Every few weeks the cousins exchanged letters. Darwin bragged about his captures, begged 'instructions about keeping Crysalises' from his 'old master,' and insisted on prompt replies. 'It is quite absurd,' he half apologized, 'how interested I am getting about the science.' Fox invited him to visit Osmaston for the first time after the reading party was over. It was too good an offer to turn down, and Darwin left Wales early, at the end of August, in time for the hunting season. So much for mathematics.

Actually he had been dying to see Fox, and, after killing a 'very contemptable [sic]' seventy-five head of game at Maer in a week, spent the rest of September with him. Osmaston Hall was a perfect menagerie, packed with creatures 'alive & dead.' Darwin was in his element. He fired off instructions to Herbert and Butler to capture certain beetles for his cousin, and promised him some of the stuffed birds. This was competition tempered by gratitude, catches conspicuously given away. But then Fox remained a paragon of generosity, and Darwin really could not thank him enough. 'Formerly I used to have two places, Maer & Woodhouse, about which, like a wheel on a pivot I used to revolve,' he enthused to him. 'Now I am luckier in having a third.'[4]

One of these places remained to be visited, his last port of call before returning to Cambridge. He could hardly wait to reach Woodhouse, with its beds of strawberries and the ones upstairs, as the girls teased, on 'Paradise Row.' It was 'a paradise,' he confided to Fox, 'about which, like any good Mussulman I am always thinking' – full of sensuous pleasures and voluptuous nymphs. Only here, he added, 'the black-eyed Houris . . . do not merely exist in Mahomets noddle, but are real substantial flesh & blood.'

All summer his imagination had run riot. Back in Squire Owen's forest, Fanny was 'as charming as ever.' They galloped through the woods again, played at billiards, and frolicked. It was a week lived to the full. After he left, Fanny chased him with a letter dated 'Paradise Row ½ past 12 – Saturday night.' She laced it with innuendo, complaining in her coquettish way that she now had '*nobody to ride with*' or to give her billiard lessons. 'I . . . shall forget all my *fine strokes*,' she purred. But her memories remained fresh. His gifts made sure of that – the books, and the swallow-tail butterfly, which she found so '*werry pecoolier*.' Nor did Charles lack for gratifying thoughts. As he rode back to Cambridge he carried a keepsake of his own, a handsome snuff box for his new habit, compliments of the Squire.[5] The outlook for romance was good.

Christ's College was now his home. It wasn't one of the older colleges, having existed for only three centuries, nor was it among the largest, with only a hundred-odd resident members. It was altogether middle-of-the-road: rather quiet, somewhat given to 'horsiness,' with a fairly high proportion of noblemen to pensioners, which made it a congenial place for men with spending money. The religious atmosphere was self-contented and relaxed, in keeping with tradition. John Milton, the poet, had been a student here; Ralph Cudworth and Henry More, the latitudinarian theologians, Master and Fellow respectively. In the elegant stone-cased front court of the college, on the south side, up G staircase to the first floor, were the rooms traditionally inhabited by the theologian best known to students for his pellucid, passionless prose, the author of their set texts, *The Evidences of Christianity* and *The Principles of Moral and Political Philosophy*, the Revd William Paley.[6] On All Saints' Day 1828, with the arrival of a new tenant in Paley's rooms, the nameplate on the door read 'C. Darwin.'

Charles was three weeks late and wasted no time settling in. He unpacked his brand-new, £20 double-barrelled shotgun – a parting gift requisitioned from his father and sisters – and dozens of boxes of beetles. A veteran Shropshire collector, the Revd Frederick Hope, had looked over the lot before Charles left home and pronounced it the richest annual haul he had seen in years. Charles was longing to tell his cousin, and when they met up at last the talk was all of trophies. This was Fox's last term before sitting the BA examination. He had been dilatory about his studies and now it was a case of cram or fail. The two of them breakfasted together daily and as the weeks passed Darwin saw his cousin grow desperate. Just before Christmas, he found Fox sitting forlornly in his rooms, wind howling at the windows, in 'awe and tribulation about his degree.' He would have to stay in college for the holidays, studying alone, but – generous as ever – he gave Charles an exotic present for the Doctor, a pair of live Death's Head hawk moths that squeaked like mice when stroked.

Charles forgot to say goodbye. Back in Shrewsbury he posted an apology, pitying his cousin's dismal state 'from the bottom of my heart.' Then in the new year he went to Fanny's mansion for a week. There was real shooting this time, and one of the Owen boys was gashed in the eye by a percussion cap. Charles had never been 'half so much frightened' at the sight of blood, even though this was an accident, and not his old bogey, surgery. When he returned home from his kissing and hunting trip he had a worrying lesion of his own, inflamed lips. They became so dreadfully painful that he began taking 'small doses' of arsenic for relief. That month he had planned to visit Edinburgh once more, 'before all my friends entirely leave.' But while Coldstream, now recovered from his breakdown, expected his arrival daily, geeing him along with news that 'the *Plinian* is flourishing most vigorously' under the same mad doctor William Browne, Darwin was laid up for weeks.[7] The trip was lost. Shortly after his twentieth birthday, his mouth finally healed, and he headed off for London, as a way stage back to Cambridge.

Erasmus had just returned to the 'dreary wilderness of houses' after his Continental tour, and Charles wanted to hear all about

Munich, Milan, and Vienna. Even more, as a man obsessed, he wanted to meet the beetle top brass. There was nowhere better. Insects were all the rage in London, where the experts had recently grouped themselves into an informal Entomological Club, breaking away from the crusty Linnean Society's constraints. His Shropshire friend, the Revd Hope, 'the most generous of Entomologists,' provided his *entrée*. Hope, in town that week, knew all the collectors. Darwin spent a day with him and came away clutching 160 new species. Another among the top brass, almost literally, was the Admiralty man James Stephens, whose *Illustrations of British Entomology* proved so useful. He had 'the best collection of British insects in the country' and kept an open house, welcoming fellow addicts. Darwin found him a 'very goodhumoured pleasant little man.' He picked up the tittle-tattle, hearing Stephens and Hope run down the Revd Jenyns, the senior beetle collector in Cambridge, as 'selfish & illiberal' (such was honour among insect men). With experts confiding in him and enriching his collection, Darwin felt his stature rising. He ordered a new £15 drawered cabinet to house his specimens in splendour, as Stephens did. And he boasted that 'only Stephens & Hope' also possessed the rare 'Diaporis Anea' (a round, broad-headed beetle, *Diaperis*), which he had taken in Shropshire over the holiday.

With Erasmus as his guide, Charles launched out and made the rounds of scientific London: 'the Royal Institution, Linnean society, & Zoological gardens, & many other places where Naturalists are gregarious.' Five days of this was the biggest 'dose of "the Science"' yet. Eras knew the tawdry venues too, places where animals were gregarious, like Cross's Menagerie, with its huge mandrill that 'indulged in a pipe & a glass of grog daily at one o'clock.' Already he had seen this massive monkey with a Union-Jack complexion nearly wrench the arm off a man who, supposing with Lamarck that it might be a distant relative, tried to shake its hand. Lamarck's notions of human ancestry were familiar enough to the Darwin brothers, but this was taking credulity too far. They behaved themselves respectfully, and Charles even planned to drop in on his old Lamarckian rambling companion, Robert Grant, now delivering his first course at London University. Then it was straight back to Christ's College and more sacred topics. He boarded the Cambridge coach at the George and Blue Boar in Holborn.

Back in college, the weather was miserable – 'rain, sleet & cold winds, alternating' – and Charles's mood matched. It was such a letdown after Woodhouse and London; so empty, dreary, and sad. Fox had scraped through his exam with an undistinguished pass and left the university. He was casting about for a curacy near Osmaston, though with such little success that a bishop was pulling strings. Darwin felt keenly for his cousin, but even more for himself.[8] He was at a loose end and missed Fox badly.

He was losing direction again, as at Edinburgh. His aimlessness was made worse by seeing his brother gallivanting about on the family fortune. Nor was Fox around to snap him into shape and talk him into holy orders. The first inkling of the problem had come during the reading party the previous summer. In a freewheeling conversation, Darwin had asked Herbert whether he really felt 'inwardly moved by the Holy Spirit' to enter the Church. When the bishop put the question to him in the ordination service, what would he reply? 'No,' answered Herbert; he could not say that he felt moved. Darwin chimed in, 'Neither can I, and therefore I cannot take orders.' He had doubts, as many did, but then he was in Wales, talking off the record. His verdict was rigorous rather than serious. He laughed off their true confessions by baiting Herbert for unbelief, dubbing him 'Cherbury' after Herbert of Cherbury, the father of English Deism.[9]

Come Lent term 1829, Darwin had real qualms. He might not have been moved by the Holy Spirit, but he hadn't been moved by his studies either. He was now a year into his degree, and his tutor warned him that he was ill prepared to attempt even the preliminary exam, the so-called 'Little Go.' He was running into trouble and seemed helpless to make amends. He marvelled at those getting on with their careers, especially Fox; his cousin still had no parish in sight, but at least he was poring over divinity books for his ordination exam. Charles begged him for advice on the subject, desperate for encouragement: 'You need not be afraid of preaching to me prematurely,' he pleaded. He latched on to others. 'Old Price,' the Darwins' Shrewsbury schoolmate, was tutoring in Cambridge and 'reading very hard' for his own ordination. Charles stuck to him so closely that it seemed to Price like 'hero worship.' One day, as they walked to the Cherry Hinton quarries south of town, Price stopped, pointed out some common plants, and proceeded to identify them. Darwin was astounded. 'Price Price,' he exclaimed, 'what w^d. I give to be such a naturalist as you'![10]

Despite this sentiment, a sort of 'scientific seediness' was setting in. Even his enthusiasm for insects was waning. He was 'sadly in want of somebody to entomologize with' and the two locals he employed to catch beetles were letting him down. In fact, one was offering first pick to a fellow collector, Charles ('Beetles') Babington, a future botany professor, who presumably paid more. Charles caught him in the act and had it out, threatening to throw the 'd - - d rascal' down the stairs if ever he came to his rooms again.

Fox's support seemed to be failing too. Charles grew exasperated. Weeks went by without an answer to his letters. 'You idle wretch,' he finally exploded on April Fools' Day, why do you not 'treat me like a gentleman'? 'If you did but know how often I think of you & how often I regret your absence, I am sure I should have heard from you long enough ago.' Charles topped it with more complaints and manipulation. Cambridge was 'rather stupid;' his lips were playing up; there was 'scarcely any one' to walk with but Whitley – and he, Charles jabbed, 'has begun to take your place.' Even the dog had to go. Sappho, the last living reminder of their beetling days together, was given away.[11]

Self-obsessed and self-pitying, Darwin was in the doldrums. Maybe Erasmus had noticed the first signs of it while they were together in London. Maybe he had warned Charles about the dangers of mid-course *ennui* – drifting into shallow company, brushing with the law, wrecking his career, and angering the Doctor. Whatever was said, Charles took it ill, and he fell out with Eras too. Now he could no more summon the courage to write to his 'injured brother' than Fox seemed able to communicate with him. It was a distressing time.

He was lonely but not alone. He laughed and sluiced his sorrows away with a crowd of drinking pals. His angry letter to Fox – soon regretted – was written while under the influence. Nor was this his first such 'debauch.' Herbert and Whitley had been 'giving some very gay parties,' with up to sixty men at each binge. They smoked and joked and gambled, and enjoyed plenty of lubrication. On the mornings after, Darwin sobered up by reading Gibbon's *Decline and Fall of the Roman Empire*, the perfect tonic for an overindulgent ordinand. It became a regular habit. He put in some hard riding too. One night the eastern sky was lit up, and he set out with three others to investigate. The blaze turned out to be eleven miles away, and they 'rode like incarnate devils' there and back. It was two in the morning and pitch black before he crept into college, violating curfew. Rustication, as he knew, was now an ace away.[12]

Others were more openly tempting the police, if not Providence. Events came to a head at the end of term in an ugly street scene, just a few hundred yards from Darwin's college. If he didn't rush from his rooms on hearing the tumult, he soon received firsthand reports.

For months resentment had been building up against the Proctors, the Revds Alexander Wale and Henry Melville. Wale, Sedgwick's successor, was zealous in his job, and Spinning House committals were his *forte*, which no doubt helped charge the air. On the morning of 9 April the storm broke. Students thronged the galleries of the Senate House, where the Proctors were marshalling undergraduates for their exams. They bellowed, 'Groans for Melville,' 'Groans for Wale,' following each with an appropriate noise. Melville cleared the galleries and marched outside with Wale to disperse the crowds, hissing and jeering in the rain. When the students spotted Wale, the real abuse began – 'Burke him!' some cried, and others, 'Stinking fish!' The Proctors retreated inside the Senate House and re-emerged fifteen minutes later only to find a well-armed mob. They bolted down Trinity Street and made for the safety of Wale's college, St John's. The mob gave chase, shouting insults and hurling turnips, dung, and dead rats. At the college gates the students tried to force their way in, but the Proctors escaped. The uproar lasted for two and a half hours.

Darwin, on the students' side, wrote to Fox the next day exulting in the scene. (Wale was Fox's friend, so Charles trod gingerly, but still he could not conceal his sympathies.) The Senior Proctor had been 'most gloriously hissed,' he reported, '& pelted with mud.' He was 'driven so furious' that even his servant 'dared not go near him for an hour.' Little did Darwin realize that revenge was already being wreaked on those, like himself, who abetted Wale's humiliation. Wale and Melville had glimpsed familiar faces in the crowd, and the culprits were summoned before the Vice-Chancellor, who was passing sentence even as Darwin wrote. For being out-of-gown and shouting abuse, four were rusticated and one was fined and admonished publicly before the Senate.[13]

By the next day Darwin and everyone else knew about the sentences. Outraged by what they considered leniency, the Proctors and Proproctors had quit *en masse*. They printed their resignation note and posted it around the colleges. The university had made examples of a few, but the students had won the victory and rid themselves of the hated Proctors. For Darwin's part, he was jolted into reflecting on the consequences of law-breaking. Other events too brought him up with a start. After weeks of abusing Fox for not writing, he opened a note from his cousin, only to learn, to his shame and sorrow, that Fox's sister was dying. And he had been selfishly pestering the man for a supportive letter. He was thrown into a sombre reassessment of his whole conduct.

That same Saturday, 11 April, another moral lesson was being taught, this time to everyone in Cambridge: a young man was being led to his death on Castle Hill. Here, in the County Gaol, men accused of capital offences – some two hundred crimes carried the death penalty in 1829 – awaited trial in the Shire Hall, above the butchers' stalls in the market-place. The guilty had their sentences carried out on Castle Hill as an example to the community. Public hanging was the ultimate deterrent in this world, just as hell-fire was in the next. The fear of the law and the fear of the Lord were all of a piece in Cambridge.

As Darwin shuddered at Fox's news, a noose was tightening. The execution had been well publicized. In an open letter, an evangelical clergyman had invited the whole county to attend and offer prayers 'for the unfortunate Culprit, that repentance and faith and so forgiveness may be granted him.' For 'highway robbery' a few miles west of town, William Osborne was hanged on the gallows.[14]

By now Charles had frittered away his entire allowance, leaving tutors' bills unpaid. Still, he sallied out with Whitley to London for the first part of the Easter break, and presumably made his peace with Eras. On returning to college, he found a grim note from Catherine in Shrewsbury. Fox's sister was dead. Charles sent his cousin a tortuous condolence. Certain that all sympathy would be useless, he set store by Fox's own 'good principles & religion' and pointed him perfunctorily to the Bible's 'pure & holy . . . comfort.' His tone was formal and detached; he was distancing himself from pain. When Fox, his spirits lifted, replied in May with an invitation to visit Osmaston, Charles sent him his itinerary for the coming months. They could not possibly see each other before September, Darwin insisted.

His devil-may-care lifestyle continued, despite recent salutary events:

> I have been in such a perfect & absolute state of idleness,
> that it is enough to paralyze all ones faculties; riding &
> walking in the morning, gambling at Van John to the most
> disgusting extent in the evenings, compose the elegant &
> instructive routine of my life. Lord help me . . .

The 'less that is said about it, the better,' he told Fox. 'What a great deal of advice I should receive were you but here.' Not that he would have paid any attention to Fox's reprimands, being too busy 'riding & Entomologizing.' 'Preaching' about divinity was the last thing he wanted; a parish was the farthest from his mind.[15] The future would take care of itself.

May saw Professor Henslow's first 'public herborizing excursion' of the year, on which students collected plants. The Revd Jenyns addressed the Cambridge Philosophical Society on the divine design of feathers. On Tuesday the 19th a pair of undergraduates ascended in a balloon with the renowned aeronaut Mr Green. Lift-off was at 6.30 a.m. from a yard in Barnwell; scores of students assembled to cheer them on, and the balloon sailed forty miles west, all the way to Castle Ashby in Northamptonshire. Darwin meanwhile was making air raids on insects. With the late spring, the netting competition was fierce. He had locals scouring pond and fen for him again, and his own success with water beetles was spectacular. 'I think I beat Jenyns' on this score, he bragged to Fox on the eve of the balloon ascent.[16]

It was a jolly, good-natured time – the calm shortly to be shattered by an outrage against the staid Anglican order. Easter term was to end in criminal convulsions, as Lent had. Again Darwin was in the thick of things, watching society take revenge. But this time the lesson to be learned was even more memorable.

On Thursday the 21st, the veteran radicals Richard Carlile and the Revd Robert Taylor tramped into Cambridge. They were notorious freethinkers, their reputations preceding them: proselytizers whipping up anti-Christian passions among the rabble. Carlile was a cobbler's son and a former tinplateman by trade. He had made his name as a fiery republican journalist and been given a six-year gaol sentence for blasphemous and seditious libel in the wake of the 1819 Peterloo Massacre (when innocent civilian demonstrators were cut down by cavalry). Taylor, his comrade-in-arms since his release, had himself just served a year for blasphemy. Blasphemy was a social crime because Christianity was part of the law of the land. By loosening the faith of 'illiterate' workers (as the Attorney General confirmed), Carlile and Taylor were lessening their ability 'to bear up against the pressure of misery and misfortune.' These demagogues, spokesmen for the secular working classes, were the bane of respectable society – clerical Cambridge not least.

In town, Taylor took the lead. He was another who had given up medicine for the Church, and he knew the university well, having been at St John's for three years. The Revd Simeon had even gained him his first curacy. But five years after ordination Taylor gave up Christianity, and his evangelical ebullience turned into eccentric anti-clericalism. He set up a Christian Evidence Society and began lecturing in London pubs. Wearing baroque vestments, he lampooned the

Anglican liturgy and lashed out at the barbarities of the Establishment and its pagan creed. The law caught up with him; he was gaoled and in his cell wrote *The Diegesis*, a biting attack on Christianity based on comparative mythology.[17]

Now, with his book hot off the press and Carlile by his side, Taylor was courting more trouble with an 'infidel home missionary tour.' That Thursday they sauntered around the colleges and sized up the opposition, bracing themselves in the evening with a hell-fire sermon from the Revd Simeon at Holy Trinity Church ('one of the worst imaginable for the morals of mankind,' they sneered). The next morning they set up their 'Infidel Head-Quarters' just off the market-place, in a lodging above a print shop in Rose Crescent. This was the heart of enemy territory, a stone's throw from the Senate House and two blocks from Christ's College. It was a shop that Darwin knew, having acquired a taste for engravings.[18] The unsuspecting landlord, William Smith, booked his guests in for a fortnight.

Four days of moral mayhem followed. By noon on Friday Taylor and Carlile had sent a printed challenge to the Vice-Chancellor, the leading Doctors of Divinity, the heads of all the colleges, and the Revd Simeon.

CIRCULAR

The Rev. Robert Taylor, A.B., of Carey-street, Lincoln's Inn, and Mr. Richard Carlile, of Fleet-street, London, present their compliments as Infidel missionaries, to (*as it may be*) and most respectfully and earnestly invite discussion on the merits of the Christian religion, which they argumentatively challenge, in the confidence of their competence to prove, that such a person as Jesus Christ, alleged to have been of Nazareth, never existed; and that the Christian religion had no such origin as has been pretended; neither is it in any way beneficial to mankind; but that it is nothing more than an emanation from the ancient Pagan religion. The researches of the Rev. Robert Taylor, on the subject, are embodied in his newly-published work, THE DIEGESIS, in which may be found the routine of their argument.

They also impugn the honesty of a continued preaching, while discussion is challenged on the whole of the merits of the Christian religion.

Here was a calculated attack on the faith 'by law established,' an outrageous ploy to rend the social fabric and raze feudal Cambridge. As a further affront, the missionaries made a mockery of etiquette, adding a postscript: 'At home, for conversation, at any appointed time. 7, Rose Crescent.'[19]

The divines went into a holy huddle late on Friday, plotting their revenge. The infidels meanwhile continued their rakish progress around town. Taylor, immaculately clad in cap and gown, paced through the sacred precincts greeting old friends, searching for freethinkers, and handing out circulars. Collegians might rattle off rote answers to his challenge – they had learned their Anglican apologetics, as Darwin had, from the likes of the Revd Sumner – but none had ever received a challenge personally, from a Cambridge-educated ex-convict, an infidel in academic robes. That fine evening the colleges were eerily silent.[20] The temperature began to rise.

Saturday brought the backlash, though not the kind Taylor and Carlile had expected. A promised article in the morning paper, advertising their mission, failed to appear. Then one of the new Proctors turned up to interrogate the landlord, Mr Smith. Soon after, another came and demanded his lodging-house licence. Smith refused to hand it over and appealed to the Vice-Chancellor, begging 'most deferentially' to know the reason. He had not violated the lodging-house regulations. Indeed, his licence had only been granted its annual renewal the day before. No reply came. Instead, that afternoon a notice was issued by the Vice-Chancellor and Proctors, officially revoking his licence. It was posted in the butteries of all the colleges, a warning to Darwin and his friends lest they fall foul of the law themselves. The lodgings at 7 Rose Crescent were now off bounds.[21]

Taylor and Carlile, infuriated by this 'paltry spite,' struck back. They posted their own notice on Sunday. It went up on the door of the University Library, next to the Senate House, in public view. Written in Latin and Greek, it carried their challenge to the university at large – a university that 'punishes the innocent,' 'crushes the weak,' 'oppresses,' and 'persecutes.' Smith, with a wife and six children, had been deprived of half his livelihood at the stroke of a clerical quill. By the next day everyone was talking about the 'iniquity' of his fate and the brash infidel challenge. It was an object lesson on the perils of religious inadvertence. Even Smith's plea for mercy fell on deaf ears.

But who was to blame? The authorities were not universally adored, yet Taylor himself could still be held responsible for the outrage, and a gang of 'young men' prepared to avenge the hapless landlord. A turncoat clergyman deserved ducking in the Cam for cloaking himself in academic attire and deceiving the tradesman about his true identity. It was dishonourable conduct, unbecoming of a gentleman. Only Proctors went incognito.

On Tuesday, when Taylor and Carlile got wind of the vigilantes, they apologized to Smith, prodded the Vice-Chancellor again to restore his licence, and slipped out of town. Not wholly empty-handed: they had uncovered 'about fifty ... young collegians, who were somewhat bold in avowing Infidelity among each other' – even an Apostle or two perhaps. But only a handful of the students, the diehards knew, would ever 'break ... the shackles' of a Cambridge education and become out-and-out unbelievers. And they would have 'a most painful conflict to endure.'[22]

One such was Darwin. In later years he would remember Taylor as 'the Devil's Chaplain,' fearing that he himself might be similarly reviled, an outcast from respectable society, a terror to the innocent, an infidel in disguise. But for now he was safe – and ready to mend his ways.

6

The Man Who Walks With Henslow

THE CHURCH OF ENGLAND was under more serious attack than this. While Darwin had been at Cambridge, Parliament had passed bills allowing Dissenters and Catholics to hold public office for the first time in centuries. The Anglican ascendancy had been snapped, aristocratic nepotism was on the wane, and a vast liberal tide was gathering to break down the ancient walls of privilege. Even in Cambridge, .cracks had appeared during Darwin's dissipations. Town and gown fought against the new freedoms, but in June 1829, after a bitter election, the 21-year-old William Cavendish – later the Duke of Devonshire – was returned for the university as Whig MP. At Oxford meanwhile, where Darwin was invited to watch the first annual boat race between the sister universities, the clergy kicked out their Tory member Robert Peel as a traitor for supporting Catholic emancipation. The boat race went easily to Oxford, a token perhaps that reform would remain an uphill struggle.[1]

Back in Shrewsbury for the summer, Charles sobered up. He had heard the warning bells as the university cracked down on moral turpitude and social deviance. He had seen the innocent suffer. Even wide-eyed beetle collectors were reminded of the shaky foundations of their leisured lifestyle. The Revd Taylor reminded the gentry, on their affluent islands, that they risked being engulfed by the ocean of miserable poor. Atheism, republicanism, and revolution swirled together in fierce working-class eddies, eroding the Establishment's defences, threatening its privileges. Freethought, as a political creed, sent a double shudder down the clerical spine. Away from the hurly-burly, Charles had time to ponder it all – more than he wanted, in fact.

He found himself laid up. He had been entomologizing with the

74

Revd Hope in North Wales in mid-June, when his lips became inflamed again, and he headed for home 'with grief & sorrow' to be tended by the Doctor and his sisters. Hope sent some stunning click beetles to cheer him up – 'bright scarlet' Elaters – but with his own mouth red and sore, it seemed like a bad joke. Charles cried on Fox's shoulder, contrasting his own paltry catches. He felt 'dreadfully stupid' kicking around The Mount, constantly reminded of life's duties. Nor had his tutor's parting advice made him feel any better: the preliminary exam for his degree next year – the 'Little Go' – would be tougher than ever.

Recovery took a fortnight, and Charles emerged a new man. These weeks would be the last of his 'perfectly idle & wandering life,' and he intended to make the most of them, 'taking care to have as little of home & as much of Woodhouse as possible.' Come term-time, all would change. 'I must read for my little Go,' he resolved, for there is 'the very devil to pay amongst all idle men & Entomologists.'[2]

So for the summer Charles cantered around Shropshire and Staffordshire, with a week out for abortive beetling at Barmouth. In Shrewsbury he stood godfather to infant nephews, the younger sons of sister Marianne and Henry Parker. At Maer he stalked insects and shot grouse. And in between, he went back time and again to Woodhouse for the wild life in Squire Owen's forest. Letters from 'la belle Fanny' had thinned out, but still he adored her. They had other ways of communicating, in summers at least. He saw her once more just before the hunting season, after which he hastened to visit Fox.[3]

Months had passed since the cousins last clasped hands. Charles had tidied up Fox's affairs in Cambridge, shipped his belongings back, captured scores of beetles for him, and generally returned many favours. Old failings were forgotten; the future hailed them both. But Fox, preparing for the Church, was clearly lagging in 'the science.' Charles was raring to go, spurred on by seeing his name in print – a capturing credit in an instalment of Stephens's *Illustrations of British Entomology*. Now no one would surpass him, not even Leonard Jenyns in Cambridge. He had Fox down on his knees like a penitent, determined to 'redeem your character in Entomology,' he quipped. They scooped up scores of insects, and Darwin catechized his cousin on the magnificent 'Fungiverous' species.[4] Their roles had reversed. Charles was now in charge.

It was only a short visit, but Charles expected Fox soon in Cambridge, where they would be 'very snug . . . together once more.' He had to hurry back to Shrewsbury to see Erasmus. His brother was giving up medicine. The Doctor considered that his 'delicate frame' could not withstand a career 'involving, if successful, a severe strain upon body & mind,' and so was pensioning him off. Eras was, quite naturally, 'very agreeable' to retirement at the age of twenty-five. He planned to settle in London, with 'an air-cushion in his rooms' to put Charles up overnight. This seemed satisfactory all round, and the brothers celebrated at the Birmingham Music Festival in early October, taking in several concerts and operatic performances by Giuseppe de Begnis and the enchanting young soprano Maria Malibran. Charles lodged near his Wedgwood cousins and 'lived entirely with them.' All told, it was the 'most glorious' cultural experience. And between the arias he managed to acquire fifteen shillings' worth of insects from a buff in town. Finally, he returned to Cambridge, anxious to be back at the beginning of term.[5]

Michaelmas was full of distractions, but Charles's resolve held. He attended tutorials and burrowed into classical texts for his Little Go. It was dry, demeaning work. Erasmus visited for a spell, and their fine arts education continued at the Fitzwilliam Museum. Charles even squeezed in a few days' hunting. But on the last one his horse had 'two such aweful [sic] rolls as nearly knocked my lungs out,' and he called a halt to it. Otherwise he kept upright in all things: he abandoned his old carousing companions and sought out a superior class. From the time of Fox's leaving, he had slighted the clerical naturalists and their genial mentor the Revd Henslow. Although he had signed up for Henslow's botany lectures in the spring, he did not so much as mention the fact to Fox, who had introduced him to the professor. Now everything was different. He became a fixture at Professor Henslow's Friday night parties and moved with a new set.

One was the Revd Jenyns, of ill repute in the beetling fraternity. The Eton-educated son of a parson-magistrate, the squire of Bottisham near Cambridge, he sprang from the old order. His father had set him up in the parish of Swaffham Bulbeck, near the family estate. Here as vicar, Jenyns 'resolved never to have anything to do with' worldly pursuits, unlike his father. Instead he spent his spare time enlarging his boyhood horde of insects. A thirty-year-old bachelor, he was retiring and austere, with a scientific mien to match: methodical in manner, fastidious about facts, and thoroughly orthodox. He kept a 'naturalist's calendar' like his hero, the Revd Gilbert White, and suffered from frequent 'sick headaches,' which further reduced his social profile. Friends pressed him to stand for a 'zoological Professorship,' but to no avail. One Friday night, however, Darwin managed a coup. He persuaded the dour young fogey to drop by

Christ's College and inspect his beetles. Although Jenyns said little about the collection, he was grateful to receive 'a good many insects' from his admirer. Maybe, thought Darwin, the man was not as bad as his 'grim and sarcastic expression' suggested.[6]

That term Fox never visited and Fanny never wrote. Charles bore their neglect with fortitude. He was becoming his own man. Active beetle collectors took precedence for him now, and big brothers. At Christmas he slept on Eras's air-bed for three weeks and did as he pleased. London turned out to be more enjoyable than he had expected, which meant quiet. He raced through Samuel Richardson's blockbuster *Clarissa*, all but finishing the seven-volume saga of ruined courtship. He considered headier matters over dinner with Sir James Mackintosh, who was still struck with him. Mackintosh pitched into phrenology, which Charles had encountered at Edinburgh. He explained that if education can alter the faculties of the brain – the compartments dealing with love, hate, reason and so on – then these faculties are not innate, so the shape of the head cannot reflect them. Charles had to agree. His faint belief in cranial bumps was 'battered down.' He went back to a sounder science, entomology. Hope was in town after Christmas to talk to, and Stephens gave up a couple of evenings to tutor his varsity friend. Darwin was introduced to a young architect, George Waterhouse, a budding collector with some brilliant captures. Waterhouse favoured him with a box of 'most glorious insects.'[7] It would not be forgotten.

Back in Cambridge on New Year's Day, a fortnight before term started, Darwin repaid Jenyns's visit. He rode out to Swaffham Bulbeck and found the vicar comfortable, snug, and smug. Darwin gave him 'an awesome lot of insects,' hoping in return for Jenyns's duplicate specimens from the fens. All he received were a couple of good beetles and '2 or 3 more common ones.' Jenyns lacked Waterhouse's generosity and it rankled. Darwin snidely noted that his own water beetles had astonished Jenyns's 'weak mind,' and he determined to work even harder to outshine him – once he had passed his Little Go.

By now the second-year men were 'all in a dreadful plight, from fear & anxiety,' with only two months left before their ordeal. They had known for almost a year what they would be examined on: prescribed texts in Latin and Greek to translate and construe; portions from the Gospels or the Book of Acts; and ten questions on Paley's *Evidences of Christianity*. They had to acquit themselves in a single day: three hours in the morning on the classics, and three in the afternoon on the New Testament and Paley. This is what now made the Little Go so strict. Candidates would be examined orally, each being called on to speak in turn. It was to be a public performance under pressure, with no scope for prevarication. 'First class' men would gain full credit; those in the 'second class' would have to try again next year.[8]

Charles force-fed himself on the ancient languages, wishing merely to pass. What really whetted his appetite was Paley. His *Evidences* was like Sumner's (which he had read in Shrewsbury), only better. Paley himself, who died in 1805 a rich rector, archdeacon, and Cambridge Doctor of Divinity, was not above suspicion for unorthodoxy, but at least his book remained a touchstone for right belief and conduct.[9] All high-minded Englishmen accepted its premises; every Cambridge ordinand swore by its conclusions. Its cold, clear reasoning proved Christianity, made apologists of young gents, and underpinned the Anglican order.

Paley's 'logic' so delighted Charles that he learnt it by heart. The sheer elegance of the deductions fascinated him: given that God exists, he would obviously reveal himself, and how else but by miracles? Nor can such miracles be dismissed as contrary to experience when there is so much historical evidence. The mere fact that early Christians suffered persecution rather than deny Jesus's miracles makes the New Testament account of the Resurrection compelling. No other miracles have been confirmed in so striking a manner. Therefore the Christian revelation is both true and unique: a 'Jewish peasant' had indeed pointed the way to God.

What difference did it make? By the time Charles finished the *Evidences*, the practical political answer was unforgettable. The Christian revelation, according to Paley, establishes the existence of 'a future state of reward and punishment.' And retribution in the next life is eminently useful for regulating human conduct in this one. Without the threat of eternal torture, men 'want a *motive*' to do their duty, and 'their rules want authority.' Promise them future rewards, on the other hand, and a perennial problem is solved: the unequal and 'promiscuous distribution' of power and wealth. The swilling masses will put up with their hardships and degrading 'stations' once they accept that any injustice will be rectified hereafter. 'This one truth changes the nature of things,' the *Evidences* declared. It 'gives order for confusion: makes the moral world of a piece with the natural.'[10]

To Charles, charmed by the argument, Paley's world was his own. Cambridge conformed to the *Evidences*, worked on the same principles. It was a microcosm where authority was vouchsafed by God, stations in life were assigned, and penalties for misconduct came with sovereign severity, just as rewards for excellence were bountifully bestowed. Here the 'truth of Christianity' depended on facts and he was about to be tested on them. Judgment day for Charles was Wednesday, 24 March 1830, when he entered the exam room. With his future at stake, he felt 'shattered,' tortured by guilty memories of 'idleness.' His inquisitors were strict and asked 'a wonderful number of questions,' but the next day, when the results came out, he let off a whoop: 'I am through my little Go,!!!. . .I am through through through'! Triumphant in his success, he could hardly wait to get back to entomology. 'Heaven protect the beetles & Mr Jenyns'![11]

Fanny was fading from his life. He was sure of it now. After a term's silence, a note from her had finally arrived while he was poring over Paley, but it was maddeningly vague. No reasons, no apology, no encouragement, just a prolix pout. 'Why did you not come home this Xmas?' Fanny demanded. 'I suppose some *dear little Beetles* . . . kept you away.' Her mocking continued. She assumed she would have to catch a strange species herself, 'a **Scrofulum morturorum**' (meaning of course a disease), before he could be 'induced to come down!' This was beyond the pale, coming from someone so devoted to her own hobby, painting, that she couldn't even write a letter! But lest Charles thought she had actually been dying to see him, Fanny resorted to riddles. The holidays had brought 'hard times,' she moaned, leaving her in the red. 'My finances are in a most pitiable state & the *Mortgages* on *my Estate incalculable.*' With creditors pressing, a debtor's prison lay ahead. 'What a **horrid disgusting thing money** is – I hate the name of it – *don't* you,' she ended disingenuously; 'it is fit for *vulgar souls* – not **Beetle** *hunters* – and *Paint brush drivers*!!!'

The message was easy to decode. Charles could read 'love' for 'money' between the lines. The silly girl had overextended her heart. Others had a claim on her affections: suitors ('creditors') besieged her, and wedlock (the 'debtor's prison') loomed. The 'Housemaid' and 'Postillion' were no more, their forest trysts were done. It was just as well that he had not gone home at Christmas. The '*dear little Beetles*' were a safer fancy than a flighty female. At least they were easier to pin down. And with his exam passed, he drowned his sorrow by doing the real thing. The new cabinet he had ordered a year before arrived at last, a 'gay little affair' with shallow drawers for displaying his specimens. He could hardly wait, and spent Easter in college, labelling, mounting, and cataloguing. 'There is not a single inducement for me to leave Cambridge,' he sighed to Fox.[12]

Another reason to stay was Henslow, who had taken a shine to him. Maybe it was the way Darwin 'hung upon' his words each Friday night, or perhaps his constant questioning. Whatever, Henslow was impressed and took him aside. By the end of term they could be seen walking the streets together, deep in conversation. Belatedly, Darwin was discovering how much he had in common with the 'goodnatured & agreeable' professor.[13]

Henslow was the scion of a prosperous professional family. Like Darwin, he had grown up dabbling in chemistry and collecting natural objects. His father had packed him off to Cambridge, emphatic on a church career. But science got in the way. As a student he excelled at maths and studied chemistry and mineralogy, while amassing the obligatory collections of shells and insects. Later he helped Sedgwick, his geological tutor, found the Cambridge Philosophical Society, to fire the undergraduates' interest in natural history. He became professor of mineralogy at the young age of twenty-six and married Jenyns's sister a year later. Only then, to augment his modest £100 annual stipend, did he take holy orders and accept the curacy of Little St Mary's Church, a short stroll from the university's Botanic Garden.

The Garden was where he taught now, and strolled with his pupil. Such were the prerogatives of the new Regius Professor of Botany, by appointment of the Crown. The post had come easily and it doubled his teaching income. His predecessor had held the post for sixty-three years, not lectured for thirty, and ceased even to reside in the university. He had neglected the Garden and left its museum in a mess. Under Henslow all this was changing. Plans were afoot to move the dilapidated garden to a prime site outside town and to set up a proper herbarium. Lectures were delivered each Easter term, accompanied by practical sessions. Here students were given plant specimens, which they 'pulled to pieces for themselves.'[14] On herborizing expeditions – now a local rite of spring – they scoured the countryside, gathering as many species as possible.

Charles first glimpsed the glad life of a clerical don on his walks with Henslow this term. He was 'awe-struck' by his mentor's versatility, just as he had been by Grant's on their seaside rambles near Edinburgh. And as the professor paced the fenland paths, he revealed other talents. Botanizing was not the only rite he attended to. He had proctorial duties as well.

In springtime a young man's fancy was easily distracted. Flowers had their charms but other beauties beckoned, and the lanes around town had many a blossom to catch his roving eye. These were the habitats the botanical proctor patrolled. Henslow had been uprooting and replanting females in the Spinning House since the previous term. In April and May, his months of wild herborizing, he was extra-vigilant, committing eight girls in the Easter break alone. He was the ideal law officer, a man of principle, motivated by 'a vigorous and determined will,' yet above 'any paltry feeling' of spite, and always 'cordial, and unpretending.' Or so said 'the man who walks with Henslow,' as the dons dubbed Charles. 'The more I see him the more I like him,' Darwin enthused. 'I have some thought of reading divinity with him the summer after next.'[15]

For now, though, plants held his fancy. Botanizing turned out to be as much fun as beetling, and even more instructive. He threw himself into Henslow's outings, soon proving his superiority over the common-or-garden students. In mid-May they all piled into stage-coaches, clutching nets and boxes, for the fifteen-mile trip to Gamlingay heath, where wild lilies-of-the-valley grew. As soon as they arrived, Darwin excelled himself. He knew it was the breeding season for toads, and that sharp, intermittent trill meant rare natter-jacks. He caught a number and passed them round, prompting Henslow to ask whether Mr Darwin intended to 'make a natter-jack pie.' Later that day, Darwin came up with another surprise, anemones never found locally before.

A week later, the naturalists floated down the Cam, their barge bound for Bottisham and the fens. Out in the wet fenlands the party disembarked and poked around. Some men chased swallow-tail butterflies across the treacherous terrain, much to Henslow's amusement. Darwin searched high and low for new plants. Across a muddy dike he spied an insect-eating bladderwort, on Henslow's most-wanted list. Showing off, he tried to reach it using his vaulting pole (one of his old beetling companions had taught him the trick). Taking a mighty lunge, he propelled himself heavenward – but with insufficient thrust. The pole stuck vertically in the ditch, with Darwin clinging to the top. Sheepishly, he slid into the mire, waded to the specimen, and returned to present it to Henslow. That night, when the party dined at a nearby inn, Darwin's bravado was toast of the term. Their annual herborizing had ended in triumph with almost 300 species bagged.[16]

Henslow's botany lectures went on five days a week. Seventy-eight men attended, including the Revds Whewell and Peacock. Darwin was clearly the 'favourite pupil.' He turned up early for the practicals and arranged baskets of plants and dissecting knives on a side-table, where the students could help themselves. And he constantly quizzed the professor. 'What a fellow that D. is for asking questions,' Henslow exclaimed, conscious that his guidance was paying off.[17]

Darwin's precocity served him well. So did his old Edinburgh interest in primitive plant-like animals, or rather the spontaneous motion of their eggs. Under Henslow he now switched his focus to pollen. One day, watching a geranium pollen grain in alcohol under a microscope, he saw 'three transparent cones' emerge from its side. One burst, spraying 'numberless granules' through the liquid with 'great violence.' Not only primitive eggs, but the matter inside seemed to have a self-activating power. He showed Henslow, only to have it explained quite differently. For Henslow the minute granules were indeed the constituent atoms of pollen – perhaps the ultimate stuff of life – but they had no intrinsic vital power. Life was impressed on matter from without; it was an endowment and ultimately derived its power from God. There were no self-activating atoms of life, whatever more 'speculative' naturalists argued.[18] Darwin had heard otherwise from Grant – that matter moved itself – and paused to reflect. He was learning to bide his time before announcing discoveries.

That summer he was expected at 'sweet-home,' as he called it through clenched teeth. Not having seen the Doctor for eight months, he had to give some account of himself, and he was not looking forward to it. For that matter, he hadn't seen Fox either, so why not have him come to The Mount? Shrewsbury was just a couple of coach rides from Osmaston, a day's travel at most. It would be immensely convenient and might cushion the debriefing. And Charles could show off his collection of minuscule, water-side beetles, the Bembidiidae, of which he now had 208 in his new cabinet, two-thirds of the British species. 'Write soon,' he instructed Fox with a wry smile, and 'be sure do not say no to [the] Shrewsbury scheme else I will never forgive you.'

Fox agreed and Charles took heart. 'The sooner you come the better,' he shot back as he packed his bags. Fox turned up at The Mount, but their reunion was spoiled. They had no time to themselves, no peace and quiet. Charles rehearsed the year's events for the Doctor – his Little Go, natural history, Henslow and divinity – but even his up-beat report did little to pacify the household. Everyone was tense. They worried about him, and the Doctor had not been well. Things eventually blew up into 'a row & confusion' that left Charles longing to escape. When Fox had gone, he went off to join Hope and some friends 'entomologizing' in North Wales.

This summer his lips played along. He spent three weeks in August among the hills, beetling on fine days, trout fishing on rainy ones, and generally becoming 'disgusted with Hopes egotism & stupidity.' As clergymen went, Hope kept a decent cabinet, but he was no field naturalist. Darwin sensed his growing superiority. With Professor Henslow as his model, he was set to become a different sort of priest, unlike Hope or Jenyns, or even Fox. His devotion to natural history would be rounded and complete. Holy orders need not detain him; a country parish might well be opportune. He began to relish the prospect again. From Barmouth he wrote to ask Fox what he was reading for his ordination exam. Then he headed off for Maer where a Wedgwood was the vicar, keen to start the partridge season with a bang and – this year for once – without 'even the least dread of the *Parish*.'[19]

The shooting was poor, but he made up for it by killing beetles and ogling cousin Charlotte, twelve years his senior. He returned home in high spirits on 10 September to be startled by a letter from Fanny. It was written 'by Papa's desire.' The stern Squire had been 'rather expecting' him to 'slay some of his Partridges' as usual; now he wanted to see him for a man-to-man talk, and within a week. Charles half-guessed and, riding over, braced himself for the worst. Sure enough, it was just a formality. He was among the first to know – not surprisingly, given the Squire's soft spot and expectations for Charles. Fanny was to be engaged. Her intended was John Hill, a clergyman, the brother of the local Tory MP. He had been with her at Brighton the winter before last, *that* winter when Charles was cloistered in Cambridge with his suspicions. Everyone called him 'The Hill.'

Three weeks later Charles was back in college. He had grumpily trampled over hill after hill getting there on his huge new horse – '16 hands & one inch' – and 'the poor beast was so tired that he hardly knew whether he stood on his heels or his head.' 'I am positively in love with him,' Charles crooned. 'Beetles, partridges & everything else, are as nothing to me.' Not even Fanny. She had rushed a letter to Shrewsbury before he left, enclosing a portrait of him that she had drawn. She promised '*really and truly*' to do a better one 'when you *next* honor the Forest with y' presence.' Wasn't that typical, playing on the emotions? But then, as she admitted, she would never learn to 'write "like a lady".'[20] No, Fanny Owen was history now. Horses were more dependable.

7

Every Man For Himself

IN THE COUNTRY political events were moving fast. England stood aghast as Paris tumbled once more towards revolution. In July 1830, the reactionary French monarch Charles X had abolished the government. Republican workers and students took to the barricades; the stock market collapsed, a *tricolore* flag fluttered atop Notre Dame. Soldiers mutinied; the Louvre was stormed, the Tuileries sacked, and a republic was declared. A week later the King fled to England, arriving as Darwin was beetling in Wales. The middle classes now held sway in France, with Louis Philippe, the 'citizen king,' on the throne.

Priests had lost power too, and Catholicism ceased to be the French state religion. With the Tory government sheltering the deposed monarch at home, Whig reformers made political capital, warning of an English 'July Revolution' if Parliament were not reformed and democracy extended. In the autumn, when Charles was back in college, the Duke of Wellington, the hardline Tory prime minister, dug his heels in and the stock market shuddered. Street radicals bellowed their rage, demanding fair wages, union power, and suffrage – and the ruination of rich English parsons. The republican atheists massed in The Rotunda, a ramshackle building on the south bank of the Thames recently reopened by Richard Carlile.

Here Carlile installed his fellow infidel missionary Robert Taylor, and the apostate priest performed in The Rotunda's auditorium several times a week. Wearing rakish canonicals, he staged infidel melodramas and preached bombastic sermons before artisan audiences. In two outrageous Sunday discourses on 'The Devil!' he pronounced 'God and the Devil . . . to be but one and the self-same being ... Hell and Hell-fire ... are, in the original, nothing more than names and titles of the Supreme God.' For this he was dubbed 'the Devil's Chaplain' – the label that stuck in Darwin's mind for life – and his sermons circulated by the thousand in a disreputable rag, *The Devil's Pulpit*. In November, when Wellington's ministry collapsed, Taylor was in his pulpit railing against the Establishment while above him, on the roof, a tricolour snapped smartly in the breeze.[1]

Anglican priests looked nervously about them. With the growing political uncertainty, many continued to see the Tories as the best defenders of Church and Crown. In Cambridge, once noted for its reformist tendencies, the dons moved decisively to the right. Out-and-out Whigs had to watch their step, even those caught in the feverish preparation for final exams.

By this time Darwin was reading in earnest, 'desperate' about his own ordeal, only two months away. Beetles were dropped and only Friday nights were left free for Henslow's parties. Nothing would induce him to miss them, and he sometimes came early to join the family for dinner. Mrs Henslow struck him as 'devilish odd' (he wasn't to know that she was pregnant for the first time). Henslow he loved. He was 'quite the most perfect man I ever met with.' They had grown steadily closer, and his walking companion was now his private tutor. Henslow's subjects were maths and theology, which was just as well for Darwin. He relished their tutorial hour together as 'the pleasantest in the whole day.'[2]

Word had it that Henslow held 'some curious religious opinions' but Darwin could find no evidence. On the contrary, their discussion of Paley's *Principles of Moral and Political Philosophy* alone must have placed his orthodoxy beyond doubt. The book had to be mastered for the exam, and unlike the *Evidences* – on which there would also be questions – it now served Cambridge more as a foil than an infallible guide. Old and outdated – published in 1785 – it was a worn-out piece of academic furniture, an heirloom to dusty traditionalists, but a piece of dilapidated junk to others. Liberal Apostles and evangelical Sims deplored it; dons like Sedgwick and Whewell wrote it off.[3] It was unspiritual and dangerous, they said.

Even Darwin, none too earnest about religion, would have realized this as he began his political education under Henslow. Paley's ideas belonged to a bygone era when Christianity was the faith of reasonable men, and reasonable men ruled the world. Then the Church sat comfortably, free to contemplate changes it knew would never come about. Paley saw the arguments for democracy but opposed them; he acknowledged that Parliament failed to represent the nation but upheld its gross inequities; he recognized defects in the administration of justice but defended a brutal criminal code. Always, he based his notions of right and wrong on purely natural reasoning, confident that all men could be brought to agree.

Thus, Darwin discovered, Paley saw no supernatural sanction for the sovereign or the State. Simple 'expediency' was his rule. One had a duty to obey the government *only* so long as it 'cannot be resisted or changed without public inconveniency.' Resistance might be justified, Paley allowed in his cosy way, if grievances become so great and the call to redress them so strong that the danger and expense to society is outweighed. And who, he asked calmly, shall make this judgment? 'We answer, "Every man for himself".'

Daring words in 1830. Nor was this Paley's only political heresy. Darwin learned that he saw nothing sacrosanct about an Established Church either. It formed 'no part of Christianity,' he declared in a notorious chapter, but was only a means of instilling the faith. Its authority lay 'in its utility,' as indeed did subscription to 'articles of religion.' The Thirty-nine Articles of the Church of England set up an exclusion zone, keeping hostile parties from ecclesiastical office. Subscribing to them might serve to maintain 'order and tranquillity,' but in stable 1785 they seemed redundant and Paley thought that they should be abolished. Nor did he think that subscription to the Thirty-nine Articles necessitated an 'actual belief of each and every separate proposition contained in them.'[4]

Here Henslow drew the line: he would have none of Paley's doctrinal laxity. Henslow might have been warming to reform, having just switched parties with the Cambridge MP Lord Palmerston, who joined Earl Grey's new Whig administration. But, he solemnly informed Darwin, he cared so much for the Thirty-nine Articles that 'he should be grieved if a single word . . . was altered.'[5] The Establishment had to remain strong, not least because the times were perilous. With Dissenters clamouring for equality and religious liberty, hasty reforms could bring about the disestablishment of the Church, an eventuality Paley did not seriously entertain. Worse, Paley's views played into the hands of the secular radicals, who saw insurrection as now the simplest expediency. 'Every man,' they cried, must decide 'for himself' whether the authorities should be obeyed.

It was a cry heard across England as Darwin attended tutorials, learning to respect authority. Massive campaigns of civil disobedience gave an eloquent answer. Falling wages and starvation were causing rage and frustration among agricultural labourers. From the Home

Counties to the Midlands and East Anglia, they went on the rampage. Landowners and parsons were threatened with a series of demands; their haystacks were torched, barns gutted, and threshing machines smashed. The uprising reached Cambridgeshire in mid-November.

As Darwin pondered Paley, the arson attacks began in outlying villages to the north. By 2 December the incendiaries had reached Coton, two miles west, and wage-riots had broken out in hamlets to the south and east. Magistrates – many of them clergymen – met in the town on Friday the 3rd and drew up plans to defend the colleges. Rumours flew that the labourers of Cherry Hinton, Bottisham, and other villages were planning to march into Cambridge on market day, if their demands were not met. They would sweep in via Barnwell, itself 'full of bad characters of all descriptions,' and take over the market square. The magistrates feared that it would spark a 'general rising of the people,' and only a show of force could stop it. They appealed for special constables, and 800 merchants, curates, dons, and students flocked to the Town Hall to be sworn in.[6]

The weekend went off without violence, and the colleges escaped attack. Deterrence worked. But then Cambridge was well practised in defending the status quo. By now Darwin realized this better than ever, but one petty incident rammed the point home. Sick of studying, he prevailed on Herbert one day to ride into the fens in search of wildlife. That night they returned exhausted, dined in Darwin's rooms, and fell asleep in lounge chairs. Herbert woke at 3 a.m. and panicked. He was in breach of curfew and feared the worst, knowing that the strict rules were never bent. He was right. The Dean of St John's was implacable. Here was Herbert, a hard-working tutor with a half-dozen pupils, never offended before, but still he was confined to college for the rest of term. Herbert's friends were in 'perfect ferment,' and Darwin's 'indignation' at the 'stupid injustice & tyranny' of the Dean 'knew no bounds.'[7]

Darwin stayed in college for the Christmas holidays, cramming – 'far too much plagued to enjoy any thing,' even a visit from Fox. Now he knew the agony his cousin had endured two years before. The final exam – three days of written papers – was scheduled for the third week in January 1831. When the time came Darwin shuffled once more on to the cold marble floor of the Senate House and sat at the appointed desk. He fretted the whole morning over Homer, and all afternoon over Virgil. But it was a mediocre performance. Next day after breakfast he tackled a dozen questions on Paley's *Evidences of Christianity*, and after lunch polished off the *Moral and Political*

Philosophy and questions on Locke's *Essay concerning Human Understanding*. Here he shone. The last day he dreaded – mathematics. He did well on the Euclidean proofs, making up for his wretched arithmetic and algebra. And the questions in physics – on statics, dynamics, and astronomy – turned out to be manageable, just.

By the end of the week, when the results were posted, he was dazed and proud. He ranked tenth in the pass-list of 178. The BA was his at last! He was also exhausted and unaccountably depressed. 'I do not know why the degree should make one so miserable,' he groaned to Fox.[8]

Still, a celebration was called for, even if he had to drag himself to it. Fortunately friends were on hand to help. Herbert and Whitley had taken their degrees already; Cameron from Shrewsbury was just through his exam. These, with Darwin and four others, had already constituted themselves the 'Glutton Club' for the purpose of dining on 'strange flesh.' The Gluttons were not gourmets, but neither were they gluttonous. Their weekly meals in one another's rooms featured some rare morsel obligingly cooked by the college staff: a bird or beast one of them had procured, which was previously 'unknown to human palate.' But the collective appetite for exotica did not last long: it came to grief one night when they tried to eat an 'old brown owl.' The Gluttons – presided over by Darwin – now resorted to more traditional fare, topped off by Van John and port.[9] Darwin began to relax.

They were a chaste bunch, and mostly old friends. Five of the Gluttons were studying for holy orders, including James Heaviside, a tutor at Sidney Sussex College with decorations in maths. Not all future priests were of this calibre. Henry Matthew was an exception. A country rector's son, he had already been thrown out of Oxford, and survived only a year at Trinity College before sidling off to Sidney Sussex, where Heaviside became his tutor and introduced him to Darwin. Matthew was a fop, a rascal, and a genius. He was elected President of the Union Debating Society that year, but he flouted respectability and refused to fit in. The model varmint, he was poised to self-destruct even before the Proctors could catch up with him.

Darwin saw it all at close quarters. Sidney Sussex was practically next door to Christ's, and he often popped over to Matthew's rooms. He was staggered by the way Matthew could reel off literary quotations, and even tempted perhaps to play the libertine himself. Never mind Matthew's chaffing at science, or his belief that Moses was 'a better authority on mundane cosmogony' than a beetle collector.

Even his gin-swilling could be tolerated – or sometimes shared. No, there was something wildly appealing about the man. Darwin felt himself being sucked into the maelstrom.

Then the truth came out. Matthew was married, and that was not the worst of it. The woman was a wench, and he loved another. He had a bastard child besides, and all by the age of twenty-three. He was in deep trouble and disappeared from town, although no one knew where. Then one day, a fortnight after Darwin's exam, a letter arrived from Matthew. He was hiding in a dingy London garret, struggling to make ends meet by selling his love poems to periodicals. His women plagued him with letters, and he had been summoned to appear before a magistrate 'about my bastard, with one sovereign in my pocket to meet Law expences [sic], arrears, and advance for a quarter.' The next stop, clearly, was gaol. Darwin took pity and sent a 'generous remittance' to spare him further punishment.[10]

Darwin's residence requirement kept him in Cambridge until June. The time was ripe to begin grooming himself for a country parish. Fox had passed his ordination exam at last and taken a curacy near Nottingham. Darwin, foreseeing 'the time . . . when I must suffer,' asked him about the state of his nerves, what divinity he had read and how closely. Other fields opened up with the start of the beetling season. Jenyns was the textbook parson-naturalist, and Darwin had learned to read friendship between the grim lines of his face. He rode out to Swaffham Bulbeck from time to time, and together they forayed into the fens, or sacked Squire Jenyns's woods at Bottisham Hall, capturing beetles for their cabinets. Ordination never came up, so intent were they on this clerical pastime.[11]

But in his mind Darwin roamed further afield, guided by Henslow. They saw each other constantly, at botany lectures, Friday soirées, and field trips. The future became more focused. Darwin had a vision of what he might become. More than anyone, Henslow was the kind of man he yearned to be – a clerical naturalist or professor – the sort that even the Doctor might approve of. Indeed, they were half-living together, which showed that Henslow's livelihood suited him well. 'I do not know, whether I love or respect' him more, Darwin confessed helplessly.[12] Who better to steer his career than one so congenial? Henslow would prepare him for ordination, see him into the Church. His advice would be indispensable.

His example would be too. Taking orders had been a leisurely affair for Henslow, something he got around to only after he married and obtained his first chair. Until then he had broadened his horizons through reading and travel, making the most of opportunities that came along. Charles thought this ideal and began to follow suit. With his exam out of the way, and only graduation to attend, he stuck his nose into books and his head into the clouds, daydreaming about how he might spend his time *en route* to a country parish.

Wide reading was vital, his passport to the wider world. He had always been struck by Paley's works. Now he picked up the last of the archdeacon's famous trilogy, the keystone of his entire system, *Natural Theology.* Here was a beautiful evocation of life abounding with goodness and joy: 'it is a happy world' teeming 'with delighted existence,' Paley enthused. 'In a spring noon, or a summer evening, on whichever side I turn my eyes, myriads of happy beings crowd upon my view.' Life was a summer's teatime on the vicarage lawn, with swarming bees and cheerful beetles testifying to God's kindness. It *was* good, life *was* happy, because all beings were adapted to their surroundings. Animals, including humans, are complex mechanisms from the divine workshop, and exquisitely fitted to their places in the world. They are so obviously designed, there has to be a Designer. For Paley such a rational proof of God's existence would make men look for signs of revelation and attend to their civic duties.

This was a different way of viewing the world for Darwin. He had even heard it ridiculed at Edinburgh. Nor did it accord with his grandfather's theory of life. Dead atoms, according to Paley, have no innate intelligence, no inherent vitality, nor does animal matter itself, as Erasmus and Dr Grant had taught. But then Erasmus's theory 'coincides with atheism' because it dispenses with 'an intelligent, designing, mind' which plans and constructs living bodies.[13] God alone creates the world, endows it with life, and keeps everything running smoothly.

Darwin nodded assent. Paley and his grandfather held radically different views, much as Henslow and Grant did. And Paley saw no evidence whatever to justify old Erasmus's science to a Cambridge man. But what sorts of 'evidence,' 'facts,' and 'laws of nature' were acceptable, and how were they established? Darwin swotted up the subject from a new, compact book by the doyen of science, Sir John Herschel, astronomer and physicist, the son of Sir William Herschel (the discoverer of Uranus). This was Sir John's year: he was knighted by the Whigs and his turgidly titled *Preliminary Discourse on the Study of Natural Philosophy* was hot off the press. It ignited Darwin. He glimpsed the limitless scope for scientific explanation and the rapid progress of every branch of knowledge. As Herschel remarked in a passage Darwin scored, 'To what, then, may we not look forward . . . what may we not expect from the exertions of powerful minds,' building on the 'acquired knowledge of past generations'? The sky was the limit. Darwin closed his eyes and exuded a 'burning zeal' for science.[14]

He also borrowed a book that Henslow heartily approved of. Darwin had picked up Alexander von Humboldt's *Personal Narrative* once before, only to put it down. Reading a seven-volume, 3754-page account of a turn-of-the-century trip to South America called for stamina. This time he summoned it up. Henslow had confided his own unfulfilled ambition to globe-trot, to 'explore regions but little known, and enrich science with new species.' For years he had longed to visit Africa, becoming 'depressed and out of spirits' when the prospect receded. Now it was out of the question, and he settled for memories of the Isle of Wight and the Isle of Man instead, where he had geologized after graduation.[15] But nothing need stop Darwin. Maybe his favourite pupil could find a suitable island to explore. He was still young and free, and in the future might regret passing up the chance. He could even take his divinity books along.

This was the incentive Darwin needed. He tore through Humboldt, still aglow from Herschel, and everything fell into place. Tropical scenery had long fascinated him, all those talks with the freed slave in Edinburgh, and the fine travellers' prints in the Fitzwilliam Museum. And Humboldt's account of Tenerife in the Canary Islands, with its lush lowland vegetation and rugged volcanic terrain, was enthralling. Why not go there? And take Henslow too – the Canaries were the next best thing to Africa, right off the coast in fact. What a view of God's world it would open up, not to mention the botanical teasers. Darwin plotted on one of Henslow's outings. He read out long passages from Humboldt to whet the party's appetite. Imagine the new species they would find on Tenerife's 'sandy, dazzling, plains,' and in its 'gloomy silent forest.' They would see 'the Great Dragon tree' and climb to the volcanic peak and . . .

The response was mixed. Only Henslow and three others were interested. But this was enough for Charles. He raced to Shrewsbury at Easter to get his father's view. The expedition would not set out for another year and would last only a month. It would not be cheap, but then Cambridge was not cheap either. The Doctor knew this only too well, as he handed Charles 'a 200£ note' to pay his debts – and with it, permission to cost out the trip. Everything spelled go.[16]

Nothing could stop Charles now, not even a simpering note from Fanny. 'Ashamed of myself for being so troublesome to you,' she asked him to pick up some artists' paint in Shrewsbury with 'half a dozen small brushes' and bring them over to Woodhouse – not forgetting 'a **juicy** Book of some kind' for her delectation. Charles caved in and made a flying visit. If it was a portrait she wanted, a portrait she could have, but he had other urgent business. Erasmus was waiting for him in London.

The capital was electric when Charles arrived on the weekend of 15 April. Six weeks before, Earl Grey had brought in the great Reform Bill, aiming to redistribute parliamentary seats to London and the industrial towns, and to extend the middle-class vote. The Whigs were now doing their utmost to contain and direct the broad-based reform movement. Carlile had been fined £200 and was serving a two-year sentence for seditious libel (writing in support of the rioting farm workers). *The Times* was full of the story; and Taylor had been nailed only the previous Monday, indicted for blasphemy in two Easter sermons. The Rotunda was on its last legs as a centre for artisan rebellion. But the Reform Bill had equally run into trouble. Its provisions appalled the Tory opposition. They were in full cry, with the outcome in the balance.

During the bill's second reading Darwin and Wedgwood supporters sat on the edges of their seats. Sir James Mackintosh's daughter Fanny (just engaged to Hensleigh Wedgwood) even went down to the House of Commons to hear the results first-hand. It passed by a whisker, only to be mangled by Tory diehards in committee stage. Everyone knew that the bill and Grey's ministry stood or fell together. So Grey left the King to decide. The choice was stark: either dissolve Parliament and cause a General Election, which would bring in enough reformers to carry the bill, or accept the government's resignation, lose the bill, and face a revolution.[17]

It was a cruel, exciting dilemma, and London was on tenterhooks. The tide for change was running high, and a General Election would demolish the Tories. Beneath the pall of smoke and soot, people held their breath.

Charles stayed with Erasmus and was plied with the latest news. Erasmus was a cosmopole, never far from Paris or some other European city, in thought if not in person. He was political and had his ear to the ground, but for all that he failed to impress his younger brother with the gravity of the hour. Charles was in the Canaries in *his* thoughts, and he found his visit to fevered London 'very fatiguing.' 'I expect Erasmus did also,' he observed with unwonted sensitivity. 'I begin to think Natural Hist[ory]: makes people Egotistical.' He was full of the expedition, his 'head . . . running about the Tropics,' his 'enthusiasm so great' he could 'hardly sit still.' There were shipping lines to contact, fares to compare, and a broker to consult. Eras proved useful in his way, advising that Spanish was the language to learn, not Italian. They did take time out for an 'Antient music' concert, but what Charles really liked was the Zoological Gardens in Regent's Park. 'On a hot day when the beasts look happy and the people gay it is most delightful,' he rhapsodized in a Paleyan way. It reminded him of the tropics.

The next weekend, as he prepared to leave, there was no ignoring the crisis. With great qualms William IV had decided to dissolve Parliament. The streets seethed with cheering crowds on Friday the 22nd as the King processed through the capital to Westminster. Cannons thundered, announcing his intention, and the people roared their approval. That night a 'general illumination' lit up the city and reform parties were held across the country. The nation returned from the brink while Charles returned to college. He arrived in plenty of time to sign the Thirty-nine Articles at his degree ceremony on Tuesday.[18]

Cambridge was gripped by election fever. No one could remember a poll held at such short notice, within a fortnight of a dissolution. Two MPs represented the university – the town itself had none. The college Tories put up Wellington's Chancellor of the Exchequer and the brother of Robert Peel as their candidates. Against them stood young Cavendish and Palmerston, the Foreign Secretary. The dons pitched in – Sedgwick, Whewell, and Peacock for the Whigs – and so did many students. Feelings ran high. The Vice-Chancellor banned a Tory election-eve rally at the Red Lion Inn, warning that students who attended would be 'proceeded against' for violating university discipline. Darwin himself went 'gossiping about town,' glad to put in a word for the Whigs (as a lodger, he had no actual voting rights). But he was fired by other things. He was dying to discuss his Tenerife plans with Henslow, grumbling because 'Henslow is Lord Palmerston's right-hand man, and he has no time for walks.' So other friends were bombarded with the 'Canary scheme' instead, and 'most wish me there,' Charles chuckled after both Tories had won, 'I plague them so with talking about tropical scenery.'

By now he was fixing to cast off, mentally at least. He accepted 'a most magnificent ... present of a Microscope' from his friend Herbert, who could not decide 'whether M^r. Darwin's talents or his sincerity be the more worthy of admiration.' He cold-shouldered Fox, postponing an overdue visit, ostensibly on financial grounds but really because of Henslow's lectures and the 'scheme.' He began 'working like a tiger' on the expedition, especially the Spanish and geology. 'The former I find as intensely stupid,' he declared, 'as the latter most interesting.' Henslow had known that Darwin would need geological skills on any island jaunt. He promised to 'cram me' with the subject, Charles said.[19] But what Henslow apparently had in mind was something simpler: introducing him to the geology professor Adam Sedgwick.

They had met before. Sedgwick, decked in stately robes, had administered his oath of matriculation. They had also seen each other occasionally at Henslow's parties on Friday evenings, and Sedgwick was familiar with Darwin's undergraduate record. Once hell-bent on becoming an 'idle man,' drinking and dabbling in field sports, Darwin was now a novice naturalist with a well-stocked cabinet and a penchant for travel. So Henslow had told Sedgwick. Geological training was what Darwin needed – fast. It would keep up his interest in natural history and prepare him for a trip to Tenerife. Sedgwick agreed, remembering how Henslow himself had responded to his tuition when he was Darwin's age. In fact, their field work together on the Isle of Wight had been a great stimulus to them both; and at the moment Sedgwick needed another such tonic. Exhausted by the general election, he was about to begin a new phase of his stratigraphic studies. A young man's enthusiasm would do him good. Darwin would be welcome to attend his lectures and accompany him on a geological tour in the summer.

Henslow introduced Darwin formally, knowing that a fellow Proctor and clergyman would look after his best interests. Sedgwick was, indeed, among Henslow's oldest and closest friends; they were of one mind on religion, politics, and morals. No better tutor could be found to take a young man into the field, shepherd and guide him on to the paths of truth.

For his part, Darwin was fired up by Sedgwick's lectures that spring. They were incomparably better than Jameson's at Edinburgh, which he had hated. Sedgwick's reminded him of Humboldt, Herschel, and Paley, wrapped into one. They opened up new vistas of God's world, exposed the grandeur of creation. 'What a capital hand is Sedgewick [sic] for drawing large cheques upon the Bank of Time!' Darwin marvelled. And as for space, the professor revealed how much more of the globe remained to be conquered. 'It strikes *me*,' Darwin reflected, 'that all our knowledge about the structure of our Earth is very much like what an old hen w^d know of the hundred-acre field in a corner of which she is scratching.'

Undaunted by his ignorance, Darwin was – as usual – anxious to please and took the initiative. When Sedgwick mentioned a local spring, flowing from a chalk hill, which deposited lime in a delicate tracery on twigs, Darwin rode out, found it, and threw a whole bush in. Later he retrieved it, an extraordinary white-coated spray, so exquisite that Sedgwick exhibited it in class; whereupon others followed suit, and encrusted branches were soon adorning rooms all over the university.[20]

The summer was to see more serious field work. Darwin left Cambridge in June for London, where he bought his first geological instrument, a clinometer, for measuring the angle of inclined rock strata. Back home he put it to use, piling 'all the tables in my bedroom, at every conceivable . . . direction' and then sizing up their angles like 'any Geologist going could do.' He even ventured into the countryside to try his hand at mapping Shropshire. Extrapolating wildly, he felt like the 'old hen' in her field, scratching in a corner, taking it for the whole. This was youthful extravagance, but then hypotheses were cheap, and his were 'such powerful ones,' he laughed to Henslow, 'that I suppose, if they were put into action but for one day, the world would come to an end.'

His mind also took flight, Daedalus-like, in visions of Tenerife. Henslow's own 'Canary ardor' was cooling. After his wife's safe delivery he found himself with new responsibilities. So 'the most likely person . . . to be my companion,' Darwin told Fox, was the last of the original enthusiasts, a college tutor of Henslow's generation, Marmaduke Ramsay. Darwin kept Ramsay informed about his plans, and meanwhile 'read & reread Humboldt.' The 'Great Dragon tree' entranced him, the volcanic hills and tropical forests too.[21] His reveries went on, accompanied by earth-shaking speculations, until 4 August, when they came abruptly to a halt. Sedgwick rattled up to The Mount in his gig, armed to the teeth with tools and climbing gear, ready for the ascent into North Wales.

For the professor it was an expedition long overdue. Wales was becoming an area of enormous geological importance. Sedgwick had run into problems sorting out the oldest rocks of northern England. Strata seemed to be missing, like pages torn out of a book, and he guessed that equivalent ones would turn up in the rugged Welsh mountains. If he could find those ancient fossil-bearing rocks below the Old Red Sandstone, he could put the opening pages back into the geological book, enabling the history of life to be read from scratch. This was territory that Henslow might have helped him map a few years before, and who better now than Henslow's prize student?

That week Sedgwick hammered his way cross country from Cambridge, preparing for the Welsh invasion by chipping at conformable strata *en route*. He arrived in Shrewsbury tired and sore, and the next day drove off with Darwin under menacing skies, heading north into the Vale of Clwyd. On the way a thunderstorm broke and they were drenched. 'As the Prince of the Air would have it, I was almost drowned,' Sedgwick declared, playing up their plight, conscious that the Devil interferes with factual research whenever he can.[22]

And serious geology was what Darwin learned in Sedgwick's on-the-spot tutorials, as well as the skills that books could never impart. The clinometer came in handy, and Sedgwick checked the accuracy of Darwin's measurements. In less than a week he learned how to identify specimens, interpret strata, and generalize from his observations. It was the best crash course in geological practice, and Darwin hardly missed a trick, developing intellectual muscle as he burnt off the flab. Sedgwick sent him off to collect rock samples and check the stratification. When they met up, Darwin reported that he found no Old Red Sandstone in the Vale of Clwyd. This contradicted the national geological map, and Sedgwick's discussions of the implications made him 'exceedingly proud.'

Before they left the hills and headed for the coast, Darwin had fallen for the romance of geology. In limestone caverns above St Asaph, along the River Elwy, the two found mammal bones embedded in mud and easily extracted after the rains. The landowner actually had a rhinoceros tooth from these caves in his collection. Here was startling evidence of a lost fauna, from an age when rhinos wandered the Welsh countryside. It had a tremendous impact. And if such discoveries could be made in Britain, what awaited him abroad?[23]

They made for Bangor on the North Wales coast and there climbed steeply towards Capel Curig, twelve miles inland, searching in vain for fossils. Along the way Darwin heard the Revd Sedgwick swear for the first time. A blunt Yorkshireman, he was sure that the 'd − − d' waiter at their inn the night before had not passed on a sixpence tip to the chambermaid. He whirled the gig around and started back, determined to see justice done. Darwin remonstrated with him, asking on what grounds would he accuse the waiter of theft. Sedgwick had none, except that the waiter was 'an ill-looking fellow.' It rather dented Darwin's faith in the former Proctor as a judge of human character. Cautiously − for he was questioning high authority − he suggested that this was insufficient reason to accuse a man of criminal misconduct. The thought slowly registered, and at last Sedgwick reversed direction again, grumbling and growling.

At Capel Curig Darwin, self-assured as never before, left Sedgwick and struck out on his own. He had a map and compass, and his wits about him. With his new geological skills, this was all he needed. He would show Sedgwick what he could accomplish by himself. His route angled south-west, through 'some strange wild places.' Thirty miles away lay Barmouth and a Cambridge reading party. He followed a straight line through the hills, avoiding the beaten paths unless they went in his direction. He identified the strata along the way, revelling in his freedom, and finished up with a hearty fortnight among Gluttonous old friends.

Partridges were next on his agenda. Not even geology would keep him from shooting his fair share at Uncle Jos's. With only days before the season opened, he was preparing to leave Barmouth when a message came: Ramsay had died. The news took a moment to sink in, and when it did, six months' well-laid plans came crashing down. His travelling companion was lost, leaving the 'Canary scheme' in limbo. Ramsay had been so young, not even forty. Darwin returned to Shrewsbury, pinching himself, unable to 'believe he is no more.' The expedition was up to him now – if he dared attempt it on his own.

Arriving on Monday night, 29 August, he found a fat envelope franked 'London' awaiting him. He opened it perfunctorily, exhausted from his trip, and found letters from Henslow and Peacock.[24] Not more bad news – far from it. Staggered, he read on breathlessly. He was being offered passage on a voyage around the world.

1831–1836

8

My Final Exit

THE HOUR WAS LATE, his body exhausted, but Charles leapt at the offer. Henslow was adamant: 'You are the very man they are in search of.' The Admirals were scouting out someone to accompany Capt. Robert FitzRoy on his two-year survey of coastal South America. FitzRoy, only twenty-six himself, wanted a young companion, a well-bred *'gentleman'* who could relieve the isolation of command, someone to share the captain's table. Better still if he were a naturalist, for there would be unprecedented opportunities. The ship was equipped for 'scientific purposes' and a 'man of zeal & spirit' could do wonders, Henslow enthused. Charles might not be a *'finished* naturalist,' but taking 'plenty of Books' would help, and he was the obvious choice.

So he was. He was well qualified scientifically, and perfectly so socially. Jameson's Edinburgh course, as luck would have it, had catered for colonial travellers. He had learned to identify minerals and disentangle strata, and Sedgwick had fired up his feeling for the subject. Grant had given him the best instruction in Britain on lowly sea life. Darwin had worked his way round Lamarck's systematics and the latest insect identification guides. And what he lacked in experience he made up for in enthusiasm. He could shoot, skin, and stuff, and Henslow had topped his training off with a grounding in botany. He was, as Henslow said, 'amply qualified for collecting, observing, & noting,' and that is what counted.

It was the chance of a lifetime – the Church could wait. The post was at his 'absolute disposal,' according to Peacock's letter, and Peacock spoke for his friend Capt. Francis Beaufort, the Admiralty hydrographer (coastal map-maker) in charge of the voyage. Anyway, the Canaries scheme was in peril, and perhaps it had always been a bit of a bubble. This one was a reality, here and now. The ship was due to sail in a month.[1] He blurted out to his sisters that he would accept. All he had to do was convince his father. Charles forced himself up to bed, dizzy with anticipation.

By the next morning, 30 August 1831, his sisters had briefed the Doctor. His refusal was a cruel blow, and neither Henslow's nor Peacock's endorsement would budge him. It was further evidence of his son's aimless preoccupation with enjoying himself. The voyage would be a useless, dangerous distraction. The unsettling years in the company of sailors would taint Charles and spoil him for the Church. It would ruin his professional chances again. Besides, why was a naturalist being sought with only weeks to spare? Something must be wrong with the vessel, the voyage, or FitzRoy. No, the whole plan looked reckless, and Susan, Caroline, and Catherine agreed.

Charles could ignore the Doctor's views if the Admiralty footed the bill. But he felt 'uncomfortable' at the thought of disobeying his father. With some sadness he declined the offer and went to Maer on the last day of August to vent his frustration on the partridges. He carried a sealed note from the Doctor to Uncle Jos, who was uncomfortable himself, with a 'buffy discharge from the bowels.' It prescribed 'turpentine pills' for his condition and then remarked on Charles's. His proposed 'voyage of discovery' was folly, the Doctor declared, but added, 'if you think differently from me I shall wish him to follow your advice.' This was unexpected, and Charles's hopes revived. Uncle Jos came out in favour of the voyage, followed by Aunt Bessy and the cousins. They were all emphatic, especially Hensleigh: he must go.

His father would listen now – he always trusted Jos's judgment, his industrialist's good sense. A jittery Charles sat up that night drafting a reply with his uncle. It might make the Doctor more uncomfortable than all of them, but he had asked for a second opinion. Far from being too dangerous or expensive, a global voyage could do him the world of good. It would shape his character, argued Jos, and might well ready him for a profession; after all, 'Natural History . . . is very suitable to a Clergyman.' Or considering him as 'a man of enlarged curiosity,' rather than an ordinand, the voyage was a golden opportunity to see 'men and things.' This alone would make it worthwhile. The Admiralty would look after him well, rump candidate or not – but, Jos ended, 'you & Charles . . . must decide.'

For his part, Charles begged 'one favor . . . a decided answer, yes or no,' and retired for a sleepless night. He tossed and turned, his mind 'like a swinging pendulum,' moving back and forth between his indulgent uncle and awesome father. If only they saw him as Henslow did. Early the next day, Thursday 1 September, the reply went off post-haste to Shrewsbury and Charles went hunting. Scarcely had he shot his first bird before Uncle Jos sent word to the field: the issue was so momentous, they should go to The Mount themselves. But it was not necessary. On arriving a few hours later, they found that their message had done the trick. The Doctor had relented. A potter's opinion had swayed him where the professors' had failed, and Charles was now to be entrusted to FitzRoy and the Admiralty. He would receive 'all the assistance in my power,' the Doctor chirped munificently.[2]

A mad scramble ensued. Charles, ecstatic, dashed off a letter of acceptance to Capt. Beaufort, worried that the post might be filled already. Then he threw some clothes in a bag, dozed a few hours, and at three in the morning started on the stage for Cambridge. He hired carriages to whisk him the last fifty miles cross country and reached Henslow by nightfall. The botanist, recovering from Charles's precipitant appearance, briefed him about the offer. True, he was not the first to receive it. The old-boy network had been buzzing for weeks: Jenyns had turned it down on account of his parish duties. Henslow himself had flirted with going, but his wife 'looked so miserable' that he withdrew. Both men then nominated Darwin, neither married nor ordained.

No sooner had Charles begun savouring his 'good fortune' than a courteous message came from FitzRoy. Regrettably, Peacock had misrepresented the offer. The Captain had already promised the place to a friend, but if this fell through Charles would have first claim. FitzRoy hoped no one had been inconvenienced.

Charles was crushed. It had been a 'tremendous, hard week,' an emotional turmoil, and all apparently in vain. He slept fitfully again that night and went to London first thing on Monday. There were contingency plans to make in case the offer was renewed, and an appointment to keep with FitzRoy. But he was no longer sanguine about the voyage. Frankly, he and Henslow had '*entirely* given it up.'[3]

London was in festive mood, with the coronation of William IV, the 'sailor king,' three days off, but Charles was glum. He elbowed his way through the streets to the Admiralty building in Whitehall, and finally met FitzRoy in Beaufort's office. FitzRoy was slight and dark, with fine features and an aristocratic hauteur. He was the grandson of the third Duke of Grafton on his father's side, and of the first

Marquis of Londonderry on his mother's – a direct descendant of Charles II. Crisp and composed, he came to the point at once. His friend had just refused the offer, not five minutes before. Was Mr Darwin still interested?

Was he? Charles felt buffeted, like a weathervane in a cyclone, but he managed a nod. Well and good. FitzRoy proceeded: the voyage would last not two years, but nearly three; it would not necessarily take them around the world. The cabin would be cramped, their dinners plain with 'no wine,' and the costs – up to £500 in all – would not be borne by the Admiralty. Seasickness could be expected, and Darwin would be free to leave for England at any time, or stay behind in 'some healthy, safe & nice country.' If he remained on board, however, he would be closely confined with the Captain for weeks or months on end, so it was imperative that they get along.

The reason for the position was becoming apparent. FitzRoy could not be familiar with his subordinates lest it weaken his command, but shunning all society was risky. Loneliness and isolation could take a terrible toll at sea. The *Beagle*'s former captain Pringle Stokes had shot himself off the South American coast. And FitzRoy feared his own hereditary disposition – in 1822 his uncle, Viscount Castlereagh, had slit his throat in a fit of depression when Home Secretary. So he had decided to take a dining companion. As long as he was a gentleman, mannered and cultivated, even a Whig would do. FitzRoy, the failed Tory candidate for Ipswich in the General Election, knew all about the Darwins' politics. (Being an unbending Tory, he probably also wondered about the grandson of the profligate Erasmus Darwin.) He had a 'horror of ... having somebody he should not like on board.' Obviously, they had to know each other better, and he advised Charles not to make up his mind 'quite yet.'[4]

Charles stayed close-by. With Erasmus out of town, he took lodgings in Spring Gardens, next to the Admiralty, and splashed out on a guinea seat for the coronation procession. He revelled in the pomp and glitter, though the subdued crowds convinced him that coronations would soon be a thing of the past. For the rest of the week he was at FitzRoy's disposal. They dined together and drove about in his gig, 'ordering things.' The Captain struck him as extravagant, though 'very scientific.' He lavished money on books, barometers, and at least £400 on firearms. Charles figured out that he would need a £5 'telescope, with compass,' and some weapons of his own. He bought a £50 rifle for the wildlife and a pair of 'good pistols' to 'keep the natives ... quiet.' 'We shall have plenty of fighting with those d – – Cannibals,' he crowed to Whitley. 'It would be something to shoot the King of the Cannibal Islands.'

It was 'capital fun,' and Charles felt as though he himself had just been crowned. He was 'happy as a king,' his 'confidence in Cap. Fitzroy' unbounded. He had taken to him 'at first sight' and begun to trust him almost involuntarily. FitzRoy became his 'beau ideal of a Captain,' and his kindness left Charles feeling as if he had been predestined to make the voyage – though he asked his sisters to refrain from chit-chat until his mind was finally made up. FitzRoy, too, liked what he saw and heard. His fears about Darwin had been unfounded; in the event, manners and breeding transcended party and family.[5]

A few things remained to be settled. Beaufort assured Darwin that he would be free to dispose of any collections he made, provided they went to some 'public body.' And FitzRoy repeated that he could leave the ship, 'as soon & wherever' he liked. He doubted that Darwin actually had the stamina to see the trip through. FitzRoy, addicted to physiognomy, judged a man's character by his face, and Darwin's nose foretold a lack of 'energy and determination.' But there was no shortage of it for the present. He was fired up, hoping that it would it be a circumnavigation. He wanted to go right around the globe, and badgered Beaufort about it without success. Finally FitzRoy promised to whisper the word in the ear of Tory friends. He told Darwin that he had 'interest enough' with people in high places 'to get the ship ordered home by whatever track he likes' – 'particularly if this [Whig] administration is not everlasting.' Charles relayed the story home, joking, 'I shall soon turn Tory!' The circumnavigation was 'all but certain.'[6]

His enthusiasm might have been checked if he had seen the size of the ship. FitzRoy knew his table-guest had no inkling of the 'square inches' he would be allotted. On Sunday the 11th he took Darwin to see her at Devonport – the long way. They left London by steam packet, chugging down the Thames, around the Kent coast into the English Channel, past Spithead and on to the safety of Plymouth Sound. The trip lasted almost three days and gave FitzRoy the chance to judge Darwin's sea legs.

He also briefed him about the Admiralty's assignment. The South American survey had begun five years ago. The continent was an open house for trade, a vast market for manufactured goods and a storehouse of raw materials. Rich Britons and their bankers had invested millions of pounds in the emerging national governments; companies had capitalized to the hilt to exploit its resources. Some of the speculation had proved ill judged, and even now the future was uncertain. That was why the Royal Navy was involved. If merchants were to beat competitors from Spain and the United States, their vessels needed easy access to South American ports. Islands and coastlines had to be mapped, harbours and channels sounded. The initial survey, which ended only a year before, had accomplished much, and FitzRoy himself – in his first command after Stokes's suicide – had served in its latter stages. But the charts needed checking and extending; tides and weather conditions remained to be logged – and FitzRoy would be the first to plot wind forces around the globe using Beaufort's scale. Parts of Patagonia and the Falkland Islands also had to be surveyed, as well as the desolate maze of channels at the continent's southern tip, in Tierra del Fuego.[7] This was his job.

He had come by it rather oddly, though, and Charles heard how. The summer before in Tierra del Fuego, while a party of his men were camping on shore, 'some Fuegians . . . approached with the dexterous cunning peculiar to savages' and stole their boat. His ship gave chase and the culprits' families were 'brought on board as hostages.' Most escaped, a few were released, and one was killed in a scuffle (his body was duly skeletonized 'for further study'). Eventually FitzRoy held two men, a boy, and a girl, none of whom could be put ashore conveniently. So he decided to try an evangelical experiment: he would civilize the savages, teach them 'English . . . the plainer truths of Christianity . . . and the use of common tools,' and then send them back to Tierra del Fuego as missionaries. The four returned with him to England. One died from a smallpox vaccination. The rest – named York Minster, age about 27, Jemmy Button, 15, and the girl Fuegia Basket, 10 – had spent the year with friends of the Church Missionary Society. In June, unable to find a ship to repatriate them, FitzRoy was on the point of sailing for Tierra del Fuego at his own expense when 'a kind uncle' interceded at the Admiralty and landed him the *Beagle* command. The Fuegians, civilized enough to be presented at Court during the summer, were joining his ship with their minder Richard Matthews, a trainee missionary himself.[8] Such was providence. The survey would be completed because the savages had been converted – the Lord was delivering native South America into English hands.

Charles marvelled at the Captain. His manners were impeccable, even towards the 'little Midshipman' he brought along, Musters, who turned out to know Charles's Derbyshire uncle, Sir Francis Darwin. By Tuesday, when the mail-boat put in at Devonport, the two of them were getting on famously. Charles had no misgivings on this account, though he sensed that his 'violent admiration' could not last. Then he saw the ship.

The *Beagle* was a ten-gun brig, eleven years old and rotting. It was being completely rebuilt as a three-masted bark in the naval dockyard. FitzRoy was personally supervising the work, and no expense was spared, even if he had to dip into his own pocket. She had a new upper deck with skylights, a reinforced copper bottom, and all up-to-date technologies: a specially designed rudder, a patented galley stove, advanced lightning conductors, and brass cannons instead of iron to avoid interference with the compasses. Charles took it in as he met the officers, an 'active determined set of young fellows.' What made him wince was the *Beagle*'s size – only 90 feet long and 24 feet wide amidships. She had only two cabins, and these were tiny. The poop cabin, behind the wheel, measured 10 feet by 11, and six-foot Charles had to stoop when inside. It held a vast chart table with three small chairs, and the mizzen-mast passed through it. The Captain's cabin was below deck, beneath the wheel, and even smaller. There were luxurious mahogany fitments everywhere, but this was no consolation. Close quarters yes, but Charles had never imagined them *this* close. His spirits sank.

He was soon buoyant again. Just before he left for London on Friday the cabin nameplates were fitted. Mercifully, his went on to the larger poop cabin (although he would also have the run of FitzRoy's cabin, and mess there too). The forward corner portside would be his part, with a few square feet of the chart table as well as a wall full of drawers, opposite the ship's library with its several hundred volumes at the rear. His cabin mate was to be the officer he liked best, John Lort Stokes, the nineteen-year-old Assistant Surveyor. They would both work here, each at his own seat, with the third place reserved for a fourteen-year-old Midshipman, Philip King, whose father had commanded the first survey. Sleeping arrangements would be awkward but adequate. Stokes's bed was in a cubicle outside the door, and King's below-deck. Charles would sling his hammock above the chart table, with his face two feet beneath the skylight.

FitzRoy took pains to make Charles comfortable in his poop cabin 'home.'[9] Charles left Devonport marginally reassured, trying to see the *Beagle* as more cosy than cramped.

Sailing had been postponed a few weeks, with FitzRoy fussing about the refit, but Charles still had to rush. His plans were 'fixed & certain' now. At last he could tell everyone, and bid them farewell. He raced up from Plymouth to London – an astonishing '250 miles in 24 hours' – and from there by night coach to Cambridge, where he talked Henslow's ear off for a couple of days. Henslow agreed to store his collections as they were sent back piecemeal and gave him a parting present, a copy of Humboldt's *Personal Narrative*. He also recommended taking the first volume of Charles Lyell's *Principles of Geology*, just published, but 'on no account' to accept all its views. Then Charles was off again, overnight to Shrewsbury, arriving early on Thursday the 22nd.[10]

The family had been at his beck and call for the last three weeks, collecting his belongings, packing his clothes, and providing bank drafts. This was his last chance to thank them in person, the dear old nay-sayers, and show his love. The Mount had often seemed like a prison but now it wore a different aspect. This great stone pile, built by his father, was home, not FitzRoy's bobbing bark. Security was a family and four solid walls, a refuge from the tempestuous world. Yet he was giving it all up, and with it 'half a chance of life.' They would be years apart; perhaps he would never see his father and sisters again. They meant more than ever to him, and he let them know. The Doctor was now 'much more reconciled' to the voyage, and his blessing made parting easier.

At the weekend Charles went to Woodhouse, only to be unnerved by the news of Fanny's broken engagement. The Revd Hill had jilted her, and she had gone away to do a 'severe Penance' for foolishly falling in love – being '*taken alive*' like some beast, as she put it. Charles scarcely knew whether to feel sorrier for himself or her. As he left, bearing a keepsake pin from Sarah, the Squire and all the family were melancholy too. At Maer the mood was brighter. He rode over and retailed FitzRoy's stories about Patagonian peat bogs and cannibals, and the 'detestable climate.' Charlotte worried that his third year at sea would put paid to 'the country parish & parsonage,' but otherwise the clan preened itself for persuading Dr Darwin and congratulated Charles on his courage.[11]

He returned to The Mount for a few days, and then on Sunday 2 October took his leave. He could hardly bear to embrace his father and sisters for the last time, but to hesitate now would betray them all. Resolve was needed. He had to prove his mettle. He choked back the tears and set his face towards London, Plymouth, and the world.

Back in London he teamed up with FitzRoy's other 'shore-going fellow,' the landscape artist Augustus Earle. Earle too was travelling in a private capacity, taken on by the Captain to provide a painted record of the *Beagle*'s stopover points. He was already well salted, having trained at the Royal Academy and then voyaged round the world, visiting and painting in Europe, North America, Brazil, and Australia. Darwin found him a bit 'eccentric.'

In the capital politics dominated life. The Whigs, swept to power with an increased majority in the General Election, had consolidated their hold on the reform movement. Rioting farm labourers had been hanged or transported; Carlile was appealing in vain against his conviction, and Taylor languished in Horsemonger-lane gaol, a broken man, his protest letters in *The Times* snubbed by the Home Secretary. A new Reform Bill was holding the headlines. It had passed its third reading ten days before and been sent to the House of Lords.

As Darwin began packing in his digs, just off Whitehall, the Lords' debate was heating up half a mile away. Everyone feared the worst. Sure enough, the next Saturday, 8 October, the peers threw out the bill and the country erupted. Gold soared; the stock market plunged. Pro-reform papers reported the death of the bill in black-edged editions. Riots and arson broke out in the major towns. Dukes were manhandled and their mansions attacked; the Tory bishops were jeered for having voted against the bill. In Cambridge Henslow feared being taken for a Tory and having his 'windows smashed.' On the 19th the King tried to calm the country by suspending Parliament, but nothing could stop 70,000 demonstrators marching through the capital, calling for fresh legislation.[12]

Darwin felt the strain. He was 'daily . . . more anxious to be off.' With introductions from Henslow, he darted around seeking specialist advice. The best display of skins and shells was at the zoo's West End museum, a short walk along Piccadilly. This was boom time for the zoo; gate takings had soared at the Regent's Park menagerie, leaving the museum curators £1000 a year to spend on anatomical specimens. Not that they needed it; exotic corpses were flooding in from the naval surveys, like Darwin's. As a result the museum, based in Lord Berkeley's town house in Bruton Street, was already packed. Darwin found it a kleptomaniac's delight, with carcasses everywhere – 600 mammals, 4000 birds, 1000 reptiles and fish, and 30,000 insects greeted him. And to this Capt. King's specimens from the previous *Beagle* survey of Patagonia were still being added.

Here Darwin met the taxidermists whose speciality was preserving, stuffing and storing. Everyone provided pointers: Benjamin Leadbeater, exhibiting cockatoos from Australia, taught him to pack skins in turpentine-soaked boxes. One of the zoo's prime movers, William Yarrell, a fellow sportsman building a fish collection, showed how to seal jars using bladders, tin foil, and varnish. Capt. King explained the use of 'Arsenical soap & preserving powder.' On marine invertebrates, though, Robert Grant was still his chief authority. He gave Darwin a list of pickling tips: crabs and the like to have their abdomens slit and gills flushed out; delicate zoophytes to be killed 'by gradual additions of fresh water,' sea anemones 'by pouring boiling water in their interiors.' Crack open 'spiral shells' to allow the preservatives to reach 'all parts.' An equal mix of water and wine spirits should do, except for crabs, which take their spirits neat.[13] At the British Museum, the top botanist in town, Robert Brown, briefed him. Brown was exceptionally shy, but a brilliant microscopist (he described the cell nucleus and Brownian motion). He advised Darwin on the best microscope to buy, and Darwin promised to pick him some Patagonian orchids.

Darwin was armed with the best advice a naturalist could carry, fully prepared (as Henslow said) for 'collection, observing, & noting.' He was on his way – or should have been.

News came of another delay. The *Beagle* would not be ready to sail until 4 November. By now Charles had assembled all his possessions, but the extra time came in handy with all the packing necessary. Shoes and slippers, breeches and boots, a dozen shirts marked 'DARWIN,' and Sarah Owen's pin – the personal items mounted up fast. His scientific gear, once crated, took on frightful proportions: specimen jars stuffed with chemicals and preservatives, dissecting tools in trays, boxed precision instruments – microscope, clinometer, telescope, compass, rain gauge, barometer – as well as an iron-chain trawling net, spare parts for the guns, his geological hammer, and of course Humboldt, Lyell and other books. 'I have *been as economical as I possibly could*,' he assured FitzRoy, but if 'the worst' came and he exceeded his allotted space, then 'two big cases' had been earmarked to be left behind.

All the crates went off by steamer in a south-westerly gale, and Charles followed on land, arriving in Plymouth late on Monday 24 October.[14] In ten days the *Beagle* would put to sea.

He was exhausted. He hadn't stayed a week in one place since August, or even a dozen days at home. He had travelled 1500 miles, spent his father's money with impunity, rubbed shoulders with naval bigwigs, and felt his life turned upside down. But now the time was near; he was about to take the plunge, leave the old world behind – make 'my final exit.' And what a relief, he wanted it over fast.

FitzRoy fixed him up in quayside lodgings with Stokes and himself, so that the *Beagle*'s intelligentsia could become acquainted. After a riotous dinner below deck in the Gun Room, the officers' mess, Darwin was glad of it. The men were 'rather rough, & their conversation . . . so full of slang & sea phrases' that it was as 'unintelligible as

Hebrew.' Among them was the Surgeon, Robert McCormick, the ship's official naturalist. He was thirty-one, hospital trained, petulant and the product of three voyages. Surgery was a menial grade in the King's navy, and only gentlemen could share the Captain's table (which is why Darwin was along). Darwin got on amicably with McCormick, even if he was 'an ass' and worried more about the *Beagle*'s paintwork than scientific pursuits.[15] There was no escaping science for Charles, or at any rate trigonometry. He began swotting again, wanting to hold his own when the talk turned to navigation. Stokes and FitzRoy primed him as they toured the dockyard, calibrating their instruments.

The gales persisted, and the sailing was postponed again. Saturday, 5 November, Guy Fawkes's Day, was to have been their first full day at sea. But while bishops were burnt in effigy across the country instead of traditional Guys, Charles sat pensively in his room, trying to read. It was a 'wretched, miserable' non-event. He went with Musters to the dockyard chapel on Sunday, took in a concert during the week, and had a geological jaunt or two. None of it cheered him up.

Next weekend, the four Fuegian missionaries arrived, laden with the trappings of civilization. Well-meaning churchgoers had inundated them with 'clothes, tools, crockery-ware, books' – everything necessary for their outpost. Somehow their cargo was stowed in the *Beagle*'s tiny hold, the sailors muttering about the crush and hooting at the toffs who sent complete sets of crockery. The missionaries had a lofty moral purpose, but they were travelling at other people's expense, in more ways than one. Darwin had paid for his passage. And having jettisoned every non-essential, he still wondered how everything of his would fit in. Claustrophobia struck, leaving him in 'continual fear.' 'The absolute want of room,' he glowered, 'is an evil, that nothing can surmount.'[16]

The sailing date kept receding. Now it was put off until early December. Alone many days, with only provisions to buy and the cabin to rearrange, he became despondent. He worried about seasickness and was tortured by thoughts of death. Ramsay's loss haunted him ominously. Then on the 21st a sailor slipped overboard and drowned. If this could happen in port, what were his chances of surviving three years – or four, as FitzRoy now mooted – at sea? Then he noticed his heart palpitating and he developed chest pains. Was it heart disease? He bottled up his fears, said nothing to surgeon McCormick, and put on a brave face in letters home.[17] If his father found out he would stop him going, Uncle Jos or no. Come what may, Charles was resolved to sail.

Through all the 'wearisome anxiety' he thought of family and friends. He was abandoning everyone he loved, and he wondered whether the voyage, if he lived through it, would compensate him for the loss. People wrote, but endearing letters only made him lonelier. Henslow preached a sermon about tolerating the crew's 'coarse or vulgar' behaviour. Fox, whom he had brushed off and had not seen in a year, was gracious, reminding him of the stories that they would swop 'by the fire' one day. Whitley brought back memories of Cambridge camaraderie and 'the simple, the elegant, Glutton club.' Those weekly meals were better by far than FitzRoy's sumptuous 'ships warming' luncheon on the 28th. 'But ... there is no use thinking about it,' Charles replied mournfully. 'It is all over.' 'Remember me ... especially to old Matthew if you see him,' and 'God bless you.'

No one touched him like Fanny, who was now pouring her heart out. It was the cruellest irony. They had passed like ships in the night, their lives headed in opposite directions. Back in September, when he was in Devonport with FitzRoy inspecting the *Beagle*, she was in Exeter, only fifty miles away, completing her 'Penance.' Indeed, they were both actually in Plymouth one day, but never met. Afterwards she heard of his plans and sent him a '*leetle* purse' as a memento, but by the time she returned to Woodhouse he was gone. Missing her had put Charles in a 'Blue devilish humour.' He wrote plaintively, hoping that she would not forget him. Her reply, for once it seemed, was candid. She pined for their tender past and longed to see him again, predicting that his return would find her 'in *status quo* at the Forest, only grown **old** & *sedate*.' 'The many happy hours we have had together from the time we were **Housemaid & Postillion** ... are not to be forgotten,' she vowed, adding provocatively, '& would that there was not to be an end of them!!'

Her last letter came on Saturday 3 December, an apt sequel giving an eager account of Sarah's wedding. But with two days before sailing, Charles determined to 'talk or think' only of the voyage.[18] And Erasmus had just arrived to help concentrate his mind.

There was so much to show Erasmus – the *Beagle* gleaming and shipshape, with its twenty-four chronometers for determining exact longitudes of islands around the globe; FitzRoy's hearty provisions, and not least that miniature, mahogany-lined compartment, his home. Things looked better, seen through Eras's eyes, and that Saturday night Charles braved staying aboard for the first time. He had the 'most ludicrous difficulty' getting into his hammock, attempting it feet first while balanced on the chart table; but after mastering the trick of seat-first entry, all went well. He even slept through a minor storm, so perhaps he would escape seasickness. Erasmus wished everyone *bon voyage* at the evening meal, and saluted his brother goodbye. FitzRoy was ready to leave in the morning.

A southerly gale blew up at midday, mocking the last-minute preparations. It kept up all week. On the morning of the 10th, while Erasmus was on board saying goodbye, the weather finally cleared, and FitzRoy gave the order to hoist sails. The effect was electric – 'Coxswains piping, the manning [of] the yards, the men working at the hawsers to the sound of a fife,' and all with breathtaking 'rapidity & decision.' At nine o'clock the *Beagle* weighed anchor and moved out as far as the breakwater, where Erasmus disembarked to a chorus of fraternal shouts.[19] Then the tiny bark ploughed through the Sound and on to the open sea.

Charles's misery began immediately. Nausea nailed him to the rail, and he spewed his breakfast into the swell. Nothing stayed down all day. In the evening a fierce gale came on from the south-west, and the *Beagle* began pitching 'bows under' into mountainous waves. It was his worst nightmare. All through the watches he swung violently in his cabin, retching helplessly, while in the blackness outside the howling wind, the 'roar of the sea, [and] the hoarse screams of the officers & shouts of the men' reached a crescendo. In the chaos FitzRoy remembered his companion. He staggered in from behind the wheel and made Charles comfortable, adjusting his hammock. The next morning the Captain admitted defeat. He headed the ship back to Plymouth, resolved to await a favourable east wind.

At anchor, the waiting went on and on. The ship was 'full of grumblers & growlers' and Charles became 'as bad as the worst.' On Wednesday the 21st the sun, the sea, and the wind were perfect. FitzRoy made a fresh start – and promptly ran the ship aground. It was low tide, and the *Beagle* could be freed only by everyone running in unison back and forth across the deck, causing the vessel to swing. They reached the Channel in the afternoon and, after a bout of sickness, Charles slept soundly overnight. In the morning he checked a pocket compass and – incredibly – it pointed back towards England. Eleven miles off the Lizard a south-westerly gale had set in. The Captain had turned the ship and was making for Plymouth Sound.[20]

Charles was past wanting anything now except to be under way, once and for all. Christmas left him cold. He went to church that Sunday and heard an old Cambridge friend preach. At four he dined in the Gun Room and thanked the Lord that he shared FitzRoy's table. The officers carried on like varmints, but with the manners of 'freshest freshmen.' Their high spirits came straight out of a bottle, just like the sailors', and without a tincture of the Gluttons' good fellowship. By nightfall no one on board was sober, not even Charles. Needless to say the next day was ideal for sailing, except for 'the drunkedness & absence of nearly the whole crew.' The ship remained in a 'state of anarchy,' with sailors in 'heavy chains' incarcerated below deck, ranting and blubbering by turn. The Captain restored order ruthlessly, and by evening the stragglers on shore had all turned up to face their punishment. Everyone settled down – to wait.

On 27 December the *Beagle*'s seventy-three souls awoke to a crystal sky washed by a light easterly breeze. FitzRoy spoke the word and the ship sprang to life, with officers barking orders and the sailors scrambling over the deck and up the masts, readying the sails. The supernumeraries kept clear, the missionaries below in their private quarter, and Charles in his cabin, scribbling last-minute letters home. At eleven o'clock, as the ship weighed anchor, he joined FitzRoy and Lieutenant Bartholomew Sulivan aboard the local naval commissioner's yacht for a farewell luncheon. While the *Beagle* warped from the shelter of Barnpool and tacked out into the Sound, the party glided on a parallel course, dining elegantly. They rejoined their ship outside the breakwater, and immediately, with every sail unfurled, she scudded slowly out to sea. The 'mutton chops & champagne,' Charles jotted in his diary, 'may I hope excuse the total absence of sentiment which I experienced on leaving England.'[21]

9

A Chaos of Delight

HE WAS SICK AGAIN, dreadfully. It started the second day at sea, while FitzRoy doled out punishments for the Christmas crimes. Four men between them received 134 lashes for insolence, disobedience, and neglect of duty. Darwin cringed as the whip hissed and the felons howled. This brutal justice turned his stomach – or was it the constant pitching and rolling?

Soon enough he knew, for the nausea remained. It went 'far far beyond' anything he had imagined. For ten days nothing stayed down but dry 'biscuit & raisins,' or when that revolted him, hot spiced wine mixed with sago. He nearly fainted from exhaustion when he tried to stand; only a 'horizontal position' brought relief. As the tiny *Beagle* bobbed through heavy seas in the Bay of Biscay he was swinging beneath the poop cabin skylight, tormented by 'dark & gloomy thoughts.' Re-reading Humboldt's 'glowing accounts of tropical scenery' bucked him up a little. And, swaying there at night, it was 'rather amusing' to watch the moon and stars performing 'small revolutions in . . . new apparent orbits.' Otherwise there was nothing but vomiting and regrets. New Year was more a time for recriminations than resolutions. The voyage was a mistake. If only he had heeded the Doctor.[1]

FitzRoy steered past Madeira, but Darwin, sick in his cabin, missed the landfall. As they made for Tenerife the air grew balmy and the swell subsided. Everyone was itching for shore leave, not least Darwin. He began to feel better, and was thrilled when the island's volcanic peak appeared above the clouds. It looked like 'another world,' 'twice as high' as he had ever dreamed. Here was compensation for the agony of seasickness. As the *Beagle* tacked into the sun-baked port of Santa Cruz on 6 January 1832, he could hardly take his eyes off the mountain, so long the 'object of my ambition.' But when the anchor dropped, a boat came alongside with urgent orders. The *Beagle* was to be quarantined for twelve days because of the cholera outbreak in England, an official shouted. No 'personal communication,' no shore going.

All eyes turned to the Captain. Would he wait? The answer came at once. 'Up Jib,' FitzRoy cried, and slowly the *Beagle* moved off into the gathering dusk. Darwin was devastated. The quarantine orders came like a 'death-warrant.' He did not have 'the slightest prospect' of visiting this tropical paradise again. The ship was becalmed a few miles off shore, and he sought solace in the night. It 'does its best to smooth our sorrow,' he confided to his diary, 'the air is still & deliciously warm – the only sounds are the waves rippling on the stern & the sails idly flapping round the masts . . . The sky is so clear & lofty, & stars innumerable shine so bright that like little moons they cast their glitter on the waves.'[2]

Two days later Tenerife disappeared. It was 'like parting from a friend,' Darwin sighed. The *Beagle* tacked south in a fine breeze and it grew hotter by the day. He lay quietly in the cabin, reading the first volume of Lyell's *Principles of Geology*. Or he ventured on to the deck to try a plankton net he had made from coarse cloth. He dropped it overboard from the poop deck and let it drag in the wake. The harvest was huge, with myriad tiny creatures 'most exquisite in their forms & rich colours.' He had never seen the like, not even with Grant. Why 'so much beauty' in the vastness of the ocean, with nobody to admire it? It seemed 'created for such little purpose.'

The weather was excellent, with light winds and puffy clouds in azure skies, and stunning sunsets. St Jago in the Cape Verde Islands, 300 miles off the African coast, was to be their first landing. A wretched place, he had read; it would not give the 'lasting impression of beauty' that he craved from the tropics.

Shrouded in thick haze, St Jago could not be seen distinctly until the *Beagle* was within three miles. It lived up to its reputation – an excrescence of desolate volcanic hills. Still, after the *Beagle* anchored off Porto Praya on the 16th, Darwin was relieved just to be walking on solid ground. He went with FitzRoy to meet the islands' Portuguese governor and the American consul. Then he finally realized his dream – he saw his first tropical vegetation. In a deep valley he came upon a scene reminiscent of Humboldt's descriptions, a lush tangle of fruit trees and palms. He was awestruck and felt like a blind man being given his sight: 'overwhelmed' and unable to 'comprehend it.' St Jago had been redeemed, and Darwin began to relish the weeks ahead on shore.[3]

While FitzRoy set up an observatory and took measurements, Darwin rushed everywhere – hiking with Musters and McCormick, pony-trekking inland with Rowlett and Bynoe (the Purser and the Assistant Surgeon), or exploring by himself. It was like a Barmouth reading party, but infinitely more exciting. Wild cats bounded past, gaudy kingfishers darted around, and he stumbled on 'the celebrated Baobob trees,' a massive thirty-six feet in girth, but as graffiti covered 'as any one in Kensington Gardens.' He carried weapons of course. 'Very good for black man,' his interpreter nodded, quite nonchalant about murder. But Darwin had never seen anyone 'more intelligent than . . . the Negro or Molatto children,' who '*immediately* perceived' and were 'astonished at the percussion guns.' 'They examine everything with the liveliest attention, & if you let them . . . will pull everything out of your pockets. My silver pencil case was . . . much speculated upon.'

Darwin was in his element. On his Edinburgh walks he had often 'gazed at the little pools of water left by the tide: & from the minute corals . . . pictured to myself those of larger growth.' Now here he was, collecting brilliantly coloured sponges and exquisite tropical corals on the coast. What most enthralled him was the volcanic terrain. Walking alone over sun-scorched plains strewn with 'black & burnt rocks' was ecstasy, his imagination running riot on nature's primeval forces. The barrenness and solitude forced all mortal thoughts from the mind: he was left facing the earth's awesome power.

He spotted something odd – a horizontal white band running through the rocks, about thirty feet above sea-level. It was made of compressed shells and corals, and continued as far as the eye could see. Obviously the whole area had once been under water, but why not now? Darwin, fascinated, took up the challenge.

Sedgwick in North Wales had inducted him into Cambridge-style geology – a science of violent crustal movements, wrenching strata, and mountain thrusts. But how had this seashell band arrived at this height above the ocean? Lyell's *Principles of Geology* could help here, even though Henslow had said to beware. Lyell pictured a world constantly and slowly changing, with the past no more violent than the present – so that today's climates, volcanic activity, and earth movements are all we need to explain the ancient world. Crustal movements balance one another: land rises in one area as it falls in another, not cataclysmically, as Sedgwick thought, but gradually.

Was Lyell right? Thousands of miles from Cambridge, Darwin thought for himself. It was impossible that the sea itself had fallen; a lower Atlantic was unimaginable in St Jago's volcanic lifetime. So had the island risen slowly or abruptly? He inspected the oyster band again. It was practically intact, showing no sign of catastrophic violence. And it varied in height above sea-level along its length, suggesting secondary subsidence in places. St Jago, at least, seemed to prove Lyell's point. Darwin started to view the world as slowly and gradually changing.[4]

With his notepads filling up, Darwin now realized that he could make a serious contribution to geology. He even imagined writing his own book on the subject, based on the countries he would visit. Only occasionally did his thoughts revert to 'England & its politicks;' the promise of tropical vistas had stopped even the sailors talking 'reform.' FitzRoy weighed anchor on 8 February. Darwin again could think of little but South American vegetation. He expected to find it even more luxuriant, though he knew that his first St Jago impressions would 'never be effaced.'[5]

'Squeamish and uncomfortable,' he described himself as the *Beagle* dashed for the Equator. Most days nausea flattened him, and he hated lying about. As he dangled in his cabin, dead animals stared at him, awaiting 'labels and scientific epitaphs.' It grew 'damp & oppressive' inside, and still he could not get up, even to air his sticky limbs. Mercifully, some nights were cool, but by day it was like being 'stewed in . . . warm melted butter.'

FitzRoy stopped for fresh food at St Paul's Rocks, 'the top of a submarine mountain' covered with nesting boobies and noddies. Darwin pulled ashore for the slaughter with Stokes and First Lieutenant John Wickham. The gulls, knowing no predators, seemed almost tame. The men filled their hats with eggs, and then laid about the birds 'like schoolboys,' crushing their skulls with stones. Darwin's geological hammer came in handy; one of the men wielded it so violently that the shaft snapped. They piled up the corpses while the sailors in the boat hooked groupers and other fish, competing for them with the sharks. It led to a glorious glut – everything the *Beagle* needed to celebrate 'crossing the line' on 16 February.

The Equator provided the traditional excuse to let off steam. Discipline was suspended and the ceremonies began that night. FitzRoy, dressed as Father Neptune, summoned each of the novices to the forecastle, where half-naked sailors daubed in paints and dancing like demons waited to perform the initiation. Thirty-two had never crossed, and Darwin was the first to be called. One look at FitzRoy and he ran down the fore hatchway, convinced that the ship had gone mad. But the demons caught and blindfolded him, stood him on a plank, and flipped him into a water-filled sail. Dragging him out, they lathered his 'face & mouth with pitch and paint, & scraped some of it off with a piece of roughened iron hoop,' then tipped him head over heels again into the water. This was light treatment, though unpleasant enough; others fared worse. Eventually the whole ship became 'a shower bath,' with water 'flying about in every direction ... Not one person, even the Captain, got clear of being wet through.'[6]

So passed 17 February too, in mummery and mayhem. Darwin awoke in the southern hemisphere, marvelling at the heavens. Out on deck he saw the sun to the north, and at night the Southern Cross and Magellan's Cloud. His stomach felt calmer now, aided by the 'variables' – the light equatorial winds. But the temperature was oppressive, and sleeping an ordeal. He took to the chart table finally – anywhere to escape the clinging hammock – but even then his heated mind worked overtime. The coming years with all their risks frightened him. A new world was beckoning, but his heart remained at home. If only he were now looking back safely on the voyage, surrounded by loved ones and friends! The yearning came over him again and again, especially on 'soft & delicious' tropical nights.[7]

A trade wind caught the *Beagle* and blew her steadily to Brazil. She hove to at Bahia (Salvador), anchoring in All Saints Bay amid a forest of large ships, and on 28 February Darwin first set foot on the continent. The old town, with its stinking wharfs and narrow streets, reminded him of student days in Auld Reekie. But here the lofty houses were 'embosomed in a luxuriant wood,' and whitewashed churches and imposing porticos glistened against the verdure. It was the rainy season, and no time better to see the forest.

At last he had his wish. Humboldt's word-pictures came to life, yet even his 'glorious descriptions' did not do justice. Darwin wandered by himself hour after hour, dazed by 'the luxuriance of the vegetation ... the elegance of the grasses, the novelty of the parasitical plants, the beauty of the flowers.' His mind was 'a chaos of delight.' Pausing in a shady nook, he listened to the droning, croaking, throbbing life. Now, as in ages past, when no human interlopers were around to hear, the forest reverberated to 'a most paradoxical mixture of sound & silence,' like some great cathedral at evensong, with the anthem fading to 'universal stillness.' Adding 'raptures to ... raptures,' he began collecting: flowers enough 'to make a florist go wild,' and countless beetles. Such 'transports of pleasure' he had never known. And imagine, he said after shooting a huge beautiful lizard, that such delight should be called 'duty'! He had to tell his father, and wrote passionately of his success, sending 'my love to every soul at home, & to the Owens.'⁴

Back in town it was the carnival season, and he braved the festive streets with Lieutenants Wickham and Sulivan, only to beat a hasty retreat under a barrage of 'wax balls full of water' and the spray of 'large tin squirts.' But there was little to celebrate here. In the merchants' warehouses, he wrote tartly, 'all the labor is done by black men.' They came so cheap that capital investment was nil; only one 'wheel carriage' was to be seen. The blacks carried everything. Still, 'when staggering under their heavy burthens,' they 'beat time & cheer themselves by a rude song.'

It was a sore point, the travails of the black man, and potentially divisive aboard ship, with FitzRoy justifying the Negroes' lot. One day he remarked that slavery was not intolerable, for Brazilians in general treat their black servants well. FitzRoy was widely travelled and Darwin was not, but in his Whig heart Darwin knew wrong from right. Slavery was the one institution that his whole family had inveighed against. It was evil, and Darwin suggested that the only solution was emancipation. FitzRoy boiled over: 'Hot Coffee' the crew called the Captain for his temper, and Darwin was scalded. FitzRoy had heard a slave-owner ask his servants whether they were unhappy or wished to be free. 'No,' they had replied – so shouldn't their wishes be respected? Darwin asked what a slave's answer in his master's presence was worth. At this FitzRoy exploded, declaring that they could not live together any longer; his word had been questioned. And then he stalked out of the cabin.

That was that. To think that Darwin had feared falling overboard when being kicked off was so easy. The news spread, and he was glad for an invitation to mess with the Gun Room officers, who briefed him about FitzRoy's flare-ups. Sure enough, a few hours later the Captain sent an apology and asked him to remain. Capt. Paget of the *Samarang*, a 'real fighting' vessel, was aboard, paying call, and Darwin was invited to eat with them. Now came sweet revenge. Paget had seen as much of the world as FitzRoy. He knew about slavery, and as a guest he could not be gainsaid. All the atrocities he could recall were trotted out over dinner. He too quoted a well-treated slave, who longed 'to see my father & my two sisters once again.' Such, Darwin fumed afterwards, was the anguish of the black men, 'who are ranked by the polished savages in England as hardly their brethren, even in Gods eyes.'⁹

*

FitzRoy put to sea on 18 March after completing a chart of the harbour. The *Beagle* ran south along the Brazilian coast, sounding near the rocky Abrolhos islets and stopping to load up with fresh fowl. Then on towards Rio de Janeiro in a 'rattling breeze,' with April Fool's jokes along the way. At midnight Sulivan burst into the poop cabin, crying, 'Darwin, did you ever see a Grampus'? Darwin bolted from his hammock to catch a glimpse of the dolphin – only to be 'received by a roar of laughter from the whole watch.'

Things were looking up. He saw his first water spout, caught his first shark, and eagerly awaited his first post from home. The mail bag came aboard on 5 April as the *Beagle* slid into Rio harbour, a mere surveying ship, raising and lowering all her canvas with split-second precision before the men-o'-war. Darwin left off helping with the display and rushed below to read his letters. Even the view of Rio, 'gaudy with its towers & Cathedrals,' and guarded by the Sugar Loaf mountain, took second place.

The gossip was overwhelming. Everyone, it seemed, was getting married: Hensleigh to Fanny Mackintosh, his sister Charlotte to a parson liked by the whole family. Charlotte longed to see Charles settled down with a wife 'in your parsonage,' and becoming a 'good active religious clergyman,' like her own Charles Langton. It was the 'happiest life in the world,' she glowed.

Another wedding was announced – Fanny Owen's. Stunned at first, Charles broke down as he read. She had been engaged since the new year, not a month after her last letter. A rich varmint-like character named Biddulph (an aspiring politician, of course) had hovered about her after the Hill affair, taken pity on her distress, and finally proposed. It had happened 'in the course of a secret ride' – shades of housemaid and postillion – and the wedding was in March. Fanny would be 'a *motherly old married woman* when you come back,' sister Catherine said, rubbing it in. Charles, tears streaming, was incoherent. He tried to be philosophical about it, but inside was 'really melting with tenderness,' and he cried 'my dearest Fanny' over and over again to himself. Oh, what a country curate's wife she would have made! – 'by the fates, at this pace I have no chance for the parsonage.'[10]

Overwrought, he plunged headlong into the interior. He teamed up with a rag-bag group of British adventurers from Rio, heading a hundred miles north, where one of them owned an estate. The ride was tortuous, the lodgings *en route* filthy, and the food meagre. Charles fell ill in the blistering heat but pressed on, 'faint & exhausted.' The sights made up for his discomfort: conical ants' nests rising twelve feet from the ground, egrets wading in salt lagoons, vampire bats supping on horses' blood, and a profusion of orchids and cabbage palms.

On arriving at the estate, he saw another 'horrible & flagrant' example of 'miserably overworked' blacks. The owner, his travelling companion, quarrelled with the foreman running the ranch, and threatened to sell the man's favourite mulatto child at a public auction. The dispute escalated, and the owner angrily rounded up all the women and children from thirty slave families, intent on selling them separately from their husbands in Rio. This was despicable. How could a man otherwise so congenial reach such depths of degradation? 'How weak are the arguments of those who maintain that slavery is a tolerable evil!'

The estate had been carved out of virgin jungle, and Charles rambled off into the steamy stillness. He was entranced again – no, profoundly moved. Alone with his gun and notebook, he knew that there was no Fanny awaiting him, no black-haired beauty to share the forest with. Seated on a mossy log, the scene reminded him of her, and his feelings flowed. 'Twiners entwining twiners,' his pencil twitched, 'tresses like hair – beautiful lepidoptera – Silence – hosannah.' It was 'sublime devotion' he felt, love displaced by nature. He felt his soul responding and thought of Nature's God.[11]

The visit lasted only a few days, and Charles headed back to Rio along a 'glaring hot sandy plain' near the coast. The *Beagle* was returning to Bahia to check the longitude, but he decided to wait here for its return. He collected his belongings and on 25 April rowed to Botafogo Bay, a good base from which he could go on collecting. As he came ashore a heavy sea crashed over the boat, knocking him 'head over heels.' When he righted himself, there, to his horror, were all his papers, 'books, instruments & gun cases' floating away in the surf. He caught everything, but the damage was done, and he wasted a whole day drying out and making repairs in a local rented cottage.

The cottage was shared with the ship's artist Augustus Earle, suffering from rheumatism but busy painting the 'beautiful spot,' and one of the civilized savages, 'Miss Fuegia Basket, who daily increases in every direction except height.' The site was idyllic, yet within walking distance of the town, where he could take in the Botanic Garden or find the aqueduct that led to the Corcovado mountain. Twice he climbed this 2000-foot 'Hunchback,' revelling in the scenery, shuddering to think what a 'horrible lovers leap' it would make.[12]

Weeks wore on with no sign of the *Beagle*. But he was absorbed in his work, trapping and shooting one day, preserving the next, with the evenings devoted to correspondence. His longest letter went to Henslow. Charles was bursting with news: geological facts to pique Mr Lyell's interest, reports of marine molluscs, octopuses with their instant colour changes, and his latest exploits around the bay. The forest inland was a veritable 'gold mine.' Here he encountered his first new-world monkey, dead. While hunting with a Portuguese padre, he saw the bearded beast hanging by its prehensile tail in an enormous tree. It had been shot the day before, and was retrieved by simply chopping the tree down. He heard chirping frogs and screaming parrots, saw glow-worms and iridescent hummingbirds, and witnessed lizards fleeing columns of predatory ants.

But what always thrilled him most was the low life. Hacking through the undergrowth, sometimes in torrential rain, he turned up 'gaily-coloured' flatworms under decaying logs. And beetles galore; on 23 June alone he caught sixty-eight species. Most of the tiny ones had never been seen in Europe, and he rallied Henslow, 'tell Entomologists to look out & have their pens ready for describing.' He was 'red-hot with Spiders' too, even finding one minuscule sort that lived on others' webs, feigning death when threatened and falling off. And one nasty parasite he was never to forget: a predatory wasp, which stung caterpillars and stuffed them into its clay cell as food for the larvae.

Geology was exciting, Fox heard, 'like the pleasure of gambling,' for one could set the odds of finding certain rocks before arriving in a locality. 'I can eat Salt Beef & musty biscuits for dinner,' he bragged to Gluttonous Herbert; 'see what a fall man may come to'! The folks in Shrewsbury received an inkling of how he viewed his prospects, now that both Charlotte and Fanny were taken. 'Maer & Woodhouse ... might as well be shut up,' he sighed, still picturing to himself 'a very quiet parsonage ... through a grove of Palms.' At least he would always have natural history. It would offer 'employment & amusement for the rest of my life,' even 'if I gain no other end.'[13]

The *Beagle* finally returned with distressing news. Three of the crew were dead. They had taken ill after a snipe-shooting party, were seized by a violent fever and had died within a week. The last to go was 'poor little Musters,' his first Gun Room friend. Only days before Musters had heard of his mother's death, Charles wrote home, ending on a tasteless pun, 'What numbers snipe-shooting has killed, & how rapidly they drop off.'

They had lost someone else just as precipitately. Robert McCormick, the ship's Surgeon-naturalist, had quit and shipped home, sick of living in a rich landlubber's shadow. He had been put out by the social preference: Darwin was allowed ashore; Darwin collected as he liked; and it was not only the Captain's table that Darwin shared. His gentleman's standing placed him with the cream of colonial society. As Darwin admitted, 'I am [the] only one in the ship who is regularly asked to the Admirals, Chargé d'affaires & other great men' – and this was important in an age when ambassadors took an interest in local geology. It was always Darwin. McCormick's own collecting had gone to pieces. Prickly about his status, he annoyed the Captain, who was glad to see the back of him. His departure suited Darwin too, now ex officio naturalist to the expedition.

Darwin rejoined the 'beautiful' *Beagle*, which had been fitted with a new gun. We are, he joked, ready to take on any 'pirate a float' or 'a thousand savages together.' As he stowed his gear back in 'my own corner,' he even felt part of the Royal Navy. 'The men foreward singing; the centinel [sic] pacing above my head & the little creeking [sic] of the furniture' were reassuring sounds.

On Sunday 1 July he attended a religious service on board the battleship *Warspite* and thrilled when 650 men doffed their hats as the band played 'God Save the King.' 'Seeing, when amongst foreigners, the strength & power of ones own Nation,' he realized, 'gives a feeling of exultation which is not felt at home.' Certainly when among Brazilians, anyway. He loathed these ill-mannered slave-owners. The men were 'ignorant, cowardly, & indolent in the extreme,' and the 'older women' full of 'cunning, sensuality & pride.' The 'monks' were as bad or worse. All degraded themselves by brutalizing the blacks, whom Darwin admired for their courage. He foresaw the day when the slaves would 'assert their own rights & forget to avenge their wrongs.'[14]

The *Beagle* tripped anchor on the 5th. She continued south in winter, along stormy coasts, further towards the treacherous tip of the continent. Everyone shivered in anticipation and grew beards to suit the 'barbarous regions,' even the officers, who began to look aptly patriarchal. The temperature dropped into the fifties a fortnight out, and the skies turned grey, sweeping the deck with squalls. Darwin was nauseous again and found his hammock tiresome. His copy of Milton's *Paradise Lost* afforded some comfort. He carried a pocket edition everywhere, inspired by its vision of a prehistoric world torn by titanic struggle. Nature and art now reached an accord as the ship approached the River Plate. Lightning split the night in a fiendish fireworks display. The *Beagle* lit up, her mast-heads shining with St Elmo's fire, as if painted with phosphorus. At the same time the

PACIFIC OCEAN

Copiapó

Guasco

Coquimbo

Rio Salado

Santa Fé

Rio Parana

Rio Uruguay

Valparaiso

Mendoza

Santiago

Mercedes

Buenos Aires

Maldonado

Montevideo

River Plate

Concepción

Bahia Blanca

SOUTH

Rio Colorado

Rio Negro

ATLANTIC

Valdivia

Patagones

OCEAN

Island of Chiloé

Chonos Archipelago

P A T A G O N I A

Darwin's South America
His main visits to the southern part of the continent from 26 July 1832 to 6 July 1835

Port Desire

Rio Santa Cruz

FALKLAND ISLANDS
Port Louis

Straits of Magellan

TIERRA DEL FUEGO

Beagle Channel

Cape Horn

Miles
0   100   200   300

0   100 200 300 400 500
Kilometres

ocean was so luminous with micro-organisms that penguins could be 'tracked by . . . their wake.' The sea offered no more 'extraordinary spectacle.'[15]

On the 26th they anchored in the River Plate at Montevideo. Charles was hoping to hear from home but no letters awaited. A political up-date would have been welcome. For weeks speculation had been rife aboard, everyone wondering the fate of the Reform Bill. Was a revolution likely, or had one already occurred? Then came word that the bill was finally passed. Herbert gleefully relayed how Tory lords had defected under pressure, allowing it to scrape through. The two-faced Tories ratting on reform now looked like a dying breed: 'you I think are amongst a Tory Crew; just put one of them in Pickle as by the time you return home, he will be more valuable as a specimen for the Cabinet of the Antiquarians, than your Fungi & Coleoptera . . . If you can get hold of one with [a] Tail, or with ears prolongated, it will be a doubly-interesting specimen.' So, the high Tory FitzRoy growled, the only question left was 'whether there is [to be] a King or a republic.'

Scarcely had Charles begun to think it over than they were caught in their own political upheaval. Montevideo had an unpredictable military government, and Buenos Aires up-river was in a state of permanent revolution. British troops had helped to destabilize the two capitals, having sacked them both twenty-five years before. They had left a bitter legacy, and the Royal Navy still prowled the Plate, protecting the interests of English merchants. To some, the *Beagle* was an intruder. As FitzRoy sailed into Buenos Aires, a shot whistled overhead from a guardship at the port. Furious, the Captain refused to accept the official explanation that it was a quarantine warning. He loaded a broadside and turned the *Beagle* around, informing the guardship as they passed its rotting hulk that next time the greeting would be answered.

More trouble lay back in Montevideo, when the ship returned. The police chief pleaded for help in quelling an insurrection among the local black troops. British residents were at risk, so FitzRoy dispatched fifty-two of the ship's complement, armed to the teeth, to occupy the fort until reinforcements arrived. Darwin accompanied them into the 'dirty town,' pistols in his belt and a cutlass at his side. The black rebels held the ammunition dump and manned cannons in the streets, and they had released and armed prisoners. The *Beagle*'s rag-tag regiment took the fort without incident and, while negotiations went on, grilled 'beefsteaks in the Courtyard.' But Darwin, crushed by a headache, retreated to the ship to watch events unfold.

He was followed by the others, when armed citizens took their place. Within days the shooting started in the town centre. Darwin wondered 'whether Despotism is not better than such uncontrolled anarchy.' Admittedly, he derived 'a great deal of pleasure in the excitement of this sort of work,' but it was not what 'we Philosophers . . . bargain for.'[16]

On 19 August Darwin shipped off his first box of specimens to Henslow, who would store them for his return. The same day the *Beagle* began the first of its charting forays up and down the Patagonian coast. The passage south was rough, but there were compensations. Off Bahia Blanca Darwin witnessed swarms of bristle-jawed worms near the surface. Millions of them, transparent, with hooked claws on their horseshoe-shaped mouths, and all distended with eggs. He had no idea what they were, but he netted huge numbers, driven on by the prospect of examining the spawn. He was back to his first love, kindled by Grant, the sea's tiniest larvae. Using his high-quality microscope, he teased open the eggs; it was precision work, they were minuscule, no bigger than one fiftieth of an inch.[17] But he managed to split them, allowing their 'molecules' to spill out, still suspecting that these were the ultimate particles of life.

He filled reams of zoological notes, with the polyp-bearing creatures dominating his thoughts. There was no blind collecting here; he was following up his Edinburgh interests. He systematically studied reproduction in encrusting sea-mats like *Flustra*. He uprooted a sea-pen *Virgularia* from the mud at Bahia Blanca and wrote page after page on the granular movement inside its stem. This wafting feather-like creature consisted of thousands of feeding polyps all moving together, but with one ovary for the lot, leading him to wonder about the very meaning of individuality.[18]

Bahia Blanca was a remote settlement. Set up as a 'frontier fort' by the government, it stood in a barren expanse of scrubby hills and pampas – 'Devil's Country' to the local Indians. The land was theirs, although seized by the Spanish. Skirmishes were frequent, and a half-caste gaucho cavalry patrolled the region, 'the most savage picturesque group' of men he had ever seen. Only their Indian captives, gnawing the bones of a 'half-roasted horse,' looked more like 'wild beasts.' He heard atrocious stories of the frontier war and its barbarities. 'The Indians torture all their prisoners & the Spaniards shoot theirs.' Even chiefs under a white flag coming to parley were summarily shot. The plains were being ruthlessly cleared, and Darwin found himself fraternizing with murderers.

Englishmen were usually safe, provided they carried guns and local dollars. Darwin had plenty of both and the gauchos were civil. They took him riding, and showed him how to bring down a fleet-footed 'ostrich' (rhea) with their bolas. Then they served roast armadillo and 'ostrich' egg dumplings around an open fire. 'The Armadilloes ... cooked without their cases, taste & look like duck' and made excellent eating, he decided. Stranger flesh no Glutton ever consumed. He spent September as he would in England, shooting. Deer were common, and he killed three, while an agouti – a twenty-pound chocolate-coloured rodent – furnished 'the very best meat I ever tasted.'[19]

He was in some trepidation whether he would find any good fossils in South America. He learned to his disgust that the French collector Alcide d'Orbigny had been working the area for six months, picking up plum specimens for the Paris Muséum. It was galling; Darwin had paid his own way here, only to find the French government sponsoring their man, allowing him to roam the pampas on a free ticket for six years. It spoke volumes for the serious French attitude towards science. 'I am very selfishly afraid he will get the cream of all the good things,' Darwin reported to Henslow.

His fears were unfounded. On 22 September he was scouring the bay at Punta Alta, ten miles from the *Beagle*. Checking some low cliffs, he spotted the fossilized bones of a colossal extinct mammal. Excitedly, he disinterred teeth and a thigh bone from the quartz and pebble gravel and loaded his pack horses. The Captain was laconic and twitted his companion, smiling 'at the cargoes of apparent rubbish' being carried up the gang plank. It was fine talk with all the Fuegians' clutter in the hold, and Darwin was not to be deterred.

Darwin returned the next day and found a huge skull 'imbedded in a soft rock.' 'It took me nearly three hours to get it out,' and it was dark before he managed to manhandle it on board. The best part of the following day was spent 'packing up the prizes.' He knew little of mammal fossils, such Brobdingnagians least of all. His best guess was that they were 'allied to the Rhinoceros' (which now lives in Africa and Asia). On the 25th he found still more bones. Many were nothing to look at, huge and shattered, and others on the beach had been rolled by the waves. But they were precious. In all England there was only one giant South American fossil – a ground sloth just acquired by the College of Surgeons.

On 8 October he was back, prying out a jawbone. Its one tooth was characteristic, and revealed it to be a megatherium, a huge ground-living relative of the sloth. Near by were six-inch polygonal bony plates, and he mentally amalgamated all the finds to come up with an 'ante-diluvial' armour-coated cow-sized sloth. He wondered how the bones had arrived there, indeed how the embedding gravels had been formed. Perhaps a flood of 'extreme violence' had swept over the pampas, washing bones and pebbles before it? Lyell might not have approved, but then Henslow had warned him off Lyell's gradualist extremism. No matter, finding them was the important part. 'I have been wonderfully lucky,' he wrote home. Some of the mammals were gigantic, and 'many of them are quite new.' Henslow heard that he had fragments of at least six animals – ground sloths, giant armadillo shells, teeth from an enormous rodent, guinea-pig relatives. He crated them ready to ship to Cambridge, *very curious* to know exactly what he had found.[20]

On 19 October the *Beagle* headed north again, back to Montevideo. She ploughed through luminous seas that reminded him of 'the regions of Chaos & Anarchy' described in *Paradise Lost*. Milton again seemed so apt as they approached the wretched River Plate, for here, with revolutions brewing around, FitzRoy would prepare for their onslaught on that Satanic stronghold, the 'land of fire,' Tierra del Fuego. He had a divine legation to land there, three Fuegians and an Englishman, and this was now the *Beagle*'s first priority. The ship slipped into Montevideo to collect the waiting missionaries and fortify herself for the southerly assault. Darwin readied himself while reading the latest mail.[21]

Cousin Fox relayed the political gossip: the monarchy was intact, although for 'some days we certainly were on the very verge of Revolution.' Still, feelings were running 'very high indeed' with a reformed House of Commons to be elected. Charles's sisters filled in the family news. Hensleigh's father-in-law, Sir James Mackintosh, was dead. Even sadder for Charles, they told of Fanny Owen – her sumptuous wedding, her *canvassing* Denbighshire with Mʳ Biddulph' (who was standing for the Whigs), and her vanquished *housemaid* spirits.' This was not what he wanted to hear. But at least the family loved his diary, which he was sending in instalments, and everyone had great expectations. Susan, echoing the Doctor, thrilled at the thought of 'the quiet Parsonage' where he would eventually settle. Catherine chimed in, baiting him with a prospective bride – Fanny Wedgwood – Charlotte and Emma's sister. A 'nice little invaluable Wife she would be,' and 'an excellent Clerg[y]man's' choice.

Erasmus, ensconced in London with a 'lab in my lodgings,' poured acid on the scheme. He was horrified to hear 'that you still look forward to the horrid little parsonage in the desert.' He wanted his brother set up in town 'near the British Museum or some other learned place.' 'My only chance,' Eras admitted, 'is the Established Church being abolished, & in some places they are beginning to demand pledges to that effect.' With bishop-baiting radicals demanding disestablishment, talk of a church career could be academic.

Eras's letter continued with screeds on politics, talk of the ballot, abolition of tithes, removal of newspaper taxes (originally brought in to cripple the radical press), and the National Political Union refusing toasts to the King. But Eras wondered if his brother was listening: 'I have written you all this politics tho' I suppose you are too far from England to care much about it. Politics wont travel.'[22]

Charles didn't know what to think. Home was constantly on his mind, especially on 'calm, delightful' days, but his old world seemed to be crumbling. Cholera, like reform, had swept across the country, even reaching Shrewsbury. Cambridge friends were acquiring their fellowships, professorships, and parishes. And he was so far away. 'Poor dear old England,' he sighed to Fox. 'I hope my wanderings will not unfit me for a quiet life & that in some future day, I may be fortunate enough to be qualified to become, like you a country Clergyman ... But the Captain says if I indulge in such visions, as green fields & nice little wives &c &c, I shall certainly make a bolt. So ... I must remain contented with sandy plains & great Megatheriums.'

He did, but only just. With the southern regions to explore, he was anxious to push on. The 'detestable' Plate depressed him. 'I would much sooner live in a coal-barge in the Cam,' he moaned to his father and sisters. Fortunately, 'a very nice gentlemanlike person,' Robert Hamond, had recently joined the *Beagle* as a Midshipman. Here was someone to pass the time with, and together he and Darwin planned their final flings ashore. At Buenos Aires the ship anchored, unmolested this time. The gents sallied into town and rode about the muddy chequerboard streets, sizing up the *señoritas*. 'Watching ... these angels gliding' by, they despaired of 'foolish English women.' Even from behind, feasting on 'their charming backs,' Darwin could not help imagining 'how beautiful' they must be.[23]

He also shopped – cigars and scissors, notebooks and pens – saw a dentist, took in a play, and still longed to be off. Each day's delay meant one less during the short summer in the south, where the winds turned vicious in winter. On Sunday 4 November he took in 'several of the Churches.' 'Idolatry' it might be, but he had to 'respect the fervor which appears to reign during the Catholic service as compared with the Protestant.' And all the more impressive for the 'equality of ... ranks' evident during worship. Before departing, he and Hamond sought to make their own peace with God. Hamond, a relative of Musters, knew as well as Darwin what perils lay ahead, and they asked the naval chaplain to give them Holy Communion. He refused a private sacrament, suggesting that, if they were sincere, they should come back with other shipmates.[24] Darwin and Hamond rejoined the *Beagle*, thrown back on FitzRoy's seamanship and other means of grace.

A treat arrived in the post at Montevideo, the second volume of Lyell's *Principles*. It was curiously different from the first. Where that had delved into the gradual changes in past landscapes, this asked whether animals and plants had been modified to match. Was there a natural mechanism for slowly transforming them to keep pace? No, was the short answer. Darwin had received a book-long refutation of Lamarck. He mulled over Lyell's view that each species of animal or plant was adapted to its birth-spot – its 'centre of creation.' Any change, any environmental stress would exterminate it, not transform it. (Darwin could appreciate this, having seen the Megatherium tombs.) Species are continually turning over; as old ones die naturally, new ones are born mysteriously.

It was a sprightly, brilliantly written book, a lawyer's book, piled with clever arguments against the idea that life had evolved and could be represented as a family tree. Can all animals trace their ancestry back to a single stem? Lyell answered no, appalled at the thought of a chimpanzee in the family, of an ape aspiring to 'the attributes and dignity of man.' He went further, arguing that the history of life on earth had been completely misunderstood. The sequence of fossils from ancient times showed no overall progress towards humanity, he argued, idiosyncratically.[25] He knew that with no progress there could be no transmutation. But Lyell had at least posed the question of how species die and are reborn, and in a more genealogical way than Darwin had ever encountered. It was food for thought.

At Montevideo Darwin did more than nose through Lyell's new book. He attended the 'grand ball' at the theatre to 'celebrate the reestablishment of the President,' and returned the next night for Rossini's *Cenerentola*. He worked hard too: two large casks of fossil bones and a small one with skins, beetles, and pickled fish went off to Henslow on the 24th, two days before they sailed. Slumped in the poop cabin, tired out, he wondered how much more he could take. 'One year is nearly completed & the second will be so before we even leave the East coast of S[outh] America. – And then our voyage may be said really to have commenced.'[26] He was desperate to press on, to reach Tierra del Fuego, and then to set off around the world.

10

Troubled Spirits from Another World

SAVAGES HE HAD EXPECTED. They were to be one of the highlights of the voyage – wild primitives, people from another age, the objects of FitzRoy's mission. But the shock of the first encounter still left him reeling.

Three weeks out of Montevideo he saw them. The air had 'the bracing *feel* of an English winter' as the *Beagle* braved the squalls and sailed into Good Success Bay, near the southern tip of Tierra del Fuego. Yet there they were, 'perched on a wild peak overhanging the sea' – naked. Raw 'untamed' Fuegians, yelling hoarsely and flailing their arms, showing their 'dirty copper' complexion beneath the scanty animal skins slung over their shoulders.

Never in his wildest imagination had he thought that the three native missionaries aboard – York Minster, Jemmy Button, and Fuegia Basket – had been like this. On 18 December 1832 he rowed ashore to meet the savages with FitzRoy and a well-armed guard. The young men were nearly his own height and powerfully built, with long black hair, painted faces, and startled expressions. Timid at first, and terrified of the guns, they jabbered and gesticulated. Then, warming to a gift of red cloth, they engaged the officers in a ludicrous charade, pulling 'hideous grimaces' at one another, back-slapping merrily, and dancing around the beach. It was 'without exception the most curious & interesting spectacle' that Darwin had ever seen, and he drew conclusions swiftly. These 'wretched looking beings' had no proper clothes, no fit language, and no decent homes or property, barring bows and arrows. 'How entire the difference between savage & civilized man is. – It is greater than between a

132

wild & [a] domesticated animal ... I believe if the world was searched, no lower grade of man could be found.'[1]

Were they even men? Their dress recalled the 'Devils on the Stage' in the opera *Der Freischütz* that he had seen at Edinburgh. Their gestures made them seem like 'the troubled spirits of another world.' He almost begrudged them the status of 'fellow-creature.' 'A wild man is a miserable animal,' he shook his head solemnly. Yet what of York and Jemmy, who – though from different tribes – also came ashore with their missionary-minder Richard Matthews? Hadn't they been civilized? Didn't their year in England show their kinship – and point up man's enormous 'power of improvement'? Dressed sensibly for an English winter, they stood apart on the beach, mocking the wild men. When the oldest Fuegian came up to York and harangued him for growing a beard, York burst into 'an immoderate fit of laughter.' Surely here was proof of the plasticity of human nature.

With everyone back on board, young Matthews remarked glibly that the savages 'were no worse than he had supposed them to be.' This was sheer sang-froid coming from one who was about to be left among them for years. And what was this callow chap's scope for comparison? Darwin remembered Cambridge – Sedgwick's and Henslow's soirées and the great guns at high table. Did these lofty moralists come from such stock too? Did Shakespeare and Newton? As he surveyed the district he was in a sombre mood. Climbing into the mountains, he collected alpine plants and insects amid 'universal signs of violence.' The 'decaying & fallen trees' harked back to the tropical forest, but here, he sensed, 'in this still solitude, death instead of life is the predominant spirit.' It was a curious Christmas vigil, held at the end of the world: he was pondering a grim outlook for man. Days later, as the *Beagle* rounded the mariner's graveyard at Cape Horn, heading for York Minster's country in the west, nature played an awful counterpoint, with 'black clouds ... rolling across the sky' and hailstones lashing the sea.

On 24 December FitzRoy ran in to Wigwam Cove on Hermit Island, further south and facing the Antarctic. All duty was suspended, and the hills resounded as the sailors shot fresh game for their feast. On the 'gala day' the grog came out while Darwin set off with Sulivan and Hamond to climb the island's principal mountain. It was an easy ascent, and along the way they added to the din, 'screaming to find out echos, Sulivan amusing himself by rolling ... huge stones' down the precipice, and 'I,' Darwin jotted in his diary, 'impetuously hammering ... the rocks.' The Fuegians were watching, it transpired. 'They must have thought us the powers of darkness,' he laughed, for fear 'kept them concealed.'²

This was his last laugh for weeks. The weather worsened. Putting to sea during a lull on New Year's Eve turned out to be a mistake. The wind veered southwesterly with a vengeance, and the *Beagle* had to fight her way along the rugged underbelly of the continent, league by agonizing league. For Darwin it was hell. Constantly retching at the rail, with the temperature in the forties and the deck awash, he knew that his 'spirits, temper, & stomach' could not 'hold out much longer.' On Saturday 12 January 1833 the gale turned into a fearsome storm. Blinded by the spray, the Captain lost track of the ship's position. He confessed that he had never seen conditions so bad.

At noon on Sunday the storm was at its height. Three gigantic rollers bore down on the *Beagle*. She 'met and rose over the first unharmed but ... her way was checked; the second deadened her way completely, throwing her off the wind; and the third great sea, taking her right a-beam, turned her so far over, that all the lee bulwark ... was two or three feet under water.' The whale-boat broke loose and had to be cut free; the sea poured into the poop cabin and below deck. Everything was in chaos. Then slowly, 'like a cask,' she righted herself, and with the ports 'knocked open,' the water drained away. Another such wave and the bark would have lived up to her class's reputation and become a 'coffin.' But the worst was over, and FitzRoy took shelter behind False Cape Horn, where Darwin checked the damage. His 'drying paper & plants' were ruined by the salt water. Terrified by the gales, he prayed 'May Providence keep the Beagle out of them.'³

Yet this was God's odyssey – his protection could be assumed. The Captain now decided to set up his mission station among Jemmy's people, as York 'from his free choice' had agreed to live there. (So Darwin said. FitzRoy noted the 'attentions' that York was paying to 'his intended wife, Fuegia,' which 'afforded much amusement.') A large party, Darwin among them, set off in a flotilla of small boats from the ship, following the Beagle Channel – discovered on the last voyage – to Ponsonby Sound, and Jemmy's home in Woollya cove. On 23 January they beached the boats and unloaded the 'wine glasses, butter-bolts, tea-trays, soup turins [sic], mahogany dressing case, fine white linen ... & an endless variety of similar things,' all of which to Darwin showed 'culpable folly.' Huts were built and gardens planted, with scores of inscrutable Fuegians looking on.

Matthews, piously resolved, bade his shipmates farewell, knowing that the Captain would pay him a final visit after the party explored further west.

The scenery was spectacular. They proceeded along the Beagle Channel, tracking a granite ridge of mountains, the backbone of Tierra del Fuego. To Darwin its horizontal tree-line looked like the 'high-water mark' on a beach, and he gloried in the 'mantle of perpetual snow.' The steep slopes plummeted straight down to the channel, where vast 'beryl blue' glaciers fed the waves with icebergs. One of the glaciers nearly marooned them. While dining on shore half a mile away, they heard a 'thundering crash' as a huge mass of ice fell from its face. The impact sent 'great rolling waves' racing towards their flotilla. Darwin was quick to act. He and others seized the boats, hauling them to safety just as the first breaker crashed down. FitzRoy was so impressed that, the next day, he named an expanse of water 'Darwin Sound.' But Darwin had acted less out of bravado than fear. Without the boats, he reflected, 'how dangerous would our lot have been, surrounded ... by hostile Savages & deprived of ... provisions.'[4]

Some Fuegians were indeed hostile. With courage 'like that of a wild beast,' they menaced the party's overnight camp, and armed guards were posted. Charles, keeping watch, shivered at his vulnerability in this land. 'The quiet of the night is only interrupted by the heavy breathing of the men & the cry of the night birds. – the occasional distant bark of a dog reminds one that the Fuegians may be prowling, close to the tents, ready for a fatal rush.' Everyone believed that they were among cannibals. Jemmy, when asked about the practice, had given the expected answer, stating tongue-in-cheek that 'in winter they sometimes eat the women.' No one questioned his authority, and the party dreaded what they might find back at 'the Settlement.' Returning along the Channel after nine days, they found that Matthews and the rest had suffered from little more than bullying and systematic looting. All their possessions had been divided indiscriminately among the Fuegians. Here was further evidence of co-operative savagery, Darwin surmised. 'The perfect equality of all the inhabitants will for many years prevent their civilization.' Until 'some chief' rises who 'by his power' can heap up possessions for himself, 'there must be an end to all hopes of bettering their condition.'

Given the mayhem, Matthews conceded defeat and rejoined his shipmates, leaving eleven-year-old Fuegia with York, and a disconsolate Jemmy, to the mercies of their countrymen. York would try to live 'like an Englishman,' Darwin believed, but none would be happy. 'They have far too much sense not to see the vast superiority of civilized over uncivilized habits.' Their only hope lay in the gardens that he had helped plant. Tilling the soil would teach them discipline and improve their diet. Eventually the example of their prosperity might alter the habits of many 'savage inhabitants,' and the whole Fuegian coast would welcome English sailors.[5]

With the added ballast of Darwin's granite and slate samples, the *Beagle* steered for the Falkland Islands, or the Malvinas, as they were called in Buenos Aires. He expected to be the guest of Argentine colonists, who had been settling them for years. But on 1 March, when the ship anchored at Port Louis, the most eastern point in the archipelago, he saw a Union Jack flying. British warships had taken the islands for the Crown in January, forcing out the Argentine army. All South America was 'in a ferment' about the British action, Darwin heard. 'By the aweful [sic] language of Buenos Ayres one would suppose this great republic meant to declare war against England!' It seemed ludicrous, the more so because only one English-man actually lived on the islands, a storekeeper named Dickson who kept the flag. But Darwin saw their strategic importance for east-west trade, and this, as FitzRoy explained, was why he intended to make an accurate survey.[6]

While the measurements went on, Darwin wandered about the country, 'breaking rocks, shooting snipes, & picking up the few living' creatures he could find on East Falkland. The region was desolate, and the weather 'cold & boisterous,' but by way of compensation he stumbled on 'most primitive looking' sandstones. He knew that Sedgwick was preoccupied with the oldest fossil-bearing rocks like these. Sure enough, they contained lamp-shells, bivalve molluscs, like the rocks in Wales. At a stroke of his geological hammer, the 'whole aspect' of the Falklands changed. Here was a fine chance to compare ancient faunas from two corners of the world. And not only fossil faunas; he was taking more interest in the spread of living animals and plants. He had never spent so long on a small offshore island, and made a memo to observe 'differences of species & proportionate Numbers,' and to relate them to their habitats.[7]

He kept returning to his first love, the tiny marine creatures, intrigued by the granules spewed from their disrupted eggs, convinced he was looking at the ultimate atoms of life. On the Falklands he collected some of 'that ambiguous tribe,' the encrusting algae: primitive, stony, branching tufts. So primitive, in fact, that even the kingdom they belonged to was debated: Grant called them plants, Lamarck animals. Darwin kept dissecting, trying to determine which. He also studied their egg-matter, like Henslow thinking it inert and acted on by some external 'creative power.'[8] Eventually he came to the conclusion that these incrustations must be strange primitive plants.

FitzRoy meanwhile had dipped into his pocket again. He bought a schooner from a swashbuckling sealer and cannibalized a wreck to refit her. It was without Admiralty approval, but it allowed him to double his charting efforts. The two ships put to sea in early April heading north, back up the Patagonian coast to the mouth of the Rio Negro, 170 miles from Bahia Blanca. For months Darwin had been keen to go ashore here, where the 'interior country is *totally* unknown.' Gliding along in 'celestial' weather, he eyed the cliffs longingly. They looked like 'an El Dorado to a Geologist.' But the Captain's plans kept changing, and at the last minute the wind, 'that omnipotent & overbearing master,' put paid to the visit. The *Beagle* tailed her sister ship all the way back to the loathsome River Plate, where she anchored at Montevideo. Nothing much had happened here during that period, 'with the exception of a few revolutions,' Darwin noted as he collected five months' post.

The schooner had to be fitted with a new copper bottom to protect it from boring worms. The work was being done at Maldonado, sixty miles away at the mouth of the estuary, and would last several months. When FitzRoy went to check the progress, Darwin accompanied him and took lodgings. The town was barren, and the hilly countryside teemed with horses, cattle, and bandits. His Spanish was bad, but he managed to find a pair of guides to show him the hinterland, and on 9 May they galloped off in 'high spirits,' rattling with 'pistols & sabres.'[9]

They spent days riding through 'endless green hills' littered with cactus and stony outcrops. He was struck by the rhea flocks, commenting on the impressive sight of thirty birds passing over the crest of a hill. They nested together, according to the gauchos. Many females lay at the same spot (Darwin himself had counted twenty-seven eggs in a clutch) and one male incubates and protects the brood. At night Darwin stayed at 'drinking shops,' where moustachioed gauchos with 'daggers at their waist' and 'great spurs clanking on their heels' stood around, swilling spirits and smoking cigars. Some evenings he had a taste of home. In Uruguayan cattle country hospitality was never refused, and though even rich landowners lived on mud floors they offered plentiful food. He repaid his hosts with gadgetry. His pocket compass was much admired for its 'powers' of showing direction, and he amazed them by striking matches with his teeth. After the antics, the men lit cigars, and 'with a little impromptu singing accompanied by the Guitar,' a pleasant day came to an end.

Two weeks later Darwin was back in Maldonado, having covered over 200 miles. The whole area was inundated, with swampy plains and swollen rivers. No one could remember electric storms of such ferocity. The power of the bolts was evident in the dunes outside town. He picked up smooth, glassy tubes, some extending five feet into the sand, where the lightning shafts had fused the grains into glass. Turning to the wildlife, he found that flashing a coin in town worked wonders, bringing every boy with a stray creature to his door. The carcasses piled up – rats, mice, snakes – and skinning them was messy nauseous work, especially the deer, which gave off an 'overpoweringly strong and offensive odour.'[10]

He took 'almost every bird in this neighbourhood,' eighty species in all, killing a dozen new ones a week – owls, cuckoos, flycatchers, mockingbirds, shrikes, and strange scissor-birds, which skim the water with their lower bill trailing for fish. He slit open stomachs, picking through the half-digested contents, and noted habits, song, and nest sites. It was too much work for one person and was made easier by the help of a sixteen-year-old sailor. Syms Covington was the *Beagle*'s fiddler and odd-job man, and no jobs came odder than Mr Darwin's. In no time he learned to shoot and skin birds. The arrangement had FitzRoy's blessing, but with the schooner almost ready and the *Beagle* about to sail, Darwin wanted to make it permanent. Having a full-time servant would enable him to step up his capture rate. He offered to take Covington on at his own expense. FitzRoy agreed, and let the boy go cheaply to Darwin, £30 a year.[11]

He and the Captain were getting on fine. Or at least FitzRoy regarded the 'Philosopher' – his new nickname – as 'a very superior young man,' with the right mix of 'necessary qualities which makes him feel at home, and happy, and makes everyone his friend.'

Darwin did not always feel as contented as his dining companion made out. In early July, pitching at anchor outside Montevideo, he was dying to 'double the Horn' and head off around the world for England. At times like this only crab larvae and the 'old bones' kept him from bolting back across the Atlantic.

Letters from home enticed him still more. The news was old of course – three months at least, but no less bracing for a reformer confined with an arch-Tory. In the December General Election Uncle Jos had stood for the Whigs in the new borough of Stoke-on-Trent and been returned with a handsome majority. Unfortunately the 'March of liberal opinion' was becoming a charge, and the whole family began to quail. Radicals were streaming into the Commons, shouting their demands for democracy and disestablishment. Jos couldn't bear them. Susan reported that they were becoming 'so fierce & licentious . . . that Papa gets more & more of a Tory every day.' Charles revelled in the political gossip, and, expecting an end to 'that monstrous stain on our boasted liberty, Colonial Slavery,' cheered 'Hurrah for the honest Whigs'! 'Thank God the cold-hearted Tories . . . have for the present run their race.'[12]

The post-bag held other surprises. The Wedgwood newly-weds were having babies, and the latest, born to Hensleigh and Fanny, had apparently forestalled a scandal. In London Erasmus had been seeing rather a lot of his cousin's wife. It was an open secret, the whole family knew. Fanny seems 'quite as much married to him as to Hensleigh,' wrote sister Catherine, 'and Papa continually prophecies a fine paragraph in the Paper about them.' But the baby put an end to Ras's 'junkitting [sic] at her house,' at least temporarily, and the family were spared from coping with dishonour.

Central to all the letters, however, was the story of Fanny Wedgwood's death. The cousin Charles had been matched with had died the previous August. Charles's sisters and cousin Charlotte relayed the whole distressing story. It was all over in a week: the fever with 'vomitings & pain,' followed by a few days' comfort, then a sudden relapse and within hours, the end. She was only twenty-six. Maer was melancholy as never before. Just two of his cousins remained there: Elizabeth the eldest, hunchbacked and only four feet tall, who was resigned to spinsterhood; and Emma, the youngest, who had been closest to Fanny and felt the loss acutely. It was expected that Charles would too. He had never been taken with Fanny – she was short and plain – but as a parson's wife, said his sisters, she would have been ideal. Everyone feared that marriage and the Church would now pass from his mind.[13]

Charles, bobbing in the Plate, never mentioned Fanny's death. He stonewalled his sisters in reply, asking for books, boots, lenses, tape measures, and more matches to astound the natives. He boasted of his hard work, adding that natural history would remain his 'favourite pursuit' for many years to come: 'doing what *little* one can to encrease [sic] the general stock of knowledge is as respectable an object of life, as one can in any likelihood pursue.' Not that he lacked a 'delightful vision' to match his sisters' happy 'day dream' of his future. He still yearned for a 'dear little lady' to take care of him and his house. But he did not confide it to his sisters, whose nannying made him uneasy. Only Fox found out his real feelings, when Charles admitted that 'so much time spent wandering' was indeed 'a serious evil.' 'I often conjecture, what will become of me; my wishes certainly would make me a country clergyman.'

One letter was left to write, to Henslow. Charles saved it until last, not having heard whether his collections had arrived safely. He sent Henslow the next consignment with trepidation: four barrels of corpses, skins, pickled fish, beetles in pill-boxes, and rocks – half his summer's haul. Henslow also received the future itinerary. Charles was itching to leave 'this stupid, unpicturesque side' of the continent and reach Valparaiso in Chile, where he could 'cross & recross the grand chain of the Andes.' Once past Tierra del Fuego finally it would 'all be Holidays.' The very thought of 'fine Coralls [sic], the warm glowing weather, [and] the blue sky of the Tropics' made him 'wild with delight.' So too did the prospect of Henslow's first letter, should it ever arrive.

FitzRoy renamed his schooner *Adventure*, and on the evening of 24 July the sister ships sailed south at last for the Rio Negro. 'The whole sky was brilliant with lightning; it was a wild looking night to go to sea, but time is too precious to lose even a bad portion of it.'[14]

After a tedious passage in adverse winds they arrived at the mouth of the river. Darwin rode upstream to the town of Patagones, where he decided to proceed overland and meet the *Beagle* back at Bahia Blanca. This was 'Devil's Country' again, full of salt lakes and sandstone and marauding Indians. Geologically it was as intriguing as it was politically dangerous. He paid £20 for a 'trusty' guide and they set off with a British trader and a band of gauchos to see General Juan Manuel de Rosas, whose army had been sent from Buenos Aires with orders to 'exterminate the Indians.' His permission was needed to pass north.

On 13 August they reached Rosas' camp on the Rio Colorado. The 'villainous Banditti-like army' and their 600 Indian allies presented the most extraordinary mix of races that Darwin had ever seen. But the most striking character of all was the General. He was 'a perfect gaucho,' with a gaudy shawl about his waist, 'fringed drawers' beneath, and a poncho. His horsemanship was as legendary as his 'despotic powers.' From keeping 300,000 head of cattle on his ranches, he knew all about rounding up and slaughtering. Darwin shook a hand soaked in blood. Rosas was grave, and the interview went off 'without a smile.' He granted Darwin a passport and even put government horses at his disposal to whisk the 'Naturalista' across the pampas.

These flat, grassy plains were the home of Indians, anteaters, and armadillos. And another, rarer creature, Darwin heard. The gauchos repeatedly mentioned a bird called 'Avestruz Petise,' a rhea – but smaller and darker than the common form, with feathered legs and blue-tinged eggs.[15] Few had seen one, but the nests had been found, and everyone confirmed that it was more plentiful further south.

Darwin was becoming quite a gaucho himself. The rough-riding suited him perfectly. At night, crouched around a fire, eating roasted game, he jotted down notes and relaxed. 'I . . . drink my Mattee & smoke my cigar, & then lie down & sleep as comfortably with the Heavens for a Canopy as in a feather bed.' Well armed, with fresh horses and ruthless companions, he had little to fear from the hostiles. Indeed, he was beginning to appreciate the 'great benefits' of General Rosas's 'war of extermination.' For landowners it promised a bonanza. 'It will . . . throw open four or 500 miles in length of fine country for the produce of cattle.'

Back at Bahia Blanca Darwin kicked around for a few days waiting for the *Beagle*. Then he bought a 'fine powerful young horse' for less than five pounds and rode back to the cliffs at Punta Alta. His luck was still holding. This time he took 'nearly an entire skeleton' from its rocky tomb: a bizarre horse-sized mammal with an enormous pelvis and a small, long face like an anteater's. This was a real prize because it had remained undisturbed, in its original place (rather than in pieces on the beach). Page after page of his notepad was filled up as he thought on the implications. It had lived before the sea shells, found in the layer above; and everything pointed to a gradual deposition of sediments and then uplift of the strata. But how old were all these megatheriums? What did the country look like in their day? And why had they all died out? He dreamed himself back to an archaic world, where bull-sized sloths roamed unimaginable plains.

The spot was secluded and the quietness 'almost sublime,' but he was living under no illusions. It was still an infernal land, where saline lakes encrusted with snow-white saltpetre baked in the blazing sun. Its conquerors were much the same. Beneath a fair veneer of civility, the gauchos were butchers. Back at the fort, he heard the latest about the General's war.

Everyone believed that it was 'the justest war' because it was being waged 'against Barbarians.' No tactic was too extreme. Prisoners were taken and treated like animals – corralled into a 'Christian's zoo,' Darwin seethed. The Indian women 'who appear above twenty years old, are massacred in cold blood,' he was informed. The younger ones too, if ugly. Tactfully he complained 'that this appeared rather inhuman,' only to be told by a soldier that 'they breed so.' Genocide was not the way God intended population growth to be checked. 'Who would believe in this age in a Christian, civilized country that such atrocities were committed?' The butchery might benefit the economy, but it would corrupt the people. 'The country will be in the hands of white Gaucho savages instead of copper-coloured Indians. The former being a little superior in civilization, as they are inferior in every moral virtue.'[16]

When the *Beagle* arrived, Covington fetched the bones from Punta Alta while Darwin made arrangements to travel 400 miles overland to Buenos Aires, where he would meet with the ship again. On 8 September he set off with his guide, heading north along the line of fortified 'postas,' left by Rosas in conquered territory. Kill or die was the unwritten law of this godforsaken plain. There was '*nothing* to eat' but what could be caught – rheas, deer, armadillos – and the vultures circled ominously overhead. Like a gaucho Darwin survived for days on nothing but meat, and enjoyed it – even 'one of the very favourite dishes of the country,' foetal puma. Still, on reaching Buenos Aires two weeks later, he was grateful to live with an English merchant's family, sip a cup of tea, and enjoy 'all the comforts' of home.

The *Beagle* was back surveying in the Plate. Darwin sent Covington out to shoot and skin birds while he stayed just long enough to stock up on sugar, snuff, cigars, gunpowder, and shot. Then he continued another 150 miles up-country to hunt for more bones. He found only one 'enormous gnawing' tooth and a few huge 'Mastodon' bones along the Rio Parana. But these were 'so completely decayed & soft' that they fell apart in his hands, and he pushed on to the 'straggling town' of Santa Fé, where he collapsed with a fever in the first week of October. Two days on his back convinced him to cut his ride short. He remembered Musters, who had died of fever within a week. Given the choice of deathbeds, Darwin preferred one in Buenos Aires; he dragged himself down to the Parana and booked passage on a pocket-sized sloop. The trip down river was tortuous, with gales and voracious mosquitoes. Darwin languished in bed, cursing, unable even to sit up in his tiny cabin. His fever left and, fed up with the boat, he paddled the rest of the way to the capital in a canoe.

A local revolution had broken out. He found the Spanish military in Buenos Aires blockaded by 'a furious cut-throat set of rebels' loyal to General Rosas. Darwin shuttled back and forth between the armies, and eventually obtained leave to enter the city on foot after he mentioned the General's former 'civility.' He bribed a man to smuggle in Covington, who had 'nearly lost his life in a quicksand & my gun completely.' Together they darted about the city for ten days, dodging the 'lawless soldiery' while arranging for their possessions to be shipped out. There was one true 'Gentleman in Buenos Ayres, the English Minister,' who came to their aid. FitzRoy in Montevideo had sent a message that he was preparing to sail. On 2 November they squeezed on to a packet crowded with refugees and fled for Montevideo as the musket volleys started. The 'utter profligacy' of dictatorship dominated Darwin's thoughts as he picked his way through sick women and children on the deck. He wished the revolutionaries 'would, like Kilkenny Cats, fight till nothing but the tails' were left.[17]

At Montevideo Darwin rushed aboard the *Beagle*, raring to go, thinking of 'the blue skys & the Bananas of the Tropics.' But no. FitzRoy was delayed by his chartwork. And the sister ship had yet to be provisioned for the treacherous passage around the Horn. He made the best of the time. He had letters to read and answer – the last, he feared, for many months. The news was all titillation and tut-tuts. Eras, still carrying on with Hensleigh's wife, was being paired off with Emma Wedgwood to avert 'an *action* in the Papers.' Fanny Biddulph, miserably married to a 'desperately selfish' ogre, had begun asking 'prettily & coquettishly' about her 'old Postillion.' And his sisters – imagine it – were 'afraid when ever we read of your enjoying yourself.'

Darwin busied himself packing two boxes and a cask, containing 'nearly 200 skins of birds & animals,' a collection of mice, a jar of fish, a case of insects, a box of stones, and 'a bundle of seeds, which,' he told Henslow, 'I send as a most humble apology for my idleness in Botany.' His fossil bones and rocks went separately to Plymouth in an immense box. Again he despatched everything with a heavy heart. Still no letter had come. For all he knew his caskets were in Davy Jones's locker. Or if not, perhaps Sedgwick and the rest were laughing at them – he had no idea. He was anxious for his collections to be applauded, desperate to find out 'whether I am going the right road.'[18]

By now the fossils meant everything to him, the romance of calling up ancient life. Nothing touched the raw excitement of the cliff face: 'the pleasure of the first days partridge shooting ... cannot be compared to finding a fine group of fossil bones, which tell their story of former times with almost a living tongue.' He decided to make a 400-mile round journey to Mercedes near the Rio Uruguay, where he had missed some curious rock formations after falling ill. Like all the 'galloping' trips since Punta Alta, it had one main object: to examine the sediments entombing the sloths – to understand the megatheriums' world and its end. He rode from ranch to ranch until he reached the picturesque megatherium country. He stayed at an estate belonging to a Mr Keen (presumably an Englishman) on 22 November. His host knew of a farm with 'giant's bones' simply lying in the yard and, four days later, they rode over. For eighteen pence Darwin came away with the best part of a perfect skull, 2 feet 4 inches long with strange curved teeth.[19] Despite the weight, he carried his one-and-sixpenny prize in triumph the 120 miles back to Montevideo.

In town, Darwin packed up and 'prepared to leave for ever.' It was an unsentimental farewell. The people of the Plate depressed him, and he had been among them too long. Robbery was rife, murder condoned, and justice at a premium. 'Every *public officer* is to be bribed,' and there were no 'Gentlemen par excellence.' Their absence was vexing, and on 5 December he was relieved to be back in FitzRoy's company as the *Beagle* made ready to sail. The artist Earle's health had 'so entirely broken up' that he quit the ship, and the Captain introduced his replacement, Conrad Martens, endorsing him in typical FitzRoy fashion, quirkily: 'By my faith in Bumpology, I am sure you will like him.' With twelve months' stores on board and the *Adventure* under the command of Mr Wickham, they were 'now on the road (though not the shortest) to England.'[20] Darwin was counting the days.

FitzRoy weighed anchor at four the next morning, and for seventeen days the sister ships sailed down the Patagonian coast. On 23 December they put in at Port Desire for the holiday, 600 miles north of Cape Horn. Darwin 'by great good luck' shot a llama-like guanaco, which fully dressed weighed 170 pounds, and a hearty Christmas dinner was had by all. Martens went one better and shot a small rhea, and it was only after the bird had been cooked and consumed that Darwin, suddenly and embarrassingly, recalled the gaucho story of the rare 'petise.' His first sight of the new bird, and he had eaten it unknowingly! Fortunately 'the Head neck legs, one wing' and larger feathers could be rescued, and they were promptly preserved and packed in the hold.

The 'stillness & desolation' here gave him inexplicable pleasure. Walking for miles on the faceless plain, he took a score of new birds. And in the shore cliffs he found 'the same great oyster bed' – just above sea level – that occurred the length of the continent, showing the recent upheaval of the land. But there were no fossils to exhume. He was already thinking of himself as a 'fossil Resurrectionist,' somewhat more respectable than the Burke and Hare variety, and when the *Beagle* dropped anchor at Port St Julian in January 1834 – 110 miles further south – he searched again. It was a wasteland, devoid of fresh water, and the only large mammal – the guanaco – could drink from the salt-lakes. Again, in the cliffs on the harbour's edge he found bits of spine and a complete hind leg of 'some large animal, I fancy a Mastodon.' 'This is interesting,' he mused; these great beasts clearly ranged far down into cold latitudes, and evidently a number of them 'were fellow brethren in the ancient plains.'[21] The old question popped up: what was the mastodon's world like, and was it as waterless and windswept as the one he tramped over?

Beating against strong westerly gales, the *Beagle* entered the Straits of Magellan on 26 January and proceeded to St Gregory's Bay, where members of a semi-civilized tribe of Patagonian 'giants' – over six feet tall – were entertained on board. 'They behaved quite like gentlemen,' despite their red-painted faces, guanaco hides, and streaming hair, and they 'used a knife & fork & helped themselves with a spoon,' Darwin noted, impressed. These Indians had long traded with the sealers, and they spoke smatterings of English and Spanish. They were 'excellent practical naturalists,' and Darwin had 'the greatest faith in their observations.' He quizzed one half-breed born in the northern provinces about the 'petise' rhea, and heard that it was the *only* rhea this far south. The two species met around the Rio Negro; otherwise the common rhea kept to the north, the 'petise' to the south. It confirmed that he had a new species with a distinct range.

Civilized savages showed how improvable humans were. Red-dyed Indians with real table manners were proof that the chasm between the brutal races and refined Englishmen could be bridged. But would the effect last – would these tame Indians turn wild again? The answer lay further south. He was curious about the fate of Jemmy, York, and Fuegia.

The ship pressed on to Tierra, anchoring at Port Famine in

'piercingly cold' gusty rain. Here hundreds of Spanish colonists had starved in the sixteenth century, and the *Beagle*'s Capt. Stokes had taken his life in 1826. On 6 February Darwin left the ship, compass in hand, to ascend 2600-foot Mount Tarn. As before, his mood matched the terrain. 'In the deep ravines the death-like scene of desolation exceeds all description,' he shuddered in the chill. 'Great mouldering trunks' lay strewn about, and 'everything was dripping with water.' 'Even the very Fungi could not flourish.' At the summit he found 'shells in the rocks' and a 'true Tierra del Fuego view:' 'irregular chains of hills, mottled with patches of snow; deep yellowish-green valleys; & arms of the sea running in all directions.' In the distance, ninety miles away, the highest peak in the south, awesome Mount Sarmiento, stood cloaked in perpetual snow.

FitzRoy threaded the ship back through the maze of waterways, past Spermaceti whales jumping out of the water. He completed his survey of the north-east region, and on 24 February anchored under Wollaston Island, just above the Horn.[22] This was Fuegian country, and everyone mingled with the inhabitants for ten days. As in his first shattering encounter with these 'troubled spirits,' Darwin was left reeling, asking questions, hard insistent ones.

What was he to make of these wretched people? Had they lived here in their present state 'since the creation'? If not, why did they leave 'the fine regions of the North' – the tropics – 'to enter upon one of the most inhospitable countries in the world'? Why did they remain naked? – he saw one pregnant woman 'absolutely so,' with the rain 'dripping from her body.' Why were they unkempt, 'their red skins filthy & greasy, their hair entangled, their voices discordant, their gesticulation violent & without any dignity'? Lyell in his *Principles of Geology* worried about Lamarck's chimpanzee ancestry crushing man's 'belief in the high genealogy of his species.' But how high the genealogy here – among aboriginals scarcely better than brutes? Where was the dignity for humans who slept uncovered 'on the wet ground . . . coiled up like animals'? Or who were locked in perpetual warfare over 'the means of subsistence'? He found these 'unbroken savages' detestable, 'more amusing than any Monkeys' but less able to enjoy their existence in this forlorn country. Yet he was helplessly intrigued. He had to find an explanation – 'Whence have these people come?'[23]

Nothing had intrigued him more, or appalled him more: 'one can hardly make oneself believe that they are fellow creatures placed in the same world.' Like animals, they were bereft of the higher pleasures:

> They cannot know the feeling of having a home – & still less
> that of domestic affection ... What is there for imagination
> to paint, for reason to compare, for judgement to decide upon.
> – to knock a limpet from the rock does not even require
> cunning, that lowest power of the mind. Their skill, like the
> instinct of animals is not improved by experience; the canoe,
> their most ingenious work, poor as it may be, we know has
> remained the same for the last 300 years.

'Although essentially the same creature,' Darwin conceded, remembering the civilized Jemmy and his friends, 'how little must the mind of one of these beings resemble that of an educated man.'

It all seemed to fly in Lyell's face – Lyell, who damned talk of monkeys and savages and philosophers linked in an evolutionary train. Lyell would have no smooth mental scale 'from "apes with foreheads villa[i]nous low,"' through savages to sherry-sipping Anglo-Saxons. Human beings might be diverse, but they showed only a 'slight deviation from a common standard.' Here spoke a man who had never seen savages; this was comforting armchair philosophy. Darwin was facing the most degraded natives, and being forced to recognize a world of difference – a world of improvement – 'between the faculties of a Fuegian savage & a Sir Isaac Newton.'

Yet for all their defects, the Fuegians were not dying out, so they must possess 'a sufficient share of happiness (whatever its kind may be) to render life worth having.' In fact, their miserable minds and manners seemed suited to their despicable environment. Nature, 'by making habit omnipotent,' had strangely 'fitted the Fuegian to the climate & productions of his country.'²⁴ The question was, did Jemmy's table manners mean that savages could be successfully civilized in only a few years? Could his old habits be broken so easily?

As Darwin pondered, the *Beagle* sailed fifty miles north, entering Ponsonby Sound to pay a final call on Jemmy. The mountains ahead were magnificent. Snow-clad and gilded in the rosy morning light, their 'broken & sharp peaks' presented 'a feast to the mind.' FitzRoy, marking the Philosopher's twenty-fifth birthday, had named the highest one Mount Darwin. They anchored near Woollya cove, where the missionaries had been left a year before. The huts were deserted, the gardens trampled and overgrown. In the distance canoes approached, a couple of the occupants anxiously scrubbing their faces. One looked familiar; it was Jemmy. But Darwin had never seen 'so complete & grievous a change.' It was 'painful to behold him; thin, pale, & without a remnant of clothes, excepting a bit of blanket round his waist: his hair, hanging over his shoulders; & so ashamed of himself, he turned his back to the ship' as the canoe came alongside. Then he looked up and raised his hand, 'as a sailor touches his hat.' A pathetic salute. FitzRoy was overwhelmed. They bundled him on board and clothed him immediately in preparation for dinner at the Captain's table. He used his cutlery properly, and, speaking 'as much English as ever,' told Darwin and FitzRoy of his companions' villainy. York Minster had persuaded him to come back to his own country with Fuegia. There one night, while he slept, the pair had absconded with all his possessions, leaving him as FitzRoy had first found him, naked.

Outside in a canoe 'a young, & for a Fuegian ... beautiful Squaw,' was crying implacably. She was pregnant, and said to be Jemmy's wife; only his reappearance on deck soothed her. The next day after breakfast Jemmy bade them goodbye. No, he had 'not the least wish to return to England.' He was 'happy and contented,' he declared, with 'plenty fruits,' 'plenty birdies,' 'ten guanaco in snow time,' and 'too much fish.' From his abundance he left gifts – a pair of 'beautiful otter skins,' arrows for the Captain, and 'two spearheads expressly for Mr Darwin.' He had made them himself. The ship got under way while he was still on board, sending his squaw into another fit of tears. Quickly he entered the canoe and dried them.

Everyone was 'sorry to shake hands with poor Jemmy for the last time,' Darwin recorded. 'I hope & have little doubt that he will be as happy as if he had never left his country; which is much more than I formerly thought.' Jemmy's habits were ingrained, it was now obvious. For untold generations his people had adapted to this wilderness, and no civilizing influence could erase his deep-seated instincts. Human differences were more profound than Lyell knew.

As his ancestors had done for centuries in this 'land of fire,' Jemmy lit 'a farewell signal ... as the ship stood out of Ponsonby Sound, on her course to East Falkland Island.'[25]

11

Shaken Foundations

THE *BEAGLE* ARRIVED at Port Louis, East Falkland, on 10 March 1834 – with perfect timing. An uprising had occurred. Gauchos and Indians had butchered British nationals, including the Union Jack keeper. 'Cold-blooded murder, robbery, plunder, suffering,' the atrocities were endless. The navy had sent in four armed sailors under a lieutenant, and they had flushed the rebels from the countryside, gaoling them ready for trial. But the 'principal murderer,' Antonio Rivero, was still at large. He was holding out on an islet in Berkeley Sound, swearing revenge, and the lieutenant, who now acted as Governor, asked FitzRoy to take him. And so the *Beagle*'s marines captured the 'villain,' clapping him in irons in the ship's hold.

Darwin viewed the whole episode with disdain. No one on East Falkland, 'this little miserable seat of discord,' deserved any praise. Of course the Buenos Aires government would call it 'a just revolt,' and talk of 'their poor subjects groaning under the tyranny of England.' For England's part, the navy's paltry police-action was unworthy of the Crown. 'Here we, dog-in the manger fashion seize an island & leave to protect it a Union jack; the possessor has been of course murdered: we now send a Lieutenant, with four sailors, without authority or instructions,' and 'the murderers have all been taken. – their [sic] being now as many prisoners as inhabitants.' What a short-sighted attitude to an island that 'must some day become a very important halting place in the most turbulent sea in the world.' Indeed, England's expanding trade only made her colonial half-heartedness seem more contemptible. 'How different from old Spain.' The Admiralty should have followed the *conquistadores*' example and turned East Falkland into a fortress.[1]

The ship that had landed the lieutenant also left the mail. Charles forgot the politics and savoured the gossip. Fanny was still asking about him; cousin Charlotte was happily ensconced in a parsonage; Erasmus was surrounded by 'all his favourites' – Hensleigh's wife and baby, and Emma Wedgwood. Talk of the parsonage continued, but Charles did not share Caroline's fear that 'the quiet clerical life you used to say you would return to' was irretrievably lost.

At last, too, he saw a letter with Henslow's handwriting, and this contained the best news. His collections were getting through safely. The plants were welcome, and the fossil megatheriums fabulously prized, revealing features never seen before. With typical diffidence, Darwin told Fox that he was 'only a sort of Jackall, a lions provider,' but the lions were roaring their approval. His megatheriums had been displayed before the cream of British science, at the Cambridge meeting of the British Association for the Advancement of Science. Your 'name is likely to be immortalized,' his beetling friend Frederick Hope said, and 'Darwin' was the word on everybody's lips. Send more bones, Henslow urged – 'every scrap of Megatherium skull you can set your eyes upon. – & *all* fossils.' Stick with the expedition; don't jump ship. 'I suspect you will always find something to keep up your courage.'[2]

Darwin was overjoyed. Nothing in two years had bucked him up so. He knew that his time had not been wasted, that all the galloping, hammering, and crating had been worthwhile. He felt proud. He had proved himself as a field naturalist and won the approval of those he respected. For the next three weeks he carried on like a man possessed. The weather was appalling, but it didn't matter. All around the island he made the rocks ring – some 'as big as Churches' – tussled with jackass penguins, and collected fragments of 'curious little Corallines.' He kept a handful of seeds too, a token of gratitude that he slipped in with a long excited letter back to his mentor.

He no longer saw himself as a random collector, a 'lions provider.' He was becoming a theorizer in his own right – a philosophical lion who could chew over old bones and explain them himself. He took fright at Henslow's talk of cleaning the megatheriums. Darwin feared that his identification numbers would be scrubbed off, making it impossible to relate the fossils to the embedding rocks. Both were needed to understand the megatheriums' world.

Their rock matrix told so much. Some fossil sloths were entombed with modern shells and agouti remains, suggesting that the bones were less ancient than he had thought. The shellfish and agoutis had obviously lived through the period of the Megatheriums' decline, making it impossible that a catastrophe had ravaged the land. The giant sloths must have died out naturally. Darwin's great diorama of the continent was changing: at the back, the coast of South America was rising out of the Atlantic – slowly, in phases, leaving a series of step-like plateaux. In the foreground, the 'ancient plains' were dominated by megatheriums and mastodons, thriving in a world no more cataclysmic than his own.[3]

Having reassured Henslow that he would 'stick to the voyage,' even if they did 'return a fine set of white-haired old gentlemen,' Darwin left the Falklands as he had arrived, on a grim note. On Sunday 6 April, while the *Beagle* was preparing for sea, a drowned English sailor was found on the beach in Berkeley Sound. FitzRoy buried him the next morning. They weighed anchor in the afternoon and tacked westward, with Rivero still chained in the hold, destined for a military court and execution. The ship headed for the Rio Santa Cruz in southern Patagonia, where the Captain planned to lead a party to the unexplored headwaters. If this 'glorious scheme' succeeded, Darwin would catch his first sight of the grandest mountain chain in the world, the Andes.[4]

The *Beagle* reached the mouth of the Santa Cruz on the 13th, and three days later the expedition set off. FitzRoy, Darwin, Stokes, Bynoe (the surgeon), and a few Gun Room men, supported by eighteen sailors and marines, were in the party. They took three whaleboats, tied together and dragged upstream by the men in teams, working hour-and-a-half shifts. It was strenuous work, pulling against water often running at seven knots; everyone took his turn, officers and ratings alike. When they weren't straining, Darwin and Stokes or Bynoe scouted ahead, walking on the embankments, rifles at the ready, always on the lookout for Indians and pumas. Neither was ever far away, as the tracks proved.[5]

They covered fifteen or twenty miles a day along the snaking stream, and were 100 miles west of the Santa Cruz estuary within a fortnight. At intervals between chasing guanacos and shooting condors, Darwin was puzzling out the geology. The river valley, five to ten miles wide, was bounded by walls over three hundred feet high. These led up to 'perfectly horizontal plains' on either side. The shells and shingle there showed that these plateaux had once been under water. It was while inspecting one with FitzRoy that Darwin plucked up courage to moot his hypothesis: that the terrace – indeed the whole Andes – had been raised slowly from the ocean bottom.

FitzRoy knew that this fitted with the latest Lyellian gradualist thought. He had been brought up with the biblical interpretation of the earth's crust – taught that the sea had risen violently a few thousand years ago at the time of Noah's flood, drowned the South American continent, and left the terraces and valleys much as they now appeared on receding. But he had not taken this 'scriptural geology' very seriously, and Darwin in his winsome way was talking him out of it. The Captain shook his head as he looked around, admitting that these raised plains 'could never have been effected by a forty days' flood.'[6]

Further on the plains were capped by a field of lava and the river entered a wild volcanic glen. Ahead lay a heavy bank of clouds, and on the 29th Darwin and Stokes climbed the cliffs to get a better view. Nine hundred feet above the river, they bellowed out their discovery: through 'the dusky envelope of clouds,' they could just make out the snowy summits of the Andes. The party, though footsore and weary, pressed on for a few days until provisions ran low. Thirty miles from the mountains, awestruck by the spectacle, they had to turn back. No matter, Darwin knew that he would reach the Andes from the other side within a year. As they raced downstream, he could think only of 'standing . . . on one of their pinnacles & looking down on the plains below.'

On 12 May the *Beagle* set sail from the eastern shores of South America for the last time. Lashed by sleet and hail, she pitched headlong into mountainous seas as FitzRoy made for the Straits of Magellan. The temperature dropped, and looking up from his hammock, where he lay 'sick & miserable' as usual, Darwin watched an inch of ice form on the skylight. Outside the Straits the *Adventure* joined them from the Falklands, bringing the mail, and the ships scudded down the famous waterway to Port Famine in ever shorter days. It was in the twenties now and snowing. How odd to receive a parcel that had been posted before Christmas. Still, it made June a festive season even at the bottom of the world, and Darwin tore into it like a child. With 'no roaring fire,' and a snow-covered upper deck, he cherished every reminder of home.[7]

There were letters and gifts galore. His sisters bubbled as usual, enjoying his diary immensely, but longing for him to be 'quite settled,' even if it meant aborting the voyage. Fanny echoed them pertly, her note a part of the orchestrated campaign. She looked forward to visiting him and his '*little Wife* in the *little Parsonage*!!' A browbeaten invalid with a six-month-old daughter, she was under the Doctor, and the Darwin sisters had clearly recruited her to their cause. Charles, feeling henpecked, put the subject 10,000 miles out of mind. Fanny's experience of marriage did not commend the institution any more than her urging enhanced the Church.

More to the point were the gifts – a purse, a chain for his pencil case, hiking boots, and a handful of books. He scanned the reading matter, always glad of additions to the ship's library. Caroline, worried by his close escapes, had sent *Scriptural Revelations concerning a Future State*, as 'we often used to find we liked the same kind' of literature. And all his sisters recommended *Poor Laws and Paupers Illustrated*, which came in several pamphlet-sized parts. Its author was 'a great Lion in London,' a fiercely independent lady, Harriet Martineau. She was the darling of the Whigs, a one-woman advertising agency, whose soap-opera novellas popularized and explained the reforms. 'Erasmus knows her & is a very great admirer & every body reads her little books & if you have a dull hour you can, and then throw them overboard, that they may not take up your precious room.'[8]

Ironic, really – here he was, in a desolate settlement called, of all things, Port Famine, distributing booklets to the men advocating sexual restraint as a way of escaping starvation. Actually they went down well. Everybody talked about her 'politico-economical tales,' homely yarns of indigence, passion, delayed marriages, and heroic prudence rescuing couples from penury and the poor house. On the ship, as in London, they were devoured as avidly as Walter Scott's novels.

Back in Britain they were doing more to pave the way for the new Poor Law than all the government propaganda. The ministers knew it; the Lord Chancellor Henry Brougham had actually commissioned them to ease in the unpopular law, feeding Martineau secret commission reports as source material. Her edifying homilies spread the word of the Revd Thomas Malthus, an economist for the East India Company. The core of his theory was bleak: as population rises faster than food supply, struggle and starvation must inevitably result. Public charities – the old poor relief – only aggravated the problem; hand-outs made paupers comfortable and encouraged them to breed. More mouths, more poor, more demands for welfare – it was a vicious circle.[9]

By now welfare was out of control and the population exploding. The 1831 census showed an unbelievable twenty-four million people in Britain, a doubling in thirty years. In bad winters one in ten was on hand-outs. Enough was enough for middle-class ratepayers; heroic surgery was needed to cut out this 'gangrene of the state,' as Martineau called it. Why should they support the work-shy? Why should they subsidize 'marriage between pauper boys and girls' and the birth of still more destitute children?

Drastic measures were sanctioned by the Poor Law Amendment Bill, just becoming law as Darwin's shipmates read the booklets. It ended relief for all but the most destitute, those so ill or old that they would enter the abominable workhouses to receive food or money. Since their prison regimes were designed to discourage entry – wives were torn from husbands to prevent breeding – few were expected to apply for relief and a vast saving was guaranteed. Martineau argued that this would benefit the paupers themselves, by making them self-reliant. But really by forcing them to compete for jobs, the Whigs were decreasing labour costs and increasing profits. By heeding the Revd Malthus, they will do 'more for the country than all the Administrations since the Revolution,' one pundit cheered. The new Poor Law will 'immortalize them.'[10]

What the *Beagle*'s shiftless seamen made of Martineau may be surmised. Charles's sisters saw the Poor Law as the 'great topic of interest,' and the Doctor argued its merits with local Tories. But Charles was too distant and kept his own counsel, although no one was to have a more crucial influence on his science than Malthus.

He was in another world, lost in wonder at the 'rugged snowy crags, blue glaciers, [and] rainbows' as FitzRoy steered from Port Famine, under the face of Mount Sarmiento, and into the Cockburn Channel. At the base of vast vertical cliffs in a tiny cove Charles saw a deserted wigwam, a reminder that man sometimes wandered this wilderness. 'Imagination,' he noted sombrely, 'could scarcely paint a scene' where humans seem 'to have less . . . authority.' The elemental forces prevail. In this desolation the 'wider power[s] of nature despise control,' as if to say 'We are the sovereign.' Here mankind 'does not look like the Lord of all.'[11]

After sailing dangerously in circles for fourteen hours in pitch darkness, the *Beagle* emerged from the Cockburn Channel on 10 June. At long last they had reached the west coast. Setting 'every inch of canvas,' she battled out into the long swell of the Pacific, the *Adventure* alongside. Here the rugged granite coast, pounded by roaring breakers, was enough to give landsmen nightmares about 'peril & shipwreck.' Howling northerly gales intensified the effect, whipping up angry seas. These were not the only sirens of death. As FitzRoy struggled at the helm, the oldest officer lay fighting for his life below-deck. Rowlett, thirty-eight, the Purser, had been Darwin's friend since trekking together on St Jago; on the 27th they watched him succumb to 'a complication of diseases.' The next day, as the ship approached San Carlos on the island of Chiloé, 1000 miles above the Horn, FitzRoy read the funeral service on the quarter-deck and Rowlett's remains were committed to the deep. To Darwin, safely through the storms, 'the splash of the waters over the body of an old ship-mate' was 'an awful & solemn sound.'

Chiloé was drenched. Only 'an amphibious animal could tolerate the climate,' Darwin moaned as he poked around. He was heartened by the 'Tropical scenery' – the best since Brazil – and the evidence of volcanic activity and recent uplift. The birds were interesting too, inviting comparison with those in Tierra del Fuego. But most curious of all was a story he heard. A whaler's surgeon told him that the lice infesting the Sandwich Islanders died in a few days if they transferred to Englishmen. How strange: what did this say about the human races? He began working through the implications in his notes: 'Man springing from one stock' - that was his axiom. From this it followed that all the human types were '*varieties*,' so were their parasites closely related too? If he could prove this, it would be a blow to the apologists of slavery, who made the blacks a separate species. Here was a line to follow up with the experts back in London.

Two weeks in the rain here and the *Beagle* moved on, 600 miles further up the coast, against an 'anything but "Pacific" Ocean.' FitzRoy planned to sit out the stormy months in central Chile while the sister-ships were refitted. On 23 July they anchored in the crowded harbour of Valparaiso, backed by steep hills with 'glimpses of the Andes' to the north. The climate here was 'quite delicious,' 'the sky so clear & blue, the air so dry & the sun so bright,' that 'all nature seemed sparkling with life.'[12]

Darwin went into town – 'a sort of London or Paris' where one was 'obliged to shave & dress decently' – and lodged with Richard Corfield, an old classmate from Shrewsbury School, now a merchant. Corfield had a fine suburban house close to open country, and Darwin rambled out to survey the scene. The hills abounded with gorgeous flowers and scrubby aromatic bushes. He found beds of modern shells at 1300 feet but, oddly enough, few insects, birds, or mammals. Perhaps none had 'been created since this country was raised from the sea.'

In the distance the Andes beckoned, or rather the foothills, which were safer to climb in winter. To take a closer look, he bought 'a small troop of horses' to use in rotation, and set off on 14 August. The landscape was like Tierra del Fuego's. No doubt these plains too had been a sea-bottom, with the distant hills marking the shoreline.

Higher up, some 4000 feet, he looked down on the 'patchwork ...
Paradise' of the valley below. At this altitude the laval rocks had
been 'frizzled melted and bedevilled in every possible fashion,' and
not so long ago. Volcanoes had spewed them up, and earthquakes
still shook and shattered them; here man was a puny being, and
Darwin hurried past massive overhangs waiting to crash down. It
was impossible not to marvel at 'the wonderful force which has
upheaved these mountains, & even more so the countless ages' that it
took 'to have broken through, removed & levelled whole masses of
them.'[13]

Darwin reached Santiago on the 27th and spent a week naturalizing
by day and dining with merchants at night. Corfield was also there
'to admire the beauties of nature, in the form of Signoritas,' and they
teamed up for the return trip to Valparaiso. At a wealthy hacienda *en
route* Darwin obliged the 'pretty Signoritas' with stories of his
travels. But the air chilled when he mentioned his sermon-sampling
in Buenos Aires. Being Catholics, the ladies

> turned up their charming eyes in pious horror at my having
> entered a Church to look about me; they asked ... why I did
> not become a Christian, "for our religion is certain"; I assured
> them I was a sort of Christian; they would not hear of it ...
> "Do not your padres, your very bishops marry" – The
> absurdity of a Bishop having a wife particularly struck them,
> [and] they scarcely knew whether to be most amused or
> horrified at such an atrocity.

It was enough to remind him of home – of sisters, parsonages, and
wives. A Catholic 'sort of Christian' he could never be, but what
about his own Church?

He did not know. Months had passed since he last conjured up
visions of 'retirement, green cottages, & white petticoats.' The voyage
had worn on, and now he felt 'like a ruined man, who does not see
or care how to extricate himself.' All he knew was that geology held
'a never failing interest.' It was of course religious in its way, giving
him 'the same grand ideas' about the earth that 'Astronomy does for
the universe.' The Revd Sedgwick had taught him as much, but now,
surrounded by 'sublime masses of snow,' he felt in his heart that it
was true.

They rode on through breathtaking scenery, still making for
Valparaiso. At an American gold mine Darwin watched pale young
men carrying 200 pounds of stone up a laddered 450-foot shaft. They
were 'allowed only beans & bread,' the proprietor explained as the

guests sipped local wine. A few hours later Darwin fell ill, and although a few days' rest seemed to cure him, once in the saddle again his stomach erupted, his appetite vanished, and he became fevered. It was that sour wine, he felt sure. By 21 September he could scarcely mount his horse. Rest-stops became more frequent, although nothing could prevent him from chipping fossil barnacles from beds along the plain – the proof positive of its marine origin. A further week of suffering and he was back in Valparaiso, a shambling wreck. He went to bed and stayed there a month.[14]

Bynoe, the Surgeon, brought medications and startling news from the *Beagle*: FitzRoy had suffered a breakdown. He was a brittle perfectionist and the obsessive chartwork had rattled him. Refitting the *Adventure* had proved too expensive and the Admiralty Lords had reprimanded him for buying her. Under a great strain, he had sold the ship – and snapped. First, he decided to return to that 'confounded country' Tierra del Fuego to check his measurements, risking a mass desertion by the crew, Darwin with them. Then, depressed and doubting his sanity, he had resigned his command. He feared his uncle's fate and remembered Stokes's suicide. Wickham was now in charge, with instructions to finish surveying the west coast and then return directly to England.

The news sent Darwin into a spin. The circumnavigation was lost, no Pacific, no Indian Ocean; his mind 'a swinging pendulum' again, downcast and homesick by turns, the gloom of a lost world brightened by the prospect of an early family reunion. Bewildered, he spent a night agonizing: should he cut and run? No, his 'geological castles in the air' came first. He would not sacrifice these for all the parsonages and petticoats in England. He decided to travel alone through Chile and Peru, cross the Andes to Buenos Aires, and sail from there for home. A fine fifteen months it would be.

FitzRoy was swinging as wildly. After some arm-twisting from the officers, he changed tack, withdrew his resignation, and announced that they would cross the Pacific after all. There was no turning back; he would hoist sails as soon as the Philosopher regained his feet. Word reached Corfield's, providing the tonic Darwin needed. 'What a revolution . . . five minutes . . . effected in all my feelings,' he exulted to his family. The *Beagle* would stay in coastal waters for several months; then 'crossing the Pacific & from Sydney home' would be a breeze. The world lay before him again.

Fired up, on 7 November he finished a long letter to Henslow, his 'father' and 'pro-proctor' in natural history, detailing his discoveries. By now Henslow's scientific son understood the Patagonian geology.

He was knowledgeable enough to query Lamarck's classification of corals; he had puzzled at the formation of the Andes, written '600 small quarto pages' of notes, and shipped two more boxes of specimens. Better was to come, for in three days he was leaving for the Chonos archipelago, where they could 'steer by the light of a Volcano.' The future looked so bright that Darwin did not know 'which part of the voyage, now offers the most attractions.'[15]

The island of Chiloé was the gateway to the archipelago. After a fair passage south, the *Beagle* arrived at San Carlos harbour on the 21st. FitzRoy took the *Beagle* off surveying, leaving Sulivan in charge of the ship's yawl and whaleboat with orders to chart the east coast of Chiloé to its southern extremity. Darwin of course went with Sulivan for the 100-mile ride. Two days out and he saw three great volcanoes billowing smoke. And, ten days later, his first petrified tree, a beautiful fossil in yellow sandstone, its trunk 'thicker than my body' and its veins transparent quartz.

Rendezvousing with the *Beagle*, they sailed along Chiloé's 'lofty weather-beaten' south coast and then tracked down to the Chonos archipelago. Christmas Day was depressing; the wind was fierce and the sodden deserted islands reminded everyone of the Horn. Not quite deserted – on the 28th they spotted a sailor wildly waving his shirt on a point of land, and a boat was sent out, with Darwin in it. They encountered five American castaways. 'I never saw such anxiety ... in mens faces,' he wrote. The wretches had deserted a Massachusetts whaler 'without knowing which way to go or where they were.' Their boat had been smashed, and for over a year they had survived on seal flesh, shellfish, and hope. In all that time they had seen sails only once, and were 'nearly jumping into the water' as the boat picked them up.[16]

FitzRoy surveyed the islands, finishing up in Low's Harbour at the northern end of the archipelago. For a week the crew stocked up on game, oysters, and potatoes. After wild people, FitzRoy thought wild potatoes were the highlight of the trip, and Darwin collected seeds for Henslow. He also set his traps and caught a 'singular little mouse.' It was common on some islands, the natives said, but absent on others, leading him to wonder why colonization was such a serendipitous affair. He also picked up dozens of conches on the beach, each '*completely* drilled' with cavities. The shells were riddled with minuscule parasites. Under the microscope, they appeared as boring barnacles, no bigger than pins' heads. These were surely the smallest, oddest barnacles in the world, and he took hundreds away to study.

The *Beagle* was back at Chiloé on 15 January 1835, anchored at San Carlos, where they were to rest up for three weeks. At about midnight on the 19th, the sentry reported 'something like a large star' slowly increasing on the horizon. By 3 a.m. Darwin and the officers were on deck, taking turns with an eye-glass: seventy miles away, volcanic Mount Osorno was putting on a spectacular show. It was one 'great red glare,' an explosion of rocks, with lava spewing down its slopes. The whole molten mass glowed so brightly that the sky was lit up and the sea reflected the display. It died down, a minor eruption, and by morning, Darwin noted, 'the Volcano seemed to have regained its composure.'[17]

While FitzRoy checked his bearings, Darwin hired a guide and spent a week criss-crossing Chiloé with Midshipman King. The weather was fine, and the beetles abundant. The settlements were surrounded by orchards. Apple trees were everywhere, along the roadsides, in the towns, he had never seen so many. At the end they climbed a hill to see the volcanoes once more and alighted on yet another bed of shells, 350 feet above the sea.[18] The west coast of the continent, no less than the east, had risen out of the ocean recently, and in the same stop-go manner.

On 5 February the *Beagle* headed north finally, and Darwin settled in to his cramped cabin to write his notes. He returned to the vexed question of the megatheriums and their demise. Lyell was right about the 'gradual birth and death of species,' Darwin jotted. After the deaths, 'successive births must repeople the globe,' replenishing species to keep the harmony established by the 'Author of Nature.'

He harked back to the 'Mastodon' found at Port St Julian. No flooding or catastrophe could have killed it; at least the rocks showed no evidence. Moreover, it was buried in a gully, in the sort of loam that overlay the shelly gravel on the plateau above. This could mean only that the animal had lived *after* these shells. And since similar shellfish thrive in the ocean today, the climate could not have changed much. Nor could the vegetation; these gravels were too poor to support anything more than scrub. At a stroke Darwin had thrown out the two commonest explanations of extinction: a catastrophic flood, or a change in climate. He still believed in Lyell's Creator but had broken with his climatic theory; he was branching out on his own.[19]

Lyell spoke of the 'succession of deaths' as part of 'the ordinary course of nature.' But what could cause a whole species to die like a single individual? Why had all the megatheriums perished?

For a novel answer Darwin now crossed over to his other interest:

the vital force in living matter. But he took a new angle. Common apples were the key – to be more exact the ubiquitous Chiloé apple trees. Even as he wrote, the *Beagle* was putting into the port of Valdivia, 150 miles up the coast, a ramshackle settlement 'completely hidden in a wood of Apple trees.' The 'streets are merely paths in an orchard,' he observed on disembarking. 'I never saw this fruit in such abundance.' He now realized what made these trees so fertile:

> the inhabitants possess a marvellously short method of making an orchard. At the lower part of almost every branch, small, conical, brown, wrinkled points project; these are always ready to change into roots, as may sometimes be seen, where any mud had been accidentally splashed against the tree.

Cuttings would root immediately, and the inhabitants were taking advantage of the fact. Whole orchards sprang from one tree. The cuttings themselves grew so rampantly in this climate that in eighteen months cuttings from cuttings could be taken.

It set him thinking about what a cutting actually was. Were all the cuttings from one tree *part* of that parent? Were they the severed pieces of one individual? If so, they should share its life span. As Darwin put it, 'all these thousand trees are subject to the duration of life which one bud contained.'[20] They would be bound by one life force, enormously extended by cutting, but still limited, or so he believed. And once it was expended, all the offshoots would die simultaneously. Darwin now took a giant leap and suggested an analogy with species. Perhaps all the megatheriums shared one life-force; perhaps sexually reproduced animals are like 'cuttings' from an original stock. Is that why all the ground sloths vanished together?

In Valdivia he nosed around, eager for excitement. The Captain threw a party on board. A boatload of blushing *señoritas* was engaged for the event and, alas, 'bad weather compelled them to stay all night.' It was a 'sore plague' to everyone, Darwin quipped. Otherwise his hours were idled away, wandering through the forest.

On 20 February he lay resting on its floor at ten o'clock in the morning when the earth moved, sending his mind into a slow-motion swirl. He had felt a tremor once before, while convalescing at Corfield's, but nothing like this. It started suddenly, became violent, and seemed to go on forever. He tried to stand but sank to his knees, dizzy and distraught. In a split second, the one abiding security of life – the firm ground – disappeared. 'The world, the very emblem of all that is solid,' he gasped, shuddered beneath our feet 'like a crust over a fluid.' The quake lasted only two minutes but encompassed an eternity; all moorings were lost, leaving him philosophically giddy for weeks. He raced into town and was greeted by the sight of wooden houses askew and 'horror pictured in the faces of all the inhabitants.' To have '*seen* as well as felt an earthquake' was an awesome experience, and he dreaded to think of the destruction in the great city of Concepción, 200 miles north.[21]

The *Beagle* stood out to sea and sailed up the coast. The shoals were treacherous and she lost two anchors, the sixth and seventh of the voyage, before gaining the harbour at Concepción. The devastation was staggering. 'The whole coast was strewed over with timber & furniture as if a thousand great ships had been wrecked.' Huge slabs of rock had been thrown up on to the beach, and the town itself looked like an ancient ruin. Houses and schools were heaps of rubble and the great cathedral lay half-razed, its four-foot-thick walls tottering on battered foundations. The quake was Chile's 'worst ever,' he heard. It gave no notice and struck with ferocity. Shock after shock hit the city, 'rumbling ... like distant thunder' and darkening the sky with a dense cloud of dust. Fires broke out everywhere. People ran screaming from their homes. Then a twenty-foot tidal wave swept across the land, carrying a schooner into the town. Scores were drowned or crushed, and even now, two weeks later, untold numbers lay buried in the rubble. Looters prowled the streets, mixing 'religion in their depradations ... At each little trembling of the ground, with one hand they beat their breasts & cried out "Miserecordia," [sic] & with the other continued to filch from the ruins.'

The carnage was inconceivable, and Darwin's thoughts turned to home. What if an earthquake struck England, with its 'lofty houses, thickly packed cities, the great manufactories, the beautiful private & public buildings?' What 'a horrible destruction there would be of human life.' The country would 'become bankrupt; all papers, accounts, [and] records ... would be lost ... Government could not collect the taxes.' It was a terrifying prospect – a revolution like no other, the violent overthrow of all that he held dear. And still worse, no one could predict when a quake might strike. 'Who can say how soon such will happen?'

Emotionally drained, Darwin began to think coolly. He found fresh mussel beds lying above high tide, the shellfish all dead – the land had risen, and by a few feet! What had he been mooting all along, but the continent's emergence from the sea? And now to have *experienced* it! Lyell had shown the same for Naples Bay, where a submerged Roman temple had been hoisted out of the water by an earthquake. It was the final confirmation that mountains are not thrown up in one colossal upheaval. Lyell was right: they grow barely perceptibly, the product of thousands of tiny rises like this over the aeons. Time, unimaginable time, that was the key; given it, anything could be achieved. Darwin now understood. He plotted the quake's epicentre and pinned down its cause to incipient volcanic action. Hot springs and 'bubbles of gas & discoloured water' percolating into the sea proved beyond doubt that 'the earth is a mere crust over a fluid melted mass of rock.'

Earthquakes and volcanoes had revealed Nature's awesome power, its driving force. But where did man – puny man – fit into her picture? It was 'bitter & humiliating' to contemplate his vulnerability, 'skating over very thin ice,' a crustal sheet, above a fiery furnace. Yet accept it he must.[22]

12

Colonial Life

THEY WEREN'T TO BE white-haired gents on their return to England. As the *Beagle* sailed into Valparaiso to fetch new anchors, FitzRoy announced that they would be home in eighteen months. At last Darwin could see the journey's 'definite & certain end.'

On 12 March 1835 he moved back into Corfield's villa, preparing for the Andes expedition that he had dreamt of for two years. While the ship finished charting, he would cross the mountains. But even while packing his 'horse cloths stirrups pistols & spurs,' he was thinking of home, planning 'the very coaches by which I shall . . . reach Shrewsbury in the shortest time.' He fired off a new set of expectant letters. Oh to be 'living quietly in Cambridge' again, he sighed to Henslow at the end of a report proving 'that both sides of the Andes have risen in the recent period.' Fox – and his new wife – received an even more wistful note. 'You a married clergyman, ave maria, how strange it sounds to my ears.' Would they have anything but memories in common by the time Darwin arrived home? He could no longer see what the future in England held. 'What I shall ultimately do with myself – Quien Sabe?' – Who knows? 'But it is very un-Sailor-like to think of the Future.'[1]

With winter approaching, his mountain trek would have to be quick. He made his way to Santiago, and from there on the 18th began the long ascent to the Portillo Pass with ten mules, a mare, two guides, and 'a good deal of food, in case of being snowed up.' With a 'strong passport from the President' of Chile, they slipped through the frontier customs, and on the 21st Darwin perched on the continental divide, panting. At 13,000 feet, the wind was 'violent and very cold,' and his head and chest felt tight. Then he looked behind him.

The atmosphere so resplendently clear, the sky an intense blue, the profound valleys, the wild broken forms, the heaps of ruins piled up during the lapse of ages, the bright colored rocks, contrasted with the quiet mountains of Snow, together produced a scene I never could have imagined . . . I felt glad I was by myself, it was like watching a thunderstorm, or hearing in the full Orchestra a Chorus of the Messiah.

Welling up with emotion, he was in 'another world.' Yet even here, in this barren wasteland with 'neither plant nor bird,' he found fossil shells in the rocks.

This was the first of the two main ridges in the Andes. The party traversed the central tract, gazing on 22,000-foot snow-covered Mount Tupungato. They plodded on through icy clouds to the Portillo, a 'narrow cleft' in the second ridge, from where the descent was short and steep. While they camped that night, sheltering from the bitter frost beneath great shattered rocks, the clouds cleared. The effect was 'quite magical.' A full moon bathed the mountains, and stiletto stars pricked the dry still air. Static electricity completed the illumination. Every 'hair on a dogs back crackled' and Darwin's flannel waistcoat glowed when rubbed, 'as if washed with Phosphorus.' Ahead lay the pampas, which he had longed to see from such a height. But come morning the view was disappointing; it was flat and featureless, broken only by rivers running 'like silver threads' before the rising sun.[2]

They reached Mendoza on the 28th after crossing more pebbly plateaux and fighting through a swarm of locusts. ('The noise of their approach was that of a strong breeze passing through the rigging of a Ship.') Giant Vinchuca bugs plagued them; it was 'horribly disgusting' to wake at night and feel them, 'an inch long . . . black and soft,' crawling over 'your person – gorged with your blood.' After resting a day in the 'forlorn & stupid' town, they turned north-west to re-cross the Andes through the Uspallata Pass. At 7000 feet Darwin came upon a striking grove of fossilized trees. 'I confess I was at first so much astonished that I could scarcely believe the plainest evidence of it' – a petrified forest, fifty fossilized trunks in a sandstone escarpment, 'snow white columns Like Lots wife,' perfectly crystallized. Even the impressions of bark were visible and the growth rings could be counted. The sandstone sediments told the full story. This 'cluster of fine trees had once waved their branches on the shores of the Atlantic, when that ocean (now driven back 700 miles) approached the base of the Andes.'[3] The land sank, drowning the luxuriant tropical forest, burying it in sand and silt thousands of feet thick. These sediments compressed into rock, crystallizing the wood, and lava overflowed it. Then slowly, inexorably, the continent began its rise out of the sea, until this eerie grove came to stand high in the freezing mountains.

He was now literally building 'geological castles in the air.' In the rarefied atmosphere, amid the towering crags and jagged ravines, he put together a theory to explain the Andes. Their granite core had been heaved up piecemeal along a north-south line, 'overturning in the most extraordinary manner the overlying strata.' These tree-entombing sandstones had been 'tossed about like the crust of a broken pie.' Powerful forces – acting with slow-motion primal violence, as it must seem to humans – had tilted and smashed the overlying rocks, leaving the trees at an angle. The sight left him gasping: 'I cannot imagine any part of the world presenting a more extraordinary scene of the breaking up of the crust of the globe.'[4]

At night he 'could hardly sleep,' for thinking of crustal oscillation and heaving continents. On 4 April, as the mule train snaked through the most treacherous passes, he was almost blasé, yet one slip would have pitched him headlong into the abyss, joining 'Las Animas' – The Souls – after whom one of the gaps was named. Beyond, the Uspallata snowstorms were overdue, but Darwin went on enjoying 'the brightest fortune' and awe-inspiring scenery, 'a fine Chaos of huge mountains divided by profound ravines.' The team descended along the valley of the Rio Aconcagua, arriving in Santiago on the 10th. A week later he was safely back in Valparaiso with 'half a mule's load' of specimens.

He packed them in two crates, which would be the last shipment to reach home before he did, and wrote Henslow an account of the expedition. This letter had top priority. 'Absurd & incredible' his discoveries seemed, still he sketched them breathlessly, with broad geological brush-strokes, painting images of fossil shells and trees that testified to the recent stuttering uplift of the continent. It was a daring performance for a novice naturalist. But he was keen for credit, eager to be thought objective and unbiased, swearing that 'no previously formed conjecture warped my judgement.'

He was equally anxious to impress his father and sisters. He boasted that his findings, if accepted, would be crucial to 'the theory of the formation of the world.' He wanted another sort of credit from the Doctor too. For the second time in six months he had 'drawn a bill for £100,' and assumed that his extravagance would be condemned. It was a 'black & dismal' subject, 'that horrid phantom money.' All his budgets had been broken. He piled up excuses like so many hypotheses, but then confessed his openness to temptation: geological field trips were as irresistible as they were expensive. Crossing the Andes alone had cost £60, and given the chance he would no doubt 'spend money in the very moon.'[5]

The extra money was of course for the next expedition. While the *Beagle* charted north towards the Peruvian capital, Lima, Darwin followed on land, starting on 27 April with four horses, two mules, and a guide. They took the road to Coquimbo, through parched valleys and over barren mountains. Prospectors roamed these hills, searching for copper and gold. Fabulous fortunes had been made and wasted; even some English workmen 'who came out as Mechanicks' had made 'some thousand pounds' and bought their own mine. Darwin visited the diggings and saw once more the dreadful labour involved.

At Coquimbo the *Beagle* was being refitted for the long haul home. After touring the countryside he washed his clothes, picked up *Paradise Lost* from the poop cabin, and set out on 1 June for Copiapó, 200 miles north, where he would rejoin the ship. This leg of the expedition was a trial for man and beast alike. Water and firewood were scarce, and the vegetation grew scantier. In the Guasco valley they had a few days' respite, but from there to Copiapó was unremitting desert. But for the joys of hammering, it would have been 'down right Martyrdom.'

He was suffering for his geology and loving it. And as if to test his pain threshold, he took one last expensive risk. Arriving in Copiapó on the 23rd, he hired a guide and eight mules for a week in the wintry Andes. Here he checked his ideas about elevation, deducing from the Indian ruins that the climate must have been more hospitable in the past. The mountains proved 'very tame,' but the night wind was ferocious. It froze the water and penetrated their clothing. 'I suffered much ... so that I could not sleep, & in the morning rose with my body quite dull & benumbed.'[6] For once he was relieved to see the ship.

The refurbished *Beagle* cast off on 6 July, for the long northern run up the coast. A week later they reached Iquique, but the town was in tumult, reflecting the 'Anarchy' of Peruvian politics, with churches looted and foreigners blamed. The jittery inhabitants had even caught and tortured some Englishmen before the authorities could restore a semblance of order. It was a foretaste of what they would find in Lima, 700 miles further north. No sooner had the ship docked in Lima harbour on the 19th than the crew was briefed: four armed factions were vying for power, and the President was 'shooting & murdering any one who disobeys his orders.' He had even been known to unfurl a black flag with a 'death's head' during Mass, and had decreed that 'all property should be at the disposal of the state.' Here too it was open season on foreigners. Three, including the British consul, had just been assaulted by renegade soldiers, stripped naked 'excepting their drawers' and robbed blind. This was an act of 'warm Patriotism.' The thugs had 'waved the Peruvian banner & intermingled crys of "Viva la Patria"; "give me your jacket". "Libertad Libertad" . . . "Off with your trowsers"'!

A young English gentleman had to tread carefully. Darwin entered the city safely but could not stray beyond its bounds. He noted the 'remarkably mongrel population,' the numbers of churches among the 'heaps of filth,' and the 'wretched state of decay.' There was faded grandeur, but only one thing turned his head. He 'could not keep [his] eyes' off the *tapadas* – the elegant ladies. Their dress and manners brought out the sailor in him. He felt as though he had fallen amongst 'nice round mermaids.'

> The . . . elastic gown fits the figure closely & obliges the
> ladies to walk with small steps which they do very elegantly
> & display very white silk stockings & very pretty feet. – They
> wear a black silk veil, which is fixed round the waist behind,
> is brought over the head, & held by the hands before the
> face, allowing only one eye to remain uncovered. – But then
> that one eye is so black & brilliant & has such powers of
> motion & expression, that its effect is very powerful.

These alluring creatures were more 'worth looking at than all the churches & buildings in Lima.'[7]

Through July and August the country lurched from crisis to crisis; the main road from the port to town became impassable, 'infested with gangs of mounted robbers.' The *Beagle* was Darwin's only haven. But time was hanging heavy, and FitzRoy, having found some 'old charts & Papers' to study, showed no sign of putting to sea. It was yet another 'grievous' delay, even though the Captain vowed to set off around the world soon enough.

Confined to the poop cabin, Darwin put the time to use, writing up notes. Whiling away the warm days, he continued to build his geological edifice. If the continent were rising, presumably the Pacific floor was sinking. This would fit with Lyell's theory of an oscillating crust, and Darwin now considered himself Mr Lyell's 'zealous disciple.' But how to prove it? The evidence, he guessed, lay in the palm-fringed coral islets dotting the Pacific. Are they sinking? Part of FitzRoy's Admiralty brief was to take soundings around these islands to determine if the coral rings really sat on 'the summits of extinct volcanoes.' Travellers knew that coral polyps required warmth, light, and shallows, and many assumed that they encrusted *rising* volcanic rims. Even Lyell did. But what if Lyell was wrong on this point?

Darwin had questioned his master before – good disciples do – and now he suspected the whole theory was topsy-turvy. It seemed more likely that the reefs encircled mountain tops which were *vanishing*. As the land sank, the coral accumulated, rising to compensate, keeping itself at the optimum depth.[8] He had an answer for the Sea Lords before he ever saw a coral island. Nothing remained but to find one and confirm it.

He fired off letters: Henslow heard about Chilean geology, and the family about his first week's appointments on arriving home. 'In truth,' he alerted them, 'I shall have a great deal to do, for a long time after we return.' Fox, his father-confessor, heard more. Fox had written extolling marriage, talking of his 'dear little wife' and child on the way. He implored Charles for a letter, a frank note about his thoughts, and it struck a responsive chord. Charles compared the happy couple beside the parsonage hearth with himself, stuck in a cramped cabin in a stinking port. He opened his heart:

> This voyage is terribly long. – I do so earnestly desire to
> return, yet I dare hardly look forward to the future, for I do
> not know what will become of me. – Your situation is above
> envy; I do not venture even to frame such happy visions. To a
> person fit to take the office, the life of a Clergyman is a type
> of all that is respectable & happy: & if he is a Naturalist &
> has the "Diamond Beetle", ave Maria; I do not know what to
> say. – You tempt me by talking of your fireside, whereas it is
> a sort of scene I never ought to think about.

He envied curate-naturalists their lives, and their wives. An 'English lady' was someone 'very angelic & good,' a type he had 'almost forgotten' about. The women here 'wear Caps & petticoats & a very few have pretty faces & then all is said.' But Darwin was trying to forget the beauty he saw in town as the *Beagle* prepared for the lonely Pacific passage. His first love, geology, would meet his emotional needs.

Anyway, to think of firesides and female company was folly.

They were about to set off at last around the world – across the Pacific to Australia, then atoll-hopping across the Indian Ocean to South Africa. And he was looking forward to the next stop, 'the Galapagos, with more interest than any other part of the voyage.'⁹

He was almost nostalgic as the ship prepared to leave South America finally. So much had he seen in three and a half years: earthquakes, volcanic eruptions, gigantic fossils, savages. He bade goodbye to the Andes, and to shipmates remaining in their graves. But there were always new faces – and not only human ones. A forecastle sailor, J. Davis, brought on board a coati mundi, a South American racoon-relative with a long flexible snout, which joined the crew for the rest of the voyage.¹⁰

A week out of Lima and the *Beagle* was 600 miles away, approaching the Galapagos Islands. It was 15 September when they first sighted the closest island, Chatham. 'We landed upon black, dismal-looking heaps of broken lava, forming a shore fit for pandemonium,' FitzRoy recorded. 'Innumerable crabs and hideous iguanas started in every direction as we scrambled from rock to rock.' Darwin was equally taken aback; the black cinders were difficult to walk on and burning hot. They glowed 'like a stove' in the overhead sun, their rugged inhospitability highlighted by the almost lifeless stunted trees. Every great squirl of lava looked as though it had been 'petrified in its most boisterous moments.' The air was sultry, the smell unpleasant, and the whole 'compared to what we might imagine the cultivated parts of the Infernal regions to be.'

These 'frying hot islands' were 'paradises for the whole family of Reptiles.' Turtles glided through the bay, popping their heads up to breathe, and inland giant tortoises gathered around water-holes. A thermometer in the black sand went off the scale at 137 degrees, which was perfect for the piles of 'disgusting clumsy Lizards' asleep on the shore rocks. The 'imps of darkness' someone christened them, and they were certainly strange sea-weed-eating creatures. But because marine iguanas in the museums had been mislabelled as mainland South American, Darwin did not realize that they were unique to the Galapagos.

The birds knew not man, nor any predator, and seemed 'tame.' Darwin approached a hawk and actually poked it with his gun-barrel. Where was the sport here? The slaughter was disgustingly easy, and eighteen giant tortoises, some weighing eighty pounds, were dragged aboard as fresh meat. The mockingbirds looked like the Chilean species; they 'are lively, inquisitive, active, run fast, [and] frequent houses to pick the meat' left to dry, but their song seemed different.[11] The flowers were ugly, like everything else. If the birds had a South American aspect, perhaps these blooms did too.

Volcanoes he had expected, and he was not disappointed. Inert cones, often sixty at a time rising fifty feet into the air, gave it the look of an industrial wasteland or 'the Iron furnaces near Wolverhampton.' Some of the more 'ancient chimneys' were covered in vegetation, others just 'naked, bare' lava streams, rough and uncolonized. The whole primordial scene was capped by the plodding tortoises, seven feet in circumference, chomping on prickly pears. He had anticipated some sedimentary strata, like those in Europe, but no. This was a new world, reflecting only its molten subterranean origins, and so alien that he might have been standing on 'some other planet.'

The strangeness was completed by the lack of insect swarms. His first thought was that the islands, so far out in the ocean, 'are effectively excluded from receiving any migratory colonists.' As a consequence the majority of birds were seed-eating finches, fitted to the lowland scrub and with short heavy-duty bills – like a bullfinch's – to peck seeds from the 'iron-like lava.'[12]

The Galapagos was a gulag, and on crossing to Charles Island on the 23rd the crew entered a settlement of over 200 exiles deported from Ecuador, run by an English acting-governor. They had chosen the best spot. Here, four miles inland and at 1000 feet, the southerly trade winds were cooling and the plantain groves as 'green as England in the Spring time.' But it was still a dicey 'Robinson Crusoe life,' cursed by lack of fresh water and cut off, except for passing whalers. Tortoise was the staple meat, huge reptiles that six men could not carry. But these were no longer so plentiful. Once a frigate's company could drag 200 to the shore, now only a fraction could be caught. Stocks were depleting fast, and the governor calculated that they would last barely twenty more years.

The prisoners believed that each island had its peculiar tortoise, varying fractionally in shell-shape from the next. Even the Vice-Governor boasted that he could tell the island by looking at the tortoise. It would have been easy for Darwin to collect representative samples: even on Charles Island empty saddleback carapaces were lying around, ignominiously used as flower pots. But he paid no heed and collected no tortoises, thinking the reptiles to be foreign imports. He assumed that the buccaneers had brought them from their real island homes in the Indian Ocean as a food source. By contrast, he *did* notice that the mockingbirds here differed from those on

Chatham. And from this time on he carefully kept his mockingbirds separate and tagged them by island.[13]

On the 28th they put in at Albemarle, the largest island of the archipelago. Here he was greeted by an even more charred smoke-stack landscape, with jets of steam hissing from laval cones. Darwin trekked off into the desolation, searching for fresh water. In this 'arid & sterile' scrub huge ragged lizards, land iguanas weighing up to fifteen pounds, scurried to their burrows with a 'quick & clumsy gait.' He thought these yellow and red iguanas 'hideous,' fit only for the pot, and on one day 'forty were collected' ('not bad eating,' was FitzRoy's most favourable comment on these unique lizards).[14] Water was rationed now, and in the baking sun Darwin could find only small pits in the rocks holding a gallon or so. These water-holes attracted all the finches, making it easy to compare them together. But he did not bother to catch any in the baking heat, assuming that – unlike the anomalous mockingbirds – they were similar on all the islands.

They sailed north to James Island, where Darwin's party bivouacked in Buccaneers' Cove and, like the old pirates, lived on tortoises fried in their own fat. He spent two days collecting, shooting mockingbirds (which looked different again), and trekking high up the fern-covered sides of the craters. Yard-long tortoises could be seen plodding along, using well-beaten paths to the permanent rain-water pools higher up the slopes. Darwin rode on one, which drank regardless of its rider. Unfortunately, his mounts here were like the tortoises on Chatham, the only others he had seen, which convinced him that their differences really had been exaggerated.

Water was at a premium on these lava outcrops. Sweltering, thirsty days were spent collecting; it was often 93° in the shade, and Darwin was parched. Were it not for a passing American whaler giving the party three casks of water, 'we should have been distressed.'[15] This American kindliness was typical of the voyage, the Yankees' 'hearty manner' a contrast to English reserve on the high seas.

On all the islands finches predominated in the lowland thickets, but Darwin had trouble telling them apart. The plumage was almost identical: the 'old cock birds' seemed to be black in his samples, and the females brown. FitzRoy, Covington, and others were making their own collections, and some caught black females, confusing him more. Nor were the birds' habits distinguishable, for 'they feed together . . . in large irregular flocks.' At the end of his stay he threw his hands up, admitting an 'inexplicable confusion.'

In all he shot six types of finch from three islands, and his samples from two of those were mixed together. Still, his difficulties left him feeling that these birds were 'very curious.' During his final days he had been told that many trees too, like the tortoises, were unique to each island. But by then his collecting was finished – he had tagged his specimens in a desultory manner and had rarely bothered to label by island. It had not seemed important. The mockingbirds were the exception; he had kept his specimens from four islands separate.

He had also caught a wren, several 'Icterus' (members of the oriole/blackbird family), and some heavy-billed 'Gross-beaks.' He had picked every plant in flower for Henslow, and he continued to wonder whether, like the mockingbirds, the 'Flora belongs to America' – whether, to use Lyell's phrase, its 'district or "centre of creation"' lay on the mainland.[16]

FitzRoy stocked up with pigs, vegetables, and thirty more tortoises from Chatham Island, enough to see them across the Pacific. Darwin and his servant Covington each came away with a baby giant tortoise, not for the pot though, but as pets.

On 20 October, after five weeks on the Galapagos, they put out to sea, thankful to be off. Darwin found it hard to imagine tropical islands 'so entirely useless to man or the larger animals.'[17] They were too hostile, too recently emerged from the sea. The birds, reptiles, and plants had seemed curious, but not riveting.

But at sea he began to examine his corpses more closely – or at least the mockingbirds. The Chatham and Albemarle birds looked similar, but the other two were different. So he had '2 or 3 varieties,' he noted as the *Beagle* sailed to Tahiti. 'Each variety is constant in its own Island. - This is a parallel fact to the one mentioned about the Tortoises.' But he still assumed that these were insignificant anomalies, and across the Pacific he ate his way through the tortoises and watched the cook dump their tell-tale carapaces overboard.[18]

Once outside the gloomy South American region, the long voyage to Tahiti was sunny and swift. 'Boundless ocean' could be boring, but to Darwin it verged on the 'sublime,' and the trade winds blew the *Beagle* the 3200 miles to Polynesia in just over three weeks. On 9 November the terns and gulls heralded the first of the Low Islands, although Darwin was not impressed. 'Uninteresting,' he called it, just 'a long brilliantly white beach' overhung by coconut palms. The monsoons and heat only aggravated his homesick mood. Even Tahiti, the jewel of the South Seas, which they saw on the 15th, looked uninviting from a distance. But he bucked up on spotting the tropical luxuriance, and the 'laughing merry faces' of the milling Tahitians in their canoes.

They were met by a missionary, and almost immediately Darwin sallied off on foot, delighting in the luxuriance. The island was 'a most beautiful orchard of Tropical plants' – bananas, coconuts, spreading breadfruit trees, and cultivated yams and pineapples. Even the delicious guavas were growing like weeds. The people welcomed him into their homes, with friendly expressions and 'an intelligence which shows they are advancing in civilization.' Their dress was advancing too, shirts and coloured cotton loin cloths. The men were still tattooed, but it was 'an elegant & pleasing effect.' The women wore camellias behind their ears and had taken to shaving their crowns, leaving just a ring of hair; quite why, Darwin laconically noted, no one knew: 'it is the fashion & that is answer enough at Tahiti as well as Paris.'

He went with a guide for a two-day climb into the craggy volcanic peaks, where he was emotionally lost among the ravines and precipices. He collected ferns for Henslow, weaved through groves of wild bananas, and was mesmerized by the view out to sea, where breakers marked the encircling reef. His guide baked strips of banana, fish, and beef in leaves, but would eat his meal only after fervent prayer. 'He prayed as a Christian should do,' Darwin noted, 'with fitting reverence, & without fear of ridicule or ostentation.'

The missions had done their work well, but then they had had plenty of time. The islands had long been visited; there were Tahitians alive who remembered Capt. Cook, and others who told stories of the mutiny on Bligh's *Bounty*. A mission printing press had been installed for almost twenty years, and an elder had spent forty years translating the Bible.[19] Also the islands were dry, alcohol was banned and drunkenness was non-existent.

Darwin was impressed by the 'high & respectable' standing of these men, and their successes were tangible. It came as something of a surprise: books he had read painted a much bleaker picture – of downtrodden natives living under a tyrannical regime. The missionaries' characters had been impugned so often that he felt bound to speak in their favour. Even their daughters had been subject to scurrilous attacks, yet their 'appearance & manners showed that they had been properly educated.' And so 'many merry, happy faces' among the Tahitians gave the lie to the slander that they were a crushed and demoralized race under the churches' heel. Given that twenty years previously, bloody wars, licentiousness, infanticide, 'human sacrifices & the power of an idolatrous priesthood' were reputed to be the norm, the present 'state of morality & religion is highly creditable' to the missioners. Even if the 'virtue of the [Tahitian] women' were still open to question, Christianity had achieved much. Would that such missions extended to wilder shores, making them safe for shipwrecked sailors.

Thinking of shipwrecks, Darwin canoed out to the reef, to collect 'the pretty branching Corals,' amazed that these 'tiny architects' could build such mountainous rings around the island. FitzRoy's work completed (he was policing the seas, collecting $3000 compensation for a ship plundered two years previously in the Low Islands), Queen Pomare of Tahiti was entertained aboard on 25 November. The *Beagle*, 'dressed with flags,' was lit up by sky rockets launched in her honour. She 'is an awkquard [sic] large woman, without any beauty, gracefulness or dignity of manners,' Darwin observed. Her Majesty had 'only one royal attribute, viz a perfect immoveability of expression.' The next evening, money collected, the *Beagle* pulled out in a gentle breeze and steered for New Zealand.

The crossing took three weeks, with nothing but deep blue sea, an immensity of it; but 'every league ... which we travel onwards, is one league nearer to England.'[20] The time was lost in writing. He drew up his coral theory in full, balancing the rise of South America with the fall of the Pacific, making the atolls mark the disappearing peaks of a drowning oceanic basin.

They sighted the northern tip of New Zealand on 19 December, and two days later were sailing in to the Bay of Islands. Darwin looked out at the verdant hills dotted with tidy whitewashed houses, interspersed by 'diminutive & paltry' native huts. The cottages were part of a twenty-year-old missionary settlement; each one, with roses around the door, a reminder of England.

The hills were a different matter: fern-covered and impenetrable, and dotted with stockades once defended by Maoris during their wars. The natives struck Darwin as a fearsome people: 'a more warlike race of inhabitants could be found in no part of the world.' But Englishmen were now safe, thanks to the missions – and to the fact that their meat was too salty, or at least 'not so sweet as Maori flesh.' Cannibalism had been stamped out in this region and, as Covington reported, heads could no longer be bought, 'though much sought after.' Still Darwin was contemptuous. These people were barely above the Fuegians in his yardstick of 'civilization.' Peering down from his privileged perch, he dismissed one chief for his 'horrid & ferocious expression,' and another as 'a notorious murderer & to boot an arrant coward.' Shifty looks betrayed a fierce cunning, and tattooed faces revealed a base nature. Was there 'in the whole of New Zealand a person with the face & mien of the old Tahitian chief'?

But that said, the English miscreants were even worse. The missionaries took him to Kororarika, a settlement dominated by escaped convicts from New South Wales and dedicated 'to drunkenness & all kinds of vice.' The missionaries had built a chapel in this den of iniquity, but such were the threats that 'the only protection which they need . . . is from the native Chiefs against Englishmen!'[21]

These 'worthy men' had done their best, and the weeks in Tahiti and New Zealand convinced FitzRoy and Darwin that the missions were a success. For both, Christianity came as a civilizing package, and most of all they applauded the noblemindedness of the missionaries. In these outposts of empire, a genteel class of white man was making shores safe for Britannia's sailors, preaching good manners and promoting good government. Their 'political agency' was needed wherever ships put in and lands were being settled.

FitzRoy and Darwin looked through Christian spectacles at the heathen hordes. Both used an inflexible 'scale' of civilization, with progress measured against the European ideal. But this was not the only way that indigenous tribes could be viewed. Some travellers, no less than the 'licentious' socialists at home, looked more sympathetically on foreign cultures, and damned the missions for foisting Christianity on peoples for whom it was ill adapted. Part of Darwin and FitzRoy's target was Augustus Earle, the artist who had shipped out in 1833, leaving a copy of his *Narrative of a Nine Months' Residence in New Zealand* on board. Written before the voyage, its attack on the local missions had Darwin and FitzRoy indignant. Darwin now knew 'without doubt' that the 'very missionaries, who are accused of coldness . . . always treated [Earle] with far more civility, than his open licentiousness could have given reason to expect.'[22]

After passing the native hovels on his walks, Darwin was always pleased to see 'an English farm house & its well dressed fields, placed there as if by an enchanter's wand.' These mission houses were surrounded by well-kept gardens of flowers, fruit and vegetables, threshing barns, forges, and 'in the middle was that happy mixture of pigs & poultry which may be seen so comfortably lying together in every English farm yard.' The Maori servant girls were 'clean tidy & healthy [in] appearance, like that of dairy maids in England.' Darwin moved between the farms, sipping tea, reminded of home. 'I never saw a nicer or more merry group: – & to think that this was in the centre of the land of cannibalism, murder & all atrocious crimes!' Thanks to the missionaries, Darwin told his devout sister Caroline, white men can now 'walk with as much safety as in England,' surrounded by tribes who 'were the most ferocious savages probably on the face of the earth.'

Where the Tahiti missions sought to improve the mind, the New Zealand ones taught farming practice, although the 'moral effect' on the Maoris was the same. It was clear that the very example 'of the Missionary is the enchanter's wand.' How could the savage radicals at home damn such enterprises and demand that the natives be left to their own devices? More missions were needed, more colonization. He was mulling this over on Christmas Day, convinced that the conversion of the 'Heathen' alone brings its reward: 'so excellent is the Christian faith, that the outward conduct of the believers is said most decidedly to have been improved by its doctrines.'

A Christmas collection was taken up. Grateful for the week's hospitality and eager to enlarge this outpost, FitzRoy, Darwin, and the officers chipped in £15 towards the building of more churches. Then they bade farewell to the missionaries on 30 December and set sail for Australia.[23]

The crossing took thirteen days and after all the hovels and filth of native New Zealand, Sydney Cove was a sight for sore eyes: large trading ships, harbour warehouses, well-stocked shops – and 'Wool, Wool ... the cry from one end of the country to the other.' The broad streets were a mad crush, 'gigs, phaetons & carriages with livery servants' clattered everywhere. After South America, so singularly devoid of gentlemen, Darwin could only marvel at Sydney's wealth and ostentation. Fortunes were for the making in this 'paradise to the Worshippers of Mammon.'

'Ancient Rome, in her Imperial grandeur, would not have been ashamed of such' a colony. Fine houses were built on shipping or construction fortunes. Land was rocketing in value to £8000 an acre – the best double that. A convict once thrashed on a cartwheel now had 'an income from 12 to 15000 pounds per annum.' Another – the 'Rothschild of Botany Bay' – was worth half a million. It left everything 'villainously dear,' Charles wrote home, punning furiously, explaining why he had drawn another 'bill for 100£.' The population of 23,000 was rising astronomically; 'not even near London or Birmingham is there an aspect of such rapid growth.' Nothing, in short, had prepared him for Sydney. It was high among the '100 Wonders of the world,' and he put it down to the 'Giant force of the parent country.' 'It is a most magnificent testimony to the power of the British nation: here . . . scores of years have effected many times more than centuries in South America. – My first feeling was to congratulate myself that I was born an Englishman.'[24]

On a sunny Saturday, 16 January 1836, he set off with a guide, heading a hundred miles into the interior. They walked on macadamized roads, one of the benefits of forced labour; and he passed convict 'Iron gangs' in their yellow and grey prison garb, hard at work in the heat. Then he noticed the ale houses, seventeen in the first fifteen miles. No wonder half of the government revenues came from duty on alcohol. (Or that the gaols were full, and stocks were appearing on Sydney streets, for confining 'ladies and gentlemen who cannot pay the usual fee for indulging too freely at the shrine of Bacchus.') Even thirty-five miles away, he still saw 'substantial houses' and fenced off pastures. The scanty-leaved gum trees left the 'woods light & shadowless.' It was high summer and everywhere was dry and parched. The crops looked precarious and he could see why they periodically failed.

He stopped a 'good-humoured' group of 'Aboriginal Blacks' who gave him a display of spear-throwing for a shilling. It was their cheeriness that left him doubting that they were 'such utterly degraded beings as usually represented.'[25] What was their fate in a civilizing world? He knew that they were being destroyed by the white man's scourges, measles and liquor, and that their children's lives depended far more on immediate food availability than in Europe. It was a question he pondered as he trekked on into the Blue Mountains, passing wool-carts and scrubby eucalyptus woods. The bay view was magnificent, and even at 3400 feet he found fifteen-bed inns, much like those he had stopped at in North Wales with Sedgwick.

He visited one of the huge, spartan, sheep stations, run by a foreman with convict labour. Here 'forty profligate men' worked like slaves, yet without the same 'claim for compassion.' He launched out one morning, hunting kangaroos with the station's greyhounds. But he managed to catch only a potoroo (a rat kangaroo), although this did give him his first good look at a marsupial. Lack of big kangaroos was a sign of how destructive these settlements were to the wildlife. And to the aborigines. His mind kept turning back to the cheery blacks. It was a sad refrain, the thought that 'the White Man . . . seems predestined to inherit the country,' dispossessing the aboriginal 'children.'

Lying on a sunny bank, he reflected on the stark divide between the marsupials here and normal placental mammals. They were so anatomically different. 'An unbeliever . . . might exclaim "Surely two distinct Creators must have been [at] work",' each producing a perfect – but unique – creation. What he saw on the riverbank that evening might have required a third Creator in the pantheon. The station manager took him 'Platypi' shooting. They glimpsed several of these 'extraordinary' web-footed, duck-billed beasts snuffling along the water's edge. The manager 'actually killed one,' Darwin exclaimed. 'I consider it a great feat, to be in at the death of so wonderful an animal.' He picked up the limp corpse, examining its bill, surprised to find it soft and sensitive, rather than hard as in the stuffed specimens. Even odder, many colonists believed that the platypus laid leathery eggs like a reptile and incubated them in a nest, although the debate was still raging in London and Paris (with his old teacher Robert Grant and the Parisian Geoffroy St Hilaire taking the colonists' side).

Of course the notion of many Creators was preposterous, fit only for the primitive Maori or Aborigine. And Nature quickly proved it. He watched an ant-lion, a huge-jawed larval insect, which lived buried at the bottom of a conical pit of sand. To catch its prey, it flicked up jets of sand, causing a sand-slide which brought unwary ants to its gaping jaws. European ant-lions did exactly the same. Now what would a 'Disbeliever say to this? Would any two workmen ever hit on so beautiful, so simple & yet so artificial a contrivance'?[26] No, it was the most telling proof of a single Creative hand at work over the globe. Darwin had argued Paley's classic case, from one perfect design to one perfect Designer.

On 20 January – after suffering 120° temperatures and oven-blast winds – he arrived at Bathhurst, a troop station on the Macquarie River. This too was sheep country, with good pastures in the river valley, although in high summer he found the land parched and the river little more than drying ponds. All around bush fires were raging, and the next day 'we passed through large tracts of country in flames.'

On the return he visited Capt. King, the *Beagle*'s former commander, having last seen him at Plymouth the day the ship sailed. King's father had been governor of the colony, and the Captain had been born here. Darwin found him on his 4000-acre farm, thirty miles from Sydney, writing an account of his own South American voyage. Young Midshipman King was here too, having left the *Beagle* to join his father and mother (who had not seen her son for ten years). The Captain's collections were extensive; Darwin had seen them at the Zoological Society in London when he picked up

King's preserving tips. They shared an interest in barnacles and molluscs, and they spent a pleasant day walking around the farm, talking over 'the Natural History of T[ierra]. del Fuego.'[27]

By the end, Darwin was beginning to pall of Sydney society. The wealth had initially blinded him to its faults. The community was split, the rich emancipists vying with the free settlers, whom they considered interlopers. Who would want to walk on streets 'where every other man is sure to be somewhere between a petty rogue & bloodthirsty villain'? The climate was splendid, but intellectual stimulation was nil. Grandfather Erasmus, celebrating the growth of Sydney forty-five years earlier, had waxed poetic:

> Here future Newtons shall explore the skies.
> Here future Priestleys, future Wedgwoods rise.

Quite how Darwin could not see, considering the tiny bookshops with empty shelves. The prospect of being waited on by convicts was abhorrent. The female servants were worst, with the 'vilest expressions' hiding 'equally vile ideas.' No attempt was made to reform the criminals' morality, and, as a young offender told him, 'they know no pleasure beyond sensuality, and in this they are not gratified.' The convicts did not know any better. What really shocked him was to see so many of the higher ranks living in the same 'open profligacy.' It was an immoral slave-run economy, generating huge profits. Nothing but 'severe necessity,' he concluded, would 'compel me to emigrate.'

Society was pleasanter in Hobart, in the newly-renamed Tasmania. This was more than could be said for weather. The *Beagle* docked in the eponymous Storm Bay on 5 February. The town itself did not live up to the 'Panorama' pictures that Darwin had viewed in London. There were few large houses, although some of the farms were appealing. Polite English society was always a relief, and here at least it was not contaminated with 'wealthy Convicts.'

The finest houses as usual opened their doors. The Attorney-General provided Italian music, beautiful décor, 'dinner most elegant with *respectable*! (although of course all Convicts) Servants.' The Surveyor-General, George Frankland, offered something even better, a tour of the ancient limestone quarries. Darwin obtained more lamp-shells to compare with those from the Falklands and Wales. He spent his twenty-seventh birthday catching skinks and snakes. He took many flatworms, and over 119 species of insects. (Among them were dung beetles that he fished out of cow pats. This itself was odd, for the dairy herds had been introduced for only thirty years. How had the beetles adapted so quickly?) Dinner at the Frankland household was the 'most agreeable evening since leaving home.'[28] Frankland was in his ninth year charting land for the immigrants, who were now flooding in. But there was a sinister underside to this colonial expansion. The land had been fórcibly cleared, and Darwin saw no Tasmanian aborigines. Their genocide was almost complete, and the last 210 had been herded on to an island. It was the most graphic evidence that white immigration was the death-knell for indigenous races.

Still, if he ever emigrated anywhere, this would be the place. But now his heart was set on home. Every merchant ship starting for England left him with 'a dangerous inclination to bolt.' The voyage was 'reduced simply to Chronometrical Measurements,' and he saw these months as 'so much existence obliterated from the page of life.' Only the thought of the atolls in the Indian Ocean kept him going. 'There never was a Ship, so full of home-sick heroes.' 'I will take good care,' he moaned to Fox, never again 'to volunteer as Philosopher (my accustomed title) even to a line of Battle Ship.'[29]

He might 'hate every wave of the ocean' but the sea was still supplying him with exotic specimens. The intrigues of colonial life ashore were as nothing to the intriguing colonial life on the shoreline. He was fascinated by the coral animals, and walked along the Hobart coast collecting marine plants. In tidal pools he turned up broken tufts of encrusting algae, budding like Chiloé apple trees. So, plants high and low could propagate by cutting. And the same was true for the branching corals, the stony reef-forming animals – they too could grow from broken stems. As the *Beagle* dropped anchor on 6 March in King George's Sound, on Australia's south-western coast, Darwin was lost in his notes on the encrusting plants and corals. He was tying these primitive life-forms ever tighter; placing them close to the zero point, where the plants and animals meet.

As for the landfall, he had never spent a 'more dull, uninteresting time' than the eight days here. King George's Sound was a neglected outpost, not ten years old, a potential penal colony that had gone to pot, eclipsed by the new Swan River settlement (now Perth). FitzRoy had even been inclined to 'put the helm up' and move on at the sight of the 'cheerless' straggling houses, but duty prevailed. Darwin did attend an aboriginal dance, performed by the white-painted 'Cockatoo men.' To an outsider it seemed like so much marching and stamping. A 'most rude barbarous scene' it might have been, with them 'all moving in hideous harmony,' but he could not help liking these 'good humoured' aborigines, so perfectly at ease and 'in such high spirits.'

In his last few days on the continent he diligently collected shells and fish, caught a native Australian bush rat, and took notes on the grass-trees and granite outcrops. But there was no disguising the disappointment. The soil was sandy and poor, the vegetation coarse, the views uninteresting, the kangaroos scarce: he had nothing good to say, except that he never wished 'to walk again in so uninviting a country.'

The *Beagle* departed in a storm and ran aground. It was a fitting end. As the ship finally refloated Darwin waved goodbye to the colony with a grand lament. 'Farewell Australia, you are a rising infant & doubtless some day will reign a great princess in the South; but you are too great & ambitious for affection, yet not great enough for respect; I leave your shores without sorrow or regret.'[30]

13

Temples of Nature

By 1 APRIL 1836 the ship had made the Keeling or Cocos Islands in the Indian Ocean – coral paradises below the equator, 700 miles from Java. These were real atolls, Darwin's first. The mountain top had submerged, leaving the reef encircling an emerald lagoon, shallow enough for the sun's rays to sparkle on the sea floor.

From the ship, nothing but 'glittering' sandy beaches fringed by coconut trees could be seen. But on shore, Darwin discovered a complete coconut economy. The islands had been colonized by British traders and freed Malay slaves, who lived off a sole export, coconut oil. In fact, everything lived off coconuts. The pigs and poultry were fattened on them, and even 'a huge land crab' specialized on a coconut diet, which was 'as curious a piece of adaptation and instinct as I ever heard of.'

The reef itself he ranked 'amongst the wonderful objects of this world.' He spent days up to his waist, making notes on brain corals and branching corals, and the fishes darting in and out. He was lost in admiration for the hues and tints, and the brilliant flashes of colour. Under the microscope these living corals posed more of a problem: however hard he looked, he could not see any discrete polyp animals. They seemed to consist of a mass of 'fleshy matter' spread 'over the whole surface.'[1] Moreover, the stony framework of the coral appeared to grow as it did in the encrusting algae. He was now convinced that the lowest animals and plants practically touched at this primitive level. He had come round to the position of his Lamarckian teacher Robert Grant ten years earlier: the plant and animal kingdoms had a common starting point.

Evenings were spent stretched out under the palms, pondering these taxonomic profundities, watching the hermit crabs. No one knows 'how delicious it is to be seated in such a shade & there drink the cool pleasant fruit of the Cocoa nut.' He was convinced about something else. Having examined an atoll, he was certain of his reef theory.

The Sea Lords had instructed FitzRoy to use any means 'that ingenuity can devise of discovering at what depth the coral formation begins.' He too was looking for clues to the reef's origin. A mile out he took soundings, but even here the sea floor had dropped away. The line was fed out 7000 feet, and still it did not touch bottom. The reef was clearly built on an oceanic mountain top. The 'circular wall' of coral had risen as the mountain had submerged, leaving only a vivid green lagoon, as Darwin's theory predicted.[2]

The *Beagle* stocked up with provisions – fresh water from the island well, coconuts, fish, and turtles to top up the diminishing Galapagos tortoise stocks – ready for its journey to Mauritius. The homesick heroes set sail once more, knowing that barely six months of the voyage remained. Darwin, keen to cover the port calls quickly, logged wearily, 'There is no country which has now any attractions for us, without it is seen right astern.'

On the high seas again, he spent three weeks 'totally rewriting' his geological notes, trying for fluency and not exactly succeeding. Even mooting the problem to his sisters left him in a syntactic mess. 'I am just now beginning to discover the difficulty of expressing one's ideas on paper. As long as it consists solely of description it is pretty easy; but where reasoning comes into play, to make a proper connection, a clearness & a moderate fluency, is to me, as I have said, a difficulty of which I had no idea.' Never mind, 'I am in high spirits about my geology.' He was feeling cut off by this point and wanting familial reassurance. No mail had reached him in New Zealand or Australia. In fact he had not received a letter in thirteen months, and he wondered how his latest geological news was being digested. 'I look forward with no little anxiety to the time when Henslow, putting on a grave face, shall decide on the merits of my notes. If he shakes his head in a disapproving manner: I shall then know that I had better at once give up science, for science will have given me up.'

He remained 'a martyr to sea-sickness.' It never let up entirely, although FitzRoy noted that 'he recovers at the sight of land.' This time the mountains of Mauritius appearing over the horizon did the trick. From far off the island had an 'air of perfect elegance,' and close up its 'beautiful scenery' and cloud-topped peaks reinforced the welcoming feeling.

Darwin toured the French-speaking town of Port Louis on 30

April, delighting in its opera and its well-stocked bookshops. After more than four years of travelling, it was wonderful to spend 'so idle & dissipated a time.' The island was exotic, full of 'glowing bewitching scenes,' the perfect place for romance. What an 'opportunity for writing love letters,' he mused; 'Oh that I had a sweet Virginia to send an inspired Epistle to.' He paced its multi-racial streets, a mélange of Europeans, 'noble looking' Indians, and Madagascar blacks. Massive sugar exports had paid for tarmac roads and Darwin was able to travel easily round the picturesque island. Not that he actually needed roads; part of his tour was by elephant, owned by a surveyor who put his house and pachyderm at Darwin's disposal.[3]

The last leg of the Pacific crossing was the longest, and on 31 May a gale blew them into Simon's Bay at the Cape of Good Hope, on the tip of Africa. The next day Darwin hired a gig and headed the twenty-two miles to Cape Town, past desert, past lumbering bullock-wagons pulled by a dozen oxen, and then past fine houses and plantations, set off against Table Mountain. Cape Town was a 'great inn' on the 'highway to the east,' its boarding houses packed with merchants and sailors of every nationality. The town was becoming anglicised, and everybody spoke English, to the consternation of the Dutch. By now Darwin was getting a sense of empire: of the endless colonies seeded around the globe in which 'little embryo Englands are hatching.' Here, as elsewhere, the indigenous peoples were retreating. He saw few Negroes and even fewer Hottentots, 'the ill-treated aboriginals of the country.' Some were in service. He actually had an impeccably dressed and mannered Hottentot groom to guide him – white gloves and all – to the outlying villages.

During his second week he met with scientific society. Army surgeons took him on geological rambles, and astronomers conducted him across the southern skies. One astronomer he wanted to meet above all others: his hero, Sir John Herschel, whose book he had devoured at Cambridge. Herschel had been here for two years, mapping the constellations, and had bought a 'comfortable country house,' situated amid firs and oak trees, six miles outside Cape Town. 'I have heard so much about his eccentric but very amiable manners,' Darwin said, 'that I have a high curiosity to see the great Man.'

He did not have to wait long. With FitzRoy he called on Herschel on 3 June. Sir John was 'exceedingly good natured,' inviting them to dinner, which enabled Darwin to confirm that his manners were 'rather awful.' The guests were given a tour of the 'pretty garden full of Cape bulbs.' They wandered the grounds, flanked by fir trees, the imposing Table Mountain looming up in the distance. All the while they talked volcanic eruptions and heaving continents, and Darwin discovered that these crustal convolutions were just as dear to Herschel's heart. Sir John was intrigued by the mechanics of subterranean movement. He had already written to Lyell explaining them, his interest too fired by the *Principles of Geology*. Perhaps Herschel and Darwin said more about Lyell's gradually evolving landscapes. In his letter, Herschel had criticized Lyell for not grasping the nettle on that 'mystery of mysteries,' the successive appearance of new species on the earth. If landscapes change gradually, shaped by forces no different from those of today, shouldn't life be understood the same way? Weren't the births of species just as natural? Sir John thought so. Whether or not they touched on this ticklish subject, the meeting struck Darwin as 'the most memorable event which, for a long period, I have had the good fortune to enjoy.'⁴

The news from home fortified his scientific resolve. At the Cape a letter from Catherine finally caught up with him, bringing the word that his name was on the tip of naturalists' tongues in England. Unknown to Charles, Henslow had edited ten of his technical letters on South American geology and *printed* them as a booklet for private distribution. Everyone had been revelling in them for six months. The Doctor was so pleased that he had given away half a dozen copies, allowing the Foxes, Owens, Wedgwoods and local gentry to read of his son's discoveries. Henslow had sung Charles's praises to the family, leaving them all enormously proud. Charles was delighted to hear it, but horrified to contemplate his dashed-off prose in print. He had 'written to Henslow in the same careless manner' as he had written home; what on earth did it read like set in type? 'But, as the Spaniard says, "No hay remedio"' – nothing can be done.

FitzRoy had more evangelical concerns. Attacks on missionaries were as common in Cape Town as elsewhere. Having seen the Pacific missions' successes, he was all for their defence; after all, Christianizing the Tierra savages had been his starting point for the voyage. In Cape Town he was asked to pen a piece for the *South African Christian Recorder*. At sea on 18 June, heading northward into the southern Atlantic, he wrote an open letter on the 'Moral State of Tahiti' for the paper. Extracts from Darwin's diary were patched in, on the manners of the missionaries, and the temperance and morality of the natives. A highlight was Darwin's description of his guide in the mountains, cooking bananas and falling to his knees before eating, praying 'as a christian should,' with reverence. As Darwin had written at the time: 'Those travellers, who hint that a Tahitian prays only when the eyes of the missionary are fixed on him, might have profited by similar evidence.'[5] The piece was finished at sea, and posted back on a passing ship for publication.

He was only four months from home, and it was time for assessments and reflections. In the Atlantic he drew up catalogues of his collections – listing specimen numbers, locations, and descriptions. He put together twelve catalogues over a few weeks, one for each class – 'Fish in Spirits of Wine,' 'Animals [that is, mammals],' 'Reptiles in Spirits of Wine,' 'Ornithology,' 'Insects in Spirits of Wine,' and so on. He was determined that his precious skins and pickled specimens would be properly named and described, each by an expert. Without names, his insect authority William Kirby had warned, the 'zoological treasures' shipped home on surveying vessels were worthless. They might as well be 'left to perish in their native deserts or forests' as grow 'mouldy in our drawers or repositories.'[6] That fate would not befall Darwin's cargo. The catalogues were to aid the specialists who took over his haul in England.

Listing his Galapagos mockingbirds, three of them different, each to its island, he began mulling over the implications.

> When I recollect, the fact that . . . the Spaniards can at once pronounce, from which Island any Tortoise may have been brought. When I see these Islands in sight of each other, & possessed of but a scanty stock of animals, tenanted by these birds, but slightly differing in structure & filling the same place in Nature, I must suspect they are only varieties . . . If there is the slightest foundation for these remarks the zoology of Archipelagoes – will be well worth examining; for such facts would undermine the stability of Species.[7]

If the buccaneers' imported tortoises varied by island, perhaps the original mockingbird colonists, blown in from Chile, had also dispersed among the islands and become adapted to each. But these were only 'varieties,' and naturalists accepted that variants of a single species could occur naturally. A slight pliancy was even necessary, to allow a species to spread out from its 'centre of creation.' Such suppleness stopped far short of transmutation, but it made Darwin wonder how far a species could be pushed. Herschel's 'mystery of mysteries' might not be arcane.

Home was on everybody's mind. They crossed the Tropic of Capricorn on 29 June – 'for the sixth & last time,' Darwin logged. Nine days later that forbidding rock, St Helena, appeared 'like a huge castle from the ocean.' Or perhaps prison was a more apt comparison, for the island's lava-stream walls seemed to augment the fort's defences and gun emplacements.

The whole island was sombre, with overcast skies and sheets of rain. Here the exiled Napoleon had died in 1821, and Darwin lodged for the five nights a stone's throw from his tomb. If old Boney's ghost haunted this dreary place, Darwin laughed to Henslow on 9 July, as rain lashed his windows, it was a perfect night for his 'wandering.' There was something quite incongruous about 'so great a spirit' – the conqueror of Europe – resting next to cottages by a roadside on this desolate rock.[8]

Even more incongruous were the English plants that surrounded him. The whole island was covered with imported species, Darwin noted: gorse and Scotch firs and blackberry brambles were running rampant over the rock fortress, wiping out indigenous species. He wandered the whole island on foot, glad to be off the ship, noting these British invaders. Nor did he miss the fossil shells at 2000 feet. Standard geology texts used these as proof that the island had risen recently. But Darwin was now enough of an expert to diagnose them as *land* shells, and of a now-extinct species.

Onward they voyaged, nearer to home. Five days' sailing brought them to Ascension Island in the middle of the South Atlantic. The only settlement here was a Marine barracks. The navy kept the island like a tightly run ship, with milestones on all roads, and water pumps, tapping natural wells. The water was needed. This was less a rock – or so an old joke went – more a 'cinder' in the ocean, and Darwin was eager to examine the butt of the joke: the red volcanic cones. He paced over the rugged island, staring at nature in all her 'naked hideousness.' Here were signs of primal violence: solidified lava streams, layers of pumice and ash, with 'volcanic bombs' strewn over the surface, white-hot missiles blown out of the exploding craters.

When they put to sea on 23 July, the *Beagle* should have been heading north. It was not. The ship's compass read WSW. FitzRoy, the infuriating perfectionist, had plotted a course back to Bahia in Brazil to check his longitude measurements. Darwin logged, with mild understatement, the crew's 'discomfiture & surprise,' and carried on cataloguing his shells. His sisters were already wondering 'whether you will have had sufficient travelling to serve you for life: & I think the Yes's Yes's generally carry it.' Certainly his frustration was apparent by this point, and he told them so. 'This zig-zag manner of proceeding is very grievous; it has put the finishing stroke to my feelings. I loathe, I abhor the sea.'[9]

Sailing time was only a week to Bahia, but it was seven days of gritted teeth. 'The novelty & surprise' were gone, Darwin lamented as he took in Brazil's 'wild luxuriance' once more. For five days in early August he twiddled his thumbs, filled his diary, and forayed into the forest, eating mangos and bananas, listening to the whining cicadas, watching the haphazard flight of tropical butterflies for the last time. The impression of the jungle, like 'one great wild, untidy, luxuriant hot house,' would remain with him for ever. He took a final walk, trying to fix the picture in his mind. Each of the 'thousand beauties' composing it would fade, yet – 'like a tale heard in childhood' – they would leave a feeling of 'the glories of another world.'

On 6 August they started for home again, and Darwin settled in to catalogue his hundreds of insects. But the weather closed in and forced them into Pernambuco further up the coast. He again whiled away his time, examining the mangrove swamps and the reef, anxious to be off. The anchor was weighed on the 17th, and the ship pitched furiously into a tropical storm. He was finally 'on the road to England' and no 'tedious misery' could dampen his spirits at the prospect. He swung in his hammock, once more planning the carriages he would take to Shropshire, and imagining the look on his sisters' faces.

They crossed the Equator on 21 August, and took on stores at St Jago early in September, mooring alongside slavers plying their evil trade. On 9 September the ship crossed the Tropic of Cancer into the temperate north. The quartermasters picked up more provisions on the island of Terceira in the Azores. While the barrels were rolling aboard, Darwin borrowed a horse from the Consul and galloped off – past Welsh scenery, country yokels, and English blackbirds – to look at an active crater. He was back on more familiar northern territory, although no fume holes at home had steam whistling from them, unless they be 'cracks in the boiler of a steam engine.' The *Beagle* sailed to the larger island of St Michael's, docking with hundreds of ships laden with oranges, many destined for England. There was still no mail, and they sailed on 25 September, plotting, 'thanks to God, a direct course' for home.

A week would see them off Land's End. In that time one thought kept flitting through his mind: 'How beautiful Shropshire will look.' He became exuberant, carried away, forgetting the lush tropics. The 'scenery of England is ten times more beautiful,' he finally exclaimed. And 'as for your boundless plains & impenetrable forests, who would compare them with the green fields & oak woods of England?' The smiling tropics, what 'precious nonsense.' 'Who admires a lady's face who is always smiling? England is not one of your insipid beauties; she can cry, & frown, & smile, all by turns.'

After five years at sea, emotions were high among the Homeric heroes. They had survived – even sailor Davis's coati mundi. At such times everybody wants to 'commit some act of uncommon folly & extravagance.' 'Man of Wars men' have the right idea, Darwin said, 'when they throw guineas into the sea or light their tobacco pipes with Pound notes, to testify their joy.'[10]

It was a choppy last week, with the blue sea-devils chasing him. Lying down, he reflected on 'the pain & pleasure of our five years' wandering.' Would he advise others to make such a hazardous journey? Yes, but only if they had a particular bent – zoology or geology – otherwise the pleasures are outweighed by the pains, the niggling irritations that assume gigantic proportions – 'the want of room, of seclusion, of rest – the jading feeling of constant hurry – the privation of small luxuries, the comforts of civilization,' and worst by far the incessant seasickness. Even then travellers must have no mere dilettante interest. They must gather and use the harvest of observations: 'some fruit,' he concluded, must 'be reaped.'

Darwin was thinking of his own. The years of sowing and tending were over for him. He had a full record, his diary, 770 pages long, written with one eye to publication and posted home in pieces. Erasmus had revelled in it, and Hensleigh, and both agreed that 'it will make a most interesting book of travels when you publish it.' His sisters had read 'it aloud, and Papa enjoys it extremely except when the dangers you run makes [sic] him shudder.' As Susan said, 'When I have corrected your spelling it will be perfect.'[11]

He had much more: notebooks on esoteric geology (1383 large pages) and zoology (368 pages), new species under his belt – not least the half-eaten carcass of his small rhea – a baby Galapagos tortoise in his cabin, still alive and two inches longer, and crates of bones and birds, rocks and corals, awaiting him at home. The haul had been enormous. His master catalogues listed 1529 species in spirits and 3907 labelled skins, bones, and other dried specimens.[12]

Would these bear fruit? He certainly expected the real labour to start now, and he looked ahead 'with a comical mixture of dread & satisfaction to the amount of work, which remains for me in England.' He knew he would have to live in London to see his specimens farmed out, so he started making plans. He wrote ahead to ask Henslow, 'my first Lord of the Admiralty,' to put him up for a fellowship of the Geological Society, and to Eras to arrange membership of some gentleman's club.[13] Friends already had his name down for the Entomological Society, where he could be lionized for his tropical insects.

He knew that skins and bones and 'isolated facts soon become uninteresting.' Something more had to be done with them. For Kirby, one of the older generation, naming was the be-all and end-all. But Darwin wanted more. He had questions, a million questions – what did the old megatheriums' world look like? Why did they die out? How do animals and birds colonize offshore islands? He already had his grand geological theories, of continental risings and coral-reef formation. He was already 'pushing ideas to their limits,' stretching his views from South America to the globe. And he prophesied that, given his views, the 'geology of [the] whole world will turn out simple.'[14] He had started a lifelong trend, extrapolating from small origins to big outcomes, from microscopic corals to huge reefs, from crustal twitches to the Andes. The world – through Darwin's Lyellian spectacles – was an accumulation of tiny changes: everything natural, gradual, and slow.

No longer the 'lions provider,' he would devour the material itself. Sedgwick had given a résumé of Darwin's conclusions at the Geological Society the previous November. Little was known of South American geology and his view that the pampas 'elevation must have been gradual, or by successive hitches,' caused a great stir. The report in the Saturday *Athenaeum* left the Doctor overjoyed at Charles's 'laurels.' Lyell himself was ecstatic: 'How I long for the return of Darwin!' he regaled Sedgwick; 'I hope you do not mean to monopolise him at Cambridge.' Sedgwick himself realized that 'it was the best thing in the world for him that he went out on the Voyage of Discovery – There was some risk of his turning out an idle man: but his character will now be fixed, & if God spare his life, he will have a great name among the Naturalists of Europe.'[15] Darwin had to justify Sedgwick's faith and live up to Lyell's expectations. He was coming home with more pertinent questions than pickled specimens, and it was up to him to answer them.

The biggest query of all concerned mankind. He could conceive of no more disconcerting sight than 'a real barbarian,' a 'man in his lowest and most savage state.' Idling in his hammock, Darwin mused, 'One's mind hurries back over past centuries, & then asks could our progenitors be such as these?' He had seen every grade in his human 'scale,' from the rude Fuegian – whose 'very signs & expressions are less intelligible to us than those of the domesticated animals' – through the Maoris, Tahitians, and pampas Indians, to the gauchos exterminating them. And all were being eclipsed by the British colonists marching under the Union Jack.

It was a 'scale' calibrated in Eurocentric units; those at the top judged those at the bottom. Darwin ranked people by their willingness to work, to better themselves, to befriend settlers, and to adopt Christian morality. Between the high and low races was a yawning gulf. 'I do not believe it is possible to describe or paint the difference of savage and civilized man. It is the difference between a wild and tame animal.' And, as Jemmy showed, the savage instincts were strong. Fuegians were well adapted to their miserable existence, as Darwin was to a sherry-sipping society. But how could this be? How could the same Creator have made man both so primitive and so sophisticated?

The questions remained, and his spiritual sentiment. He had climbed the Andes, stood on volcanic rims, seen glaciers crashing into the sea, waded along coral reefs, but, with all said and done, none of these exceeded 'in sublimity the primeval forests.' He had sat enraptured in lush creeper-strewn jungles, 'temples filled with the varied productions of the God of Nature.' He had been filled with religious awe: 'No one can stand unmoved in these solitudes, without feeling that there is more in man than the mere breath of his body.' And this is what he now looked forward to, adoration in a new temple.

The parsonage was being crowded out by Nature – overtaken, overgrown. His sisters had guessed as much. 'Papa & we often cogitate over the fire what you will do when you return, as I fear there are but small hopes of your still going into the Church.'[16] Indeed, Charles was already worshipping elsewhere. He had felt the awesome power beneath the fragile crust, in Concepción where the cathedral collapsed, and in the elemental forces that raise and lower continents – forces that reduce man's puny efforts to 'insignificance.' Here indeed was something venerable, even numinous: the very grounds of life itself. His Cambridge professors had placed devotion to Nature's God among the highest. He would go beyond them – study Nature for its own sake, explain its powers, understand its wisdom, justify its ways.

As Falmouth hove in sight on the stormy night of 2 October he had questions enough for a career.

1836–1842

14

A Peacock Admiring His Tail

CHARLES RACED FROM Falmouth to Shrewsbury, dying to
see everyone, bursting, his head 'quite confused with so much delight.'
At full speed the journey took two days, the sweaty horses galloping
past West Country woods and orchards, more 'beautiful & cheerful'
than he ever remembered. 'The stupid people on the coach did not
seem to think the fields one bit greener than usual,' he mused, but –
having seen the tropical forests, the scrubby pampas, the mighty
Cordilleras – he knew 'that the wide world does not contain so
happy a prospect as the rich cultivated land of England.' He finally
reached The Mount late on Tuesday night, 4 October 1836. So late,
in fact, that the family had gone to bed. Even though he had been
away for five years and two days, he slipped quietly into his room
exhausted, without waking them.

The first they knew was when he walked in for breakfast. Surprise
led to ecstasy, with 'poor Charles so full of affection & delight' at
the sight of his father and sisters after so many years. They hugged
and kissed, and the servants got drunk to celebrate Master Charles's
return. The girls worried that he was thin, eighteen pounds
underweight, but no matter, he was home. The endless journey had
ended. Caroline was quietly pleased that the awful swell in the Bay of
Biscay had left his 'hatred of the sea . . . as intense' as ever. But even
she allowed that the trip had served its purpose, for 'he has gained
happiness & interest for the rest of his life.'

In his delirious 'dead and half alive state,' he fired a salvo of letters
to relatives, the smiles practically rising from the page. 'I am so very
happy I hardly know what I am writing,' he burbled to Uncle Jos.
Before he had even found his landlegs Squire Owen had invited him
over with his gun, to see 'whether you are *improved by your travels*'

– and perhaps a spot of shooting was the best way to become a landlubber again.[1]

But was it the same Master Charles? Five years and a world separated him from his old flustered, directionless, insecure self. There was a new confidence, a new earnestness; he had survived on his wits in inhospitable climes, encountered wars and savages, and trekked across the Andes. He was pleased just to be alive. He had become his own man, thinking for himself, confident enough to challenge authority. He had made his mark, proved his worth, and he was proud of what he had achieved. It made him the centre of family attention and he loved it. For the first time he had the unqualified approval of his loved ones. He was scarcely the same person; he had undergone his own reform.

And what had he returned to? What of the country? He was the first to admit that 'all England appears changed.' The reforms had been extensive, entrenching the power of the new urban and industrial centres. So much had the Whigs altered, one wag said, that they obviously 'mean not only to change everything on the earth, but to alter the tides, to suspend the principle of gravitation, and to tear down the solar system.'[2]

Little had been left untouched. The Reform Bill was already four years in place. Only the previous year the Tory town councils had been democratized and invaded by the Whig Dissenters, who were even now electing Unitarian mayors in some cities. Things certainly had changed. Power was tilting, as the iron Duke of Wellington complained, from decent Tory Anglicans to Whig manufacturers, shopkeepers, and atheists.

Also in place was the New Poor Law, so abominated by the swelling army of paupers. Darwin was returning to a re-energized Malthusian world – Malthus's words had finally been acted on: the old outdoor charity had been scrapped, and the poor made to compete or face the workhouse. The workhouses were going up, despite firebrands railing against them as the sign of a vicious law that 'punishes [unfortunates] for being poor.' The New Poor Law was slated as 'a Malthusian bill designed to force the poor to emigrate, to work for lower wages, to live on a coarser sort of food.' The first riots had broken out in the southern counties in May 1835, with poor-law commissioners pelted and magistrates reading the Riot Act. Resistance was ferocious that winter; workhouses were razed and running battles fought with the police.[3]

This Whig restructuring was an assertion of middle-class Malthusian values. Darwin found that Malthus had acquired a new meaning. His name was on everybody's lips, as either Satan or Saviour. His doctrine of population, progress, and pauperism was no longer academic. It was the very kernel of poor-law policy: the stuff of inflammatory oratory, popular defiance, and government propaganda.

Darwin actually encountered a deceptive calm, the eye in the hurricane. The situation was simmering, cooled by the bonanza harvest and railway boom during the summer. Even so, the government had not yet dared to introduce the New Poor Law into London or the industrial north. And a recession was already setting in, with massive unemployment in prospect.

Off the *Beagle*, he was back in his Whig element. Having humoured the staunch Tory FitzRoy aboard, he now informed him just as good-naturedly that 'by the time we meet, my politics will be as firmly fixed and as wisely founded as ever they were.' With his own party commanding the ship of state, it was now his turn to be cool and inflexible. FitzRoy, for his part, did anything but behave predictably. He astonished Darwin by promptly getting married. For five years he had kept his lady a secret, even from his daily dining companion.

Darwin could barely contain himself at home. The person he longed to see was Henslow, and he rushed off a note, still 'giddy with joy & confusion': 'I want your advice on many points, indeed I am in the clouds.' He had no idea what to do with the *Beagle* specimens, many still aboard, carefully numbered and listed, ready for the experts. He wanted them described, but which specialists should he approach? Ten days on land, 15 October, and he was back among the spires of Cambridge, picking Henslow's brains. Here at least was someone to take the plants. Professor Sedgwick also got in touch, and they breakfasted together, talking over geology and catching up on Cambridge politics. Darwin received introductions to the best London naturalists – and warnings that they were overwhelmed with work. He could but see.[4]

From the quiet of Cambridge he plunged into bustling London on the 20th, staying with Erasmus in Great Marlborough Street, off the new Regent Street. London: the 'modern Babylon,' daunting in size, so large that 'a pedestrian could not encompass [it] in a day's time.' The enormous population of two million overawed visitors, who found themselves engulfed in great 'waves of people silently surging through the gloom.' He found a city in transition. Euston Station was being built, London Bridge was finished, but nighttime revealed the sight of sights, when the town was 'magically lit by its millions of gas lights.' Lights on every street, so bright that from the high point of Hampstead Heath the city transmogrified into a shimmering constellation. Road works were a constant complaint: sewers going in, gas mains being laid. Some of the gutting had been unintended, the charred shell of the House of Commons was a sorry sight, but most of the works signified expensive renovation.[5] This was true of the wealthiest scientific institutions, the British Museum and the Royal College of Surgeons, sporting an impressive new portico behind a shield of scaffolding.

He spent days traipsing from institution to institution – the Zoological and Geological Societies, the Linnean and British Museum – all a short walk from his brother's house. He introduced himself, and dined out on his South American stories, trying to tempt the experts with his collections. He was strutting, a celebrity; the geologists had read his printed letters, and many had seen his megatherium fossils. Everyone wanted to meet the tropical traveller and hear his tales of savages and rain forests and giant ground sloths. Charles Bunbury, a fellow Cambridge-educated squire-naturalist, was typical in trying to corner him. Darwin 'seems to be a universal collector,' Bunbury reported enthusiastically, discovering new species 'to the surprise of all the big wigs.' Here Darwin was, a month after landing, moving 'in most exciting dissipation amongst the Dons in science.' At first he had mixed results in placing his specimens. The geologists seized on his South American rocks, but, as Henslow had predicted, 'the Zoologists seem to think a number of undescribed creatures rather a nuisance.'[6]

Not surprisingly, for they were inundated by shells and skins from the four corners. The Zoological Society, having solicited exotic species from émigrés and military surveyors, was now drowning under the torrent. Despite its new West End museum, it could hardly keep pace. So many colonials contributed that, Darwin realized, collections outnumbered competent naturalists to describe them.

The old museum had long been a bone of contention with the zoologists. Zoo officials had just taken over the great surgeon John Hunter's museum in Leicester Square to mitigate the problem. It was extensive, twice the size of their old building, with 'well arranged rooms and galleries, lighted from the top.' When Darwin arrived, £1200 had just been spent on fittings, giving it 460 feet of exhibition space. But it was already crammed. The walls were lined with endless glazed cases, a cornucopia of colonial mammals, birds, reptiles, and fish – 6720 as he walked round, the largest exhibition 'open to public view in this kingdom.' So many species, in fact, that half had yet to be named or labelled. Assistants could still be seen taking pickled fish and reptiles out of temporary storage jars. What hope did he have when the museum was 'nearly full & upward of a thousand specimens remain unmounted'?[7] He could see why they were loath to take still more.

Something else was obvious: the electric atmosphere. The society had been buffeted by the political winds, with rowdy democrats – led by Darwin's old tutor Robert Grant (now at University College) – trying to usher in a new zoological era. Not for them the aristocrats' interest in raising game for the rich man's table (one of the zoo's original aims). They wanted the society run by paid experts. They were out of sympathy with the old zoology, presided over by rich amateur dabblers – the parsons, dilettantes, and noblemen. The new museum was one result of their campaign, a monument to serious, imperially useful zoology. Reformers had fought to have it sited in the West End, away from the aristocrats' promenading Zoological Gardens in Regent's Park. These battles for reform left bitter feelings, as Darwin noticed. 'I am out of patience with the Zoologists,' he snorted, 'not because they are overworked, but for their mean quarrelsome spirit. I went the other evening to the Zoological Soc[iety]. where the speakers were snarling at each other, in a manner anything but like that of gentlemen.'

Darwin was beginning to get Grant's measure: his old teacher's politics had become fiercer since the Edinburgh days. Grant, like so many radicals in the turbulent, reforming 30s, was a democrat, a Church-critic, a Cambridge-hater, always attacking privilege. A comrade said that 'whenever a good, honourable, generous, and liberal cause was in agitation,' there you 'would find the name of Professor Grant.' But these honourable causes were not necessarily Darwin's. His friends were Cambridge clerics. As a Whig gentleman on a private fortune, he relished his freedom to follow his own pursuits, to make his home a lab, as the rich had done for centuries. He was not one for salaried science, or making the zoo's aristocratic grandees accountable to members. He *was* concerned with standards of behaviour, however, and he shared his family's abhorrence of the 'fierce & licentious' radicals.[8]

Not only zoologists suffered. Other institutions faced challenges to their traditional leadership. Even the British Museum was in turmoil. It was the subject of a bruising Parliamentary inquiry in 1836, instigated by radicals who wanted to oust the titled Trustees and turn it into a research institution along French lines. There again was

Grant, slamming the museum's incompetent aristocratic governors under the Archbishop of Canterbury. All this made Darwin wary of depositing his collection there. 'I cannot feel, from all I hear, any great respect even for the present state of that establishment.' It also began to make him chary of Dr Grant. More and more the prickly secularist, Grant was slated by Tories for backing the 'reptile press,' well known for its 'blasphemous derision of the sacred truths of Christianity.'[9] To the gentlemen of science, pillars of the Establishment, his gutter-press flailings were anathema.

All this rushing around, trying to place specimens, listening to weary political harangues, left Charles exhausted. 'I am quite tired,' he sighed to Caroline, '& long to be living quietly with dear old Henslow.' Cambridge was a sanctuary, away from the bickering as much as the smog and soot. Better to break the collection in Cambridge, he thought, and parcel bits out. His father's support and promise of continued backing meant he could do just that, put Church and career out of mind and do the job. The Doctor duly gave him an allowance plus stocks, bringing in about £400 a year. Comfortably off, he could pursue an independent lifestyle, unburdened by guinea-grabbing academic needs. Four hundred pounds was enough to sustain a single gentleman, pay for his servant – Covington was kept on – and more. He could actually afford to buy the help he needed. 'About the fossil shells. Is Sowerby a good man?' he asked Henslow. 'I understand his assistance can be purchased.'[10] Darwin was to bankroll a number of such specialists over the years, the illustrator and shell-trader George Sowerby among them. He could settle down as a self-financed naturalist, subcontracting his work.

But where? He squared up to the choice of life options: amid the dissipations of London with the 'Dons in science' or quietly at Cambridge with the clerical naturalists. Should he emulate Lyell and Eras in the city with its intellectually bracing atmosphere, moving in their circles of advanced intellectuals – freethinking, political, exciting? Here were the freshest fish and the freshest news, the latest shows, and the largest pool of scientific talent in the country. Eras was still enjoying his life of literary leisure, his week revolving around intellectual dinner parties. Lyell was a perfect role model, a self-financed specialist making his mark famously. Or should he retire to the pastoral fields like Henslow, giving him the quiet to think? He was torn, but it was clear that he would have to settle in the smoke eventually, to see his precious specimens farmed out, however much he blanched at the prospect.

*

In London he did have Eras for company. Or at least some of the time, for his brother was taken with that literary lioness Harriet Martineau. In these weeks he would drift back in the evening, tired 'from driving out Miss Martineau.' Martineau herself was London's prime literary apologist for the whole gamut of Whig reforms. She had even been introduced to the old Revd Malthus.[11] It might have been a meeting of minds, but neither had expected much more. With her ear trumpet and his cleft palate, it was a surprise anything transpired, but they transcended their impediments and made perfect contact. She heard every word without her trumpet, and gratifying words they were: he praised her poor-law tales as the very epitome of his views.

But she met virulent opposition. She was slammed by Tory paternalists as a Malthusian 'who deprecates charity and provision for the poor!!!' On the other side, more radical doctors than Eras were unionizing to protest at the pestilential workhouses. Yet again, here were Grant and his fanatical friends in 1836, founding the militant pressure group, the London-based British Medical Association, to hamper the poor-law commissioners and refute Malthus's statistics.[12]

But Martineau was ensconced in Whig high society, Darwin's society, where she was fêted for her Malthusian sense. She was practically one of the family. Eras was smitten, but Charles wondered about such a threateningly assertive lady. 'Our only protection from so admirable a sister-in-law is in her working [Eras] too hard. He begins to perceive . . . he shall be not much better than her "nigger". – Imagine poor Erasmus a nigger to so philosophical & energetic a lady . . . She already takes him to task about his idleness.' Martineau had just returned from a whirlwind tour of America, and was full of married women's property rights, as Charles heard. 'She is going some day to explain to him her notions about marriage – Perfect equality of rights is part of her doctrine. I much doubt whether it will be equality in practice. We must pray for our poor "nigger".'

The 'nigger' wasn't enslaved, and Martineau didn't become a Darwin. But there were other connections tying the family to Malthus. Hensleigh Wedgwood's father-in-law, the economist Sir James Mackintosh, had been Malthus's fast friend (and fellow lecturer at the East India College at Haileybury), and Malthus's daughter Emily had been a bridesmaid at Fanny and Hensleigh's wedding.[13] Darwin was becoming enmeshed in a close and personal Malthusian circle.

Lyell, fired by Darwin's reports from South America, was eager to meet his disciple. Darwin too was expectant. On Saturday 29 October they finally met, when Darwin came to dinner. He found Lyell boiling with enthusiasm beneath his hushed tones, and watched bemused as Lyell sank into his chair, almost ending on the floor as he listened to Darwin's earthquake stories. Lyell was the most adventurous geologist in town, and the most famous after the *Principles of Geology*. He had a barrister's way with words and a beautiful command of foreign languages; he was courtly, and at ease in high circles. He was also politically aware, a friend of the Whig Lords, with his finger on the pulse of reform. Then there was Mrs Lyell, Leonard Horner's daughter: pretty as a picture and a model of patience. Darwin was overawed by their kindness, praising the 'heart & soul' way they were ready to help. Lyell bent over backwards with advice about specialists, and all in the '*most* goodnatured manner.' Darwin gravitated to him, heeding his advice to stay in London and get his projects off the ground. Nor should he waste his energy running societies (Lyell, losing time as President of the prestigious Geological, told him to 'tell no one I gave you this advice').[14]

That October evening Lyell invited others to meet the globe-trotter. He introduced Darwin to a tall, striking figure with glittering eyes, Richard Owen. Owen was man of the hour, the new Hunterian Professor at the Royal College of Surgeons in Lincoln's Inn Fields. He seemed a bit diffident, even awkward, but he came supported by his best friend from the other end of Lincoln's Inn, the magistrate William Broderip. These two, Tories to the core, had just voted the 'malcontent' Grant out of a post at the Zoological Society, and doubtless over dinner Darwin heard all about the rumbles.[15] Owen now stood triumphant at the zoo, its reigning anatomist, dissecting whatever died in the Gardens without hitch or hindrance. No one was more versatile or prolific, and he already had a string of papers on the zoo's corpses under his belt. For his part, Broderip kept an impressive cabinet of shells in his Lincoln's Inn chambers. During dinner he must have salivated at Darwin's description of his exotic haul, and he offered to look them over.

Lyell had made the right choice of dining companions. Owen shared Darwin's interest in fossils and invertebrates. He lived on the top floor of the College of Surgeons, looking out over the rooftops. When Darwin later visited, he found the new library and ninety-foot museum almost finished, with workmen rushing around putting on the final licks of paint. Partly this rebuilding had been forced by the political attacks on the college, which had led to probing Parliamentary questions about its role as a repository of national treasures. In the van as always was Grant, denouncing college corruption from his soapbox.[16] The grave, moralistic Owen was more than a little suspicious of his jaundiced rival.

Owen was on the up-and-up, and ready to topple the 'great Grant' as the city's leading comparative anatomist.[17] At the college Darwin found Owen charming, vehemently opposed to Grant's evolution, and well versed in the latest German science. (Owen was busy synthesizing German ideas on the forces regulating life and growth, preparing his first lectures – ideas which were to stimulate Darwin in his own search for the laws of life.[18]) But for the moment Darwin was concerned to place his precious pampas relics. Owen took some of the animals preserved in spirits. And Darwin persuaded him to look over his fossil bones.

At this time Grant volunteered his help. He was one of the few who actively offered to examine the haul, and presumably one of the few actively turned down. Ten years earlier in Edinburgh, he had introduced the teenage Darwin to Lamarck's views and the study of corals. Now he offered to sift through the seafarer's tropical spoils. But Darwin had become a competent and competing coral expert, and he had his own plans. He was interested in the polyps' reproduction, and of course reef formation. He roped in Erasmus instead, putting him to work translating German papers on coral banks. So, at the end of the day, ironically, the corals were not monographed.[19] Nor, it seems, did Darwin and Grant have anything more to do with one another.

Darwin might have wanted his specimens described quickly, but not by a disreputable dissident, one spitting venom at Henslow's Cambridge for its 'monastic ignorance.' A compelling need for quiet respectability dominated Darwin's life. His inclination to 'take offence at rudeness of manners & any thing bordering upon ungentlemanlike behavior' had made even Henslow chide him years ago. He hated loudmouthed radicalism, and Grant was now beyond the pale.

Others were too tardy. If anyone looked like laying a 'dead hand' on his specimen Darwin manoeuvred them out of sight. When he spoke to the shy Robert Brown, botany keeper at the British Museum, the pitfalls became apparent. He 'asked me in rather an ominous manner, what I meant to do with my plants. – In the course of conversation, Mr Broderip who was present remarked to him, "you forget how long it is since Capt: King's expedition." He answered, "Indeed I have something, in the shape of Capt: Kings undescribed plants to make me recollect it".'[20] Brown had been sitting on a hoard of Galapagos plants for six years. It was no inducement for Darwin to hand his over.

By the end of October FitzRoy had brought the *Beagle* around to Woolwich and berthed her alongside the other ten-gun brigs. Here, on the Thames near London, he took his last chronometric reading, and the ship was paid off. The docks were bristling with sailors, redcoats, quartermasters, and suppliers when Darwin came down to fetch his crates. It deflated him rather, seeing all the specimens packed by Covington. He was 'at an utter loss to know how to begin.' He sent a box of Galapagos plants to Henslow by coach, followed by four crates of rocks, bird skins, insects, and spirit bottles. Everything was already arranged into groups, but he foresaw an uphill struggle. 'All I know is, that I must work far harder, than [these] poor shoulders have ever been accustomed to do.'[21]

All this time, he had practically ignored the Wedgwoods, still waiting patiently to see him. He finally got to Maer on 12 November and suffered an endless round of visiting relatives. The girls thought him better for being thinner and were not above a bit of back-handed flattery: 'it has improved his looks, and his countenance is so pleasant that his plainness does not signify.' Round the fire he regaled them with stories of his giant fossils and the wild, women-eating Fuegians.

He was still thinking of publishing a book of his travels. The whole family rallied to the idea. Fanny and Hensleigh had read his five-year diary and loved it, especially the sections on Tahiti and New Zealand. In their view it bettered '99.100^{ths} of the travels that are published.' Dr Henry Holland, a distant cousin and self-important society physician, disagreed, but that only left Hensleigh taking a dim view of the doctor's faculties. Nor did Emma Wedgwood believe that cousin Henry was 'any judge as to what is amusing or interesting.' She thought it would make a wonderful book, and she was ploughing through unfamiliar fare – rival accounts of pampas crossings – ready to engage Charles. FitzRoy wanted a three-volume narrative of his and King's expeditions, with King, himself, and the 'Philosopher' contributing one each, and he drew up a contract with Colburn the publisher to that effect. Everyone at home entered into the spirit, and Charles – back at The Mount on the 16th – found his sisters deep in travelogues, picking up tips.[22]

On 2 December Darwin returned to London, and began to find takers for his prized specimens. The new zoology professor at King's College in the Strand, Thomas Bell, came forward, intrigued by the reptiles. The seaweed-eating Galapagos iguanas fascinated the Oxford geologist the Revd William Buckland. The zoologists also were turning up trumps, and experts were looking over 'whole tribes of animals, of which I know nothing.' Most required the specialist touch, beyond his competence. So much so that he was left red-faced by a botanist in the Linnean library:

> I felt very foolish, when [he] remarked on the beautiful appearance of some plant with an astoundingly long name, & asked me about its habitation. Some one else seem[ed] quite surprised that I knew nothing about a carex from [I] do not know where. I w[as] at last forced to plead most intire [sic] innocence, & that I knew no more about the plants, which I had collected, than the Man in the Moon.

Being unsure of his botany, he worried again about how the experts would react to his haul. 'Tell me whether you are disappointed with the Galapagos plants,' he pressed Henslow; 'I have some fears.'[23]

His real trophies, though, were the fossil mammals, which he had unpacked at Owen's College of Surgeons. The museum still had decorators in, and when Hensleigh dropped by he was horrified to find the huge skull that Darwin had picked up for eighteen pence near Mr Keen's ranch 'in a room with workmen.' This was the first fossil Owen diagnosed, and his conclusion was surprising. It belonged to a huge rodent, a hippo-sized capybara relative, which Owen called *Toxodon*. And the Punta Alta skeleton with an enormous pelvis and pointed snout came from a horse-sized anteater. The fossils 'are turning out great treasures,' Charles boasted to Caroline.[24] Rhino-sized rodents! 'What famous cats they ought to have had in those days!'

These spectacular fossils were his *entrée* into the world of high science. The College sent casts to the Geological Society and the British Museum; Cambridge received some, as did Oxford, where Buckland – Sir Ammon Knight himself – wanted to figure them in a new edition of his *Geology and Mineralogy*. At the end of the day no savant was ignorant of Darwin's pampas giants.

The social whirl continued. He felt duty bound to call in on Erasmus's belle, Harriet Martineau. 'She was very agreeable,' he admitted, 'and managed to talk on a most wonderful number of subjects, considering the limited time.' Martineau was writing *Society in America*, on her trip to the United States, where she too had seen new social and natural worlds in the making. She was full of American democracy, women's rights, and the horrors of slavery. At Niagara Falls she had marvelled at the 'process of world-making,' where nature sculpted scenery with an awesome 'blind and dumb' force. She too had witnessed the 'grandeur and beauty' of the earth's own 'workshop,' and it gave them a perfect talking point.[25]

'I was astonished to find how ugly she is,' Charles conceded, noting that 'she is overwhelmed with her own projects, her own thoughts and abilities.' Her literary threat was met by male hauteur: 'Erasmus palliated all this, by maintaining one ought not to look at her as a woman.' Martineau captured her beau's brother far more succinctly: 'simple, childlike, painstaking, effective,' she called Charles Darwin.

Charles thought back on his own loves. He sent Fanny Biddulph – four years unhappily married and cooped up in a Welsh castle expecting her third baby – a present of flowers, which left her lost for words.[26]

Two months home and he was already cursing 'dirty odious London.' He could not face winter in the city. It might have been 'the real capital of the world' for the fashionable set bored with Paris. But Charles was choked by the fog and smoke. Dark clouds descended from chimney-stacks like 'a soft black drizzle, with flakes of soot in it as big as full-grown snow-flakes – gone into mourning, one might imagine, for the death of the sun.' Coal smouldered in every grate. Coal, 'hell's own fuel, torn from the bowels of the earth.' It left the streets enveloped in freezing smog. It 'admits only a wan daylight and casts a funereal pall over all things. In London one draws gloom with every breath; it is in the air; it enters every pore . . . one's head is heavy and aching, one's stomach has trouble functioning, breathing becomes difficult for lack of pure air.' Mud-splattered pavements, freezing pea-soupers rising from the infernally smelly Thames: he hated it. On the cobbled roads the clatter of hoofs and iron-rimmed cartwheels was deafening. He knew he would have to settle here for a time, especially if he had to continue hawking his skins and bones around, as Lyell advised.[27] But he yearned for a few months first at Cambridge, breathing fresh air – living with the Henslows, or so he hoped.

So back he went to Cambridge on 13 December. He did manage three days with a house full of Henslows before finding 'solitary lodgings' in Fitzwilliam Street. Cambridge was a quiet, clean contrast with London. Nothing much had changed. Not even the reforms had penetrated its Anglican exterior (the bill to admit Dissenters without subscribing to the Thirty-nine Articles had failed). He could reflect on the teachers he had not seen for so long. There was kindly Henslow, growing fatter, with five children now. While still on the *Beagle* Darwin had been asked to stand godfather to the latest, and he felt for Henslow the way he did for a close relative. Sedgwick was another matter. Darwin gave a talk to the Cambridge Philosophical Society on the glassy tubes in the Maldonado sand dunes, caused by lightning fusing the sand into black shiny funnels. He discussed these over tea with Whewell and Sedgwick, the 'talking giants,' and something happened to cause an odd reflection on Sedgwick's temperament. 'I really sometimes think he will go mad,' Charles told Caroline, without explanation; the old bachelor was 'so very absent & odd,' although a 'more high-minded man does not anywhere exist.'[28]

Cambridge might not have changed, but Darwin had. There was no chance of his sinking back into old ways, even if he did spend the odd merry evening reminiscing with Herbert, and lose the occasional bet in Christ's College common room. Now he was committed to his haul, and to gilding his scientific reputation in the eyes of the Lyells and Henslows. His cold winter days were cut out, sniffling with flu as he sorted his specimens. Each evening he retired to write his first paper, proving that the Chilean coast – indeed the whole South American landmass – was rising slowly. Those inland sea shells, found at increasing heights above sea level, clinched his case.

Lyell loved the paper, but then it was he who had made mountain elevation compensate for drowning continents. Darwin was taking a partnership in Lyell's geological business, throwing himself into its operation with gusto. From the first his geology was creative, speculative, and written in ponderous English (causing Sedgwick to plead for sharper prose). Darwin had a Lyellian sense of balance, his rising Andes offset by a sinking Pacific. He extended Lyell's earthquake-cause of mountain uplift, and – on the down side – he pointed to coral reefs as the last relics of disappearing mountains. This 'knocked' Lyell's own reef explanation 'on the head.' But still Lyell was ecstatic: 'Coral islands are the last efforts of drowning continents to lift their heads above water,' he crooned, giving way gracefully. He egged Darwin on to report his South American findings, revelling in the 'idea of the Pampas going up, at the rate of an inch in a century.' 'What a splendid field you have to write upon!'[29]

Owen was struck too, and Darwin gladly sent a further crate of fossil bones from Cambridge. He followed these down in the new year, and another hectic round commenced: dining with Lyell, discussing his paper, unpacking the fossils at the College of Surgeons.

The real red-letter day was 4 January 1837. In the evening he read his paper to the Geological Society, on Chile's coast as uplifted sea floor. It was his début, and friends and family rallied round. Hensleigh was present, and of course Lyell. Many of the geologists were brilliant orators who could enliven the dullest subject. But

Darwin was a novice, and nervous. Standing in front of Lyell, the President, with rows of expert geologists on benches either side, huge maps and diagrams of mountain sections behind them on the walls, he read his paper, heart in hand, pounding furiously. On the table were his oyster fossils and other pampas samples, collected a world away. Lyell lapped up the talk, but, he cautioned, 'do not flatter yourself that you will be believed, till you are growing bald, like me.' Darwin did not have to lose his hair first. In fact, his Cordilleras and coral reefs were so well received that he felt 'like a peacock admiring his tail.'

Darwin was ambitious and the Geological was to be his forum. Elected soon after the *Beagle* docked, he was at ease here among the urban gentry, more so than with the squabbling zoological salariat. (Two years would elapse before he became a Zoological Fellow.) His public persona was as a 'hammerer' gent. He still worried about falling short in his father's eyes, but here, with hard work, he would amount to something. These were boom times for the science. The recalcitrant older strata were being conquered, rocks that revealed the first created forms; and Cambrian, Silurian, and Devonian were becoming household words. Geology provided spy-holes into a dim, distant past, a view on the comings and goings of continents as much as the fortunes of fossil dynasties. Lyell's *Principles of Geology* was read by thousands: 'every ambitious young man studies geology; so members of Parliament are made, and churchmen' – and even divines were getting used to seeing 'the *coup de grâce*' given 'to the deluge.'[30] It was a growth industry, and Darwin was about to join the captains.

Darwin's rising and falling lands had other – more covert – consequences. They raised tantalizing questions about the inhabitants; about annihilation and repopulation, about Creation itself. On this key question he was still moving away from Lyell. The Galapagos finches, all feeding in flocks together (or so he thought), suggested that Lyell was wrong – that conditions did not strictly determine what was created where.[31] So what could explain these variants? There had to be another solution.

He had one other engagement on 4 January. At the zoo's headquarters in Leicester Square, he presented 80 mammals and 450 birds to the Society. Knowing the zoologists' museum, he wisely added the proviso that all were to be mounted and described. Actually, the men in the museum were proving their worth. He popped down Regent Street from Eras's house to meet them on many days. He became friendly with George Waterhouse, an old beetle enthusiast and former architect, who – as the new curator – had finally achieved his goal of a paid post in zoology. Waterhouse was already cataloguing the museum's 870 mammals when he agreed to take on Darwin's.

It was the birds that intrigued others, if not Darwin. He remained confused by the Galapagos finches, believing that they fed indiscriminately together, unaware of the importance of their different beaks. Come to that, he still had trouble identifying the species, or their locations; and he still thought that his collection contained finches, wrens, 'Gross-beaks', and 'Icteruses' (blackbird-relatives). He had no sense of a single, closely related group becoming specialized and adapted to different environmental niches. The birds did not even seem that important when he donated them to the Zoological Society, rather badly labelled, on the 4th.[32]

The expert he turned them over to was the ornithologist, artist, and taxidermist John Gould, already making a name for himself through his lavish bird books. Gould was a prolific describer of the skinned specimens shipped to the Society. He had studied wrens, toucans, and Australian, Himalayan, African, and European birds. Unlike Darwin, he was not a leisured gentleman; a gardener's son, he had graduated to the poorly paid post of 'Animal Preserver' at the Society in 1828. Five years later he earned the grand title 'Superintendant' of the stuffed birds, but the pay was still only £100 a year. As a result he was having to print and sell a string of illustrated books to make up the shortfall. His output was prodigious, as Darwin realized that January: the fifth and last volume of his *Birds of Europe* was just appearing, and the first of his *Birds of Australia* about to be published. (In fact, these were so lucrative that he had just gone on half-pay at the zoo to concentrate on his prints.) As Darwin deposited his corpses, Gould was continuing to describe the exotic parrots shot in the New South Wales settlements.[33] If anyone could disentangle Darwin's wrens and finches and blackbirds, Gould could.

Interrupting his paying work, he quickly realized that Darwin's Galapagos birds were not so diverse at all. The reverse, in fact: the beaks were deceptive and the birds, astonishingly, were closely related. 'Gross-beaks,' 'blackbirds' – they were all in truth finches. By the next meeting, on the 10th – only six days later – Gould had linked them as 'a series of ground Finches which are so peculiar' as to form 'an entirely new group, containing 12 species.'[34] They were close-knit, despite their range of bills – although the significance would only become apparent later to Darwin. Darwin's birds and mammals were set out for display, and reporters from the dailies heard Gould's news. The papers ran the story, so that even Catherine could read about Charles's finches in the *Morning Herald*.

Meanwhile, revelations were startling the geologists. Owen, working through the fossils, had made out a gigantic ground sloth and an ox-sized armoured *Glyptodon* in Darwin's new batch. There was more: the leg and neck bones taken at Port St Julian in January 1834 turned out, judging by the arteries in the spine, to be 'fragments of a Gigantic Llama!' So Darwin could at last picture the scene – on the waterless, windswept plains dominated by the llama-like guanaco today, enormous llamas had once roamed. Lyell realized the implications. Just as the wombats and kangaroos of Australia had giant precursors, on the ancient plains of Patagonia llamas, capybaras, sloths, and armadillos had their own gigantic forebears. Lyell saw a 'law of succession' in play here: mammals are replaced by their own kind on each continent.[35]

Lyell paraded Darwin's skeletal 'Menagerie' across the stage in his presidential address to the Geological Society on 17 February. He drew out the conclusions from Owen's findings: that fossil faunas are closely related to their living replacements. At Lyell's request, Darwin came down to hear the talk. He knew of Owen's results, but the speech brought home the real importance of his fossils for the first time. He sensed the close relationship between extinct megatheriums and glyptodons and the modern sloths and armadillos.[36] Darwin had never expected this; on the voyage he assumed that he had found European and African mastodons and rhinos, not exclusive South American species. It pulled him up sharp, causing him to ask the key question: why is present and past life on any one spot so closely related?

His stock was rising, and at the same meeting he was elected to the Council of the Geological Society. Fossils were not the only things of importance to Lyell; he valued an ally, and he considered Darwin 'a glorious addition to my society of geologists.' His society was a crack corps. All were gentleman specialists, most wealthy or with Oxbridge chairs. Together they constituted a self-referential (and self-reverential) élite. These were the last of the virtuoso scholars in an age before the salaried class moved in. They were rich careerists, with no professional paymaster to pull the strings, and duty only to scientific integrity, social stability, and responsible religion. The Geological Society was the most stimulating and envied in town. The science touched the age of the earth and the Days of Creation; it was fashionable, difficult and dangerous, and as such under close 'public surveillance.' Here Darwin lived up to Lyell's expectations. He showed that he could hold his own: 'I really never saw that bore Dr. Mitchell so successfully silenced or such a bucket of cold water so dexterously poured down his back as when Darwin answered some impertinent & irrelevant questions about S[outh]. America,' Lyell grinned after one spat.[37] Darwin was now the resident expert on the subject.

All this encouraged Darwin to begin working 'tooth and nail' at a book on South American geology. His French rival Alcide d'Orbigny, back two years earlier, had already started a multi-volume account of the continent, but Darwin and Lyell had withering words for d'Orbigny's cataclysmic explanation of mountain formation. It was time for a rival account, a Lyellian one. Darwin's public career was being mapped out. A country curacy, a 'parsonage in the desert,' was fading from view. His was to be the horrid desert of cobbles and concrete, the clatter of cartwheels and choking smog. He was steeling himself for London. 'The only evil I found at Cambridge,' he said, 'was its being too pleasant.' He could never say the same for the capital. But 'I am pretty well resigned to my fate.'[38]

15

Reforming Nature

IT WAS AN IRONY that nowhere was so good for natural history as 'this odious smokey town,' because no one could see any real nature here at all. But he had to be on the spot to supervise his collections.

Lyell told him to arrive in time for one of Charles Babbage's Saturday soirées in the West End, where he would meet 'the best in the way of literary people in London,' and, more to the point, plenty 'of pretty women.'[1] The season was in full swing, so, on Friday 6 March 1837, Darwin came down from Cambridge and moved in with Eras.

At Babbage's parties you could 'see the *World*.' You could also sense the way science was going: pick up the tittle-tattle, hear remarks off the cuff. They were glittering affairs, 'brilliantly attended by fashionable ladies, as well as literary and scientific gents.' Bankers, politicians, and industrialists mixed with well-heeled savants – Lyell, Owen, Broderip, the 'King of Siluria' Roderick Murchison, and now Darwin himself. The polymathic Babbage was a mathematician, apologist for industry, advocate of the division of labour, and builder of the costly 'Difference Engine,' or calculating machine. He was a reformer (and a failed Whig Parliamentary candidate), so there was plenty of political banter. The turbulent times demanded it. The town halls were currently being democratized and the Church reformed. Even as Darwin arrived the Church looked like losing its tithes, and the clergy had lost their monopoly on the rites at birth, marriage, and death. No longer would Dissenters have to be married by Anglican parsons (or Unitarians have to perjure themselves by affirming the doctrine of the Trinity). Staunch Tories called these the worst reforms since the English Civil War of the 1640s, when Parliament tried to abolish bishops. Of course, this became the butt of the best jokes. Babbage, omnipotent himself, was once taunted, 'What do you mean to be when the revolution comes?' and replied, 'Lay Archbishop of Winchester.'[2]

In keeping with the period, Babbage had written his cheekily named *Ninth Bridgewater Treatise*, already in proof. The title gave away his target. It was a snub to the eight officially sanctioned 'Bridgewater' books. This lavish series had been financed by the late Earl of Bridgewater, in atonement for an impious life, and overseen by the Archbishop of Canterbury. The *Bridgewater Treatises* played endlessly on the theme of God's wisdom and goodness deduced from nature. Hardly a stone was left unturned in the search for divine design, even though the enterprise was positively passé to the cynics and secularists. By now the run of books had appeared and world-weary Londoners – like freethinking Erasmus – were 'somewhat *saturated*' with the subject. Critics doubted that even the buffoonish Buckland in his Bridgewater – *Geology and Mineralogy* – could add to 'so threadbare and exhausted a topic.' Babbage by contrast could. In his unofficial *Ninth*, he laughed to Lyell, 'the Devil is to have his due.'[3]

Of course, he wasn't. The book presented God as a divine programmer, and Babbage used his hand-cranked calculator to prove the point. He set out to undermine the conservative view of God as a tinkering miracle-monger. He was a divine legislator, far-seeing, not a feudal monarch acting on whim. Out went the notion of 'Creative Interference,' as Buckland called it; no more *ad hoc* miracles each time a minor mollusc or fossil feline was needed. Such nonsense undermined rational science and sound religion, denying God 'the highest attribute of omnipotence,' foresight. On Babbage's smart machine any sequence of numbers could be programmed to cut in, however long another series had been running. By analogy, God at Creation had appointed new sets of animals and plants to appear like clockwork throughout history – he had created the laws which produced them, rather than creating them direct. Babbage's God displayed 'a degree of power and of knowledge of a far higher order.'[4]

A host of geologists had been poring over Babbage's proofs. Lyell had only put down his copy in January when Darwin's South America paper arrived. Babbage's position was well known to the cognoscenti. Lyell thought that his 'philosophical speculations' were majestic. They reinforced his own views.

No doubt some people would not like any reasoning which makes miracles more reconcilable with possibilities in the ordinary course of the Universe & its laws; but you do not write to please them . . . I think your estimate of the Creator's attributes much higher than theirs.

So did Darwin's medical cousin, Henry Holland, who was struck by Babbage's 'originality & ingenuity.' When the book came out in late spring, Babbage presented a copy to Princess Victoria, summing it up as a 'work written in defence of Science and for the support of Religion.'[5]

The *Ninth Bridgewater* had people talking. Even before it appeared, Darwin would have known all about the book, perhaps even from Babbage (whom he called a rather cold 'calculating machine' himself). He realized that a 'lawful' approach was carrying the day. Reformed nature was the product of careful legislated change, a rational plan. The prophets were proved right: the radical Whigs really were intent on changing heaven and earth.

Darwin's other heroes were making a similar point, including John Herschel, whom Darwin had met at the Cape. Herschel openly alluded to the problem, the 'mystery of mysteries,' as he called it: what caused new species to appear in place of the extinct ones? Was it miraculous? He doubted it. In his view, the same natural causes that have sculpted the earth over the aeons must explain the coming and going of life on its surface. God does not intervene personally, by supernatural meddling. He set up laws at the creation of the universe, and these have operated throughout geological history, producing species. Awesome as the birth of a species must be, it was no more miraculous than the birth of a child.[6]

Herschel was not thinking of one animal actually *transmuting* into another, nor did he envisage man as an ape descendant, which was abhorrent. In fact he could visualize no actual process. But he guessed that a good naturalist would sooner or later clear up the mystery.

Though still resident at the Cape, Herschel was influential, the de facto head of science in Britain. (Babbage had put him up as a presidential candidate at the Royal Society in 1830, although the post went to the King's son.) His letter to Lyell on the 'mystery of mysteries' was well thumbed, Lyell having passed it around. Darwin could see its impact on Babbage, who extracted it in his *Ninth Bridgewater*. It was an injunction to seek the explanation of the ultimate mystery. The searcher had to be bold. Herschel prefaced his remarks with the couplet:

> He that on such quest would go must
> 　　know nor fear nor failing
> To coward soul or faithless heart the
> 　　search were unavailing.

To some it looked like the holy grail's quest. But it taught Darwin that nature too needed 'reforming' and reappraising – that it had to be brought under the rule of law.[7]

Darwin also knew that any search for the cause of species would lead into deep and difficult waters. It would be a far more dangerous voyage of discovery than the *Beagle*'s had been, and anyone undertaking it would stir up 'a host of prejudices.'

Herschel's epistle was huge, and it showed how much a new historical sensitivity was spreading through the sciences. The origin of language or the origin of rocks, both had to be seen as a gradual development.

> Words are to the Anthropologist what rolled pebbles are to
> the Geologist – Battered relics of past ages often containing
> within them indelible records capable of intelligible
> interpretation – and when we see what amount of change
> 2000 years has been able to produce in the languages of Greece
> & Italy or 1000 in those of Germany France & Spain we
> naturally begin to ask how long a period must have lapsed
> since the Chinese, the Hebrew, the Delaware & the Malesass
> [from Madagascar] had a point in common with the German
> & Italian & each other. – Time! Time! Time! – we must not
> impugn the Scripture Chronology, but we *must* interpret it in
> accordance with *whatever* shall appear on fair enquiry to be
> the *truth* for there cannot be two truths. And really there is
> scope enough: for the lives of the Patriarchs may as reasonably
> be extended to 5000 or 50000 years apiece as the days of
> Creation to as many thousand millions of years.

Darwin knew this passage well. He cited it to Caroline, explaining Herschel's view of the ages 'since the first man made his wonderful appearance on this world.' It was nowhere near 6000 years: 'Sir J. thinks that a far greater number must have passed' to account for the divergence of languages 'from one stock.'[8]

But what if animals, like Lyell's pebbles and Herschel's words, were also 'relics of past ages,' a living record 'capable of intelligible interpretation'? What if they were just as natural and had slowly diverged 'from one stock'? This was the up-and-coming approach, and Darwin must have realized it: the present held the genealogical key to the past. It was the high road to historical truth.

Charles was in and out of his brother's house this spring. He never strayed far from Eras. When he did move in mid-March into lodgings of his own, they were only a few doors down, at 36 Great Marlborough Street. Eras's was a hive of intellectual activity. After five lonely years at sea, Charles embraced his brother's ready-made circle of friends, revelling in his intimate dinners with Eras and Harriet Martineau. Here the buzz was radical and Dissenting and 'heterodoxy was the norm.'[9] He gained reassurance from this home circle.

Hensleigh also joined them. He was himself a philologist, looking for the 'laws' by which alphabets slowly change. He praised the Germans for understanding the 'organic' development of language and for tracing 'every descendant' of their own Gothic tongue. Languages had to be anatomized, their underlying unity exposed, ancestral sounds teased out. The analogy with Charles's zoology was overt. Just as he uncovered fossil sloths, Hensleigh was listening for 'fossil remains' in speech. Hensleigh's job was even harder; the sloths had lain undisturbed in their tombs, but sounds, because of their 'everyday use . . . have been worn, until, like pebbles on the beach, they have lost every corner and distinctive mark, and hardly a vestige remains to indicate their original form. Yet even here we are not left entirely without traces' of parentage.[10]

Through Hensleigh and Herschel, Charles grasped the historical analogy. These modern developmental ideas could be stretched to do more heretical work, to explain new life, new species. The issues were probably thrashed out during Eras's literary dinners. Here the sardonic Eras counterbalanced the serious Hensleigh, with the Unitarian, necessitarian Martineau listening in on her ear trumpet. Eras and Harriet were now so close that Fanny Wedgwood, feeling left out, thought they already seemed entirely married. (The Doctor did not approve. The liaison was sparking gossip, and Emma Wedgwood wondered how Susan and Catherine were weathering it.) All were interested in German biblical criticism and language studies, and devoted to Whig Malthusian ideals. All were better read than Charles, and he relished their conversation. As at Lyell's or Babbage's, politics, science, and literature were all of a piece here.

Not that the coteries were distinct; Lyell would call on Harriet and Erasmus, and Martineau loved Babbage's 'glorious soirees.' But, given their intimacy, Charles preferred Eras's affairs. They were 'worth all other, & more brilliant kinds, many times over,' even when Thomas Carlyle was sounding off 'in high force,' as he usually was. Charles recalled one 'funny dinner at my brother's, where among a few others, were Babbage and Lyell, both of whom liked to talk. Carlyle, however, silenced every one by haranguing during the whole dinner on the advantages of silence. After dinner, Babbage, in his grimmest manner, thanked Carlyle for his very interesting Lecture on Silence.'

Back home the Doctor worried about Martineau's radicalism and its influence on the boys. As a potential daughter-in-law she was bad enough, but her politics were too extreme. Reading a piece in the *Westminster Review* on the need for the radicals to break with the Whigs and give working men the vote, he got thoroughly steamed up 'before he knew it was not hers, and wasted a great deal of good indignation, and even now can hardly believe it is not hers.' She was polluting the others. 'Poor Martineau seems going down the hill with Hensleigh and Erasmus,' Emma laughed to Fanny Wedgwood, 'so I hope you will stick by her.'[11]

Martineau's scientific attitude was typical of radical Unitarians. She saw nature as predictable, predetermined, invariant. It was subject to law and order, not the province of miracle. Among Unitarians such 'determinism' encouraged views on life's self-development. Take Dr Southwood Smith, who had studied at the same Unitarian school as Martineau and worked for the poor-law commission. His *Divine Government* pictured nature as upward-striving, with needs driving organisms higher and higher. Animals and people were all of a piece, subject to the same everlasting ascent, 'continually advancing from one degree of knowledge, perfection and happiness to another.' Self-help in society – and here Malthusians were thinking of paupers pulling themselves up by their bootstraps – was part of a larger self-developing nature: 'all reasonable beings, however inferior the condition in which they commence their existence, are destined to rise higher and higher in endless progression, and to contribute to their own advancement.'[12]

Such a view demanded that the trammels be removed, that religious and civil disabilities be lifted, to allow everyone to compete freely to realize their God-given potential – to rise as nature and God intended. The Anglican priests were keeping the people down. This, of course, was why some radical Unitarians saw reform and evolution as going hand in hand. A self-developing nature held no terrors for them. Eras's group, with Martineau at its centre, gave Charles the licence to work out his own deterministic theories.

217

Darwin was learning Malthusian Whig ideals: his family and friends were justifying the reforms, rationalizing middle-class values, underpinning competition, arguing for free trade, factory expansion, and the removal of religious disabilities. They saw their social world as part of nature, itself struggling and progressing in accordance with God's laws. As at Eras's, so at Lyell's, language, genealogy and development were the hot topics. Fossil bones were chewed over at dinner, with Whig grandees and suave savants gnawing on the more arcane points. After the ladies departed, the talk would turn to Herschel's letter, or the origin of 'new species, and that mystery of mysteries, the creation of man.'

These discussions took place as Darwin was pondering the divine government himself. He too came to accept that 'the Creator creates by . . . laws.' Law ruled the earth, as it did the heavens; anything else was demeaning to God. Darwin complained that 'we can allow satellites, planets, suns, universe, nay whole systems of universe[s,] to be governed by laws, but the smallest insect, we wish to be created at once by special act.'[13] It was absurd; just as the winds in the Andes obeyed regular laws, so did the comings and goings of animals on the planet's surface. Dining at Lyell's, dancing at Babbage's, he found the idea of miraculous, catastrophic interruptions increasingly deplored. The rule of law had to be upheld.

By 1837 attacks on the Anglican miracle-mongers were barbed. Up-and-coming Dissenters wanted *more* reforms, furious at being barred from jobs in the hospitals, the law courts, Oxford, and Cambridge. They fulminated against Anglican privilege, indicting the Established Church of the 'filthy crime' of adultery with the state. The 'harlot' had to be wrenched from her caress.

These fierce Dissenters saw nature as a product of self-adjusting laws, initiated by God and proclaimed to everyone through His Word and Works. All men were therefore equal before Him, and no state-endowed priests were needed to interpret life or control science. The Church should be disestablished, its privileges stripped. With the four million Dissenters making political headway under the Whigs, their lawful explanation of nature was beginning to challenge the Anglicans' supernatural one.

Conservative Anglicans saw the whole world as ruled directly by God's will, immediately upheld 'by the word of His power,' and the Church as the divine agency on earth. If it were overthrown, everything would collapse. As someone joked: 'Many of our clergy suppose that if there was no Church of England, cucumbers and celery would not grow; that mustard and cress could not be raised. If Establishments are connected so much with the great laws of nature, this makes all the difference.' Reduced to the comical, it did seem unlikely to those outside the vicarage gate.

Others weren't laughing. They considered a manikin nature dancing to the tune of Creative whim risible. The sight of the Revd William Kirby's Universe moved by angelic demigods caused one commentator to snap: 'No no. – The Almighty laid down general laws at the beginning, for man, for animals, for the elements, and even the Universe around them. The laws, being founded in infinite wisdom, require neither revision nor supervision. They are eternal and immutable.' Darwin had read Kirby's Bridgewater book on animal instincts aboard ship, and now he found it causing wry amusement ashore. The sight of Kirby's puppet creation had everyone hopping: the 'silly and superstitious nonsense' to which men 'of Mr. Kirby's class' descend![14]

Darwin – with his Unitarian family and friends – stood at the crossroads. As he pondered life's progression on the earth he continued to hear a chorus of complaints about the old miraculous explanations.

The onslaught on the corrupt Church was accompanied by new questions. Could God's goodness be deduced from the perfect adaptation of animals? Darwin had loved Paley's logic at Cambridge – which moved from the wise design of animals to the existence of a wise Designer. But it was beginning to look suspect. Some spurned the superstitious divines who encircled animal structures 'with a spiritual halo; as if truth could be more sacred when thus surrounded.' Reforming zoologists saw animals not as contingently created by God to fit their niches, but related through a unity of plan: the bat wing and whale flipper had the same bones as a human arm.

Darwin found the old design arguments in tatters in London. The medical schools were brimming with dissident ideas. The Bridgewater books were written off as 'Bilgewater.' Demagogues warned clergymen not to meddle in mental and moral speculation. These were bullish times. Things had reached such a head that most medical men were now talking of nature as a legislated '*process* of change.'[15]

Some medical men actually toyed with 'transmutation' (the mutation or change of one species into another). Grant lectured on the 'metamorphoses' of fossil species yearly at University College. And James Gully, another Edinburgh graduate and editor of a radical London newspaper, translated the Heidelberg embryologist Friedrich Tiedemann's evolutionary treatise on *Comparative Physiology*. Gully

– who in later years became Darwin's physician – endorsed what one incensed critic called 'that most extravagant of all suppositions, that most grovelling of all religions – the self-created, self-endowed, and self-creating powers of Nature.'[16]

So in Darwin's London, there was a new fuelling of excitement. Natural theology was in crisis, and many expected a new life science to arise like a phoenix from its ashes. Here Darwin could make his mark. He could see the need to solve the great 'mystery of mysteries.' Lyell was bold; he would be bolder. He would provide the sort of reforming, developmental science so admired in his brother's circle.

Almost imperceptibly, he glided towards transmutation himself. It was easy because he had been habituated to it, in his grandfather's writings and Grant's talks; because London provided a conducive environment; and because he had the time and patience and love for intractable theoretical problems. He had been wondering about the stability of species since the last leg of his voyage. Now the experts were to supply the zoological rivets to hold his ideas together. And the first of these was hammered home by the bird painter John Gould.

A few days after arriving from Cambridge, he met Gould again in the zoo's museum and learned more of his finch revelations. Gould now realized that even Darwin's Galapagos 'wren' was a finch, giving him thirteen species in all. Darwin's mixed bag of birds was in fact a unique flock of finches.

It was a surprise, but because Darwin had neglected to label most of them by island he missed the import. Gould's conclusions about the other birds were what really rocked the boat. Darwin *had* labelled the four mockingbirds by island, and he had idly speculated that if they turned out to be true varieties it 'would undermine the stability of Species.' It would suggest that castaways, cut off from their mainland stock, could start to change. They turned out to be more than varieties; Gould told him that three were distinct *species*.[17] Moreover they had relatives on the American mainland; close relatives, but not identical species.

Darwin had his intractable problem: how to explain a crop of new related species, each to its island. The evidence of separate island species was mounting. Thomas Bell confirmed that the giant tortoises *were* native to the Galapagos, not food brought in by the buccaneers. This, with the finch and mockingbird findings, made it likely that the Vice-Governor had been right – that each island did have its own indigenous tortoise. But it was too late to prove the point: Darwin

2
The Mount, where Charles grew up, built by Robert Darwin after his marriage in 1796.

3
To the manor born:
Charles and his sister
Catherine, the babes of
the family.

1
Dr Robert Darwin, Charles's father: 'the largest man … I ever saw'.

Fuegian could be 'essentially the same creature,' from the hand of the same Creator.

He remembered Jemmy Button and his friends. Two years after being presented at Court they had reverted to a naked, filthy existence and were apparently happy. Jemmy had shown how difficult savage habits were to break. Fuegian savages seemed as well adapted to their waterless wastes as sophisticates were to European cities. But how could this be? Again it was as if two Creators were at work. How had *one* God produced this cultural spread? Had he personally locked the Fuegian into his miserable environment? Surely he could not intend that man remain a savage? How much better to see the one God using evolution to spread the human races naturally. And how much more reassuring; evolution for Darwin posed none of Lyell's bestializing threat – the gentlemen were at the top in their rightful place. They were the evolutionary successes.

To everyone's surprise, the first fossil monkeys were announced this spring. Two had turned up simultaneously, one from the foothills of the Himalayas, the other from the south of France. Both were immensely old, contemporaries of long-extinct mammals, and this, Lyell admitted uncomfortably, bought Lamarck the time he needed. (Lamarck had mooted the slow evolution of a stooping chimpanzee into an erect human.) Lyell gritted his teeth and conceded that from 'Lamarck's view, there may have been a great many thousand centuries for their tails to wear off, and the transformation to men to take place.'[20]

The Indian monkey was baboon-like, but larger than anything living today. A 'nearly perfect head' had been found, to everyone's astonishment, and it was announced at the Geological Society on 3 May. This was the meeting at which Darwin read his next paper, on the pampas. Both he and Lyell were aware of the ancient monkey's potential. Lyell dashed off a letter to his sister that night, laughing about tails wearing off, but Darwin did what petrified his mentor most: within months he was viewing the 'wonderful' monkeys in an evolutionary light.[21] Human ancestry was on the cards from the first moment that Darwin expressed a belief in transmutation.

Richard Owen was pushing Darwin hard, making him rethink the laws governing living matter.

In the museum of the College of Surgeons Owen and Darwin talked over fossil skulls and the meaning of life. It was the perfect place: the renovations at the college were complete, and the builders were out. It had been officially reopened in February in a typically had missed the opportunity, or rather eaten his way through it. Only his baby tortoise had survived, and that lacked the distinguishing features of the adult.[18]

By mid-March he realized that the original immigrants had become altered somehow, and that the alteration had actually produced an array of new species. He had joined the '*infidel* naturalists,' as Sedgwick castigated them, those adopting 'false theories' of Creation. For Anglicans such transmutation (or evolution as we call it today) threatened Christian Britain at its core. If life was self-made, what became of God's delegated power holding together a precarious paternalist society? Even for Lyell the prospect was appalling, because he feared that an ape ancestry would brutalize mankind and destroy his 'high estate.' Darwin was staring heresy in the face.

So why did he opt for transmutation? True, the zoologists' findings surprised him; the mockingbirds and tortoises *could* be seen as immigrants that had settled in differently on each island. The living llamas *could* be seen as diminutive descendants of the Patagonian giants Darwin had disinterred. But they need not have been. No one else saw them this way, not Gould nor Lyell – who were reverently reticent on such matters. Nor would Darwin's Anglican mentors like the Revds Henslow and Sedgwick have baulked at using such discoveries to applaud the providential distribution of beautifully-designed island and mainland species.

He was sailing close to the edge of his intellectual world. What drove him to live so dangerously? Why did he opt for a physical transformation of animals, so horribly bestializing in Lyell's view? His colleagues denied it pointedly, and the exception – Robert Grant – was being cold-shouldered for his reckless abandon. It required intellectual courage, and a sort of bull-headed character, pushing on determinedly to make his mark, proving he had no 'coward soul or faithless heart.' It took a certain type of person to be receptive; to see nothing heretical, nothing incompatible with his moral or social values. A person for whom there could even be something gained.[19]

Darwin had seen savage man in the flesh, in all his naked, revolting crudeness, and Lyell had not. This made much of the difference between them. For Lyell, transmutation and an ape ancestry threatened to bestialize man, drag him down to gutter-level, raze his 'high estate.' But Darwin had come face to face with men reduced to the lowest meanest level, wild, stupid, murderous, amoral – men barely above the beasts. Here was the real threat; here was man *already* brutalized and degraded. The point for Darwin was not to protect civilized gentlemen, but to explain how they and the

4

His first school, run by Mr Case, minister of the Unitarian chapel in Shrewsbury. The classroom windows overlooked a graveyard. In August 1817, a month after his mother's death, Charles was traumatized by the sight of a dragoon soldier being buried here.

5

Edinburgh University, where Darwin abortively studied medicine.

6
The best of rambling companions: Darwin's Edinburgh mentor, the radical Lamarckian Robert E. Grant.

7
The Plinian Society minutes of 27 March 1827, recording Darwin's short talk before the censored debate on the material basis of mind. The transcription reads:

> Mr. Darwin communicated to the Society two discoveries which he had made –
>
> 1. That the ova of the Flustra [a 'sea-mat' composed of tentacled hydra-like polyps] possess organs of motion.
> 2. That the small black globular body hitherto mistaken for the young Fucus Lorius [a seaweed], is in reality the ovum of the Pontobdella muricata [a leech that infests skates].
>
> At the request of the Society he promised to draw up an account of the facts and to lay ~~them~~ it, together with specimens, before the Society next evening.
>
> Dr. Grant detailed a number of facts regarding the Natural History of the Flustra.
>
> ~~Mr. Browne then read his paper on organization as connected with Life & Mind – in which he endeavoured to establish the following propositions.~~

[There then follow four propositions, which culminate in the heretical conclusion:]

> ~~And V.   That mind as far as one individual sense, & consciousness are concerned, is material.~~
>
> ~~A discussion ensued between Messrs. Binns, Greg, Dr Grant, Ainsworth, & Browne~~ – after which the Society adjourned.

Mr. Darwin communicated to the Society two discoveries which he had made —

1. That the ova of the Flustra possess organs of motion.
2. That the small black globular body hitherto mistaken for the young Fucus Loreus, is in reality the ovum of the Pontobdella muricata.

At the request of the Society he promised to draw up an account of the facts and to lay ~~them~~ it, together with specimens, before the Society next evening.

Dr. Grant detailed a number of facts regarding the Natural History of the Flustra.

~~Mr. Browne then read a paper on experiments as connected with life & mind in which he endeavoured to establish the following propositions.~~

~~I. That all activity is acquired~~

~~II. That it is the quality to increase proportion in the amount of the parts constituting organization,~~

~~which in the case of the Animalcules possible in the cause of development and progress of power.~~

~~III. That life is the abstract of the qualities inherent in the modes of energising matter.~~

~~IV. That mind is to be distinguished from life, being neither one of the functions nor a combination of functions, by the consideration of which life is constituted, nor arise to individuality a similar mode.~~

~~And V. That mind as of some individual never terminates after an onward, in activity.~~

~~A discussion ensued between Professor Kirner, Grey, Mr. Gould, ~~ sennett, Browne~~ — after which the Society adjourned.

The members present were. Messrs.

8
Christ's College, Cambridge: the view from Bacon the tobacconist's where Darwin first lodged.

9
Darwin's second cousin, who started him beetling at Cambridge, Revd William Darwin Fox.

10
Revd Robert Taylor, the 'Devil's Chaplain'. In May 1829 he publicly challenged his old Cambridge teachers to debate the truth of Christianity.

12
The botanist Revd John Stevens Henslow. He gave up the chance to sail on the *Beagle* and proposed Darwin instead.

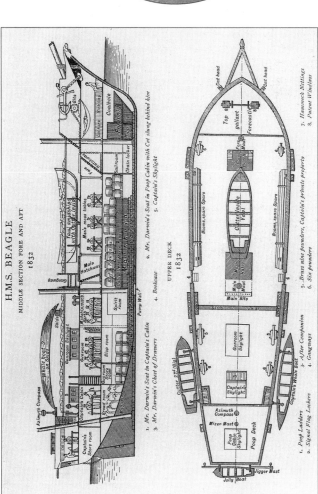

H.M.S. BEAGLE
MIDDLE SECTION FORE AND AFT
1832

Coalhole

Azimuth Compass

White boat on Skids

Skids

Gunroom Skylight

Captain's Cabin

Gunroom

Gunroom Coal room

Slop room

Gunroom Steward's room

Spirit room

Main Hatchway

Men's mess tables

Pump Well

Boobies

Chain locker

Sail room

Captain's Store room

Captain's Cabin

Bits

Bitts

1. Mr. Darwin's Seat in Captain's Cabin
2. Mr. Darwin's Seat in Poop Cabin with Cot slung behind him
3. Mr. Darwin's Chest of Drawers
4. Booboxes
5. Captain's Skylight

UPPER DECK
1832

Cat head

Top gallant

Forecastle

Cat head

Fore Mast

Boom, spare Spars

Cutter inside Boat

Boom, spare Spars

Main Hatch

Main Mast

Main Bits

STERN   STERN

Gunroom Skylight

Captain Skylight

Azimuth Compass

Mizen Mast

Poop Cabin Skylight

Poop Deck

Cutter 2nd Gig

Captain's Whale Boat

Jolly Boat

Jigger Mast

1. Poop Ladders
2. Signal Flag Lockers
3. After Companion
4. Gangways
5. Brass nine founders, Captain's private property
6. Six pounders
7. Hammock Nettings
8. Patent Windlass

11
Darwin's home afloat, after a drawing by his former shipmate Philip King.

13
'Naked miserable' Fuegians, 'stunted in their growth... red skins filthy &
greasy... hair entangled... gesticulation violent & without any dignity': a far cry
from high table at Christ's College.

14
Nature's indiscriminate power: the cathedral at Concepción after the earthquake
of 1835, 'the grandest pile of ruins' Darwin had ever seen.

lavish way with the Duke of Wellington, Sir Robert Peel, and 500 guests. Visitors flocked to the magnificent new museum, with its three-storey galleries packed with exhibits and supported on Doric pillars. Everything was on show, from an eight-foot Irish giant to chimpanzee skeletons, platypuses to fossil armadillos. It was as though 'the whole earth has been ransacked to enrich its stores.'

Here Owen and Darwin got down to fundamentals. On a major point Owen differed from Darwin's old teacher Henslow. Owen followed the Berlin physiologist Johannes Müller, believing that there was no *outside* creative force animating 'inert' matter. On the contrary, the simplest living matter, like the embryonic germ, had a unique, intrinsic 'organizing energy.' This directed growth, enabling tissues to be built according to plan. The force was concentrated in the germ, but waned as it diffused into the developing tissues, thus slowing growth with age. There was a reciprocal relationship between degree of organization and strength of the force. Darwin accepted this 'organizing energy' but began to modify it in his speculations on species.[22]

When Darwin came to tea with Owen one day they discussed the basics of life over a microscope in the drawing-room. Darwin undoubtedly kept quiet about his real leanings; after all, his goal was anathema. *He* now wanted a way of turning one species into the next. But Owen abominated talk of chimpanzee-ancestry or life's self-development. With the life-force limited, no individual can stretch beyond the organization marking out its species. A mollusc cannot spontaneously increase its vital force to 'develope new organs' or mutate into a mackerel.[23] Darwin was stymied.

Others were more pliant than Owen. The shy botanist Robert Brown thought that even the granular matter *inside* the germs was 'self-moving.' Break open minuscule polyp eggs and the atoms gush out, rushing around like 'bees swarming.' An acceptance of 'living atoms' was almost universal among the flaming democrats. It gave a scientific basis to their belief in free men controlling their own destinies, so important in an age of democratic demands. It provided the perfect political analogy – power from below, 'mandating' upwards, rising from the 'social atoms' – the people – rather than reigning down from a godhead or monarch. The notion of self-organizing atoms was spreading like wildfire through the democratic press. Looking at Brown's swarming atoms Darwin too became convinced. He ventured beyond Owen's position, accepting that the atoms themselves were alive. He was switching a Cambridge tradition of inert matter powered by God for a more secular one.[24] Living atoms were an essential step towards his understanding of nature's self-development.

Owen was a conservative Anglican. He denounced transmutation as subversive and anti-Christian: it would submerge man in a brutal quagmire, destroy his responsibility – and the atheist agitators showed where it would all end. (Owen met this street threat in a more immediate way. He drilled with the Honourable Artillery Company, the urban gentry's own volunteer regiment, which backed up the police during riots.) Bestializing man was reprehensible; people were not super-apes. To destroy mankind's unique status by stretching the life-force was like throwing muskets to the rabble. But Darwin, with his reforming Unitarian circle, treated nature's self-development quite casually. Apes failed to frighten him; the brutalization threat passed harmlessly overhead. What angered him was quite the reverse, the arrogance of those who put mankind on a pedestal.

He was still tussling with extinction. Unlike Owen, Darwin suspected that individuals were analogous to species. He thought that they both had fixed life spans, limited by the vital force. At sea he had compared the individuals of a species to the cuttings of a rampant Chiloé apple tree. They all perish together. How else to explain the deaths of the giant sloths?

From changing conditions perhaps? Darwin spewed out counter-facts in his miscellaneous 'Red Notebook,' which he had begun on the *Beagle*. Domestic animals can live under any conditions, he noted: 'Dogs. Cats. Horses. Cattle. Goat. Asses. have all run wild & bred. no doubt with perfect success.'[25] Where is the adaptation to local conditions here? And his fossil llamas showed that species can die without the climate changing. Again, it pointed to the conclusion that their time had just run out.

He drew out other life-and-death implications. Mammals, being complex and with a more diffused life-force, must have shorter lives as species than simple microscopic creatures. These are almost immortal; they continue today as they must have in the hot primeval seas. By contrast mammals have gone extinct one after the other, hence the succession of fossils in the rocks. Darwin told the Geological Society that his own pampas mammals had much shorter lives than their molluscan contemporaries. He mooted it too in his *Journal of Researches*, the book he was writing based on his *Beagle* diary. In his account of Patagonia he threw down a cryptic teaser to his readers. His former giants were not extinguished by climatic change, he said. So maybe, 'as with the individual, so with the species, the hour of life has run its course, and is spent.'[26]

What, then, of repopulation, the birth of new species to fill the gaps? If the 'organizing energy' is limited in each species, how could more complex forms be generated?

His deeper speculations were probably kept secret from everybody, except perhaps Eras and his dining circle. Darwin listened to Owen and Lyell, but let on little.

In his Great Marlborough Street study he continued to puzzle over the Galapagos. He became impatient to know what else besides mockingbirds, finches, and tortoises were derived from South American colonists. He asked Henslow to look at the Galapagos plants first, hoping he would pinpoint equivalent but different species on each island ('representative species,' as they are called – the descendants of the same immigrant). He pressed his dour friend the Revd Jenyns, who had received the *Beagle* fish by default, when no one else wanted them. But he was too slow, having to work up the subject from scratch. Darwin was eager, and prodded him to get on with the Galapagos fish first.

He continued collaborating with Gould, speaking with him at the Zoological Society on the South American rheas. Gould confirmed that the remnants of Darwin's Christmas dinner at Port Desire was a new species, smaller and fluffier. And to 'commemorate' Darwin's gifts to the Society, he christened it *Rhea Darwinii*.[27] It set Darwin thinking about these Patagonian birds. The Galapagos islands illustrated the importance of isolation for forming new species. But how to explain the two rheas, whose ranges overlapped near the Rio Negro? No barrier separated them, so how had they evolved?

Soon the first tantalizing transmutatory notes began appearing in his Red Notebook. Cryptic notes: 'Speculate on neutral [i.e. overlapping] ground of 2. ostriches [rheas],' he scribbled. Why were there no intermediates between the big and small species at the Rio Negro? He speculated that 'change not progressif: produced at one blow.' Meaning that perhaps one sprang fully formed from the other. One was born a mutant from the other's egg. Such fetal sports – 'monsters' or 'freaks' they were called – were well known to medical men; there were bottles of them in the Hunterian Museum. Owen himself was writing on these mutants from the womb, deformed by an unknown process. Whatever the cause, Darwin jotted, these deformed babies 'present an analogy to production of species.'[28]

Was it the same with the llamas? Did the extinct giants give birth to freaks – to today's small guanacos and llamas, which remain on the same arid plains? Whatever happened, Darwin looked on the mutations as dramatic.

On other points the evidence was contradictory. Galapagos life had diversified because of its island isolation, and the finches showed a 'perfect gradation' in their bills. But no isolation was necessary for the rheas – they roamed free on the mainland. It showed how much more thought was needed.

Time was the problem, or the lack of it; he had to finish the *Journal* first. He began shunning parties to get on with the travelogue, grumbling about overwork and groaning with a bad stomach. He ploughed on, augmenting his diary account with bits and bobs from his *Beagle* geological and zoological notebooks, lacing it with the latest from his bevy of specialists. Everything, he told his cousin Fox, was going in: the habits of animals, the geology and the natives, and the scenery 'will make the hodge-podge complete.'

Not quite everything; the finches were barely mentioned. He simply noted his suspicions that they were probably 'confined to different islands.' He continued to believe that these birds had similar habits. This and the similar terrain on the islands left him baffled as to how they could have evolved so differently – perhaps they too had appeared at a 'blow.'[29]

He tore on, trying to meet the deadline for his book. As if the *Journal* were not enough, he began toying with a new project: to collect the experts' reports on his *Beagle* animals and edit a multi-volume *Zoology*, a spotter's guide for future travellers. He relished the idea of seeing 'the gleanings of my hands, after having passed through the brains of abler naturalists collected together in one work.' The *Zoology* looked impossibly ambitious, unless the government stepped in with a grant (at least to cover the cost of the 150 engravings, estimated at £1000). All the zoologists – Bell, Waterhouse, Owen, Gould – came out in favour; but as museum staff, they cut little weight when it came to funding.

Here great patrons were needed. Darwin arranged an interview with the Earl of Derby, President of the Zoological Society – an aristocrat who was more interested in his menagerie than debating in the Lords (where he had been placed to stack the House in the Whigs' favour). The antiquarian Duke of Somerset, President of the Linnean, was also approached, and of course the Revd Whewell at the Geological was ready to canvass government help. Darwin wondered how others had obtained sponsorship. He asked John Richardson, the naturalist who published an account of Captain Franklin's search for the Northwest Passage, and whose specimens were also stowed in the zoo's museum.[30]

Darwin might not have had an inside track to the Chancellor of the Exchequer, but he knew someone who did. Henslow could tap the old-boy network. The Chancellor was Thomas Spring Rice, the Whig MP for Cambridge, and Henslow had campaigned for him. Both men had also helped in 1836 to get a charter for that great Whig initiative, the University of London. Henslow's friends in the Cabinet had just engineered him a 'Crown Living' at Hitcham, in Suffolk, worth £1000 a year. So he was well known, and he put out feelers. Spring Rice summoned Darwin for an interview and, instead of grilling him, coolly told him to make the most of the Treasury money! Henslow had done his work. 'You have been the making of me,' Darwin acknowledged. 'If it had not been for you *alone* I should never have got the 1000£.'[31] The cash spoke eloquently for Darwin's status, contacts, and potential, even though his scientific credentials were negligible. Social inferiors had inordinate difficulty prying grants out of a retrenching government, but Darwin's came easily. It enabled him to dispense his own patronage, to act as taskmaster and paymaster, chivvying a Gradgrind work force of white-collar museum men. The *Zoology* was secured.

It meant an inordinate amount of work, cooped up in this 'vile smokey place.' He was still apportioning his precious relics. Edible fungi from Tierra del Fuego and fossil wood from the Andes went to the shy Robert Brown, causing him to open up. 'I think my silicified wood, has unflintified Mr Brown's heart,' Darwin jibed. Beetles went off to the Revd Hope, in memory of those far-off insect-hunting days, and Chonos potatoes to Henslow, now so preoccupied with his parish that he hardly seemed to notice. A rural parish: the mere thought reminded Darwin of how much he missed the countryside. He felt trapped in his Marlborough Street 'prison,' staring at the dingy walls of the house opposite. He gave a quiet inner scream, 'I do hate the streets of London.'[32]

He was becoming obsessed by transmutation. Everything kept resolving into tantalizing questions. How did plants reach the Galapagos, let alone mid-oceanic outposts like Keeling Island? What species were in his Keeling samples, he asked Henslow, and could their seeds 'endure floating in salt water'?

Continuing to collaborate with Gould, Darwin became more embarrassed by his lack of proper labels. He belatedly set out to prove that each finch had its island home. He examined FitzRoy's scrupulously documented skins, deposited in the British Museum, and contacted crewmen who had made their own collections. Even his servant,

Syms Covington, had three Galapagos finches, each with its island noted. The replies helped him to rack his memory and reconstruct his own finches' localities, although the by-guess-or-by-God approach led to errors. At the end of the day he was convinced that the finches, like the mockingbirds and tortoises, were island-specific. That allowed him to see them as the diversified descendants of mainland stock.

On 20 June the country went into mourning as William IV died. With the flags at half-mast Darwin finally finished the *Journal*. His account of the voyage had been written in record time, seven months from start to finish. Given his uncommon trouble expressing himself in 'common English,' he declared that he would 'always feel respect for every one who has written a book, let it be what it may.' As he left for ten days with the family at Shrewsbury on the 26th he looked forward to the future as an author. And as a geologist, judging by the way his third paper, on coral reefs, had been received. The applause of the 'great guns,' he conceded, 'gives me much confidence.' It encouraged him to put his 'shoulder to the wheel' and plan a book on South American geology.[33]

He also put his shoulder to another, more massive, wheel. He threw himself into a study of transmutation.

16

Tearing Down the Barriers

IN MID-JULY 1837 Darwin took the plunge and opened a clandestine transmutation notebook (called his 'B' Notebook). He was entering an intense and lonely new world of monologues and musings. The brown-covered pad was small, and on the title page he inscribed in bold letters the word *Zoonomia*, to signal that he was treading the same path as his grandfather. He then burst into a continuous series of notes covering twenty-seven or so pages, a breathless machine-gun-like effusion of telegraphic jottings, representing hurried and excited trains of thought on the laws of life. Transmutation was a fact, and these scribblings set the framework for his exploration of the ways animals and plants changed.

Odd and obvious questions litter the text. 'Why is life short' and sexual reproduction so important? Because sexual mixing produces variants and a fast turnover spreads them through the population. Sex causes variety, which is necessary to enable species to meet new conditions. If climates alter, species can respond quickly, generating new adaptations automatically.[1]

But Owen had denied that simpler species could grow more complex. They were unable to stretch up with new vitality, summon up new stocks of 'organizing energy' or life-force. Frustrated, Darwin kicked against Owen's life-force limiting each species. Darwin knew that something must 'alter the race to [fit a] *changing* world.' As he kept saying, species *must* 'become permanently changed.' They *must* pass on and build on their modifications.

One problem could be circumvented. Clearly, any varieties generated were normally blended back into the population as a result of 'intermarriages,' or crossings. This normally contained the changes, keeping a species looking uniform. It explained why classifiers had always assumed that species were fixed and immutable. Isolation of varieties was the way round this. In-breeding finches or mockingbird castaways facing a brave new world on some 'fresh isl[an]^d.' would accentuate their new traits.[2] A slightly thicker beak on one Galapagos island could not be lost by being blended back into the mainland American stock. The bill could continue growing thicker as the finches in-bred. Islands allowed the possibility of rapid, permanent deviation. The longer a country was separated – like Australia with its peculiar platypuses – the more different its mammals would be.

He then flirted with some of Lamarck's basic tenets. If the simplest monads – the building blocks of life – are spontaneously emerging from inorganic matter, they would *push* the escalator upwards. They would provide the pressure from below, forcing life onward – or, as Darwin doodled, 'the simplest cannot help . . . – becoming more complicated.' Like individuals maturing, perhaps the species stand on an escalator and are carried effortlessly upwards. As they move on, the creatures below rise to fill their old shoes. He joked about it: 'If all men were dead then monkeys make men. – Men make angels.'[3] It was a joke with terrifying consequences for the old élite, playing on a bestial image of monkey origins. It showed that this ancestry held no horrors for him.

Owen was pushing on with the *Beagle* haul. He now recognized five giant, archaic armadillos and sloths and was describing them in *Fossil Mammalia*, his contribution to Darwin's *Zoology* series. These huge herbivores must have lived on the pampas plains as African game does today. 'What an extraordin[ar]^y. mystery it is,' Darwin puzzled to Lyell, 'the cause of the death of these numerous animals, so recently, & with so little physical [i.e. environmental] change.'

The blitz of thoughts continued as he squared up to extinction in his notebook. He kept recycling Owen's idea that the complexity of a species was inversely related to its life span. He sketched an '*irregularly branched*' tree to convey the genealogical history of animals and plants. If life was like a huge old oak, growing through the ages, the fossil mammals were the 'terminal buds dying,' their life-force decayed. The trunk symbolized the ancient common ancestor, the stock from which all animals sprang. And the single trunk must have had a single origin. Darwin realized that life's initial spontaneous appearance from inorganic matter on the earth must have been a one-off affair, buried in the dim, distant past. Living molecules cannot be emerging constantly, everywhere, or millions of unrelated trees of life would be springing up, making the whole image 'excessively complicated.'[4] The origin of life was a once-only event, lost somewhere in pre-Silurian times.

The scrawling continued furiously as he worked through the implications. If everything came from one set of living atoms or 'monads' in the primeval past, then these particles could not have lifespans related to complexity; otherwise *everything* on each branch would die simultaneously, whole classes would collapse – mammals, birds, reptiles, or whatever. It didn't happen. Suddenly he saw the light. 'Monad has not definite existence.' There was *no* limited life-force holding species back. He had broken through Owen's barrier.

Life had originated only once, then ramified through history, an endless growth, terminal buds dying as others appeared. No revitalizing was necessary, no creative re-energizing. He dashed off pages exploring the family-tree image. The deaths of terminal twigs produced the gaps, between birds and mammals, or between families of beetles. The more distant two groups, the further down the stem their common ancestor, and the more dead wood must have fallen off in between.[5] With extinction no longer from old age, he became convinced (contrary to his former view of the giant llamas' demise) that it resulted from conditions changing too fast. Adaptation – the fit of an organism to its niche – was back on the agenda. If the environment changed gradually, animals adapted, transmuting to keep themselves synchronized; if they failed to keep pace, extinction was inevitable.

Adaptation was not alone in explaining an animal's make-up. There was also a 'heredetary [sic] taint.' The 'taint' was the general plan bequeathed by the first common forebear. All fishes, reptiles, birds, and mammals share a vertebrate plan. All snails, slugs, and cuttlefish conform to a molluscan blueprint. Adaptation was simply stamped on top of this structural plan.

But how do adaptive changes match the climatic rhythms? Does the climate modify the reproductive process, causing offspring to emerge ready-adapted? He assumed that all variants emerge perfect, but then he was still living in Paley's perfect world. Even so, it was not a use of Paley that his Cambridge mentors would have condoned. The idea of an organism continually adjusting itself was anathema, perfection or no. This was dynamic self-sufficiency.

His reflections became startling. Because life followed the vagaries of climate, there was no yardstick to measure progress. For Grant, the cooling planet drove life upwards towards higher, hotter-blooded forms. But Darwin forswore any unidirectional change; life adapted to the quirks of habitat. It sprawled everywhere; animals were not climbing a mythical ladder, stretching up to the highest human rung. Even races of people were spreading laterally into their peculiar niches: Jemmy Button's Fuegians into a desolate, windswept wilderness, civilized Englishmen into their factory cities. Darwin was left with a shockingly relative outlook. 'It is absurd to talk of one animal being higher than another,' he mused. '*We* consider those, where the intellectual faculties most developed, as highest. – A bee doubtless would [use] ... instincts' as a criterion.[6] In his bee's-eye view man was no longer the crown of creation. Even the radical Lamarckians kept a human-topped chain, and allowed an imperious man to look down on life. Darwin's non-human orientation was a total departure from radical wisdom, let alone religious convention.

Through a hot August he continued 'stewing in this great den of a place,' jotting down heretical notes. In September he was still teasing at the problem, while continuing to correct the *Journal* proofs, complaining that he was 'tied by the leg, hard at work as any galley slave.'

He switched to transport problems, devising ways of shipping creatures out to islands to start the process of speciation. He knew it was a serendipitous affair from the fact that there were mice on some Chonos islands and not others. Ingenuity was the key: 'Owls. transport mice alive?' he queried. Well, that might explain rodents. Seeds were easier; they could have been blown or washed ashore. Or thrushes and coots might fly out to islands and 'bring [them] in stomach.' He left a memo to look into it. What else would survive a sea crossing? He started devising tests to find out. 'Experimentise on land shells in salt water & lizards d[itt]o.,' he scrawled, hoping to try it in the future. Perhaps the extreme conditions of the crossing would themselves alter the floating seeds. 'It would be [a] curious experiment to know whether soaking seeds in salt water' changes them.[7] Perhaps the owls, and coots, and seeds did not have to travel as far as supposed. They could have hopped across island arcs that subsequently sank beneath the waves. His theory of subsidence allowed him to summon up island chains as migratory stepping-stones.

Thinking about blue seas took him back to the voyage. During those years island-hopping himself, he would have given his right arm to be home. Now he was dreaming himself back to sea again. He had missed his family so much afloat, yet here he was, trapped in his London prison, far from the Shrewsbury countryside. All that longing, all the planning, and what had come of it? He had seen his father and sisters for only nine days since his return!

He was stuck indoors, wrapped up in his covert notebook. 'What a waste of life to stop all summer in this ugly Marlborough Street &

see nothing but the same odious house on the opposite side.' He turned down Elizabeth Wedgwood's invitation to a concert in order to finish the *Journal* proofs. They were dragging on, cumbersome prose and recalcitrant commas only increasing his misery, leading to the groan: 'What a very difficult thing it is to write correctly.' His *Zoology* volumes also needed planning and Darwin lost more time liaising with authors and editors. The Treasury grant was to keep the cover price down and make the books useful to the public. Given it, the publishers calculated that they could bring out the whole 800-page edition, including 250 plates, for £9.

His cackhanded language in the *Journal*'s preface immediately landed him in trouble. FitzRoy, a stickler for etiquette, was 'astonished at the total omission of any notice of the officers' for their help, let alone the offhand way he himself was mentioned. It was tactless of Darwin, but prickly of FitzRoy. 'I esteem *you* far too highly to break off from you willingly,' FitzRoy announced in his hoity-toity way.[8] The connection of Darwin's volume with his own was 'one of feeling and fidelity – not of *expediency*.' Darwin made immediate amends, giving fulsome thanks, and honour was restored, but it showed that he still had to step lively with the Captain.

The work and worry were compounding. He had performed prodigious mental and manual feats during the voyage with no obvious ill effects. But now, deep into his clandestine work, compiling notes that would shock his geological compatriots, his health was breaking. He was living a double life with double standards, unable to broach his species work with anyone except Eras, for fear he be branded irresponsible, irreligious, or worse. It began to tell in the pit of his stomach. On 20 September he suffered an 'uncomfortable palpitation of the heart,' and his doctors urged him '*strongly* to knock off all work' and leave for the country.[9] Two days later he finished the *Journal* proofs and headed to Shrewsbury for a rest.

He did not get much of one. He returned via Maer, where Emma and the family wore him out with questions about gaucho life. Emma, at twenty-eight, was a year older than Charles and talented. She knew French and Italian, and more than a bit of German (which was a bit more than Charles). She played the piano fluently (after lessons from Chopin) and was keen on outdoor sports, being a 'dragonness' at archery. While Charles was at sea, she had parried four or five marriage proposals. Then her mother had suffered a seizure and become bedridden, requiring her constant presence at home. Her courting days seemed to have ended – despite the precedent of her brother Jos's marriage in August to Charles's sister Caroline, herself thirty-seven.

But Emma kept up hope while serving the family as nurse, caretaker, and aunt. For diversion she read the latest novels and worked in the garden. Here Charles now strolled, and Uncle Jos showed him some disused ground where lime and cinders, spread years before, had disappeared into the soil, leaving a layer of loam. Jos assumed that worms had done the work, although he thought such gardening trivia of little consequence to a young man working on a continental scale.[10] Charles disagreed, and from this unprepossessing beginning sprang a lifelong interest in the humble earthworm – a tiny unsung creature which, in its untold millions, transformed the land as the coral polyps did the tropical sea.

Darwin returned to London on 21 October but his palpitating heart remained in the Shropshire countryside. His talk on worms and their castings to the Geological Society on 1 November only highlighted his growing idiosyncrasies. This august body expected something grander than *worms*. Darwin knew it; he now steeled himself and began planning a technical book on South American geology. Separate papers on Chile's coastline, the fossil-tombs, and coral reefs were not enough. He had to bring them together in a rounded volume. The thought suffocated him more than the November fog. He hankered after a rural retreat of his own. He viewed his Cambridge friends, Henslow, Fox, and Jenyns in their country rectories with envy. In November he finally took a few days out from the tropical lagoons to visit Fox in his Isle of Wight parish. The contrast with his palm-fringed beaches was stark – these were bitter wintery days and the Channel was choppy and more black than blue. But he was just happy to be out of the 'abominable murky atmosphere of London.'[11]

He had a rather idealistic image of vicarage life. Jenyns was 'bitterly complaining of his solitude' at Swaffham Bulbeck. It wasn't only the isolation. 'Henslow tells me he hears a groan occasionally escape from you, when you mention my fishes,' Darwin consoled Jenyns. This was an understatement. His friend was staggering under the weight of pickled fish. Even though half the catch had deteriorated during the voyage, he was left with 137 species to describe, 75 of them new. The *Fish* volume in the *Zoology* series was coming out in parts, and Darwin hoped that he could squash sixteen fish into each number. But Jenyns was having trouble meeting the quota. Darwin was learning to cajole in his beguiling way: 'for the credit of English zoologists, do not despair and give up,' he pleaded, even if 'you have undertaken [the job] chiefly out of kindness . . . for me. – I am sure I am very much obliged to you.' Then he about-faced and floored his friend with an alternative strike: 'you must not for a moment *hesitate* about throwing it up, if your health or want of time prevents your taking any satisfaction in the employment.'[12] Darwin got what he wanted, and what he expected; Jenyns struggled on to confirm that all the Galapagos fishes were new.

Things were moving faster on the fossil front. Owen had christened the 'llama' *Macrauchenia* and worked steadily on it through Christmas and New Year 1838. His reputation for speed was deserved, and his instalment was the first of any of the *Zoology* volumes. This opening eight-shilling part of *Fossil Mammalia*, with its full-size, pull-out illustration of the two-foot skull of the rodent *Toxodon*, appeared in February. It came at an opportune moment. At the anniversary meeting of the Geological Society on the 16th Owen was 'wonderfully pleased' to receive the Society's Wollaston Medal for diagnosing Darwin's hippo-sized fossils.

Darwin himself basked in the reflected glory. But it did not pay to look too closely at Owen's conclusions, which were straying from expectation. Less a llama, *Macrauchenia* was turning out to be more a tapir 'with a soupçon of camel' thrown in.[13] This was a mite inconvenient; Darwin actually wanted a llama ancestor for his pampas guanacos. No matter, he ignored Owen's fine print. He persisted in looking at the bones through a naturalist's eyes. Because the spot where he found the fossils betrayed a harsh, arid environment, he continued to visualize them as camel-like llamas.

Darwin took Lyell's advice and turned down Geological jobs to get on with his projects. The President William Whewell had asked him to become a Secretary in 1837, and Henslow thought it his duty 'as a follower of science.' But Darwin declined, ostensibly on account of his ignorance of English geology. More embarrassing still, 'it would be disgraceful to the Society' to have a Secretary who could not pronounce a word of French. Imagine the *faux pas* as he fumbled with foreign papers! And written English was barely less mysterious to him, so the prospect of abstracting manuscripts was hardly appealing. If these weren't excuses enough, he topped them off by adding that 'anything which flurries me completely knocks me up afterwards and brings on a bad palpitation of the heart.'

By 1838 his resolve was crumbling. He was having trouble avoiding official posts, time-wasters or no. On 5 February he accepted the Vice-Presidency of the Entomological Society (founded by fellow beetle aficionados Waterhouse and Hope in 1833). Whewell's pressure was now relentless. He was still trying to recruit Darwin to the geologists' *sanctum sanctorum*. In his presidential address, he praised Owen's results and extolled Darwin's circumnavigation 'as one of the most important events for geology which has occurred for many years.' With such flattery from the podium Darwin had to succumb. He was coerced into becoming a Secretary. 'I could not refuse with fairness,' he lamented to Henslow, 'although it is an office which I do not relish.'[14]

One excuse he could never mention. He was joining the star chamber of Britain's best geologists, urban gentry and Anglican clergy mostly, upright men who execrated evolution as morally filthy and politically foul. This was no exaggeration: Sedgwick, a past President, damned Lamarck, Geoffroy, and the revolutionary French for their 'gross (and I dare say, filthy) views of physiology.' How could Darwin rub shoulders with the excitable old Proctor if he found out? Sedgwick saw science provide moral uplift in a turbulent age. It should raise men's eyes heavenward, while reminding them of their station on earth. The geological élite had to provide spiritual leadership, not spread depraved 'doctrines of spontaneous generation and transmutation of species, with all their train of monstrous consequences.'[15]

On 7 March, before Whewell, Sedgwick and the rest, Darwin read his longest paper, on the devastating Concepción earthquake. He explained how the same crustal movements were responsible for thousands of miles of volcanic and earthquake activity along the length of the Andes, which were rising slowly as a consequence. Lyell was delighted at this support for his gradualist tenets, and Darwin saw his 'geological salvation' in Lyell's principles. The new Secretary was not only reading his own papers, but other people's. Yet he remained edgy, despite hours of practice, whispering the lines to himself in private. 'I was so nervous at first, I somehow could see nothing all around me,' he recalled, '& I felt as if my body was gone, & only my head left.'[16]

This was the red public face of an ambitious young geologist, wending his way into the corridors of geological power. But his identity was split; privately he had unmitigated contempt for the arrogance of the dons. Secretly, at home, he lurched into undisguised sneers at them for bending the universe to fit man and then pronouncing a panegyric on God's design. He scorned anyone who found Whewell 'profound, because he says length of days adapted to duration of sleep of man.!!! whole universe so adapted!!! & not man to Planets. – instance of arrogance!!' This was Darwin, Whewell's right-hand man, schizoid, scorning in private, smiling in public.

His notetaking became more secretive as his public position strengthened. The deterministic talk at Eras's dinner table was a world removed from the Revd Whewell's miraculous human-centred science. Darwin pressed on, stomach notwithstanding, cleansing a corrupt science, convinced he was right, dying to make his mark – his moral sanction coming from the huge shift to Dissenting values in the country. He was leading a crusading reform, breaking Whewell's old Tory Anglican dynasty, stripping the privileges it accorded man in the cosmos, as the Whigs were stripping the clergy's privileges on earth. Darwin became more and more frustrated by an arrogant theology. 'People often talk of the wonderful event of intellectual Man appearing,' he sniffed, smashing another idol, yet 'the appearance of insects with other senses is more wonderful.' Human chauvinism now outraged him.

Yet he was desperate to earn the respect of his scientific elders. His double life became more nerve-racking as the months passed, setting off an inner turmoil. What if they saw through his false face? He took so much pleasure in unravelling the enigmas of natural history, but his thoughts were becoming dangerous, his brooding masochistic. The pandemonium in his mind made a subtle and complex counterpoint to the public turmoil in urban Britain. (The country was now deep in an economic depression, and ahead lay the grimmest five years in the nineteenth century, with massive unemployment, starvation, and riot.) What he was mooting was disreputable in Anglican eyes, and socially subversive. His vision was no longer of a world personally sustained by a patrician God, but self-generated. From echinoderms to Englishmen, all had arisen through a lawful redistribution of living matter in response to an orderly changing geological environment.

He dashed off cryptic notes with increasing confidence. Everywhere he left the prominent stamp – 'my theory' – and he was in no two minds about its importance. He exuberantly claimed that 'my' theory 'would give zest to recent & Fossil Comparative Anatomy.' It would revolutionize the 'study of instincts, heredetary. [sic] & mind,' and transform the 'whole [of] metaphysics.'[17] It would – but not yet. The *ancien régime* had to give way first, the reactionary Church-and-corporation men, the sort now being swept out of the town halls countrywide as the radical Dissenters infused a new improving, secular, industrial spirit into society.

Darwin's secret notes left him looking like a radical Unitarian. They expressed the ethical feelings of a wider Dissenting community, sick of slavery, demanding equality, against privilege. His abhorrence of slavery in this emotive period coloured his evolutionary fervour. He scribbled:

> Animals – whom we have made our slaves we do not like to consider our equals. – Do not slave holders wish to make the black man other kind? Animals with affections, imitation, fear. pain. sorrow for the dead.

Pain and suffering united enslaved man and the miserable beasts. As he wrote in 1838 abolitionist passions were being fired by the Whigs' former Lord Chancellor Henry Brougham, who was fighting for the immediate release of the Jamaican slaves. Martineau too was writing more moral tales after her American trip, of the beating and murder of slaves, and the heroism of the abolitionists – tales that Emma Wedgwood found stirring, despite the 'little Harrietisms' littering the text. Darwin was reflecting what fellow anti-slavers felt, and he was not alone in extending the ethical net from oppressed men to the forlorn brutes. The Quaker doctor John Epps – a London phrenologist, homoeopathist, and disestablishment campaigner – had come 'to consider all creatures as being equally important in the scale of creation as myself; to regard the poor Indian slave as my brother.'[18]

This Dissenting mood gave Darwin his sanction as he filled his heretical pages. Radical Dissenters were openly discussing mind and pain in nature. Many were adamant that all creation was conscious and suffering. Theirs was no 'happy world' admired through Paley's rose-tinted spectacles, teeming with 'delighted existence.' It was John Wesley's bleaker image, in which 'the whole creation travaileth and groaneth.' This was Epps's reading of St Paul. He was adamant that '*animals enjoy* MIND' – and with it personality, desires, and pain.[19]

But this mental egalitarianism absorbed by Darwin had disreputable doctrinal associations. Even though some Anglicans – like old William Kirby – accepted that animals showed a modicum of reason, demagogues like Epps mixed their views so promiscuously with anti-Anglican polemics that they acquired a dangerously heretical mystique. And however much reason Kirby granted to the worms, Darwin gave them something infinitely more abominable, a place in the dirt among the roots of man's family tree. Here he was, scratching breathlessly:

> if we choose to let conjecture run wild then animals our fellow brethren in pain, disease death & suffering & famine; our slaves in the most laborious work, our companion in our

amusements. they may partake, from our origin in one
common ancestor we may all be netted together.

The dangerous point was that man's mind had emerged from the
worm's in the first place. This was the crux.[20] By subjecting mind
and morality to self-evolving forces, he threatened the ideals so
cherished by the geological gentry: human dignity and accountability.
If man was only a better sort of brute, where was his spiritual
dignity, and if he had self-evolved, what of his moral accountability
to God, no more his Creator? Since moral accountability, with
eternal punishment and rewards, was part of the fabric binding
society, that too would crash.

Had Lyell or Owen or Sedgwick or Whewell known his beliefs,
they would have found them utterly demoralizing. Darwin could
expect a furore among his geological friends if they discovered his
secret. No more 'hail fellow, well met.' He could be labelled as a
traitor. His respectability would be compromised. Not only would
his science be impugned. He himself would be accused of reckless
abandon.

17

Mental Rioting

THE NEW SECRETARY continued brainstorming, 'mental riot-ing' he called it. By February 1838 he was ploughing through a second pocketbook (the maroon 'C' Notebook).[1]

He was mulling over fancy and farmyard breeds. He traipsed down Regent Street on crisp spring mornings to talk pedigree dogs and pigeon-fancying at the zoo museum. The subject seemed mundane, set against the platypuses and pythons, bottled snakes and spirit-dripping bats. But the landed gents had more esoteric lore about dogs than about all the zoo animals put together. William Yarrell's were the best brains for picking. Yarrell was a gun-and-dog man himself – or rather a newspaper wholesaler, but in a town with fourteen dailies he could afford to indulge his country passions. He was a mine of facts on domestic varieties, crosses, hybrids, and foreign escapees, and his tips littered Darwin's notes. He taught Darwin about crossing farmyard stock, and how older, established breeds always dominate the hybrid offspring. Darwin fidgeted in his Marlborough Street study that spring, jotting anecdotes of blood hounds, gun dogs, and horse crosses, while dreaming of galloping over Shropshire fields.

All along, he had assumed that wild variants appeared ready-adapted, but the breeders were leaving him uneasy. What if 'in course of ages ten thousand varieties' are produced '& those alone preserved which are well adapted'? It was a discordant but interesting idea. Not *all* offspring need be a good fit; think of the grotesque, the runts. He now conceded that two types were possible, 'adaptations' and 'Monsters,' the good and the bad, with the latter leading to the ugly. To produce the fanciers' whimsies, the top-knotted pigeons, hairless dogs, tailless cats, and deformed pigs, breeders were picking

240

the 'monsters.' They were cutting across nature's grain. He asked Yarrell outright: weren't breeders going *against* nature? Their way of 'picking varieties' was surely 'unnatural.'[2]

Humans not only selected animals, they were self-selectors. People picked and chose mates, favouring certain traits; they were in the mêlée, part of nature's process. Darwin was convinced that *Homo sapiens* was a single species split into climatically adapted clusters. He damned slave-owners for setting themselves up as a superior species, and he whittled away at their arguments, looking at the subject from every odd angle. Since the day on Chiloé in 1834 when a whaler's surgeon mentioned that the Sandwich Islanders' lice died on Englishmen, he was fascinated, and collected parasites from the various races to try to prove the 'origin of man one.'[3]

He came up with a new word for the process of development by transmutation at this time. 'Descent' he called it, and the descent of man was as legitimate a subject as the descent of cats and cows.

As the weather warmed, he began to reassess nature's perfection in his picture of descent. The whole theology of 'perfection' had been lambasted by the secularist fanatics as a sort of justification for the status quo – the notion that everything is as it should be. It had reigned supreme in Cambridge circles, and Darwin had never doubted it. But he began to see that perfect adaptations were not the whole story. Nature herself was eliminating the 'monsters' that breeders fancied. How did her scythe work, how were the freaks killed? In one instance he actually mooted a struggle to decide the fittest. He imagined a 'chance offspring' that had 'a little more vigour' – a head start – by virtue of some peculiarity. Then he cut to talk of strutting male combat, 'warlike' cocks, and females preferring the 'victorious' males.[4] It was a flash whose light dimmed for the moment.

He was pulling away from Cambridge theology: his example suggested that perfection *might* be the serendipitous product of chance. In fact, fitness had to be chancy given the quirks of climate. A gargoyle in one environment might be a godsend in another. His doodlings became fascinating at this point. 'If puppy born with thick coat then [in warm climates it would be a] monstrosity, [but] if brought into cold country . . . [it would be a good] adaptation.' Even good and bad, adaptation and deformity, were not the absolutes they once seemed. Their value fluctuated with the environment. Again it was another brilliant flash that faded.

He overturned it all by considering a better – and more goal-directed – way to produce adaptations. How did flippers appear on land animals whose homes were frequently flooded? He followed

Lamarck in suggesting they met the challenge by altering their habits. The ancestors of ducks and otters had begun by paddling, fishing, and exploiting the new resources. These habits, repeated incessantly, became ingrained; the animals now instinctively swam, stretched the skin between the toes, strengthened the muscles, and ultimately ended up with webbed feet. This was the pure, unadulterated Lamarckism that Lyell lampooned, Sedgwick execrated, and the geologists damned as rubbish. Darwin was now deep in his Lamarckian phase. Quietly, to himself, he praised the Frenchman's 'prophetic spirit in science –. the highest endowment of lofty genius' – words he would never repeat in public.[5]

He started firing questions at breeders, not singly of course, but whole *lists*, querying the way babies take after one parent and whether females 'prefer certain males.' Being interested in the 'Effects of habit' on the body he also wanted to know about 'trades affecting form of man' – whether blacksmiths' biceps are passed on to their boys.[6] Be it Mr Wynne, his father's gardener and an oracle on farmyard breeds, or the back-room zoologists, everyone suffered his strange quizzing. He tried any and every tack to get a handle on the inheritance of peculiarities in animals and man.

He was now in and out of the zoologists' museum continually, tapping Gould's brains on birds and Yarrell's on the barnyard. He heard a French visitor announce that the Galapagos tortoises were so many distinct species, finally confirming what he suspected. Gould and Waterhouse were in the midst of describing the *Beagle* specimens, with Darwin managing the whole operation. But the Treasury money remained tight. He restricted Gould to fifty illustrations of birds, to keep within budget, and even then he could only afford five pence each to have them coloured. He turned down a naturalists' dinner with Henslow, apologizing that he was 'tied firmly by the leg' as a result of co-ordinating the *Zoology*.[7]

FitzRoy was making his own apologies. Darwin's *Journal* was printed and awaiting the Captain's volume before it could be published. But FitzRoy's was late: 'I am rather old fashioned in habits as well as ideas – Ergo – a slow coach,' he explained. Darwin was frustrated, and also a bit wary after FitzRoy's splenetic outburst about the preface. Still, he was a landlubber now. He no longer shared the Captain's table. He did not have to smile sweetly and stay silent. The FitzRoys invited him over to tea at the end of March, and Darwin told his sister: 'The Captain is going on very well, – that is for a man, who has the most consummate skill in looking at everything & every body in a perverted manner.' He began to wonder about the quality of FitzRoy's work. The third volume – Capt. King's – was frankly impenetrable; 'no pudding for little shool [sic] boys [was] ever so heavy. It abounds with Natural History of a very trashy nature. – I trust the Captain's own volume will be better.' The Secretary of the best scientific society in town was imposing his own high standards.

Darwin's geology book was taking shape by now. He raced on through the spring, mentally splashing around in blue lagoons as he wrote up coral reefs. He was 'covering so much paper' that it would be impossible to contain his ideas in a single volume. At first he thought he could keep coral atolls and volcanic islands together and follow up with another volume later, but even these two topics took on lives of their own and had to be divorced. He marched on resolutely, describing the Atlantic Islands and the Cape of Good Hope, talking on earthquakes at the Geological, managing the *Zoology*, scribbling on descent.[8]

On the question of descent, mankind was now his focus. He had reached the walls of the citadel. Evolution, he believed, explained every mental tic, every bodily posture: not only the spine and spleen, but people's habits, instincts, thoughts, feelings, conscience, and morality. 'Man – wonderful Man' must collapse into nature's cauldron. Man, 'with divine face, turned towards heaven,' – 'he is not a deity, his end under present form will come ... he is no exception. – he possesses some of the same general instincts, & feelings as animals.' Plumbing the radical depths Darwin saw the cataclysmic consequences. 'Once grant that species ... may pass into each other ... & whole fabric totters & falls.'[9] The Creationist 'fabric' and all it entailed was his target. He peered into the future and saw the old miraculous edifice collapsing, even as Sedgwick saw Anglican society crumbling as a consequence.

The refrain was reinforced by his first sight of an ape. It was an unseasonably warm day, 28 March, when he rode to the zoo, and 'by the greatest piece of good fortune' it was hot enough for the rhino to be turned out. 'Such a sight has seldom been seen, as to behold the rhinoceros kicking & rearing' in high spirits, he told his sister. But what really enthralled him was Jenny, the first orang-utan ever to go on display at the Gardens. Jenny caused a sensation, with the savants as much as the socialites, and she had just been presented – in appropriate feminine apparel – to the Duchess of Cambridge. The entrepreneurial Council had bought the three-year-old in November 1837 for £105 and installed her in the specially heated giraffe house.

Here Broderip described the youngster's 'grave' though 'sage deport-ment' (he had obviously caught her in a sullen mood).[10] Darwin too saw her full range of passions, and he regaled Susan with her antics:

> the keeper showed her an apple, but would not give it her, whereupon she threw herself on her back, kicked & cried, precisely like a naughty child. – She then looked very sulky & after two or three fits of pashion [sic], the keeper said, 'Jenny if you will stop bawling & be a good girl, I will give you the apple.['] – She certainly understood every word of his, &, though like a child, she had great work to stop whining, she at last succeeded, & then got the apple, with which she jumped into an arm chair & began eating it, with the most contented countenance imaginable.

His first ape made a profound impression, but this anecdote belied the deeper importance of Jenny's human-like emotions. He was struck by her comprehension; it became another missile in that cockshy he had made of human arrogance: another hard-hitting fact to knock mankind off its pedestal. He exclaimed in his notes:

> Let man visit Ourang-outang in domestication, hear expressive whine, see its intelligence when spoken [to]; as if it understands every word said – see its affection. – to those it knew. – see its passion & rage, sulkiness, & very actions of despair; let him look at savage, roasting his parent, naked, artless, not improving yet improvable & let him dare to boast of his proud preeminence.

Of course he had never seen a cannibal feast, but, compared to Fuegians and Maoris, Jenny Orang came off well in her civilized cell.[11]

'So much for Monkeys, & now for Miss Martineau,' he wrote home. They were all ears for the gossip, and things between Erasmus and Harriet were shameless. Charles reported that she had been 'as frisky lately as the Rhinoceros. – Erasmus has been with her noon, morning, and night: – if her character was not as secure, as a mountain in the polar regions she certainly would lose it.' They were clearly living in each other's pockets (presumably to the Doctor's disgust), and she admitted as much without blushing. 'Lyell called there the other day & there was a beautiful rose on the table, & she coolly showed it to him & said "Erasmus Darwin" gave me that. – How fortunate it is, she is so very plain; otherwise I should be frightened.'

It pushed Charles into thinking about marriage himself, and the future. He was twenty-nine, his heart was troubling, and he faced life alone. 'We poor bachelors are only half men, – creeping like caterpillars through the world, without fulfilling our destination,' he joked as his Cambridge crony Charles Whitley was married.

> Of the future I know nothing I never look further ahead than two or three Chapters – for my life is now measured by volume, chapters & sheets & has little to do with the sun. As for a wife, that most interesting specimen in the whole series of vertebrate animals, Providence only know[s] whether I shall ever capture one or be able to feed her if caught.[12]

The *Journal* would soon be published, the *Zoology* was under way, the specimens farmed out. In the foreseeable future he would finish the task that had brought him to London. What then? He began a cool deliberation, counting his life options again, applying his telegraphic technique to the prospects of marriage and money. Like everything else, they had to be analysed and abstracted in an obsessively orderly fashion. He listed the pros and cons on the back of an old letter.

The advantages of staying single were manifold: 'Travel. Europe, yes? America????' He circled Europe in pencil; it was a nice idea. He had been round the world but knew almost nothing of the Continent. What he would give to make an 'exclusively geological' tour of the 'United States'! Or else 'If I dont travel. – Work at transmission of Species' and get back to the 'simplest forms of life.' That was it, days of scientific leisure with Eras pointing the way. 'Live in London for where else possible in small house, near Regents Park – keep horse – take Summer tours.'

Marriage was the down side of the equation. All this would go by the board, and the options were stark. He might have to 'work for money.' Could he continue his science 'with children & [being] poor?' 'No,' he answered poignantly. And without his zoological avocation to keep him sane, 'could I live in London like a prisoner?' Obviously not; so he would have to look out of town. What better way of earning a living than in a 'Cambridge Professorship, either Geolog[y]. or Zoolog[y].' A chair like Henslow's would suit nicely, providing an income and an agreeable lifestyle. The incongruity of a transmutationist holding a chair at an unreformed Anglican seminary did not strike him. 'Then Cambridge Professorship, – & make the best of it,' he added with a flourish.

But suppose he married and didn't get a chair? This alternative was the bleakest scenario. He would again end up in 'poverty;' and without a scientific sideline he would be a 'fish out of water' in Cambridge, an idle down-at-heel gent with a nagging wife. No, this wouldn't do either. To keep up his science he would require both independent means and a place out of town. Lyell twitted him often enough that the country dulled the intellect, no doubt believing that the shire 'mists' would extinguish his 'volcanic speculations.' But Lyell's lifestyle was losing its attractions in the wretched, dirty metropolis. At last he reached a conclusion.

> I have so much more pleasure in direct observation, that I could not go on as Lyell does, correcting & adding up new information to old train & I do not see what line can be followed by man tied down to London.
>   In country, experiment & observation on lower animals, - more space.[13]

He had his line to follow, a threatening new theory to pursue, not a book like Lyell's *Principles* to go on safely revising. Accordingly, if his father would indulge him, he would marry and follow the Revds Henslow, Jenyns, and Fox into the country and continue his research.

Money was the operative, but the Doctor had considerable investments and income. His £20,000 in government bonds was dwarfed by the capital loaned as mortgages to Shropshire's first families. This brought a handsome return: by the 1830s some £7000 a year, showing that the Doctor was 'as financially agile as he was physically ponderous.' Charles was reminded of it in April, when he was invited to dinner by the 'awesomely polite Robert Clive' (a Shropshire Tory MP, son of the Earl of Powis, and grandson of the empire builder, Robert Clive of India). He had no illusions about the offer. 'It really is very civil of him, as it is of course all meant to show his friendship to my Father.' The Doctor – having no scruples about subsidizing local Tories – had lent the Earl £50,000, and even now kept the mortgage deeds under his bed.[14] If wealth could buy Charles aristocratic friends, it could certainly buy him a leisurely future. He could live life to the full, one of the last generation of self-financed scientific gents, whose home was his laboratory.

But Cambridge still appealed. On 10 May he took four days out to visit Henslow. He was lionized at Henslow's party the first night, and rode over to talk fish with Jenyns the next morning. Then back to talk plants with Henslow, to ask why oceanic islands should have so many unique species (although knowing by now that these were the descendants of mainland immigrants). After this he threw himself into the serious business of parties and bowls on a college green. Having been driven mad for months by the cart-wheel clatter of cobbled London, he was pleasantly 'deafened with nightingales singing.' He dined in Trinity and gloried in Haydn's *Creation* in the chapel – 'the last chorus seemed to shake the very walls' – before moving on to Sedgwick's party.[15] This was the life: more and more he saw himself set up in Cambridge, his heresies on the creation tucked away in a private drawer. It was a tonic that put a new spring in his step.

Coming back down, he continued to mull over domestic breeds. He looked at the way show pigeons were pinched and pulled, bustled and bonneted, like the ephemeral female fashions. At this stage he believed these had nothing to do with 'real' nature, but the process of producing fancy animals was oddly instructive.

This move into the farmyard was natural given his interest in gun-dogs and game birds. He had grown up in the agricultural heart of England, where horticulture and husbandry magazines lay around every manor house. His mother had kept pigeons; Uncle Jos was a leading sheep breeder who had introduced short-haired Spanish merinos into his flock. Uncle John Wedgwood cultivated dahlias and advised him on plant crosses. Landowners had a wealth of knowledge about producing domestic breeds to order; they were the people to quiz, not the closet taxonomists. Look at the way Lord Orford increased his greyhounds' stamina, by 'picking out finest of each litter & crossing them.' Breeders were *selecting* their traits.

He located a pamphlet that made the point exactly. It was by that most liberal of squires, Sir John Sebright: a retrenching, free-trading Whig who had ushered the Reform Bill through Parliament. The seventy-year-old Sebright knew Yarrell. He owned land in three counties and was a brilliant bird breeder, who boasted he could 'produce any feather in [three] years & any form in [six].'[16] His pamphlet provided the key to picking and choosing. But it also went further to distinguish Nature's scythe:

> A severe winter, or a scarcity of food, by destroying the weak and the unhealthy, has had all the good effects of the most skilful selection. In cold and barren countries no animals can live to the age of maturity, but those who have strong constitutions; the weak and the unhealthy do not live to propagate their infirmities.

Darwin scored this passage with its 'excellent observations of sickly offspring being cut off' before they could breed. He was beginning to appreciate the darker side of nature. Experienced breeders like Sebright also laid emphasis on the sexual struggle. He talked of the females falling to 'the most vigorous males' and claimed that 'the strongest individuals of both sexes, by driving away the weakest, will enjoy the best food, and the most favourable situations, for themselves and for their offspring.'[17] Here was evidence of the natural wastage that Darwin had begun mooting.

The way farmers mated select animals exposed the 'whole art of making [domestic] varieties.' But Darwin did not see the breeders mimicking Nature. For him the farmyard remained an unnatural laboratory, and sheep and dogs had unnatural histories. Nature was expunging runts and thrusting the fit forward; fanciers were rescuing the freaks to breed from. The laws of the jungle were not those of a gentleman's game park. Transmuting nature and producing an ornamental duck were asymmetrical acts. The latter was a 'mere monstrosity propagated by art.'[18]

He fired questions at his cousin Fox about crossing domestic breeds. 'It is my prime hobby & I really think some day, I shall be able to do something on that most intricate subject species & varieties.' This was his first admission that he was working on more ticklish aspects.

Dogs and ducks, if nothing else, gave him strategic ammunition, and he was always trawling for facts to floor the expected opposition. He devised ripostes using these farmyard and fireside examples. There must have been 'a thousand intermediate forms' between the otter and its land ancestor, he ruminated. 'Opponents will say, show me them. I will answer yes, if you will show me every step between bull Dog & Greyhound.'[19]

The *Journal* was left sitting, waiting for FitzRoy's volume, but there was action on other fronts. He had something to show for the London sojourn, both in his *Zoology* (the first number of Waterhouse's *Mammalia* was now out), and his geology of the voyage, already up to New Zealand. The transmutation still told in the pit of his stomach, but he had learned to take long rides as a restorative, and was 'astonished to find there is in truth pretty country within three miles of London.'

In town, he restricted his party-going to Erasmus's 'brilliant' dinners ('as all his invariably are'). Eras's life of 'literary leisure' was still sustained by salmon suppers with the Hensleighs, Martineau, and Carlyle. A penny-pinching Charles reeled at their expense. After one he reported home that 'I should . . . be sorry to pay for it.' 'NB. tell the Governor [the Doctor] the desert alone cost $8^s : 6^{d.}$' At the time Martineau was starting her three-volume novel of common folk, *Deerbrook*, with its surgeon-hero. Charles waylaid her at table, flabbergasted that such fluent prose should trip off her tongue, or at least her pen, when he was stumbling and grumbling, befogged by grammar and confused by commas. He was disgusted that she 'never has occasion to correct a single word she writes.' He only salvaged something of his self-respect on discovering that she was 'not a complete Amazonian, & knows the feeling of exhaustion from thinking too much.' 'I forgot to say,' he reported to Susan, deliberately putting the cat among the pigeons (knowing the Doctor would get to hear of it), 'Miss Martineau is going to pay me a visit some day, to look at me as author in my den, so we had quite a flirtation together.'[20]

In his den life was degenerating. He continued mutating species, but each conceptual leap turned the screw on his stomach. Just down from Cambridge, he was feeling jumpy about the hysteria his views would unleash among his clerical friends. He had gone far beyond Lamarck – Lamarck, so despised by Sedgwick and Whewell, who were blowing the revolutionary storm clouds back across the Channel. He switched to a disarming tactic: 'Mention persecution of early Astronomers,' he scribbled. 'If I want some good passages against, opposition of divines to progress of knowledge. see Lyell.' His friend had written on Galileo's fate during the Inquisition, and on astronomy dealing a death blow to religious obscurantism to 'set posterity free.'[21] Darwin saw himself in the torture chair, suffering to set the future free, waving Lyell's words at the Whewells of the world.

That spring Darwin was in his deepest radical phase, playing with inflammatory issues as the country slid further into depression. His notes were acquiring a compulsive quality. He had reduced life to its starkest, to its living elements – self-organizing atoms. This sort of flaming science was favoured by street agitators, the people trying to overthrow the undemocratic state. It petrified clerical society; self-sufficiency was tantamount to atheism. With Christianity part of the law of the land, and used to keep the lower orders in check, anything that undermined it was seditious. If living atoms had the power of self-development, the divine influence of Sedgwick's God was lost. And since that influence worked through the Church, the chain of command from God down through the priesthood into nature would be snapped. And with that, Sedgwick believed, came the end of civilization.[22]

Darwin had boxed himself into a corner. He was not chaffing at Anglican thraldom, or champing at clerical iniquities, whatever the secular talk around Eras's table. Personally he envied his mentors' privileged lifestyle. But he was repeating radical talk: mind a product of matter, living atoms organizing themselves. And it did provide a ready-made solution to one problem: the evolution and inheritance of instincts. How do a father's instincts pass to a son, or a hen blackbird's to her chicks? How do mental traits pass from one generation to another? He needed some sort of physical code for thoughts and feelings, something material that can be handed on. If instincts are products of neural organization, they will be inherited as part of the brain. And if altered instincts modify the brain's physiology, these changed behaviours will be transmitted.[23] It was a solution, but it required the kind of mind-matter identity favoured by freethinkers and the most extreme Dissenters.

His notebooks were now alive with the shocking metaphors wielded by the medical hellions. He equated all mental activity with brain states. 'Thought' was inherited; 'it is difficult to imagine it anything but structure of brain,' he declared. Habits and beliefs had evolved, inextricably linked to the mental machinery. Every instinct, every desire could be located here, each an evolutionary inheritance – even the adoration of God: 'love of the deity [is the] effect of organization. oh you Materialist!' he whispered.[24] Such crudities were the stock-in-trade of the swelling ranks of secularists, slapping the faces of tithe-rich priests. He had heard this kind of challenge from the censured Plinian phrenologists ten years earlier; he could still hear it on any street corner.

He approached the inflammatory subject with a mixture of dread and exhilaration. 'Materialism' itself was a pejorative label. Technically it meant nothing but matter existing (and certainly no spirits), or thought being a function of the brain, but it was indiscriminately used to damn anyone looking for the laws of mind or the mutability of species.

It terrorized the Anglican anatomists, who saw it slooshing through the medical underworld like sewage, especially in disease-ridden London. London was sin city, the 'modern Tyre.' It was taught in the fiercer medical schools, and the artisan atheists championed a soulless self-sustaining universe.

The materialist man of the moment was the flamboyant professor of medicine at University College, John Elliotson. A self-proclaimed 'cockney,' Elliotson displayed astonishing bravura. He championed the London University over the 'barbarous' Oxford and Cambridge, and colleagues considered him the 'strongest materialist' of his day. His stock provocation was that the brain exudes thought as the liver does bile. It was Darwin's *bon mot* exactly: 'thought, however unintelligible it may be, seems as much function of organ, as bile of liver.' But Darwin's goading had a sting that even Elliotson's lacked. Everyone accepted that gravity was an intrinsic 'property of matter;' no one made it a spiritual adjunct. So 'Why is thought' not seen as 'a secretion of [the] brain' in the same way? 'It is [because of] our arrogance, it is our admiration of ourselves.'[25]

Charles tried this out on Hensleigh, the safest of sparring partners, when his cousin arrived back in town. Hensleigh had been away at Maer after resigning his magistrates' post over the swearing of unnecessary oaths, which he considered unChristian. He had made a huge financial sacrifice for his principles, and in debating the dualism of mind and body he showed similar scruples. Charles's theory of the brain was, he declared, 'nonsense.'

The talk was frank. 'Hensleigh says the love of the deity & thought of him or eternity, only difference between the mind of man & animals,' he recorded. How could this be? Savages were a living disproof – 'how faint [is this idea of God] in a Fuegian or Australian!' If God had planted the knowledge of his existence in humans, all would possess it.[26] There was no need for the Fuegian-European gradation in religious belief – unless, of course, it had evolved.

Darwin's words were private, but Elliotson's showed what could happen if he went public. The professor's lectures in the later 1830s were greeted with howls by the medical Tories. They trashed his cynical 'Spinozaism,' which denied free will and a soul and took from the 'thousands of the despised and the miserable' their 'consoling' Christian hopes in a future recompense.[27]

Darwin's materialism was no less rank and reviled, and he knew it. His geological confrères saw the social fabric being torn apart by such provocative babble. It was all that Lyell hated in Lamarck, all that upright Tories deprecated in street atheists. There were blasphemy laws and sedition acts to curb it, and courts to prosecute it. Darwin had seen harassment. He could recall the Plinian fracas, and Taylor and Carlile being hounded out of Cambridge. The clampdown was continuing, with disgraced materialists falling like London flies. No wonder he was brooding about persecution. At this point he might have begun his morbid interest in any 'curious trial' reported in the dailies, when he began to find court cases 'the most interesting part of the paper.'[28]

Medical loudmouths, Dissenting extremists, and artisan activists were not the sort of company he wanted to keep. They were up on their soapboxes to contest medical or clerical privileges. All had run-ins with the authorities, and for some prison was a short step away. The cocky Elliotson hit the headlines again this June. He was carpeted by University College when his female patients ran amuck in mesmeric trances. His resignation was now inevitable. (It came at the end of December.) Whatever the cause, many heaved a mighty sigh of relief when he came crashing down.[29] *This* was where material-ism was located – on a sliding scale between disgraced doctors and loutish low-life. And it wasn't a slippery slope that Darwin wanted to be caught on.

In June his illness intensified as he sank deeper into the quagmire. Bad stomachs and headaches accompanied a fluttering heart, and all the while he transformed animals and materialized thought. He was now overworked, worried, and laid up for days on end. He faced three years' grind to finish the *Beagle* geology before he could escape the rat-race, and it would be an uphill struggle. 'I hope I may be able to work on right hard during the next three years . . . but I find the noddle & the stomach are antagonistic powers, and that it is a great deal more easy to think too much in a day, than to think too little – What thought has to do with digesting roast beef, – I cannot say.'[30]

His developing science had social implications that were just as radical. Because thoughts and actions are inherited, it was essential to educate working men *and* women – which would double the benefits passed on to the children. 'Educate all classes,' he scribbled amid the evolutionary notes, 'improve the women. (double influence) & mankind must improve.' On paper it looked similar to the demands of the red Lamarckians (who wanted women properly schooled because both parents passed acquired traits to the children). But in fact the whole Wedgwood-Darwin family was committed to limited female education, and Martineau even more so.[31] Still, it was the strongest stand on environmental conditioning that Darwin would take.

He was now sounding like a dissident. 'Man in his arrogance thinks himself a great work. worthy the interposition of a deity, more humble & I believe true to consider him created from animals.' No stone was left unturned to understand how this could have come about. He made his first forays into the origin of facial expressions at this time. Charles Bell, so mauled by Darwin's classmates in Edinburgh, had seen grinning as originally designed to expose the canines. Darwin twisted the stiletto in: 'no doubt a habit gained by formerly being a baboon with giant canine teeth,' he scoffed, taking the mauling to an unprecedented degree. It was an intriguing way of tackling human ancestry, and he saw its potential. 'Laughing modified barking., smiling modified laughing. Barking to tell [troop] . . . good news. discovery of prey. – arising no doubt from want of assistance. – crying is a puzzler.'[32]

Such a slap at human pride would leave his theories – if they became known – ripe for exploitation by the extremists. The pauper presses were adept at pirating. Any grist to their mill could be churned out cheaply and find its way to every street corner. And there was a real danger of it with the militants using materialism to underwrite their anti-clerical propaganda.

Censored works were routinely pirated, none more so than the surgeon William Lawrence's. Lawrence was a republican whose scientific rhetoric achieved a pyrotechnical brilliance. He had been forced to resign his post at the College of Surgeons and recant his views after a vicious attack in the Tory *Quarterly Review*. The *Quarterly* execrated his materialist explanations of man and mind. The Court of Chancery ruled his *Lectures on Man* blasphemous, which destroyed its copyright. This was a ringing endorsement to atheist ears. Six pauper presses pirated the offending book, keeping it continuously in print for decades. The latest disreputable edition had only just hit the streets, advertised by flyposters 'sneering at the clergy.'[33] As a result, although officially withdrawn, Lawrence's *magnum opus* could be found on every dissident's bookshelf.

Darwin had his own rough-edged edition of the *Lectures*, sandwiched in cheap boards, the sort that could be picked up for a song in any working-class bookshop. His copy had been pirated by the notorious shoemaker-turned-publisher William Benbow, who financed his flaming politics by selling pornographic prints.[34] Darwin only had to stare at this shabby tome (which he was currently using) to see the fate awaiting him. He was no atheist, nor would he countenance being highjacked by sleazy fanatics. Lawrence was a reminder of how one's good name could be dragged through the mud.

Darwin's schizoid existence intensified as he moved towards the centre of literary society. With Lyell's help, he was elected to the Athenaeum Club on 21 June (along with Charles Dickens) and found it very agreeable. He dined here daily, confessing that it made him feel 'like a gentleman, or rather like a Lord.' 'I enjoy it the more, because I fully expected to detest it,' he conceded, rather alienating Eras; 'one meets so many people there, that one likes to see.' An inveterate society watcher, he relished spying the Good and Great. A gentleman had certain obligations, his science underpinned certain values. It was an age, one teacher said, when 'not *knowledge* alone, but *character* is power; when knowledge without character can procure no more than temporary and very transient pre-eminence.'[35] Of all the clubs, the Athenaeum stood for knowledge and character, and Darwin was not about to sacrifice one on an altar to the other.

Midsummer in Marlborough Street was a time for celebration. The Hensleigh Wedgwoods had moved in next door to Erasmus, and Catherine Darwin and cousin Emma were staying a week with them. Charles popped over from time to time, and they were 'a very pleasant merry party.' One evening Thomas and Jane Carlyle came for dinner. Emma missed most of what the sonorous Scot said, although she found him 'remarkably pleasant and . . . straightforward.' For his part, Charles was noticing Emma's own remarkably pleasant manners.[36]

Still, London was full of 'smoke, ill health & hard work,' and when the party at the 'Darwin & Wedgwood Arms' broke up, he resolved to recuperate. He needed a tonic and travel promised it. Illness finally drove him out of town, and out of England. He took his first hammering holiday since the voyage, travelling to the Scottish Highlands.

On 23 June he set off in a steam boat for Edinburgh, and the old sea-dog 'enjoyed the spectacle, wretch that I am, of two ladies & some small children quite sea sick, I being well.' He spent a day in Edinburgh, his first since dropping out of medical school in 1827, and took 'a solitary walk on Salisbury crags' to 'call up old thoughts of former times.'[37] That was another age, separated by a gulf. He was changing, Britain was changing: here he was, on 28 June 1838, the day a slip of a girl, a month past her eighteenth birthday, was crowned Queen Victoria.

He pushed on into the remote Highlands, past Loch Leven and north through Fort William to the mouth of Glen Roy, arriving a week after leaving London. Here he enjoyed 'the most beautiful weather, with gorgeous sunsets, & all nature looking as happy' as he felt. He wandered up a dirt track, through a wide green valley, and into the rolling hills. The Glen stretched on for miles, but well before he reached the half-way point he could see the famous 'parallel roads,' three of them, running along its sides. These were among the great geological riddles, and what he had come to see. They were not actually roads. Standing on the middle one, he realized that it was not flat. It was a slanted shelf, 60 feet wide with a twenty-degree tilt. The same for the other terraces, 200 feet below and 100 feet above him. These 'parallel roads' went right around Glen Roy as far as the eye could see, while behind him, twelve miles away, Ben Nevis, Britain's tallest peak, completed the panorama, a snow-clad sentinel guarding the enigmatic formation.

None of his geological sightings – 'not even the first volcanic island, the first elevated beach, or the passage of the Cordillera' – had been so intriguing. He knew that the 'roads' had lured geologists to this remote spot for years. Were they traces of an ancient lake, which had dropped on three occasions, each time leaving a shore-line cut into the mountain side? Some thought so and assumed that the valley had once been dammed to hold the lake water.

Darwin approached the Glen armed with his theory of an oscillating earth's crust. He had seen terracing in Chile; there the 'roads' were littered in shells – they were obviously old beaches. If the mountains around Glen Roy had also risen stepwise out of the sea, old shores would be a tell-tale sign. Proving the parallel roads to be sea margins would in turn confirm his global geological theory. He was convinced that they must be old sea beaches, even if he could find no tell-tale barnacles or sea-shells. They had been formed at sea-level, after which the land had risen in three stages.

Satisfied, he started for home, his notebook bulging. 'Eight good days in Glen Roy' had done the trick. 'My Scotch expedition answered brilliantly.'[38] He was feeling on top of the world.

18

Marriage & Malthusian Respectability

FORTIFIED AND full of optimism, Charles came back via Shrewsbury in July 1838. So much had been boiling up in his mind as he thought on the religious implications of his theories that he decided to discuss everything with a sage old freethinker, his father. Marriage was also on the cards, more than ever. Three weeks after Emma Wedgwood caught his eye in Great Marlborough Street he was weighing up his options, looking for advice.

The Doctor foresaw the problems ahead. Charles could be walking into a trap. The Darwins and the Wedgwoods were united by marriage and divided by religion. Ever since old Erasmus scorned grandfather Josiah's Unitarianism as 'a featherbed to catch a falling Christian,' religion had been a sore point, so if Charles was serious about cousin Emma, he had better watch his step. The Doctor advised him to conceal his religious doubts lest they cause 'extreme misery.' His father spoke from experience. 'Things went on pretty well until the wife or husband became out of health,' he said, 'and then some women suffered miserably by doubting about the salvation of their husbands, thus making them likewise to suffer.'[1] The Wedgwood women in particular feared for their menfolk's eternal destiny.

In a way the Doctor's counsel seemed prophetic, with Charles now doubting many sacred truths and beset by debilitating illness.

Money was another desideratum, equally affecting wedded bliss. Here too the Doctor had to be consulted and Charles refined his cost/benefit analysis of marriage while at home. He plunged once more into the pros and cons of having children, balancing outgoings against obligations, future security against lost leisure. His calculations were typical of the wealthy classes, if rather blunt. Having jotted daily on animal breeding, it seemed natural that he should approach his own domestic crossing in the same fastidious way – and with the same utilitarian detachment.

On a blue scrap of paper, he filled up 'for' and 'against' columns, rambling in a self-centred way:

Marry	*Not Marry*
Children – (if it Please God) – Constant companion, (& friend in old age) who will feel interested in one, – object to be beloved & played with. – better than a dog anyhow. – Home, & someone to take care of house – Charms of music & female chit-chat. – These things good for one's health. – *but terrible loss of time.* –	Freedom to go where one liked – choice of Society & *little of it.* – Conversation of clever men at clubs – Not forced to visit relatives, & to bend in every trifle. – to have the expense & anxiety of children – perhaps quarelling – **Loss of time.** – cannot read in the Evenings – fatness & idleness – Anxiety & responsibility – less money for books &c – if many children forced to gain one's bread. – (But then it is very bad for ones health to work too much)
My God, it is intolerable to think of spending ones whole life, like a neuter bee, working, working, & nothing after all. – No, no won't do. – Imagine living all one's day solitarily in smoky dirty London House. – Only picture to yourself a nice soft wife on a sofa with good fire, & books & music perhaps – Compare this vision with the dingy reality of Grt. Marlbro' St.	Perhaps my wife wont like London; then the sentence is banishment & degradation into indolent, idle fool.

Marry – Mary – Marry Q.E.D.

The balance had shifted in marriage's favour – decisively.

What the frustrated 'neuter bee' needed was a soft unsociable wife with a dowry, to allow him to work undisturbed. Without a wife there was no living on through children, 'no second life,' as he called it. The bee decided to change his caste, even though it meant 'I never should know French, – or see the Continent – or go to America, or go up in a Balloon.' 'Never mind my boy – Cheer up – One cannot live this solitary life, with groggy old age, friendless & cold, &

childless staring one in ones face, already beginning to wrinkle. –
Never mind, trust to chance – keep a sharp look out.' It could not
be that bad, after all, 'There is many a happy slave.'[2]

Better if his wife was 'an angel & had money' – like Emma. She
was Josiah Wedgwood's granddaughter, Hensleigh's sister (and Eras's
old companion), and about the only eligible daughter left in his small
circle of acceptable family acquaintances. More importantly, her
money would come as a dowry, making her more attractive than an
independent breadwinner such as Martineau. Emma was safer, she
offered security, and being his cousin he could accurately count the
cost. Uncle Jos had given his son Josiah III a bond for £5000 and an
allowance of £400 a year when he married Charles's sister Caroline
the year before. With so many first-cousin marriages, Charles would
not so much be tying the knot as adding another lucrative loop to the
cord binding the Darwin-Wedgwoods together.

Marriage it was – a wife rather than a dog. To the obvious question,
'When?' his father advised 'soon,' and he agreed. Emma was perfect,
already a model of domesticity. She could be a nursemaid, a matron, a
protector, providing the comfort and seclusion he craved within four
walls. Thinking himself so 'repellently plain' he actually doubted that
she would accept, but, he said, 'I determined . . . to try my chance.'[3]

He recorded that he was 'very idle at Shrewsbury,' which meant
working furiously to no avail. The time passed without any bombshell
solutions to his problems of descent. But work he did; secure at home
he opened two new leather-bound notebooks, one in the transmutation sequence ('D') and the other ('M') on its wider consequences. He
was squaring up to the materialist conundrums, and setting out to
explore the evolutionary basis of moral and social behaviour. Sixty
pages of the 'M' notebook were filled in the 'idle' fortnight, with the
opening words 'My father says . . .' setting the tone.

His shorthand scribblings became frenetic. He was still trying to
explain how instincts pass from generation to generation, coded
somehow in the brain. He taxed the Doctor over his demented
patients, the effect of strokes, senility, the manifestations of madness,
and the quirks of memory. He listened to anecdotes about old folks
who could not remember anything, yet who could sing childhood
songs almost instinctively, in a way that might almost 'be compared
to birds singing.' A memory lying dormant throughout life, with the
person unaware of it, made the idea of 'memories' passing across the
generations as instincts seem less 'wonderful.'[4] Perhaps that was all
instinct is: an unconscious memory physically written into the brain.

Fresh from his talks with the Doctor, and ready to take the plunge after his costing of matrimony, he rode over to Maer on 29 July in 'high spirits.' Emma too hoped that, if Charles saw more of her, 'he would really like me.' They whispered long and grew closer, later chewing a 'sentimental fat goose ... over the Library fire' (a 'goose' being a comfy intimate chat). Nothing was said about marriage – it was too soon, or perhaps Charles lost his nerve – but they both looked forward to 'another goose.'

Unfortunately, at the sight of Emma, Charles threw his father's advice out of the window. The cousins had known each other for too long to keep secrets. He was still mulling over his heterodox brain science. At The Mount he had confessed that free will had no place in his determined world-system, and he carried his materialism with him to Maer. Neural matter acted under the iron rule of law, so how could thought have any freedom? He seemed to be sinking deeper, and it scared him. Writing notes on the psychology of panic, he turned inwards. 'I have awakened in the night. being slightly unwell & felt so much afraid.' 'The sensation of fear is accompanied by troubled beating of heart, sweat, trembling of muscles.' He must have opened his heart in more ways than one during their talks, unable to resist letting Emma in on his secret. His scribblings at Maer, in a new ink and in a new vein, suggest that he was taken aback by her response. He began devising ways of camouflaging his materialism. Don't mention it, he admonished himself, talk only of inherited mental behaviour: 'To avoid stating how far, I believe, in Material-ism,' he scrawled in a rush, 'say only the emotions[,] instincts[,] degrees of talent, which are heredetary [sic] are so because brain of child resemble[s], parent stock.'[5] He was learning to guard his words.

He should have listened to his father. The Doctor said conceal, Emma made him reveal. But that was probably easy, for he had the one quality Emma prized above all others: 'he is the most open, transparent man I ever saw, and every word expresses his real thoughts.' And so, it seems, he mooted evolution too, but again she must have startled him by asking awkward questions about ultimate origins. Whatever was said, he realized the difficulty of carrying conviction and returned to his notebook chastened, warning himself to limit his remit. He must steer clear of first origins and explain only how organs or animals *change*; otherwise 'it will become necessary to show how the first eye is formed.'[6] And that he could not do.

He trained back to town on 1 August. He stood on the threshold, ready to shroud himself in family life as he up-ended conventional Anglican wisdom. He was convinced that his science was not only right, but as shattering as Galileo's. 'Mine is a bold theory,' he admitted – a profound view of human ancestry that would revolutionize philosophy and ethics. Or, as his words blared: 'Origin of man now proved. – Metaphysic must flourish. – He who understands baboon would do more towards metaphysics than Locke.' These intimations of immortality had more mundane repercussions. A rising self-importance led him to start dating his notes and to open a journal to record the key events in his life. He also penned a 1700-word recollection of his childhood, from the age of four to eleven, recording odd memories and incidents. It added up to a change, a new confidence that his pioneering research would not go unrecognized.[7]

After a few days in London he was enthralled by a review of the French mathematician Auguste Comte's *Positive Philosophy*, which convinced him that his view of the world was the right one. He sat absorbed in it at the Athenaeum, revelling in the covert swipes at Whewell, praising its tone as 'capital.' Mature science for Comte was characterized by belief in the rule of law, as Darwin himself held. All other approaches were mere relics – from the 'theological or fictitious' stage of human development (Comte was an atheist), relying on the hand of God, or the medieval 'metaphysical' stage, which had a world ruled by subtle emanations and mystic influences. This historical progression to modern science had a universal ring to it; Darwin even wondered whether children pass through similar stages, mentally recapitulating the cultural progress.

Comte believed that only 'positive' facts should make up true knowledge (hence his followers were called 'Positivists'). His notion of a 'theological state of science' was a 'grand *idea*,' Darwin jotted. And eminently exploitable; it provided a new pejorative tag for the Cambridge science to be superseded. 'Zoology itself is now purely theological,' Darwin declared. Savages like York Minster, who 'consider the thunder & lightning the direct will of the God,' were scarcely less primitive than the miracle-mongering 'philosopher who says the innate knowledge of creator has been implanted in us . . . by a separate act of God,' rather than evolving according to 'his most magnificent laws.'

Divine anthropomorphisms and animisms were out; Comte was content in 'tracing facts to laws.' The review that Darwin sat reading in the Athenaeum baulked at following Comte *too* far, lest his rampant positivism end up 'poisoning the springs' of morality and religion. But Darwin was already one jump ahead, doing what the reviewer dreaded. Even 'our will may arise' from the 'laws of organization,' he declared; 'it is what my views tend to.' A few days later he reread the review so intently that he developed a headache from the stress. Dipping into Dickens cured it. But his migraines were getting worse, and he later visited Woolwich dockyards, 'trying to unbend my mind.'[8]

Others were taken by Comte's Positivism. Martineau went on to translate his book and wrote ecstatically: 'We find ourselves suddenly living and moving in the midst of the universe . . . not under capricious and arbitrary conditions . . . but under great, general, invariable laws, which operate on us as part of a whole.' Darwin had already indulged in similar flights, and Positivism simply intensified them. 'What a magnificent view one can take of the world,' he exclaimed. The vast sweep of law controlled the climate, the landscape, the changes in animals and plants, with everything synchronized 'by certain laws of harmony.'[9]

It was 'far grander' than the perverse idea of God individually crafting every slug and snail. The Almighty – personally creating 'a long succession of vile Molluscous animals – How beneath the dignity of him'! Darwin was working out a persuasive strategy, like Babbage giving God back his omnipotence, like the Dissenters giving the Creator some consistency: after all, what were miracles, but God interrupting himself? His laws stood supreme, no subsequent tinkering was necessary. Unitarians knew this, and so did Darwin. Only a 'cramped imagination' would have God 'warring against those very laws he established in all organic nature.'[10] Privately, Darwin was plugging into the larger Unitarian movement, summoning up Dissenting support, preparing to fire a wider audience with familiar clarion calls.

Darwin's denial of free will edged him closer to the metaphysical abyss. He now routinely reduced thought and behaviour to cerebral structure, boiling it down to bits of the brain. If wishes are a consequence of neural organization – evolving under the constraints of 'circumstance & education' – then anti-social behaviour can be inherited. 'Verily the faults of the fathers, corporeal & bodily are visited upon the children.' *That* was frightening. Acknowledging that patterns of behaviour and thought were inherited 'would make a man a predestinarian of a new kind, because he would tend to be an atheist.' But Darwin was no atheist. He accepted that all this resulted from God's natural laws, and if it looked like leading to a godless conclusion, a 'Man . . . would more earnestly pray "deliver us from temptation".' On the other hand, accepting this evolutionary determinism could transform human conduct, for a father would 'strive to improve his organization for his children's sake.' Men 'would only marry good women & pay detail[ed] attention to education & so put their children in way of being happy.'[11]

As he wrote this he was reading a predestinarian of the old kind,

Harriet Martineau. She was arguing against any 'universal moral sense,' claiming that among humans 'right' and 'wrong' are culturally conditioned, not spiritual endowments. Such moral relativism was common among radical Dissenters, and Darwin was primed to appreciate it after the *Beagle*'s visits to Tierra del Fuego and New Zealand. He accepted Harriet's axiom that moral norms are formed by external influences, that all vices and virtues depend on their social context.[12] Virtue could lie in slaughtering men in tribal war, or in altruistically saving life; it manifested in bizarre and unpredictable ways across the globe.

What if Polynesian mothers drown their children out of duty, or Eastern potentates laugh at English kings for lacking a hundred wives? This moral spectrum was no odder than dog breeds exhibiting different instincts. And the fact that all humans have some sort of morality (however expressed) was because 'man, like deer,' was a 'social animal.' Moral acts were as instinctive as a deer's warning bark. They had evolved from the social instincts to aid the cohesion of the human ancestral troop. They were socially useful, helping to cement relations. Even the Christian precepts, 'do unto others as yourself,' and 'love thy neighbour as thyself,' had evolved naturally out of our ancestors' 'sexual, parental & social instincts.'

He saw that his evolutionary prescriptions and the New Testament's morality 'come very near each other.' Both led to similar behaviour. Both demanded that people act morally out of 'dread of misery of future' – in this life for the evolutionist worried about his children, and in the next for the Christian. For both, duty before God meant providing for future happiness.[13] By the autumn of 1838 he had thrashed out all the social and moral issues with Hensleigh, Harriet, and Erasmus, and worked them into his evolutionary formula, enormously expanding its scope.

He had so much on the front burner that things were beginning to boil over. His geology book, now restricted to *Coral Reefs*, was grinding on slowly; he was trying to prove Glen Roy a former arm of the sea; and the *Zoology* numbers 'murder much of my time.' The notebooks were draining his energy and the *Journal* still was not out. Lyell had cannibalized the proofs for the '*juicy*' new edition of his textbook *Elements of Geology*, and Darwin was gratified that he had 'made such infinitely more use of my journal than I could have anticipated.' But there was no sign of FitzRoy's volume or a publication date. Lyell complained of the hold-up in his own preface, and Darwin recorded that FitzRoy 'looked rather black' and 'made a kind of growl' as he read it. 'I never cease wondering at his character,' he reported back to Lyell, 'so full of good & generous traits but spoiled by such an unlucky temper.' 'Some part of the organization of his brain wants mending,' he concluded, covertly introducing a topic dear to his heart.

Other ugly expressions intrigued him. He spent long hours peering at the zoo's baboons, trying to decipher their eyebrow movements. He teased monkeys by withholding nuts to induce 'peevish' expressions. Similarly tormented, the new orang-utan 'threw itself down on its back & kicked & cryed like [a] naughty child.' He climbed into the orang's cage to study her bashful, scheming, quizzical countenance close up. She would pout at her reflection, use straw as a tool, play the harmonica, and hide after disobeying her keeper.[14] The pouting and shame-face were eminently human, reflecting similar mental states, which left her cell-mate to conclude once again that there was no great gulf between a Fuegian savage and a civilized ape.

Even the human tantrum had evolved. We have emotions like 'revenge & anger,' however sublimated, because they have benefited our ape ancestors. 'Our descent, then,' is the root 'of our evil passions!!' he jotted. Good and evil were not moral absolutes so much as monkey attributes. Or, to put it more graphically: 'The Devil under form of Baboon is our grandfather!' Evolution explained the passions in a way nothing else could. Erasmus joked that Plato thought 'our "*necessary ideas* [of good and evil]" arise from the preexistence of the soul' – and that they 'are not derivable from experience' – which Darwin capped by adding 'read monkeys for preexistence [of the soul].'[15]

On 6 September he finished the important Glen Roy paper, destined for the Royal Society. He started reading voraciously, singling out books on human statistics that emphasized the law-like moral and social behaviour of populations. Religion, morality, and descent now dominated his thoughts. He still ploughed a lonely furrow, bottling up his feelings and fears. Mid-month he did timidly tell Lyell that he was ruminating 'on the classification & affinities & instincts of animals – bearing on the question of species – note book, after note book has been filled, with facts, which begin to group themselves *clearly* under sub-laws.'[16] Lyell could not have known the direction of his research, but it was a pointer.

Darwin was isolated. He needed an ally of Lyell's stature. He was also vulnerable, and a week later, on 21 September, his fear of persecution translated into a strange dream of execution. No sombre nightmare, this; it was almost flippant as he recalled it. Yet the execution was vivid enough to be remembered the next day. He dreamed 'that a person was hung & came to life, & then made many

jokes. about not having run away &c having faced death like a hero.'
Here was Darwin, standing his ground scientifically, still languishing
in his Marlborough Street 'prison,' waiting to plead that his views
were not actionable, perhaps recalling the poor devil hanged while he
was at Cambridge. Then he remembered from his anatomy days that
a person could not recover from hanging. So he switched mid-dream
to decapitation, the victim taking delight in 'showing [the] scar
behind [his neck]' where his head had been cut off, proving that 'he
had honourable wounds.'[17] The transmutationist was in the highway-
man's place, pleading honourable motives, but paying the price for
his treachery.

The condemned man continued reading, still interested in human
statistics. Late in the month he picked up the sixth edition of
Malthus's *Essay on the Principle of Population* – the polemical
account of humanity outstripping its food supply, and the weak and
improvident succumbing in the struggle for the available resources.

Malthus had rarely been more topical. In the depth of the depression, with unprecedented distress, the poor law and pauper riots
were on everybody's lips. Workhouses were still being attacked,
commissioners still being pelted. Malthus had denounced charity,
and the rioters abominated anything Malthusian that propped up the
New Poor Law. By now the dissident groups had come together
under an umbrella organization known as Chartism: they supported
the People's Charter, a list of demands for universal suffrage, annual
elections, and salaried MPs. This was a countrywide mass movement,
and the New Poor Law was one of its prime targets. Christian
Chartists denounced a system that would deny 'the distressed poor
their God-given right to a dignified support on their native soil.'
They were marching under banners in September that proclaimed
with the Psalmist, 'Dwell in the land, and verily thou shalt be fed.'
Chartist speeches, lambasting the 'cruel and detestable doctrines of
the Malthusians,' were heard by tens of thousands in the manufacturing towns, and reported in *The Times*.[18] Love him or loathe him,
Malthus could not be ignored.

Darwin knew the theory. With Martineau his dinner guest, how
could he not? Getting the poor off welfare increased competition among
working men and reduced taxes. Competition was paramount, making
Malthus a Whig free trader's godsend in the 1830s. But it was Malthus's
statistics that struck Darwin with a vengeance in his primed state.
Malthus calculated that, with the brakes off, humanity could double in
a mere twenty-five years. But it did not double; if it did the planet would

be overrun. A struggle for resources slowed growth, and a horrifying catalogue of death, disease, wars, and famine checked the population. Darwin saw that an identical struggle took place throughout nature, and he realized that it could be turned into a truly creative force.

He *had* thought that only enough individuals were born to keep a species stable. Now he accepted that wild populations, too, bred beyond their means. Like the architects of the poor law, nature showed no charity; individuals had to scrimp and struggle, like the growing gangs of scavengers on London's refuse heaps, with starvation staring them in the face. Darwin gained a unique understanding from Malthus. Others such as the botanist Augustin de Candolle wrote of plants being 'at war one with another.' But nobody, Darwin said, conveys 'the warring of the species' so strongly as Malthus.[19] Even then de Candolle meant only one species fighting another for space – no one had suggested that this was a civil war fought among members of the *same* species. In society and nature, paupers and brutes were both struggling, the best alone surviving. The face of nature was no longer smiling; it scowled at a gladiatorial arena, strewn with the corpses of the losers.

This population pressure became 'a force like a hundred thousand wedges' rammed between the members of a species, forcing 'gaps by thrusting out weaker ones.'[20] The best adapted varieties survive to breed, expanding at the expense of the rest, changing the whole species slowly. The same 'grand crush of population' that shook men from their indolence kept life at its peak of perfection.

In Darwin's nature, the many fall that the few might progress. Death acquired a new meaning, and there was enough of it around: with rising joblessness and homelessness, medical statisticians were compiling their 'ledgers of death' (mortality statistics) among the slum dwellers.[21] Nature's ledgers were always open; the Reaper sat, draped in black, with scratch pen permanently in hand. Progress was not so much a hymn to divine beneficence as a dirge accompanying the savage struggle. Both Darwinian science and poor law society were now reformed along competitive Malthusian lines. Ruthless competition was the norm; it guaranteed the progress of life and a low-wage, high-profit capitalist society.

Emigration surged in 1838 as the factories closed and lay-offs grew. The 'surplus' workers shipped to the colonies rose exponentially. Malthus sanctioned such an escape in his sixth edition, which differed strikingly from the unrelentingly bleak first edition. That had been a frontal assault on William Godwin's visions of utopian progress. (It was also an attack on the nonsense of the 'noble savage,' and Darwin knew from experience how ignoble the Fuegian really was.) Malthus had used the population crush to prove that co-operative progress was pie-in-the-sky. But Godwin's threat and the egalitarian evils of the French Revolution had long passed, and in the sixth edition Malthus allowed that the population explosion might be mitigated by education, celibacy, and emigration. That said, the price of 'progressive improvement in . . . society' was still a terrible struggle for existence.[22]

Malthus's followers in the 1830s circumvented death by deportation and shuffled the poor out of the country. Another free-trading evolutionist, Patrick Matthew, was showing the way. His *Emigration Fields*, being written at this moment, directed the paupers who lost out to the colonies. Huge numbers were leaving as the Depression deepened, 400,000 annually – to America, Australia, the Cape – and radical MPs planned to side-step government bureaucracy and open up New Zealand as well. Indeed, 'the whole of the unpeopled regions of the earth may now be said to be British ground.' Shipping out the surplus would reduce poverty at home, raise wages, and the Malthusian 'curse, will become . . . a blessing.' The emigrants would create new markets abroad, so that '*our paupers would be transformed into rich customers.*' The race itself would be invigorated, because

> change of place . . . seems to have a tendency to improve the
> species equally in animals as in plants, and agricultural and
> trading occupations are far more congenial to health and
> increase, than manufacturing occupations. It cannot therefore
> be doubted that the increase of the British race . . . and their
> extension over the world, and even the vigour of the race
> itself, will be more promoted by this colonizing system.

Like Darwin's, Matthew's social and organic evolution were all of a piece, dominated by Malthusian competition and selection.[23]

Emigration might solve the pauper problem at home, but others saw these boatloads of rejects wreaking havoc abroad. Dire predictions accompanied this tidal wave of flotsam. European settlers had always been 'harbingers of extermination to the native tribes,' and it was prophesied that all the 'aboriginal nations' would be wiped out within a century. At every outpost the *Beagle* crew had witnessed the destruction: the Tasmanians were all but exterminated, the aborigines were dying from European diseases, General Rosas's policy was deliberate genocide. But Darwin believed that colonial warfare was necessary 'to make the destroyers vary' and adapt to the new terrain.

Destruction was becoming integral to his Malthusian view of humanity:

> When two races of men meet, they act precisely like two species of animals. – they fight, eat each other, bring diseases to each other &c, but then comes the more deadly struggle, namely which have the best fitted organization, or instincts (ie intellect in man) to gain the day.

The 'stronger [are] always extirpating the weaker,' and the British were beating the lot. This imperial expansion ended the isolation of the indigenous races, and thwarted their development in other ways. As whites spread out from the Cape, the black tribes were pushed together in the interior, blending races and ending their species-making isolation. Had this not happened, Darwin speculated, 'in 10,000 years [the] Negro [would] probably [have become] a distinct species.'[24]

With emigration in the headlines, Lyell was convinced that animals too are driven by overpopulation to migrate. He agreed with Darwin that burgeoning species become colonizers, invading new terrain and defeating the natives. But Darwin's population pressure was pushing species to the limit in other ways. The crush was a creative force. The overcrowding that sent boatloads to the colonies meant that only animals with a competitive edge survived.

Darwin's biological initiative matched advanced Whig social thinking. This is what made it compelling. At last he had a mechanism that was compatible with the competitive, free-trading ideals of the ultra-Whigs. The transmutation at the base of his theory would still be loathed by many. But the Malthusian superstructure struck an emotionally satisfying chord; an open struggle with no hand-outs to the losers was the Whig way, and no poor-law commissioner could have bettered Darwin's view. He had broken with the radical hooligans who loathed Malthus. Like the Whig grandees – safe, immune, their own world characterized by *noblesse oblige* – Darwin was living on a family fortune, and thrusting a bitter competition on a starving world for its own good. From now on he could appeal to a better class of audience – to the rising industrialists, free-traders, and Dissenting professionals.

Paley's 'happy nature' was losing its Arcadian benignity. Life wasn't a vicarage garden on a summer's afternoon, but a battle among the down-and-outs on London's mean streets. From this conflict came continual adaptation. Progress from perpetual strife: it seemed like a paradox, but it was the conundrum of the age, 'an age of beauty, yet deformity, – an age of darkness, and yet of brightness.

Steam, iron, smoke, egoism, doubt, and *distrust*, are all alike in
colour.' Darwin was asking momentous questions and was confident
of the answers, even if they threw up still more doubt. His brazen
speculations seemed characteristic of an entrepreneurial society pushing
to extremes. 'The charm is broken – chivalry, charity, the church, lie
cold,' someone summed up the spirit of the age; 'we interrogate a
new godhead – we interpret it in our own way – it may be for good,
it may be for evil – it may be a deity, it may be a demon.' As much
could be said for the Malthusian strife at the core of Darwin's new
evolutionary theory.

Eyes were turning to the citadel. 'Man has been called a
microcosm,' a reviewer wrote, yet 'we have as yet no great key to
unlock those secret chambers where the great laws of his nature are
revealed; we are still fumbling at the door.'[25] Darwin, his stomach
shouting 'no,' his head countering 'yes,' was quietly turning the key.

Darwin was approaching the Victorian dilemma, becoming 'destitute
of faith, yet terrified at scepticism.' His new Malthusian evolution
might have been implicitly secular, but it was not atheistic. How could
it be, he asked, when God's laws have produced so 'high a mind' as
ours? This pointed to a purpose behind the whole messy process. To
deny it was to deny that descent was geared to the 'production of
higher animals' or that 'we are [a] step towards some final end.'[26]

None of this was incompatible with Unitarianism, not even his
denial of a 'superadded' soul. (Unitarians like Harriet Martineau also
held that matter was spiritually endowed, obviating the need for a
separate spirit world.) So much underlying Darwin's transmutation
smacked of this creedless rational faith in a law-giving God – from
the cultural conditioning of morality to the mental continuum
between humans and brutes. Even so, it is debatable how many
Unitarians would actually have accepted a monkey ancestry or have
found hope in a higher life form rather than a material heaven.
Indeed, as Darwin shifted on these grounds his own religious beliefs
were shaking. All he knew was that children are visited with rewards
and punishments in this life for the actions of their parents. What
happens 'when we turn into angels' was immaterial, he shrugged.[27]

October saw him start two new notebooks, 'E' in the transmutation
series and 'N' on metaphysics. It was a time for polishing his views
and practising his rhetorical skill. He started grandly:

To study Metaphysics . . . appears to me to be like puzzling at
Astronomy without Mechanics. – Experience shows [that]

the problem of the mind cannot be solved by attacking the citadel itself. – the mind is function of body. – we must bring some *stable* foundation to argue from.

'Descent' was that foundation; it offered a rational key to the mind. Human conscience was perhaps the hardest nut to crack, and he looked for its origin in the pack behaviour of dogs and baboons. He argued in a typically anthropomorphic way that a deviant dog, going against its 'social & sexual instinct' and harming the pack, would feel remorse *if* it could reflect on its act. Such a reasoning dog would have acquired a conscience. But this hypothetical 'dogs conscience would not have been same with mans because original instincts different.' He was now fully convinced that, from troop instincts alone, he could derive 'all that is most beautiful in the moral sentiments.'[28]

Thus were character and conscience formed, not from reading the Bible, but from an ancestral ape's family feelings. Conscience lay outside a person's control. 'A man ... may be congratulated [for doing good],' but the act is conditioned and 'deserves no credit.' By the same token 'wickedness is no more a man's fault than bodily disease!!' This cultural determinism extended even to our knowledge of God, and here Darwin leaped beyond most Dissenters. Our 'innate knowledge of [the] creator' had evolved as a consequence of 'his most magnificent laws.'[29] It was a grand instinct, developed because of its social utility.

Worries about his heresies made him repeatedly ill, and on 25 October, pondering the origins of shame and beauty, he visited the salubrious castle town of Windsor for two days' rest, making the most of the 'glorious weather.'

Shame and beauty were recurrent thoughts as he prepared to ask for Emma's hand. After an excruciating early November, he was well enough to set off for Maer. The 11th was 'The day of days!,' he noted in his new journal. He did the deed and proposed. It took Emma by surprise. She had 'thought we might go on in the sort of friendship we were in for years.' Her acceptance left Uncle Jos in tears of joy. Fanny, Hensleigh's wife, twigged at once what had happened, and the women sat up all night giggling and talking. Others had a more direct insight; Aunt Jessie, being a palm-reader, had known it all along. Emma now carried out her own calculus, praising Charles's openness and honesty. He is so 'perfectly sweet tempered, and possesses some minor qualities ... such as not being fastidious, and being humane to animals.'[30]

Charles galloped to The Mount the next day, where Caroline congratulated him on having 'secured the very sweetest . . . of wives.' The engagement was kept private, Lyell being one of the few outsiders to hear. Emma was Hensleigh's and Josiah's sister, Darwin told him, 'so we are connected by manifold ties, besides on my part, by the most sincere love & hearty gratitude to her, for accepting such a one, as myself.' Letters went off to all the relatives, although one became confused, thinking that Emma was marrying Dr Darwin, and panicked about their 'disparity of age.'

For his part the Doctor was mightily pleased, the more so because Emma's mother continually teased him that Charles would end up with Harriet Martineau, and the thought gave him apoplexy.[31] Not that Charles had the chance, with Erasmus monopolizing her day and night. Eras himself heard the news as he was about to escort Harriet out, and they turned their jaunt into a house-hunting foray for the happy couple.

These idyllic days at Maer had a down side, for Emma was still privately troubled. Unable to conceal his doubts, Charles had again broached the prickliest subject of all with her, religion. Now she could not contain her anxiety:

> When I am with you . . . all melancholy thoughts keep out of
> my head but since you are gone sad ones have forced
> themselves in, of fear that our opinions on the most important
> subject should differ widely. My reason tells me that honest
> & conscientious doubts cannot be a sin, but I feel it would be
> a painful void between us. I thank you from my heart for
> your openness with me & I should dread the feeling that you
> were concealing your opinions from the fear of giving me
> pain. It is perhaps foolish of me to say this much but my own
> dear Charley we now do belong to each other & I cannot
> help being open with you. Will you do me a favour? yes I am
> sure you will, it is to read our Saviours farewell discourse to
> his disciples which begins at the end of the 13th Chap[ter] of
> John. It is so full of love to them & devotion & every
> beautiful feeling. It is the part of the New Testament I love
> best. This is a whim of mine[,] it would give me great pleasure,
> though I can hardly tell why.[32]

Unwittingly, Emma had pointed him to the Gospel that Caroline suggested he read a decade earlier at Edinburgh. It was Jesus's emotive farewell before his crucifixion, with its 'new commandment' to 'love one another.'

In the discourse Jesus assures his disciples that after his death he will 'prepare a place' in heaven for them and then return 'to receive you unto myself.' But doubting Thomas asks the way to the place being prepared: Jesus replies, 'I am the way, the truth, and the life.' Emma wanted Charles to remember the way lest she lose him for ever, and recalled Jesus's words:

> I am the vine, ye are the branches ... If a man abide not in
> me, he is cast forth as a branch and is withered; and men
> gather them, and cast them into the fire, and they are burned.

The farewell discourse might have been full of love but this was the fiery underside, and Charles could hardly have missed the warning. He doubted the existence of hell, he doubted the existence of a soul, and in fact this Gospel would always stand between them. But he sent Emma a warm reply, and she took comfort that at least he had entered into her heart's concern 'a little more.'[33]

Charley wanted to rush the ceremony and he repeated his opening notebook gambit to Emma, 'remember life is short.' But she was used to caring for invalid parents and worried about leaving her tiny hunchback sister Elizabeth to cope. She hoped he would 'take things leisurely.' Elizabeth did too, sad at the prospect of losing her sister. She wrote to Catherine, 'Do dear Catty clog the wheels a little,' let Emma glory in being a fiancée. Get Charles to 'wait till Spring & fine weather!'

Back at Maer on the 17th, Charley had more sentimental 'gooses' by the fire, discussing practical matters, the 'question of houses, – suburbs versus central London,' and such. 'My chief fear is, that you will find ... our quiet evenings dull,' he alerted Emma. 'You must bear in mind, as some young lady said, "all men are brutes", and that I take the line of being a solitary brute.' Solitary and wealthy now, for Emma's father promised a dowry of £5000 plus £400 a year, to which the Doctor added £10,000 for Charles, the sum to be invested, with Eras and Josiah III as executors. The family fortune would be secure.[34]

The couple took the Doctor's advice and opted for a London house until, Charles said, 'I have wearied the geological public with my newly acquired cacoethes scribendi [itch to write].' Then they would 'decide, whether the pleasures of retirement & country ... are preferable to society.' Charles scouted out houses, traipsing the misty November streets. The West End was out, the traffic noise was deafening (so much so that trials with wood block road surfaces were about to start in Oxford Street). Bloomsbury, near the British

Museum, was quieter and its leafy squares preferable. Emma gave Charley his marching orders: to investigate 'the back lanes about the Regents Park' or nearer to Covent Garden 'if it is not too dear.' But the astronomic rents came as a shock. The 'landlords are all gone mad. they ask such prices,' £150 a year was nothing. (And Charley remained canny, even with £15,000 in prospect.) He and Eras decided that the Bloomsbury squares were the most affordable.

Meanwhile Emma's 'old curmudgeon' was doing the social rounds and getting in as much snuff as possible before his bachelor days ended. He dined with the Lyells and Henry Holland, and Eras took him to tea with Thomas Carlyle (whose wife Jane he considered not 'quite natural or lady-like,' with her 'hysterical sort of giggle'). The invitations were already coming in for the married couple. Sedgwick invited them to his house, suitably impressing Emma. 'What an honour for the great Sedgwick to invite me to his house. *Me* only think of it! I feel a greater person already for it & how my head will stand it when I am really Mrs D.'[35]

At night, after house-hunting, the cogitations on Malthus continued. Darwin was pulling the implications out like stretched wire. By this point he had every tissue, every organ, 'capable of innumerable variations,' with nature selecting the best. More and more he realized the irony of perfection arising from cut-throat competition. The perfect adaptive nuance was 'the surviving one of ten, thousand trials. – each step being perfect or nearly so . . . to the then existing conditions.'[36] Out of the millions that perish comes the one perfect being.

Or as perfect as inheritance allowed, for nipples on the male were hardly functional adaptations. Selection could only sculpt the existing model, the basic groundplan, and even then animals retained useless vestiges, like the human coccyx (the tail). Darwin scorned the common idea that God had created these rudimentary bits and pieces to round out the vertebrate plan, following his 'original thought, or design . . . to its utmost exhaustion.' 'What bosch!!' he exploded – 'the designs of an omnipotent creator, exhausted . . . Such is Man's philosophy. when he argues about his Creator!' These were inherited holdovers, ancestral remnants, diminishing and disappearing slowly. The traces of limbs in whales reveal their land ancestry, and on the coccyx hung an interesting tale.

In the absence of human fossils, rudimentary organs provided the pointers to 'the parent of man.' The tail stump indicated a monkey. Nor need one stop there. He followed this reasoning to its rather slimy conclusion. The clue to our lowly ancestry lay in the skull, which London medical men considered a modification of the spine: 'The head being six metamorphosed [expanded and welded] vertebrae, the parent of all vertebrate animals,' Darwin concluded, 'must have been like some molluscous bisexual animal with a vertebra only & no head-!!'[37] We had come from a squid-like animal with a cuttlefish backbone.

Nothing was sacrosanct in his notebooks, and analysing his own feelings set off new trains of thought. Courting Emma, he began considering sexual arousal, slobbering and kissing, tracing them to our animal ancestors. As he jotted, breathing heavily:

> November 27th.- Sexual desire makes saliva to flow[,] yes *certainly* – curious association: I have seen Nina [the dog] licking her chops. – someone has described slovering teethless-jaws. as picture of disgusting lewd old man. ones tendency to kiss, & almost bite, that which one sexually loves is probably connected with flow of saliva, & hence the action of *mouth* & jaws. – Lascivious women. are described as biting: so do stallions always.

Blushing too must be sexual, because it intensifies when men and women interact. Perhaps thinking of 'one's appearance' drives 'blood to surface exposed, face of man ... bosom in woman: like erection.'[38]

Still Malthus was being digested, and it was a slow bovine process. Even now, two months after reading the book, Darwin was breaking new ground. He had assumed that habitual behaviour becomes instinctive and causes the necessary changes in mind and body: that is how variations occur. Now he introduced a strikingly different image, suggesting that odd variants might be thrown up by *chance*.[39] Perhaps even instincts appear randomly, with selection keeping only the useful ones.

There was a bonus. If nature was sifting the fit from the random variants, then she mimicked the breeders more than he had imagined. Fanciers built their pigeons and pigs by discarding all but the desired traits. Nature was evidently doing the same. She was a supreme selector, a superior Sir John Sebright, more vigilant, ruthless, and efficient. Think of her as 'a being infinitely more sagacious than man,' he suggested, though 'not an omniscient creator.' The gentry selected greyhounds the way Nature sifted jackals – except that, while the breeders looked to one or two points, Nature juggled a million variations, making sure that 'every part of [every] newly acquired structure is fully practised & perfected.' By December he admitted that this similarity between natural and artificial selection was the most 'beautiful part of my theory.'[40] He had his theory, and a fancy animal analogy; but in these riot-torn years they were safely tucked away in his secret notebooks, and only in the very distant future would he even think of publishing.

His thoughts were now swinging between Malthus, marriage, and house prices. The *Zoology* was still a burden. Owen's mother had just died, causing him to halt work on *Fossil Mammalia*, and Darwin was lumbered with the half-finished *Birds* after Gould sailed for Tasmania: 'What can a man have to say, who works all morning in describing hawks & owls; & then rushes out, & walks in a bewildered manner up one street & down another, looking out for the word "To let".' Emma could see how stressed he was:

> I want to persuade you dear Charley to leave town at once
> & get some rest. You have looked so unwell for some time
> that I am afraid you will be laid up . . . I want you to cast
> out of your mind all anxiety about me on that point & to feel
> sure that nothing *could* make me so happy as to feel that I
> could be of any use or comfort to my own dear Charles when
> he is not well . . . So don't be ill any more my dear Charley
> till I can be with you to nurse you.

It was the beginning of the pact, with Emma willingly exchanging an invalid mother for a dyspeptic husband. She did not want a 'holiday husband' putting on a brave face. She expected to continue nursing and he was happy to oblige.

Emma came to town on 6 December to help with the house-hunting. She stayed with the Hensleighs and spent her days 'galivanting' with Charley 'in the flies [one-horse cabs] & omnibusses,' checking Bloomsbury's squares, buying pots and pans, and theatre-going. At the end she felt quite 'cockneyfied.'[41]

At the Geological Society this month Darwin was reminded of his predicament. The geologists' seething hatred of evolution erupted into the open on the 19th, when his old teacher Robert Grant's views were finally given the 'coup de grace.'[42]

Darwin found himself trapped between the devil and the deep blue sea. Grant had been lined up for summary justice because he insisted that the world's oldest mammal, an 'opossum' known only from four inch-long jaws found in Oxford's rocks, was in fact a reptile. This fitted better with Grant's Lamarckian image of an upward-sweeping evolution from lower to higher forms. These Oxford rocks were laid down as sediments during the age of reptiles. They were too old; mammals should not have existed that far back. The first real marsupials only appeared much later, Grant believed, during the age of mammals. By contrast the clerics, with their contingently active Creator, could accommodate mammals anywhere, anytime. They opted for an ancient opossum and put Grant's view down to his deviant Lamarckism.

They set Grant up. Conspiratorial letters flew between Buckland and Owen about how he was to be nailed. Egged on, Owen – now London's marsupial expert – postponed the second number of Darwin's *Fossil Mammalia* to do the deed. There was even backroom talk about how to publicize the coup, and Buckland cannily invited the omniscient Lord Brougham along 'to witness our Skirmish.'

The irony was complete. Darwin – from his Secretary's chair – watched the polite company convene to bury Grant's fossil heresy. Here he sat, a silent witness, before Sedgwick, Buckland, and the rest, most of them Oxbridge-educated, many Anglican divines, all loathing Lamarckism. Yet even as he watched the spectacle unfold, he was hatching his own evolutionary scheme. True, he had outgrown Grant's nonsense. Owen had convinced him that this *was* a true opossum. And yet Darwin did not doubt that its ancestors lay among the extinct reptiles. As Owen and Buckland lashed Grant, Darwin in his notebook was secretly calling their primitive opossum 'the father of all Mammalia in ages long gone past,' a blast to send tremors under the Creationist edifice.[43] What was he thinking as Grant was trounced? Did his heart bleed on hearing Grant's spirited defence? Probably not, for he was out of sympathy with the ultra-radical, and he went off to dine with the 'élite' at the Crown and Anchor tavern that night, as they gloated over their victory.

He could salvage something from the episode. It pushed him further from the Lamarckian minefield. He had already dumped the idea of an inexorable, upward-sweeping nature: 'in my theory,' he scribbled, 'there is no absolute tendency to progression.' Environments change only 'slowly & insensibly,' and life follows suit. Conditions might remain stable, in which case species would not alter at all. Not even man was exempt; he had shown no improvement since ancient Greek times. Some animals – parasites, for example – had even simplified, and if these died out, others would 'degenerate' to fill their niche.[44] So inexorable ascent and guaranteed progress was a radical myth.

Darwin's new way of viewing nature was defiantly at odds with

Grant's utopian notions. It kept faith with the competitive, capitalist, Malthusian dynamics of a poor-law society, Brougham's society. At the time Darwin was actually reading Brougham's lordly *Dissertation on Subjects of Science*. The former Lord Chancellor was renowned for his encyclopaedic knowledge; some called it 'encyclopaedic ignorance,' but the book further undermined Darwin's old ideas. Brougham convinced him that many instincts could not have originated from conscious purposeful habits. What about a parasitic wasp paralysing a caterpillar and placing it with its own eggs? Darwin had seen these wasps in Brazil doing exactly that. The caterpillar might have been food for the grubs, but the wasp could not have known it. The grubs hatch only after the wasp's death. No adult lived to see its young. So how could this instinct have originated as a knowingly purposeful act?[45] It must have appeared at random and been found useful.

This had crucial ramifications. If conscious habits had ceased to drive his evolutionary machine, then it was irrelevant whether or not they were coded in the brain. He could drop the argument about the conscious mind being synonymous with the brain. He could ditch the mental materialism that was associated with ultra-radicalism, and which – if he ever published – would cost him votes. He was back hunting with the urban gentry, rather than running with the radical hounds.

As chance crept into the picture the idea that man was a divine forethought became less tenable (did God plan chance events?). Babbage's programmed nature took a battering as Darwin resorted to haphazard variations. Contingency and unpredictability became the norm. But Darwin remained muzzy on the subject and never really let go of his harmonious law-based system. Sometimes he viewed 'chance' as the unintentional intersection of causal chains, an idea woolly enough to allow any number of accommodations. At others he spoke as deterministically as Martineau, calling it an event with an unknown cause, or meaning that the variations were not ready-directed.[46] It was the making of future confusion.

Confusion was exchanged for chaos as Emma left town on 21 December. With the wedding a month away, Charles shut his 'E' notebook to sort out somewhere to live. They had their heart set on a terraced house in Upper Gower Street. The estate was ideally quiet, with no pubs or shops, and almost no mews. University College was down the road, but here the street turned into a private track and was closed off by a gate. The house was gaudily furnished and ugly, but it had the advantage of being cheap. 'Gower St is ours, yellow curtains & all,' he rejoiced to Emma on the 29th.[47] The rent was 'extraordinarily low' and the furniture and crockery a snip at £550, even if there was an unseemly dead dog in the back garden.

Sunday, New Year's Eve, Darwin and Covington spent packing books and rocks, and New Year's Day 1839 two vanloads were taken over to Gower Street. He reported to Emma:

> I was astounded, & so was Erasmus at the bulk of my luggage
> & the Porters were even more so at the weight of those
> containing my Geological Specimens. – The dining room,
> hall, & my own room are crammed & piled with goods –
> One servants room up stairs, & my own charming room
> below will hold all most admirably. There never was so good
> a house for *me*, & I devoutly trust you will approve of it
> equally . . . My room is so quiet, that the contrast to
> Marlborough is as remarkable, as it is delightful.

By six in the evening the house was looking suitably like a museum.

Out of the blue Charles suddenly recalled having been in the house before. Leonard Horner – the erstwhile Warden at the university – had lived here, and Charles had dropped in before the voyage. But since Horner's day the décor had degenerated atrociously. 'Macaw Cottage' they dubbed it, and the reason for the gaudiness soon became apparent. The 84-year-old owner Colonel Irvine had lived here with his beautiful 30-year-old second wife. The azure walls and garish yellow curtains said something about her taste, 'which, like her character,' Charles chuckled, 'I presume, is none at all.' The horrified Hensleighs ordered them to send the curtains 'to the dyers at once.'

Still it was perfect after the West End noise. Uncle Jos thought it 'the quietest place he had ever been.' The dog removed, Darwin took to pacing the ninety-foot narrow garden daily, starting a trend that lasted for life. And he planned to plant laburnums to shelter them from the neighbours.[48]

Macaw Cottage was a stone's throw from Grant's college classroom, but by now the threads were irrevocably broken. Darwin wanted nothing more to do with this soapbox Lamarckian, nor his guinea-grabbing zoology. More to the point Gower Street was only a few hundred yards from Regent's Park, where Charles could parade with Emma in her best bonnet.

Days were now spent piling up crates in the front attic, 'hence forward to be called the Museum.' So much hefty work left him feeling 'stupid & comfortable, so dull in the noddle & weary in the legs.' In that state he cabbed to the Athenaeum for his evening meal, or Eras made him break to dine with the Hensleighs and Carlyles, although the talk inevitably turned to the difficulty with domestics. Likewise discussions with Lyell were now less about the origin of coal, than the best coal merchant in the neighbourhood.

He eased off and grew grumpy on hearing that the Wedgwoods had put the wedding day back from 24 to 29 January. He squeezed in a few notebook jottings, analysing love in an outrageously unromantic way. Only a clinical naturalist could ask, 'What passes in a man's mind, when he says he loves a person'! Then it was off for a final round at Shrewsbury and Maer on 11 January, and back to London on the 18th, making last-minute preparations. It only remained for him and Eras to scour the Baker Street bazaar for cheap furniture for the servants to make Macaw Cottage complete.[49]

He recognized that five years of solitude had left him inward-looking, as he candidly apologized to Emma.

> I was thinking this morning how on earth it came, that I . . . should so entirely rest my notions of happiness on quietness & a good deal of solitude; but I believe the explanation is very simple, & I mention it, because it will give you hopes, that I shall gradually grow less of a *brute*, – it is that during the five years of my voyage (& indeed I may add these two last) . . . the whole of my pleasure was derived, from what passed in my mind . . . I think you will humanize me, & soon teach me there is greater happiness, than building theories, & accumulating facts in silence & solitude.

He had found his 'nice soft wife on a sofa,' or rather a soft nursemaid while he lay on the sofa. Already he was giving her full-blooded accounts of his 'stomachic disasters' and relishing her coming to 'take final charge of me.' 'Thank Providence,' he sang out, 'I shall not be a free agent much longer.'

Emma was to humanize the brute, care for him, take charge of the sofa. Her role from the first was narrowly circumscribed – the solitary beast did not want an intellectual soul-mate. She tried to dip into Lyell's *Elements of Geology* only to be told not to bother. Lyell's treatment of his long-suffering wife was a paradigm. Charles sent an account of the couple's visit: 'we talked for half an hour, un-sophisticated geology, with poor M[rs] Lyell sitting by, a monument of patience. – I want *practice* in illtreating the female sex.' Another joke of course, but women were spectators in the male preserve of science, as unwanted here as at the Athenaeum. They had to tolerate this masculine preoccupation, and Emma would prove his equal in forbearance.

Charles was itching to get the ceremony over with. On 24 January 1839, the original date, he took consolation in being elected a Fellow of the Royal Society – still largely a privilege of the wealthy, well-connected, scientific élite. The next morning he trained to Shrewsbury, where he heard from Emma, dreaming of the big day:

> I shall always look upon the event of the 29th as a most happy one on my part . . . There is only one subject in the world that ever gives me a moments uneasiness & I believe I think about that very little when I am with you & I do hope that though our opinions may not agree upon all points of religion we may sympathize a good deal in our *feelings* on the subject.

He arrived at Maer on the 28th and the following day they were married at St Peter's Church by the vicar, their cousin John Allen Wedgwood.

The service, although Anglican, was by special arrangement, so as not to offend Unitarian sensibilities. Emma wore a 'greenish-grey rich silk [dress] . . . and a white chip bonnet trimmed with blonde and flowers.' Charles was nervous and escaped the relatives' clutches by whisking Emma off to the railway station afterwards with undignified haste. She barely had time to change her bonnet, and their precipitous departure raised eyebrows and upset sister Elizabeth. The couple ate their 'sandwiches with grateful hearts' on the train and toasted the future from a 'bottle of water.' Emma took comfort from knowing that her bedridden mother had slept through the service, sparing them both 'the pain of parting.'

Never mind. They were back at Macaw Cottage. Darwin jotted in his journal: 'Married at Maer & returned to London 30 years old.' But his real obsession did show on this, his wedding day. He re-opened his secret 'E' notebook specially to record Uncle John Wedgwood's views on turnips.[50]

19

The Dreadful War

A SHADOW FELL over the couple from the start. Forty-eight hours after the ceremony, on 31 January 1839, Charles's sister Caroline lost her first baby, six-week-old Sophie. There could have been no sadder end to a happy month, and it clouded their first weeks together. Emma longed for 'news of poor Caroline,' knowing that few infant deaths 'have caused more bitter grief than hers.' Caroline was thirty-eight, her husband Josiah (Emma's brother) forty-three. The child was weakly from birth, 'a poor puny little delicate thing,' the first-born of a first-cousin marriage, like Charles and Emma's.[1] It did not bode well.

Emma found solace in her snug urban 'cottage' and new life. They lived at the back overlooking the garden. It was much quieter here, and the month was spent settling in, with her shopping for morning gowns, plates, and a mahogany pianoforte.

But her fears about Charles's future life kept returning. On finding herself pregnant a few months later she set down her anxieties. She found it easier to express herself in a letter to Charles, for 'when I talk to you . . . I cannot say exactly what I wish to say.' Of course he was 'acting conscientiously' in 'trying to learn the truth' about nature, but equally she knew it could not be the whole truth. His scientific pursuits excluded 'other sort of thoughts,' religious thoughts. And always there was the wretched example set by Eras, who had 'gone before you,' removing 'some of that dread & fear' that accompanies doubt.

Charles had lost any qualms about scepticism, dismissing them in his notes as 'an unreasonable or superstitious feeling.' Emma realized that his private work was leading him into perilous waters. The habit of 'believing nothing till it is proved' had prevented him from considering 'other things which cannot be proved in the same way, & which if true are likely to be above our comprehension.' She was tortured by the thought of him giving up Christ's revelation of eternal life and sacrificing his salvation. Ever since losing her beloved sister Fanny she had lived in hope of 'being with her again, never to part.' She hoped to spend eternity with her precious husband too, but his doubts threatened to separate them at death. It would be a nightmare, she finished, 'if I thought we did not belong to each other forever.'[2]

Emma's Christianity was a simple evangelical prescription to gain everlasting life by believing in Jesus. Eternal life 'cannot be proved;' it might not even be comprehensible but, with so momentous an issue, she implored her Charley to be 'careful, perhaps even fearful' of 'casting off' what Jesus had 'done for your benefit as well as for that of all the world.' The letter reduced him to tears, and he was never to forget it.

As they grew closer, she would take him on Sundays to King's College church on the Strand. (There was, needless to say, no church attached to the godless college of Gower Street.) At the same time his illness increased, and her anxieties only exacerbated his own. 'The question' that divided them, as Emma called it, was not whether the Bible was an unimpeachable divine revelation. He already doubted that, understandably, given his integration into Erasmus's circle. It was whether he would spend eternity in heaven or hell.[3]

Still, the present life went on happily enough. The home was run, like all upper-middle-class households, by a retinue of domestics. They carried on a back-breaking daily grind, trudging up and down stairs with coal and water, laying out clothes, serving meals, cleaning hearths – ministering, as Darwin might have said, to the king and queen termite for little succour. The faithful Syms Covington, with Darwin since the voyage, stayed a while after the nuptial flight to London, and then left in February with a £2 golden handshake. A few months later he emigrated with the hordes to Australia, working his passage as a cook, and carrying Darwin's letter of introduction to Capt. King. The new manservant was the redoubtable Joseph Parslow, who carried Aunt Jessie's accolade as 'the most amiable, obliging, active, serviceable servant that ever breathed.'

The vetting of domestics was obviously fraught. Charles depended on friends and family for recommendations, with little success: 'The Cook from Shrewsbury is a failure as she cannot cook, & has a drunken husband. I am fearful of getting a converted Jewess from Miss Farrer.' Emma was just as pernickety about her attendants. The new cook was 'too cute' and had to go, the maid 'vulgar and plain,' although some better excuse was needed to sack her.

It was a very proper house, with the proprieties observed to the last detail. Charles was even more of a stickler for etiquette than Emma. Permitting her maid to forgo a bonnet led to a terrible tiff. He was horror-struck, as was everyone at Shrewsbury: she was a *lady*'s maid not a grocer's girl, inviting men to take liberties. Nor was Parslow's long hair tolerated, and the Doctor gave him a public and sarcastic dressing-down about his judicial locks, unbecoming in one so lowly.[4]

Darwin was freed for the pleasures of untrammelled thought. His paper on Glen Roy at the Royal Society in January 'crowned the series' on global elevation. But there was no sign of the published *Journal* and Whewell at the Geological Society had to be dissuaded from protesting publicly, so as not to rile FitzRoy. The Captain ploughed on, and to be fair his own volume would top Darwin's at a thousand pages, when it eventually appeared in print.

In private Darwin was now watching the way horticulturalists worked. They certainly capitalized on chance peculiarities. He noted growers talking of the '*accidental production of seedling*[s] *with hardier constitution*[s],' and himself saw the 'vigorous battle between strong & weak' leading to 'the preservation of *accidental* hardy seedlings.'[5] His whole habit-driven mechanism was irrelevant to plants anyway; he was now adamant that hardier seeds could only be produced by chance.

In smoky London he remained a country gent at heart, writing to farmers on their methods of selection, and moving far from the concerns of the closet zoologists and academic botanists. He opened a 'Questions & Experiments' notebook, cramming it with queries and plans for rearing daisies in rich soils, sowing seeds under coloured glass, hybridizing cabbages, crossing dogs, skeletonizing ducks, and comparing blood corpuscles, all ingenious approaches to the enigma of variation. Indeed, they were bizarre by contemporary standards. No Cambridge don expected peach-nectarine crosses to hold the key to Creation.

He printed queries, a sheaf for each specialist, framing his *Questions about the Breeding of Animals* in such a way as to elicit the required responses. They went out to gentlemen farmers, for their nurserymen and gamekeepers, quizzing them on the way they crossed varieties or picked offspring to achieve the 'requisite qualities.' This blitz of queries plainly proved too much. Only three replied, and one

of these was overwhelmed, despairing that 'Mr Darwin's questions
... require a longer course of experience than the life of one man ...
can furnish.'[6]

Darwin's Malthusian specs were beginning to fit comfortably, and
peering through them revealed 'the dreadful but quiet war of organic
beings. going on the peaceful woods. & smiling fields.' Or rather, on
the capital's dirty, disease-ridden streets, because he was hardly
seeing nature at all any more. His increasingly bleak image of nature
was a counterpoint to a society in the grip of depression, with the
war in London's slums forcing the starving poor to emigrate or
march in protest.

He entertained the visiting Swiss botanist de Candolle to dinner
and was able to talk over nature's 'war' face to face with the man
who had first mooted the idea. The contest was paramount, with
nature a charnel house, strewn with losers. For each tiny gain, many
must die. Consider the ages it would take for small advantages to
carry through to an entire population of dogs: suppose 'that one out
of every hundred litters is born with long legs & in the Malthusian
rush for life, only two of them live to breed.' If the terrain is hard
and the prey swift, 'the long legged one shall rather oftener ...
survive' and 'in ten thousand years the long legged race will get the
upper hand.' But look at how many had to perish to achieve that
end!

It seemed so obvious that he tried it out on Hensleigh. Knowing
his cousin's developmental approach to language he surely would see
the subtlety of it. But no, Hensleigh 'seemed to think it absurd ...
that [a] tiger springing an inch further would determine his preservation.' Even transmutation itself was baffling.[7] Java and Sumatra were
similar islands, he protested, yet each had a unique rhino. Why? Of
course, this was the nut Darwin had already cracked with the
Galapagos, but it was clear that others would need persuading.

It wasn't only his cousin he went beyond, but Hensleigh's late
father-in-law Sir James Mackintosh. As a tyro Charles had first met
Sir James at the Wedgwood mansion, but a world had passed since
then. Now, in May, he looked again at Mackintosh's *Ethical
Philosophy* while visiting Maer with Emma. Mackintosh thought the
moral faculties inborn, and the knowledge of right and wrong instinctive. This fitted Darwin's scheme wonderfully, but he wanted to
know how these moral instincts appeared.[8] Miraculously was no
answer. They must have emerged from herding and bonding instincts
that were useful in cementing relations in the ancestral troop.

Hensleigh was a regular at the dinner parties, and Emma endured the scientific ones stoically. On 28 March Sedgwick called, and even she recognized that 'there is something remarkably fresh and odd about him.' By April her bemused feelings were making themselves known. Keeping the conversation flowing on Easter Monday with the likes of Lyell and Robert Brown taxed her to the limit. Lyell's whispers were 'enough to flatten a party' and Brown was so shy that he looked as if 'he longed to shrink into himself and disappear entirely; however, notwithstanding those two dead weights, viz., the greatest botanist and the greatest geologist in Europe, we did very well and had no pauses.'[9] But then Emma struck everybody as reserved and grave – it was Charles who disgraced himself by cracking all the jokes.

Late May 1839 – two and a half years after the *Beagle*'s return – was a time for jubilation. His first book, the *Journal* of the voyage, finally went on sale. For the new author these were nail-biting days as the reviews appeared. Capt. Basil Hall's in the *Edinburgh Review* was complimentary and applauded FitzRoy for spending 'considerable sums from his private funds to complete the survey of the Peruvian coast.' Even so, FitzRoy found the piece 'very shilly shally and self-contradictory.' What struck everybody about Darwin's volume was its 'spirit of bold generalization.' For the Saturday *Athenaeum* this was meant as a rebuke in an age recruiting facts. Why, exclaimed the hack, on Mr Darwin's slow elevation theory, 'at least one million of years must have elapsed since . . . the sea washed the feet of the Cordillera of the Andes!'[10] *This* was the shilly-shally review, which criticized the publishers for lumping the three volumes together and causing endless repetitions. (It was taken to heart, and on 15 August, after the three-volume set had been given a ten-week run, Darwin's *Journal* was issued separately.)

His colleagues were much more gracious, particularly Owen: 'It is as full of good original wholesome food as an egg, & if what I have enjoyed has not been duly digested it is because it has been too hastily devoured.' What another liked (digging at the French) was 'the tone of kind & generous feeling that is visible in every part.' He meant that 'it is the work of a plain English gentleman – travelling for information, and not for Effect. – & viewing all things *kindly*.' Even the thin-skinned FitzRoy, combing through the luxuriant forests for lapses of etiquette, doubted that he would find 'an expression in it – referring to me personally – which I could wish were not in it' and he expected to 'be thoroughly at ease in that respect.'

By contrast, FitzRoy's tailpiece had Lyell and Darwin in fits. FitzRoy, at home now and with a religious wife, had turned into a scriptural literalist and closed his tome with an exegesis of Genesis. He regretted doubting the existence of the Deluge in Darwin's presence. Now he could plainly see how wrong the geologists were: all Darwin's high-and-dry shells, all his fossil trees in the Andes, all the gravelly pampas plateaux, all the fossil bones attested one thing only – a great catastrophic flood. It was a direct hit at Darwin's science and Lyell's *Elements of Geology*. Lyell thought it 'beats all the other nonsense he has ever read on the subject.' 'Although I owe very much to FitzR[oy],' Darwin admitted, 'I . . . am anxious to avoid seeing much of him.' He was too peppery, his wife too patronizing, 'but then this cannot be wondered at from so very beautiful & religious a lady.'[11]

Darwin's hero Alexander von Humboldt wrote a paean of praise. He called the *Journal* one of the most remarkable travelogues published. Even 'a young author cannot gorge such a mouthful of flattery,' Darwin replied. Humboldt repeated the praise later in London, fulsomely; Darwin listened to him talk for three hours nonstop, coming away more wearied than worshipping. Always first off the mark, the Germans wanted a translation, and Carl Hartmann, the Brunswick commissioner of mines who had translated Lyell's *Elements*, offered to do the job. But it eventually fell to Ernst Dieffenbach. He was surgeon to the New Zealand Colonization Company (founded this year by radical MPs to ship surplus labourers to the new country), and he got to work after arriving back in Berlin.

The praise was opportune. In June Darwin closed his last major notebook and continued *Coral Reefs* with the thought: 'it is very pleasant easy work putting together the frame of a geological theory, but it is just as tough a job collecting & comparing the hard unbending facts.'[12] As the reviewers recognized, Darwin was a theorist in an age concerned with detail. Hypothesizing was tainted. Understanding God's handiwork in nature was time-consuming and Truth could only emerge from a collation of dry facts, according to the Revd Sedgwick. Any attempt to circumvent this toilsome process with a quick hypothesis or a priori guess was sinful.

The criticism would strike even harder at Darwin's evolutionary theory. The frame for this was also in place, the facts stretched across it in a Malthusian manner. Was it true? Truth for the Cambridge dons led from nature to God, and was moral, conservative, and guarded by the élite. Darwin's speculation served quite different masters, the up-and-coming industrial and professional middle classes. And what was to stop out-and-out dissidents from appropriating his theory for real revolutionary ends?

*

By summer the disorder on the streets was impossible to avoid. The arming of Chartist mobs was discussed in the House of Commons. At the first Chartist Convention in London, the moderate Perth delegate Patrick Matthew, the Malthusian evolutionist, was ousted as a 'middle-class traitor.' The radical workers, having lost out in the Reform Bill, were taking matters into their own hands. A national petition demanding universal manhood suffrage containing 1.3 million signatures had been rejected by Parliament in July. In August, when Darwin attended the week-long jamboree of the British Association in Birmingham, he found a city almost under martial law. The Chartist Convention had switched to the town. Socialists had joined them – some of them red Lamarckians – distributing half a million pamphlets, denouncing marriage, property, and the unco-operative state. Rioting had broken out the month before, and the scientific gentlemen had been ready to call off the event. Darwin arrived in a city that was 'feverish quiet' with peace preserved by 'men in green and men in red, police staves and cavalry sabres.'[13]

Darwin was sick with worry. Yet he felt compelled to confess to the priests vilified by the mob – or at least to the orthodox Henslow – that he was 'steadily collecting every sort of fact, which may throw light on the origin & variation of species.' It would have been music to the ears of street atheists, but not of course to Henslow. Darwin desperately hoped that his old mentor would understand. In Shrewsbury for ten days in September he was 'so languid & uncomfortable' that he laid low and saw no one. Emma was six months pregnant and ill herself many days, and they cocooned themselves more and more, retreating into the home.

Entertaining grew uncomfortable: 'we are living a life of extreme quietness ... We have given up all parties, for they agree with neither of us; & if one is quiet in London, there is nothing like its quietness – there is a grandeur about its smoky fogs, & the dull distant sounds of cabs & coaches.' Gower Street was now a sanctuary: 'we see nothing, do nothing & hear nothing.' The old circle had lost its charm, and members were drifting away. Harriet, fearing she had a tumour, had moved to Newcastle, to be near her medical brother, although she and Eras still wrote. Eras, left in his own hazy world, 'sticks to his opium with many groans.' Hensleigh had become trying, and Carlyle was even more of a bore: Darwin had 'become quite nauseated with his mysticism, his intentional obscurity & affectation.'[14]

The days became alike 'as two peas:' up at seven leaving Emma asleep, tinker with *Coral Reefs* until ten, 'eat our breakfast, sit in our arm-chairs – and I watch the clock as the hand travels sadly too fast to half past eleven – Then to my study & work till 2 o'clock luncheon time.' Off to town after lunch, back in time for dinner at six. 'Sit in an apoplectic state, with slight snatches of reading till half past seven – tea, lesson of German, occasionally a little music & a little reading & then bed-time makes a charming close to the day.' It was monotonous but, he comforted himself, 'how much worse it would have been if I had been in any business.'

As Emma's confinement approached his sickness increased, and he suffered from migraines daily. On Christmas Eve he 'became unwell, & with the exception of two or three days remained so' for a couple of months.[15] As his sickness grew worse and the country careered towards ruin (the Welsh Chartist uprising had just been crushed and its leaders sentenced to death), he began thinking again of escaping London. A morbid air settled over the family; Emma was even more sickly, although he was getting the attention. His theorizing portended grave consequences; he was frightened for his respectability, and he would soon have the added worry of a family.

After Christmas, Emma's sister Elizabeth arrived to assist with the delivery. The grisly business upset a peaky Charles. 'What an awful affair a confinement is: it knocked me up, almost as much as it did Emma herself.' A baby boy, Charles's 'little Prince,' was born at 9.30 a.m. on 27 December – 'a prodigy of beauty & intellect.' William Erasmus he called the boy, after a great grandfather who had unearthed an ichthyosaurus before such a thing was dreamed of, 'so that *we* have a right of hereditary descent to be naturalists & especially geologists.'[16] He was baptized but without godparents, Charles and Emma objecting to religious proxies. Immediately the baby with his scrunched face and instinctive movements became the object of obsessive notetaking, his doting father peering over the cot at this convenient source of facial contortions. Willy Darwin's response to a looking-glass was compared with Jenny Orang's, and his first signs of anger, fear, pleasure, and reason were recorded.

Other work in 1840 ground to a spluttering halt. He missed deadlines for his *Birds* numbers and put *Coral Reefs* aside. Sickness finally sent him to Dr Holland, to no avail. 'Is it not mortifying [that] it is now nine weeks, since I have done a whole day's work,' he wailed to Lyell in February. 'But I wont grumble, any more.' The slightest excitement laid him up, so he shunned it, opting for quiet isolation. His 'little animalcule of a son' learnt to smile half-way through February, but his father saw less and less to smile about. He skipped four Geological Society meetings in a row and tried to resign his Secretary's job on 24 March, only to be talked out of it. It was soul-destroying for Emma. He was 'constantly in a state of languor that is very distressing.' At least he was 'not like the rest of the Darwins, who will not say how they really are; but he always tells me how he feels and never wants to be alone . . . so that I feel I am a comfort to him.'[17]

Emma nursed him, and Willy, while reading Carlyle's pamphlet on Chartism – this 'bitter discontent grown fierce and mad,' seethed the Scottish prophet. Botany Bay and heavy-handed policing were no solution; nor the workhouse a way of ridding society of its problems. Parliament, Church, and Aristocracy must cease abdicating their responsibilities, cease their obsession with game laws, cease their high-flown, dreary Malthusian apologetics, and start facing the grievances. Emma thought it 'full of compassion and good feeling but utterly unreasonable.' On his sick bed Charles too kept on 'reading and abusing him.'

Fanny and Hensleigh had moved to Gower Street, four doors down, making visiting and helping easier, yet life remained grim in Macaw Cottage. Willy was vaccinated, protecting him against smallpox, but nothing could protect his father, who had lost eight pounds in as many months. When he went home to Shrewsbury in April, the Doctor was unable to diagnose the problem.[18]

Charles began to pick up in May, and he was evidently strong enough to accept a seat on the Council of the Royal Geographical Society, even if he did then decamp to Maer and Shrewsbury to recuperate for five months. Although he thought furiously about evolution he managed only a couple of desultory notes on bees, and in August he suffered a relapse, forcing him back to bed. It was a long, idle, lost summer, the summer of '40.

He returned to London on 14 November and was in the Zoological Society the next day, examining snake skulls. Looking at the pickled exotica, he faced up to some seemingly insuperable problems. How on earth had bats evolved? Envisaging a half-way house was nonsensical, a *half*-winged bat! 'It is not possible to imagine what *habits* an animal could have had with such structure.' But he perked up as he thought of the mangrove-climbing mud skippers, with a fan-like fin on their back: 'Could anyone. have foreseen, sailing, climbing & mud-walking fish?'

His other problem was the fossil evidence for evolution. There was hardly any to speak of. But he was optimistic; the fossil scraps that we possess are 'a mere vestige' of what once existed, and more will turn up to plug the gaps. Even now, 'wonderful discoveries' were being made, none more so than a fossil ape, larger than a chimpanzee, found in Brazil. Just let detractors try to rubbish an ancestral 'monkey-man' now, he whooped defiantly.[19]

Darwin's outstanding problem was his audience. Ironically, he was dying to tell his old Anglican friends. But more unsympathetic ears could not be imagined, especially in this era of mounting class hostility. The clergy was under siege; the barbarians were at the gate. Talk of 'monkey-men' recalled the filth spouted by gutter atheists. None of the zoologists would have been appreciative, so what chance of finding allies in vicarage drawing-rooms? Yet the obsessions he shared with his cousin Fox – for Abyssinian cats and bizarre birds – overrode his caution. He told Fox that he was hammering away at 'Varieties & Species,' and begged crumbs of information on dog crosses and 'domestic birds.' Skeletons were his latest thing, so if Fox wanted to ship him a 'little hamper,' his dead 'half-bred African Cat' or any cross-bred fowl carcass would be 'more acceptable than the finest haunch of Venison or the finest turtle.'[20]

His own 'poor carcase' was improving in 1841. He could work for an hour or two a couple of days a week, and he devoted the time to a paper on the transport of boulders by ice-floes in South America. 'I am forced to live, however, very quietly and am able to see scarcely anybody & cannot even talk long with my nearest relations. I was at one time in despair & expected to pass my whole life as a miserable useless valetudinarian but I have now better hopes of myself.' He was still skipping the Geological Society (and he finally resigned his post in February), but it was easy to have Hensleigh read his iceberg paper and relay the comments.[21] He had begun delegating in a way that was to become characteristic. Proxies were quite acceptable here.

Emma was happy to be 'debarred from all London's gaieties' herself while attending to her ailing husband. Indeed, her second pregnancy made this exclusion easier. It was again a worrying time, but Anne Elizabeth was born safely on 2 March, a fair sunny-hearted rival to 'Doddy,' as Willy was now called. Charles doted on his first daughter from the start. She was a normal restless baby but a touch could soothe her as nothing else, and he delighted in cuddling and kissing her. One day, he knew, all his love would be returned, and more. Annie would be their 'solace in old age,' his nurse to the end.[22]

Even now her father was becoming delicate, 'bad & shivery,' as he put it, with headaches and sickness. Alarmed that he was sinking back into 'my old beggarly self,' he sojourned alone at Maer and Shrewsbury for June and July. Here he was 'scandalously indolent,' ignoring letters and dabbling with vegetable experiments. He had the Doctor's gardener try pea crosses, to obtain new varieties, but without much joy. 'I have gather the seed Peas,' the grower drawled in his Shropshire accent, 'but i dount see heney new kinds at all in them as the came up true to the sorts.'[23] At Maer during his strolls he was more successful in understanding the relationship between bees and flowers.

It was all he could do these summer days, drained of 'mental energy.' The doctors thought that 'it will be some years, before my constitution will recover itself.' He was miserable and wanted mollycoddling. His *cri de coeur* went out to nursing Emma: 'I was very very desolate & forlorn without my own Titty's sympathy & missed you cruelly.' And fate had another trick in store. His fears about first-cousin marriages were realized when the Doctor diagnosed Willy 'a very delicate child,' needing a special diet. A melancholy air now settled over the whole family; father and son were both afflicted. In the 'Malthusian rush' they were losing, the unhealthy results of inbreeding. The Doctor doubts 'that I shall become strong for some years – it has been a bitter mortification for me, to digest the conclusion, that the "race is for the strong" – & that I shall probably do little more, but must be content to admire the strides others make in Science.'

Comfort and quiet were what he needed, a rural retreat away from the urban tumult and calls on his time. Others had already gone. FitzRoy had moved fifteen miles out of town. Herschel, back from the Cape, had taken a country seat in the hop-picking county of Kent. This summer Charles persuaded his father to buy him a house, something about twenty miles away near a railway line, he fancied.[24]

In July he returned to the smoke and picked up the coral atoll book after a thirteen-month interval. He managed to spend a couple of hours each morning on the volume, and that, plus a short walk or ride, was his day.

He started to house-hunt in August, scouring the south-east along the chalk Downs. His Cambridge friends – Fox, Henslow, and Jenyns – had parishes, which seemed to suit them. Henslow was 'happy & flourishing – giving lectures, displays of fireworks, initiating agricultural prizes, & I do not know what besides, for his Parishioners.' It was the life; just switch the public lectures for private science, which Henslow had all but given up. Still, Henslow was turning up fossil footprints of extinct amphibians, which had Darwin green with envy.

In the depression London's streets were running sores, and he

longed 'to be settled in pure air, out of all the dirt, noise vice &
misery of this great Wen, as old Cobbett called it.' He read William
Cobbett's sprightly *Rural Rides*, the demagogue's diary of a
horseback trip through southern England. Bloody old Cobbett hated
London too, but his book offered little comfort. It was culled from
his 'twopenny trash' newspaper, the *Political Register*, and mixed
serene sights and political diatribe. Between images of Kent's pretty
villages he sniped at the clergy, Sir James Mackintosh, 'PARSON
MALTHUS,' and the corn laws.[25] There was no escaping the spirit of
the age.

Charles was unfit and unwilling to go out or receive visitors. By
his own admission he had 'grown a dull old spiritless dog.' Owen
was one of the few scientific friends who still came to tea, and when
he turned up on 10 November, he found Darwin handicapped more
than usual, with his arm in a sling. The two got on well; they mixed
in the Geological star chamber, and could snooze after confabs at the
Athenaeum. Both moved behind the scenes at the zoo, but Owen was
more interested in the apes' anatomy than in their expressions, and
he carved his way through the rare carcasses. He was petted and
patronized by the Anglican élite, who were scheming to obtain him a
Crown pension even now, at the age of thirty-seven. In August he
had been fêted at the British Association for his talk on fossil reptiles,
in which he created the concept of the 'dinosaur.' But in the same
speech he received even bigger cheers for castigating Lamarck's
fancies. He damned the notion of life's 'self-developing energies,' and
would have been horrified at Darwin's closet beliefs.[26]

Friendships had foundered on less. Owen execrated talk of an ape
ancestry. He denied it emphatically when describing the first adult
chimpanzee skeleton, which was unlike the appealing, wide-eyed
baby ape, and more of a beetle-browed, dog-jawed beast. Strip away
man's soul, make him a hairless ape, and he will sink degraded. But
Owen had done the *Zoology* proud, and his College of Surgeons was
always welcoming. It was filling with South American relics, many of
them Darwin's. The library had an enormous shell of an extinct
armadillo at one end, and workmen were about to set up a giant
ground sloth. The Owens had Darwin to breakfast in their rooms
here, unaware that he was a transmutationist. For Darwin this
double life was the stuff of inner confict, as his sickness confirmed.
Any moment his confidants could turn on him as they had on Grant.
He tried to re-join Owen and the others at the Geological Society, but
he finally gave up the attempt 'as I must remain quiet in the evenings,
or be utterly knocked up next day.'[27] Self-preservation came first.

Yet he was always on the verge of spilling his secret from sheer excitement. He knew his theory's sophistication and power; he knew that it was the way of the future. To cover up and disguise his three-year struggle had not been easy, nor had living a lie. Just as he had blurted out his doubts to Emma against good advice, he could not resist telling Lyell. The temptation was too much. Lyell could be trusted to keep a secret, however much he loathed Lamarck. In January 1842, Darwin let the cat out of the bag, probably cautiously, cryptically, and with some trepidation.

Lyell was on his American tour at the time, escaping the Boston winter by travelling south to geologize. Before sailing for the New World, he had heard that Darwin was leaving London. He doubted that 'a congenial soul so occupied with precisely the same pursuits & with an independance enabling him to pursue them will [ever again] fall so nearly in my way.' In America Darwin's letter must have stunned him. His geological twin a transmutationist! He was surely disappointed, but he merely noted on a fly-leaf that Darwin 'denies seeing a beginning to each crop of species.'²⁸ They did not have such parallel interests after all; on the most fundamental point of all they disagreed. Transmutation destroyed the biological base of Lyell's *Principles of Geology*, built to resist the Lamarckian onslaught. Perhaps it was better that the Darwins were moving away.

Charles was still panicky. After finishing the *Coral* proofs, Emma convinced him to go to Shrewsbury 'to see if a change would shake me right again.' But even as he arrived at The Mount on 7 March he was vomiting and shivery, and that night Susan nursed him to sleep. He was no better.

Throughout the spring he searched for a house, wanting one no more than five miles from a station, which, he laughed, was 'the length of my tether.' His work was finally finishing. In May *Coral Reefs* came out. He had lived with it, on and off, for three years and seven months, but it was a technical book that no 'human being will ever read.' (Not that it made any financial difference. His *Journal* had sold 1337 copies, but he had not seen a penny.) The huge *Fish* volume was finished too. The grant for the rest of the *Zoology* was petering out, and he wondered how to get the remaining bits of the *Beagle* haul into print without dipping into his own pocket.²⁹

On 18 May they left town for two months, visiting the folks at Maer, where Charles continued bee-watching, before moving to Shrewsbury on 15 June. Taking advantage of the seclusion, he finally fleshed-out a thirty-five-page sketch of his evolutionary theory in pencil. He drained it of all references to the origin of conscience and morality, but the remaining body of work was far from anaemic. It looked good on paper, pieced together for the first time.

He described how farmers selectively bred race or dray horses, beef or tallow cows, according to need, before describing Nature as an analogous super-selectionist. By now he had it down pat: overpopulation and competition led to a '*Natural Selection*,' as the victors emerged triumphant from the 'war of nature.' This was the mechanism of descent. Everything at the present day was related. But animals were not steadily advancing up a Lamarckian ladder, one behind the other, with each grading into the next. Life had a tree-like pedigree; we could relate mammals – say the 'horse, mouse, tapir, elephant' – by searching back through the genealogy for the 'common parent.'

Then he piled on the arguments for 'descent' in general. The old fossils became common ancestors of diverse modern groups. He explained island colonization and diversification. Classification became as simple and natural as a gentleman's genealogy. So much was explicable: the rudimentary organs – remnants of once-functioning parts; and the unity of plan, where wings, hands, and flippers reflected a common inheritance.

He now had his sub-headings, and the format would remain constant. He also had his strategy: 'We no longer look on [an] animal as a savage does a ship,' he wrote, 'as a thing wholly beyond comprehension.' Wild animals are not a product of God's whim any more than planets are held up by his will. Everything results from grand laws – laws that 'should exalt our notion of the power of the omniscient Creator.' This was a modified Unitarian view of the divine government. And like a Unitarian Darwin (with a certain amount of double-think) argued that it got God off the hook for evil and suffering, bundling the blame on to 'natural law.' He finished with a flourish:

> It is derogatory that the Creator of countless systems of worlds should have created each of the myriads of creeping parasites and [slimy] worms which have swarmed each day of life on land and water on [this] one globe. We cease being astonished, however much we may deplore, that a group of animals should have been directly created to lay their eggs in bowels and flesh of other [parasitic wasps] – that some organisms should delight in cruelty . . . that annually there should be an incalculable waste of eggs and pollen. From death, famine,

rapine, and the concealed war of nature we can see that the highest good, which we can conceive, the creation of the higher animals has directly come.

Here was realism and reverence combined, a theological advance on Paley's rose-tinted Creationism. 'There is a simple grandeur in [this] view of life with its powers . . . being breathed into matter under one or a few forms.'[30]

But grandeur to him was heresy to the geologists and blasphemy to the parsons. Were this not so, he could have planned to publish. The *Journal* was acclaimed, *Coral Reefs* in the shops, and the *Zoology* on its way, so why not follow these up with a book on evolution? He had enough material, but absolutely no intention of going ahead – at least not in this hysterical climate.

Consider, who would read the book? There was a genteel audience for his geology, but not for his species theory.

At most his science might tempt the odd breeder. But the best of them believed that domestic races had already been stretched to the limit. And anyway the salts of the earth wanted farming manuals, not arcane treatises. There *was* an audience in the wider sense. Some medical men and Dissenting industrialists might have applauded. More and more these oligarchs of new wealth were occupying the back benches of the learned societies: mining engineers, empire builders, improving doctors, and London professors.[31] Darwin's Nature sanctioned no privilege; everything was thrown into competition, and talent was rewarded. The new meritocrats wanted nothing more.

Further, law and order in science and society was the Dissenters' creed. A legislative harness guaranteed John Bull's freedoms and prevented social upheaval. For Darwin, too, law kept populations in their place and a capricious Deity out of earthly matters. Revolutionary upheavals were as illegitimate in civil as in geological history. Evolution was the key. The 'regular laws [of development],' he noted, 'baffles idea of revolution.'[32] And with Chartists massing, it was time for middle-class Malthusians to stand up and show that nature was on the side of the bosses.

On the religious side, the book would have sat beside Southwood Smith's *Divine Government*, which promised natural progress, civil liberties, and freedom to compete, everything Unitarian reformers wanted. But these social improvers were envious of Anglican power and trying to oust the privileged élite. Darwin thought like a Unitarian but felt for the Cambridge clerics. Henslow, Sedgwick, and Jenyns had all helped to make his career and reputation; he coveted

their lifestyle and respectability. His theory – with its improving nature and cut-throat competition – would have armed their urban enemies. And ultimately – the crux of course – at its core stood a damnable transmutation that would make man a beast and throw their world into confusion. How could he unleash such a work?

Nor was this the worst scenario. Imagine if it fell into the hands of the gutter snipes. The pauper presses might have execrated his weak-to-the-wall ethic. They might have hated Malthus, loathed the poor laws, and damned Darwin's 'base, brutal and bloody Whigs.' For these socialist tykes, nature could never condemn the co-operatives or condone the workhouses. Competition and exploitation were anathema.[33] But they *could* have cut up and cannibalized his book for their own ends. There was a real risk of this.

The atheists had already founded an illegal penny paper, the uncompromising *Oracle of Reason*, a year old and still selling in its thousands. It vilified the rich priests and armed infidel missionaries with geological tidbits to use against them. One of the cadre, the working-class printer William Chilton, fashioned a revolutionary Lamarckism, driven from below, pushing nature and society towards a higher, brighter, co-operative future (a meaningless concept to the port-swilling nobility). The hard-bitten editors were fitting evolution into their militant credo. Materialism was given revolutionary class overtones. Man was just a collection of organized atoms. 'Life is nothing and nothing life' was Chilton's slogan, tailored to the poor and downtrodden.[34]

The *Oracle* cynics denigrated Paley's 'happy' nature. It was a 'pernicious' way to justify the status quo. Chilton's nature had a satanic air that would have shocked even Darwin. Where was the design? Had God existed, he would have planned 'less suffering and more enjoyment, less hypocrisy and more sincerity, fewer rapes, frauds, pious and impious butcheries.'[35] It was raw, rough, and calculated to insult. Accordingly, a succession of *Oracle* editors were jailed for blasphemy after well-publicized trials.

Their evolution was a world removed from Darwin's. His suited the rising industrial professional classes. Theirs was for socialist workers. His was stabilizing, theirs revolutionary. And yet, they would have relished seeing simians substituted for souls. Nothing could have stopped them from pirating his book and playing up a monkey ancestry. No one escaped their democratic depredations. Lyell, Southwood Smith, Elliotson, Lawrence – all were grist to their mills, all plagiarized. Darwin's lawful chains would be even better to truss up the Anglicans' meddling God.

Of course Darwin could not publish. Materialism petrified him, and one can see why, with it condemned by the forces of Church-and-State as a blasphemous derision of the Christian law of the land. He was too worldly-wise not to sense the danger, the damning class implications. He had no illusions about how he would be treated. Carlile and Taylor had been hounded, Lawrence's trial was notorious, Elliotson was being trashed in the Tory press, and Grant had been humiliated before his very eyes. By netting man and ape together he risked being identified with atheistic low-life, or with extreme Dissenters cursing the 'fornicating' Church. The 'whole fabric' was ready to be ripped apart without his help. As the old world 'totters & falls,' he could not be seen aiding the demolition.

Ultimately he was frightened for his respectability. For a gentleman among the Oxbridge set, priming itself to guard man's soul against the socialist levellers, publishing would have been tantamount to treachery – a betrayal of the old order. It was a terrifying predicament. His crisis might have been precipitated by an industrializing society, but it was the stuff of nightmares. He might have been formulating a science for the expanding market economy. But for the moment it threatened the existing élite – the Church leaders, who were resisting change, suspicious of a greedy capitalism destroying the old order.[36]

On 18 July Darwin returned to London and started copying his evolutionary sketch, revising and over-writing until it was barely legible. He found the city a cauldron. The ledgers of death were filling up, Malthusian hatreds were festering, the northern diehards were resisting a second onslaught by London poor-law commissioners, wage-cuts and unemployment were swelling the Chartist ranks. Society was teetering.

The Darwins' house-hunting acquired a new urgency, and within days they found a place, a former parsonage, in the rural hamlet of Down, near Farnborough in Kent, 'a quiet most rustic spot on the chalk.' They spent 22 July exploring the village and outlying district with its thatched barns, spending the night in the local public house. Emma – pregnant again – was 'a good-deal disappointed' with the North Downs, thinking how 'desolate' they would look on a bleak wintery day. The house was 'square and unpretending, built of shabby bricks,' but it came with a smallholding. And the village was 'extraordinarily rural & quiet,' away from trouble spots, with an old-world charm where the locals still tipped their hats as the great folks passed.[37] Moreover it was cheap: Charles talked the price down to £2000.

In mid-August the country was paralysed by a general strike called by the Chartists. Half a million workers were out, fighting wage cuts and demanding the vote – what the Attorney General damned as the 'most formidable conspiracy ever.' Leaders declared it permanent, until the People's Charter was accepted. The Cabinet went into emergency session and put the troops on alert. The Riot Act was read in many cotton towns, and in some the troops shot and killed demonstrators.

For three days, from 14 – 16 August, battalions of Guards and Royal Horse Artillery marched up through central London to the new Euston Station to put down the riots in Manchester. The troops were trailed by jeering crowds. The commotion was terrible as they passed Darwin's road, with screams of 'Remember, you are brothers,' and 'Don't go and slaughter your starving fellow countrymen.' By the time the battalions reached Gower Street the demonstrators were hemming them in and the soldiers had fixed bayonets. The Darwins were also hemmed in, with gangs everywhere. The streets were frightening, even with a huge police presence. Each day the situation worsened. On the 16th the station (only a few hundred yards from the house) was actually blocked and the troops repeatedly charged the crowds to clear a way in.[38]

The geological squires damned the Chartists for 'trying to extort concessions by the terror of civil war,' and were thankful that 'the insurgents do not seem to have any good leaders.' Those they had were being rounded up. Following *The Times*'s law reports, Darwin might have caught the unfolding drama as the *Oracle* editor George Holyoake was tried on 17 and 18 August. Holyoake's blasphemy was to deny God's existence and to consider the people too poor to support parsons during the depression. Trial provided a public platform, and Holyoake defended himself in style, rhapsodizing on atheism, socialism, and other 'wretched sophistries and absurdities' continuously for eight hours. These agitators sought respectability in martyrdom, and he was duly convicted of the 'heinous offence' and given a six-month term. During this, *The Times* added, 'he will have ample opportunity of reflecting upon the enormity of his guilt, and of discovering the futility of the impious doctrines which he has the effrontery to avow.'[39] What he did discover was bitterness, when his elder daughter died of malnutrition while he was inside. It left him with an abiding hatred of Christianity.

A week later the Duke of Wellington so feared an uprising in London that he called for the Guards to return and special units of police were put on stand-by. The gentlemen of science also stood their ground. Darwin's *Zoology* collaborator Richard Owen drilled with the Honourable Artillery Company, and it was called out to back the police. For days on end, up to ten thousand demonstrators massed on the commons all over the capital. Working men and women milled about the streets, shouting and cheering. Even scientific institutions were preparing to resist attack. The worst was expected. In the north troops were refusing to fire on the people. In London the Home Secretary kept an enormous police and military presence on the streets.

Emma, her confinement almost due, was overseeing the packing. It was now the fourth week of the general strike, and the transportation of the ringleaders had begun. The Darwins were thankful to be getting out. Willy, Annie, and Emma left on 14 September and two days later the last trunk was ready for removal. 'I long for tomorrow,' Charles wrote excitedly. 'I feel sure I shall become deeply attached to Down.'[40]

1842–1851

20

The Extreme Verge of the World

THE DAY ARRIVED, 17 September 1842. Charles dressed, collected his valuables, and slammed the door on 12 Upper Gower Street for the last time. The traffic was worse than when he moved in four years ago – students streaming back to University College, barristers bustling up to Euston Station to catch trains to the north, where 1500 strikers awaited prosecution. It was no place for a growing family, or for a couple who loved the country. Certainly it was no place for an ambitious young naturalist with a secret. Fond memories, yes – Macaw Cottage had been his and Emma's first home. But he was leaving none too soon.

In the street his new 100-guinea horse and carriage stood at the ready. The quickest way out of town lay due south, over Waterloo Bridge, past the gin shops and brothels to the Elephant and Castle. On the right in the distance, the Palace of Westminster. On the left, the Rotunda and Horsemonger-lane gaol, with prisoners' relatives outside, a reminder that this was radical territory. Still further and the great landmarks vanished. At New Cross Gate they left the smoke behind and breathed country air. The traffic thinned out past Bromley as they made for Keston. The horse was working harder now, plodding up the chalky North Downs. Flinty fields surrounded them on either side. Countless millions of years ago these vast chalk slopes had been eroded to form flat-bottomed valleys – 'bottoms,' the locals called them – separated by strips of woodland that provided fringes of autumn colour. Near Keston the road became a narrow stony lane.[1] Slower now, rising 200 feet in the last two miles, the lane led through beech woods into the village of Down.

Two hours out of London, sixteen miles from St Paul's, this was the perfect rural retreat: a parish like Henslow's at Hitcham, or Fox's new one in Cheshire – a parish like the one Charles himself had dreamt of aboard the *Beagle*, the one in which the Doctor would have installed him all those years ago. The scene struck a responsive chord. He breathed an enormous sigh of relief. Here he was at a safe distance from society. No more worrying about what people might say; the rustics would respect him for the gentleman he was, not judge him by what he thought or wrote. He would see everyone on his own terms, when and as he pleased. The nearest train station, Sydenham, was eight miles away, and the hilly drive cut Down off, secured its inhabitants, preserved their past. A parish set in aspic – the ideal habitat for a gentleman evolutionist. 'Down, near Bromley, Kent,' was the address he sent his old servant Covington in Australia. 'N.B.,' he added, 'this will be my direction for the rest of my life.'[2]

The lane went straight to the centre of the village. There, against the churchyard wall, stocks had stood until recent years. The great yew at the lychgate was centuries old. The flint-walled parish church of St Mary dated from the fourteenth century. A 29-year-old curate, the Revd John Willott, had charge of Down's 444 souls, but it was a meagre living, his income from rents and tithes barely topping £100 a year. The Baptist chapel lay a stone's throw away, and for thirty years its little band of members had lived patiently under the Anglican regime.[3]

The parishioners were agricultural labourers and tenant farmers mostly. Scattered over two and a half square miles, they worked with their hands and walked everywhere. Their life centred on the village. In that cluster of forty houses lay all their essential services: a butcher, a baker, a carpenter, as well as the grocer's shop, a post office, and a pub. The George and Dragon Inn stood conveniently opposite the church. What could not be obtained here the 'carrier' would fetch on his weekly run to London. It was a stable, closely knit community, like ten thousand hamlets in Victoria's England.

Down had its great folks too. Some twenty men owned property enough to qualify as voters, but few were really wealthy. The better-off lived in houses that bore the names of old village families, such as Petleys and Trowmers. The occupants of Down Court, a 'most beautiful old farm-house with great thatched barns' and traces of a moat, were successors to the lords of the manor.[4]

On the outskirts was a 3000-acre estate with a mansion being built. This was High Elms farm, with Sir John Lubbock, his wife and four children in residence. A third-generation City banker – of Sir John William Lubbock, Forster & Co. – he was less interested in money than science. For his work in astronomy and mathematics he had been elected a Fellow of the Royal Society. The folk at Down knew nothing of this. To them the money was what counted, and Sir John obliged them by spending it. The mansion building and estate gave jobs to dozens of local craftsmen, staff, and tenants. Sir John was the chief landowner and employer in the area. Naturally, the squire's friends would be great folks too. Sir John had already announced the good news to his eldest son John, aged seven: 'Mr. Darwin is coming to live at Down.'[5]

With villagers peering quizzically, touching their hats as he passed, Charles drove his carriage to the right at the church, down Luxted Road, past the village pond and gently up into open country. On the right, a few hundred yards along, was a plain brick building hugging the road – Down House.[6] This would be home.

For a parsonage it was modest enough – 'oldish & ugly' but 'largish & ... cheap.' Built as a farmhouse and extended some sixty years before, it comprised kitchen, scullery, and stores in the oldest part; drawing-room, dining-room, and study on the main ground floor; and bedrooms enough for half the Darwin–Wedgwood clan on the two floors above. Down's previous incumbent had lived there for three years and made various improvements. Not that these were obvious now. Two years standing empty had taken their toll, and the faded musty rooms were due for refurbishment. But with all his furniture '& chattel' in place, the fires lit, and Willy 'in ectasies,' tearing around 'country ouse,' Charles thought it good enough to be going on with.[7] Alterations could wait.

Besides, with Emma at full-term, the first priority was to make life comfortable for her and the baby. No sooner done than the confinement began, six days after Charles arrived. The village surgeon rushed over from 'two fields off' and delivered a girl, Mary Eleanor. The baby, though small and feeble, helped relieve Emma's anxiety about her father, who she now heard was dying. And her recovery was quicker than ever, owing to the 'country air,' Darwin assumed. At nine days old, on a Sunday, Mary was baptized in the parish church. Erasmus came down for the event. Afterwards the baby went on 'fairly well,' but she lived only another fortnight. On 19 October Charles, Emma, and the Revd Willott gathered in the churchyard to inter the body. Charles soldiered through the funeral, which he had dreaded. Emma's grief was worse. She had hoped that the baby's 'likeness to Mamma,' now an elderly invalid, 'might run through her mind as well as face.'[8] Both of them took comfort from the fact that the child had not lived longer and suffered more.

It was a grim start to their new life. They threw themselves into the house, and Willy and Annie distracted them. Charles rejoiced to Fox that 'our two little souls are better & happier' than in London. He omitted to explain why there were not three. Fox still had not come to terms with his wife's death in childbirth the previous spring; not even a trip abroad had healed his heart. 'Strong affections,' Charles consoled him, 'have always appeared to me, the most noble part of a man's nature . . . Your grief is the necessary price for having been born with . . . such feelings.' 'But,' he added, 'I am writing away without really being able to put myself in your position – you have my sincerest sympathy & respect in your sorrow.'⁹ Losing Mary was the closest that death had touched his adult life.

Other children, too, distracted Charles and Emma, though not without bringing their own heartaches. That autumn Emma's brother Hensleigh had a long illness. To relieve the strain on Fanny, they agreed to take in the older cousins, Snow aged nine, Bro eight, and Erny five. With their own, aged three and two, it was quite a houseful. One day in early November Emma sent them out for a hike with the nursery maid Bessy, herself only a teenager. They had permission to explore Cudham Wood, but Bessy took them in the wrong direction, across a sprawling bottom into the 'Big Woods,' full of giant oaks with a tangle of hazel coppices cut by footpaths. It was wintery, with frosty fields. Snow and Willy got separated and turned up at home, their feet caked in clay. Fighting back the tears, Snow told Uncle Charles that the others were lost. He set off urgently with Parslow, and after asking at a farmhouse, tracked them down, huddled together, cold and frightened, Erny and Bro and Bessy, who had been carrying Annie for three hours. The men scooped up the little ones and took them all to the farmhouse for a reviving snack, then, with the neighbour's help, brought the babes back home safely.¹⁰

Charles and Emma were learning about Kentish country ways. Down was nothing like London, more like Maer. The rural economy was as different from the urban cash nexus as the Big Woods were from Gower Street. People here were closely interdependent. They bartered and bargained as familiars if not equals. Relationships were all-important, and these began at home. As the Darwin home itself began to take shape, with Parslow as their most trusted servant, other household staff would have to be found locally, and hiring could be difficult unless the family observed the proprieties and kept on good terms with the neighbours. A cook was vital for Emma, as a coachman was for Charles. A footman would assist Parslow at door and table. In the spring a gardener would have to be found; and, soon afterwards, another nurse.

Emma was pregnant again, a few months after Mary's death. With the prospect of three children under the age of four, young Bessy required expert help. Enter Brodie, a staunch Scottish lass with 'carrotty hair, china-blue eyes,' and a face made memorable by smallpox. She had proved her worth by spurning a suitor to tend the deranged wife and children of the impoverished writer William Makepeace Thackeray. Down House was like a holiday compared to the Thackerays' ménage in Paris. True, there was a problem of Bessy's 'pertness' towards her, but Emma – a stickler for tranquillity – used a 'sledge-hammer' to keep the peace.

While Emma ran the household, Charles passed the winter survey-ing his new estate. He did make a start on the 'second very thin part' of the *Beagle* geology, on volcanic islands. And he intended to spend a night or two in London every month 'to keep up my communication with scientific men,' so as not to 'turn into [a] complete Kentish Hog.' Even so, the thought of it turned his stomach. Going there 'so generally knocks me up, that I am able to do scarcely anything.'[11] But the country got the better of him. Like Henslow in Hitcham, criticized for neglecting his botany, Charles took to pottering around the parson-age.

Down House sat high and exposed, with a 'desolate air.' The old clump of stunted trees beside it – yew, fir, mulberry, chestnut – accentuated the bleakness rather than giving any shelter. To the rear lay the rest of the property – fifteen acres of hayfield – with only a hedge separating the house from a 'rather ugly distant horizon.' The public footpaths were too close. Charles's only real protection was the primeval terrain: a great chalk escarpment to the south, cutting off the estate from the low country of Kent; a deep valley to the north between the village and the road to London; and to the east and west 'impassible' valley bottoms. 'We are absolutely at [the] extreme verge of [the] world,' he boasted to Fox – but even this was not safe enough for him.

The wind was vicious. In the south-westerly gales the children could taste the salt on the drawing-room window-panes, although the sea was forty miles away. And that winter the exposed north face of the house took a brutal beating. He craved solitude, a 'quiet routine.' Nothing must happen out of the ordinary, nothing unexpected. 'I cannot dine out or receive visitors, except relations with whom I can pass some time after dinner in silence.'[12] For such a man, artifice had to help nature; fortifications had to be built.

Charles was full of home-improvement schemes. The Doctor put up the money – 'a cool 300£' to start – against his future inheritance. Upstairs the bedrooms needed a rethink. Emma would have a 'truly magnificent' one of her own, and there had to be some for relations. A schoolroom was also imperative – soon there would be a governess to give the children lessons. Downstairs the kitchen and pantry were not quite right. The drawing-room, and master bedroom above, were large but undistinguished spaces. They overlooked the garden in the direction of the Big Woods, towards the setting sun. What each needed was a handsome bow, with three windows to catch the light and warmth.[13] And after all the structural work was done, complete redecoration.

Bricklayers and carpenters moved in as spring arrived. 'A most deceptious property to buy Sir,' one said, meaning a compliment. His architect was right on how much cheaper labour was here than in London. Outside, security arrangements were being stepped up. The kitchen garden would be re-designed, with a high wall running 100 yards along it to form the northern boundary of the property. Other 'great earthworks' would be undertaken to embellish the grounds and raise a large mound outside the front door, to 'make the place much snugger.' Beyond the mound an orchard would be planted. And further still lay a slip of land beside Luxted Road, which Charles would have to buy.[14]

That road was a problem. Though only a cart track, it permitted easy access from north and south, skirting the frontage just yards from his study window. As things stood passers-by could peer right inside. 'The publicity of the place is at present intolerable,' he declared, and in April 1843 he sought leave from the parish vestry to lower the road and build a perimeter wall. The officials were 'as civil, as civil could be,' and work began immediately. He hired 'a sort of jack of all knowledge' named Vinson to help him. 'I suspect he is an old rogue, but he is a useful one.' The 'effects of a 1£ present & the hopes of another' set him calculating the volume of earth to be moved – some 200 cubic yards. Then the heavy spadework began. It was a mammoth undertaking: from 18 to 24 inches of flinty clay were laboriously dug from the road along a 500-foot stretch, the flints being used to build a wall over six feet high, running from the far end of the house to the northernmost point on the property. But the whole job cost only £110.

These projects dragged on for many months, although the worst of the disruption – everyone hoped – would be over in time for the new baby. When eventually the walls were up and Charles felt secure, he added the finishing touch: a mirror outside his study window, so that callers could be spied approaching the front door.[15]

The 'capital study 18 x 18,' as Charles called it, was the focal point. Two great shuttered windows lit the corniced room with clear, white northern light, ideal for writing, dissecting, and microscopy. The fireplace, surrounded by milky marble, made up for the absent sun, with a chimney-breast separating ample alcoves for books and files. An arm-chair sat in one corner, between hearth and window, and tables were placed within easy reach. In the corner opposite, the door opened on to a long hallway leading from the front entrance to the kitchen. Life went on far above, in the children's rooms, and in the servants' quarters at the other end of the house.[16] In his insular laboratory, cut off from the world, he could think clear thoughts and contain the contradiction that was tearing him apart. It was an Archimedean point from which, given time, he would move the world.

Not that much earth-moving was going on at present, except outdoors. He tried dabbling with his species sketch in the spring, but the commotion made it impossible. Indeed, he spent a desultory first year at Down, only occasionally getting to grips with the greater upheavals in the past. He worried that his explanation of the strange parallel roads of Glen Roy – as prehistoric sea beaches – was already crumbling. The Swiss naturalist Louis Agassiz, promoting his novel idea of a former Ice Age, was suggesting that a glacier had once blocked Glen Roy, damming it to form a lake – making these 'roads' old lake margins. Agassiz's icy catastrophism made Darwin shiver; gentle rising and subsidence of the land was the key.[17]

For years his manuscript on volcanoes had kicked around; now, as he picked up the subject again, he was mortified to discover just how much remained to be done. He rummaged through his old *Beagle* notes and called in the specialist reports on his 'beastly rocks.' He even made a couple of flying visits to the Geological Society, imploring the curator to have books, maps, and nodules of glassy obsidian '*ready for my inspection, as my time is short.*' The whole process took him back to those seasick days of discovery, when he set foot on the Galapagos, St Helena, and St Jago; and his first sight of the obsidian beds and lava 'bombs' strewn over Ascension. How much more those romantic places had meant to him than his turgid 150-page *Volcanic Islands* would mean to the geological community. 'I hope you will read my volume,' he despaired to his preceptor Lyell, 'for if you don't, I cannot think of anyone else who will!'[18]

He craved recognition from his fellow geologists – approval shored up his respectability – and it drove him to finish the *Beagle* reports. Other writings that year hinted at more heretical concerns. Reproduction, such a fact of life in Down House, was still fascinating for the light it shed on descent. He penned a short paper on the spawning arrowworms he had trawled from Brazilian seas ten years before. His interest in their eggs was never-failing, and the granular matter they released when disrupted. In another note, on peculiar double-flowered gentians, posted off to the *Gardeners' Chronicle*, he showed that the flowers on a single plant can be arranged in 'a series ... by which the stamens are seen to become deformed, and gradually to pass into small petals and scales.' Perhaps some alteration of the environment determined this 'metamorphic change ... early in the plant's life.' 'Is there any shadow of truth in this theory?'[19]

Coy but provocative, he concealed much more than readers realized. 'Metamorphic changes,' environmental causes, these terms had double meanings. They referred to individual development, but evolutionists gave them wider connotations – tadpoles metamorphosed into frogs, but evolutionists also talked of fish 'metamorphosing' into reptiles, and apes into men. Language was a screen; metamorphosing plants could be mooted safely, but they pointed up Charles's contradiction. He had unselfconsciously assumed the guise of an orthodox clerical-naturalist, a pottering, parsonage-living harmless soul, and it was making his quandary worse. And he wasn't just *living* in a clergyman's house; he was actually beginning to emulate the most eminent of parish naturalists, the Revd Gilbert White.

For almost fifty years White's *Natural History and Antiquities of Selborne* had inspired clergymen and country folk to observe the rhythm of the seasons. It taught them to record nature's trifling phenomena, even – as White did so famously – to compile a country diary. Charles had pored over the *Natural History* as a teenager; in February 1843 he had read it again in the edition just published by his friend, the Revd Jenyns. Then in May he reacquainted himself with two of the best known books to have come from rectories, Paley's *Natural Theology* and *An Introduction to Entomology* by the Revd William Kirby and William Spence. And that month he started a country diary of his own.[20] He called it 'The General Aspect.'

His observations were largely geological, made during extensive rambles. Flints, footpaths, farmhouses, each was discussed. The 'slippery red clay' from October to April, the brilliant flowers of early spring, the 'quite extraordinary' humming of hive bees in the summer were also mentioned, showing that in his first cycle of seasons he made the parish his own, took charge of its natural-history aspect, became nature's 'parson' (as rustics liked to say) to Lubbock's new-model squire. With the gentlest condescension, so like a man of the cloth, he noted the prevalence of error among the yokels concerning the overhead humming heard on hot days. 'The labourers here say it is made by "air-bees," and one man, seeing a wild bee in a flower different from the hive kind, remarked: "That, no doubt, is an air-bee".'[21]

With renovations going on all around and workmen to keep an eye on, Charles filled up the idle moments by bestowing favours and good advice. 'Get up your steam . . . & have a ramble in Wales,' he jollied Fox, still down in the dumps; 'its glorious scenery must do every one's heart & body good.' Covington in Australia was going deaf, and Darwin sent him an ear trumpet. Like a true country curate, he was dispensing patronage everywhere. He interceded with FitzRoy, recently appointed Governor of New Zealand, on behalf of the émigré son of his successor as Secretary of the Geological Society. He gave a glowing reference to the sacked Assistant Curator of the Zoological Society George Waterhouse – the man who had described the *Beagle*'s mammals – to help him obtain a post at the British Museum. He even stood godfather, with Richard Owen, to Waterhouse's son (who was christened Charles Owen Waterhouse). Most portentous of all (though he did not know it), he heard news of a young ship's surgeon and botanist named Joseph Hooker. Hooker, sailing with Capt. Ross's Antarctic expedition, was the son of the Director of the Royal Botanic Gardens at Kew, Sir William Hooker. Darwin told Sir William that, when Joseph returned, his own plants from 'T[ierra]. del. Fuego & of Southern Patagonia will be joyfully laid at his disposal.'[22] Such generosity would be rewarded.

In the first week of July 1843 word came that Emma's father was dying. Charles and Emma, seven months pregnant, set off immediately on the long, sad, anxious farewell journey to Maer, arriving with just days to spare. At seventy-four, Josiah was the ghost of his former self. Once the commanding industrialist and Whig statesman, he had become a hallucinating bedridden wreck, clutching at the last threads of life with quivering, senile hands. This was the revered uncle – 'so high, so pure, so true and so engaging by his exquisite modesty' – whose intervention had smoothed Charles's path aboard the *Beagle*. His wife Bessy, too, was now a total invalid, and scarcely able to grieve for her pathetic husk of a husband. Her life seemed 'sadder than death;' Maer was melancholy as never before. Only Elizabeth was left, Emma's hunchbacked eldest sister, who cared unstintingly for their parents. The old days of autumn shoots and parties were gone for ever. Josiah died on the 12th, peacefully. The women sought religious consolation, the more earnestly because they all worried about their father's indifference to God. Charles lingered, then made his usual summer pilgrimage to Shrewsbury before heading home.[23]

He returned to find letters from Waterhouse waiting. Waterhouse wanted advice on that be-all and end-all of British natural history, classification. Conventional classification meant ordering nature, all living things in their place, each given its due rank, slotted into a fixed hierarchy. Classifiers, legions of them, were taming a chaotic world, providing a rock on which an immutably Creative biology could be built. They were revealing God's Plan. Darwin had struggled with the problem of a 'natural classification' ever since he opened his species notebooks. It was obvious to him that few were taking the right approach, and Waterhouse least of all. 'It has long appeared to me, that the root of the difficulty in settling such questions as yours,' Darwin told him, 'lies in our ignorance of what we are searching after.' Why construct a classification? What was it designed to show?

Waterhouse was poor and powerless, a minor salaried official. When Darwin praised him in his testimonial as 'so infinitely my superior' he meant in his stock of zoological facts. Waterhouse was above all a describer. Beyond this, Darwin saw him wandering in circles. Waterhouse's nature consisted of clusters of wheels. All groups – species, genera, families – sat on circles. The circular classification kept nature safely and aimlessly revolving. There was no 'chain of life,' no linear piling of creature upon creature; thus it was safe from the Lamarckian evolutionists, who might turn the chain into an escalator, and set it gliding upwards towards man.

Darwin had Waterhouse's confidence. Now was the moment to try to turn him. Indeed, a week back from seeing his sage old freethinking father, a fortnight since his beloved uncle died, he was feeling bloody-minded. 'Most authors,' Charles snapped, referring to classification,

> say it is an endeavour to discover the laws according to
> which the Creator has willed to produce organized beings –
> But what empty high-sounding sentences these are – it does
> not mean order in time of creation, nor propinquity to any

> one type, as man. – in fact it means just nothing. According
> to my opinion, (which I give every one leave to hoot at . . .)
> classification consists in grouping beings according to their
> actual *relationship*, ie their consanguinity, or descent from
> common stocks.

He had tipped his hand to a colleague; he was out in the open now, a
new brusqueness masking his fear. He believed in a real genealogy, a
pedigree, a bloodline.[24] He was proposing a system far less aesthetic,
and much messier and more contingent, with a proper historical
aspect supplied by fossils. He had exploded with a force that
surprised even himself.

Nor was that the last word. A few days later he skewered
Waterhouse with another well-honed letter. He rammed the same
point home. '*All rules for a natural classification are futile until you
can clearly explain, what you are aiming at.*' He protested that
anything less than an actual genealogical relationship is useless as a
criterion. Then he chanted his credo:

> I believe (though why I should trouble you with my belief,
> which must & ought to appear the merest trash and
> hypothesis?) that if every organism, which ever had lived or
> does live, were collected together . . . a perfect series would be
> presented, linking all, say the Mammals, into one great, quite
> indivisible group – and I believe all the orders, families &
> genera amongst the Mammals are merely artificial terms highly
> useful to show the relationship of those members of the series,
> *which have not become extinct.*

Charles had broached the heretical subject, but then trembled. Why,
indeed, tease Waterhouse on the genealogy of mammals and man
when he knew it would appear 'the merest trash' to an anti-evolution-
ist?[25] He was exposing himself and felt torn.

'But it is no use my going on this way,' he quickly added, and he
turned the spotlight back on to Waterhouse, challenging him: 'I beg
you to think clearly . . .' 'What do you exactly mean . . .' 'I shall be
curious to hear . . .' Then, farewell, and a P.S.: 'Will you . . . keep
this *one* letter of mine to be returned; as at some future year, I shall
be curious to see, what I think now.' Security was of the essence, and
Waterhouse complied. But he did not like the ungodly way his son's
godfather had treated him. He felt browbeaten – no, downright
crucified. 'You nail me to the stake and grumble because I wriggle a
bit. . . . Well, I *will* explain what I am aiming at.' He carried on,

discussing how nature can be 'symbolically represented,' and how spiritual man was the 'standard of perfection.'[26]

The summer wore on, with workmen gravelling walks – 'Ave Maria how the money does go' – and Emma grieving the loss of her father with sister Elizabeth, who had come for the confinement. September was sunny; the great wall was up and, a year since leaving London, Charles's health had improved. On the 25th, almost on poor Mary's birthday, Henrietta was safely delivered, much to his relief. Then October saw delivery of the fifth and final part of the *Zoology*, at long last. Charles celebrated with a trip to Shrewsbury, where he rambled leisurely around old haunts and felt 'very much in love with my own dear three chickens' and their nursing mother, 'My dear old Titty.' He saw something of his own mother too, finding two of her 'very old letters ... such kind & considerate ones,' written in a hand 'very like that of the Wedgwood family.'

Waterhouse got the job, but his ensuing article showed that he had gone his own way. Worse, in fact. In print Waterhouse, cued by Richard Owen, attacked the heretics who believe that all groups of animals 'blend perceptibly into each other.' Darwin assumed that he was being fingered as 'one of the very guilty ones' who accept *living* 'links' between the groups, whereas he only acknowledged *ancestral* intermediates. Anyway, Waterhouse's own mammals sat on circles, with no links between them, and this explained nothing about their real relationships.

'*Vicious* circles,' Darwin spat back; they had done 'infinite harm.' Of course the descriptive approach was important, and Waterhouse had 'done good service in pointing out how rare half-way-links are, if indeed they [now] exist.' This was grist to Darwin's mill in a way, because for him the 'half-way-links' were *extinct*: they were the common ancestors, sitting at the forks in a family tree, not half-way houses among living animals. Classification was a genealogical task, not a geometrical one, and it could only be explained by evolution. Darwin had to get rid of those symbolic circles, which stood in his way. 'I admire my own impudence in criticising you,' he strutted at the end; 'as for your wicked circles, I wish they were all d – – d to-gether.'[27]

21

Murder

A 'MURDER,' Darwin compared it to. He was writing to his new friend, the botanist Joseph Dalton Hooker, just back from four years at sea. It was 11 January 1844, and he was talking about the transmutation of life. *Volcanic Islands* had just gone off to the printers and Darwin was mulling over his 1842 pencil sketch again. Hooker – young, buoyant, fresh from abroad – had promise. Darwin waylaid him. From behind his great wall at Down he plucked up courage and confessed his awful secret, his belief that all animals were descended from common stocks.

Hooker was unprepared for the revelation. As a boy 'croaky Joe' had been brought up in Puritan strictness, taught to despise the 'scoffer and the sceptic' and accept 'the hand of an overruling Providence in every turn of events.' Glasgow medical studies were perhaps liberating – even Charles's brother Erasmus had been horrified to see Glasgow students playing football inside college. And Hooker's stint as an assistant surgeon in the navy must have broadened his outlook still further.[1] But his was still a pretty disciplined evangelical background, with none of the male Darwins' history of freethought.

Why, then, did Darwin confide in Hooker? He hardly knew the man, addressing him as 'My Dear Sir.' (It would be another six weeks before he threw aside 'old-world formality' and adopted the bluntly familiar 'Dear Hooker.') Maybe it was because Hooker, too, was 'well salted.' He had returned in September 1843 from his 'long & glorious' Antarctic voyage aboard HMS *Erebus* under Capt. Ross. Maybe it was because he was a prolific worker, familiar with island flora, and delighted to accept Darwin's offer of plants from the *Beagle*.[2]

Darwin had met Hooker a couple of times fleetingly, long before, in 1839. Hooker, then twenty-one and getting ready to sail, was walking in Charing Cross with Robert McCormick, the *Erebus*'s surgeon (and the *Beagle*'s as far as Rio). They bumped into Darwin, who impressed Hooker with 'his animated expression, heavy beetle brow, mellow voice, and delightfully frank and cordial greeting to his former shipmate.'[3] He was eight years Hooker's senior, with his own expedition behind him. Of course there was an obvious difference in their circumnavigations: Darwin travelled as a self-financed companion to the captain, Hooker as a salaried assistant surgeon, a menial grade in young Victoria's navy. Darwin had a magnificent *Journal* to show for his trip. Unknown to him, Hooker had actually read the proofs of the *Journal*. Lyell's copy passed to Hooker's father as Joseph prepared for his voyage; he had slept with them under his pillow so that, at first light each day, he might 'devour their contents.' The proofs made him despair of ever following in Darwin's footsteps, 'at however great a distance.' But they also increased his 'desire to travel and observe.' 'A copy of the complete work was a parting gift from Mr Lyell on the eve of my leaving England,' Hooker remembered, 'and no more instructive and inspiring work occupied the bookshelf of my narrow quarters throughout the voyage.'[4] This too – youthful adoration – played its part in winning Darwin's confidence.

These two young salts, having seen the world and its ways, gravitated towards one another in late 1843. It was really Darwin's doing. In a long letter welcoming Hooker home, Darwin urged him to think on the broader implication of the South American flora, and compare it to the European. He made the request seem like a 'trust,' and Hooker hoped that he would not be 'unworthy' of it. He drafted a paper immediately showing the striking similarities in the plants across the whole of the Southern Hemisphere, from Tasmania to Tierra del Fuego.[5] Hooker exuded confidence and had total command of the data. Darwin was impressed; and in reply he blurted out his confession, wrapped in his usual disarming prose.

For seven years he had been 'engaged in a very presumptuous work,' perhaps 'a very foolish one.' Having been struck by Galapagos life and the South American fossils, he said, he had 'blindly' collected everything bearing on species, including 'heaps of agricultural & horticultural books.' Slowly, reluctantly, he had been forced to a conclusion. 'I am almost convinced (quite contrary to the opinion I started with) that species are not (it is like confessing a murder) immutable.' Murder it might have been, but in his plea nature was to blame. He had *blindly* collected; there was no intention to commit a crime – to *deliberately* come up with something so gross as evolution. Puritanical young Hooker, placed in a judicial seat, was asked to weigh up the mitigating circumstances. Not murder, his correspondent was pleading, but helpless manslaughter. Darwin was angstridden. 'You will groan, & think to yourself "on what a man have I been wasting my time in writing to".'[6]

Why a 'murder,' the ultimate affront to society? Transmutation in January 1844 was still associated with riot and revolution – in other words, the gutter press. Even as Darwin incriminated himself, extremists were touting their penny papers around London's streets. That week's *Movement*, a scurrilous atheistic rag printed by George Holyoake – now out of gaol – and the *Oracle* evolutionists, ran attacks on Christianity and Paley's natural theology. True, theirs was a different evolution, one in which life strove for its own betterment. No Malthusian weak-to-the-wall mechanism here. Still, transmutation was being touted by street atheists intent on smashing the Anglican state. Darwin's clerical friends – the Foxes, Jenynses, and Henslows – stood to be stripped of their tithes by the red Lamarckians. The fat clergy, the revolutionaries screamed, would have to prove that they had something worth bartering for the products of labour.[7] So these were the subversives who were associated with evolution in January 1844. This is why Lamarckism had murderous overtones.

Darwin distanced himself more and more from Lamarck. 'Heaven forfend me from Lamarck['s] nonsense of a "tendency to progression" "adaptations from the slow willing of animals" &c.' Darwin's own Malthusian 'means of change' was unlike anything coming from the revolutionary French. In short, he told Hooker, 'I think I have found out (here's presumption!) the simple way by which species become exquisitely adapted to various ends.'

He posted the confession, hoping his faith in Hooker was not misplaced, and waited and waited. Two weeks passed with no word; Hooker was busy, collating his pressed flowers and looking for his land legs. Then at the end of the month a long unruffled response arrived. Hooker sent screeds as usual on South American plants. He seemed flattered and a bit chary of Darwin's attentions; aware that Darwin was hanging on to his every word, and worried that he would not come up to snuff. 'You take so much notice of me, that I am almost afraid of saying too much, & of destroying the illusory character you give of my little notes.' He did not say too much on species, but what he did was encouraging. He went as far as he would for the next decade, bending over backwards to preserve their budding friendship. There may have been 'a gradual change of species. I shall be delighted to hear how you think that this change may have taken place, as no presently conceived opinions satisfy me on the subject.'[8]

Darwin could not have asked for more; his faith had been vindicated. From this time on transmutation became a ghostly presence in his letters, always there but never quite seen. Hooker knew full well why his brains were being picked. Given the all-clear, Darwin started setting his young friend tasks, pushing him to look at island faunas through Darwinian eyes. The Galapagos birds and shells were all distinct species, he said, but related to South American stock – was the same true of Galapagos plants? Hooker became a sounding board for a thousand such queries, a co-opted assistant in Darwin's quest for the laws of life.

After this effectual absolution, Darwin looked over his two-year-old species sketch again, relieved. He had been tinkering with it continually. Now he decided to flesh it out properly, make it more fluid, less telegraphic, less crabbed. He followed the same format: the first part spelled out his mechanism – variation and selection – based on what breeders had done with domestic animals, and the second covered the proofs of descent in general. As he reworked it, he still saw natural selection operate only intermittently. Normally, he believed, animals and plants do not vary much in the wild. They remain well adapted so long as conditions are steady; only as the environment changes does the reproductive system become affected. This has a destabilizing effect: 'the organization of the beings' becomes 'plastic,' as it does 'under domestication.'[9] New variants are thrown up, competition occurs, and selection picks out the best. In 1844 he understood it as a sort of automatic feedback loop, which restored the balance.

Through the spring the sketch expanded into a full 189-page essay. Darwin sensed its power and he saw its truth.[10] He also knew, grinding away month after month, that he could not publish – he would be accused of social delinquency, or worse.

Transmutation was still a weapon wielded by militants, angrily eyeing the islands of gentrified opulence. The first week in July, when Darwin entrusted the finished manuscript to the local schoolmaster to be copied, the feminist Emma Martin published her inflammatory pamphlet *Conversation on the Being of God*, arguing that evolution needed no Creator. She then toured the country, lecturing in markets and socialist Halls of Science, and was summoned for causing disturbances at churches. The old infidel order might have been passing, indeed the 'Devil's Chaplain,' the Revd Taylor, had died in exile only the month before. But others were emerging to carry on the crusade, shocking prim Victorians by their behaviour. Mrs Martin was held up as an example. She had left her Baptist husband for the socialist cause; she was hard up, living on hand-outs, and carting her children around with her. She was hounded from town to town, harassed by rectors and magistrates. This was no way for a mother to behave. But like her friend Holyoake, she was a mesmerizing orator, who criss-crossed the country smashing the '*thraldom* of religion,' drawing crowds of 3000 whenever she challenged the clergy.[11]

No, publishing would be suicidal. Clergy-baiting was on the increase, and country parsons were among Darwin's friends and family. He risked being accused of betraying his privileged class.

On 5 July, with the evolution essay gone, he wrote his wife a difficult letter, one he would hide away, to be opened in the event of his 'sudden death.' Maybe his constitution would break, or cholera could carry him off. (Epidemics still raged periodically. He later copied out an opium-based prescription to ease the symptoms of cholera.) The letter contained his 'most solemn & last request' – that she should publish the essay posthumously. Maybe he half-hoped that he would die first. He reposed a terrible trust, for they differed grievously on religion. But he was so sure of the essay. 'If, as I believe that my theory is true & if it be accepted even by one competent judge, it will be a considerable step in science.'[12] She was to give a good editor £400 plus his books and clippings, to enlarge and publish the work, and he hoped that she or her brother Hensleigh would promote it.

He ran through possible editors, scrubbing some, adding others. Lyell should be approached first. Or perhaps Edward Forbes, a good all-rounder – a biogeographer and botanist, a pioneer of deep-sea dredging with a book on starfishes behind him. No, probably Henslow was 'best in many respects,' but then again Hooker was a 'very good' choice. Owen's name went on, then came off as Darwin thought of his abomination of transmutation. This was the trouble. He would be placing each man in a moral quandary: Lyell had devoted his *Principles of Geology* to refuting Lamarck, Forbes was a High Anglican who hated materialism, Henslow a clergyman, Owen a Tory who was combating radical propaganda on nature's 'self-development.'[13] One studied comparative anatomy, Owen proclaimed, to eradicate such pernicious theories; no amount of bribe would have persuaded him to *publish* one. Darwin was expecting his nominees to be impossibly impartial, to ignore their social duty and do something deeply repugnant.

And why should they? How far did friendship extend? Forbes believed that an 'ill book well written is like poisoning a fountain that runs for ever.' How could any of them contemplate polishing Darwin's prose to make a poisonous philosophy attractive? – to make it what Sedgwick called one book on evolution a few months later, a 'rank pill of asafoetida and arsenic, covered with gold leaf.'[14] Darwin's was a terrible trust. He wondered if anyone would accept.

He did not tell Hooker of the essay, but he was dying to discuss its contents. At times, he tended to forget Hooker's youth and lack of fortune, which gilded a gentleman's path. He kept urging him to put his name down for the Athenaeum Club, where they might discuss the world's plants in plush surroundings, only to learn that Hooker had done so long ago, and could not get in. Nor could they meet at the Geological Society, whose six-guinea admission fee and three-guinea annual dues deterred the young botanist. With the essay finished Charles got up his 'steam & courage' and went with Emma one fine July day to visit Hooker at Kew Gardens. At last they met properly. Hooker really was 'a most engaging young man,' Lyell heard.[15] Soon Emma was exchanging recipes with Hooker, still a bachelor, trying his apple preserve and cakes.

A week later Darwin started his third geological book based on the *Beagle* voyage. *Geological Observations on South America* would describe the pampas, the plateaux, the Andes, showing how they had been pushed up with Lyellian slowness. Not for him D'Orbigny's nonsense about catastrophic upheaval. Darwin knew that the pampas had been built up gently in fresh water, not cataclysmically as the sea invaded the land, sweeping animal carcasses before it. He had written sixty pages by September 'on the elevation & great gravel terraces & plains of Patagonia & Chile & Peru,' and they were 'pretty good.'[16]

In his weekly epistles to Hooker, he was releasing equally tantalizing matter from his essay. Why for instance were species numerous in some spots and not in others? The production of species on islands was the key, as the Galapagos had shown. Here the bird and reptile colonists had diversified into varied niches created on the newly emerged volcanic outcrops. Each had its peculiar fauna. Elsewhere submerging continents were breaking up into islands, isolating species, encouraging new adaptations as habitats changed. He could not go into details, but

> with respect to original creation or production of new forms
> . . . isolation appears the chief element: Hence . . . a tract of
> country, which has oftenest within the later geological periods
> subsided & been converted into isl[an]^{ds}, & reunited, I sh[oul]^{d}
> expect to contain many forms.

Hooker mooted the exceptions: the Falklands and Iceland, which had hardly anything indigenous. *Their* plants were identical to South America's or Europe's. And even granting the point, how does a species reaching the outlying islands radiate into the diverse forms? Are we to believe 'Lamarck's twaddle' or the other 'mad' theories doing the rounds? Species may be mutable 'but I should not think they set about it themselves so systematically as he says.' Darwin agreed that Lamarck was 'veritable rubbish' and the others no better, but then none of them had 'approached the subject on the side of variation under domestication.'[17] Another tantalizing clue, did Hooker but know it.

By late September the evolution essay was back in Down House. Charles broke off from *South America* to correct the fair copy, which had grown to 231 pages in the schoolmaster's hands. It was a month of recuperation after a summer that had played havoc with his stomach. Emma made him comfortable with a holiday at home. She now had the house in perfect order – 'pretty, brilliantly clean, quiet,' her Aunt Jessie observed on a visit, with Emma 'the dearest little hostess in the world.' The furnishings were plain and dignified. In the 'charming drawing room,' which she made specially her own, were some gifts from Shrewsbury – an arm-chair, an ottoman, a sideboard – and her prized wedding present, the Broadwood grand pianoforte.[18] She liked to sit there in the afternoon while Charles worked, watching Willy and Annie play with the nurses in the garden. One day he came in, carrying the essay. With trepidation, he asked her to read it.

He could never hope to convert her. And the last thing he intended was to rub salt into old wounds. But since Emma would be entrusted with the manuscript if he died, why not ensure that it would not offend her? Her opinion was conventional and safe, the gentlest foretaste of what the world would say one day. She sat with the pile of papers, pointing out unclear passages, leaving tell-tale notes in the margin, showing where she disagreed. 'A great assumption/E.D.' she scribbled against his claim that the human eye 'may *possibly* have been acquired by gradual selection of slight but in each case useful deviations.' He softened the passage still more; but, from then on, the piecemeal evolution of a complex, integrated organ like the eye left him in a cold sweat.[19] On the other hand, he never doubted the viability of his theory, even if Emma withheld her blessing.

By the mid-forties transmutation was moving off the streets, out of the shabby dissecting theatres, and into the drawing-rooms. No longer was it to be the province of socialist revolutionaries and republican physicians. One book was responsible for this sea-change more than any other. In October 1844 the Edinburgh publisher of popular periodicals, Robert Chambers, galvanized the intelligentsia with his anonymous *Vestiges of the Natural History of Creation*.

A golf-playing, overworked, man of the people, Chambers knew of the advanced anatomy and evolution floating around the medical schools and he determined to make this 'alternative scientific vision of progress' more accessible. The book was brilliantly written and marketed; it was also highly impressionistic. Nature's self-development was treated journalistically in a way never tried before. He surveyed the whole of cosmic evolution, from the coalescence of planets, through the chemico-electrical generation of first life, to the fossil series – the 'vestiges' of the title – and the emergence of man. He made this progression not just exciting, but titillating in an earnest, evangelical society. This was reforming science, not ornamental knowledge for an old élite. He deplored the scientists' specialist approach and static nature, which consecrated a paternalist set of values. He wanted to reach 'ordinary readers.'[20] He provided what many clamoured for in an age of progress and aspiration, the reassurance of an upwardly mobile nature.

By contrast the élite remained Darwin's target: the rulers of the learned societies, the shepherds of parish folk. Those 'dogs of clergy,' as Chambers vilified them, were Darwin's warmest friends. He would never dream of alienating vicar-naturalists like Fox, Henslow, and Jenyns with a rabble-rousing production. His would be 'responsible' knowledge. It would respond to the needs of a new scientific aristocracy, the aristocracy of talent. Darwin's would be a 'palace coup.'[21]

Vestiges caused a sensation when it hit the high streets. It was a massive seller and passed into a new edition immediately. Even Hooker thought it good value for a hack-work, despite its egregious blunders. But what a 'funny fellow' the author must be! Darwin was less amused. The prose was perfect, but the 'geology strikes me as bad, & his zoology far worse.' Hooker labelled it a '9 day wonder,' but the nine days dragged on, and it was already heading for a third edition as he spoke. Each edition was patched and polished, cutting out more mistakes, leading one Tory naturalist to fume that his 'deformities no longer appear so disgusting.' Critics thanked God that the author began in 'ignorance and presumption.' Had he begun with the revised versions 'he would have been more dangerous.'[22]

In an unsettled Chartist age, when science had a moral dimension, it *could* be dangerous in the wrong hands. As a result the clergy, benefactors of the old paternalism, met the work head-on. A few responses were cranky; as Hooker laughed to Darwin – 'a funny thing. Some Liverpool Parson, after reading "Vestiges," had written to all Geologists for proofs on the contrary, & rather coolly, printed all the answers.' But that was not the most telling part. All the geologists, bar one, 'referred said parson to their own works!' It showed how widespread anti-transmutatory sentiments were among the wealthy specialists. Anglican dons believed that God actively sustained the natural and social hierarchies from on high. Destroy this overruling Providence, deny this supernatural sanction for the status quo, introduce a levelling evolution, and civilization would collapse. And, more to the point, Church privileges. The Revd Adam Sedgwick, an honest Dalesman used to calling a spade a spade, apocalyptically predicted 'ruin and confusion in such a creed.'[23] Picked up by the querulous working classes, 'it will undermine the whole moral and social fabric,' and will bring 'discord and deadly mischief in its train.'

Those querulous classes disagreed. Sedgwick told the British Association that new species appeared 'not by the transmutation of those before existing – but by the repeated operation of creative power.' What was he, 'God's reporter,' one atheist shouted. How did he *know* this? Where was his evidence? The gutter presses were fizzing with anger. Embittered artisans fighting for a secular state ignored *Vestiges*' providential veneer and saw its science represent 'the transition state at which the religious world will presently arrive,' after which 'men will glide into atheism.'[24]

Even Darwin thought that Sedgwick's over-the-top review of *Vestiges* smacked of the 'dogmatism of the pulpit,' and he knew it was 'far from popular with non-scientific readers.' Radical Quakers and Unitarians demurred too. But they eyed the opulent Anglican Church financed by feudal tithes with disdain, and denounced the corrupt privileges brought by Establishment. They favoured more emancipating forms of knowledge. Many liked *Vestiges*; it might have been badly marred, but it was 'a very beautiful and a very interesting book,' Darwin's physiologist friend William Carpenter said, and he went on to help Chambers patch it up. Some were pleased to see it choke the 'bigoted saints,' others thought the idea of Creation by natural law more ennobling. Unitarians like Carpenter doubted that 'the great-grandfather of our common progenitor [was] a chimpanzee or an orang-utan,' but on the rule of law he was adamant – God with his 'perfect knowledge of the future' had unleashed one law at the Creation and the universe has gone on unfolding ever since.[25]

Radical Quakers and Baptist doctors argued that nature had to be naturalized – spiritually unfrocked. Evolution for many of them was a better way for God to operate. The Almighty had instituted moral and physical laws at the Creation and made them known to everyone through nature and the Bible. No hierarchy of priests was necessary, no Established Church. Like Tom Paine, they lambasted the Church's 'adulterous connection' with the State; 'fornication' with aristocratic government one called it, and they tried to tear her from this 'illicit embrace.' Sedgwick responded in kind, equal to this sexual rhetoric. In *Vestiges*, he growled, evolution and spontaneous generation coupled in an 'unlawful marriage' and spawned a hideous monster; it would be merciful to crush 'the head of the filthy abortion, and put an end to its crawlings.'[26]

Sedgwick's review was his first ever, and it showed. 'Unmitigated contempt, scorn, and ridicule are the weapons to be used,' he seethed, but this sledge-hammer approach partly defeated the object. Darwin read his outburst with 'fear & trembling.' This was Sedgwick the Cambridge Proctor who had once slept at The Mount and taken Darwin on a geological tour of Wales. The whole sordid affair made it impossible to view *Vestiges* dispassionately. Sedgwick's histrionics only harmed his cause. When 'Mr. Vestiges' replied in the temperate *Explanations: A Sequel to the 'Vestiges'* (another bestseller), Darwin thought his 'spirit,' though not his 'facts, ought to shame Sedgwick.' All in all he had mixed feelings. He alternately decried *Vestiges* for muddying the waters and welcomed it for drawing the poison; if it stole his thunder, it also habituated people to nature's development. It did teach him one lesson, which was to avoid detailing specific genealogies – of pigs, or horses, or men: they simply presented a barn-door target.[27]

The author's anonymity increased the *frisson* of excitement. Wild rumours abounded. Sedgwick initially ascribed it to the frail intellect of a woman – privately he pinned it on to wicked Byron's daughter, Ada Lovelace. But fingers were pointing in all directions, and with Darwin's predilections known, at least by a few, some began pointing at him. 'Have you read that strange unphilosophical, but capitally-written book, the Vestiges,' he asked Fox; 'it has made more talk than any work of late, & has been by some attributed to me. – at which I ought to be much flattered & unflattered.' London geologists quickly had Chambers pegged as the author; letters flew thick and fast comparing *Vestiges'* errors with those in his other works. The case was actually clinched for Darwin a couple of years later.[28] He dropped in for an hour's chat with Chambers one day when he was in London – to talk over Glen Roy, which Chambers was working on. Lo and behold, a complimentary copy of the sixth edition of *Vestiges* arrived through the post shortly afterwards, convincing Darwin that Chambers was the man.

A future son-in-law once asked Chambers why he never owned up to his 'greatest work.' Chambers 'pointed to his house, in which he had eleven children, and then slowly added, "I have eleven reasons".' By 1845 Darwin had three reasons of his own, with another on the way. He also had public esteem to forfeit. The *Journal* had made him well known. It had given him an *entrée* into scientific society worldwide, and a reputation among travellers. His success was tangible. Animals and plants were routinely named after him, anything from the giant sloth *Mylodon Darwinii* to the imponderably tiny *Asteromphalus Darwinii*. Global travellers could fish in Galapagos waters for *Cossyphus Darwini* or pick a shelly *Pecten Darwinianus* from Patagonian rocks.[29] Among London's savants, too, he rated high. He was a Vice-President in the Geological Society in 1844, and was targeted by aspiring geologists wanting to get their papers into print. An ill-spoken word and all this could be jeopardized.

Then there was the company he kept, which made his quandary worse. His parish friends were as eager as Sedgwick to keep science on the straight and narrow. Darwin understood this conservative moral attitude – he knew what gave offence. Hence his self-condemning talk of the 'sin of speculation.' It was a sin denounced by many: Hooker censured naturalists for taking speculation as the easy route, and his shaft struck hard.[30] So while Darwin was dying to divulge his secret to Fox and Jenyns, he was reticent. He moved forward tactfully.

The month *Vestiges* came out, he was quizzing Jenyns on mortality rates among song birds, the Malthusian 'checks' that prevented populations from exploding. He had the right person. Jenyns was the compleat parson-naturalist, an antiquarian fact-gatherer. But Darwin was always supportive. Jenyns's 'trifling facts' – whether on bird territories or beak sizes – provided spy holes into Nature's innermost workings. Darwin delighted in snuffling through such trifles, collecting clues, the oddball, the unnoticed, the incongruous – becoming, he laughed, 'a complete millionaire in odd and curious little facts.' Jenyns's tidbits, the sort disdained by deskbound taxonomists, were the stuff of a new science. And this, Darwin intimated, was what he was engaged on – studies that would explain Jenyns's 'trifling points.'

He broached the inflammable subject gently. Jenyns's observations on bird mortality were part of a 'grand body of facts' from which he could draw morally unimpeachable conclusions. Honesty of intent was the key:

> The general conclusion at which I have slowly been driven
> from a directly opposite conviction is that species are mutable
> & that allied species are co-descendants of common stocks. I
> know how much I open myself, to reproach, for such a
> conclusion, but I have at least honestly & deliberately come
> to it.

Jenyns found the Malthusian 'checks' quite explicable. The surviving young were driven out of parental territories into those where the death-rate had been high. He viewed the process as a static system of curbs and balances, not competition and progress. Like any parson supporting the Creative stasis of nature, he damned talk of life's self-development. He saw through all Darwin's cagey talk and accused him of implying that his 'conclusions were inevitable.'[31]

Darwin flinched: 'In my wildest day-dream, I never expect more than to be able to show that there are two sides to the question of the immutability of species, ie whether species are *directly* created, or by intermediate laws, (as with the life & death of individuals.)' Darwin was polarizing the issue: either supernaturalism or natural laws, which he, at least, equated with the mutation of organic forms (although many others didn't). He repeated that the results had been forced on him, and that he was sensitive to stepping on hallowed ground: it must all look 'absurdly presumptuous,' he admitted. 'I am a bold man to lay myself open to being thought a complete fool, & a most deliberate one.'[32] His motives were pure. His image as an objective, neutral 'scientist' – a neologism that still seemed faintly foreign – was in the making. If 'the fabric falls,' it was Nature's doing, not his. If this spiritual unfrocking, this secularizing of nature, seemed uncomfortable, Nature was to blame. Darwin offered Jenyns his newly copied essay, which explained his theory in full. The offer was never accepted.

He did not give up on his clergymen friends, but he could at least keep the dialogue going with the younger career-naturalists. Hooker was eager to help, showering Darwin with books, rooting out obscure ones. Darwin put in his orders:

> When you tell me not to buy Kingdons trans[lation]. of Decand[olle's]: veg[etable]: organ[ography]: do you mean you can *sometime* lend it me. I will order Jussieu: I hope you will not forget the French pamphlet on variation. & I sh^d like to see the iceberg-paper in Boston Journal. I have got Couthouy's paper on Coral-Reefs.

Hooker spilled out information on plant distribution, wanting nothing for himself and resting 'content to be a gatherer of facts for you.' Darwin thought 'a little vanity' would not go amiss; after all, 'say just what you please, I am sure no one could put them to better use than yourself.' But it did not stop him firing questions, in order 'to screw knowledge' out of his compliant friend. Hooker's assistance, he claimed, was more 'than I have received from anyone else, & is beyond valueing [sic] in my eyes.'[33]

He came to rely on this help, constantly inviting Hooker to Down, almost to the point of pestering him. Eventually Hooker did plan to 'run down and look at your habitat.' On his first visit, the weekend of 7 December, Darwin picked his brains on island floras, milking him mercilessly – 'pumping' he called it – and it became a regular feature of their get-togethers. After breakfast he would take Hooker into the study for twenty minutes and bring out a list of questions. Some Hooker answered on the spot, a few required consideration, and others protracted research in Kew Gardens. The answers came on slips of paper, which Darwin deposited in pockets that hung against the study wall near his chair, each one devoted to a special topic.[34] From then on, secure on home ground, he plagued his young assistant with requests to come down, refusing Hooker's return invitations on health grounds.

The obsessive questioning continued in letters. Hooker, himself neutral, had become so inured to talk of evolution that he routinely laughed at the ways *Vestiges*, Lamarck, and others would describe an ugly fact – like the same plants turning up in Tasmania and across the globe in Tierra del Fuego. But it was such anomalies that Darwin had to explain; he refused to sweep them under the carpet. If the élite were to be turned, it would be on *these* grounds, not by sinful speculation or a piece of racy journalism. Anything on distribution and variation was ruthlessly hunted down. He followed up reports, fired off letters, set a thousand hares running, intoning all the time 'every variation must have some cause.'

But what? Was it external, the environment? He was no longer so sure, and beginning to gravitate to some internal cause of the change. He needed more case studies. He sniffed out the unusual, collecting factual knick-knacks until it became a kind of kleptomania. Hooker said he had 'the power of turning to account the waste observations ... of his predecessors,' and he had.[35] Whether it was the Earl of Enniskillen's odd yew tree, Dorking fowl in the farmyard, Galapagos snakes' tails, or variegated plants, every variation was fastidiously followed up.

Other naturalists were taxed, especially those setting off on exploratory voyages. With the distribution of animals and plants the 'keystone of the laws of creation,' he needed precise geographical information. Biogeography was a very British concern, which is why Darwin's was a very British science. It reflected the nation's maritime ambitions, at a time when the Royal Navy was busily mapping the world. Every year a batch of raw assistant surgeons sailed on Her Majesty's surveying ships, doubling as naturalists and filling up journals, becoming 'well salted,' like so many of the Hooker-Darwin circle. The Admiralty's Capt. Beaufort actually told Darwin to list any facts he wanted checking anywhere in the world and he would see to it; sooner or later a brig would be passing by.[36] Indeed, this year – 1845 – young Harry Goodsir, working away on crustaceans, set off with Capt. Franklin in Hooker's old ships *Erebus* and *Terror* to search for a Canadian north-west passage to the Pacific, carrying Darwin's list of requirements in his trunk.

In six short months Hooker had become a mainstay. He worried that Darwin was too attached, that his expectations were too high, his sentiments 'too flattering.' The fall came in February 1845, when Hooker was invited to teach botany at Edinburgh, standing in for old Professor Graham, then 'on his last legs' (he had been there since Darwin's day). It was a blow; Hooker might be furthering his career, but Darwin could only 'most heartily deplore it.' 'There is something so chilling in a separation of so many hundred miles ... You will hardly believe how deeply I regret for *myself* your present prospects – I had looked forward to seeing much of each other during our lives. It is a heavy disappointment.' He worked himself up into such a state that he even talked of visiting his friend that summer in Scotland. Darwin was 'awe-struck' by the idea of lecturing, but then Hooker too thought that his heart might not take the strain. Darwin's fatherly advice was to take care, and go for 'walks, like a good boy.' 'I dread the thought of your breaking down.'[37]

*

The previous autumn a long 'parchment talk' with his father left Darwin convinced that he should invest in land. Sir John Lubbock, Down's chief landowner, agreed that it was a wise buy, providing insurance against a stock-market crash. Properties around the village were 'absurdly dear,' he learned from Sir John, so Charles followed the example of his father and sister Susan; he planned to plough his inheritance into the fertile farmland of Lincolnshire. 'How very grand we shall be,' he wrote Susan in anticipation, 'when we go arm & arm & astonish our tenants.'

Lincolnshire was a county of few squires, lax parsons, and absentee landlords. (The advice from the future Bishop of Oxford, Samuel Wilberforce, to the local squires was to take the yokels' education in hand, lest they learn a 'smattering of science' and forget their God-given duties.) Charles's own agent found him an estate of 324 acres near the village of Beesby, a few miles from the coast. It had outbuildings and a modest farmhouse occupied by an 'industrious good Tenant.' The annual tithes due to the incumbent were about £70, the parochial charges 'very moderate'; the church had just been rebuilt and 'the money borrowed . . . paid off.' Local obligations would thus be minimal, and it promised a better return than government bonds: a 'steady clear Rental of 3¼ Prcent, free from deductions,' on an outlay of £12,500.

In March 1845 Charles snapped it up. Or rather the Doctor did and passed it to Charles, for father took charge in such matters. The farm would have been a sound investment, producing about £400 a year – but for a national calamity. Still, that was months away and unforeseeable; for the moment Charles gloated to Fox, 'I am turned into a Lincolnshire squire!' He was thinking of the future. The family was growing. Emma was pregnant and 'as bad as she always is,' and a 'Boy-Baby' was born on 9 July. George, Darwin christened him, recalling the 'pleasant associations' of Henslow's son George. Maybe, he said wistfully, he will 'turn out to be a Naturalist' like his father.[38]

His father, meanwhile, was working furiously. Darwin interrupted *South America* to revise his *Journal*, after John Murray suggested a cheaper edition for his Colonial Library. The offer was welcome – Darwin had 'never received one penny' from the old publisher, despite selling 1400 copies.[39] Murray knew how to treat an author; he gave Darwin £100 for the copyright, and upped it £50 on request.

All summer Darwin revamped the book, incorporating the latest on the *Beagle* specimens. It was ten years since he had visited the Galapagos, and he was still reconceptualizing the islands. By now he had had ample time to reinterpret the fauna in the light of John

327

Gould's work on the birds and his own theory. 'The archipelago is a little world within itself, or rather a satellite attached to America, whence it has derived a few stray colonists,' he explained. It was a new lava-strewn Eden of 'aboriginal creations.' Here 'we seem to be brought somewhat near to that great fact – that mystery of mysteries – the first appearance of new beings on this earth.'

But finches were still a minor part of his evolutionary proof. Admittedly he now illustrated the various types, showing their range of beaks. 'Seeing this gradation and diversity of structure in one small, intimately related group of birds,' he hinted, 'one might really fancy that from an original paucity of birds in this archipelago, one species had been taken and modified for different ends.' It was a broad clue, and as much as he would ever say on finch evolution. He also now nailed down the evidence for the differing island tortoises. Or rather, he disinterred it from an older book. Capt. Porter, recounting his voyage in the United States ship *Essex* in 1815, had reported saddleback tortoises from Charles and Hood Islands, and 'rounder, blacker' and better-tasting ones from James Island. There were further vindications. Hooker, who had slept on the proofs of the first edition, now found himself botanical adviser for the second. He confirmed that the flowering plants, too, were mostly 'aboriginal productions.' Why, Darwin teased as he rewrote the Galapagos chapter, all these 'new birds, new reptiles, new shells, new insects, new plants'? Why, on these tiny islands so recently emerged from the sea, were so many beings created slightly different from their South American counterparts?[40] It was rhetorical; he already had the answer.

He took the opportunity to repay another debt while revamping. *Coral Reefs* and *Volcanic Islands* had both come 'half out of Lyell's brains.' Swearing everyone to secrecy, Darwin dedicated the new edition of the *Journal* to Lyell, as a sign, he said, of 'how much I geologically owe to you.' But the compliment came with a nasty sting.

Lyell dropped by early in June, accompanied by Mrs Lyell. ('You ought to have a wife,' Darwin advised Hooker, 'to stop you working too much, as Mrs Lyell peremptorily stops Lyell.') Lyell's *Travels in North America* was just coming out, and he was planning a new trip to the United States. Perhaps the mention of America swung the discussion to slavery. Certainly when Darwin glimpsed the *Travels* he was horrified. Unlike Martineau, who supported the 'martyr' abolitionists, Lyell saw them doing no good. Darwin might have owed the world 'geologically' to Lyell, but on this subject he stood back, aghast. After a sleepless night in August, pent-up with rage, he exploded on this 'odious deadly subject.' How could Lyell relate 'atrocious' tales of slave children being taken from their parents and then 'speak of being distressed at the Whites not having prospered'?

Darwin distilled his feelings, pushing a slamming indictment of slavery into the last pages of his *Journal*, just as they were leaving his hands:

> I thank God, I shall never again visit a slave country. To this day, if I hear a distant scream, it recalls with painful vividness my feelings, when passing a house near Pernambuco [Brazil], I heard the most pitiable moans, and could not suspect that some poor slave was being tortured . . . Near Rio de Janeiro I lived opposite to an old lady, who kept screws to crush the fingers of her female slaves. I have stayed in a house where a young household mulatto, daily and hourly, was reviled, beaten, and persecuted enough to break the spirit of the lowest animal. I have seen a little boy, six or seven years old, struck thrice with a horse-whip (before I could interfere) on his naked head, for having handed me a glass of water not quite clean.

His catalogue of 'heart-sickening atrocities' continued – deeds 'done and palliated by men, who profess to love their neighbours as themselves, who believe in God, and pray that his Will be done on earth!' 'It makes one's blood boil,' he stormed. He cursed those who, seeing only the well-fed slaves of the 'upper classes,' call it a 'tolerable evil.'[41] He claimed that these last-minute additions were not in answer to Lyell, just an 'explosion of feeling,' but it sounded hollow.

Murray was delighted with the new edition, and did well with it. He continued courting his new author, softening him up with twelve complimentary copies. One went to Lyell, just leaving in September for America; another to Hooker in Edinburgh. By now Hooker was standing for the botany chair – Graham having died – and finding canvassing 'detestable work.' Darwin wrote him a reference, half-grudgingly, wondering who would now show him 'a daisy from a Dandelion.'[42] He was quite relieved when Hooker did not land the job.

Hooker's letters continued full of recommended reading. Hewett Watson was the author he particularly pushed – Edinburgh-trained, a phrenologist, and Graham's gold medallist in 1831. Hooker rated him 'at the very head of English botanists,' with an unrivalled knowledge of plant distribution. In 1845 Watson was still publishing the results of his trip to the Azores three years earlier. More controversially, he was in the midst of a series of articles on 'Progressive Development,' prompted by *Vestiges*. Hooker said Watson had a 'philosophical' cast of mind, meaning he was that rare breed, a plant geographer with a statistical bent. The 'demography' of species was his forte; he treated plants like a Public Records officer carrying out a census, trying to understand plant population trends. As a radical, he sympathized with the great Victorian demographic surveys. More than a radical, he was an atheist, touchy, and a transmutationist to boot – in short, a 'renegade,' said Hooker, intriguing Darwin no end.

What did that make Darwin then? 'You will be ten times hereafter more horrified at me,' he replied; his own renegade 'views of descent' were just as heretical. Hooker was unimpressed; the more he looked at island floras, the less he accepted mutation. It might be an 'active agent,' but only in 'perturbating' species, causing them to wobble slightly. But then he still had no inkling of Darwin's 'sublimely grand' mechanism for magnifying the wobble, natural selection. Only two months later would Darwin finally offer him his 'rough sketch (well copied) on this subject' for comments. Even then he thought it 'too impudent a request.'[43] Perhaps it was.

Over and over Darwin invited Hooker to Down. Eventually in December, a year after his first visit, he came for a weekend with an up-and-coming bunch of naturalists. An all-round group they were: Hooker covered botany, Waterhouse zoology; Edward Forbes astonished all with his biogeography, and the agreeable Hugh Falconer – currently working on Indian fossils in the British Museum – spoke for palaeontology. Darwin revelled in this kind of occasion, on home ground, where he was able to 'pump' the young bloods. 'I shall have the four most rising naturalists in England around my table,' he chortled.[44]

It was the first time for Forbes. Breezy and likeable, he was six years Darwin's junior and another Edinburgh product (he had even lodged in Darwin's old digs, with Mrs Mackay).[45] He had sailed with an expedition in Mediterranean waters, where he dredged for deep-sea creatures, and now, back in London after his father's bankruptcy, he was attached to the Geological Survey. He could be breathtakingly speculative, and Darwin wanted to hear of his lost continent – a sunken supercontinent supposedly stretching from Ireland to Portugal and out into the Atlantic past the Azores.

Forbes had conjured it up to explain the distribution of related plants, and even the fickle Hooker, to Darwin's chagrin, seemed to be leaning Forbes's way. Actually he was swinging to and fro, 'as unstable as water,' but currently arguing that Darwin's means of plant dispersal – sea-transport, wind, and so on – 'has been ridden to death.' Hooker accepted that each species migrates from one 'centre of creation,' rather than being created in many centres. But how did animals and plants, seeds and eggs, spread and ultimately colonize islands? Did dry land – continental extensions – once stretch out to embrace them, as Forbes suggested? If so, where has this land gone? The notion of a lost Atlantis staggered Darwin. It was an appallingly 'bold step ... to sink into the depths of *ocean, within the period of existing species*, so large a tract of surface.' He was flabbergasted. Island-making, oceanic subsidence, and marooned species were the stuff of Darwin's evolutionary theory all right, but he envisaged a much slower process. Sinking supercontinents in one species' lifetime was rash to the point of reckless, when dispersal by sea currents and birds would do. Forbes 'will injure his reputation' with this wild speculation.[46] Getting him to Down, Darwin could confront the issue head-on.

The weekend went off brilliantly, with 'raging discussions' on all the hot topics. Falconer and Darwin presumably tried to scupper the supercontinent, with the good-natured Forbes giving as good as he got. Species were probably skirted; all the guests were anti-transmutationists, Forbes not least. He refused to see the fossil succession prove the '*real or bodily change*' of one animal into another.[47] Fish and reptiles and apes could not transmute themselves; they had no power of self-development. He was an extreme idealist: species were divine ideas incarnate, and only in God's mind did any real change occur.

Like many materially minded Unitarians Darwin hated this other-worldly Platonism, where species change only in the Creator's mind, where genera are 'God-born thoughts that become manifest in living shapes.' It stopped all attempts at finding a physical mechanism. Nor could he extract anything more positive from the others. Hooker held 'aloof from all speculation on the origin of species.' He plumped for 'the old assumption that each species has one origin [and] is immutable,' and stuck with it. Darwin bridled a bit at this unyielding fudge and wondered 'whether we shall ever be public combatants.'[48] The lack of allies was beginning to frustrate him.

Not that he was unappreciative of Hooker's help. Far from it. He said over and over that he had extracted more from him 'than from any other person.' As a result in the new year, 1846, he even contemplated the 'bold step' of staying at Kew with his friend – bold because he '*literally*' had 'not slept out of *near* relations house or inn for five years!!' (What he confided to Fox was even stronger: that he had not slept out of a safe house since he married.) It was a sign of his growing dependence, even if he did not eventually go.

He kept up the pressure on his friend. He rejoiced on hearing of Hooker's appointment in February as botanist to the Geological Survey, where he was to join Forbes and that 'loose set of dogs' gathered loyally round the Director Henry de la Beche. It meant he would be based in Charing Cross, two hours from Down. So when, Darwin asked, would he be down to look at the Kent Chalk? – a horse and a bed were waiting. And with the British Association meeting coming up, he wanted to know 'why cannot you come here afterwards & work.'[49] These lures, and refusals to make a return journey, showed that he was less a recluse, more a man who needed to control the situation; he needed to be at home with his problems, or in familiar surroundings.

Darwin was still Henslow's student in parish matters, learning how to look after his villagers by example. He saw Henslow 'doing wonders' for his Suffolk labourers, organizing horticultural shows, lectures to the farmers, fireworks on the rectory lawn, as well as setting up a savings club, a benefit society, a library, and a school. 'How you are astonishing all the clod-hoppers,' Charles enthused. And to think that none of this had 'aroused the envy of all the good surrounding sleeping parsons.'[50]

Most clergymen lacked Henslow's enterprise and tact. Young 'Mr. Willott' – the Darwins always avoided 'Reverend' – had Charles's confidence, and he subscribed £5 towards redecorating the parish church. But the feeble man had trouble handling village disputes. One day Willott came out to Down House seeking advice, only to be silenced by his companion, the Rector of Hayes. The Rector gossiped 'grand nonsense' about the schoolmaster being religiously 'unsound,' then looking around in an awesome voice declared, 'and we all know what that will come to.' Immorality, of course; but Charles demurred at his conclusion that 'unsound religion was worse than none at all.'[51]

The Revd Willott died suddenly in March, leaving his two innovations, a Sunday School and a Coal and Clothing Club, to another callow curate, the Revd John Innes, who came from neighbouring Farnborough. Innes, a product of High Church Oxford in its heyday, was Hooker's age; Darwin had actually met him years previously, soon after moving to Down. Now, thanks to his own 'dear patron' Henslow, Darwin could help Innes educate the clodhoppers and insure them against the need for winter coal and clothing.[52]

As an improving Lincolnshire landlord, there was a thing or two he might try himself. Beesby farm, like Down, gave new scope for proving his social worth. In the previous September, when Darwin went to see his father, he had looked over his estate and authorized contractors to demolish the old buildings and put up a new farm house. This cost the Doctor another £1000, but modernizing was necessary, his agent insisted, to keep 'a Tenant of respectability.' When he heard how Henslow was trying to assist his parishioners by letting them small allotments, Darwin did the same. Self-sufficiency had to be encouraged, as much in Lincolnshire as Tierra del Fuego, where he had helped to plant gardens for the savages. (And it would reduce the rates that he paid to maintain the local poor.) While Beesby was being rebuilt, he instructed his agent to arrange a cottage garden for every labourer on his land. And he started supporting Beesby school, contributing £10 a year to its upkeep from his rent.[53]

By now, though, something more than allotments was needed. In 1845 the country's potato crop had failed, killed by a virulent fungus disease. It was the first of many failures and, with the poor subsisting largely on bread and potatoes, famine and devastation followed. Ireland was worst hit; here 700,000 were to die and one million emigrate over the next five years in the greatest natural disaster of the nineteenth century. Shielded at first, Darwin, like Henslow – an expert on crop diseases – saw the blight as a 'painfully interesting subject.'[54] An intriguing problem, or so it appeared to a squire-naturalist who could do without potatoes for a while. But the parish poor were starving.

Famine and death crept closer to Down House. Charles's own workmen, with only a few weeks' supply of potatoes laid in, and those diseased, were alarmed. Matters were made worse by the price of flour, forced up by the corn import duty. His handyman was having to spend over a shilling more a week from his twelve shillings wages on it. 'This would be nearly as bad,' Darwin calculated, as if 'we had to pay an additional 50 or 100£ for our bread: how soon in that case, would those infamous corn-laws be swept away.' His squire's fortune sustained him. Having tightened his belt, he was managing to live on £1000 a year, and the saving made the family feel 'as rich as Jews.' But he remained worried as the rural economy collapsed, and he tried to play his part. He agreed with Henslow 'about gentlefolk not buying potatoes,' and Emma probably told the cook to stop. She even started giving away penny bread tickets at the door, which could be exchanged with the village baker. Charles put his naturalist's mind on the problem, suggesting that his potato seeds from Chile might be used to replenish affected stocks – but he found that these too were infected.[55]

The disaster confirmed his free-trade principles. Protectionism had to be abolished, whatever Disraeli and diehard farmers thought. The duties on imported corn which kept bread prices high were iniquitous. As a free-trading Malthusian he also hated primogeniture, that is, inheritance by the eldest male; this had to be destroyed 'to lessen the difference in land wealth & make more small freeholders.' It would create more competition and sift out the clever, ingenious, 'fittest' sons. The stamp duty also had to go. It was so 'atrociously unjust,' rendering it difficult 'for the poor man to buy his ¼ of an acre, it makes one's blood burn with indignation.'[56] Darwin remained a competitive free-trader, in science and out.

No fortune could shield him from the human cost of the tragedy. During the unseasonably stormy June, while Emma took Willy and Annie to her aunts' in Tenby, more alterations were carried out to the house. At last there would be a schoolroom and two more bedrooms upstairs. And a new back door would help keep traffic out of the kitchen; after all, it seemed 'selfish making the house so luxurious for ourselves and not comfortable for our servants.' Charles, taking opium pills, feeling sick, watched the domestic dramas unfold as walls came down and workmen fell out. John Lewis, the Down builder and foreman, eventually became fed up with the bickering and fired the lot. With the famine biting and no pay, one labourer broke down in the half-renovated rooms. Charles, gripped by the trauma, gave a blow-by-blow account to Emma: his 'wife had come from a distance with a Baby & is taken very ill – The poor man was crying with misery.' It was too much for an emotional household and the Darwins 'persuaded Lewis to take him back again.'[57]

That month Parliament finally acted. The famine had intensified calls for the repeal of the Corn Laws. After the disaster in Ireland, the Tory Prime Minister Sir Robert Peel was converted to free trade and the corn duty was slashed. Ironically it hit Darwin in the pocket, for as corn prices fell, so did farm incomes and therefore the rent his Beesby tenant could afford to pay. He agreed a fifteen-per-cent rent reduction, grumbling to his agent that it seemed 'unusually large.' How much had the 'great landowners' in the district – Lord Yarborough, Robert Christopher, MP – cut their rents? he wanted to know. Suddenly he realized that he was comparing himself with Tory protectionists, and he backpedalled at once: 'Although I am on principle a free-trader, of course I am not willing to make a larger reduction than necessary to retain a good tenant.' He reconciled himself to the drop. While hardline Tories and hard-up farmers wanted a return to the old protectionism, he 'saw no cause whatever to despair.' He rallied his tenant, telling him to 'hope for better times.'[58]

He was vomiting again; the old sickness was as virulent as ever. His stomach had not really been right for a single night since his move to Down and left him fit for only a few hours' work a day. Friends thought him a hypochondriac, because he routinely trotted it out as an excuse. He dreaded going anywhere, especially 'horrid' London, that 'old Babylon,' whose choking smogs rose straight from the 'subterranean kingdom of his Infernal Majesty.' Trips left him 'knocked up' and good for nothing. He had avoided the British Association at Cambridge the previous year because he 'expected more mortification than pleasure.' When he went to visit his father he kept quietly out of the way if the house was full.

But he was no malingerer. The sickness was real and distressing, although no one knew what caused it. He experimented with all manner of remedies. His father put him on a non-sugar diet, and he tried bitter 'Indian Ale.' He sacrificed snuff for a month, only to be told by an unsympathetic Hooker to 'knock it off altogether.' He even resorted to quackery. He laughed at the dupes taken in by mesmerism, and at Harriet Martineau for mesmerizing young girls, muttering about the 'diseased tendency to deception in disordered females.' Yet he was galvanizing his own insides using plate batteries for an hour a day, which he knew was an equal 'piece of quackery.' These crazes sweeping the country – mesmerism, galvanization – were the 'Devil's laws,' in Carlyle's view, as disreputable as any that made men the sons of monkeys.[59] They all oozed from the same quagmire on the lunatic fringe. Darwin tried them, but he had little faith in alternative medicine and doubted that he would ever be cured.

Self-absorbed, some thought self-centred, Charles demanded constant attention. In the midst of everything else that spring – neighbours starving, builders hammering – Emma's elderly mother gently slipped away. The Wedgwood household would be broken up, Maer sold. Elizabeth would move to a new place of her own. Forty years of family life, their golden age, was at an end. But Emma never went back to her childhood home, staying to pamper and protect Charles. When she did finally get away with the children in June, going to see her favourite Aunt Jessie (a 'most unusual' thing for her to do), Charles felt bereft. He longed to have her back, urged her to cut her visit short, complained day after day of feeling sick. Then one afternoon, sitting alone in the summer-house watching the thunderstorms, he half-came to his senses and counted his blessings. 'I am an ungracious old dog to howl, for I have been . . . thinking what a fortunate man I am, so well off in worldly circumstances, with such dear little children & . . . more than all with such a wife.' A selfless wife; as her sister Elizabeth said, she had never heard a complaint pass Emma's lips. More and more Charles felt that 'I can . . . say so & shall say so on my death-bed, – bless you my dear wife.'[60]

Down was more than ever a sanctuary. Its rurality was invaluable. Hooker wondered why he plumped for such 'an impracticable part of the country,' but Darwin purposely chose it. Down provided his retreat, and it was continually made more secure. He rented a one-and-a-half-acre strip of land at the back from Lubbock early in 1846, which he fenced and replanted with bushes and trees to shelter the house. In this plot he marked out his quarter-mile thinking path, the 'Sandwalk,' on which he would plod henceforth on his midday constitutional. He was still a creature of habit. Life was now totally 'Clockwork,' a tick-tock routine of breakfast – work – mail – work – walk – lunch – letters – nap – work – rest – tea – books – bed. He liked life humdrum, and the pace of Down provided it. He told everyone that 'I am fixed in the spot where I shall end it.' Emma too liked the solitude, and bore the dull life with her 'poor old sickly complaining husband' with great forbearance.[61]

He pushed on with *South America* all year. The Treasury grant had by now run out, so the book had to be subsidized by Darwin and his publishers. Both forked out, even if it did not promise much of a return. By August two-thirds had passed through the press and he expected to 'be a comparatively free man' again soon.[62] In September, finally, he penned the Preface, then ventured out with Emma to the British Association at Southampton.

As usual he found the sessions dreary. Not surprisingly so in this case; the proceedings were dominated by Owen's numbingly technical paper comparing the homologous bones in fish, reptiles, and mammals. Owen was the anatomical 'master mind' who awed Hooker, and even Darwin confessed himself an 'ignoramus' on the technicalities. There was the odd interesting item. Later Owen described some new fossil mammals, including llama-sized toxodons, shipped to the College of Surgeons by Capt. Sulivan (formerly of the *Beagle*) at Darwin's suggestion. Darwin was just one of the milling delegates, an élite geologist and gentleman, but hardly perceived in Owen's category. He never cared much for conferences, but it was a chance to meet friends and glimpse the up-and-coming men. He thought Jenyns looked thin, and cursed missing that 'renegade' Hewett Watson, who had been there in person to face down Forbes with accusations of plagiarism. Best of all were the convivial tours that went with the occasion. He took a Sunday jaunt to Winchester Cathedral with a party that included the Dean of Armagh and 'never enjoyed a day more in my life.'[63]

The next month Sulivan and his family came to stay – 'a real good rattling fellow,' whooped Darwin, trying to tempt Hooker into joining their 'reunion of naturalists.' They nattered about old times, meaning the Falklands, fossils, and FitzRoy. Sulivan had done sterling work in South America, returning home with six crates of fossils from Patagonia. Coincidentally, a letter from FitzRoy arrived while he was at Down. FitzRoy, too, was home, dismissed as the Governor of New Zealand. Sulivan put FitzRoy's fall down to his 'old *Aristocratic*' hauteur. It was the 'Beagle all over again, *temper violent* saying *any thing* to any body, doing most hasty and extraordinary things.' Once he was 'so violent as even to cause a *deputation* to take up their hats and walk out of his room in the middle of his *attack* on them, leaving him storming.' He was 'in fact, being the Captⁿ. of a ship over again.'[64]

Darwin got FitzRoy's address from the Admiralty and dropped him a line. But he realized that it was the end of an era even as he wrote. The *Beagle* work was all but finished. Nothing had been wasted; not even the dust from the decks, or the soil stuck to roots – it had been posted to Christian Ehrenberg in Berlin, on the look-out for micro-organisms. Darwin was finishing his last book of the journey, on the pampas and land elevation, and it would be, he warned FitzRoy, 'geological & dull.' Nor was he sanguine about sales. Look at *Volcanic Islands*, he moaned to Lyell, 'it cost me *18 months!!!*,' yet few had bought it. It left him feeling that geologists did not actually read each other's books and that the only reason to write one was to show 'proof of earnestness.' Darwin had convincingly proved his. He was now a fully accredited geologist, no longer the tyro scrambling alongside the Captain. There were other changes, too, he told FitzRoy: 'I am a different man in strength and energy to what I was in old days, when I was your "Fly-catcher", on board the Beagle.'

On 1 October he returned the final proofs of *South America*. That was almost it. The binders did have one last *'stupid* trick' to play –

they bound the only coloured plate of geological sections back to front, and it had to be cut and repasted in the entire stock.[65] But then that was an author's lot.

22

Illformed Little Monsters

O F THE *BEAGLE* SPECIMENS, only a single barnacle species was left to describe. 'You cannot think how delighted I feel at having finished,' he told Henslow on 5 October 1846. But the time it had taken – ten years. Henslow's prediction had not been so far off the mark: 'Your words, which I thought preposterous, are come true, that it w^d take twice the number of years to describe, that it took to collect & observe.'

The barnacle beckoned. He anticipated a short descriptive paper. It would not take long; the house was tranquil now, the refurbishment complete, his study freshly painted. And he had only one species to describe, after all, even if it was bizarre: 'some months,' he optimistically reckoned, 'a year' at most. Then, finally, he would begin sifting his 'accumulation of notes on species.' Writing them up 'will take me five years, & then when published, I daresay I shall stand infinitely low in the opinion of all sound naturalists – so this is the prospect for the future.'[1]

The barnacle was that 'illformed little monster' he had collected from the shores of southern Chile in 1835. Hooker heard that it was 'quite new & curious' and was intrigued. Aberrant was the word: it was the world's smallest barnacle and lived as a parasite, boring inside the conch-shell of the mollusc *Concholepas*. Darwin could not imagine how to classify the unique creature. Even christening it foxed him, loathing Latin as he did: 'how to invent a name completely puzzles me,' he said, dragooning Hooker. It seemed to be articulated when they looked under the microscope, so they opted for *Arthrobalanus* ('Jointed Balanus' – *Balanus* being a common conical-shelled barnacle on sea shores), although Darwin was not entirely happy with it.

He began dissecting 'M^r. Arthrobalanus' and Hooker helped, despite the crush of his Kew work (he was still describing the Galapagos plants). Darwin's microscope left something to be desired, so Hooker also contacted a good optician, and a new 3s. 6d. lens worked wonders. Darwin perfected his technique: he cut down the strain of dissecting for long periods by putting woodblocks under his wrists. It was not only technical advice that Hooker fed his friend; jars of his homemade relish also arrived at Down. 'The porcupine quills better than the glass tube; the Chutney Sauce capital,' Darwin replied after one parcel. Hooker's willingness to drop everything and assist had Darwin crowing with delight: 'You really are the most goodnatured man I ever knew.' They grew still closer. It had been only three years since Hooker's return, but Darwin felt as if they had been friends for 'fifty years.'[2]

Progress reports went out to interested parties. He told FitzRoy that he had spent two weeks 'dissecting a little animal about the size of a pin's head' from Chile '& I could spend another month on it, & daily see some more beautiful structure!' After so many years devoted to grand geological projects – coral reefs, parallel roads, volcanoes, and icebergs – he relished the idea of using his 'eyes & fingers' again in filigree anatomical work.

Arthrobalanus was odd, but only a comparison with normal species could show to what extent. So Darwin began borrowing other barnacles. He sent Owen his notes and asked for the loan of comparable specimens from the College of Surgeons. Not only other species; he began looking at other growth stages, especially the barnacles' larvae. What started as a trickle of specimens soon became a torrent. Conchologists – who specialized in every conceivable type of seashell, from exotic conches to boring barnacles – offered to lend him entire collections. Many explorers traded commercially in shells. These were big business in mid-century. The bizarre and unusual fetched high prices at auction as the gentry and collectors outbid one another to augment their showy cabinets. Shells even attracted *hoi polloi* now that the new trains could whisk them to the seaside.[3] As a result sellers were eager to see their specimens classified expertly, to increase their value. Darwin was sucked in deeper; the whole enterprise snowballed uncontrollably.

He began to contemplate other barnacle groups. Not that this worried him, for a comprehensive study would boost his reputation. An up-to-date reference work on barnacles was cried out for; Louis Agassiz, the new professor of natural history at Harvard in 1847, told the British Association that it was 'a pressing desideratum.' As things stood, the whole subject was in a 'state of chaos.' Until recently barnacles had been totally misunderstood; indeed, they had just been transferred lock, stock, and barrel from one division of the animal kingdom to another. Originally barnacles – being shell-covered – had been thought molluscs, relatives of mussels and snails. But in 1830 an army surgeon, John Thompson, had penetrated their 'disguise' by studying, not the immobile adults, but their free-swimming larvae.[4] They turned out to be crustaceans – relatives of crayfish and crabs. It was an astonishing revelation. No one had imagined that the barnacle cemented to its seaside rock was cousin to the crabs that scuttled beside it, or that those feathery filaments wafting through the water were modified feet. A barnacle was like a shrimp lying on its back waving its legs in the water. Moving the barnacles in with the crabs and shrimps necessitated a complete reappraisal of their anatomy. The field was wide open.

There was another reason, closer to home, why he was happy to embark on a larger study. Hooker, grumbling about the French botanist Frédéric Gérard's book *On Species*, told Darwin that no one had the right to 'examine the question of species who has not minutely described many.' This stung. Darwin took it personally, as an attack on his right to speak on the origin of species. What did it matter, he answered, if he had not described his 'due share of species.' It did 'not alter one iota my long self-acknowledged presumption in accumulating facts & speculating on the subject of variation.' The work had at least given him 'the greatest amusement' for 'nine years.' It was a sad refrain; Darwin had not expected this sort of criticism. Actually Hooker was not thinking of Darwin at all, and he was embarrassed when he realized the misunderstanding. And yet, privately, he *did* believe that Darwin was 'too prone to theoretical considerations about species.' If anything could dampen his speculative ardour, Hooker reasoned, it would be an exhaustive study of one group.

It made Darwin more determined than ever. If only museum curators who handle hundreds of specimens and produce ponderous monographs could speak on the great questions, he would earn that right. Barnacles would establish his credentials. And like Gérard, he would be on the look-out for variations.[5] A thorough examination of all the barnacle varieties could put him in a commanding position when discussing natural selection.

So barnacles were not totally irrelevant to his evolutionary work. In fact, as he proceeded, he began to uncover the most extraordinary proofs of his notebook speculations.

He pushed deeper into the subject, only to be limited by his equipment. His simple lens just could not resolve the detail in his pin's-head dissections. He took advice from Carpenter, an adept microscopist, and ordered a good compound microscope. Even then, he found it wearisome work, and tiring on the wrists and eyes. 'I have been nearly 3 months,' he complained to Hooker, '& have done only 3 genera!!!'[6] Four months later he had finished only two more. It really was taking an age, and he wondered whether it was worth it.

By late 1847 the conchologists were pushing him hard. The most flamboyant, Hugh Cuming, agreed that he should study the entire barnacle group. Cuming was laid up quietly, partly paralysed after a heart attack; but from 1827 until the early 1840s he had been a sort of conchological privateer. Immensely wealthy, he had built himself a schooner, the *Discoverer*, fitted out to hold the world's natural treasures. He had roamed the seven seas plundering islands of their pearls, exotic birds, tropical plants, and prized shells. Sometimes he took the last of their kind – at least one species went extinct after he passed through. From Polynesia, South America, and the Philippines he had shipped back tens of thousands of shells. He traded in this booty, and one can imagine 'what a bull market in conchology set in when Cuming's molluscs reached the auction room.'[7] He was an acute financial operator. His mercenary tactics looked to many like plain '*meanness*,' leaving Hooker, at least, with a low opinion of the man. Darwin had always found him fair. He had known Cuming since 1845, and had examined his Galapagos seashells (so complete a series, of course, that Cuming had advised him to ignore all previous books on the subject). Forced to rest up now, Cuming put his 'whole magnificent collection' – a treasure trove of barnacles – at Darwin's disposal and urged him on.

More scholarly systematists, particularly J. E. Gray at the British Museum, also thought a monograph was needed, and Gray pledged his public collection. Darwin was convinced. He made a formal – and highly irregular – request to the Trustees of the British Museum. Specialists were expected to work inside the museum, but he asked that the barnacles be sent to his home. He was not prepared to travel to Bloomsbury; he wanted them at Down, and in stages, for it took at least two days to soak, clean, dissect and describe each one. As a sweetener he promised the Trustees his own prepared specimens after finishing, and they accepted.

He called in specimens from far and wide. Even Sir James Ross – Hooker's old Captain – setting off to search for the missing Franklin expedition, was cajoled into gathering Arctic barnacles on his melancholy voyage. (The *Erebus* and *Terror* had been caught in the Canadian pack ice and were lost with all hands.) With the empire expanding – the quest for the Northwest Passage was a reminder of how much Britain needed this route to the Pacific – the flow of new animal species to the imperial capital was unabated; the natural world lay at John Bull's feet. Darwin, well connected through the Zoological and Geological Societies and with time to spare, was perfectly placed to carry out the definitive study: to name and describe every species of one sub-class.

Even this had its imperial ramifications. Naming is possessing, said the old insect specialist William Kirby. Science was a sort of metaphoric appropriation: when an animal 'is named and described, it becomes . . . a possession for ever, and the value of every individual specimen of it, even in a mercantile view, is enhanced.' Hence the glory seeking, as describers rushed into print. Here Darwin drew the line. Where was the scientific 'disinterest'? he asked Hugh Strickland, looking into new procedures for naming animals. Darwin thought it pure vanity that a naturalist should suffix his name to every species he describes, as though he owned it personally. The practice led to too many hasty 'baptisms' in the race for priority.[8] Darwin's own study would be conducted at a more dignified pace.

To be definitive a monograph would have to embrace fossil barnacles as well. Darwin had originally turned down a collection from the Bristol Institution. Now he wrote accepting it, and he notified the Geological Society of his needs. It was dogged, grinding work. The modern species had to be dissected, the fossils disarticulated or sectioned. He was inundated with so many species that the labour became exhausting and the smell of spirits nauseating. 'I hope to Heaven I am right in spending so much time over one subject,' he exclaimed to Hooker.[9]

From that day in 1844 when Darwin bared his soul, Hooker had come to play an increasingly important role. He was Charles's confessor, his confidant, a sounding board on the 'criminal' subject of species, an endless source of geographical lore. Their friendship blossomed. Darwin revelled in Hooker's weekend visits, and even more his longer working stays.

By now Hooker was spending 'a week at a stretch' at Down. He brought his work, which he set out on the dining-room table, and Emma made him feel at home. Walking through the room to her store cupboard, 'she would take a pear or some good thing, and lay it by my side with a charming smile as she passed out. Then in the evening she always played [the piano] with me and sometimes asked me to whistle to her accompaniment of some simple airs!'[10] Clearly, he was becoming one of the family.

Hooker spent the third week of January 1847 at Down. Here he polished off papers and polished up fossils, finishing his account of the coal plants and their living relatives for the Geological Survey. The subject gave the two men plenty to argue over as they paced briskly through the grounds. But the deterioration in Darwin's health was evident. Even pumping Hooker took its toll: the half-hour sessions forced Darwin to take 'a complete rest, for they always exhausted him, often producing a buzzing noise in the head, and sometimes what he called "stars in the eyes," the latter too often the prelude of an attack of violent eczema in the head, during which he was hardly recognisable.'[11]

On this occasion Hooker – finally – came away with a copy of the evolution essay. Goodness knows Darwin had dropped enough hints over fourteen months. Now the moment had arrived. Hooker's would be the first expert opinion. Darwin was apprehensive; he would finally be able to talk it over with his friend, tease out his views. If, that is, he could get to town: he made date after date, only to cancel, sick, debilitated, and infuriated. Eventually Hooker scribbled a page of telegraphic notes and posted it to Down.

And what did he make of this 231-page manuscript? London's freethinkers all accepted that some natural law or other explained the appearance of new species of fossil animals in the rock strata. But what this law was, few could say. Some, like the 'renegade' Watson or reprobate Robert Grant (Darwin's old tutor), were radical transmutationists. Others professed ignorance and simply spoke of 'Creation' out of convention. Or in Hooker's case, default: he had long agreed that it was a 'fair & profitable subject,' but that, having 'no formed opinion' of his own, he opted 'for immutability, till I see cause to take a fixed post.' Darwin was now giving him cause, and wondering which mast he would nail his colours to. Hooker would not say. But he did argue that Darwin's tirade against the continual Creation of life was 'uncalled for:'

> All allusions to superintending providence unnecessary – The Creator [who is] able to make first [organisms is] able also to go on directing & [it is a] matter of moonshine to [the] argument whether he does or no.

All he wanted to know was the mechanism of 'Creation.' He rather mistook Darwin's intent. If Darwin really wanted to show Creative foresight, he should point out the reason for 'retaining [those] *useless* organs' which in later species might be turned into something useful.[12] *This* would illustrate God's intentions. This would demonstrate nature's design aspect. It would also scupper Darwin's strategy entirely.

At last Darwin was getting feedback. Calm feedback, with no sign of Sedgwick's histrionics, or the savagery meted out to the hapless *Vestiges*. But Darwin was not dealing with an unreconstructed Anglican cleric. Hooker lived up to his expectations by providing the 'highly suggestive,' geographically precise criticisms he needed. And more: Hooker annotated the copy before giving it back – 'very good,' he thought the arguments against multiple centres of creation for the same species. 'Goodish,' he scribbled alongside the summary on artificial selection bending species into 'infinitely numerous races.' But the way domestic races were derived from one or more wild species was 'not clear' at all.[13]

Darwin had groomed young Hooker for just this: a series of detailed discussions on nature's way of making species. Hooker might have been unimpressed by the overarching argument – much later, with a modicum of hindsight, he admitted that he 'failed to grasp its full significance' – but this did not stop him feeding Darwin a stream of geographical tidbits.[14]

Hooker's next move was totally unexpected. The very day he took away the essay he dropped a bombshell: he was planning another voyage. After his 'Antarctic herborizations' in 1839-43, he had always wanted to see the Tropics. But no one had expected him to be off so soon, and even he thought he might crack 'like a glass tumbler' on bouncing from the polar ice to the palm beaches. He had only been home for four years; it hardly seemed possible. Darwin had come to know him so well, he had grown so close, so reliant. Suddenly all talk of the essay was overshadowed. It left Darwin confused, casting a pall over their relationship. He was deflated and groaned on being told the news. Without Hooker's help he would be 'lost.' He kept trying to come up to town, to tax Hooker over the essay, fearing that he would 'forget all about' it, anxious lest he leave England suddenly. But he was now retching non-stop. For weeks through March and April he was almost continuously ill, tormented by 'boils & swellings,' and signing off his apologetic notes 'Ever yours rather wretchedly C. Darwin.'[15]

Their first tiff, in May, only aggravated the situation. Considering the ideological issues at stake – murders, confessions, creations – it is ironic that the flare-up was ignited by coal. For months they had disagreed over the origin of coal, which Hooker was analysing for the Survey. (With Britain the 'workshop of the world,' mining over half the world's output of coal to fuel its growing industries, the publicly funded Survey paid particular attention to mapping the coalfields.) Darwin imagined the ancient coal-plants growing in warm shallow seas like mangroves. He twitted Hooker that coal was a sort of 'submarine peat,' betting him '5 to 1 that in 20 years this will be generally admitted'; 'sneer away,' he said, misjudging the mood, goading him with his mangrove theory. Hooker's temper snapped. Darwin was 'mad' for thinking the ferns of the coal seams marine; these were terrestrial, unequivocally so. He could speculate on species as wildly as he wanted, but on fossil plants Hooker was the expert. The 'savage onslaught' left Darwin reeling. Hooker's short fuse had shown itself. He was quick to snap, soon to make up. Not that Darwin didn't deserve it. A few days later he tried his long-shot on Falconer, the expert on Indian fossils, who thought 'such infernal nonsense ought to be thrashed out' of him. But it gave Darwin an inkling of Hooker's darker side. There was no 'man more lovable,' and none more 'peppery,' he later said, even if 'the clouds pass away almost immediately.'[16]

Another pet theory was taking a pounding at the time – his ancient sea beaches running along the Glen Roy valley. Louis Agassiz had already convinced almost everybody that a glacier had dammed the valley, forming a meltwater lake. Now the Scottish geologist David Milne added new evidence. He had gone to Glen Roy convinced that Darwin was right, and come away a sceptic: these were ancient lake margins. But Darwin clung to his seashores, holding tight because of his *idée fixe* with bobbing landmasses. Dry sea beaches on the mountain sides testified to a risen land. Lose this evidence of rising and subsiding continents and his whole geological edifice was at risk – including his island-making mechanism. Continents must sink to make isolated islands, cutting off species which start to adapt differentially. 'M^r. Milne will think me as obstinate as a Pig, when I say, that I think' his Glen Roy theory 'more utterly impossible than words can express.' Privately he was sensitive to the criticism. He wobbled precariously over Agassiz's glacial lake. Anxiously, he fired off a succession of letters supporting his side. 'I have been bad enough for these last few days,' he grumbled to Hooker, 'having had to think & write too much about Glen Roy (an audacious son of dog (Mr Milne,) having attacked my theory) which made me horribly sick.'[17]

His condition worsened. Every trip was 'stomacho volente,' and invariably deferred. But illness had its consolations. It provided psychological security, allowing him to cry off visits, escape jury service, turn down dinners. And dining clubs; in April he refused a nomination for the Royal Society's élite Philosophical Club. Not that society do's were unappealing. He was half-tempted by Lord Northampton's soirées, where the literati danced and élite geologists plumed themselves. Here Roderick Murchison would strut, discussing the military precision of his Silurian campaigns, and the haughty Owen would boast of moas and megatheriums; here William Broderip, who had sorted the *Beagle* shells, would show the ladies his sponge the size of Cardinal Wolsey's hat.[18] At these fashionable galas, rich patrons could meet their young protégés. Hooker even offered to escort Darwin, as one would an invalid. But no, he was too 'stomachy.' The undiagnosed sickness and swellings were his release. And yet, however useful an excuse, they were no less real, no less debilitating, and he dosed himself with bismuth or opium. He retreated further into the family fold, revelling in Emma's care, refusing to believe that his own protégé was really leaving.

Hooker had finished his *Flora Antarctica*, and the coal plants for the Geological Survey. He was making his mark; even Darwin had heard the Survey's head, De la Beche, heap praise on Hooker's 'coal-doings.'[19] He was also publishing voluminously and elected a Fellow of the Royal Society that April as a consequence. He turned thirty in June and should have been settling down. The more so because of his attachment to Henslow's eldest daughter, Frances, which became obvious to all during the British Association meeting at Oxford the following month.

Darwin planned to attend Oxford, with his evolution essay, determined to probe Hooker more deeply on his reaction to it, even though Emma – about to give birth again – would be left at home alone. It was the supreme sacrifice, not so much on Emma's count, but because he had not slept in a stranger's house for five years. He was breaking his own most solemn rule. He felt awful, but here he was, asking to lodge with Hooker's relations. He still stipulated rooms which would guarantee peace and privacy. Only a 'secure solitary retreat' would do, he said, aware that he was making a 'ridiculous fuss' about his 'precious self.' Following some juggling, he boarded with Hooker's uncle, the Vice-Principal of Magdalen Hall, but again, only after reassurances that 'I can have my meals to myself & a room to be by myself in.'[20] And that is what he did: dined in and refused evening invitations, even from Capt. Ross, who had already proved himself by turning over his Antarctic barnacles.

Darwin attended the geological section, only to be made painfully aware of how anathema evolutionary speculation was to the gentlemen present. For the moment, though, they had easier prey in their sights. Robert Chambers was down from Edinburgh to give a talk on ancient beaches. This was Darwin's subject, so he must have sat in and have seen Chambers mugged by his friends. According to an observer, Chambers

> pushed his conclusions to a most unwarrantable length, and got roughly handled on account of it by Buckland, De la Beche, Sedgwick, Murchison, and Lyell. The last told me afterwards that he did so purposely that C[hambers]. might see that reasonings in the style of the author of the *Vestiges* would not be tolerated among scientific men.[21]

And not only scientific men. On Sunday Samuel Wilberforce, the new Bishop of Oxford, delivered a cautionary sermon in St Mary's Church on the wrong way of doing science. It was a brilliantly aimed blow at the 'half-learned,' at those seduced by the 'foul temptation' of specula-tion. In other words, at Chambers, with his drawing-room notion of development. The scholars loved it. The church 'was crowded to suffocation' with geologists, astronomers, and zoologists, all feeling that Wilberforce had hit his mark. Science was the province of quiet, cloistered, respectable thinkers. The demagogues, Wilberforce said, looked for a self-sustaining universe, one they could praise in a 'mocking spirit of unbelief.' Such deluded souls do not understand the 'modes of the Creator's acting,' nor the grave responsibilities of a gentleman. This warning about humility before the facts was another slap in the face. Chambers, fuming in his pew, denounced it as an attempt to stifle progressive opinion. He must have gone home, the geologist Andrew Ramsay guessed, 'with the feeling of a martyr.'[22]

Darwin missed this; Sunday was probably the 'Heavenly day' he spent with Henslow's party looking over the great house and grounds of Dropmore. But for the rest of the week, there he was at Oxford, essay in hand, chasing up Hooker for his opinions, watching his colleagues come crashing down on Chambers. There was an irony to the situation. But no surprise: the Association was a coalition of clergy and gentlemen, whose geological science provided the bedrock for the established order. It wasn't that they were slating an outsider. Lyell himself could invite the Archbishop of Canterbury to Geological Society dinners. They objected to sloppy science with evil consequences coming from a magazine publisher. The sloppiness also allowed Darwin to abuse *Vestiges* in Lyell's presence, in order to dis-tance himself from it. He deplored the author's 'poverty of intellect,' and dismissed the book as a 'literary curiosity.'[23]

Still, for all that, here he was, surreptitiously touting an essay that would bruise many a gentleman's virtuous view of nature. Darwin achieved his aim in coming. He met up with Hooker and dragged him off to hear the organ at New College Chapel, where the celestial music sent a tingle 'up and down' his spine.[24] He led Hooker point by point through key parts of the essay. He heard at first hand Hooker's objection to the natural colonization of islands: to the wind-and-waves dispersal of seeds and plants. Hooker responded with his identical mountain plants in Tasmania and Tierra del Fuego, at opposite ends of the globe. How could migration account for this astonishing distribution? How indeed; Darwin determined to work on it, but for the moment he feared that Hooker's objection would reinforce Forbes's sunken supercontinent nonsense.

More than one knot was being tied at this meeting. Hooker broke the news that he was to become a Henslow-in-law: he and Frances were engaged. This bound him ever tighter to Charles, who saw a trusted scientific circle closing round himself. Everyone noticed how happy Hooker was in these weeks. But not even Frances could cure his wanderlust. Charles did not know 'whether to be glad or sorry,' balancing the betrothal against Hooker's determination to travel – glad 'for your sake,' or sorry 'for mine.'[25]

Hooker was unsettled because the government had not given him a post at Kew, under his father, and he was loath to canvass aristocratic patronage. (Kew was still a promenading park for noblemen and their ladies.) Sir William wanted him to kick his heels, perhaps write up his diary of the Ross expedition – indeed, John Murray even offered to publish it as a companion to Darwin's *Journal*. But Hooker said no. He was itching to travel again. Any voyage would do, he told Capt. Ross in desperation. He applied for an Admiralty expedition to Borneo, and an East India Company trip to Goa. But each time money proved the obstacle. 'I wish I had a private fortune,' he wailed, knowing how Darwin's had put him at the Captain's table. By now he was 'ready to make any sacrifice to get to the tropics.'[26] Before he knew it he was on a team planning to trek through the Sikkim valley and Tibet, the exotic land of 'Lama worship' and soaring peaks that he had dreamed of as a boy. Just as precipitously he obtained a Treasury grant to collect Himalayan plants for Kew. It was all so sudden; he was rushed off his feet. The needs of Down were now forgotten.

What his fiancée thought we do not know. Darwin was dejected, even despite Emma's safe delivery of Elizabeth in July. He had repeatedly tried to get to Kew through the summer and autumn, treating his own twenty-mile trek with grim determination – 'I *must* go over the remainder of my species sketch' – but each occasion found him face down on a sofa, with 'fiercely reinflamed' boils or debilitating sickness. In the event, he saw Hooker only once more, on 20 August, when he was finally strong enough to make the carriage drive to Kew. Darwin wished him well. The terms were touching, but there was no disguising his remorse: 'It will be a noble voyage & journey but I wish it was over, I shall miss you selfishly & all ways to a dreadful extent.' His only consolation was that Frances, that 'beautiful magnet,' would bring him back.[27]

With that, Charles went off to Shrewsbury, where his father's condition was giving cause for concern. Here for days he lay writhing on a sofa, 'groaning & grumbling,' plagued by bursting boils, immersed in Bulwer-Lytton's epic of tragedy and disaster, *The Last Days of Pompeii*. Hooker tried to get to Down in early November. The attempt was seen by Charles 'as the greatest proof of friendship I ever received from mortal man' – hyperbole which reflected his emotional state.[28] A few days later Hooker was aboard ship, HMS *Sidon*, sharing a suite with Lord Dalhousie, on his way to India as the new Governor-General. Darwin never did clasp him in a fond farewell.

23

Al Diabolo

CHARLES WAS ON his own now. Yet he was not lonely – the patter of little feet up and down the corridor outside the study made sure of that. Seven-year-old Annie often popped in, her face aglow. She would give him a naughty pinch of snuff from the jar that had been moved upstairs to break his habit. He loved her the more for it. And Emma was expecting again, her seventh. With an influenza epidemic gripping London, Charles – ever careful of disease – had another reason to avoid town, and went up for little more than the obligatory meetings of the Geological Society. Anyway, with Emma and babies and barnacles, as well as the genial new incumbent of the parish, the Revd John Innes, who was fast becoming a friend, he had all the company he wanted at Down. But he missed Hooker. Their months apart were dragging and it would be years before they met again – if indeed Hooker survived his perilous Himalayan expedition. Charles would have to bottle up his feelings about the origin of species until then.

Not that he could get back to species with the barnacles snowballing out of control. He had expected to be finished now and back to natural selection. Instead, he was bracing himself for another two years of smelly dissections. Each one took longer than planned, leaving him little time for anything else. But some calls had a royal ring about them and could not be refused. In February 1848, he was contacted by the leader of British Science, Sir John Herschel. Writing at the behest of the First Sea Lord, he invited Darwin to join an élite team drawing up instructions on scientific field work for sailors. When Sir John crooked a finger, scientists jumped. Just let him finish a dissection, Darwin replied; it would take a week or so, then he would oblige. As he put it to Richard Owen, 'When men like

351

Herschel & yourself give up your time to the task, I could not of course refuse.'[1]

In the Admiralty manual, Darwin explained that any gentleman could geologize abroad. It required slight preparation and little apparatus, in fact only the sort of curiosity and systematic habits that the officers of a man-of-war were expected to possess. Aboard ship they were ideally placed to observe those slow 'still active causes' that had shaped the geological past: sedimentary deposition, erosion of cliffs, icebergs, coral reefs – just the things Darwin himself was interested in. They should collect dust that settled on the deck, and, ashore, concentrate on fossils, volcanoes, and coal samples. The writing cost him five weeks, to his dismay, but it was worth it to train future Sea Lords to be good Lyellians – indeed good Darwinians.

At home the tensions were mounting, along with the barnacles. He fretted about the family, and his perennially wretched stomach. The condition of his 81-year-old father was grave; Charles was horrified to see how much he had 'changed bodily during the last six months.' And Emma's condition was always uncertain. These were matters of life and death, and the thought of them made a grim counterpoint to the fetid corpses he was dismembering. Outwardly, all seemed well on the weekend of 12 February, when the Lyells and Owen, along with those young Turks of the Geological Survey, Edward Forbes and Andrew Ramsay, stayed at Down to celebrate Darwin's thirty-ninth birthday. Ramsay had never enjoyed himself more. Darwin struck him as an 'enviable man,' with 'a pleasant place, a nice wife, a nice family, station neither too high nor too low, a good moderate fortune, and the command of his own time.'[2] Little did he realize his host's inner turmoil. But then Darwin gave little away, merely begging off a post-prandial promenade around the Lubbock estate on Sunday.

Darwin's was a privileged life, as Ramsay recognized, and it stood on a precipice in the dark days of 1848. That weekend the insurrection sweeping Italy was threatening to explode nearer home. France – in Alexis de Tocqueville's phrase – was 'sleeping on a volcano.' Sure enough, the barricades went up in Paris on the 22nd; protesters were shot, the troops mutinied, and an interim ministry was installed under the moderate reformer Adolphe Thiers. The French King abdicated on the 24th and headed for exile in England. In London the rumours flew. At the Tory leader Sir Robert Peel's party on Saturday the 26th, Darwin's colleagues – Lyell, Owen, Buckland, and De la Beche – were given a graphic account of the Paris uprising by the

Prussian ambassador, a member of whose staff had escaped through the revolutionaries' lines. They heard of the '30,000 communists in Paris who are for property in common and no m...riage, and who are much to be feared by those who have aught to lose.'[3] After the ladies retired, there was hectic talk of the revolution, and how, with a few sensible reforms, the throne could have been saved. Peel told Lyell he feared a financial crisis in Britain as the measures of the new Republican government – to be proclaimed the next day – frightened capitalists on both sides of the Channel.

Peel's guests were the gentlemen and clergy who rubbed shoulders with Darwin at his clubs, the Geological and the Athenaeum. Some had shared his hospitality at Down the fortnight before. All were concerned to see stabilizing reforms put into place and to police the radical masses, now demanding total suffrage at home. Darwin's friends were fearful. Lyell had long deplored 'mob-rule.' Forbes, the son of a banker, was himself shortly to take up his baton against rioters. And Owen's Honourable Artillery Company had seen service during the working-class demonstrations.[4]

After the initial bloodletting in Paris, when the populace took the city, Emma's aunt sighed with some relief that the revolution had become 'more a social than a political one.' She still wondered whether the new leaders would be 'able to realise their promises to the working classes,' and dreaded the 'vengeance of the monster they have unchained' if they could not. But while French workers had gained concessions, British unions were frustrated over the government's intransigence. There was nothing like the French 'Right to Work,' and unemployment remained high during the 40s. Worse, no promise was held out of an extended franchise. The British monster began seeking its own vengeance. The 'Marseillaise' was sung and the Parisians praised in radical London. The uprising across the Channel gave a new impetus to the Chartist leaders, spurring them to plan a huge demonstration.

Panic spread among the wealthy. With 150,000 Chartists expected to converge on Kennington Common on 10 April, there was feverish activity in the capital. No one knew what would happen as they tried to take their petition demanding suffrage to Parliament. The Queen left the Palace for her own safety, and plans were drawn up to 'quell the insurrection by force.' Eighty-five thousand special constables were sworn in over some weeks – mostly gentlemen and their employees and servants – and 7000 troops were mobilized. The Bank, Downing Street, the Foreign Office, and all public buildings were sandbagged, and their officials sworn in as specials. Those at the

General Post Office were issued with hand grenades; some at the British Museum had muskets.[5] Everything was done to ensure that demonstrators did not occupy any buildings, as they had in Paris.

The jitters were as pronounced among Darwin's colleagues, who mounted guard in the scientific institutions. At Charing Cross, Ramsay, sworn in as a special, patrolled with Forbes at the Geological Survey, shouldering his truncheon in defence of his trilobites. The Director, De la Beche, brought in an armful of cutlasses and prepared for a siege. Owen took his watch at the College of Surgeons; big and burly, he was ready for the rioters, and afterwards he set off for Peel's house to make sure the Tory leader was safe. The Revd Buckland, Dean of Westminster, waited at the Abbey, armed with a crowbar. Darwin might have thought him an amusing 'fool' for flapping like a pterodactyl during his geological lectures, but the tomfoolery stopped now, and Buckland threatened to bludgeon any rioters who broke in through Poet's Corner. His protégé, William Broderip (Darwin's shell identifier), sentenced Chartists in the Thames Police Court, where he was a magistrate.[6]

The air of frantic preparation left everybody panicky, Darwin not least. His reading took on a new aspect. In March, as fears of the Chartist demonstration turned to hysteria, he read Thiers's *History of the French Revolution*, only to throw it down as 'dull & poor.' Later he tackled Mary Wollstonecraft's inflammatory *Vindication of the Rights of Women* and the libertarian William Godwin's *Memoirs* of Wollstonecraft, although he was far happier with De Tocqueville's *Democracy in America*. During this unsettled period his nausea increased, which prevented him from attending the March Council meeting of the Geological Society.[7] London was now up in arms, anyway. The agitators' demands – for land taxes, property taxes, wealth taxes – would have hit him hard. Here he was, a member of the despised gentry, a leisured gentleman, living, as the extremists would say, off the backbroken poor. His father was ill, he had a growing family to fend for, and, if events took a nasty turn, his investments could be wiped out.

He was a closet evolutionist besides. This was the heart of the matter. His Anglican friends were quelling the rioters, some of whom were armed with transmutation and godless sciences. Owen and Forbes were holding the line and protecting his privileges. But wouldn't they condemn him as a fifth-columnist if they uncovered his secret? When he had cried 'the fabric falls!' ten years before, he did not have this sort of insurrection in mind. Anyhow, he had been a tyro then, speculating privately. Now he was a squire, a family man, a member of the geological élite. For all his theory's middle-class Malthusian core, and its capitalistic roots, he could still be branded a traitor by the Tory diehards.

Ensconced at Down, with the world around him threatening to tear itself apart, Darwin kept up the tedious dissections. 'It's dogged as does it,' he would mutter to himself. In late March, as his Creationist colleagues made plans to resist the radicals, he made a crucial breakthrough. Many of his specimens appeared to be infested with tiny parasites. He had always picked these off and thrown them away, but now he looked closer. Barnacles are usually hermaphrodite (each animal has both male and female sexual organs), but among Cuming's Philippine species was an exception. It was undescribed and Darwin christened it *Ibla cumingii*. Not only did it have separate sexes, but the males and females were so different as to appear almost unrelated.

Henslow was the first to hear the news:

> the female has the ordinary appearance, whereas the male has
> no one part of its body like the female & is microscopically
> minute; but here comes the odd fact, the male or sometimes
> two males, at the instant they cease being locomotive larvae
> become parasitic within the sack of the female, & thus fixed
> & half embedded in the flesh of their wives they pass their
> whole lives & can never move again.

Here was a reproductive set-up almost unparalleled in the animal kingdom. And how had Darwin uncovered it? He told Henslow that he felt an 'instinct for truth,' akin to 'the instinct of virtue;' and this had helped him.[8]

It seemed like a veiled challenge. What virtue could an Anglican Creationist be expected to find in parasitic polyandry among barnacles? If true, there was little in it to praise God for. Nature could hardly have moved further from 'Time's Noblest Offspring,' Man. A dominant female, tolerating a clutch of dependent, degenerate males clinging to her skirt-tails! 'Is it not strange,' Darwin prodded his old friend, 'that nature should have made this one genus unisexual, & yet have fixed the mates on the outside of the females.' Later he taunted Lyell with similar evidence: an *Ibla* female with a pocket in each valve of her shell in which 'she kept a little husband.' These half-inch-long females were apparently 'parasitized' by their own tiny mates. The males were a tenth of the size and remained almost embryo-like. In their 'flattened, purplish, worm-like' bodies most of the thoracic segments were vestigial and, in fact, useless. 'Truly,' he jibed, 'the schemes and wonders of nature are illimitable.'[9]

All this revived Darwin's flagging interest; he announced he had found the most interesting barnacle 'in the world.' And the surprises continued. In a second species of *Ibla* – this time a hermaphrodite – he also detected parasitic males, 'supplemental' males he called these hermaphrodite-companions. They were tiny larva-like sacs, sixteen hundredths of an inch long. This was even more unexpected: a *hermaphrodite*, in which the male organs were dwindling, accompanied by a tiny, embryonic mate, rudimentary in all but its sex organs. Suddenly he became suspicious of all those parasites he had thrown away. He looked closer. Some, it turned out, were true, unrelated parasites. But those on a similar genus, *Scalpellum*, were yet more minuscule males.

He went on to identify six species of *Scalpellum*, all showing different degrees of sexual differentiation. This came as a splendid vindication of his earlier evolutionary hypotheses. In an 1838 notebook he had speculated on the way the 'sexes separate in some of the lowest tribes:' from ancestral hermaphrodites had evolved the molluscs, in which the males and females retained 'abortive traces' of one another's sexual organs.[10] But he needed a fuller series to illustrate this divergence of the sexes. Now he had it. Barnacles suggested the sequence of events: from hermaphrodites proper, to those with reduced male organs and minute 'supplemental' males, to females that had obliterated their male organs entirely and acquired 'simple' male companions.

Curiouser and curiouser, he wrote in reply to Hooker's welcome first letter from India. He told Hooker of his *Ibla* males in order 'to boast of my species theory, for the nearest & closely allied genus to . . . these parasites, I can now show, are supplemental males,' living on hermaphrodites, whose own male organs are tiny.

> I never sh[d]. have made this out, had not my species theory convinced me, that an hermaphrodite species must pass into a bisexual species by insensibly small stages, & here we have it, for the male organs in the hermaphrodite are beginning to fail, & independent males ready formed. But I can hardly explain what I mean, & you will perhaps wish my Barnacles & Species theory al Diabolo together. But I don't care what you say, my species theory is all gospel.[11]

Hooker did not rise to this outburst. Nor did he wish him to the devil; in fact he thought the evidence staggering. Darwin was convincing them both of the value of his taxonomic work. They could now see what needed to be done: sex and ancestry took top place on the hidden agenda being drawn up as work proceeded. A new 'gospel' was in the making.

Darwin remained enthralled. His minute males were 'truly wonderful.' They were 'rudimentary to a degree, which I believe can hardly be equalled in the whole animal kingdom.' Breathlessly he told Hooker the latest: 'they have no mouth or stomach' and the larva 'fixes itself on the hermaphrodite, [and] develops itself into a great testis!' They grew up as 'mere bags of spermatozoa.' Nor was there necessarily a one-to-one relationship; he found up to ten supplemental males embedded in some hermaphrodites. These tiny mouthless hangers-on never ate, but died off quickly to be replaced by others. So there was a swift turnover in mates. Hooker, taking it all in his stride, replied from Darjeeling that ten mates were commonplace. 'The supplemental males of Barnacles are really wonderful,' he conceded, 'though the supplemental males in the Bhothea families' – the 'uncouth' Himalayan tribe which provided his coolies and where 'a wife may have 10 husbands by Law' – 'have rather distracted my attention of late.'[12] He had caught the Darwinian drift. Primitives of all sorts lacked the virtues innate to gentlemen of the highest Victorian class.

While Darwin marvelled at his barnacle bonanza, the Chartist demonstration on 10 April passed off peacefully. In May, as he told Hooker about the barnacles, fully expecting to be sent 'al Diabolo' for his efforts, he suddenly cut away to the hoary subject of coal. Coal, that old bugbear, the one thing they disagreed on most. Hooker had been seeking evidence for its origin in India, hoping to solve the problem once and for all. Good, replied Darwin: 'I shall never rest easy in Down church-yard' if it is not solved 'before I die.' This sounded glib, but mortality was now a sombre undercurrent in his thought. 'Talking of death,' he went on, 'my confounded stomach ... has been rather worse.' His sickness increased alarmingly as he watched his father sink.

The corpulent Doctor was now breathing with difficulty and suffered a sort of 'dyeing sensation.' Charles travelled to Shrewsbury with a heavy heart a week later, fearing the worst. Emma stayed at home, pregnant, but she received daily health reports on both Charles and his father. The Doctor's prognosis of his own condition was good and bad: he would live a little longer, he said, but then die suddenly. Charles was only slightly sick during his first few days at

The Mount. He took comfort in Emma's letters, egging her on to write 'all I like to hear.' She posted him newspapers, although he only relished the 'damnable' *Globe*, with its vitriolic reports on the new Frankfurt Parliament and the French National Assembly. But his health slowly deteriorated and within a few days he could not forget his 'stomach for 5 minutes.' The mollycoddling continued, with a simpering Charles caressed from a distance.[13]

The Doctor began to have trouble talking and his legs became weak; his health, Charles realized, was finally failing. Two weeks passed in this way, two weeks of anxiety. As he kept vigil, he too began cracking under the strain. He came over faint and had shivering and vomiting fits, after which he was listless and drained. 'My attack was very sudden,' he wrote home; 'it came on with fiery spokes & dark clouds before my eyes; then sharpish shivery and rather bad . . . sickness.' Feeling vulnerable, he longed to be home. The 'sounds of the town & blackguards talking & want of privacy' left him crying for his rural retreat. 'I did yearn for you,' he wailed to Emma, and continued plaintively: 'Without you, when I feel sick I feel most desolate.' Away from her – even in his birthplace – he lacked security, he missed the caring hands. Oh to be the centre of attention again: 'Oh Mammy I do long to be with you & under your protection for then I feel safe.'

He stayed to celebrate the Doctor's eighty-second birthday, on 30 May. Then, with some relief, he returned to Emma's care. Life at Down ticked on, although his heart was not in the barnacle work. Nor can it have been pleasant, gutting tiny corpses while constantly retching himself. With Emma now seven months pregnant, he began to worry about his own scientific gestation. 'Never will a mountain in labour have brought forth such a mouse as my book . . . It is ridiculous the time each species takes me.' Emma's time grew closer. Charles, extraordinarily sensitive to the slightest pain, planned to have the new anaesthetic, chloroform, administered during the delivery. Ever since his sickening surgical experience as a teenager, he had hated the sight of suffering. Chloroform was a godsend, and he never ceased extolling it. No sooner had the Edinburgh professor James Simpson knocked himself out by inhaling it in 1847 – in the very hospital that Charles had fled from in such terror twenty-one years earlier – than Charles was trying it out for himself. He doctored the Revd Innes, telling him to put a drop of it on his gums for toothache, and he took advice from a London physician on its use in childbirth.[14] His third son, Francis, was born on 16 August, presumably painlessly.

The summer passed, with Darwin hardly seeing a soul. His condition worsened almost daily. As his work slowed to a spluttering, vomiting snail's pace, he saw his friends getting on famously: Lyell was knighted by Queen Victoria at her new Scottish castle, Balmoral, in September. Hooker was making great gains in the Himalayas, discovering new roses, magnolias, and rhododendrons. He was engaged, and Forbes now married. So 'no more of the old *bachelor* parties,' Darwin joked.[15] He remained at Down, a captive to his stomach, attending only the Geological Society Council meetings as required, although they wearied him. More and more, he cried off dinner invitations. Trapped in his self-imposed exile at Down, he lived vicariously through books, trawling them for facts, escaping to exotic locations. With death hounding him, he turned to religious literature again.

Charles and Emma read together almost every day. Novels, travels, histories, biographies – the turnover was immense. Many came by post from the London Library; some were borrowed from Erasmus. As Charles toppled headlong into depression, fearing for his father, Emma must have swayed his reading. For her *The Evidences of the Genuineness of the Gospels*, two fat volumes of cold erudition by Andrews Norton, the late Harvard professor of sacred history, provided hope. Norton, dubbed the 'Unitarian Pope' by Thomas Carlyle, insisted that the Gospels were genuine, untouched, and 'ascribed to their true authors.'[16] If Emma wanted to give Charles reasons for believing in Jesus's promise of eternal life, these were they.

But with the onset of 'swimming head, depression, trembling, [and] many bad attacks of sickness,' he plunged back into heterodoxy. He became absorbed in the life of John Sterling, a young clergyman who had succumbed to chronic illness. Perhaps he saw a reflection of himself: Cambridge, a curacy in rural Sussex, illness, doubt and disillusion. Sterling had moved in the same Carlyle circle in London, and, as with Darwin, this period saw his 'greatest moral and intellectual energy.' By 1840 Sterling was as hopeful as Darwin would ever be of resting his 'faith in the possibility of deep and systematic knowledge on the laws and first principles of our existence.' Darwin's deeper fears too were reflected in Sterling's life. Sterling saw his wife die in childbirth, and died himself prematurely in September 1844, assuring his friends that 'we shall meet again ... Christianity is a great comfort and blessing to me, although I am quite unable to believe all its original documents.'

Darwin, desperately ill himself, was absorbed in this account of a fallen curate, critical only of Sterling's continued emotional attachment to Christianity. 'I simply feel, that I *cannot* believe,' he confessed to his clergyman-cousin Fox, 'in the same spirit . . . that ladies do believe on all & every subject.'[17] Maybe he could no longer believe at all.

He was following the religious journeys of others, dreading his father's death. He read Coleridge too this summer. Emma's father had been taken with Coleridge. He was another Cambridge drop-out who had flirted briefly with religious and political radicalism until the Wedgwoods became his literary patrons. He then made his way back to Anglican conservatism of a sort, and documented his journey in *The Friend* and *Aids to Reflection*, which Darwin read. Christianity for Coleridge was not a theory to be proved but 'a life and a living process.' It required a leap of faith that Darwin could not make. For Coleridge religious feeling was innate to the soul and had nothing to do with inherited instinct, but Darwin's heretical notebooks belied this. Coleridge was wrong.

And what of unbelievers? Darwin thought of his dying father, himself even. Coleridge ascribed their lack of feeling for Christianity to an 'enslaved will.' Leave these '*enfans de Diable*,' he said, to suffer divine retribution. Will 'any of you,' he asked doubters, 'be cured of that common disease, the fear of death?'[18] He answered with a paraphrase of the Gospel of John, Emma's favourite.

Darwin was unmoved, even as he watched his father subside. There was no cure in Coleridge's books. He had learned his Christianity too well from the likes of Paley and Norton – Christianity based on evidence – to think that its doctrines could survive based on vague emotion. He had long abandoned Coleridge's distinction between soul and body, reason and instinct. For all his protestations, Coleridge ended up sounding like an evangelical. Hellfire still put the steam in his religious appeal. The Doctor – Erasmus too, perhaps Charles himself – stood to be eternally burnt. This was a monstrous doctrine.

Death was close for the Doctor. Charles travelled to Shrewsbury on 10 October. He stayed a fortnight, ill himself. As he turned to leave, he saw his father 'serene & cheerful,' a memory he would cherish ever after. On Monday, 13 November, while Emma was away visiting relatives, Charles heard from Catherine that the Doctor was sinking fast. After a number of bad nights, he seemed to be past pain – the suffering had stopped, and his face, she said, was not 'so distressed,' even though he could barely speak and gasped for breath. He was now resigned to death. To see him, enormous and immobile, sitting in the greenhouse was 'one of the most beautiful and pathetic sights that can be imagined.' The next day the inevitable note arrived. The Doctor had died at 8.30 in the morning, propped up in his chair, with Susan 'close to him the whole time.'[19] After so much suffering, it was a peaceful end.

Five-year-old Henrietta – Etty – too young to comprehend death, was 'awe-struck' by the effect the news had on her father and cried 'bitterly out of sympathy.' Charles was devastated and Emma rushed home. Her 'sympathy & affection' was beyond all value. He was now so miserable that he could not even attend the funeral on Saturday. He did set off for Shrewsbury, worrying that he had exhausted Emma with his emotions. But he arrived after it had started, and stayed at The Mount with his sister Marianne who was so distraught that she too could not attend. It was 'only a ceremony,' he admitted, yet he grieved at missing it. Nor was he well enough to act as an executor a few weeks later.[20] For the rest of the year and well into the next, he hid from the world at Down.

He felt unable to see anybody, except perhaps Sir John Lubbock's teenage son John. The boy's fascination for his microscope helped rescue Charles from total despair. He escaped with the lad into an unimaginable microscopic world, teeming with life. He became John's scientific father, in a way, obtaining for him an identical instrument.[21] He was carrying on the Doctor's practice – giving the wise guidance that his father had given him.

Nine months of nagging fears and obsessive work had taken their toll, leaving Charles chronically depressed. Waves of dizziness and despondency swept over him. Through the winter he suffered dreadful vomiting fits every week. His hands started trembling and he was 'not able to do anything one day out of three.' There were disquieting new symptoms: involuntary twitching, fainting feelings, and black spots before his eyes. For the first time he became convinced that he himself was 'rapidly going the way of all flesh.' When his melancholy maiden sisters, Susan and Catherine, came to stay, he avoided them and never talked about their mutual loss. He could not bear to tell them of his numbing fear: that he was the next to go.

Emma alone was left to comfort him. Ever since her sister Fanny's tragic death at the age of twenty-six, she had found deep consolation in the Scriptures. She now drew from her inner source of strength, binding Charles to herself with cords of love, ministering to his daily needs and praying for him. They failed to see eye-to-eye on the question of eternal life – the Gospel of John still stood between them. In fact, Charles was entertaining many more religious doubts than

Emma knew about. But she could bear Christian witness in this stressful time and help him rest.

Three miserable months after the Doctor's death, in February 1849, a maudlin Darwin immersed himself in Harriet Martineau's new book. He and Eras had grown impatient with her scientific credulity. It was her 'Mania' over mesmerism that prompted Darwin to decry the way ladies believe everything. Now Martineau redeemed herself. Her *Eastern Life, Present and Past* contained an unholy guide to the Holy Land. Unholy enough for John Murray to throw it out, objecting to its 'infidel tendency.'[22] So far had Martineau departed from the manner in which, conventionally, ladies believed.

The travelogue was a thinly disguised critical history of religion, and more to Darwin's taste. The dominant note is death; the text is littered with tombs. The 'black pall of oblivion' followed her from Egypt across the Sinai desert to Palestine. There, at Easter, she visited the grave of Lazarus, the Dead Sea, the tombs of the prophets on Mount Olivet, the Potter's Field necropolis where Judas Iscariot hanged himself, and the Valley of Gihon 'where the worm died not, and the fire was not quenched.' All are set against the paschal 'puppet-show' in the Church of the Holy Sepulchre. Darwin was intrigued by Martineau's message, that Christian beliefs about reward and punishment were based on heathen superstitions. And how little the world had moved on. Martineau marvelled at the untouched tomb of a rich Egyptian, painted with scenes of his family, his deeds, his expected hereafter. 'How like ours were his life and death!' 'Compare him with a retired naval officer made country gentleman in our day, and in how much less do they differ than agree!'[23]

But some country gentlemen had moved on. Darwin had done with superstition, and he enjoyed Martineau's excursus. Even so thoughts of death still filled him with foreboding, and his fortieth birthday, a week away, augured no lessening of the gloom. Having shunned society for so long, he could barely answer letters or do anything that required effort. 'Incessant vomiting,' he told Owen, explained why the barnacles were taking so long. 'I have,' he added, 'lost for the last 4 or 5 months at least 4/5 of my time.' Clearly, enough was enough.[24] Something had to be done.

24

My Water Doctor

FRIENDS WORRIED about him. His old *Beagle* companion Capt. Sulivan, on three-year's leave and about to sail with his family to the Falklands, had dropped in to say goodbye and found Charles in a dreadful state: frail and hardly able to walk. He recommended that the 'Philosopher' try Dr James Gully's Water Cure Establishment, which had worked for others.

Charles toyed with the idea. Fox had heard good reports about Gully's fashionable hydropathic home in the beautiful Malvern hills. It had been open seven years, and was already the top watering hole for the gout-ridden rich. During the summer months the charming, erudite Gully would take in a hundred or more dyspeptic patients. Literary figures and loungers alike paid their two guineas a week for the tonic: Tennyson had tried it; Carlyle, Macaulay and Dickens would follow. Charles could see that Gully was making a fortune, which did not exactly instil faith. He was also sceptical about the treatment itself and inclined to dismiss it as so much quackery. Nor would his London consultant, Dr Henry Holland, vouch for it. In fact, Holland was baffled by Darwin's case. He had never seen one like it and diagnosed it as a sort of 'suppressed gout.'[1] Unlike his father's gout, Charles's acted internally, on the stomach. It was, Holland thought, caused by poisons in the blood activating a hereditary disposition. But there was still nothing he could do for it.

If his condition baffled the specialists, then, as his father had said before he died, nothing was to be lost. Charles read Gully's book *The Water Cure in Chronic Disease* to learn about it for himself. Cold water over the body was used to stimulate the circulation and draw the blood supply away from the inflamed nerves of the stomach. But Gully warned that dyspepsia took time to cure and recommended a two-month stay, with no miracles guaranteed. Emma thought that he sounded like a sensible man. With some trepidation, Charles decided to take the plunge. Only experiencing it would prove whether 'there is any truth in Gully & the water cure,' he concluded, as experimental as ever. 'It will cause a sad delay in my Barnacle work, but if once half-well I c^d do more in 6 months than I now do in two years.'[2] Little did he realize just how long a delay it would be.

The whole household would have to move, and Emma quailed at the prospect of transplanting six children, 'bag and baggage,' all the way to Malvern. 'It is a great trouble . . . but we think he could not give Dr Gully's treatment a fair trial under 6 weeks or 2 months & that would be too long to leave the children even with their Aunts.' Everyone decamped to foggy Worcestershire on 8 March 1849, the older children in the care of their new governess, Miss Thorley, and the servants, Charles and Emma separately with baby Francis. The 150-mile journey took two days and Francis screamed all the way. Great Malvern lay in an undeveloped no man's land, fought over by railway companies competing to extend their lines into south Wales. From London they took the Cheltenham and Great Western line to Gloucester, where a special coach set off over turnpikes on a nerve-rattling three-hour trip to the spa. By the time they arrived, the whole family was in need of recuperation. The village had several thousand inhabitants, but its white stone buildings, clustered on the steep slope beneath the Worcester Beacon, had a clean genteel appearance, and the atmosphere was one of 'peaceful solitude.'[3] The Darwins rented a house, The Lodge, a quarter of a mile out on the Worcester Road. There the children could romp on the wooded slopes of the North Hill. And Charles could maintain his accustomed privacy while being in touch with Dr Gully. His spirits began to rise.

Charles and Dr Gully were an interesting mix. They were almost direct contemporaries. Both had matriculated at Edinburgh in 1825. Gully, though, had gone on to Paris and had graduated in 1829. Like so many medical radicals coming out of Edinburgh at this time, he was devoted to heterodox science, and had evolutionary sympathies himself. He had a radical's faith in all manner of unorthodox practices – homoeopathy, hydropathy, mesmerism – none of which Charles shared. Charles never overcame his distrust of homoeopathy, nor did he have much to say for the rest. It was a 'sad flaw' in Gully's character that 'he believes in everything.'[4] But for all that, Gully was cautious in his diagnoses. He was also caring, and Charles, his father gone, his nerves shattered, appreciated this more than anything.

So he began the cold water cure. He sent his sister Susan a splash-by-splash account of the regime.

¼ before 7. get up, & am scrubbed with rough towel in cold
water for 2 or 3 minutes, which after the first few days, made
& makes me very like a lobster – I have a washerman, a very
nice person, & he scrubs behind, whilst I scrub in front. –
drink a tumbler of water & get my clothes on as quickly as
possible & walk for 20 minutes . . . At same time I put on a
compress, which is a broad wet folded linen covered by
mackintosh & which is 'refreshed' – ie dipt in cold water
every 2 hours & I wear it all day.

He was kept off sugar, salt, bacon and stimulants, in fact 'anything
good,' although, against the rules, he was allowed the odd pinch of
snuff. Gully dosed him with homoeopathic medicines, which Charles
took 'without an atom of faith.' The family liked Gully, and Charles
thought he sounded a lot like the Doctor, authoritative but benign.
The bond grew very quickly and he even referred to him later as 'my
beloved Dʳ Gully.' 'He is very kind & attentive,' Charles noted from
the start, and even if he had been 'puzzled with my case,' Charles
was responding well to treatment.[5]

So was everyone else. Paralytic gentlemen, female invalids, and
emaciated children could be seen all over the village. They had come
– at great trouble and expense – expecting a cure, and most believed
it was occurring. 'Malvern is always merry,' noted a contemporary.
'The patients . . . are generally given to intoxication – sure to be tipsy
with water.' This had a beneficial effect on their families, the Darwins
not excepted. With spring in bloom, it was turning out to be a
glorious holiday. They always remembered it as a happy time.
Charles took four-year-old Georgy to a toy bazaar and bought him a
musical instrument. Emma went shopping for gifts and hiked on the
hill with Annie and Willy. Annie in her large leghorn hat and black
polka jacket took dancing lessons and learned to do quadrille duets.
Francis was christened in the Priory Church. The festive atmosphere
further buoyed Charles's spirits. He began to calm down and feel idly
content. He went beetle hunting 'for auld langsyn,' and reminisced to
Henslow about their fenland botanical outings. He even bought a
horse and relived those 'delightful days.'[6] His sickness subsided, the
tremors vanished, his strength returned, and he put on weight. Soon
Emma was expecting again.

His stomach trouble was diagnosed as nervous in origin – the
result of excessive mental exertion – and the resulting bad circulation
was remedied by the compress. He told Hooker, sweating away in
India, how 'I am heated by Spirit lamp till I *stream* with perspiration,

& am then suddenly rubbed violently with towels dripping with cold water: have two cold feet-baths, & wear a wet compress all day on my stomach.' By mid-April he had been free of sickness for a month and was walking seven miles a day. By early May Gully believed that a full recovery would be made. Feeling good, Charles had to admit that the water cure was no quackery after all. Whatever else it achieved, the regime stopped him from working and deflected his overcharged mind from anxieties about persecution and death. This was no mean feat, quackery or not, although the months of enforced idleness were beginning to tell in other ways. Soon he complained that his mind was stagnating.[7] Down and his 'beloved Barnacles' beckoned; he was dying to get home.

The retinue finally arrived back on 30 June. Charles had been away longer than he intended – longer, indeed, than he would ever be away from Down again. We 'staid 16 instead of 6 weeks', he told Fox. But it was worth it; the nausea had passed, his head was clear, his hands steady – he was ready to pick up the dissecting needles again.

He continued the cure at home, 'though in a somewhat relaxed degree, so as to avoid bringing on a crisis.' In the garden, near his spectacular well – 100 yards deep – he had the village carpenter build a miniature church-shaped hut to contain a tub with a platform in it and a huge cistern above holding 640 gallons of water. The carpenter's son, John Lewis, remembered,

> I had to pump it full every day . . . Mr. Darwin came out and
> had a little dressing place, and he'd get on the stage and . . .
> pull the string, and all the water fell on him through a two-
> inch pipe. A douche they called it.

Young Lewis, fifteen, also helped with Darwin's other regime, the morning plunge.

> He used to get up . . . at seven, and I had to have the big
> bath outside the study on the lawn . . . and Mr. Darwin would
> come down [into his hut] and sit in a chair with a spirit lamp
> and all rolled round with blankets till the sweat poured off
> him in showers when he shook his head . . . I've heard him
> cry to . . . Parslow, 'I'll be melted away if you don't hurry!'
> Then he'd get into the ice-cold bath in the open air.

Parslow the butler served as bathman, scrubbing Darwin until he was red and raw. He already considered himself 'absolutely cured,' but it was better to play safe, and he now opened a health diary to keep a check of his day-to-day progress. Hydropathy certainly was 'a grand discovery' – if only he had tried it 'five or six years' earlier.[8]

First on the agenda after settling in were the barnacles. He continued sending out requests for specimens. Even at Malvern he had written to ask his old *Beagle* servant Syms Covington, now in New South Wales, to collect in the colony – which he did expertly. But processing them all was slow work so long as he remained a 'slave to treatment.' Gully permitted at most two or three hours of intellectual activity a day, and then only with a minimum of 'mental excitement.' He understood his patient well.

Still, some engagements were pressing, such as the Birmingham meeting of the British Association in September. He could hardly avoid this, having been elected one of the Vice-Presidents, and anyway he wanted to comment on a paper by Albany Hancock on burrowing barnacles. Emma went along too, to keep an eye on him. But the meeting was not 'brilliant.' He grew weary 'of all the spouting,' and got irritated by 'Sir H. Delabeche's harsh loud voice & empty noisy speeches.' The whole place was 'so large & nasty,' and to cap it all his retching returned with the excitement. In desperation, he made a flying visit to Dr Gully at Malvern. Then he returned home, where he spent a day in bed feeling dreadful. Obviously the treatment was only going to work so long as he lived the 'life of a hermit.' Two weeks afterwards his stomach still had not recovered. He had learned his lesson: even though he was elected a Council-member of the Royal Society a few weeks later, he shamefully attended only once the next year.[9] Such absenteeism was not condoned by the Society's young reformers, and he was not re-elected.

Through all, Darwin continued to be fascinated by 'Mr. Arthrobalanus.' This 'ill-formed little monster' had started him on his onerous dissections and even after three years it still held surprises. In fact, the 'Mr.' was a misnomer, for his specimens turned out to be females with minute males clinging to their shells – as in *Ibla* and *Scalpellum*. Here the reduction was just as drastic: the male was a 'mere bag, lined by a few muscles, enclosing an eye,' antennae, and a gigantic sexual organ. To Darwin, it seemed, the member came first and the male followed. 'Mr. Arthrobalanus' himself was little more than a rudimentary head atop an 'enormous coiled penis' – with no vestige of the other fourteen segments of a normal barnacle body.[10]

Having worked out this segmentation, he knew how barnacles had diverged from their crab-like relatives. With other comparative anatomists in the 1840s, he accepted that all animals were constructed according to a few basic patterns. These were the 'archetypes' of life. By studying these blueprints, zoologists could work out homologies among different creatures. In mammals and birds, for instance, arms, wings, and flippers are homologous: they are derived from the same part of the blueprint. Richard Owen championed this approach. Darwin himself had been dealing with homologies since studying under Grant at Edinburgh, but he interpreted them very differently from Owen.

Although Darwin praised Owen's work, and coyly told him that he too had deciphered homologies 'on a very **small** scale,' he never let on about his own private interpretation. This he scribbled in Owen's new book *On the Nature of Limbs*:

> I look at Owen's Archetypes as more than ideal, as a real
> representation as far as the most consummate skill & loftiest
> generalization can represent the parent form of the Vertebrata
> – I follow him that there is a created archetype, the parent of
> its class.

Darwin believed in a Creator, as Owen did. But Owen was a Coleridgean idealist; his 'archetype' existed only in the divine Mind. Darwin was heir to a rival Unitarian tradition that rooted itself in material events. He was thinking of real, historical parents.[11] Homologies for him indicated blood ties, and he used them to work out how barnacles were actually related to crabs and lobsters.

In Paris Henri Milne-Edwards had shown that the archetypal crustacean had twenty-one segments. This primitive shrimp-like creature, Darwin believed, gave us an idea of the common ancestor of the various crabs, lobsters, and barnacles. Using Milne-Edwards's model, Darwin could show how they diverged. He deduced that everything visible externally in barnacles was equivalent to the first three segments of a crab's head, but 'wonderfully modified,' and 'so enlarged as to receive the whole rest of the body' inside them.[12] Fourteen body segments – the last four had vanished altogether – were tucked up inside this shell, and only the animal's feathery feet protruded occasionally to strain the water for food. In the miniscule males, even these body segments were reduced to a remnant.

Darwin was 'cock-a-hoop' at having cracked this relationship. It also helped him to work out the barnacles' life-cycle. Their metamorphosis, he told Louis Agassiz, was odd to say the least. In the free-swimming larva a part of the reproductive system, the ovarian tube, becomes 'modified & glandular & secretes a cement.' Even stranger, these ducts open, of all places, at the tip of the antennae. The larva pours cement from its head and glues itself to the rock and thus begins its sedentary adult life upside down. It all sounded 'extremely improbable,' Darwin was the first to admit, but barnacles were improbable beasts.[13] From a crab's oviduct to a cement gland: this was far more surprising than feet turning into feeding nets. It provided Darwin with his most dramatic evidence of the way an organ could change function as an animal exploited new conditions.

Darwin was now internationally known through his *Journal* of travels, and he traded off his name. He fired off letters far and wide. The American response was munificent. Agassiz shipped a crate of barnacles. His co-author, Dr Augustus Gould, the real expert, currently describing the shells collected by the United States Exploring Expedition, also sent one. In return both received up-to-the-minute reports of supplemental males and cement glands. By the autumn, too, major European collections were arriving at Down. Milne-Edwards arranged for Darwin to have specimens from the Paris Muséum, and the physiologist Johannes Müller sent some from Berlin. He already had Sir James Ross's polar specimens. Others came from the Continent. Or didn't in one case: Professor Johan Forchhammer's, sent from Copenhagen University, vanished coming across the Channel. Darwin was now drooping, weighed down by the 'odiously tedious job' of compiling descriptions. It rubbed off on Hooker. Letter after letter he endured, crammed with barnacle news, and he was beginning to wilt. On reflection, he said, he really did prefer to hear the evolutionary speculations after all. The irony was not lost on Darwin. Now 'this is too bad,' he snorted, for it was 'your decided approval of my plain Barnacle work' that led 'me to . . . defer my species-paper' in the first place.[14]

The test of his new-found stamina came with approaching winter. All his morbid symptoms had gone – the muscle spasms, fainting feelings, spots before the eyes – as well as the vomiting. Indeed, after Etty's and Willy's brief fevers in the summer, the whole family was 'flourishing.' But Charles had to keep up the water torture. 'Lamp 5 times per week & shallow bath for 5 minutes afterwards; douche daily for 5 minutes & dripping sheet' was the rigmarole. The water got colder with the onset of winter. 'Sharp work my Baths have been for 5 minutes under 40°.' But it was wonderfully invigorating and had other advantages. It provided an excuse, and not only to cut down work. He had already given up 'all reading, except the newspapers.' Now he had the medical authority for avoiding personal contacts. 'I have never been so much cut off from all scientific friends,' he consoled Hooker in his mountain bivouac.[15]

Cut off was not the word. But at least Darwin had his freedom. Hooker by this time was a prisoner. One day Darwin was 'indolently skimming through the Paper' when he read, to his horror, that his friend had been kidnapped. On 7 November, Hooker and the government agent to Sikkim were returning from Tibet through a Himalayan pass, when they were seized by a local anti-British ruler. It was a common tactic to express grievances and wring concessions, and Hooker was not badly treated. Still Darwin, who knew his priorities, 'feared that his collection' would go 'to rack & ruin.' In fact, the reverse was true, comically so: Hooker was allowed to collect rhododendron seeds even as he was marched south. The group was held for six weeks, and released just before Christmas after threats from Lord Dalhousie, who moved a regiment up to Darjeeling. To stop such banditry and show – in Hooker's words – that the rajahs 'could not play fast and loose with a British subject,' southern Sikkim was promptly annexed for the Crown, with Hooker advising the expeditionary force. In future, botanizing would be a safer business in the Himalayas. For Darwin, the adventure was a little too close for comfort. He feared losing his confidant. 'Heaven grant that poor Joseph Hooker may be spared,' Lyell prayed – after hearing that four of Hooker's colleagues had died on the trip – to which Darwin would have added 'Amen.' Darwin hoped that at least some good would come of this skulduggery, namely, he said, that 'Sir William and Lady Hooker will insist on your coming home.'[16]

Nor was Hooker's captivity the end of Darwin's concern. At the close of 1849 the causes for disquiet were mounting ominously. In November, first Annie, then Etty and two-year-old Elizabeth – Lizzy – came down with scarlet fever. Forchhammer's fossils had still not turned up, and he waited on tenterhooks. They did eventually arrive, but only after some nail-biting weeks. He was also keen to obtain some rare fossil barnacles from Robert Fitch, a Norwich pharmacist and amateur geologist. But when Fitch's parcel came early in the new year, one of his specimens was shattered into thirteen fragments. Darwin painstakingly gummed it back together, petrified that the accident would reflect ill, on him and kill Fitch's co-operation. Meanwhile, as Darwin worried about the fossils and fever, his theory of coral reefs was under scrutiny in the United States, by a geologist 'as "d – – d cocked sure" as Macaulay.' Darwin regained his composure on discovering that James Dwight Dana at Yale differed only a little from him. But for one who confessed himself 'as tender of his theories as of his child[ren],' reading Dana's *Geology* was an emotional ordeal. It left him in a lather, the sort that came over him whenever he thought his work slighted.

To cap it all, Emma was about to deliver again – her eighth. On 15 January Charles was just patching up Fitch's fossil when her contractions started. He sent for the doctor, but he was delayed, and 'her pains came on so rapidly & severe,' he told Fox, 'that I c$^{d.}$ not withstand her entreaties for Chloroform.' He had to administer it himself, which was 'nervous work not knowing from eye-sight anything about it or of midwifery.' He placed a soaked pad over Emma's nose, and the effect was instantaneous. Unfamiliar with the procedure, he kept her unconscious for a dangerously long time – one and a half hours. The doctor arrived with ten minutes to spare and she woke knowing nothing of the ordeal to be told that it was a boy. They called him Leonard, after Henslow's firstborn and the Revd Jenyns. Chloroform was 'the grandest & most blessed of discoveries,' Darwin informed Henslow.[17] It had worked for Emma as the water cure was working for him. Together, thanks to medical science, they had got through the winter's worst perils almost painlessly. He now felt better than he had for months.

A few days after Leonard's birth Darwin started to describe the fossils. So often fossil barnacles consisted of nothing more than disarticulated shells, which had separated soon after the animal's death. But a few, a very few, held out the promise of something more. Fitch had built up his 'unrivalled collection' over a period of twenty years, and in all that time he had managed to find only two that were whole (and not broken into pieces before they were fossilized). Darwin now crowed with delight at the sight of Fitch's rare fossil *Pollicipes* from the Norfolk Chalk, which still had its shells complete, suggesting that a cast of the animal might exist inside. It left him drooling: Fitch had '*incomparably* the best specimens' he had ever seen 'from any Secondary rock.'[18]

He also removed the surface valve from one of James Bowerbank's intact fossils to expose the interior, which made it 'a **hundred**-fold more instructive.' Bowerbank was a distiller by trade, a sponge expert by avocation. He owned a brewery, Bowerbank & Co., but devoted much of his time to natural history, and his *Fossil Fruits of the London Clay* was definitive. He had an excellent collection of barnacles, now in Darwin's hands. More to the point, he ran a new specialist society – the Palaeontographical – dedicated to publishing monographs on British fossils. In February he recruited Darwin and the Society paid his illustrator, James de Carle Sowerby, to engrave the plates. Darwin, always cost-conscious, was grateful to be saved the expense. (He already had Sowerby's brother George on the payroll, drawing his dissections and translating his descriptions into Latin.)

With two publishers in hand – the Ray Society had agreed at the outset to publish his monograph on the living species – he still had a way to go. Boxes of fossils were coming in by the week, and he continued to open them with trepidation. Two more specimens, he reported to Fitch in 'grief & shame,' were 'broken slightly but can be **perfectly** repaired: a third is rather more injured.' Then began the hard work of describing each species in the minutest detail. He finally settled into a routine: a spartan douse for five minutes in freezing water, later two hours of barnacles. But two hours – the doctor's limit – meant that the work dragged on. Fitch became anxious as time passed. In letter after letter Darwin wriggled and apologized for his snail's pace. 'I **cannot** work quicker,' he finally exploded, promising to return his fossils just as soon as he could.[19]

Four years into the barnacles, and it seemed like an eternity. Some days he had to force himself to go on, working his way through the sub-class, species by species. 'I groan under my task,' he sighed to Lyell. 'Heaven only knows' when he would finish. The work was never-ending. He had started the year with forty or fifty fossils, now he had two hundred. Down House was beginning to look like a museum. It dawned on him, with some horror, that a one-volume monograph was no longer feasible. Each of the books on fossil and living barnacles would have to be a two-volume affair. The first, to be published straightaway, would concentrate on the stalked barnacles – those which attach themselves by a leathery stem to driftwood or the hulls of ships. Such types were geologically the oldest; the earliest known, *Pollicipes*, lived in Jurassic and Cretaceous seas, a contemporary of the dinosaurs.[20] In June 1850 Darwin had almost finished his descriptions for this volume, although James Sowerby was dragging his feet over the engravings.

That month Charles went back to Malvern. With Emma dividing her time between him and the baby, the pressure of barnacles had been his undoing. He had begun to lose whole working days, to complain again of 'excitement & fatigue,' to cancel trips to London. Varying his treatment had made some difference – alternating heat lamp and douche – and he never vomited now. His weight indeed was up to nearly 170 pounds. But still something was amiss. A week together with Emma, cheered by Dr Gully's optimism, would clear it up. 'My Water Doctor continues to give me hopes,' Charles beamed, and everybody at Malvern told him that he looked 'blooming &

beautiful.'[21] The refresher week at the spa also gave him time to reflect, to stand back and assess his taxonomic odyssey. What was his major conclusion after scrutinizing so many specimens? Hooker – now safely delivered from his captors – asked this. Darwin's answer, as he slapped himself with wet towels, was that barnacles were infinitely variable.

At the time Hooker was actually trying to test Darwin's ideas in the Himalayas. He was looking for terraces and parallel roads, guided by Darwin's geological books; and, knowing Darwin's fascination with domestic breeds, he sent back a flood of details on dogs, elephants, and cattle. In return he received a string of new marching orders: bring home silkworms, and don't forget a local beehive. But there was a more subtle influence too. Hooker now admitted that Darwin's evolutionary ideas 'have possessed me, without however converting me.' In fact, the Indian evidence was not encouraging. He was looking for a graded sequence of floras on passing from the tropics up the temperate hills to the snowy Himalayan heights.[22] But without success, so he asked whether the barnacle work had caused Darwin to modify his theories. He had expected it to make Darwin more cautious.

But no. Rather than undermining his theory, it had proved to Darwin that variation was ubiquitous. Ten years earlier he had thought variation the exception in nature, but barnacles had changed that. Wide-ranging barnacle species were '*eminently* variable.' Every part 'of every species' was prone to change; the closer he looked, the more stability seemed an illusion. While many curators accepted that varieties were natural productions, he went further to see them as incipient species. Yet however reassuring in one respect, all this variation made a mockery of his attempt to define each species precisely. Where did the varieties end and new species begin? Half the time he found it impossible to tell. This 'confounded variation' was a mixed blessing, he told Hooker, rubbing his nose in it rather. It 'is pleasant to me as a speculist though odious to me as a systematist.'[23]

Indeed he was hopping. So often he had described specimens as separate species, had second thoughts and made them all variants of one species, changed his mind, torn up his paper, and started all over again. And each time 'I have gnashed my teeth, cursed species, & asked what sin I had committed to be so punished.'[24] Since today's species were yesterday's varieties, he ended up cutting the Gordian knot by simply lumping the variants into recognized species. None of it mattered. There were no absolute, unvarying forms, so a precise classification was, in any case, impossible.

Still, he remained coy about it. Years earlier he had lectured Waterhouse on classification, telling him it was 'a logical process,' or rather genealogical: it 'consists in grouping beings according to their actual *relationship*, ie their consanguinity, or descent from common stocks.' But this was easier to preach than practise, and anyway the *Vestiges* had warned him off presenting a tree-like target. When it came to the crunch in the monograph, he conventionally listed the genera of each barnacle family. He did moot relationships in the text, but he made no effort to picture a genealogical tree.[25] That would have been a give-away.

The second stay at Malvern had perked Charles up. He admitted that he had grown quite fond of his aquatic habits, 'except the dressing & undressing.' His stomach was still never 'right for 24 hours,' and he went back to his garden privy for 'douching &c &c' in a spirit of patient resignation. 'I have given up all hopes of ever being a strong man again,' he rather plaintively wrote to Covington, acknowledging his rich crop of pickled specimens. But now at least the Grim Reaper was held at bay. The 'wondrous Water Cure' seemed cheap at any price. Even partial health 'is, compared to my state two years ago, of inestimable value.'[26]

25

Our Bitter & Cruel Loss

AFTER CHARLES ARRIVED HOME from Malvern, a cold shadow crept over the household once again. He was petrified that his ailment was a heritable defect. Now, he thought he could detect a glimmer of it in the children.

At the end of June 1850, as he sat scratching his fossils, a clutch of Wedgwood cousins came for a visit – there were now fourteen of them under the age of twelve, besides Charles's and Emma's seven. They romped together and enjoyed an outing in Knole Park at nearby Sevenoaks. But Annie, the Darwins' eldest daughter, complained of feeling sick. She was not just a clever nine-year-old seeking attention. When the others left she was miserable for weeks on end. Her lessons became an endurance test, for her and the governess Miss Thorley. She sometimes burst into tears for no apparent reason and often woke at night crying pitifully. Charles began to fear that the problem was 'wretched digestion' again.[1] Clearly, the child was no longer herself.

In the last two years she had won her father's heart in a special way. The Doctor had had a favourite daughter, Susan, who lavished attention on him until the end. Charles, fearing he would soon die, naturally grew attached to his eldest girl for the same reason. And Annie reminded him of Emma. Tall for her age, with long brown hair and greyish eyes, she had a sunny, affectionate disposition. She delighted in straightening his clothes, combing his hair and 'making it beautiful,' before joining him on the Sandwalk. She loved being kissed, and showed a wonderful sensitivity to others' feelings, which made her the apple of her father's eye. At Malvern the year before, she gave Miss Thorley a little lesson on the rigours of the water cure. 'And it makes Papa so angry,' she added with a pout, at which Papa, who was present, had to admit that it did sometimes make him feel rather cross.[2]

Now all that had changed. Annie's bright spirit was beginning to break. She picked bilberries at Leith Hill near Dorking with Jos and Caroline Wedgwood's girls, but these few pleasant days in August failed to restore her. In October Miss Thorley took her to the seaside – Ramsgate – with the other children for three weeks. Charles and Emma joined them briefly at the end, but Annie became so feverish and headachy that Emma had to stay on with her when the others left. In November and again in December Emma took her to London to see Dr Holland, who believed that Charles's stomach troubles were inherited. He could do little for the child, who clung more and more to her parents. Her nights became worse; she cried and complained, and it upset her to go any distance from home.[3] Dr Holland had been Charles's last port of call before taking the water cure. If Annie's condition persisted, he would take her to Malvern too.

By this time Emma was pregnant yet again. Charles was 'working like a wretched slave,' mindlessly describing barnacles, without the 'heart to begin work of interest.' He remained as well as could be expected, though Annie worried him a good deal. Emma, once over her usual morning sickness, enjoyed the intimacy of a visit with him to her sisters at Hartfield in East Sussex.[4] At home their life together went on like clockwork, eased by the loyal domestic staff. When Charles was not shut up in the study, hunched over his brittle beasts, he and Emma had ample time to read. He continued to dip into religious books. His health had improved dramatically since his last such reading; his mortal fears had subsided. Still, he would not countenance anything remotely orthodox now. He had begun to look beyond Christianity.

He turned to Francis Newman, the Latin professor at University College. Among Unitarians and freethinkers he was the man of the hour: an evolutionist – following *Vestiges* – calling for a new post-Christian synthesis. Charles had already read *The Soul*. Its later chapters came 'with the shock of a shower-bath,' complained a pious aunt of Emma's; but Charles must have found them as invigorating as his daily douche. In the book Newman gave up trying to prove human immortality from the Bible. Such proof was inaccessible 'to the great mass of mankind' whose salvation is supposed to depend on it. And he rejected 'the dreadful doctrine of the Eternal Hell.' Real assurance of a blessed hereafter, he maintained, came only through 'a full sympathy of our spirit with God's Spirit.'

That was how Emma felt, but Newman's intuitive spirituality made Charles uneasy. When he opened Newman's *History of the Hebrew Monarchy* after returning from Leith Hill, his misgivings were confirmed. For all its criticism of Old Testament history based on advanced German scholarship, the book left 'the relations between the divine and the human mind . . . the same as ever.' But how could that be? How could faith in 'the Holiness of God' have arisen amid the death, famine, and wars of Semitic tribes? No, Charles insisted, the religious instinct had evolved with society. The primitive Jewish God, whose atrocities had 'lit up hell-fires in Christendom,' could be nothing but a barbaric tyrant.

Newman was consolidating Charles's doubts. With the restoration of England's Catholic dioceses in 1850 many saw religious barbarism making a come-back. It was an opportune moment for Charles to reflect – with Newman's help – on what he actually believed. He could admit the religious thrust of his old notebook speculations on morality and the afterlife, at least to himself, in the privacy of Down. Certainly, two years after his father's death, he was not tortured by anxiety as he contemplated the fate of unbelievers. His reading and the water cure had calmed him, and Newman's freethinking example helped to restore his sense of security.[5]

Annie, though, was still not out of danger. Christmas came and went with little respite from her vague stomach complaint. Charles, his spirits lifted by the tidings that Hooker was heading home, felt confident enough to experiment with medications. In the new year, 1851, he began rubbing tartar emetic ointment on his stomach and perhaps on Annie's too. By March she was well enough to play outdoors and ride on horseback for the first time. Charles meanwhile began returning borrowed barnacles. He sent Fitch's back at last and saw his first fossil volume through the press. Then, shortly after Annie's tenth birthday, influenza struck the household. Both of them were laid low. Annie stayed beside Emma in bed, weak and miserable. Charles lay propped up on his sofa dosing himself with tonics and reading Newman's powerful, agonizing, spiritual autobiography *Phases of Faith*.[6]

Here were shades of Charles again: Newman's odyssey saw him destined for the Church, suffering qualms about the Thirty-nine Articles, rejecting hell, and passing through Unitarianism (knowing it 'could never afford . . . a half-hour's resting-place') to end up on the fringes of free religion. Its potent, emotional tone struck Charles at this moment. If a person deserves infinite punishment for offending an Infinite Being, Newman reasoned, 'the fretfulness of a child is an infinite evil!' Charles looked at poor Annie.

Religiously he had moved on, and, as with Newman, the Bible had disintegrated in his hands – the Old Testament with its Creation legends and moral monstrosities, the New Testament bristling with inconsistencies and myths. The Gospel of John, Newman's 'impregnable fortress of Christianity,' collapsed with the evidence that Jesus may never have uttered the words attributed to him there, and the simple Jewish Rabbi 'melted into dimness' and vanished from Newman's faith, even as he had from Charles's. 'I felt no convulsion of mind, no emptiness of soul, no inward practical change,' Newman recalled.[7] The glide to a purely theistic religion, combining Christian virtue with the rigour of modern science, was as anodyne as it was complete.

Charles finished *Phases of Faith* and snapped the covers shut. It was 'excellent,' he jotted in a notebook – fit reading for a Sunday while Emma was at church. The story of a gentleman with the courage to pursue an enquiry to its end. Emotional attachment to Christianity was not enough; faith had to comply with reason, morality, and historical evidence. There was no stopping short at Unitarianism, that 'feather bed to catch a falling Christian,' as Charles's grandfather said. Christianity had to be rejected once and for all. The moral logic that condemned eternal punishment could not condone the New Testament where the monstrous doctrine was taught. Evolution – the new 'gospel' – explained mind, morality, and religious beliefs as part of the social development of the human species.

Lying on his back, recovering from the flu, Charles had several days to ponder such thoughts. But although he began to feel stronger, Annie remained downcast. Nothing Emma did seemed to help, so they decided to take her to Dr Gully. On Monday, 24 March, Annie sat crying on the sofa beside Emma. Her bags were packed, the carriage was ready, and it was time to set off. Etty was going along to keep her company, with Brodie the nurse. But Annie clung to her mother, sobbing. It would be so lonely in Malvern without her – a whole month away.[8] Mama would soon be having a baby, yes, and Papa would leave her in good hands. But as Charles bundled Annie into the carriage for Sydenham station, it felt as if she was going away for ever.

As the Great Western coach clattered up the Severn valley, through the toll gates, and into the Malvern Hills, Charles could feel relieved. Annie, nestling beside him and Etty, would soon be safe in the care of his trusted physician, the man who all but saved his own life.

Spring dappled the fields and hedgerows, reminding Charles of the first trip to Malvern just two years before. How precarious human existence again seemed.

Safely in Malvern, Charles settled his charges in lodgings with Eliza Partington at Montreal House, overlooking the village and the vale of Worcester. Once Annie got better, she and Etty could play together on the hillside where Emma used to take them hiking. On examining Annie, Dr Gully recommended that she be seen by a clairvoyant. Charles was highly sceptical but tolerated the expense. Hydropathy, after all, had originally seemed like quackery too; and once when Gully's own daughter was gravely ill, he had employed a far-sighted female to report on her internal state and – somehow – the girl recovered. But Charles first put Annie's clairvoyant to the test. He offered her a banknote sealed in an envelope if she could reel off its number. The woman scorned the trick as beneath her professional dignity, dismissing it as something her 'maid-servant at home' could do. Whereupon she turned, peered long and hard, and described in lurid detail the horrors she saw in Annie's innards. Charles assumed that she was following 'some unconscious hints' from Gully.[9]

Still, there was no doubt that Annie's stomach was the root of the problem, and that Gully would cure it if anyone could. Charles stayed on until he saw all was well. On Friday the 28th he kissed the girls goodbye for a month, promising that Miss Thorley would come soon, and set off for London. The next morning he called on Lyell in Harley Street. Word had it that Hooker was back in town. On Sunday the Darwin brothers dined in palatial splendour at Hensleigh and Fanny Wedgwood's, overlooking Regent's Park. It became an impromptu reunion – Carlyle dropped in, joining Emma's seventy-year-old maiden aunt, Fanny Allen, and a clerical friend. Only Harriet Martineau was missing from the old circle. And just as well, for Aunt Fanny would have roasted her for dinner. Martineau's correspondence with a garrulous, self-styled scientist named Henry Atkinson had just been published. Already these *Letters on the Laws of Man's Nature and Development* were outraging literary London. Martineau now preened herself as a mesmeric evolutionary atheist. Aunt Fanny blanched at the boldness of 'these two criminals' with their 'miserable' book. Charles was intrigued. He made sure to borrow it from Erasmus.[10]

Back at Down on Monday, things were looking up, and his health was back to normal. Annie had the best medical supervision he could buy. The precious barnacle collections were being returned, intact, to their long-suffering owners. And the first fruits of five years' work, volume one of his monograph on fossil barnacles, printed by the Palaeontographical Society, arrived in the post. More auspicious still, Hooker was indeed back, safe and well, loaded with specimens and full of facts about Indian species.[11] Of course he would soon be married – Fanny Henslow now took pride of place in his life. Still, it was a relief to know he was home at Kew, and able to visit Down. Charles settled in and expected to be on hand for weeks.

It was not to be. Late on Tuesday 15 April came an urgent message: Annie had relapsed, seriously. She was feverish and vomiting. Brodie was beside herself. Miss Thorley was distraught. Someone was needed from home, and Dr Gully called for Charles. The news sent Down House into a whirl. Emma, now eight months pregnant, dared not think of going, and Charles would not hear of it anyway. She prepared for the worst, providing everyone with emotional support. She asked sister-in-law Fanny Wedgwood to meet Charles at Malvern. What about Fanny's six children, and Etty? She arranged for cousins Jos and Caroline to take them all at Leith Hill. And the baby? An early confinement was unlikely, but already Emma felt overwhelmed. Just in case, ask Aunt Fanny to come down from London, and send for sister Elizabeth to take the 'first good steamer' from Jersey – and fetch chloroform.[12]

Charles collected his belongings, some books for diversion, and a mass of painful thoughts. The next day he set off. Once before he had rushed this way to the Severn valley, too late for a funeral. Afterwards he had fled to the Malvern hills fearing he was going to die. Those hills loomed up before him again as the carriage sped along the turnpike, the rocks laced with extinct shells and trilobites. It was Maundy Thursday when he arrived.

Montreal House was in an emotional spin. Annie seemed a trifle better but Brodie and Miss Thorley were wringing their hands. Dr Gully, with eighty-eight patients, had little time to spare. Etty had to be jollied constantly to prevent her fretting about her sister. Everyone was anxious and exhausted. Keeping up hopes all round meant that no one really knew what was happening. Charles stepped into the vortex at Annie's bedside. It was a scene where his ragged medical knowledge, his ability to become like Doctor Darwin, would be tested to destruction. When he first saw Annie he completely broke down, flinging himself on a sofa, agonized and desolate. The pinched face and withered body, the smell of camphor and ammonia – he had been there once before.[13] At Edinburgh he had run in terror from the scene of a tortured child. This time the child was his own. He must compose himself, maintain everyone's spirits, serve as orderly, nurse, and locum. Emma, soon due, was to be kept informed, but with calm discretion; more than one life was at stake. Much as Charles longed for her protective presence, as he had in Shrewsbury at his father's bedside, he had to prop her hopes up. She would hear what was necessary about their poor child, but never know how much he was suffering.

That night the crisis deepened. Wishing for the best, Charles had fallen for Gully's early optimism. Now he was violently cast down. Annie's pulse became irregular and she sank into semi-consciousness. Gully rushed to her side, watching anxiously for the restlessness and chill that precedes death. He thought it would probably be all over before the morning and agreed to stay the night. At 6 a.m. Annie vomited, showing she still had strength. Charles was in a wretched state. Choking back what remained of his tears, he described to Emma the hourly 'struggle between life & death.' 'Oh my own it is very bitter indeed,' he let on, then added anxiously, 'God preserve & cherish you.' Throughout the day Annie failed to keep down the brandy and gruel they gave her. Once she alarmed them by vomiting the 'bright green' contents of her gall bladder. By early evening the child was 'dreadfully exhausted' – but no worse, said Gully. 'He yet has hopes – *positively he has Hopes*,' Charles rejoiced to Emma as the sun set on Good Friday. 'Oh my dear be thankful.'[14]

As Emma pored anxiously over Charles's letter the next morning, taking what comfort she could, Fanny arrived in Malvern, with a servant to escort Etty to her cousins. The sisters kissed farewell, never dreaming it might be their last. Annie had rallied overnight – 'turning the corner,' Gully said – and Charles dared to picture 'my own former Annie with her dear affectionate radiant face.' He sent word by telegraph to Emma. The message came mid-afternoon, while she was outside looking for a blossom in Annie's flower patch. 'What happiness! How I do thank God!' she replied in haste. Now she could 'wait very well' until Monday for his next report.

Even as she wrote, Annie was improving. Charles and Fanny had been watching hopefully all day. Her fever was gone and her pulse was quickening; her food was staying down. She lay tranquilly – perhaps too tranquilly – and looked more comfortable by the hour. Fanny told Emma that Charles himself appeared 'sadly overcome & shaken,' but not ill. He was loath to leave his child, though twice that day he did go out to wander alone on the hillside, confident of Fanny's care. The wind, the view, the freshness everywhere felt like life made new. Tomorrow Emma would be thanking God in church.

When he got back Dr Gully came. Annie had vomited a little, but there was 'decided improvement in the tongue,' he announced, 'a most important point.'[15]

All night Fanny and Charles kept watch by the bedside. 'Poor dear devoted Miss Thorley' had her first unbroken sleep. Annie vomited slightly a second time and took less of the gruel. As Brodie sponged her face and hands, she put her arms round the nurse's neck and kissed her. Then she slept peacefully. In the small hours Charles sat circled in candle-light and poured out his heart to Emma. 'Whilst writing to you, I can cry; tranquilly,' he confessed. Otherwise 'I . . . am constantly up & down: I *cannot* sit still.' First thing in the morning, Dr Gully came. Annie had brought up another mouthful, but he hastened to assure them that she really was no worse. If only she could last two more days, there would be every chance of recovery. But as the Priory Church bells rang out that Easter Sunday, Annie began vomiting again. Her bladder was now paralysed, and a catheter had to be used, though she put up a pathetic struggle. Afterwards, exhausted, she took a little brandy and water. 'I quite thank you,' she breathed. Gully examined her and reported that her pulse was 'rather better, certainly not worse.' In the evening he pronounced her 'decisively better.' Charles no longer knew what to think. 'These alternations of no hope & hope sicken one's soul,' he groaned to Emma.

Monday brought little relief. Early in the morning Annie's bladder and bowels acted spontaneously, which Charles thought an excellent sign. He was 'foolish with delight' and pictured her whirling merrily about the garden at Down – 'making custards,' she used to say. He told her that he thought she would get better. 'Thank you,' she replied meekly. But Gully came at 8 a.m. and dashed his hopes. The diarrhoea was ominous, he declared, and Annie's pulse was faltering. Then the mail arrived and suddenly Charles felt overwhelmed. On reading how Emma had gone to Annie's garden for a flower, he burst into tears. 'I wish you could see her now,' he sobbed to his wife, 'the perfection of gentleness, patience & gratitude, – thankful till it is truly painful to hear her. – poor dear little soul.' In the afternoon Annie weakened, rambling incoherently, and then fell asleep. On waking she called out, 'Where is poor Etty?' Later at dinner she thanked Fanny for a spoonful of tea, exclaiming in a strong voice, 'It is beautifully good.' One more day on this form, as the doctor said, and Annie would be in the clear. Charles assured Emma that she was 'going on very well.'

At Down Emma was helpless except to save the life within her. She hung on to the words of the telegraph message, and prayed. By post time on Monday morning she felt desperate. She tore open the reports from Charles and Fanny but hardly knew what to make of them. Annie's ups and downs pointed nowhere. She tried to feel hopeful and told Charles that she and baby remained well. 'I . . . have considered every thing in case I should be taken short, but I don't the least expect it.' On Tuesday came better news. Now she detected a note of 'progressive improvement' in Charles's letters and became more hopeful. Just before post time on Wednesday morning she let herself go, revelling in 'the pleasure of fancying I have something to do for her.' She sent Charles some simple recipes for Annie 'when she can take a little food.' And then came a letter from Fanny which plunged Emma into despair. 'Alas my own how shall we bear it,' she added to her recipes. 'It is very bitter.'[16]

Tuesday had been the turning point, as Gully predicted. But Annie did not improve. Violent diarrhoea set in, and with each bout she lost strength. Charles was fatigued, Fanny told Emma, sparing her the awful truth. As Annie lay writhing helplessly, his own stomach gave way, and he ran from the room, convulsed and retching. The attack lasted all day. By evening father and daughter were both prostrate. He could not bring himself now to write a single line to Emma. Annie was sinking. Even Dr Gully admitted it.[17]

While Emma wept at home over the news, her hopes crushed, the struggle in Malvern was ending. Annie continued to sink throughout the night, only now and then regaining consciousness. Twice amid her wanderings she made pathetic attempts to sing. Southerly winds blew storm clouds across the hills and it was unseasonably warm. By the morning, Wednesday 23 April, she lay tranquilly, her breathing soft and gentle, her wasted body a jagged outline beneath the sheets. The wind played at the curtains beside an open window. Charles sat motionless, drained, quietly waiting and weeping. He stared out past the bed into the grey immensity beneath the Worcester Beacon. His thoughts were racked and torn, like the Poet Laureate's in Emma's favourite, *In Memoriam*.

> Are God and Nature then at strife,
>   That Nature lends such evil dreams?
>   So careful of the type she seems,
> So careless of the single life.

Annie's breathing became shallower. Fanny came in with Brodie and Miss Thorley. The wind picked up. Charles and Fanny moved closer to the bed. Annie lay still, unconscious. It was just twelve o'clock midday. Thunder began to sound, great peals far above them, the mighty knell of Nature. They edged nearer and heard the breathing stop. She was dead.[18]

Brodie went to pieces. Miss Thorley had an attack and collapsed. Fanny rushed to help them, quite overcome herself, while Charles kissed the shrunken little face one last time and hid himself by the window. It was raining now, pouring. The sodden landscape, a graveyard of extinct life, made a mockery of his bitter tears.

> 'So careful of the type?' but no.
>   From scarpèd cliff and quarried stone
>   She cries, 'A thousand types are gone:
>   I care for nothing, all shall go.'

This was the end of the road, the crucifixion of his hopes. He could not believe the way Emma believed – nor *what* she believed. There was no straw to clutch, no promised resurrection. Christian faith was futile.

Dragging himself to his room, he lay agonized in bed for hours, his stomach churning. He stopped crying long enough to see Dr Gully, who gave the cause of death as a 'Bilious Fever with typhoid character.' But when writing to Emma, he broke down again. Annie had gone 'to her final sleep . . . without a sigh.' How desolating to think of her 'frank cordial manners.' It was impossible to recall 'ever seeing the dear child naughty.' 'God bless her,' he sobbed at last. 'We must be more & more to each other my dear wife.' Towards six o'clock Fanny went in and found Charles still crying bitterly. It kept the nausea at bay, he said. But there was something else tormenting him now. He longed to be with Emma, yet how could he go until his beloved child was buried? The rites, the graveside, would break him completely. Fanny urged him to go – to take the first coach in the morning.[19] She would attend to the funeral.

This was what Charles wanted to hear. He rose early on Thursday, still ill, and left instructions: Brodie was to pick up the washing, Miss Thorley to bring the books, Fanny to return to Erasmus one by the atheistic 'Miss Martineau.' And 'once again my dearest Fanny God Bless you & thank you.' Then he turned his back on Malvern with all its memories, picturing to himself once more Annie's precious ruined face, and fled. He travelled directly to Down with hardly a delay, arriving in the early evening.[20]

When no word had come on Wednesday, Emma knew that the struggle was over and felt 'as if it had all happened long ago.' She bore the blow 'gently & sweetly,' crying 'without violence.' Her 'only hope of consolation' was to have Charles back, but her power of hoping seemed to be gone. She knew he would be ill, perhaps gravely ill. To her horror, she began to think the unthinkable – that he might actually die. But these were unreasonable fears, she chided herself; and when he appeared unexpectedly at the door, some of the light returned. They clung to each other and wept.[21]

The next morning at nine o'clock Annie was buried in the Priory Churchyard. Fanny herself had chosen the final resting-place, beneath a cedar of Lebanon, not far from the magnificent north transept window depicting the joys of Mary. The vicar performed the last offices; Fanny was joined at the graveside by Hensleigh, who helped support Brodie and Miss Thorley. 'There never could have been a child laid in the ground with truer sorrow round her than your sweet & happy Annie,' Fanny told Charles and Emma. And Dr Gully had come afterwards to enquire kindly how the two of them were.[22]

Once the family was reunited, the older children realized the severity of their loss. Willy, eleven, had been grief-stricken for days. Seven-year-old Etty had a special burden to bear, the last of the playmates to see their sister. She had been told the tragic news already, at Leith Hill, but when she returned and heard how Annie had called for her just two days before the end, she sobbed as if her heart would break. The whole experience marked the child for life, much in the way Emma herself was affected by her elder sister's death. Not long afterwards Etty began to be distressed about seeing Annie again. 'But Mamma,' she once cried while Miss Thorley was singing at the piano, 'where do the women go to, for all the angels are men?' Emma, seeing that she was upset, asked her whether she had been thinking about Annie. Etty let go with floods of tears. She knew about Annie's reputation as a 'good' child, never needing punishment; now she wanted to be as good herself. Emma wondered why she was so concerned. Etty answered one night at bedtime, 'I am afraid of going to hell.' Emma reassured her that she 'thought Annie was safe in heaven.' The next night Etty asked, 'Do you think you shall come to Heaven with me?' 'Yes,' Emma sighed, 'I hope so & we shall have Annie.'[23]

The truth was that both Emma and Charles had been severely shaken. It was easier to give religious reassurance to a child than to take it for oneself. 'Poor Emma is well and bodily firm,' Charles wrote to Eras in London, asking him to insert obituary notices in *The Times* and 'any other one or two Papers of largest circulation.' But, he added, she 'feels bitterly, & God knows we can neither see on any side a gleam of comfort.' For Emma the wound never healed. She hoped 'to attain some feeling of submission to the will of Heaven,' but it is doubtful whether she ever managed it.²⁴ The small keepsakes she put away and cherished through the years – the childish notes, the half-finished woolwork, the locks of hair – were a constant reminder of her favourite daughter, wrenched away at Easter.

Charles's reaction was more decided. He had borne the brunt of their 'bitter & cruel loss,' as he told Fox on 29 April. He had watched helplessly as a 'low & dreadful fever' took its toll. He had stood by in that awful passion scene, high on the Malvern hillside, and witnessed Annie expire 'as tranquilly as a little angel.' For him the death marked an impasse and a new beginning. It put an end to three years' deliberations about the Christian meaning of mortality; it opened up a fresh vision of the tragic contingency of nature. The day after writing to Fox, exactly a week after Annie was gone, he struck the new note in a brief memoir of the child, written solely for himself and Emma 'in after years, if we live.' Free of all taint of bitterness, it was the most beautiful – and certainly the most intensely emotional – piece he would ever write.

He portrayed Annie as an example of all the highest and best in human nature. Physically, intellectually, and morally she was all but perfect: her movements 'elastic & full of life & vigour;' her mind 'pure & transparent;' her conduct 'generous, handsome & unsuspicious; . . . free from envy & jealousy; good tempered & never passionate.' He repeated that 'she hardly ever required to be found fault with, & was never punished in any way whatever.' 'A single glance of my eye, not of displeasure (for I thank God I hardly ever cast one on her,) but of want of sympathy would for some minutes alter her whole countenance.' It was this fine sensitivity that left her 'crying bitterly . . . on parting with Emma even for the shortest interval' and that made her exclaim when very young, 'Oh Mamma, what should we do, if you were to die.' The perfection of Annie's character was shown by her physically affectionate ways. From infancy she would fondle her parents, much to their delight. And 'she liked being kissed.' Indeed, 'every expression in her countenance beamed with affection & kindness, & all her habits were influenced by her loving disposition.' Charles remembered Annie's face above all, her tears and kisses, her 'sparkling eyes & brindled smiles,' her 'dear lips.' Again and again he summoned the innocent features before his mind, comparing them with the daguerreotype taken two years before. 'Oh that she could now know how deeply, how tenderly we do still & shall ever love her dear joyous face,' he ended. 'Blessings on her.'²⁵

Annie had not deserved to die; she had not even deserved to be punished – in this world, let alone the next. 'Formed to live a life of happiness,' as Charles put it, she had stumbled on ill health and nature's check fell upon her, crushing her remorselessly. The struggle was 'bitter & cruel' enough without the prospect of retribution. Yet, against the odds, he still longed that she might survive. He was haunted by her face, her loving kisses, and her tears when leaving Emma. Eventually he must part from Emma too.

That very day Emma's contractions started. Childbirth, even aided by chloroform, was a risky business, especially for a mother two days short of her forty-third birthday. It was a false alarm. Emma, who had endured so much, still had a fortnight to wait. She was so looking forward to the event. Taking care of an infant, she said, would be a 'very soothing occupation.' When Horace arrived safely on 13 May, however, she found her sorrow did not diminish. New life had come to Down House but she missed a pair of helping hands. And the baby would have to be her last.

Annie's cruel death destroyed Charles's tatters of belief in a moral, just universe. Later he would say that this period chimed the final death-knell for his Christianity, even if it had been a long, drawn-out process of decay. He was also freer to hold his beliefs in the home. Through nine pregnancies, always difficult and dangerous, Emma had needed the security of thinking that they belonged to each other for ever.[26] With no more babies, the threat of separation lifted. They would certainly be together for many years to come. Charles now took his stand as an unbeliever.

1851–1860

26

A Gentleman with Capital

THE SUMMER SUN of 1851 beamed reassuringly on Victoria's England, a pledge of peace and progress for the richest empire in the world. Gold had been discovered in Australia, Livingstone had just reached the Zambesi, and the first successful cross-Channel cable was being laid. A new era was dawning, bright with imperial promise, and the signs were no less auspicious nearer home. Free trade and *laissez-faire* had brought unparalleled prosperity to the few, with rising expectations for the rest. Old political allegiances were crumbling and from the old Whigs a new 'liberal party' had emerged. The storms that swept away half the governments of Europe had passed harmlessly over the British Isles, and the last lingering fears of domestic conflict now vanished like morning dew. There was 'just as much chance of a revolution in England as of the falling of the moon.'[1]

The Great Exhibition was Britain gloating in its success. It was the first international showcase of arts and manufactures, held in London's Hyde Park. It opened on 1 May, housed in a vast new glass-and-iron edifice, the Crystal Palace. Strong but brittle, capacious but combustible (it burned in 1936), Joseph Paxton's masterpiece was the architectural symbol of English economic supremacy. Its towering nave and transept promoted a sense of reverential awe. Inside, like a gargantuan hot-house, it displayed the first fruits of thriving free enterprise, the enormous engines and myriad manufactured goods that had been forced from native soil. Here the industrial dreams of the Lunar Society – of Boulton and Wedgwood, Priestley and Erasmus Darwin – came abundantly true. Half of all the exhibits came from British factories. Albert, the Prince Consort, presented them to his Queen on opening day as a tribute, the outcome of social harmony 'aided by . . . modern science.'[2]

391

Victoria's nation flocked as one to the dazzling spectacle. Three weeks after the opening, the weekday admission price was reduced to a shilling. The railways issued concessionary fares and day-tripping became the rage. More people made their first rail journey in 1851 than had ever travelled by train before. Landowners, shareholders, businessmen, and the masses met on common ground. They all seemed 'ruled and subdued by some invisible influence ... Not one loud noise was to be heard, not one irregular movement seen; the living tide rolls on quietly.'³ New deference and respectability were springing from a science-based industry.

While religious pundits praised God for the Exhibition, the literary freethinkers were otherwise inspired. Many had been lured to London by the more mundane need for a job. They were poets and professors, doctors and lawyers, novelists and naturalists, journalists and politicians. Some of them had independent means, but many struggled to survive. Most were in their thirties or early forties and on the make. All believed that the new age of the Crystal Palace demanded liberal, progressive reforms; that nature's interpreters had a fair claim to the status and rewards enjoyed by the Anglican Establishment. They formed an uneasy coalition whose creeds ran the gamut of Positivism, Republicanism, Secularism, Materialism, and even the more extreme '-isms' of unbelief. This intellectual élite began recasting nature as a competitive market-place. They were the new constituency for evolution, committed to progress, technology, and the naturalizing of morals and man. As the champions of change, they were making the world safe for Darwin.

The focus of their alliance was the house of John Chapman at 142 the Strand. Chapman was a medical man by training – once Dr Gully's homoeopathist in fact – and a publisher by vocation. Not yet thirty, he had built an impressive list of the latest dissolvent literature, including titles by Newman, the Atkinson-Martineau *Letters*, and brash first books by Darwin's student friend, the retired millowner W. R. Greg, and by a budding journalist named Herbert Spencer. The catalogue was put together by the brilliant but unknown Marian Evans – later George Eliot – with whom Chapman and his wife shared an awkward *ménage*. Chapman had acquired the ailing *Westminster Review* and was refurbishing it as a platform for his authors. They came to his Friday soirées that summer, full of support for the new flagship of freethought and reform. Other dissidents joined them, 'the world's vanguard,' as Evans called them: there was the philosopher John Stuart Mill and the Unitarian physiologist William Carpenter, the author of *Vestiges*, Robert Chambers, and even the mellowing atheist Holyoake, just preparing to launch 'Secularism' as a moderate movement.[4] Soon an angry young ship's surgeon would join them, Thomas Henry Huxley.

As the warm weeks passed Evans laboured over a prospectus for the new journal. Chapman needed a document that would do justice to the common beliefs of his circle – beliefs in progress, melioration of ills, and rewards for talent. The four-page flyer went out to the intelligentsia at the end of August. This was a vital moment. For the first time, progressive evolution had collective middle-class support. What artisan agitators had risked gaol to proclaim now became 'the fundamental principle' of one of the nation's leading literary reviews. Chapman and Evans called it the 'Law of Progress.' The editors declared that 'the institutions of man, no less than the products of nature, are strong and durable in proportion as they are the results of gradual development.'[5]

But what sort of 'development' were the *Westminster* reviewers plumping for? There was no unanimity beyond the belief that evolution consisted of a perfectly natural, unbroken process. *Vestiges* conformed to this view, and Newman and Carpenter had thrown their weight behind the book. But it was still a hack-work, and flawed. None of the Chapman circle found it adequate now, certainly not Chambers himself, who was engaged in a major revision for the tenth edition. A smart, sophisticated, and scientifically reputable notion of evolution was an urgent need, and the dissidents were casting around for one. Chapman asked Richard Owen, but got nowhere. Anyhow Owen's idea of development was a Platonic ideal, something that existed in the divine Mind. The 'Law' of evolution would have to explain human life rather more materially. It would have to account for the magnificent sights of the Crystal Palace – industrial achievement, English supremacy, and above all progress.[6] Only one of Chapman's friends was grasping the nettle.

Herbert Spencer had been living on the cheap in the offices of *The Economist* where he worked. This was opposite Chapman's house, amid the 'eternal rattle' of the Strand, and Evans consulted him about the prospectus during the summer. He came from Derby, from Methodist and Unitarian stock; his *Social Statics*, published by Chapman the year before, was an attempt to recast the Dissenters' moral universe as a beneficent natural process. Spencer had long accepted evolution, seeing it as an accumulation of changes acquired and passed on by each individual. Progress was a necessity. It was a 'law underlying the whole organic creation;' civilization was 'a part of nature; all a piece with the development of the embryo or the unfolding of a flower.' It was a guarantee that evil will ultimately disappear and man 'become perfect.'[7]

By the summer of the Great Exhibition he realized that progress meant something more. George Lewes, another of Chapman's circle, introduced him to the French zoologist Henri Milne-Edwards's concept of the 'physiological division of labour.' And Carpenter convinced him that evolution was a continuous change from the 'general' to the 'special;' it honed organisms to their environments, adapted each to its task, as in Milne-Edwards's industrial analogy. Spencer now believed that what was true for animals held for society: progress came through specialization. Was it not Prince Albert who said that the 'great principle of the division of labour' was the 'moving power of civilization,' and that the Great Exhibition was a 'living picture of the point of development at which the whole of mankind has arrived'?[8]

However, a great stumbling block still had to be overcome, one that had damped down belief in human perfectibility for half a century. There were always too many mouths to feed, with never enough food to go round; a painful struggle for existence was inevitable. This was the Malthusian 'principle of population' and for most liberals its status was sacrosanct. Humanity's only hope lay in abstinence from sex until each couple had the means to support children. But such 'moral restraint,' as the Revd Malthus called it, had never been practised by the great mass of humanity.[9] If past experience counted for anything, Spencer's visionary faith was doomed.

In fact, the *Westminster* reviewers were deeply divided over Malthus. To those, like Holyoake, with working-class sympathies, Malthus's principle was an evil invention. It was the ideology of the workhouse, blaming poverty on the poor and blessing the rich. But to those who sided with the cotton kings and their apologists – like Greg and Martineau – the Malthusian principle was a beneficent law of nature, encouraging responsibility and self-improvement. Chapman was so concerned about the lack of unanimity that, on acquiring the *Review*, he asked Spencer to write about population in the first issue.

Spencer's 'Theory of Population deduced from the General Law of Animal Fertility' actually appeared in the second number. It had something for everyone – but the lion's share was for the comfortably well-off. In his view the painful Malthusian principle is both true and self-correcting. People who multiply beyond their means take 'the high road to extinction;' they die off in droves, as 'we have recently seen exemplified in Ireland.' Those who remain are 'the select of their generation.' Having exercised moral restraint and foresight, they bequeath their powers of 'self-preservation.' Progress is ensured, and eventually human wants and needs will be perfectly balanced: there will be no more mouths to feed than food.[10]

The Darwin family waited two months before going up to the Exhibition. Charles wanted to finish his volume on the stalked barnacles and deliver it to the publishers by hand. Emma also needed ample time to recover from Horace's birth. They all arrived mid-week, on 30 July, at Erasmus's Park Street town house in fashionable Mayfair. The Crystal Palace was only a short cab ride away, and just as well. Several trips were needed to take in all the exhibits. Etty and Georgy, aged eight and six, got bored; Uncle Ras plied them with sweets, and they stayed at home after that. But Charles and Emma had never seen anything like it. Only nature itself – an earthquake, a rain forest, a Fuegian savage – provoked greater awe. Vast whirling pumps and presses, loud clattering looms, stately boilers and hissing engines; glass-covered velvet stands decked with gold and silver finery; closely guarded caskets bearing a queen's ransom in gems – all this came from other worlds. But Charles tired easily. It was hot, the great glasshouse was packed, and he returned with headaches. Then his stomach erupted and pestered him for days.[11]

He missed Hooker. Hooker, like Lyell, was an Exhibition 'juror' – a scientific judge asked to draw up reports on the exhibits – and he took the job for the £100 as much as the kudos. By the time Charles came up, he was off in Paris with his bride, wining and dining with the other jurors at Louis Napoleon's expense. In London Charles had a servant deliver his only copy of the huge barnacle manuscript to the Ray Society. It was five years' work and he was 'very unwilling to trust it to the tender mercies of a public conveyance.' Nor could he leave for Downe‡ until he made sure others handled it with the same care. Send it to the printer by some 'trustworthy messenger,' he urged the Society, and confirm the fact at once. '*Forgive* my silly particularity,' he added, understandably concerned.[12]

Back in Downe life went on, one day like the next. An early breakfast, then barnacles until the post arrived; afterwards more barnacles, a brisk walk, and lunch; the afternoon for recovery, with

‡ The village changed its spelling to Downe in mid-century, to avoid confusion with County Down in Ireland. Down House retained the old spelling.

reading, letter-writing, and a nap; then another bout of barnacles until tea-time, followed by backgammon and bed. Nights for Charles were '*always* bad.' He could never clear his mind. Thoughts, or things he had seen, haunted him: an awkward dissection, a social indiscretion, a troublesome letter. Safe at home, the Exhibition still made him feel unwell.[13] The future troubled him too. A gentleman had to plan ahead. Prudent foresight had brought him the security he craved, including moderate wealth. But with seven small mouths to feed, his responsibilities were greater than ever. The family was now complete – 'send only condolences' if another child comes, he told Fox. It was the long-term he had to plan for.

The girls would take care of themselves under suitable governesses and Emma's example. The boys were the main concern – the five of them. They required solid, upstanding professions to enable them to live in the manner to which they were accustomed. Charles was in more than a pother about this 'bug-bear.' In their future hands lay the family fortune – if indeed there would be a fortune to pass on.[14]

Money was the root of the matter. On paper Charles and Emma were doing nicely. Their joint annual income had just passed £3000, putting them in the top few per cent of *rentiers* nationwide. It came from shrewd investment of their inherited capital. Besides the Beesby farm in Lincolnshire, valued at some £14,000, Charles had acquired assets worth about £40,000 on his father's death. The Doctor left him another Lincolnshire farm at Sutterton Fen, a £13,000 mortgage to the Earl of Powis, and sufficient other funds to enable him to invest massively in British and American industry. Emma, too, had profited handsomely from her father's will. Her assets were held in trust by brother Josiah and Erasmus Darwin, a contemporary caution to shield a wife from her husband's creditors. This Wedgwood wealth came to something over £25,000, including an interest in the family firm, canal and railway shares, and a big mortgage to the son of a Shropshire squire.[15] In all she and Charles had more than £80,000 in investments.

A large and growing proportion was in securities, mostly railway stock. Charles was financing the new age of iron and steam. Britain in 1851 had 6800 miles of track, seven times the length of all the rail networks of the five countries of western Europe put together. This achievement, like the building of the pyramids or the Great Wall of China, had cost dear. The railway boom had been a free-for-all, fuelled by mad speculation and condoned by laissez-faire. Fortunes were made overnight, then lost – and so were lives. Savants might

travel in sixty-mile-per-hour expresses to British Association meetings, but the carnage was awful with all the unregulated companies
competing to get there faster. Crashes became so common that the
papers reported only the major disasters. Carelessness was sometimes
to blame. Charles's friend Hugh Strickland was killed near Retford
station on his way home from the Hull meeting of the British
Association in 1853.[16] Geologizing his way through the railway
cuttings, he stood watching a coal train pass in one direction when
an express hit him from the other.

Charles himself was too cautious to make a killing on the railways.
He and Emma came into their money as the boom was subsiding, but
he still bided his time, bought when the market was sluggish, and
went in for low-risk loans. In 1847, after the spring panic and the rise
in interest rates, he began pouring thousands into the Leeds and
Bradford Railway. A few years later he got out of London and North
Western shares too late and lost about £800, but in 1854 he put
£20,000 into the Great Northern Railway and lived on the
proceeds for years. He had become an astute financier. 'The present
low prices of Guaranteed Railway shares,' he reasoned with his
Lincolnshire land agent, who was then scouting another farm for
him,

> has put it into my head, that I should act wiser in investing
> . . . in such shares; for supposing I could get nearly 5 per cent,
> the extra interest beyond what I shd. get from land, would
> during the rest of my life (as I do not spend my whole income)
> make up a depreciation fund at compound interest, to
> compensate for any fall in Gold.

That year his income went up to £4600 in all, half of which was
reinvested.[17]

But Charles did not come by this financial know-how easily. For
years he had read the news, watched the markets, taken expert advice.
Often he felt jittery too. On paper he and Emma were set up for life,
but in practice their future – and the boys' – could be jeopardized at a
stroke. Most of their income was vulnerable to stock-market fluctua-
tions. When shares fell, companies – the railways notoriously – went
to the wall, taking their investors with them. One panic could lead to
another and the railway bubble burst. He began to consider land a
safer bet. 'With my *large* & growing family,' Charles explained to
his land agent, asking him to look out a property worth
£5000, 'it behoves me to do my best in making safe & wise investments.'[18]

The Darwins weren't the only big family needing security in Downe. The villagers with their thriving broods far outnumbered the 'great folks,' and Charles – his 'patron' Henslow's example before him – was also giving them a stake in the economy. He now served as treasurer of the local Coal and Clothing Club, which the Revd Innes had asked him to take over. The kindly curate was a regular visitor to Down House, and one day as they exchanged pinches of snuff Charles had proposed starting a benefit society. It would teach 'our Clodhoppers' thrift, encourage them to lay up against sickness, old age, and death. A small monthly premium would bring them a few shillings weekly to live on and £5 to be buried with. Innes welcomed the plan, and in 1850 the Down Friendly Society was duly founded, with its 'clubroom' at the George and Dragon Inn, across from the parish church. Henslow helped them draw up the rules and regulations – a 2s. 6d. fine for swearing in the clubroom, 5s. for drunkenness or fighting, and expulsion from the Society for drinking, gambling, or working while receiving benefits. Darwin became guardian and treasurer, investing the men's pennies in the Bank of England.[19] His paternal responsibilities now extended far beyond the home.

He kept scrupulous accounts. It was his own insurance against public disgrace and private penury in uncertain times. Indeed, the signs were ominous in the early 1850s. Another 'bug-bear' was haunting him, gold. It caused mass migrations. In 1849 the glittering stuff was discovered in California; two years later came Australia's turn. People rushed to seek their fortunes – over 80,000 were lured from England to Australia in 1852 alone – and the fear was that capital would follow. With the price of gold rising, a surge of share-selling would follow. Once the rush started it would be too late. His and Emma's portfolios would be wiped out, the family ruined. The boys would have to move and he would 'certainly emigrate' with them. For without a comfortable inheritance, their prospects in England were nil. They could all 'slave for years in any profession and not make a penny.'

'Though I am a rich man,' he wrote to his old ship's servant Covington, long since relocated down-under, 'when I think of the future I very often ardently wish I was settled in one of our Colonies ... Tell me how far you think a gentleman with capital would get on in New South Wales ... What interest can you get for money in a safe investment? How dear is food ... How much land have you?' Actually, the place Charles said 'I fancy most' was 'the middle States of N. America.' The Empire also held out promise, a bolthole if the

15
Emma Wedgwood at the time of her marriage to Charles in 1839.

16
Charles and Emma's first home, 'Macaw Cottage', 12 Upper Gower Street. Darwin finished devising his theory of evolution here in 1839.

17
Troops marching through hostile crowds to Euston Station, on their way to suppress the Manchester riots in August 1842. For three days the battalions passed close by Darwin's house.

18
Charles and his eldest
son William in an
1842 daguerreotype:
the only known
photograph of Darwin
with a member of his
family.

19
Darwin's old study: to the right his tiers of working files, to the left a curtained
privy. His book-lined back wall is reflected in the mirror on the mantelpiece.

20
The photo Darwin wept over for life, his beloved Annie (b. 1841), at the time of her first trip to Malvern. Her tragic death at Easter 1851 destroyed the final shreds of Darwin's Christianity.

21
Charles's freethinking elder brother Erasmus, after a decade of 'literary leisure' and opium-eating.

22
Emma aged about fifty, after bearing her tenth child.

23
Revd John Brodie Innes, Tory High Churchman, Darwin's vicar and confidant: 'one of those rare mortals' from whom 'one can differ and yet feel no shade of animosity'.

24
Darwin in 1854, finished with barnacles at last. The strain had begun to show.

already showed the 'hereditary principle' in his passion for collecting butterflies. Charles paid the school a visit. It looked good, and it was 'cheap *with extras* about 80£' per annum. But it seemed an 'awful experiment' to make on one's eldest son. Charles was already paying the Vicar of Mitcham in Surrey, Henry Wharton, £75 a term to drill Willy in nothing 'but the Latin grammar.' Willy was getting on swimmingly. If a boy who can conquer Latin can conquer anything, as Charles believed, why disrupt the process? There was 'so much novelty' at Bruce Castle – who could predict the result?

Better to play safe and follow the example of his eminent neighbour Sir John Lubbock. He had sent his eldest to Eton, one of the 'great schools,' and already the seventeen-year-old could be seen setting out each morning from High Elms with his father to catch the train for the City, where they were banking partners. Worse fates could befall a firstborn. And young John was turning into an excellent naturalist. Charles helped him with dissections and found him 'a remarkably amiable pleasant young man.' No, one of the public schools it was. It was an agonizing decision. Charles hated the 'old stereotyped stupid classical education,' which he remembered all too well from Shrewsbury.[23] Such was his aversion that he even dispensed with the wretched Latin descriptions in the second volume of his Ray Society monograph, on the acorn-shell barnacles. But it was better to be safe than sorry: Willy would follow his Wedgwood uncles to Rugby. At £120 per annum all-in, it was still cheaper than his tutor. Willy started in February 1852.

He fitted in perfectly. At the Revd Wharton's he had learned to overcome his adolescent awkwardness, to put away 'grave & gruff manners' and strive to 'please *everybody*' he met. Charles never regretted sending him to the genteel old school. Rugby remained Anglican through and through: the headmaster's predecessor and successor both became Archbishops of Canterbury. But the reforms of Thomas Arnold a generation earlier had paid off, and the school was now grooming future bankers, industrialists, and politicians – an oligarchy for the Empire. Formation of character, development of moral muscle, and a sense of duty were all implicit within the curriculum, and Charles heartily approved. If anything, he wished Rugby did more to develop character. Altogether he felt sure that the risk of exposing a boy to 'the temptations of the world' would be reduced once he had 'undergone the milder ordeal of a great school.' His only regret was in tearing Willy from 'the affections of the family' at so tender an age. He missed his son. And it was not long before he noted that Willy's 'steady attention to classics' was having economy plunged. 'The English certainly are a noble race,' he added, 'and a grand thing it is that we have got securely hold of Australia and New Zealand.' Covington's reply egged him on, and soon they were back in regular correspondence. Charles wanted to hear about the gold. He was amazed to learn that 'all great and novel schemes' for working the mines were 'planned & executed' by American immigrants. The colony was 'getting decidedly republican,' Covington said. This struck Charles as the best of both worlds, and before long he was reading every book he could on Australia.[20]

There was another reason to emigrate. On 2 December 1851 Louis Napoleon seized power in a *coup d'état*. The spectre of a new Napoleonic empire sent the patriotic British into a spin. 'The fall of France seems decreed by Heaven,' Emma's Aunt Jessie mused. 'Now I think everything may be possible, even an invasion.' Over dinner at Downe Capt. Sulivan frightened everybody with his scenario for a French landing and occupation of the home counties. It left Charles with a recurrent nightmare of the French army sweeping up 'the Westerham & Sevenoaks roads' in a pincer movement and surrounding Downe. Seeing the village cut off by Napoleon – the 'Beast' as Jessie called him (from personal acquaintance) – was not total paranoia. Charles's friends were equally vehement. The anti-Catholic Lyell cursed the dictator 'and his pretorian guards and Jesuits.' There was enough of a threat to set England cleaning 'old rusty cannons' and Prince Albert begging his brother for 'a Prussian needle-gun.' The government actually fell in the new year after Lord Palmerston forced a debate on whether a local or national militia should be revived.[21]

Of course the French did not invade, and the Darwins remained safe at Downe. The family fortune grew by leaps and bounds while the sons prepared to take it over. The boys' education as much as anything ensured that Darwin stayed put, and his moans about 'bugbears' rapidly became a ritual. 'Oh the professions, oh the gold, & oh the French,' he stuttered to Fox. Really there was only one nagging uncertainty.[22] 'The worst of my bugbears,' he complained, 'is heredetary [sic] weakness.'

Twelve-year-old Willy, the future head of the family, was 'backward for his age.' Darwin agonized over the boy's education. He toyed with the Bruce Castle School in Tottenham, north of London. Founded by Rowland Hill, inventor of the penny post, it reinforced class distinctions, emphasized rigid discipline, and gave scope to modern languages and science. This might be good for Willy, who

26
Alfred Russel Wallace,
the young animal
collector from the Malay
Archipelago. His letter
prompted Darwin to
start writing the *Origin
of Species*.

27
Ilkley Wells hydropathic hotel on the North Yorkshire moors, where Darwin
was 'living in Hell' as he sent out advance copies of the *Origin*.

25
His sounding board, the botanist Joseph Hooker, photographed at the same
time.

a 'contracting effect' on his mind, 'checking interest in anything in which reasoning & observation come into play.' He vowed to send his other boys to a 'smaller school, with more diversified studies,' and nearer home.[24]

Willy came home for the summer, and everybody had a splendid time. The main attraction was gangly Uncle Ras, who stayed for weeks. The children had never seen him for more than a few days at a time, when they visited London. Now they had him all to themselves, to drag around their garden haunts, to pommel into submission. Such excitement – Eras was totally unused to it. He lived on his own except for servants, at forty-seven a confirmed bachelor. His demeanour was languid, his disposition melancholic, as if he had resigned himself to some unmentionable fate. But he shone at dinner parties, where his playful wit made him the 'universal solvent,' and he delighted his nieces and nephews. He loved them dearly – especially Hensleigh and Fanny Wedgwood's six – as only a man could who longed for a family of his own. And the children adored him. Romping with them, he escaped his world-weariness. He got down on his hands and knees and became a playmate.[25] The little Darwins never forgot the fun.

Three of them had birthdays in those months – Georgy and Lizzy on successive days in July – and celebrations were held. But no school chums joined them, no village friends dropped in. The children's life was self-contained, with only Uncle Ras and the household staff on hand. Charles did take at least one of them round the Sandwalk each day, but for hours on end he was secreted away with his barnacles. The boys began to look on the study as a 'sacred place,' not to be entered 'without some really urgent cause.' One of them finally resorted to bribery – Emma's ploy for getting their co-operation – by offering him sixpence if he would come out and play.[26] Of course Charles could not resist. But still, after Uncle Ras left the children felt bored; their usual inventiveness had to be rediscovered.

Horace hurled toys in the playroom watched by the new nurse – Brodie never recovered after Annie's death – and Lenny, now two, tottered menacingly, throwing his considerable weight around. The older boys stuck together. Willy took the lead, when his nose was not in a book. Georgy and four-year-old Franky struggled to keep up. They leapt from the banisters over the top-floor stairwell, swinging precariously on a trapeze suspended from the ceiling, with much 'crashing and banging and shouting.' In the garden a swing was suspended between the twin yew trees, suitable for the girls. Stilts came in two styles, short ones on which 'even girls had been known to walk,' and the pair that made a boy as big as Uncle Ras. These were for outdoor use, for scaling the humpy landscape like Papa's friend Mr Hooker in the Himalayas.[27]

Etty and Lizzy usually stayed near the house. They were born four years apart, and Emma did little to bridge the gap. She had Charles to look after, and the babies to attend at intervals; so the girls attached themselves in turn to the cook, governess, or nurse, with Etty helping Mama as allowed. Sometimes they traipsed over to great-aunt Sarah Wedgwood's in the village. Her huge house, Petleys, lay just opposite the pond, only a quarter-mile across the fields. She had come there in 1847, a spinster in her seventies, waiting to die. Encounters with her were 'rather awful but rare events.' But her servants were the real attraction. Ringing the back door always brought a cheerful welcome. Martha Hemmings taught them catchy tunes and Mrs Morrey served heavenly gingerbread. The girls could wander about the garden, where the flowers had a 'mysterious charm,' picking the plums in autumn.[28]

But none of this made up for the girls' lack of stimulus at home. With busy grown-ups on the one hand, babies on the other, and a gang of brothers in between, they had to fend for themselves – separately too often. Rare trips to Jos and Caroline's at Leith Hill in Surrey, where there were three female cousins, helped a bit. The family went for a week in September. Etty renewed old friendships but Lizzy, the youngest, behaved like a stranger. Now that she was five, her isolation was beginning to tell. She easily became tongue-tied, using words in the oddest way, and she seemed increasingly self-absorbed. When concentrating on something, Lizzy had begun by 'twiddling her fingers as Charles used to do,' but now she had grown into the habit of 'talking to herself for an hour.' And 'she does not like to be interrupted,' her worried mother noted. The little monkey 'shivers & makes ... extraordinary grimaces,' Charles observed. 'Poor little dear.'[29]

One thing they did do together was attend the parish church. Lizzy, Lenny, and Horace had been christened there; Emma regularly took the sacrament. On Sunday the boys put on their best jackets, Etty and Lizzy their frocks, and they all trooped up the Luxted Road, past Aunt Sarah's, to the centre of the village. Charles sometimes went along, but nowadays he left them at the lychgate and set off on a stroll. The Revd Innes understood perfectly. He enjoyed Charles's backing in parish business, but only Mrs Darwin and the children were to be expected. Emma led her brood into the large family pew at the front, just beneath the lectern. Its green baize covering, the whitewashed walls, the organ now sounding better than ever – all owed something to Charles's largesse. When the Creed came to be recited, however, Emma kept faith with her heritage. The congregation turned to face the altar but she faced forward, refusing any truck with Trinitarianism.

Outside was the one sure chance each week to see new faces. The children gawked, but scarcely mixed. There were labourers in smocks – some the worse for Saturday night – with wives and babes in arms and the children scrubbed clean; tradesmen with their families exchanging friendly gossip; the awesome Sir John Lubbock, High Sheriff of Kent, followed out of church by eight sons.[30] The Darwins observed the differences and stood apart, on Sundays not least.

For an upwardly-mobile ex-Methodist such as Spencer, large, well-fed families like the Darwins represented the cutting-edge of progress – 'the select of their generation.' This is what his theory predicted – a theory of human ascent that was moving closer towards Darwin's own. Ideas on progress, population, and evolution were catching on among the literary freethinkers in London. A social network was forming, and one day it would serve Darwin well.

Spencer went fishing for proofs of evolution in Owen's lectures at the College of Surgeons. But Owen abhorred transmutation, the more vehemently because High Church 'reptiles' had accused him of pantheism and of promoting the infidel doctrine himself, which he adamantly denied. Spencer tried Owen again with his new theory of human population. Or rather Chapman did. Would the great comparative anatomist lend his weight to the dissenters' cause? Owen had read Spencer's *Westminster* article, he told Chapman; but no, he would not pronounce on its merits. Given Owen's 'known caution as to new views,' Spencer took consolation and he continued to canvass support.[31]

Copies of Spencer's article went out to 'leading men,' who acknowledged them politely. One went to an astute, dark-eyed young naturalist, making his name with a series of technical studies on sea-squirts. This was Thomas Huxley. Twenty-seven years old and fiercely ambitious, he had returned from a four-year stint on the surveying ship HMS *Rattlesnake* just in time for the Great Exhibition. Angry, down on his luck, out of money, he had been ekeing out an existence, searching in vain for a job. Universities turned him down; the Admiralty refused to pay him to write up his shipboard research and the Royal Society wouldn't either. He was on the point of badgering Owen (yet again) for a testimonial, this time to send to the Secretary of State himself.

Huxley was livid: in science England wanted all the credit without paying the cost. One had to be an independent gentleman to make a vocation of it. Here he was, a newly elected Fellow of the Royal Society, living in tawdry St John's Wood. He could not even afford decent lodgings, let alone bring his fiancée from Australia where they had parted three years before. Talk about Malthusian 'moral restraint' – this was ridiculous; it drove him 'wild.' Months of lecture-grubbing and other profitless pursuits left him in despair. How he had envied Hooker at the British Association a year ago, destined to succeed his father as the Director at Kew, and engaged to Professor Henslow's daughter, who was sitting by his side. Huxley's mother had just died, leaving his own father a dependent mental wreck.[32] When Spencer's article arrived in September, Huxley was close to a break-down.

Something sparked between them. Maybe it was Spencer's sanguine theory, maybe his ingenuous accompanying note. Huxley called on him straightaway and they rapidly became friends. Spencer, five years older, was a schoolmaster's son like himself and had already tasted success. At least he lived adequately by his pen. They both were bachelors with lady problems, although Spencer's were quite different: he could not get away from Marian Evans, who was infatuated with him. Huxley and Spencer spent afternoons at the zoo, evenings at Covent Garden – and Spencer moved to St John's Wood to make their meetings easier. They became sparring partners too. Huxley was a freethinker like the *Westminster* set but his approach to natural history was idiosyncratic. He would have none of Owen's etherial 'archetype' – that mythical ideal of vertebrate structure – still less of evolution. He dismissed the author of *Vestiges* as a crackpot and thought that Spencer, the evolutionist he knew best, needed a dose of expert advice. It was bad science, Huxley warned him, and harmful to one's career. There was no inexorable ascent in nature. Those who toyed with a '*chain* of beings' always ended up in shackles. Spencer, riding back with him from Lewes's house in Kensington, past the Crystal Palace, retorted that he no more accepted that symbol than Huxley did. The 'true symbol' was a tree.[33]

27

Ugly Facts

DARWIN'S HEALTH was holding up – just. He was still keeping a running record. Every day, morning and night, he scratched cryptic notes in a foolscap diary. Using minuscule handwriting, he made one cramped page cover a whole month. He had code-words for the water cure, special terms for how he felt, and left spaces in between for the nasty symptoms. It was obsessive work. 'Very well,' with double underlining, meant he was comfortable enough for a three-hour stint of barnacles. 'Poorly' meant he was incapacitated by some ache or pain, or plagued by his stomach. Towards the end of 1852 the number of hale 'double dash' days was on the increase. He totted them up each month, a rough index of his well-being. For over a year the index had hovered in the teens – half the time he had been under the weather – but by December there were twenty-four double dashes, his second best month. Nights were still bad, 'wakeful' was how he described them.[1] Yet the days had become pleasantly productive. He was in the pink and decided to take a risk.

He stopped the water cure. The aquatic ritual had been performed religiously until Annie died. Morning baptisms in the garden hut were his salvation, and even when away from home he had begun his day in a shivery shower or dripping sheet. But the trauma of his last trip to Malvern had tainted everything connected with the ritual, right down to the snuff allowed by Gully, which Annie used to fetch. And Gully himself, having failed to save the girl, was no longer his patron saint. Charles went on dowsing himself intermittently, his faith faltering. He experimented with other remedies, including 'electric chains' made of brass and zinc wires. He looped them around his neck and waist, then drenched his skin with vinegar. They did nothing for him but tingle and leave unsightly marks. Finally he

405

decided that his health index was more or less water-resistant, and at the end of November he turned off the tap. Hydropathy only helped to ease his mind; when he felt really agitated, it was useless.

And what really agitated him was still London. A day trip to the city brought on violent vomiting. Even the prospect of going made him unwell. Painful or intense thoughts had similar effects, regardless of where he was, or with whom. When Hooker came to Downe for a week, Charles was ill half the time. They tangled over species and the stress left him on the sofa. On 18 November they were due to meet to attend the Duke of Wellington's funeral at St Paul's Cathedral. It was the fourth anniversary of his own father's funeral, which he had missed through illness, and the memory left him doubled up the night before. Alone with his thoughts, he was miserable for the first time in weeks.[2] But the next day the state spectacle monopolized their attention, and Charles – who revelled in pomp – felt fine again.

Tens of thousands braved the damp and cold to pay their last respects to the 'Iron Duke,' among them young Huxley. Arriving early at the cathedral, he got a 'capital seat' at the front, and remained there frozen from eight until three. Darwin would not have recognized him – they had never met – but Huxley had sent him a scientific paper or two, and they were now in correspondence. A testimonial from Darwin failed to get Huxley a post at the University of Toronto, and he was still doing odd jobs, cataloguing the sea-squirts in the British Museum and so on. He was also taking an interest in other marine invertebrates. Darwin had sent him the first barnacle volume. (The price – a subscription to the Ray Society – was beyond Huxley's means.) Technical quibbles aside, Huxley thought the monograph was one of the 'most beautiful and complete' of its kind, and 'the more remarkable' coming from a distinguished geologist, 'not an anatomist *ex professo*.'[3] When he and Darwin finally came face to face, at the Geological Society in April 1853, he mooted reviewing it.

Darwin was pretty shrewd. Years of cajoling correspondents for barnacles – a bit like extracting money from his father – had taught him how to get what he wanted, and what he wanted now was a good press. So he baited Huxley.[4] On the shelf were some splendid sea-squirts in spirits – 'it would give me *real pleasure* should you wish to have and examine them.' And how about a copy of Johannes Müller's German book on echinoderms, 'which is really wasted on me, and would be at the service of *anyone* who would value it'? By the way, 'it would give me *great* pleasure to see my work reviewed by any one so capable as you.' 'Upon my honour I never did such a

thing before as suggest ... a review to any human being. But ...' –
and, having done so, he went on to specify those 'most curious
points' he wanted mentioned: the cement glands, the homologies, the
'sexual peculiarities.' 'I daresay I *greatly* exaggerate their curiosity,'
he half-apologized, 'for I have become a man of one idea,' barnacles
'morning & night.'

Huxley did not bite, but the contact was good for future reference.
Here was an established gentleman-naturalist who wanted his support. Patronage had stranger guises. There could be something in it
for them both.

Darwin was pleased to see his first volume in print, announcing
'my little friends, the complemental males.' 'I greatly feared that no
one w^d believe in them,' he told Albany Hancock, '& now I know
that Owen, Dana & yourself are believers, I am most heartily
content.' Besides, there were further curious discoveries to report in
volume two, on the acorn-shell barnacles. Darwin was bedevilled by
the sheer unpredictability of these beasts, just as he had been by their
stalked cousins. Every time he hit an abnormal type, like Hancock's
Alcippe, he was 'almost driven mad.' To his surprise, he found this
parasitic barnacle nothing like *Arthrobalanus*, despite the presence of
tiny males. It was 'one of the most difficult creatures' he had ever
attempted to make out. Females had the most uncongenial life – and
presumably felt like Darwin on a bad day: 'after a good meal,' he
said, they have 'to vomit forth the residuum, for there is no other
exit!' The males, of course, were even odder, he prodded Lyell,
and 'the most negative creatures in the world; they have no mouth, no
stomach, no thorax, no limbs, no abdomen, they consist wholly of the
male reproductive organs in an envelope.' He had found twelve of
these living negations '*permanently* attached by cement to one female!'[5]

Yet, for all their sex appeal, the barnacles remained a chore.
Darwin had come to hate them 'as no man ever did before, not even a
Sailor in a slow-sailing ship.' He was 'working like a slave,' chained
to his desk, seeing almost no one except Sowerby the engraver, going
up to London once a month or less, and only when forced. He kept
missing deadlines – his health index dropped – and the seventh year
of his odyssey was speeding by. The younger children saw it as his
life's work; they had never known Papa do anything else. Indeed, they
began to think all adults must be similarly employed, leading one to
ask of a neighbour, 'Where does he do *his* barnacles?' The end,
though, was now in sight. In the autumn the 'everlasting barnacles'
were all but through.[6] Darwin felt quietly proud, but nothing prepared
him for the news in November as he was finishing off.

He was summoned to London. The Royal Society wished to bestow on him that 'Philosophic Order of Knighthood,' the Royal Medal. Traditionally awarded to a naturalist who had published in the Society's journal, the Royal Medal that year – for the first time – was thrown open to all comers. It was initially intended to honour Darwin's three volumes on the geology of the *Beagle* voyage plus his invertebrate research; but at the final meeting of the Council, Hooker reported ecstatically, there was 'such a shout of paeans for the Barnacles that you would have [sunk] to hear.' The news brought tears to Darwin's eyes. And hearing it from 'one that is loved … made me glow with pleasure till my very heart throbbed.' Of course, self-effacing as ever, he thought it '*ridiculous*' that his rival for the award, the botanist John Lindley, had not got the medal 'long before me' (and he was careful to nominate Lindley himself in subsequent years). But it suddenly made his whole prodigious project worthwhile. 'When work goes badly & one ruminates that all is vanity,' he beamed to Hooker, 'it is pleasant to have some tangible proof, that others have thought something of one's labours.'[7]

Darwin received the medal in person at the anniversary meeting of the Royal Society on 30 November 1853. It was traumatic as always, going to the podium to express a few words of thanks, faced by the serried rows of savants. He stood flanked by the two Secretaries, with the President sitting behind; above him was a huge chandelier, hanging from the ornate ceiling, and on the walls all around two centuries of British scientific gentlemen captured in oils, staring at him. The medal was a great 'nugget,' he boasted to Covington, out in the Australian gold fields, having to dig the hard way for his; 'it weighs 40 sovereigns.' But the command performance sent him back to the bath for a spell, after a year's break. The water did the trick, his health index shot back up and the *matins* ceased. Then, with an enormous, protracted sigh of relief, he put his second, 900-page barnacle manuscript to bed.

What had started as a few months' work in 1846 on one strange, boring barnacle ended almost eight years later in two technical treatises overhauling the entire sub-class. It was the longest piece of sustained research he would ever undertake; and it was punctuated by the worst illness, tragedy, and despair he would ever endure. Had he gone 'the way of all flesh' at this point, he would have been remembered as a tropical traveller and gentleman geologist who had withdrawn into his lonely shell to conquer the least archetypal of crustaceans. (Indeed, the novelist Bulwer-Lytton would immortalize him as the blinkered boffin 'Professor Long' who had written 'two huge volumes on Limpets.') He had persevered, Job-like, to become the world's authority on barnacles. His was a monumental, definitive work, with a hundred printed pages on the fossil forms and over a thousand on the living ones. It established him as a zoological specialist, and no longer just the geological expert. More important, it was his licence to speak on species.[8] He had taken Hooker at his word all those years ago and earned this right. No one deserved it more.

After so much wrist-aching, eye-straining work, Darwin some days yearned for the old romance of geology. He liked a humdrum life, but he still experienced a twinge of envy as friends came and went. Lyell, back from America, turned him green with his talk of exhuming '3 skeletons of Reptiles out of the *Carboniferous* strata.' He was setting sail again for Madeira in December. Darwin was left at Downe, building air-castles: 'It really makes me quite envious to think of you clambering up & down those steep valleys ... I often think of the delight which I felt when examining volcanic islands; & I can remember even particular rocks which I struck – & the smell of the hot, black, scoriaceous cliffs.' He daydreamed of more exotic places: 'Tasmania has been my head quarters of late,' he said after hearing that the colonial government was financing Hooker's *Flora Tasmania*; 'I feel very proud of my adopted country.'

There was vicarious pleasure in Hooker's *Himalayan Journals*, with their vivid descriptions of the perilous mountain terrain: 'one can feel that one has seen it,' Darwin reported after devouring the book, '& desperately uncomfortable I felt in going over some of the Bridges.' His complimentary copy arrived in February 1854, and with it another shock – it was dedicated to him. Since the Antarctic voyage Hooker had wanted to honour his friend in a book, 'out of love for your own "Journal".' And he had gone about testing the waters in a devilish way: he had asked Darwin how *Lyell* would like it dedicated to him. 'You *bad* man,' Darwin laughed when he twigged, 'who ever would have dreamed of you being so *crafty*?'[9]

His voyages complete, the wanderlust over, Hooker was now happy to stay at home and 'jog-trot at Botany till the end of my days.' He was at last settling down: 'the craving of 30 years is satisfied.' He was mellowing into a family man, with a son, born in 1853, and a thumping daughter – eleven pounds at birth – in June 1854. 'Did you administer the Chloroform?' inquired Darwin, an old hand; it is 'very composing to oneself as well as to the patient.' Hooker's star was rising and becoming brighter all the time. Darwin mentioned him to an acquaintance, saying 'we shall see him some day the first Botanist in Europe,' only to be pulled up sharp: 'Sir, he is decidedly *now* the first Botanist in Europe.' The first botanist was a fast friend, everything Darwin had hoped for. He dug out the secret letter to Emma, concerning the £400 to edit his ten-year-old essay, and scribbled on the cover definitively: 'Hooker by far best man to edit my Species volume.'[10]

Another potential editor was rising fast. In London that year Darwin again met the jovial Edward Forbes and found him looking well. Forbes was hoping to take the natural history chair at Edinburgh. Jameson, now old and creaky, had hung on to it too long – fifty years – and not without some unkind cuts. Darwin, who never forgave his dull lectures, described him as an 'old brown, dry stick;' others called him 'a baked mummy.'[11] Forbes had long wanted the chair, and when Jameson died in April, he got it.

By now Darwin was relatively hearty. As an insurance he sucked lemons, whole ones twice a day, which were supposed to be good for the stomach, and he felt safe enough to come out into society. In the spring of 1854 he finally accepted an invitation to join the Royal Society's élite Philosophical Club. In years to come it would be the powerhouse of evolutionary science, but for the moment Darwin was to rub shoulders with the young guard: a whole cadre – Huxley, his good friends George Busk and the pugnacious Irish physicist John Tyndall among them – were elected the following year. The Club suited Darwin perfectly. 'Only two or three days ago,' he told Hooker in March, 'I was regretting to my wife, how I was letting drop & being dropped by nearly all my acquaintances, & that I would endeavour to go oftener to London.' Now he could see fresh faces, be lionized, catch the gossip among the new men – the ones, he hoped, who would swing behind his species work. To his surprise, he rather enjoyed his trips to town. They 'suit my stomach admirably,' he admitted in May. 'I begin to think, that dissipation, high-living, with lots of claret is what I want, & what I had during the last visit. – We are going to act on this same principle & in a very profligate manner have just taken a pair of Season-tickets to see the Queen open the Crystal Palace.'[12]

Paxton's huge iron-frame, glass-curtain building had been dismantled and re-erected at Sydenham in south London, where it occupied a spacious site, laid out with beautiful gardens, artificial lakes, and even Owen's life-size concrete dinosaurs. The Hookers could visit Downe and take in the Crystal Palace grounds on the way home: 'paradisaical,' they called it after one weekend – 'We both of us said we had never spent 5 happier days since our marriage.' The

Queen visited time and again, once even escorting Louis Napoleon when Charles and party attended, although on this outing 'Aunt Elizabeth fainted dead away' which was rather 'frightening & disagreeable.'[13]

Generally Charles loved these social occasions. He preferred strolling around the Palace to attending Royal Society meetings, and given the choice – 'pray conceal the scandalous fact,' he ordered Huxley – he did just that. Huxley, intent on stamping out the Society's old amateur ethos, was the last person he should have confessed to. But Charles remained a country gentleman at heart, so different from the rising generation, who clamoured for professional reforms. In many ways he kept both feet in the old school. When Huxley talked of his 'scientific young England,' he envisioned new standards, new status, new rewards: a science seized from the old clergy's hands and revamped – naturalized – and made serviceable to new mercantile masters. The spider-stuffers, the 'old buffers,' the country parsons – all had to go.[14] But the professionals still needed a new legitimating philosophy, a new competitive, capitalist sanction in place of Anglican Oxbridge paternalism; a dynamic biological science to replace the old static, creative hierarchy. And Huxley at this stage had no idea who would provide it.

The societies were transforming rapidly, with great stirs inside the Royal and even the soporific Linnean, which Darwin joined in 1854 in the hope of new times. The Royal Society was now awash with fresh blood, and it showed in the way the medals were falling. Huxley took the Royal Medal in 1852; Tyndall was named with Darwin in 1853, and Hooker in 1854, for his work on 'the origin and distribution' of plants. The pushing and prodding on Darwin's part had paid off for Hooker too. These young bloods were all destined to be 'scientific giants,' Darwin prophesied; and he thought it only right that the young men should get the accolades, to spur them on.[15]

In fact, the fast non-Oxbridge set were already sliding into positions of power. Huxley got his break in November 1854 and started regular teaching at the Royal School of Mines in Jermyn Street, Piccadilly. Then, 'sick of the dilettante middle class,' he began his famous working men's lectures a year later. Tyndall had taken the chair of natural philosophy at the Royal Institution in 1853, and was soon helping Huxley run the science section of the *Westminster Review*. Hooker, following in his father's footsteps, was shortly to become ensconced at Kew Gardens. All of them swore by London, 'the centre of the world.'[16] Here they would stay and make their mark.

*

Biology was liberalizing, along with society. Looked at from inside or out, there was real change. Even one man of the cloth, the Revd Baden Powell, Savilian Professor of Geometry at Oxford (and father of the Chief Scout), was sympathetic to evolution. Admittedly, he was an extreme liberal and his argument theological: God is a lawgiver – miracles break the lawful edicts issued at Creation, therefore belief in miracles is atheistic. QED. A clever riposte to miracle-mongering Creationists. He was an idiosyncratic Anglican apologist. 'These parsons,' Hooker complained, 'are so in the habit of dealing with the abstraction of doctrines as if there was no difficulty about them whatever . . . that they gallop over the [science] course . . . as if we were in the pews and they in the pulpit. Witness the self confident style of . . . Baden Powell.'[17]

Hooker was coming around. He had not embraced Darwin's new gospel but, 'Oh dear, oh dear,' he sighed to the botanist Asa Gray at the Harvard Herbarium, 'my mind is not fully, faithfully, implicitly given to species as created entities *ab origine*.' In fact, he could see that 'Creation' was empty verbiage. 'It is very easy to talk of the creation of a species,' he agreed with Darwin, 'but the *idea* is no more tangible than that of the Trinity & . . . is neither more nor less than a superstition – a believing in what the human mind cannot grasp.'

The problem Hooker still faced was a common one: the origin of life itself. He could follow Darwin 'back to the vital spark' – and then what? Surely *this* involved 'a vis creatrix or whatever you may call it; which is a fact as inscrutable as a full blown species.' But unlike the atheists, seeking an alternative to Anglican Creationism in a chemical soup, Darwin kept ultimate origins out of the picture. Life's initial appearance on the earth was inscrutable, he implied to Hooker. All that should concern the naturalist was its subsequent change. The origin of the first living globule was as irrelevant as the origin of matter was to the 'laws of chemical attraction.' At its starkest, he insisted, the only question was 'whether species of a genus have had a common ancestor.'[18]

This narrow focus left his project looking more professional, less ideological. It had to, if he was to bring about a *coup d'état* in science. It distanced his study from the shabbier cosmological works, the sort that left his Church mentors foaming. Rival evolutionists all betrayed their reforming, anti-Anglican intent. Herbert Spencer's 'law' of progress in *Social Statics* had been generalized in 1852 as 'the development hypothesis' in a disreputable rag, *The Leader*. Robert Chambers's *Vestiges* had been relaunched a year later in a slick tenth edition. Robert Grant, now a melancholy sixty-year-old, laughed at by Huxley and Forbes, was still insisting on the 'direct generation' of one species from another. Then again, stop on a street corner in 1854, or drop into a newsagent around Fleet Street, and pick up the scurrilous *London Investigator* for a penny and read its shocking revelations on the 'origin of man.'[19] Here, in a crusading atheistic paper, the emphasis was on co-operation rather than the fit and rich killing the weak and wan. Each of these offered a cosmic alternative to 'Creation' – an upward-sweeping progression, powered from below, underwritten by strict laws. And all promoted, as part of a naturalistic package, the atomic origin of life. They were levelling, progressive, democratic works.

And that is what petrified Lyell. Man would lose his 'high estate,' his special status in creation. He would be reduced to gutter level. Lyell was still shoring up human dignity, protecting it from radical degradation. He was still denying any progress (or therefore transmutation) in the history of life. No species had a genealogy, least of all the noblest one, on whom God had conferred immortality. As late as 1851 he had reaffirmed to the Geological Society that there had been *no* 'gradual advance towards a more perfect organization . . . resembling that of man.'[20]

Sir Charles Lyell was an urbane Whig, Unitarian by conviction, wealthy by inheritance. He called Harley Street his home when not travelling on the Continent or occupying his Scottish family seat. Politics to him was all of a piece with religion, and religion with science. The 'high estate' of man was his own, and he guarded it jealously. Back from Madeira, he and Lady Lyell spent several days at Downe with Hooker and his wife. Species were on the agenda, and the party cost Darwin two nights' sleep. Lyell boggled at Darwin's 'ugly facts.' It was these anomalous facts, he warned his brother-in-law afterwards, 'which will figure in C. Darwin's book on "Species".'[21] Lyell saw the writing on the wall and began mulling over mutability again, worrying once more about mankind's place in nature.

Darwin's strategy, as old as his own notebooks, was to stick to species and let Creation collapse by itself. And his Malthusian, capitalist, competitive mechanism was quite unlike any rival evolutionary theory. He pooh-poohed the attacks of libertarians and socialists on Malthus's 'most logical writings.' Many doubted that more food led to more animals, which were therefore doomed to struggle. Some claimed the reverse: that potting plants in rich soil actually *lessened* their fertility. Darwin thought this absurd and experimented with seed-beds and compost to prove it.[22] Not for him old William Godwin's optimism of a naturally progressive meliorating society. Darwin's version of evolution promised no inevitably rosy progress based on utopian co-operation. On the other hand it did underwrite many reformers' demands: for free trade and unfettered competition, for a breaking of the old 'unnatural' monopolies and privileges. It made Nature an ally of the middle-classes.

But could he convert a tyro such as Huxley, who was contemptuous of the rabble-rousing, evolutionary pot-boilers? Huxley scorned the 'cynics who delight in degrading man.' He thought that Grant had missed his vocation and that Spencer misunderstood science. While his fellow writers on the *Westminster Review* were sympathetic to a meliorating evolution, Huxley was not. He savaged the *Vestiges* so badly as to cause him qualms later. Progressive transmutation was 'pretentious nonsense,' he pronounced in his brash way. The rancour stemmed partly from his own predicament; he was disgusted to see an author making a mint from his 'charlatanerie.' Huxley hated the book because it explained nothing. To his mind *Vestiges*'s theme – 'creation by law' – was gibberish. Natural law, conceived as a divine edict causing the development of life, had no 'intelligible meaning at all.' It offered no '*explanation* of creation,' short of saying that it was an 'orderly miracle.'[23]

'How capitally you analyse his notion about law,' Darwin cooed, knowing that such shafts could not be aimed at him. But for the rest he had mixed feelings, and ultimately thought Huxley too hard on the hapless book. 'I am perhaps no fair judge,' he teased, 'for I am almost as unorthodox about species as the Vestiges itself, though I hope not *quite* so unphilosophical.' Huxley's review was clever, he agreed with Hooker; nay, the best review 'I have seen, on poor Vestiges, but I think he is too severe, – you may say "birds of a feather flock together," & therefore I sympathise with the author.'[24] Maybe he did; maybe he saw himself, a few years on, in the same boat. Huxley would have to be won over.

By September 1854, when Darwin read Huxley's review, the second volume of his monograph on living barnacles, huge at 684 pages, was out, and he was busy dispatching copies to friends. Huxley, *au fait* with French and German zoology – dissecting barnacles himself in the light of Darwin's work – supplied the addresses of authorities who should receive a copy, garnished with spare pickled specimens. On the 7th Darwin told Hooker that he had 'been frittering away my time for the last several weeks in a wearisome manner, partly idleness, & odds & ends, & sending ten-thousand Barnacles out of the house all over the world. – But I shall now in a day or two begin to look over my old notes on species.'

At last the way was clear to carry on with natural selection. The time was ripe to begin; with the young reformers on the rise, the *Westminster* evolutionists already in place, the social basis of science was visibly changing. And Darwin now had his licence. Two days later he jotted in his pocket diary, 'began sorting notes for Species Theory.'[25]

The next month Lyell and Hooker came down to find out how Darwin was getting on with his 'ugly facts.' Lyell was shaken, Hooker teetered, and Darwin took heed. Caution was still imperative – the question was too momentous for anything else. Though fifteen years had passed since he closed his notebooks, the supernatural fabric of creation in shreds around him, he was still telling Hooker that he would 'give the arguments on *both* sides.' He would not plump for 'the mutability side alone.' Unsure on so touchy a subject, even of intimates, he tied himself in knots of self-abnegation. To his clerical cousin Fox he disclosed his plan to

> view all facts that I can master (eheu, eheu, how ignorant I
> find I am) in Nat[ural]. History, (as on geograph. distribution,
> palaeontology, classification Hybridism, domestic animals &
> plants &c &c &c) to see how far they favour or are opposed
> to the notion that wild species are mutable or immutable: I
> mean with my utmost power to give all arguments & facts on
> both sides. I have a *number* of people helping me in every
> way, & giving me most valuable assistance; but I often doubt
> whether the subject will not quite overpower me.[26]

Balance and doubt were a public mask. Despite appearances, he knew exactly what he was doing. For fifteen years he had committed himself unequivocally to one side.

In-coming books were routinely tested, to see how his theory explained their data. He was characteristically modest about it. The exercise left him, as he growled to Hooker on reading his essays, having to 'gnash my teeth & abuse you for having put so many hostile facts so confoundedly well.' There was no 'for and against' here; he was singling out hostility to his own view. Hooker still had botanical doubts about the '*Elastic* theory,' as he dubbed it. Darwin took it all on the chin: 'what a villain you are to heap gratuitous insults on my *elastic* theory; you might as well call the virtue of a lady *elastic*, as the virtue of a theory accommodating in its favours.'

But then, regretting it, he begged off as usual: 'I feel deadly sick, & decidedly an animal of low development.' That week, with a houseful of guests, his special plague was boils. Your 'cautions on the species-question ought to overwhelm me in confusion & shame,' he reproached himself to Hooker another time; 'it does make me feel deuced uncomfortable.'[27]

Confusion and shame: the old thoughts were there, but the words rang hollow. Uncomfortable he may have been – sick in fact – but Darwin felt more assured with the barnacles and the Royal Medal under his belt. He was internationally known from the *Journal*, the geology books, and the barnacles, enough for Professor Asa Gray – sending information on American plants – to invite him to Harvard, all expenses paid. (Of course he turned it down on health grounds.) He was emboldened by each step Hooker took in his direction. And Hooker was quickening his pace, informing Gray that he now had 'an utter disbelief in the stability of my own genera and species.' Or, as he admitted to Darwin, he no longer cared a hoot whether species 'are all pups of one generic type or not.'[28]

28

Gunships & Grog Shops

BARELY HAD DARWIN put his barnacles away than the great Crimean struggle began. War preparations had been going on steadily throughout 1853. In November, as he received his medal, Russia – wanting a toehold in the Ottoman Empire – was blasting Turkish ships in the Black Sea port of Sinop. At stake was not merely the protectorate of the Christian holy places, which had been ceded to France, but control of the Mediterranean and the trade routes to India and the Near East. The British could not afford to lose these. Her Majesty's fleet had lain at anchor outside the Dardanelles during the summer. In autumn it had moved opposite Constantinople, awaiting orders.

The country was on a war footing, not least the great folks at Downe. Young John Lubbock, now a published naturalist (thanks to Charles), marched off to Dover to train with the Kent Artillery Militia. The Darwin family went with the Harry Wedgwoods to the Chobham army base to see the manoeuvres. There were twelve small cousins in the party, eight of them boys; and who should be on hand to show them around but Capt. Sulivan, recently returned from the Falklands. Battle had already commenced, with the bloodcurdling shouts and thundering mounts of over 10,000 men: the grandest war games yet staged by a peacetime British army. For a moment, in fact, it became all too real. The Darwin-Wedgwood contingent found themselves being charged by the 13th Light Dragoons and had to flee for their lives. It was part of the thrill that made three happy days unforgettable. And the one who enjoyed them most was Charles.[1]

Back at home the mood changed as the flotilla put to sea again. 'We are all much afraid of war with Russia, which, pray God, may be prevented,' wrote Charles to Covington. It could not. With the papers howling for revenge against the Tsar, the fleet passed through the Bosporus under orders to clear the Black Sea of Russian warships. The French joined in, and on 28 March 1854 the allies declared war. Charles kept in touch with Sulivan, who was returning to active service in the Baltic in command of HMS *Lightning*.[2] The slaughter was dreadful – 15,000 allied dead alone – and still the Russian naval base at Sebastopol lay intact.

The young Darwins were bitten by the warfare bug, and Emma abetted them with 'galloping tunes' on the piano. With William away at school, Georgy was now in charge. He had dismissed the Duke of Wellington with a seven-year-old's sang-froid – or was it Papa's gloss on immortality that he captured when he jotted in his funny, cryptic way, 'The Duke is dead. Dodos are out of the world'? But, now, after the Chobham manoeuvres he too became a hot-headed little soldier. With himself as sergeant, to Franky's private, they mastered the childhood arts of war.

They took on men's names and measurements. Georgy constructed a short foot-rule so that, on the cloakroom wall under the stairs, he could conscientiously record his height as six feet, and Franky's as something less, in accordance with his age and rank. They learned the parts of guns, practised drills, and then, donning knapsacks, hoisted toy rifles and trooped down the Sandwalk to pitch camp. Georgy built a touch-wood fire for warming the gingerbread and milk; Franky stood guard until released by his brother's bugle. No one dared interfere. When Papa came out for his daily stroll and went to kiss the guard, Franky bristled and presented his homemade bayonet. Indoors the fantasies continued. There was much playing with tin soldiers – ferocious troopers with swords raised and a regiment of French dragoons whose coats Emma laboriously reddened with sealing wax to make them thoroughly British. Upstairs in the long hallway the boys attacked each other with lead-weighted darts, which crashed harmlessly against their wooden shields. Their sisters were dumbfounded, even shy Lizzy. 'Georgy is such a soldiery boy,' she pouted. 'He never speaks to a single girl.'[3]

At Sebastopol the siege had started. Then came Balaclava, Inkerman – news of the carnage was being flashed by telegraph from war correspondents in the field for the first time. As the nation faced up to reports of 3000 British dead, news came of another loss: on 18 November 1854 Forbes, the genial soul who had shown Hooker how to summon up a supercontinent, died of kidney failure. In a time of heightened emotions, Darwin and his friends were stunned. Huxley had 'never felt so crushed by anything before.' Ramsay could 'scarce realise it. My grief breaks out in short fits, and then I struggle to suppress its signs.' It was a cruel and ironic twist; Forbes had fulfilled his lifelong ambition to take the Edinburgh chair, only to die seven months later. For Lyell it was 'the greatest loss of an active scientific friend I have ever sustained, and he was but thirty-nine.' It was 'dreadful,' Darwin lamented, recalling his own mortal fears at the same age.[4] 'What a loss to his singularly numerous friends & to Natural Science!' 'As for his poor wife I pity her from my soul; I have lost a child, & I can, therefore, in some degree realise what death in its worst form is.'[5]

Darwin was thinking about the parallel warfare of nature, and how sea-borne invaders, seeds and fruit, frogs and snails, could establish a beachhead on alien terrain and oust the occupiers. More and more he concentrated on the idea of struggle; how it took place, and with what result.

The last major rethink of the theory was underway. Faced with grim reports from the Crimea and the tragic news of Forbes's death, he sat uncomfortably at Downe in November – only fifteen 'double dashes' that month, with a week of 'wakeful' nights – pondering the diversity and extinction of animals. He looked at aberrant species, those out on a limb, like the peculiar egg-laying platypus, far removed from the rest of creation. Were they ill adapted and dying out? Had intermediates, connecting them with normal animals, already become extinct?[6] This brought a flood of new questions. How did animals radiate into every conceivable form – even into broody, duck-billed mammals? What caused a species to split into two? How could *selection* generate this branching 'tree' of life – the one he had first sketched in his 1837 notebook? And if animals are diverging along lateral branches, away from one another, what of the old notions of 'high' and 'low' in nature?

The tree was the key. By the 1850s it was the accepted metaphor among naturalists: gnarled branches, forking, spreading. Even from Calcutta, the curator of the Asiatic Society's museum, Edward Blythe – 'a very clever, odd, wild fellow,' who sent Darwin reams on Indian domestic animals – compared life to a tree that 'branches off, & still divides & subdivides & resubdivides.' It was Darwin's image exactly: he had long visualized nature as '*irregularly branched.*' But why should offspring depart from their parents and go a different way? How to explain this forking?

'I can remember the very spot in the road, whilst in my carriage, when to my joy the solution occurred to me,' he later recalled – the cause of the forking. A eureka moment maybe, but he was now to spend three years refining and applying his solution.[7]

Just as his Malthusian insight had come from population theory, so his mechanism for creating diversity looked like a blueprint for industrial progress. Darwin was a heavy investor in industry. His Wedgwood cousins were among the pioneers of factory organization. They created a production-line mentality with a marked division of labour among the work force, pushing up productivity by giving each operative a single, specialized function.[8] This mechanisation of the labour force, and its effect on output, was totally familiar to Darwin. Endless trips to Uncle Jos's house as a young man had ensured that, and the Darwin library was stocked with books on economy and manufacture.

Every gentleman living off his industrial shares understood 'division of labour.' It was synonymous with specialization and speed in a steam-powered society. It promised wealth and booming markets, and the industrial metaphor seemed to stretch to nature herself. It was the catch-phrase of the age; Prince Albert called it the engine of civilization, thundering through every aspect 'of science, industry and art.'[9] Herbert Spencer, that erstwhile railway surveyor, thundering down his own branch line, was not alone in importing it into science.

Darwin recognized that, just as industry expanded when the workers specialized, so did life. But Nature had the 'more efficient workshops.' He argued that natural selection would automatically increase the 'physiological division of labour' among animals caught in competitive situations. Stressful competition in overcrowded areas – what he called Nature's 'manufactory of species' – favoured variants that could exploit free niches. These individuals would seize on new opportunities, exploit the available openings on that spot.[10] Isolation on islands was clearly not so crucial as he had thought. Competition pried apart dense local populations, fanning them out and forcing a greater number to escape the rat-race by finding their own unpressured nook. New varieties were actively pushed away from the parental stock, thus mitigating the blending effects of cross-breeding. Just as a crowded metropolis like London could accommodate all manner of skilled trades, each working next to one another, yet without any direct competition, so species escaped the pressure by finding unoccupied niches in Nature's market place. The greater the functional diversity of animals, the more an area can support.

The metaphoric extension was complete. Nature was a self-improving 'workshop,' evolution the dynamic economy of life. The creation of wealth and the production of species obeyed similar laws. Division of labour was nature's way as well as man's. But economic doctrine was promiscuously mixed with partisan politics in Britain, and Darwin introduced the subject by citing the zoologist Milne-Edwards's use of the term 'division of labour' rather than an economist's.[11] A political taint would have made natural selection too much of a target. To be successful, evolution had to be seen standing on the solid rock of science.

With progress guaranteed in Nature's workshop, as much as it was in Uncle Jos's, Darwin's self-evolving Nature was like the expanding, diversifying empires of the Dissenting cotton kings and pottery patriarchs. And indeed, the 50s were a decade of accelerating production; the boom years when economic laws seemed as iron-clad as Nature's own. But the masters' views were very unlike those from the shop-floor. Darwin was siding with the factory bosses and his fellow investors, and he would have no truck with any other.

He dismissed critics who saw mechanization beggar the workforce, and those included Emma's uncle, the economist Jean Sismondi. Brutal competition, a dehumanizing division of labour, the 'unjust' distribution of profits: Sismondi had slated them all as 'scourges.'[12] So Darwin *did* have alternative models available. But he rejected them. He accepted that Nature's struggle, like the nation's in the Crimea, took a terrible toll. This was the price of progress and diversification, and there was no bucking it. This rift with Sismondi ran deep, right down to the ownership of land. Sismondi thought that those who worked it should own it. Hardly surprising that Darwin rejected his theories, when he was himself an absentee landlord in Lincolnshire.

Evolution and utilitarian economics were perfectly attuned, and to many Dissenting industrialists this seemed natural. But few were investing so heavily in both areas as Darwin. Economists had called for a specialized work force, free markets, and a rail network to reduce transport costs. Their utilitarian ethos had led to the railway mania as much as a *laissez-faire* Nature. Darwin put his mouth where his money was. He spent tens of thousands of pounds on railway companies, and twenty years of his life revealing the competitive, specialized, and labour-intensive aspect of Nature's 'workshops.' He was placing Nature on industry's side.

Christmas that year was gloomy. Franky and Lenny had fevers and on the 22nd Franky threw a fit. To buck them all up, Charles decided to ring in the changes and spend a month in town. They took a house off Baker Street on 18 January 1855, only to have the weather close in behind them. It was that 'terrible Crimean winter,' with bitter, below-zero temperatures, when even the Thames froze over. Charles, like Emma, felt the cold acutely and regretted ever setting foot in 'dirty and snowy' London.[13]

While they were there Lord Aberdeen's government fell, censured for mismanaging the war, and Palmerston, who had helped instigate the fiasco, became Prime Minister. A dirge was playing in society. Britain lost 30,000 men in all, half of them to disease and the cold. The Wedgwood women collected clothes for the troops, and then threw themselves into the 'playful gaiety' of Sydney Smith's *Memoirs* to shake the 'stern reality of life' staring at them from every newspaper. But it was no good; nor did London society seem pleasanter knowing what 'the noble Flo Nightingale' was enduring. There were parties at the Horners and Lyells but the talk was of a half-million dead on all sides.[14] The family returned to Downe on 15 February, relieved to be snowed in at home.

While the fleet were besieging Sebastopol, Darwin kept worrying at the sea-borne dispersal of species: how they migrated, whether they could compete successfully with occupying plants when they beached. He was still looking for a way to scupper Hooker's supercontinents. According to Hooker, Tierra del Fuego had plants in common with Tasmania and Kerguelen Land, a remote island midway between Australia and South Africa. These similarities were 'far more than can be accounted for by any known laws of migration – I am becoming slowly more convinced of the probability of the southern flora being a fragmentary one – all that remains of a great Southern Continent.' Darwin hated hypothetical continents almost as much as another alternative, that God had created identical life in different places, or 'multiple centres of creation.' Plants could cross the oceans to conquer new lands and he would prove it.

Islands and castaways were important to Darwin for another reason – how else to explain species like the Galapagos finches and tortoises, each peculiar to its own island?[15] If islands and continents were where they had always been, at least for untold millions of years, the only question was how animals and plants had colonized them.

Darwin was in no two minds: plants, seeds, eggs, and animals made the journey by accident, carried by wind, water, and rafts. But he needed evidence. So off went letters, as usual to the oddest places. He tracked down a sailor who had been shipwrecked on Kerguelen, to see if he recalled driftwood on the beach, which might give a clue to colonization. He tried other tacks, asking if naturalists had found seeds in ducks' stomachs; or if, as a Hudson's Bay man told him, seeds were carried out to sea on ice-floes. But still, he grumbled, Hooker's facts were 'the greatest anomaly known in the distribution of beings over the whole world.'[16] The trouble was, everybody – Hooker included – assumed that seeds were killed by sea-water. But were they?

Late in March 1855 Darwin resolved to find out. Like a country vicar, with the time and patience and a love of pottering, he set up a series of experiments brilliant in their mundanity. He bought sea-salt from a chemist. Seeds from the kitchen garden – cress, radish, cabbages, lettuces, carrots and celery – were placed in small bottles of brine. Some he left in the garden, others in a tank of snow in the cellar, to check whether the cold would make any difference. He took a few from each bottle at intervals and planted them in glass dishes on the study mantelpiece, where he could watch for signs of life. It worked. Almost everything came up after a week in sea-water, a fact he delighted in telling Hooker. He twitted the poor man, telling him to send the seeds that he expected 'to be *most easily killed*,' and to guess at their survival times.[17] Two weeks later and the vegetables still sprouted.

Hooker took it 'like a good Christian,' as befitted the new Assistant Director-elect of Kew Gardens. He suggested that Darwin experiment on a massive scale, plying him with exotic seeds for the purpose. But Down House lacked Kew's facilities. Darwin was already coping with forty or fifty bottles. He could not manage any more; as it was, the chimneypiece was covered and the water had to be changed every other day, or it 'gets to smell horribly.' And he was having to cancel engagements if they fell on days when his salted seeds 'come due.'[18]

The whole thing became a vicarage industry. He had the Revd Henslow paying schoolgirls sixpence a time to collect seeds, and Miles Berkeley, the Northamptonshire curate who had described the *Beagle* fungi, sending bags of seeds to Ramsgate to sit in Channel water. Meanwhile the stalwart Revd Fox was posting reward notices to encourage boys to find lizard and snake eggs – there was nothing Darwin would not try, however ludicrous. What other objects he was testing he would not say. 'If you knew,' he told Hooker, 'you would have a good right to sneer for they are so *absurd* even in *my* opinion that I dare not tell you.'[19]

In the *Gardeners' Chronicle*, he announced that cress, lettuce, carrot, and celery had germinated well after forty-two days' immersion, radishes less well, and cabbages hardly at all. He also explained *why* he was experimenting; he did not mind audaciously dismissing

Forbes's Atlantis 'in a temporary publication like a newspaper.' A quick calculation followed. His atlas gave the average current in the Atlantic as thirty-three nautical miles a day – so in forty-two days a seed might cover 1400 miles. This was highly convenient, for it just happened to be the distance to the mid-Atlantic islands, the Azores. No Atlantis need have risen from the sea floor. To suggest that it had was reckless; 'it cuts the knot instead of untying it.' He was untying the knot slowly and deliberately. Seeds of European plants could have drifted out to conquer the Azores. At least, the distance was no problem. He went one stage further. 'The real interesting thing would be to get a list of the Azores plants, & try & get the seeds of as many as I could, & test them; & by Jove I will!'[20] And he did. He wrote to the British consul asking what seeds came ashore on the Azores and had Henslow's schoolgirls collect the British equivalents.

That pods could travel these distances was also proved by tropical seeds washed up by the Gulf Stream in Norway. The British consul forwarded two types to Darwin. Hooker identified them as coming from Caribbean plants; he sowed them at Kew and to his 'unutterable mortification' they germinated. And still the records fell. Some celery and onion seeds actually sprouted after eighty-five days. Even odder, the celery came up faster than seeds spared the trial. But the prize went, surprisingly, to the sensitive pepper plant, which germinated after almost five months in cold salt-water. Once again, Darwin's experiments, so simple, seemed so obvious. Gray at Harvard, reprinting Darwin's newspaper article in the *American Journal of Science*, kicked himself, wondering why no one had thought of them before.

But the real problem as Darwin presented it was not dispersal. He finished his *Gardeners' Chronicle* tally of survival times on a deliberate teaser. When the seed reaches its 'new home then,' he said, 'comes the ordeal.' Will it be able to establish a beachhead? Will 'the old occupants in the great struggle for life allow the new and solitary immigrant room and sustenance?'[21] With the British fleet still battling at Sebastopol it must have seemed curiously topical: as though warfare ran through nature and society, and colonialism was all of a kind. But Darwin was actually smuggling in one of the major themes of his theory, and the subject would vex more than gardeners and arm-chair admirals in the years to come.

The war dragged on. The nation wanted dramatic victories, not a drawn-out struggle; and to Charles it did seem as if the whole conflict was being conducted 'very badly.' But Capt. Sulivan came home, full of valiant tales, and was preparing to set off again for the Baltic with a new command. Charles saluted him. 'The men and officers have behaved most nobly, and have made the name of Englishmen a prouder thing than ever,' he rejoiced to Covington. Out in his 'clay fort,' Georgy felt much the same. When Sebastopol fell at last, in September 1855, the guns of thanksgiving boomed out across the country. He would never forget the sound.[22]

Struggle and selection – these were the guiding themes of Darwin's system. But examples were still needed to underpin this ramifying view of nature, and his picture of specialization continued to raise new questions. For example, however diverse mammals, reptiles and fishes, their embryos, if traced back, quite clearly converged in appearance. Foetal mammals and fishes were much more alike than the adults. It was wonderful proof of 'community of descent,' he believed, but how to *explain* it by natural selection?[23]

From the first he had wanted to bring such embryological evidence into the fold and make it work for him. But he had long departed from conventional wisdom. Medical men had always assumed that freaks were formed in the womb, and that this is where all variations originated. But was it? What if in some cases only dispositions to vary were inherited, and the actual variations manifested later, in the youngster or adult? Selection could only act later, when they appeared, sustaining or quashing them. After all, people had hereditary dispositions towards illness that only manifested at a certain age. The embryos in this case, being left unaltered by selection, would look more alike than the adults: the changes – the divergence – would remain hidden until the individual began to grow. In the wake of Annie's death, Darwin became more and more convinced that his own affliction was inheritable, and even now lay dormant in the children. 'My dread is hereditary ill-health,' he told Fox. 'Even death is better for them.'[24] It was morbid confirmation that he was on the right track.

He needed a graphic demonstration of this embryonic similarity and selection of emerging variants. He turned to domestic animals. Fanciers copied nature by breeding from the best of their stocks and drawing out new strains. How did they operate? There was one way to find out: he had been reading up on domestication since his notebook days. Now he would knuckle under and study fancy animals first-hand. 'Get young pigeons,' he had scribbled on his evolution essay a year or so before.[25] Expose the similarities among the hatchlings of the breeds cropped and coiffed by man – breeds that were derived from a single ancestral stock – and the model of nature would be complete.

In March 1855, just as the seed experiments were beginning, he started asking around. He cornered Fox: 'As you have a noah's ark, I do not doubt that you have pigeons; (how I wish by any chance they were fantails!) Now what I want to know is, at what age nestling pigeons have their tail feathers sufficiently developed to be counted. I do not think I ever even saw a young pigeon.' At first he just wanted information, not to get too closely involved. He needed fledglings 'to see how young, & to what degree, the differences appear.' He could either breed them himself, which would be 'a horrid bore,' or buy the young, and – this being a pleb's hobby – he wanted to be genned up before he put his money down so as 'not to expose my excessive ignorance, & therefore be excessively liable to be cheated & gulled.'[26]

Domestication had always fascinated transmutationists. In Paris and Edinburgh they had seen its potential, and even detractors believed that it was the best evidence of a 'plastic' nature. But few deskbound scientists had ever got their hands dirty, leaving it to tree cultivators like the curmudgeonly Patrick Matthew to prove the point. Darwin on the other hand had never ceased collecting scraps and facts. He followed up hearsay stories of exceptional hounds, silkworms, hybrid geese, feral and farm animals in the colonies – anything in fact on selection, inheritance, and breeding. For fifteen years he had ploughed through manual after manual on pigs and poultry, and the more he studied the bizarre types, the odder it seemed 'that no zoologist sh^d. ever have thought it worth while to look to the real structure of varieties.'[27]

It was hard to realize the novelty of his move. Most naturalists disdained pigeons and poultry. Science was not done in the farmyard. The gentry might have kept ornamental ducks on shooting estates. They might have founded zoological gardens to celebrate Britain's colonial control over nature. But such gamekeeping was a world removed from contemplative philosophy. It was this elevated pursuit – of wild species and their order and meaning in God's Creation – that commanded the philosopher's attention. Hence the scientist's disdain: no one expected pigs and pigeons to hold the key to the mystery of mysteries.[28]

But unconventional science required unconventional support, and Darwin strayed far beyond the normal bounds. He looked anew at the gamekeepers' familiar fare; agricultural shows, animal husbandry, farmhouse lore, and the *Poultry Chronicle*. And he began quizzing those who knew most about breeding and inheritance: fanciers and nurserymen.

Even before Christmas 1854 he had begun boiling up wild and domestic ducks to compare their skeletons, although sometimes with a lingering gastronomic interest: 'oh the smell of well-boiled, high Duck!!' But it was pigeons, to his surprise, that became his passion in the summer of '55. Like barnacles, seeds, and so much else, the enterprise took on a life of its own. All talk of cheating tradesmen ceased. Once inside the 'fancy' he was drinking with breeders, joining their clubs, picking up the lore and the gossip. And what a change: he built a pigeon house in the garden, bought choice fantails and pouters for £1 a pair, and declared them an 'amusement to me, & a delight to Etty.' He ordered almond tumblers and runts and soon had quite an aviary. Come, he told Lyell, see the pigeons, 'which are the greatest treat . . . which can be offered to [any] human being.'[29] He stocked up with books on the 'Art': how to judge proportion, carriage, and the beak, and how to select and breed from those offspring that show the desired combination.

His enthusiasm soon got the better of him. Boiling and measuring were now daily routines, and he became adept at judging the breeds and their young. His letters acquired a ghoulish air: I 'am watching them outside,' he said, eyeing his birds, '& then shall skeletonise them & watch their insides.' It was not only pigeons. Fox showered him with dead ducklings and chicks, and volunteered mastiffs and turkeys. 'Very many thanks for your offer,' Darwin responded. 'I have puppies of Bull-dogs & Greyhound in salt. – & I have had Carthorse & Race Horse young colts carefully measured.' Horses, dogs, ducklings – 'I am getting out of my depth.' He tried all means of killing his pigeons: chloroform took too long and he squirmed at the sight. Better was potassium cyanide in a bottle; the prussic acid gas it gave off was quick and painless. But however swift, the death of his pigeons affected him; 'I love them to that extent that I cannot bear to kill & skeletonise them,' he wailed to Hooker. Seeing his funny gawky chicks lose consciousness was always sad. 'I have done the black deed & murdered an angelic little Fan-tail & Pouter at 10 days old.' The corpses mounted, skeletons, measured and unmeasured, lay everywhere; cadavers were arriving by post, boxes crushed and intestines hanging out. Even he admitted it was becoming 'a chamber of horrors.'[30]

Etty might have been entranced by the birds, but what Emma thought of the stench as their remains rotted in a witches' brew of potash and silver oxide no one knows. At first Charles was overcome, the putrid flesh 'made my servant and myself (we not having had much experience in such work) retch so violently, that we were compelled to desist.' 'It really is most dreadful work,' he admitted, taking expert advice, and the following year he sent the birds out to be skeletonized professionally.[31]

Fox – the 'kindest of Murderers' – dispatched all the duckling varieties he had and began purloining farmyard animals from neighbouring estates. The fossil-collecting Sir Philip Egerton, whose Cheshire manor adjoined Fox's parish, was ever ready to help. But Egerton became intrigued. Running into Darwin at the Glasgow meeting of the British Association in September 1855, he inquired – Darwin related to Fox – 'why on earth I instigated you to rob his Poultry yard?'[32] As a shire Tory MP, patron of Richard Owen, and spokesman for respectable Anglican science, Egerton might not have appreciated the true answer.

Darwin wanted to show nature composed of myriad tiny variations, invisible to all but experienced fanciers. These enthusiasts could judge to one-sixteenth of an inch. And the differences that only they could spot formed the raw material to be accentuated through generations of selective breeding. From such minute aberrations, enormous sculpted changes had been wrought by fanciers, leading to today's pouters, fantails, runts, and tumblers. So enormous, in fact, that had these birds been wild, zoologists would have classified them as different species, perhaps different genera: 'Darwin finds, among his fifteen varieties of the common pigeon,' Lyell reported, astounded, the equivalent of 'three good genera and about fifteen good species.' Even their red blood corpuscles were differently shaped, as Darwin discovered when he had an expert examine samples. The same diversity was apparent in other domestic breeds. He pointed out the variations in domestic rabbit skeletons to Waterhouse at the British Museum, and asked whether 'they were not as great as between species.' More so, was Waterhouse's reply.[33] Here, then, were single species, so modified as to fox even the best zoologists. From infinitesimal variations, common rabbits and pigeons had been stretched to the extent of emulating whole new genera.

Darwin believed that similar imperceptible variations held the key to Nature's own Malthusian selection. Weak, ill-adapted variants were discarded by Nature, as they were by the fancier. The good ones thrived and over the generations particular trends were encouraged. Adaptive features were drawn out, as if by an invisible breeder. 'Artificial selection' showed the craftsman sculpting nature; Nature's own 'selecting' hand was infinitely superior.

He had seen the 'selecting hand' – but it was rather a grubby one. The feathers he admired were largely the handiwork of artisans.

Working men had always taken pride in their pigeons and sought solace in the loft after the drudgery of the day. 'I am hand & glove with all sorts of Fanciers, Spital-field weavers & all sorts of odd specimens of the Human species,' he said.[34] Of course, not really hand-in-glove; there was always a certain detachment. Even educated fanciers and poultry journalists who plied him with information were reimbursed their expenses. They were treated as paid technicians, offered cash to check his facts and read his manuscripts. These fanciers, appalled at the indifference of the scientific nobs, welcomed his interest in their prize breeds. His kindly paternalism gave their backyard hobby a certain cachet. But to the end he remained imperturbably a gent among working fanciers.

This also showed in his favoured club. He was easiest in the exclusive Philoperisteron, which met up in town at the Freemason's Tavern. It had all the snobbish appeal of a Piccadilly club, and its shows attracted hundreds of exhibitors, despite a lack of prizes. The 'Philo' was an attempt to escape the grimy associations of the fancy. This ruffled a few feathers, and the vulgar thought it fit only to 'bird-lime the House of Lords.'[35] The velvet waistcoats cut no ice with ordinary breeders. They preferred the cheap feather clubs of the City and Borough, in south London. Darwin joined the Borough club himself. In fact, the 'Squire,' as he became known here, visited them all, high and low, with a sense of anthropological mission: from the rowdy beer-halls of Spitalfields to the posh venues of the West End, he was attempting to see nature through the eyes of the natives.

Grog shops were not his normal haunt, yet here he was, eavesdropping:

> I sat one evening in a gin palace in the Borough amongst a set
> of pigeon fanciers, when it was hinted that Mr. Bult had
> crossed his Pouters with [larger] Runts to gain size; and if you
> had seen the solemn, the mysterious, and awful shakes of the
> head which all the fanciers gave at this scandalous proceeding,
> you would have recognized how little crossing has had to do
> with improving breeds.[36]

Darwin could see no substitute for hob-nobbing with fanciers. It was the only way to pick up the lore.

And with the lore came the initiation. The Borough club, he told William, a world away at Rugby, was populated by a 'strange set of odd men.' After dinner one

handed me a clay pipe, saying 'Here is your pipe' as if it was
a matter of course that I sh^d. smoke. – Another odd little man
(N.B. all Pigeon Fanciers are little men, I begin to think) . . .
showed me a wretched little Polish Hen, which he said he
would not sell for £50 & hoped to make £200 by her, as she
had a black top-knot.[37]

But these odd little weavers and costermongers were skilled at
finishing pigeons to exacting standards. They could pinch, bustle,
and crown birds, creating forms scarcely less marvellous than the
changing female fashions. It was they who gave the squire his first
sight of artificial selection at work.

On the other hand, it was Darwin's own dedication to the fancy –
visiting the beer-halls, buying the *Poultry Chronicle*, breeding his
own pigeons – that gave such authority to his comparison of Art and
Nature. He had found analogies of selective transmutation in the
grubbiest, most unsuspecting quarter.

29

Horrid Wretches Like Me

BY 1856 THE YOUNG GUARD was organizing. Huxley, Hooker, Tyndall and their fellow travellers were discussing strategy and marking out enemies. First on their list of priorities was to claw more power for London's science lecturers and gain a greater 'command over the public' – and the public purse.[1] They saw themselves as grossly underpaid compared to the clerical naturalists of Cambridge and they bitterly resented it.

Huxley was rising fast: a specialist on molluscs, medusae, and other marine creatures, teacher at the School of Mines, and now – in 1856 – Fullerian Professor at the Royal Institution (which he accepted for the £100 pay). This year, too, with Darwin's and Sir John Lubbock's help, he followed Carpenter as an examiner at the University of London. He was accumulating posts as a clergyman collected livings, and the pay rose with the overwork. He was razor-sharp; a 'very clever man,' Darwin recognized, the sort he was counting on to convert quickly. Fearsomely clever, in Hooker's view. He found Huxley's lectures 'overwhelming,' his facts 'revolutionary,' to the extent that he could not master the half of them. Darwin did not attend the lectures, but he was just as daunted, claiming to know no more about Huxley's molluscs 'than a man does, who has only eat[en] oyster patties.'[2]

Huxley's London teachers were scientific outsiders who sneered at the cloistered Cambridge mentality and the privileged, old-boy network. Yet incongruously, here Darwin was, playing Huxley's 'Father confessor.' Little did the group know that the Downe recluse, once educated to the cloth, was to supply the iconoclastic science to match their ambitions.

For the moment they had their own strategy, which involved

creating a new tightly knit, highly regulated 'profession.' It meant selling themselves to the public as 'scientists,' a respectable white-collar body who should be decently paid for providing a public utility – however novel 'knowledge' was as a commodity. The profession had to be self-validating. Science could owe no allegiance to theology, and Huxley rushed around, baiting bishops, making a public show of dissociation. Proper pay, too, would bring in talent and push out the dilettantes. The science section of the *Westminster* was proving too cramped; soon the coterie was agitating for a house journal and a club of its own – an 'intellectual resort' where these traders in science could sup and scheme without being bothered by the 'pitiful botchers.'[3]

Ties were strengthening all the time. Huxley, now in regular employment, had brought his fiancée Henrietta from Australia in 1855. After six years apart, they were married, with Hooker, Tyndall, and the Carpenters in attendance. Darwin sent his blessing, although warning that 'happiness, I fear is not good for work.' Holidays were spent together, with mountain climbing the manly rage. The dreaming spires they admired were not Oxford's, but the Tyrol's. Huxley would join Tyndall in the Alps, or spend Christmas with Hooker and George Busk, a naval surgeon friend, on Snowdon, glorying in the scenery. Huxley, bellicose, brash, a good hater and a fast friend, knew the value of men like Hooker, Tyndall, and Darwin, and admonished them all to 'pitch into me when necessary.'[4]

Already the young bloods were mugging old hands like Owen, the newly appointed Superintendent of the Natural History collections at the British Museum in 1856. Owen, the darling of Oxbridge divines and politicians, symbolized all that they despised. New standards were needed, not deference to old vanities; a new accountability to one's peers. The clique cringed at Owen's deferential mysticism, never mind his personal quirks. Huxley, that 'Roundhead who had lost his faith,' with his flashing eyes and lacerating wit, smeared Owen physically and mentally. A 'queer fish,' he called the vertebrate specialist, and 'not referable to any [known] "Archetype" of the human mind.' Cronies sniped continuously at the 'Autocrat of Zoology.' Almost literally at times – when Owen hit back at Huxley's 'blindness,' Carpenter told Huxley 'to put a bullet into some fleshy part' of his enemy to prove his eyesight. What the tyros lacked in respect they certainly made up for in bravado. Owen might have published more than all of them put together, but they wanted the Superintendent superintended. Make him answerable, Carpenter urged, 'to a body of scientific men, who are competent to estimate and criticize his proceedings.'⁵ A body, of course, that would be Huxley-led, and responsible to no man. The chill winds of professionalism were blowing across the old order.

All this was brewing in April 1856, when Darwin called a meeting at Downe. 'I am very glad that we shall meet at Darwins,' Hooker wrote to Huxley. 'I wish that we could there discuss some plan that would bring about more unity in our efforts to advance Science.'⁶

Darwin desperately wanted to get Huxley to Downe for other reasons. His anatomy was brilliant, but he seemed to be drifting in the wrong direction. He hated evolution and damned talk of a progressive fossil record. Like everyone else he dismissed *Vestiges*'s uninterrupted ascent of life. But he went on to repudiate Owen's vision of progress as well, which baffled Darwin. Owen imagined fossil animals as less specialized than today's. Trace each lineage back and the more general the animals become. Eventually we must arrive at the original archetype – the ideal mould from which they were all forged. Owen gave an example that became a classic. Today's thoroughbred horse stands on tip-toe – a single toe – but it was preceded by the smaller, extinct *Hipparion* with two small extra toes in each foot, while further back the tapir-like *Palaeotherium* had a full three-toed foot. He believed that this kind of specialization typified the ascent of life.⁷ So did Darwin.

Huxley did not. He hated Owen, hated his 'metaphorical mystifications,' and denied the whole progressionist kit-and-caboodle. Worse, the horses made their début during Owen's onslaught on Lyell's non-progressionist geology. Owen was so vicious that it made Hooker sick. It further angered Huxley, who greatly respected Lyell and his science. Darwin too had done with Owen's mysticism and 'detested' his murky Platonic thinking.⁸ But he appreciated the great man's fossil framework. He realized that Owen, for all his wishy-washy rationalizations, had simply traced the bloodline of the horse. His whole scheme could be translated into evolutionary terms; the genealogy was perfect. Darwin was happy for it to be left intact, ready for his own new explanation. Huxley's gleeful demolition was not appreciated.

Huxley's own views were disquieting, inscrutable even. He thought of species in a strange way. He saw them clustered as if on the surface of a sphere, each the same distance from the archetypal centre. There was no place for intermediates, and no possibility of higher and lower forms. Darwin was baffled – it was all geometry again, not genealogy. 'I am,' he said, 'surprised at what you say.' He was dumbfounded at Huxley's denial of any progression – and nonplussed by his archetype, the central abstraction. This appeared Ptolemaic in its crudity, in its unyielding, unchanging form. It bore no relationship to the ancestor Darwin had in mind when he continued: 'I sh^d. have thought that the archetype in imagination was ... capable & *generally undergoing* further development.'[9] But if Darwin was disbelieving, Huxley must have found an *evolving* archetype positively absurd.

Darwin annotated Huxley's reviews, trying to gauge the strength of his anti-evolutionary argument.[10] He needed to probe further. This was why he invited Huxley to his Downe gathering, to get his objections first-hand.

Hooker and his wife were to arrive on Tuesday 22 April. Also invited was the punctilious T. Vernon Wollaston, a quiet, cultured Cambridge man, an insect-specialist '& very nice & pleasant into the bargain.' Here, surely, was someone after Darwin's own heart. At the time Wollaston was arranging his beetles in the British Museum. His new book *On the Variation of Species* was dedicated to Darwin and made the strongest case yet for 'a legitimate power of self-adaptation' in insects – for their tendency to vary '*within fixed specific bounds.*'[11] He shared Darwin's interests, and his ill health. His own work on Madeira (where he had gone to recuperate) had shown that island isolation and climatic change were major causes of variation in beetles, and he repeatedly cited Darwin's *Journal* to prove the point. He seemed to be leaning the right way.

To complete the party Darwin invited the renegade, Hewett Watson. He had met the fiery atheist and phrenologist the previous August, and found him 'a bit sarcastic.' This at first made him suspicious, as he always was of radicals. But the more Watson plied him with plant statistics, the more Darwin came to value his 'clearness of mind & acuteness,' and he soon had the '*highest* opinion' of the man. Watson too opened up, confiding his own evolutionary views.

As it turned out, Watson could not come that weekend. There was also doubt about Huxley. He was exhausted, and his wife ill with morning sickness – she could hardly have wanted to go anywhere. Tuesday was also his day for lecturing. Darwin was not sanguine, although he suggested that a 'little change' might do them both good. Emma promised that Henrietta 'could be as quiet as she liked, & sh^d. have a comfortable arm-chair in her bedroom, so as to live upstairs' if she preferred.[12] The Huxleys eventually came on the Saturday – their first trip to Downe – probably taking the train to Sydenham, where Darwin's carriage met them.

It was one of those occasions relished by Hooker, with 'long walks, romps with the children on hands and knees,' and strolls through the garden. They ambled out to the Sandwalk, Hooker and Huxley planning the reformation of science, Wollaston full of beetles. Darwin, with his 'hearty manner,' led the way in his grey shooting coat, staff in hand, pointing out his pigeons. John Lubbock, just married, joined them for dinner on the 26th, the night the Huxleys arrived. In the morning, after breakfast, came the 'interviews' one by one in the study, like a doctor's surgery, when Darwin brought out a pile of slips with questions needing answering. The slips were now ready for Huxley.

Lyell was astonished to hear of the events that weekend. 'When Huxley, Hooker, and Wollaston were at Darwin's last week,' he informed his wife's botanical brother-in-law Charles Bunbury, 'they (all four of them) ran a tilt against [immutable] species farther I believe than they are deliberately prepared to go. Wollaston least unorthodox. I cannot easily see how they can go so far, and not embrace the whole Lamarckian doctrine.'[13] In truth the tilting was Darwin's and Hooker's. Wollaston had been expected to join in. From his talk of 'legitimate variation,' Darwin had thought that he was a potential convert. But no. 'Least unorthodox' was an understatement. His views were as fixed as his species: he made exceptions only for minor variations.

Darwin reckoned that his exceptions would eventually get the better of him. He twitted Wollaston mercilessly and threw grandfather Erasmus's adage at him:

> I have heard Unitarianism called a feather-bed to catch a falling Christian; & I think you are now on just such a feather bed, but I believe you will fall much lower & lower. Do you not feel that 'your little exceptions' are getting pretty numerous? It is a funny argument of yours that I (& other horrid wretches like me) may be right, because we are in a very poor minority! anyhow it is a comfort to believe that *some others* will soon be with me.

Wollaston's 'funny argument' – the minority might be right after all – was meant as a mock concession. It was drawn from the Gospel of Matthew: 'strait is the gate, and narrow is the way, which leadeth unto life, and few there be that find it.' But twisting a text like this played straight into Darwin's post-Christian hands. If he and 'other horrid wretches' who believed in evolution were such a minority, perhaps they had found the way of life; the damned were those like Wollaston who equivocated.[14] Maybe Darwin could even be credited with saving '*some others*' – Hooker and Huxley, he hoped.

But as a wealthy rector's son Wollaston was shocked at these implications. While he allowed insects to vary 'to a much greater extent' than most, he still insisted that their power of change was 'positively circumscribed.' Each species had 'only certain *limits* to vary between,' he told Darwin, 'beyond which ... it cannot pass.' This posed no 'danger,' he boasted, because 'it does not touch the question of development in its *larger* sense.' To him the idea of transmutation was 'monstrous.' Darwin was thwarted. It is pretty 'rich,' he groused, 'considering how very far he goes,' that he denounces 'those who go further, "most mischievous" "absurd", "unsound". Theology is at the bottom of some of this. I told him he was like Calvin burning a heretick.'[15]

Theology was never behind Huxley's opposition. Hadn't he slammed *Vestiges* for making nature an 'orderly miracle'? And yet he was even more adamant that progressive transmutation was pernicious nonsense. Later he recalled his 'first interview' with Darwin, and how he argued for the 'sharpness' of species and 'the absence of traditional forms, with all the confidence of youth,' and then puzzled over Darwin's smiling response 'that such was not altogether his view.' Darwin of course knew Huxley's position; he had annotated and 'grieved' at his reviews and speeches. He was frankly dismayed at the brilliant tearaway.[16] Darwin now fired a series of questions at him – although without tipping his hand on natural selection.

In the study, Huxley ran through his objections. He pointed out that even ancient fossil animals have little-changed living relatives, that crustaceans could not pass into fishes, that intermediate forms were missing, and that fossil history did not mirror an individual's embryonic growth. As soon as Huxley had gone Darwin scribbled a series of notes, picking at Huxley's quibbles, unravelling his fallacious reasoning, reconceptualizing his static spherical nature as a dynamic, ramifying tree: in short, knocking his objections down, one by one.[17]

More strategic differences were also emerging. While Darwin was looking for a bloodless coup in science, Huxley had other ideas. He was pugnacious to a degree. And iconoclastic, rushing into scientific citadels, slaying emperors – Cuvier, Owen, and Agassiz – and challenging their minions. Hooker wanted to get Huxley elected to the Athenaeum, as he himself had been five years before; but Darwin worried about Huxley's brazenness. Whatever the strengths of his science, his tone was 'too vehement.' Two weeks after the meeting, Darwin decided against putting Huxley's name up, guessing that Owen would only blackball him anyway: 'Cannot you fancy him, with a red face, dreadful smile & slow & gentle voice, asking, "Will

[you] tell me what M^r. Huxley has done, deserving this honour; I only know that he differs from, & disputes the authority of Cuvier, Ehrenberg & Agassiz".' We 'had better pause,' Darwin cautioned Hooker; 'to try in earnest to get a great Naturalist into [the] Athenaeum & fail, is far worse than doing nothing.'[18] He would mellow out, they guessed, given a couple of years.

The new men were closing ranks, like any cadre: identifying outside 'aggressors,' forcing cohesion, a common policy, common enemies. All were sympathetic to Darwin, with his technically excellent science, uncontaminated by theology. Owen was alienated and excluded, for his hauteur as much as his idealist heresies. Morality came into it too, as it always did with Huxley. Owen delivered guest lectures in Huxley's School of Mines in 1856-57. They were, by all accounts, a roaring success and attended by a smattering of lords and ladies, who were shown 'the power of God in His Creation.' The Duke of Argyll (the Postmaster General) scarcely missed one, nor Dr Livingstone, back from Africa. The lionizing alone must have galled Huxley, who was forced to watch the socialites parade through his institution to applaud his enemy. But Owen also craftily advertised himself as the 'Professor,' usurping Huxley's position in the school. At this Huxley hit the roof. 'Of course I have now done with him, personally. I would as soon acknowledge a man who had attempted to obtain my money on false pretences.'[19]

But Owen gave as good as he got. Better sometimes, and even Hooker realized that Huxley's hotheadedness could catch him out. He reported the latest to Darwin breathlessly:

> Owen I hear committed a cutting telling & flaying alive assault on Huxleys adaptation views at the Geolog[ical]. Soc[iety]. & read it with the cool deliberation & emphasis & pointed tone & look of an implacable foe. – & H. I fear did not defend himself well (though with temper) & perhaps had not a popular champion in Carpenter who barbed him – These embroglios are very bad indeed & must insensibly have a bad effect upon Huxley.

Darwin, who also derived a jot of guilty pleasure from Huxley's antics, nonetheless warned him again, 'for Heaven sake do not come the mild Hindoo to Owen (whatever he may be): your Father confessor trembles for you.'[20]

Shortly after the Downe gathering Darwin began working out a strategy for presenting his theory. Lyell, intrigued by Darwin's speculations (though not realizing their extent), egged him on to write and publish, fearing that he would be scooped.

What had alerted Lyell was a cryptic, guarded paper on the 'introduction' of species, published in the workaday *Annals and Magazine of Natural History*. He had tipped Darwin off, as had the ebullient Edward Blythe, raving about it, 'Good! Upon the whole!' A self-financed globetrotter – a specimen-hunter selling bird skins, beetles, and exotic butterflies for a living – Alfred Russel Wallace, had composed it in Borneo, idling away his time trapped indoors by a tropical monsoon. In Blythe's words, 'friend Wallace' had 'put the matter well' – and in a way which suggested that 'the various domestic races of animals have been fairly developed into *species*.'

This ought to have shaken Darwin out of his complacency. But Wallace's guarded language threw him: his statement that '*Every species has come into existence*' coincident in space and time with an earlier allied one could have been Owen's 'ordained continuous becoming,' or a cryptic gloss on Creative continuity. Darwin missed its import, as did others. It is 'nothing very new,' he scribbled on his copy of the *Annals*. 'Uses my simile of tree,' but 'it seems all creation with him.'[21] Darwin misread Wallace's coded talk, putting him down as just another alert young Creationist.

Lyell did not. He was considerably shaken, enough to open a notebook on species, where he mulled over the consequences for humanity, frightened that the world was again tumbling towards transmutation. Lyell churned the subject over and over, peering at it from every angle. How had the 'Author of Nature' introduced species on to the earth? Did a new species look like its predecessor because 'Omnipotence' was fitting it to similar conditions?[22] Lyell was now grappling with the issues directly.

At Downe Darwin, knowing he could trust Lyell implicitly, watching him waver, finally spelt out the full details of natural selection. Lyell toured Darwin's pigeon house, admiring the runts and tumblers and, by now, almost every other breed known in England. He did not really agree in his heart of hearts, but he urged Darwin to publish, for priority's sake.

Lyell went away staggered. As always, he saw the starkest implications. At home, pondering the selectively bred pigeons, he extrapolated to man's selected origin 'from an Ourang.' He cut to the heart of the problem; animals did not really matter – but was *man* only a better sort of brute? Was he 'improved out of' some Old World ape? It seemed unthinkable; humans differed in kind. And yet, if Darwin was right, 'the whole geological history of the globe is the history of Man.' It was a sublime and sobering thought. Lyell, the mentor who had refuted Lamarck a quarter of a century earlier, was playing with fire, hesitant yet hypnotized, tantalized by Darwin's 'species-making' mechanism. His quandary increased when he raised the issue at the Philosophical Club. Talking to the young bloods, it was obvious that fixity was a thing of the past, even if they had 'no very clear creed to substitute.' Natural selection was ripe. It would fall into their hands, Lyell realized; 'whether Darwin persuades you and me to renounce our faith in species,' he prophesied to Hooker, 'I foresee that many will go over to the indefinite modifiability doctrine.'[23]

Pushed by Lyell, Darwin began collating his notes. Other gentrified naturalists spurred him on, not realizing the consequences. Bunbury, Lyell's in-law, was intrigued by his 'speculations on species' and delighted that he intended to press on with publication. He knew Darwin went further than most, but even Darwin, he insisted, 'would not assert an *unlimited* range of variation: he would hardly ... maintain that a Moss may be modified into a Magnolia, or an oyster into an alderman.' Many an alderman, too, eating his oyster patty, would have been startled at the prospect. Bunbury advised Darwin to show 'caution & candour,' to avoid the dogmatism which so easily creeps into discussions 'of *multiple* creation, & of transmutation.' Give 'every fact & argument on any side,' he advised.[24] This, of course, is what Darwin planned.

But when nip came to tuck, it was a tall order. For the first time Darwin began to face up to the logistical problem, and his own partiality. 'To give a fair sketch would be absolutely impossible' because of the welter of facts. Perhaps he should 'only refer to the main agency of change, selection.' But a skimpy paper would hardly spark a *coup d'état* in the scientific citadel, among the people he really wanted to convince. Only a commanding tome – sizeable, abstruse, and referenced – stood any chance of converting them. But if he did not seize priority, it could be twenty years wasted. And with so much transmutationist talk about – in *Vestiges*, all over the gutter press, among the *Westminster* crowd – time was running short. He was flurried: 'I do not know what to think: I rather hate the idea of writing for priority, yet I certainly sh^d. be vexed if any one were to publish my doctrines before me.'

And then, where to publish? 'I positively will *not* expose myself to an Editor or Council,' so an academic journal was out. Maybe a modest monograph was best after all. 'If I publish anything it must be a *very thin* & little volume, giving a sketch of my views &

difficulties,' he told Hooker, imploring his advice; 'but it is really dreadfully unphilosophical to give a résumé, without exact references, of an unpublished work.'[25] And, anyway, how could he? He would 'sneer at any one else doing this.'

In the end proprietorial fears won out, and on 14 May 1856 he started a sketch, putting off the decision whether to publish until later. Hooker could see the advantage of getting out a 'Preliminary Essay,' but wondered if it would not destroy the impact of his full tome. Fox too evidently counselled against a slight work. No, no, said Watson, go ahead, publish now and perfect it later. 'This I have begun to do,' Darwin announced, 'but my work will be horridly imperfect.' His self-doubt set in again: the traumatizing feeling, the 'wibber-gibbers,' as he called it. 'I begin *most heartily* to wish that Lyell had never put this idea of an Essay into my head.'[26]

It was an auspicious time to start. The Crimean War was over at last, and two weeks later, on the night of 29 May, when Charles was in town for a Royal Society meeting, he saw 10,000 coloured rockets launched simultaneously to celebrate the peace-treaty. Russia had been defeated, the eastern trade routes secured. The future for Britain was looking bright, the age of sterling imperialism and Pax Britannica. And the young bloods were determined to make a new 'science, pure and free, untrammelled by religious dogma' part of her success story.[27]

30

A Low & Lewd Nature

AT FIRST HIS MIND was not totally on the book. Emma, now forty-eight, had had nine children, and they confidently expected no more. Then in 1856, as he began writing, she found herself pregnant again. It came as a complete surprise. Horace's birth, her last, had been five years earlier. Now Emma was once more 'as wretched as ever.' Through May and June she was sick, and by July 'general oppression' had replaced the nausea.[1]

He also became het up again about supercontinents as more naturalists jumped on the bandwagon. Wollaston was connecting Madeira to the mainland, others were conjuring up a lost Pacific land, and the old Atlantis was still below the waves. Darwin 'fairly exploded' on the subject: 'my blood gets hot with passion & runs cold alternately.' It was so absurd. Add up all the lost continents and 'half the present ocean was land within the period of living organisms.' And did the extensions help? Why the absence of Australian Banksia plants in New Zealand if they were formerly connected? And couldn't ice-sheets pushing animals and plants down from the Arctic explain the common American and European forms? And why were old continental strata never found on mid-oceanic islands? He was now 'fairly *rabid*' on the subject, admonishing himself to become more 'humble,' and allow the miscreants 'to make continents, as easily as a Cook does pan Cakes.'[2]

By mid-July he had drafted forty pages on the migration of Arctic species. On paper his ideas looked good, 'but Lord knows it may be all hallucination.' He had finally stopped vacillating on the book's size. No skimpy précis would do; it had to be a full-blooded work, although little did he realize how full that would make it. He asked Lyell to be allowed to dedicate the volume to him. Sir Charles –

considering his old loathing of Lamarck – was squaring up well; 'he is coming round at a Railway pace on the mutability of species,' Darwin told Hooker, and allows 'me to put some sentences on this head in my preface.'[3]

That was in public; the private Lyell was still tormented. What really racked him was an issue that never bothered Darwin, the threat of human degradation. By 1856 Lyell was desperately assuring himself that a brute ancestry was only ignoble or 'lowering' to people who denied an after-life. He kept trying to persuade himself that the future was important, not the past. Where was man's dignity anyway, given 'the hundreds of millions of savage or semi-barbarous races' and 'the millions of idiots & of the insane' born barely a step above the brute level? 'If a race of savages of the lowest capacity exist for 1000 years without progress, why not a race intermediate between them & the Chimpanzee.'

Lyell turned the issues over and over in his notebook, agonizing about the moral consequences. For all his twisting and turning, he still feared that humanity would lose its noble 'rank' and submerge in brutal nature. Could nature 'evolve the rational out of the irrational'? This was the crux. Fighting off feelings of 'moral repugnance,' he sought to rationalize man's ape ancestry. Think of a 'sensible Man . . . born of two idiotic parents.' Surely this was no different from a savage born of brutes? Think of Shakespeare's birth from ordinary mortals. He kept reworking it into his own terms – the emergence of genius, of greatness. And what heralded the birth of this exalted being – Man – on the earth? No one believed that the 'front of heav'n was full of fiery shapes.' But the more he tried to see man stealing quietly into the world, the more he wanted a miraculous moral moment when 'a responsible soul' first appeared.[4]

The rise from savagery to Shakespearean nobility was a comforting crumb to the Victorian gentry. But it was a short step to the racist slurs that Darwin was already hearing. Given the dinner-table wisdom that genteel Anglo-Saxons towered above their black butlers, evolution cast a shadow over ancestral purity. Lyell himself was irresistibly drawn to the theme: go back umpteen generations and would blacks and whites find a common ancestor? Itself the descendant of an ape? The very idea 'w^{d}. give a shock to . . . nearly all men.' No university would sanction it; even teaching it 'w^{d}. ensure the expulsion of a Prof. already installed.' Race was blowing up as an emotive issue in the 1850s. The hardbitten Robert Knox (he of the Burke and Hare scandal) achieved a new notoriety by his doom-mongering about coming racial wars. He made the races separate species. Others like

Louis Agassiz made them separate Creations; and one of Darwin's contacts thought it 'fortunate for those of us who respect our ancestors & repudiate even the contamination of Negro blood – that Agassiz remains, to do battle with the transmutationists.' Darwin instantly confessed his evolutionary 'heresy' as a rebuke, declaring himself 'as bad as the worst.' But this deep-rooted racism left no doubt that evolution threatened more than one cultural taboo. He knew that Agassiz 'will throw a boulder at me, & many others will pelt me.'[5]

It wasn't only Lyell who was moving. Others were cautiously coming round. Darwin was struck by 'the change in Hookers & Huxley's opinions on species during the last few years.' Like Lyell, Hooker still put up objections, wondering why duplicate species did not evolve under similar conditions, but Darwin swept them aside, repeating that he attributed 'very little to the direct action of climate.' By now he had no truck whatever with the radicals' environmentalism; life neither lifted itself nor was moulded by its surroundings. His brand of competitive evolution would not have appealed to the Hookers and Huxleys if he had. But he was still edgy, his nerves jagged; it was a terrifying feeling, knowing that he was about to break ranks with the Anglican élite and go public. He could not stop thanking Hooker for all his help: 'my Book may be wretched,' but 'you have done your best to make it less wretched. Sometimes I am in very good spirits & sometimes very low about it. My own mind is decided on the question of origin of species but good Heavens how little that is worth.'[6]

He was focusing again on his original target audience: it was not to be a flimsy paper, nor a racy, unreferenced pot-boiler like *Vestiges*. Only a technical treatise would do, one that piled on cumulative layers of evidence. Nothing less would convert the reforming tyros making their way up the Royal Society ladder.

All the while he kept his teeth in the continent-makers, especially in an impenitent Hooker. He fretted and fumed, unable to 'get the subject out of my head.' While continents rise and sink, willy-nilly, 'scarcely anything is known of means of distribution.' As he worked up the section on dispersal he ploughed on with his counter-experiments. He was not past salting frog spawn, or floating snails' eggs, however unsuccessfully. Eventually he noticed that hatchling snails will crawl on to a dead duck's foot, where they can live for a day or so out of water. It set off another train of experiments. Snails were not floating, he guessed; birds were flying them to their island destinations. As for plants, he was still trying to show how Hooker's

Edwardsia and other species could end up in New Zealand and South America but nowhere else. Hooker plied him with exotic seeds, goaded on occasions: 'I believe you are afraid to send me a ripe Edwardsia pod,' Darwin chivied him, 'for fear I sh^d float it from N[ew]. Zealand to Chile!!!'[7]

But difficulties were piling up all around. The salting had already hit a serious snag. Although many seeds survived, almost all of them had sunk. Without being able to stay afloat, they could not drift to distant shores. It seemed insuperable, and he cursed the 'horrid seeds.' 'I have been taking all this trouble in salting the ungrateful rascals for nothing.' He adopted a fall-back position; branches buoyed up by fruit and pods, he assumed, were washed down the rivers and out to the islands. Even this hypothesis was soon in tatters. He kept fruit-laden plants in sea-water 'with sorrowful result.'[8] Within a month they were rotting at the bottom of his tank. He was becoming disconsolate.

He began casting around for other mechanisms; perhaps ice-floes. Or ducks' feet again – it sounded laughable, but from a 'table-spoon-full of mud' out of a pond he raised twenty-nine plants. Once word got around, the strangest things started arriving by post. 'I have just had a parcel of partridges feet well caked with mud!!!,' he reported, triumphant. Eight-year-old Franky suggested ghoulishly that he try floating a dead well-fed bird. 'No sooner said, than done: a pigeon has floated for 30 days in salt water with seeds in crop & they have grown splendidly.' Of course, he admitted, scavengers would eat the corpse '999 [times] out of a thousand' but 'one might escape: I have seen dead land birds in sea-drift.' Nature was not looking quite so recalcitrant.

Seed-eating birds suggested another line of off-beat experiments. He began collecting birds' droppings. He poked through them microscopically, tweezered out the undigested seeds and germinated them. And there were still more tortuous methods of transport to be investigated. He fed oats to fish, and imagined herons flying off with their catches to some distant island. While many tests went well, others were a wash-out. Everything 'has been going wrong,' he exclaimed on one occasion: 'the fan-tails have picked the feathers out of the Pouters in their Journey home – the fish at the Zoological Gardens after eating seeds would spit them all out again – Seeds will sink in salt-water – all nature is perverse & will not do as I wish it.'[9]

The first chapter – on stock breeding and artificial selection – was left unfinished as he carried on measuring and experimenting. He kept buying pigeons – scanderoons, and polands, and laughers (who wouldn't laugh) – and now had ninety or so. Skins were arriving from every continent, and sometimes birds too: 'I have just had Pigeons & Fowls *alive* from the Gambia!' he informed an astonished Fox. The 'blessed Pigeons' were invaluable, providing him with a wonderful analogy of descent. He waded through innumerable old records to 'trace the gradual changes in the Breeds,' searching, in effect, the fancy's own 'fossil' record, tracking the races back to a wild ancestor.

The next chapter stayed with domestication and was complete by 13 October. The fragment on distribution was ready, too, and he warned Hooker, 'you unfortunate wretch,' that it was about to land in his lap. Three days later he handed it over during a Royal Society meeting, wanting to know, in his disarming fashion, 'how *atrociously* bad it is,' for it was certainly 'too long, & dull, & hypothetical.'[10] He would finally learn whether his pottering had paid off, and if his ideas could satisfy the 'King of Sceptics.'

While in town he took the opportunity to test another of his grisly dispersal ideas at the zoo. He had brought up some dead sparrows, their crops stuffed with oats, and fed them to a bateleur eagle and snowy owl, whose regurgitated pellets he then took home. 'The Hawks have behaved like gentlemen,' he reported to Hooker, and a few seeds survived the eagle's gastric juices. 'Hurrah!,' he shouted after planting a whole owl's pellet, 'a seed has just germinated after 21½ hours' in its stomach. This, he announced, with a mite less than his usual precision, 'w^d carry it, God knows how many miles.' Here, then, was 'an effective means of distribution of any seed eaten by any Birds.' Seeds did not have to blow across a mythical land mass; they could hitch a macabre lift.

Hooker wobbled and wavered as he read the manuscript, 'delighted & instructed,' suddenly getting Darwin's drift, and a clearer picture 'of *change*.' 'I never felt so shaky about species before,' he finally confided. He pencilled comments, and found bits 'rather stiff reading,' but he did not, as Darwin feared, suggest the lot be burnt. Ice-age migrations he was not sure about, but iceberg transport he accepted. The verdict was '*incomparably* more favourable' than Darwin had anticipated. He came up to town one lunchtime – not for long, Emma was soon due – to talk more. He continued pressing points that Hooker had still not grasped. The critical one was that 'external conditions do *extremely* little.' It was the selection of '*chance*' variations that resulted in a new species. Selection in dense-population struggles depended more on competition among 'associates' than the environment.[11]

The book was progressing, but it exacted a mental toll. Having gone for a huge tome, he now groaned at the prospect. 'I find to my sorrow it will run to quite a big Book.' He was palling, complaining that the labour 'tries me a good deal & sets my heart palpitating.' As he staggered under its weight, the old symptoms began to return. 'Charles's health,' as Emma had long recognized, was 'always affected by his mind,' and his mind was in turmoil.[12] He feared he would break down, swamped with work. He was on a knife's edge and in need of the water cure.

But Emma, who now found even writing a letter 'a considerable exertion,' came first, at least until the baby was born. Other duties were also pressing. Her octogenarian aunt Sarah (the last of the elder Josiah Wedgwood's children), who still lived shut away in the village, had become crippled on fracturing her thigh in September. She died suddenly on 6 November, leaving Charles to arrange the funeral and cope with a house full of uncles. At the graveside, he reported sadly, the Revd Innes 'did not read [the] very impressive service well' and the old servants cried a lot. Then everyone went back to Petleys for the reading of the will. Aunt Sarah's property was to be sold, with Charles seeing to the auction. On the 22nd all the children but William, who was still at Rugby, traipsed down to the grand old house one last time for a farewell tea party. How they would miss the place, with Mrs Morrey's gingerbread and Martha Hemmings's songs. Etty felt specially bereaved; it was her first big emotional loss since Annie. Now thirteen, she had a cold that weekend, and it got worse. The doctor said it was a 'low fever' and recommended that she should have breakfast in bed for a spell.[13]

Two weeks later, just before the sale, Emma had her sixth son, Charles Waring. Her sister Elizabeth was again in attendance, and it was, as always, a tense time. With all the talk now of chloroform's dangers, Charles gave Emma less than usual – nothing like the hour-and-a-half's worth he had used at first. In fact, 'I never gave it till she shri[e]ked out for it,' he confided, comparing notes after Hooker's fourth child was born some months later. Wollaston congratulated Darwin on 'the addition of another ♂ to your vivarium.' As it sank in that the child was 'born without its full share of intelligence,' Darwin must indeed have felt trapped in capricious Nature's cage, one of her monstrous experiments in fertility and futility.[14]

The auction of Aunt Sarah's property took place on 9-10 December, admission by ticket only. He watched her carriage go for £11, her 'American clock' for twice its purchase price, then vases, an arm-chair . . . a lifetime's prized possessions. She had lived in 'Spartan simplicity,' dispensing her fortune to the needy, and thus she died. No tablet was to be erected; her *largesse* would perpetuate her memory. The remnant of Josiah Wedgwood's wealth, the last legacy from England's first great industrialist, was to be passed on to numerous charities, with a bit for the servants. Such was the time-honoured obligation of the rich: to sustain life's casualties, without regard for the necessity of Nature's wastage.[15]

Through the births and deaths and illness Darwin ploughed on with chapter three. By now any 'satisfaction in writing' was destroyed by the 'tiresome' length of the manuscript. However brutally he chopped and condensed, it grew hopelessly. This latest chapter on 'fertility & sterility,' he grumbled to Hooker, had 'run out to 100 pages M.S., & yet I do not think I have put in anything superfluous.' He had. He threw in everything, from Huxley's hermaphrodite jellyfish to bees and cross pollination – example after example, the whole designed to wear down resistance by attrition, to prove that outbred offspring fare better in the 'severe struggle for existence.'[16] But then it was a subject close to his heart.

Family inbreeding had long worried him. There were now four first-cousin marriages between the Darwins and Wedgwoods, with his and Emma's own. Of the ten Darwin children, two had died young from natural causes and the signs were ominous for the rest: George was sick and home from school, Etty languished in bed every morning, Lizzy still behaved strangely, and the baby was not normal. Charles believed that the main problem was hereditary: that his own constitutional weakness had been passed on, accentuated by Emma's Wedgwood blood. The struggle for existence had already set in, and he expected the children's health to fail at any time. Nine or so was the critical age; that was when Annie became so ill. Since her death the thought had put him through agonies, and he waited for nature to exploit the fatal flaw. All of them except William, who was nearly seventeen, were potential victims.

In the book he belaboured the 'evil' effects of inbreeding and the good effects of crossing. As always, he was looking for moral meaning: birth, death, and chronic illness needed some rationale, and Nature provided it. 'When relations unite,' there is a 'decrease in . . . general vigour' and an increased likelihood of 'infirmity' among the offspring. The struggle for existence then inevitably takes its toll, and the Darwin children were not immune. It was often hard to see the good, but Nature was working for a better world. 'The survivors' were the more 'vigorous & healthy, & can most enjoy life.' He finished chapter three the week after the auction, rounding off by debunking the radicals' benign population studies and vindicating Malthus's pessimistic work.[17] There was no escaping Nature's ruthless scythe, and no virtue in the attempt.

He knew he was overworking. His nerves were stretched, his heart still palpitating. Fox had tried Gully's water cure for his lumbago a few months earlier and had checked Annie's headstone while he was there. Charles had never even seen 'our poor dear child's grave,' and the thought of Malvern brought back such bitter memories that he went off the water cure. He tried alternative remedies, sipping concoctions of acids on the chance that his gastric juices needed strengthening. But still he was overwhelmed. The book was growing out of all proportion; pigeon skins were 'flocking in from all parts of the world,' and snails, too.[18] He wondered how long he could hold out.

Just before Christmas he cannibalized his twenty-year-old transmutation notebooks, sorting the pages into thirty or forty large portfolios, ready to be reworked. It was indeed a season for reflection, and a quiet one too. Lady Lubbock had offered to take the noisy younger boys after the baby was born, but the staff managed to subdue them, allowing Emma to recover peacefully. Etty, too, remained in her bed each morning; Lizzy was as silent as a mouse. William and George spent Christmas in London with Fanny's and Hensleigh's boys, returning on the 27th for William's birthday. George was full of first-term talk from Clapham Grammar School, where he had been sent in August to get a grounding in maths and science under the Revd Charles Pritchard (his father's Cambridge contemporary). As 1856 waned, they all said goodbye to their governess Miss Thorley. After ten years, it was her last holiday with them.[19]

Darwin pushed on into 1857, analysing the plant data supplied by Hooker, Watson, and Gray. He filled 300 foolscap sheets with tabulations to prove that wide-ranging 'large genera,' those containing many species, were expanding and the 'manufacturing' sites of varieties. The chapter on variation, finished at the end of January, was another case of bludgeoning by bountiful instances. But then, 'I am like Croesus overwhelmed with my riches in facts,' and the overwhelming was intended to carry over.[20]

A week on and he was well into 'The Struggle for Existence.' Here he would show how the variants were weeded, how endless numbers fell in the 'War of Nature.' His new theory of divergence created a chilling image. Nature became a seething slum, with everyone scrambling to get out, rushing to break from the rat-pack. Only the few survived, bettering themselves by creating new dynasties. Most remained trapped on the breadline, destined to struggle futilely, neighbours elbowing one another aside to get ahead, the weak trampled underfoot. Sacrifice and waste were endemic, indeed necessary. Nature was abortive, squandering, profligate. Her failures were discarded like the breeder's runts to rot on some domestic dump. In Victorian poor-law society, the image did not seem unduly sombre.

There was a baseness about it all. At one point, he was trying to prove that hermaphrodite jellyfish cross-fertilize (rather than impregnate themselves). It had to happen, he believed, to keep the species vigorous – just as cross-breeding was good for human beings. He taxed Huxley, suggesting that the water washing into the mouths of jellies contained the sperm. This was a soft lob from a straight man. 'The indecency of the process is to a certain extent in favour of its probability,' Huxley shot back in his ribald way, 'nature becoming very *low* in all senses amongst these creatures.' Darwin shared the lewd remark with Hooker. Nature's depravity cried out against a noble Providence; good grief, Darwin spurted in the next breath, 'What a book a Devil's Chaplain might write on the clumsy, wasteful, blundering low & horridly cruel works of nature!'[21]

But he was the one in the mocking surplice now, perched in his Down House pulpit; and the protracted sermon he was writing would read like a grim indictment: progress through pain, life from death. He had seen it all at first-hand. So had others, if they were honest. It should not be hard to convince a Church Establishment of the savagery beneath Nature's surface, any more than of the brutishness of London's slum dwellers. (Everyone had been reading Henry Mayhew's monumental dossier, *London Labour and the London Poor*, even Darwin.) Look at the carnage in the Crimea – it was finally sinking in, vividly brought home by the gaslight photographs being exhibited in London. Who could doubt old Erasmus Darwin's line 'One great slaughter-house the warring world!' Even Tennyson's 'Nature, red in tooth and claw,' was shrieking against a complacent creed.[22]

How different from Archdeacon Paley's 'happy' nature in his *Natural Theology*. The world had been turned upside down in fifty years. Seen through Paley's rose-tinted spectacles, it was a continual summer's afternoon, with the rectory garden buzzing with contented life. But no longer. An expanding industrial society meant that more and more people were herded, hungry and angry, into factory towns.

Those on the sharp end had been hammering away at Paley's image for ages. Working-class agitators had denounced Paley's pernicious justification of the status quo. George Holyoake had long ago written *Paley Refuted in His Own Words*, after his two-year-old daughter died of malnutrition.[23] At Downe Darwin peered hard into nature's 'horridly cruel' face; the time had come for him too to challenge Paley, whose words he had once embraced.

Seen through Malthusian spectacles, the parsonage garden became a battlefield. 'One may well doubt this,' he allowed, when viewing 'the contented face of a bright landscape or a tropical forest glowing with life;'

> ... & at such periods most of the inhabitants are probably living with no great danger hanging over them & often with a superabundance of food. Nevertheless the doctrine that all nature is at war is most true. The struggle very often falls on the egg & seed, or on the seedling, larva & young; but fall it must sometime in the life of each individual, or more commonly at intervals on successive generations & then with extreme severity.[24]

It had to if reproductive rates were totted up. When one sea-slug could lay 600,000 eggs (he had calculated the figure on the Falklands), only wholesale destruction could stop the South Atlantic being overrun.

He was writing up his Malthusian case on 23 February when Capt. FitzRoy and his new wife came to lunch. FitzRoy had known enough grief – his first wife had died, and recently his only daughter – but believing in a beneficent Providence who ordains nature's economy, he could hardly have sympathized with this harsh view. Others fully shared if not sympathized with Darwin's secret now. Fox remained a mainstay, warning him against overworking and recommending holidays, fearing that nature's scythe would cut down his cousin. Of course Darwin could not leave his salted snails and frogs, his pigeons and seeds. The book, Fox heard, was huge, and even Darwin wondered if he would survive to see it in print.

He was in a dilemma: desperate for recognition, yet fearing it; dreading death, yet looking for a form of release. 'I wish I could set less value on the bauble fame, either present or posthumous,' he maundered, 'yet, if I know myself, I would work just as hard, though with less gusto, if I knew that my Book w^d be published for ever anonymously.'[25] In short, he felt a sense of mission; he believed implicitly in his self-imposed task.

31

What Would A Chimpanzee Say?

HIS FEARS WERE hardly assuaged by the mandarins of science manoeuvring around him. Before getting a word into print, obstacles were appearing in his path. Lyell might have reconciled himself to humans stealing into the world, born – somehow – of ape parents, but Owen had not.

Richard Owen had probably dissected more apes than any man, and he had always used his results to crush treacherous theories of human origins. He met the threat again in 1849, shortly after the missionary Thomas Savage announced that West Africa housed another, still unknown ape, huge and 'indescribably fierce' – the gorilla. By now Owen was being pestered by a new class of dissidents, the Chapmans and Spencers, and the author of the *Vestiges*. Evidently some stronger antidote was needed, and he reassured audiences that the 'villainous low' ape-features, as Lyell called them – the overhanging brows and stabbing canines – were not modifiable. Man was not an ape descendant.

Owen had acquired four gorilla skulls, covered in sacred tribal marks, from an old sea captain. The taints of barbarism were easily washed off, but not the feeling that this was a 'peculiarly forbidding' creature, with a 'scowling physiognomy' that mocked humanity in sinister caricature. The gorilla became a crucial pawn. Owen's whole speech before the British Association in 1854 centred on the impossibility of apes standing erect and being counted men. The brute could not transmute; man was safe, his dignity assured. But the pressure continued. Even Darwin had sounded Owen out on transmutation (and found him 'vehemently opposed'), and by 1857 Owen must have known that he was writing a book on the subject.[1]

'Gorilla' suddenly became a household word in the late 1850s.

There was a flurry of interest in this new black-skinned ape, whipped up by salacious stories, macabre tales of ferocity and woman-snatching. To glimpse any ape in captivity was a thrill. Because of the East India Company trade, baby chimps and orangs had arrived intermittently at Bristol docks, to be snapped up by zoos. But never a gorilla; in fact nobody in Europe had seen one alive. Only in 1855 could crowds finally gawk at this grotesque beast. Wombwell's travelling menagerie, which paid the top prices at the docksides to ensure star attractions, managed to obtain a young female.[2] The show trooped hundreds of miles that year, from the West Country through Oxford up to Yorkshire. At the head marched a brass band, with trumpeting elephants, and the noisy parade attracted huge crowds.

But the gorilla's début, among the milling, unwashed masses, could only heighten fears about the bestialization of man. Respectable savants disdained the razzmatazz and worried about the consequences. As well they might, judging by the gutter press. Already working-class militants, latching on to anything to back their cry that 'man is nothing' in an impersonal universe, were heralding his monkey origin.[3]

This kind of provocation needed a firm rebuff. Like Lyell, Owen feared that man would lose his high-born status in creation. And the scholars who dabbled in transmutation only inflamed the situation, arming the militants. This was treachery. Such faulty science had to be stamped on with an iron heel, and Owen was the one to do it. By now he had a European reputation; he had just taken the Royal Society's Copley Medal, Oxford University had awarded him an honorary Doctorate, and the French government the Légion d'Honneur. He was well connected, attending ex-Chancellor Gladstone's breakfasts, and hob-nobbing with bishops and earls to an extent that infuriated the young Turks. (He was already living in a 'royal house' in Richmond Park, granted him by the Queen.)[4] In 1857 he was President-elect of the British Association. Naturally it was to Owen – the trusted authority on apes – that the squires of science turned. They wanted reassurance about the gorilla.

Owen was no reactionary. He now announced that Creation was constantly sustained, an ongoing event. Clumsily, he called it a process of 'ordained continuous becoming,' without going into particulars. This looked like a sort of providential evolution. Yet he was loath to let a gorilla transmute into a human. He envisaged more of a Creative leap, but he needed proof. Others wondered where he was going to find it. Worried divines would question him about the gorilla's similarity to humans. What 'places man so far above brutes?'

one asked. Do the nerves and muscles make the human hand and tongue unique, 'or is the mind working on almost the same anatomy?'[5] It was a morally loaded question, and he had to handle it carefully.

Owen needed some factor that would allow him to classify man apart, and he found it in the brain. He had been studying ape brains for a generation, and being 'so great an authority,' Darwin scoffed, he 'ought to be right.' In 1857 he announced that humans possess a unique lobe, the hippocampus minor, and cerebral hemispheres that are larger than any other mammal's, completely covering the cerebellum. Because of this, man should stand in a special sub-class, one reserved for him alone. He was as different from a chimp as the ape was from a platypus. Darwin was incredulous and threw up his hands: 'I cannot swallow Man' being *that* 'distinct from a Chimpanzee.' Then he asked, in his blithely brilliant way, 'I wonder what a Chimpanzee w^d. say to this?'[6]

Darwin's pace was now visibly slackening. Illness cut his working day 'ridiculously short,' and he despaired of finishing. He plodded on with chapter six, 'Natural Selection.' This looked at which of the competing variants 'shall live & which die.' At the font of life – in the expanding, huge genera moving out across the world – Nature was ruthless, sifting and selecting, picking the most 'profitable.' She was the paramount pigeon-fancier, a supra-mundane snail selector. Infinitely superior to the little Spitalfields weavers, 'she cares not for mere external appearance; she may be said to scrutinise with a severe eye, every nerve, vessel & muscle; every habit, instinct, shade of constitution ... The good will be preserved & the bad rigidly destroyed.' Her 'productions bear the stamp of a far higher perfection.' 'By nature,' he put in as an afterthought, 'I mean the laws ordained by God to govern the Universe.'[7]

He was on to the causes of variation when the crunch came. Croesus was suffocating under his riches, with no one to rescue him. In March Etty's complaints worsened; Emma took her to Hastings for a month to breathe the sea air, leaving him alone. Finally, after a few days, the 'everlasting species-Book' just overwhelmed him. 'It is beyond my powers,' he cried to Lyell. A year before, Fanny Allen had seen him as 'fresh and sparkling as the purest water.' Now he was washed out, a wreck, in need of a tonic, slapping towels and slooshing baths to invigorate the system. He needed to top up with mineral water (being bottled commercially at Malvern by this time). He could not think of going to Malvern, though; the thought of Annie stabbed his heart.[8]

He settled on a 'fortnight of hydropathy & rest' at Dr Edward Lane's establishment closer by. It was on the rolling Farnham heathland, about forty miles away across the patchwork-quilt landscape of the south of England. At the luxurious Moor Park estate, once home to Jonathan Swift, patients could rest up, relax, and wander the warm sandy heaths. Lane was another Edinburgh medical man, like Gully, but still in his early thirties, and an MD of barely three years: 'too young,' Darwin reckoned, but 'that is his only fault.' More to the point, 'he is a Gentleman & very well read.' Nor did he 'believe in all the rubbish which D^r. G. does,' the clairvoyance and clap-trap, even if Darwin had to endure his dottier patients' crotchets. Darwin became attached very quickly. The doctor had made a good marriage, to Lady Drysdale's daughter, and Darwin thought them 'some of the nicest people, I have ever met.'

Lane found Darwin much as Gully had, and was as surprised at his condition. 'I cannot recall any [case] where the pain was so truly poignant as his. When the worst attacks were on he seemed almost crushed with agony.' But they were so stoically borne, and Darwin's 'sweetness and gentleness' showed in the 'gratitude with which he received the most ordinary services.'[9] Lane made him give up snuff but, despite that, away from the pressures of home and the crippling workload, Darwin rather enjoyed himself. The walks were wonderful among the secluded pines and silver birches bordering the heath. He dismissed the patients as a dull lot, but Lane remembered him roaring at jokes around the dinner table, and taking to a garrulous Irish lady and her ghost stories, because she also put salt on the tablecloth to pinch with her bread.

A week into the treatment and he was effervescing. What 'an amount of good,' he burbled to Hooker. It is 'quite unaccountable. – I can walk & eat like a hearty Christian; & even my nights are good. – I cannot in the least understand how hydropathy can act as it certainly does on me. It dulls one's brain splendidly, I have not thought about a single species of any kind, since leaving home.' Then followed a screed on hairy Alpine plants that rather belied the point. Still, he was now sure of his science: 'I sometimes despise myself as a poor compiler,' he mused, 'though I do *not* despise my whole work, as I think there is enough known to lay a foundation for the discussion on origin of species.'[10]

Others did too. Alfred Russel Wallace had been in touch from the opposite side of the world and was now working for Darwin, sending him the skins of domestic fowl. 'The carriage is costing me a fortune!' Darwin moaned, but that was the price of having a first-rate collector in the Far East. He wrote a cheery letter to Wallace from Moor Park, thanking him for his encouragement. 'I can plainly see that we have thought much alike & to a certain extent have come to similar conclusions.' This was to reassure Wallace, feeling rather cut off and fearing that his paper on the introduction of species (which Darwin was partly going on) had been ignored. But the pleasantry had a deeper motive too. He continued:

> This summer will make the 20th year (!) since I opened my
> first-note-book, on the question how & in what way do species
> & varieties differ from each other . . . I am now preparing my
> work for publication, but I find the subject so very large, that
> . . . I do not suppose I shall go to press for two years . . . It is
> really *impossible* to explain my views in the compass of a
> letter . . . but I have slowly adopted a distinct & tangible
> idea, – whether true or false others must judge.[11]

Wallace – Creationist or not – was receiving the nicest kind of trespass notice. Shrewdly, Darwin staked his claim without giving his case away.

Like the blessed chloroform, the hot heathlands anaesthetized Darwin's brain. And yet, he began to see them as no other patient did. The sanatorium had been deliberately sited on the heath for its serenity. But what was serene to most was a battle zone to him. He began to notice that fenced areas had tall sapling firs, whereas those on the open heath were stunted, browsed by the cattle. He was ruminating again on the checks and balances, the turbulence beneath the tranquillity. One gnarled fir, grazed for twenty-six years (he counted the growth rings), was still only three inches high. 'What a wondrous problem it is, – what a play of forces, determining the kinds & proportions of each plant in a square yard of turf!' Not even a sanatorium could provide an escape from the killing fields. There was no safe haven; his obsession was transforming the world around him.

He came home with a cold in early May ready for a fresh assault. He pushed on into his huge chapter on variations, trying to find some reason for their appearance. Even when he mooted one in animals – noting that it was the abnormally developed organs in barnacles that tended to be most variable – he had to run Hooker's gauntlet to prove it in plants.[12] He also looked with fresh eyes on his own meadow, experimentally seeded with sixteen kinds of competing plants. They were smothering one another on such a scale that he doubted whether more than one would survive to flower.

A few days later Emma arrived back from Hastings with Etty, clearly 'not one bit better.' They were just in time to celebrate Horace's sixth birthday and begin receiving a house full of guests. A troop of Wedgwood cousins were due, and Charles's sisters Susan and Catherine. A week afterwards Down House was groaning. There were ten children and six adults, not counting the staff and extra servants who catered for the crowd. 'A good lot too many,' Charles lamented, 'now poor dear Etty is so indifferent.' They had all come for the christening of his namesake, the defective baby Charles, which took place on the 21st in the parish church. Darwin's cold 'suddenly turned into my old vomiting,' and he was back to square one. It was all 'very disheartening.' The work, the worry, the crush – it destroyed in a fortnight all 'the wonderful good which Moor Park did me.' His health had vanished 'like a flash of lightning.'[13]

There was only one thing to be done. Both invalids had to go back to Dr Lane's: first Etty with Emma on the 29th, and when Emma returned two weeks later, Charles would 'relieve guard' and join Etty, who was staying there all summer. Still he pressed on, piecing together one after another of 'my *many* horrid puzzles,' declaring that 'I would sooner be the wretched contemptible invalid, which I am, than live the life of an idle squire.' He dropped a letter to the *Gardeners' Chronicle* about dun-coloured ponies, trying to fathom the origin of the domestic horse, and then readmitted himself to the sanatorium.

Here he continued his half-begging, self-mocking letters, eliciting information while converting the donor – softening up breeders to obtain gulliver runts (pigeons) and softening up old presbyterians like Asa Gray at the Harvard herbarium: 'It is extremely kind of you to say that my letters have not bored you very much, & it is almost *incredible* to me, for I am quite conscious that my speculations run beyond the bounds of true science.' Or, at least, true science as then was. He played backgammon with Etty every day, watching her tenderly for fear that he would have to relive the Malvern tragedy all over again. But no, she seemed to be getting her strength back, and Charles returned to Downe on 30 June much happier.[14] Back to the grindstone; back to the old problem – the laws of variation.

It was turning into a long, hot summer – the time of the Indian Mutiny: an 'Indian Summer' when he should have been in his meadow, watching his pigeons, salting his snails, not sitting indoors. He finally finished 'variation' in July and posted pages to Huxley for checking. He was still trying to relate foetal divergence and the distinctness of species – trying to put some embryological muscle behind his theory. Huxley agreed that the more distinct the adults, the earlier their embryos begin to differ. But Darwin had also cited French opinion that the specialized organs appear first in the foetus. Huxley would have none of this. The body is like a house, he laughed; the builder starts with the walls and rafters, not 'the cornices, cupboards, & grand-piano.' The point was taken. With a sigh Darwin expunged the passages, 'which I rather grieve about, as I wished it to be true; but alas a scientific man ought to have no wishes, no affections, – a mere heart of stone.'[15]

Clearly, it was a case of two steps forward, and one back. He was still tabulating the ratio of varieties in plants a week later when young Lubbock spotted 'the grossest blunder' in one of his assumptions, which cost him '2 or 3 weeks lost work.' He had to borrow the plant catalogues and start all over again. 'I am the most miserable, bemuddled, stupid Dog in all England,' he howled. From then on he paid Downe's 'laboriously careful Schoolmaster,' Ebenezer Norman, to do the tabulating in his free time.[16] And Hooker too went to pains to help.

Others offered aid. Gray supplied details on American plants. He was not only a 'cautious ... reasoner,' but clearly a 'loveable man;' and Darwin, at the risk of seeming 'horribly egotistical,' now told him what he was up to. He ran through his twenty-year labour, ending up: 'As an honest man I must tell you that I have come to the heterodox conclusion that there are no such things as independently created species – that species are only strongly defined varieties. I know that this will make you despise me.' How species changed from their ancestral stock, he had come to understand from the 'agriculturists & horticulturists.' 'I believe I see my way pretty clearly on the means used by nature to change her species and *adapt* them.' Hooker, he said, had already read his section on geographical distribution and 'had never been so much staggered about the permanence of species.'[17]

Gray was fascinated, admitting his long-held belief 'that there is some law, some power inherent in plants,' causing variants to appear. 'I suppose this is your starting point,' he ventured – and then asked 'can you get at the *law* of variation'? This was Darwin's cue. He knew that Gray had not cottoned on; they had similar interests but were working on separate lines. On 5 September he did what he told Wallace was impossible in a letter. He sent Gray a detailed account of his views, explaining the difficulties he faced, the 'frightful' problems of embryology, facts which had kept him orthodox the longest, and the impossibility of 'climate or Lamarckian habit' explaining them. He included an abstract of *Natural Selection*, as he had decided to call the book, copied out legibly by the schoolmaster. Gray digested it and warned him against personifying 'Natural Selection,' making it a causal agent – Nature's Guiding Hand – when it simply described ways of winning life's race.[18]

Darwin swore Gray to secrecy, for fear that someone 'like the Author of the Vestiges' hear of his views and 'work them in.' Transmutation might no longer be rogue's terrain, but he was still afraid of a hack queering his pitch. Natural selection could be discredited for good. Darwin had to present it properly. He had to address the leaders of science with an original, authoritative tome. This was now more important than ever, because the 'mode of creation' was on their own agenda for the first time: teasers were appearing, questions being asked. The subject was even turning up in addresses to the Geological Society; quietly, perhaps, but it was there. Liberal Presidents were calling for unbiased attitudes towards the origin of new life: 'it is a speculation worthy of the exercise of the highest intelligence,' one had said earlier in 1857 – but 'let us avoid the fatal error of connecting the results of scientific enquiry with the articles of religious belief.' He admitted that the 'mode of creation' had once been 'proscribed from inquiry.'[19] But perhaps no longer. If the Geological, once a bastion of Oxbridge orthodoxy, was hearing rumbles, then things were really changing.

Darwin knew that he had to address this august body. He had to convince his peers that 'natural selection' was the evolutionary mode. He had the scientific standing to do it, and his words carried weight. Indeed, his status was increasing – the German Academy of Naturalists this autumn was the first European society to elect him a member. It made his job easier and harder: his words would command attention from the élite. They could not write him off as a crank, as they had his teacher Grant; or point out blunders, as they had in *Vestiges*. But that actually made him more dangerous in some eyes. His big book was aimed at the new specialists. He was recruiting treacherously, like a mole with impeccable old-boy credentials. This is how others judged it: 'my dear old friend Falconer,' he complained, 'attacked me most vigorously, but quite kindly, & told me "you will do more harm than any ten naturalists will do good" – "I can see that you have already *corrupted* & half-spoiled Hooker"(!!).' As he told Gray, 'when I see such strong feeling in my oldest friends, you need not wonder that I always expect my views to be received with contempt.'[20]

On the other hand the young guard – those who would support him – were becoming a force in their own right. Fired by Hooker, they were re-energizing the Linnean Society. This had just moved to Burlington House, Piccadilly, in the same prestigious block as the Royal Society. Huxley, Tyndall, and Hooker were still planning their own journal, and Huxley was busy arranging them a column in the *Saturday Review*. Darwin was held in high regard by the whole group. Huxley's praise for the barnacle books was unbounded: some of the most 'admirable' monographs ever published, he announced in his lectures in 1857. Here was the best sort of support; 'you will turn my head,' Darwin cooed.[21]

Huxley did not know the details of natural selection, but Darwin never missed a chance to push his pedigree approach. While Huxley retained strange views of nature's symmetry, embedding circles within circles, like a taxonomic Chinese puzzle, Darwin told him that the natural system of classification was 'simply genealogical.' And, he added, 'whenever heterodoxy becomes orthodoxy,' the realization 'will clear away an immense amount of rubbish about the value of characters ... The time will come I believe, though I shall not live to see it, when we shall have very fairly true genealogical trees of each great kingdom of nature.' But a pugilistic Huxley was looking another way. He was still squaring up to Owen, looking for a fight. He doubted that a sound zoology was possible until the 'servile' Owen's science was scotched. Only then could a new phoenix rise from the ashes 'of the old Comparative Anatomy.' As for classifying, he missed the point entirely. The 'pedigree business' might be a matter of 'profound interest,' he granted, 'but to my mind it has no more to do with pure Zoology – than human pedigree has with the Census.'[22] Classification was a count of the living, not a family tree of the dead.

During the Indian summer carcasses continued to arrive (rabbits were now his passion) and the skeletonizing went on as usual. But Darwin was finishing up with pigeons. He even thought he might give his birds away the following year. Seeds were his new passion. He was trying 'to break their constitutions,' rearing them under coloured glass, trying to create 'monsters.' Minor monsters – mere varieties – nothing as grand as the deformed creatures aimed at by Geoffroy and his son Isidore in France. He asked Hooker if his botanical friends had ever tried '*inducing varieties* by playing tricks with plants? as by high manuring wild species; plucking all their flowers off for several years; pruning; &c.' After raising a plant with green flowers, Darwin reckoned he 'could make any flower in some degree monstrous in 4 or 5 generations.'[23]

The younger generation became involved. In Papa's spare time the boys helped him keep track of the flowers' friends, the humble bees, and to play tricks on them too. On Sandwalk strolls Charles had noticed that the bees interrupted their journeys and buzzed momentarily at the same places among the shrubs. He wondered what flight paths they took and why they stopped to buzz. This was the fourth summer he made observations with the children. Warm days around lunchtime were best. The boys crawled on their tummies like trainee cadets, tracking the bees under hedges and brambles. They mapped out the buzzing places, stationed themselves along the flight paths, and yelled 'Here is a bee!' as one passed. The calls carried down the line until the bee reached Charles. He found that the flight paths were the same year by year, and the buzzing places 'fixed within an inch.' Pulling up the undergrowth, or sprinkling white flour on a spot, made no difference.[24] The bees stayed on track. He never did fathom why they adopted fixed flight paths.

The boys were coming on. Franky was his father's shadow, good for all kinds of odd jobs in a house full of skinned animals and experimental plants. George, back from Clapham, would certainly be an engineer if homesickness did not get the better of him. And William was headed for Cambridge after another stint of tuition with a clergyman. Charles saw him as a barrister, the 'future Lord Chancellor of all England.' His annual allowance of £40 – 'nearly as much as Parslow's wages' – was only for basic expenses. Artistic outings, desk supplies, and his latest indoor hobby brought extra calls on the exchequer. The craze this summer was photography, and it was not cheap. Charles forked out for the equipment when William returned from Rugby in July. A room upstairs was set aside, and soon the boy was 'rushing up & down the House' grasping glass plates with 'dirty hands,' or poring over containers of chemicals.[25] In the autumn he would take up painting again.

Emma had her hands full too, even in Etty's absence. Horace was learning to read, using the story book that Emma had written for her Sunday school at Maer. All the children had heard about Jane doing Sally a good turn; about Mary and her mother going to market; about the lying child who was to ask God's forgiveness. Emma had sat patiently with each of them, instilling duty and literacy. But Horace it seemed would be the last, for baby Charles was backward and showed no sign of walking or talking. Though 'remarkably sweet' and affectionate, with a 'wicked little smile,' he was totally passive, and 'made strange grimaces & shivered, when excited.' He had a 'passion for Parslow,' and a special claim on his mother.[26]

Emma's kindness was known throughout the neighbourhood, however much her rectitude set her apart. The parish folk felt they could depend on her. Like a parson's wife, she ministered to them, giving bread tokens to the hungry, and 'small pensions for the old, dainties for the ailing, and medical comforts and simple medicines.' Having lost her sister Fanny and nursed her crippled mother, having married a broken-down gent and been almost permanently pregnant into her forties, she understood human suffering. Indeed, since Annie's death, sickness had been a way of life – illness was normal. She lived to make others comfortable, to soothe their pains. Down House was like a hospital for the occupants, and a dispensary for the parish, with Emma the staff nurse. She used Dr Darwin's old prescription book, translated with Charles's help, and offered her own remedies for croup, 'pain of cancer,' and 'weakly girls of 15 or 16.' The servants delivered the medicines, which the children would help make up; and all who received Emma's house-calls found her 'like a rock to lean on.'[27]

Charles, too, had acquired a reputation locally and was taking on new duties. While Emma prescribed opium and gin cordial, he was preparing to dispense justice. He had been approached by the Kent Commission of the Peace to join the ranks of squires and parsons on the bench. He accepted, even though it would cost time and energy he could ill afford. (Ironically, he had evaded jury service, 'incapable of the fatigue' of a single trial.) Becoming a Justice of the Peace consolidated his sense of worth; it spoke eloquently for his responsibility. It did for his social standing what the Royal Medal had done for his science. With testimonials from the Revd Innes and the former High Sheriff, Sir John Lubbock, he became a magistrate. On 3 July he swore on the Bible to 'Keep the Peace of one said Lady Queen in the said County, and to hear and determine divers felonies and also trespasses and other misdemeanours in the same County perpetrated.'[28] Who could 'despise' an evolutionist who pledged himself thus?

As if this were not enough for an overstressed man with an overstretched family, September found him extending the house. The crush of children, never mind the squash when the cousins came, made expansion imperative. Workmen began building a huge new dining-room with a bedroom above, essentially creating a north wing, and making them all 'jolly & big.' 'I often feel dreadfully ashamed of my extravagance,' he told everyone, but it was mock modesty. The £500 costs were easily absorbed by his £4200 investment income that year. The labourers had to keep the noise down outside the study as he pushed on with the book. 'I have been writing an audacious little discussion,' he said, alerting Hooker to a major point, 'to show that organic beings are not perfect, only perfect enough to struggle with their competitors.'[29] The fog over 'perfect adaptation' had long cleared and he explicitly rejected the idea. New adaptations could not be perfect, as the old theologians had taught, or there would be no competition, no selection, and no progress. Imperfection was Nature's rule – it seemed so obvious now.

And, lest he forget, Nature gave him a poignant jolt. A few days later, in the 'midst of brick & rubbish,' with labourers everywhere, seven-year-old Lenny collapsed. Emma rushed him upstairs to bed. Charles took his pulse and found it 'extremely irregular & feeble.' It was the wretched inheritance again, what Papa experienced as 'palpitations.' The 'darling little fellow' was failing '*exactly* as three of our children have before,' Hooker heard. Hoping it was 'something temporary,' but knowing how ruthlessly Nature targeted imperfections, Charles felt 'bitter' for weeks.[30]

What with the sanatorium, the children's health, the tabulations, seeds, and skeletonizing, two chapters had taken him six months: 'Pleasant prospect!' he said of the future. Nor was it getting any easier, with the house in a shambles. The plasterers left and the scaffolding came down half-way through a chapter on hybrids. Etty returned, better but still weak, and Lenny now had only occasional 'attacks,' so Charles indulged in a bit of luxury. He took himself off again to Moor Park in November for a week's recuperation. 'I only wanted rest,' he admitted to Hooker, and that he got in plenty. He 'took quite long walks & enjoyed the scenery like a gentleman at large.'[31] He tramped the countryside, enjoying the solitude, away from the children, the work, and the worry.

By Christmas Day 1857 the *Natural Selection* manuscript was piling up. 'I have just finished a tremendous job, my chapter on Hybridism,' he wrote to Hooker; 'it has taken me 3 months to write, after all facts collected together!' But he suffered from one chill feeling, which Lyell understood well. Wallace did too, even at the other end of the empire. He wrote from the Malay archipelago to ask whether *Natural Selection* would delve into human origins. For Darwin, discretion was imperative. He was sensitive to Lyell's fears about bestialization. He could see Owen tinkering with the brain, making man an impregnable fortress, a fit repository for an immortal soul. 'I think I shall avoid the whole subject, as so surrounded with prejudices,' Darwin replied, 'though I fully admit that it is the highest & most interesting problem for the naturalist.' Others knew that the subject could not be shirked. Lyell was asking crucial questions in his notebook: 'Mind & the Soul of Man will be found to be a development of the instinct of Animals?' Even Darwin found it difficult to keep man out. In his 'Instinct' chapter just starting, humans were thrown in pell-mell among the puppies, bees, and parasitic wasps. Infant habits, sneezing, old ladies dropping stitches, instinctive piano playing, all crept in almost unintentionally.[32] And yet the chapter continued the theme: instincts were inherited and modified by selection. If these examples stood, the implications for people would be obvious.

Darwin praised Wallace's collecting in the Far East. And he encouraged his theorizing, for 'without speculation there is no good & original observation.' But he did not really catch Wallace's drift and continued to assume that 'I go much further than you.' His proprietary attitude was also still clear. For twenty years he had been working on species; his book, 'about half written,' would contain 'a large collection of facts with one definite end,' but it remained 'too long a subject to enter on my speculative notions.' Secure in his non-competitive niche, Darwin added in leisurely fashion, 'I do not suppose I shall publish under a couple of years,' and he closed with the warm sentiment, 'May all your theories succeed.'[33] Not surprisingly, Wallace had now targeted him as a sympathizer, eager to hear speculations on the subject.

Expansive, bold books were cried out for in the age of empire and progress. Darwin, like the rest of Britain at the beginning of 1858, revelled in Henry Buckle's breathtaking *History of Civilisation in England*. The first volume, with 500 fancy-footnoted pages, caused a sensation. It 'is *wonderfully* clever and original,' Darwin thought. Buckle, the son of a wealthy merchant, was as devoted to London as Darwin was to Downe. He hitched history to the capital's mid-century mood. Barbarism, priestcraft, superstition were on the way out – 'the signs of the time are all around,' he announced. True religion was to believe in the 'one glorious principle of universal and undeviating regularity' taught by physical science.[34] All this made him a man after the *Westminster*'s heart. Social improvement and morality were statistically and scientifically explicable without recourse to divine caprice. It was a song secularists had been singing for a long time, and now – as with *Vestiges* – Buckle's *History* was attracting huge high street sales.

Erasmus thought it wonderful: 'a clear, flowing, easy style,' the sort to aim for in *Natural Selection*. Charles eventually read the

History through twice, and once met 'the great Buckle' at Hensleigh Wedgwood's. But he was not too taken with the man, who was glib and garrulous and dominated the conversation. They were discussing the 'astonishing number of references' in the book when Charles miffed him by jumping up to hear pretty young Effie Wedgwood sing. 'Well Mr Darwin's books are much better than his conversation,' Buckle whispered, which Darwin topped by adding, 'What he really meant was that I did not properly appreciate his conversation.'[35]

All the scientific parvenus had heard Buckle, or knew him. He joined Spencer and Huxley on their Sunday afternoon strolls, and debated the emergence of morality with Tyndall. For Spencer the evolution of life and civilization was all of a piece. His second book, *Principles of Psychology*, already dealt with 'the genesis of mind in all its forms, sub-human and human.' Now he planned a ten-volume treatise that would take in everything else – all knowledge was to be systematized from 'the evolution point of view.'[36]

And yet Buckle's lionizing was not without its backlash. There was an unsettling cost for 'setting people thinking,' as Lyell recognized. Old fogies were 'up in arms,' frightened of the new secularism. Hooker had only just got Huxley into the Athenaeum in January, and now the two of them planned to introduce the rest, Tyndall, Busk, and Buckle. But the old gents blanched at the thought of Buckle and threatened to blackball him.[37]

If Darwin was comforted by the changing ethos, he sensed the greater uproar that would greet his own bold book. Buckle's unfinished epic was as massive, but nowhere near so controversial. It was the work of a dusty dilettante who had broken ranks with no one. *Natural Selection* would bear the name of a Royal Medallist, a county magistrate, a squire who had once trained for the Church. And in March it was nearing completion. After twenty-three months, Darwin had done with chapter ten. That put him two-thirds of the way through, with a quarter of a million words.[38] The finished book would out-weigh Spencer's leaden works and out-class Buckle's sprightly ones; it would find a fitting rival only in Lyell's multi-volume *Principles of Geology*.

Elsewhere, too, the social lines were becoming sharper. The future protagonists over apes and ancestry were striking up their positions. In March Huxley attacked Owen's human sub-class. Owen could be crucified on the question; Huxley knew it, and he relished a propaganda victory.

Owen had already delivered his stock talk on man and apes at the

Royal Institution. Spencer had heard the lecture here in 1855 and called it 'anything but logical.' Now Huxley took a diametrically opposing line on the very same platform. In his own Royal Institution lecture in March 1858 on 'The Special Peculiarities of Man,' he compared the baboon, gorilla, and man, and emphasized their complete continuity. Man was no further from the gorilla, structurally speaking, than the gorilla was from a baboon. 'It is true that we are in possession of the links between the [baboon] & the Gorilla which we have not between the latter & man – but that does not affect the question. No one will pretend that, of two roads, one is shorter than the other because it has milestones along it.' Huxley was prepared to go even further, wondering just how much he could get away with: 'Nay more I believe that the mental & moral faculties are essentially & fundamentally the same in kind in animals & ourselves.' 'I can,' he continued, 'draw no line of demarcation between an instinctive and a reasonable action.' It left only one conclusion: 'to the very root & foundation of his nature man is one with the rest of the organic world.'

Of course, in another sense, there was an 'infinite' gap. Man had speech, and thus tradition, which made him the 'only organic being in whose very nature is implanted the necessary condition for unlimited progress.' But while Huxley admitted this, there was no disguising his iconoclastic intent; he was rushing towards a collision with Owen. Man was finding his own polemical way into the picture of progress and evolution.

This tit-for-tat antagonism did not augur well for *Natural Selection* being considered dispassionately. But it did ensure the gorilla's central role in the coming debate. With Huxley and Owen at one another's throats, apes and morality were to become explosively intertwined. And Huxley's heterodoxy, fired by hatred for Owen, was easing him towards evolution. Indeed, in his next Royal Institution lecture he tackled the species problem in a more open way than ever before. He still believed that 'the question is at present insoluble.' But if a solution *is* possible, it 'must come from the side of indefinite modifiability.'[39] He had never admitted that much before.

Huxley knew virtually nothing of natural selection, but he did know that Darwin was well into his big book. And he was beginning to realize that he had been wrong-footed. The more he argued that 'Theology & Parsondom' are the 'irreconcilable enemies of Science,' the more he sensed that a certain type of evolution could serve his purpose well.[40] Indeed, having squared up to Owen and seen him slip on a pickled brain, he sensed the pay-off in adopting an antagonistic theory of mind and morals. His gladiatorial attitude was at last pushing him Darwin's way.

As Huxley spoke, Darwin was still cranking out calculations on 'large genera,' not without some tribulations. The work was 'turning out badly,' he groused to Hooker, 'and I am sick at heart.' It was getting on top of him again, and in April, with his stomach in 'a horrid state,' he returned to Moor Park. Here he rested and relaxed, and wrote to reassure Emma:

> The weather is quite delicious. Yesterday . . . I strolled a little beyond the glade for an hour and a half . . . At last I fell fast asleep on the grass, and awoke with a chorus of birds singing around me, and squirrels running up the trees, and some woodpeckers laughing, and it was as pleasant and rural a scene as ever I saw, and I did not care one penny how any of the beasts or birds had been formed.

Indoors he perfected his billiards, read novels, and devoured *The Times*'s reports on the attempt on Napoleon's life. He also dispensed advice to William, now occupying his old rooms at Christ's College, warning him against the 'temptations there are at Cambridge to idleness' – ones that Charles remembered well. He visited the barracks near by at Aldershot, loving military manoeuvres, and watched Victoria review the troops. It gave him another lease of life, and by the time he came home in early May he was fit for anything. The cure 'made a man of me for a short time,' and he was determined to take advantage of it.[41]

He threw himself into work once more. Chunks of *Natural Selection* went off to Hooker, with the warning that it was 'tough and obscure.' As usual he expected Hooker to call it 'bosh,' which of course he did not.[42] Day in, day out, he continued, cursing species, tightening up the prose. Then on the 18 June, as the postman arrived, the bottom dropped out of his world.

All those years, the terrifying ordeal, the mental destruction he had endured worrying about the reaction, let alone his respectability. All the sickening delays, the soul-searching as he touched the untouchable, and finally, after twenty years, getting so close to publishing. Now, on a quiet Friday morning, a packet arrived from half-way around the world. Inside were a score of pages from Wallace, responding – ironically – to Darwin's encouragement.

Darwin saw his life's work 'smashed,' in pieces. 'Your words have come true with a vengeance,' he cried to Lyell. He had been 'forestalled.'[43]

32

Breaking Cover

DARWIN'S CAREFULLY ORDERED world started to crumble. Etty was seriously ill with diphtheria. *The Times* was running daily more lurid reports of Dr Lane's trial for adultery. His health deteriorating yet again, Darwin stood to lose his favourite hydropathist, destroyed by the notoriety. (Like the doctors testifying, he supported the defendant, convinced that the lady patient's sensational testimony of their affair was a morbid case of erotic delusion.) Baby Charles Waring, severely retarded, was a constant worry; on the night of 23 June 1858, he came down with the scarlet fever raging through the village. Darwin had to fight his way through an emotional tangle just to think about Wallace's letter.

True, his evolutionary mechanism seemed identical. Dolefully, almost disbelievingly, Darwin wrote to Lyell, 'If Wallace had my MS. sketch written out in 1842, he could not have made a better short abstract!'[1] Unknown to him, there were significant differences, if not on the pages.

Alfred Russel Wallace came from another world, betrayed by his specimen-haggling, socialist origins. He was no independently wealthy squire-naturalist, nor one of Huxley's career teachers, but an impoverished lawyer's son, born on the Welsh borders, and apprenticed to a builder in London at fourteen. His nights were spent in the socialists' 'Hall of Science' just off the Tottenham Court Road. The coffee was free and the 'social missionaries' stirring in their tirades against private property and religion. Here he picked up the political values that stayed with him on and off for life. Many were reinforced by his work. As a trainee land-surveyor back in Wales in the early 1840s, he had been paid to redraw property boundaries after the commons were fenced and divided among the squires

467

following the Enclosure Act. It was, he later said, 'a legalized robbery of the poor.'

As a self-taught socialist Wallace saw humanity as part of a progressive world governed by natural law; and in his Hall of Science he had learned to see morality as a cultural product, equally valid in any race. Like so many with his background, he was instantly drawn by the 'ingenious' *Vestiges*, delighting in its vision of an upward-sweeping nature. It set him pondering the problem of species. The 21-year-old was left with 'an intense appreciation of the beauty, harmony and variety in nature . . . and an equally strong passion for justice as between man and man.'[2]

Fired by Humboldt's *Narrative* and Darwin's *Journal*, he scrimped and saved the money to pay his passage to the tropics to collect specimens and test *Vestiges*: to the Amazon in 1848, and (after a two-year spell in London in 1852-54) to the Malay archipelago, a vast group of equatorial islands, including Borneo, the land of orang-utans, where he hoped to gain clues to man's ancestry. His shipments of beetles, butterflies, and bird skins to a London dealer paid his way. He had to pack a thousand labelled beetles per box, but it was a living. From here he had sent Darwin long screeds and consignments. His latest letter, dated February, had been posted from the volcanic island of Ternate. Wallace had reached the Moluccan Group, the Spice Islands, *en route* to New Guinea.

Here, in a feverish fit, he had conceived his evolutionary theory. Malaria was not the only sign of derangement; the world was turning upside down for socialists. Malthus had been their bogey man, but by the late 1850s his population *Essay* was less taboo. A new generation was changing tactics to make his evidence for overpopulation underline the need for birth control (another socialist hobby-horse).[3] Wallace had read Malthus's sixth edition, and in the Spice Islands, bed-ridden by hot and cold flushes one afternoon, he too switched its logic on overpopulation from man to the animals.

Still, the ensuing theory differed from Darwin's. Wallace's idea of selection was the environment eliminating the unfit, rather than a cut-throat competition among individuals. Moreover, he viewed his Dyaks, not as Darwin had his bestial Fuegians, but in an egalitarian socialist light. And Wallace was to pose the question dismissed by Darwin – what was the *purpose* of natural selection? Evolutionary forces worked towards a just society, this was the point – 'to realize the ideal of perfect man.'[4]

Darwin accepted nothing so utopian. But for the moment, in 1858, all he had in front of him was Wallace's stark twenty-odd page letter

– and it did look very much like an abstract of *Natural Selection*. It mooted 'variations' being pushed 'further and further' from parent species by a 'struggle for existence.' Here was talk of overpopulation: how a pair of birds would increase ten-millionfold in fifteen years if not checked, how the weak succumb, leaving 'the most perfect in health and vigour.' The system works, Wallace said, like 'the centrifugal governor of the steam engine, which checks and corrects any irregularities almost before they become evident.'[5] But nature was a self-chugging steam engine; the variations build up, pushing the superior varieties past their parents.

Darwin 'never saw a more striking coincidence,' partly because he read his own thought into it. Wallace asked him to send the paper to Lyell, which he did, with a wailing note. Wallace did not mention publication, but Darwin would 'of course, at once write and offer to send [the paper] to any journal' of Wallace's choice. Yet 'all my originality, whatever it may amount to, will be smashed.' Lyell mulled over the problem and came up with the solution; they should announce their discoveries jointly. Darwin concurred, trying to suppress the niggling fear that this might look suspicious, as though he were stealing Wallace's credit. Hooker had seen his 1844 essay, Asa Gray at Harvard had a long abstract of it,

> so that I could most truly say and prove that I take nothing
> from Wallace. I should be *extremely* glad **now** to publish a
> sketch of my general views in about a dozen pages or so. But
> I cannot persuade myself that I can do so honourably . . . I
> would far rather burn my whole book than that he or any
> man should think that I had behaved in a paltry spirit.

No more sickening piece of scientific misfortune could have befallen him, even if Lyell had prophesied it.

With three children dead from scarlet fever in the village, he was preoccupied with baby Charles. He wanted Lyell to ask Hooker for a second opinion, fearing it unethical to put out a preemptive paper, given his insider's knowledge. But he was in a state beyond caring. Baby Charles died two days later. On the 29th Hooker wrote, but Darwin responded, 'I cannot think now . . .' Later that night he tried again: 'I am quite prostrated, and can do nothing, but I send Wallace, and the abstract of my letter to Asa Gray . . . I hardly care about it . . . I will do anything. God bless you.' And he threw the whole affair into Hooker's and Lyell's hands.[6]

They agreed on a joint paper. The venue was quickly settled – the Geological Society was inappropriate and anti-theoretical, Owen held court at the Zoological, and that only left the Linnean, fresh in its premises in Piccadilly. Hooker was still trying to revive the venerable old lady, and a controversial communiqué by Darwin and Wallace would be a shot in the arm. Under its new President, Thomas Bell (describer of the *Beagle* reptiles), meetings were livelier. There was a *Journal* now, and papers were discussed at meetings rather than simply read to a stony-faced audience.

How to slip it in with the summer recess looming? An ill wind finally blew some good these gloomy June days. To make up for a meeting postponed when Darwin's shy old friend Robert Brown died, the Council fitted in an extra one before the break, on Thursday 1 July. At the eleventh hour – on 30 June – Hooker and Lyell inserted the Darwin-Wallace papers on to the agenda. The next evening the Secretary read them to thirty-odd nonplussed fellows: extracts from Darwin's 1844 essay, part of his 1857 letter to Gray, and Wallace's paper – followed by six scheduled papers from the postponed meeting, ending on the vegetation of Angola. ('New facts' rather than novel theories were still the society's *raison d'être*.)[7] Darwin stayed at home, grief-stricken and ill, but also continuing a trend of absenteeism that would see him through the next stormy decade.

He had finally gone public. After twenty years of fret and frustration, he had exposed himself. But no fireworks exploded, only a damp squib. The meeting was overlong, the talks rushed, and the whole was greeted in silence, although listeners left muttering 'with bated breath.' Bell was hostile, but the fellows were evidently flummoxed by Hooker's and Lyell's tacit approval.

For Darwin's peace of mind such a lack of response was probably best. But it was cold comfort. The President had walked out of the meeting lamenting, as he later put it, that the year had not 'been marked by any of those striking discoveries which at once revolutionize, so to speak, [our] department of science.'[8] (Although, tellingly, the Vice-President promptly struck out all talk of immutability from his own pending paper.)

Not that Charles cared. While the Linnean meeting went on he and Emma were burying their son in the parish churchyard, comforted by the Revd Innes. And by now their fears about an epidemic had 'almost driven away grief.' The next morning Charles evacuated all the children except Etty to his sister-in-law's in Sussex. Four days later he collected his thoughts and informed Hooker that the family was

less panic-struck, now that we have sent out of the house
every child, and shall remove H[enrietta]., as soon as she can
move. The first nurse became ill with ulcerated throat and
quinsy, and the second is now ill with the scarlet fever, but,
thank God, is recovering. You may imagine how frightened
we have been [six children were eventually to die in the village
of the fever]. It has been a most miserable fortnight.

And not only a fortnight. His eldest sister Marianne died on 18 July,
aged sixty, her five grown-up children being adopted by Catherine
and going to live at The Mount. Charles remembered Marianne as
an 'admirable woman,' but they had not been close. After her 'long
continued & latterly severe suffering,' he could 'thank God' that she
was at rest.[9]

Still, he was '*more* than satisfied' with the Linnean proceedings.
The stunned silence augured well for a fuller statement of his theory,
which would have to be rushed into print before the book was
finished. He took his ailing children and stomach off to the Isle of
Wight for sea air, and here, at the King's Head Hotel in Sandown on
20 July, he began an 'abstract' of *Natural Selection*. At first he simply
anticipated a paper, condensed 'to the utmost,' intended for the
Society's *Journal*. But it was the same old story: the condensation
expanded out of all proportion. By August he had forty-four folio
pages on domestic animals alone, and this while he was still at the
seaside. By October the manuscript was an 'inordinate length,' and
inevitably it turned back into a book. Indigestion plagued him
constantly. He was aiming to finish by the spring and anxiety played
havoc with his stomach. At last he returned to Moor Park and the
water cure. His wails resumed their eerie familiarity: 'It is an accursed
evil to a man to become so absorbed in any subject as I am in
mine.'[10]

Wallace's approval for the whole proceedings arrived in January
1859. Not only was he gracious; he was gratified to have galvanized
Darwin. He told Hooker that he would have suffered 'much pain &
regret' if they had published his paper alone. Darwin, still sheepish,
reassured him that 'I had absolutely nothing whatever to do in
leading Lyell and Hooker to what they thought a fair course of
action.' Wallace was curious about Lyell's views on evolution. 'I
think he is somewhat staggered,' Darwin replied, 'but does not give
in, and speaks with horror . . . [of] what a job it would be for the
next edition of "The Principles," if he were "perverted." But he is
most candid and honest, and I think will end up by being perverted.'

Darwin never grasped the depths of Lyell's difficulty. His mentor, tormented by transmutation, was still struggling to rationalize immortal man's origin from the beast. Was kinship limited to 'the animal nature of man,' with his 'Moral & Intellectual & Progressive part' created unique? Lyell mooted it to Huxley and Tyndall, only to find them opting for transmutation, body and mind. He came away wanting a 'moral' flash at the birth of the species; a sacred instant when the gift of immortality was bestowed. It was hard for a knighted geologist from the older generation. Still Darwin was pleased. 'Considering his age, his former views and position in society, I think his conduct has been heroic on this subject.'[11]

The young bloods were manoeuvring fast. Fresh from hammering Owen, Huxley now seized on transmutation as a solid wedge to split science from theology. It fitted his campaign for a decently salaried scientific civil service, a new professional authority at the call of an imperial nation. Authority came with a single voice, and any clerical dilution of the message was abhorred.

His parson-hating was at its height. The 'origin of man' question allowed him to skewer 'whatever dares to stand in the way' of a secular biology, and whoever doubts that 'it is as respectable to be modified monkey as modified dirt.' This militance moved him further into Darwin's camp. He did not *want* reconciliation with the clergy. It defeated his object: hence his desire to push the debate in more inflammatory directions. If the orthodox were allowed to prove that Genesis was compatible with geology, then 'I for my part,' he announced that January, 'will undulate to prove that rape, murder & arson are positively enjoined in Exodus ... Depend upon it there is no safety in trying to put new wine into old bottles.' He wanted to make the old curates uncomfortable and vacate their chairs for his new specialists. A 'new Reformation' was dawning, a fresh revolt against ecclesiastical privilege. 'If I have a wish to live thirty years, it is that I may see the foot of Science on the necks of her enemies.'[12] There spoke a man who had scrimped and struggled, trying to make ends meet, only to see the Cambridge clergy on a thousand pounds a year.

Huxley was swinging into line with Spencer, Chapman, and the *Westminster* crew, most of whom believed in evolution. On other points they were aligning too. Spencer was castigating Richard Owen's rival science of ideal archetypes, of divine thoughts made incarnate, words made flesh in the stately procession of animal life through the ages. 'Terrible bosh,' Spencer called this, a sop to the priests, and he set out to make a 'tremendous smash of it.' Simpler, material explanations were called for. Animals had developed gradually, by the piling '*of adaptations upon adaptations.*'

For years Huxley had been lampooning Owen's philosophy, using comparative anatomy. The previous June (1858), at the prestigious Royal Society, he had pulled off a coup, smashing Owen's majestic etherial archetype while Owen himself was in the chair. On the morning Darwin received Wallace's paper, Huxley was regaling Hooker: 'I wonder how Richardus, "Rex anatomicorum" feels this morning. I am deuced seedy but that is just punishment' for us 'democrats.'[13] Owen was being alienated, squeezed out – the future Darwinian generals were making any accommodation with Darwin's old friend impossible. Hatreds were already festering, a public fight over evolution was assured. It made Darwin's predicament worse as he agonized over his book.

He was back to his 'old severe vomiting' and swimming head. Towel-slapping during another Moor Park stay in February perked him up for his fiftieth birthday, but by March he had sunk again. Hooker checked the chapters of his 'abstract' one by one. 'You have not attacked it nearly so much as I feared,' Darwin rejoiced, receiving one back on 15 March. 'You do not seem to have detected *many* errors. It was nearly all written from memory, and hence I was particularly fearful.' 'P.S. I shall to-morrow finish my last chapter (except a recapitulation) . . .' The labour was not eased by Hooker's children, as a disconsolate Hooker relayed to Huxley:

> I proposed ending the week by finishing Darwin's MS when to my consternation I find that the children have made away with upwards of ¼ of the MS., By some screaming accident., the whole bundle, which weighed over 1 lb when it came (Darwin sent stamps for 2 lbs) got transferred to a drawer where my wife keeps paper for the children to draw upon – & they have of course had a drawing fit ever since. – I feel brutified if not brutalized for poor D. is so bad that he could hardly get steam up to finish what he did. – How I wish he could stamp & fume at me – instead of taking it so good naturedly as he will.

The family tried every trick to keep Charles's spirits high during this period. He even sold his father's gold watch and Wedgwood pottery to buy a billiard table, which was installed next door to the study. He resorted to it daily to drive 'the horrid species out of my head.'[14]

He struggled on through April, stripping off the references, smoothing the text, and removing the umpteen illustrations of every esoteric point. Finally he had boiled down *Natural Selection* to its core theory in 155,000 words. It was a most atypical science book for the age, turgid but saleable.

Lyell agented it, selling the idea to John Murray. Murray had one of the best back lists in London, with the *Principles of Geology*, Hooker's *Himalayan Journals*, Darwin's *Journal*, Layard's *Nineveh*, Grote's *Greece*, and even a *Muck Manual* for farmers, and he was already planning his autumn leads – an account of the search for Sir John Franklin's lost expedition, Wellington's dispatches, and Samuel Smiles's *Self-Help*. 'Does he know at all the subject of the book'? Darwin asked. There was some worry; after all, Murray had rejected Martineau's *Eastern Life* for its 'infidel tendency.' Darwin added a PS to Lyell. 'Would you advise me to tell Murray that my book is not more *un*-orthodox than the subject makes inevitable'? – by which he meant that 'I do not discuss the origin of man. That I do not bring in any discussion about Genesis, &c. &c.' Murray was reassured by Lyell, and indeed broke his cardinal rule and agreed to publish the manuscript sight unseen, offering Darwin two-thirds of the net proceeds.

Being a practical man, Murray was more concerned with the title. Darwin was set to call it *An Abstract of an Essay on the Origin of Species and Varieties through Natural Selection*, and even with the Victorians' propensity for top-heavy titles Murray saw the profits draining away. Sample chapters went off to him, including the 'dry and dull' one on distribution that Hooker's children had enjoyed, accompanied by the squeal, 'God help him if he tries to read it.' Darwin thought it 'will be popular to a certain extent ... amongst scientific and semi-scientific men,' but not with the literary set; and it was too 'intolerably dry and perplexing' to sweep *Vestiges*-like through the novel-grubbing middle class.[15] Murray must have agreed because he anticipated printing only 500 copies.

In late May Darwin's health failed again, but a week's hydropathy fortified him for the proofs. He needed it; the prose appalled him in print, and he made drastic revisions, blackening pages and pinning notes to the smudged mess, offering to defray the cost. Through late June he continued chopping and changing; 'my corrections are terrifically heavy,' he told Lyell. He bemoaned the 'miserable' mire to Hooker; but the man was 'deep in the mud' of his own proofs, writing up the flora of Darwin's favourite colony, Tasmania. Here Hooker publicly signalled support for Darwin. Not that he would compare his effort with the *Origin of Species*. That, Hooker beamed, would be like putting 'a ragged handkerchief beside a Royal Standard.'

Huxley too was generous. He had only one cavil: that domestic races originating from a single stock (say bulldogs and greyhounds, descendants of the same wild dog) do not produce sterile offspring when crossed, as distinct wild species do. Until breeders achieved this degree of separation – actually made new species from a single stock – the analogy with natural selection remained incomplete. 'You speak of finding a flaw in my hypothesis,' Darwin rallied him, '& this shows you do not understand its nature. It is a mere rag of an hypothesis with as many flaw & holes as sound parts.' But 'I can carry in it my fruit to market for a short distance over a gentle road; not I fear that you will give the poor rag such a devil of a shake that it will fall all to atoms; & a poor rag is better than nothing to carry one's fruit to market in.'[16]

Darwin was 'as weak as a child' by September and barely able to carry anything, however delicately. He planned a long sojourn at a spa when it was all over, perhaps the new one beside the bleak Yorkshire moors, at Ilkley, suitably remote from anywhere. Through fits of sickness and gloom he trudged on, scrawling on the revised sheets, driven by 'an insanely strong wish to finish my accursed book' and 'banish the whole subject from my mind!' Murray absorbed the enormous £72 bill for corrections and upped his estimate of the *Origin*'s saleability, fixing to print 1250 copies and setting the publication date for November. The title continued to evolve under Murray's selective pressure. It had slimmed down to *On the Origin of Species and Varieties by Means of Natural Selection*, when Darwin improved matters more by docking '*and Varieties*.'[17]

Clean sheets of the 'abominable volume' went off to Lyell. Darwin remained 'foolishly anxious' about his verdict, keen for him 'to come round,' more so than for 'any other dozen men.' Lyell did indeed give Darwin 'very great *kudos*,' and others noted 'how eager Charles Lyell is . . . about Darwin's forthcoming book on Species.' But then, as Lyell's relative Bunbury admitted, it is 'sure to be very curious and important . . . however mortifying it may be to think that our remote ancestors were jelly fishes.' Lyell was still grappling with imponderables, still sensing that 'the dignity of man is at stake.' How to accept a soulless ape ancestor while saving human face? Darwin had little sympathy. 'I am sorry to say that I have no "consolatory view" on the dignity of man. I am content that man will probably advance, and care not much whether we are looked at as mere savages in a remotely distant future.'[18]

A ghastly fifteen months was capped on 1 October, when Charles finished the proofs amid fits of vomiting. During that whole time he had rarely been able to write free of stomach pains for more than twenty minutes at a stretch. The next day, in torrential rain, he took himself off to Ilkley, there to sit out in his bath the calm before the storm. Not wanting to be alone in his new hydropathic home, he cajoled amusing Miss Butler to accompany him (the old Irish lady full of ghost stories at Moor Park). With her there, he confided, it would 'feel safe & home-like.'

Ilkley Wells House was a grand palazzo set in ornamental grounds on the edge of Rumbold's Moor, commanding sweeping views over the village and wooded Wharfedale. Opened only three years before, it offered the ultimate in civilized seclusion, with bowling alleys, billiard tables, and teams of consultants to meet every genteel whim. The baths were at the spring, in a stubby brick terrace on a nearby hill dappled with deciduous trees. Donkeys bore the invalids there from the mansion, a twenty-minute ride. As Charles jolted up the narrow dirt track, the gorse and heather rattled in the north-west wind, chilling him even before he took the awful plunge. Winter came early that year, and when the family joined him on the 17th they were unprepared. Everyone remembered it as a time of 'frozen misery.'[19]

His two months' stay at Ilkley was one of relapses and recoveries, occasionally crashing to awful depths. With only ten days to go before the proofs were bound, he moaned to Hooker: 'I have been very bad lately; having had an awful "crisis" one leg swelled like elephantiasis – eyes almost closed up – covered with a rash & fiery Boils: but they tell me it will surely do me much good. – it was like living in Hell.' Job-like in his torture, he sought reassurances from friends. Convince Hooker, Lyell, and Huxley about natural selection, he believed, and the 'subject is safe.' Beyond these intimates he expected a rough ride; ridicule at least, being 'execrated as an atheist' at worst, with its damning implication of social irresponsibility.

On 2 November Murray sent a specimen copy, in royal green cloth, the text printed on heavy cream paper, price fifteen shillings, tickling Darwin with 'the appearance of my child.' On the 11th and 12th, two weeks before the launch, he faced the moment he had dreaded for twenty years: he wrote notes from the spa to accompany the complimentary copies. All were laced with disarming self-deprecations: two went to Harvard, to Louis Agassiz (it was not sent in 'a spirit of defiance or bravado') and Gray ('there are very many difficulties'); others to Henslow ('I fear you will not approve of your

University College, put out a slim book on classification and dedicated it euphorically to his former companion: 'With one fell-sweep of the wand of truth, you have now scattered to the winds the pestilential vapours accumulated by "species-mongers".'[30]

The Times's anonymous review on Boxing Day. The staff reviewer, 'as innocent of any knowledge of science as a babe,' had turned the book over to Huxley. How 'did you influence Jupiter Olympus and make him give three and a half columns to pure science? The old fogies will think the world will come to an end.' Darwin cherished the piece more than 'a dozen reviews in common periodicals.' But it contained the usual 'naughty' snipe at Owen, which Huxley was constitutionally incapable of avoiding:

> Upon my life I am sorry for Owen [Darwin piped up]; he will be so d – – d savage; for credit given to any other man, I strongly suspect, is in his eyes so much credit robbed from him. Science is so narrow a field, it is clear there ought to be only one cock of the walk![27]

Damned savage or no, Owen was an arbiter of London science and received a string of complaints about the book. Sedgwick in Cambridge, Livingstone in the Sudan, the Duke of Argyll in government, and Jeffries Wyman at Harvard, all contacted him. Livingstone could see no struggle for existence on African plains, Sedgwick could not see the point in a world without providence; Argyll thought Darwin might have caught 'a few *bits* of the truth,' but Wyman knew that these certainly did not include chance variations.[28]

Five days after Huxley's, Hooker's review appeared in the *Gardeners' Chronicle*. Darwin was well known to its readers, and the piece was carefully tailored to the sons of the soil. Hooker treated the *Origin* as an extension of horticultural lore. Like strawberry varieties, created by the 'gardener's skill,' prize species have been picked by nature – and he added the chauvinistic thought that the book would 'fructify' first in the agriculturalist's mind.

Hooker made it sound like easy meat. But even he had to chew on it for weeks. He praised Darwin for publishing the *Origin* first, 'for the three volumes [of *Natural Selection*], unprefaced by this, would have choked any Naturalist of the nineteenth century.'[29] In fact the book's very toughness made it seem more respectably scientific, a hand's remove from the flighty *Vestiges* pandering to the lowest taste.

But the real enthusiasts were the radical atheists, like Hewett Watson and old Robert Grant; transmutationists of course, and more concerned with the scale and power of Darwin's opus than his mechanism. Watson hailed Darwin as 'the greatest revolutionist in natural history of this century' (and it was the first time anybody had said that). Grant, sixty-eight and still teaching evolution weekly at

Darwin told him that he was 'inclined to look at everything as resulting from designed laws' (as he told Asa Gray a few months later). By this he meant that God had appointed natural laws to evolve life rather than intervene himself; but Owen, seizing on 'designed laws,' presumed that they shared common ideological ground, both believing in an immediate 'Creative Power.' Hence his politeness, and Darwin's impression that 'he goes at the bottom of his hidden soul as far as I do!'[24]

But Darwin's 'design' was a far cry from Owen's 'ordained' nature. Like Carpenter, Southwood Smith, and other Unitarians, Darwin made nature an immutable chain of material causes and effects. There was no providentialism; natural causes did not express the 'continuous operation' of God's will. There was none of Sedgwick's Anglican view that the Creator designs and updates each dragonfly personally. Darwin told Lyell that if each step in evolution was providentially planned, the whole procedure would be a miracle and natural selection superfluous. To Gray, Darwin mooted 'designed laws,' but he had 'the details, whether good or bad, left to the working out of what we may call chance.' Like a good Unitarian, Darwin saw a rational, lawful nature offer a solution to the problem of evil. Why the 'misery' if everything is ordained? he asked Gray. 'I cannot persuade myself that a beneficent and omnipotent God would have designedly created the Ichneumonidae [parasitic wasps] with the express intention of their feeding within the living bodies of Caterpillars.' Such adaptive accidents merely happened in a world governed by laws; they were not God's responsibility.[25]

Here spoke an old Unitarian who had fallen off the feather-bed. He was holding to a semi-respectable theism and packaging it under a designer label for the Owens and Grays. But his God was an absentee landlord, and nature self-sufficient.

Not unexpectedly, Carpenter came over, convinced that only a world of 'order, continuity, and progress' befitted an omnipotent Deity. He was writing on the *Origin* for the Unitarian *National Review* in December. 'Any theological objection' to the derivation of one breed of dog or one species of slug from another was 'simply absurd,' he announced, and he ridiculed the '"most straitest" sectarian organs' for their dogma on such matters. Human evolution was no obstacle, though he shelved the issue. It was enough that the struggle for existence tended 'inevitably . . . towards the progressive exaltation of the races engaged in it.'[26]

At this point Darwin's carefully built bridge with Owen was dynamited, and of course it was Huxley's doing. Darwin revelled in

1860–1871

33

More Kicks Than Halfpence

TWENTY YEARS after its inception, Darwin's theory was in print. To some it looked like a belated piece of Reform Age business. Its bleak, uncharitable survivalism seemed more suited to the poor-law 1830s than the optimistic 1860s. Ironically Malthus was passing out of vogue. So even where evolution was accepted, natural selection – the 'law of higgledy-piggledy,' in Herschel's words – usually was not.

A 'bitter satire' on man and nature, Marx and Engels called the *Origin of Species*, detesting Malthus. Darwin's secular, struggling nature might have served Marx 'as a basis in natural science for the class struggle in history,' but he laughed at the way 'Darwin recognizes among beasts and plants his English society.' This was nature in the technology age, with divisions of labour, manufactories, and workhouse losers. Worst of all it was 'Hobbes' *bellum omnium contra omnes.*' Others were appalled at the implicit message of this 'war of all against all.' *Laissez-faire* run amok, throat-slitting competition: one press squib had Darwin proving that '"might is right," and therefore that Napoleon is right, and every cheating tradesman is also right.' Another knew that the *Origin* would gratify the free-market fanatics 'who reduce all the laws of action and human thought habitually to the lowest and most sordid motives.'[1]

But closer to home the old 30s Malthusian circle was ecstatic. Erasmus thought it 'the most interesting book I ever read,' and he posted a copy to his old flame Harriet Martineau, now fifty-eight and living in the Lake District, still reviewing and sprightly enough to be receiving champagne from anonymous admirers. There was plenty of time to read the *Origin* that January 1860. Cold north-easterlies brought blizzards from Siberia, keeping the nation huddled around the fireside. Martineau sat in her 'snow landscape' revelling in the book, unable to thank Eras enough: 'one might say "thank you" all one's life without giving any idea of one's sense of obligation.' She had often praised

> the quality & conduct of your brother's mind, but it is an
> unspeakable satisfaction to see here the full manifestation of
> its earnestness & simplicity, its sagacity, its industry, & the
> patient power by w^h. it has collected such a mass of facts, to
> transmute them by such sagacious treatment into such
> portentious knowledge. I sh^d. much like to know how large a
> proportion of our scientific men believe that he has found a
> sound road . . . It does not very much matter; for it is the
> next generation that effectively profits by such books.

Who wrote *The Times*'s review? she asked, and what did Owen think of the *Origin*? – not that anybody 'trusts Owen's manners or speech on such occasions: but there is some wonder about what he thinks.'[2]

Harriet read it as an atheist and simplistically summed it up to fellow campaigner George Holyoake: 'What a book it is! – overthrowing (if true) revealed Religion on the one hand, & Natural (as far as Final Causes & Design are concerned) on the other. The range & mass of knowledge take away one's breath.' Other rationalists were equally taken. The 'great Buckle highly approves,' Darwin chortled. And John Chapman spoke for many when he called it 'one of the most important books of this century,' which was 'likely to effect an immense mental revolution. The sagacity, knowledge and candour displayed in the work are unusually great and wonderful.'[3]

Martineau demurred at only one point. Darwin had traced all animals and plants back to an ancient 'progenitor.' To avoid stirring up a secondary storm with spontaneous generation to start the process, he talked of this having been 'created,' of life having been 'first breathed' into it. 'I think it is a pity that 2 or 3 expressions' seemed theological, Harriet complained. She assumed that they were used colloquially, 'without reference to their primitive meaning. If so, they ought not to have been used: but the theory does not require the notion of a creation; & my conviction is that Charles D. does not hold it.'[4]

She dropped a note to Fanny Wedgwood to make the same point.

> I rather regret that C.D. went out of his way two or three
> times . . . to speak of "the Creator" in the popular sense of

the First Cause . . . It is curious to see how those who w^d. otherwise agree with him turn away because his view is "derived from" or "based on" "Theology" . . . It seems to me that having carried us up to the earliest group of forms, or to the single primitive one, he & his have nothing to do with how those few forms, or that one, come there. His subject is the "Origin of Species," & not the origin of Organisation; & it seems a needless mischief to have opened the latter speculation at all. – There now! I have delivered my mind.[5]

The Unitarian approval, secular glee, and young Turks' optimism was a world removed from the distress felt by Darwin's Cambridge mentors. Old patrician Anglicans still feared that a nature not actively upheld by God's Word boded ill, threatening the command structure of a paternalist society, just as a vicious free-for-all capitalism destroyed its harmony. Sedgwick spoke bluntly. Old and lined, he was now marginal to the world of London science, but his anguish was real. He had received his copy

> with more pain than pleasure. Parts of it I admired greatly, parts I laughed at till my sides were almost sore; other parts I read with absolute sorrow, because I think them utterly false and grievously mischievous. You have *deserted* . . . the true method of induction, and started in machinery as wild, I think, as Bishop Wilkins's locomotive that was to sail with us to the moon.

The old proctorial hackles rose: he accused Darwin of trying to sever the link between material nature and its moral meaning. Only this indication of divine love can keep the social fabric secure. 'Were it possible . . . to break [the link], humanity, in my mind, would suffer a damage that might brutalize it, and sink the human race' into a cesspit. He called himself 'a son of a monkey and an old friend of yours' but then signed off with a sentiment that stung Emma. 'If you and I' accept God's revelation in nature and the Bible, he told Charles, 'we shall meet in heaven.' This questioning of Charles's future life upset her and she refused to show the letter to Henrietta.[6]

Henslow was more magnanimous. He told his brother-in-law, the Revd Jenyns, that 'the Book is a marvellous assemblage of facts & observations – & no doubt contains much legitimate inference – but it pushes *hypothesis* (for it is not real *theory*) too far. It reminds me of the age of astronomy when much was explained by Epicycles – & for every fresh difficulty a fresh epicycle was invented.' He showed better grace than Sedgwick, but in the end he too dissented: 'Darwin attempts more than is granted to Man, just as people used to account for the origin of Evil – a question past our finding out.'[7] Publicly he admitted that the *Origin* was 'a stumble in the right direction,' but when his name was linked with Darwin's supporters he protested to the papers.

This Anglican censure had more personal repercussions. Darwin may even have lost a knighthood. Lord Palmerston, the incoming Liberal Prime Minister in June 1859, had apparently mooted Darwin's name to Queen Victoria as a candidate for the Honours List. Prince Albert concurred; he was a friend of science, a friend of Owen's, President of the British Association in September 1859, where Lyell had spoken of Darwin's forthcoming work, and he had seen Sir Charles similarly honoured. Darwin would have been delighted and astonished. But then came the *Origin*. The Queen's ecclesiastical advisers, including the Bishop of Oxford Samuel Wilberforce, scotched it. The honour would imply approval, and Palmerston's request was turned down.[8]

Not that all Anglicans stood in opposition. Charles Kingsley, as eager to side with the evolution *avant garde* as he had been with the Chartists, struck up a dialogue with Huxley, who admitted in February 1860 that Kingsley

> is a very real, manly, right minded parson but I am inclined
> to think on the whole that it is more my intention to convert
> him than his to convert me. He is an excellent Darwinian to
> begin with, and told me a capital story of his reply to Lady
> Aylesbury who expressed her astonishment at his favouring
> such a heresy – "What can be more delightful to me Lady
> Aylesbury, than to know that your Ladyship & myself sprang
> from the same toad stool." Whereby the frivolous old woman
> shut up, in doubt whether she was being chaffed or adored
> for her remark.[9]

But generally the young guard had no time for priests; their strategy called for confrontation, for edging out the men with dual callings.

Huxley's gladiatorial attitude was being noticed. In February he lectured at the Royal Institution on Darwin's theory of 'Species and Races, and their Origin.' He arrived at the theatre armed with Darwin's drawings, skulls of pouters and tumblers, and sheaves of the *Natural Selection* manuscript. He left in an 'ocean of hot water,' having 'disappointed & displeased' everybody by trying to be even-handed. Or so he said. In fact some of the disappointing was deliberate. 'I had a Bishop & a Dean among my auditors, and, to please *them* I wound up with the most' confrontationist appraisal 'of Science *versus* Parsonism that is likely to have reached their ears.'[10]

He was openly goading the prelates, exploiting the *Origin* to wrench science from ecclesiastical control, leaving those in the audience like Owen seething. Huxley perfected his stock-in-trade metaphors – about clerical oppositions being 'crushed and maimed in every battle' since Galileo's day, about 'Canutes of the hour enthroned in solemn state, bidding the great wave to stay,' about the *Origin* heralding a 'new reformation.' He damned the pious 'meddlers' and ended on a question. Would England play a noble role in this 'revolution' of thought?

> That depends upon how you, the public, deal with science. Cherish her, venerate her, follow her methods faithfully and implicitly in their application to all branches of human thought, and the future of this people will be greater than the past. Listen to those who would silence and crush her, and I fear our children will see the glory of England vanishing like Arthur in the mist.

Secular expertise was being wedded to Britain's technological and imperial salvation. The nation's health was linked to the professional scientist's own. It was a self-serving plea on behalf of the new white-collar specialist, standing at arm's remove from the dog-collared dogmatist. In his first public lecture on the *Origin* Huxley had prepared the future ground. Not that Darwin, the Downe squire and anything but white-collar, really appreciated it. He thought the flashy rhetoric so much 'time wasted.'[11] The talk should have been on the *Origin*'s arcana, not Canute and Arthur.

Yet by March Darwin was typically drawing up lists of supporters. He too had a polarized view of events: everybody was for or against him, on 'our side' or with 'the outsiders.' Huxley became his 'good and kind agent for the propagation of the Gospel – *i.e.* the devil's gospel.' The camaraderie between Huxley, Hooker, and Darwin strengthened, fired by a sectarian spirit which manifested in mock religious metaphors – despite some doubt as to whose side Satan was on: 'the alternative, for men constructed on the high pressure tubular boiler principle, like ourselves,' Huxley told Hooker, 'is to lie down and let the devil have his own way. And I will be torn to pieces before I am forty sooner than see that.'[12]

Owen was the unknown quantity. His public verdict on the *Origin* was anxiously awaited, and indeed the Superintendent of the natural history collections at the British Museum was being forced to grapple with the book. Owen told a Parliamentary Committee, inquiring into the feasibility of erecting a purpose-built Natural History Museum, that 'in the present phase of natural history philosophy' expansion was more necessary than ever:

> The whole intellectual world this year has been excited by a book on the origin of species; and what is the consequence? Visitors come to the British Museum, and they say, "Let us see all these varieties of pigeons: where is the tumbler, where is the pouter?" and I am obliged with shame to say, "I can show you none of them" . . . As to showing you the varieties of those species, or any of those phenomena that would aid one in getting at that mystery of mysteries, the origin of species, our space does not permit; but surely there ought to be space somewhere, and, if not in the British Museum, where is it to be obtained?

But however useful the *Origin* might have been as a lever to pry open government coffers, Owen viewed it as a dangerous weapon in the wrong hands. Huxley's religious provocations and goading on apes were hitting the mark. When Owen's *Edinburgh* review of the *Origin* appeared in April Darwin, hypersensitive, was so shocked that he lost a night's sleep. 'Spiteful,' he called it: 'extremely malignant, clever, and . . . damaging.'[13]

Owen himself was now furious, alienated by Huxley's pugnacious posturing. His review boiled at the *Origin*'s crude caricature of 'creationists,' fumed at Darwin's asking whether they really believed that animals appeared out of thin air, as 'elemental atoms suddenly flashed into living tissues.' ('Preposterous and unworthy' he was to call this, especially with Darwin *himself* writing of the first 'progenitor' having been 'created'! How were they created? Owen snapped – from 'elemental atoms'?) Left prickly by Huxley, Owen took Darwin's talk of 'the blindness of preconceived opinion' to heart. He accused Darwin of setting up straw men. Was Owen's own ugly 'axiom of *the continuous operation of the ordained becoming of living things*' to be ignored? Didn't most modern geologists believe that the 'mystery of mysteries' had a natural explanation? That none accepted transmutation was beside the point. Darwin had fallen into the error of assuming that selection was the only possible natural Creative law.[14] There was a more godly, less chancy, alternative: new species appeared at a stroke, by natural birth.

Others joined the fray, nailing their colours to Owen's mast. Angered by Huxley, many gentlemen of substance believed it their duty to steer science in a respectable direction. The Duke of Argyll, the Lord Privy Seal in Palmerston's government, currently defending the Budget with its repeal of the newspaper tax, saw Owen's distinction as crucial. Creation by natural selection was inconceivable – bloody, wasteful, and chaotic – whereas '*Creation by Birth*' harmonized with experience; the reproductive process was 'the only "Law" which we know of as capable of "Creating".'[15] Of course Huxley and Hooker, with their secular professional needs, treated this distinction as pernicious. It threatened to fragment their scientists' coalition and let the priests and princes back in.

Owen's bitterness was exacerbated by Huxley's conclusion that 'man might be a transmuted ape.' In his review he slated Darwin's 'disciples' for their 'short-sighted' adherence. He mauled Hooker. Then he turned to Huxley's Royal Institution lecture, having sat through it in utter disgust. England owed its 'greatness' to books like the *Origin of Species*! Owen thought that it more accurately symbolized an 'abuse of science,' the sort 'to which a neighbouring nation, some seventy years since, owed its temporary degradation.' This would not be the last time that revolutionary France was thrown in Darwin's teeth.

The cadre of disciples bunched up for protection. 'He is atrociously severe on Huxley's lecture,' Darwin lamented on reading the review, 'and very bitter against Hooker. So we three *enjoyed* it together.' Huxley had calculated well. Owen stood ostracized and caricatured, and it was too much for his overweening pride. Everyone knew why he retaliated. An admirer put it to Huxley, 'You had some forecast of what was to happen I suppose as you have given him as good.' Darwin had a different, rather glib, explanation. 'The Londoners say he is mad with envy because my book has been talked about,' he told Henslow. 'It is painful to be hated in the intense degree with which Owen hates me.'[16]

The disciples continued to stake claims. Huxley, reviewing for the *Westminster* in April, first uttered the rallying cry 'Darwinism.' He gave them a flag to march under; no longer would they be a stateless nation, they were set to conquer scientific Britain. Huxley slated Owen, hailed the *Origin* as a 'Whitworth gun in the armoury of liberalism,' and projected 'the domination of Science' over 'regions of thought into which she has, as yet, hardly penetrated.' It was clear by April that Darwin's and Huxley's fates were now irrevocably entwined. Huxley's was 'a *brilliant* review,' Darwin admitted, 'with capital hits.' It no longer mattered that he hardly 'advances the subject.'[17]

Darwin took the knocks very personally. Most reviewers wrote with great respect, however dumbfounded that a squire of science should have turned to heresy. But his older friends were often negative. Wollaston insisted with Coleridge that Nature is a 'pestilent abstraction' and can select nothing. The pannings depressed Darwin. The attacks were raining down 'hot and heavy.' Few were grasping natural selection, which left him cursing that 'I must be a very bad explainer.' Selection for most implied a Selector, and they wondered why Darwin did not see it. 'I suppose "natural selection" was a bad term,' he admitted. 'Natural Preservation' might have been less anthropomorphic. He tried it out on Lyell. But Lyell could not read his abysmal handwriting and read it as 'Natural Persecution,' which, considering the fraught circumstances, raised a laugh at Downe.[18]

Love it or loathe it, at least nobody was ignoring the *Origin*. Three publishing houses in America tried to pirate it (there was no international copyright protection), but Gray at Harvard twisted arms, made two withdraw, and closed with a five per cent royalty from Appleton's in New York, on the adage that 'all got is clear gain.' Darwin had hoped that Gray's review in the *American Journal of Science* could be bound in at the head, making it a joint publication (and mollifying the opposition). He was happy to have the botanist 'baptize' the *Origin* 'nolens volens, which will be its salvation.' It was not to be. The US *Origin* stood alone on its publication in May, in a print run of 2500 copies. But he was mightily pleased. 'I never dreamed of my book being so successful' with Yankee readers, he chortled, offering Gray a cut of the £22 revenue. Once 'I should have laughed at the idea of sending the sheets to America.'[19]

Every potential triumph was now talked up by the evangelical Darwinians. Feeling themselves beleaguered, they needed visible gains. Thus it was that a witty bit of repartee on Saturday 30 June 1860, at a section meeting of the British Association for the Advancement of Science, was destined to be blown out of all proportion to become the best known 'victory' of the nineteenth century, save Waterloo.

Oxford was the venue in 1860, the home of High Anglicanism, Bishop Samuel Wilberforce's diocese. There was no set-piece debate on Darwinism, but Professor John William Draper of New York University was slated to talk on Darwin and social progress, so no one doubted that the bishop would eloquently vent his spleen, if called upon. But much had changed since the last Oxford meeting in

1847, when Soapy Sam floored Chambers for his *Vestiges*: dissident scientific Londoners were seizing the reins of power and Wilberforce was no longer guaranteed unanimous support. To start with he was in a brand new museum, not St Mary's Church; even in Oxford, science now had its own house. On the other hand, this *was* still Oxford, and the gothic revival museum was a shrine to nature's God. An angel stood over the entrance. The dons, on passing through, were transported into the light glass-roofed atrium. Here they imagined themselves in a 'temple of science,' glorying in all the designs of nature, 'by which the Author of the universe manifests himself to His creatures.'[20]

That Saturday was a routine 'Botany and Zoology' meeting, but Draper and the bishop drew a large crowd, seven hundred at least. The clergy gathered in the middle, undergraduates at the back; Oxford dons, science teachers, and gentlewomen clustered around. The make-up might have ensured an anti-Darwin consensus, but these were uncertain times. Some of the same Londoners were here as in 1847, but thirteen years had taken their toll. Many felt out of place among the spires and out of sorts with the dons.

Consider the Geological Survey corps. These were young middle-class salaried professionals, jealously guarding their autonomy. Andrew Ramsay was a Survey careerist. In 1847 he had applauded Sam's slap at those succumbing to the 'foul temptation' of speculation. But he had been lecturing alongside Huxley and Hooker for years. In their School of Mines lines of ancient shells were glued to boards around the walls to indicate pedigrees. Ramsay told Darwin that he had long done with a 'succession of small miracles' and come over to transmutation.[21] This wasn't the Ramsay of 1847. In 1860 he was working specifically to plug the embarrassing gaps in Darwin's geological evidence.

The London audience might have changed, but it was the same loquacious, plum-in-mouth Wilberforce. He was no supple Kingsley, prepared to follow Darwin's 'villainous shifty fox of an argument, into whatsoever unexpected bogs and brakes he may lead us.' The liberal *Daily Telegraph* abused the bishop as one of the 'old style Tories,' men who 'have not advanced one iota beyond their ancient notions.'[22] Owen, lodging with Wilberforce the night before, was suspected of priming him. He probably did; during the port the talk undoubtedly turned to Darwin's book. But Owen believed in the 'continuous creation' of life, so he was probably pushing Sam beyond Genesis miracles to a more enlightened view; not Darwinian, but not traditional.

Huxley had been spoiling for a fight. He was razor-sharp; but his shaking temper could still reduce his effectiveness, and Owen had bettered him on occasions. Hooker was cooler and clearer, if less cutting. Later legends depicted a bloody clash, with Wilberforce scotched if not slain. But the first play-by-play account received by Darwin painted a very different picture.

Darwin had settled into Dr Lane's new hydropathic home, in Sudbrook Park, Richmond. (Lane had been acquitted of adultery and moved premises.) Here he sat, 'utterly weary of life,' reading Hooker's long letter. Hooker remembered when they were together at the last Oxford meeting of the Association, but he too noticed the changes. Clerical Oxford no longer held its attractions: 'without you & my wife I was as dull as ditch water & crept about the once familiar streets feeling like a fish out of water. I swore I would not go near a Section,' and indeed he did not enter a meeting room for two days, lazing about the colleges instead, admiring the gardens.

Clearly nothing had been premeditated that Saturday. Huxley was not even going to wait for the meeting, until Robert Chambers – of all people – ran into him in the street the day before and remonstrated about his 'deserting them.'[23] Of course Chambers, once ritually humiliated, was hoping for vicarious revenge. Hooker too was lackadaisical. He wandered to the meeting door, he told Darwin, not in the best mood, '& swore as usual I would not go in; but getting equally bored of doing nothing I did.' He described the scene in his letter:

> A paper of a Yankee donkey called Draper on "civilization according to the Darwinian hypothesis" or some such title was being read, & it did not mend my temper; for of all the flatulent stuff & all the self-sufficient stuffers – these were the greatest, it was all a pie of Herb[ert]ᵗ Spenser [sic] & Buckle without the reasoning of either.

In fact Draper was English-born and London University-educated, even if he had lived in America for twenty-eight years. He was the star attraction, because he was applying Darwin's theory to society. But his numbing speech droned on for an hour, although he 'was listened to with the profoundest attention, no one went out indeed no one stirred.'[24] Hooker continued to Darwin:

> however hearing that Soapy Sam was to answer I waited to hear the end. The meeting was so large that they had

494

adjourned to the Library which was crammed with between
700 & 1000 people, for all the world was there to hear Sam
Oxon. Well Sam Oxen got up & spouted for half an hour
with inimitable spirit[,] uglyness & emptyness & unfairness. I
saw he was coached up by Owen & knew nothing & he said
not a syllable but what was in the Review [Wilberforce's
Quarterly Review diatribe on the *Origin*, just out] – he
ridiculed you badly & Huxley savagely.

What Hooker did not say was that the bishop, after two hours of
boring speeches in a stuffy room, tried to lighten the proceedings
with a joke that palpably missed its mark. He turned to Huxley and
asked whether it was on his grandfather's or grandmother's side that
he was descended from an ape.[25] Whereupon Huxley retorted to the
'savaging'

> & turned the tables, but he could not throw his voice over so
> large an assembly, nor command the audience; & he did not
> allude to *Sam*'s weak points nor put the matter in a form or
> way that carried the audience. The battle waxed hot. Lady
> Brewster fainted, the excitement increased as others spoke.

Hooker mentioned no names, but 'a grey haired Roman nosed
elderly gentleman' then stood in the centre of the audience to protest
at 'Mr Darwin's book' and 'Prof. Huxley's statement.' It was FitzRoy,
now head of the Government's Meteorological Department and at
Oxford to read a paper on storms. With military bearing the Admiral,
'lifting an immense Bible first with both and afterwards with one
hand over his head, solemnly implored the audience to believe God
rather than man.'[26] He admitted that the *Origin of Species* had given
him 'acutest pain.' It was a sad sight as the crowd shouted him
down. Hooker continued:

> my blood boiled, I felt myself a dastard; now I saw my
> advantage – I swore to myself I would smite that Amalekite
> Sam hip & thigh if my heart jumped out of my mouth & I
> handed my name up to the President (Henslow) as ready to
> throw down the gauntlet. I must tell you that Henslow as
> president would have none speak but those who had
> *arguments* to use, & 4 persons had been burked [silenced] by
> the audience & President for mere declamation: it moreover
> became necessary for each speaker to mount the platform &
> so there I was cocked up with Sam at my right elbow, &

there & then I smacked him amid rounds of applause – I hit him in the wind at the first shot in 10 words taken from his own ugly mouth – & then proceeded to demonstrate in as few more 1 that he could never have read your book & 2 that he was absolutely ignorant of the rudiments of Bot[anical] Science. I said a few more on the subject of my own experience, & conversion, & wound up with a very few observations on the relative positions of the old & new hypotheses, & with some words of caution to the audience. Sam was shut up – had not one word to say in reply & the meeting *was dissolved forthwith* leaving you master of the field after 4 hours battle. Huxley who had borne all the previous brunt of the battle & who had never before (thank God) praised me to my face, told me it was splendid, & that he did not know before what stuff I was made of. I have been congratulated & thanked by the blackest coats & whitest stocks in Oxford.[27]

This was certainly not the old Hooker of 1847. He had acquitted himself splendidly, faced down a bishop in his own diocese. Darwin trembled reading this, secure at Sudbrook Park, hearing about his absent body being tugged this way and that. The body itself was falling apart. 'I have been very poorly,' he replied, 'with almost continuous bad headache for forty-eight hours, and I was low enough, and thinking what a useless burthen I was to myself and all others, when your letter came.' 'It is something unintelligible to me how any one can argue in public like orators do ... I am glad I was not in Oxford, for I should have been overwhelmed.'

It looked as if Hooker had carried the day, not Huxley. Darwin asked for *his* account of the 'awful battles.' 'I often think that my friends (and you far beyond others) have good cause to hate me, for having stirred up so much mud ... I honour your pluck; I would as soon have died as tried to answer the Bishop in such an assembly.'[28]

Huxley's version, however, was substantially different. On being asked about his ancestry, 'I had said that I could not see what difference it would make to any moral responsibility if I *had* had an ape for a grandfather.' This was flat, as Hooker said; 'saponaceous Samuel thought it was a fine opportunity for chaffing a savan' and he pitched into Huxley.

However he performed the operation vulgarly & I determined to punish him, partly on that account & partly because he talked pretentious nonsense. So when I got up I spoke pretty much to this effect – that I had listened with great attention to the Lord Bishops speech but had been unable to discern either a new fact or a new argument in it – except indeed the question raised as to my personal predilection in the matter of ancestry – That it would not have occurred to me to bring forward such a topic as that for discussion myself, but that I was quite ready to meet the Right Rev. prelate even on that ground. If then, said I, the question is put to me would I rather have a miserable ape for a grandfather or a man highly endowed by nature and possessed of great means & influence & yet who employs these faculties & that influence for the mere purpose of introducing ridicule into a grave scientific discussion I unhesitatingly affirm my preference for the ape.

Whereupon there was inextinguishable laughter among the people, and they listened to the rest of my argument with the greatest attention. Lubbock & Hooker spoke after me with great force & among us we shut up the bishop & his laity.

Huxley insisted that he 'said my say with perfect good temper,' but eye-witnesses reported that he was 'white with anger,' too wrought up to 'speak effectively.' His hot-head had stymied him again.

Soapy Sam, a Tory bishop who 'presumed on his position' to pronounce on science, was everything the new men despised. Huxley had the 'most unmitigated contempt' for 'the round-mouthed, oily, special pleading of the man.' Anyway, like Hooker, Huxley came away believing that he was himself 'the most popular man in Oxford for full four & twenty hours afterwards.' Faced by the conflicting propagandist claims, Darwin did not know who had triumphed exactly, except that it must have been 'our side.' (On the other, Wilberforce went away happy that he had given Huxley a bloody nose, while many in the crowd adjudicated it an entertaining draw.)[29]

Mooting an ape for a grandmother was a risky gambit, playing on Victorian sensibilities about the sanctity of the female sex. Had it not been so clever, it would have been in shocking taste. Sedgwick had tried a parallel tack against the *Vestiges*, saving 'our glorious maidens' from such depravity. Maidens stood for the Church and the chaste against the sordid evolutionists. Wilberforce might have succeeded in his ploy, but for Huxley's righteous riposte. He reformulated the issue as one of rectitude. He co-opted Darwin's clean unsullied 'truth' for the New Model Army of scientists. He brought an earnestness to the rhetoric that the bishop lacked, but then, of course, 'no man ever manifested more of the moral presuppositions of a Puritan evangelicalism.'[30]

Huxley's strategy was to portray a morally regenerative science combating a corrupt Church. He was taking over an old radical ploy and using it to advance the career scientists. No one with a double calling was henceforth to be granted a hearing. Clerical geologists like Sedgwick, Hooker said, 'are like asses between bundles of hay.'[31] Wilberforce was something worse. The asses had to choose their trough, science or theology. Scientific power was being closely circumscribed by the new professionals.

Darwin at Sudbrook Park pored over Hooker's account 'with infinite pleasure.' He re-read Huxley's letter, sent it home to Emma, and 'when I get home shall read it again.' Having had 'more "kicks than halfpence",' he was thankful for champions, and voluble ones; but he would still have preferred a calm discussion about pouters and poultry. From his Richmond rest home he twitted Huxley: 'how durst you attack a live bishop in that fashion? I am quite ashamed of you! Have you no reverence for fine lawn sleeves?'[32] But for all the mock heroics, he knew the die was cast, and that his old mentors were not to be reconciled now.

More colourful stories began to circulate, sealing the legend. William Darwin – following his father at Christ's College – heard from one of the tutors that after the meeting blind Henry Fawcett (a Darwin sympathizer, shortly to become professor of political economy at Cambridge) and another Cambridge man 'happened to be near the B[ishop]. of Oxford; and the one asked Fawcett whether he thought the Bishop had ever read the Origin' and the blind man shouted out in a loud voice '"Oh no, I would swear he has never read a word of it." The Bishop bounced round with an awful scowl and was just going to pitch into him, when he saw that he was blind, and said nothing.'[33]

One hopes Sam read the *Origin*, because he was paid £60 to write it up for the Tory *Quarterly*. This completed the trinity of heavy-weight reviews (with Owen in the *Edinburgh* and Huxley in the *Westminster*), and in late July Darwin caught up with Wilberforce's article. It was slick. The bishop had even disinterred a sixty-year-old parody of grandfather Erasmus's evolutionary prose, to show that a Darwin never changed his spots. (The political message was obvious – the parody came from the reactionary government-sponsored *Anti-Jacobin*, cracking down in the aftermath of the French Revolution.) But the day of arbitrating Tory bishops was over. Darwin took his pencil to the piece, out of all sympathy. If 'transmutations were actually occurring,' Wilberforce argued, we should see them today in the rapidly reproducing invertebrates; since we don't, why believe that 'the favourable varieties of turnips are tending to become men.' Darwin slashed 'rubbish' in the column. This was truth sacrificed for a slippery style, like Soapy Sam's jibe at Huxley. The bishop's explanation of animal classification left Darwin in even higher dudgeon: 'all creation is the transcript in matter of ideas eternally existing in the mind of the Most High'!! 'Mere words' Darwin scribbled, the sort spouted by Owen, and anathema to lapsed Unitarians with their feet on the ground.[34]

34

From the Womb of the Ape

WHATEVER THE FURORE over Darwin, liberal theologians were generating even fiercer passions in their own world. Seven – 'seven against Christ' – responded to the likes of Wilberforce by issuing a manifesto with the deceptively innocuous title *Essays and Reviews* only three months after the *Origin* appeared. They were a miscellaneous lot, Oxford professors, country clergymen, the headmaster of Rugby School, and even a layman. But Anglican divines declaring miracles irrational whipped up unprecedented anger in a country still hardly touched by German biblical criticism. *Essays* sold 22,000 copies in two years (as many as the *Origin* in two decades) and provoked a ferocious paper war. Four hundred books and pamphlets contested and defended the issues over five years, hardening attitudes on both sides.[1]

With *Essays and Reviews* deflecting the clerical mind, the *Origin* escaped behind the smokescreen. Some related the two books. The most scientific of the seven, Baden Powell, slipped a sentence into his *Essays* proofs commending 'Mr. Darwin's masterly volume,' while restating his argument that belief in miracles was atheistic. An unbroken causal nexus was proof of Creative intent, and the *Origin* therefore a boon to faith: it 'must soon bring about an entire revolution in opinion in favour of the grand principle of the self-evolving powers of nature.' Darwin's detractors turned on Powell. Sedgwick scowled at his 'greedily' adopting such nonsense. Tory reviews charged him with joining 'the infidel party.' (Time ran out before he had the chance; he died of a heart attack two weeks before the British Association debate, in June 1860, otherwise he would have been on the platform at Oxford facing the bishop.) After slating Darwin, Wilberforce retrained the *Quarterly*'s sights on to *Essays*.

His iron fist came down again in a letter to *The Times*, signed by the Archbishop of Canterbury and twenty-five bishops, which threatened the heretics with the ecclesiastical courts.[2]

This many prelates were never to be trusted. Darwin rattled out his favourite proverb, 'A bench of bishops is the devils flower garden' – then, a bottle of anaesthetic in hand, went about the latest Satanic experiments in his own beds, chloroforming carnivorous sundew plants. With Lubbock, Busk, Lyell, Carpenter, and others (including the mathematician and Queen's printer William Spottiswoode), he signed a counter-letter supporting the *Essays* for trying to 'establish religious teachings on a firmer and broader foundation.' Hooker declined (as did Huxley), arguing that if the signatories were 'chiefly men of one way of thinking, in such matters as "Origin of Species",' it would give the impression that science had dictated 'our religious views.'[3] But there was no disguising the fact that pro-*Origin* scientists – with a strong flank of Unitarians – were aligning with liberal churchmen. Not that it was to any avail. Two of the *Essays*' authors were indicted for heresy and out of a job by 1862.

In science the lines were also sharpening as Huxley indicted Owen again. Perjury was the charge, ape brains the issue, and the brawl was every bit as rancorous as the *Essays* débâcle. At the British Association Owen had repeated his view that human and ape brains differed on two points. Humans had a peculiar lobe, the hippocampus minor, and their enormous cerebral hemispheres were unique in covering the underlying cerebellum. Huxley denied both distinctions, and promised to prove it. The outcome might have had nothing to do with evolution, but, with these two involved, nobody doubted that the squabble was over Darwin's 'absent body.'[4]

The bloodletting began in Huxley's new *Natural History Review*, which made Owen its *bête noire*. This was the first Darwinian house organ, bought and refurbished by Huxley, Lubbock, Busk, and other 'plastically minded young men' (a code for Darwin's men). The tone 'will be mildly episcophagous,' Huxley gloated to Hooker, 'and you and Darwin and Lyell will have a fine opportunity if you wish it of slaying your adversaries.' The first issue in January 1861 set the scene with Huxley's paper on man's relationship to the apes (which he duly posted to Wilberforce out of bravado). 'What a complete and awful smasher (and done like a "buttered angel") it is for Owen!' Darwin cooed. How 'Owen is shown up' by the whole issue, '"this great and sound reasoner"!'[5]

Through the excitement Darwin continued quietly at home, cutting the early chapters out of his unfinished 'big book,' *Natural Selection*. Nothing was wasted, everything recycled at Downe; just as the carpets were well worn, so old manuscripts were continually re-read, and every trifling fact re-deployed somewhere. It was back to pigeons and poultry, the pages to be worked up into a separate volume on the way breeders made domestic animals. This was more necessary than ever. Lyell and Gray still believed that variations were providentially planned – that nature's course was steered. The pigeons alone should scotch this. Their ruffs and frills were not supernaturally selected, so why was a wild bird? As he explained to Gray:

> you believe 'that variation has been led along certain beneficial lines.' I cannot believe this; and I think you would have to believe, that the tail of the Fantail was led to vary in the number and direction of its feathers in order to gratify the caprice of a few men. Yet if the Fantail had been a wild bird, and had used its abnormal tail for some special end, as to sail before the wind . . . everyone would have said, 'What a beautiful and designed adaptation.'

He asked Lyell if 'the shape of my nose was designed.' If it was, 'I have nothing more to say. If not, seeing what Fanciers have done by selecting individual differences in the nasal bones of pigeons . . . it is illogical' to suppose that variations in nature have been planned. Noses were no less natural than fancy beaks. The new book would hammer the point home: it would illustrate 'what an enormous field of undesigned variability there is ready' in the farmyard and the forest.[6]

Not that he was above exploiting Gray's providential defence of 'my deity "Natural Selection".' Over the winter he let go the pigeons to organize a third edition of the *Origin*. He added a perfunctory historical sketch, a cursory list of 'precursors,' and prefaced it with a clever piece of self-promotion. Asa Gray had published three supportive articles in the *Atlantic Monthly*. Darwin persuaded him to reprint them as a pamphlet, and even to have its title reflect their providential tone. When Gray came up with 'Natural Selection Not Inconsistent with Natural Theology,' Darwin was delighted, paid half the cost, and imported 250 copies into England. He was rubbing balm on to the theological rash. He advertised the pamphlet in the periodicals, and posted a hundred copies to scientists, reviewers, and theologians, not forgetting Wilberforce. In the new edition, before the 'Historical Sketch,' he recommended it to the theologically squeamish, to be purchased for 1*s*. 6*d*. from Trübner's in Paternoster

Row. Yet, happy as he was to run this religious endorsement, afterwards he went 'crawling on' with his fancy animal book, trying to convince the Grays of the world that natural selection was actually self-sufficient.[7]

The Huxleys and Darwins grew closer in these years. The Down House doors were always open, Emma ever ready to help. The Huxleys lost their first son Noel from scarlet fever three months after the British Association meeting. He was almost four, and his sudden death prostrated Henrietta, six months pregnant, and brought her husband to the edge of a breakdown. Huxley tried to rationalize the 'holy leave-taking' as he stood over the body, with its staring blue eyes and tangled golden hair, but the tragedy left a deep scar. At the funeral, 'with my mind bent on anything but disputation,'

> the officiating minister read, as a part of his duty, the words, "If the dead rise not again, let us eat and drink, for to-morrow we die." I cannot tell you how inexpressibly they shocked me. [The parson] had neither wife nor child, or he must have known that his alternative involved a blasphemy against all that was best and noblest in human nature. I could have laughed with scorn. What! because I am face to face with irreparable loss . . . I am to renounce my manhood, and, howling, grovel in bestiality? Why, the very apes know better, and if you shoot their young, the poor brutes grieve their grief out and do not immediately seek distraction in a gorge.

A desolate Henrietta Huxley brought her three infants to Down for a fortnight in March 1861, where Emma lavished consolation. Huxley remained in town to start his working-men's lectures at the School of Mines. But he sent reports on his men-and-apes talks, and the cloth-cap crowd which lapped them up. 'My working men stick by me wonderfully, the house fuller than ever,' he regaled his recuperating wife. 'By next Friday evening they will all be convinced that they are monkeys.'[8]

A few days later his slanging match with Owen spilled over into the *Athenaeum*. The 'slaying of the slain' continued week in, week out in this emotionally charged period, Huxley's refutations becoming more acrimonious with each resuscitation of the corpse. He was joined by the entire Darwinian camp, which turned out ritually to refute Owen. Some put his ape-brain blunder down to his use of brains deformed in their preserving spirits, others to his poor dissectors. The Christians who sided with Huxley maintained that cerebral differences bore no relation to psychology, or the debate to human ancestry. But Owen tried to whip up sympathy by tarring Huxley as an 'advocate of man's origin from a transmuted ape.' Eventually the *Athenaeum* even printed one of Owen's ripostes under the head 'Ape-Origin of Man as Tested by the Brain.' The ruse backfired. In private Huxley had already talked provocatively of 'pithecoid man' – ape-like man – delighting Darwin, who called the term 'a whole paper & theory in itself.' (But then he had been mooting 'monkey-men' in secret for twenty years.) Now Huxley could go public on the issue, accepting Owen's terms of debate.[9] By turning a question of brain structure into one of human ancestry, Owen had ensured that Huxley would proclaim his defeat as a vindication of Darwinism in its most sensitive aspect.

Darwin sat down to each Saturday's *Athenaeum*, crowing with delight at Huxley's ridiculing responses; 'well done, but almost too civil,' he gleefully replied after one. 'It is a good joke, that since Owen attacked me, I do not feel at all a good monitor, & feel more inclined to clap anyone on the back, than to cry hold forth! I wonder whether he will answer you. Oh Lord what a thorn you must be in the poor dear man's side.'[10] Mock concern, of course; he now evinced no shred of sympathy for the poor dismembered man. Darwin's 'demoniacal' hatred of Owen grew like a boil and burst into the open as he egged Huxley on.

In this hysterical atmosphere Huxley's anatomical compatriots forlornly tried to disentangle the issues. One of his Oxford protégés declared that 'our higher and diviner life is not a mere result of the abundance of our convolutions.'[11] But this wasn't the point for Huxley. Owen was being indicted for perjury, and it was made to seem symptomatic. His whole toadying ideology was in the dock. Huxley intended to create a spectacle, promising, 'Before I have done with that mendacious humbug I will nail him out, like a kite to a barn door, an example to all evil doers.' As prosecuting attorney, he was exposing the incriminating evidence: religious contaminants had led to Owen's blindness and evil doing. He was another, like the priests, who 'prostitute Science.' Darwin's new professionals were the more faithful followers of Nature.

It was a powerful call: a denunciation of Owen and Wilberforce designed to appeal to the up-and-coming meritocrats who despised the Anglican *ancien régime*. In the eyes of older chivalrous souls Huxley had stepped well beyond the bounds of good taste, and they loathed his 'offensive manner.' But he deliberately trumpeted his efforts to 'get a lie recognised as such.' Moralizing served his group well. Sucking up to 'the "peace & make-things-pleasant party"' promised no return. He would dump these reconcilers in a 'hot locus in the lower regions' if he 'were Commander in Chief in their universe.'[12]

The campaign was devastingly effective, with each 'slaying' followed by a recruiting drive by the Darwinians. The sniping lasted two years and left a festering cancer for life. When Huxley joined the Zoological Society Council in 1861, Owen left. A year later Huxley moved to stop Owen being elected to the Royal Society Council, on the grounds that no 'body of gentlemen' should admit a member 'guilty of wilful & deliberate falsehood.'

Huxley's belligerence worried Lyell. He was equally troubled by what Huxley was advocating, an ape ancestry. For years he had denied such bad blood in the family; now he was forced to confront the problem head on. He decided to face it in a book, to reconcile himself – somehow – to the artefacts and fossils that proved man's ancient pedigree. Darwin had little sympathy for the loss of human 'dignity,' teasing his old friend: '*Our* ancestor was an animal which breathed water, had a swim bladder, a great swimming tail, an imperfect skull, and undoubtedly was an hermaphrodite! Here is a pleasant genealogy for mankind.' Even pleasanter, 'mankind will progress to such a pitch' that nineteenth-century gents will probably be looked back on 'as mere Barbarians.'[13]

Huxley was even less help on dignity or design. He was too happy to pit the 'anthropomorphism' of Providence against 'the passionless impersonality of the unknown and unknowable,' itself becoming the commanding orthodoxy of the secular Darwinians. Nor would he disentangle men and apes. He told Lyell that there was more difference in size between the brains of people than between small-brained men and gorillas. 'Under these circumstances it would certainly be well to let go the head [as a way of distinguishing the species] though I am afraid it does not mend matters much to lay hold of the foot.'[14]

By April 1861 Lyell had toured the archaeological sites in England and France to confirm that stone tools occurred alongside extinct hyaenas. He had denied such human antiquity for thirty years, but the evidence was now overwhelming. Falconer had found pre-glacial scrapers in 1858 in a cave in Brixham, a fishing village on the Devon coast; and in 1859, after touring the Abbeville flint site in France, Lyell had signalled his conversion. Examining flints in a Bedford gravel pit he had a clearer picture of the pre-Ice Age dating for ancient man. Darwin was ecstatic. 'It is great. What a fine long pedigree you have given the human race.' Others were stretching it further. A new fossil human had opportunely made his début, a Neanderthal skull from a cave near Düsseldorf, described by the anatomist Hermann Schaaffhausen in 1858. It had a swept-back forehead, overhanging brow ridges, and brutal looks. Lyell questioned Huxley about it, intriguing him too. Busk translated Schaaffhausen's paper for the *Natural History Review* in April, and Huxley set to, examining the cast of the 'degraded' cranium at the College of Surgeons.[15] Now he had a new line of lectures in mind, on fossil man.

That spring Henslow lay dying of heart disease. Hooker stood vigil at his father-in-law's bedside, watching him bid 'farewell to his friends, parishioners and little botanical school children, one by one.' For two months Hooker sent harrowing reports of Henslow's decline. They threw Darwin into agonies of indecision, and he finally apologized about not visiting, on 23 April. It was a melancholy moment. Ten years to that day Annie had closed her eyes for the last time. Darwin had everything to thank Henslow for: his *Beagle* trip, his grants, his support, his parish advice – Annie, George, and Leonard even bore his own children's names. But he declined a last call: 'I sh[d]. not like to be in the House (even if you could hold me) as my retching is apt to be extremely loud.' His own health was precarious, and a few minutes speaking at the Linnean Society that month had brought on '24 hours vomiting.' The decision racked him with guilt: 'I never felt my weakness [a] greater evil.'[16] He did not see Henslow again. After his death on 18 May, Darwin penned a short, clinical note for the family *Memoir*, but it could not assuage his feelings.

He went his sick way, worrying about the children. His youngest, Horace, was Annie's age when she died, and Charles waited for the hereditary weakness to show. Lenny, eleven, was being tutored by a local vicar and seemed 'slow & backward' in his lessons. His deficiency, Charles feared, was only 'in part owing to loss of time from ill-health.' Sixteen-year-old George came home from Clapham School for surgery on his decaying teeth. As he passed out under the chloroform, so death-like in its effect, Charles relived old memories and was overcome with nausea.

Henrietta's condition upset him most. She remained weak and wan, an invalid at eighteen. A typhoid infection the previous year had left her dangerously close to death; for months she had required three attendants around the clock. Her fevery spells and indigestion caused Charles such 'incessant anxiety' that sometimes his 'tender sympathy and emotion' were too 'agitating' for her, and she could 'hardly bear to have him in the room.' The lack of recovery left Emma at her wits' end. 'I have succeeded pretty well in teaching myself not to give way to despondency,' she sighed, but she could only 'live from day to day.'[17]

Amid this backdrop of painful thoughts, lost children, lost friends, Emma poured her heart out in another touching letter to Charles, reminiscent of the one she had written after their marriage. The strength of her pleading reflected her own painful experience: the 'only relief' was to take affliction 'as from God's hand' and 'try to believe that all suffering & illness is meant to help us to exalt our minds & to look forward with hope to a future state.'

> When I see your patience, deep compassion for others[,] self command & above all gratitude for the smallest thing done to help you I cannot help longing that these precious feelings should be offered to Heaven for the sake of your daily happiness . . . I often think of the words 'Thou shalt keep him in perfect peace whose mind is stayed on thee.' It is feeling & not reasoning that drives one to prayer.

Charles had done with Christianity, damned hell's torments, but Emma was now urging prayer for his present happiness, not as insurance against future suffering. She wished him to find the meaning of his pain in an after-life, where their love would go on for ever. But the hope of heaven was dim. He only scrawled 'God Bless you' on the bottom of the note. In the end all that stood between his grief and thoughts of oblivion was Emma's unshakeable faith. He became twitchy whenever she left him alone.[18]

Huxley's spring lectures on men and apes to the labourers and shopkeepers were a roaring success. Lyell, boning up for his book, sat among the cloth-caps and was 'astonished at the magnitude and attentiveness of the audience.' The scene might have been his worst fears realized, teaching a gorilla-ancestry to the great unwashed, yet the carters and cabbies were polite, and they would, he conceded, 'devour any amount of your anthropoid ape questions.'

The lecture was rapturously received because human origins had been trailed in the radical press for decades. (Even as Huxley was talking, the secularist *Reasoner* was running an evolutionary series combating 'Theological Theories of the Origin of Man,' arming infidel missionaries with human fossils and Darwin's book.) Radical workers were evolutionists long before the neophyte addressing them. Inflammatory tracts had sought to undermine priestly power with materialist explanations of man's ancestry. The *Origin* was grist to their mill, like *Vestiges* and French Revolutionary science before it. One tailor offered Darwin services in exchange for an inscribed copy; a baker plagued him with a whole manuscript assessing the *Origin*. This audience was prepared for any anatomist who would stand on their ground and relate man to the 'under-world of life.' Gutter-press hacks gleefully turned up pad in hand to report Huxley's 'exciting and even solemn' words.[19]

Huxley was capturing a new constituency for Darwin. Each talk was carefully tailored. He started off iconoclastically, like one of their own infidel missionaries, praising those 'cursed with the spirit of mere scepticism' and casting off tired traditions. As on so many radical broadsheets, he intimated that man was made in the image of an ape. 'Brought face to face' with chimpanzees, 'these blurred copies of himself, the least thoughtful of men is conscious of a certain shock.' The clinical anatomy was dressed with a bit of artisan cynicism. 'It is as if nature herself had foreseen the arrogance of man,' he said, speaking of the mirror held up by the gorilla, 'and with Roman severity had provided that his intellect by its very triumphs, should call into prominence the slaves, admonishing the conqueror that he is but dust.'

Yet he distanced himself from the gutter cynics bent on degrading mankind. Man might have come from the brutes, but 'he is assuredly not *of* them.' A common origin implies no 'brutalization' – man is not 'degraded from his high estate' by his descent from a 'bestial savage,' Huxley pleaded, mindful of Lyell sitting incongruously among the carters.

Rather, he promoted evolution as a form of self-betterment, urging that the downtrodden masses, 'once escaped from the blinding influences of traditional prejudice, will find in the lowly stock whence Man has sprung, the best evidence of the splendour of his capacities; and will discern in his long progress through the Past, a reasonable ground of faith in his attainment of a nobler Future.' This 'lowly-origin, noble-future' picture would have fallen flat among the port-swilling aristocracy, but the idea of promotion through the ranks was devoured by the aspiring sweeps and enterprising shopmen. Others caught Huxley's drift. One correspondent fleshed the pedigree out. 'Man's descent reads very much like a Law Lords pedigree in the Peerage, a remote ancestor temp. Will. 1 [in William the Conqueror's time]. Seventy fourth in descent a Wig-maker – and then the full-blown Chancellor or Chief Justice.'[20] Exactly; evolution bestowed scientific dignity on lowly parentage and promised better things.

It might not have been Darwin's image; Huxley mentioned no callous competition, no going to the wall. But the lecture served a purpose, blowing aside the smoke on the burning human question. Where once it was taboo, the subject now seemed obligatory, and the question was carved and apportioned in every way. Lyell was plotting human antiquity, Lubbock publishing on Danish shell mounds, and Falconer finding more Brixham tools, including an extinct bear's arm bone carved as a stave. There was no doubt among Darwin's group that humans could be pushed into the fossil past, or that man lived alongside extinct hippos, even if Huxley's dinosaur-spearing *Homo ooliticus* was a bit strong.[21]

Given the excitement, Darwin's continuing obsession with stewed rabbit bones verged on the mundane. He was now deep in his domestication book, borrowing collections of fowls' skulls, and posting pleas for more carcasses: 'get me, if you can, another specimen of an old white Angora rabbit,' he asked one breeder. 'I want it dead for the skeleton; and not knocked on the head.'

He stopped for July and August to take Henrietta to the fishing village of Torquay, opposite Brixham on the Devon coast. Here in the warm sun Charles spent hours on his hands and knees, watching insects visit wild orchids. Bizarre petals guided the bees to the nectaries, enticing them into position. Pollen sacs were then glued to their probosces, precisely where they could be removed by a stigma of another flower. Since the late 30s, in the gardens at Maer and The Mount, he had speculated on the ways bees cross-pollinate, convinced by his theory that crossed plants give stronger offspring. Orchids offered the most exquisite devices for achieving that end. Coming home from Torquay, he searched for little orchids on the hillocks around Downe. In the idyllic sun it seemed infinitely preferable to stewing pigeons. The lure was too strong; he put 'the confounded cocks, hens and ducks' down and switched.[22] He was side-tracked again.

There was a flourishing orchid fancy in Victorian Britain. But no back-street, grog-shop hobby this; it was an élite fancy. Wealthy enthusiasts gave over hot-houses to the fantastic flowers and dispatched orchid hunters to the tropics. Darwin shot out feelers and was showered with rare specimens. Orchids proved the ultimate test case. What more glorious example of floral whimsy could exist? 'Who has ever dreamed of finding an utilitarian purpose in the forms and colours of flowers'? Huxley had once asked incredulously. Darwin of course. He took the hardest case and cracked it. Orchid petals were exquisite devices for guiding bees and moths to particular spots for dobbing or docking pollen. Every ridge and horn served this end. Natural selection could not explain useless or frivolous or pretty flowers; it *could* explain functional ones.

He became lost in the floral intricacies, delighting in the outrageous. The orchid *Catasetum*, peculiar enough for having three flowers – male, female and hermaphrodite (themselves thought to have been three species until his study) – was actually sensitive to insects and fired arrows with a sticky pollen head as they brushed past. He described the preposterous mechanism to Huxley, to be greeted by, 'Do you really think that I can believe all that!'[23]

The subject was genteel and a perfect foil. He worked out the homologous parts of every flower, making them 'modifications of one and the same ancestral organ.' As in barnacles, each homologous organ twisted and turned to a different role, switching tactics as needs arose, adopting any contingency to deposit the packet of pollen. He talked Murray into taking a book, selling it as a fashionable subject seen through evolutionary eyes. And if that wasn't enticement enough, it would be a new 'Bridgewater Treatise' for the old fogies. But a Bridgewater with a kick: a glorious lampoon on design, pointing not to God, but a series of accidents. It was 'a "flank movement" on the enemy,' he twitted Gray. Darwin was following his grandfather yet again. But this was to be no *Loves of the Plants*, nothing as salacious; 'any woman could read it,' and Murray was wise enough to see that many would. With German and Dutch translations of the *Origin*, and a French one in press, Darwin was rising up the list.

He still wondered whether the whole venture wasn't the 'most ridiculous thing.' And no sooner had he sold the idea in September than he fell ill again; the work piled up, the prose proved intractable, his stomach erupted, and he seethed through gritted teeth 'I ought to be exterminated.'[24]

Friends proved a mixed blessing, and bulldogs infuriating. Huxley continued to cavil about sterility: breeders had not produced infertile hybrids by crossing fancy breeds. Until they did, Huxley argued – until they produced, in effect, separate species – the analogy between artificial and natural selection was incomplete, and the *Origin*'s theory unproved. So Darwin ended up experimenting, losing hundreds of hours pollinating plants and sifting seeds. He was collating his results on primroses in January 1862, and trying to persuade Huxley to mute his criticisms. He showed that primroses and cowslips, nearly identical in structure and long thought to have been varieties, produced sterile hybrids.[25] Sterility, he suggested, evolved to allow close species like these to diverge. It was a mechanism to stop them both being blended back to some unadapted middle line. Huxley was half-convinced.

While Darwin sifted seeds, his letters chased Huxley to Edinburgh, where the evangelist was 'preaching Darwinism pure & simple as applied to man to the Scotch presbyterians. Whats more I made 'em listen . . .'

He 'found sinners enough in "Saintly Edinburgh",' as in London. But then the tabloid talk was all of salacious apes, thanks to the French-American traveller Paul du Chaillu, whose chilling gorilla hunts were sensationalized in his *Explorations and Adventures in Equatorial Africa*. Du Chaillu was in England lecturing and talking, visiting Owen and exhibiting skins and skeletons. The tall stories of women-snatching gorilla males and screaming females clinging to their babies amid a hail of bullets dominated the gutter press; everybody was talking gorillas, every Irishman in a *Punch* cartoon was a 'Mr. G. O'Rilla' or 'Mr. O'Rangoutang.' More and more, audiences flocked to Huxley's serious talks, lapping them up, not realizing, the Free Church *Witness* said, the 'foul outrage' being committed upon them. When 'their kindred to the brute creation was most strongly asserted, the applause was the most vigorous,' it reported, appalled. Given the anti-slavery furore during the American Civil War, the *Witness* expected the hood-winked workers to form a 'Gorilla Emancipation Society.' The 'vilest and beastliest paradox ever vented in ancient or modern times amongst Pagans or Christians,' was the kindest cut.[26]

This was what Huxley had planned. He gloried in the provocation, sending press cuttings to Hooker and Darwin. 'I told them in so many words that I entertained no doubt of the origin of man from the same stock as the apes.' He was revelling in the Darwinian jingoism: 'Everybody prophesied I should be stoned and cast out of the city gate,' he reported to Darwin, but 'I met with unmitigated applause!!' The gung-ho mood was infectious. 'By Jove,' Darwin responded, 'you have attacked Bigotry in its strong-hold. I thought you would have been mobbed.'[27]

Still he pottered on with orchids, refusing to enter another side-show. The flanking-movement became obvious on 15 May when his book appeared under the unpromising title, *On the Various Contrivances by which British and Foreign Orchids are fertilised by Insects*. This was the first of his books on beauty and the bizarre, the evolution of the inexplicable. It also proved the benefit of crossing; orchids were engineered to receive pollen-bearing insects. Only the odd one held out; the bee orchid, which seemed to be a self-fertilizer, and predictably doomed to extinction. Darwin must have been the only man on the planet who wanted to live a thousand years just to see the bee orchid's demise.

Orchids was published just in time to give the newly returned Wallace a complimentary copy. Wallace announced his arrival in England with a present of a wild honeycomb from Timor. He was home finally after eight years in the East, and lodging on the fringe of London's West End, where he could get 'doctored,' read the backlog of reviews, and recover from exhaustion. Through the summer he sifted and organized his six-year tally of 125,660 specimens, as Darwin had done in more salubrious surroundings so long ago.[28]

Huxley gathered his lectures on apes, origins, and Neanderthals into a slim book on *Man's Place in Nature*. No fat, two-volume tome for him, but the effect was just as devastating. Although reading the proofs was a 'great treat' for Lyell in August 1862, he worried about parts and warned that they were 'not in good taste & will do no good.' But advising Huxley 'to write as if you were not running counter to . . . old ideas' was like dragging a bull backwards out of a china shop. He was too intent on smashing Owen's providential pots and humiliating him at every turn. And anyway Lyell's tall order was countermanded by the militant strategy of the younger naturalists.

Huxley and Darwin had forced the agenda on apes and origins, unsettling more orthodox Anglicans who looked to Owen for a response. Even the *Athenaeum* goaded Owen. The Darwinians on their side had said enough 'to freeze us.' Darwin had spoken and 'found a bold and able advocate in Prof. Huxley. Is Prof. Owen, then, to be reserved?'[29]

Owen was taking a very different approach. He believed that jellyfish and liver flukes and the like, which pass through complex life cycles involving different forms, each one 'giving birth to another,' held the key. He was pressing for sudden jumps, for the analogous birth of one species direct from another. What did this mean for man? The Revd Gilbert Rorison, a Scottish Episcopalian minister, writing his orthodox article on the Genesis 'Creative Week' for the *Replies to 'Essays and Reviews'*, wondered just this. Did Owen believe that man was 'produced by *Creative Law* (& in so far supernaturally) *through* the lower: e.g. the womb of the Ape'? Did the 'special Creative Energy' work on the gorilla's reproductive system to create the first human?

Owen would only admit some pre-ordained natural cause of man's birth; he intimated that it did not matter religiously if the ape's womb were the mediating organ, or, astonishingly, if '"original sin" should prove to be only the remnant of the untransmuted ape still lingering in our constitution.' If 'God's ministers' *were* natural causes it would not diminish our duties and responsibilities. Rorison published Owen's letter in the *Replies*, failing to see it as a chide to literalists.[30] But, of course, ending up in the reactionary *Replies* – edited by Bishop Wilberforce – and contributing to Rorison's 'theological hash' only damned Owen further in Darwin's and Huxley's eyes.

Owen did not deny that man might change, even hinting that *Homo sapiens* might be replaced by higher species 'at an inconceivably remote date,' only that transmutation was the mechanism. Nevertheless he was ostracized, dumped by the Darwinians *en masse*, who were making sure he was by-passed by history. Darwin thought Owen 'so dishonest that I really now care little what he says,' eventually confessing to Huxley, 'I believe I hate him more than you do.'[31]

At Downe the grind continued, and the summer saw Darwin 'slaving on bones of ducks and pigeons.' Unable to let Huxley's cavil go, he delegated as his health deteriorated, offering breeders £5 to cross Spanish cocks with white Silk hens to check the chicks' fertility. He was going against the fancy grain, coercing breeders to undo their varieties by producing sterile hybrids. No mind, he reassured them, they will always 'do for the pot.' By now he had gardeners experimenting at Kew and Edinburgh Botanic Gardens, apiarists and fanciers shipping hives and corpses, and breeders examining every cross, from melons to mastiffs.

When Sulivan and Wickham visited on 21 October for a *Beagle* reunion, they found the philosopher inundated in orchids, sundews, and interminable trays of seeds, with farmyard bones everywhere, and dead ornamentals brewing in foul-smelling spirits. The old dyspeptic himself had aged badly. They caught him at a low moment, after Emma's and Lenny's scarlet fever attack in the summer, and typically sipping the latest quack remedy, 'Condy's Ozonized Water Cure.'

He was so wrapped up in orchids now that he had Sir John Lubbock's gardener build him a hot-house over winter, and he sent a tax-cart to Kew for plants to stock it. It was the pigeons over again: 'You cannot imagine what pleasure your plants give me,' he thanked Hooker. Henrietta 'and I go and gloat over them.' It was his only consolation in another uncomfortable winter. His skin inflammation left him sloughing like a reptile. He gruesomely related to his friend

Falconer how eczema had 'taken the epidermis a dozen times clean off.'[32]

Falconer, the only fossil expert in London to rival Owen, cheered him with a tip-off in January 1863 about a 'sort of mis-begotten-bird-creature,' a part-reptilian feathered fossil from Solenhofen in Germany, and by all accounts a prize ready to drop into his lap. Owen had bought the exquisitely preserved bird for the British Museum. Darwin's old friend George Waterhouse had been dispatched to Pappenheim in Bavaria, to pay the unheard-of sum of £450 (increasing the fossil's notoriety). Darwin had predicted that a proto-bird would one day turn up with unfused wing fingers, but this exceeded all expectations. He pressed Falconer for more 'about the wondrous bird.'[33] As the news dribbled in he pieced together an astonishing picture. It was as old as the dinosaurs, with a long, lizard-like tail, and Owen had detected four free fingers in each wing, clawed.

'The fossil bird,' he agreed, 'is a grand case for me.' Others feared as much and were trying to forestall him. At the Munich Natural History Museum the ageing Andreas Wagner guessed that Darwin, lost in his 'fantastic dreams,' would hail it as an ancestral bird. He dismissed it on hearsay as an aberrant reptile to ward off 'Darwinian misinterpretations.' Owen was also worried. He officially described the fossil, christening it *Archaeopteryx* in a paper read to the Royal Society. He called it unequivocally a bird, but primitive, its fingers and tail placing it closer to the primal vertebrate archetype.[34]

Darwinians rushed to regain the initiative. The beak was detected on the slab, and most controversial of all, four, perhaps five, teeth, the lustre of the enamel still visible. Announced in the *Natural History Review*, the discovery of teeth left no doubt about the archaic bird's relevance to 'the great question of the Origin of Species.' Hooker saw another great lesson. He caught part of Owen's paper and realized that the fossil, suddenly turning up in a lithographic quarry, proved Darwin's point about the bittiness of the fossil record. Darwin, at home sipping his 'Ozonized Water' and sifting strawberry varieties, revelled in the splendid 'bird-creature with its long tail and fingers.' A note was filed away for the next edition of the *Origin*.[35]

Huxley's lectures to the labourers this winter popularized Darwinism. His ensuing little book, sewn together from six fourpenny pamphlets (published by an enterprising hack taking notes in the audience), appeared in December. Darwin was full of praise; it was 'capitally written,' 'simply perfect.' So good, in fact, that 'I may as well shut up shop altogether.' As for the substance, the talks flew high and low. Huxley might have vindicated Mr Darwin's science, which was no 'modern black art;' he might have scotched the humbug about the *Origin*'s speculative method.[36] But he *still* overcalled the sterility objection. The ferocity of newshounds Darwin expected, but not the continual nipping of a friendly bulldog.

None of his friends moved far or fast enough for him. He coveted their public praise, and craved their emotional support to dispel his perennial fears. On 4 February 1863 Lyell's *Antiquity of Man* arrived. Darwin cheered 'the great book,' then took it to Eras's for ten days to read. Sir Charles's endorsement would be the most important to date; he expected his old mentor to give 'the whole subject of change of species' an enormous boost. But apes and immortality gnawed at the sexagenarian, and Hooker knew that he would 'have a pretty job to reconcile all his old Geology and Biology to the new state of things.' Even so 'the sale of his work will be *prodigious*.' 'What a sale!' Darwin exclaimed; 4000 went into the shops on publication day. Hooker was right, 'he has the ear of the public.'[37]

The *Antiquity of Man* was tame, and Darwin despaired at Lyell's timidity, even if the book as a whole produced a striking effect. Much was said, but so much more was missing. Part was a stale hash, a 'compilation' from archaeologists far ahead of him in the game, although Lyell covered his tracks by implying that 'nothing is to be trusted until he has observed it.' Part – a small part – was a feeble summary of the evidence for transmutation. He attacked Owen's brain work (cued by Huxley) but nowhere said 'openly that he believed in change of species, and as a consequence that man was derived' from an ape-like ancestor. Lyell was visibly straining, but unable to move. He made man old but refused to degrade him, reverting to 'new and powerful causes' to explain the spiritual part of human nature.[38]

Back at Downe, Darwin's patience ran out. The Lyells were coming to stay for a few days and he braced himself for a confrontation: 'I dread it,' Hooker heard, 'but I must say how much disappointed I am that he has not spoken out on species, still less on man. And the best of the joke is that he thinks he has acted with the courage of a martyr of old.' But Lyell *had* struggled, and no martyr moved so far from accepting man as an 'archangel ruined' to seeing him as an elevated animal. As he explained to Darwin, 'I have spoken out to the full extent of my present convictions, and even beyond my state of *feeling* as to man's unbroken descent from the brutes.' It had been unrealistic to expect Lyell to 'go the whole orang,' one who had devoted thirty years and nine editions of the *Principles of Geology* to refuting bestial transmutation. 'Your judgment would have been an epoch in the subject,' Darwin groaned; now 'all that is over with me.'³⁹ He felt so sick that he cancelled the Lyells' visit.

No wonder he shouted 'Hurrah the Monkey Book has come' as Huxley's *Man's Place in Nature* arrived later in February. It was more to his taste, and to Hooker's – 'amazingly clever' he called it. The frontispiece spoke more loudly than the text. It showed a line of skeletons, as though they were standing at a tram stop, with a gibbon at the rear, stooping apes in the middle, and a man at the head. 'It is a grim and grotesque procession,' the Duke of Argyll squirmed, thankful that their brains could not be similarly queued. This line of 'gibbering, grovelling apes' set the *Athenaeum*'s teeth chattering. It lumped Lyell and Huxley as cynical degraders; the one making man 'a hundred thousand years' old, the other giving him 'a hundred thousand apes for his ancestors.'⁴⁰

Man's Place mined the last ounce of gold from the Owen debate. Owen was his own worst enemy; his tongue-twisting expressions invited parody. His 'continuous operation of the ordained becoming of living things' simply meant that God was an '*anticipating* Intelligence' constantly re-fitting species to the world by means of natural law (itself a sort of divine edict). Huxley, however, treated it as a piece of semantic pandemonium. Such providential platitudes galled the swelling ranks of rationalist Darwinians. Owen's words even sounded evasive, and it was Huxley who extracted the capital in *Man's Place*:

> though I have heard of the announcement of a formula
> touching 'the ordained continuous becoming of organic forms,'
> it is obvious that it is the first duty of a hypothesis to be
> intelligible, and [this] . . . may be read backwards, or forwards,
> or sideways, with exactly the same amount of signification.

Darwin relished the 'delicious sneer.' The theatrics used in nailing Owen boosted sales, and the 1000 copies of *Man's Place* sold quickly, requiring a reprint within weeks.⁴¹

But nothing made up for his disappointment over Lyell. While reading the *Antiquity of Man* Charles was vomiting so badly again that Emma resorted to drastic measures. 'It breaks my heart,' he sighed to Hooker, 'but Emma says . . . that we must all go for two months to Malvern.' He had avoided the spa for twelve years, the memories cut too deep. Even now he thought 'a good severe fit of Eczema ... might save me' from the trauma. But no, a mild one simply delayed his departure and left him languid. In desperation he tried visiting the family, hoping that the change would cure him. He only grew worse, and by June was confined to his couch, fit only to watch his new tendril-bearing plants. Gray had started him off with a packet of wild cucumber seeds, which had sprouted and rather hooked the patient. Day and night, from his sickbed, he observed the long lasso-like tendrils sweeping around in a circle, first one way then the other. 'I am getting very much amused by my tendrils,' he told Hooker, requesting more exotic ones to watch, 'it is just the sort of niggling work which suits me.'[42]

The eczema cleared up, but then word came that Dr Gully was ill, and the Malvern trip was postponed once more. Charles lived a 'hermit's life' all summer, more so 'than ever.' 'Devilish headaches' set in and by August he was retching again every morning. He posted off vials of vomit for analysis, but to no avail. As the partridge season opened in September, Emma finally had her way. She took him off to the sounds of shooting, reminding them of the 'old times.' In Malvern they avoided their former lodgings, but there was no escaping the sad associations of the town. Charles and Emma had never seen Annie's grave. It was hard enough for Emma to venture into the churchyard, but soul-destroying not to find the headstone. Charles jumped to the conclusion that it had been stolen in a despicable act of vandalism. Fox, who had seen it once, was contacted and he directed Emma to the overgrown spot.[43]

By the most crushing coincidence, within days – on Tuesday 29 September – they received a note from Hooker, sobbing 'My darling little 2^d girl died here an hour ago.' Hooker's six-year-old Minnie was carried off 'after a few hours *alarming* illness.' He was given three minutes' warning by the doctor, and spent the precious moments by her bedside. 'I have just buried my darling little girl,' he wrote a few days later. She was

> the flower of my flock in everyone's eyes, the companion of
> my walks, the first of my children who has shown any love
> for music and flowers, & the sweetest tempered affectionate
> little thing that ever I knew. It will be long before I cease to
> hear her voice in my ears – or feel her little hand stealing into
> mine, by the fire side & in the Garden – wherever I go she is
> there.

The memories came flooding back at Malvern. 'I understand well your words: "wherever I go she is there",' Charles answered mournfully. 'God bless you my best of friends.' Re-reading the letter, he cried again 'over our poor darling.' But time heals, and the tears had 'lost that unutterable bitterness of former days.'[44]

35

A Living Grave

GULLY ORDERED SIX MONTHS' rest, but all Charles managed was six months' sickness. He became too weak even to raise a pen, and Emma took dictation. The good news, an Italian translation of the *Origin*, was not enough to rally him. Nor the family news enough to shock him – even though widower Charles Langton's marriage to Darwin's poorly, 53-year-old sister Catherine struck everybody else as an act of futility. Darwin was spreadeagled every day on a sofa, 'steadily going downhill,' wishing he were dead on one, wanting 'to live to do a little more work' the next. Visitors were banned, friends and pilgrim freethinkers put off. Harley Street doctors came and went with vials of urine. Nothing worked; nobody could find anything wrong with his 'brain or heart.' He sank lower, unable to walk 100 yards to the hot-house, unable even to cope with *The Times*, and Emma had to move on to 'trashy' novels. He vomited after every meal, and several times nightly – at one point for twenty-seven days in a row. Washed out and wiped out, he hoped he could 'crawl a little uphill again' or, if not, that 'my life may be very short.'[1]

The debilitating sickness lasted until spring 1864. April was merciful and found him on the mend, sitting in the greenhouse. For years, on and off, he had been breeding purple loosestrifes (*Lythrum*), struck as always by the oddities of nature, and there was nothing odder than their triple sexuality.[2] He loved sexual enigmas because they bore so closely on sterility and evolution – and provided the ultimate excuse to potter. He had induced all manner of 'illegitimate marriages' among loosestrifes, attempting to determine the reason for their peculiar flowers. As his strength returned, he tweezered seeds and planted a new generation.

Lythrum has three kinds of flower. The female (pollen-receiving) stigma can be either tall, medium, or short-styled; and whatever its size, two sets of male (pollen-producing) stamens occupy the remaining two slots – so if the female stigma is tall, the male stamens will be medium and short-sized. Nobody had asked why nature had resorted to such a peculiar arrangement, and nobody had thought in functional terms. Darwin revelled in inducing the eighteen possible sexual combinations, brushing pollen from every sized stamens on to every sized stigma, counting the seeds and growing them in dozens of pots to test their fertility.

He sorted hundreds of seeds this April, tabulating the results and writing them up for the Linnean Society. Only six 'marriages' proved 'legitimate,' and in each case the stamens and styles proved to be the same height. His tables clearly revealed that the greater the disparity in height, the greater the 'illegitimacy' and frequency of sterility. Tall styles and short stigmas (which occurred in the same plant) produced sterile seeds: it was another of nature's ad hoc mechanisms to ensure cross-pollination.

Talk of illegitimacy might have shocked the ladies' guilds, at least coming from Erasmus Darwin's grandson. (Grandfather's own bastardizing experiments were still supplying tittle-tattle. At this moment Darwin suspected the widow of a botanical friend, Francis Boott, to be an illegitimate granddaughter of old Erasmus.) But Darwin was stolid and methodical, reducing the loves of the plants to cold, clinical calculation. Sterile seed counts somehow fitted an unromantic, data-crunching age. Not for him Erasmus's flowery personifications, as styles and stamens bent to embrace in a kiss:

> Two knights before thy fragrant altar bend,
> Adored Melissa! and two squires attend.

Still he could tease. Solicited by a Mrs Becker for something edifying for her ladies' literary society, he posted 'On the Sexual Relations of the Three Forms of *Lythrum salicaria.*' Goodness knows how many red faces left after hearing that 'nature has ordained a most complex marriage-arrangement, namely a triple union between three hermaphrodites, – each hermaphrodite being in its female organ quite distinct from the other two hermaphrodites and partially distinct in its male organs, and each furnished with two sets of males.'[3]

By the time Darwin had finished with *Lythrum* the bedroom, study, and greenhouses were choking with climbers and coiling tendrils. Everywhere was covered with Hooker's exotics and commercial creepers: Queensland wax flowers, *Cerepegia*s from Ceylon, passion flowers and bryony. And never of course just one, but seven species of clematis, eight species of Indian cress . . . As he sat down to pen a short paper on the sweeping tendrils in May, others were tending rather more warily to the varieties of man.

Lyell's *Antiquity* and Spencer's *Social Statics* had spurred Wallace to speak out on human evolution. That month Darwin pored over Wallace's first paper, delivered to the unpleasantly ultra-racist, pro-slavery Anthropological Society.

The Society itself was an abomination, and the American Civil War only heightened Darwin's detestation. Despite Gray's dispatches on the 'dreadful carnage' during the Battle of the Wilderness, he remained adamant 'that the destruction of Slavery would be well worth a dozen years war.' There was no scientific justification for slavery, and the entire rival Ethnological Society agreed. London partisans were now busy shoring up positions on the race question with the inalienable truths of biology. The white supremacist Anthropologicals were at the throats of the abolitionist Ethnologicals (led by Huxley, Busk, Lubbock, Galton, and Wallace, with Darwin an honorary fellow and Eras on the Council), and the reviews provided cover for literary assassination.[4] Wallace, the co-operative peace-broker, was trying to engineer a truce based on a daring evolutionary compromise. He proposed that the races had long been separate (pleasing the Anthropologicals), yet had emerged from a single stock just after the ape stage (pleasing the Ethnological Darwinians).

As a good – or at this time rather wobbly – socialist Wallace started on the social differences of men and animals. Even primitive societies had a 'division of labour:' members of a tribe hunt or fish, others gather or plant. 'Mutual assistance' is all-important: the sick are cared for, food is shared, internal competition is reduced for the good of the group. As social organization strengthens, these shared 'moral' qualities will be honed to perfection by natural selection.

Competition was not between individuals, but the groups themselves. The hardiest races with the greatest ingenuity and co-operation would prevail, while the struggle 'leads to the inevitable extinction of all those low and mentally undeveloped populations with which the Europeans come into contact.' This Darwin could agree with; he marked the passage heavily. Imperial expansion from the north was wiping out the indigenous tribes. The *Beagle* voyage had shown him as much. He scribbled at the top of the page: 'natural selection is now acting on the inferior races when put into competition with the New Zealanders – high New Zelander[s] [sic] say the [Maori] race dying out like their own native rat.'[5] The hordes of

European colonists, rats and rural farmers, were wreaking havoc in the colonial bywaters.

So far a co-operative ethic was compatible with Darwinism in Wallace's political vision – indeed, mutual care was the product of natural selection. But then he changed tack: the advent of building, fire, clothing, and agriculture had made man master of his environment. The human physique, with its basic racial differences, was no longer subject to natural forces; the intellect prevailed over selection. Man's body had stopped evolving, except for aspects of skin colour or hair, while over hundreds of centuries intellectual progress had continued unabated, leaving humans with the body of an upright ape but the mind that could fashion a utopia.

Wallace's naturally selected group morality was leading society in a very unDarwinian direction. The old socialist peered optimistically at the millennium under this moral regime: everybody will 'work out his own happiness;' policing will be unnecessary, freedom will be the order of the day, 'since the well balanced moral faculties will never permit any one to transgress on the equal freedom of others;' coercive governments will wither ('every man will know how to govern himself'), the lot to be 'replaced by voluntary associations for all beneficial public purposes.'[6] On that upbeat, oddly anarchist note – intelligent selection leading to an egalitarian society – Wallace closed.

Darwin was presumably nonplussed to find the path to utopia paved by his science. He told Wallace that the brain/body dichotomy was 'grand and most eloquently done,' but he demurred on the abating of selection and played dumb on the politics. As he reasoned, the Australian savage is subject to selection, given his 'constant battles.' And English society will stay vital and progressive only through unimpeded competition. The sickly and degenerate deserve to be scythed down, he believed, even as he sent subscriptions to the Downe charities to maintain his own paternal order and worried about his sons' in-bred ailments. He decried 'primogeniture for destroying Natural Selection' even as he had Lubbock set up his eldest William in the banking business.

Wallace shook his head. Wars did not pick the fit, for the 'strongest and bravest' die first. Nor could he see much to 'sexual selection,' with each race choosing mates according to its own standards of beauty – nor, come to that, Darwin's claim that the European aristocracy is handsomer than the middle classes. Mere '*manner*' and refinement among the leisured classes were being 'confused' with beauty.[7] Politics was coming between the two men.

*

Wallace was brimming with ideas. He convinced Lyell that the caves of Borneo might reveal 'our progenitors.' Erasmus tipped off his brother that Lyell was for sending an expedition, and trying to whip up support among the Brixham Cave excavators. Lyell even set up a meeting with Sir James Brooke, the government-appointed Rajah of Sarawak, spurring him on with the thought that they might get 'extinct ourangs, if not the missing link itself.'[8] But no money was forthcoming and the British consul agreed to scout out the giant caverns himself.

What cave fossils there were seemed to confuse the issues. Neanderthal man was tugged this way and that. He was a 'poor idiot' to some, a primal human with brutish 'thoughts and desires' to others – *Homo neanderthalensis*, the first non-sapient man. Fossil skull-caps coming on top of antediluvian tools pushed the religious press to new exegetical lengths. Even granting a 'pre-Adamite' man, the Quaker *Friend* reasoned, there was no telling that he 'had any closer connection with the descendants of Adam than have the possible inhabitants of the Moon.' The Low Church *Morning Advertiser* wondered if this was 'the "man" who is without the "living soul," spoken of in Genesis.' Probably he was a brute-man, a 'mere animal, and of no more account than the bats and lizards of those long-past times.' The speculations and Huxley's attempt to turn the moral tables led Cardinal Wiseman to issue a Pastoral, appalled that 'a solitary cranium' or 'an antiquated fishbone' could be 'put in the scale against the doctrines of Scripture.' He condemned professors who teach that man has 'the matured intelligence,' and woman the 'ripened graces,' of a baboon. Shall we, he asked in *The Times*'s paraphrase, 'submit our belief in moral and spiritual truth to the judgment of those who claim to hold the key of scientific truth?'[9]

Through all of this the *Essays and Reviews* debate dragged on, its liberal Anglicanism a national scandal. Prelates fumed at the authors' dynamic, non-miraculous Christianity. Tolerate it and the Thirty-nine Articles mean nothing; the very Establishment would be imperilled. The two clerical essayists convicted of heresy for loose views on the Bible and eternal punishment had appealed to the Judicial Committee of the Privy Council, which now overturned the judgment, 'dismissing hell with costs.' Wilberforce was furious, as no doubt were the 137,000 laity who signed a letter of thanks to the Archbishops of Canterbury and York for voting against the Committee. With legal channels exhausted, churchmen united in public protest; evangelicals and High Church prelates buried their feuds and clasped hands. A declaration in favour of biblical inspiration and eternal torments was drawn up at Oxford and circulated to the 24,800 clergy. Wilberforce, armed by the 11,000 signatories, went to the Convocation of Canterbury and in June secured a 'synodical condemnation' of *Essays and Reviews*.[10] A backlash was brewing, and it boded ill for evolution.

Not that Darwin himself took much notice. While society grappled with imponderables, he hacked through creepers, trying to figure out how they evolved. Tables and sills were an entangled mass of twiners and tendrils; pots perched on every ledge as he timed sweeps and tested the effect of light. Warm summer days were spent in the hop fields watching the plants snake up their poles. He brought hops indoors, and sat ill in bed, tying weights to their tips in an attempt to slow their ascent. Around the house the vines took on a surreal appearance, covered in paint markers as he timed their twisting movements.

Clematis also clamped tight using its hooks, and since Darwin's studies were nothing if not inclusive, he started examining these leaf-climbers as well. He guessed that they were evolutionary links between the stem-twiners and tendril-waving plants. They served his purpose: he showed that hooks were modified leaf stems, and that tendrils were leaves or flower stalks drawn out drastically to form lassoes. The alterations aided a plant in its grappling, gyrating struggle for existence. Like the orchids' reproductive apparatus, they ensured the species' survival. His *divertissement*, as always, had grown into a major project. For four summer months he had been sidetracked as a result of Gray's wild cucumber seeds, and his paper, finished on 13 September, had grown so large that the Linnean Society published it as a 118-page monograph, 'The Movements and Habits of Climbing Plants.'

The next day he crept back to his domestic ducks and geese. He was not totally well; the slightest flurry could floor him. In October ten minutes with the Lyells gave him an 'awful day of vomiting' and he felt 'confined to a living grave,' showing how much he still resented Lyell's failure to support transmutation. From his mausoleum he continued cajoling fanciers and dispensing his largesse. He supported distressed breeders, helped a horticulturalist buy his ticket for India, and sent admirers his autograph.[11] He needed this humdrum existence – he preferred dealing with the world by post.

He lived vicariously through letters, especially his sons'. George, a Cambridge fresher, kept him up on collegiate life, and Frank at Clapham School recalled the agony of maths, bemoaning the tedious 'logrithmic calculations' set by the Revd Wrigley, the headmaster. Lenny and Horace, slow and frail, were still at home, being tutored by local clergymen. Everyone coddled them, dreading a breakdown. Charles also feared for their future, even despite the sound advice on suitable schools from Downe's old vicar, the Revd Innes.

Innes was now a correspondent, with a new name, Brodie Innes. He had changed it on inheriting property in the Scottish Highlands and had retired there with his wife and sickly son, putting the parish in the dubious hands of his curate, the Revd Thomas Stephens. Without a vicarage it proved impossible to attract a priest of calibre to Downe. Brodie Innes, still the patron, relied on Darwin as his deputy and informant. For years they had been pillars of the Coal and Clothing Club and the Friendly Society; and, on leaving, the vicar had made Darwin treasurer of the village school. The Revd Henslow's old protégé took on the job gladly, despite his own work. Tending the temporal needs of poor neighbours was as much a duty as meeting their spiritual ones, and he plied Brodie Innes with the parish politics even as Stephens reported on religious matters. They were a good combination. Liberal and Tory they might have been, but Darwin and Brodie Innes, as landowners, saw their interests coinciding. From the wilds of Elgin, Innes regaled Darwin with hunting stories while deploring his crofters' morals. 'They are certainly far from honest, but ... all as full of pious talk as an English Dissenter. What can I say more?'[12]

As Huxley's ring encircled defensively around Darwin, he began to feel easier. It tightened dramatically in 1864, but by then a militant upsurge was evident on all sides. At the Anglican Convocation evangelical scientists presented a declaration reaffirming their faith in the harmony of God's Word and his Works, which they tried to make a 'Fortieth Article' of the Church of England. They carried it to the British Association, where Huxley's 'dangerous clique' was spreading its heresies 'as a prop to the scepticism which has of late years met with disciples even in the ranks of duly authorised Christian ministers.'[13] Schisms and splits appeared as they evangelized the delegates and destroyed the Association's decades-old veneer of religious neutrality.

The Darwinians and radical Dissenters strained on the other side. Outraged at a blinkered Toryism that would crush the 'new reformation,' they united in defence of evolutionary naturalism. On 3 November, at St George's Hotel in Albemarle Street, Huxley, Hooker, Tyndall, Busk, Spencer, Lubbock and two others constituted themselves into a sort of masonic Darwinian lodge, invisible to outsiders: a dining club devoted to science 'untrammelled' by any theology. Spottiswoode joined them, making nine, but they never recruited a tenth for what came to be called the 'X Club.' They would free nature from a reactionary theology, free science from aristocratic patronage, and place an intellectual priesthood at the head of English culture. Manoeuvring inside the Royal Society, they altered the election procedures to get their allies elected and were soon pulling the Presidential strings.[14]

The X's first act was to bestow 'the ancient olive crown of the Royal Society' on Darwin – the Copley Medal. Busk and Falconer nominated him, and despite furious politicking, with the Cambridge men putting up old Sedgwick in opposition, the votes ran 10 to 8 in Darwin's favour. It shocked some old members, who dreaded 'crowning anything so unorthodox as the "Origin",' Lyell reported back. As an indication, the President slipped a debilitating disclaimer into his address on 30 November, announcing that the Council 'expressly omitted' the *Origin* 'from the grounds of our award.' This caused fury; Lubbock, Hooker, Huxley, and Busk complained (and it miffed Darwin too, when he heard). Huxley called for the minutes, to prove that the Council had agreed no such thing, and he tried to have the offending statement struck from the record. The snub was mitigated somewhat by Lyell, who declared in his speech that he had been 'forced to give up' his 'old faith' in fixed species, even if he could not see his 'way to a new one.' The medal exhilarated Darwin, fortified the X, and incensed the evangelical Anglicans; no wonder Huxley told Darwin of the 'satisfaction the award has given to your troops of friends.'

Darwin stayed away, his stomach erupting at the mere thought of the pomp and ceremony. Busk accepted the medal and dropped it off at Eras's. Darwin feigned surprise that 'so old a worn-out dog as I am is not quite forgotten,' although 'such things,' he said, 'make little difference.' Huxley's and Hooker's congratulations 'are the real medal to me, and not the round bit of gold.' His coyness was topped by Eras, who had the last word on his younger brother's accolade. He reported the medal's arrival, but 'it is rather ugly to look at, & too light to turn into candlesticks.'[15]

The *Natural History Review* had failed to 'appeal to the masses,' as Huxley had hoped, so the X Clubbers ploughed their energies and money – £100 from each shareholder – into a new weekly review, *The Reader*. Darwin gave his blessing, but Spencer wanted more, the odd publishable letter at least to give the journal a boost. The *Reader* supported Darwin in turn, printing the Copley presidential address (minus the offensive disclaimer). The *Reader* was probably the last attempt in Victorian England to keep together liberal scientists, theologians, and men of letters. Galton acted as editor, as did Huxley, who penned a crushing leader on 'Science and Church Policy' in the last number for 1864. Here he made his famous claim that a deep sense of religion was compatible with the total absence of theology. Religion was important, and he advised secularists against 'burning your ship to get rid of the cockroaches.' But still the ecclesiastical pests had to be eradicated. In a blistering provocation he warned that science had no 'intention of signing a treaty of peace with her old opponent, nor of being content with anything short of absolute victory and uncontrolled domination' over theology.[16]

A sarcastic Tory opposition outdid even Huxley in polarizing the issues. Benjamin Disraeli, the Jewish defender of the Church, the witty littérateur who had satirized *Vestiges* in his novel *Tancred*, stood at the Oxford Diocesan Society in an outlandish black-velvet shooting coat and wideawake hat to tell Wilberforce: 'The question is this – Is man an ape or an angel? My Lord, I am on the side of the Angels.' With that, thoughtless Toryism made its stand. Darwin had no love of literary Tories, even less of Jewish jokes, and he looked back in scorn on *Tancred*. He was pleased to see its parvenu author – that 'blank page between the Old Testament and the New' – deliver himself to Mr *Punch*, who rendered him a suitably Jewish angel.[17]

Three weeks later opposition took a more serious turn. Pope Pius IX issued an encyclical with an appended Syllabus of Errors announcing the Catholic Church's hostility to everything that the new English-man held dear – 'progress . . . liberalism, and . . . modern civilization.' It was the first step towards the proclamation of papal infallibility. Huxley answered with a rival 'encyclical' in the *Reader*, a 'slashing' rejoinder which effectively scuppered the paper's broad church.[18] This militance coupled with editorial incompetence brought the publishing venture to an end, and the proselytizing Darwinians went their own way, looking for a partisan periodical.

With X Clubbers answering the Pope, Darwin had all the troops he needed. He could afford to drop his older conciliationist allies. He had reached an impasse with Gray over design and stopped advertising his pamphlet in the *Origin*. Lyell continued to disappoint. It was infuriating to hear him agree with the Duke of Argyll that selection was not the real 'creational law.' It was even more irritating to hear His Grace maintain in a well-dressed speech that life is led from above, and that the shimmering iridescence of hummingbirds demolished Darwin's crude view of nature's utility. Glorious beauty defied such a base explanation. Owen agreed; through Darwin's pessimistic Malthusianism he could perceive the pure light of Nature's goal – 'One true soul, like one seed of corn that grows and one egg of spawn that develops,' he told Argyll, might be 'a rare exception – for "narrow is the gate."' But if 'it pleases the Great First Cause' to usher in a moral order by this roundabout route, so be it. All concurred – selection was directed; nature was not a blind, accident-prone cripple.

Darwin was dismayed. His Grace's talk of beauty for beauty's sake showed that, like any politician, he was all mouth and no ears. 'The Duke, who knows my Orchid book so well,' he complained to Lyell, 'might have learned a lesson of caution from it.' As for minute variations in the beak and wings making no practical difference, that was preposterous. He demurred at Argyll's belief in the dramatic appearance of species or his calling them 'new births.' 'That may be a very good theory, but it is not mine, unless indeed he calls a bird born with a beak 1/100th of an inch longer than usual "a new birth".'[19] Darwin's variants crept forward, and sideways, by infinitesimal stages, but it took a pigeon-fancier rather than a politician to see it.

Behind all the cavils lurked the human question. Neanderthals, apes, black ancestors – it was emotionally fraught and for many frightening. The old certainties were threatened, the rules that had governed conduct for centuries. This is why Huxley in his lay lectures substituted Nature's laws for religious dictates, and saw obedience to science lead to the same end, social order and right morality. But there was no escaping the traumatic upheaval – or the surge of messianic materialism. From the gutter to the Palace, man's standing in nature was the issue. Back from a three-week trip to Berlin in January 1865, Lyell recounted how he had engaged the Princess Royal of Prussia in 'an animated conversation on Darwinism,' and found her 'very much *au fait* at the "Origin" and Huxley's book, the "Antiquity," &c. &c.' Darwin, with his 'instinctive reverence for rank,' lapped it up.[20]

By February Darwin was so weak that even the weight of Lyell's new *Elements of Geology* was intolerable in bed. He broke it in half and ripped off the covers. There he lay, amid a chaos of shredded pages, lost in morbid thoughts brought on by Falconer's agonized death from rheumatic fever. Years earlier Hugh Falconer had been one of the privileged few at the Downe gatherings. Only weeks before he had helped engineer the Copley Medal. Darwin was stunned by a spate of existential nightmares, Hooker adding to them by maundering on about 'meeting in a better world.' 'Personal annihilation,' Darwin answered wryly, paled into insignificance alongside his own 'pet horror,' the ice-death of the whole planet. Listen to the physicist Sir William Thomson on the cooling of the sun, and the inescapable refrigeration of earth at some determinable date! What solace for men with no faith in the divine society? The slow evolution of mankind hardly mattered, Darwin added, with 'the sun some day cooling and we all freezing. To think of the progress of millions of years with every continent swarming with good & enlightened men all ending in this . . . Sic transit gloria mundi with a vengeance'![21]

By April he was horribly ill again. He dropped the ducks and geese, doubting if he would ever finish the domestication book. He sacked his Harley Street consultant and cast around for a better one. Busk recommended a specialist on 'gouty complaints,' but none really seemed able to do anything about his 'suppressed gout.' At best his faith in the medical profession was shaky, and Hooker did not help. 'What the devil is this "suppressed gout" upon which doctors fasten every ill they cannot name?' he inquired. 'If it is *suppressed* how do they know it is gout? If it is apparent, why the devil do they call it *suppressed*.'[22] It was hardly reassuring coming from an Edinburgh MD.

Nor was it a laughing matter. Darwin now slumped into an appalling period of sickness, lasting the best part of eight months. 'What a life of suffering his is,' Emma's aunt sympathized. 'Oh! that a pure sunshine would rise for them.' But the summer sun did not shine; it was a penumbral shadow, where death again seemed a release. He lay in bed for weeks on end, with Emma reading aloud to him: novels from the London Library, so long as they had happy endings, and more esoteric matter if the postbag provided it. She gave a running translation of Fritz Müller's powerful apologia *Für Darwin*, and Friedrich Rolle's *Der Mensch*, which traced the roots of the human race to South African bushmen. Charles's ideas, dubbed *Darwinismus*, were racing ahead in Germany, with its long liberal traditions of biblical criticism and unabashed materialism.

He sank again on hearing that Lubbock was throwing himself away on politics, standing for the Liberals in the West Kent constituency – 'oh, dear! oh, dear! oh, dear!' he moaned at the prodigious mental waste. Only in *The Times*'s 'poor short-sighted view' was politics more interesting than science. Emma tried to stir him with Lubbock's book, *Prehistoric Times*, and he did perk up at the talk of savages. He rallied even more on hearing that Lubbock was trounced by the sitting Tory member, saving a great brain for science. But then science had been his undoing. *Prehistoric Times* had appeared midway through the campaign and unnerved the floating Kent voters, who considered expertise on stone-age savages inappropriate for solving Maidstone's traffic problems.[23]

Wanting release himself, he was unprepared for FitzRoy's escape. In the first days of May news came of the Admiral's end. FitzRoy, pressured at the Meteorological Department, his weather forecasting ridiculed, had fallen into one of his black moods. Darwin had seen them on the *Beagle*, the rages, the mental collapse. Everything conspired: FitzRoy had been passed over, Sulivan, his subordinate, taking the post he craved as Chief Naval Officer in the Marine Department. He brooded over the *Origin*, suffered fits of depression, and overworked; his health failing, his hearing going, he became caught up in one of his own tempestuous storms. On Sunday 30 April he walked into his bathroom in a melancholy fit and slit his throat.

The news pulled Darwin up sharp. 'I never knew in my life so mixed a character. Always much to love & I once loved him sincerely; but so bad a temper & so given to take offence, that I gradually quite lost my love & wished only to keep out of contact with him. Twice he quarreled bitterly with me, without any just provocation on my part. But certainly there was much noble & exalted in his character.'[24]

A few days later Darwin contacted John Chapman – the *Westminster* and book publisher – now a qualified specialist in dyspepsia, sickness, and psychological medicine. Chapman was Spencer's and Huxley's intimate, and the nub of a neurosis-ridden circle of dissidents. He had seen them all 'knocked up' one time or another as they pressed their rationalist claims in a hostile society. He specialized in the highly strung, those 'whose minds are highly cultivated and developed, and often complicated, modified, and dominated by subtle psychical influences, whose intensity and bearing on the physical malady it is difficult to apprehend.' Darwin the heroic evolutionist was the ultimate challenge. Chapman sent his book *Sea-Sickness* ahead, giving Darwin a foretaste. His treatment – ice-bags in the small of the back – assumed that nervous complaints could be affected by freezing and anaesthetizing the spine.

Darwin invited Chapman to Downe, listing his symptoms in gory detail:

Age 56-57. – For 25 years extreme spasmodic daily & nightly flatulence: occasional vomiting, on two occasions prolonged during months. Vomiting preceded by shivering, hysterical crying[,] dying sensations or half-faint. & copious very palid urine. Now vomiting & every passage of flatulence preceded by ringing of ears, treading on air & vision. focus & black dots[,] Air fatigues, specially risky, brings on the Head symptoms[,] nervousness when E[mma]. leaves me . . .

The list went on. Dr Chapman must have been as astonished as his predecessors: the patient was not highly strung but stretched taut. He fitted Darwin with a spinal bag, freezing him three times a day for ninety minutes a time.[25] Darwin felt sprightlier to start with and, given the ray of hope that Emma's aunt had prayed for, he wrote the most controversial chapter of his domestic animal book.

Frozen-backed, he finished forty pages on his novel hypothesis about heredity. He ended them in a flutter. Even christening his theory ruffled domestic feathers: trying to convey his idea that every bodily cell buds off a representative part of itself, he called it 'pangenesis.' The 'pan' was supposed to convey the idea that these bits – or gemmules – came from the whole body and congregated in the reproductive organs, but 'my wife says it sounds wicked, like pantheism.' The ice seemed to work, and he posted 'pangenesis' to Huxley as proof. Only Huxley was shown and then Darwin cringed, calling it 'rash and crude.' It was a rough-hewn hat-stand on which to hang all his favourite hats. Pangenesis could explain buds on a plant, or a newt regenerating a severed foot, or the strengthening and shrivelling of organs from use or disuse, or sexual generation – it was an all-purpose descendant of those ancestral unifying ideas of his London days. Not least he needed it to explain how tissues altered by selection can be transmitted. Why do pouters – pigeons coiffed and coutured by backyard breeders – hatch little pouters?

The gist was 'that each cell throws off an atom of its content or a gemmule, and that these aggregated form the true ovule or bud.' Every region of the body is democratically represented in the egg. In fact he compared the whole body to a colony (like his colonial polyps of old), where each individual buds off a representative bit of 'generative protoplasm.'[26] Forty years on, his student fascination with the granules composing pollen and eggs was still there.

After a month spent carrying ice-packs four hours a day, he was wearying in every sense. With pangenesis off his hands, he was lying prostrate, hoping Huxley would be tender with his baby Pan. Huxley donned his 'sharpest spectacles and best thinking cap' and weighed his words. He was dubious; but, having been wrong-footed by the *Origin*, he was cautious about throttling Darwin's embryonic god. 'Somebody rummaging among your papers half a century hence will find *Pangenesis* and say, "See this wonderful anticipation of our modern theories, and that stupid ass Huxley prevented his publishing them".'[27] But the message was clear enough. Don't.

Darwin was as sick as a dog again, and Huxley's deicide did not help. Despondent, he dropped Chapman and the ice-packs in July, realizing that nothing worked, and he returned to bed for the rest of the year.

Here he watched the world revolve and old friends fall out. Lyell was embroiled in a furious row. In the *Antiquity of Man* he had lifted whole paragraphs from Lubbock's paper on Danish archaeology. This sort of 'compiling' was despicable even in Darwin's eyes. 'Lyell took and forgot whole sentences from Lubbock,' he admitted. 'It is horrid.' Hooker explained what really lay behind the rancour. 'And now my dear D. shall I tell you what is at the bottom of it all? Perhaps you won't believe it, it is just this – that Lady Lyell will not call on Mrs Busk nor invite the Busks to her parties. This the Lubbocks and Huxleys resent.' Busk was routinely 'pumped dry of his knowledge' by Lyell (who lived in the same street), even while his lower-class wife was snubbed. It was a sign that not all members of the X (or at least their YVs, as the joke went) fitted the old social bill.

But times were changing, and with them the control of official science. The Xs continued to penetrate the British Association, manipulating its byzantine political machinery. They themselves were climbing into positions of power. Following his father's death, Hooker had been appointed Director of Kew Gardens, and Lubbock's Parliamentary career looked set.[28]

Huxley's power came from his ability to draw huge crowds. Two thousand were turned away in January 1866 as St Martin's Hall overflowed with Londoners wanting to hear him inaugurate the 'Sunday Evenings for the People.' Jenny Marx (Karl's daughter) squeezed in and found it 'packed to suffocation.' She had waltzed in the hall on the anniversary of the First International, but to hear a 'genuinely progressive' scientific lecture here was something new, especially at a 'moment when the flock are supposed to be grazing in the house of the Lord.' Huxley's was a hymn to material salvation. He had humanity escaping the 'fine-spun ecclesiastical cobwebs' to a bright new world of Tyndall's deterministic physics, Buckle's progressive history, and Darwin's evolving life. It was a world no longer static; a world in Heraclitan flux, like Turner's *Rain, Steam, and Speed*, a blur of movement, 'a world thrown out of focus by the driving motion of the steam engine.'[29]

The rhetoric was brilliant, and to outsiders bellicose. Owen was livid at Huxley's 'extremist views,' peddled in the hall to the 'youth of both sexes.' Having hoodwinked workers that they were the sons of gorillas, he was now inflaming them by 'attacks on the common basis of beliefs.' Lyell was just as appalled at Carpenter's subsequent Sunday speech, which 'rudely assailed' Calvinistic doctrines. The scandal of lay sermons on the Sabbath was too shocking and the Lord's Day Observance Society shut the hall. Huxley tediously fended off accusations of atheism, complaining that such a position was absurd where the 'possibilities of nature are infinite.' But with every year he felt the need for some new label, some new '-ism,' which would legalize doubt in the absence of evidence and leave faith in the realm of the 'immoral.'[30]

It was all Darwin could do to marvel from a distance. He was now 'half starved to death' on a crash diet (scanty amounts of 'toast & meat') under a new doctor. The slightest reading left his head beginning 'to sing violently.' So his 'good womenkind' did their duty, stroking his vanity by reading him 'advanced' books. Emma's self-sacrifice was tested as she read aloud Lecky's *Rise of Rationalism* and Tylor's evolutionary account of culture and religion in *The Early History of Mankind*. Left to his own devices for fifteen minutes, Charles's idea of entertainment was to skim back numbers of the middle-brow *Annals and Magazine of Natural History*. The diet seemed to work; he lost fifteen pounds and the doctor had him up and walking. Hopping in fact; he put on his magistrate's hat and threatened a neighbouring landowner with action over the mangy state of his horses.[31]

But the ravaging months had done their damage; Darwin's new photograph revealed a haggard figure, glazed and drawn. A year earlier he had been rugged and venerable, with a passing likeness to Moses in the fresco at the House of Lords, according to Hooker. Burn it and try again, was Eras's unhelpful suggestion on the latest effort. 'Cartes' (photographic calling cards) were *de rigueur* and Darwin had a wretched yearly record of his facial deterioration. He collected cartes enthusiastically, and posted his own wan physiognomy to English and German scientists. They might not have done much for his profile, but in Germany, they put a craggy face to the terrible *Darwinismus*.[32] This was fast becoming the face of evolution – and well-enough known for his calling card to be seen on sale in a shop window.

There was a stony sadness also in his reflection. Sister Susan, still at The Mount caring for Marianne's orphans, was suffering from fainting fits. In January 1866 Catherine wrote her farewells, knowing she was dying. Death came easily a few weeks later. Hers was the 'great soul,' as the Doctor long ago called it; but her life was one of unfulfilled ambitions and discomfort. Her passing was 'a blessing, for there was much fear of prolonged and greater suffering.' 'Sad, sad Shrewsbury! which used to look so bright and sunny,' Emma's aunt lamented, and Charles and Eras felt it as they met to arrange Catherine's estate and modify their wills.[33]

The doctor's walking and dieting regime at least had Charles on his toes, and he re-emerged into society protected by a bushy beard. His patriarchal face disappeared behind the hirsute mask. Fashion was the excuse; even Huxley sported a black beard (only to realize his error). But now the author of the *Origin* could travel incognito – no more alarms as strangers recognized him among the Crystal Palace crowds. Unfortunately his friends were equally stymied. He was sprightly enough to put in an appearance at a Royal Society soirée on 27 April, appearing like Moses down from the mountain. Hooker was staggered. So was everyone else, once they realized. The bearded gent with the drawn features was forced to introduce himself to friends and strangers alike, including the Prince of Wales. The young Prince said something *sotto voce*; Darwin failed to pick it up. Flustered, he 'made the profoundest bow he could' and fled.[34]

He might be crumbling bodily but it was galling to be attacked for scientific blindness. The Grays, Lyells, Owens, and Argylls all marvelled at his failure to see that nature's selection required as much thought and direction as the farmer's. Darwin's Nature 'preferred' and 'favoured,' his writings proclaimed it. The selecting hand was intelligent and could only evince God's long reach. Darwin was being painfully hoisted on his own petard.

Spencer offered an easy escape, and Wallace alerted Darwin to it. The socialist was now swept up by Spencer's cosmic optimism, indicating as much by calling his son Herbert Spencer Wallace. 'I hope he will copy his father's style and not his namesake's,' Darwin politely replied, taken aback. In his *Principles of Biology* Spencer had coined 'survival of the fittest' as a replacement for 'natural selection.' It avoided the anthropomorphism of 'selecting' and 'favouring' – and

Wallace went through his copy of the *Origin* striking out 'selection' and substituting 'survival,' arguing the advantages.

Darwin had struggled through the turgid tome – deterred by its 'detestable style,' thinking that Spencer must be 'very clever' and himself very dense, for he was no wiser at the end. If only Spencer observed a little more and thought a little less he might have something to say. 'Noisy vacuity' was Hooker's description of Spencer's numbing *Synthetic Philosophy*. Darwin subscribed to the endless volumes, but he had to agree. 'Survival of the Fittest,' he told Wallace, lost the analogy between nature's selection and the fanciers'.[35] Still, the phrase might stop the churlish criticisms and get him off the anthropomorphic hook, and he planned to use it judiciously in his *Variation under Domestication*.

36

Emerald Beauty

IN 1866, FOR THE first time, Darwinism – or descent at any rate – dominated the British Association meeting at Nottingham. The newspapers were full of it. The Anglican *Guardian* reported that Darwin's theory 'was everywhere in the ascendant.' It was 'impossible to pass from Section to Section without seeing how deeply those views have leavened the scientific mind of the day.' The President, physicist and barrister W. R. Grove, took a judicious view of nature's continuous constitutional change. Soon to sit on the judge's bench, he practised summing up in robes and wig, advising the scientific jury that evolution did on balance serve the Crown's interest. Continuity was the key, from the swarming specks on a microscope slide to the greatest galaxies, and we should be prepared 'to see it in the history of our own race:'

> the revolutionary ideas of the so-called natural rights of man
> . . . are far more unsound . . . than the study of the gradual
> progressive changes arising from changed circumstances,
> changed wants, changed habits. Our language, our social
> institutions, our laws, the constitution of which we are proud,
> are the growth of time, the product of slow adaptations,
> resulting from continuous struggles. Happily in this country
> practical experience has taught us to improve rather than
> remodel; we follow the law of nature and avoid cataclysms.[1]

England had found that Nature did things her way. The Wilberforces and Sedgwicks were stood on their heads: evolution threatened no bloodcurdling cries at the enthronement of the Goddess of Reason, only the security and peace of a progressive reform.

Darwin felt gypped because the speech about natural progress and social order 'dealt in such generalities.' But Grove had avoided the *Origin* by arrangement. He had called Hooker to the bench in advance and counselled him to 'carry Darwinism through the ranks of the enemy.' With Huxley President of the biology section, Hooker talking on island colonization and 'blessing Nat[ural]. Selection,' and Wallace President of the new anthropology sub-section, the best addresses went Darwin's way.

Hooker's ended on a savage allegory, satirizing the anti-evolution savants at the 1860 Oxford British Association as an uncivilized tribe who regarded 'every month's moon as a new creation of their gods.' They devoured 'the missionaries of the most enlightened nation' for explaining its real motion. 'The priests first attacked the new doctrine, and with fury, their temples were ornamented with symbols of the old creed, and their religious chants and rites were worded and arranged in accordance.' 'The medicine men, however ... sided with the missionaries – many from spite to the priests, but a few, I could see, from conviction.' Now six years were as six centuries, and the elders were duly baptized in the faith, and applauded their 'presiding Sachem' (Grove) for leading them out of the wilderness. Two thousand listened agog to all this, and were 'sent into fits by the conclusion,' Hooker boasted to Darwin. Darwin had heard as much; Fanny Wedgwood had been there, and she graphically described the stunned silence at the start of the lecture, followed by 'roars of laughter.'[2]

No guffaws greeted it in the religious press. The *Methodist Recorder* was 'surprised and grieved' by Grove's address. So was Owen, but then it left him out of the picture. He complained that scoffing was 'in fashion at that meeting,' and ranting and ridicule were the Darwinians' stock 'weapons.' They showed a 'contemptuous relegation' of design arguments and deliberately trampled on higher feelings. It reflected ill on the Downe naturalist: 'Darwin is just as good a soul as his grandfather,' Owen conceded, 'and just as great a goose.'[3]

Ironically, as Huxley's and Tyndall's parson-bashing appeals to the labourers reached a materialist pitch, the radical audience itself was splintering, with factions drifting off in totally different directions. After the collapse of Chartism many middle-aged agitators were swept along by the tide of spiritualism. The American fad of table-turning and spirit-rapping had taken hold by the 1860s; rooms were darkened, hands held as the dead signalled. No 'science,' not even phrenology, was more popular – or more directly accessible. Robert Chambers was won over and started revamping *Vestiges* in a more spiritual light. For old radicals, if not old ladies, it was a democratic outlet, a new dissident healing religion – the human spirit had progressive tendencies, driving society to its co-operative conclusion.[4] Unseen forces were undermining capitalism and ushering in the millennium. The doyen of socialists Robert Owen was won over, and even the reprieved leader of the 1839 Welsh Chartist uprising John Frost saw the light.

Séances also started in the capital's genteel drawing-rooms, to the annoyance of the hard-nosed scientists striking out on their own priest-free path to the New Jerusalem. Huxley's evolutionary probabilities now had to vie with spiritual certainties in the Mechanics' Institutes. *The Reader* in 1864 ran a slashing piece, 'Science and Spirit Rapping,' intriguing Darwin as to the author (Hooker confirmed that it was Tyndall's response to a séance). Huxley had already exposed a medium at his brother George's house, although he admitted that spiritualism could be advantageous in cutting the suicide rate: 'Better live a crossing-sweeper,' he laughed, 'than die and be made to talk twaddle by a "medium" hired at a guinea a *séance*.'[5]

But Wallace – the best sort of scientific crossing-sweeper – stood apart. Phrenologist, mesmerist, and old socialist, he had a self-help mentality shaped by millennial ideals. He attended his first séances with Mrs Marshall, England's most famous medium, in 1865. Darwin's cousin Hensleigh knew of this, and within a few years so did everyone else when Wallace acknowledged a higher spiritual reality. At home his own table tilted, and fresh flowers appeared from the other side to adorn it (he typically analysed them, '15 chrysanthemums, 6 variegated anemones, 4 tulips . . .' to trace their provenance). He printed a pamphlet, *The Scientific Aspect of the Supernatural*, and began importuning. Huxley declined to attend his séances, not wishing to be bored by the 'disembodied gossip.'[6] Having seized power from the priests, he was loath to see it devolved on dotty ladies. This spiritual legerdemain diluted the serious message that sober scientists were the new moral authority. But the worst of it was to come. Wallace was revamping evolution to take account of these unseen spirits.

In October the Darwins met Charles's most bombastic, prolific German admirer, the zoologist ultimately to be designated the 'German Darwin,' Ernst Haeckel. It was a meeting of opposites. Haeckel, thirty-two, was the son of Prussian civil servants. His evangelical upbringing and admiration for Goethe's pantheistic philosophy had led him to a mystical Nature-worship at the University of Würzburg. He was a superb field naturalist with a string of publications, but he and Darwin came from different worlds.

For years Haeckel had sent long flattering accounts of the progress of Darwinism in Germany – *Darwinismus* – listing converts. Huxley had vouched safe the new Extraordinary Professor of Zoology at Jena, confirming that he was 'one of the ablest of the younger zoologists of Germany.' Haeckel was turning liberal Jena, Goethe's university, into a 'citadel of Darwinism.' Here, Darwin heard, he had built up huge classes of 150 students for his lectures on *Darwinismus*. His pupils were taught to venerate the Downe naturalist. One, Anton Dohrn, immersed in barnacle larvae, considered a letter from Darwin like being granted a 'scientific knighthood.' These students looked back on 1859 as a year of crowning significance in the century; the war with Lombardy or the end of the Papal States paled beside the publication of the *Origin*. No wonder that Darwin told William Preyer, an English physiologist teaching at Bonn (and soon to take a chair at Jena) that the German response was the 'chief ground for hoping that our views will ultimately prevail.'[7]

The *Origin* had 'profoundly moved' Haeckel as well. He rushed in where Darwin feared to tread. It was Haeckel who started the debate in Germany by extending selection and struggle to society, seeing it 'drive the peoples irresistibly onward ... to higher cultural stages.' Progress was a natural law that 'neither the weapons of the tyrant nor the anathemas of the priest' could rescind. To Haeckel the *Origin* was a political document affecting everyone's 'personal, scientific and social views' – and he was proving it. As a way of drowning his sorrows after the tragic death of his young wife in 1864 (whose photo he touchingly sent Darwin) he had thrown himself heroically into a systematic rearrangement of all biological knowledge along Darwinian lines.[8] The *Generelle Morphologie* was a monumental work astonishingly written in a year, and Darwin had the first proof sheet in hand by August 1866.

Their meeting at Down House was a religious experience for Haeckel. From the moment Darwin's hand gripped his, he felt his heart being taken 'by storm.' Darwin to him was

> tall and venerable ... with the broad shoulders of an Atlas
> that bore a world of thought: a Jove-like forehead, as we see
> in Goethe, with a lofty and broad vault, deeply furrowed by
> the plough of intellectual work. The tender and friendly eyes
> were overshadowed by the great roof of the prominent brows.
> The gentle mouth was framed in a long, silvery white beard.

Overawed, Haeckel began jabbering in broken English. Darwin said something and found that Haeckel did not understand him either. They stared at each other for a moment and then burst into laughter. Speaking slowly worked wonders, and over lunch communication was finally established – until Haeckel became excited again. Waving his arms, he railed against 'the stubborn and bewigged professors who still held out against the luminous truth of the theory of evolution.' No one could make out what he was saying and Emma looked impatient. Darwin just put his hand on Haeckel's broad shoulder, nodded and smiled. To Haeckel it was a benediction.

Darwin had 'seldom seen a more pleasant, cordial, and frank man.' Links were quickly cemented with the whole group: Lubbock came over from High Elms to meet Haeckel, and Darwin introduced him to Hooker. There was much mutual back-slapping; Haeckel praised Huxley as 'the most eminent English zoologist' and was in turn hailed as a Coryphaeus among German naturalists.[9]

Within a few weeks Darwin, still pounding away at *Variation under Domestication*, had knocked the chapter on pangenesis into shape. The theory left him in jitters – it would be 'classed as a mad dream,' or worse. 'Wildly abominably speculative,' he called it to a head-scratching Hooker, staggered by all the hypothetical gemmules, which were 'worthy even of Herbert Spencer.'

Not that Spencer's speculations weren't useful. He was generalizing evolution to explain the universe in his *Synthetic Philosophy*, projecting the social ambitions of his X Club friends on a cosmic scale. And politically he was a brick. In November he roped Darwin into the Governor Eyre debate, then racking the English intelligentsia. A year earlier the Jamaican Governor's troops had brutally crushed a local peasant revolt – over 400 blacks executed, 600 flogged, 1000 suspect houses razed. Anti-slavery radicals and liberal politicians formed the Jamaica Committee to bring Eyre to justice; Wallace, Lyell, Huxley, and Spencer had joined, and now Darwin added his name with a £10 donation towards the prosecution. An Eyre Defence and Aid Committee also had a fund, enlisting scores of clergymen, peers, and members of the armed forces. Tyndall chipped in, the Revd Kingsley jumped on the bandwagon, and even Hooker seemed sympathetic. The principles of Governor Eyre's prosecutors, Hooker told Darwin, were 'fiddlesticks.'[10]

Darwinian emotions flared, fanned by the *Pall Mall Gazette*'s nasty jibe that Huxley's and Lyell's views on the 'development of species' had 'influenced them in bestowing on the negro that sympathetic recognition which they are willing to extend even to the ape as "a man and a brother".' Huxley lashed back, boiling everything down to the constitutional proposition that 'English law does not permit good persons, as such, to strangle bad persons, as such.' If it did, he would 'take the first opportunity of migrating to Texas or some other quiet place.' For Darwin's part, the issue ran deeper. He detested all forms of cruelty; the Eyre defenders' attitudes to blacks reminded him of FitzRoy's defence of slavery. He burned at their arrogance and wondered that some of his friends could agree. Once his feelings even overpowered him when an Eyre lobby turned up at home.

William, twenty-six, was now a banking partner in Southampton; his sympathies had been under suspicion since August, when his name was published 'by accident' as having attended a banquet in Eyre's honour in the town. So incensed was Charles that he actually wrote to the Lord Chancellor to rectify the error. But now the truth came out. At Ras's in November, William made a disparaging remark about the Jamaica Committee raiding the prosecution fund for its own dinners. Charles turned on him with a blistering fury and bellowed that if he felt that way, then he 'had better go back to Southampton.' William stayed another night, and at seven the next morning his father came in and sat on his bed. He hadn't slept one wink, he said; his anger had been cruel, and he was sorry.[11]

This was Charles's first visit to Ras since Susan's terrible lingering death at the beginning of October. They had lost two sisters this year, and it was an emotional time. Susan's effects were being distributed, and Charles had first refusal on her Indian chessmen. Ras had just returned from The Mount, which was being sold. Charles heard about the auction from Hooker, who had also been there. Hooker was a fanatical collector of Wedgwood ware, and could be seen poking around London's dingy bric-à-brac shops searching for pieces. He had visited The Mount hoping to buy a few medallions, knowing that the Darwins were – as Charles laughed – 'the degenerate descendants of old Josiah W.' He came home empty-handed.[12] The Mount was bare, the last ties with Shrewsbury severed, and Hooker had been there at its break-up.

At Downe the two 500-page volumes of Haeckel's *Generelle Morphologie* thumped in Darwin's letterbox. They were designed to daunt, and Darwin was duly humbled. He struggled through the thicket, losing his way in the profusion of genealogical trees, sagging under the weight of neologisms. 'The number of new words, to a man like myself, weak in his Greek, is something dreadful:' 'ontogeny' for the course of foetal growth, 'phylogeny' for the evolutionary history of the race, and 'ecology.' Nor was his German much better. Word after word was extracted with the pain of pulled teeth, using a dictionary. He knew 'no grammar whatever' and so read each sentence over and over until at last the meaning dawned. (The constructions infuriated him – he was convinced that Germans 'could write simply if they chose.')

By this dogged means, he snatched painful glimpses of Haeckel's ambition, pushing evolution beyond its legitimate bounds. For Haeckel selection was only a fragment of a 'universal Theory of Development, which embraces in its vast range the whole domain of human knowledge.' Darwin's quintessentially English light – an incandescence of Paley's design, Malthus's pessimism, pigeon lore, and maritime life – was being passed through a distorting lens. Here was *Darwinismus* shaped to suit Bismarck's unifying Germany. Priest-baiting patriotism formed a backdrop to anatomy and embryology, and the whole was blended into a unitary evolutionary cosmology. It was pushy and provocative, unnecessarily so in Darwin's view.[13]

But then Haeckel's books had a political punch. His liberal *Darwinismus* was associated with calls for a national state that would guarantee free speech and free trade. At its crudest, an ape ancestry could level the privileged aristocracy – noblemen and dogs were all of a kind in the womb, he once commented. On another level, the laws of biological and national evolution offered hope for a new Teutonic superiority in a unified Germany. Haeckel had an almost Messianic idea of the German *Volk*, the spirit binding all to the fatherland, and he was busy underwriting it. Welcoming Bismarck to Jena, he declared: 'While the booming of guns at the Battle of Königgrätz in 1866 announced the demise of the old Federal German Diet and the beginning of a splendid period in the history of the German Reich, here in Jena the history of the phylum was born.'[14] The *phylum*, a higher group whose racial integrity was explained by evolution, had developed through the same struggle and selection as the new Prussian state.

The polemical *Morphologie* was impressive and galling. Darwin grappled with it for weeks. 'I see he often quotes both of us with praise,' he told Huxley. 'I am sure I should like the book much, if I could read it straight off instead of groaning and swearing at each sentence.' By Christmas he had conquered 'a page or two here and there.' His only hope was a translation, but however much Huxley revelled in Haeckel's attempt 'to systematise biology' along Darwinian lines, he thought it hopeless 'without too great an outlay.'

The real problem was that Haeckel's *Darwinismus* came wrapped in an anti-clerical package, and the wrappers would have to be stripped off. The immutability of species was 'a colossal dogma ... empowered by blind belief in authority' – Christian authority, a crude backward religion whose Creator-God was a 'gaseous vertebrate.' Nothing was more guaranteed to raise hackles. Huxley took vicarious satisfaction in its 'polemic *excursus*,' sympathizing that 'it is a good thing for a man' once in a while 'to perform a public war-dance against all sorts of humbug and imposture.'[15] But he knew that English propriety too easily took fright.

True, Haeckel was less scurrilous than Darwin's other admirer, the socialist Carl Vogt. Vogt, a German exiled after the revolution of 1848 to Geneva (where he translated *Vestiges*), was now bidding to translate *Variation*; but Darwin knew enough to opt for Huxley's man Victor Carus, the Leipzig professor who had translated *Man's Place in Nature*. Carus himself warned Darwin against letting a church-baiting revolutionary like Vogt do the job. Indeed, there was a real worry about Vogt's language. No one outside the gutter press in England would have dared call certain 'simious' skulls from the Dark Ages 'Apostle skulls' on the assumption that they belonged to degraded Christian missionaries.

Not that Carus was totally happy with Haeckel either – a man who could point to the 'pious inquisition' as proof that the cosmos lacked moral order. Only Darwin could put a stop to such mischief, Carus said; Haeckel would heed no one else. Darwin did try pulling in Haeckel's horns, advising that to lance the theological boil 'will excite anger, and that anger so completely blinds every one.' Do not 'unnecessarily make enemies,' for 'there is pain and vexation enough in the world.'[16] But Haeckel was uncompromising, replying that only a vigorous assault could overcome prejudice and usher in a radical reform.

Just before Christmas Darwin sent *Variation* to the printers – all except the last chapter. He was popping in a special present for Gray, a knock-down argument against his notion of divinely guided variation. So many had seized on Gray's leading idea (thanks partly to the advertisement for his pamphlet in the *Origin*) that it seemed 'shabby to evade' it any longer.

He presented an analogy that he had been perfecting for years. Consider the stones at the base of a cliff, each having broken off naturally; suppose that an architect uses these to build a house. 'Can it be reasonably maintained that the Creator intentionally ordered

... that certain fragments of rock should assume certain shapes so that the builder might erect his edifice?' Obviously not. So, Darwin asked, 'can it be maintained with any greater probability that He specially ordained' the minuscule variations that breeders work on to make their fancy races? No. Well, nor were they ordained in nature. Variations arise by 'general laws' and some *happen* to be useful. Natural selection – the architect – picks them to improve plants and animals, 'man included.'[17]

'Man included' was a hint that no heavens opened to herald mankind's birth. He was just as natural, just as accidental. Darwin had wanted to add a chapter on the subject to *Variation*, but the book was now so 'horridly, disgustingly big' that Murray was already making two volumes of it, each over 400 pages. The referee found the tome indigestible, and Murray planned only 750 copies. In March 1867, after the compositors had come up with a better title, *The Variation of Animals and Plants under Domestication*, Murray did double the print run, but by then Darwin had decided to turn his man chapter into a separate 'short essay,' concentrating on ape ancestry, sexual selection, and human expression. He would finally speak out, tired of being 'taunted that I concealed my views' on human origins.[18]

Translations were sewn up quickly. Carus would do the German and Vladimir Kovalevsky the Russian. Considering how much Darwin had suffered from polemically packaged foreign editions of the *Origin*, he reposed some faith in Kovalevsky. Bronn's translation, the first in Germany, came with critical notes and appendix; Clémence Royer prefaced hers in France with an anticlerical harangue, and added insult to injury by changing the title. Kovalevsky, fiery and only twenty-five, was translating Huxley and Lyell in style, so he should have been all right. On the other hand he was using evolution in his Nihilist crusade against Russia's Orthodox autocracy. Darwin had proofs hot off the press sent to St Petersburg – and Kovalevsky, translation notwithstanding, pulled out all the stops and beat Murray's publication date. The earliest edition of *Variation* was Russian.[19]

Darwin struggled with sexual selection this spring, explaining the causes of variation in that 'eminently *domesticated* animal,' man. Why do the races differ in their physical and emotional features and yet all belong to one species? Why do males and females have different hair and habits? He could see no evolutionary advantage in beards, big lips, or large buttocks – nothing for natural selection to work on – so he put it down to the mating game. Nature does not select, individuals do; their racial and sexual differences show what is successful in winning wives and attracting husbands. Aesthetic preferences are translated into anatomy.

He called in evidence from molluscs to monkeys, but concentrated on the glorious plumage and mating rituals of birds. He had the bower birds in London zoo given a choice of worsted to test their colour preference; he had breeders trimming and daubing game cocks to see whether the mutilation would make them less 'successful in getting wives;' he had male pigeons dyed magenta to see how far 'it excited in the other pigeons, especially the females, admiration or contempt.' By analogy, Darwin believed that insect colours had also been sexually selected, and he once even had a dragonfly 'painted with gorgeous colours,' though the experiment never got off the ground.[20]

The Duke of Argyll's *Reign of Law* rammed home the need for a book on sexual selection. The Duke, or 'Dukelet' as Huxley demoted him ('how can you speak so of a living real Duke?' Darwin wondered), rounded up the providential criticisms of the *Origin* and rehashed them in a pot-boiler. Darwin was rather annoyed. 'The Duke's book strikes me as very well written, very interesting, honest, & clever & very arrogant,' he told Kingsley. He whittled away at it, wrote to Lyell about it, and complained to William.[21] Clearly his own book would have to crush this dilettante nonsense, and provide a thousand counter illustrations for every clever flick of Argyll's pen.

Argyll's intellectual heritage showed. He had attended Owen's lectures and learned the lesson well. Natural selection explains the 'success and establishment and spread of new Forms when they have arisen,' but gives no clue to their origin. The *Origin* was a misnomer; the book should have been called *The Selection of Species*. So what causes the variations? Argyll captured the new consensus on design, in which species were preordained, and natural laws the outcome of God's legislative will. Judicial rule still held, Argyll announced in the *Reign of Law*, chaos and anarchy had not descended on nature; the back-street slum hordes had not overrun the citadel.

The Duke had put his chapters together while trying to juggle Gladstone's new Reform Bill through the Commons in 1866. He envisioned nature controlled by a similar guided meliorative reform, ordered from above. Like Owen, he could never accept that random variations were the font of progress. He talked of some unknown cause steering the 'variations in a definite direction.' Lyell agreed, so did Gray. So did Owen; in fact it could have been Owen speaking through Argyll's mouth in the *Reign of Law*, talking of a force guiding life, 'working to order, subject to direction, and having that direction determined by foresight.'[22]

But the real sting in the book came with Argyll's discussions of hummingbirds. He asked the crunch question, the one that made Darwin flinch. Why should a topaz crest be selected in shimmering hummingbirds in preference to sapphire? Or a frill end in emerald spangles rather than ruby? This was beauty for God's sake – there was no earthly reason for it, no struggle could explain it.

Argyll accused Darwin of giving mindless natural selection the credit. But for Darwin selection *was* creative. His Grace

> depreciates the importance of natural selection, but I presume he w[d] not deny that [husbandry experts] had in one sense made our improved breeds of cattle, yet of course the initial variations have naturally arisen; but until selected, they remained unimportant, & in this same sense natural selection seems to me all-important.

He protested in vain. Argyll's sort of Creative evolution was immensely appealing to non-Darwinians. With Owen, they hailed the Duke's 'healthy' intervention as 'a timely & wholesome antidote' to Darwin's 'mischievous fallacies.' No one was better placed to refute Darwin's and Huxley's belief that everything is 'governed by invariable Laws with which no volitions, natural or supernatural, interfere."[23]

Huxley did not even bother to read the *Reign of Law*. Hooker skimmed it 'with utter disgust and uncontrollable indignation.' Imagine, he fumed, 'God being compelled to dab on rudimentary organs *to keep up appearances*,' the divine architect adding useless bits to conform with Owen's blueprints. Darwin agreed, scorning Argyll's picture of God as 'a man, rather cleverer than us.' But then it was a Duke writing, 'no common mortal.' Perhaps he was 'not to be judged by common rules.'[24]

Wallace countered Argyll chapter-and-verse in a razor-sharp review, delving into hummingbird splendour. There was a pitfall in putting it down to God's beauty – how to explain stink bugs and snakes? He pulled up His Grace on the gaudy orchids too, which functioned in attracting bees, reminding him that continual interference implies a lack of Creative foresight. Petty tinkering might do for Reform Bills, but nature got it right from the start.

How nature got things right was another matter. Wallace and Darwin were differing more and more. Darwin had sexual selection replacing God the artist, just as natural selection ousted God the architect. Brutes were their own breeders, forming fancy varieties; humans sculpted themselves by selecting mates. But for every brilliant bird that Darwin ascribed to sexual selection, Wallace described another that was due to natural selection. Dull-coloured female birds are camouflaged to survive sitting in an open nest. Gaudy moths, distasteful to their predators, wear warning colours; still others mimic them.

Wallace rejected sexual selection as the 'main agent' forming the human races. Natural selection was quite equal to the task. To Darwin this came as 'the heaviest blow possible.' No amount of evidence on birds and insects would turn Wallace. Darwin now played the apostate devil, arguing against the very theory that he had spent his life supporting. Wallace for his part was turning out the more single-minded adherent of natural selection, more Darwinian than Darwin.[25]

For each Wallace reply to Argyll came a clutch of new criticisms, and worse was in store. Darwin's most prestigious opponents were physicists with close ties to the Glasgow professor Sir William Thomson (later Lord Kelvin). Thomson was recalculating the earth's age, putting crippling limits on the time a clumsy, wasteful natural selection had to work in. In June his partner in the submarine cable business, the engineer Fleeming Jenkin, applied an even crueller logic. He showed that no single variation could survive being blended back into an ocean of normal peers. Blood always mixes; a white sailor with a black wife has 'mulatto' children. No old salt marooned on African shores, however resourceful and superior, was going to 'blanch a nation of negroes.' Boat-loads of whites were needed. As Jenkin said, only if many simultaneous 'sports' or mutations appeared and bred true could a species change.

But that was tantamount to a 'theory of successive creations' – or at least a divinely directed evolution. Jenkin had turned the tables. He convinced Darwin that 'freak' variations could not survive, only a wave of them appearing simultaneously.[26] Others cut the knot and sought refuge in Argyll's 'creation by birth,' with each sport preplanned and fixed. It was a retreat on all fronts.

In July Lyell was in despair, working on a tenth edition of the *Principles of Geology*, trying in vain to turn what was an anti-Lamarckian opus into a pro-Darwinian fudge. Darwin, ever hopeful, rejoiced that he was going to 'speak out plainly about species' for the first time, even if his proof chapter on man, 'who thinks too much of his fine self,' was a flop. It was 'too long . . . and too orthodox, except for the beneficed clergy,' a remark not guaranteed to put the seventy-year-old Lyell at ease.

Lyell for his part loved Darwin's proofs of *Variation*, on the exotic pigeons and rabbits and the ways the breeds have fanned out from their wild ancestors. All this would be 'most persuasive to real naturalists,' he replied magnanimously, pushing them further towards the *Origin of Species*.[27]

Darwin needed this reassurance. *Variation* was his biggest book and the proofs were killing him, with every page 'greatly altered.' Twice that summer he downed pen and went to Eras's for a week, but it was no use. Back at Downe he worked overtime to make up for the breaks. There were endless letters from Carus and Kovalevsky, regular queries about the index, fresh batches of revised proofs, and always the obsessive fact-finding and fact-filing on sexual selection and man.

For all Darwin's fears and phobias, and Lyell's procrastination, and Argyll's aggravation, the world was turning. Kingsley symbolized its comically elliptical orbit. Here was a parson who preached that God created beauty for its own sake, but who crowed that 'the best and strongest men' in Cambridge were 'coming over' to 'what the world calls Darwinism, and you and I and some others, fact and science.'

> The younger M.A.'s are not only willing, but greedy, to hear what you have to say; and . . . the elder (who have, of course, more old notions to overcome) are facing the whole question in quite a different tone from that they did three years ago. I won't mention names, for fear of 'compromising' men who are in an honest but 'funky,' stage of conversion: but I have been surprised . . . at the change since last winter.

Fancy evolution all the go at Cambridge! Kingsley knew that Darwin made man's ancestors 'hairy beasts' – did no one else? Or was the idea now as debatable at Oxbridge as it was desirable among the secularists? Once Darwin's worst nightmare might have been to turn up in a rogues' gallery like Holyoake's secularist tract *Half-Hours with Freethinkers*. Now his potted biography was included there, cheek-by-jowl with those of Emma Martin, Robert Owen, and Lucretius, even while the Revd Kingsley, the Cambridge professor of modern history, sang his praises.[28]

He pushed on with *Variation*. After seven months of scratching and correcting, the proofs were finished on 15 November. Emma wished that he would relax and 'smoke a pipe or ruminate like a cow,' but 'enjoying leisure' was hard work. He worried whether anyone would read his mammoth volume. Still, he breathed a sigh and exhaled his relief to Hooker, telling him how to get through the two volumes: 'Skip the *whole* of Vol. 1., except the last chapter (and that only to be skimmed) and skip largely the 2nd volume; and then you will say it is a very good book.'[29]

37

Sex, Politics, & The X

THIRTEEN YEARS AFTER breeding and brewing up his first pouters the book was in the high-street shops – the book that rammed home the real plasticity of species: *The Variation of Animals and Plants under Domestication*. Of course now it also had multiple other functions: it pointed up the 'evil from interbreeding,' introduced Darwin's latest deity, the 'great god Pan,' and put paid to Gray's divine designer as the cause of variation.

On publication day, 30 January 1868, Darwin advised Fritz Müller, 'The great part, as you will see, is not meant to be read; but I should very much like to hear what you think of "Pangenesis".' Every recipient was so cajoled and Darwin was deflated by the response. Hooker thought the 'gemmules' and what not were better left mysterious. 'This power of packing into a cell the potentiality of an infinite number of the indefinite properties of its ancestors, is as much beyond our comprehension as atoms, or ethics, or time, or gravity, or God.' Darwin began to agree. And still he was expecting a 'blowing up' from Huxley, who put pangenesis in the same category as Genesis. Suddenly the sight of the book sickened him; his old insecurities resurfaced, his fear of rejection and loss of status: 'if I try to read a few pages I feel fairly nauseated.' He was protective about Pan, but for the rest, 'The devil take the whole book.'[1]

The public thought better, and even Murray underestimated demand. The 1500 copies vanished in a week. Demand was so high that eleven days found the presses reprinting. That afternoon George Lewes in the *Pall Mall Gazette* gave it a wonderful send off, praising the 'noble calmness' of its exposition. To read of himself 'undisturbed by the heats of polemical agitation' made Darwin laugh, and all in all the review left him 'cock-a-hoop.' As usual the *Athenaeum* jumped in with a panning; but that was par for the course and Darwin was inured to its Saturday morning sneers, if not quite hardened. 'The writer despises and hates me,' he flinched, half-suspecting his identity.[2] Only one man could 'cut me up so severely' – Owen.

Still, he worried about pangenesis. He doted on it like a 'beloved child,' believed in it like a god. It was the offspring of his fertile imagination, a *deus ex machina* to explain the phenomena of inheritance. Fearing that it would 'expire unblessed and uncursed by the world,' he was determined to 'stick up' for the theory; but like God and his children's health, its status was constantly in doubt. He blew hot and cold. Hooker's and Huxley's reactions made him want to give up 'the great god Pan as a still-born deity.' Then Wallace's enthusiasm made him sanguine again. Later, when Gray treated the theory sympathetically Darwin fancied that the 'infant . . . will live a long life. There is parental presumption for you!'[3]

Parental presumption was on the rise. For years he had never been sure whether his sickly sons would succeed in life's struggle. William, the fittest, was succeeding in managing his bank, a safe sedentary occupation. But what prospects for the rest? Would they follow their father and take to science or would the family weakness hold them back? Leonard, eighteen and minding Horace at Clapham School, had just been placed high on the Sandhurst list and was headed for the Royal Military Academy at Woolwich, where he came second in the entrance exam. 'Who would have ever have thought that poor dear old Lenny would have got so magnificent a place,' Charles exclaimed, doubting its significance. 'I shall be curious to hear how many tried.' Lenny would have a solid engineering education but limited scope for attainment. It suited him actually, the son in whom 'the collecting mania' had taken 'the poor form of collecting Postage stamps.'

Horace, a year behind Lenny, remained an enigma. He had a mechanical bent; if his health held, he might follow Frank to Cambridge and read natural science. George was proving what a feeble Darwin could achieve there, and now his father's eyes were on him. At twenty-three he was only just finishing a maths degree. He stood at the crossroads. Just as pangenesis reached the reviewers a telegram came: he had done magnificently, runner-up in his class. Charles's hand trembled as he penned congratulations. He had 'never expected such brilliant success as this.' At Clapham, where the Revd Wrigley had prepared the new Second Wrangler, there was a 'regular saturnalia.' Everyone was given a half holiday and packed off to the nearby Crystal Palace. George was offered a science mastership at Eton but turned it down to read for the bar. He could hardly refuse a fellowship of Trinity College, which Uncle Ras thought 'the most enviable position on earth.'[4]

Darwin too was collecting accolades. The *Origin* had been translated half-a-dozen times. Everywhere naturalists grappled with its arguments, intellectuals debated their implications. Love it or loathe it, the book was a work of genius. A few days after George's telegram, and while congratulations were flooding in, he heard that the King of Prussia had conferred the Order *Pour le Mérite* on him. Only weeks later the Imperial Academy of Sciences at St Petersburg elected him a Corresponding Member. He rushed a note to the revolutionary Vladimir Kovalevsky, hoping to lard the title-page of the Russian *Variation*. There was plenty of time, with Kovalevsky temporarily dropping his translations and travelling 1000 miles a week on a relief committee for Russian agricultural distress.[5]

The day after hearing from the Prussian Embassy he picked up sexual selection again. On a normal day he fired off eight or ten letters, garnering information, becoming a billionaire in bizarre facts: the manes of macaque monkeys, the antlers of deer, the breeding plumage of scarlet ibises or the hue of a toucan's beak – no frill or eyespot was lost that might have been favoured by a mate. He even plucked up courage to contact Louis Agassiz at Harvard. Agassiz was back from the Amazon, where he had travelled searching for evidence of former glaciers to prove that his Ice Age had been global, thus cutting off the old Creation from the new. Everyone knew that his apocalyptic ice-shroud was intended to stifle 'Darwinian views' and was so much 'wild nonsense.' Darwin considered him 'glacier mad.' But that did not preclude his pumping Agassiz on spawning Amazonian fishes – turning the poor man's anti-Darwinian gains into serviceable spoil, pickpocketing him so gently that he was none the wiser.

Darwin's sexual selection, like the fish, was transmuting and taking on a life of its own. It had grown to a 'gigantic subject.' He dropped on to his knees to scrutinize the Kingdom's lowliest inhabitants. Old helpers from the barnacle days were reactivated: Albany Hancock sent reams on gaudy sea-slugs, others on breeding crabs, the courtship of blind beetles, sadistic spiders, and brilliant butterflies. Come to that, 'how low in the scale [do] sexual differences occur which require some degree of self-consciousness in the males'? There were questions that only he could ask; were cricket chirps sexually selected? Could 'dumb' *Cicada*s breed?[6]

He started cornering commercial breeders, and he soon had them daubing, damaging, and docking prize specimens – pigeons were painted, game cocks had their tail feathers plucked, and he looked for a fancier to buff a bullfinch's rose-pink breast and spy on its sexual prowess. And still he cast around for a wealthy gent, willing to snip the eyes out of a peacock's tail – 'but who would sacrifice the beauty of their bird for a whole season to please a mere naturalist?'

Worrying and working obsessively, he left scant room for anything else. Hearing Hooker one day in ecstasies after taking in Handel's 'Messiah,' Darwin declared his soul 'too dried up to appreciate it as in the old days.' Orchids moved him more than pipe organs, corals more than the Hallelujah Chorus. 'I am a withered leaf for every subject except Science.'[7] But he had enough paper science for an entire civil service. His one-man collation agency was as usual out of control. By March he was inundated by daily bundles of letters from fanciers, farmers, fisheries experts, census statisticians, collectors, and colonists.

Partly he was being pushed by Argyll to explain jewelled hummingbirds, goaded by His Grace's claim that 'mere ornament or beauty is in itself a purpose, an object, and an end,' a Creative whim to please man. Wallace too was looking at scales and plumage, and the way leaf-like moths or camouflaged brooding birds were selected, and how the rest, the brilliant snakes or iridescent insects, were announcing their venom – or mimicking those that did. But this left the topaz and emerald nectar-sippers, and that was Darwin's terrain. The eye spots on a caterpillar might mimic a snake's face, but the eyes on a peacock's tail enamoured the hen. They had to be the result of conscious choice.

Did minuscule variations make any difference to star-crossed admirers? Wallace was dubious. Would 'an inch in the tail of the peacock, or ¼-inch in that of the Bird of Paradise . . . be noticed and preferred by the female'? Darwin was convinced of it.

> A girl sees a handsome man, and without observing whether his nose or whiskers are the tenth of an inch longer or shorter than in some other man, admires his appearance and says she will marry him. So, I suppose, with the pea-hen.

An extra fleck added to the effect, but what was appreciated was the 'gorgeous appearance.' Mates were selecting, with beauty in the eye of the beholding peahen. 'It is an awful stretcher to believe that a peacock's tail was thus formed; but, believing it, I believe in the same principle somewhat modified applied to man.'[8]

He brought his work along when Emma and the girls took him to London in March for four weeks' rest. His gardener sympathized: a month away was certainly a 'terrible thing' for his experiments. Still, after a week with Eras they took over Elizabeth Wedgwood's Regent's Park house, ten minutes' stroll from the zoo. Here, apart from entertaining luncheons and popping 'over the way' to Hensleigh's to discuss mankind's descent with the freethinking feminist Frances Power Cobbe, his time was spent in the zoo, carousing with keepers, making the elephants trumpet (to see if tears formed), and watching the pheasants display. Even more, he was retracing the steps of his old metaphysical notebooks, investigating the social instincts of monkeys – or at least putting snakes into their cages to test the communal reaction.

The unnaturally hectic trip was a sign of improving health. He thanked Grove at the Royal Institution in Piccadilly for helping George enter Lincoln's Inn to study law, talked pigs at the British Museum, sat in on an X Club meeting, and almost made it to Kew Gardens.[9]

Perhaps he also had a confab with John Murray about a new promotional scheme. Darwin was an adept self-publicist, but importing the Gray pamphlet was small fry compared to the plan he now had in mind. Whatever the rash of Germanic *Darwinismus*, no single, satisfactory book had appeared in England to support the side. He was greeted by a thundering silence. Lyell's *Antiquity of Man* was namby-pamby and off-beam; Huxley's working-men's pamphlets had a tiny sale, and surrounded Darwinism with caveats; his *Man's Place in Nature* was splendid on apes but silent on natural selection. With Argyll's wretched *Reign of Law* garnering the laurels, drastic measures were demanded.

Darwin had to cast his net wide – all the way to the Amazon – for a real chapter-and-verse disciple. He tried to interest Murray in translating Fritz Müller's *Für Darwin*. Müller was another radical exiled after the abortive 1848 revolution, but to Brazil, where he studied prawns and barnacles and scraped by as a schoolteacher. Murray feared the financial risk, so Darwin commissioned the book, subsidizing it to the tune of £100. He arranged the translator, oversaw the operation, picked up the advertising tabs, and organized the review and presentation copies. What to title it? The translator impertinently suggested *A Lift for Darwin*, a joke too near the knuckle. Lyell came up with *Facts and Arguments for Darwin*, which won the day – and the compositors took it upon themselves to set '*Darwin*' in larger type than 'Müller' on the title-page. Murray printed 1000 copies at six shillings apiece, and both publisher and patron did quite well by it.[10]

*

Through the spring one of Huxley's protégés plied Darwin with esoteric notes on breeding newts. St George Mivart was a zoological sophisticate and a convert of twenty-five years to Catholicism. He was a suave Old Harrovian, stately in manner, brought up among the swells who flocked to his father's 'Mivart Hotel' in Grosvenor Square (later Claridge's). He had qualified as a barrister at Lincoln's Inn, only to throw over a law career after hearing Owen lecture next door at the College of Surgeons. But the turning point came when he met Huxley in 1859. Compared to the ponderous, taciturn Owen, Huxley was frank, exciting, and zoologically nimble. Mivart was mesmerized by the 'deep-set dark eyes,' the quick wit, and awed by his relentless debunking. He found himself between David and Goliath; and a reference each from Owen and Huxley had been enough to gain him the lectureship in zoology at St Mary's Hospital in Paddington in 1862. He continued to sit Huxley's lectures at the School of Mines and to visit the family.[11] And under Huxley's tutelage, he gained Darwin's ear.

Darwin fired strings of questions at him, tapping his brains on the colour, crests, and courtship of spawning newts. Mivart bent over backwards to help. He was a brilliant technical anatomist and could talk on the muscles of newts or the limbs of apes. But on grander issues, of man and morality, his position was becoming ambiguous. He had been a 'hearty' Darwinian, or so he said. In the wake of Huxley's *Man's Place* he had studied monkeys and lemurs and debated life and mind. 'As to "natural selection" I accepted it completely,' he told Darwin. But anyone who could add that, whatever the similarity of man's 'dead body' to a gorilla's, our 'intellectual, moral & religious nature' set us farther 'from an Anthropoid Ape than such an Ape differs from a lump of granite' was not going to sit docilely in Huxley's class for long.

Mivart's conversion and lapse were probably not blindingly Pauline. He had hedged his bets, kept faith with his Church. Deep down a love of Owen's science persisted, along with fears for a degraded humanity, and in fact he confessed to Darwin that his 'doubts & difficulties were first excited by attending Prof. Huxley's lectures.'[12] In 1868 Mivart hovered equivocally on the Darwinian fringes.

By now Darwin had reached Argyll's bottom line as he wrote his book: bedazzling birds. Enthusiasts were still buffing bullfinches and dyeing white doves for him, testing female ardour to its limit. The situation had a new urgency with Argyll's criticisms snowballing through the press. What of Darwin's vaunted selection if it could not produce 'the japanned peacock and Bohemian pheasant'? wondered the *Edinburgh Review*, musing on the *Variation*. Selection required utility, but there was none in gaudiness. Darwin had to prove that birds could choose their mates' fine feathers to prevent a holy Haberdasher from being invoked.

Hooker was sizing up Argyll's *Reign of Law*, ready to pounce on it as President of the British Association this year. The Duke's cockiness left him in 'utter disgust.' 'I like a man to sneer at me out of malice and envy, but cannot stand a man's sneering at me from atop of a high horse.' It all smacked of Owen, right up to Argyll's lofty remarks on rudimentary parts, which were 'very droll.' Owen's belief that rudiments related an animal to a Plan, rather than an ancestor, was squashed by the Darwinians with a vengeance. As a critic laughed, when Darwin pointed out our monkey bits, like 'the persistent tips in our ears, he did more to discomfort' his enemies than with a million other facts. Rudiments were easy; the real problem was to prove that iridescence and showy eyes are not similar pieces of Creative whimsy.

Talking to Hooker, watching the reviews, reading the likes of Lubbock and Tylor, it was clear that the new book – which he had decided to call *The Descent of Man* – would have to range widely, from sexual selection and ape ancestors to the evolution of morality and religion. His old notebooks had covered the ground. Indeed, Hooker thought that 'morals and politics would be very interesting if discussed like any branch of natural history.' Nor were he and Darwin the only ones to view these fields in the light of natural selection. Darwinizing about society was now a booming intellectual business.[13]

The quality magazines bulged with offerings. Darwin read them all, pencil in hand, culling ideas for his book. Wallace, the old socialist, had been the first to argue that co-operation made groups compact and fitted them to survive life's struggle. This was questionable meat and drink to Darwin – but evidence at least of inherited moral qualities. His cousin Francis Galton served up richer puddings. Of Quaker stock, heir of an arms manufacturer and a Birmingham banker, he had profited by Darwin's example and abandoned medicine to take a Cambridge maths degree before settling for a life of travel and scientific leisure. 'Hereditary Talent and Character' were his forte, and his *Macmillan's Magazine* article galvanized Darwin. It stressed the inheritance of every moral and mental trait, from drunkenness and stupidity to sobriety and genius. Races and classes assume the character of their individual members, and Galton called for better breeding, as with 'horses and cattle,' to ensure that the 'nobler varieties of mankind' prevail over the feebler. Above all, advancing civilization was to be saved from 'intellectual anarchy' by the rise of scientific 'master minds' to power.[14]

Galton's line was shared by Darwin's old Plinian Society friend, now a retired Lancashire millowner, W. R. Greg. His article in *Fraser's Magazine* on natural selection in society raised sinister fears about the 'unfit.' Darwin read it assiduously, pondering the problem of the upper middle classes – those who delayed marriage until they had the means to support a family – being swamped. The idle rich outbred them because they could afford to, the idle poor because they lacked Malthus's 'moral restraint.'

> The careless, squalid, unaspiring Irishman multiplies like rabbits: the frugal, foreseeing, self-respecting, ambitious Scot, stern in his morality, spiritual in his faith, sagacious and disciplined in his intelligence, passes his best years in struggle and in celibacy, marries late, and leaves few behind him. Given a land originally peopled by a thousand Saxons and a thousand Celts – and in a dozen generations five-sixths of the population would be Celts, but five-sixths of the property, of the power, of the intellect, would belong to the one-sixth of Saxons that remained. In the eternal 'struggle for existence,' it would be the inferior and *less* favoured race that had prevailed – and prevailed by virtue not of its good qualities but of its faults.

Whither progress, when society was being genetically drained? The dynamic, competing, improving part of the population was strangled by its own success. Natural selection failed them. Darwin was brought up sharp on the ultimate Malthusian dilemma.

Military help arrived with Walter Bagehot's essays on 'Physics and Politics' in the *Fortnightly Review*. Darwin had his pencil out again. To Bagehot, a comfortable banker and editor of *The Economist*, progress depended on a society's command structure. Civilization began with obedience, a respect for law, and a 'military bond.' The greater a tribe's disciplined coherence, the better its chances of triumphing in battle and carrying on its success. Through imperial blood-contests, new human racial and national types emerge, honed and heightened by selection, and this is a moral boon. 'The characters which do win in war are the characters which we should wish to win in war.' Darwin was fascinated. Thinking of the colonial English no doubt, he jotted the proviso, 'nations which *wander* & cross would be most likely to vary' – because they would face unceasing competition. But he agreed with Bagehot's analysis of 'prehistoric politics' and commended it to Hooker.[15]

Hooker was the first Darwinian to take the British Association Presidency. It was a sure sign that, in the 'Parliament of Science' at least, Darwin's statesmen were moving across to the government benches. Hooker moaned at the prospect of his 'Queen's Speech.' The address was crucial, with the hacks reporting it as if it were 'a budget speech by Mr. Gladstone' (which caused only marginally more of a furore). Darwin was even more appalled. 'I pity you from the bottom of my soul about the address: it makes my flesh creep.' Hooker's own flesh was wobbling. 'I would give 100 guineas that it were over, even with a failure, a fiasco, or worse.' At first he thought he would talk on the 'non-acceptance of Natural Selection.' Darwin cued him, reminding him that Newton's theory of gravitation was rejected by the 'extraordinarily able' Leibniz. Word crept out that the speech would be a party pronouncement, and Wallace hoped that it would 'promulgate "Darwinianism"' pure and simple.[16] The X Clubbers seized the opportunity, and it was arranged at party headquarters that Huxley would move the vote of thanks and Tyndall second it.

With the party preparing and Hooker rehearsing, the Darwins trooped off on holiday. They took the train and ferry to the Isle of Wight, with Eras in tow and even old Tommy, Charles's huge horse. Charles himself was a wreck, but the sea air braced him. It was wretched away from home, divorced from his experiments, and he grumbled at having to 'live the life of a drone.' They leased a cottage at Freshwater for six weeks from the photographer Julia Cameron. The haggard evolutionist provided a perfect subject for a portrait in her elemental and manic sepia shades (the Darwins pronounced the shot 'excellent'). Her more poetic subjects appeared on Darwin's doorstep; Tennyson visited several times, as well as the Americans Longfellow and Thomas Appleton. And the Irish poet William Allingham wrote:

> . . . to the Darwins. Dr. Hooker in lower room writing away at his Address; going to put 'Peter Bell's' primrose into it and wants the exact words. Upstairs Mrs. Darwin, Miss D. [Henrietta] and Mr. Charles Darwin himself –, yellow, sickly, very quiet. He has his meals at his own times, sees people or not as he chooses, has invalid's privileges in full, a great help to a studious man.[17]

Hooker had joined them, composing his speech to the greater glory of the yellow sickly soul upstairs.

The Darwinians minus Darwin assembled at Norwich for the Association jamboree. From far and wide they came, a rallying of evolutionary pilgrims of every persuasion. The fiery materialist Carl Vogt travelled from Geneva, telling fellow socialist Wallace that the 'Germans are all becoming converted' by the *Variation*. Victor Carus arrived from Leipzig, hoping to pay homage at Downe afterwards. With so many sects gathered, each holding aloft the *Origin*, friction was inevitable. Mivart came with his confessor Father Roberts, currently leading an austere life in a Drury Lane slum and weaning St George off a Darwinian explanation of ethics. What hope of Huxley's 'new reformation' if the old had yet to take effect? Huxley stumbled upon the two in the nave of Norwich cathedral and expostulated with a wink: 'Oh! for the time when the king shall have his own again.'

Hooker's address was a wild success for the Xs, a stew of hot topics cooked in a Darwinian pot: orchids, tendrils, origins, and 'Tom Tiddler's Ground,' a prehistoric diorama on which he observed the rise of ancient man and demise of archaic theology. He praised Lyell's heroism, and Darwin's more, and damned 'that most dangerous of all two-edged weapons, Natural Theology.' The *Variation* was applauded, the *Athenaeum* abused, and natural selection made out to be part of the mental equipment of every 'philosophical naturalist.'[18] No President could have said more.

Darwin arrived home from holiday on 21 August carrying that day's *Times*, *Telegraph*, *Spectator*, and *Athenaeum*, all running the address. And having devoured them he ordered another bundle of newspapers. The Tory press kicked up a fuss about the theology. *John Bull* bridled at Hooker's 'puffing Mr. Darwin's latest hallucinations,' slating the speech as 'a melancholy exhibition of verbose mediocrity in excelsis,' which increased Hooker's stock no end. He told Darwin that he felt like 'the Turk in Hogarth's picture, calmly smoking his pipe as he gazes in through the window of a Church where the congregation are in a state of religious excitement.'

But who was inside and who out? Party spirit was high as the Darwinians invaded the church scientific with Hooker. Wallace gloated to Darwin that 'Darwinianism' was 'in the ascendant.' The 'worst of it is that there are no opponents left who know anything of natural history, so that there are none of the good discussions we used to have.' The liberal *Telegraph* backed Hooker to the hilt, the Anglican *Guardian* acknowledged that Darwinism's 'reign was triumphant,' and even the grumpy *English Churchman* conceded that 'rank infidelity' was now the scientific norm.[19]

Everywhere the press noted that Darwin's disciples were ready to 'push their consequences more fearlessly than the master himself.' Huxley rubbed the point in, dropping Darwin a note:

> The only fault was the terrible 'Darwinismus' which spread over the [biology] section and crept out when you least expected it, even in Fergusson's lecture on 'Buddhist Temples.' You will have the rare happiness to see your ideas triumphant during your lifetime.

Even in the physics section Tyndall held out hope that eventually science would resolve the 'mystery' of the relation between mind and brain, making them identical. He was too sanguine for Huxley, who genially summed up Tyndall's question for a future physics: 'Given the molecular forces in a mutton chop, deduce Hamlet or Faust therefrom.'[20]

But Darwin revelled in Tyndall's speech. Tyndall and Huxley led the new breed of star performers, their lectures enrapturing audiences and leaving the religious press in a lather. (True to form, Huxley 'offended the clergy twice without cause or warrant,' Hooker tittered to Darwin.) They were persuasive and visionary, hell-bent on dominion, sweeping aside the remnants of privilege and dilettantism. Science was losing its strictures; the old Oxbridge restraints were being shaken off. The X Clubbers with an evolutionary axe to grind deplored 'the stream of cold water which has steadily flowed over geological speculations.' Tyndall despised the 'Tories . . . in science who regard imagination as a faculty to be feared.' Their protest was aimed at lifting sanctions against Darwin's new naturalism, enabling Tyndall to issue a hands-off demand, warning scientists 'to be cautious in limiting [Darwin's] intellectual horizon.'

Tyndall's appeal was universal, which made him dangerous. In these combative years he initiated the Association's working-class talks, and outrageously. Faces were agog with teasing talk of babies built from chemicals, and the thinking capacity of robots. His gloriously deterministic cosmological system left every priest and pauper a soul of fire and child of the sun. All bowed to the same unyielding necessity. He captured its beauty and inescapability, exulting that 'at the present moment, all our poetry, all our science, all our art – Plato, Shakespeare, Newton, and Raphael – are potential in the fires of the sun.'

Darwin's New Model Army had inherited the ethical rigour of the evangelicals. They were positivists in part, Darwinians at heart, and X Clubbers to a man, but they weren't atheists, or materialists, and in fact they lacked any identifying label. They wielded biblical metaphors but were anti-theological. They embedded morality in acquiescence to positive facts, and crucified their enemies for the 'sin of faith.' They retained 'a scientific hell, to which the finally impenitent, those who persist in rejecting the new physical gospel, might be condemned,' and portrayed the Darwinian scientist as the real heir to the Reformation – all of which made Mivart doubly contemptuous of Tyndall's 'new creed – "I believe in One Force".' The 'terrible "Darwinismus"' was being hitched to a pantheistic superstructure and underwritten by its aggressive middle-class exponents.[21] Darwin could only watch in wonder.

In Haeckel's work, *Darwinismus* became even more terribly encompassing, taking in life, mind, society, politics, and knowledge itself. Darwin was still agitating for an expurgated translation of his *Generelle Morphologie*. He offered to defray some of the cost, and at Norwich the Ray Society agreed to publish it with the 'aggressive heterodoxy' toned down. Savage cuts were needed, Huxley insisted; the God-as-gas jibe had to go and the book be 'condensed to the uttermost.' 'We don't much mind heterodoxy here if it does not openly proclaim itself as such,' he warned incongruously, meaning that in England unbelief had to be polite. Haeckel actually prepared a shorn version, ready for translation. But still they met insuperable problems and the scheme eventually fell through. The book was just 'too profound and too long.'[22]

It was also eclipsed by Haeckel's *History of Creation*. Darwin was astonished at another thumping tome arriving on his doorstep, wondering at the 'indomitable worker' who could gestate books at Herbert Spencer's speed. Haeckel rushed in once more with a ream of ancestral pedigrees, precisely where Darwin feared to tread. There was a breathlessness to it, and so much scintillating speculation. 'Whether one agrees or disagrees with him,' Huxley conceded, it was 'more profitable to go wrong than to stand still.' Huxley finally bowed to the inevitable and adopted Haeckel's approach. At the Zoological Society he drew up a heraldic tree for the partridges and pigeons, doing what he once told Darwin was impossible and wrong. He produced 'a *genetic classification*,' signifying the route by which 'all living beings have been evolved one from the other.' He carried on, pushing birds back, past their ostrich-like ancestors to the dinosaurs themselves.[23] After a decade of cavils and caveats, he had finally come round to Darwin's position.

No doubt it was Haeckel's doing, and Huxley paid his debt. He named a primal slime creature *Bathybius Haeckelii*, an enucleate organism dredged from the deep by a sounding ship preparing for the transatlantic cable. Unfortunately it proved less a creature than a creation of the preserving fluid; but the homage was indicative, a tacit admission that the Germans were stealing a march. Huxley also sought audiences for German pilgrims who wanted to pay their 'devotions at the shrine of Mr Darwin' – or 'Pope Darwin,' as he appeared in one accompanying sketch, complete with thurible-swinging acolyte. At Downe Parslow ushered the professors into the study, where they glowed and gloated about the impact of *Darwinismus* in German universities. Jena, where Haeckel taught, was rapidly becoming the centre of the subject. At Bonn Wilhelm Preyer was outdoing even Haeckel, attracting up to 500 students for his lectures. Days after being elevated by Huxley to the papal throne, Darwin received a greater honour: an honorary doctorate from Preyer's university.[24]

The autumn was memorable for the garlands, the touching dedications from one side of the world to the other. French fossil tomes with lavish family trees; an account of the Smithsonian Institution's expedition to the Amazon; Wallace's *Malay Archipelago* – all were dedicated to Darwin.[25] With *Orchids* about to be translated into French, Hooker reckoned that even the French Académie would eventually cave in and elect him a member.

These were the most sociable months the children could remember. Asa Gray, overburdened at the Harvard herbarium and 'half dead with drudgery,' arrived in England with his wife for a long rest in mid-September, after a fast steamship crossing of two weeks. He spent his time in the Kew greenhouses with Hooker, who took the Grays to visit Downe, with Darwin roping in Tyndall on one occasion. On these weekend trips the Grays observed the Darwins at home – the casual untidiness, the worn furniture, the unvarying routine. Emma's and Charles's evening backgammon battles became a spectator sport, with Mrs Gray cheering Emma's gains and her husband consoling the loser. ('Bang your bones'! Charles would explode in mock anger at his wife.) Darwin struck Mrs Gray as 'entirely fascinating,' tall, craggy, with 'a full grey beard cut square across the upper lip.' But not even 'the sweetest smile, the sweetest voice, the merriest laugh' could disguise the ravages. His 'face shows the marks of suffering and disease . . . He never stayed long with us at a time, but as soon as he had talked much, said he must go & rest, especially if he had had a good laugh.'

It was like the old gatherings. Gray's friend Charles Eliot Norton, editor of the *North American Review*, was staying at nearby Keston rectory and dropping into Downe for lunches with his wife and her nineteen-year-old sister Sara Sedgwick (who caught William's eye). On another occasion Wallace and Edward Blythe visited, both tropical travellers to be pumped on hummingbirds and brilliant butterflies. Down House had not seen so many comings and goings for a decade. 'I shall enjoy it immensely,' Darwin chortled before one dinner, 'if it does not kill me.'

Gray, among the natives, found himself rather swamped by Hooker, Huxley, and Tyndall. He was theologically stalemated by the *Variation*, and realized that the *Origin* was irretrievably in the X Club's court. He could hardly condone Hooker's address, or Tyndall's fantasies, and while he took one English fashion back to Harvard (a 'venerable white beard'), he left behind any remaining desire to indulge in '*Darwinian* discussions,' not wishing 'to be at all "mixed up" with the Huxley set.'[26]

A million first-time voters helped rout the Tories in the November General Election and sweep the new Liberal leader, William Gladstone, into 10 Downing Street. The X Club also came within a hair's breadth of getting its own Parliamentary representative. Lubbock fought West Kent again, with Darwin giving moral support (as well as the loan of his carriage), and almost turned out the sitting Tory. It was a crumb of comfort for Downe's old vicar Brodie Innes, who had twitted Darwin for trying to get the Birmingham MP and working-class hero John Bright 'made Dictator.' Innes, however, now had rather more urgent local politics to contend with. From his family estate in Scotland he was making common cause with Darwin to sort out Downe's sitting curate.

It was a sad saga of an 'impoverished benefice' ill served. The lax curate Brodie Innes had left in charge, the Revd Stephens, had departed the previous year, and Innes had been keen to rid himself of responsibility for the living. He even offered to sell the 'advowson' – the right to appoint Downe's priest – to Darwin (who replied that 'it w^d not be in my way'). Stephens's replacements were worse, and Brodie Innes plied Darwin with anxious letters about their conduct. The Revd Samuel Horsman had lasted only three months. He ran up a string of debts and made off with the school's cash after Darwin mistakenly shared the treasurer's duties with him. Horsman was 'more an utter fool than knave,' Darwin pronounced, and Innes could only 'think he is mad.' But no sooner had he been forced out, vapouring threats of litigation, than his successor, the Revd John Robinson, proceeded to disgrace himself by 'walking with girls at night.'[27]

Or so it was rumoured that autumn, according to Brodie Innes's eyes and ears in Down House. Darwin wrote:

> My wife found Mrs. Allen very indignant about Mr. R.s
> conduct with one of her maids. I do not believe that there is
> any evidence of actual criminality. As I repeat only second
> hand my name must not be mentioned. – Our maids tell my
> wife that they do not believe that hardly anyone will go to
> church now . . .

Brodie Innes replied with a written 'challenge' to be circulated in the parish, urging Robinson's accusers to come forward. This put Darwin in a pother – passing on the challenge might expose him to 'an action for defamation of character.' But still, something had to be done.

Rumours were now 'rife against Mr R.' Darwin dug deeper, acting like a sleuth around the village. Brodie Innes heard the magistrate's verdict just before Christmas.

> Mr Allen knows nothing from his own observations. The name
> of the girl is Esther West. Mr Allen's cook saw Mr R. talking
> to her in the road near the house. He had heard from Mrs
> Allen that the mother of the girl (who has left Mr Allen) had
> written to Mr R. forbidding him to call at her cottage; also
> that Mr R. had been seen to go into some house in the village
> where some girl supposed to have a bad character lives. Mr
> Allen said that he believed this 2nd story came from Mrs
> Engleheart, & about the girls mother thro' Mrs Buckle the
> wife of the bailiff.

All hearsay evidence. So Darwin cross-examined Mrs Allen, who had started the story, observing her emotions with a practised eye.

> Judging by her manner, [she] knew a good deal, but said she
> was nervous & w^d not commit herself – accordingly she said
> she c^d not remember who had told her any one single thing;
> or the name of the girl in the village; & further that her
> cook did not want to commit herself & declined to say
> whether it was in the daylight or after dark that M^r R.
> talked with the girl.

The 'only evidence worth any thing c^d be obtained from the girl's mother' but 'perhaps she w^d refuse to commit herself,' Darwin summed up, and so returned the circular, 'sincerely sorry for all this vexation & trouble.' Brodie Innes thanked him profusely for helping 'an old friend out of a most distressing dilemma.' Robinson's days were numbered. 'I hope there may very soon be a resident vicar.'[28]

At home sexual sleuthing of a different kind was gathering pace. Down House had become the hub of a correspondence network across the Empire, its tentacles touching every little England. The sack of mail brought gems daily to aid his sexual selection. Botanists from Ceylon to Calcutta sent reports on monkey manes and bearded Indians; mining engineers from Malacca to Nicaragua told of indigenous customs; tile manufacturers in Gibraltar attended to merino lambs; wine exporters in Portugal followed the local tailless dogs; Laplanders measured reindeer horns; New Zealanders heroically tackled the Maori's sense of beauty; and missionaries and magistrates from Queensland to Victoria ceased converting and incarcerating to observe aboriginal ways – with even an old *Beagle* shipmate Philip King helping out.[29] This is what Darwin excelled at: collecting and collating, tracking down facts, verifying, extending his old notebook speculations to embrace the globe.

38

Disintegrating Speculations

WHATEVER THE GROWING appreciation of evolution, friends and foes alike opposed Darwin's blind, stumbling, accident-prone mechanism: Lyell and Gray stood on the same ground as Owen and Argyll; not one could reconcile himself to it. Where was the time for man to have evolved by Darwin's 'higgledy-piggledy' process – where one accidental variation in ten thousand was usable – with Scots physicists crimping millions from the earth's age? Waiting for chance variants was time-consuming, and time was running out. Lyell had once called up almost infinite reserves; Darwin in 1859 had mooted 300 million years alone since the dinosaurs' reign. But William Thomson's latest calculations, based on the earth as a cooling globe, suggested 100 million years since crustal condensation, which was 'preposterously inadequate' for Darwin's slow, hit-or-miss method.[1] Not for providentialists of course; they were happy to speed up the process, using 'guided' rather than random variations, keeping the flow under Creative control. The physicists' monkey was now on Darwin's back.

Thomson loomed 'like an odious spectre' from one of Wallace's séances. Darwin was appalled at this curtailing of the time available for the evolution of life. His own mathematical geology being wobbly, he asked George, fresh from Cambridge with his maths degree, to check Thomson's figures, incredulous at the 'brevity of the world.' Endless ages *must* have preceded the earliest Silurian sea creatures 'else my views w^d be wrong, which is impossible – Q.E.D.' How could the thousands of feet of sediments have been laid in such short time? Or the old strata have been weathered away? It was absurd.

Nonetheless he met the criticisms with cosmetic surgery to a new (fifth) edition of the *Origin* through the winter of 1868-69. Sometimes the cutting went a little deeper. He had the environment cause a greater number of useful variations to appear. This sped up the process and cut down the risk of new varieties being blended back into a population by intercrossing. And he reactivated the old notion that excessive use of an organ causes its growth (as in the case of a blacksmith's biceps), and that this change can be passed on ('use-inheritance').[2] All this gave a more focused direction to the variations, accelerating evolution, allowing the wonderful richness of life to be a product of a mere 100 million years. He finished on 10 February 1869, two days before his sixtieth birthday.

A week later Huxley turned 'attorney-general' and advised the Geological Society as its President on the time question. His brief was to lift spirits, Darwin's not least: 'Biology takes her time from geology,' he announced, speaking for the evolutionary lobby. 'If the geological clock is wrong, all the naturalist will have to do is to modify his notions of the rapidity of change accordingly.' And it appeared a big 'if' after he had finished with the vagaries of solar heating and terrestrial cooling.

Darwin thought the talk wonderfully 'brilliant,' but shafts rained down on Huxley for compromising the queen of sciences, physics. He was like his execrable 'Trades-Unionists,' another of Thomson's co-workers wrote, smashing the sophisticated machinery supplied by the physicists which would make the biological drudges redundant. 'That educated scientific men should thus fall into the wretched fallacies of handloom-weavers . . . is surely a very singular psychological phenomenon, worthy the attention of sensational writers on obscure diseases of the mind and brain.' If anything, Thomson had been too generous to these biological yahoos, '*ten* or *fifteen* millions' was the *real* age of the earth. This figure, were it true, would have scotched any evolutionary accommodation.

Reading this, Darwin 'felt very small,' and his earth shrank even smaller. Frankly, he did not believe the figure for a moment. He took comfort in the review's 'severe fling' at Hooker and fatuous remarks about Huxley, knowing that he was not alone. 'This review shows me – not that I required being shown – how devilish a clever fellow Huxley is, for the reviewer cannot help admiring his abilities.' George guessed that this latest estimate was by a Thomson co-worker, P. G. Tait, a Bible-toting Edinburgh professor of natural philosophy. He also impressed on his father the gravity of Thomson's case. 'Tell George from me not to sit upon you with his mathematics,' Hooker rallied him. 'Take another dose of Huxley's . . . Address, and send George back to college.'[3]

Darwin's discomfort was more than scientific this spring. In April he was riding Tommy on Keston Common when his favourite old horse tripped, threw him on to the ground and rolled over him. The bruising was extensive, and the doctors advised him to rest for a few months. He mended within weeks and resumed work under Emma's watchful eye, but they agreed that Tommy was unreliable.[4] At sixty, Charles needed a sure mount, but he never found one and his riding days came to an end.

Huxley, who had instructed Haeckel on metaphysical rectitude, found himself charged with heresy after preaching a Sunday 'lay sermon' in Edinburgh 'on the physical basis of life.' It *sounded* like materialism – life and mind a glorified chemical process – although he insisted that materialism was as absurd ultimately as spiritualism. To no avail. His lecture, published in the *Fortnightly Review*, caused a sensation and the issue ran to an unheard-of seven editions. The religious hacks foamed. Was he not Darwinism personified, the high priest of the new secular faith, conducting 'Sunday Evenings for the People,' canvassing for 'scientific Sunday schools,' and chairing London's 'Sunday Lecture Society'?[5] They portrayed him as a man of matter without a soul, an atheist and immoral.

He was none of these, even if there was some dispute as to what he was. He came clean in April, when a group of liberal churchmen made a last attempt to reach a religious consensus among the nation's feuding intelligentsia. Their monthly discussion group, the 'Metaphysical Society,' was a menagerie of faiths and heresies; bishops and archbishops mingled with Positivists, deists, and Unitarians, and for spice there was even the odd atheist. Huxley joined with Tyndall and Lubbock, representing the Darwinian faction, but before anyone could pin him down he came up with a new identifying label – he coined the name 'agnostic.' An agnostic did not deny or affirm God's existence; he did not pretend to know whether the world is made of matter, spirit, or whatever. Like 'lunar politics,' the subject was endlessly and pointlessly debateable. Darwin's science stood above such squabbles, dealing with the knowable world. To Huxley Darwinism was 'not only "unsectarian" but . . . altogether "secular".'[6]

Huxley loved military issues and he needed a reactionary enemy. Catholicism provided it. He constantly vilified the Roman Church as 'our great antagonist,' the supreme foil. He pictured it as a Jesuitical militia, whose priests, trained to combat scientific change, were, next to the Dad's army of Dissenters, like 'the trained veterans of Napoleon's Old Guard.' These strategic attacks racked his Catholic admirer St George Mivart to breaking point. To hear of 'Pithecoid Man' was distressing; to be told that the Catholic Church 'must, as a matter of life and death, resist the progress of science and modern civilization' was too much – even if recent papal condemnations seemed to imply it. (Mivart was too liberal to take Pius IX's 'Syllabus of Errors' seriously.) Nor had crusading Continental works like Vogt's inflammatory *Lectures on Man* and Haeckel's *Generelle Morphologie* helped. Mivart was torn; his letters to Darwin became a desperation of pleasantries.

> For my part I shall never feel anything but gratitude & sincere esteem for the author of 'natural selection' but I heartily execrate some who made use of that theory simply as a weapon of offence against higher interests and as a means of impeding Man's advance towards his 'end' whatever may have been his 'origin.'

He had Huxley in mind. In his 'wandering about Italy' he had been 'amazed and saddened' to see Huxley's *Man's Place in Nature* on sale at 'most of the railway stations amongst a crowd of *obscenities*.'[7] Huxley's aggressive posturing was losing Darwin followers.

Darwin also knew that trouble was brewing with Wallace, and he awaited his review of Lyell's tenth-edition *Principles* with trepidation. The High Church *Guardian* had already smiled on Lyell's mild Darwinism. 'Really,' Wallace wrote, 'what with the Tories passing Radical Reform Bills and the Church periodicals advocating Darwinianism, the millennium must be at hand.' But it was Wallace's spirit-driven evolution that worried Darwin. 'I shall be intensely curious to read' the review. 'I hope you have not murdered too completely your own and my child.' Poignant, anxious words. The review appeared in April and Darwin identified the child's corpse, horrified at the disfiguring torture. He stabbed exclamation marks at Wallace's text, and triple underlined 'No.'[8]

Wallace had plucked mankind's expansive consciousness from the realm of selection altogether. Savages have a mental capacity far beyond their needs. Little more than a gorilla's brain would suffice; as it is they possess the egg-head of an Englishman, and as such an intellectual over-capacity. Selection, which deals in the immediately useful, could not have given it to them, but the spiritual forces could. Having gone native while collecting in the Amazon and Far East, the socialist held savages in high esteem. He did not share Darwin's defamatory view, based on the crafty, cannibalistic Fuegians. 'The more I see of uncivilized people,' Wallace had said while living with the Dyaks in Borneo, 'the better I think of human nature.' The brain was an over-endowment, but some tribes had used it to develop a higher morality than the colonists trying to exterminate them.

The big brain was an essential prerequisite for the development of civilization. But selection had no foresight – it provided for day-to-day existence, not future needs. And judging by the 'social barbarism' of Victoria's England, morally crippled by a cut-throat capitalism, selection had no power to enhance civilization. No, for Wallace higher spiritual powers guided human destiny. They were responsible for the brain, and they would be man's salvation, putting him on the path to the millennium.

'I differ grievously from you,' Darwin wrote, 'and I am very sorry for it.' It was sad, the stoutest defender unaccountably calling in other-worldly intelligences. It was also 'incredibly strange.' Not knowing better, Darwin 'would have sworn' the brain passages 'had been inserted by some other hand.' An invisible spiritual hand, as Wallace explained by return; his opinions had been modified, he confessed, after studying 'the existence of forces and influences not yet recognized by science.'⁹

The spring of defections was turning into a summer of despair. On 3 June, with Huxley's help, Mivart gained his Fellowship of the Royal Society. It was a crowning testimony to his studies of monkeys, and gave no indication of the cruel blow to come. Twelve days later, he turned traitor. He told Huxley face to face that he was going to publish his objections to Darwinian views of human nature and morality. 'As soon as I had made my meaning clear, his countenance became transformed as I had never seen it before,' Mivart recalled. 'Yet he looked more sad and surprised than anything else. He was kind and gentle as he said regretfully, but most firmly, that nothing so united or severed men as questions such as those.' Mivart had been groomed, ready for the charmed inner circle. His desertion was viewed as treachery, and the Darwinians closed ranks as a period of bitterness and recrimination set in.

The breach had already opened, with Mivart placing anonymous articles in the Catholic *Month* criticizing natural selection. He raised a host of difficulties: how could selection explain a placental dog and marsupial wolf converging so miraculously? And can it explain an incipient wing? What use is half a wing, yet selection is supposed to keep the animal functional at every stage? These were puzzlers. 'How incipient organs can be useful is a real difficulty,' Wallace admitted to Darwin after reading the *Month*, 'so is the independent origin of similar complex organs.' Darwin heavily annotated the anonymous reprint. He could not accept Mivart's inner force working to a definite end. Nor could he see life swept forward on a wave front according to God's will, any more than he could agree with Lyell, Gray, and Argyll.[10]

While Mivart and Wallace muddied the waters, Argyll stirred the sediment. The result was more best-selling froth. The new Secretary of State for India found time to push Gladstone's Irish policies, organize the Indian railways, and, like everyone else, publish on man. *Primeval Man* was no more than one might expect from a Liberal duke charged with running India from a desk in Whitehall, but the public loved such things.

Argyll took on Lubbock, admitted a long prehistory, but saw no signs of original bestiality. Mankind could not rise unaided from 'utter barbarism.' But he could have sunk from some higher state. Modern savages were not Stone Age relics but degenerates, forced into the worst regions by fitter races. Nor were our ancestors morally barbarous. And how could selection produce all this? Look at man's pink skin and puny frame – how could selection evolve greater weakness without the counter-balancing gift of reason being bestowed first? Where would such a helpless savage stand in the struggle for existence? One newspaper knew exactly: 'Place a naked high-ranking elder of the British Association in [the] presence of one of M. de Chaillu's gorillas, and behold how short and sharp will be the struggle.'[11]

Argyll was adamant: 'Man must have had the human proportions of mind before he could afford to lose bestial proportions of body.' And just because Sir John's savage had no knowledge of metal did not mean 'he was also ignorant of duty or ignorant of God.' Darwin found it all immensely clever and rather tedious. He ploughed on with the real *Descent of Man*, pointing out that, in the absence of ancestors, no one can assume that we are 'smaller and weaker.' Anyway, he added, standing Argyll on his head, man's vulnerability encouraged social cohesion and with it the moral sense. Lubbock prepared to restate the case at the British Association, that savage customs are stone-age hold-overs, which 'tell a tale of former barbarism.'[12] And – armed by Darwin on the Fuegians – he hammered the point home in his second edition of *Prehistoric Times*.

While Lubbock prepared for the bustling Association, Darwin was spirited away by 'his ladies' on holiday, grumbling and grousing as he got over his riding accident. They started on 10 June for Caerdeon in the Barmouth valley, sleeping at Shrewsbury on the way. He revisited The Mount, but the new owners dutifully followed him around. 'If I could have been left alone in that green-house for five minutes,' he whispered with a melancholy sigh, 'I know I should have been able to see my father in his wheel-chair as vividly as if he had been there before me.' The purple-heathered hills of North Wales, full of old memories, depressed him. He longed to pound up to the peaks as he used to as a student, but he could barely walk half a mile from the house. 'It is enough to make one wish oneself quiet in a comfortable tomb,' he mumbled, and he joined George on a sick-bed while the other children larked and posed for a group photograph.

The resort drew other notables. Plodding up a gentle rise one afternoon, he was stopped by a shout. He peered through the 'impenetrable brambles' to see, on the road sixty feet away, the redoubtable Miss Cobbe, the women's and animals' rights campaigner, bursting to tell him about Mr Mill's emancipationist book *On the Subjection of Women*. It was perfect for his study of human descent, she yelled, especially the chapters on sexual selection. Darwin bellowed back that Mill 'could learn some things' from biology. Men's superiority was the product of the 'struggle for existence;' their special 'vigour and courage' came from battling 'for the possession of women.' Hearing that, Cobbe offered her copy of Kant on the 'moral sense' to sort out his obvious ethical problems. He politely refused.[13]

The X Club gained their permanent press outlet in November when *Nature* was founded. While Hooker used it to review, and Huxley to extol Goethe, Darwin was reading another *Nature* supporter, Francis Galton's *Hereditary Genius*. He wrote in praise to his cousin: 'you have made a convert of an opponent in one sense, for I have always maintained that, excepting fools, men did not differ much in intellect, only in zeal and hard work; and I still think [this] is an eminently important difference.'[14]

Darwin ended the year as he came in, at the grindstone, 'putting ugly sentences rather straighter' and struggling to finish sexual selection, 'weary of everlasting males and females, cocks and hens.' It left him as 'dull as a duck.' And still the colonists and empire builders showered scraps on him: sons off to China acted as his eyes; from the Colonial Office in Cape Town came information on African moths; and natives were scrutinized from India to Sierra Leone in response to his printed 'Queries about Expression.' If nothing, the *Descent of Man* would carry the mark of empire.

All eyes were turning to Darwin. Everybody had spoken on the rise or fall of man but him. He was expected to clear the mud with a definitive pronouncement. Murray's new literary monthly, *The Acad-*

emy, trailed the work in the opening issue. As always the Germans were quick off the mark and competing to translate the *Descent of Man*. Darwin felt secure with Carus, but the fiery Vogt was bidding for the rights, to Darwin's horror. At Eras's he told Frances Cobbe that Vogt in London 'gave a lecture, in which he treated the Mass as the last relic of that *Cannibalism* which gradually took to eating only the heart, or eyes of a man to acquire his courage.' Darwin's only comment was 'how much more *decency* there was in speaking on such subjects in England.' He could never let the *Descent* go to such a sneering cynic.

The prospect of speaking out on this contentious issue filled Darwin with dread. This time his critics were lying in wait, forearmed. 'Whenever I publish my book,' he told Mivart half-accusingly, 'I can see that I shall meet with universal disapprobation, if not execution.'[15]

Charles kept the study fire stoked and wrote through the long hard winter, wrapping up the chapters on man's 'mental powers' and 'moral sense.' He posted them to Cannes, where Henrietta, twenty-seven and rather eligible, had swanned off for a reconnoitre. A stylist and petty moralist, she touched up his prose and guarded the proprieties. Parts were too evangelical, he feared; they read like a sermon. 'Who w^d ever have thought I sh^d turn parson'!

An infidel parson at that, given his argument's atheistic overtones. As he saw it, the 'feeling of religious devotion' was not basically different from a monkey's affection for its keeper, or Henrietta's dog Polly's 'deep love' for her. Nor was the 'ennobling belief in God' innate and universal, merely the highest sanction for keeping society in order. All beliefs and mores had originated in animal instincts and savage superstitions. These were old views, from Charles's notebook days. But even now, ten years after the *Origin* furore, publication might injure the family; Henrietta had to ensure that the wrong inferences would not be drawn. As she preened the text, her own guardian angel – Emma – jogged her. The treatment of morals and religion might be 'very interesting,' Emma wrote, but she would still 'dislike it very much as again putting God further off.'[16]

Soon he was exhausted and Emma carried out her threat to 'force him off somewhere' for a break. He went willingly this time, to Cambridge. Frank was graduating with a good maths degree and Horace had joined him at Trinity. It was mid-May and the backs of the colleges were 'paradaisical.' When better to visit the ancient town after more than thirty years? Henrietta came along with her sister Bessy to check on Horace's health, and they all stayed at the Bull

Hotel. Besides the bustling market and teeming shops, there was a new chapel at St John's, refurbishments in Great St Mary's, and museums and lecture rooms where the old Botanic Garden once stood. Charles, recalling his student strolls, was haunted by 'dear Henslow.' Cambridge was just 'not itself' without him.

The day before leaving they ran into Professor Sedgwick. Elderly and 'living in cheerless solitude,' he was 'overflowing with joy' to see Charles in 'a dear family party' and sat him down for a long chat. He carried on as if the *Origin of Species* had never been published – in politeness perhaps, but Charles thought his brain 'enfeebled.' He then proposed to show off his pride and joy, the Woodwardian Museum, full of fossils and rocks. It was late but a refusal unthinkable, and the old Proctor, hobbling on his stick in flowing robes, frogmarched him through the streets for the geological tour. By the end Charles was 'utterly prostrated;' the next morning he could barely drag himself to the train. 'Is it not humiliating,' he sighed, 'to be thus killed by a man of eighty-six, who evidently never dreamed that he was killing me?'[17]

Safely home, he carried on nailing down the coffin of Sedgwick's divinely created man. Some did not realize what he was up to. The new Tory Chancellor of Oxford, Lord Salisbury, invited him to the June commencement to receive an honorary Doctorate of Civil Laws. Darwin, fit enough for Cambridge, invoked poor health and refused. An honour from the High Church stronghold was dubious at best, and anyway, as Huxley squealed, he had been a compromise candidate. When the venerable Revd Edward Pusey, Regius Professor of Hebrew, got wind of the nominations there had been a 'tremendous shindy.' He agreed to 'your being doctored' only 'to keep out seven devils worse than the first.' But 'I wish you could have gone,' Huxley grinned wryly, 'not for your sake, but for theirs . . . oh Coryphaeus diabolicus.'[18]

Other titles suited better. Moscow's Imperial Society of Naturalists elected him an honorary member, and the South American Missionary Society offered to do the same. His last sight of bedraggled Jemmy Button left him swearing that wild Fuegians were untameable; FitzRoy's failure proved the impossibility of breaking their habits. But Sulivan, believing that no humans were 'too low to comprehend the simple message of the Gospel,' and reeling off the Society's record, had made Darwin repent. An Anglican outpost had been established in Tierra del Fuego, the natives converted and clothed, and the strategic Cape Horn region secured for English shipping. As proof, Sulivan had sent a photo of Jemmy's upright-looking son. Darwin, keen to spread the blessings of civilization, had made small

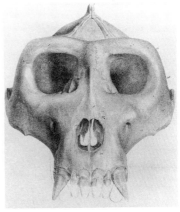

28
Richard Owen had been Darwin's friend, but the relationship turned sour.

29
A gorilla skull, pictured by Owen in 1849, when he first described the beast. The ape's novelty ensured its emotive role in the Darwinian debate.

30
Owen lecturing at Huxley's School of Mines in 1857. The deed caused a breach of diplomatic relations.

31
T. H. Huxley, lecturing on the gorilla. He made evolution serve his secular interests.

32
Pope Darwin, a lightning sketch on a letter from Huxley. He sought an audience for a visiting German naturalist, who wished to pay 'his devotions at the shrine of Mr. Darwin'.

33
The haggard
paterfamilias in the
1860s, contemplating
the *Descent of Man*.

34
The family at home about 1863: from left to right, Leonard, Henrietta, Horace,
Emma, Elizabeth, Francis, and a visitor.

35

Down House from the rear in the 1860s. (The earliest known photograph.)

36

The Down House staff in the late 1870s: included are Jackson the butler and his wife, John the coachman, Fred the groom, Tommy Price the under-gardener, Mrs Evans the cook, Jane the head housemaid with Harriet her assistant, and Mary Anne the nurse. The boy on the pony may be Charles's grandson, Bernard, who lived at Down.

THAT TROUBLES OUR MONKEY AGAIN.

Female descendant of Marine Ascidian :—"REALLY, MR. DARWIN, SAY WHAT YOU LIKE ABOUT MAN; BUT I WISH YOU WOULD LEAVE MY EMOTIONS ALONE!"

37
Darwin with his finger on the pulse of femininity. In *The Expression of the Emotions in Man and Animals* he wrote that 'a pretty girl blushes when a young man gazes intently at her' because she immediately thinks about the 'outer and visible parts' of her body, and this alters their 'capillary circulation'.

38
Charles Lyell just before his death in 1875, a blind widower obsessed with the problem of an afterlife. Darwin admitted that, similarly placed, the same fears would strike him 'in the dead of the night with painful force'.

39
Darwin on the verandah at Down House, about 1880, dressed for his daily constitutional on the Sandwalk.

40
John Lubbock, Darwin's neighbour and childhood protégé, in his study at High Elms near Downe. As a Liberal MP and scientific polymath he helped to engineer Darwin's burial in Westminster Abbey.

41
Darwin immortalized among the nation's heroes: the graveside scene in the Abbey, with the leaders of science, state, and Church in attendance.

42
A saintly Darwin icon, based on a photo from the early 1870s: the kind of serene and untroubling image that the family sought to substitute for the anxious 'Devil's Chaplain'.

donations to the mission for several years. Yes, he would be proud to be an honorary member. Only, he warned Sulivan, 'I shall ... publish another book partly on man, which I dare say many will decry as very wicked.'[19]

The election that most pleased him was Lubbock's. In February 1870 his neighbour had been returned for Maidstone, squeaking into the Commons by 100 votes, and Darwin wasted no time in putting him to work. The telegraph service to Downe was paltry; 'all the inhabitants' wanted their new MP to lean on the Post Office to make improvements. Also there was a census coming up. With his old protégé's help, it could turn into an anthropological questionnaire. Darwin had sent out scores of printed queries over the years, pestering farmers, surgeons, missionaries, and colonial travellers for first-hand reports. Here was his chance to turn the nation into a network of informants on the vexed question of in-breeding.

Darwin had crossed pigeons *ad infinitum*; even now he was running growth trials on crossed and self-fertilized plants. But on humans he drew a blank – the *Descent of Man* lacked evidence. The country was experimenting daily, the population booming, yet no one had investigated the fertility of inbred families. With four first-cousin marriages in his generation of Darwin-Wedgwoods, the question was personal. If his own frail children were victims, then surely the nation's stock suffered likewise. Would it not pay to find out whether defects like 'deafness, and dumbness, blindness, &c.' were associated with close intermarriage?[20]

The question was this: did married cousins have as many surviving children as unrelated parents? Bigger families were fitter, he reasoned; size would tell. Lubbock asked the House of Commons on 22 July during the second reading of the Census Bill: since naturalists held that 'consanguineous marriages were injurious throughout the whole vegetable and animal kingdoms,' would it not be 'desirable to ascertain whether that was ... the case with the whole human race'? In the bill's committee stage Lubbock moved an amendment 'to insert the words, "whether married to a first cousin",' in the relevant census question. A furious debate erupted. It was 'inquisitorial,' howled the opposition, and 'the grossest cruelty ever thought of.' If 'the philosophers' had their way, it would naturally lead to 'further inquiries as to the number, health, and mental condition of ... children.' Parliament might even be called on to decide whether first cousins could marry, causing 'mental torture' to couples.[21] The amendment was defeated by a margin of two to one.

*

Charles gnashed his teeth and pressed on to finish the manuscript, by which time Parliament was forgotten and the talk was all of France's war with Prussia. Tens of thousands were dying daily, and in August the family thought about nothing else. Leonard at Woolwich declared himself a staunch Prussian, even though his fellow soldiers, itching for a fight, supported the French, knowing that war with England would be more likely if they triumphed. Emma stoked her pro-Prussian ardour by reading up on the intrigues of Napoleon I. In France she saw 'no national value for truth.' 'What an enormous collapse it is,' a nation self-deceived, 'tumbling headlong into ... war, without a notion of what the enemy was capable of'! Charles joined in the chorus of condemnation, but worried about his allies, Haeckel, Preyer, and Carus. The war would 'stop all science ... for a long time.'[22]

War games started at Downe, like those during the Crimea, but with a new battalion of troops. The seven little Huxleys came for a fortnight so that the 'General' – as Huxley senior was known – could attend the British Association at Liverpool. The people's scientist had taken the Presidency, after a lot of politicking, although it outraged *The Times*. The popular press hooted at the 'thunderer': 'Mr. Huxley is so indiscreet,' they roared in imitation. 'If only we had an "indiscreet" Archbishop!' Failing that the tabloids hoped for an 'indiscreet President' and some fun. But a sobered-up Huxley reassured everyone that the agnostic was no hell-raiser and gave a guarded address on the origin of life, which was hissed at by the tabloids as 'not naughty enough.' Darwin, agonizing over his 'accursed proofs,' suddenly missed his old hellion. Tyndall was still performing though, justifying the use of hypothesis and metaphor in science, much to Darwin's pleasure.[23]

Darwin was rattled by the war. By now, late September, Napoleon had surrendered at Sedan. Paris, besieged, was in pandemonium and Strasbourg had fallen. The carnage was awful, the country overrun, and yet the French spurned Prussian peace terms and fought on for *la gloire*. 'I have not yet met a soul in England who does not rejoice in the splendid triumph of Germany over France,' Darwin boasted to Fritz Müller in Brazil. 'It is a most just retribution against that vainglorious, war-liking nation.' In Leipzig Carus astonished him by his readiness to translate the *Descent of Man* while the conflict raged. It would not hurt sales, he reported, though he wished the struggle between the 'Romanic' and 'Teutonic' races could be conducted less primitively. Darwin, sharing the sentiment, promised to rush him the corrected proofs. Kovalevsky had earlier written from Berlin bemoaning England's Prussian sympathies; now, his proofs not having arrived, he feared that he had committed some political infelicity in speaking out. He had to finish the translation quickly, he told Darwin, because he wanted to go to his sister-in-law's in besieged Paris.[24]

Darwin worked on at his 'frightful' corrections, sensitive to the offence his book would give. It 'half kills me by fatigue,' he told Wallace in November as he came to the last page of proofs, and 'I much fear will quite kill me in your good estimation.' Family and friends would feel worse. For all Henrietta's pruning, he knew the *Descent* would offend them. Already Fox had heard 'sad tales' circulating about the book and denied the existence of illegitimate apes in his family tree. And Sulivan; he and the mission would be up in arms. 'Ailing and grumbling,' Darwin warned him again at Christmas that the *Descent of Man* would 'disgust you & many others.'[25] He was battening down for the storm.

The proofs went off on 15 January 1871. He doubted that the book was 'worth publishing' and launched straight into his next one, using the left-over materials on emotional expressions. Others doubted it too. Within a week Mivart's clever critique *On the Genesis of Species* arrived, the most devastating all-round attack on natural selection in Darwin's lifetime. It was also a pre-emptive strike on the *Descent of Man* and, coming from a man close to the inner circle, it left Darwin badly 'shaken.' He was so angry he could barely speak.

Like an Old Bailey barrister, Mivart – trained at Lincoln's Inn – shrewdly caricatured Darwinism as natural selection 'pure and simple.' He put it in the dock and produced such a welter of counter-evidence as to overwhelm the jury. Much of it was unimpeachable at the time, and it was certainly persuasive, judging by book sales. He piled on refutation after refutation, aiming for a cumulative effect: he conjured up Thomson's time spectre, laid waste to pangenesis, lampooned the notion of a half-evolved wing, raised the problem of convergent species, exploited the differences between Darwin, Huxley, and Wallace, and ended by slating Darwinians for meddling in metaphysics. This was his real object, to show that selection was not only false, but dangerous applied to morals and religion – and he knew that Darwin was about to apply it.

Privately Mivart professed nothing but 'sympathy and esteem' for Darwin himself. He wrote earnestly, looking forward to a chat. He blamed the reckless extension of Darwinism on its overzealous supporters, though he regretted that 'you do not more protest against [their] unnecessary irreligious deductions:'

the acceptance of your views means with many the
abandonment of belief in God and in the immortality of the
soul together with future rewards & punishments . . . I think
that the destruction of such beliefs is most important viewed
from the . . . standpoint of the temporal happiness of mankind
. . . God grant we in England may not be approaching a
religious decay at all similar to that of the middle of the 18th
century in France which Frenchmen are now paying for in
blood & tears!

Atheism, anarchy, and national ruin – as Darwin winced at the old
equation, Paris was under siege. Dogs and cats were being eaten, and
rats brought a franc each in the starving streets. Some in Mivart's
circle were affected more directly. Owen, an investor in the *Jardin
d'Acclimatation* (which was modelled on London zoo), saw his
holdings wiped out as the exotic mammals, even the beloved
elephants, were slaughtered to feed the citizens. Darwin's old
nightmares began to return. In the hysterical climate he expected a
backlash. Not only would 'the pendulum swing against' natural
selection; the author of the *Descent of Man* would be depicted as a
black-caped anarchist.[26]

Advance copies went out, to Mivart, Wallace, Cobbe, and a host
of other critics. While Darwin awaited the reviews, he faced further
ignominy. The parish was now in the good hands of the Revd Henry
Powell, but his predecessor Robinson, despatched to a nearby curacy,
had teamed up with the previous curate Horsman, who was on the
point of suing Darwin for defamatory remarks about absconding
with the school's cash. Robinson, it seemed, was the informant. 'I
really think being examined in court could half-kill me,' Darwin
moaned to Brodie Innes, now valuing his vicar's friendship more
than ever. The case would 'never come to trial,' Innes assured
Darwin. The incongruity of their soothing alliance struck Innes: 'dear
me! if some of your naturalists, and my ritualist friends were to hear
us two saying civil things to each other, they would say the weather
was going to change, or Paris to be relieved, both [of] which I wish
might happen.'

But *belle* Paris did fall and was thronged by Prussian troops.
Charles and Emma, with old memories of the city, felt for the people.
Emma even had words with a German guest, who resented it: 'we
each spit our spite,' she told Aunt Fanny, 'and then made peace.'
Letters with Continental franks were opened with bated breath.
Carus was getting on with the German edition, delayed only by a

bout of illness. Haeckel reported the birth of a daughter, named Emma. Kovalevsky and his wife had actually carried the proofs of the *Descent of Man* twenty-five miles through the Prussian lines into Paris, losing only a few sheets on the way. He kept on translating, even though knowing that the Russian interior minister had banned the 'materialistic' book and threatened to impound copies. A 'fearful piece of tyranny,' Darwin fumed.[27]

The *Descent of Man* went on sale at such a time, two portly 450-page volumes retailing for twenty-four shillings. A second edition was called for within three weeks; by the end of March 4500 copies were in print and Darwin was almost £1500 better off, a 'fine big sum,' he boasted to Henrietta, offering her a £30 memento for her labours. The early response was astonishing. 'Everybody is talking about it without being shocked.' Few howls of abuse, few anti-Darwinian rants; it was so perplexing that he asked Murray to note reviews in 'out-of-the-way papers, especially the religious,' to confirm his worst fears. Nothing turned up. Most reviewers let out a low moan, and that was it. Like the *Edinburgh* critic, they conceded that the book was 'raising a storm of mingled wrath, wonder, and admiration' among the populace. They grudgingly admitted some sort of evolution but denied that man's 'spiritual powers' were selected from brute instincts, otherwise 'earnest-minded men will be compelled to give up those motives by which they have attempted to live noble and virtuous lives.'

Inured to monkey-men and materialism by Huxley and Tyndall, informed by Galton, Greg, and Bagehot about the struggle for civilization, people seemed to be snapping up the *Descent* simply because it carried the name 'Darwin.' The subject was less bad news than old news. To Darwin, immensely relieved, it was 'proof of the increasing liberality of England.'[28]

It was, and more. In many ways the book *was* the man – pudgy and comfortable, sedate in its seniority, full of anecdote and rather old-fashioned. There was little fire and flair about it, nothing of Huxley, Haeckel, or Vogt. Like a doting uncle, it did not tax one's tolerance so much as entertain. It told an arm-chair adventure of the English evolving, clambering up from the apes, struggling to conquer savagery, multiplying and dispersing around the globe. In Darwin's early anxious jottings such a story seemed dangerously implausible; his secret assault on man's ancestry had been a brazen act of faith, fit only for radicals and their ilk. But now, habituated to material progress, social mobility, and imperial adventure, the *arriviste* reading classes lapped it up. A romantic pedigree suited them, an epic genealogy. Disregarding the apes, as many did, they found the *Descent* a tremendous family saga.

All Victorian life was there, from the Fuegian savage York Minster up to 'our great philosopher, Herbert Spencer.' Each race moves along the ladder of civilization, propelled by natural selection, aided by use-inheritance, with selfish instinct giving way to reason, morality, and English customs. Fidelity and courage are on the rise, chastity in women, temperance in men; slavery, superstition, and senseless conflict are passing away, so that 'virtue will be triumphant.' Yet it is an undeniable tale of Malthusian struggle. Always there are heroes and the hapless, victorious civilizations and vanquished 'barbarians,' expanding nations and exterminated ones, large families and small. The 'intellectually superior' out-breed the inferior, the better classes out-distance the 'intemperate, profligate, and criminal classes,' and even the rich tend to leave more offspring than the swelling poor, who are cut down in infancy. And yet through it all a lofty humanitarianism prevails. The 'noblest part' of human nature dictates sympathy for the 'inferior members of society.' The 'bad effects of the weak surviving and propagating their kind' are to be borne 'without complaining.'[29]

The Darwins fitted the picture perfectly. The *Descent* was essentially their story. Natural and sexual selection had made and maimed them. Charles had strutted like 'a peacock admiring his tail' courting Emma. Coy and impressionable, she had selected him, admiring his 'courage, perseverance, and determined energy' after a voyage around the world. Her 'maternal instincts' and feminine intuitions had been the mainstay of their marriage (even if partly a hold-over from 'a past and lower state of civilization'). Endowed with wealth, they had a head-start in the struggle – and an 'accumulation of capital' was essential if civilized Westerners were to spread and subdue the lower races. The wealthy 'who have not to labour for their daily bread' were vital to society. 'All high intellectual work is carried on by them, and on such work material progress of all kinds mainly depends.' Their sons, however, must be exposed to competition, kept up to nature's mark, and 'the most able should not be prevented by laws or customs from succeeding best and rearing the largest number of offspring.'

Darwin ended the book on a personal note, still telling tales, still praising the real heroes, the animals. He told of the 'heroic little monkey, who braved his dreaded enemy in order to save the life of his keeper,' and the old baboon who saved 'his young comrade from a crowd of astonished dogs.' 'For my own part,' he confessed, 'I would as soon be descended' from them as from a naked, degraded savage.[30]

In Paris peace had come and the Prussian troops were gone. But an insurrection had broken out, with angry citizens attacking the army. Led by socialists and republicans, they drove the troops from the city, repudiated the national government, and on 26 March elected their own, the Commune. A week later came the second siege of Paris, this time by French forces, and the butchery began once more. The English papers railed against the Communards, and *The Times* against Darwin. He was undermining authority. If his views of moral development were accepted, the eternal principles of right and wrong would lose their force. Conscience would fail to check 'the most murderous revolutions.' In France 'loose philosophy' had rotted moral principles with dreadful results. A 'man incurs a grave responsibility when, with the authority of a well-earned reputation, he advances at such a time the disintegrating speculations of this book.'[31]

Darwin dismissed the hack as a 'windbag full of metaphysics and classics,' even while worrying about its impact on sales. From the 'thunderer' to the Welshman who called him 'an old Ape with a hairy face,' the cranks could no longer hurt him. Nor could Brodie Innes: 'Man was made a man,' the old Tory taunted, and he split 'into niggers who must be made to work' and into 'better men able to make them,' or such was God's scheme before being thwarted by the interfering 'radicals.' Darwin replied, 'I consider myself a good way ahead of you, as far as this goes.' Not even the 200,000-circulation, down-market *Family Herald*, shrieking 'society must fall to pieces if Darwinism be true,' could touch him. There were simply too many plaudits, too much weighty discussion for such silly jibes to matter. The serious magazines were now chocked with essays 'on Darwinism and Religion, Darwinism and Morals, Philosophy and Darwinism,' and he devoured them all.[32]

He shrugged off Cobbe's kind but untutored defence of the supernatural conscience. He praised the brilliant editor of the *Fortnightly Review*, John Morley, for agreeing that 'the foundations of morality, the distinctions of right and wrong, are deeply laid in the very conditions of social existence.' Wallace's review in the *Academy* had little impact; its objections seemed 'almost stereotyped' by now. But, in Eras's words, it was a 'perfectly beautiful' piece of controversy, generous and polite. 'In future histories of science,' he predicted, 'the

Wallace-Darwin episode will form one of the few bright points,' a shining example of how gents managed their disputes.[33]

By contrast, the Mivart fracas was an ignoble tale, which Darwin took too personally and Mivart too casually. Darwin was watching himself shudder in a mirror, wrestling with his manuscript on facial expressions, when Mivart's letter arrived. He was being stalked. Mivart laid down the terms of engagement, while wishing 'with all my heart we did *not* differ so widely.' The debate was to be on metaphysics, on the basic assumptions of science. And he repeated that, 'while combatting (as duty compels me to do) positions you adopt, I am not so much combatting *you*, as others to whose views your scientific labours give additional currency.'

Darwin felt irritatingly targeted, and by a turncoat. Mivart could not be written off as a windbag, though theology made him moralize. A few days later Darwin threw down his expressions manuscript, the rough draft done, and began planning a new edition of the *Origin*. A cheap one, he told Murray: working men in Lancashire were clubbing together to buy the fifth at fifteen shillings.[34] He wanted them all to have copies. The sixth would take on Mivart. It would challenge his assumption that a half-evolved wing was an absurdity, and that selection cannot explain the similarity of marsupial and placental wolves. It would destroy his claim that some unplumbed inner force drives evolution to its goal.

May and June shot by, and he raced into the summer, plundering old notes, building defences, shoring up his reputation. Paris was ravaged and the Communards crushed. And while they were making themselves 'everlastingly infamous,' as Darwin wrote to Kovalevsky, Mivart's wretched *Genesis of Species* was 'producing a great effect against Natural Selection, and more especially against me.' He was determined to defend himself, hold his ground, and wait for philosophical reinforcements. Mivart's *ancien régime* would not be revived.

A week at Eras's in June brought news from the United States. Ras's dinner guest, Edward Youmans, was America's top scientific salesman. He was over from New York to recruit big names – Huxley, Tyndall, Spencer, Lubbock – to write for his new popular library, the 'International Scientific Series.' Darwin insisted that Youmans's plans be canvassed at a fringe meeting of the British Association at Edinburgh in August. He was 'all curiosity' about the progress of science in the States, where he was sending George and Frank on holiday this summer. Youmans told him about lecturing on the descent of man to a 'clerical club' in Brooklyn. The topic seemed less surprising than the audience. 'What!' Darwin burst out. 'Clergy-men of different denominations all together? How they would fight if you should get them together here!'[35]

At Downe another American cheered him. One of Gray's students, Chauncey Wright, a shy young philosopher ekeing out a living compiling the Nautical Almanack, sent a damning analysis of Mivart's *Genesis of Species*. It was due out in the *North American Review* and Darwin realized that it could prove useful to neutralize his keenest critic at home. He was a dab hand at pulling in support from abroad. He asked Wallace, 'an incomparably better critic than I am,' whether he should import the article, only to be told that it was heavy and obscure. He mooted the idea to Henrietta, who thought the piece merely 'interesting.'[36] He dithered.

Then Mivart's review of the *Descent of Man* arrived. It was a long, deadly dissection, laced with accusations of 'dogmatism,' question-begging, and spurious metaphysics. It was also anonymous, but Darwin knew the 'wonderfully clever' anatomist's hand behind it, scissoring him into shreds. Work on the new *Origin* made him 'sick of everything;' this left him in despair.

Here was the Catholic convert in the *Quarterly Review*, exposing 'the entire and naked truth as to the logical consequences of Darwin-ism.' Mivart roused the slumbering Tories against his former mentor. The *Descent of Man* was calculated to disturb time-honoured convic-tions held by 'the majority of cultivated minds.' It would unsettle 'our half-educated classes.' Morality was no 'development of brutal instincts;' if it were, who would know whether society 'is right or wrong,' or even 'why we should obey society at all.' People would do as they please, breaking laws and customs as they liked. No, man is a 'free moral agent,' created with a supernatural soul. He has 'a consciousness of an absolute and immutable [divine] rule *legitimately* claiming obedience.'[37]

Darwin saw himself an offender, a villain. 'I shall soon be viewed as the most despicable of men,' he burst out, 'the most arrogant, odious beast that ever lived.' Mivart's 'bigotry arrogance illiberality & many other nice qualities' made him furious, and the bile built inside, eating at his intestines. Wright's review of Mivart suddenly seemed perfect. It turned the tables, took natural selection as a model of good science and Mivart as a case of bad metaphysics. His inner driving force would take evolution nowhere.[38] With Wright's help, Darwin would see to it.

He dashed off a letter asking Wright for permission to reprint his article as a pamphlet. Then Emma took him away for a month to recuperate. He was in a mess, so 'giddy and bad' at Croydon Station that she could not leave him for a moment. They rested in the North Downs hamlet of Albury (where Malthus had once been curate), looking out on the sandy fern-covered hills and pine forests. It was a sunny August, with nothing to do but sit or stroll. But Charles's head remained 'rocky and wretched.' He read a little – Lubbock's latest work on insects, Thomson's snubbing of natural selection in his British Association address – but his mind kept drifting back to Mivart. Wright's permission came and Darwin wrote to Murray about running off 750 copies of the pamphlet. His damage-limitation exercise began. 'Some 200' would see every scientific journal and society supplied, together with 'clubs & . . . all private individuals' he could think of.[39] That would leave plenty for the public.

They returned for Henrietta's wedding on the 31st. The courtship had been a brief whirlwind. Her fiancé Richard Litchfield was a stout, shortsighted barrister who worked for the Ecclesiastical Commission, managing Church property, and in off hours he taught music, maths, and science at the Working Men's College in London. Singing was his passion, conducting his *forte*, and Henrietta had fallen for the artist in him, not to mention his 'sweet' smile and 'long thick brown beard.' The ceremony was simple and without festivity afterwards. Nor were friends or relations invited, for Charles had to be kept calm. However, on arriving with his old butler Parslow he found strangers in the pews. Parslow, ever protective, was thunderstruck; he thought that he knew 'every face' in the village. A handful of Litchfield's working men had discovered the time of the service, trained out from London, and walked four miles from Orpington Station to surprise him.

Henrietta, taking her trousseau to London, left her fox terrier Polly behind. From now on Polly would trot dutifully behind Charles.[40]

Murray posted copies of the pamphlet in September. *Darwinism*, it was called, a 'somewhat sensational title' that Wright thought would sell. The word had Darwin's blessing; it would set his seal of approval on a safe notion of science, above the metaphysics and religious mumbo-jumbo. Huxley received his copy in Scotland, where he was on holiday. He thought it would 'do good,' but by chance he had already done better, having just taken a few days off from golfing to castigate Mivart's *Genesis of Species* and *Quarterly* article in a review. Mivart, though not a 'bad fellow,' was 'poisoned with . . . accursed Popery and fear for his soul' and had sinned unpardonably by being 'insolent to Darwin.' Worse, his arguments were actually swaying people. Punishment was called for, Huxley snarled, and 'the devil has tempted me' to administer it.[41]

Darwin, disconsolate and sick, slaving away at the *Origin*, sprang to life when Huxley's news came. 'The pendulum is swinging against our side, but I feel positive it will soon swing the other way; & no mortal man will do half as much as you in giving it a start in the right direction.' Huxley's proofs arrived a week later, further fortifying him.

Huxley indulged in what he loved most, religious exegetics. He effectively side-stepped science and came crashing down on the Catholic Church – showing that Mivart's position was as pernicious theologically as it was disastrous scientifically. Mivart had suggested that evolution could be reconciled with the Catholic fathers – Augustine, Aquinas, and the last great scholastic, Suarez. Huxley denied it and upstaged him with pages of painstaking Latin exegesis, proving that his wayward pupil did not understand scholastic philosophy any more than Darwin's.

> If Suarez has rightly stated Catholic doctrine, then is evolution utter heresy. And such I believe it to be ... Indeed, one of its greatest merits in my eyes, is the fact that it occupies a position of complete and irreconcilable antagonism to that vigorous and consistent enemy of the highest intellectual, moral, and social life of mankind – the Catholic Church.

Huxley revelled in these military matters, pitting Church against Evolution, and the *Genesis* had simply offered another unbridled opportunity. Mivart, the lapsed protégé, was told that he could not be 'both a true son of the Church and a loyal soldier of Science.'[42] Face to face, the cut was unkinder; he was ordered to stop running with the hare and hunting with the hounds.

Huxley spoke *ex cathedra*, the way Owen used to. Such had the world changed. 'How you do smash Mivart's theology,' Darwin crowed, 'Nothing will vex him so much as this part of your review ... He may write his worst & he will never mortify me again.' To Hooker, laid low by his mother's health, the essay was a 'god-send,' and Huxley the 'defender of the faithful.' Surely though, he wrote his friend at Downe, you are 'not the happier' for Mivart's humiliation. 'I am not so good a Christian as you think me,' Darwin fired back, 'for I did enjoy my revenge.'[43]

He was not out of his misery. Science had gone by the board; the defence of natural selection was ignored. Huxley had simply chipped at the bedrock of Mivart's metaphysics, smiting Amalekites with his usual dexterity. Natural selection had to be shored up somehow, given the 'impression Mivart's book has made.' And the omens were worrying. Wright's pamphlets had not shifted – only fourteen had sold by the end of October.[44] The way ahead looked daunting.

1871–1882

39

Pause, Pause, Pause

HE STILL PACED the Sandwalk. A quarter-century had seen it worn smooth, his private turnpike beneath the full-grown trees – this thinking path leading his mind to untold destinations. In 1871, as the autumn days closed in and the beeches shed their leaves, he plodded on, reflecting and recuperating.

The year had aged him. Stooped and grisled, he felt older than sixty-two. The children were grown, leaving him and Emma alone with Bessy. William, a banking partner in Southampton, George reading for the bar, Frank studying medicine in London, Leo training for the Royal Engineers, Horace taking the Little Go at Cambridge, all destined for great things. If, that is, their health held, for they still came home often enough for nursing. Not Henrietta, though. Losing her to the solemn fop Richard Litchfield was 'awful and astonishing,' and life would never be the same. Only Emma was left to pamper Charles. 'Keep her as an example,' he advised his daughter, 'and then Litchfield will in future years worship and not only love you, as I worship our dear old mother.'[1]

His stomach had aged him most. Even now, each turn around the Sandwalk made his insides spin. Emma might distract him but she failed to stay his thoughts, and ruminating had led to retching as Mivart's challenge unfolded. He knew that he was vulnerable. Evolution had triumphed, but only time would tell about natural selection. And what about 'the citadel itself,' human mind and morality? In the *Descent of Man* he had stormed this last religious redoubt and explained the most sacred human traits. Yet the citadel had not fallen; man, guarded by Mivart, stood proud and impregnable. It was Darwin's crowning frustration. Would defeat be added to his notoriety for making men out of monkeys? Perhaps he should have kept his worst heresy to himself. Perhaps publishing the *Descent* had been a mistake.[2]

But the vicious secret was out and he had to stand by it. One lap to go. He strode back to his study to finish revising the *Origin*. In December, after months of fitful progress, he was finishing the herculean task. Over two thousand sentences had been added or rewritten, including a new chapter against Mivart. The word 'evolution' appeared for the first time. A helpful glossary was added. Most encouraging of all, Murray planned a new sales drive based on a popular half-price edition.[3] This would be Darwin's last chance to answer Mivart, and he knew it.

It was a virtuoso thrust. He slashed at the strongest thread running through Mivart's *Genesis of Species*, cutting the knot that the Argylls and Owens thought secure, and whose strength worried even Wallace. Were partially evolved structures – half a wing, an incipient eye – functional absurdities? Could the whole structures have appeared only in a single Creative leap? Darwin piled fact upon fact with effortless effrontery. He showed some organs switching function, obviating the problem: swim bladders becoming amphibian lungs, and breathing tubes extending into lacey insect wings. Mivart had missed the point: incipient lungs and eyes and wings need not have breathed or seen or flapped. As always Darwin paraded nature's oddities – whale baleen, the migrating eyes of flatfish, prehensile tails, and the pinching forceps on starfish – showing how each had gradually developed. He buried Mivart under a plethora of details, while hedging and wriggling himself, downgrading natural selection in some cases, backpedalling to admit 'spontaneous variations in the right direction' or a growth from increased use in others. What he could never admit was Mivart's emasculating inner force, or his monstrous jumps to ready-made wings and lungs.

The stakes were high, and Mivart was enlisting the same starfishes and whales to guard the sacred citadel: the 'intellectual powers' and moral disposition of man. Darwin's sword was also aimed at his opponent's metaphysical heart. A million odd facts were showered not simply to vindicate natural selection, but to discredit Mivart's allegiance to theology. Mivart's benign relationship with his master had turned poisonously sour, with Darwin convinced that Catholic fanatacism was at root. Mivart never understood why: his 'natural laws' were divine edicts, as were Owen's, Argyll's, and Gray's – expressions of Will Power, guiding and directing. They kept a proper scientific order in the universe, pushing life forward on a co-ordinated wavefront. But for Darwin, Mivart's directed, guided jumps from one beautifully co-ordinated fish or frog to another were unnatural and intolerable: science was entering 'the realms of miracle.'[4]

The debate nudged Darwin further into once taboo areas. As he ploughed through the *Origin* proofs, he posted a ringing endorsement to a leading freethinker, himself safely distanced in the United States.

Francis Abbot was editor of *The Index*, weekly voice of the radical wing of the Free Religious Association, a ginger-group of disaffected Unitarians and philosophical unbelievers. They were on the look-out for contributors who would foster 'the spirit of reform' without 'deference to the authority of the Bible, the Church, or the Christ.' Charles Eliot Norton, who had lunched at Downe, was a founder of the Association, and Abbot had sent Darwin his manifesto *Truths for the Times* and asked for a paper. 'I do not feel that I have thought deeply enough [about religion] to justify any publicity,' came the lame reply. Yet Darwin did subscribe to *The Index*, pore over the issues, and approve of Abbot's tract. Brazenly, in fifty pungent propositions, it augured 'the extinction of faith in the Christian Confession' and the development of a humanistic 'Free Religion' in which 'lies the only hope of the spiritual perfection of the individual and the spiritual unity of the race.' These were evolutionary 'truths' and Darwin responded warmly, 'I admire them from my inmost heart, & I agree to almost every word.'

'Almost' was an insertion, an afterthought. Just as he had casually subscribed to the Thirty-nine Articles on graduating from Cambridge, so now, as he angrily penned his last words on evolution, he held by the fifty propositions of a post-Christian creed. Uncharacteristically, he allowed Abbot to print his endorsement in *The Index*. It appeared in the Christmas issue, an ocean away from English eyes. Nor did he let up in his support: a few years later, when *The Index* fell on hard times, Charles and William sent a generous gift by courtesy of William's bank, a token of deep sympathy 'in your noble & determined struggle' for free religion.[5]

Charles cheered another infidel supporter abroad, Ernst Haeckel, whose anti-clerical bombast had once unnerved him. That was long ago, and the situation had changed. Most of what Haeckel stood for had been presentably packaged in the *Descent of Man*. And Darwin was retiring slowly, handing on freedom's flame. 'I doubt whether my strength will last for much more serious work,' he confided to the zoologist. 'I shall continue to work as long as I can, but it does not much signify when I stop, as there are so many good men fully as capable, perhaps more capable than myself, of carrying on our work; and of these you rank as the first.'[6]

Darwin had reached an impasse. Religious controversy had deflated him and he hated it. Ten years and he was running out of answers, tired of repeating himself. After the last revisions to the *Origin*, what more was there to say? The world knew all that was worth knowing about his views. Speaking out further would incur yet more abuse and might injure Emma, who still differed grievously from him on religion. In future he would keep his counsel.

With the changes to the *Origin* in hand, Murray put his plan into practice. He reset in tiny type. This left the edition riddled with errors, but it did cut 142 pages, saving sixpence a copy on paper alone. He sold the plates to Appleton in New York for £50, and as a result projected a six shillings cover price, putting it within reach of working people.[7]

Controversy ended, natural selection defended, Darwin turned to unfinished business in January 1872. Nothing would deflect him. Mivart did try to prod him once more. Breezily 'wishing you very sincerely a happy new year,' he wanted a disclaimer of the 'fundamental intellectual errors' in the *Descent of Man*. Their letters were now fraught, the pleasantries more desperate than ever, laced with denials of ill intent yet exuding mistrust. Darwin had had enough. He cut him dead. Further communication would be futile; life was too short. They went their own ways. While Mivart worried over the highest member of creation, Darwin worked at the lowest, the worm. With 'the little strength left to me,' he was turning to uncontentious subjects.[8]

Correspondents obliged, and earthworm anecdotes began surfacing in his mountain of mail. Everyone answered his queries – not just colleagues on three continents, but Wedgwoods, Darwins, and even Frank's Welsh girlfriend Amy Ruck. Darwin had kept a soft spot for the recyclers of the soil since his first fishing days at The Mount and flirting days at Maer. Now he was stuffing an old folder with notes, the prelude to another book. Having started his geological career by speculating on continents, he would end it digging in the garden. The evolutionist was working his way down to worms.

Worm-like himself, he moved slowly; writing up took endless time. Even now there was an another unfinished book, hived off from the *Descent of Man*, and nine months delayed by the Mivart crisis. After a break, completing *The Expression of the Emotions in Man and Animals* would be his first priority. He spent five weeks in London, visiting Erasmus and arranging for the new *Origin of Species* to be reviewed favourably with Mivart's *Genesis*. Publication day was 19 February, and even though the torrent of revisions had pushed the cover price to 7s. 6d., sales still soared from 60 to 250 a month. He went back to the *Emotions* manuscript, knowing that he was reaching a wider audience.[9]

The book was the amputated head of the *Descent* that had assumed a life of its own. And just as well, for it would prove popular. Responses to his questionnaires asking how the races expressed joy and grief, pleasure and pain, had flooded in from missionaries, entrepreneurs, and government colonials. He collated his bundles on Bombay beards and gaucho gestures, Aboriginal habits and Sinhalese signs. Like a phrenologist of old, he showed evidence for human descent on the face of everyday life. And like the Plinian phrenologists in particular, forty-five years before at Edinburgh, he made Sir Charles Bell's pious *Anatomy and Physiology of Expression* his prime target. Man's facial muscles had not been divinely created to express his exquisite feelings. They had evolved – look at nature, at monkey's faces, look at savages, idiots, and the insane to appreciate their social origins. Any sympathetic observer could see that man and animals shared not only feelings, but the means of expressing them.

Long ago Jenny Orang had shown her human side, behaving 'precisely like a naughty child.' His studies on the terror, rage, and noiseless laugh of chimps led to a fatherly fascination with his own infants. He had peered over numerous cots noting every squint and squall, as a succession of smiling, scowling, down-turned mouths witnessed their own ape ancestry. Latterly, he used the latest technology to capture these images. Hundreds of photographs had poured in to Down House, of actors cringing and babies wingeing and 'dreadful . . . imbeciles' in a Yorkshire asylum, their 'degraded' features evoking an ape-like primevalism.[10]

The manuscript swelled with the evidence. And as he cursed his convoluted prose, cancelled and recast his paragraphs, he also wrote helplessly of himself. He remembered his feeling of horror when a child had been 'exposed to . . . instant and crushing danger;' his 'frantic grief' and 'despair' following a family death; and his subsequent tearful thought that 'long-past happy days' will 'never return.' Englishmen, he owned, 'rarely cry, except under pressure of the acutest grief.' Yet he had known this feeling, watched himself weep, and had learned to read strangers' faces.

> An old lady with a comfortable but absorbed expression sat nearby opposite me in a railway carriage. Whilst I was looking at her, I saw that her *depressores anguli oris* [muscles at the corners of the mouth] became very slightly, yet decidedly,

contracted; but as her countenance remained as placid as ever, I reflected how meaningless was this contraction, and how easily one might be deceived. The thought had hardly occurred to me when I saw that her eyes suddenly became suffused with tears almost to overflowing, and her whole countenance fell. There could now be no doubt that some painful recollection, perhaps that of a long-lost child, was passing through her mind.[11]

No detached observer, Darwin. He perceived with pathos, and the thought of his own long-lost child still moved him to tears. In death as in life, Annie opened his heart.

All spring he wrestled with the book, braced by the news of his election to national academies in the Netherlands and Hungary. The proofs were no less a nightmare, and farmed out to Leo and Henrietta, with instructions to make cosmetic changes. As usual this proved impossible. His intractable style called for major surgery. He groaned at the humiliation and delay, 'sick of the subject, and myself, and the world.' The *Expression* had seven heliotype plates, making it one of the first books with photographs. But the production problems were horrendous – and the cost. At £75 per 1000 sets, and with a print run of 7000 copies, the plates would poke 'a terrible hole in the profits,' Murray warned.[12] Worrying, that was all he was good for. It clouded his week's holiday in August at Leith Hill with sister Caroline and Emma's brother Jos, but at least he finished the proofs there.

Back home a letter from Wallace awaited; it emphasized the gulf that had grown up between the joint inventors of natural selection. Wallace had moved twenty miles east of London, using his surveying skills to help build a new family house. Still surviving on royalties and reviews, he had failed to gain full-time work as a museum director, even with Darwin's backing. Their differences over spiritual forces and sexual selection had become irreconcilable. Each was dogged, but Wallace remained an enthusiast, irrepressible, always lapping up the latest.

And the latest was H. Charlton Bastian's *The Beginnings of Life*. The Victorians liked their shocking science in two laboured volumes, and the professor of pathology at University College provided it. Germs and their origin was the unlikely subject. These must have first appeared in a chemical soup on the archaic earth, starting evolution off, and Bastian proved that the process continues today. (He was one of eighty-year-old Robert Grant's students, and there was no stopping them, still marching defiantly along their own evolutionary path.) 'Nothing more important has appeared since your "Origin",' Wallace announced, hoping to spark Darwin's interest, and he declared himself a 'thorough convert.'

Not Darwin. Spontaneous generation, he admitted tactfully, would be 'a discovery of transcendent importance' if it really were proved. Huxley was less polite, scoffing at Bastian's alchemical brew of boiled phosphates and escaping bugs: 'Transubstantiation will be nothing to this if it turns out to be true.' Once, on the earth, yes, in primeval soups, but not today. Too many facts told against Bastian. And Darwin had spent too many decades examining minutiae to be taken in. Anyway he was swearing off controversial science, preferring to sit instead with his sun-dews. He had waited twenty years to tease these insect-eaters properly and was in no mood to be diverted. 'I have taken up old botanical work,' he informed Wallace in a peremptory PS, 'and have given up all theories.'[13]

By the end of September he was nearing collapse again. He never felt comfortable except at work or in bed, and sleep was not restoring him. Emma blamed it on the 'fatiguing and unwholesome' microscope and called George, Frank, and Horace to the rescue. She sent the boys scouting for lodgings, hoping that she could get him away from his wretched work. Horace located a house on Sevenoaks Common, only a few miles away, and between them they managed to pry Charles out of the study. He had to admit that three weeks away worked wonders. A spell like this every couple of months would keep him sane, slow his slide into oblivion. He was no longer sick, only 'growing old and weak,' and dreading the day when his intellectual powers began to fail.[14]

Friends awaited his convenience. Kovalevsky, translating the *Expression* into Russian, delayed a trip to Downe while Darwin recuperated. Even Hooker was put off, though he had his own preoccupations as Director of Kew Gardens.

For over a year Hooker had been 'in the most detestable position that a scientific man, or an officer, or a gentleman can be with my Lord and Master.' His Lord and Master was the Commissioner of Works in Gladstone's government, Acton Smee Ayrton, an acid-tongued, thick-skinned, heavy-handed cost-cutter. He was a no-nonsense populist, known for his 'reckless toughness,' elected on a platform of keeping down the proliferating 'architects, sculptors, and gardeners,' and intent on pruning Kew. The gardens were publicly funded, and Hooker believed that Ayrton's secret aim was to close down Britain's premier plant collection – built by the Hookers with sweat and tears over thirty years – discard the scientific research, ignore the imperial need, and turn it into a cheap public park.

Hooker had appealed to the Prime Minister and denounced Ayrton to the First Lord of the Treasury, to no avail. So the X Club swung into action, determined to raise Kew's political profile. A petition was drawn up, signed by Darwin and other scientific sympathizers, and handed to Gladstone. Lubbock raised the matter in the Commons. However, among the papers tabled in Parliament was an official report on Kew that Hooker himself had never seen. The author's name gave the game away, Richard Owen – it had been drawn up at Ayrton's request by the X's *bête noire*. The old autocrat, loathing Hooker and his henchmen, was angling to bring the plant collections under his own control at the British Museum. Darwin seethed, 'I used to be ashamed of hating him so much, but now I will carefully cherish my hatred & contempt to the last day of my life.'[15]

Ultimately Hooker's post was secured, although in October he still squirmed under Ayrton's heel as he sent Darwin sun-dews and Venus's fly-traps for experiment. He was deflated enough, but he then suffered a blow which poisoned any desire to fight on. His aged and bedridden mother died, leaving him 'a man of 55,' feeling 'as if *orphaned*.' At Sevenoaks Darwin was touched by the news and tried to empathize. Unable to recall his emotions at his own mother's death, he thought on other losses: 'with the exception of ones wife, it is the greatest that a man can suffer; – though God knows the loss of a child is bitter enough & overwhelming.' Between them, Hooker and Darwin had watched five young ones die. They had shared their deepest feelings for years and would do so more and more. Age was no barrier to their intimacy. As Darwin weakened he needed Hooker's strong 'affections' to keep him going, to breathe life into his work.[16]

In November Darwin put his insect-eaters through their paces, looking for nervous and digestive similarities between plants and animals. What strange chemistry made the sticky tentacles of the sun-dew contract and hold their prey? He dabbed on all manner of household substances: milk, urine, saliva, alcohol, even strong tea. And what could the tentacles digest? He served them roast beef, vegetables, hard-boiled egg – there was nothing an old dyspeptic on odd diets would not try. Amazingly, the plants flourished. They took their food like animals, secreting similar digestive juices, itself 'a new and wonderful fact.' So he poisoned them. Strychnine, quinine, and nicotine were all more or less fatal, but morphine had little effect and cobra's venom acted as a stimulant. Proof, he laughed at last, that the sun-dew was not a 'disguised animal' with a nervous system.

Even so, it was extraordinarily sensitive, more than 'the most delicate part of the human body.' He marvelled that 'so inconceivably minute a quantity as the one-twenty-millionth of a grain of phosphate of ammonia' made a tentacle bend through 180 degrees.[17]

Fly-traps, bladderworts, and butterworts were similarly wined, dined, and poisoned. They arrived from around the world to be held on remand in the garden hot-house. They presented a rogues' gallery in their pots, displaying every devious means of gluing, trapping, and drowning their prey. Darwin's torture and trickery was fitting for them. As the experiments proceeded he began writing *Insectivorous Plants*. Inevitably, the strain proved too much. The news that the *Expression of the Emotions* had sold over 5000 copies – tickling a shocked, blushing, eyebrow-raising Victorian generation – failed to spur him on. (Even the *Athenaeum*, giving a deep swallow, thought the notion of 'forcing Expression into the service of the Evolution Theory . . . a brilliant one, worthy of the acumen and ingenuity of its author.') He was exhausted and more than ever a 'confirmed invalid.' Decamping to Eras's for a week before Christmas did nothing for him. He sat engulfed in fog, downhearted, drawing up his will. One sixth of his estate for each of the boys, Ras suggested; one sixth between the girls – that would be 'as much as is good for them.'[18]

Seeing Huxley in town did not help. The old bulldog was himself feeling mangy, crushed by overwork and in the throes of moving the family to a new house. Incessant dyspeptic nausea signalled that he was juggling too many jobs – Secretary of the Royal Society, lecturer in biology at the new Normal School in South Kensington, Hooker's second in the Ayrton affair – while countering criticism for opposing the medical education of women. The doctors warned him that 'all sorts of wonderful things will happen if I do not take some more efficient rest,' he told Haeckel's student Anton Dohrn, himself in a more congenial climate on the Mediterranean. On top of it, Huxley had just been elected Lord Rector of Aberdeen University (after Darwin declined), but when the two met no toasts were raised. Huxley was struggling to survive on 'strictly ascetic principles,' drinking water only. Not that he was in a mood to celebrate anyway, with a neighbour taking out a lawsuit over his damp basement, threatening to ruin him with legal costs.[19]

Charles had his own troubles. George and Horace were ill and home for nursing. To spare his own health Charles stopped writing on insect-eaters and began a more leisurely update of his old monograph on climbing plants. The family seemed cursed, blighted by biology. Only when Galton sent his latest deliverance on 'hereditary improvement' did Charles perk up. Society, cousin Galton proposed, should breed out feebleness in body and mind by creating 'a sentiment of caste among those who are naturally gifted.' Register their families, have their children intermarry, and offer them incentives to reproduce – the genetic drain would be plugged and the nation's stock must improve. Charles wondered about the practicality of creating such racial supermen. Only the odd child in each 'large superior family' would be the breeders' pick, like the choicest pigeon – William alone of the Darwins enjoyed good health. These would naturally refuse to be listed and 'stick to their own families,' scotching the whole enterprise. The alternative, compulsory registration, gave Charles the political jitters. It was an illiberal 'utopian' nostrum, even if the 'sole feasible' one for 'improving the human race.' Better simply to publicize 'the all-important principle of inheritance' and let people pursue the 'grand' objective for themselves.

Galton's scheme came too late for the Darwins. What they needed was short-term relief. By March 1873 Charles was unwell again. He would 'much rather stay at home, but knows his place and submits,' Emma bustled, dragging him to a West End town house for a break. The city held no terrors, provided that he was cosseted and secure. The Litchfields and the Hensleigh Wedgwoods were safe company, always solicitous of his health. Now reports of Huxley's deterioration were rife. The court action was breaking him in every way. The X men's YVs suggested taking up a collection, and Emma floated the idea to Charles. He primed the pump with £300 of his thousand-guinea royalties for the *Expression of the Emotions*. He called on the Xs – Hooker, Tyndall, Spencer, and Spottiswoode – who passed the hat, and an attractive stove-pipe it turned out. Over £2000 was raised from eighteen colleagues. Darwin put the money directly into Huxley's account through Lubbock's bank. It was to enable 'an honoured and much loved brother' to take a 'complete rest,' he informed Huxley on 23 April. 'We are convinced that we act for the public interest.'[20]

Fate mocked the fraternity, bereaving them the very next day. Lyell's wife succumbed to typhoid fever. She was twelve years younger than her husband, who at seventy-five had not expected to survive her. Erasmus broke the news to Emma, leaving her to tell Charles gently. Hooker increased his anguish by tenderly describing 'that most lovable face shrouded in flowers in the coffin – looking so calm and beautiful.' Darwin could picture her perfectly, a model of patience, listening to the men talk geology over thirty years before. His feelings welled up, but words failed him. He drafted and redrafted a condolence, settling at last to assure his old friend that 'you are now suffering . . . the greatest calamity, which a man can endure in the world. God grant that you may have strength to bear your misery.'[21]

At the end of May, Fanny's and Hensleigh's daughter Effie married her persistent suitor Thomas ('Theta') Farrer at Little Portland Street Unitarian Chapel in London, where the Lyells had attended. He was twenty years her senior, a powerful Secretary to the Board of Trade, and a botanical barrister, one of Charles's informants and a contributor to the Huxley fund. The couple settled at Abinger Hall, not far from the Wedgwoods of Leith Hill, offering the Darwins yet another convenient retreat.

In June Charles resumed work on his sun-dews, not without distraction. Huxley brought his entire brood to Downe in advance of his expenses-paid holiday. Emma served the 'public interest' and took the seven children to give his wife a break. No sooner had Huxley left with Hooker for the Continent than the young ones were poking into every greenhouse, investigating every experiment.

It was like summers in the fifties, children clambering everywhere. Old toys came out, old games were played, and Emma basked in memories. The Huxley children joined in greater festivities on Sunday 6 July, when Down House played host to Litchfield's singing class from the Working Men's College. It was a 'brilliant day with the roses full out, hay in the fields,' and Charles and Emma in rare form. Some seventy came, many young labourers walking from Orpington station, others arriving with Henrietta and her husband in horse-drawn carts. All were received in the drawing-room and directed out to the new verandah – Charles's pride and joy – and the garden. 'There were long tables . . . for tea and strawberries, singing under the lime trees, dancing on the lawn, and games in the field.' Everyone joined in, heartened by their host's 'cordiality and warmth.'[22]

The Huxleys were dutifully indulged, with Mr Darwin rumpling curly heads at breakfast and bidding them to 'take large mouthfuls.' Then out to the Sandwalk, where they played at 'Red Indians . . . armed with javelins of hazel from the gardener's store of bavins behind the pigeon-house.' Just before lunch Mr Darwin would join them, his 'blue eyes beaming' as he took his turns with Polly trotting at his heels. Tea-time might find the Huxleys 'roasting potatoes in the embers of a real gipsy fire' when the same tall figure would return, clad in a wide black cloak and soft felt hat, always with a 'cheery word.' Evenings were serene. Portly Parslow, 'white-haired and apple-faced,' saw to the children's needs, while Mr and Mrs Darwin played their ritual backgammon matches beside a bright lamp in the parlour.[23]

Down House was heaven, but the parish was purgatory. A staunch new vicar had taken charge in November 1871, the Revd George Sketchley Ffinden. He was a reforming High Churchman, not an emollient type like Brodie Innes. He believed in architectural improvements, liturgical finesse, and the renewal of priestly authority. His theology made the parish his command, rather as the *Beagle* had been FitzRoy's; and it had set him at odds with the Darwins even before they met. In truth, they belonged to different worlds. Ffinden had been ordained in 1861 by Bishop Wilberforce and served as domestic chaplain to Lord Carington. He ran with top Tories and ecclesiastical toffs, and was tapping them to pay for a new vicarage and church restorations.[24]

Downe's great families went along with Ffinden as far as possible. The Darwins had given the church £50 the previous year and donated £35 towards the vicarage. In the winter Charles took time off to advise on Ffinden's purchase of a meadow from Emma's sister Elizabeth, now living in Trowmer Lodge. But the vicar was manoeuvring. First his restoration plans upset the vestry, and Brodie Innes – the hapless patron – had to ask Darwin why. Then Ffinden usurped control of the village school. For years it had been run for the parish poor by an informal committee consisting of Darwin, Lubbock, and the incumbent. Even after the Education Act of 1870, which brought in rates support and government inspectors, the committee maintained much of its independence. It still insisted on a 'conscience clause,' which protected the children from Anglican indoctrination. Ffinden ended that. He was now chairman and treasurer of the committee and had designs on the curriculum. In future Downe's eighty urchins would have lessons on the Thirty-nine Articles from the vicar.

Ffinden was acting within his rights but he trod on too many toes, and Anglican indoctrination really was the last straw. Darwin dropped off the school committee and slashed his annual donation to the church. Except for the Friendly Society, his parish responsibilities were winding up, like his public controversies, and he was 'half killing' himself instead with *Insectivorous Plants*.[25]

On 5 August the Darwins drove to Abinger to join the newly-wed Farrers for a few days. This itself was a milestone, the first time in twenty-five years that Charles had been anyone's house guest outside the immediate family. The last thing they expected was a morgue, or

Effie's and Theta's grisly greeting. Two weeks before, it transpired, the servants had been called to an accident. They found the leader of the Lords, Earl Granville, distraught, doubled over a dead body, slumped on the ground. His riding companion had been bragging about his horsemanship when his mount stumbled, hurling him over its head. The corpse was laid out in the drawing-room, where they now sat. It was Samuel Wilberforce. Here the bishop had remained, flat on the floor, vested in his robes of office, his Garter ribbon, and a cross of roses in place of his jewelled crucifix. For two days he lay in state, while an inquest was held and dignitaries paid their respects. Gladstone knelt beside his friend's cold smiling face, sobbing audibly. Then as village church bells tolled, the bishop was borne away.

Wilberforce had always thought Darwin a 'capital fellow,' whatever his dismay at evolution, and there was no satisfaction in such an end. Huxley of course cried crocodile tears and wise-cracked to Tyndall, 'For once, reality and his brain came into contact and the result was fatal.'[26] But others knew more of equestrian accidents. Charles recalled his own fall in '69, when Tommy rolled over him. He and Emma expressed dismay at the bishop's fate, and left for ten days with William in Southampton.

At home Hooker dropped in, burbling about Huxley's recuperation and expecting to be cross-examined on Darwin's latest hobby-horse, the waxy 'bloom' on certain plant leaves. Darwin was sure that this protected them from burning when watered in direct sunlight and wanted the authority of Kew's Director – and now President of the Royal Society – on his side. They hammered at the subject too hard, for it left Darwin prostrate. He agonized in bed with a 'severe shock continually passing through my brain,' his memory gone, unable to recall anything Hooker had said. Nothing like it had ever happened and Emma feared an epileptic fit. They called Huxley's doctor, Andrew Clark, who put him on an 'abominable diet' and pronounced that 'the brain was affected only secondarily.' By mid-September Charles was back at his insect-eaters. 'Thank God,' he sighed to Hooker; 'I would far sooner die than lose my mind.'[27]

His mind was indeed still nimble and working overtime. Between trips to the greenhouse he wrote to *Nature* about barnacles, posted £75 to help found Anton Dohrn's marine biological station at Naples, and acknowledged countless gifts. Karl Marx sent the new edition of *Das Kapital*, inscribed from a 'sincere admirer.' It was a 'great work,' Darwin realized, as he cut open the first few dozen pages. But the German language befuddled him and the tenor of the book seemed 'so different' from his own. He wished that he was 'more worthy to receive it, by understanding more of the deep & important subject of political economy,' he wrote to Marx darkly. But no doubt their respective efforts towards 'the extension of knowledge' would 'in the long run . . . add to the happiness of mankind.'[28]

Haeckel's *History of Creation* was different. Charles had ploughed through rather more of it in the German and praised the new edition fulsomely, knowing it would 'do a wonderful amount of good in spreading the doctrine of Evolution.' But then 'young and rising naturalists,' the ones appealed to in the *Origin*, needed every encouragement.

And Darwin was adept at giving it, experienced at pushing and prodding his own sons. Even now Frank's medical studies were flagging. He had been living with Uncle Ras, whose dilettante culture was contagious (not that Charles had set a better example in medicine). They agreed that Frank should finish his thesis on animal tissues and then assist at Downe with botanical ones. The old first-floor nursery was duly fitted out as a lab in anticipation.[29]

George was also floundering. Tense, his stomach in knots, he had spent the best part of two years travelling to spas, scuppering his legal career. Back in Cambridge at the begining of October, he was desperate to make his mark and began writing topical essays. One had appeared in the *Contemporary Review*, backing Galton's eugenic proposals for a family register, and advocating legal changes that would permit divorce on the grounds of insanity, criminality, or vice – all hereditary defects. His father applauded it, but George's latest offering was another matter.

It pooh-poohed prayer, divine morals, and 'future rewards & punishments,' all issues his father had carefully skirted in public. The problem was strategy.

> I w^d. urge you not to publish it for some months, *at the soonest*, & then consider whether you think it new & important enough to counterbalance the evils; remembering the cart-loads which have been published on the subject. – The evils on giving pain to others, & injuring your own power & usefulness.

Hadn't Voltaire found that 'direct attacks on Christianity . . . produce little permanent effects,' that 'good seems only to follow from slow & silent side attacks'? Or take Lyell: he had 'shaken the faith in the Deluge &c far more efficiently by never having said a word against the Bible.' Even John Stuart Mill, England's greatest philosophical unbeliever, had seen his writings become 'text-books at Oxford' by keeping his 'religious criticisms' quiet. The author of the *Origin of Species* had been circumspect too.

> It is an old doctrine of mine that it is of foremost importance for a young author to publish (if with his name) only what is very good & new; so that the public may have faith in him, & read what he writes . . . I have marked one or two passages in which you give your own conviction: remember that an enemy might ask who is this man, & what is his age & what have been his special studies, that he sh^d. give to the world his opinions on the deepest subjects? This sneer might easily be avoided . . . but my advice is to pause, pause, pause.

Charles, with one eye on the 'enemy,' had delayed for decades. Nor should George act impulsively, go public with damaging views that might reflect ill on the family. 'I wish that you were tied to some study on which you could not hope to publish anything for some years.'[30]

The 'moral problem' of speaking out on religion was 'frightfully difficult,' and Darwin had 'never been able to make up my mind' about it. Although he had used theological language freely in the *Origin* and discussed the evolution of religion in the *Descent of Man*, he only mooted his personal beliefs with the utmost discretion. Even now the most he would say, to a student admirer in Holland, was that the question of God's existence is 'beyond the scope of man's intellect.'[31]

Many of his admirers had come to the same conclusion. This November he received a whirlwind visit from the corpulent cosmic theist John Fiske, the genial Harvard philosopher-turned-popularizer, touring Europe to glimpse his heroes. Fiske, having rebelled against the New England Congregationalism of his youth and finished his *Outlines of Cosmic Philosophy*, was kneeling at Spencer's shrine to the Unknowable and Unthinkable. He ingratiated himself with the X set through his infectious humour, keeping even Tyndall in stitches. 'There is nothing so pleasant as *seeing* these men, after one has known them in a shadowy way so long,' Fiske wrote home. 'Reading their books doesn't give you the flesh-and-blood idea of them.'

And flesh and blood was what the earthy New Englander was after. He had been warned about Huxley by an expatriate cockney in New York. 'What, that 'orrid hold hinfidel 'Uxley?' Fiske related to roars of laughter, trying to bend his tongue around the London accent. 'Why, we don't think *hanythink* of 'im in Hingland! We think 'e's 'orrid!' While the big and little 'Uxleys were used to hearing of the headman as a 'cannibal,' Fiske was happy to report the ogre among the most 'charming and lovely' of men and as 'tender as a woman.'

> I am quite wild over Huxley. He is as handsome as an Apollo
> . . . I never saw such magnificent eyes in my life. His eyes are
> black, and his face expresses an eager burning intensity . . .
> He seems earnest, – immensely earnest, – and thoroughly frank
> and cordial and modest. And, by Jove, what a pleasure it is
> to meet such a clean-cut mind! It is like Saladin's sword which
> cut through the cushion.

The pilgrimage to Downe was his highlight. The ebullient Fiske reported that

> old Darwin is the dearest, sweetest, loveliest old grandpa
> that ever was. And on the whole he impresses me with his
> strength more than any man I have seen yet. There is a
> charming kind of quiet strength about him and about
> everything he does. He isn't burning and eager like Huxley.
> He has a mild blue eye, and is the gentlest of gentle old
> fellows.

Fiske pictured him in the Galilean mould, his 'long white hair and enormous white beard' making him 'very picturesque.' Overriding everything was the 'guileless simplicity' of this savant shut away from society. 'I am afraid I shall never see him again, for his health is very bad . . . Of all my days in England I prize today the most.'[32] However Darwin and Emma took this whirlwind sweeping through Downe – it must have nonplussed Emma and knocked up Charles – jovial John Fiske, a Spencerian so typical of America's Gilded Age, certainly went away happy.

Darwin recovered to tackle a new edition of the stolid *Descent of Man*. With two or three books on the boil, he hated another interruption, and without help he saw the changes taking him for ever. He thought of Wallace, struggling as a self-financed writer and in need of work.

Darwin approached him rather sheepishly in November, hating to see colleagues turn ignominiously into hired hands (although familiar with buying dissectors and draughtsmen since his London days). Seven shillings an hour, Wallace quoted; he had helped Lyell edit his

Principles for five, but that was low pay for 'the class of work.' A good deal of revision might be needed and Darwin's abominable handwriting doubled the labour involved. He would keep a record of the hours put in and not even 'think of offering criticisms' of substance. Labour was money for the socialist, and he hired it out in any good cause. You 'have perhaps seen that I am dipping into politics'? he asked Darwin. In fact he was submerged in it, arguing in the *Daily News* that the country's coal reserves should be made a national trust, or the mines be taken out of private hands altogether.

Emma put a stop to Charles's deal. She had him give George the job; he lacked nothing but literary direction and would do it free. Charles agreed – never mind that the subject was technical and outside his scope. An even more sheepish Darwin told Wallace that if 'my son could not do the work, I will write again and *gratefully* accept your proposal.' But meanwhile 'I hope to Heaven that politics will not replace natural science.'[33]

Not that the Darwins could keep out of parish politics themselves. While Charles rose in the middle of the night to watch his twitching Indian telegraph plant – 'it was dead asleep, all but its little ears, which were having most lively games' – Emma lay awake planning a winter reading room for local labourers. Previous ones had proved a great success. They were a model of quiet parish paternalism, the sort practised in a thousand sleepy hamlets. 'Respectable newspapers & a few books were provided & a respectable householder was there every evening to maintain decorum.' The men subscribed a penny a week and came to smoke and play games, 'without the necessity of resorting to the public house.' The schoolroom had been an ideal venue and Lubbock was prepared to loan it again. Emma hoped the vicar would join them in petitioning the school committee.[34]

Ffinden had tolerated the reading room for two winters, but no longer. 'Coffee drinking, bagatelle & other games' had been allowed, and 'the effects of tobacco smoke & spitting' were evident when the children returned in the morning. This was a 'perversion of the building' and he opposed it. Not to be outdone by an unfeeling Tory, Emma had Charles contact the education inspectorate in London. He received a favourable reply, with the proviso that the room be tidied before the next day. The Darwins and the Lubbocks – Elizabeth Wedgwood too – laid this before the committee, offering to pay for any repairs.

The confrontation came just before Christmas. Emma drafted a final plea to the committee, which Charles signed. It was essential, they believed, 'to afford every possible opportunity to the working class for self-improvement & amusement.' Indeed, 'the working men of this country have so few amusements, beyond the brutish one of drinking, that even if the Reading Room be looked at merely as a place of amusement, it is *desireable* [sic] to grant them' the facility. The committee ruled in Emma's favour, as Ffinden was obliged to report in the curtest of notes. He was furious that Darwin had contacted the education department behind his back. 'As I am the only recognized correspondent of the School according to rule 15. Code 1871, I deem such a proceeding quite out of order, especially as I myself had undertaken to communicate with the Office.'[35]

Pulling rank came easily for a gentleman of Darwin's position. And it was a trifle after petitioning the Prime Minister in the Ayrton affair. Still, the parish was a fragile political world and damage had been done. If the clergy and great folks did not stand shoulder to shoulder, how would the rural order hold? Given the kerfuffle, it was as well that moving plants still mesmerized him, diverting his mind from Ffinden's pettiness.

40

A Wretched Bigot

Feeling 'OLD & HELPLESS,' Charles trained to London with Emma on 10 January 1874 to consult Dr Andrew Clark. He toured the publishers, talking to Murray about the *Descent of Man* and Smith Elder about a new edition of *Coral Reefs*, wearing himself out. The afternoons with Erasmus should have offered a respite. But no, Ras too had become fascinated by séances.

London's polite parlours had reverberated to rapping spirits for ten years or more. Noble ladies hosted the 'manifestations' and the cream of society came, keen for the latest *divertissement*. True to form, Huxley had stonewalled a high-level inquiry into the possibility of spirit-produced phenomena. But Wallace still saw nature manifest a progressive spirit, and William Crookes, a prominent chemist (who discovered the element thallium), had conducted experimental séances to prove the power of 'psychic force.' Francis Galton attended one and the goings-on 'confounded him.' No 'vulgar legerdemain,' he told Charles, something queer was happening.[1]

Darwin could dismiss Wallace's low-brow credulity with a twist of the wrist, but not Galton. And now his own brother was about to be swayed by the spirits and duped in front of friends. They all gathered around Eras's dining table one afternoon: Galton and the Litchfields, Hensleigh and Fanny Wedgwood with their eldest daughter Snow, George Lewes and Marian Evans (George Eliot) – Snow's literary mentors – Charles and Emma, who had been eager to meet the author of *Middlemarch*, and son George, who had hired the medium, Charles Williams. One more held hands in the chain, Huxley, 'incognito, so far as the medium was concerned,' at Darwin's urgent request. George and Hensleigh sat on either side of Williams, securing his hands and feet. The curtains were drawn and doors shut. Everyone sat silently in the dark – except Lewes who cracked jokes – waiting for the spirits to move.

With two dozen eyes and ears straining, the room grew stuffy. Charles found it 'so hot and tiring' that he broke the spell, made his excuses, and dragged himself upstairs to lie down. The show began without him. It 'took away all their breaths' – a bell ringing, a candlestick jumping, the sound of wind rushing, sparks flashing, and then the table moving. When he returned he heard that it had risen above everyone's heads, with the chairs ending up on top, as he could see. Understanding how Williams performed these 'astounding miracles, or jugglery,' was beyond him. Galton called it a 'good séance' but Charles had no sympathy. 'The Lord have mercy on us all, if we have to believe in such rubbish,' he moaned to Hooker from the safety of Downe.[2]

While Erasmus dabbled in 'spirit photographs,' Huxley rushed to prop up Darwin's wobbling faith. He joined George in arranging another séance with Williams. They sat beside him and detected subtle movements, proving that he was nothing but 'a cheat,' much to Darwin's relief. He had already told Emma that the events at Ras's were 'all imposture.' It would take 'an enormous weight of evidence' to convince him otherwise. Emma detected the creak of a closing mind. Neutral herself about a psychic explanation, she told Snow that 'he *won't* believe it, he dislikes the thought of it so very much.' A disillusioned Snow recalled that Uncle Charles 'used to look upon it as a great weakness if one allowed wish to influence belief.' 'Yes,' Emma nodded, 'but he does not act up to his principles.' 'Well,' Snow retorted, 'that seems to me what one means by bigotry.' 'Oh, yes,' Emma smiled; 'he is a regular bigot.'[3]

The winter wore on with little to show for it. Darwin did talk Lubbock into selling him the Sandwalk, rented all these years, but Lubbock charged top price and chilled their friendship. Otherwise Darwin trudged about a humdrum existence, moving between plant experiments and book revisions. Henrietta helped with *Coral Reefs*, but the later chapters had to be substantially rewritten. He seemed to be getting nowhere in his race against time. The botany books were languishing and so was he. Dr Clark's regime could not be kept up. The diet proved impossible and his 'strychnine' preparation 'did me harm.' Little wonder that it had killed his sun-dews.[4]

The *Descent* was being doctored too, not as extensively as the *Origin of Species* but with equal pains. While George pieced together the manuscript and made a new index, Charles scribbled scores of insertions – suicide among savages, courtship among butterflies, and the effects of castration on sheep. Anecdotes from correspondents vied for place with snippets from magazines, and his hoarded references tricked out the already copious notes. Sexual selection remained powerful but natural selection was somewhat curbed. 'With highly civilised nations continued progress depends in a subordinate degree on natural selection,' he jotted optimistically; 'for such nations do not supplant and exterminate one another as do savage tribes.' Yet the winnowing still went on, less violently perhaps but no less effectively. Galton's work on mental inheritance had convinced him. 'The more intelligent members within the same community will succeed better in the long run than the inferior, and leave a more numerous progeny, and this is a form of natural selection.' Progress now depended on 'a good education during youth whilst the brain is impressible' combined with 'a high standard of excellence, inculcated by the ablest and best men.'[5]

His own brain was good for settling old scores. 'What a demon on earth Owen is. I do hate him,' Darwin ranted to Hooker after hearing of the latest shenanigans. A conspiracy to oust the superannuated Darwinian President of the Linnean Society, the botanist George Bentham, was supposedly masterminded by the botany keeper at the British Museum, spurred on by Owen. Since Bentham had Hooker's backing, it looked like spite for Owen's failure to control the Kew collections. The old wounds, left festering after Huxley's slashes, had not healed in a decade. Tyndall did once try to mediate, only to be pulled up short by Owen, who demanded that the 'base and mischievous' Huxley first retract his charge of perjury.

Given this new duplicity Darwin was not above aggravating the sore. He resurrected the ape-brain debate for one final reslaying of the slain. An update in the *Descent*'s final edition would enshrine Owen's defeat and put paid to recent critics. Huxley obliged on spec with a stringent reassertion of his old views. It 'pounds the enemy into a jelly,' he strutted, although 'none but anatomists' would know it.[6]

Darwin dropped the *Descent* manuscript off in April. Fired by the success of the cheap *Origin*, Murray planned a half-price edition, at twelve shillings. That was it; Charles had finally washed his hands of evolution – he could not even face the proofs, which went to George. No more books on the subject, he told Fox, now retired to the Isle of Wight. His remaining strength was to be devoted to the genteel savagery of his insectivorous plants.

He roped in all hands: Hooker and his assistant William Thistelton-Dyer at Kew; the physiologist John Burdon Sanderson at University College, who ran lab tests on their digestive juices; Asa Gray at the Harvard herbarium, still defending him against the theologians; even old John Price from Shrewsbury, who offered a rare bladderwort. Through the spring specimens arrived, cluttering up the greenhouses, to be fed scraps from the family's table. He never lost his knack of winkling out information. He only had to drop a note to *Nature* on greenfinches severing his primrose nectaries to receive a fresh crop of mail. [7] At least Frank was now helping, which made the load lighter.

The other sons were away, making successes of themselves. Horace had his degree and an engineering apprenticeship, and Leo had been posted to New Zealand with the Royal Engineers to observe the transit of Venus. Frank was the mainstay, and had settled in to Brodie Innes's old house in the village, preparing for his marriage to Amy Ruck. The wedding took place on 23 July just as another 'scientific son' was joining the family, like Lubbock long ago. This was George Romanes, one of Burdon Sanderson's students, who had been with Frank at Cambridge. Wealthy, twenty-six, and once destined for the Church, he had a penchant for marine invertebrates and an inquisitive mind – it was all agreeably familiar. [8]

George, still sickly, kept his nose in the proofs and carried out statistical analyses of first-cousin marriages. (He found them to be three times more frequent in 'our rank' than the lower.) He took up Galton's human-breeding scheme and had already published an article on 'beneficial restrictions to marriage.' Mivart read it with alarm. Having broken with Darwin, he saw George's essay as a perfect pretext to renew the attack on the *Descent of Man*. What better proof of Darwinian social tendencies, Mivart sniped anonymously in the July issue of the *Quarterly Review*, than George's proposals to loosen the bonds of marriage – widen the grounds of divorce – for the sake of better breeding? This was moral anarchy. Mivart had composed the piece in Dresden from hasty notes and misconstrued thoughts. George advocated divorce in cases of criminality or vice, but Mivart garbled this to accuse him unaccountably of standing for 'the most oppressive laws, and the encouragement of vice in order to check population.' Shades of national degeneracy, of revolutionary France and pagan Rome. Indeed, 'there is no hideous sexual criminality of Pagan days that might not be defended on the principles advocated by the school to which this writer belongs.'

'Vice,' 'sexual criminality,' 'oppressive laws,' this was slanderous. It slurred George's father, impugned the family's respectability, and cast the whole Darwinian 'school' into a moral cesspit. Charles was seething – even without knowing who wrote the piece. He told George to seek legal advice while he tackled the *Quarterly*'s publisher, John Murray. It would be a 'dreadful evil' if they 'came to a quarrel,' but either the *Quarterly* printed George's reply in the next number or he would take his business elsewhere.[9]

The affair overshadowed his August holiday at Southampton, even though William was a brick. Charles drafted a reply for George and tried to divert himself with the proofs of the Orangeman John Tyndall's address to the British Association, due in Belfast that month. It was to be an X Club jamboree, with Huxley, Hooker, Lubbock, and Tyndall – half the *Quarterly*'s damned 'school' – making speeches. Tyndall's clarion call only served to emphasize how much militancy was on the upsurge on every side: 'We claim,' he announced in his Irish brogue, 'and we shall wrest from theology the entire domain of cosmological theory,' which led to calls for his prosecution for blasphemy. Set against these evangelical demands by the new 'sect of the Darwinian evolutionists,' Mivart's postures seemed less threatening than defensive. Reviewers were already castigating the religious dogmatism, 'missionary zeal,' and Puritan fervour of the Darwinians, in which enthusiasm 'has a tendency to outrun discretion' and a 'spirit of latent intolerance' is 'tinged with sectarian bitterness.' In sectarian Belfast Darwin was appointed the head of a reformed biology. 'He moves over the subject with the passionless strength of a glacier,' Charles read of himself; 'and the grinding of the rocks is not always without a counterpart in the logical pulverization of the objector.'[10]

Quite so, as the Catholic Mivart was about to find out. Murray, anxious not to lose a bread-and-butter author, leaned on the *Quarterly*'s editor, and in the October issue George's flat contradiction appeared beside an 'apology' from his traducer. It bore all the hallmarks of Mivart's ingenuous backstabbing. Without implying that the younger Darwin had 'approved of anything which he wishes to disclaim,' it ended, 'we must still maintain that the doctrines which he advocates are most dangerous and pernicious.' This was sophistical nonsense – damning the sin but not the sinner. Darwin was livid and took it personally. 'He has gained his object in giving me pain, and, good God, to think of the flattering, almost fawning speeches which he has made to me!' To what depths Mivart had stooped in the name of Christianity.

Even as he seethed, his antipathy to religion was tempered by thoughts of Lyell. Now almost blind and in parlous health, Lyell had generously applauded Tyndall's fillip to 'you and your theory of evolution,' whatever his qualms about the 'fearless out-speaking.' More than ever he was absorbed in the question of a future life, and he let it show. Darwin could offer little comfort. Many accepted it by intuition, '& I suppose that I must differ from such persons' – Emma included – 'for I do not feel any innate conviction.' Still, to be 'circumstanced as you are' was a ghastly thought. Darwin knew that if he were blind, without Emma, and facing the end, the problem of the hereafter would 'recur in the dead of the night with painful force.'

Back at the microscope by day, he thrust it out of mind. He lost himself in his plants and plotted Mivart's downfall. Huxley and Hooker would know best what punitive action to take. Meanwhile he let off steam at the Revd Ffinden and formally resigned from the school committee on health grounds.[11]

On 13 November the new *Descent of Man* was hot off the press, priced down to nine shillings, though Murray conceded that it would cut the profits to the bone.

That day Hooker's wife Fanny died suddenly. Hooker was at the pinnacle of his career and already severely strained: he sat on fifteen committees at the Royal Society and was struggling with the new Disraeli government to increase Kew's funding. At home he had six children, three young. Fanny had held the household together, helped him write and proof-read, and escorted dignitaries around Kew, being a botanical Henslow herself. She had been the perfect partner for twenty-three years, since his return from the East. Now he felt as though he were wandering again in the Himalayas, cut off, desperately alone. He entered 'a sort of trance,' scarcely able to fathom the calamity. The prospect of returning home after the funeral stunned him, and he begged refuge at Downe. The house as so often turned into a hospice, with Hooker staying for a few days and leaving the children to Emma's care. Returning home he was unable to function. 'Utter desolation' overcame him as he stepped into his house at Kew, and his first impulse was to return to the Darwins. Charles passed on his own remedy, encouraging him to banish harrowing thoughts 'by hard work.'[12]

But Hooker kept 'stumbling into pitfalls of recollections.' Darwin waited a couple of weeks and then raised Mivart's iniquity. Hooker agreed that the so-called apology was abominable and proposed forcing him to admit to the anonymous piece and to recant. A joint letter from X Club members should twist his arm. For Huxley it was another excuse to pitch into his old pupil's split loyalties, to evolution and the Church, and he took the opportunity in a book review. 'Unless I err,' he bristled, the '*Quarterly Reviewer*' is 'good enough to include me among the members of that school whose speculations are to bring back ... the gross profligacy of Imperial Rome.' With his usual sensual pleasure in smiting Amalekites – now sitting oddly against Darwin's unsmiling earnestness – Huxley rehearsed his sectarian theme: that 'misrepresentation and falsification are the favourite weapons of Jesuitical Rome' and that 'anonymous slander' culminates not in 'the profligacy of a Nero or of a Commodus, but the secret poisonings of the Papal Borgias.'

The X Club were closing ranks, forming a protective circle. 'You ought to be like one of the blessed gods of Elysium,' Huxley counselled Darwin before Christmas, 'and let the inferior deities do battle with the infernal powers.' He himself passed word to Mivart via a Catholic priest that scurrility of this sort was unacceptable. Mivart was being pinned out, like Owen before him, and he knew it. He erupted with pleas and protestations, and in confidence asked Huxley how to go about making amends.

Huxley plotted Mivart's excommunication from the church scientific with Darwin: 'the severest and most effectual punishment for this sort of moral assassination is quietly to ignore the offender and give him the cold shoulder.' Darwin, not brimming with seasonal spirit, drummed his fingers. Emma, his X friends, and even George backed Huxley's advice, but he was itching to do the 'manly thing' and speak his mind. Malicious twisting of the truth and stabbing at the family was unforgivable. On 12 January 1875, when no further apology had come, Darwin acted. He sent a note with icy formality, vowing never to communicate with him again.[13] Mivart's worm twisted on the Darwinian hook and died of its improprieties. There was never any spirit of forgiveness; years later Huxley and Hooker were still blackballing Mivart's application to join the Athenaeum Club.

Darwin sprinted on with *Insectivorous Plants*, plagued by the interminable manuscript. The prose was muddy, and by February he was bogged down and gasping. He hardly helped George's low spirits by commiserating, 'I know well the feeling of life being objectless & all being vanity of vanities.' He was even 'ready to commit suicide,' a startled Hooker heard, and the death of an old, sad Lyell on the 22nd left him feeling 'as if we were all soon to go.'

After Lyell's failure to back the *Origin*, their camaraderie had cooled. It was a grim end to a once famous friendship. Hooker arranged for Lyell's place in Westminster Abbey but Darwin declined to be a pall-bearer. 'I should so likely fail in the midst of the ceremony, and have my head whirling off my shoulders.'

In March he clambered out of the mud, throwing his finished book down, sick of his insect-eating companions. He gazed at his oil portrait by Walter Ouless, a birthday present. It showed 'a very venerable, acute, melancholy old dog,' he decided, which fairly reflected his mood. But the old dog had a bone or two to bury yet. He carried the manuscript to Murray and spent a fortnight with Eras and Henrietta in town. With Lyell departed, an April Fools' day séance at the Hensleigh Wedgwoods' seemed ill judged, a tragic joke if it were not so tasteless, so much 'rubbish' to please the dreary dictates of fashion.[14]

Life was wearying on so many fronts. The parish added to his woes with the Ffinden fiasco chuntering on. For a year the vicar had cut every member of the family, making Darwin the parish Mivart. He felt 'so grossly insulted' that any word now had to go through an intermediary. Lubbock had asked on Darwin's behalf for the loan of the schoolroom to hold two evening lectures for the village. The committee consented, but Ffinden demurred. He refused to co-operate with an infidel who impugned his authority, adopting a sugar-of-lead smile:

> I had been long aware of the harmful tendencies to the cause
> of revealed religion of Mr. Darwin's views, but on coming
> into this parish I had fully determined, as far as lay within my
> power, not to let my difference of opinion interfere with a
> friendly feeling as neighbours, trusting that God's Grace might
> in time bring one so highly gifted intellectually & morally to
> a better mind.

This Sir John diplomatically side-stepped as he tried to patch up the schoolroom quarrel. With Henrietta beside him, Charles drafted a tortuous self-vindication, designed to elicit another clerical climb-down. 'If M^r F bows to Mrs D. and myself, we will return it,' he condescended, showing that High Church Tories had no monopoly on hauteur. With no parish X Club to extort an apology, restoring peace was going to be a 'herculean task.'

The asperity was evident. Having forsworn public controversy, he found his private hostility to Christianity increasing. Ffinden and Mivart had stretched his tolerance to breaking point.[15] Dogmatism of their sort needed a dose of liberal humanitarianism; closed minds needed to be opened by the rush of a reforming science.

Scientific progress was his other preoccupation during his spring break in London. He was master-minding a rear-guard action against the rising anti-vivisectionist movement. Henrietta, a confirmed hypochondriac, had jumped on the bandwagon. Like so many closeted Victorian matriarchs, she identified with suffering life. Victoria's maidens formed the anti-vivisectionist core and 'read their own misery into the vivisector's victims.' Henrietta supported a petition drawn up by the women's campaigner Frances Power Cobbe. Cobbe was marshalling lay support for a crackdown on live animal experiments. Her petition – signed by archbishops, poets, and politicians – even threatened legislation that would take the moral decisions out of the hands of the experimenters. Darwin was atypically British, an animal lover who loved his colleagues' autonomy more. 'Physiology,' he warned Henrietta, 'can progress only by experiments on living animals.' These must be conducted freely, 'in the search for abstract truth.' Any abuses should be corrected by 'the improvement of humanitarian feelings.' In other words, legislation would be fatal. If the hare-coursing, hypocritical House of Commons passed Cobbe's 'puerile' law, physiology in England would 'languish or quite cease.'[16]

The more he thought, the more he worried. Cobbe's meddling had to be trumped. He toyed with a counter-petition, but it was Huxley who recognized that the fox-hunting Commons would have to save science, fearing for their own skins. 'If physiological experimentation is put down by law, hunting, fishing and shooting, against which a much better case can be made out, will soon follow.' To preserve liberty all around, let the physiologists propose their own legislation. In London Darwin frantically mustered support for a pre-emptive law. There was 'not a day to lose' if his 'Vivisector's Bill' – as opponents dubbed it – was to be introduced in the current session.

Neither he nor Huxley had conducted experiments on live animals, but friends who had, like Burdon Sanderson, were easily won over. Darwin even swayed Henrietta, and her lawyer-husband helped draft a bill. Regulation, not restriction, was its aim. Licensing experimenters would ensure their freedom and minimize animal suffering. Darwin sent it to Hooker for the rubber stamp, so that he could 'say that it meets with your approval as President of the Royal Society.' Then he offered it to Lord Derby, the Foreign Secretary, urging him to have a word with select members of the Tory cabinet in order to head off 'hasty legislation versus science.'[17]

It was a splendid piece of lobbying. His name opened doors and, Derby told him, placed the scientists' bill on the Home Secretary's desk. At Downe Ffinden was still buzzing about 'uncalled for interference,' like a gnat on a rhino's back; now Darwin, surrounded by insect-eaters, had shown what interference could do. When Huxley and Romanes, Darwin's new protégé, came out on 17 April there was only the bill's mechanics to arrange – who would sponsor it and when. At home the topic remained a male preserve. The bumptious Romanes, on his first visit, was told by Darwin not to 'talk about experiments on animals' in the 'presence of my ladies.'

One lady got the better of them. On 4 May Cobbe's bill was presented in the Lords. The scientists' alternative, with its 'more humanitarian aspect,' as Darwin put it, reached the Commons eight days later. The Home Secretary reacted by announcing a Royal Commission of inquiry into 'the practice of subjecting live animals to experiments for scientific purposes.' In the event it was opportune, with the physiologists falling out over their bill's intent. Darwin pinned his hopes on Huxley, co-opted on to the Commission, and they 'let the present madness subside.'[18]

Darwin was a man trapped on a literary treadmill, walking faster and faster towards the grave. One book led to another, and there were always a couple on back burners should he feel bored. *Insectivorous Plants* sold out quickly, and in July a 1000-copy reprint vanished within a fortnight. The name 'Darwin' was a draw now, however odd the subject. Who could imagine a 450-page catalogue of plant experiments selling faster than the original *Origin of Species*?[19] A new edition of *Variation of Animals and Plants* followed, its additions culled from the hundreds of letters and scores of monographs that had swamped Downe over seven years. Even more idiosyncratic, this piece of science; he changed his mind about the hairy throats of goats, added bits on the selection of goldfish during the Sung Dynasty, and discarded Robert Chambers's hexadactyl daughter, whose amputated extra finger had appeared to be regrowing ('we are manifesting a tendency to return to the reptilian type,' the six-fingered Chambers had once joked, and in the first edition Darwin had taken him literally).[20]

Then he re-throned his 'great god Pan,' altering his appearance but leaving his powers intact. The deity had not acquired many worshippers, though Romanes presented himself at the altar. Overawed by Darwin's father-figure, Romanes had set aside his jellyfish and started grafting vegetable plants, miscegenously mixing the 'gemmules' (or so he hoped) to produce a hybrid with the characters of both the scion and stock. Darwin knew that 'the world will be much more influenced by experiments on animals,' but success with plants would be a start.

He also knew that Galton had tried and failed. Galton's house had been overrun with rabbits as he experimented on blood transfusions, intrigued by 'pangenesis.' But pure-bred silver-grey bucks and does given the blood of common rabbits still bred true – eighty-eight offspring in thirteen litters showed no adulteration. Darwin protested that he had never mentioned 'gemmules' in the blood, but his brave face was getting a little stiff. Galton suspected that heredity was not a democratic process: gemmules do not convene from all over the body in the egg and sperm. Instead, those in the reproductive cells are sovereign, governing all. Offspring are determined by the genetic make-up of these cells, not by changes in their parents' bodies.[21]

But Darwin was loath to let go of the notion that a well-used and strengthened organ could be inherited. For decades he had amassed evidence that tradesmen's physiques were passed on – that blacksmiths' children are born with hammering biceps, or that parental scars reappear on a baby. More and more he fell back on this, making pangenesis essential. In the *Descent* such inheritance was presented as a powerful factor in human evolution. Nothing would induce him to emulate Huxley and strangle his baby god. So he left Pan essentially intact, allowing organisms literally to grow from their inherited gemmules. Bitter experience had taught him that the children shared his weakness. It was pleasanter to think that they shared his mental strengths, and that the modified gemmules of his young over-worked brain had passed on his peculiar psychological gifts.[22]

For proof there was Frank. His love of natural history was like Charles's at the same age. Frank came down from the village most days and was always pottering in the greenhouse, experimenting on plant fertilization, or tinkering upstairs in the lab. Charles, proud of his new assistant, put him up for a Fellowship of the Linnean Society.

Fame left Darwin pestered by every fool with a thought. He was plagued by sermon-senders and soul-savers, by foreigners wanting papers published, or just wishing for his *imprimatur*, by lecturers wanting chairs and scientists their fellowships. Most were treated graciously, a few received grudging treatment. Some refused to give up. The brash Birmingham surgeon Robert Lawson Tait currently had his foot in Darwin's door. Just thirty, Tait specialized in removing ovaries and wombs, with a side-line in plant physiology. His reputation was on the rise and he wanted a Fellowship of the Royal Society to garnish his gynaecology practice. After months of shameless sycophancy, he forced Darwin in October to send his paper on pitcher plants to the Royal Society for publication. It seemed to be an 'important contribution to science,' not that Darwin read it carefully.[23]

His own publications took every waking hour. There were endless negotiations with Murray about prices, print runs, and rights. His translators Victor Carus in Leipzig and Giovanni Canestrini in Padua were straining to catch up with him, working on several of his books simultaneously. And they were losing. The *Variation of Animals* was at the printer's; an old botanical essay was due out in November – *The Movements and Habits of Climbing Plants* – with 'illustrations . . . drawn by my son, George.' And Charles was already scribbling 'vile' screeds for *The Effects of Cross and Self Fertilisation in the Vegetable Kingdom*. Only a noble invitation from London stayed his hand. Lord Cardwell asked him to testify before the Royal Commission on vivisection.[24]

Huxley demanded he attend. A young Austrian physician, Edward Klein, had outraged the panel, muttering in broken English about his 'entire indifference to animal suffering.' 'He only gave anaesthetics to keep animals quiet!' Huxley spat. Klein tarred everyone with the same brush, sickening the committee by his deliberate probings and torturings. 'He has done more mischief than all the fanatics put together' – but 'don't mention' it 'outside the circle of discreet Darwindom.' High authority was needed to counter Klein's testimony, and an 'astonished and disgusted' Darwin agreed to testify. He made a flying visit on 3 November. Cardwell met him at the door, sat him in a special oversized chair, and treated him 'like a Duke.' They wanted his 'confession of faith' about the importance of physiology and 'the duty of humanity' towards animals, that was all. Ten minutes from him was worth two hours of risky vivisectionist apologias. It was a painless episode, but the cab left him at Ras's that night 'unwell.'[25]

This was the first Christmas at Downe without Parslow. Darwin had set him up in the village with a £50 pension and the rent of Home Cottage in Back Lane, his reward for thirty-six years' unfaltering service. Jackson, a comic little man 'with red cheeks [and] . . . loose curly wisps of side whiskers' took over, but no one could really replace the redoubtable old butler. Other servants came and went; there was always a coachman and a footman, a pair of housemaids and at least two gardeners. Mrs Evans, the cook, was second in seniority to Parslow, though her cuisine in Charles's view left something to be desired. But she was cheap, less than £8 a quarter. Actually no one bar Jackson received more, and this year the total servants' wage bill came to only £86.

This was a fraction of their outgoings. At Christmas Emma balanced the books. Charles was full of 'dismal forecasts' as usual, predicting penury and ruin. He worried about his fortune, even as it swelled, and begrudged every penny of household expenditure. With the children away, expenses hit a five-year low, with meat – the biggest item – down to £221. The total was just £900, or ten per cent of their earnings and interest. Rates and income tax were negligible, less than the servants' pay, but even after deductions for beer and brandy, sweets and champagne, and the boys' allowances, they had the second-best surplus ever of £4658 to reinvest.[26]

Typically, everything was listed and accounted for in the house, from fat drippings, £3, to the village Friendly Society. Their clockwork lives ran by calculations; balances were continually totted. Even games were recorded religiously. Charles kept the account in a notebook tucked away in the parlour. Each evening, after precisely two games of backgammon, he and Emma entered their scores, a practice that amazed and amused their guests. It had tickled Mrs Asa Gray on her husband's visit years before and on 28 January 1876 Charles posted the current tally, as 'she likes to hear men boasting, it refreshes them so much.' Emma, 'poor creature, has won only 2490 games, whilst I have won, hurrah, hurrah, 2795 games!'[27]

But then notebooks were nothing new. Since his shooting days at Maer every aspect of life was entered on a list. He had counted and classified, sifted and sorted – beetles at Cambridge, birds on the *Beagle*, books to be read, and 'double dash' days in his health diary. All was to some end. Since 1866 he had kept records on thousands of plants hand-reared from seed, and his pollination experiments now reached a climax in *Cross and Self Fertilisation*.

From his first jottings on evolution, he had guessed that the offspring of self-fertilized plants would be weaker. In the *Origin* he made the point, but then it was personal to him. For plants or marriages, outbreeding was best. Self-pollinators and first-cousin offspring suffered in life's struggle. *Orchids* had illustrated the bizarre adaptations ensuring that bees could only cross pollinate, and for a decade he had been crossing plants under controlled conditions, trying to prove statistically that it was beneficial.[28]

This was his most prodigious, painstaking series of experiments.

The plants had to be protected from insects by sheets of gauze. He cross-fertilized some batches and selfed others. Seeds were carefully collected, labelled, and grown to maturity under identical conditions. These were themselves bred to test for sterility: crossed plants had to be crossed again, the others self-pollinated. For up to ten generations this went on, with records kept at every stage of the lengths of plants, times of flowering, the number and weight of seed pods, and the quantity of seeds in each. Nor was just the odd species involved; morning glories, foxgloves, violas, poached-egg plants, petunias, and dozens of others were all tested simultaneously, the greenhouse bursting and space so restricted that many were crammed into the same pot. Then Chinese primroses, French poppies, and hothouse exotics were tried . . .

Thousands of paintbrush pollinations took place, tens of thousands of seeds were counted. It was obsessive work: each seed became 'a small demon trying to elude him by getting into the wrong heap or jumping' from under the microscope. Now, peering over his pince-nez spectacles, ledgers of data lay before him as he tabulated the results. Galton checked his statistics, and the figures quantified the 'selective force' at work in modifying flowers. Crossed plants came out markedly superior to self-fertilized ones in height, weight, vigour, and fertility. And why, Darwin asked at the end? Because nature blesses 'legitimate marriages' – among those from different backgrounds.

People or plants, it was all the same, and the personal dimension was too evident. After the fruitless effort to get a census question on cousin-marriages, George had followed up with an analysis of data culled from lunatic asylums and wedding announcements in the *Pall Mall Gazette*. According to his statistics, which Darwin cited, the evils produced by first-cousin marriages might be 'small' but they could be condoned 'amongst the upper classes,' among gentlefolk brought up in richly different environments.[29] And Charles and Emma? Theirs was a fertile union with sickly seedlings. Evidently the beds at Maer Hall and The Mount had been too alike. The couple had not been well crossed.

Cross and Self Fertilisation was turning out to be his biggest plant book and the writing dragged on into the summer. Charles paced himself with short breaks – or rather Emma did – and made the most of the time, revelling in 'my sole pleasure in life,' work.

Not even the setbacks destroyed that pleasure. Haeckel came out against pangenesis. Tait's paper was ignominiously rejected by the

Royal Society. Romanes started secret inquiries into spiritualism, though Darwin confessed himself 'a wretched bigot on the subject.' And a 'cruelty to animals' bill was introduced in Parliament that went far beyond the Commission's recommendations and fell into Cobbe's lap. Darwin vented his spleen in *The Times*, the old patrician targeting those women who 'from the tenderness of their hearts and . . . their profound ignorance' oppose all animal experiments.

He let none of it get him down. By May the first draft of the fertilization book was finished and, unable to relax for a moment, he promptly threw himself into a new edition of *Orchids*.[30]

Emma dragged him away almost before he started. Hensleigh and Fanny had built a house in the Surrey countryside, and Charles and Emma accepted an invitation to visit, dying to tell them the good news.

41

Never an Atheist

THEY WERE TO BE grandparents! Frank's wife Amy was five months pregnant. Charles and Emma had been expecting the announcement – the marriage was after all two years old – and Hensleigh and Fanny celebrated with them. In their seventies, the Hensleighs longed for their own grandchild, and they spent the weeks with the Darwins thinking on the future.

For Charles time was running out, with so much left to do. He had *Orchids* to revise and two more plant books in prospect. Earthworms still intrigued him and he hoped to write on their habits before joining them. He would have a grandchild to see him buried. And what then? He imagined himself 'a dead man in another world' looking back. He pictured the baby growing up, haunted by his name, wondering about the author of the *Origin of Species*. Hadn't he often wished to know more about his own grandfather Erasmus?

Basking in the sun with new life swarming about him, he decided to compose a posthumous message to the family. He started on Sunday, 28 May 1876, scrawling 'Recollections of the Development of my mind and character' across a fresh foolscap sheet. The paragraphs poured out quickly, racing through his naughty childhood and wasted schooldays, his Edinburgh apprenticeship under Dr Grant, his extramural interests at Cambridge and walks with Professor Henslow, his tangles with FitzRoy on the *Beagle* and growing love for science. None of this was for publication: there were too many casual comments about old friends, not to mention the intimacy and mild self-criticism. This was for the family's eyes.

Off to a flying start, he wrote for an hour most afternoons at Downe. It was easy going, unlike the hair-tearing revisions to *Cross and Self Fertilisation*, which he laboured over after breakfast. The story reached London – geology, his *Journal*, and Lyell – when he broke off to start a section headed 'Religious Belief.' Chronologically, it stood on the threshold of his marriage, but Charles ranged far beyond. Just weeks before Amy's confinement, he was tackling his long dispute with Emma.

Nothing curbed his candour; these were private pages. At first he had been unwilling to give up the faith, and had even tried to 'invent evidence' to bolster the Gospels, which had prolonged his indecision. But, just as his clerical career had died a slow 'natural death,' so his belief in 'Christianity as a divine revelation' had withered gradually. There had been no turning back once the death-blow fell. His dithering had crystallized into a moral conviction so strict that he could not 'see how anyone ought to wish Christianity to be true.' If it were, 'the plain language' of the New Testament 'seems to show that the men who do not believe, and this would include my Father, Brother and almost all my best friends, will be everlastingly punished. And this is a damnable doctrine.'[1]

Hard heartfelt words, they recalled the bitter months and years after the Doctor's death. But what about the wider issues? How could belief in God and immortality be justified, given the conflicting evidence? 'Inward convictions and feelings' were unreliable because the human mind had evolved. Blind nature had given them a survival value, like other instincts. So while he sometimes felt himself a theist, at others he distrusted his own feelings, let alone anyone else's.

Altogether it was a grim indictment of Emma's sentimental, Bible-based faith. The enormity of what he had written shook him. It exposed their intimate conflict, laid it bare before the family. As he wrote on, his affection turned to tears. 'You all know well your mother,' he added, 'so infinitely my superior in every moral quality ... my wise adviser and cheerful comforter.' He recalled her 'beautiful letter' after their marriage, with its fear for his eternal destiny. Here was her side of the story, and he wanted the family to know it. Then his melancholy thoughts turned to Annie, and how she would now 'have grown into a delightful woman ... Tears still sometimes come into my eyes, when I think of her sweet ways.'

Anxious memories flooded back. Twice he had tended dying loved ones while awaiting a confinement: his father a few months before Frank was born, and Annie just before Horace. Now he looked back on his own life like a 'dead man' as Amy prepared to give birth.

Through July he continued the autobiography. He piled on anecdotes from the Gower Street years and relived writing the *Origin of Species* and his other books. After *Cross and Self Fertilisation* was published 'my strength will . . . probably be exhausted,' he closed. Like the devout old priest Simeon, on seeing the infant Jesus, 'I shall be ready to exclaim "Nunc dimittis".'[2]

He finished the manuscript on 3 August, ready for his grandchild, and returned to his perennial *Orchids* and parish responsibilities. He pumped £25 into the Revd Ffinden's 'vicarage endowment fund,' matching Lubbock's subscription.[3] Nothing but solid respectability for the second squire of Downe, building for the future. The baby – Bernard – arrived on 7 September, born at the house. He was fine but his mother contracted a fever, which turned into convulsions. She fell unconscious, and on the third day the prognosis was bleak. Frank stayed the night at her bedside, stroking her raven hair and slender face. On the 11th, at seven in the morning, Charles came in, and they watched her die. Amy was just twenty-six.

Frank went into shock. Bessy collapsed and Emma herself was almost overcome. For Charles it was 'the most dreadful thing' that had ever happened – worse for Frank than 'poor Annie's death' for him. Comfort came in the knowledge that Amy 'never knew she was leaving her beloved husband for ever,' but that was a 'miserable consolation.' His son was enduring what he himself most feared. Surviving Emma was unthinkable.[4]

Months passed before anything like normal life resumed. Frank, distracted by grief, moved into Down House with the baby. He did mechanical chores for his father, making a fair copy of his autobiography and correcting the proofs of *Orchids*. Charles extended the house for him, which meant more upheaval. It had been twenty years since contractors vied with a crying child to disrupt the daily routine. A two-storey extension was added on the north side of the house, with a purpose-built billiard room downstairs and a bedroom-cum-dressing-room for Frank above. The old billiard room became Frank's study, next to his father's, and down the hall the workmen made a new front door.[5]

In October Charles and Emma braced themselves for another of Haeckel's whirlwind visits, which Emma dreaded. Again he stormed the house, bellowing enough 'bad English' to leave them 'nearly deafened,' but for all that she found him 'hearty and affectionate.' Charles regaled him with the quirky news. Huxley's protégé, the stormy Ray Lankester, a good fossil fish man and now Grant's successor at University College, had exposed a marauding American medium in *The Times*. As a result Henry Slade had been sentenced to three months' imprisonment with hard labour – despite the defence calling Wallace as a witness! Emma was scandalized, believing that the credulous deserved the rogues. But not Charles; the affair was a 'public benefit,' and he had secretly sent £10 towards the prosecution's costs.[6]

Parish politics still bedevilled them, even if they scored some successes. A reading room was opened before Christmas, cheering Emma because Ffinden had tried everything to oppose it. Charles, on to his next book on flowers, saw *Orchids* and *Cross and Self Fertilisation* published, and in February 1877 won a small victory of his own. During the farm slump, with wages down and jobs in jeopardy, the village labourers wanted to disband the Friendly Society and share out the proceeds. Only Mr Darwin as treasurer stood in their way. A deputation duly called at Down House and an extraordinary general meeting was convened, at which Mr Darwin would speak.

Donning his black overcoat and soft felt hat, Charles trudged to the George and Dragon one frigid Saturday night and sat surrounded by his tipsy cottagers in the reeking smoke-room. He harangued them about their losses if the society were dissolved, about thrift, about exchanging long-term security for a few pounds in hand. What if the distress got worse? Without the society, who would provide for their families? The room erupted into quarrels and Charles left in a haze of blue smoke, his 'bombshell' demolishing the spendthrifts.[7] The men compromised, agreeing to distribute their surplus funds while keeping the books open.

A parish paternalist, he was promoting the self-help values of his fellow Murray author Samuel Smiles. Darwin had been impressed by *Self-Help* and later gloried in Smiles's biographies of self-made men – stories of heroic prudence, industry, and enterprise, not unlike Martineau's mythic poor-law tales. Smilesian values had made England and evolution great. The unfettered individual, pursuing his self-interest in a freely competitive society, had been the political ideal for half a century, since the days of the radical Whigs and free-traders. It was Darwin's manifesto in the *Descent of Man*, and he himself remained a 'thorough Liberal.'[8]

That meant a thorough Gladstonian. Darwin followed the Grand Old Man even in his opposition foreign policy. In December he had signed up as one of the convenors of the great St James's Hall demonstration against the bloody 'Bulgarian horrors,' the massacre of 15,000 Bulgarian rebels by Turkish troops. He also contributed to the relief effort – £50 all told – and backed Gladstone's call for the Russians to secure Christian Bulgaria against the Muslim Turks. This slavish support did not pass unnoticed. Freethinkers branded Gladstone an opportunist for rousing the religious rabble against the pro-Turkish Tories. To Marx he was just a hypocrite, a High Anglican putting his Christianity before his Liberalism, who preferred an Orthodox Tsarist oppressor for a Turkish one. Marx expected more of Darwin and lashed his support for the 'piggish demonstration.'

But political loyalty paid off, and the Olympian deities of Victorian Liberalism shortly descended on the sleepy village of Downe. Gladstone was making the rounds of his backbenchers, spending the weekend with Lubbock at High Elms. With them were Lyon Playfair MP, with a brief for science and a supporter of the vivisection bill; the *Fortnightly*'s John Morley, who had puffed the *Descent of Man* so helpfully; and even Huxley, his black eyes flashing scorn at Gladstone's biblical bombast. On Saturday 10 March the deities turned up on Darwin's doorstep and settled into his drawing-room. The Grand Old Man took for granted his host's interest in Turkish terrorism and like Zeus himself 'launched forth his thunderbolts with unexhausted zest,' reading from the proof of his latest pamphlet. Darwin was stunned into a bemused silence for almost two hours. Before sweeping out, Gladstone asked what evolution held in store. Did the future belong to America as the Eastern civilizations decayed? A better question perhaps for Disraeli, but after mulling it over Darwin ventured, Yes. As he watched Gladstone's 'erect alert figure' walking back towards the village, he murmured to Morley, 'What an honour that such a great man should come to visit me!' That night in his diary Gladstone noted merely his host's 'pleasing & remarkable' appearance.[9]

Even Tories were not above paying Darwinians tribute, though not, understandably, for their Darwinism. While the Duke of Argyll had failed to honour Hooker as the head of Kew Gardens because 'he don't like my Darwinism,' the new Secretary for India in Disraeli's cabinet, the staunch Anglican Lord Salisbury, put his name up for a knighthood, a very specific, complimentary honour, the Star of India, acknowledging Hooker's monumental, decades-long work on the Himalayan flora. Hooker told Darwin he 'would rather go down to posterity as one of the "Star of India" than as of any other dignity whatever that the Crown can offer,' and he accepted the investiture.[10] Sir Joseph, President of the Royal Society, showed that Darwinism was no longer a social hindrance.

As the disciples tended to exalted circles, Darwin was even more loath to become mixed up with disreputable radicals. They appealed in vain for his support. Charles Bradlaugh, a big boisterous solicitor's clerk from London's East End, was the dominant Secularist of the day. A militant atheist, he had stood as an unofficial Liberal candidate for Northampton in every election since 1868 – unsuccessfully, but with the best political machine of any radical outside the trade unions. His hard-hitting demands for electoral reform were matched by a commitment to contraception: birth control would rescue working people from the Malthusian poverty trap, free them from domestic slavery. Two weeks after Gladstone's visit, Bradlaugh outraged the genteel nation by publishing do-it-yourself contraceptive advice from an American doctor, James Knowlton. The sixpenny pamphlet, *Fruits of Philosophy*, was branded a vicious obscenity. Bradlaugh and his co-publisher Annie Besant (a latter-day Emma Martin – an atheist mother-of-two who had left her parson-husband) were committed for trial at London's Central Criminal Court, the Old Bailey, on 18 June – the day Darwin heard of Hooker's honour.

The case was splashed all over the press. Nothing so notorious had hit the headlines since Holyoake's trial thirty years earlier. It split the radicals themselves – even old, cigar-smoking, respectable Holyoake fumed that it compromised them before a Christian public, who damned such 'neo-Malthusian' nonsense as immoral and subversive. Contraception was 'vice' and execrated by Malthus as a way of checking population. Who in their right minds would divorce sex from babies and invite women to become wanton, to corrupt men and to destroy the family? The defendants fought back by calling medical and scientific authorities to testify that 'the doctrine of the limitation of the family' was freely discussed in other publications.[11]

Darwin was appalled to be subpoenaed two weeks before the trial. Bradlaugh and Besant, defending themselves, had made a gigantic miscalculation, assuming that the author of the *Descent of Man* would back them. Had not he liberated mankind from superstition? Darwin replied instantly, protesting his years of illness, his forced withdrawal from 'all society or public meetings,' and the 'great suffering' that a court appearance would entail. Underneath he was a flurry of old fears, for his family, his reputation, his status as a justice of the peace. If compelled to testify, he finished, he would have to denounce the defendants, for he had 'long held an opposite opinion' on birth control.

As proof, he sent an extract from the *Descent of Man*: 'our natural rate of increase, though leading to many and obvious evils, must not be greatly diminished by any means.' Plain speaking, that meant any 'artificial means of preventing conception.' Otherwise he spelt out the nightmarish consequences – such practices would 'spread to unmarried women & w^d destroy chastity on which the family bond depends; & the weakening of this bond would be the greatest of all possible evils to mankind.' No compromise could be struck; 'my judgment would be in the strongest opposition to yours.' He passed on addresses at Leith Hill and Southampton where he was holidaying that month, should the subpoena be renewed. But he hoped not, and he wanted to know immediately, 'as apprehension of the coming exertion would prevent the rest which I require doing me much good.'

'Rest' of course meant working furiously away from home. Mercifully, the atheists withdrew their subpoena and left him in peace with his worms.

He was back on the ground, exalting the humble in his own peculiar way. As with all his work, he moved from minuscule, unnoticeable changes to their global consequences. Worms burying castles, earthquakes throwing up the Andes, flecks and specks adding up to an eye or wing: he looked for tiny effects that were cumulative and creative. From William's he made a day-trip to Stonehenge – his first – to see how worm castings had buried the ancient monoliths. Emma thought that the two-hour rail trip and twenty-four-mile drive would 'half kill' him, but even after digging in the blazing sun he was in wonderful form.[12]

Fifteen years tampering with the sex-life of plants culminated in *The Different Forms of Flowers on Plants of the Same Species* in mid-July – with a fetching and rare dedication, to Asa Gray. This book continued another old theme, strategies for safe sex and fertile reproduction. No 'little discovery' ever gave him 'so much pleasure' as cracking the *raison d'être* of double- and triple-sexed flowers – it was like the *frisson* of finding the barnacles' 'complemental males:' each female in heterostyled plants was most fertile with the same-sized males, which always occurred on another flower.

Forms of Flowers capped his work on nature's complex 'marriage arrangements.' It was a botanical voyeur's diary. He had contrived all sorts of liaisons among the blossoms, spying on them through his eyeglass. After endless manual pollinations, myriad microscopic seed-counts; and he described the results with due delicacy, showing how 'legitimacy' was conferred in cross-fertilizations.[13] Even before the first reviews appeared, he was wrapped up in his next book on plant movement. No time could be lost, nor could he 'endure being idle.'

Not that idleness was on the cards. He continued collecting seeds and specimens, scrounging all he could from Hooker and Thistelton-Dyer at Kew. He kept up a massive correspondence, on everything from worm lore and butterflies to drunken monkeys. In October he even found time to dodge Gladstone's thunderbolts and dared to criticize him on the colour-sense in Homeric Greece. Politically, though, he was steadfast. A young Russian botanist, Kliment Timiriazev, dropped by one afternoon and heard Darwin declare unqualified support for the Tsarist war against Turkey. But months later, when Russia threatened to overstep her bounds and trench on English interests, Darwin toed Gladstone's neutral line: he endorsed a public 'Declaration against War' and put his name forward to collect signatures.[14]

Every month or two Emma still winkled him out of the study for a break, although it was getting harder. They missed their usual visit to Southampton this autumn – William, just engaged, received a gift of £300 – but a week at rustic Abinger on the North Downs made up for it. Wallace was living at Dorking, a few miles away, having had to sell his idyllic new house. Darwin avoided him. They were out of tune after the spiritual Slade trial, and hopelessly discordant over sexual selection. Wallace seemed as incorrigible as Mivart, though infinitely more pleasant. It was futile arguing with him on any 'difficult subject.' A reunion would have ruined the holiday, though Darwin phrased it more politely. 'I . . . wished to come over to see you, but driving tires me so much that my courage failed.'[15]

In November Darwin did trek to Cambridge, to be honoured. By now even his Alma Mater had come round. Here robed Darwinians taught, organized the new labs, and placed their protégés in posts, while Hooker and his fellow examiners taxed students on natural selection. Nothing was left but to capitulate and award Darwin an honorary Doctorate of Laws. On the day of the ceremony, Saturday the 17th, the Senate House was packed, everyone wanting to catch sight of the bearded sage. Undergraduates spilled out of the galleries, perched on statues, and stood in the windows. They strung a cord across the chamber and sent a monkey-marionette dangling above the waiting crowd. A Proctor climbed up and snatched it to antiphonal cheers and groans. Then a real 'missing link' appeared, a fat ring garnished with gaudy ribbons, which remained suspended in mid-air throughout the ceremony. Darwin was ushered in, robed in red, and a mighty roar went up from the students. He beamed back. The Vice-Chancellor followed in his scarlet and ermine gown and with two mace-bearers marched him up to the front, where he had taken his oath of matriculation fifty years before.

The Public Orator came forward and uttered his panegyric to occasional 'shouts and jeers.' 'Most unmannerly,' Emma hissed, sitting in the audience with Bessy and the boys, even if it was a 'tedious harangue.' Coral reefs, pigeons, fly-traps, barnacles, climbing plants, and volcanoes – all things Darwinian were decked in the purplest Latin prose. When the Orator paused for breath, a breezy voice in the crowd rang out, 'Thank you kindly,' which brought the house down. This was Cambridge still, rowdy but respectable; and the Orator, like the zealous Proctor, kept up the dialectic, distancing the dignitaries from 'the unlovely tribe of apes.' 'We may yet have the consolation of saying with the Roman orator, who was a great philosopher too, "Mores in utroques dispares"' – the moral nature of the two races is different.[16]

The ritual conferment followed, and afterwards feasts and celebrations. Emma had a headache, so Charles backed out of dinner with the Cambridge Philosophical Society, even though he was the guest of honour. Hooker could not attend, but laughably his new wife sent a bunch of bananas from Kew. Romanes and all the Darwin boys except William stood in to hear Huxley take the toast with a dulcet attack on the university for failing to honour Darwin twenty years earlier. On Sunday there was a 'brilliant luncheon' with George at Trinity College and guided tours of the new university buildings. Emma felt 'very grand walking about with my LL.D. in his silk gown.' She watched with amusement as wide-eyed dons met the renowned recluse. 'A strong ... looking man with iron grey hair,' marvelled the engineering professor James Stuart, who took Darwin around his workshop. He seemed to have been 'rough hewn from a rock with a heavy ... hammer.' He had an aura about him, like an ancient megalith, which cast Huxley and all the other celebrities 'into the shade.' 'A man of genius' this, 'indeed one of "the few".'[17]

Amy's death still haunted him. 'Life would be a most weary blank without a dear wife to love with all one's soul,' he told William's fiancée, Sara Sedgwick. The wedding at the end of November helped him to bury the past. Sara bashfully proclaimed herself 'so American,' but the Darwins loved her anyway, and they had already taken to her Boston brother-in-law, Charles Eliot Norton. She had an openness that Charles always admired about Americans, and a 'readiness to trust and confide' that made her presence like a balm.

The family settled in for a quiet winter, with Frank's baby Bernard – 'Abbadubba' – everyone's favourite. So possessive were the family that Charles complained of not seeing enough of him. The grown-up children appeared from time to time: George, studying mathematical astronomy beyond his father's ken, Leo, now teaching chemistry for the Royal Engineers at Chatham, and Henrietta, who stayed on beyond Christmas while her husband recuperated from appendicitis. In the drawing-room Litchfield catalogued all Emma's piano music, a grateful 'labour of love,' while across the corridor Charles and Frank toiled from morning to night on moving plants.[18]

This too was a labour of love. Spring turned the study into a pungent jungle, with seeds sprouting in biscuit tins on the chimneypiece, cabbages and runner beans in floor pots, and nasturtiums, cyclamens, cacti, and telegraph plants scattered on tables. Charles was in his element, infatuated with every rootlet and blossom. All these were his companions; he had a feeling for their 'aliveness.' He talked to them unselfconsciously, praising their ingenuity or twitting the 'little beggars' for 'doing just what I don't want them to.' Sometimes a flower caught his eye, and he would stroke it gently, childlike in his 'love for its delicate form & colour.' The plants moved him, like the romances Emma read aloud in the afternoons, and when the plants moved themselves they stirred him most of all.[19]

How did they do it? Alone in the Brazilian forest, he had felt the seething life, vines twisting, palms aquiver, snagging barbs dangling. In his study too the plants lassoed and grappled, but here he and Frank could catch them at it. They devised ways for mapping the movements and even making the plants perform. They grew seeds upside down and watched their root-tips hour-by-hour tracing minute zig-zags as they turned back to the ground. Faced by obstacles, the roots twisted to and fro, searching for the way. They tied up, tampered with, and tormented sprouts and found that the upward spiralling persisted, even in total darkness. Darwin at first thought that the zig-zags might be a response to vibration. But Frank's bumping the table, slamming doors, and serenading them on his bassoon proved that wrong. Every part of every plant was constantly and spontaneously on the move, in a continuous rhythmic rotation, or 'circumnutation,' as they called it.

At night they followed the sleeping movements, catching plants drooping or folding their leaves. And they proved that these were necessary for survival. By March 1878 he and Frank had killed dozens of plants by tying their leaves to prevent them from hanging or closing at night. They observed house plants, which slept only if left outside during the day, and tropical ones that did not need to sleep at all. A whole series of intricate experiments had led them to conclude that exposure was the critical factor. In every case the leaves adjusted spontaneously, protecting their upper surfaces.[20]

The work went on non-stop. 'I shan't be easy till I've tried it,' Charles would announce on dreaming up another 'fool's experiment.' To Frank it seemed 'as if an outside force were compelling him.' Needless to say, the strain proved too much – the old sickness set in. In March he saw Dr Clark in London about the attacks of dizziness, which were an 'intolerable bother.' The doctor's 'dry diet' left him panting for a 'wine-glass of water,' but it seemed to do good. Clark refused to charge his famous patient, so Darwin, flush as ever, sent £100 towards the development of a fungus-proof Irish potato – making sure first that the Belfast breeder in question was 'highly respectable.'

His old shipmate Sulivan, now Admiral of the Fleet, was less concerned with respectability, and more with savages. He wanted help in supporting an orphan, and all the *Beagle* officers were chipping in. Darwin obliged as always, struck with the civilizing successes of the South American mission. The boy was the grandson of Jemmy Button.[21]

Romanes was now Darwin's leading protégé. A dyed-in-the-wool Darwinian, he had worked with Hooker at Kew, backed Huxley on vivisection, and even impressed crusty Spencer with his work on the nervous reactions of jellyfish. Huxley, Hooker, and Darwin had him elected to the Linnean and Royal Societies. More than a high-flier, Romanes was a kowtowing convert, and little wonder. At Cambridge he had been an out-and-out evangelical. All the zeal of his prize-winning undergraduate essay *Christian Prayer and General Laws* was now laid on the altar of evolution. Darwin was his new deity.

Romanes shadowed his master, writing long letters and currying favour. His 'respect and affection' were genuine enough, and Darwin could not help but like him, for all his 'superficial faults.' He admired Romanes's brashness, his determination to test hopeless hypotheses, and he egged him on with his motto, 'It is dogged as does it!' The pangenesis experiments were flopping, but Darwin still offered his kitchen garden for onion graft trials. Spiritualism was another dead-end, Romanes having failed to settle 'between Ghost *versus* Goose.' Darwin welcomed his negative results with mediums, including the 'clever rogue' Williams, believing their deceptions to be 'wicked and scandalous.'[22]

But in private Romanes's new faith too was faltering. With his sister delirious on her deathbed that spring, he yearned for some assurance that they would meet again. He sought out an eminent spiritualist, one of the defence counsel in the Slade trial. It was a pathetic meeting. Romanes, looking 'terribly ill and cut up,' poured out his awful doubts. He wanted conviction, pleaded for facts, but went away empty-handed. Days later his sister died.[23] When Darwin heard the news he invited Romanes to Downe.

The situation was emotionally fraught. Four years since joining the Darwinian set, Romanes had reasoned himself into an unrealistic scepticism. His head belonged to evolution but his heart would not co-operate. He was a perambulating paradox, the embodiment of Charles's and Emma's dilemma. Darwin talked of his own moral outrage at the doctrine of eternal damnation. Christianity was no longer an option for either of them, but try as he would, Romanes simply could not believe in God and immortality either. To make matters worse he was courting, and soon to acquire a devout wife of his own. He asked Darwin's help.

It was the old 'frightfully difficult' problem of 'speaking out on religion.' In his first flush of evolutionary enthusiasm a couple of years earlier Romanes had penned a strident refutation of theism, but then followed Darwin's advice to pause. Now he felt driven to publish, certain of his convictions, sad perhaps, but eager for an audience. There was no stopping him, any more than the Doctor could once keep Charles from opening his heart to Emma. Darwin counselled him to publish anonymously, leaving the argument to be judged on its merit. It also helped, as Darwin knew, to think on the way religious reasoning had evolved. He turned over his notes and unused chapter on instinct from *Natural Selection*, launching Romanes on the study of comparative psychology.[24]

Darwin's prodding paid off, and Romanes was given a standing ovation for his talk on mental evolution at the British Association in August. In the absence of actual ancestors, *The Times* reported, he lined up an ugly ersatz collection of 'savages, young children, idiots, and uneducated deaf-mutes.' These dubious stand-ins seemed to show that 'man and brute have much more in common intellectually, and perhaps, even morally, than is dreamt of.' Each was 'arrested' at some lowly stage. Darwin savoured it all, especially the eulogium in the 'grand *finale*.' Try 'keeping a young monkey, so as to observe its mind,' he advised. Frank added a less than practical suggestion. 'Frank says you ought to keep an idiot, a deaf mute, a monkey, and a baby in your house!'

Idiots were unnecessary with the family offering its own throw-backs. Hensleigh daftly clung to spiritualism even though his favourite medium Williams was exposed as a charlatan in September. Even sillier, he now called Williams a charlatan *with* supernatural powers, and he claimed to have seen a ghost, dirty clothes and all, at one of Williams's séances. Is this not a 'psychological curiosity!' Darwin marvelled. He tried to expose Williams in the press in the hope that the story would snowball. He detested mediums, triflers with the transcendent. Imagine manipulating people's fear and grief for a handful of loose change![25]

In November Romanes, new book in hand, drove to the Litchfields, where Charles and Emma were staying. He introduced his fiancée, and presented them *A Candid Examination of Theism* by 'Physicus.' Darwin was not sanguine. One might as well try to 'illuminate the midnight sky with a candle' as throw the light of reason on metaphysics. But he agreed to browse it, and back home found that he could not put it down. Romanes was a tragic spirit. He had embraced the 'lonely mystery of existence' with the 'utmost sorrow,' more a convert to unbelief than Darwin ever was. The universe without God had 'lost its soul of loveliness,' and the biblical precept to 'work while it is day' took on a frightful force from its closing words, 'the night cometh when no man can work.' Philosophy had become 'a meditation, not merely of death, but of annihilation.'

Darwin rushed a note to Romanes. His tolerance for religious literature was low, but he had read *Candid Examination* with '**very great interest**.' Not that it convinced him. Romanes's arguments did not rule out God creating matter and energy at the beginning of the universe with a propensity to organize and evolve. Nor was it necessarily 'more *human*' to doubt God's existence, just because this seemed more 'rational.' If theism is true, 'reason may not be the only instrument for ascertaining its truth.' Our instinctive feelings might point to heaven – though who could say? But Romanes, just engaged, was in an '"idiotic" state of mind,' unfit to ponder imponderables. 'You will wish me at the Devil for bothering you,' Darwin apologized, tucking a photo of himself in the letter for 'the future Mrs Romanes.'[26]

The world wanted to know Darwin's religious views. With public honours showering on him, he had entered his Delphic Oracle phase. The audacity of the sermon-senders, the evangelists, and the spiritual Peeping Toms was excruciating. 'Half the fools throughout Europe write to ask me the stupidest questions,' he groaned. He sometimes managed a terse retort – 'I am sorry to have to inform you that I do not believe in the Bible as a divine revelation, & therefore not in

Jesus Christ as the Son of God' – or infrequently a guarded response, especially if his interlocutor was eminent.[27]

No, he answered a young count studying with Haeckel, he did not 'believe that there ever has been any Revelation. As for a future life, every man must judge for himself between conflicting vague probabilities.' No, he responded to the prelate E. B. Pusey's sermon, the *Origin* had no 'relation whatever to Theology,' although when he wrote it his own 'belief in what is called a personal God was as firm as that of Dr. Pusey himself.' No, he stonewalled the Archbishop of Canterbury, he would not attend a 'Private Conference' of devout scientists at Lambeth Palace to harmonize science and religion, for he could 'see no prospect of any benefit arising' from it.

Dodges and denials were safer than declarations. He was unwilling to be drawn or exposed. Huxley might bait bishops, Tyndall might indulge in pantheistic pyrotechnics, and he would cheer them for it. But he intended to keep the peace – to his vicar's applause. Brodie Innes (who had sent Pusey's sermon) deplored the 'unwise and violent' theological attacks on the amiable sickly squire. They were opposed on most things except the parish, and Innes had some inkling of his friend's contempt for Christianity. And yet, he smiled, 'How nicely things would go on if other folk were like Darwin and Brodie Innes.'[28]

What Charles actually believed was of 'no consequence to any one but myself.' Outside Down House, only Eras and a few intimates knew. Only *The Index* in America carried his endorsement of a creed. But in early 1879 he did open up a little more as he turned his hand to family history.

It began with a glowing essay on his grandfather Erasmus. This appeared in the German scientific periodical *Kosmos* as a seventieth-birthday tribute to Charles. In March he arranged with the author, Ernst Krause, for it to be translated in book form, enabling him to add a biographical preface. Setting his grandfather's record straight was urgent now, with the appearance of Samuel Butler's wretched *Evolution Old and New* – which elevated old Erasmus to the head of the Darwinian pantheon and threw out the *Origin* as an 'intellectual sleight-of-hand.' Charles sent Butler's book to Krause, urging him not to 'expend much powder and shot' on it, as Butler knew no science.

He set into the biography with gusto. Rummaging through dusty letters and manuscripts, he was almost 'having communion with the dead.' By May old Erasmus had materialized on his side. Not that his science was much use, too wildly theoretical. But they shared a larger social and evolutionary world view. Erasmus was a humanitarian liberal, devoted to educational reform and technological advance. His intellectual and moral qualities were outstanding, and he too was traduced as a radical atheist. It was reassuring.[29]

Fortified, Charles returned to his own biography, which had lain fallow for three years. He scribbled fond notes about his father: his prodigious powers of observation and memory, and his marvellous business sense. He 'formed a theory for almost everything,' though his mind was not strictly scientific; and his sympathy and sagacity made him a moral beacon for his sons. Charles recalled especially his father's ways with women, how he handled their emotions, and his premarital advice about concealing religious doubts – good advice as it turned out. Too often wives agonized over the salvation of their freethinking husbands, causing them to suffer in turn.

Charles saw no salvation and suffered for it. Now he absolved himself on paper. As one with 'no assured and ever present belief in the existence of a personal God or of a future existence with retribution and reward,' he had not lived in fear of divine wrath. Instead he had followed his inherited 'social instincts' with a clear conscience. A freethinking Darwin ancestry had left him with neither moral obliquity nor guilt. 'I feel no remorse from having committed any great sin,' he assured Emma and the family. 'I believe that I have acted rightly in steadily following and devoting my life to science.'

As he wrote, another prying letter came. Did he believe in God? Were theism and evolution compatible? He replied that a man undoubtedly can be 'an ardent Theist & an evolutionist,' look at Charles Kingsley and Asa Gray. For himself, he had 'never been an atheist in the sense of denying the existence of a God,' but he still felt profoundly uncertain. If he had to wear a label, Huxley's suited better. 'I think that generally (& more & more as I grow older), but not always, that an agnostic would be the most correct description of my state of mind.'[30] Even if, in his clear-headed confusion, he was agnostic about his agnosticism on occasions, in ten years it had become the respectable thing.

Biography was not his *forte*. The sketch of his grandfather was hard enough. It was terminally boring, and he mutilated proofs all summer. It was worse than that, Henrietta said, too long and too frank. While Krause tinkered with the German text, she snipped at her father's, removing the religiously *risqué*. John Murray was the only one satisfied with the end-product, and he offered to issue 1000 copies of

Erasmus Darwin on spec and split the profits. Charles, feeling a 'perfect fool' for taking on the job, swore 'never again' to be 'tempted out of my proper work.'[31]

42

Down Among the Worms

HE WAS TIRING faster now and resigned to it, though still working hard at shoots and roots for several hours a day. 'I have nothing else to do,' he sighed to his old *Beagle* shipmate Admiral Sulivan, 'and whether one is worn out a year or two sooner or later signifies but little.' Emma, spry as ever, kept an eye on him. Without her supervision he would work himself to death.

She dragged him to Dorking for a weekend in June 1879 and in August joined forces with the Litchfields to haul him to the Lake District for a month.[1] Having recovered his 'horrid sinking feeling' at leaving home, Charles enjoyed himself. They made their headquarters at the Waterhead Hotel on Coniston Water, and took trips to Furness Abbey and Grasmere. Several times they crossed the lake to meet Litchfield's friend from the Working Men's College, John Ruskin.

Ruskin had just retired from the Slade Professorship at Oxford and settled into Brantwood Cottage, to concentrate on his art. Darwinism was nonsense to him, so much gratuitous conflict, but he greeted 'Sir Charles' with politeness and gave him a tour of the Turners in his bedroom. Darwin did his best to screw up interest. He could make 'absolutely nothing of what Ruskin saw' in the paintings, although he disliked a Titian, for which his host was 'very glad.' Then the bedroom conversation turned delicately to sexual selection, with talk of peacocks, primates, and courtship. When the party left Ruskin chased them with some fine studies of peacock's feathers, hardly appreciating how sick the furore about such objects made his guest. The prickliness cut both ways. Ruskin's sexual difficulties – his failure to consummate his marriage after the appalling discovery that his young bride had pubic hair – rather flavour his observation that

Darwin had a 'deep & tender interest' in the 'brightly coloured hinder half of certain monkeys.' He was right, Darwin laughed on hearing it.[2]

Haeckel came to Downe when they returned and wore Darwin out by '*roaring*' for an hour about the freedom of science. Even if foppish Litchfield found 'something pleasant in his . . . exuberant muscularity,' Emma was not so sure. Charles retreated to his blessedly silent plants. He hired another gardener, and fretted over the Belfast potato trials, on which he had lavished £100 the previous year. The breeder was now in 'much distress,' with all his work in jeopardy. Maybe the Board of Trade would come up with money to help feed the Irish? He approached the Permanent Secretary, 'Theta' Farrer – Effie Wedgwood's husband – but to no avail. It was 'very difficult for Ministers to decide what to do in such cases,' Theta prevaricated; they were always meeting 'cavillers in the H[ouse]. of Commons.' Charles fumed at the way 'politicians waste their time squabbling and neglect doing any good.'[3]

In truth, Farrer's thoughts were elsewhere. With only one daughter (from his first marriage) he was determined to see her well matched. Ida had fallen for Horace, the youngest and feeblest of the Darwin boys. He had a mechanical bent but no career, and was still kicking around machine shops, living on an allowance. His prospects looked dismal, or so Theta had whispered loudly from the time Horace and Ida first mooted an engagement. Ida was too good for him. Her father, a worldly man – Eton, Balliol, Lincoln's Inn – had hoped for a banker or barrister. A sickly, unsuccessful Darwin would not do.

Emma and Charles felt 'terrible,' the Hensleighs were embarrassed, and the besotted couple adamant. But they had their way and before Christmas the marriage settlement was reached. Darwin assured Farrer that his son would inherit enough to retire on comfortably, and he gave Horace £5000 of railway stock as proof. The wedding took place on 3 January 1880 at St Mary's, Bryanston Square, in London, next door to the Litchfields. But the relations remained frosty, and at the reception the families were still not speaking to one another.[4]

More petty tempests were in store. Frank, now serving on the Downe school committee, was embroiled in a bid to oust Ffinden as chairman. The vicar did not go quietly. As the '*legally* constituted head' of the parish, Frank heard, he would not deign to serve under another's authority. Nor was it 'a becoming part of a Priest's Office "to serve tables," if you can understand what I mean as a High Churchman.' Democracy was too much for Ffinden, and he tendered his resignation from the committee. For spite, he sent the note to Frank's father.[5] This grated, but Emma and Bessy had long worshipped at the neighbouring parish of Keston.

Priests might lie like strangled snakes beside the cradle of Hercules, but new enemies were rising as if sown from dragon's teeth. Apostates worried Darwin most, those disciples-turned-enemies: Mivart, and now Samuel Butler. And it did not help to imagine these ostracized evolutionists hobnobbing together. 'Have you read Butler's "*Evolution Old & New*"?' Mivart asked Owen. 'There is method in his madness & it will I think help to burst the inflated bubble of "Natural Selection".'[6] Owen, Mivart, and Butler now constituted the demonic Trinity.

Samuel Butler was the grandson of Darwin's old Shrewsbury headmaster. His father had been at Cambridge with Darwin, preparing for holy orders, and had joined his beetling expeditions. Destined himself for the Church, Butler had read the *Origin* and become a devout Darwinian and an unbeliever. His anonymous novels, *Erewhon*, an anti-Christian satire, and *The Fair Haven*, a sly attack on the Resurrection, had won Darwin's praise. He had visited Downe twice, dined with Charles and Eras in London, and even helped with illustrations for the *Expression* book. But Mivart's dissenting *Genesis of Species* left him disillusioned with natural selection, and the materialists' exploitation alienated him further: 'It is not the bishops and archbishops I am afraid of,' Butler admitted. 'Men like Huxley and Tyndall are my natural enemies.' He re-read the *Origin* and moved rapidly away, convinced that Darwin had humbugged the world by slighting his evolutionary predecessors, whose cause he espoused in *Evolution Old and New*. It was to set the record straight, to place Dr Erasmus Darwin over his degenerate grandson, to propose that mind is the moving force in nature, not matter. Life evolves consciously through changing habits, he insisted, not mechanically through natural selection.[7]

Butler was primed to take *Erasmus Darwin* personally. And not surprisingly; in his preface Darwin vouched for the accuracy of the translation of Krause's article. He indicated that it had come out in German *before* publication of *Evolution Old and New*. But Butler pointed to passages in translation that could only have been written *after* his book – including a dismissal of attempts to rehabilitate Erasmus as showing 'a weakness of thought and a mental anachronism which no one can envy.' Darwin admitted that Krause had revised his German text before translation, 'so common a practice' that it had not seemed worth mentioning. Butler took this to mean that the affront had been deliberate. He protested to the *Athenaeum* (once the home of vitriolic anti-Darwinism) that Darwin had disguised a condemnation of *Evolution Old and New*, putting the words into the mouth of an 'unbiassed' third party.[8]

Emma fulminated at Butler's 'odious spiteful letter.' Charles hated it. Ignorant theological attacks he could bear, but to be accused of 'duplicity and falsehood' before the literary world was too much. He would as soon be known as an atheist or neo-Malthusian. It sent him into a tailspin of tortured self-acquittal. For a week in February he drafted replies, posting them to the family for advice. Nobody liked the first, opinion was divided on the second, and Litchfield's legal advice was to forget Butler altogether. It would bring about '*exactly* the result he most wants . . . a "Butler-Darwin affaire" as the French w[oul]d say.' Huxley agreed, suspecting that Mivart had 'bitten him and given him Darwinophobia.' 'Its a horrid disease and I would kill any son of a [bitch] I found running loose with it.'

Suffocation by silence was the answer. Darwin took Huxley's advice, thankful to be spared the agony of self-defence. 'I feel like a man condemned to be hung who has just got a reprieve,' he exhaled wearily. Butler naturally felt like one of his pre-Darwinian evolutionists, deliberately ignored. To him Darwin's silence was a tacit admission of guilt.[9]

Spring 1880 brought a sad reminder that a generation was passing. Word came of Josiah's death. Emma's brother was eighty-five. No man with a 'sweeter disposition' ever lived, Charles consoled Hensleigh. Emma missed her brother's funeral because Charles was feeling under the weather. He was not well enough to see Fox buried either. They had drifted apart over the decades, but were sustained by vivid memories. Charles looked up from his *Movement in Plants* manuscript, closed his eyes, and travelled back fifty years. He pictured Fox's 'bright face, so full of intelligence,' at their breakfasts in Christ's – he could even make out his cousin's voice 'as clearly as if he were present' in the study.[10]

Time had to be passing for Huxley to title his Royal Institution talk 'The Coming of Age of the Origin of Species.' Had twenty-one years passed since the *Origin*'s publication? Charles thought that the title referred to 'the maturity of the subject' until Emma tipped him off. Of course Huxley was presenting the key of science's door to Darwin. It was propaganda, and as such a fair piece of distortion, which argued that 'great and sudden physical revolutions, wholesale creations and extinctions' had been the order of the day in 1859 before the *Origin*. (They had not; Owen had advanced the world dramatically by the 1850s with his uniform continuous creation.) It was the bulldog at his best. Charles read the reports on holiday at Abinger with the Farrers. With the families speaking to one another again, he chortled to Theta about the press coverage. Then he read the text. It was a distortion in more insidious ways. His great leading idea – natural selection – the theory that he had given half his life to, was not even mentioned.

Huxley had always been non-committal about selection. Now Mivart and other critics were winning. It was ignominiously jettisoned, an impediment to a belief in the actual 'fact of evolution.' The bulldog's tail should have been between his legs. Darwin admitted that he sometimes saw natural selection 'of quite subordinate importance.' At others, when he discovered the survival-value of some 'useless' part of a plant, he knew that it was all-pervasive. But never for a moment had he doubted that his 'deity "Natural Selection"' existed at all. He was sad that true believers were so few. He had turned the world to evolution, and practically no one to natural selection, not even his champions.[11]

Much the best news in April was the Tories' crushing defeat after Gladstone's brilliant campaign. At seventy Gladstone launched his second ministry as a moral crusade; the Union Jack flew for all humanity, in Egypt and the Transvaal, in Ireland and the Middle East. 'Mercy and profits had met together, economy and peace had kissed.' Emma and Charles were ecstatic, despite the boys' waywardness. Frank 'hardly cares,' Emma shrugged. 'George cares a little the wrong way,' and the Litchfields' opinions were 'diametrically opposite.' But she and Charles had the country behind them and Aunt Elizabeth in the village shared their 'mental champagne.' Charles, buoyed by the Liberal tide, sent a large subscription to Abbot's 'excellent Journal' *The Index*, 'most heartily' wishing him success in his 'admirable endeavours in the good cause of truth.'[12] 'Free religion' was still the Darwin creed.

But Liberalism had limits. On the extreme edge of the party Bradlaugh was finally elected MP for Northampton. After losing the Knowlton trial, his mastery of legal procedure kept him and Besant out of prison, but it had done nothing to redeem his reputation. The Christian nation now faced the prospect of an avowed atheist and convicted purveyor of obscenity swearing on the Bible in order to take his seat in the House of Commons. MPs erupted at the outrage. Every trick of parliamentary procedure was used to exclude Bradlaugh. He was forbidden to take the oath of allegiance, which referred to God, and prevented from 'affirming' like Quakers. Atheists were by nature immoral; their word meant nothing, the Commons could not accommodate them. Northampton would have to vote again – responsibly.

By the end of May atheism was a burning political issue. Select committees were smouldering, the press fanned the flames, and 'Bradlaugh' was a household word. Secularists pitched into the fray. Edward Aveling, a young anatomy lecturer and popularizer of evolution, had joined up with Besant (in more ways than one, though both were married) and they stumped the country, haranguing crowds about Christian hypocrisy and the curtailment of civil liberties. Aveling wrote for Bradlaugh's paper, the *National Reformer*. In fact he was running a series on 'Darwin and His Works' when the parliamentary struggle began, a continuation of articles he had published in a student magazine two years before. Darwin had written to thank Aveling for these first offerings and asked to see future instalments.[13]

That was two years earlier. Now Darwin was worried that his letter to the newly-prominent Aveling would return to haunt him – scruffy infidels of dubious morality were not above printing private correspondence. For a gentleman of the parish, public association with these reprobates was intolerable. He was taking no risks. He packed *Movement in Plants* off to Murray and went to William and Sara's in Southampton at the beginning of June. He talked with William about the freethought *Index*, supposedly safe from prying English eyes in America. They both read it avidly but agreed that after nine years – with the English papers now kicking up a pother about atheism – Charles's weekly endorsement of Abbot's *Truths for the Times* should be scrubbed. It could be appropriated by these English headline-grabbers and republished in Britain. Charles, having just sent Abbot a generous subscription, found it a bit embarrassing, so William took on the task. He posted a letter, larded with cordiality, but he blundered in stating that 'My Father . . . had no intention that his words should be used for this purpose.' The words had of course been sent expressly as advertising copy – Abbot held the proof.[14] But Abbot complied anyway.

At Downe work was piling up, but Charles liked it that way. Worms were his chief occupation again, and he co-opted the family, even having Theta send soil samples from Abinger's Roman ruins to make up for his mud-slinging. He was inundated in requests for advice, and loans, and audiences. It was nothing to donate £25 to a Birmingham committee as a prize to encourage local research, or welcome the Lewisham and Blackheath Scientific Association to Down House. But his work came first, Emma made sure of it. After forty years his priorities had become her own, and 'if it was a condition of his living, that he sh[oul]d do no work, she was willing for him to die.'[15]

By August he needed a break, and Horace and Ida, settled in Cambridge, invited them. For the old man the trip was daunting. With no command performance to galvanize him, no silk gown in store, he started niggling about the seventy-mile ride. A panic started at the prospect of negotiating London's tumultuous train stations. So Emma planned a piece of unadulterated luxury. She and the boys booked a special railway carriage for him to travel in style. Here he could remain with his entourage, without changing, like the Queen on her sweeps through the country. On the day, he royally got on at Bromley, six miles away, and at London's Victoria Station his carriage was shunted across town to the Cambridge line out of King's Cross. They sat in plush first-class comfort, watching the slums and gasometers pass by. So unfamiliar now was Emma with the city that she even mistook 'some small church' for St Paul's Cathedral.

The trip was set off by a leisurely week in Cambridge, being shown the latest sights by Horace and his 'charming wife.' Emma heard the organ at Trinity Chapel and had a private demonstration of the stops. Charles took her arm-in-arm through the courts of St John's to admire the gothic 'grandeur' of King's College Chapel, which reminded him disgracefully of old Herbert and the Gluttons. Cambridge still played hard, drank long, and dodged the Proctors – the new women's colleges notwithstanding. Everywhere Charles gazed wistfully on 'scenes of my early life,' half-suspecting that this would be his last view.

At home in September he polished off the proofs of *Movement in Plants*, a gargantuan job. With 600 pages and 196 wood-cuts, it was his largest botany book and, he suspected, as dull as ditchwater. 'I am turned into a sort of machine for observing facts & grinding out conclusions,' he was heard to sigh. Never mind, he arranged for a German translation and set into the next book, on the homely earthworm. Meanwhile the correspondence mounted – facts to file, honours to acknowledge, invitations to refuse – and he dashed off a half-dozen replies most afternoons, seated in a huge horse-hair chair by the fire.[16]

On 13 October the letter he feared arrived, Aveling's. He had not forgotten Darwin's encouragement. Aveling was collecting his evolution articles from the *National Reformer* into a book and asked permission to dedicate it to Darwin. It was to appear in the 'International Library of Science and Freethought' under the editorship of 'my friends Mrs. Annie Besant and Charles Bradlaugh, M.P.' Enclosed was Besant's translation of a pamphlet by the German physician Ludwig Büchner (whose fierce materialist literature was already on Darwin's shelves), with an advert explaining that the aim of the Library was to 'spread heresy' among the English 'reading masses.'

Heresy was nothing new. The *Origin* and *Descent* had spread it politely for years. What set off a tremor was the company he would be keeping. He replied by return, a four-page letter marked conspicuously 'Private.' No, he would not permit the dedication, 'though I thank you for the intended honour.' It would imply 'to a certain extent my approval of the general publication,' the International Library – 'about which I know nothing,' Darwin dissembled, knowing the editors full well.

> Moreover though I am a strong advocate for free thought on all subjects, yet it appears to me (whether rightly or wrongly) that direct arguments against christianity & theism produce hardly any effect on the public; & freedom of thought is best promoted by the gradual illumination of men's minds, which follow[s] from the advance of science. It has, therefore, been always my object to avoid writing on religion, & I have confined myself to science. I may, however, have been unduly biassed by the pain which it would give some members of my family, if I aided in any way direct attacks on religion.

Here spoke one who had been hand in glove with Christians all his life, one whose entire well-being depended on his devout wife and daughters. 'Gradual illumination' had always been his luxury, religious reticence his practice. Now even Aveling's proofs were too hot to handle. 'I am old & have very little strength, & looking over proof-sheets (as I know by present experience) fatigues me much.' He was still his own man.[17]

That autumn life began closing in as he saw his relatives failing. Sister Caroline at Leith Hill was plagued by heart trouble and crippled with arthritis. She welcomed him and Emma for a visit but found it difficult to cope. Fanny Wedgwood too had a heart condition, although when they visited Ras she still came trundling down Queen Anne Street in a bath chair to hold his hand at tea. Ras himself was poorly. His effete existence had gone on too long. Time and opium had ravaged him and he was in constant pain, scarcely able to leave home. Emma's last sister, the tiny hunchback Elizabeth, also kept indoors, blind and mostly bedridden. Her bent figure, tottering around on a stick, had been a fixture in Downe for a dozen years, but now she lay in Trowmer Lodge, wizened and forlorn, her servants driving off the 'beggars and imposters' who sought to tap her Wedgwood wealth. She died on Sunday, 7 November, aged eighty-five. A small family circle gathered in the churchyard to hear the Revd Ffinden read the burial service. Emma took it calmly, feeling 'nothing but joy' at Elizabeth's release.

Natural selection continued under a barrage of criticism, and Mivart's ghost hovered about the zoological report of the government's latest scientific circumnavigation, conducted by Sir Wyville Thomson. Thomson, knighted for his efforts aboard HMS *Challenger* (an honour that Darwin would have loved), made a point of slighting 'the theory which refers the evolution of species to extreme variation guided only by natural selection.' Darwin was wounded, and let it show. 'Can Sir Wyville Thomson name any one who has said that the evolution of species depends only on natural selection?' he seethed in a letter to *Nature*. No one had paraded such a plethora of additional causes as himself in the *Variation of Animals*, including 'the effects of the use and disuse of parts' and of the 'direct action of external conditions.' Evolution was a multi-causal affair; he had admitted it. These crude caricatures would not do. Thomson's was 'a standard of criticism not uncommonly reached by theologians and metaphysicians, when they write on scientific subjects.' Darwin was tempted to use 'irreverent language,' and only Huxley stopped him swearing.[18]

Through the carping and cavilling Darwin continued to shower patronage. Wallace was still out of a job, his meagre investments drying up in the depression, and he had moved to Croydon to find a day school for his two children. On a fixed income of about £60 a year with tiny supplements from his writing, he had barely enough to support his family 'in the most economical way.' It was a source of 'ever-increasing anxiety,' and some embarrassment to a naturalist in his fifties. A year earlier, when the superintendency of Epping Forest eluded him, despite support from Darwin, Hooker, and Lubbock, he had become so depressed that his friend Arabella Buckley, Lyell's old secretary, pleaded for him. She asked Darwin whether some 'modest work' might not be found.

Darwin thought of a Crown pension, in recognition of Wallace's services to natural history. Hooker pooh-poohed it. Wallace had 'lost

caste terribly,' both for his spiritualism and for dishonourably pocket-
ing a bet won from a rich flat-earth fanatic for proving that the
planet was a globe. (Litigation over the case had dragged on for a
decade, costing Wallace the entire £500 and more.) Anyway, Hooker
jabbed, 'a man not in absolute poverty has little chance,' and 'Wallace's claim is not that he is in need, so much as that he can't find
employment.' Darwin caved in – Wallace's misdemeanours had 'never
once' crossed his mind – and he informed Buckley it was hopeless.[19]

He may have cringed at Wallace's credulity and 'quite doubted' his
scientific sanity – indeed, Romanes had returned from his first visit
to Wallace laughing that he was 'rather queer on . . . astrology' – but
Darwin never forgot Wallace's magnanimity over natural selection.
Now, in November, there was a further reason to reopen the pension
file. Wallace's 'best book' to date, *Island Life*, was acclaimed by the
critics. The incongruity struck Hooker: 'that such a man should be a
Spiritualist is more wonderful than all the movements of all the
plants.' Hooker thought the book 'splendid,' as well he might, for it
was dedicated to him. Darwin seized the moment. He knew that
Lubbock was on his side, another admirer of Wallace's 'characteristic
unselfishness;' he won Huxley over and they twisted Hooker's arm.
Huxley took the case to fellow X Clubber, William Spottiswoode,
President of the Royal Society, who drafted a request to Gladstone.
Having entertained Gladstone at Downe, Darwin even anticipated
returning the honour. He had 'seldom wished for anything so much'
as the pension to be granted and would 'gladly come to London' and
present the petition in person at 10 Downing Street.[20]

He composed his own moving testimonial, pointing up Wallace's
'love of natural history,' his jobless situation, failed investments,
pitiful return on his publications, and his weak health caused by
'tropical exposure.' (And there, but for the grace of God and a family
fortune, went Charles.) The final draft was ready before Christmas,
and he collected signatures feverishly. Emma saw him 'so full of
Wallace's affair [that] he has no time for his own,' referring to his
worm book. The memorial had to reach Gladstone before Parliament
reopened in the new year. While Emma did the annual accounts over
the holidays, Charles enlisted his old sparring partner on the 'beauty'
question, the Duke of Argyll, ex-Secretary of State for India. His
Grace urged the Prime Minister to assent, and the memorial reached
the Grand Old Man in the first week of January 1881. Twelve
Darwinians good and true had signed.

Before the Queen's Speech on the 6th, Gladstone wrote to Darwin
that he would recommend Wallace for a modest civil list pension of

£200 a year, backdated six months. An overjoyed Darwin relayed the news to Wallace on his fifty-eighth birthday, and tutored him in the proprieties of returning thanks.

As Wallace received his £200, Emma finished the family accounts, allowing Charles to distribute the surplus from the year's £8000 investment income to the children.[21]

Still old controversies returned to haunt him. Butler had been busy rewriting history, like Huxley, only portraying himself and other evolutionists as the victims of a Darwinian conspiracy. His *Unconscious Memory* repeated the charges against Darwin – 'duplicity and falsehood' – and compounded the injury by printing their private correspondence about old Erasmus's biography.

Darwin writhed while the family wrangled. The boys wanted an explanatory slip inserted in the unsold copies of *Erasmus Darwin* stating that the German text had been altered in translation. (They now realized that Krause had actually borrowed whole passages from Butler.) But the Litchfields cautioned silence. Their friend Leslie Stephen, editor of the *Cornhill Magazine*, an uncassocked clergyman who had lost his faith as a result of the *Origin* and now 'admired Darwin as a god,' arbitrated and settled the matter: silence was the very 'slap in the face' that Butler deserved. But one 'scientific son' was not bound by the family's compunctions. Romanes, knowing Darwin's feelings, administered a loud slap in public. Now living with a monkey in his nursery, he was an authority on lesser intelligences. Butler was a 'psychological curiosity' to Darwin, but to Romanes he was a 'lunatic beneath all contempt – an object of pity were it not for his vein of malice.' 'Punishment' was due, and he dished it out in *Nature*, arraigning Butler as a character assassin.[22]

Charles returned to more dignified subjects, worms and pigs, which were easier to deal with. Swine disease was rife around the village and a strict quarantine in force. Snowed in at Downe, he had to issue a magistrate's order daily just to allow farmers to move their animals across the road. He felt the burden of public responsiblity more than ever as the days ticked by. 'My life is as regular & monotonous as a clock,' he droned to Kovalevsky, thanking him for a huge box of Russian tea. 'I make sure, but wofully [sic] slow progress, with my new book.'[23]

The twilight years brought back strange memories. Late in February Charles went to town with Emma, staying with the Litchfields. Charles had heard from Sarah, one of the Owens of his Woodhouse youth, that her sister Fanny was living in town, now seventy and a widow. He hoped for a short reunion, maybe their last. More august first-time visits were arranged on this trip. He called on the Duke of Argyll, a critic for so many years. The butler ushered him into Argyll House where the Duke welcomed him warmly and accepted his heartfelt thanks for assisting Wallace. There were political talking-points aplenty – the conflict in the Transvaal, land reform in Ireland, Gladstone's health after a fall in Downing Street – and they had a long and 'awfully friendly' discussion. The Duke was 'not at all cocky,' as Darwin had feared, but inevitably the talk swung to religion.

Sitting before Argyll was the man who had convulsed English science, who had made beasts of men and taken Mind out of nature. Argyll, like everyone, wanted to know what the sage of Downe really believed. He harked back a dozen years, picking up the threads of tattered debates. Orchids and their wonderful design: did Darwin really suppose them a chance evolution? Surely now, Argyll insinuated, it was 'impossible to look at these without seeing that they were the effect and the expression of Mind'? Darwin looked at him 'very hard' before replying. Yes, he could see how this view might have 'overwhelming force.'[24] But, he shook his head gravely, he could no longer accept it.

Back at Downe Darwin did see a million individual minds at work – or, to be precise, 53,767 per acre. Worms were clever creatures, how so he was beginning to find out. He experimented indoors, in the new billiard room, now turned into his study to make more space. Worms littered it, triturating through earth in glass-covered pots. Darwin stumbled around at night and flashed lights at them – candles, paraffin lamps, and even lanterns with red and blue slides. Only an intense beam brought a reflex response, when they bolted – 'like a rabbit' lisped Bernard – into their burrows. Heat made little difference, even a red-hot poker held near by. Nor were they sensitive to sound. Bernard blew a whistle, Frank played his bassoon, Emma performed on the piano, and Bessy shouted, but no worms were roused. Touch was different – a puff of breath sent them into headlong retreat. Charles tested for their sense of smell by exhaling gently into the pots while chewing tobacco or sucking on scented cotton wool. Their culinary sense was assessed and their preferences determined – green to red cabbage, celery to both of these, and raw carrots above all.

What struck him most was their mentality. They seemed to 'enjoy the pleasure of eating,' judging from their 'eagerness for certain kinds of food,' and their sexual passion was 'strong enough to overcome

. . . their dread of light.' He even found 'a trace of social feeling,' for they tolerated 'crawling over each other's bodies' and touching. He observed how they dragged leaves into their burrows. The habit was instinctive, but what of the technique? All sorts of leaves were tried, and finally triangular slips of stiff paper. Digging the objects out of the burrows, he discovered that the great majority had been pulled in the easiest way, by their narrower end or apex. It was clearly not a trial-and-error learning process. Worms somehow acquired a 'notion, however rude, of the shape of an object,' probably by 'touching it in many places' with their bodies. This heightened sense was like that of 'a man . . . born blind and deaf.' It enabled them to solve geometrical problems. Intelligence was there.[25]

Not quite Argyll's notion of supramundane intelligence, but then more earthy matters had preoccupied Darwin for fifty years. He retired to write the last chapters of *The Formation of Vegetable Mould through the Action of Worms*. It would be 'a small book of little moment,' he told Victor Carus in mid-March, and certainly his last. 'I have little strength & feel very old.'

As he finished, the vivisection debate boiled up again and he fired off letters to *The Times*. Cobbe was in the thick of it, as he knew women always were. They committed a 'crime against mankind' by retarding the 'progress of physiology.' They were too soft on suffering, too squeamish about death. Death now entered his thoughts as he stared into his pots of dirt. The old worm was turning as he contemplated the endless sculpting of the earth's surface by myriad slimy, semi-intelligent beings. Worms buried and preserved our past, like Theta's ruins at Abinger. They ploughed farmers' fields, as Uncle Jos first mooted at Maer. We 'ought to be grateful' to them. And they bore into the earth 'five or six feet,' even 'here at Down,' at which depth he expected to be consumed soon.[26]

Darwin packed the manuscript up on the weekend before Easter and found himself at a loose end. He had no 'heart or strength . . . to begin any investigation lasting for years,' which was all he really enjoyed. 'Never happy except when at work,' he was facing his first fortnight in a quarter-century without a manuscript to complete.

Then he remembered his autobiography. With Ida and Horace expecting a baby there was another reason to leave a good record. After Easter he picked up the pieces, inserting his notes about his father and reworking the passages on religion. He thought of Emma and their religious differences. Her anxiety lest they should not 'belong to each other forever' had made him suffer, just as the

Doctor had predicted, and now he was sorry. At the end he slipped in a coded reminder to Emma – a date. Beside the paragraph with his father's advice about concealing doubts he jotted, 'copied out Ap[ri]l 22, 1881.'[27]

It was the Friday of Easter week, thirty years to the day since Annie was laid in the Priory Churchyard at Malvern. Whenever he pictured her beaming face, 'her sparkling eyes & brindled smiles,' her 'dear lips' and kisses, her 'crying bitterly . . . on parting with Emma,' his emotions would overflow.[28] Now, looking over his autobiography for the last time, he had her daguerreotype beside him. He read on – of Emma, his 'wise adviser and cheerful comforter,' of her 'beautiful letter' to him after their marriage, of their grief, and Annie's 'sweet ways.' He had written these words as if he were 'a dead man . . . looking back.' Emma would be left behind, still longing for a reunion. He was helpless to reassure her, to ease her pain.

Tears were flowing again – tears at the thought of their parting, the tears that Annie had shed, kissing her mother goodbye before going to die. He reached for Emma's beautiful old letter, preserved with the other mementos beside his manuscript. He read again of her fears for him, and her undying love. Dwelling a moment on Annie's face, he scratched miserably at the bottom, 'When I am dead, know that many times, I have kissed & cryed over this.'[29] It was the only comfort that he could give.

43

The Final Experiment

HIS REASON FOR LIVING was gone. Without a fresh mountain of facts to conquer, without a new experimental odyssey to embark on, nothing seemed worthwhile. One look at the proofs of *Worms* and he passed the pile to Frank, unable to face the revisions. He turned down Gladstone's invitation to become a Trustee of the British Museum. He listened to Hans Richter at Emma's piano, but even the visiting conductor of the Vienna Opera, who had taken London by storm, only roused him for an hour. Charles gritted his teeth and pulled up plants to look at the cell-structure of their roots. It was paltry work compared to barnacles, species, and flowers but it helped fend off despondency.

At the start of June Emma and the Litchfields took him to the Lake District. With Bernard and William along, it should have been a happy family time, cosy in a big house on Ullswater. But Charles brought his troubles. Bernard's cavorting and the lakeside strolls with Emma did little good, nor the stunning scenery. The weather was bitter, the sky 'like lead,' and the lake 'as black as ink.' An attempt to climb left spots before his eyes; almost fainting, he stumbled back down and they called a doctor. He diagnosed angina, called his heart condition 'precarious,' and ordered relaxation, not mountain climbing. 'Idleness is downright misery to me,' Darwin groaned to Hooker. 'I cannot forget my discomfort for an hour' and 'must look forward to Down graveyard as the sweetest place on earth.'[1]

The unlikeliest 400-page tome perked him up, *The Creed of Science*, by the Irish philosopher William Graham. Housebound, he read it from cover to cover and puffed it to Romanes. Graham was reassuring, adamant that many traditional beliefs – in God, free will,

652

morals, and immortality – could survive the fad for materialism. Darwin doubted many of Graham's conclusions, though he was swayed by one, telling him, 'You have expressed my inward conviction . . . that the Universe is not the result of chance.' But even on this a 'horrid doubt' crept back in, as it always did. What value any such belief if the mind has evolved? 'Would any one trust in the convictions of a monkey's mind, if there are any convictions' in it? The issue was insoluble, and there he took his stand.

Less welcome was Graham's down-playing of natural selection as the engine of social progress. Darwin still fought on this score. What a struggle had gone on between Spaniards and South American Indians, between English settlers and Australian Aborigines, between colonists and the colonized everywhere. 'Remember what risk the nations of Europe ran, not so many centuries ago of being overwhelmed by the Turks, and how ridiculous such an idea now is! The more civilized so-called Caucasian races have beaten the Turkish hollow in the struggle for existence.' Packing for home, he assured Graham that the elimination of 'lower races' by 'higher civilized races' was inevitable as the Malthusian struggle pushed mankind onward.[2]

At Downe a letter from Wallace showed that he too would remain a social missionary to the end, although a world separated them now. He was promoting the American Henry George's socialist tract *Progress and Poverty*. 'It is the most startling novel and original book of the last twenty years,' he enthused to Darwin; its impact would probably be 'equal to that made by Adam Smith a century ago.' Wallace, President of the Land Nationalization Society, was prepared for George's remedy for chronic poverty and unequal wealth – 'make land common property.' The 'ultimate defence' of private land, the notion of inevitable struggle, was wrong, and the belief that 'some have a better right to existence than others' immoral. Malthus might apply to animals, but not to people. Wallace remained at a political distance. An abyss stood between him and Darwin, as it really had that fateful day in 1858 when his Ternate letter arrived.

Squire Darwin, the Lincolnshire landlord, parried him politely, but refused to be censured and complained that such books had 'a disastrous effect' on his mind. Of course 'something ought to be done' about land and poverty, but he hoped that Wallace would not 'turn renegade to natural history.' The two men, seemingly so close, had spent a lifetime missing one another's point. Darwin was past caring, an absent-minded old naturalist who thoughtlessly admitted to the astute-minded old socialist, 'I have everything to make me happy and contented.'[3]

It was a time of tranquil recollection, abetted by a stable stomach. 'Pleasant memories of long past days,' he told Hooker, when they had 'many a discussion and . . . a good fight.' Hooker was pushing on with the world's plants, still not too proud to lean on his oldest colleague, craving his criticism 'as your pupil.' Darwin remained a sounding board, able to reel off facts, pick holes, and 'pour out my idle thoughts.' They had mellowed, but neither had lost his edge. 'As iron sharpeneth iron,' they had forged the toughest friendship. Hooker, longing to 'throw off the trammels of official life' and retire from Kew, felt for Darwin's misery at having no projects to 'fall back upon.' In his sixties now, Hooker too was facing the end of his useful days and found it 'difficult to resist the pessimist view of creation.' But 'when I look back . . . to the days I have spent in intercourse with you and yours,' he consoled his 'beloved friend,' 'that view takes wings to itself and flies away.'[4]

Darwin's was a twilight contentment, spent not only with his plant roots. With the Litchfields he sat under the limes at Downe and whiled away the summer afternoons. He was in his 'happiest spirits' and chatted 'deliciously' for hours. In the evenings, reclining on the sofa, he asked for Bach and Handel to be played over and over. Romanes would stop by with his wife and new baby, and left the old man as 'grand and good and bright as ever.' But in the small hours, with Emma breathing softly beside him, he felt the rot inside.

Time was running out and of course he worried about his *Worms*. He urged Murray to bring publication forward, even if it meant a loss.[5] The book, forty years in the making, hung over him like a pall.

Honours crowned his dotage. An oil portrait was commissioned by the Linnean Society. He went to London to sit for Huxley's son-in-law John Collier in the first week of August, and by common consent the painting was his 'best likeness.' He stayed with Eras, melancholy and wasted, dwelling on the death of his old companion Thomas Carlyle. On the 3rd Charles dined by special invitation with the Prince of Wales, the Crown Prince of Germany, and eminent physicians at the start of the Seventh International Medical Congress.

As he sipped port with the regal heads that day, the real atheists – those who plagued him, those he had always feared being associated with – were out on the streets, literally. Bradlaugh, re-elected MP for Northampton after his seat was declared vacant, had arrived at the Commons with Aveling and Besant, only to be dragged down the lobby stairs and flung into Palace Yard by a mob of messengers, policemen, and Tory MPs. Darwin walked on eggshells with such people, aware of the prejudices they stirred. A week later Aveling sent his collected articles, *The Student's Darwin*, minus a dedication, with a note apologizing for his atheistic extrapolations. Darwin replied with a cool thanks, admitting that he could hardly stop writers from taking his views 'to a greater length than seems to me safe.'[6]

Erasmus became gravely ill within days. The Litchfields rushed over. So did Fanny Wedgwood, 'the true love of his life,' and she stayed at his bedside until the end. He died quietly on the 26th. A telegram came for Emma, who broke the news to Charles. He had seen Ras dying slowly 'for many years.' He was not 'a happy man,' but always kindhearted, clearheaded, and affectionate. There was no consolation. Indeed, Hooker thought it worse to lose such a lifetime's companion than a brother when young, as he had. No, Darwin replied, missing the point. The death of a child, 'where there is a bright future ahead, causes grief never to be wholly obliterated.' Always he thought of Annie.

The funeral took place in Downe churchyard on 1 September with the whole family present. Ffinden stood aside for Charles and Emma's 85-year-old cousin John Allen Wedgwood, who had married them. It was wretchedly cold; frost dusted the graveside as he performed the last offices in the pale morning light. Charles, looking 'old and ill,' huddled in a long black funeral cloak, a picture of 'sad reverie' as the coffin was lowered. On the marble slab were to be Carlyle's words, 'one of the sincerest, truest, and most modest of men.'[7]

London would never be the same. The house in Queen Anne Street was sold within a week and the contents dispersed quickly. Jolted by the 'heavy loss,' Charles looked to his own death. With half of Ras's estate and his own investments, he was worth over a quarter of a million pounds, an astonished William announced, and this *without* mother's' fortune. Charles redrafted his will. He planned to bequeath £34,000 to each of the girls and £53,000 to the boys. This would leave them 'beyond want' should their health give way. And he thought of others, colleagues who had seen him through the hard times, old friends who had protected him when the *Origin* was published: Hooker and Huxley were to receive £1000 each, 'as a slight memorial of my life long affection and respect.' The will was signed on the 7th, with Jackson the butler as witness. Afterwards there was a subdued party. It was Bernard's fifth birthday.

Charles sent a sad note to Caroline about her half of Eras's estate. Only the two of them remained to recall the childhood days. He enclosed a miniature of their mother. It showed a 'most sweet expression' – if only he could remember her face as vividly as his father's. He did recall her 'black velvet gown' and the 'death scene,' and how they cried together, but little more. Maybe he had forgotten that precious face because no one had been 'able to endure speaking about so dreadful a loss.'[8]

His reverie was interrupted by a cryptic telegram:

> Doctor Ludwig Büchner Germany is in London could he have Honour of interview Wednesday or Thursday at hour most convenient to you leaves Friday Pardon abruptness and Boldness of request.

It threw the family into commotion. The wire was from Aveling, attending the Congress of the International Federation of Freethinkers in the capital. Büchner, President of the Congress, was fifty-seven and renowned; Aveling, thirty and notorious. As a land nationalizer and leader of the workers' movement, Büchner might have descended on Wallace; as a zealous materialist he might have singled out Tyndall. But no, Darwin for German physicians had assumed heroic status, elevated by a crusading *Darwinismus*. Büchner thought that he was greeting a noble ally. The gentle squire of Downe had always feared such a grotesque misunderstanding.

Charles asked Emma: how could he refuse the distinguished Büchner, atheist or no? And Aveling had always treated him civilly. They could come for lunch, stay an hour or so, and that would be that. An appalled Emma, expected to play hostess to notorious atheists, bargained for something better. Since Brodie Innes was near by, shouldn't he be invited too? And she trusted that Herr Büchner 'talks English & will refrain from airing his very strong religious opinions.'[9]

The next afternoon, Thursday the 28th, Jackson ushered everyone to the dining-room table at one o'clock. (A nervous Bessy stayed upstairs.) At the head sat Emma, her serene face haloed in sunlight from an Indian summer day. Opposite her, near the door where the servants passed with steaming platters, was Frank, and beside him Bernard and some friends. Across from the children, in a single imposing row, sat Charles and the atheists. Between Aveling and Emma, as if to shield her, was the white-haired Revd Brodie Innes, amiable and upright. The table became an embodiment of Darwin's life-long dilemma. It was less a lunch, more a last supper; everybody he had loved, everything he had feared, every paradox of his career had come together in a penultimate act. Here, his disapproving evangelical wife, his kindly Tory vicar, his genetically weak children, and his atheistic disciples, Büchner to his right and Aveling on the left, gloating in his physical repulsion, a malevolence emanating from his presence 'as from a diabolical source of being.' In the middle sat the parish naturalist, the failed ordinand, the Devil's Chaplain, damning and defying all expectations.

Some explanation of the parson's presence was evidently required. Mindful of the mixed company, Charles put it masterfully: 'B[rodie] I[nnes] & I have been fast friends for 30 years. We never thoroughly agreed on any subject but once and then we looked hard at each other and thought one of us must be very ill."[10] Nerves were jangled, the situation fraught. It would have been a nightmare, but for the funny turn.

Worms came up during the first course. Aveling expressed pious horror that the author of the *Origin* had stooped to a 'subject so insignificant.' The freethinking missionaries had the great Victorian social problems in mind. Neither expected to find their hero obsessed by the sods rather than sons of the soil. Turning gravely, Charles stated, 'I have been studying their habits for forty years.' For him the humble explained the great, but not in a way that Aveling – soon Marx's 'son-in-law' – could appreciate. After the sweet, which he was forbidden but ate anyway, Charles adjourned with Frank and the guests to the smoking room, his old study, where he had written the *Origin*.

They lit cigarettes and Darwin, completely out of character, pitched in. 'Why do you call yourselves atheists?' In his dotage, forty years since his covert notebook days, he finally dragged the issue into the open. He preferred the word agnostic, he said. '"Agnostic" was but "Atheist" writ respectable,' Aveling replied, searching for common ground, 'and "Atheist" was only "Agnostic" writ aggressive.' But, Darwin retorted, 'Why should you be so aggressive?' Is anything to be gained by forcing new ideas on people? Freethought is 'all very well' for the educated, but are ordinary people 'ripe for it?' Here spoke the comfortable squire, seeking not to disturb the social equilibrium.

The atheists realized this, and Aveling rounded on him. What if 'the revolutionary truths of Natural and Sexual Selection' had been addressed only to 'the judicious few'? What if he had delayed publishing the *Origin* until the time was 'ripe'? Had he 'kept silence,' where would the world be in 1881? Surely 'his own illustrious example' was encouragement to every freethinker to proclaim truth 'abroad from the house-tops'! Still they missed the real Darwin. He *had* buried evolution for twenty years, petrified for his respectability, upholding the paternalist order for a generation before being forced into the open.

Only one subject could they agree on, Christianity. Darwin admitted that it was not 'supported by evidence.' But – he dug at his guests – he had reached this conclusion only slowly. He did not force new ideas even on himself but waited until the time was ripe. In fact, he told them openly, 'I never gave up Christianity until I was forty years of age.'[11] It had taken his father's and Annie's deaths to make him shake off the last shreds. And even then he had refused to speak out, or violently to assail people's faith. He never was a comrade at arms.

Worms appeared in October and sold phenomenally, thousands within weeks. But the 'laughable' number of letters, especially the 'idiotic' ones! Everyone had a query, a theory, a petty observation. Worms were, after all, the commonest of beasts. 'Worn out,' he escaped to Cambridge with Emma, trying to follow orders and relax. They spent a 'happy week' with Horace and Ida, who was shortly to give birth to a boy, baby Erasmus. The trip 'quite set up' Darwin, and he went home ready to section his roots.

He had them standing in an ammonia solution. Did a struggle for existence take place among the cells in this environment? Had the cells clogged with 'effete matter' become 'unfitted,' or was collecting it their job – evidence of a root's 'physiological division of labour'? He was working 'all the harder now,' extending natural selection to the tiniest living entities, rounding out his life's work. Not a second was wasted; his head bobbed from microscope to notes. He fumbled for his spectacles, tugging at his waistcoat with 'violent confoundings.'[12] He lost himself for hours in the ammonia vapour. He even forgot his heart.

Charles and Emma stayed with Henrietta in London before Christmas, their first trip to town since Ras's death. It should have been a time of shopping and presents. Strangely the West End seemed empty, subdued, despite the holiday crush. On the 15th Charles called unannounced at Romanes's house in Cornwall Terrace, opposite Regent's Park. Romanes was not at home. The butler realized that the old gent at the door was having trouble. His face was pale and contorted, he was gripping his chest. Darwin declined an invitation to rest inside and stumbled away to take a cab back to Emma. He crossed over and tottered towards Baker Street, the butler watching apprehensively. As he neared the corner, a few hundred yards off, he staggered and clutched the park railings. He turned and started back as the butler ran towards him, then stopped, turned again, and hailed a cab.

Dr Clark came at Emma's call the next morning, but Charles seemed better and the doctor pronounced him fine. Emma took no chances, keeping him indoors under a watchful eye. Invitations were sent out instead, and a galaxy of scientific stars turned up to pay court – Romanes, Hooker, Huxley, Galton, Burdon Sanderson, and the geologist John Judd. Darwin seemed bright and animated, if 'perhaps a little forced.' Nonetheless, he told Judd, he had 'received his warning.'[13]

It was too easily ignored by a man absorbed in cells. At home he drove himself relentlessly into 1882. He rose early, breakfasted with Bernard, and paced the day with turns around the Sandwalk – fewer now and slower, his iron-tipped walking stick ticking against the flints. In the mornings he wrote technical papers about the effect of ammonium carbonate on roots and leaves. At lunch there were sometimes guests, including Graham, whose religious book he still touted. Afterwards came endless letters – arguing with an American feminist that women are 'inferior intellectually,' sponsoring a translation of August Weismann's *Studies in the Theory of Descent*, promising Hooker £250 a year towards a catalogue of all known plants, the great *Index Kewensis*. Then a cigarette at three while Emma read aloud, another at six before tea, two games of backgammon with perhaps a pinch of snuff and he was ready to retire. The new study was his dressing room. At 10.30 p.m. sharp he blew his nose loudly and mounted the stairs with a 'slow tired step.'[14]

A cough left him 'miserable to a strange degree' in February. Emma prescribed quinine, which helped, but a week after he turned seventy-three he vomited badly and the chest pain returned. It stopped him walking for a while. Through the torment his fascination with nature's revealing oddities never wavered. Someone sent him a water beetle with a bivalve stuck to it. He planned to take it to the British Museum for identification when he was well, welcoming this example of hitch-hiking to his pond-hopping methods of dispersal. For Darwin, old hobby-horses were ridden to death.

On 7 March, hobbling around the Sandwalk, he had another seizure. He was alone and terrified, 400 yards from the house. Somehow he picked his way back, lurching from tree to tree, and collapsed in Emma's arms. Dr Clark confirmed angina and prescribed morphia pills for the pain. Charles froze. He felt condemned, a prisoner of his body, an innocent about to be hanged. He gave in to despair. For days he lay on the drawing-room sofa staring blankly at a display of old family china, 'Henrietta's shrine.' He was terminally ill. His mind reeled, his stomach churned. When he rose the pain came on with 'half-fainting feelings' and Emma rushed to his side. She suggested sitting on the verandah, but he refused. Nor would he dine with the family, preferring to eat in his bedroom alone. Prostrate, he could hardly sleep.[15]

Dr Norman Moore, a young and rising physician, assured him that his heart was only weak. Within days Charles rejoined the evening meals, played backgammon, and caught up with correspondence. The London trip was abandoned; instead he posted the shell-encrusted beetle. And he wrote a note to *Nature* on how beetles disperse their hitch-hikers, flying from pond to pond with bivalves hanging on tight. It rekindled old memories, of Cambridge collecting and his seed-floating experiments. Maybe he had more time. The thought put a spring in his step. One day he forgot himself and walked quickly upstairs, without pain.

Company heartened him too. Leo stopped by with his fiancée on 23 March and seeing how '*very* happy' she was, he chaffed her with gentle jokes. Henrietta arrived, accompanied by her friend Laura Forster (aunt of the young E. M. Forster), herself convalescing after an illness. Laura's rapid recovery made him hopeful. Day after day he described his symptoms to her, pouring out his feelings. It eased Emma's lot, which 'made her more cheerful & bright for him.' The exquisite spring weather helped. Emma and Henrietta coaxed Laura out past the pigeon house to the kitchen garden, then through the gate in the great wall to the orchard. As they sat under the trees in the still sunshine, a blaze of crocuses about them, Charles emerged and eased himself on to the grass. He put his arm around Emma's shoulders and pulled her to him, murmuring, 'Oh Laura, what a miserable man I should be without this dear woman.'[16] An eternal moment, it seemed to augur a return to health.

Charles knew better and could feel the changes, almost hourly. He observed his body with morbid interest, uncertain yet calm. He shuffled from the study one afternoon to lie on the drawing-room sofa, and found Laura seated by the fire. 'The clocks go so dreadfully slowly,' he groaned. 'I have come in here to see if this one gets over the hours any quicker than the study one does.'

Laura and Henrietta left on Tuesday 4 April because Emma wanted a quiet Easter together. That day and the next Charles had dreadful attacks. With habitual cold-blooded precision, he began making notes. 'Much pain,' he jotted clinically. Emma sent for Dr

Moore and a local physician, Dr Allfrey, who urged her to get a special chair for carrying him upstairs. On the 6th Charles was very tired, with pain in the evening, and he took two amyl nitrite capsules, an antispasmodic. The weekend brought a reprieve. On Monday the 10th George arrived and helped Frank and Jackson move him to and from the bedroom. He was glad for the extra company but had no breath to talk long. The next two nights were excruciating. 'Stomach excessively bad – went to bed at 2° but no pain & no dose,' he scrawled on Thursday. And on Friday, '1 attack slight pain 1 dose.' He was running his final experiment.[17]

The Litchfields came for dinner on Saturday the 15th. Everyone sat at table, with Bernard in his high chair. After the meat was served Charles felt a violent stab in his head. 'I am so giddy I must lie down,' he croaked, and staggered into the drawing-room. He braced himself for a moment against the mantelpiece, then fell face down on the sofa. He was unconscious for only a minute. George gave him a tot of brandy and helped him to the study, while Emma shooed the servants away. 'Dropped down,' he recorded before retiring, as if he were some night-drooping plant.

Emma, 'calm & self possessed,' refused to summon the doctors, who flustered him. He survived Sunday with 'very slight pain several times' and no drugs. 'It's almost worth while to be sick to be nursed by you,' he petted Emma. Monday saw further improvement. He even walked as far as the orchard, supported on both sides. He seemed 'fully up to his average,' so the next day the Litchfields left and George set off for Cambridge. Charles continued to eat well and in the evening stayed in the drawing-room later than usual, chatting with Bessy.[18]

The pain came on just before midnight. It was brutal, gripping him like a vice, tightening by the minute. He woke Emma and begged her to fetch the amyl from the study. She darted from the bedroom and became confused, finally calling Bessy. They took minutes to find the capsules. Charles, in agony, felt that he was dying but unable to cry out. As he slumped unconscious across the bed, Emma and Bessy returned. They rang for a servant and, propping him up, gave the brandy. It trickled through his beard and down his nightdress on to the quilt. Struggling, they forced his head back and poured it into him. Emma was distraught, thinking it was the end.

Seconds later he spluttered and retched; his eyes flickered open. She pressed close to him, searching his face for some sign of recognition. 'My love, my precious love,' he whispered, barely audible. 'Tell all my children to remember how good they have always been to me.'

He choked and grimaced. Emma clasped his hand tightly – it was so awful, words failed her. He started again, fully conscious now, looking into her eyes, 'I am not the least afraid to die.' He became calm.

She sent for Dr Allfrey, who arrived at two o'clock. He applied mustard plasters to Charles's chest, which gave some relief. Just after seven the servants brought breakfast up and he managed to take a few mouthfuls before falling asleep. Allfrey, finding his pulse stronger, wondered that he had ever regained consciousness. The doctor left at eight.

Immediately Charles started vomiting. It was violent and prolonged. When there was nothing left the nausea kept on in waves, overpowering him. His body heaved and shuddered, as if possessed by an outside force. An hour passed, then two. Still he gagged and retched. 'If I could but die,' he gasped repeatedly, 'if I could but die.' Emma clung to him, trembling, as another spasm started. He was cold, clammy, his skin grey and ghostlike. Blood spewed out, running down his beard. She had never seen such suffering.

Frank returned from London before ten. Bessy sent Jackson for Henrietta, who arrived by one. She ran upstairs to find her father sleeping and Emma about to break down, trying to comfort Frank. Henrietta insisted that she take an opium pill and rest, which she did without a murmur. She had slept less than two hours in twenty-four.

Charles awoke in a daze, and asked to be propped up. He recognized the children and embraced them with tears. Frank spooned soup and brandy for him while Henrietta lightly rubbed his chest. Then the nausea struck and convulsed him again. 'Oh God,' he cried helplessly, 'oh Lord God,' and began to faint. Henrietta gave him smelling salts, which he sniffed eagerly, falling back exhausted. 'Where is Mammy?' he called in a thin, hollow voice. They said that she was resting. 'I am *glad* of it,' he sighed. 'You two dears are the best of nurses.' He grew drowsy. It confused him; he thought that he was sinking, and with a 'feeble quivering motion' held out his hands to be lifted. But as Frank raised him, the pain came on. He begged for a little whisky, remembering that Dr Allfrey had suggested it.

Time stood still for Henrietta. Frank, taking his father's pulse at intervals, knew that the hour was near. At twenty-five minutes past three, while sitting up, Charles groaned 'I feel as if I sh^d faint.' They called Emma, who came immediately and held him. His face dropped, but after a few teaspoons of whisky he revived, and she helped him to lie down. But the pain was excruciating in any position. Rising, he began to faint again. The doorbell rang – the doctors. Henrietta raced downstairs to meet them as Charles clutched at Emma. Frank shouted for them to come instantly, and Bessy.

He lost consciousness. They saw it was hopeless. There was only the deep stertorous breathing that precedes death. Emma cradled his head on her breast, swaying gently, her eyes closed. His life ended at four o'clock in the afternoon, Wednesday 19 April, 1882.[19]

Frank, choked with grief, fetched Bernard from the nursery. They walked into the garden, slowly, hand-in-hand, past the drawing-room window, where Bernard saw his aunts together. 'Why are Bessy and Etty crying?' he asked; 'because Grandpa is so ill?' They were by the kitchen garden before Frank could speak. 'Grandpa has been so ill that he won't be ill any more.' When they reached the Sandwalk, Bernard gathered a bouquet of wild lilies.[20]

44

An Agnostic in the Abbey

THE NEXT DAY the papers announced that Darwin would be buried in St Mary's churchyard at Downe. Interment would take place in the 'family vault,' on the following Monday or Tuesday. He would lie under the great yew that had stood sentinel for six centuries at the lychgate – next to his infant children and beside Erasmus. Darwin had expected to be placed here, glimpsing his death the previous summer, and it was clearly the wish of the family and village folk.

Brodie Innes offered to perform the burial rites. William and George, Leo and Horace, hurried home to join the others. John Lewis, the village carpenter, who as a lad had helped with Darwin's cold garden baths, was already at work on the coffin, and the body was placed in the inner shell, 'composed and almost lifelike.' The family gathered round. Emma found her sons' grief 'so violent and affecting' that she finally broke down and wept.[1]

Letters, so difficult at this time, had to be penned. They were a duty and provided their own sort of catharsis. Emma and Henrietta wrote touchingly to female friends and relatives, relating intimate details and last words. Frank and George contacted their father's scientific colleagues, breaking the news of the heart attack in a more clinical manner.

Galton and Huxley had received their black-edged notes by Thursday afternoon. Both were consummate publicists. They acted immediately out of love and loyalty for their old friend. Huxley spent hours anguishing over a short memorial notice for *Nature* before taking the sombre news to the Athenaeum. Galton set off for the Royal Society, which met that day.

Both were part of that influential group within the Society that had struggled to usurp the clergy's role. A new 'scientific priesthood,' Galton called these new professionals, whose duties affected 'the health and well-being of the nation,' and whose growing social prestige reflected it. One of the priesthood's functions, Galton believed, was to emphasize 'the religious significance of the doctrine of evolution,' and what grander way of doing so than a fitting commemoration of Darwin's death? The scientific priesthood had lost a great fellow naturalist, and Galton his first cousin and spiritual father. 'There was no man who I reverenced or to whom I owed more, *spiritually*, than to him,' Galton consoled George Darwin. 'His *Origin of Species* first put me so to speak in harmony with Nature.'[2] For such a man, a 'royal character,' the ultimate remembrance was necessary.

Galton tackled William Spottiswoode, the President of the Royal Society, and arranged for him to telegraph the Darwins asking if they would consent to burial in Westminster Abbey. The request was more official coming from the scientific 'Woolsack,' and more proper from a scientist unrelated to the family. Spottiswoode was influential, by virtue of his office and as printer to Her Majesty. A fellow member of the Athenaeum and an X Clubber, he was one of the Huxley-Galton group and perfectly placed to expedite the plan. Everything was to be done properly, with no risk of upsetting public proprieties. A careful word in the right quarters would have the required effect. Could the Revd Charles Pritchard, a Fellow of the Royal Society who had prepared George and Frank Darwin for Cambridge, write urging the family's assent? Perhaps someone might arrange for a leading conservative newspaper like *The Standard* to call independently for an Abbey burial?[3]

Word was passed to Huxley, Hooker, and Lubbock, tipping off the scientific curia and members of the X. Hooker, forty years Darwin's friend, was grief-stricken and depressed. For days he had been suffering angina pains himself and was now 'utterly unhinged and unfit' for any sort of work. He at first demurred, having 'no fancy for the bitter taste of these ceremonials.' But Huxley and Lubbock were enthusiastic. They knew how much Darwin had rejoiced at Lyell's interment in the Abbey in 1875.

The next day, Friday, Huxley and Spottiswoode discussed Galton's plan at the Athenaeum. They were joined by the Revd Frederic Farrar, Canon of Westminster, and the former headmaster of Marlborough School. In the sixties Farrar had chaired – and Huxley had served on – the British Association's committee on public-school education. Spottiswoode and Huxley respected Farrar as a friend of the new sciences and a critic of the classical curriculum. Darwin, no lover of classics, had also warmed to Canon Farrar, praising his work on the origin of language and supporting his successful candidacy for the Royal Society. Farrar asked why the scientists had not approached the Dean of Westminster, Revd George Granville Bradley, with a request that Darwin be buried in the Abbey.

Getting a freethinker into the Abbey was not easy. A couple of years earlier Huxley had actually refused to ask Bradley's liberal predecessor to allow George Eliot's burial there, thinking it unfair to press him to do 'something for which he is pretty sure to be violently assailed.' But Darwin had not lived openly in sin as Eliot had. This time he reckoned that the Dean could be persuaded, and he knew the way to go about it. He goaded Farrar, intimating that there was little point in making a request, for it would surely be turned down. This was devilishly disingenuous. After all, Huxley knew Bradley well. He had even been offered his post of Master of University College, Oxford, the previous November, when Bradley became Dean. And he was aware of Bradley's strong interest in science, having discussed Oxford science fellowships with him. It was actually because of this interest that Galton, Huxley, and Spottiswoode had supported Bradley's election to the Athenaeum in 1873. He felt sure that, with the right overtures, the Dean would acquiesce.[4]

The ruse worked. Farrar informed them that if a petition were sent, the Dean would no doubt look kindly on it, and he went off to make sure. Meanwhile Spottiswoode sent a note on Athenaeum stationery to William Darwin, now the head of the family:

> I consulted with Huxley, one Bishop, 2 canons (one of whom has a very extensive acquaintance with clergy metropolitan & other), one public school master. All heartily encouraged the proposal being carried out. I saw the L[or]d. Chancellor who was naturally rather more cautious. Lord Aberdare, on his own part, & on that of the Geograph[ical]. Society, was most urgent that the thing should be done, & expressed his sincere hope that your family would consent. –
>
> There is a place beside Lyell where your father could be laid; arrangements could, so far as would be done in & from London, be easily completed for Wednesday next.

That Friday evening Huxley jumped the gun, telling Hooker, 'I think the Westminster Abbey business is all settled though it is unfortunate the Dean is out of town.'[5]

While Spottiswoode approached the family, and Farrar the Dean of Westminster, Lubbock summoned support in the corridors of power. He was President of the Linnean Society, and when word of Darwin's demise reached him on the Thursday, he adjourned the Society out of respect. His own wish had been for a local burial, among their friends and neighbours. But duty came first. He bowed to 'the will of the intelligence of the nation,' as Huxley called it in his *Nature* eulogy – and as a City banker and Liberal MP he had long since deferred to professional middle-class opinion.[6] On Friday, hearing that a petition would be needed, he went to the Houses of Parliament. In the Commons, Ireland had been dominating the debates. The Liberal Party was divided as Fenian atrocities continued, and Gladstone was deeply involved in his Irish Land Act. That Friday, with 150 members on the benches, Lubbock moved among his colleagues collecting signatures, and Ireland was pushed aside for a moment in favour of Darwin and English pride. Lubbock left the House with a petition stating that 'it would be acceptable to a very large number of our countrymen of all classes and opinions that our illustrious countryman Mr. Darwin should be buried in Westminster Abbey.'[7]

'It was very influentially signed,' he told Frank Darwin after sending the petition to the Dean the next morning. Leading the twenty-eight signatories in this essentially Liberal document were four Fellows of the Royal Society, including the education minister, and Lyon Playfair, now the Deputy Speaker. Also down were the Under Secretary of State for Foreign Affairs, and Sir G. O. Trevelyan, Secretary of the Admiralty. There followed the Solicitor General, the Postmaster General, a Sea Lord, and the Speaker of the House. Arthur Russell, a silent member of the Commons, was the cousin of a schoolboy named Bertrand Russell. Another signatory, Henry Campbell-Bannerman, would one day be Prime Minister. As Lubbock confirmed, 'If there had been time many other signatures would have been added.' He now told William Darwin that the Abbey interment was 'very right.'[8]

Following Spottiswoode's telegram and letter, the family was showered with letters urging them to consent. On Saturday, *The Standard* made an emotive plea – a request, as it were, from ordinary people to Emma and the children.

> Darwin died, as he had lived, in the quiet retirement of the country home which he loved; and the sylvan scenes amidst which he found the simple plants and animals that enabled him to solve the great enigma of the Origin of Species may

seem, perhaps, to many of his friends the fittest surroundings for his last resting place. But one who has brought such honour to the English name, and whose death is lamented throughout the civilized world, to the temporary neglect of the many burning political and social questions of the day, should not be laid in a comparatively obscure grave. His proper place is amongst those other worthies whose reputations are landmarks in the people's history, and if it should not clash with his own expressed wishes, or the pious feelings of the family, we owe it to posterity to place his remains in Westminster Abbey, among the illustrious dead who make that noble fane unrivalled in the world.'

Other papers also latched on to the crusade. Patriotism was the paramount theme. Who was the Abbey's hallowed ground for, if not those who had made Britain great, extended her Empire, civilized new worlds at home and abroad? David Livingstone and the heroes of the Indian Mutiny lay there beside the engineers, Stephenson and Telford, whose feats had paved the way for the iron-clad Victorian age. And near by were memorials to others who had harnessed nature's forces – Watt, Trevithick, and Brunel. Towering above them all stood Sir Isaac Newton, still the man against whom all others were measured; and by his standard Darwin was not found wanting. Was he not 'the greatest Englishman since Newton'? Had he not given 'exactly the same stir, the same direction, to all that is most characteristic in the intellectual energy of the nineteenth century, as did Locke and Newton in the eighteenth?'[10]

The obituarists alone almost ensured an Abbey interment by their comparisons with Newton. The demand became even more pointed as the foreign tributes poured in. The Prussian, French, and American newspapers gushed praise, highlighting Britain's neglect of her own native genius. The Prussian king – the *Telegraph* pointed out – had honoured Darwin with a knighthood of the Order 'Pour le Mérite' a full fifteen years earlier, yet England had shabbily ignored her first son. She had failed to 'honour herself' by conferring a title. Unlike the Lyells, Herschels, and Newtons, Darwin had gone to his grave, like the muddy engineers, a plain 'Mr.' Amends had to be made, before it was too late. Britain must not be outdone by her foreign rivals. Comparison with the immortal Newton would ring hollow unless it was acted upon; Newton's honour had to be Darwin's.[11] The State must take and enshrine the body.

*

Canon Farrar had done his work well. Even before receiving the Parliamentary petition, the Dean, then in France, telegraphed his cordial acquiescence. The family was told. By Saturday afternoon, they had all but relented, accepting that Charles was destined to lie beside his old mentor Lyell at Westminster. Still, they made it clear that they would not consent if there were 'any opposition or discussion.'[12] And they felt anxious lest the proposal be thought to have come from them. Their fears were allayed, even if, as X Clubbers knew, the instigator had indeed been a relative, Galton.

The sudden switch in arrangements left little time for mourning. Pall-bearers had to be selected, guests invited, and the former funeral arrangements cancelled. New undertakers were engaged, Messrs T. and W. Banting of 27 St James's Street, who had organized the Duke of Wellington's funeral. They were to collect the body and lay it out for burial on Wednesday. William and George lined up the pall-bearers. Lord Derby and the Dukes of Devonshire and Argyll represented the State, and Devonshire was Chancellor of Darwin's Alma Mater, Cambridge University. They were to be joined by the American ambassador, James Russell Lowell, in 'grateful recognition of the interest taken by Americans in Mr. Darwin's works.' And from English science, the X Club stalwarts Spottiswoode, Lubbock, Huxley, and Hooker would help bear the coffin. Canon Farrar, who had done so much to ease the way, was to accompany them. Stupidly, Huxley forgot to ask Wallace. Wallace, that perennial afterthought in the Darwinian story, was hastily contacted and it was agreed that he would bring up the rear. The undertakers dispensed tickets of admission. Mrs Huxley and the boys received theirs – Leonard, now in his twenties, was Darwin's godson after all. There was a problem with pernickety Herbert Spencer, who wanted to sit with friends rather than scientific dignitaries. But even he was allotted his chosen seat – in the choir – after Huxley hinted that his Dissenting views might otherwise stop him from attending.[13]

Through all the hurry and bustle, Emma stayed outwardly calm, Henrietta and Bessy beside her. But she thought on the future, and how she would cope in a world now 'so empty and desolate.' She poured out her feelings to Fanny and Hensleigh.

> You will hear about West[minster]. Abbey wh[ich]. I look
> upon as nearly settled. It gave us all a pang not to have him
> rest quietly by Eras –; but William felt strongly, and on
> reflection I did also, that his gracious & grateful nature w^d
> have wished to accept the acknowledgement of what he had

done . . . I am sure dearest Fanny that you w^d have wished to attend if you had been in London; but it will be long & agitating & prob[ably]. cold & considerable risk & I am sure this applies to Hensleigh too.

In the event, 79-year-old Hensleigh braved the cold and emotion on Wednesday and walked down the aisle with the rest.[14] Emma stayed at Down House alone. She felt closer to Charles there.

Apparently no villagers journeyed to Westminster either. Old Parslow did go. But he was practically a part of the family he had served so faithfully since the days in Gower Street. As a downstairs-man close to the 'great folks,' he blended the sentiments of locals and family alike. Not long afterwards, he recalled the 'great disappoint-ment' among the people of Downe that Darwin had not been buried in the village. 'He loved the place, and we think he would have rested there had he been consulted.'

The tradesmen were peeved. The publican at the George and Dragon accused the chiselling politicians of undermining local busi-ness. 'All the people wished to have Mr. Darwin buried in Downe, but the Government would not let him. It would have helped the place so much, for it would have brought hosts of people down to see his grave.' St Mary's churchyard could have become a shrine, providing a steady stream of customers for his pub across the road. The joiner John Lewis was equally put out. His reward would have been more than financial; it would have been the knowledge that his coffin held the mortal remains of his illustrious neighbour, Mr Darwin. But after the rough oak box had been made and the body had reposed in it for a day, a smart Piccadilly undertaker had turned up with a resplendent and expensive coffin. Nothing less, he said, would suffice for a state funeral. 'I made his coffin just the way he wanted it,' Lewis lamented, 'all rough, just as it left the bench, no polish, no nothin.' But when they agreed to send him to Westminster . . . my coffin wasn't wanted, and they sent it back.' The replacement one 'you could see to shave in.' Lewis thought it was an outrage. 'They buried him in Westminster Abbey, but he always wanted to lie here, and I don't think he'd have liked it.'[15]

None of the papers saw any religious obstacle to an Abbey burial. *The Standard*, in proposing the honour, maintained that 'true Christians can accept the main scientific facts of Evolution just as they do of Astronomy and Geology, without any prejudice to more ancient and cherished beliefs.' *The Times* on Friday had declared the clash between Huxley and Bishop Wilberforce in 1860 a piece of 'ancient history'; and the Liberal *Daily News* added that Darwin's doctrine was quite consistent 'with strong religious faith and hope.'[16] On Sunday the preachers outbid one another to prove the hacks right.

Morning, noon and night, the pulpits resounded with praise for Darwin. At the Abbey, Canon George Prothero, the Queen's chief Chaplain-in-Ordinary, toed his usual Broad Church line and inveighed against extremism and superstition. However one viewed the new science, it was certainly born of Mr Darwin's moderation, impartiality, and patient industry in pursuing truth. In scholars like him lived 'that charity which is the essence of the true spirit of Christ.' That evening at the Abbey, Canon Alfred Barry echoed the weighty sermons on politics and business that he had delivered the previous autumn. These had sanctioned the time-honoured assumptions implicit in Darwinism. He had dismissed equality as unnatural, an 'impossible figment,' and assigned each person his station – professional, merchant, trader, or worker – to help England work with God for the progress of 'all mankind.' Every man was still in his place, and Darwin's death provided the excuse for a more particular appreciation. Natural selection was 'by no means alien to the Christian religion' – not if it was rightly understood, with selection acting 'under the Divine intelligence' and governed by 'the spiritual fitness of each man for life hereafter.'[17]

The star attraction that Sunday afternoon was Canon H. P. Liddon at St Paul's, lauding Darwin for 'the patience and care with which he observed and registered minute single facts.' In this way he had brought about a 'revolution' in modern thought and shed 'high distinction upon English science.' It did not show, but Liddon's sermon masked a deep anxiety. Privately he felt queasy and confided that the occasion had caused him some 'discomfort and misgiving.' Nevertheless even an awkward emphasis on Darwin's facts could only swell the chorus of demands for his burial in the Abbey. The *Guardian*, voice of Liddon's High Church party, acquiesced in his authority and discarded 'any misgivings lest the sacred pavement of the Abbey should cover a secret enemy of the Faith.' The Abbey service was to be a visible sign 'of the reconciliation between Faith and Science.' On this point, the Anglo-Catholics at St Paul's and the latitudinarians at Westminster were as one. The 'new truths' of biology were 'harmless,' their discoverer a secular saint.[18]

With Darwin's canonization assured, the newspapers played up their role in the affair. *The Standard* congratulated itself that 'the suggestion which we threw out on Saturday has been acted upon.' Evidently tolerance was 'the latest evolved and not the least satisfactory mode of clerical thought.' The thinking public would be able to honour the memory of a man who had 'set the stamp of his individual intellect on the age.' Professional gentlemen and their families would find it easy to obtain admission cards to the funeral. These, the papers said, could be collected from Banting's in St James's Street during office hours on Tuesday.[19]

So many applied that the undertakers did not complete the preparations for the burial until early the next morning. All day Tuesday the hearse, drawn by four horses, had progressed slowly, sombrely, the sixteen miles from Downe to Westminster. The weather was awful, drizzling rain, with temperatures in the forties. Frank, Leo, and Horace, who had followed the hearse, were chilled, spiritually and bodily. William and George had been in town all day making final arrangements. They hastened to the Abbey, just in time to meet their brothers. It was late, eight o'clock at night, before they bore the coffin through the cloisters. The cortège was led into the Chapel of St Faith, a bare, formal chamber dimly lit by two old lamps. In this cold, sepulchral room, the feeling of death was overwhelming. Guards took up their posts to protect the body overnight.[20]

On Wednesday 26 April Queen Victoria was at Windsor Castle, preparing for Prince Leopold's wedding the next day. Gladstone remained in Downing Street, wrapped up in Irish politics. Neither would attend the funeral; neither had been an avid reader of the *Origin of Species*. But elsewhere that grey day committees adjourned, judges put on mourning dress, and Parliament emptied as members trooped across the road. From embassies, scientific societies, and countless ordinary homes they came. Under leaden skies they converged on the Abbey, anticipating the awe and spectacle of a state occasion. The Darwins and Wedgwoods queued in the Jerusalem Chamber, thirty-three in all, including Galton. William, the principal mourner, stood at their head, Parslow and Jackson behind the family. In the Chapter House, where Parliament had once met, the elders of science, State, and Church, the nobility of birth and talent, stood waiting to file through the cloisters, behind the coffin. They were 'the greatest gathering of intellect that was ever brought together in our country,' said one. The transepts were filled with friends and guests; the south side of the nave with the bearers of black-edged admission cards. The Lord Mayor of London took his place in the sacrarium, before the altar, with still more family members. In the choir, Spencer sat forlornly among the distinguished ladies, now regretting that he was simply 'one of the spectators.' Finally, the doors opened to the multitudes without tickets.[21] They flooded into the dank, gaslit building, filling the less desirable seats on the north-west side of the nave.

Then, at midday, the moment arrived. As the Abbey bell tolled, Canon Prothero entered from the West Cloister door, leading the procession, with the choristers singing 'I am the resurrection.' The train of family and dignitaries shuffled past the tombs of the famous and made their way slowly through the candle-lit choir to the centre of the transept. There the coffin, draped in black velvet and covered in a spray of white blossoms, was placed beneath a lantern. A specially commissioned hymn was sung after the lesson. Composed by the Abbey's deputy organist, it was sensitive to the occasion. The lyrics were taken from the Book of Proverbs. The opening line, 'Happy is the man that findeth wisdom, and getteth understanding,' paid tribute to Darwin's lifework. The closing refrain, sung by the cassocked choirboys, left a sacrilegiously unDarwinian image of nature: 'Her ways are ways of pleasantness, and all her paths are peace.' William, seated at the front, felt a draught cross his bald pate. Worrying, as all Darwins did, about ill health, he perched his black gloves on top of his head and sat there incongruously, with the nation's eyes upon him, until the service ended. Then the family, with the pall-bearers carrying the coffin, made its way to the north-east corner of the nave, to the accompaniment of Schubert and Beethoven.[22]

In the end – fitting though it would have been – Darwin was not laid beside Lyell, but beneath the monument to Newton at the north end of the choir screen, and next to another mentor, Sir John Herschel. The floor was draped with black cloth, which dropped away into the dry, sandy grave. Henrietta, Bessy, and the ladies sat down, while the others crowded around. American freethinkers rubbed shoulders with orthodox churchmen; Romanes and agnostic X men stood next to devout old Fellows of the Royal Society; and Liberal lords closed ranks with the Tory leaders Sir Stafford Northcote and Lord Salisbury. The coffin was lowered, and the choristers sang 'His body is buried in peace, but his name liveth evermore.' Then, to the 'Dead March' from *Saul*, the mourners filed past, sombre, sable-suited figures, lit by coloured beams from the overlooking stained-glass panes commemorating the railway pioneers, George and Robert Stephenson.[23] The sky outside was clearing.

Galton was satisfied at this reverence for the new scientific priest-hood. The country's rulers were seen honouring a ruler of nature, and the ritual served as a visible reminder of evolution's 'religious significance.' But work was still to be done. The next day, in the *Pall Mall Gazette*, Galton suggested that at church services the following Sunday the 'Benedicite' should replace the regular 'Te Deum.' Its invocation of praise – 'O all ye Works of the Lord: bless ye the Lord: praise him and magnify him for ever' – underscored what clergymen 'would probably wish to say afterwards from the pulpit' regarding Darwin. Galton perhaps raised the point directly when he coached Canon Farrar for his Sunday evening sermon at the Abbey. Nor was this the end of his commemorative scheme. He suggested a bust be erected, and also the incorporation of a new stained-glass window in the Abbey. Its panels would symbolize the works of nature praised in the Benedicite – the rocks, plants, fish, birds, and beasts – each to be contributed in Darwin's memory by a different country.[24]

The dignitaries of science and State liked the idea of worldwide homage to an English naturalist. One told the Bishop of Carlisle that the whole splendid pageant made him 'thankful for his native land.' The bishop assured his congregation at the Abbey that Sunday that the great scientist had been placed there 'in accordance with the judgment of the wisest of his countrymen.' He went on to strike the same patriotic note: 'Had this death occurred in France, no priest would have taken part in the funeral, or, if he had, no scientific man would have been present.' It was Galton's view entirely. He was the first to grasp the cultural significance of Darwin's burial in such hallowed ground. He talked of the higher 'feeling promoted by the ceremony,' the thrill of 'national honour and glory.' It proved that the scientists' moral duty in furthering human evolution was best exercised in harmony with the old religious ideals 'upon which the social fabric depends.'[25]

Nothing came of the evolution pane. But the idea of a bust had taken root and, at a meeting of scientists at Burlington House on Saturday, it was decided to start a fund. At the Royal Society two weeks later, a provisional committee was appointed, with Spottiswoode as chairman.[26] It decided on a bronze plaque in the Abbey. But the committee also commissioned a statue to stand on the central sweeping staircase in that great new Romanesque cathedral of science, the Natural History Museum at South Kensington.

Huxley took over the presidency of the Memorial Committee after Spottiswoode's own death and Abbey burial in 1883. He was aided by Galton, Lubbock, and Hooker, a cluster of sixty-one FRSs, the Lord Chief Justice, five MPs, and a phalanx of prelates led by the Archbishop of Canterbury. The High Church cried off – Canon Liddon declined to serve out of deference to his anti-Darwinian superior, the aged E. B. Pusey. Another conspicuous by his absence was Wallace. Nor did he contribute to the fund. The money began to pour in, and the scientists chivied their colleagues overseas, who started similar committees, making this a truly imperial endeavour. At home the largest individual contributions, £100 each, came from the instigators of the Abbey affair, Galton, Spottiswoode, and Lubbock. Emma and the family gave £200, and the X Club subscribed to a person – even Spencer, perennially penny-pinching, chipped in £2.

In all £4500 was raised, half of which went on the statue for the Natural History Museum. This 'Temple of Nature,' as *The Times* called it, had been completed only in 1880. The figure of Adam stood high over the entrance (he fell during World War Two) and an unapproving Richard Owen was still the towering presence. The unveiling of the Darwin statue had to wait until 1885, after Owen's retirement. Again the occasion was one of pomp and ceremony. The Prince of Wales was present, as were the family – except Emma – and Charles's close friends, Hooker, Galton, Romanes, Theta Farrer, and Admiral Sulivan. But it was the scientists, in the person of 'Pope' Huxley, who now occupied the pulpit.[27] And standing at the back among the congregation, scarcely noticed, was an old man, Parslow.

The Abbey interment gave tangible expression to the public feeling that Darwin, in his life and work, symbolized English success in conquering nature and civilizing the globe during Victoria's long reign.

Religious writers of all persuasions now testified to his 'noble character and his ardent pursuit of truth.' The *Church Times* was lost for epithets – patience, ingenuity, calmness, industry, moderation. Others added the Pauline graces perseverance and faith, and depicted him as a 'true Christian gentleman.' Even the evangelical *Record*, cagey about the burial itself, noticed his defence of missionaries as harbingers of civilization. And it reported the Bishop of Derry's speech at the annual meeting of the South American Missionary Society, in which he revealed, to some hear-hears, that Darwin had subscribed on a regular basis. The *Nonconformist and Independent* rang the changes on the 'moral influence' of his example.

But the most tireless supporters were the Unitarians and free religionists, proud that Darwin had been brought up in their rational Dissenting tradition and always appreciative of his naturalistic views. His trusted friend William Carpenter carried the entire British and Foreign Unitarian Association with his resolution applauding Darwin for unravelling 'the immutable laws of the Divine Government,' and

for shedding light on 'the progress of humanity.' He sent the resolution to Emma, trusting that a Wedgwood would approve. Others too
welcomed 'the most emphatic lesson' of Darwinism, 'the gospel of
infinite progress.' They gloried in the 'universal applicability' of
Darwin's teaching, which had brought 'order . . . and peace into life
and thought.' From New York city, a Unitarian preacher, John
Chadwick, described the momentous day at the Abbey in profanely
Messianic language: 'The nation's grandest temple of religion opened
its gates and lifted up its everlasting doors and bade the king of
science come in.'[28]

The elegies stressed Darwin's exemplary character, his simple
'everyday virtues,' and his wealthy respectability. Mr Darwin's was
'an ideal life,' according to the *Saturday Review* – a private fortune,
a great opportunity capitalized on the *Beagle*, 'immense labours,
wisely planned and steadily executed,' amid scenes of 'quiet domestic
happiness,' and all crowned by a 'sweet and gentle nature blossomed
into perfection.' Many found Darwin's homeliness especially attractive. It was 'difficult to imagine a more beautiful picture of human
happiness than that which he presented in his Kentish home, working
at those great books which are acknowledged to have been a priceless
gift to humanity, surrounded by a devoted family.'

Some even inverted the honour of official burial. Westminster did
not bestow dignity on the naturalist from Downe – his body was
hallowed already. 'The Abbey needed it more than it needed the
Abbey,' thundered *The Times*. This saintly man, who had 'borne the
flag of science,' extended the boundaries of knowledge, and
'established new centres whence annexations of fresh and fruitful
truths are continually to be made,' gave the Abbey 'an increased
sanctity, a new cause for reverence' on being laid beneath its stones.
'The Abbey has its orators and Ministers who have convinced
reluctant senates and swayed nations. Not one of them all has
wielded a power over men and their intelligences more complete than
that which for the last twenty-three years has emanated from a
simple country house in Kent.'[29]

Above all, the national and imperial theme was trumpeted in the
press coverage. The *Pall Mall Gazette*, staunchly Liberal under John
Morley's editorship, and staple fare for London's professionals,
proclaimed that Great Britain had 'lost a man whose name is a glory
to his country.' It noted Darwin's support for Gladstone and pictured
him an equal world statesman. This emphasis on Darwin's global
status – particularly by Liberals – came in final recognition of his
politically comforting science. His image of biological and social

progress, resting on individual competition, free trade and fair selection, had risen to dominance alongside the party that gave it political expression in mid-Victorian Britain.

'The Darwinian creed ... runs through almost all the best thought of our time,' boasted Morley's Liberal rag on the day of the ceremony.

> It tinges our unformed public notions; it reappears under a
> hundred disguises in works on law and history, in political
> speeches and religious discourses, in artistic theories and vague
> social speculations. Our very novels and poems are full of
> latent Darwinian gems. If we try to think ourselves away
> from it we must think ourselves entirely away from our
> age.[30]

So Darwin's body had to be appropriated and buried with ecclesiastical pomp. The Abbey interment celebrated the vast, unfinished social transformation that England was undergoing. There were new colonies, new industries, new men to run them – not least a 'new Nature,' as Huxley called it, speaking through new priests, promising progress to all who obeyed.[31] Darwin's body was enshrined to the greater glory of the new professionals who had snatched it. The burial was their apotheosis, the last rite of a rising secularity. It marked the accession to power of the traders in nature's marketplace, the scientists and their minions in politics and religion. Such men, on the up-and-up, were paying their dues, for Darwin had naturalized Creation and delivered human nature and human destiny into their hands.

Society would never be the same. The 'Devil's Chaplain' had done his work.

Abbreviations

Annotated Calendar	Carroll, *Annotated Calendar of the Letters of Charles Darwin*, 1976.
APS	American Philosophical Society Library, Philadelphia.
ARW	Marchant, *Alfred Russel Wallace*, 2 vols., 1916.
Autobiography	Barlow, *Autobiography of Charles Darwin*, 1958.
BL	British Library, Department of Manuscripts.
BM(NH), OCorr./OColl.	British Museum (Natural History), Owen Correspondence / Owen Collection.
Calendar	Burkhardt and Smith, *Calendar of the Correspondence of Charles Darwin, 1821-1882*, 1985.
CCD	Burkhardt and Smith, *Correspondence of Charles Darwin*, 7 vols., 1985-91.
Charles Darwin	Barlow, *Charles Darwin and the Voyage of the 'Beagle'*, 1945.
Companion	Freeman, *Charles Darwin: A Companion*, 1978.
CP	Barrett, *Collected Papers of Charles Darwin*, 2 vols., 1977.
CUL	Cambridge University Library.
DAR	Darwin Archive, Cambridge University Library.
Darwin's Journal	De Beer, 'Darwin's Journal,' *Bulletin of the British Museum (Natural History), Historical Series*, 2 (1959), 1-21.
Descent	Darwin, *The Descent of Man*, 2 vols., 1871; rev. ed., 1 vol., 1874.
Diary	R. Keynes, *Charles Darwin's 'Beagle' Diary*, 1988.

DON	Barlow, 'Darwin's Ornithological Notes,' *Bulletin of the British Museum (Natural History), Historical Series*, 2 (1963), 201-78.
Down House	Charles Darwin Museum, Down House, Downe, Kent.
ED	Litchfield, *Emma Darwin*, 2 vols., 1915 (otherwise 1904 private edition).
EUL	Edinburgh University Library.
Foundations	F. Darwin, *Foundations of the 'Origin of Species'*, 1909.
Journal	Darwin, *Journal of Researches*, 1839; rev. ed., 1845/60.
KAO	Kent County Archives Office, Maidstone, Kent (collection transferred to Central Library, Bromley, Kent).
LJT	Eve and Creasey, *Life and Work of John Tyndall*, 1945.
LLAS	Clark and Hughes, *Life and Letters of the Reverend Adam Sedgwick*, 2 vols., 1890.
LLD	F. Darwin, *Life and Letters of Charles Darwin*, 3 vols., 1887.
LLJH	L. Huxley, *Life and Letters of Sir Joseph Dalton Hooker*, 2 vols., 1918.
LLL	K. Lyell, *Life, Letters, and Journals of Sir Charles Lyell*, 2 vols., 1881.
LLR	E. Romanes, *Life and Letters of George John Romanes*, 1896.
LLTH	L. Huxley, *Life and Letters of Thomas Henry Huxley*, 2 vols., 1900.
LRO	R. S. Owen, *Life of Richard Owen*, 2 vols., 1894.
MLD	F. Darwin and Seward, *More Letters of Charles Darwin*, 2 vols., 1903.
Narrative	Stanbury, *Narrative of the Voyage of H.M.S. 'Beagle'*, 1977.
Natural Selection	Stauffer, *Charles Darwin's Natural Selection*, 1975.
Notebooks	Barrett *et al.*, *Charles Darwin's Notebooks, 1836-1844*, 1987.
Origin	Darwin, *On the Origin of Species by means of Natural Selection*, 1859.
Pedigrees	Freeman, *Darwin Pedigrees*, 1984.
PRO	Public Record Office, Kew, and Quality Court, London.
RBL	Litchfield, *Richard Buckley Litchfield*, 1910.
RFD	Recollections of Francis Darwin, Darwin Archive 140.3, Cambridge University Library.
TBI	Colp, *To Be an Invalid*, 1977.

THP	Thomas Huxley Papers, Imperial College of Science and Technology, London.
UCL	University College London.
W/M	Wedgwood-Mosley Collection, Keele University Library.
Wedgwood	B. and H. Wedgwood, *The Wedgwood Circle*, 1980.

NOTES

A DEVIL'S CHAPLAIN?

1. For a survey of previous studies: Colp, 'Charles Darwin's Past and Future Biographies.'
2. Greene, 'Reflections;' Churchill, 'Darwin.'
3. J. Moore, 'Darwin's Genesis.' The Darwin Industry is analysed in Ruse, 'Darwin Industry,' and J. Moore, 'On Revolutionizing.'
4. Oldroyd, 'How did Darwin arrive at His Theory?' 334ff; La Vergata, 'Images,' 953-58; R. Young, *Darwin's Metaphor*, 23ff.
5. Churchill, 'Darwin,' 62; Kohn, *Darwinian Heritage*, 4; Lenoir, 'Darwin Industry,' 115-16; Desmond, 'Kentish Hog' and 'Darwin;' R. Young, 'Darwinism;' Schweber, 'Correspondence.'
6. J. Moore, 'Freethought,' 293; Desmond, *Politics*, 373-414; R. Young, 'Darwin,' 71; Lenoir, 'Darwin Industry,' 117; Rudwick, 'Charles Darwin,' 186 n. 2.
7. Colp, 'Charles Darwin's Past and Future Biographies,' 167; *ED*, 2:203.

1 CATCHING A FALLING CHRISTIAN

1. Krause, *Erasmus Darwin*, 45; also *LLD*, 2:158.
2. The words of grandson Charles, referring to those like himself who had gone beyond Unitarianism: Darwin to T. Wollaston, 6 June [1856], EUL, Gen. 1999/1/30.
3. King-Hele, *Doctor*, 289 and *Letters*, 127.
4. Darwin to Reginald Darwin, 4 April 1879, in Colp, 'Relationship,' 11; J. Moore, 'Of Love,' 204–205.
5. *Pedigrees*, 35; King-Hele, *Doctor*; McNeil, *Under the Banner*; R. Porter, 'Erasmus Darwin;' J. Browne, 'Botany.'
6. Corrected proof sheets of Darwin's 'Preliminary Notice' to Krause, *Erasmus Darwin*, DAR 210.20; Wedgwood, 239; *Autobiography*, 93.
7. King-Hele, *Doctor*, 73, 77, 89, 100–101, 106, 130 and *Letters*, 35–37, 54, 65, 130; McNeil, *Under the Banner*, 9–15; McKendrick, 'Josiah Wedgwood;' *Wedgwood*, 36, ch. 6.
8. Holt, *Unitarian Contribution*, ch. 2; Seed, 'Theologies,' 108–14; King-Hele, *Letters*, 38.
9. McNeil, *Under the Banner*, 83; King-Hele, *Doctor*, 93-94, 135, 142-43 and *Letters*, 284, 286; *Wedgwood*, 8, 11, 16; *Memorable Unitarians*, 166–67; McKendrick, 'Role,' 297–302; Brooke, 'Joseph Priestley,' 12.
10. King-Hele, *Letters*, 8-9, 43; Rowell, *Hell*, 33–38; Willey, *Eighteenth Century*

Background, ch. 10; Brooke, 'Sower,' 439–48; Webb, 'Unitarian Background,' 10–13.

11. R. Porter, 'I Live too Chaste. 'Tis Not a Common Fault,' *Independent* (London), 28 July 1990, p. 27; King-Hele, *Letters*, 91, 297 and *Doctor*, 121–22, 131, 134, 136, 138–40, 172; *Wedgwood*, 74; Woodall, 'Charles Darwin,' 9; *Pedigrees*, 35; *Autobiography*, 30.

12. King-Hele, *Doctor*, 123–24, 176–78 and *Letters*, 164–65; Woodall, 'Charles Darwin,' 11; *LLD*, 1:8–9.

13. H. Gruber, *Darwin*, 46–47; King-Hele, *Doctor*, 204, 211–13, 217, 230, 232–33 and *Letters*, 166, 204–205, 215–16, 225–26; McNeil, *Under the Banner*, 79–85; *Wedgwood*, 98, 101–104.

14. *Wedgwood*, 102–103, 108; Keith, *Darwin*, 4; *Autobiography*, 29–30; *LLD*, 1:9; King-Hele, *Doctor*, 258.

15. D, 'Death;' *LLD*, 1:9; *Companion*, 209; King-Hele, *Doctor*, 273–74, 284–85; *Pedigrees*, 10.

16. *Wedgwood*, 132–38; *ED*, 1:26.

17. Colp, 'Mrs. Susannah Darwin,' 4–6; Woodall, 'Charles Darwin,' 1; *Autobiography*, 28, 40; *Pedigrees*, 34; *Wedgwood*, 116–17.

18. Woodall, 'Charles Darwin,' 12; E. Thompson, *Making*, 529–42; King-Hele, *Doctor*, 264–65, 297.

19. Broadbent, *Story*, 5, 9, 12; Woodall, 'Charles Darwin,' 11–12; *Autobiography*, 22; recollections of W. Leighton, DAR 112. In 1798, when a minister was being sought, Samuel Taylor Coleridge had stood as a candidate, but then Susannah's father granted him a fat £150 annuity to pursue his literary interests, and the post fell to Case.

20. *Autobiography*, 22–24, 26–27; CCD, 1:537, 2:438; Woodall, 'Charles Darwin,' 14; *Wedgwood*, 117.

21. Mansergh, 'Charles Darwin;' Bowlby, *Charles Darwin*, 56; recollections of W. Leighton, DAR 112; *Autobiography*, 23, 27; CCD, 2:439–40.

22. CCD, 2:439–40; *Autobiography*, 22, 24; Colp, 'Mrs. Susannah Darwin,' 7–11; Colp, 'Notes on Charles Darwin's *Autobiography*,' 364; *Wedgwood*, 181.

23. *Autobiography*, 30, 32, 39; *ED*, 1:60; *Charles Darwin*, 8–9.

24. CCD, 1:537; *Wedgwood*, 165; *ED*, 1:139–40; E. Richards, 'Darwin,' 82.

25. CCD, 2:440; Bowen, *Idea*, 213.

26. Recollections of W. Leighton, DAR 112; *Autobiography*, 27–28, 43.

27. E. Craddock to F. Darwin, 10 July 1882, DAR 112:16–17; *Autobiography*, 25, 42, 44; Colp, 'Notes on Charles Darwin's *Autobiography*,' 363–64.

28. CCD, 1:538; 2:440–41; *Autobiography*, 44–45; Bowlby, *Charles Darwin*, 64; recollections of W. Leighton and of J. Price, DAR 112.

29. CCD, 1:1–15; *Wedgwood*, 112; Chaldecott, 'Josiah Wedgwood.'

30. Green, *Address*, 36, 41–42.

31. *Autobiography*, 45–46; CCD, 1:1–15.

32. *Autobiography*, 44, 46; *Wedgwood*, 138, 195–96.

33. *ED*, 1:56, 61, 141–42, 160–61; *Wedgwood*, 195, 198; E. Wedgwood, *My First Reading Book*; Thackray, 'Natural Knowledge,' 679–80.

34. *Autobiography*, 28, 36, 39; CCD, 1:14–15.

2 THE NORTHERN ATHENS

1. *Autobiography*, 47-48; TBI, 3-4.

2. CCD, 1:15–16; Shepperson, 'Intellectual Background,' 17–20; Audubon, *Audubon*, 1:210.

3. *Report from the Select Committee on Medical Education* . . . (Parliamentary Papers, 13 Aug. 1834), pt 1, 93; Chitnis, 'Medical Education;' Parry and Parry, *Rise*, 105–107.

4. CCD, 1:15, 18–19; Mudie, *Modern Athens*, 23.

5. Mudie, *Modern Athens*, 252–53; CCD, 1:19, 28.

6. *Pedigrees*, 10, 31; King-Hele, *Doctor*, 123.

7. CCD, 1:25, 28–29, 41; *Autobiography*, 52; Audubon, *Audubon*, 1:206.

8. Mudie, *Modern Athens*, 185; CCD, 1:38–40, 44.

9. McMenemey, 'Education,' 138–39; Desmond, *Politics*, 166; CCD, 1:34.

10. CCD, 1:16, 39, 45; Shepperson, 'Intellectual Background,' 27.

11. CCD, 1:25; *Medico-Chirurgical Review*, 20 (1833–34), 315–19; Morrell, 'Science;' Mudie, *Modern Athens*, 220; A. Grant, *Story*, 2:389–90.

12. In 1826–27 Knox taught 207 anatomy students, compared to Lizars's 104 (the next highest) and Monro's 78: Struthers, *Historical Sketch*, 92. On Robert Knox: E. Richards, 'Moral Anatomy.'

13. CCD, 1:25; *Autobiography*, 47; Audubon, *Audubon*, 1:146, 174. Knox lectured at 10 Surgeons' Square, Lizars at No. 1: Cathcart, 'Some of the Older Schools,' 775–78.

14. CCD, 1:iv, 25, 36; A. Grant, *Story*, 2:424–5; *Evidence*, 1:220–22.

15. *Autobiography*, 39–40, 47–48; recollections of G. Darwin, DAR 112; Richardson, *Death*, 41.

16. Morrell, 'Science,' 54–55; Ashworth, 'Charles Darwin,' 98; CCD, 1:25, 29; *Autobiography*, 47.

17. CCD, 1:29; Freeman, 'Darwin's Negro Bird-Stuffer;' *Autobiography*, 51. Waterton had a flair for notoriety. He had just launched his sensational hoax, the 'Nondescript' – a Red Howler Monkey with a face recast in grotesque caricature of the Secretary to the Treasury: Aldington, *Strange Life*, 112–14.

18. CCD, 1:22, 36–39, 41.

19. Diary for 1826, DAR 129; *Autobiography*, 45. Darwin's copy of White's *Natural History of Selborne* (2 vols., 1825) is in the Darwin Library, CUL.

20. R. Porter, 'Erasmus Darwin,' 58; *Autobiography*, 49.

3 SEA-MATS & SEDITIOUS SCIENCE

1. *Autobiography*, 46; Peterson, 'Gentlemen,' 462.

2. *Evidence*, 1:146.

3. W. Browne, 'Observations.'

4. Plinian Minutes MSS, 1:ff. 34–36, EUL, Dc.2.53; G. Bell, *Letters*, 251; Kirsop, 'W. R. Greg,' 377–83; Desmond, *Politics*, 210, on the deterministic science and theology taught at Lant Carpenter's Unitarian school in Bristol, which Greg attended.

5. *Phrenological Journal*, 5 (1829), 141; Kirsop, 'W. R. Greg,' 378–83; Shapin, 'Phrenological Knowledge,' and Cooter, *Cultural Meaning*, on phrenology's social appeal.

6. Ainsworth, 'Mr. Darwin.' William F. Ainsworth, later to become famous as an Oriental scholar, was a Plinian President who sometimes accompanied Darwin on his coastal walks.

7. *Autobiography*, 48; Balfour, *Biography*.

8. Desmond, 'Making,' 163, 167; Corsi, *Age*, chs. 3–4.

9. Audubon, *Audubon*, 1:149, 223; R. Grant, 'Notice of a New Zoophyte.' The details of Grant's life are from 'Biographical Sketch of Robert Edmond Grant,' *Lancet*, 2 (1850), 686–95; Poore, 'Robert Edmond Grant,' 190; Desmond, 'Robert E. Grant' and *Politics*. For his zoology: Sloan, 'Darwin's Invertebrate Program,' 73–87.

10. Beddoe, *Memories*, 32; Godlee, 'Thomas Wharton Jones,' 102; Poore, 'Robert Edmond Grant,' 190; *Autobiography*, 49.

11. Wernerian Society Minutes, 1:f. 272, EUL, Dc.2.55; 'Edinburgh Zoology Notebook,' DAR 118, in *CP*, 2:283–91.

12. R. Grant, 'Notice regarding the Ova.' Darwin exhibited the leech's eggs at the 3 April Plinian meeting: Ainsworth, 'Mr. Darwin'. On the Wernerian Society: *Evidence*, 1:146; *Autobiography*, 51; Audubon, *Audubon*, 1:186. Despite Grant's patronage, his seniority remained paramount, judging by the fact that he once warned Darwin against seizing priority and publishing on *his* subject: Jesperson, 'Charles Darwin,' 164–65. Grant, like so many naturalists before professional standards were introduced into science, was bedevilled by 'plagiarists:' Desmond, *Politics*, 401–402.

13. 'Edinburgh Zoology Notebook,' DAR 118, f. 6, in *CP*, 2:288. His transcription of Lamarck can be found in DAR 5. See also Egerton, 'Darwin's Early Reading,' 454–55; *CCD*, 1:22.

14. Plinian Minutes, 1:ff. 56–57, EUL, Dc.2.53; H. Gruber, *Darwin*, 479; Desmond, *Politics*, 67–69, 402. Greg, Browne, Grant, and Ainsworth joined in the *mêlée* at the end of the talk.

15. McMenemey, 'Education,' 145; Desmond, *Politics*, 120, 264–67.

16. Wernerian Society Minutes, 1:ff. 241–43, EUL, Dc.2.55; Desmond, *Politics*, ch. 2 and Desmond, 'Lamarckism' for Grant's friendship with Geoffroy and the radical basis of his philosophical anatomy. Grant was in the Geoffroyan mainstream. Appel, *Cuvier-Geoffroy Debate*, ch. 5, describes the excitement in Paris at this time as Geoffroy's disciples announced all manner of homologies between insects, crustaceans, molluscs, and vertebrates.

17. Jameson, 'Observations.' Jameson's authorship was ascertained by Secord, 'Edinburgh Lamarckians.' See also: R. Grant, 'Structure,' 283–84; Desmond, 'Robert E. Grant's Later Views,' 405–406; Desmond, *Politics*, 59–81, 398–403; *Autobiography*, 49; and Corsi, *Age*, ch. 8 on French science in this period.

18. R. Porter, 'Erasmus Darwin,' 39; R. Grant, *Dissertatio Physiologica*, 8; R. Grant, *Tabular View*, v; Shepperson, 'Intellectual Background,' 27.

19. Sloan, 'Darwin's Invertebrate Program,' 78–84; Jameson, 'Observations,' 295.

20. Matthew, *On Naval Timber*, 364–69; Dempster, *Patrick Matthew*, 98–99. Wells, 'Historical Context,' discusses Matthew's *laissez-faire* radicalism and evolutionary views.

21. Hugh Miller, in Hodge, 'England,' 11; Corsi, *Science*, 273; Balfour, *Biography*, 7–12, 39.

22. *Evidence*, 1:145; Secord, 'Discovery;' Mudie, *Modern Athens*, 221 on Jameson as one of the immortals.

23. *Evidence*, 1:141–42, App., 115–18; Secord, 'Discovery.'

24. Jameson's testimony, *Evidence*, 1:141–42. The course included 'Instructions and Demonstrations as to the mode of collecting, preserving, transporting, and arranging objects of Natural History' (App., 118), something that was to

prove immensely important to Darwin during his *Beagle* voyage. See also Sweet, 'Robert Jameson.'

25. Ainsworth, 'Present State,' 271, 276; 'Phrenology and Professor Jameson,' *Phrenological Journal*, 1 (1824), 56; *Evidence*, 1:142, 144–45; Chitnis, 'University of Edinburgh's Natural History Museum,' 86–88, 90–93.

26. *Evidence*, 1:223; *Autobiography*, 52. Duncan opposed the botany professor Robert Graham's rival – and rather antiquated – Linnean system. On De Candolle's botany: J. Browne, *Secular Ark*, 52–57.

27. Kirsop, 'W. R. Greg,' 377–78; Coldstream, *Sketch*, 10–11; Balfour, *Biography*, 38; Desmond, *Politics*, 81; *ED*, 1:194.

4 ANGLICAN ORDERS

1. *CCD*, 1:58, 539; *ED*, 1:198.
2. Brent, *Charles Darwin*, 56; *ED*, 1:183, 200-202, 208.
3. *ED*, 1:139–40, 227; *CCD*, 1:22, 24, 28, 40–41, 44.
4. *ED*, 1:206–10, 227; *Autobiography*, 55; *Wedgwood*, 200.
5. Such a place of last resort was also in Squire Owen's mind when, years later, he asked Darwin about a tutor for his third son, 'a very honorable, & well disposed Boy,' but immature and rather slow, 'who if nothing better offers I intend for the Church:' *CCD*, 1:528–29; *Autobiography*, 56-57.
6. Trollope, *Clergymen*, ch. 5; Addison, *English Country Parson*; Hart, *Country Priest* and *Curate's Lot*; Colloms, *Victorian Country Parsons*; Evans, 'Some Reasons,' 85-101; Halévy, *History*, 342-52; J. Moore, 'Darwin of Down,' 441–42.
7. *Companion*, 116, 296; cf. *Wedgwood*, 198.
8. *Autobiography*, 56–57; Darwin's notes on Sumner's *Evidences of Christianity*, DAR 91:114–18. Cf. H. Gruber, *Darwin*, 125–26 and Dell, 'Social and Economic Theories.' Darwin's notes are undated, but they appear for the most part on the same kind of paper he used for his 'Early notes on guns and shooting' (DAR 91:1–3), datable between 1825 and 1827 (*Autobiography*, 44, 54). A later dating is also possible: J. Moore, 'Darwin of Down,' 478 n.3.
9. *Autobiography*, 58; *CCD*, 1:48, 51, 70–71.
10. *Cambridge Guide*; E. Evans, 'Some Reasons;' E. Thompson, *Making*, 246ff; Hobsbawm and Rudé, *Captain Swing*, ch. 4.
11. *Cambridge Guide*, 9-10; Brace of Cantabs, *Gradus*, 83–84; Winstanley, *Unreformed Cambridge*, 22–24; Parker, *Town and Gown*, ch. 15.
12. *Cambridge Guide*, 29–35; Brace of Cantabs, *Gradus*, 90; Winstanley, *Unreformed Cambridge*, 197–203.
13. *Cambridge Guide*, 18; Winstanley, *Unreformed Cambridge*, 16–33.
14. Parker, *Town and Gown*, 142–43; Stokes, *Cambridge Parish Workhouses*, 27; Winstanley, *Later Victorian Cambridge*, 92–93.
15. *LLD*, 1:163; *CCD*, 1:1–18.
16. Brace of Cantabs, *Gradus*, 14, 121–31; cf. Winstanley, *Unreformed Cambridge*, 203ff.
17. Peacock, *Observations*, 76.
18. *CCD*, 1:3; *LLAS*, 1:317; Speakman, *Adam Sedgwick*, ch. 5; Secord, *Controversy*, ch. 2.
19. Spinning House committals, 1823–1836, CUL, University Archives, T.VIII.1, esp. 149-96. Cf. Marcus, *Other Victorians*, esp. 100–103.
20. *CCD*, 1:48–49, 53–55.

21. Reid, *Life, Letters,* 1:75; Pope–Hennessy, *Monckton Milnes,* 10ff; Preyer, 'Romantic Tide,' 43-46; P. Allen, *Cambridge Apostles,* ch. 1; CCD, 1:112.
22. Gascoigne, *Cambridge,* 252–62; Reid, *Life, Letters,* 1:51; W. Carus, *Memoirs,* 641, 648ff; Smyth, *Simeon,* 98ff, 202ff, 296–98; Barclay, *Whatever Happened,* ch. 1; O. Chadwick, *Victorian Church,* 1:110, 442, 449.
23. J. Cameron to F. Darwin, 15 Sept. [1882], DAR 112:14; *Autobiography,* 61–62; J. Herbert to F. Darwin, 26 May and 12 June 1882, DAR 112:50–51, 58–59; CCD, 1:58.
24. CCD, 1:539; D. Allen, *Naturalist,* 101–103; Barber, *Heyday,* chs. 1-2.
25. *Pedigrees,* 15, 28; LLD, 1:322; *Autobiography,* 63; RFD, 110; CCD, 1:74, 82.
26. CCD, 1:57, 91; Blomefield, *Chapters,* 54; *Autobiography,* 62–63.
27. CCD, 1:58–59 and cf. *Autobiography,* 62; Samouelle, *Entomologist's Useful Compendium,* 160; K. Smith, 'Darwin's Insects,' 7ff.
28. CUL, University Archives, C.U.R. 39.16.6–7 and O.XIV.109; [Blomefield], *Memoir,* 29-30, 49–51; Todhunter, *William Whewell,* 1:36–37.
29. CCD, 1:7; *Autobiography,* 64, 66–67; CP, 2:72.

5 PARADISE & PUNISHMENT

1. CCD, 1:56, 59, 61, 72, 325, 430; J. Heaviside to F. Darwin, 15 Sept. 1882, DAR 112:56–57.
2. CCD, 1:59, 61; recollections of J. Herbert, DAR 112; *Autobiography,* 58.
3. CCD, 1:62, 64–65.
4. CCD, 1:62–67, 70.
5. CCD, 1:51, 54, 66, 69, 71–72.
6. *Cambridge Guide,* 145–49; LLD, 1:165; *Companion,* 55; CCD, 1:70.
7. *Cambridge Guide,* 29; CCD, 1:68, 70–77, 98; *TBI,* 7–8.
8. CCD, 1:73–76, 78, 80, 539; [Blomefield], *Memoir,* 8; recollections of J. Price, DAR 112; *Cambridge Guide,* 304. On entomological society in London: D. Allen, *Naturalist,* 103–106; Desmond, 'Making,' 157ff.
9. Recollections of J. Herbert, DAR 112; LLD, 1:171; CCD, 1:64, 67.
10. Recollections of J. Price, DAR 112; CCD, 1:76, 79.
11. CCD, 1:79, 81–82.
12. CCD, 1:79–82; *Autobiography,* 60.
13. Acta Curiae, 1822–1835, CUL, University Archives, V.C.Ct.I.19:146–51; Cooper, *Annals,* 561–62; CCD, 1:82–83.
14. CUL, University Archives, UP 7.234; Cooper, *Annals,* 560–63; CCD, 1:8. On Castle Hill: *Cambridge Guide,* 232, 235–36; Parker, *Town and Gown,* 143.
15. CCD, 1:79, 82, 84–85.
16. *Cambridge and Hertford Independent Press,* 9 May 1829, p. [2], col. 1, and 16 May 1829, p. [2], col. 1; Joseph Romilly diary, 1829, CUL, Add. 6810; Cooper, *Annals,* 563; Reid, *Life, Letters,* 1:65–67; CCD, 1:85.
17. Royle, *Victorian Infidels,* 34–39; J. Wiener, *Radicalism,* esp. 130ff, 463; Desmond, 'Artisan Resistance,' 82; Royle, 'Taylor, Robert;' W. Carus, *Memoirs,* 308; Hole, *Pulpits, Politics,* 190–93, ch. 14.
18. *Lion,* 3 (24 April 1829), 519 and (29 May 1829), 673–74, 678, 682, 684. On Darwin's print purchases: CCD, 1:70–71; *Autobiography,* 61; RFD, 95–96; recollections of W. Darwin and of J. Herbert, DAR 112.

19. *Lion*, 3 (29 May 1829), 674–75; J. Moore, 'Freethought,' 290–93.

20. *Lion*, 3 (29 May 1829), 673, 675, 678, 682, 686.

21. *Lion*, 3 (29 May 1829), 682–83; CUL, University Archives, UP 7.244 and C.U.R. 124 for the regulations, and Rose Crescent lodging houses as late as 1854; Winstanley, *Early Victorian Cambridge*, 59–60.

22. *Lion*, 3 (29 May 1829), 678, 685, and (5 June 1829), 705–707; Joseph Romilly diary, 1829, CUL, Add. 6810; CUL, University Archives, UP 7.245; R. Taylor, *Devil's Pulpit* (1881 ed.), 2:vi.

6 THE MAN WHO WALKS WITH HENSLOW

1. Briggs, *Age*, 227ff; Hole, *Pulpits, Politics*, ch. 16; Cooper, *Annals*, 559–60, 563–64; Gascoigne, *Cambridge*, 236; C. Wordsworth to J. Brogden, 28 Mar. 1829, CUL, University Archives, UP.5; *LLAS*, 1:341–49; Brilioth, *Anglican Revival*, 93–96; CCD, 1:85–86.

2. CCD, 1:88–90.

3. CCD, 1:90–93; *Pedigrees*, 11.

4. CCD, 1:90, 93–94, 96; *Autobiography*, 63; K. Smith, 'Darwin's Insects,' 7–9.

5. CCD, 1:93–94; recollections of J. Price, DAR 112.

6. CCD, 1:95–96; 'Names of Men who attended the Botanical Lectures . . .,' CUL, University Archives, O.XIV.261; Blomefield, *Chapters*, 10, 12, 23; Blomefield, *Naturalist's Calendar*; Leonard Jenyns, '[ta peri emauta]' MS diary, commonplace books, and notes in possession of R. G. Jenyns, Bottisham Hall, Bottisham, Cambridgeshire; *Autobiography*, 66–67.

7. CCD, 1:96–97.

8. CCD, 1:98; CUL, University Archives, C.U.R. 28.11 (2 July 1829), 8; Examination Papers, 1830, CUL, L952.b.1.7.

9. Clarke, *Paley*, ch. 4; LeMahieu, *Mind*, ch. 1; Gascoigne, *Cambridge*, 241–44; Cole, 'Doctrine, Dissent.'

10. *Autobiography*, 59; Paley, *View*, 2:24–25, 395, 410. On Paley and revelation: Clarke, *Paley*, ch. 8; LeMahieu, *Mind*, ch. 4.

11. Paley, *View*, 2:395; CCD, 1:101; Previous Examination, 1824–1843, CUL, University Archives, Exam.L.67.

12. CCD, 1:99–102.

13. CCD, 1:102; recollections of J. Rodwell and of W. Leighton, DAR 112

14. [Blomefield], *Memoir*, 4–7, 13, 16–21, 30–39, 46–47; *Cambridge Guide*, 13; Walters, *Shaping*, 47–58.

15. CP, 2:72–73; Spinning House committals, 1823–1836, CUL, University Archives, T.VIII.1, esp. 209–97; *Autobiography*, 64–65; CCD, 1:104.

16. CP, 2:72–73; [Blomefield], *Memoir*, 41; recollections of J. Rodwell, DAR 112; CCD, 1:80; 'Plants gathered in five herborizing expeditions . . .,' CUL, University Archives, UP.5.

17. Sloan, 'Darwin, Vital Matter,' 373; 'Names of Men who attended the Botanical Lectures . . .,' CUL, University Archives, O.XIV.261; [Blomefield], *Memoir*, 39; recollections of J. Rodwell and of W. Leighton, DAR 112.

18. 'Edinburgh Zoology Notebook,' DAR 118 f. 13; *Autobiography*, 66; Sloan, 'Darwin, Vital Matter,' 373–87, 395 and 'Darwin's Invertebrate Program,' 86–87.

19. CCD, 1:95, 103–106, 272. The Bembidiidae beetles (Stephens, *Systematic Catalogue*, 1:36–41) are now the Family Bembidiini.

20. *CCD*, 1:50, 100, 105–109, 115, 192–93, 208, 255, 634. What Fanny enclosed was 'some scrawl of mine . . . out of my Book.' Her offer to 'do you another' was contingent on Charles's next visit. For her portrait: *Calendar*, 8917, 8926.

7 EVERY MAN FOR HIMSELF

1. R. Taylor, *Devil's Pulpit* (1881 ed.), 2:79; E. Thompson, *Making*, 843–44; J. Wiener, *Radicalism*, 164–70; Royle, *Victorian Infidels*, 39–40.
2. *CCD*, 1:109–11, 123, 180; *Autobiography*, 59, 64; [Blomefield], *Memoir*, 48, 57–58.
3. *CCD*, 1:110; Sedgwick, *Discourse*, 95–102; Todhunter, *William Whewell*, 2:174–78.
4. Gascoigne, *Cambridge*, 241–44; Paley, *Principles*, 1:217, 2:138–39, 302; Francis, 'Naturalism;' Clarke, *Paley*. chs. 5–6.
5. [Blomefield], *Memoir*, 60–61; *Autobiography*, 65.
6. E. Thompson, *Making*, ch. 7; E. Evans, 'Some Reasons;' Hobsbawm and Rudé, *Captain Swing*, 165–67; *Cambridge Chronicle and Journal*, 3 Dec. 1830, p. [3], col. 4; 10 Dec. 1830, pp. [1], col. 4 and [2], col. 5.
7. Recollections of J. Herbert, DAR 112.
8. *CCD*, 1:111–12; Examination Papers, 1831, CUL, L952.b.1.8; *Autobiography*, 59.
9. Recollections of J. Herbert, DAR 112; F. Watkins to F. Darwin, 18 July [1882?], DAR 112:111–14; *LLD*, 1:169–70; *CCD*, 2:125–26.
10. J. Heaviside to F. Darwin, 15 Sept. 1882, DAR 112:56–57; Monsarrat, *Thackeray*, 42; *CCD*, 1:113–19.
11. *CCD*, 1:112, 124; Blomefield, *Chapters*, 54; L. Jenyns to J. Hooker, 1 May 1882 (copy), DAR 112:67–68.
12. 'Names of Men who attended the Botanical Lectures . . .,' CUL, University Archives, O.XIV.261; *CCD*, 1:123.
13. Paley, *Natural Theology*, vii, 465, 490; Francis, 'Naturalism,' 212–16; Gillespie, 'Divine Design;' Clarke, *Paley*, ch. 7; LeMahieu, *Mind*, ch. 3.
14. Paley, *Natural Theology*, 465; Herschel, *Preliminary Discourse*, 350, 353 in Darwin Library, CUL; *CCD*, 1:118; *Autobiography*, 68; Ruse, 'Darwin's Debt,' 160ff; Schweber, 'John Herschel.'
15. [Blomefield], *Memoir*, 11, 13–15; Cannon, *Science*, 86ff; *CCD*, 1:539. Henslow later presented Darwin with Humboldt's book: *CCD*, 1:120.
16. *Autobiography*, 67–68; *CCD*, 1:120, 122–23, 125, 539.
17. J. Wiener, *Radicalism*, 174–79; Royle, 'Taylor, Robert,' 469; *The Times*, 31 May 1831, p. 4, cols. 1–2; *ED*, 1:234.
18. *CCD*, 1:121–22, 147; *Autobiography*, 68; Halévy, *Triumph*, 32–33.
19. Cooper, *Annals*, 570; *CCD*, 1:122–24; *LLAS*, 1:374–76; Todhunter, *William Whewell*, 2:118; Gascoigne, *Cambridge*, 236.
20. *LLAS*, 1:204, 376; [Blomefield], *Memoir*, 13–14; Secord, *Controversy*, 45–47; recollections of J. Rodwell, DAR 112; *CCD*, 1:25, 125.
21. *CCD*, 1:125–27.
22. Secord, *Controversy*, 47–53; *LLAS*, 1:378–80; *Autobiography*, 69; *CCD*, 1:540.
23. Secord, 'Discovery;' *LLAS*, 1:381; Barrett, 'Sedgwick–Darwin Geologic Tour,' 147–48, 157–58.
24. *Autobiography*, 69–71; *LLAS*, 1:381; recollections of G. Darwin, DAR 112; *CCD*, 1:127–31; Barrett, 'Sedgwick-Darwin Geologic Tour,' 149, 161–62.

8 MY FINAL EXIT

1. CCD, 1:127–30; *Diary*, 3.
2. CCD, 1:132–35, 151, 165, 382; *Diary*, 3; Graber and Miles, 'In Defence,' 99; cf. *Autobiography*, 71–72.
3. CCD, 1:135–16, 139–41, 145; L. Jenyns to J. Hooker, 1 May 1882 (copy), DAR 112:67–68; *Diary*, 3.
4. CCD, 1:140–41, 144, 146; Mellersh, *FitzRoy*; Burstyn, 'If Darwin wasn't;' Stanbury, 'H.M.S. *Beagle*,' 82; S. Gould, 'Darwin.'
5. CCD, 1:140, 144, 148–50, 156; Barlow, 'Robert FitzRoy,' 496; F. Darwin, 'FitzRoy,' 547.
6. CCD, 1:144, 146, 149; *Autobiography*, 72; Hyman, 'Darwin Sidelight.'
7. CCD, 1:154; F. Darwin, 'FitzRoy,' 547; Basalla, 'Voyage;' Nicholas and Nicholas, *Darwin*, 3–5.
8. CCD, 1:154; *Narrative*, 27–33; Barlow, 'FitzRoy,' 501–502; Stanbury, 'H.M.S. *Beagle*,' 76–78.
9. CCD, 1:154–56, 177, 553–54; B. Sulivan to [F.] Darwin, 12 Dec. 1884, DAR 112; K. Thomson, 'H.M.S. Beagle,' 665–66, 670–71; Stanbury, 'H.M.S. *Beagle*,' 86–92; R. Keynes, *Beagle Record*, 21, 39.
10. CCD, 1:155–57, 161, 167; *Autobiography*, 110. Henslow's gift, inscribed 21 September 1831, is in the Darwin Library, CUL.
11. CCD, 1:163, 165, 168–69, 171, 192–93, 540; *Wedgwood*, 215.
12. J. Wiener, *Radicalism*, 176–80; 'Trial of the Rev. Robert Taylor,' *The Times*, 5 July 1831, p. 4, col. 3; 9 July, p. 3, col. 1; 21 July, p. 5, col. 3; 23 July, p. 3, col. 5; Halévy, *Triumph*, 40; Briggs, *Age*, 251–53; CCD, 1:172, 174–76, 393; E. Thompson, *Making*, 888ff.
13. Notes on preserving specimens, DAR 29.3:78ff; *Reports of the Council and Auditors of the Accounts of the Zoological Society of London, read at the Anniversary Meeting, April 30th 1832* (London: Taylor, 1832), 9–10; Desmond, 'Making,' 232; CCD, 1:146–48, 171, 173; *Autobiography*, 103.
14. CCD, 1:143–44, 148–50, 172, 175.
15. CCD, 1:172, 176–77, 180, 182; J. Gruber, 'Who,' 271ff; *Diary*, 4–7. So wretched was the navy surgeon's lot that passions were flaring. A riot actually broke out in the London College of Surgeons over the snubbing of ships' surgeons in 1831: *London Medical Gazette*, 7 (1830–31), 765.
16. CCD, 1:175, 177–80; *Diary*, 6–7, 133; *Narrative*, 35.
17. CCD, 1:163, 179–80, 183, 186; *Diary*, 8–9; *Autobiography*, 79–80; Colp, 'Pre-Beagle Misery.'
18. CCD, 1:127, 145, 168–69, 173–74, 181–84, 186; *Diary*, 9.
19. CCD, 1:177, 182; *Diary*, 7–8, 10–11.
20. CCD, 1:187; *Diary*, 11–12, 13–15.
21. CCD, 1:180, 190; *Diary*, 15–17; F. Darwin, 'FitzRoy,' 547.

9 A CHAOS OF DELIGHT

1. *Narrative*, 40–41; *Diary*, 17–18; CCD, 1:201.
2. *Diary*, 19–20; CCD, 1:201–202; *Narrative*, 44–45.
3. *Diary*, 21–25; CCD, 1:202; *Narrative*, 46.
4. Secord, 'Discovery;' *Diary*, 24–26, 30, 33; *Charles Darwin*, 156–57.
5. *Autobiography*, 81; *Diary*, 27, 34.

6. *Diary*, 36–37; *Narrative*, 49–52; *CCD*, 1:203, 240.
7. *Diary*, 37–41, 48; *CCD*, 1:206; *Charles Darwin*, 158.
8. *Diary*, 41–44; *CCD*, 1:205; Cannon, *Science*, 87; Paradis, 'Darwin,' 95ff.
9. *Diary*, 43–46; *Narrative*, 56; *Autobiography*, 73–74.
10. *CCD*, 1:192–93, 197–98, 219–20; *Diary*, 46–51.
11. *Diary*, 52–60, 74; *Journal* (1839), 21–28, 605; *CCD*, 1:247, 252; *Charles Darwin*, 164–65.
12. *Diary*, 61–78; *CCD*, 1:226.
13. *Diary*, 64–77; *CCD*, 1:227, 230, 232, 237–38, 241, 247; *CP*, 1:182–85; *Journal* (1839), 35, 38.
14. *Diary*, 71–72, 77–80; *CCD*, 1:225, 231–32; J. Gruber, 'Who,' 275–76; Burstyn, 'If Darwin wasn't,' 67–68.
15. *Diary*, 81–83; *CCD*, 1:247, 248, 251–52; *Autobiography*, 85; Schweber, 'John Herschel,' 52–55.
16. *CCD*, 1:222–23, 248–50, 261, 277; *Diary*, 78, 84, 87–91, *Narrative*, 74–78; Parodiz, *Darwin*, 76–78.
17. Sloan, 'Darwin, Vital Matter,' 388–91; *CP*, 1:181. These were arrowworms, the chaetognaths.
18. *Journal* (1839), 117–18; Sloan, 'Darwin's Invertebrate Program,' 87–91; Thomson and Rachootin, 'Turning Points,' 26–27.
19. *Diary*, 92–94, 99–101, 104–105, 121; *CCD*, 1:276; *Narrative*, 83; Parodiz, *Darwin*, 99–102.
20. *CCD*, 1:276, 280–81; *Narrative*, 82; *Diary*, 106–110; *Charles Darwin*, 166; *Journal*, 204; Gruber and Gruber, 'Eye,' 195; H. Gruber, 'Going,' 18. The Punta Alta fossils were identified by Richard Owen after Darwin had returned to London: Owen, *Fossil Mammalia*, 7–9, 29 (the huge rodent *Toxodon*), 68–69 (the ground sloth *Mylodon*), 107–108 (a cow-sized armadillo or glyptodont).
21. *Diary*, 111; Schweber, 'John Herschel,' 55–56; *Narrative*, 95–96; cf. Bush, *Milton*, i:180–88.
22. *CCD*, 1:222–23, 235, 245, 255–59; *Diary*, 111–12, 117.
23. *Diary*, 113, 115; *CCD*, 1:222, 245, 257, 277–78, 281, 286.
24. R. Hamond to F. Darwin, 19 Sept. 1882, DAR 112:54–55; *Charles Darwin*, 167–69; *Diary*, 114, 116–18.
25. C. Lyell, *Principles*, 2:2, 10; Bartholomew, 'Lyell;' Desmond, *Politics*, 327–30.
26. *Diary*, 117–18; *CCD*, 1:281–82, 308.

10 TROUBLED SPIRITS FROM ANOTHER WORLD

1. *Diary*, 120–25; *CCD*, 1:306, 397.
2. *Diary*, 122, 124–29, 444; *CCD*, 1:303, 307, 316; *Narrative*, 102–103.
3. *Diary*, 130–32; *Narrative*, 105–106; *CCD*, 1:303; Stanbury, 'H.M.S. *Beagle*,' 84.
4. *Diary*, 133, 138–40; *Narrative*, 115, 124–25; *CCD*, 1:304.
5. *Diary*, 135, 139, 141, 143, 224; *CCD*, 1:303, 305; *Narrative*, 127–28.
6. *Diary*, 144–45; *CCD*, 1:304, 307; *Narrative*, 134–36; Parodiz, *Darwin*, 85, 106–108.
7. *Diary*, 145–47; *Narrative*, 139–40; *CCD*, 1:307; *Charles Darwin*, 178–79.
8. Sloan, 'Darwin, Vital Matter,' 391–92 and 'Darwin's Invertebrate Program,' 98–100; *Diary*, 149; *CCD*, 1:307, 399–400.

9. CCD, 1:247–48; *Diary*, 148–54; *Narrative*, 158–59.

10. *Diary*, 154–60; CCD, 1:321; *Charles Darwin*, 182–83; *Journal* (1839), 55, 69–70, 105–107.

11. *Diary*, 160–61; DON, 214–24; *Journal* (1839), 54ff; CCD, 1:311–12, 315, 321.

12. CCD, 1:288, 290–91, 299, 309, 311, 313, 320; F. Darwin, 'FitzRoy,' 548; A. Mellersh to F. Darwin, 10 June 1882, DAR 112:83; *Diary*, 167; *Wedgwood*, 219.

13. CCD, 1:266, 269, 271–72, 274–75, 291, 299, 309; ED, 1:61; *Wedgwood*, 155.

14. CCD, 1:311–12, 314, 316, 320–22, 398; *Diary*, 162.

15. DON, 273; *Journal* (1839), 108; *Charles Darwin*, 199; *Diary*, 99–100, 163–71; Parodiz, *Darwin*, 103ff; CCD, 1:330–31.

16. CCD, 1:330–31, 343; *Diary*, 172, 175, 178–81; *Charles Darwin*, 194–98; Gruber and Gruber, 'Eye,' 195–96. The long-snouted skull was identified by Richard Owen later in London as a giant anteater-like *Scelidotherium*: Owen, *Fossil Mammalia*, 73–74.

17. *Diary*, 182–98; *Charles Darwin*, 199, 206–13; CCD, 1:336, 342–43, 352; Parodiz, *Darwin*, 108–10, 116–17.

18. *Diary*, 198–99; *Narrative*, 173; CCD, 1:230, 318, 323–25, 328–30, 344–45, 351–53.

19. *Diary*, 203–204; CCD, 1:344, 378–79; *Journal* (1839), 180–81; LRO, 1:119–20; Owen, *Fossil Mammalia*, 16ff. Later in London Owen identified it as a hippo-sized rodent *Toxodon*, an antecedent of the South American capybara.

20. *Diary*, 205–209; CCD, 1:335, 354, 359. The asthmatic Earle died in London in December 1838.

21. *Diary*, 208–12, 215; DON, 229, 271; *Journal* (1839), 108–109, 208–209; CCD, 1:369–70, 2:373; Owen, *Fossil Mammalia*, 35–36. Later in London Owen called this camel-sized llama-forerunner *Macrauchenia*: Rachootin, 'Owen and Darwin.'

22. *Diary*, 213–22; *Narrative*, 177; CCD, 1:358, 370; *Journal* (1839), 109–10; DON, 272, 273.

23. *Diary*, 222–24; C. Lyell, *Principles*, 2:21.

24. *Diary*, 222–24; C. Lyell, *Principles*, 2:60–62; Herbert, 'Place of Man, Pt 1,' 227–29.

25. *Diary*, 226–27; *Narrative*, 182–83, 185; CCD, 1:378, 380.

11 SHAKEN FOUNDATIONS

1. *Diary*, 228; *Narrative*, 185–87; CCD, 1:378, 380.

2. CCD, 1:316, 327–28, 333–34, 359, 363; Morrell and Thackray, *Gentlemen*, 165–75 on the Cambridge BAAS meeting in June 1833, under Sedgwick's Presidency.

3. CCD, 1:368–71, 398; DON, 246; *Charles Darwin*, 218–19; *Diary*, 229–31; Herbert, 'Darwin,' 492–93; Sulloway, 'Darwin's Early Intellectual Development,' 132–44.

4. *Narrative*, 188; CCD, 1:370, 381; *Diary*, 232.

5. R. Keynes, *Beagle Record*, 199, 203; *Diary*, 231–33; *Narrative*, 193–96.

6. R. Keynes, *Beagle Record*, 202, 210; *Diary*, 232–37; *Charles Darwin*, 221–22; *Narrative*, 196ff, 369.

7. *Diary*, 236–40; *Narrative*, 198–200; *Charles Darwin*, 222.

8. CCD, 1:336–42, 345–47, 356–58, 392–93.

9. LLL, 2:33; CCD, 1:345–46, 392; Erskine, 'Darwin,' 261–63; H. Martineau, *Autobiography*, 1:218–19, 260–63, 327; *Diary*, 240–41; Wheatley, *Life*, 95–97.

10. Austin, *Memoir*, 2:383; Harrison, *Early Victorian Britain*, 23, 73, 107–12; H. Martineau, *Autobiography*, 1:211–12, 219; Hilton, *Age*, ch. 3 on religious Malthusianism.

11. CCD, 1:338, 389; *Diary*, 243; *Charles Darwin*, 223.

12. *Diary*, 244–49; *Narrative*, 205–207; CCD, 1:392, 3:38; DON, 250–53; Gruber and Gruber, 'Eye,' 193.

13. *Diary*, 249–50, 253–55; CCD, 1:393, 405–406, 419.

14. *Diary*, 257–63; *Charles Darwin*, 226; CCD, 1:396–97, 410; Parodiz, *Darwin*, 123–25.

15. CCD, 1:312, 397–402, 410–11, 418–20; *Narrative*, 210–11; *Diary*, 263.

16. *Diary*, 264–71, 274–76; *Charles Darwin*, 229; *Narrative*, 216–18.

17. *Diary*, 275–80; *Narrative*, 221–23; *Journal* (1839), 351; CCD, 4:258, 389, 436.

18. *Diary*, 247, 269, 280–86; CCD, 1:432, 434, 437; Parodiz, *Darwin*, 126–27.

19. Hodge, 'Darwin and the Laws,' 18–22; Kohn, 'Theories,' 70–71; H. Gruber, 'Going,' 16–18.

20. Sloan, 'Darwin, Vital Matter,' 393–95; Hodge, 'Darwin and the Laws,' 22–27; *Diary*, 287; *Journal* (1839), 363–64.

21. CCD, 1:419, 434; *Diary*, 286–93. Cf. *Autobiography*, 75.

22. *Diary*, 293–302; *Narrative*, 229–30; CCD, 1:434, 436; Parodiz, *Darwin*, 127–28; Rudwick, 'Strategy,' 4, 16. Cf. Darwin's copy of Humboldt's *Personal Narrative*, 2:207 in Darwin Library, CUL.

12 COLONIAL LIFE

1. *Narrative*, 235; CCD, 1:432–37.

2. *Diary*, 304–13; CCD, 1:440, 445–46.

3. *Diary*, 314–18; *Charles Darwin*, 236; CCD, 1:442; *Journal* (1839), 354–55. The Vinchuca insect hosts a trypanosome parasite that causes Chagas's disease in humans. But Darwin did not mention coming down with the fever that accompanies the initial infection, and it is now doubted that the Vinchuca bite was the cause of his later recurrent sickness: *Diary*, 315; TBI, 126ff. Leonard Darwin, recalling his father's opinion, did not attribute the illness to anything that happened on the voyage: L. Darwin, 'Memories,' 121.

4. CCD, 1:440, 445; *Diary*, 321; *Charles Darwin*, 232–33.

5. CCD, 1:419, 435, 440, 443, 445–48; *Diary*, 318–19, 322–23; *Charles Darwin*, 237; Parodiz, *Darwin*, 119–21.

6. *Diary*, 324–43; *Charles Darwin*, 238–43; CCD, 1:449, 457–58.

7. *Diary*, 343–50; CCD, 1:458, 462, 466; *Charles Darwin*, 244.

8. Stoddart, 'Darwin, Lyell,' 200–204; C. Lyell, *Principles*, 2:290; R. Keynes, *Beagle Record*, 350–51; *Charles Darwin*, 243–44; *Autobiography*, 98–99; CCD, 1:460, 567–68.

9. CCD, 1:416, 460, 462, 465–66; *Diary*, 350.

10. Davis presented it to the zoo after arriving back in England. See the entry for 4 November 1836, 'Occurrences at the Gardens,' Zoological Society of London: 'Rec[d]. A brown Coati Mundi Pres. by J. E. Davis Esq RN H.M. Sloop Beagle, off Woolwich.' J. Davis is one of the forecastle men listed in CCD, 1:549.

11. DON, 262; *Diary*, 354, 362–63; *Charles Darwin*, 247; *Narrative*, 270, 272; CCD, 1:489; Sulloway, 'Darwin's Conversion,' 339 n. 23 on the museum mislabelling of the marine iguana.

12. *Narrative*, 286; *Diary*, 351–54; *Charles Darwin*, 247–48; CCD, 1:485.
13. Sulloway, 'Darwin's Conversion,' 338–44; *Journal* (1839), 465; DON, 262.
14. *Narrative*, 279; *Diary*, 357–59; Sulloway, 'Darwin,' 19.
15. *Diary* 360–63.
16. *Diary*, 355–57; DON, 261–62; Sulloway, 'Darwin,' 6–19; CCD, 1:485.
17. *Diary*, 360; *Narrative*, 277, 283, 286. Much later he admitted that 'it never occurred to me, that the production of islands only a few miles apart, and placed under the same physical conditions, would be dissimilar. I therefore did not attempt to make a series of specimens from the separate islands:' *Journal* (1839), 474–75.
18. Sulloway, 'Darwin,' 12, 19; DON, 262.
19. CCD, 1:471; Pennington, 'Darwin,' 4; *Narrative*, 295–98, 302; *Diary*, 365–73.
20. *Diary*, 376–79; CCD, 1:569; Stoddart, 'Darwin, Lyell,' 205.
21. *Diary*, 380–87; Pennington, 'Darwin,' 5-8; *Narrative*, 322.
22. CP, 2:20–21, 34–37; CCD, 1:472, 485, 560; *Diary*, 384–85.
23. *Diary*, 389–93; CCD, 1:472. We are grateful to David Stanbury for information about the collection, including a copy of FitzRoy's letter that accompanied it.
24. *Diary*, 395–96; Nicholas and Nicholas, *Charles Darwin*, 20–21; CCD, 1:482, 484–85, 492.
25. *Diary*, 396–400; Marshall, *Darwin*, 11; Nicholas and Nicholas, *Charles Darwin*, 22–44.
26. *Diary*, 401–403; CCD, 1:481; Nicholas and Nicholas, *Charles Darwin*, 45–54. Desmond, *Politics*, 279–87.
27. *Diary*, 403–405, 408; Desmond, 'Making,' 247 n. 169; CCD, 1:483; Nicholas and Nicholas, *Charles Darwin*, 18, 63–64.
28. *Diary*, 406–10; CCD, 1:485, 490; King-Hele, *Letters*, 190; Nicholas and Nicholas, *Charles Darwin*, 83–104; Darwin, *Volcanic Islands*, 138, 158; *Journal* (1839), 583n.
29. CCD, 1:490–91; Nicholas and Nicholas, *Charles Darwin*, 86–87.
30. *Diary*, 410–13; *Narrative*, 339; Nicholas and Nicholas, *Charles Darwin*, 105–17; P. Armstrong, *Charles Darwin*, 17–19, ch. 4; Sloan, 'Darwin's Invertebrate Program,' 104–108.

13 TEMPLES OF NATURE

1. Sloan, 'Darwin's Invertebrate Program,' 108–109; P. Armstrong, *Charles Darwin*, 31; *Diary*, 413–16.
2. *Diary*, 416–18; CCD, 1:495, 570; R. Keynes, *Beagle Record*, 350–51; *Narrative*, 344.
3. CCD, 1:492–93, 495–96; *Diary*, 419–22; F. Darwin, 'FitzRoy,' 548.
4. *Autobiography* 107; CCD, 1:497–98, 500; Kohn, 'Darwin's Ambiguity,' 222; *Notebooks* RN32; Cannon, 'Impact,' 304–11.
5. CP, 1:3–16, 19, 24–25; CCD, 1:473–74, 487, 498–99; *Diary*, 422–27.
6. Kirby, 'Introductory Address,' 5; Desmond, 'Making,' 168. Sulloway, 'Darwin's Conversion,' 332–37, argues from Darwin's spelling pattern that the ornithology catalogue (published as DON) was drawn up between the Cape and Ascension Island, that is between 18 June and 19 July 1836.
7. DON, 262. Unlike Sulloway, Hodge thinks that Darwin was already looking favourably on transmutation by this time: Hodge, 'Darwin, Species,' 236.
8. CCD, 1:500, 502; *Diary*, 424–30.

9. Darwin had known at least since Mauritius that FitzRoy intended to put in at Bahia, but that did not soften the blow: CCD, 1:488, 495, 503; *Diary*, 431–32.

10. CCD, 1:492, 501; *Diary*, 432–42.

11. CCD, 1:469; *Diary*, 441–42.

12. Sulloway, 'Darwin's Conversion,' 333 n. 17; D. Porter, '*Beagle* Collector,' 979–88; Gruber and Gruber, 'Eye,' 189; *Narrative*, 286.

13. CCD, 1:492, 495, 499–500.

14. *Notebooks* RN18, 72; H. Gruber, 'Going,' 25; *Diary*, 446.

15. CCD, 1:469, 474–75, 503; *LLL*, 1:460–61; CP, 1:18.

16. CCD, 1:488; *Diary*, 443–47.

14 A PEACOCK ADMIRING HIS TAIL

1. CCD, 1:504–507.

2. Austin, *Memoir*, 2:352; CCD, 1:506; Halévy, *Triumph*, 56; Holt, *Unitarian Contribution*, 23, 132, 217–41.

3. Edsall, *Anti-Poor Law Movement*, 21, 59; Harrison, *Early Victorian Britain*, 28; Berman, *Social Change*, 109–10; E. Thompson, *Making*, 904.

4. CCD, 1:507–509, 512.

5. Tristan, *London Journal*, 1–2; Harrison, *Early Victorian Britain*, 26. For a graphic illustration of the metropolitan works under way on Darwin's return: Jackson, *George Scharf's London*, 70–71, 100, 112–13, 131–36. Darwin was told of the gutting of Parliament while on the *Beagle*: CCD, 1:413.

6. CCD, 1:509, 514, 516; Bunbury, *Life*, 1:147.

7. *Reports of the Council and Auditors of the Zoological Society of London, Read at the Annual General Meeting, April 29, 1836* (London: Taylor, 1836), 20; (1837), 15; (1838), 10; Zoological Society, Minutes of Council, 4:396–7; Desmond, 'Making,' 233; CCD, 1:512. The Society had moved from its old museum, Lord Berkeley's former town house at 33 Bruton Street, to Hunter's museum on 11 July 1836: cf. CCD, 1:514 n. 2.

8. CCD, 1:299, 513–14; Desmond, 'Making,' 224–25, 232–41; *Lancet*, 1 (1840–41), 117.

9. *London Medical Gazette*, 13 (1833–34), 293, 676; Desmond, 'Robert E. Grant,' 217; Desmond, *Politics*, 122, 149; *Report from the Select Committee on British Museum* (Parliamentary Papers, 14 July 1836), 133; Gunther, *Founders*, ch. 8; CCD, 1:512.

10. CCD, 1:510, 534; Keith, *Darwin*, 221–22.

11. *LLL*, 2:33; CCD, 1:345–46, 2:518; Erskine, 'Darwin,' 261–63; H. Martineau, *Autobiography*, 1:218–19, 260–63, 327.

12. Quoted in Erskine, 'Darwin,' 109; Martineau, *Autobiography*, 1:204–209; Desmond, *Politics*, 126–27 on the BMA.

13. CCD, 1:518–19; Erskine, 'Darwin,' 260–61.

14. CCD, 1:514, 532; *LLL*, 1:474–75.

15. Broderip, 'Zoological Gardens,' 321; LRO, 1:96, 102, 169; Desmond, 'Making,' 238, 240–41; CCD, 1:515; Bunbury, *Life*, 1:187.

16. R. Grant, *Study*, 17–19; Desmond, *Politics*, 126–33, 385, 402–403.

17. As the radicals hailed him: *Lancet*, 2 (1841–42), 246; LRO, 1:102.

18. Sloan, 'Darwin, Vital Matter,' 399ff.

19. CCD, 1:512, 520; D. Porter, '*Beagle* Collector,' 1006–1007. Particular polyps are mentioned in *Journal* (1839), 552–53 and Darwin's *Coral Reefs*, esp. ch. 1.

20. *CCD*, 1:14, 183; Herbert, 'Place of Man, Pt 1,' 241, and 'Place of Man, Pt 2,' 174–75; Desmond, *Politics*, 122.

21. *CCD*, 1:511–12, 514–15; D. Porter, '*Beagle* Collector.'

22. *ED*, 1:272–74; *CCD*, 1:513, 519, 524, 526, 530, 533, 535; 2:2.

23. *CCD*, 1:515–16, 2:14, 23.

24. *CCD*, 1:518, 527–28, 531, 534. Darwin left Owen fifty-odd preserved mammals and birds in addition to the fossil bones.

25. Quoted in David, *Intellectual Women*, 36–37; *CCD*, 1:524.

26. H. Martineau, *Autobiography*, 1:355; *CCD*, 1:524, 2:1, 5; *LLL*, 2:34.

27. Tristan, *London Journal*, 7; Dickens, *Bleak House*, 1; Raumer, *England*, 1:7; Jackson, *George Scharf's London*, 75; *CCD*, 1:511–13.

28. *CCD*, 1:395, 421, 525; 2:8; *Journal* (1839), 69.

29. *LLL*, 2:12; Stoddart, 'Darwin, Lyell,' 206–207; Herbert, 'Darwin,' 490–94; Rudwick, 'Charles Darwin,' 195ff; Babbage, *Ninth Bridgewater Treatise*, 209–20; Cannon, 'Impact;' *CCD*, 1:532, 2:1; *LLD*, 1:278–79, 2:12; *CP*, 1:41–43.

30. Gillispie, *Genesis*, 140; Dean, 'Through Science,' 121; Herbert, 'Darwin,' 485.

31. *CCD*, 2:4, 29; Sulloway, 'Darwin,' 6ff; Hodge, 'Darwin and the Laws,' 47.

32. *DON*, 261; Sulloway, 'Darwin,' 6, 8–9, 13–19 and 'Darwin's Conversion,' 356–57; *CCD*, 2:2; Zoological Society, *Reports* (1837), 15.

33. *Proceedings of the Zoological Society*, 4 (1836), 142; 5 (1837), 7; on wrens, vol. 4 (1836) 88–89; J. Gould, *Birds of Europe* and *Birds of Australia*. On Gould's position in the museum: Desmond, 'Making,' 231, 246 n. 164.

34. Zoological Society, Minutes of Scientific Meetings. Oct. 1835 – Aug. 1840, f. 120. The final draft of Gould's 10 January paper was not submitted for publication until 3 October that year (as explained in *Proceedings of the Zoological Society*, 107 [1937], 79), by which time he had designated fourteen species, and this figure appears in the printed version: J. Gould, 'Mr. Darwin's Collection,' 4. Sulloway brilliantly disentangles Gould's maturing views in 'Darwin,' 21 n. 32 and 'Darwin's Conversion,' 358–61. Ultimately Darwin's 'Icterus' turned out to be a cactus finch, his 'wren' a warbler finch, and his 'Gross-beaks' heavy-billed finches.

35. Wilson, *Charles Lyell*, 437–38; C. Lyell, 'Address,' 510–11; Rachootin, 'Owen,' 156–59. Owen called this llama-forebear *Macrauchenia*.

36. *CCD*, 2:4, 8; C. Lyell, 'Address,' 511; Sulloway, 'Darwin's Conversion,' 252–55.

37. Wilson, *Charles Lyell*, 441; R. Porter, 'Gentlemen,' 810, 821–24.

38. *CCD*, 1:259, 516, 2:11, 13; Rudwick, 'Charles Darwin.'

15 REFORMING NATURE

1. *CCD*, 2:8, 11.

2. *LLL*, 1:466, 472; *Hansard*, 3rd ser., 32 (1836), 162; 34 (1836), 491; *CCD*, 2:175. In March 1837 the Parliamentary debates over Church tithes were furious (Bunbury, *Life*, 1:149). Darwin already knew these soiréeing guests; he was attending the geologist Roderick Murchison's lavish dinners with Babbage and Owen as early as 5 Nov. 1836: *LRO*, 1:103.

3. *LLL*, 1:467; 'Geology and Mineralogy,' *Athenaeum* (1837), 79.

4. Babbage, *Ninth Bridgewater Treatise*, 25, 45–47, 92; Desmond, *Archetypes*, 214–15.

5. C. Babbage to Victoria, 24 May 1837, BL, Add. MSS 37,190, f. 147; H.

Holland to C. Babbage, 26 May 1837, f. 153; C. Lyell to C. Babbage, 6 Jan., 17 Feb., May 1837, ff. 8, 37, 185.

6. *CCD*, 2:106; Schweber, 'John Herschel,' 33; Cannon, 'Impact,' 305.

7. Cannon, 'Impact,' 305, 312; Wilson, *Charles Lyell*, 438–39. Because it contained some controversial geological points, the letter was finally read aloud to the Geological Society on 17 May 1837: *LLL*, 2:5, 11; Babbage, *Ninth Bridgewater Treatise*, 226–27. On the Royal Society: MacLeod, 'Whigs,' 64–65; Desmond, *Politics*, 225–26. And on the Herschelian high road: Kohn, 'Darwin's Ambiguity,' 222–23.

8. *LLL*, 1:467, 2:5; Bartholomew, 'Lyell;' Cannon, 'Impact,' 308; *CCD*, 2:7, 8–9.

9. Erskine, 'Darwin,' 34; *CCD*, 2:13.

10. Wedgwood, 'Grimm,' 170, 175; *Notebooks*, N31, 39 for Charles's discussion with Hensleigh on the parallel evolution of sounds.

11. *CCD*, 2:155; H. Martineau, *Autobiography*, 1:355; *ED*, 1:277, 284; *Autobiography*, 112–13; Erskine, 'Darwin,' 106.

12. Southwood Smith, *Divine Government*, 109, 111. By the depression year of 1837, though, even Smith was losing his rosy view of inevitable progress. He alerted the Poor Law Commissioners to the epidemics in London's East End and he showed Dickens the squalor, shaking him to an extent that he based episodes from *Oliver Twist* and *Bleak House* on Smith's report.

13. *LLL*, 2:8; *Notebooks* N36, B98; Brooke, 'Relations,' 46–47; Ospovat, *Development*, 30–33; Cornell, 'God's Magnificent Law,' 387–89.

14. Epps, *Church of England's Apostacy*, 3; *CCD*, 1:259; Austin, *Memoir*, 2:384; *Medico-Chirurgical Review*, 23 (1835), 413; Jacyna, 'Immanence,' 325–26.

15. *British and Foreign Medical Review*, 5 (1838), 86–100; Rehbock, *Philosophical Naturalists*, 56; Epps, 'Elements,' 100; Desmond, *Politics*, 110–17, 199.

16. *Medico-Chirurgical Review*, 30 (1839), 450. Gully, like so many Edinburgh graduates, had studied at the republican Hôtel Dieu in Paris (in 1828). He helped run the Dissenting *London Medical and Surgical Journal* in the mid-1830s (Mann, *Collections*, 5–6, 10), which supported many of the heterodox sciences: Desmond, *Politics*, ch. 4, esp. 175.

17. Sulloway, 'Darwin,' 12, 21–22 and 'Darwin's Conversion,' 359–62; Kottler, 'Charles Darwin's Biological Species Concept,' 281; Herbert, 'Place of Man, Pt 1,' 236–37; J. Gould, 'Three Species.'

18. What happened to Darwin's tortoise is not known. There is no record in the 'Occurrences at the Gardens' ledger, held at the Zoological Society of London, of it being presented alive to the Zoological Gardens in 1836 or early 1837; nor is it mentioned in Flower, *List*, 3:33.

19. *LLL*, 2:36; C. Lyell, *Principles*, 2:20–21; Bartholomew, 'Lyell;' Desmond, *Politics*, 328–29; Schweber, 'Origin,' 265; H. Gruber, 'Going,' 10.

20. *LLL*, 2:10–11; *CP*, 1:44–45; *Notebooks* B94, 126, 133. The Indian monkey, from the Siwalik Hills, was found in Pliocene to Lower Pleistocene strata (in today's terminology). It was found in the same deposits as the tapir-like *Anoplotherium* and huge *Sivatherium*, with their four foliated antler-like horns. The monkey's discoverers, Hugh Falconer of the Bengal Medical Service and Capt. Proby Cautley of the Bengal Artillery, had only ten weeks earlier received the society's Wollaston medal for their Himalayan work: D. Moore, 'Geological Collectors,' 404; Cautley and Falconer, 'On the Remains,' 569.

21. *Notebooks* B126; Cautley, 'Extract,' 544.

22. Knight, *London*, 3:200–203; Bunbury, *Life*, 1:186; Sloan, 'Darwin, Vital Matter,' 405ff; Desmond, *Politics*, 346ff. Owen was borrowing from Müller's *Handbuch der Physiologie*.

23. Sloan, 'Darwin, Vital Matter,' 418–19, 425–30; *CCD*, 2:32; *LRO*, 1:108; Desmond, *Politics*, 291–93, 347.

24. Sloan, 'Darwin, Vital Matter,' 424, 434; *Notebooks* RN inside front cover; Jacyna, 'Immanence,' 314–327; Desmond, 'Artisan Resistance,' 95–104 and *Politics*, 265–66.

25. *Notebooks* RN 129–30, 133; Hodge, 'Darwin on the Laws,' 19–28; Kohn, 'Theories,' 75, 77–78; cf. C. Lyell, *Principles*, 3:85; Sloan, 'Darwin, Vital Matter,' 433ff; *Journal* (1839), 212.

26. *Journal* (1839), 212; *CP*, 1:45; Sloan, 'Darwin, Vital Matter,' 434; *Notebooks* RN inside front cover.

27. *Notebooks* RN 127; *CCD*, 3:14; Blomefield, *Chapters*, 29 on Jenyns's fish; J. Gould, 'New Species;' *CCD*, 2:11.

28. *Notebooks* B161, RN 127, 130, 153; Herbert, *Red Notebook*, 6–12; E. Richards,'Question,' 148; Kohn, 'Theories,' 73–76; Sulloway, 'Darwin's Conversion,' 371ff; Hodge, 'Darwin and the Laws,' 44–45, 48–49.

29. *CCD*, 2:11, 14; *Journal* (1839), 462, 475; Sulloway, 'Darwin,' 33.

30. *CCD*, 2:15–17, 20–21, 24, 38; Zoological Society, *Reports* (1832), 9–10 on Richardson's Arctic species.

31. *CCD*, 2:26, 31 n. 4, 37, 59; Desmond, *Politics*, 384.

32. *CCD*, 2:16–18, 27.

33. *CCD*, 1:14, 31, 2:29; *CP*, 1:40, 46–49; Sulloway, 'Darwin,' 23–29; *LLL*, 2:12.

16 TEARING DOWN THE BARRIERS

1. *Notebooks* B2–3; Kohn, 'Theories,' 81–87; Ospovat, *Development*, 40ff. Hodge, 'Darwin and the Laws,' 38–39, 80 calls these early pages a discrete 'Zoonomical Sketch.'

2. *Notebooks* B3–6, 15; Sloan, 'Darwin, Vital Matter,' 436–39; Kohn, 'Theories,' 88–92.

3. *Notebooks* B18, 169; Hodge, 'Lamarck's Science,' 343–45, on Lamarck's escalator of life. Herbert, 'Place of Man, Pt 2,' 196 on man's animal ancestry holding no terrors for Darwin (but then neither did it for many Unitarians and secular radicals in London in the late 1830s).

4. *Notebooks* B21, 23, 25–26; *CCD*, 2:32, 41, 48; Kohn, 'Theories,' 109–13; Hodge, 'Darwin and the Laws,' 78–79; H. Gruber, *Darwin*, ch. 7.

5. *Notebooks* B29, 35, 38, 39, 42; Sloan, 'Darwin, Vital Matter,' 442–43; Kohn, 'Darwin's Ambiguity,' 223–24.

6. Ospovat, *Development*, 33–37; Kohn, 'Darwin's Ambiguity,' 224; Kohn, 'Theories,' 86, 98–99, 104–105; *Notebooks* B46, 74.

7. *CCD*, 2:39; *Notebooks*, B82, 92, 125, 224, 248; Grinnell, 'Rise,' 264–71.

8. *CCD*, 2:39–40, 44–45, 49, 58.

9. *CCD*, 2:47–48, 52; *TBI*, 14–16.

10. *ED*, 1:216, 220, 255, 266, 273, 278–79; *Companion*, 293; E. Richards, 'Darwin,' 82–83, 87; *Pedigrees*, 11; *Wedgwood*, 221; *CP*, 1:49–52.

11. *CCD*, 2:55 n. 1, 70; *CP*, 1:49–53.

12. *CCD*, 2:61–63, 86; Jenyns, *Fish*, v–vi; he was to produce the fattest of the books in the *Zoology* series.

13. *LLL*, 2:37, 39; *LRO*, 1:121; Owen, *Fossil Mammalia*, 16, 55; Freeman, *Works*, 28; Rachootin, 'Owen,' 166; *CCD*, 2:66.

14. *CCD*, 2:10, 13, 50–52, 69–70; Whewell, 'Address,' 643; D. Porter, '*Beagle* Collector,' 994.

15. Sedgwick, 'Address,' 206, 305; Napier, *Selections*, 491.

16. *CCD*, 2:104–105, 6:344; *LLL*, 2:39–40, 43–44; *CP*, 1:53–86.

17. *Notebooks* B207, 215, 224, D49.

18. Epps, *Diary*, 61; H. Martineau, 'Right and Wrong,' 2, 58; *CCD*, 2:148; Halévy, *Triumph*, 239; *Notebooks* B231, C154.

19. Epps, 'Elements,' 118; Paley, *Natural Theology*, 490; Desmond, *Politics*, 184–85, 407–408.

20. *Notebooks* B232; Desmond, *Politics*, 184; *Notebooks* N62 n. 1; R. Richards, 'Instinct,' 213–16, 227 and *Darwin*, 130–42; H. Gruber, *Darwin*, 202.

17 MENTAL RIOTING

1. *CCD*, 4:40; *Notebooks* C1–2; Ospovat, *Development*, 46–47.

2. *Notebooks* B90, C4, 52, 120.

3. *Notebooks* B142, C60, 233–234; *CCD*, 3:38, 53.

4. *Notebooks* C61; Kohn, 'Theories,' 124–25.

5. *Notebooks* C65–66, 119; Kohn, 'Theories,' 131–2; R. Richards, 'Instinct,' 196ff and *Darwin*, 91ff. But, as Richards shows, Darwin was still distancing himself from the maligned Lamarck. Where Lamarck, Darwin mistakenly thought, attributed changing habits to will-power, Darwin made unconscious instincts the cause of new structures.

6. *Notebooks* C inside front cover; *CCD*, 2:70–71; H. Gruber, *Darwin*, 424–25; Wynne is identified as The Mount's gardener in *Calendar*, 5583.

7. *CCD*, 2:72, 79; *Journal* (1839), 628; *Notebooks* C54; Sulloway, 'Darwin's Conversion,' 345.

8. *CCD*, 2:69, 75, 80, 85.

9. *Notebooks* C76.

10. Scherren, *Zoological Society*, 65, 85; Flower, *List*, 1:4; *CCD*, 2:80. The zoo had purchased other orangs, but none had lived long enough to be exhibited. Because of the new heated giraffe house, Jenny was the first to survive a winter.

    An orang named 'Jenny,' seen sipping tea by the Owens in 1842, and presented to Queen Victoria that year, was a different ape, purchased on 13 Dec. 1839. Darwin's 'Jenny' died after an illness on 28 May 1839: 'Occurrences at the Gardens, 1839,' MS, Zoological Society of London; *LRO*, 1:193–94, 206.

11. *CCD*, 2:80; *Notebooks* C79, also M138.

12. *CCD*, 1:510, 2:80, 7:Supplement.

13. *CCD*, 2:105, 443.

14. *CCD*, 2:83; Brent, *Charles Darwin*, 17–18.

15. *CCD*, 2:86; *Notebooks* C100.

16. *Natural Selection*, 36; *Notebooks* C120, E13; Secord, 'Darwin,' 525; Ruse, *Darwinian Revolution*, 178.

17. Sebright, in *Notebooks* C133; Ruse, 'Charles Darwin,' 344–49.

18. *Notebooks* C133, D107; Kohn, 'Theories,' 137–39; Herbert, 'Darwin, Malthus,' 212–13; Cornell, 'Analogy,' 316–18.

19. *CCD*, 2:92; *Notebooks* B216–217.

20. *CCD*, 2:84, 86, 431; H. Martineau, *Autobiography*, 2:115–18.
21. *Notebooks* C123, N19; H. Gruber, *Darwin*, 38.
22. Jacyna, 'Immanence;' Desmond, *Politics* and 'Artisan Resistance.'
23. R. Richards, 'Instinct,' 198–99 and *Darwin*, 94–98.
24. *Notebooks* C166; Kohn, 'Darwin's Ambiguity,' 224–25; Manier, *Young Darwin*, 56, 129–30; H. Gruber, *Darwin*, ch. 10; cf. Ospovat, *Development*, 67.
25. De Morgan, *Memoir*, 325; Elliotson, 'Address,' 33; *London Medical Gazette*, 11 (1832–33), 213–21; *Lancet*, 2 (1832–33), 341; *Notebooks* C166, OUN 37.
26. *Notebooks* C244, M61, OUN 39–41; Manier, *Young Darwin*, 129–31, 220–23; Erskine, 'Darwin,' 216ff.
27. Robertson, 'Dr. Elliotson,' 205, 256–57; Elliotson, *Human Physiology*, 39; Elliotson, 'Reply,' 289–90. Darwin read Elliotson's *Physiology*: *Notebooks* OUN 10v.
28. RFD, 23; also recollections of William Darwin, DAR 112.2 and *LLD*, 2:114.
29. *Lancet*, 1 (1838–39), 561–62. Elliotson was not alone. Martineau's Unitarian schoolfellows had all run into similar trouble. W. B. Carpenter was declared 'unfit for the duties of a Public Instructor' after suggesting that 'one simple law' impressed on matter at the Creation controlled the emergence and peopling of the planets. Southwood Smith was upbraided for saying that 'Life is nothing but organization in action.' C. Bell to T. Coates, 2 Sept. 1829, UCL, SDUK Correspondence; Carpenter, *Remarks*, 1–3.
30. *CCD*, 2:85, 431; *TBI*, 16–17.
31. H. Martineau, *Autobiography*, 1:401; *Notebooks* C220; E. Richards, 'Darwin,' 91. Erasmus and Hensleigh went on to become Chairman and Trustees of Bedford College for Women (founded in 1849 by Elizabeth Reid, Martineau's friend): Erskine, 'Darwin,' 166. On the socialist Lamarckians' education policy: W. Thompson, 'Physical Argument,' 250–54.
32. *Notebooks* C196, 243.
33. *London Medical Gazette*, 17 (1835–36), 783; Desmond, 'Artisan Resistance.'
34. Darwin's copy of Lawrence's *Lectures on Man* (London: Benbow, 1822) is in Darwin Library, CUL; *CCD* 2:142, 4:535; McCalman, 'Unrespectable Radicalism,' on Benbow's pornographic sideline; Desmond, *Politics*, 120 on Lawrence's pirates.
35. *Lancet*, 1 (1828–29), 50–52; *Notebooks* E52; *CCD*, 2:94, 97.
36. *CCD*, 2:91; *ED*, 2:287; *Wedgwood*, 232.
37. *CCD*, 2:95–96, 432.
38. *CCD*, 2:96, 432; Rudwick, 'Darwin,' 114–17, 153–57, 161–65; *Notebooks* GR29ff.

18 MARRIAGE & MALTHUSIAN RESPECTABILITY

1. *Autobiography*, 95.
2. *CCD*, 2:444–45; Macfarlane, *Marriage*, 8–9 for Malthus's description of these sorts of upper–class calculations.
3. *CCD*, 2:114, 445; *ED*, 2:1; H. Martineau, *Autobiography*, 2:175–77.
4. *Notebooks* M7–8; R. Richards, *Darwin*, 96–97; *CCD*, 2:432.
5. *CCD*, 2:95; *ED*, 1:5; *Notebooks* M54, 57; Kohn, 'Darwin's Ambiguity,' 225, reveals that these notes were written at Maer.
6. *Notebooks* D21; *ED*, 2:6.

7. *Notebooks* D26, M84; Herbert, 'Place of Man, Pt 2,' 208; Colp, '"I was born",' 20; *CCD*, 2:438–41.

8. Brewster, 'M. Comte's Course,' 274, 278, 280; *Notebooks* M69–70, 81, 89, 135–136, N12; *CCD*, 2:104; Manier, *Young Darwin*, 41; Schweber, 'Origin,' 245.

9. *Notebooks* D36–37; Ospovat, 'Darwin,' 215; Schweber, 'Origin,' 255; Martineau, in Burrow, *Evolution*, 106.

10. *Notebooks* D37. For a Unitarian who held similar views: Carpenter, 'On the Differences' and *Remarks*, 3.

11. *Notebooks* M73–74, OUN 25 n. 1.

12. *Notebooks* M75–76, 142, 151; R. Richards, *Darwin*, 112; Manier, *Young Darwin*, 140; Desmond, *Politics*, 182, and 'Artisan Resistance,' 91ff, for this moral relativism in radical circles.

13. *Notebooks* M76, 120–21, 132, 150, N3–4.

14. *CCD*, 2:92, 95, 98; *Notebooks* M107, 129, 138–40, 151, 153, N13.

15. *Notebooks* M122–23, 128.

16. *CCD*, 2:107, 432; Schweber, 'Origin,' 283ff.

17. *Notebooks* M143–44; Colp, 'Charles Darwin's Dream,' 287–88.

18. Erskine, 'Darwin,' 271; E. Yeo, 'Christianity,' 111.

19. *Notebooks* D134; C. Lyell, *Principles*, 2:131; J. Browne, *Secular Ark*, 52ff; Herbert, 'Darwin, Malthus,' 214–17; Bowler, 'Malthus,' 632–36.

20. *Notebooks* D135, E9; Hodge and Kohn, 'Immediate Origins,' 195.

21. E.g., the activist William Farr at the General Register Office used the mortality statistics in 1839 to attack the Malthusian basis of the Poor Law and embarrass the government about urban squalor and slum disease: Farr, 'Medical Reform;' Desmond, *Politics*, 130, 132; Kohn, 'Theories,' 144.

22. H. Martineau, *Autobiography*, 1:399; Malthus, *Essay*, 2:440–41; R. Young, *Darwin's Metaphor*, 26; Bowler, 'Malthus,' 637–38, 642; Erskine, 'Darwin,' 251–55.

23. H. Martineau, *Autobiography*, 1:210; Malthus, *Essay*, 1:94–95; Matthew, *Emigration Fields*, vii, 3, 6, 9; Wells, 'Historical Context,' 242ff. The proposed new steam passage to New Zealand and the west coast of America would cut the journey time to a month.

24. Prichard, 'On the Extinction,' 169; *Notebooks*, TAN81, D38, E64–65; *Journal* (1839), 520.

25. Herbert, 'Darwin, Malthus,' 214; Hodge and Kohn, 'Immediate Origins,' 195; *Notebooks* D135; Gallenga, 'Age,' 3, 4, 7; Gale, 'Darwin,' 327–31; Kohn, 'Darwin's Ambiguity,' 229; Keegan and Gruber, 'Love, Death,' 17–20.

26. Carlyle, in Harrison, 'Early English Radicals,' 206; *Notebooks* OUN30, 37.

27. *Notebooks* OUN32, 36. On the Unitarian tradition: Willey, *Eighteenth Century*, ch. 10; Rowell, *Hell*, 33–57; O. Chadwick, *Victorian Church*, 1:396–98; Brooke, 'Sower,' 446ff. See also Murphy, 'Ethical Revolt' and J. Moore, '1859.'

28. *Notebooks* E49, N2–3, 5; R. Richards, *Darwin*, 118–19.

29. *Notebooks* M136, OUN 25 n. 1; H. Gruber, *Darwin*, 409 n. 50.

30. *ED*, 2:5, 6, 9; *CCD*, 2:432; *Notebooks* N25–27.

31. *CCD*, 2:114–16, 123.

32. *CCD*, 2:123; Brooke, 'Relations,' 68.

33. John 14:2–3, 5–6; 15:5–6 (AV); *CCD*, 2:126. Three weeks later Henslow sent Darwin some kindly pre–nuptial advice, asking him 'to remember daily that

our greatest earthly blessings may be taken from us in a moment:' *CCD*, 2:141.

34. *CCD*, 2:116–19; *ED*, 2:12; Davidoff and Hall, *Family Fortunes*, 209.

35. *CCD*, 2:120, 123, 125–26, 128–29; Jackson, *George Scharf's London*, 74–75.

36. *Notebooks* Mac58v, E57; Ospovat, 'Darwin,' 221; Kohn, 'Darwin's Ambiguity,' 229–32.

37. *Notebooks* Mac54v, E66–68, 89; Brooke, 'Relations,' 58.

38. *Notebooks* N41, 51–52.

39. *Notebooks* N42; Hodge and Kohn, 'Immediate Origins,' 197–200; R. Richards, *Darwin*, 102.

40. *Notebooks* D104 n. 5, E63, 71, 75, 136; *Foundations*, 6; Hodge and Kohn, 'Immediate Origins,' 199; Cornell, 'Analogy,' 320.

41. *CCD*, 2:131, 133, 144, 150, 432; *LRO*, 1:140–41; E. Richards, 'Darwin,' 80.

42. W. Buckland to Henry Lord Brougham, 14 Dec. 1838, UCL, Brougham Papers 1957. These events are reconstructed in detail in Desmond, *Politics*, 308–18.

43. *Notebooks* B88, D62; *CCD*, 2:106.

44. *Notebooks* N47, E4, 95–96, TAN19. In 1839 Edouard Lartet (who had found the French fossil monkey) unearthed a fossil musk shrew identical to the living Pyrenean one. This evidence of a mammal undergoing no alteration over untold aeons was, Darwin said, 'valuable because it shows [that species have] no *innate* power of change:' *Notebooks* TAN41, Frag 4ʳ.

45. *Notebooks* N62; R. Richards, *Darwin*, 135–39; Kohn, 'Darwin's Ambiguity,' 228; Stewart, *Brougham*, 198.

46. Ospovat, *Development*, 220; Brooke, 'Relations,' 59–60; Schweber, 'Origin,' 266ff; Manier, *Young Darwin*, 121.

47. *ED*, 2:16, 18; *CCD*, 2:147–49; Freeman, *Darwin and Gower Street*, 5.

48. *ED*, 2:30, 33, 50; *CCD*, 2:148–49, 151, 155, 159–60.

49. *Notebooks* N59; *CCD*, 2:151, 155–57, 159, 161, 165.

50. *CCD*, 2:169, 171, 433; *ED*, 2:17, 26, 28; *Notebooks* E98 for Darwin's wedding–day notes on propagation.

19 THE DREADFUL WAR

1. *CCD*, 2:157, 169, 235; *ED*, 2:31.

2. *Notebooks* C244; *CCD*, 2:171–72; *ED*, 1:251, 2:29.

3. *ED*, 2:38. Emma's Christianity, in which Jesus's revelation of a future life is not to be proved from Scripture but simply to be believed through the transforming power of the Gospels on the individual heart, was being defended at the time by the Unitarian theologian James Martineau, Harriet's brother: J. Martineau, *Bible*, 8–9, 39–44.

4. *ED*, 2:39, 55; Freeman, *Darwin and Gower Street*, 5; *CCD*, 2:147, 194, 296. Nicholas and Nicholas, *Charles Darwin*, 119 on Covington, who took a clerk's job with King's powerful Australian Agricultural Company.

5. Rudwick, 'Charles Darwin,' 197; *CCD*, 2: 174, 178; *Notebooks* E111–12; Hodge and Kohn, 'Immediate Origins,' 200–201; Cornell, 'Analogy,' 323–25.

6. *CCD*, 2:179, 182, 187–89, 446–49; Vorzimmer, 'Darwin's *Questions*;' Freeman and Gautrey, 'Darwin's *Questions*.'

7. *Notebooks* E114, 144, TAN51, Mac28v; *CCD*, 2:237–38; Hodge and Kohn, 'Immediate Origins,' 201–202.

8. *Autobiography*, 55; *ED*, 2:42; *Notebooks* OUN42–55; R. Richards, *Darwin*, 114–18.
9. *ED*, 2:40–41, 45.
10. 'Narrative of the Surveying Voyages,' *Athenaeum*, no. 607 (15 June 1839), 446–49; B. Hall, 'Voyages,' 485–86, 489; *CCD*, 2:178.
11. *CCD*, 2:197, 199, 236, 255; *Narrative*, 372–74.
12. *CCD*, 2:207, 214, 218–22, 230 n. 4, 372; *ED*, 2:67; Halévy, *Triumph*, 232. In July 1839 he did begin what has subsequently been characterized as the *Torn Apart Notebook* on transmutation.
13. Morrell and Thackray, *Gentlemen*, 252; Desmond, *Politics*, 331; Wells, 'Historical Context,' 241; *Hansard*, 3d ser., 48 (1839), 33.
14. *CCD*, 2:233, 234, 236–38; H. Martineau, *Autobiography*, 2:145ff.
15. *CCD*, 2:236, 249.
16. He was mistaken. It was actually unearthed by Robert Darwin of Elston Hall (1682–1754), his great-grandfather, who thought it a 'human Sceleton.' This Robert was the *son* of William Darwin of Elston (1655–1682): *CCD*, 2:235 n. 6, 250, 269–70, 303; *Pedigrees*, 26–27; *ED*, 2:44; H. Gruber, *Darwin*, 465–74.
17. *ED*, 2:51; *CCD*, 2:253, 255, 260–61; *TBI*, 21.
18. *ED*, 2:52; *CCD*, 2:262; *Wedgwood*, 236; Carlyle, *Chartism*, 4, 12, 32. Darwin was a stickler for vaccinations, and kept up with the medical breakthroughs. Willy was vaccinated against smallpox twice in 1840, chicken pox in 1845, measles in 1855, and scarlet fever thrice (1853–55), according to the inside cover of the family Bible, Down House.
19. *CCD*, 2:268, 269, 434; *Notebooks* TAN55–57, 63, 79, 177, D60.
20. *CCD*, 2:279; Herbert, 'Place of Man, Pt 2,' 189; Rudwick, 'Charles Darwin,' 203. The gutter presses did indeed pick up on the fossil monkeys and throw them in the face of the priests: Desmond, 'Artisan Resistance,' 100.
21. *CCD*, 2:279, 289; *CP*, 1:145–63 for the paper on erratic boulders read by Hensleigh.
22. *ED*, 2:56; *CCD*, 2:294, 315–16, 319, 399; 5:540, 542.
23. *CCD*, 2:292–93, 306; *Notebooks* TAN91–135, 151. On 22 June he finally finished taking notes on species, closing the *Torn Apart Notebook*.
24. *CCD*, 2:292–94, 296, 298, 300 nn. 2–3, 303.
25. Cobbett, *Rural Rides*, 170–225; *CCD*, 2:304–305, 4:459.
26. Owen, 'Report on British Fossil Reptiles,' 196–99, 201–202; *LRO*, 1:168, 184, 188–89; Desmond, 'Making,' 230–41 and *Politics*, 325–26, 333, 351–58; *CCD*, 2:303, 305.
27. Owen, 'On the Osteology,' 343; Knight, *London*, 3:198; Bunbury, *Life*, 1:186; *CCD*, 2:307.
28. Annotation, 26 Jan. 1842, on Lyell's copy of his *Elements of Geology*, 2d ed., Down House; *CCD*, 2:299; *LLL*, 2:59.
29. *CCD*, 2:312–13, 318–19; *ED*, 2:70.
30. Herbert, 'Place of Man, Pt 2,' 191; *CCD*, 2:435; *Notebooks* Summer 1842; *Foundations*, 51–52; also 3, 6–8, 17, 23–24, 27, 35–36, 38, 45–47.
31. On Darwin's utilitarian audience: Desmond, *Politics*, 408–11. The utilitarian grip on London science is discussed in Berman, *Social Change*, ch. 4. One receptive breeder was the tree grower Patrick Matthew. He openly brought his Malthusian evolution to the aid of capitalist society.
32. *Notebooks* E6.
33. E. Yeo, 'Christianity,' 113. While the militants were abominating Malthus,

Hensleigh was entertaining the Darwins and Malthuses to dinner: CCD, 2:312. Obviously, Darwin read Adam Smith and the classical economists, not William Thompson and their socialist rivals. Hence his framework was always one of individuals in competition, not communities in co-operation: Schweber, 'Origin' and 'Darwin.'

34. Chilton, 'Regular Gradation,' *Oracle*, 19 Feb. 1842, 27 Nov. 1841, and *Oracle of Reason*, 12 Feb. 1842; Desmond, 'Artisan Resistance,' 85ff.

35. Southwell, 'Is There a God,' and Chilton, 'Regular Gradation,' *Oracle*, 11 Nov. 1843.

36. *Notebooks* C76; H. Gruber, *Darwin*, 202; S. Gould, 'Darwin's Delay;' J. Moore, 'Crisis,' 66.

37. Kohn *et al.*, 'New Light,' 424–26; CCD, 2:324, 326, 328, 332, 435; ED, 2:75.

38. Jenkins, *General Strike*, 19, 95–104, 165–71; *Illustrated London News*, 20 Aug. 1842; Goodway, *London Chartism*, 106.

39. *The Times*, 11 June 1842, p. 9; 17 Aug., p. 7; 18 Aug. 1842, p. 7; Royle, *Victorian Infidels*, 80–81; Desmond, 'Artisan Resistance,' 85; Bunbury, *Life*, 1:220–21. Holyoake's fellow editor, the rough–edged Charles Southwell, was already serving a two-year stretch at Bristol.

40. LRO, 1:167, 198, 321; Desmond, *Politics*, 332; CCD, 2:332.

20 THE EXTREME VERGE OF THE WORLD

1. Jenkins, *General Strike*, ch. 10; CCD, 2:324, 332; Tristan, *London Journal*, 74–75; Howarth and Howarth, *History*, 82; B. Darwin, 'Kent,' 83; Atkins, *Down*, 7–8, 22.

2. CCD, 2:324, 350, 395.

3. Howarth and Howarth, *History*, 10–11, 34; J. Moore, 'Darwin of Down,' 477; 1851 religious census, Parish Church of Down, PRO HO.129/49.

4. Howarth and Howarth, *History*, 48, ch. 7; CCD, 2:324.

5. Howarth and Howarth, *History*, ch. 8; Hutchinson, *Life*, 1:2–4, 15.

6. CCD, 2:324; ED, 2:75.

7. CCD, 2:326, 332, 335–36, 345; Atkins, *Down*, ch. 2; Howarth and Howarth, *History*, 76–77.

8. CCD, 2:332, 334–36, 338; 'Register of baptisms . . .,' KAO P123/1/10; Death Certificate, Mary Eleanor Darwin, General Register Office, London; 'Register of burials . . .,' KAO P123/1/14; ED, 1:255, 2:78.

9. CCD, 2:315–16, 352.

10. CCD, 2:345; ED, 2:80–81; B. Darwin, *World*, 19, 21.

11. *Companion*, 126; Freeman, 'Darwin Family,' 15; CCD, 2:345, 348, 350, 355; Monsarrat, *Thackeray*, 113–19; ED, 2:85–86.

12. CCD, 2:324, 336, 345, 348, 352–53; ED, 2:76; J. Moore, 'Darwin of Down,' 460–61.

13. CCD, 2:326, 332, 352, 360–61, 414; 3:248; Atkins, *Down*, 25; Freeman, 'Darwin Family,' 13–15.

14. CCD, 2:352, 360, 409, 418; 3:134, 248; Atkins, *Down*, 34.

15. CCD, 2:360, 387; *Historical and Descriptive Catalogue*, 21; Gay, *Bourgeois Experience*, 403–62 on 'fortifications for the self.'

16. CCD, 2:325; Glastonbury, 'Holding,' 31.

17. CCD, 2:285–86, 321–22, 338, 387, 435; CP, 1:163; Wilson, *Charles Lyell*, 496–502.

18. *CCD*, 2:105, 339, 341, 389–90; Darwin, *Volcanic Islands*, 36, 61–65.
19. *CP*, 1:175–82.
20. *CCD*, 3:67; 4:466; Darwin's 1826 diary, DAR 129; J. Moore, 'Darwin of Down,' 460.
21. Atkins, *Down*, 24; Trollope, *Clergymen*, 54; *MLD*, 1:33–36.
22. *CCD*, 1:97, 2:330–31, 351, 354, 359–60, 371, 373, 387, 395; Stearn, *Natural History Museum*, 210.
23. *ED*, 2:82–83; *CCD*, 2:333–34, 345, 374, 435; Freeman, 'Darwin Family,' 13; E. Darwin to H. Wedgwood, April 1837, in Kohn, 'Darwin's Ambiguity,' 226.
24. *CCD*, 2:373, 375–77; Waterhouse, 'Observations,' 399 for the circles; Desmond, 'Making,' 161ff on the circular classification as a buffer against Lamarckism.
25. *CCD*, 2:378; Colp, 'Confessing,' 12–13.
26. *CCD*, 2:377–79, 381–82.
27. *CCD*, 2:387, 389, 397–99, 405, 415–16; Waterhouse, 'Observations,' 403, 406.

21 MURDER

1. *CCD*, 1:34, 3:394; *LLJH*, 1:20.
2. *CCD*, 2:408, 3:10; *LLJH*, 1:161; D. Porter, 'Darwin's Plant Collections,' 520.
3. Hooker, 'Reminiscences,' 187; *LLJH*, 1:41–45; *LLD*, 2:19; D. Porter, 'Darwin's Plant Collections,' 519. Hooker does not mention McCormick by name, only that it was one of Darwin's crewmates who 'had accompanied him in the *Beagle* to Rio.' McCormick befriended Hooker in 1839 and took him in tow before the *Erebus* trip, which leaves little doubt that it was he who introduced him to Darwin.
4. Hooker, 'Reminiscences,' 187; *LLJH*, 1:41; *LLD*, 2:19.
5. *CCD*, 2:408, 410–11, 419.
6. *CCD*, 3:2; Colp, 'Confessing.'
7. Desmond, 'Artisan Resistance,' 90 n. 47.
8. *CCD*, 3:2, 5, 7, 11.
9. *Foundations*, 85, 91; Ospovat, *Development*, 82–3; Kohn *et al.*, 'New Light,' 427. According to Ospovat, Darwin believed that species were 'perfectly' adapted in these stable periods, and that he had still to shake off the old theological framework. Kohn ('Darwin's Ambiguity,' 230) disagrees, maintaining that 'relative' adaptation had been Darwin's working concept since writing his 'E' Notebook. The 'imperfection' of nature's contrivances in Paley's own natural theology has also recently been emphasized: Francis, 'Naturalism,' 214.
10. *Foundations*, xix.
11. B. Taylor, *Eve*, 131; Martin, *First Conversation*, 5–6; *Movement*, 6 July 1844, p. 239 and 31 Aug., p. 315; Royle, *Victorian Infidels*, 88.
12. *CCD*, 3:43–44; *TBI*, 158.
13. Desmond, *Politics*, chs 6–8, p. 376; *CCD*, 3:43–44; Colp, 'Confessing,' 16–19.
14. Napier, *Selections*, 492; Forbes, *Literary Papers*, 120.
15. *CCD*, 3:28, 42, 47–49, 57, 79, 83, 310. John Thackray of the Geological Society supplied the figures for GS membership.

16. Darwin, *South America*, chs 1–4; D'Orbigny, 'General Considerations,' 367; CCD, 3:56, 59, 162, 193, 391.
17. CCD, 3:61, 70–72, 79; *Foundations*, 183–94.
18. CCD, 2:413–14, 3:56, 67; ED, 2:88; Raverat, *Period Piece*, 142.
19. CCD, 3:396; Colp, 'Confessing,' 19–20; Kohn, 'Darwin's Ambiguity,' 226; *Foundations*, xvii; LLD, 2:12, 296; Eng, 'Confrontation.'
20. Secord, 'Behind the Veil,' 166, 168; R. Yeo, 'Science,' 25–27; Desmond, *Politics*, 175–80.
21. Secord, 'Behind the Veil,' 166, 173. The vast conceptual differences between Darwin's science and *Vestiges* are explored in Hodge, 'Universal Gestation.' Chambers rejected *common* ancestry, picturing life as a series of parallel – but unrelated – lineages, each originating in a spontaneously generated base.
22. Words of the dour Episcopalian professor at Edinburgh, James D. Forbes. Forbes was an expert on glacial movement; Darwin thought him clever, civil, and 'as frigid as one of his glaciers:' Shairp *et al.*, *Life*, 178; CCD, 3:103, 108, 166.
23. Gillispie, *Genesis*, 169–70; CCD, 3:184.
24. Chilton, 'Vestiges,' 9; Chilton, 'Regular Gradation,' *Movement*, Nov. 1844, 413; Desmond, 'Artisan Resistance,' 102.
25. Carpenter, 'Vestiges,' 155, 160, 180; Desmond, *Politics*, 195; CCD, 3:258.
26. Napier, *Selection*, 492; Epps, *Church of England's Apostacy*, 3; Desmond, *Politics*, 178–79 for the deeper context.
27. CCD, 3:253, 258, 289; Egerton, 'Conjecture'; Napier, *Selections*, 494.
28. CCD, 3:181, 289, 4:19, 36, 152; A. Sedgwick to M. Napier, 17 April 1845, BL, Add. MSS 34,625, ff. 113–19; Napier, *Selections*, 491–93; Desmond, *Archetypes*, 210.
29. Chambers, in Secord, 'Behind the Veil,' 186. For the species named after Darwin: CCD, 3:46, 196, 232, 276; Darwin, *South America*, 92, 253; *Companion*, 82–86.
30. CCD, 3:65, 168.
31. CCD, 3:67–68, 332, 354; LLD, 3:27.
32. CCD, 3:85; Ospovat, 'Perfect Adaptation,' 39ff; Gillispie, *Charles Darwin*, ch. 5.
33. CCD, 3:164, 166, 177.
34. Hooker, 'Reminiscences,' 187–88; CCD, 3:88–90, 399–403.
35. Hooker, 'Reminiscences,' 188; CCD, 3:34–35, 62, 149, 167, 181–82, 288.
36. CCD, 3:140, 149, 167–68, 177, 207.
37. CCD, 3:139, 147, 166, 186; LLJH, 1:191, 194.
38. Hill, 'Squire,' 337, 342, 344–45; Ashwell and Wilberforce, *Life*, 1:130; CCD, 3:68, 86, 157, 181, 214, 216, 229, 256, 260; Beesby estate papers, DAR 210.25.
39. CCD, 3:169, 176.
40. *Journal* (1845), 360–61, 363, 375, 376; Sulloway, 'Darwin' and 'Darwin's Conversion,' 345; Hooker, 'Reminiscences,' 187.
41. CCD, 3:55, 203, 213, 233, 242; *Journal* (1845), 469–70.
42. CCD, 3:208, 240, 339; LLJH, 1:204.
43. CCD, 3:211, 217, 264, 336–37; J. Browne, *Secular Ark*, 65–68, 77–80; Egerton, 'Hewett C. Watson,' 89, 92.
44. CCD, 3:274, 289.
45. Mills, 'View,' 372.
46. CCD, 3:71, 149, 163, 245, 250, 253, 291, 294–95, 300, 304–305; *Foundations*,

168–71; Sulloway, 'Geographic Isolation,' 30–49. For Forbes's science: Rehbock, *Philosophical Naturalists*, 157–75, 186–87; J. Browne, *Secular Ark*, 114ff.

47. E. Forbes to R. Owen, 2 Nov. 1846, BM(NH), OCorr.; Desmond, *Politics*, 365; CCD, 3:274.

48. CCD, 3:282–83, 287; Mills, 'View,' 377; Rehbock, *Philosophical Naturalists*, 72–73.

49. CCD, 3:141, 285, 287, 339.

50. CCD, 2:346, 353, 306; Russell–Gebbett, *Henslow*, ch. 3; J. Moore, 'Darwin of Down,' 466–67.

51. CCD, 3:248; 'Subscription towards embellishments of the Church . . .' and copy notebooks, KAO P123/6/1–3.

52. KAO P123/2/1, 5 and P123/5/26; Stecher, 'Darwin–Innes Letters,' 255; CCD, 2:406; J. Moore, 'Darwin of Down,' 477.

53. CCD, 2:406, 3:49, 192, 228, 256, 260, 321, 377; 4:256–57, 304; Barnett, 'Allotments.'

54. CCD, 3:260; Harrison, *Early Victorian Britain*, 27.

55. CCD, 3:248, 259–60, 347–48; ED, 2:309.

56. CCD, 3:228.

57. CCD, 3:325.

58. CCD, 4:290, 337; 5:94; Crouzet, *Victorian Economy*, 165. In fact, Darwin had started paying for the first free-trade reforms in 1842, when Peel introduced his income tax to make up the lost revenues. Darwin's tax bill was about £30 in 1842.

59. CCD, 3:68, 84, 86, 95–96, 141–42, 166, 181, 215, 264, 311–12, 327; ED, 1:250.

60. CCD, 3:312, 326; ED, 2:98–99, 102–103.

61. CCD, 3:68, 141, 246, 277, 331, 345; Atkins, *Down*, 28 and RFD.

62. CCD, 3: 307, 332, 390.

63. CCD, 3:111–12, 164, 346, 4:127; Owen, 'Notices,' 66; Rehbock, *Philosophical Naturalists*, 176–84.

64. CCD, 3:124, 323, 345–46, 359. Ministers were riled by FitzRoy's maverick action; he adopted 'free trade in *every thing*,' dropped customs duties, gave up the Crown rights to the land and allowed settlers to buy direct from the Maoris, slashing the government fee from ten shillings to a penny an acre. The colonial office might have baulked, but even Sulivan agreed that his decisive action had saved New Zealand.

65. CCD, 3:331, 338, 345, 356.

22 ILLFORMED LITTLE MONSTERS

1. CCD, 3:346, 350.

2. CCD, 3:356–58, 365–66.

3. CCD, 3:359, 363; D. Allen, *Naturalist*, 124–31; LLL, 2:129.

4. J. Thompson, *Zoological Researches*, 71–73, 79; Winsor, 'Barnacle Larvae,' 295–98; Huxley, 'Lectures,' 238; CCD, 4:100, 178; Ghiselin, *Triumph*, ch. 5. For the best analysis of Darwin's work on barnacles, containing many fresh insights, [M. Richmond], 'Darwin's Study of Cirripedia,' CCD, 4:388–409.

5. LLJH, 1:190; CCD, 3:251, 253, 256, 4:327. Hooker and Darwin tellingly disagreed over Gérard's worth. Hooker thought Gérard's listing of hundreds

of variations of species wretched. Hooker was a 'lumper,' determined to 'cut down ... all the intermediate forms' and parcel them out to 'everyday' species. But Darwin, concerned with change rather than taxonomy, sympathized with Gérard's enterprise. It gave the information he needed: the variations on which selection acted.

6. *CCD*, 3:375, 4:38.
7. Quoted in Dance, 'Hugh Cuming,' 477; Darwin, *Monograph on the Sub-Class*, 1:v–vi; *CCD*, 3:137, 231, 297, 4:98–100; *Journal* (1845), 372–73.
8. Jardine, *Memoirs*, clxxiv–v; Kirby, 'Introductory Address,' 5; Desmond, 'Making,' 168; Gillespie, 'Preparing,' 102; *CCD*, 4:187, 189, 192. In 1842 Darwin had served with Strickland on the British Association committee on Zoological nomenclature: *CCD*, 2:311.
9. *CCD*, 4:11.
10. J. Hooker to [a Darwin son], 19 Feb. 1905, BL, Add. MSS 58,373 (unbound).
11. Hooker, 'Reminiscences,' 188; *LLJH*, 1:213–14; *CCD*, 4:10–11, 25, 382.
12. *CCD*, 3:254, 4:21.
13. *Foundations*, 71–74, 80, 170–71; Colp, 'Confessing,' 30–31; *CCD*, 4:25.
14. Hooker, 'Reminiscences,' 187.
15. *CCD*, 4:11, 29–30; *LLJH*, 1:167.
16. *Autobiography*, 105; *CCD*, 4:37, 40, 44, 5:300; Secord, 'Geological Survey,' 233–34.
17. *CCD*, 4:71, 74; Rudwick, 'Darwin,' 131–45, 153–65; Barrett, 'Darwin's "Gigantic Blunder",' 25–27.
18. Desmond, *Politics*, 296–97; Secord, *Controversy*, 123; Morrell, 'London Institutions,' 137; *CCD*, 4:25. The opium and bismuth are mentioned in *CCD*, 3:247, 325.
19. *CCD*, 4:48; Secord, 'Geological Survey,' 253; *LLJH*, 1:210, 221.
20. *CCD*, 4:44–45, 47, 51, 53; *LLL*, 2:130.
21. Geikie, *Memoir*, 103.
22. Andrew Ramsay, diary for 1847, f. 59, Imperial College Archives, London, KGA Ramsay/1/8 (we thank Jim Secord for giving us this reference); Wilberforce, *Pride*, 15–20; *Illustrated London News*, 3 July 1847, p. 10. Ramsay approved the sermon; the Owens also thought it 'very fine': LRO, 1:299.
23. *CCD*, 4:152, 269; *LLL*, 2:154; Morrell and Thackray, *Gentlemen*, on the BAAS's social ethos.
24. Hooker, 'Reminiscences,' 188; *CCD*, 4:49–50.
25. *CCD*, 4:55, 61; *LLJH*, 1:219.
26. *LLJH*, 1:216, 219.
27. *CCD*, 4:56, 61, 87.
28. *CCD*, 4:92–93.

23 AL DIABOLO

1. *CCD*, 4:107, 109.
2. *CP* 1:227; *CCD*, 4:24, 383; Geikie, *Memoir*, 130.
3. *LLL*, 2:139, 141. Buckland and Owen had acted as Peel's scientific advisers while he was Prime Minister (1841–46), and they were personally close to the Tory leader. Sir Robert had given Owen a huge Civil List Pension in 1842, and he appointed Buckland Dean of Westminster and offered Owen a

knighthood in 1845, shortly before leaving office: Gordon, *Life*, 220; Desmond, *Politics*, 354–58.

4. Desmond, *Politics*, 328, 331–32; *LRO*, 1:167; *LLL*, 1:291; *CCD*, 4:108–109.

5. *ED*, 2:115; Goodway, *London Chartism*, 68–96; Wilson and Geikie, *Memoir*, 432.

6. *CCD* 4:151, 157; Geikie, *Memoir*, 129; Wilson and Geikie, *Memoir*, 433; *LRO*, 1:320; W. Broderip to R. Owen, 13 Mar. 1848, BM(NH), OCorr.

7. *CCD*, 4:128, 476–78.

8. *CCD*, 4:128; *MLD*, 1:370–71; Darwin, *Monograph on the Sub-Class*, 1:186, 189, 198, 202. The barnacles' hermaphroditism made them even odder crustaceans; crabs are single sexed: J. Thompson, *Zoological Researches*, 80–81.

9. *CCD*, 4:252–53.

10. *CCD*, 4:249; Darwin, *Monograph on the Sub-Class*, 1:205–208, 231–32; *Notebooks* D157, 162.

11. *CCD*, 4:140, 159.

12. Darwin, *Monograph on the Sub-Class*, 1:232, 291; 2:23; *CCD*, 4:169, 180, 204 (Darwin in his *Monograph* eventually reported seeing 'as many as fourteen adhering on one female!'); Hooker, *Himalayan Journals*, 2:206; *LLJH*, 1:270, 312.

13. *CCD*, 4:139, 142, 144–46.

14. *CCD*, 4:102, 145, 147, 154; *TBI*, 38.

15. *CCD*, 4:169–70, 269; *LLL*, 2:146.

16. Norton, *Evidences*, 1:11; *CCD*, 4:476; Stevens, 'Darwin's Humane Reading.'

17. *CCD*, 3:141, 4:384, 477; Hare, *Essays*, 1:lxxxii, cvi, cl, ccxiv.

18. Coleridge, *Aids*, 1:89–90, 133, 144–45, 152, 157, 194–96, 245, 281, 333 (cf. Barth, *Coleridge*, 137, 191–93); *ED*, 2:284; *CCD*, 4:477.

19. *CCD*, 4:178, 181–82, 209.

20. *ED*, 2:119; *CCD*, 4:183; 5:9; *Autobiography*, 117; *Wedgwood*, 249–50; Will of Robert Waring Darwin, PRO 11/2084.

21. Hutchinson, *Life*, 1:22–25.

22. *CCD*, 3:96, 4:223, 225–27; Wheatley, *Life*, 264.

23. H. Martineau, *Eastern Life*, 1:67, 277, 2:9, 3:158, 162, 167.

24. *CCD*, 4:209, 219, 228, 478.

24 MY WATER DOCTOR

1. *CCD*, 4:209, 234; Mann, *Collections*, 12–21; *TBI*, 39.

2. *CCD*, 4:219; *TBI*, 39–40.

3. Billing, *M. Billing's Directory*, 412; B. Smith, *History*, 194; RFD, 85; *CCD*, 4:209, 223.

4. *CCD*, 4:354; Mann, *Collections*, 5–6, 12ff; Desmond, *Politics*, 175 n. 81.

5. *CCD*, 4:224, 354.

6. 'Malvern Water,' *Household Words*, 11 Oct. 1851, pp. 67–71; E. Darwin's recollections of Annie, DAR 210.13; recollections of G. Darwin, DAR 112; Baptismal Register, Parish of Great Malvern, 5 June 1849, County of Hereford and Worcester Record Office, Worcester; *CCD*, 4:234, 236, 239–40.

7. *CCD*, 4:227; *TBI*, 40.

8. *CCD*, 4:246, 5:78; *TBI*, 43; RFD, 84; 'A Visit to Darwin's Village: Reminiscences of Some of His Humble Friends,' *Evening News* (London), 12 Feb. 1909, p. 4.

9. *CCD*, 4:247, 256–57, 269, 311, 314; *CP*, 1:250–51; *TBI*, 49; Morus, 'Politics of

Power,' on the reform of the Royal Society (cf. MacLeod, 'Whigs').

10. Darwin, *Monograph on the Sub-Class*, 2:26.

11. *CCD*, 4:127, 219; Ospovat, *Development*, 146, 150 and Owen, *On the Nature of Limbs* in Darwin Library, CUL; Desmond, *Archetypes*, 50 and *Politics*, ch. 6, esp. 216, 267–68 on specific antagonisms between the Unitarian materialists and Coleridgean idealists; Di Gregorio, 'In Search,' 249.

12. *CCD*, 4:179, also 156, 169; Darwin, *Monograph on the Sub-Class*, 1:2, 25–28 (cf. T. Huxley, 'Lectures,' 238, 241 for a rejigging of Darwin's barnacle homologies); Desmond, *Politics*, ch. 8, on the prevalence of archetypal thinking in London in the 1840s.

13. *CCD*, 4:179, 314; Darwin, *Monograph of the Sub-Class*, 1:34–7.

14. *CCD*, 4:270, 273.

15. *CCD*, 4:269, 272, 303, 311.

16. *LLJH*, 1:312–20; Hooker, *Himalayan Journals*, 2:206–14, 233, 247; *CCD*, 4:294, 310, 478; *LLL*, 2:153.

17. *CCD*, 4:282–83, 289, 293, 300–303; Trenn, 'Charles Darwin.'

18. Darwin, *Monograph on the Fossil Lepadidae*, v, 1; Trenn, 'Charles Darwin,' 471, 479; *CCD*, 4:300, 305; *CP*, 1:251–2.

19. *CCD*, 4:304–305, 310–11; Trenn, 'Charles Darwin,' 481–82.

20. *CCD*, 4:319, 323, 349, 361; Darwin, *Monograph on the Fossil Lepadidae*, 3.

21. *CCD*, 4:312, 315, 319, 321, 335, 344; *TBI*, 44.

22. *CCD*, 4:114–15, 139, 268–69, 327–28.

23. *CCD*, 4:344; Darwin, *Monograph on the Sub-Class*, 2:155; Gillespie, 'Preparing,' 107–108.

24. *CCD*, 5:155–56.

25. *CCD*, 3:376; T. Huxley, 'Lectures,' 240 on Darwin's classification. Ghiselin and Jaffe, 'Phylogenetic Classification,' 137, have subsequently constructed a dendrogram of barnacle relationships according to Darwin's known views. Such diagrams were common in Darwin's day (Ospovat, *Development*, 161), but it was telling that Darwin did not draw one.

26. *CCD*, 4:344, 353, 369.

25 OUR BITTER & CRUEL LOSS

1. E. Darwin's recollections of Annie, DAR 210.13; *CCD*, 4:369, 5:9.

2. *CCD*, 4:225, 5:540–41; *ED*, 2:184; *TBI*, 149.

3. E. Darwin's recollections of Annie, DAR 210.13; *CCD* 4:385–87.

4. *CCD*, 4:379–80, 386–87.

5. Corsi, *Science*, 262–65; Robbins, *Newman Brothers*, 107–16; *CCD*, 4:479; *ED* 2:125; Newman, *Soul*, 227, 230, 233, 258; Newman, *History*, iv, 210, 370; O. Chadwick, *Victorian Church*, 1:291–301.

6. *TBI*, 45; E. Darwin's recollections of Annie, DAR 210.13; *CCD* 4:479, 5:69.

7. Newman, *Phases*, 78, 81, 101, 141, 172, 188, 200, 233.

8. *CCD*, 4:479, 5:519; *LLD* 2:158; E. Darwin's recollections of Annie, DAR 210.13.

9. Billing, M. *Billing's Directory*, 415; *CCD*, 4:354; RFD, 85; Colp, *TBI*, 44–45. Francis and George Darwin recalled that Gully wanted the clairvoyant to report on their father. If true, this family tradition can be only part of the story. Charles was feeling fairly well in March 1851; Gully had already successfully diagnosed his ailment. Annie was now their prime concern. Since

Gully's own daughter had been helped by a clairvoyant, it stood to reason that Annie should also be seen. Clairvoyant females were supposed to have special insight into female patients.

10. M. Lyell to F. Wedgwood, 28 April [1851], W/M 310; *LLJH*, 1:332; Froude, *Carlyle*, 2:67–77; Fielding, 'Froude's Second Revenge;' *ED*, 2:128–29; *CCD*, 5:25. Charles did not indicate reading the book until August 1852 (*CCD*, 4:488). But Erasmus and Fanny were close friends of Martineau and held decided views on the 'priestess' and her outrageous book (Calder, 'Erasmus Darwin,' 38; Arbuckle, *Harriet Martineau's Letters*, 113). It is inconceivable that the first time Charles was in Eras's and Fanny's company after the book's publication (in early February), they did not discuss it and arouse his reading interests.

11. *CCD*, 5:10, 13.
12. C. Thorley to E. Darwin, [14 April and 15 April 1851], DAR 210.13; *CCD*, 5:13, 16–17, 22; *ED*, 2:132–33.
13. *ED*, 2:132; *CCD*, 5:13, 16.
14. *CCD*, 5:13–15, 21.
15. *CCD*, 5:16–17; F. Wedgwood to E. Darwin, [19 April 1851], DAR 210.13.
16. *CCD*, 5:18–23.
17. *CCD*, 5:23–24. F. Wedgwood to H. Wedgwood, [23 April 1851], W/M 310.
18. F. Wedgwood to H. Wedgwood, [23 April 1851], and to K. E. Wedgwood, 25 April 1851, W/M 310; 'Thunderstorms,' *Barron's Worcester Journal*, 1 May 1851, p. [3]; *ED*, 2:286; H. Montgomery, 'Emma Darwin;' Ricks, *Poems*, 910 (lv:5–8).
19. F. Wedgwood to H. Wedgwood, [23 April 1851], W/M 310; F. Wedgwood to E. Darwin, [23 April 1851], DAR 210.13; Ricks, *Poems*, 911 (lvi:1–4); Death Certificate, Anne Elizabeth Darwin, General Register Office, London.
20. *CCD*, 5:25; E. Darwin to F. Wedgwood, [25 April 1851], W/M 310.
21. *CCD*, 5:24–26; F. Allen to F. Wedgwood, 23 Ap[ril 1851], and E. Darwin to F. Wedgwood, [25 April 1851], W/M 310.
22. *CCD*, 5:28–29; F. Wedgwood to K. E. Wedgwood, 25 April 1851, W/M 310; Burial Register, Parish of Great Malvern, 25 April 1851, County of Hereford and Worcester Record Office, Worcester.
23. *CCD*, 5:25, 542–43; S. E. Wedgwood to F. Wedgwood, [27 April 1851], W/M 310.
24. *CCD*, 5:26–27; *ED*, 2:137, 139; E. Darwin to F. Wedgwood, [24 April 1851], W/M 310; Annie's keepsakes, DAR 210.13.
25. *CCD*, 5:32, 540–42; Colp, 'Charles Darwin's "insufferable grief";' J. Moore, 'Of Love.'
26. *CCD*, 5:33; *ED*, 2:140; Darwin to J. Hooker, 6 June [1868], DAR 94:69–70.

26 A GENTLEMAN WITH CAPITAL

1. Best, *Mid-Victorian Britain*, 252; T. Macaulay, in Golby, *Culture*, 3.
2. McNeil, *Under the Banner*; Prince Albert, in Harvie *et al.*, *Industrialization*, 234-38.
3. Charlotte Brontë, in Jennings, *Pandaemonium*, 262.
4. *CCD* 4:354; Haight, *George Eliot*, 20ff, 60; Rosenberg, 'Financing,' 169-72; Van Arsdel, 'Westminster Review,' 544-49; Heyck, *Transformation*, 17; Corsi, *Science*, 204; Holyoake, *Sixty Years*, 1:239.

5. Rosenberg, 'Financing,' 175; J. Moore, *Religion*, 432.

6. Corsi, *Science*, 273-76; Desmond, *Archetypes*, 29-32.

7. Spencer, *Autobiography*, 1:348, 394ff; Rosenberg,'Financing,' 174; Spencer, *Social Statics*, 80; J. Moore *et al.*, *Science*, 6ff.

8. Spencer, *Autobiography*, 1:377, 384; Prince Albert, in Golby, *Culture*, 1-2.

9. R. Young, *Darwin's Metaphor*, 23-55.

10. Spencer, *Autobiography*, 1:372, 388; J. Moore, *Religion*, 406, 408; R. Young, *Darwin's Metaphor*, 51-52.

11. CCD, 5:49-52, 55, 538; ED, 2:142; TBI, 49.

12. CCD, 5:54, 57.

13. CCD, 5:55, 81, 83; RFD, 17, 38; TBI, 48.

14. CCD, 5:83; Davidoff and Hall, *Family Fortunes*, 205-207, 360-65.

15. Hobsbawm, *Industry*, 156; Keith, *Darwin*, 222, 225; CCD, 3:375-77, 4:xx, 52, 62-63, 154-55, 185, 375-77; 5:119, 183-84.

16. Austin, *Memoir*, 2:472; Jardine, *Memoirs*, cclix; Crouzet, *Victorian Economy*, 285-87; LLL, 2:129; CCD, 3:303-304; Burn, *Age*, 30; Schivelbusch, *Railway Journey*, chs 8-9.

17. CCD, 4:62-63, 375; 5:99, 101, 190-91; Atkins, *Down*, 97.

18. CCD, 4:377, 378; 5:40, 94, 143, 191.

19. CCD, 4:138, 264-65; 5:222-23; 'Down Coal Club: Honorary Subscriptions, 1841-1876 Inclusive,' Down House; recollections of J. Brodie Innes, DAR 112; registration document, 'N° 3043 Down Friendly Society . . .,' PRO FS1/232/643, pp. 12-13, 18, 32; cf. J. Moore, 'Darwin of Down,' 466-69.

20. Briggs, *Age*, 388; CCD, 4:362, 369; 5:85-6, 163, 174.

21. CCD, 5:83-84; ED, 1:144; LLL, 2:172; H. Bell, *Lord Palmerston*, 2:58.

22. CCD, 5:83, 100, 104, 111.

23. CCD, 4:353-54, 362; 5:51, 52, 55, 63, 83, 147-48; TBI, 49; Hutchinson, *Life*, 22-24, 29-30.

24. CCD, 5:63, 97, 100, 112, 147-48, 536; Duman, 'Creation,' 120-23; F. Darwin, *Rustic Sounds*, 157.

25. CCD, 5:96; ED, 2:146-50.

26. L. Huxley, 'Home Life,' 6; recollections of G. Darwin, DAR 112; ED, 2:81.

27. CCD, 5:81; F. Darwin, *Springtime*, 60-62 and *Rustic Sounds*, 154.

28. ED, 2:105-106, 154.

29. CCD, 4:425; 5:81, 141-42, 536.

30. ED, 2:173; Foote, *Darwin*, 20; F. Darwin, *Springtime*, 51-53; 'Register of baptisms . . .,' KAO P123/1/10; Hutchinson, *Life*, 1:32.

31. Duncan, *Life*, 64, 541; E. Richards,'Question;' Desmond, *Archetypes* 30ff.

32. Duncan, *Life*, 62-63; Spencer, *Autobiography*, 1:402; LLTH, 1:81, 83, 90; Desmond, *Archetypes*, 25-29.

33. Duncan, *Life*, 65, 543; Spencer, *Autobiography*, 1:350; Schoenwald, 'G. Eliot's "Love" Letters;' LLD, 2:188; Desmond, *Archetypes*, 37ff, 99.

27 UGLY FACTS

1. Health diary, Down House; TBI, 43–53.

2. TBI, 45–46; Freeman, 'Darwin Family,' 17; Health diary, Down House, April, Aug.–Nov. 1852; CCD, 5:96, 98, 100, 194.

3. LLTH, 1:89, 102, 107; CCD, 5:49, 64, 75, 131. T. Huxley, 'Lectures,' 238–39 adopted the terminology of Darwin's 'very admirable' monograph, accepted

his views on the tiny males, but had reservations about the cement glands and thought that Darwin had mistaken the site of the 'true ovaria.'

4. *CCD*, 5:130.
5. *CCD*, 5:103, 105, 108, 110, 113–15, 117–18.
6. *CCD*, 5:82, 100, 123, 147, 212; *MLD*, 1:38.
7. *CCD*, 5:165–66, 225, 307; 6:406. The Royal Medal is likened to a scientific knighthood in 'The Royal Society,' *Lancet*, 1 (1846), 635. On the reforms: MacLeod, 'Of Medals,' 92; Morus, 'Politics of Power.'
8. Health diary, Down House; *CCD*, 3:253, 5:157, 163, 172, 536, 539; 6:55; *Autobiography*, 117. Bulwer–Lytton parodied Darwin as the crusty 'Professor Long' in *What Will He Do With It?*, 1:284–96.
9. *CCD*, 5:113, 174–75, 177, 179–81.
10. *CCD*, 3:45, 5:113, 178, 196–97, 215.
11. *CCD*, 5:174, 195; Geikie, *Memoirs*, 165.
12. *CCD*, 5:186, 194, 331.
13. *CCD*, 5:224, 321; *LRO*, 2:5–6.
14. *CCD*, 5:351; *LLTH*, 1:133; MacLeod, 'Whigs,' 79–80; Morus, 'Politics of Power.'
15. *CCD*, 5:224–25, 278, 6:408; *LJT*, 45–48; *LLTH*, 1:101ff; Gage and Stearn, *Bicentenary History*, 53.
16. *CCD*, 5:424; *LLTH*, 1:85, 114–15, 119, 137–38; *LJT*, ch. 4.
17. *LLJH*, 1:477–78; Corsi, *Science*, ch. 17.
18. *CCD*, 5:345, 350; *LLJH*, 1:474.
19. 'Origin of Man: Science *versus* Theology,' *London Investigator*, 1 (1854–55), 8ff; Desmond, 'Robert Grant's Later Views,' 402, 404; Beddoe, *Memories*, 32–33; E. Forbes to T. Huxley, 16 Nov. 1852, THP 16.170; *LLTH*, 1:94.
20. C. Lyell, 'Anniversary Address,' xxxiii, xxxix; Corsi, 'Importance,' 224, 241; Bartholomew, 'Lyell' and 'Singularity.'
21. *CCD*, 5:537; *LLL*, 2:199; Desmond, *Politics*, 327–30.
22. *CCD*, 5:416; *Natural Selection*, 89.
23. T. Huxley, 'Vestiges,' 425–27, 429; Huxley's notes on *Vestiges*, THP 41.57–63; Bartholomew, 'Huxley's Defence,' 526–28; Desmond, *Archetypes*, 49; *LLD*, 2:188–89; *LLTH*, 1:224.
24. *CCD*, 5:213–14; Pearson, *Life*, 2:204.
25. *CCD*, 5:212–13, 215, 537.
26. *CCD*, 5:155, 294, 379.
27. *CCD*, 5:159, 186, 201; Health diary, Down House.
28. *CCD*, 5:322, 334, 348, 372; 6:196, 209; *LLJH*, 1:374.

28 GUNSHIPS & GROG SHOPS

1. Hutchinson, *Life*, 30, 36; *CCD*, 5:105; *ED*, 2:154; *TBI*, 49–50; recollections of G. Darwin, DAR 112; Health diary, Down House.
2. *CCD*, 5;164, 182, 187, 265.
3. F. Darwin, *Rustic Sounds*, 154–55 and *Springtime*, 59–60; G. Darwin's 'manual exercise' and diary, 1852–54, DAR 210.7; *CCD*, 4:427.
4. *LLTH*, 1:116; Geikie, *Memoir*, 224; *LLL*, 2:201; *CCD*, 5:241.
5. *LLL*, 2:202.
6. *CCD*, 5:196–97, 199, 201, 230, 247–49; Ospovat, *Development*, 177–78; Kohn, 'Darwin's Principle,' 251; J. Browne, *Secular Ark*, 205–16.

7. *Autobiography*, 120–21; *Natural Selection*, 249; *Notebooks*, B21; *CCD*, 4:139, 5:475; Ospovat, *Development*, 171; Kohn, 'Darwin's Principle,' 250.

8. McKendrick, 'Josiah Wedgwood,' 30–34.

9. Prince Albert, in Golby, *Culture*, 1–2; Schweber, 'Wider British Context,' 64–65; Schweber, 'Darwin,' 258–59, 265; *Autobiography*, 55.

10. *Origin*, 56, 380; *Natural Selection*, 228ff. Schweber, 'Darwin,' 212; Ospovat, *Development*, 181–83; Kohn, 'Darwin's Principle,' 250; *CCD*, 5:197; J. Browne, *Secular Ark*, 210–16. In today's language, Darwin was developing a theory of sympatric speciation, where the parents and (different) offspring inhabit the same area, rather than being isolated by geography.

11. Even though Milne–Edwards acknowledged his debt to the economists openly: Schweber, 'Darwin,' 197, 213, 255–56, 285; *Natural Selection*, 233; cf. Conry, *Introduction*, 387.

12. Seed, 'Unitarianism', 1–3; Schweber, 'Darwin and the Political Economists,' 269–70; *CCD*, 4:473.

13. *CCD*, 5:253, 265; *ED*, 2:156.

14. *ED*, 2:155–56; *CCD*, 5:537–38; Ereira, *People's England*, 78–85.

15. *CCD*, 5:68; *LLJH*, 1:445; *CP*, 1:255; Sulloway, 'Geographic Isolation,' 41–47.

16. *CCD*, 5:237, 241, 263.

17. *CCD*, 5:299, 305, 308; *CP*, 1:256–57; J. Browne, *Secular Ark*, 198. Although these experiments came as a response to the supercontinent threat, they had actually been on the cards for fifteen years: *Journal* (1839), 541–42; *Notebooks*, Q10, where he jotted, 'Soak all kinds of seeds for week in Salt. artificial water.'

18. *CCD*, 5:305, 308, 321, 328; *LLJH*, 1:352.

19. *CCD*, 2:282, 5:320, 331, 364; *CP*, 1:265; D. Porter, '*Beagle* Collector,' 1015.

20. *CCD*, 5:338–39, 364–67, 374–75; *CP*, 1:257.

21. *CCD*, 5:363, 370, 440–41, 477, 483, 500; 6:122; *LLJH*, 1:494; *CP*, 1:257–58, 261–62.

22. *CCD*, 5:265; F. Darwin, *Springtime*, 53.

23. Ospovat, *Development*, 153–57.

24. *CCD*, 5:84, 100, 147, 194; Ospovat, *Development*, 153ff. He first gave hint of this embryological view in *Notebooks* Summer 1842, 7, where he jotted: 'You can select cattle & sheep for horns & yet no difference in calves – how is this in young pigeons – dogs – cattle? ... as in trades there is no reason, why the peculiarities sh^d be born, – may come in corresponding time of life of offspring ... may just as well be born a tendency to alter or assume some form late in youth, – only facts can decide.'

25. *Foundations*, 221; Ospovat, *Development*, 156.

26. *CCD*, 5:288.

27. *CCD*, 6:217, also 3:9, 4:18, 30, 63–64, 89–90, 231 and Colp, 'Darwin and Mrs. Whitby;' Wells, 'Historical Context,' 228–29; Desmond, *Politics*, 310; Secord, 'Darwin.'

28. Secord, 'Darwin;' Desmond, 'Making,' 224–29.

29. Secord, 'Nature's Fancy,' 166; *CCD*, 5:250, 321, 337, 359; *Notebooks*, Q3, p. 493.

30. *CCD*, 5:326, 352, 386, 492, 497.

31. Darwin, *Expression*, 259; *CCD*, 5:508.

32. *CCD*, 5:415, 482.

33. *CCD*, 5:528, 6:24, 217; *LLL*, 2:213; Secord, 'Nature's Fancy,' 164, 170.

34. CCD, 6:236; Secord, 'Nature's Fancy,' 165, 175, 178 and 'Darwin,' 537.
35. Secord, 'Nature's Fancy,' 173.
36. Secord, 'Nature's Fancy,' 177; LLD, 2:281–82.
37. CCD, 5:509; ED, 2:157.

29 HORRID WRETCHES LIKE ME

1. LLJH, 1:368-69.
2. CCD, 5:282, 425, 6:114; LLJH, 1:375; LLTH, 1:138-39, 148.
3. J. Hooker to T. Huxley, 4 April 1856, THP 3.23; LLJH, 1:369-70, 412.
4. LLTH, 1:128-29, 144, 157; CCD, 5:442.
5. T. Huxley to E. Forbes, 27 Nov. 1852, THP 16.72; W. Carpenter to T. Huxley, 16 July 1855 and 22 Oct. 1858, THP 12.78, 94; LLTH, 1:95; Baynes, 'Darwin,' 505-506; Desmond, *Archetypes*, 22, 123. Macaulay engineered Owen's job at the British Museum, and the £800 pay that went with it: LRO, 2:13-15.
6. J. Hooker to T. Huxley, 4 April 1856, THP 3.23.
7. Owen, 'Lyell,' 448-50; Ospovat, *Development*, 129-40; Desmond, *Archetypes*, 42-46; Bowler, *Fossils*, 101-106; E. Richards,'Question,' 145-46.
8. CCD, 5:68, 133; Desmond, *Archetypes*, 42; Bartholomew, 'Huxley's Defence,' 527-29.
9. CCD, 5:133; T. Huxley, 'Contemporary Literature,' 243; Ospovat, 'Darwin on Huxley;' Winsor, *Starfish*, 90-97.
10. Darwin made notes on Huxley's attack on W. B. Carpenter's enunciation of the principle (T. Huxley, 'Comparative Literature,' 243-46): Ospovat, 'Darwin on Huxley,' for the transcription from DAR B.C.40f.
11. Wollaston, *Variation*, 186, 189; CCD, 5:268-70, 6:100.
12. CCD, 5:403, 498-99; 6:66, 74, 361.
13. LLD, 2:26-27; CCD, 6:87, 89; LLL, 2:212. Like Lyell, Bunbury had married one of Leonard Horner's daughters, Frances, whom Darwin knew well from his London days.
14. Darwin to T. Wollaston, 6 June [1856], EUL, Gen. 1999/1/30 (cf. CCD, 6:134); Matthew 7:13-14 (AV); J. Moore, 'Of Love,' 220-23.
15. CCD, 5:270; 6:147; Wollaston, *Variation*, 186, 188; Darwin's notes on Wollaston, DAR 197.2
16. LLD, 2:196 (Huxley was undoubtedly referring to this April 1856 meeting; he confused the dates in his reminiscences); CCD, 5:351. Darwin's dismay was caused by Huxley's Royal Institution talk in April 1855 denouncing progressive development, an abstract of which Huxley posted to him: T. Huxley, 'On Certain Zoological Arguments.'
17. Ospovat, 'Darwin on Huxley,' 11-16, transcribing DAR B.C. 40e.
18. CCD, 3:83, 6:103, 106, 111-12; LLTH, 1:150.
19. CCD, 6:147, 175-76; LLJH, 1:427; T. Huxley to F. Dyster, Dec. 1856, THP 15.80; LRO, 2:60.
20. CCD, 6:260, 484.
21. CCD, 5:519, 522; Wallace, 'On the Law;' Brooks, *Just Before*, ch. 5.
22. Wilson, *Sir Charles Lyell's Scientific Journals*, 6-7.
23. LLL, 2:213-14; CCD, 6:58, 90, 152, 236; Wilson, *Sir Charles Lyell's Scientific Journals*, 54-57, 60: Lyell talked species with Busk, Carpenter, Hooker, Huxley, and John Stuart Mill at the 28 April meeting of the Philosophical Club.

24. *CCD*, 6:78; Bunbury, *Life*, 2:90, 99-100.
25. *CCD*, 6:100, 106.
26. *CCD*, 6:109, 130-31, 135, 142, 238.
27. Jensen, 'X Club,' 63; *CCD*, 6:122-23.

30 A LOW & LEWD NATURE

1. *CCD*, 5:83, 6:87, 151–52, 191.
2. *CCD*, 6:140, 143–44, 147, 153, 155, 193; *Natural Selection*, 534–44.
3. *CCD*, 6:169, 179, 193.
4. Wilson, *Sir Charles Lyell's Scientific Journals*, 86–87, 102, 119–20, 153, 233, 259, 279; *LLL*, 2:215; *CCD*, 6:194; Bartholomew, 'Lyell.'
5. *CCD*, 6:184, 189, 236; Wilson, *Sir Charles Lyell's Scientific Journals*, 57–58, 94–95, 97–98; E. Richards, 'Moral Anatomy,' 391–96, 406–10; Lurie, *Louis Agassiz*, ch. 7; Lorimer, *Colour*, ch. 5; Bolt, *Victorian Attitudes*, ch. 1.
6. *CCD*, 6:100, 199, 201.
7. *CCD*, 6:198, 200–201, 239, 385, 408.
8. *CP*, 1:258, 262, 268; *CCD*, 5:329–30, 500, 6:244.
9. *CCD*, 5:326, 6:100, 174, 248, 305.
10. *CCD*, 6:152, 218, 234, 238, 247, 409.
11. *CCD*, 6:248, 250, 259, 266–67, 274, 282; *LLJH*, 1:449.
12. *ED*, 2:132; *CCD*, 6:238, 267.
13. *CCD*, 6:238, 264, 268–69, 303, 285, 301, 385; *ED*, 2:105, 161; Raverat, *Period Piece*, 122; *Wedgwood*, 260.
14. *CCD*, 6:305, 438; *ED*, 2:162.
15. *ED*, 2:105, 162; *CCD*, 6:268–69, 274–75, 286, 303; Roberts, *Paternalism*, 115–16, 151–52.
16. *CCD*, 6:304; *Natural Selection*, 73, 89.
17. *CCD*, 5:84, 100; *Natural Selection*, 35–36, 89, 208.
18. *CCD*, 6:335, 237–38, 249; *TBI*, 57.
19. *Natural Selection*, 6; *CCD*, 5:112, 6:218, 301, 303–304; J. Moore, 'On the Education,' 53–54.
20. *CCD*, 6:335; *Origin*, 57; *Autobiography*, 137; *Natural Selection*, 92–94; J. Browne, *Secular Ark*, 204–205.
21. *Natural Selection*, 172–75, 569; Darwin to J. Hooker, 13 July [1856], DAR 114.3:169 (cf. *CCD*, 6:178); Colp, 'Charles Darwin's Reprobation.'
22. *CCD*, 4:479; *LRO*, 2:12; *Natural Selection*, 172; Ricks, *Poems*, 912 (lvi:15–16).
23. Desmond, 'Artisan Resistance;' Holyoake, *Sixty Years*, 1:166–70; McCabe, *Life*, 1:85–87, 95–96; Royle, *Victorian Infidels*, 80–81.
24. *Natural Selection*, 175–76.
25. *CCD*, 6:345–46.

31 WHAT WOULD A CHIMPANZEE SAY?

1. *CCD*, 3:253; Owen, 'On the Anthropoid Apes' and 'Osteological Contributions,' 414–17; Desmond, *Politics*, 288–94 on the 1830s debates. Thomas Savage discussed the gorilla's discovery in a long letter to Owen, 24 April 1847, BM(NH), OCorr. 23.103.
2. Flower, *List*, 1:2; Middlemiss, *Zoo*, 10–11, 23; Barnaby, *Log Book*, 36–37.

The German comparative anatomist Carl Gustav Carus saw his first living orang–utan in London: C. Carus, *King of Saxony's Journey*, 62.

3. Chilton, 'Geological Revelations;' 'Origin of Man: Science *versus* Theology,' *London Investigator*, 1 (1854–55), 8–122 *passim*; Desmond, 'Artisan Resistance,' 100.

4. *LRO*, 1:377, 2:73, 385; Argyll, *George Douglas*, 1:408–11; Desmond, *Archetypes*, 62–64.

5. W. Whewell to R. Owen, 3 April 1859, BM(NH), OCorr. 26.285; Owen, 'Presidential Address,' xlix–li and *Classification*, 62–63.

6. Owen, 'On the Characters,' 19–20; CCD 6:367, 419; Desmond, *Archetypes*, 74–76. Owen had first begun casting alcohol–hardened ape brains in 1830, so he was extremely experienced in the matter: R. Owen, Notebook 1 (Oct.–Dec. 1830), BM(NH), OColl.

7. *Natural Selection*, 214, 223–24; CCD, 6:366.

8. CCD, 6:368–69, 372–73, 377, 385–86, 394; ED 2:159.

9. CCD, 6:377, 385, 395, 416; TBI, 59–60.

10. CCD, 6:384, 389.

11. CCD, 6:290, 387–88, 457.

12. CCD, 6:395–96, 407; *Natural Selection*, 307–12, 570–71.

13. CCD, 6:394–95, 404, 407; 'Register of baptisms . . .,' KAO P123/1/10.

14. CCD, 6:412, 416; CP, 1:274; ED, 2:163; LLD, 1:137; CCD, 6:524 and Emma Darwin's diary, 9 April 1857 *et seq.*, on deposit in DAR, for the travel movements that spring. (We thank Anne Secord for alerting us to the diary.)

15. CCD, 6:420–21, 424–28; *Natural Selection*, 275–79, 303–304; ED, 2:163.

16. CCD, 6:429, 443; *Natural Selection*, 94; LLJH, 1:496.

17. CCD, 6:325, 412, 432–33.

18. CCD, 6:437, 445–50, 492. He was writing chapter eight, 'Difficulties on the Theory of Natural Selection,' at this time. Although not mentioned in the letter to Gray, the instincts of bees were among Darwin's more pressing problems. So pressing, Robert Richards believes, that they were the stumbling block holding up publication of his entire theory through the 1840s and 1850s (R. Richards, 'Why' and *Darwin*, 144–52; also Prete, 'Conundrum'). The problem was the sterile worker bees: not breeding, they had no offspring to select from. So how did their instincts evolve?

Whether this technical teaser prevented Darwin from publishing is another matter. To start with, he only recognized the conundrum on reading Kirby and Spence's *Introduction to Entomology* in 1843, so it could not have spiked his 'Sketch' of 1842. Moreover, no sooner had he spotted the problem than he had an answer. He guessed that ancestral bees had all been working queens, and through the generations the majority had turned into sterile workers, retaining their instincts. In 1848 he still accepted this for wasps and humble bees, but in addition he toyed with the novel notion of 'family' selection (today called kin selection) for sterile soldier ants, whose body and behaviour are quite unlike the queen's. He thought that the whole colony stood to be selected if new armaments or protective instincts appeared by chance among the soldiers.

He did not doubt that the neuter castes offered 'the greatest *special* difficulty' (quoted in R. Richards, *Darwin*, 146). But it was not so overpowering as to stop him writing *Natural Selection* in the meliorative 1850s. This is the crux: he had no new solution in 1856, and yet he began his 'big book.' Neuter insects did not delay him, nor need they have in the 1840s. His strategy in 1856 was, as in 1848, to pose the problem and suggest plausible mechanisms. Only in 1857, well into the big book, did he finally plump for kin selection as *the* mechanism.

Strategic presentation was Darwin's forte. He singled out sterile insects as potentially 'fatal' to his theory in the *Origin* (236) in order to disarm critics before confronting them with his 'family' selection mechanism. But all along he had had one theory or another in mind, and he could have published at any point. Had insect sterility truly been lethal he would never have laid himself on the line by beginning *Natural Selection* in 1856.

19. Portlock, 'Address,' 1858, clvii–iii; 1857, cxliv–v; *CCD*, 6:445–50. In Portlock's words: if Creation was 'an act imposing laws upon nature, and calling into existence organisms subject to the controlling and modifying action of physical circumstances, why should not an alteration in these circumstances produce the same change in a created being'?

20. *CCD*, 6:445–46.

21. *CCD*, 6:108, 454; *LLTH*, 1:139; Gage and Stearn, *Bicentenary History*, 53. T. Huxley, 'Lectures,' 238.

22. *CCD*, 6:456, 461–62.

23. *CCD*, 5:376, 6:459, 467, 489; *LLJH*, 1:452; Appel, *Cuvier–Geoffroy Debate*, 125–36 on the Geoffroys' attempts to create 'monsters' in Paris.

24. Freeman, 'Charles Darwin;' cf. *CCD*, 2:300–303.

25. *CCD*, 5:253, 537, 6:345–46, 394, 451, 475–76, 478.

26. *ED* (1904), 1:183–84; E. Wedgwood, *My First Reading Book*; Darwin's memoir of Charles Waring Darwin, DAR 210.13.

27. *ED*, 2:45–48, 164–65; *TBI*, 161–64; Healey, *Wives*, 148–68.

28. *CCD*, 4:103; Marsh, 'Charles Darwin;' Zangerl, 'Social Composition.'

29. *CCD*, 6:451–52, 460, 477; Atkins, *Down*, 28, 97; *Natural Selection*, 380; Ospovat, 'Perfect Adaptation;' Ospovat, *Development*, ch. 9; Kohn, 'Darwin's Ambiguity.'

30. *CCD*, 6:460–61; *TBI*, 120–21; *Darwin's Journal*, 14.

31. *CCD*, 6:461, 475, 487; *Natural Selection*, 339.

32. *CCD*, 6:515–16; *Natural Selection*, 387, 467–68, 477, 481; Wilson, *Sir Charles Lyell's Scientific Journals*, 85; R. Richards, *Darwin*, ch. 3. It was well known that habits, and 'even the trifling peculiarities of an individual, have a tendency to become transmitted' (Lewes, 'Hereditary Influence,' 162). Darwin's innovation was to see the best adapted selected, so that change would take place over time.

33. *CCD*, 6:514–15.

34. *LLD*, 2:110; G. Allen, *Miscellaneous and Posthumous Works*, 1:3ff; Buckle, *History*, 1:174–77; 3:481–82; Ruse, *Darwinian Revolution*, 146; Irvine, *Apes*, 166.

35. *Autobiography*, 110; *LLD*, 2:110; Bunbury, *Life*, 2:138–39.

36. Spencer, *Autobiography*, 2:4, 10, 15–16; *LJT*, 76l; Duncan, *Life*, 85, 97, 550.

37. J. Hooker to T. Huxley, 26 Jan. 1858, THP 3.28; *LLL*, 2:279–80.

38. *Natural Selection*, 10, 463. The nine extant chapters of *Natural Selection* were finally published in 1975.

39. T. Huxley, Royal Institution Lecture 10, 'On the Special Peculiarities of Man,' 16 Mar. 1858: Lecture 11, 'Modifiability of Vital Phenomena,' 22 Mar. 1858, THP 36.98–100, 114; Spencer, *Autobiography*, 1:462.

40. T. Huxley to F. Dyster, 30 Jan. 1859, THP 15.106.
41. *LLD*, 2:103, 112–14; *TBI*, 61–63; *ED*, 2:166.
42. *MLD*, 1:109; *LLJH*, 1:458; *LLD*, 2:107.
43. *LLD*, 2:116. On the dating of the letter's arrival: Brooks, *Just Before*, 251–57; Brackman, *Delicate Arrangement*, ch. 3; and especially the response by Kohn, 'On the Origin.'

32 BREAKING COVER

1. Darwin to J. Hooker, 23 [June 1858], DAR 114:238; Colp, 'Charles Darwin, Dr. Edward Lane,' 205, 210; *LLD*, 2:116.
2. Wallace, *My Life*, 1:87, 224; Durant, 'Scientific Naturalism,' 35ff; Hughes, 'Wallace;' Brooks, *Just Before*, ch. 1; Desmond, 'Artisan Resistance,' on the Halls of Science.
3. Durant, 'Scientific Naturalism,' 39; Brooks, *Just Before*, ch. 4.
4. R. Smith, 'Alfred Russel Wallace,' 178, 182, 184ff; Kottler, 'Charles Darwin,' 374. Kohn, 'Origin,' 1106, discusses Darwin's and Wallace's differences on divergence in 1858.
5. Wallace, *Natural Selection*, 27–36, 42.
6. *LLD*, 2:115–20; *MLD*, 1:119; Darwin's memoir of Charles Waring Darwin, DAR 210.13; *Calendar*, 2295; Brooks, *Just Before*, 264.
7. *LLD*, 2:126; Gage and Stearn, *Bicentenary History*, 53–57.
8. *LLJH*, 2:301; Moody, 'Reading;' Gage and Stearn, *Bicentenary History*, 57; *LLD*, 2:294.
9. 'Register of burials . . .,' KAO P123/1/14; Darwin to W. Fox, 2 July [1858], 21 [July 1858], and 30 [July 1858], Christ's College Library, Cambridge; *LLD*, 2:126, 132; *TBI*, 63ff; *Companion*, 116.
10. *LLD*, 2:128, 131–32, 137–39, 143; *TBI*, 64.
11. Wilson, *Sir Charles Lyell's Scientific Journals*, 195, 198–99, 202; *LLD*, 2:146, 326; *ARW*, 1:134–35; *Calendar*, 2337.
12. T. Huxley to F. Dyster, 30 Jan. 1859, THP 15.106; Desmond, *Archetypes*, 81; Turner, 'Victorian Conflict,' 359ff.
13. T. Huxley to J. Hooker, 18 June 1858, THP 2.153; *LLTH*, 1:161; Duncan, *Life*, 87; Spencer, 'Owen,' 415; Spencer, *Autobiography*, 1:368, 462; 2:24; Desmond, *Archetypes*, 97–98. On the way the Positivist in the Chapman group, George Eliot's lover G. H. Lewes, dumped the 'Archetype,' see S. Bell, 'Lewes,' 288–90.
14. J. Hooker to T. Huxley, [Mar. 1859], THP 3.47; *LLD*, 2:149–50; RFD, 75; *TBI*, 64ff.
15. Peckham, *Origin*, 13–16; *LLD*, 2:151–54, 160; Paston, *At John Murray's*, 169–70.
16. *LLJH*, 1:510; *LLD*, 2:159, 160, 163; Darwin to T. Huxley, 2 June [1859], THP 5.65; *MLD*, 1:137.
17. *Calendar*, 2488; *LLD*, 2:163–65, 171, 178.
18. *LLD*, 2:166–68, 262; Wilson, *Sir Charles Lyell's Scientific Journals*, 330–32, 335–36; Bunbury, *Life*, 2:185.
19. *Calendar* 2489; *TBI*, 66–67; Judd, *Coming*, 117; Peckham, *Origin*, 16; *ED*, 1:172; *LLD*, 2:170; RFD, 86; *Denton's Ilkley Directory*, 46; *Shuttleworth's Popular Guide*, 50–51.
20. Darwin to J. Hooker, [27 Oct. or 3 Nov. 1859], DAR 115:25; *Calendar*, 2515, 2521; *LLD*, 2:166, 175, 215–20, 230; Peckham, *Origin*, 16–17

21. Peckham, *Origin*, 17, 748; *LLD*, 2:287–88; *MLD*, 1:174.

22. *LLD*, 2:229, 266; *Calendar*, 2542; *Athenaeum*, 19 Nov. 1859, pp. 659–60; Ellegard, *Darwin*, 41, 43, 294.

23. *LLTH*, 1:176; Carlyle, *On Heroes*, 96; *LLD*, 2:228–29, 232; *LLL*, 2:325; *LLJH*, 1:510; Himmelfarb, *Darwin*, ch. 12.

24. *MLD*, 1:149; *Calendar*, 2526, 2575; *LLD*, 2:240, 312; Owen, 'Presidential Address,' li; Wilson, *Sir Charles Lyell's Scientific Journals*, 227 on humans as the 'offspring of anthropoid species,' but somehow created at conception; Desmond, *Archetypes*, 60–62 for Owen's philosophy of Creation; Ellegard, *Darwin*, 65 on the status of Presidential Addresses to the BAAS.

25. *LLD*, 2:303–304, 312; cf. Southwood Smith, *Divine Government*; Gillespie, *Charles Darwin*, chs 5–6.

26. *LLD*, 2:239, 262; Hull, *Darwin*, 93–94, 114; Ellegard, *Darwin*, 35–38, 362–67 on the Unitarian response.

27. Darwin to T. Huxley, 28 Dec. 1859, THP 5.92; *LLD*, 2:235; *MLD*, 1:135; *LLTH*, 1:176.

28. D. Livingstone to R. Owen, 29 Dec. 1860, BM(NH), OCorr. 17.415; A. Sedgwick to R. Owen, 1860, vol. 23.268, 308; J. Wyman to R. Owen, June 1863, vol. 27.254; Argyll to R. Owen, 2 Dec. 1859 and 27 Feb. 1863, vol. 1.230.

29. *LLD*, 2:242; Hull, *Darwin*, 81–84.

30. R. Grant, *Tabular View*, vi; Desmond, 'Robert E. Grant's Later Views;' *LLD*, 2:226.

33 MORE KICKS THAN HALFPENCE

1. Ellegard, *Darwin*, 56; *LLD*, 2:241, 262; Marx and Engels, *Selected Correspondence*, 9:125-26; Engels, *Dialectics*, 19; R. Young, *Darwin's Metaphor*, 52; Durant, 'Scientific Naturalism,' 45 n. 75.

2. H. Martineau to E. A. Darwin, 2 Feb. 1860, W/M 32974-57. We thank Fiona Erskine for showing us transcriptions of this and the Harriet-Fanny letter; cf. Erskine, 'Darwin,' 92, 108 and *LLD*, 2:234.

3. Poynter, 'John Chapman,' 7; *LLD*, 2:315; H. Martineau to G. Holyoake, Friday [1859], BL, Add. MSS 42,726, f.26.

4. H. Martineau to G. Holyoake, Friday [1859], BL, Add. MSS 42,726, f.26; *Origin*, 484, 488. Darwin did indeed regret having 'truckled to public opinion' in resorting to the word 'creation,' 'by which I really meant "appeared" by some wholly unknown process:' *LLD*, 3:18.

5. H. Martineau to F. Wedgwood, 13 Mar. 1860, W/M 32975-57.

6. A. Sedgwick to Darwin, 24 Nov. 1859, DAR 98.2:17-18; *LLD*, 2:250; *ED*, 2:172, 196. Sedgwick, 'Objections,' 335 gave a blow-by-blow refutation in the Mar. 1860 *Spectator*, using 'Dame Nature's old book' to damn talk of 'the bestial origin of man.'

7. J. Henslow to L. Jenyns, 26 Jan. 1860, Bath Reference Library, Letters from Naturalists, &c to Rev. L. Jenyns, 1826-1878, vol. 1, 1 (9); Ellegard, *Darwin*, 45.

8. Bunting, *Charles Darwin*, 88-89, based on evidence apparently found while researching Parliamentary history. The sources have not been located and the author is deceased.

9. Huxley to F. Dyster, 29 Feb. 1860, THP 15.110.

10. Huxley to F. Dyster, 29 Feb. 1860, THP 15.110; Huxley's draft notes of the Royal Institution lecture, THP 41.9-56; *LLD*, 2:251, 281; *MLD*, 1:130-31.

11. *LLD*, 2:282-4; *MLD*, 1:139-40; Desmond, *Archetypes*, 110.

12. *LLTH*, 1:222-23; *LLD*, 2:293, 331.

13. *LRO*, 2:39; *LLD*, 2:300.

14. Owen, *Palaeontology*, 403 and *Anatomy*, 3:796, Hull, *Darwin*, 176, 181, 191.

15. Argyll to R. Owen, 27 Feb. 1863, BM(NH), OCorr. 1.230; Argyll, *George Douglas*, 2:ch. 23.

16. Hull, *Darwin*, 177, 182, 201, 202; G. Rolleston to T. Huxley, 13 April 1860, THP 25.142; *LLD*, 2:300; *MLD*, 1:149.

17. T. Huxley, *Darwiniana*, 23, 78, 79; *LLD*, 2:300; Barton, 'Evolution.'

18. *MLD*, 1:171-72; *LLD*, 2:316-18; *Calendar*, 2809; Hull, *Darwin*, 134; R. Young, *Darwin's Metaphor*, ch. 4.

19. *Darwin's Journal*, 15; Dupree, *Asa Gray*, 271; Loewenberg, *Calendar*, 17-25; *LLD*, 2:269-70; J. Moore, *Post-Darwinian Controversies*, 270-71.

20. Morrell and Thackray, *Gentlemen*, 395-96.

21. Wilson, *Sir Charles Lyell's Scientific Journals*, 355; Geikie, *Memoir*, 276-77; *LLD*, 2:291, 293, 366-67; *Calendar*, 2711, 2787; Secord, 'Geological Survey,' 260.

22. *Daily Telegraph*, 10 April 1863, p. 4; *LLD*, 2:287; Desmond, *Archetypes*, ch. 2; E. Richards,'Question,' 145-48.

23. *LLTH*, 1:187; *LLD*, 3:270.

24. 'Recent Acquisitions of the Manuscript Division,' *Quarterly Journal of the Library of Congress*, 31 (1974), 257.

25. Jensen, 'Return,' 166-67 and *LLL*, 2:335, on this equivocal point. One London weekly, *The Press*, did report this specific jibe.

26. G. Stoney to F. Darwin, 17 May 1895, DAR 106/7:36-39; *Athenaeum*, 14 July 1860, p. 65; Burton, 'Robert FitzRoy,' 151-61.

27. J. Hooker to Darwin, 2 July 1860, DAR 100:141-42 and *LLJH*, 1:525-27. Lucas, 'Wilberforce,' emphasizes how these on-the-spot accounts differ from the later legend of Huxley's triumph.

28. *LLD*, 2:323-24.

29. Huxley to F. Dyster, 9 Sept. 1860, THP 15.115; Tuckwell, *Reminiscences*, 54-55; Poulton, *Charles Darwin*, 155; Jensen, 'Return,' for an assessment of Huxley's rejoinder. Huxley's actual letter to Darwin is lost, but this to Dyster undoubtedly reflects its content.

30. Brown, *Metaphysical Society*, 139; Lucas, 'Wilberforce,' 327; Jensen, 'Return,' 166-67; cf. Gilley, 'Huxley-Wilberforce,' 333; J. Browne, 'Charles Darwin – Joseph Hooker Correspondence,' 361-62.

31. *LLJH*, 1:520.

32. *MLD*, 1:152, 158; *Calendar*, 2856.

33. Darwin to T. Huxley, [Aug. 1860?], DAR 145 and *Calendar*, 2887.

34. Wilberforce, 'Darwin's Origin,' 239, 255, 259, Darwin Reprint Collection, R.34, CUL; *MLD*, 1:156; *ARW*, 1:144.

34 FROM THE WOMB OF THE APE

1. Ellis, *Seven*; Crowther, *Church Embattled*.

2. Church, *Life*, 188; Corsi, *Science*, 283-84; Powell, in *Essays*, 139; Ellis, *Seven*, 62; *MLD*, 1:174-75; *LLJH*, 1:514.

3. RFD, 69; *LLJH*, 2:55; J. Moore, *Religion*, 425, 437; *MLD*, 2:266-67. For the political significance of this 'whig-liberal' alliance: Parry, *Democracy*, ch. 1.

4. J. Hooker to Darwin, 2 July 1860, DAR 100:141-42; *Athenaeum*, 7 July 1860, p. 26.

5. *MLD*, 1:177-78; T. Huxley to S. Wilberforce, 3 Jan. 1861, THP 227.101; *LLTH*, 1:210.

6. *LLD*, 2:353-54, 373, 378; Dupree, *Asa Gray*, 296-97; *MLD*, 1:191.

7. Dupree, *Asa Gray*, 298ff; Loewenberg, *Calendar*, 100, 103, 134; Peckham, *Origin*, 57; *LLD*, 2:351, 355-56, 361, 370-71, 373; *MLD*, 1:166, 169-70; *Darwin's Journal*, 15; J. Moore, *Post-Darwinian Controversies*, 270ff, 389 n. 48.

8. *LLTH*, 1:152, 190, 220, 225; *Calendar*, 3066, 3085; *ED*, 2:177.

9. Darwin to T. Huxley, 1 Nov. [1860], THP 5.141; *MLD*, 1:460; Owen, 'Gorilla,' 395-96; Owen, 'Ape-Origin,' 262; T. Huxley, 'Man,' 498; Desmond, *Archetypes*, 75. Huxley's Christian compatriots included the Oxford anatomist George Rolleston and William Henry Flower at the Royal College of Surgeons.

10. Darwin to T. Huxley, 1 April 1861, THP 5.162; *MLD*, 1:185; Huxley, 'Man,' 433.

11. G. Rolleston to ?, 1 Oct. 1861, Wellcome Institute, London, AL 325619. Rolleston, who pitched into Owen on anatomical grounds, was promoted at Oxford with Huxley's help, but he was too cautious for Hooker, who saw him living 'in fear and trembling "of God, man, and monkeys":' *MLD*, 1:185.

12. Huxley to F. Dyster, 11 Oct. 1862, THP 15.123; *LLTH*, 1:192; 'Professor Huxley on Man's Place in Nature,' *Edinburgh Review*, 117 (1863), 563.

13. T. Huxley to W. Sharpey, 13 and 16 Nov. 1862, UCL, Sharpey Correspondence MSS Add. 227 (no. 122, 124); *MLD*, 2:30; *LLD*, 2:264, 266.

14. T. Huxley to C. Lyell, 26 June 1861, THP 30.35; *LLTH*, 1:239.

15. *LLD*, 2:364; *LLL*, 2:341, 344; *LLTH*, 1:197; C. Lyell to T. Huxley, 26 Nov. 1860, THP 6.40; T. Huxley, *Man's Place*, 168, 178; Bynum, 'Charles Lyell's *Antiquity*,' 161ff; Grayson, *Establishment*, 212 etc.

16. Darwin to J. Hooker, 23 [April 1861], DAR 115:98; *LLJH*, 2:60; *Calendar*, 3101 *et seq.*; *CP*, 2:72-74; *TBI*, 71.

17. J. Moore, 'On the Education,' 57; *TBI*, 69; *LLD*, 1:136; *ED*, 2:176-77; *MLD*, 1:460.

18. E. Darwin to C. Darwin, [June 1861], DAR 210.10; *ED*, 2:174; *TBI*, 83; Healey, *Wives*, 173-74.

19. C. Lyell to T. Huxley, 5 July 1860 [sic, 1861], THP 6.36; *LLTH*, 1:190; T. Huxley, *Man's Place*, 81; 'Professor Huxley at the Royal Institution,' *Reasoner*, 25 (1860), 125; Watts, 'Theological Theories,' 119, 134; *Calendar*, 3466, 4464, 4468.

20. R. Godwin-Austen to T. Huxley, 30 Mar. 1863, THP 10.183; T. Huxley, *Man's Place*, 81, 144, 146, 152-55; *LLTH*, 1:224.

21. Bynum, 'Charles Lyell's *Antiquity*,' 161, 170-71; *LLTH*, 1:174; Desmond, *Archetypes*, 83-86.

22. *MLD*, 1:181, 2:270, 278; *Calendar*, 3070; Darwin, *Orchids*, 113; Allan, *Darwin*, 195ff; *LLD*, 3:262-63

23. Basalla, 'Darwin's Orchid Book,' 972; *LLD*, 3:255; *MLD*, 2:280, 373; Darwin, *Orchids*, 178-79; *CP*, 2:63.

24. *Calendar*, 3662; *MLD*, 1:195, 202; Ghiselin, *Triumph*, 136; *LLD*, 2:267, 383; 3:254, 266; Darwin, *Orchids*, 233.

25. *LLTH*, 1:194-95; *Calendar*, 3386; *MLD*, 1:252; *CP*, 2:60-61. *LLD*, 2:384.

26. T. Huxley to F. Dyster, [Jan. 1862], THP 15.113; Ellegard, *Darwin*, 295; *LRO*, 2:115-23 (Du Chaillu set off for West Africa again, intending to capture Owen a live specimen: P. du Chaillu to R. Owen, 19 Aug. 1864, BM(NH), OCorr. 10.173); *LLJH*, 2:25; *LLTH*, 1:192-95; *Witness*, 11 and 14 Jan. 1862.

27. Darwin to T. Huxley, 14 Jan. 1862, THP 5.167; *LLD*, 2:384; *LLTH*, 1:194-95; Huxley to J. Hooker, 16 Jan. 1862, THP 2.112.

28. *LLD*, 3:276; *ARW*, 1:143-44, 146; Brooks, *Just Before*, 69.

29. C. Lyell to T. Huxley, 9 Aug. 1862, THP 6.66 (reply *LLTH*, 1:200); 'Palaeontology,' *Athenaeum*, 7 April 1860, pp. 478-79.

30. G. Rorison to R. Owen, 25 April 1860, BM(NH), OCorr. 22.379; Rorison, 'Creative Week,' 322, 517; Hull, *Darwin*, 182-83; Desmond, *Archetypes*, 78; E. Richards, 'Question,' 147; *MLD*, 2:341.

31. Darwin to T. Huxley, 14 Jan. and 10 Dec. 1862, THP 5.167, 183; Ellis, *Seven*, 121-22; Owen, *Monograph on the Aye-Aye*, 62.

32. *Calendar*, 3728, 3741, 3763, 3775, 3809, 3972; *TBI*, 72; *MLD*, 1:200, 223-26; *LLD*, 3:269; Atkins, *Down*, 29-30.

33. *MLD*,1:228-29; *Calendar*, 3899, 3909; Owen, 'On the Archaeopteryx.'

34. Owen, 'On the Archaeopteryx,' 46; Wagner, 'On a New Fossil Reptile,' 266-67; *Calendar*, 3905, 3928.

35. Peckham, *Origin*, 509; *MLD*, 1:234, 472; *LLD*, 3:6; *LLJH*, 2:32; *Calendar*, 3926; J. Evans, 'On Portions,' 418, 421. On the initial interpretations of *Archaeopteryx*: Desmond, *Archetypes*, 124-31.

36. T. Huxley, *On Our Knowledge*, 56; *MLD*, 1:216-17, 229-30; *LLTH*, 1:206.

37. *Calendar*, 3905, 3967; *MLD*, 1:472; *LLJH*, 2:32.

38. Bynum, 'Charles Lyell's *Antiquity*'; *MLD*, 1:472; *LLD*, 3:8-9; C. Lyell, *Geological Evidences*, 405ff, 429.

39. *LLD*, 3:9, 12; *LLL*, 2:361-65, 376; *TBI*, 74.

40. 'Evidence as to Man's Place in Nature,' *Athenaeum*, 28 Feb. 1863, p. 287; *LLTH*, 1:201; *LLD*, 3:14; Argyll, *Reign of Law*, 265; T. Huxley, *Man's Place*, 76; *LLJH*, 2:32; Darwin to T. Huxley, 18 Feb. 1863, THP 5.173.

41. T. Huxley, *Man's Place*, 147; *MLD*, 1:237; Owen, 'Summary,' 115; Desmond, *Archetypes*, 64; Huxley to F. Dyster, 12 Mar. 1863, THP 15.125; *LLTH*, 1:201. .

42. Darwin to J. Hooker, 5 Mar. [1863], DAR 115:184; *Darwin's Journal*, 16; *TBI*, 74-75; *LLD*, 3:312-13; Allan, *Darwin*, ch. 12.

43. Darwin to J. Brodie Innes, 1 Sept. [1863], APS, Getz Collection B/D25.m; Darwin to W. Fox, 4 Sept [1863], and E. Darwin to W. Fox, [29 Sept. 1863], both Christ's College Libary, Cambridge; W. Fox to E. Darwin, 7 Sept [1863], DAR 164; *TBI*, 74-75.

44. *LLJH*, 2:62; Darwin to J. Hooker, [4 Oct.] and [22-23 Nov. 1863], DAR 115:206, 211; J. Hooker to Darwin, [28 Sept.] and [1 Oct. 1863], DAR 101:159, 160-62.

35 A LIVING GRAVE

1. *Calendar*, 4334, 4338, 4347, 4367, 4368; *ED*, 2:180–81; *LLD*, 3:3; *MLD*, 1:247, 2:338; *TBI*, 76–77.

2. *CP*, 2:106; Allan, *Darwin*, 271–72.

3. *Calendar*, 4389, 4667, 5316, 5391; *CP*, 2:106; J. Browne, 'Erasmus Darwin,' 602.

4. Loewenberg, *Calendar*, 55; Colp, 'Charles Darwin: Slavery,' 487; E. Richards, 'Moral Anatomy,' 415–24 and 'Huxley,' 261ff.

5. Greene, *Science*, 103.

6. Wallace, *Natural Selection*, 303–31; Schwartz, 'Darwin, Wallace,' 283–84; R. Smith, 'Alfred Russel Wallace,' 179–80; Durant, 'Scientific Naturalism,' 40–45; Kottler, 'Charles Darwin,' 388; Vorzimmer, *Charles Darwin*, 190; ARW, 1:150.

7. *MLD*, 2:31–37; *LLD*, 3:89–91; *Calendar*, 3158 *et seq.*; ARW,1:152–59.

8. *Calendar*, 4458; *LLL*, 2:382–83; ARW, 1:152.

9. *The Times*, 25 May 1864, pp. 8–9; King, 'Reputed Fossil Man,' 92, 96; Ellegard, *Darwin*, 165; Bowler, *Theories*, 33–34.

10. Ellis, *Seven*, 109–11, ch. 4.

11. Allan, *Darwin*, ch. 12; *MLD*, 1:251; *Calendar*, 4527, 4582, 4607, 4619; TBI 80.

12. J. Moore, 'On the Education,' 59–60 and 'Darwin of Down,' 468–69; F. Darwin, *Springtime*, 63; Stecher, 'Darwin–Innes Letters,' 215–17.

13. Brock and MacLeod, 'Scientists' Declaration,' 41, 48.

14. Barton, 'Influential Set,' 61ff; Jensen, 'X Club,' 63; MacLeod, 'X Club.'

15. *Calendar*, 4671, 4686, 4689, 4690, 4696, 4700–712, 4719; *MLD*, 1:252–56, 258; *LLD*, 3:28, 29; *LLTH*, 1:255; *LLJH*, 2:75–76; *LLL*, 2:384; MacLeod, 'Of Medals,' 83; Bartholomew, 'Award.'

16. Huxley, in Barton, 'Evolution,' 263–64; Roos, 'Aims,' 164; *Calendar*, 4817; *LLL*, 3:28; X Club Notebook, Tyndall Papers, Royal Institution; T. Huxley to J. Hooker, 21 July 1863, THP 2.120.

17. *Calendar*, 4712; Ashwell and Wilberforce, *Life*, 3:154–55; Ellis, *Seven*, 136.

18. T. Huxley to F. Dyster, 26 Jan. 1865, THP 15.129; J. Hooker to Darwin, 1 Jan. 1865, DAR 102:1–3; Barton, 'X Club,' 225; J. Moore, *Post-Darwinian Controversies*, 25; Huxley–Rolleston correspondence, THP 25.171–74, 180–84, for the divisive effect of the leader.

19. Argyll, *George Douglas*, 2:167; *LLL*, 2:384–85; *LLD*, 3:32.

20. *LLL*, 2:385; *LLD*, 3:32; Desmond, *Archetypes*, 159; Paradis, *T. H. Huxley*, chs 2, 3.

21. *LLD*, 2:35; J. Hooker to Darwin, 3 Feb. [1865], DAR 102:8–9; Darwin to J. Hooker, 9 Feb. [1865], DAR 115:260; W. Thomson, *Popular Lectures*, 1:349ff.

22. *LLJH*, 2:72; *Calendar*, 4820.

23. Hutchinson, *Life*, 1:74; *LLD*, 3:36–38, 40–41; *ED*, 2:183; *Calendar*, 4829, 4986.

24. J. Hooker to Darwin, 2 May 1865, DAR 102:20–21; Darwin to J. Hooker, 4 May [1865], DAR 115:268; B. Sulivan to Darwin, 8 May 1865, DAR 177; TBI, 82; Burton, 'Robert FitzRoy,' 164ff; *Narrative*, 26.

25. TBI, 82–84; Poynter, 'John Chapman,' 15–17; *Calendar*, 4834, 4837, 4846; *ED*, 2:182.

26. Hodge, 'Darwin as a Lifelong Generation Theorist,' 227–36; Olby, 'Charles Darwin's Manuscript;' *MLD*, 1:281; *LLD*, 3:43–44; *Calendar*, 4837.

27. *LLTH*, 1:267–8; *Calendar*, 4841.

28. Bynum, 'Charles Lyell's *Antiquity*,' 178, 182; *LLD*, 3:39; *Calendar*, 4858, 4860, 4883, 4892.

29. Paradis, *T. H. Huxley*, 75; *English Leader*, 13 Jan. 1866; T. Huxley, *Method*, 38. We thank Simon Schaffer for providing a translation of the Jenny Marx letter from Lefebvre, *Marx–Engels*.

30. Owen, 'The Reign of Law,' Autograph Manuscripts of Sir R. Owen, BM(NH), OColl. 59.1–2; C. Lyell to T. Huxley, 22 Jan. 1866, THP 6.120; *English Leader*, 3 and 24 Feb. 1866.

31. *LLD*, 3:39; *TBI* 86; Irvine, *Apes*, 166; Bowler, *Theories*, 52; *Calendar*, 4963.

32. *Calendar*, 4529, 4942, 4971, 4973, 4985, 4990. Haeckel distributed them in Germany.

33. *ED*, 2:184; E. C. Langton (*née* Darwin) to Charles and Emma Darwin, [Jan. 1866], W/M 444; Darwin to J. Hooker, 21 [Jan. 1866], DAR 115:280; *Calendar*, 5009–10; *MLD*, 1:477.

34. *Calendar*, 5089; RFD, 70; *ED*, 2:184–85;

35. Paul, 'Selection,' 413–16; *Calendar*, 4794; Spencer, *Autobiography*, 2:102, 484; *LLD*, 3:46, 56; *Calendar*, 4645, 4650; *ARW*, 1:170, 188, 191; *MLD*, 1:267–69.

36 EMERALD BEAUTY

1. Grove, *Correlation*, 346; Morus, 'Politics of Power;' Ellegard, *Darwin*, 78-79.

2. *LLJH*, 2:98-99, 100-106; *Calendar*, 5165, 5167, 5201-202, 5229; *LLD*, 3:47-48; 'British Association for the Advancement of Science,' *Journal of Botany*, 5 (1867), 29-30.

3. Hutchinson, *Life*, 1:92; Owen, 'The Reign of Law,' Autograph Manuscripts of Sir R. Owen, BM(NH), OColl. 59.7, 18, 24; Ellegard, *Darwin*, 79.

4. Barrow, *Independent Spirits*, chs. 2, 6; Oppenheim, *Other World*, 276; Harrison, 'Early Victorian Radicals,' 198-99, 212 n. 3.

5. *LLTH*, 1:419-20; *LJT*, 115; *Calendar*, 4742-43; Kottler, 'Alfred Russel Wallace,' 170, 171-72; T. Huxley, in *Report*, 230.

6. Kottler, 'Alfred Russel Wallace,' 164-65, 167-72; Wallace, *My Life*, 2:277-81; *ARW*, 2:187-88.

7. *Calendar*, 4646, 4555, 4934, 6540, 6676; *LLTH*, 1:266; Weindling 'Ernst Haeckel,' 314, 317; Groeben, *Charles Darwin – Anton Dohrn Correspondence*, 10, 22; *LLD*, 3:88.

8. *Calendar*, 4555, 4586, 4646, 4934, 4973, 5193; Bölsche, *Haeckel*, 133ff, 150; Corsi and Weindling, 'Darwinism,' 694; Bayertz, 'Darwinism,' 297-98.

9. Bölsche, *Haeckel*, 242; RFD, 36; *RBL*, 159; *MLD*, 2:350; *Calendar*, 5252, 5257, 5262; T. Huxley, 'Natural History,' 13-14; Haeckel, *History*, 2:248.

10. *LLD*, 3:53, 73; *Calendar*, 5051, 5265-66, 5281; Spencer, *Autobiography*, 2:143; *LLTH*, 1:278; Lorimer, *Colour*, ch. 9; Bolt, *Victorian Attitudes*, ch. 3; Semmel, *Governor Eyre*, chs 4-5.

11. *LLTH*, 1:279-82; recollections of W. Darwin, DAR 112.2 (cf. *LLD*, 3:53).

12. *Darwin's Journal*, 17; Darwin to J. Hooker, 25 Sept. 1866 and [4 Oct. 1866], DAR 115:300, 302; *LLJH*, 2:77-79; *Calendar*, 5230, 5238, 5283-84, 5487.

13. *MLD*, 1:274; RFD, 37-39; Haeckel, *History*, 1:1-2; Haeckel, *Generelle Morphologie*, 2:451. On Haeckel and Darwin: Altner, *Charles Darwin*; Schwarz, 'Darwinism;' Kelly, *Descent*; Roger, 'Darwin.'

14. Gasman, *Scientific Origins*, 17-18; Corsi and Weindling, 'Darwinism,' 689; Weindling 'Ernst Haeckel,' 311; Haeckel, *History*, 1:295; S. Gould, *Ontogeny*, 78.

15. *MLD*, 1:274, 277; *LLTH*, 1:288; Haeckel, *Generelle Morphologie*, 1:90, 173-74n; *LLTH*, 1:288.

16. Vogt, *Lectures*, 378; Gregory, *Scientific Materialism*, ch. 3; *Calendar*, 5256, 5269, 5489, 5495, 5499-500, 5503, 5506, 5533; W. Montgomery, 'Germany,' 82-83; *LLD*, 3:69.

17. *LLD*, 3:62; Darwin, *Variation*, 2:426-28; Loewenberg, *Calendar*, 53 and De Beer, 'Some Unpublished Letters,' 40-41 for early formulations.

18. *MLD*, 1:277, 2:40; *LLD*, 3:59-60, 72, 98; *Calendar*, 5380, 5382, 5448, 5450.

19. *Calendar*, 5443, 5446, 5464; *LLD*, 2:279, 3:72-73; Vucinich, *Darwin*, 62ff; Vucinich, 'Russia,' 249; Freeman, *Works*, 123. On Royer: Miles, 'Clémence Royer;' Stebbins, 'France,' 125-27; Conry, *Introduction, passim*.

20. *ARW*, 1:179, 181; *MLD*, 2:57-58, 65.

21. Darwin to C. Kingsley, 10 June [1867], APS, Getz Collection B/D25.165; *MLD*, 1:277, 282-83; *LLD*, 3:65; *Calendar*, 5466.

22. Argyll, *Reign*, 219, 259-60; Mozley, 'Argument of Design,' 162; *LLL*, 2:431-2; Gillespie, *Charles Darwin*, 93-104. Bowler has emphasized the prevalence of this non-Darwinian view: Bowler, *Charles Darwin*, ch. 9 and *Non-Darwinian Revolution*, 90ff.

23. Darwin to C. Kingsley, 10 June [1867], APS, Getz Collection B/D25.165; Owen, 'The Reign of Law,' Autograph Manuscripts of Sir R. Owen, BM (NH), OColl. 59.1-2, 26.

24. *LLJH*, 2:114; *LLD*, 3:62; *MLD*, 1:302.

25. Wallace, *Natural Selection*, 34-90, 280, 282-85; Durant, 'Ascent,' 298; *ARW*, 1:178-80, 183, 185, 189; *Calendar*, 5522; Kottler, 'Charles Darwin,' 417ff.

26. Russell, 'Conflict Metaphor;' Burchfield, *Lord Kelvin*, 27ff, 70ff; Jenkin, 'Origin,' 289, 291-94; *LLD*, 3:107-108; *MLD*, 2:379; Vorzimmer, *Charles Darwin*, 27-30, 44-45.

27. *LLD*, 3:71-72; *MLD*, 1:272; *LLL*, 2:415-16.

28. *MLD*, 1:300; *Darwin's Journal*, 17; Kingsley, *Charles Kingsley*, 2:248-49; *Calendar*, 3427, 3439; Watts and [Holyoake], 'Charles R. Darwin.'

29. *Darwin's Journal*, 17; *ED*, 2:187; *Calendar*, 5781; *LLD*, 3:74-75.

37 SEX, POLITICS, AND THE X

1. *LLD*, 3:75, 84; *MLD*, 1:287; *LLJH*, 2:113; *Calendar*, 6036.

2. *Calendar*, 5844, 5874, 5885, 5915, 5918, 5972; *LLD*, 3:76-77; *ARW*, 1:199. The *Athenaeum* reviewer was evidently Berthold Seemann: *Calendar*, 5931, 5951.

3. *LLD*, 3:78, 80, 84; *Calendar*, 5914.

4. *Calendar*, 5773, 5843, 6047, 6127, 6219, 6289, 6294; *ED*, 2:187-88, 190-91; Loewenberg, *Calendar*, 42; J. Moore, 'On the Education,' 63-64.

5. *Calendar*, 5836, 5938, 5976, 5979; Vucinich, *Darwin*, 62ff.

6. *Calendar*, 5198, 5217, 5852, 5864, 5870-71, 6009, 6082, 6382; *LLD*, 3:77, 97, 99-100, 103, 111-12; *MLD*, 2:68, 90, 103, 159; *LLL*, 2:410; Agassiz and Agassiz, *Journey*, 15, 33, 399, 425; Lurie, *Louis Agassiz*, 353ff, 382.

7. *MLD*, 2:64-65; *LLD*, 3:92.

8. *MLD*, 2:63, 90; Wallace, *Natural Selection*, ch. 3; Ellegard, *Darwin*, 251.

9. *LLD*, 3:82; *ED*, 2:188-89; *MLD*, 2:69, 71, 99 and *Calendar*, 5885, 6042, 6052, 6062, 6067, 6070, 6127; *Descent* (1871), 1:43; X Club Notebook (5 Mar. 1868), Tyndall Papers, Royal Institution.

10. *Calendar*, 5919, 6107, 6114, 6629, 6635; *LLD* 3:86; *MLD*, 1:312, 2:92; W. Montgomery, 'Germany,' 83-85.

11. Mivart, 'Some Reminiscences,' 988-89; J. Gruber, *Conscience*, chs 1-2.

12. St G. Mivart to Darwin, 20 May 1868, 22 April 1870, and 10 Jan. 1872, all DAR 171; *Descent* (1871), 2:24-25; J. Gruber, *Conscience*, 31ff.

13. Dawkins, 'Darwin,' 436; Durant, 'Ascent,' 298-99; Ellegard, *Darwin*, 284-85; *LLJH*, 2:114; *LLD*, 3:98-99.

14. Forrest, *Francis Galton*, chs 1-2; Greene, *Science*, 102-106.

15. Greene, *Science*, 106-11; Greg, in *Descent* (1871), 1:174; Helmstadter, 'W. R. Greg;' Bagehot, *Physics*, 215.

16. *ARW*, 1:219; *MLD*, 1:297, 302, 305; *LLJH*, 2:114; Ellegard, *Darwin*, 65.

17. *TBI*, 87; *ED*, 2:190; *ARW*, 1:219; *Companion*, 276.

18. *ARW*, 2:221; *Calendar*, 6321; Mivart, 'Reminiscences,' 994; *LLJH*, 2:115-18; Hooker, 'Address.'

19. Ellegard, *Darwin*, 82-83; *LLJH*, 2:121; *LLD*, 3:100; *ARW*, 1:121.

20. 'The British Association,' *Guardian*, 23 (2 Sept. 1868), 977; *LLTH*, 1:231, 297; *MLD*, 1:297; *LLJH*, 2:119; Tyndall, 'Address,' 6.

21. *Calendar*, 6327, 6333, 6413; *LLD*, 3:100; Mivart, *Essays*, 228; Baynes, 'Darwin,' 505-506; Tyndall, *Fragments*, 92-93, 163-64, 130, 198, 441; Cockshut, *Unbelievers*, 91; Lightman, *Origins*, ch. 5; G. Young, *Portrait*, 116; Barton, 'John Tyndall;' T. Huxley, *Discourses*, 319-20; Mivart, 'Some Reminiscences,' 987.

22. Uschmann and Jahn, 'Briefwechsel,' 15, 17-19; *Calendar*, 6239; E. Haeckel to T. Huxley, 28 Feb. 1869, THP 17.198; *LLD*, 3:104; *MLD*, 1:277-78; *LLTH*, 1:305; Darwin to T. Huxley, THP 5.239.

23. T. Huxley, in *Ibis*, 4 (1868), 357-61; T. Huxley, 'Natural History,' 41; Foster and Lankester, *Scientific Memoirs*, 3:303-13, 365; E. Haeckel to T. Huxley, 27 Jan. 1868, THP 17.183; *LLTH*, 1:294-95, 303; *LLD*, 3:104-105; *Calendar*, 6450; Di Gregario, 'Dinosaur Connection,' 413-17; Desmond, *Archetypes*, 127-30, 156-58.

24. *LLTH*, 1:295-96; T. Huxley to Darwin, 20 July 1868, DAR 221; Weindling, 'Ernst Haeckel,' 317; Rehbock, 'Huxley;' Rupke, *'Bathybius Haeckelii.'*

25. *Calendar*, 6561, 6655; *ARW*, 1:232-33, 235; Wallace, *Malay Archipelago*, [v]; *Calendar*, 6542 on James Orton's *The Andes and the Amazon*; *Calendar*, 6454 and *MLD*, 2:235 on Albert Gaudry's *Animaux fossiles et géologie de l'Attique*, with its dynastic charts of horses, elephants and pigs, and praised by Darwin as 'the most striking which I have ever read on the affiliation of species;' Desmond, *Archetypes*, 165.

26. *ED*, 2:191, 221; *Calendar*, 6424; Dupree, *Asa Gray*, 337-41; Loewenberg, *Calendar*, 94; *MLD*, 1:309.

27. Stecher, 'Darwin-Innes Letters,' 219-20, 223, 226; Darwin to J. Brodie Innes, 15 June [1868], APS, Getz Collection B/D25.m. On curates as a contemporary problem for the Church: Halcombe, 'Curate Question.'

28. Darwin to J. Brodie Innes, 16 Dec. 1868, APS, Getz Collection B/D25.m; Stecher, 'Darwin-Innes Letters,' 227-29; J. Moore, 'Darwin of Down,' 470, 477.

29. India: *Calendar*, 5872, 6080, 6160, 6184, 6285, 6295, 6420, 6514, 6815, 7030; Nicaragua: 6546; Gibraltar, 6547, 6553; Portugal, 6577; Lapland, 6430, 6438, 6517; New Zealand, 6520; Australia, 5899, 5916, 6314, 6374, 6419, 6635; Nicholas and Nicholas, *Charles Darwin*, 136; for the rest, Darwin, *Expression* 19-20.

38 DISINTEGRATING SPECULATIONS

1. Jenkin, 'Origin,' 301; W. Thomson, *Popular Lectures*, 2:64; Sharlin, *Lord Kelvin*, chs 9–10; Burchfield, *Lord Kelvin*, 32ff; *Origin*, 285–87.

2. *Calendar*, 5974, 6496; *MLD*, 1:312, 2:163–64, 379; *LLD*, 3:107, 109; Vorzimmer, *Charles Darwin*.

3. Tait, 'Geological Time,' 407, 438; *Calendar*, 6688; *LLD*, 3:113; T. Huxley, *Discourses*, 306, 329; *MLD*, 1:314–16, 2:6–7.

4. *ED*, 2:195; *Calendar*, 6705, 6716, 6718; Loewenberg, *Calendar*, 63; *Annotated Calendar*, 369.

5. T. Huxley, *Method*, 155; Paradis, *T. H. Huxley*, 100ff; Block, 'T. H. Huxley's Rhetoric,' 379–81; Bibby, *T. H. Huxley*, ch. 8.

6. Hutchinson, *Life*, 1:101; A. Brown, *Metaphysical Society*, 50–56; T. Huxley, *Method*, 162; T. Huxley, 'On Descartes' "Discourse",' 79–80; Lightman, *Origins*, 10ff; R. Young, *Darwin's Metaphor*, ch. 5.

7. St G. Mivart to Darwin, 25 April 1870, DAR 171; T. Huxley, *Science*, 120.

8. Annotations on Wallace, 'Principles,' DAR 133; *MLD*, 2:39–40; *LLD*, 3:114, 117; *ARW*, 1:232–33.

9. R. Smith, 'Alfred Russel Wallace,' 181–84, 193–94; Wallace, *Natural Selection*, 335–43, 351–60; Wallace, *My Life*, 1:342; Kottler, 'Alfred Russel Wallace,' 150–56; Durant, 'Scientific Naturalism,' 46–47; *ARW*, 1:227, 243–44.

10. Mivart, 'Difficulties,' in Darwin Reprint Collection, R.145, CUL; *ARW*, 1:246–47; Mivart, *On the Genesis*, 67–73; Mivart, 'Reminiscences,' 988–93; Root, 'Catholicism,' 162–70.

11. Ellegard, *Darwin*, 308; Argyll, *Primeval Man*, 4–5, 33, 66–68, 124ff; Argyll, *George Douglas*, 2:246–47, 272–73.

12. Gillespie, 'Duke of Argyll,' 48; *Descent* (1871), 1:65–69; Argyll, *Primeval Man*, 70, 133; *Calendar*, 6433, 7024.

13. *LLD*, 1:11, 3:106; *ED*, 2:195; *RFD*, 82; F. Darwin, *Rustic Sounds*, 162; *MLD*, 1:313; Cobbe, *Life*, 488–89; *Calendar*, 7145, 7149.

14. *MLD*, 1:317, 2:41; *LLJH*, 2:146–47.

15. *MLD*, 1:316; *Calendar*, 6897, 6900, 6947, 6954, 6956, 6960, 6995, 7022, 7030, 7036; *LLD*, 3:119; *Annotated Calendar*, 375; Cobbe, *Life*, 490.

16. *Calendar*, 7107; Darwin to H. Darwin, [Mar.– June 1870], BL, Add. MSS 58373; *Descent* (1871), 1:34, 67–68, 106; *ED*, 2:196.

17. *LLD*, 3:125; F. Darwin, *Springtime*, 67; *Calendar*, 7200; *MLD*, 2:236; *LLAS*, 2:402, 464.

18. *Calendar*, 7222, 7225, 7246; *LLD*, 3:126; *LLTH*, 1:330.

19. *Calendar*, 5873, 5889, 7195; *LLD*, 3:126–28; 'Speech of His Grace the Archbishop of Canterbury . . .,' DAR 139.12.

20. *Calendar*, 7057, 7117, 7182–83, 7257; *LLD*, 3:129.

21. *Calendar*, 7277 et seq.; *Hansard Parliamentary Debates*, 3d ser. (22 July 1870), 817; (26 July 1870), 1006–10.

22. *ED*, 2:198–99; *MLD*, 2:92; Ensor, *England*, 6–7.

23. *ED*, 2:186; T. Huxley, *Discourses*, 257; *MLD*, 1:323; Ellegard, *Darwin*, 85.

24. *MLD*, 1:324, 2:92; *Calendar*, 7332–33, 7340, 7342, 7381, 7389, 7442, 7485.

25. T. Huxley, *Discourses*, 271; *Calendar*, 7374, 7376, 7400; *ARW*, 1:254.

26. *Darwin's Journal*, 18; Stecher, 'Darwin–Innes Letters,' 233; Mivart, *On the Genesis*, 211; St G. Mivart to Darwin, 22 Jan. and 24 Jan. 1871, both DAR 171; *ARW*, 1:258; Owen, 'Fate.'

27. Stecher, 'Darwin–Innes Letters,' 232–34; *ED*, 2:202; *Calendar*, 7485, 7488, 7510, 7583, 7735; Vucinich, *Darwin*, 66. Three Russian translations of the *Descent of Man* were published at St Petersburg in 1871–72: Freeman, *Works*, 140.
28. Freeman, *Works*, 129; *ED*, 2:202; *LLD*, 3:138–39; Ellegard, *Darwin*, 296; Dawkins, 'Darwin,' 195.
29. *Descent* (1871), 1:67, 101, 104, 167–80, 238; G. Jones, 'Social History;' Durant, 'Ascent,' 293ff; J. Moore, 'Socializing,' 46–51.
30. *Descent* (1871), 1:169, 2:326–27, 403–4; E. Richards, 'Darwin;' Bowler, *Theories*, 7ff.
31. 'Mr. Darwin on the Descent of Man,' *The Times*, 8 April 1871, p. 5, cols. 4–5.
32. *LLD*, 3:139; *Calendar*, 7705; *ED*, 2:203; Stecher, 'Darwin–Innes Letters,' 235, 237; Ellegard, *Darwin*, 101; Fiske, *Life*, 267.
33. Cobbe, *Life*, 489; *MLD*, 1:329; *ARW*, 1:260; *ED*, 2:202–203.
34. *LLD*, 3:142; *ARW*, 1:262; St G. Mivart to Darwin, 23 April 1871, DAR 171; *Darwin's Journal*, 18; *Calendar*, 7730, 7755, 7798; Peckham, *Origin*, 22.
35. *Calendar*, 7761, 7796; *ARW*, 1:264; *Darwin's Journal*, 18; Fiske, *Life*, 266, 276; MacLeod, 'Evolutionism,' 65–69.
36. *Calendar*, 7829; P. Wiener, *Evolution*, ch. 3 and App. A; *ARW*, 1:264–65, 268.
37. *ARW*, 1:268–69; *Calendar*, 7878; Mivart, 'Descent,' 47, 52, 81–90.
38. *ARW*, 1:269; *MLD*, 1:333; *Calendar*, 7963; Wright, *Darwinism*, 9, 13, 15, 37, 43.
39. *LLD*, 3:149; *ARW*, 1:265, 270; *ED*, 2:204; *MLD*, 1:329–32; H. Litchfield to F. Darwin, 18 Mar. 1887, DAR 112:79–82; Darwin to C. Wright, 13–14 July and 17 July [1871] (copies), both DAR 171; *Calendar*, 7907, 7916.
40. *Wedgwood*, 299; *RBL*, 121, 124–25; *ED*, 2:210.
41. C. Wright to Darwin, 1 Aug. 1871, DAR 181; *LLTH*, 1:363; T. Huxley to Darwin, 20 Sept. 1871, DAR 99:39–42; T. Huxley to J. Hooker, 11 Sept. 1871, THP 2.181.
42. *Darwin's Journal*, 19; *LLD*, 3:152; Darwin to T. Huxley, 21 Sept. [1871], THP 5.279–82; T. Huxley to Darwin, 28 Sept. 1871, DAR 99:43–46; T. Huxley, *Darwiniana*, 145, 147, 149.
43. Darwin to T. Huxley, 30 Sept. [1871], THP 5.283–87; *LLJH*, 2:130; *MLD*, 1:333; Desmond, *Archetypes*, 141.
44. *LLD*, 3:148; Darwin to T. Huxley, 9 Oct. 1871, THP 5.289–90; R. Cooke to Darwin, 1 Nov. [1871], DAR 171; Bartholomew, 'Huxley's Defence,' 533–34.

39 PAUSE, PAUSE, PAUSE

1. *Autobiography*, 163; *ED*, 2:204–205.
2. H. Litchfield to F. Darwin, 18 Mar. 1887, DAR 112:79–82; *TBI*, 87; *Darwin's Journal*, 19; *Calendar*, 7964, 8013, 8199; *LLD* 3:133.
3. Peckham, *Origin*, 22–23; Freeman, *Works*, 79–80; *MLD* 1:332.
4. Peckham, *Origin*, 242–67; Vorzimmer, *Charles Darwin*, 246–49; *Origin* (6th ed.), ch. 7. In the same way he controverted Mivart on the impossibility of explaining convergence. He cited example after example – from electric organs in unrelated fishes to placental and marsupial mice (chs 6, 14) – to show how selection, not some converging inner force, had caused similar structures under similar conditions.

5. *Calendar*, 7924, 8070, 8099, 8110, 8145, 9105; Darwin to F. Abbot, 6 Sept. [1871] (copy), DAR 139.12; RFD, 23; Abbot, *Truths*, 7–8; *CP*, 2:167; J. Moore, 'Freethought,' 303–304; W. Darwin to F. Abbot, 20 Dec. 1875, University Archives, Harvard University Library.

6. *Descent* (1871), 1:4; *MLD*, 1:335–36.

7. Peckham, *Origin*, 22–24; Freeman, *Works*, 79–80; *MLD* 1:332; *Calendar*, 8209.

8. St G. Mivart to Darwin, 6 Jan. 1872, DAR 171; Darwin to St G. Mivart, [6–10 Jan. 1872], DAR 96:141; *MLD*, 1:335; *Calendar*, 8186.

9. *Darwin's Journal*, 19; *Calendar*, 8168 etc., 8209, 8212; *MLD*, 1:335; *Descent* (1871), 1:5; Peckham, *Origin*, 22–24.

10. Darwin, *Expression*, 15–19; *CCD*, 4:410–30; Freeman and Gautrey, 'Charles Darwin's Queries;' *Calendar*, 7698; J. Browne, 'Darwin;' Ritvo, *Animal Estate*, 39–40.

11. Darwin, *Expression*, 80, 155, 179, 195–96, 217, 305.

12. *Calendar*, 8302, 8383, 8404, 8427, 8435, 8567, 8473–75; *LLD*, 3:171; *Darwin's Journal*, 19.

13. Wallace, *My Life*, 2:90ff; ARW, 1:273–78; *LLTH*, 1:333; Bastian, *Beginnings of Life*, 2:165–66, 584; R. Grant to H. Bastian, 26 June 1872, Wellcome Institute, London.

14. *Calendar*, 8533, 8585; *ED*, 2:210; *Darwin's Journal*, 19; *LLD*, 3:171.

15. *Calendar*, 8406, 8449, 8525, 8533, 8577; *LLJH*, 2:131, 159–77; MacLeod, 'Ayrton Incident.'

16. *Calendar*, 8542, 8586; J. Hooker to Darwin, 19 Oct. 1872, DAR 103:124–25; Darwin to J. Hooker, 22 Oct. [1872], DAR 94:231–32.

17. Darwin, *Insectivorous Plants*, 76–84, 92ff, 134–35, 199–209, 232–33, 272; *MLD*, 2:267; Allan, *Darwin*, 235ff; Ghiselin, *Triumph*, 198–200.

18. *Calendar*, 8616, 8620, 8675; *Annotated Calendar*, 425; *Darwin's Journal*, 19; 'The Expression of the Emotions,' *Athenaeum*, 9 Nov. 1872, p. 591.

19. *Calendar*, 8606, 8682; *LLTH*, 1:367–89; E. Richards, 'Huxley,' 277ff. We assume that a meeting could have taken place before Darwin left town.

20. *MLD*, 2:43; *Darwin's Journal*, 19; *Calendar*, 8747, 8761, 8763, 8799, 8839, 8843 *et seq.*, 8870; *ED*, 2:212; *LLJH*, 2:183–84; *LLTH*, 1:366–67.

21. *LLL*, 2:450–51; E. A. Darwin to E. Darwin, 24 April [1873], DAR 105.2:88–89; *LLJH*, 2:188; Darwin to C. Lyell, [after 27 April 1873], DAR 96:167.

22. Register of Marriages, 1854–74, Little Portland Street Unitarian Chapel, Dr Williams's Library, London; *Wedgwood*, 303; *Calendar*, 8855, 8956; *Companion*, 170; *RBL*, 139; RFD, 103.

23. L. Huxley, 'Home Life,' 3–4.

24. J. Moore, 'Darwin of Down,' 470, 478; 'Downe Parsonage House Building Fund,' KAO 123/3/5; 'Downe Vicarage Endowment Fund,' KAO 123/3/6.

25. 'Contributions Received,' KAO P123/3/7; *Calendar*, 8842, 9000; S. Wedgwood to G. Ffinden, 14 Mar. 1873, KAO P123/3/4; Stecher, 'Darwin–Innes Letters,' 238; school regulations and annual reports, KAO P123/25/5; parish of Down, PRO Ed. 2/234, no. 4431; *CCD*, 5:161–62; accounts and letters, KAO P123/5/7.

26. Ashwell, *Life*, 3:424–27; T. Huxley to J. Tyndall, 30 July 1873, THP 9.73 and in Blinderman, 'Oxford Debate,' 127; *LLD*, 2:325, 3:340; *ED*, 2:214; ARW, 1:243; *Darwin's Journal*, 19.

27. *LLJH*, 2:152–53; *LLD*, 3:339–40; *Calendar*, 8839, 9040, 9052; H. Litchfield to F. Darwin, 18 Mar. 1887, DAR 112:79–82; *TBI*, 88–89.

28. *Calendar*, 9061, 9148; *CP*, 2:177–82; Colp, 'Contacts,' 393; presentation copy of *Das Kapital*, Down House.
29. *LLD*, 3:180; *Calendar*, 9060, 9069; F. Darwin, *Springtime*, 67–68.
30. F. Darwin, *Rustic Sounds*, 162–63; *Calendar*, 8997, 9088; Darwin to G. Darwin, 21 Oct. 1873, DAR 210.1.1.
31. Darwin to G. Darwin, 24 Oct. 1873, DAR 210.1.1; Darwin to N. Doedes, 2 April 1873 (copy), DAR 139.12 and *LLD*, 1:306.
32. Fiske, *Personal Letters*, 121–22, 147–48.
33. *Calendar*, 9149; *ARW*, 1:281–84, 2:261; Wallace, *Studies*, 2:138–44.
34. *ED*, 2:216; E. Darwin to G. Ffinden, [Nov.–Dec. 1873], and Darwin to Downe School Board, [Nov.–Dec. 1873], KAO P123/25/3.
35. G. Ffinden to Privy Council office, 1 Dec. [1873]; Darwin to Downe School Board, [Nov.–Dec. 1873] and 19 Dec. 1873; G. Ffinden to E. Darwin, 24 Dec. 1873; G. Ffinden to J. Lubbock, 8 Feb. 1875, all KAO P123/25/3; Hart, *Parson*.

40 A WRETCHED BIGOT

1. *Calendar*, 8173, 8256, 8258, 8263, 8293, 9229, 9236; Oppenheim, *Other World*, ch. 1, 293–94; Barrow, *Independent Spirits*, 125; Crookes, *Researches*.
2. Oppenheim, *Other World*, 291–92; Wedgwood, 298, 305; *Calendar*, 8831, 8832; *LLTH*, 1:419; *ED*, 2:216–17; *LLD*, 3:186–88.
3. *LLTH*, 1:419–23; *LLD*, 3:187; *ED*, 2:217; J. [Snow] Wedgwood to E. Gurney, 9 July 1874, in *Wedgwood*, 305. Snow recalled a conversation with her uncle twenty years earlier when he had explained his belief in evolution as an alternative to special creation. She had expressed 'extreme repugnance to this idea & the sense of loss in giving up' the traditional doctrine. He replied, 'I cannot conceive any *wish* about the matter one way or another.' His manner and tone of voice left her with the profound impression 'that he was confronting some influence that *adulterated the evidence of fact*:' J. Wedgwood to F. Darwin, 3 Oct. 1884, DAR 139.12.
4. RFD, 64–65; Atkins, *Down*, 28; *Calendar*, 9310, 9318, 9325, 9327, 9333, 9373, 9386; *TBI*, 89; H. Litchfield to F. Darwin, 18 Mar. 1887, DAR 112:79–82.
5. *Descent* (1874), v–vi, 143.
6. *Calendar*, 9333, 9376, 9409 (cf. 9510); *LLJH*, 2:114; J. Hooker to Darwin, 3 Mar. [1874], DAR 103:189–92; Darwin to J. Hooker, 4 Mar. [1874], DAR 93:313–16; *LLTH*, 1:419; R. Owen to J. Tyndall, 14 June 1871, BM(NH), OCorr. 21.28; *Descent* (1874), v, 199–206; Desmond, *Archetypes*, 143.
7. *Calendar*, 9388, 9402, 9446, 9454, 9474, 9496 etc.; *CP*, 2:183–87.
8. *Calendar*, 9234, 9227, 9417 *et seq.*, 9440, 9475, 9529, 9550; *ED*, 2:217; *Pedigrees*, 12; Stecher, 'Darwin–Innes Letters,' 239; *MLD*, 1:352–54; *LLR*, 1–18.
9. *Calendar*, 9568, 9579, 9596, 9598; J. Gruber, *Conscience*, 99–100.
10. *Calendar*, 9580 *et seq.*, 9597–98; Tyndall, *Address*, 44, 61; Barton, 'John Tyndall;' *LJT*, 187; Baynes, 'Darwin,' 502–505.
11. J. Gruber, *Conscience*, 100–101; *ARW*, 1:292; *Calendar*, 9685, 9687, 9720; *LLL*, 2:455; Cobbe, *Life*, 449–50; Darwin to C. Lyell, 3 Sept. [1874], APS 448 and *MLD*, 2:237.
12. *Calendar*, 9717; *LLJH*, 2:139–40, 189–90; Turrill, *Joseph Dalton Hooker*, 191; Darwin to J. Hooker, 22 Nov. [1874], DAR 95:342; J. Hooker to

Darwin, 25 Nov. 1874, DAR 103:228–29; Darwin to J. Hooker, 26 Nov. [1874], DAR 95:345–46.

13. *LLD*, 2:186; *LLJH*, 2:191; *Darwin's Journal*, 19; J. Gruber, *Conscience*, 102–10; *LLTH*, 1:426; *Calendar*, 9757 *et seq.*, 9785, 9807, 9809, 9812–13; *ARW*, 1:291–92.

14. *LLD*, 3:195, 197, 328; *Calendar*, 9851, 9869, 9911.

15. Grant Duff, *Life-Work*, 15; G. Ffinden to J. Lubbock, 30 Jan., 8 Feb., 29 Mar., 3 April, and 23 June 1875 (drafts); and J. Lubbock to G. Ffinden, 4 Feb., 9 Feb., 31 Mar., and 12 April 1875, all KAO P123/25/3; Darwin to J. Lubbock, 8 April [1875] (draft), DAR 97.3:15–17; J. Moore, 'Darwin of Down,' 471–72; J. Wedgwood to F. Darwin, 3 Oct. 1884, DAR 139.12.

16. Lansbury, 'Gynaecology,' 426; *RBL*, 143–45; Ritvo, *Animal Estate*, 164; Rupke, *Vivisection*.

17. *LLTH*, 1:437; *Calendar*, 9923, 9933–34, 10251; *LLD*, 3:204; *RBL*, 143, 145; French, *Antivivisection*, 62–75.

18. G. Ffinden to J. Lubbock, 23 June 1875 (draft), KAO P123/25/3; *Calendar*, 9916; *Annotated Calendar*, 465; *LLR*, 22; French, *Antivivisection*, 69, 73, 79; *LLTH*, 1:438–39.

19. *Calendar*, 10024, 10044, 10071; *TBI*, 89; *Darwin's Journal*, 19.

20. *Calendar*, 7620, 10096–97, 10106, 10114, 10119, 10124; Darwin, *Variation*, 1:106, 312, 459; R. Chambers to R. Owen, 6 Mar. 1849, BM(NH), OCorr. 17.19 on Chambers's six-fingered joke.

21. *MLD*, 1:359–62, 2:71; *LLR*, 32, 39–42; *LLD*, 3:195; Galton, *Memories*, 294–98.

22. *MLD*, 1:360; *Calendar*, 10241, 10243; Darwin, *Variation*, 1:xiv, 2:389, 398.

23. *Calendar*, 10011, 10080, 10091, 10098, 10168, 10190, 10193, 10200, 10268, 10279–80; *LLR*, 34; Shepherd, 'Lawson Tait.'

24. *Darwin's Journal*, 20; Darwin, *Movements*, v; *Autobiography*, 137; *Calendar*, 10231–32, 10234; Pancaldi, *Darwin*, ch. 3.

25. *LLTH*, 1:439–40; *Calendar*, 10231–32, 10234, 10242; *ED*, 2:221; *Darwin's Journal*, 20.

26. RFD, 71; Atkins, *Down*, 97–99.

27. Atkins, *Down*, 99; L. Huxley, 'Home Life,' 4; *ED*, 2:221.

28. *Notebooks* B96; *Origin*, 92.

29. Darwin, *Effects*, 10ff, 448–49, 465–66; RFD, 7, 125; F. Darwin, 'Botanical Work,' xv; Allan, *Darwin*, 250–62; G. Darwin, 'Marriages.'

30. *Darwin's Journal*, 20; *LLR*, 50, 61; *Calendar*, 10452, 10462, 10501, 10506, 10522, 10530, 10546; *Annotated Calendar*, 488; French, *Antivivisection*, 114; F. Darwin, *Rustic Sounds*, 164; *ED*, 2:221; *Wedgwood*, 308.

41 NEVER AN ATHEIST

1. *Darwin's Journal*, 20; *Autobiography*, 21, 57, 78, 85-87, 145; Colp, 'Notes on Charles Darwin's *Autobiography*.'

2. *Autobiography*, 91-93, 96-98, 133; J. Moore, 'Of Love,' 196-97, 206-208.

3. Darwin to G. Ffinden, 5 Sept. 1876 (draft), DAR 202; 'Downe Vicarage Endowment Fund,' KAO P123/3/6.

4. Darwin to J. Hooker, 11 Sept. [1876] and 17 Sept. [1876], DAR 95:417-20; *ED*, 2:255; E. Darwin to W. Darwin, [13 Sept. 1876], DAR 210.6; Darwin to E. Haeckel, 16 Sept. 1876, Ernst-Haeckel Haus, Friedrich-Schiller-Universität,

Jena; Darwin to W. Darwin, 11 Sept. [1876], and to L. Darwin, 11 Sept. [1876], both DAR 210.6; Darwin to W. Thistleton-Dyer, 16 Sept. 1876, Royal Botanic Gardens, Kew.

5. E. Darwin to W. Darwin, [13 Sept. 1876], DAR 210.6; *Calendar*, 10611; Atkins, *Down*, 29; *Annotated Calendar*, 499-501.

6. *Darwin's Journal*, 20; *ED*, 2:223; Milner, 'Darwin, Pt 1,' 29; Oppenheim, *Other World*, 23.

7. Stecher, 'Darwin-Innes Letters,' 242, 248; *Darwin's Journal*, 20; Freeman, *Works*, 157; Crouzet, *Victorian Economy*, 166ff; *Calendar*, 10853, 11057-58, 11064-65, 11079.

8. Vorzimmer, 'Darwin Reading Notebooks,' 153; *Calendar*, 10720; *LLD*, 3:178; recollections of W. Darwin, DAR 112.2; cf. Beer, *Darwin's Plots*, 23 on Smiles.

9. Colp, 'Notes on William Gladstone;' Royle, *Radicals*, 209-10; J. Morley, *Life*, 3:562; *Wedgwood*, 307.

10. *LLJH*, 2:147, 150.

11. Royle, *Radicals*, 12-24, 254ff; Bonner, *Charles Bradlaugh*, 2:23.

12. Darwin to C. Bradlaugh, 6 June [1877] (draft), DAR 202, transcribed with the kind help of Peter Gautrey; *Descent* (1874), 618; J. Moore, 'Freethought,' 305-307; *ED*, 2:225-27; Ghiselin, *Triumph*, 201.

13. *LLD*, 3:295-96, 306; *Autobiography*, 128, 134; Darwin, *Different Forms*, 276; F. Darwin, 'Botanical Work,' xvi; Allan, *Darwin*, 263-76.

14. *LLD*, 3:309; *Calendar*, 11134, 11148, 11163; De Beer, 'Further Unpublished Letters,' 88-89; H. Gruber, *Darwin*, 53; Colp, 'Notes on William Gladstone,' 183; *ED*, 2:234-35.

15. *Darwin's Journal*, 20; *Calendar*, 11169; Wallace, *My Life*, 2:98; *ARW*, 1:298-300.

16. *Calendar*, 10822, 10958, 10974, 10991, 11211; *ED*, 2:230-31; 'Speech delivered by the Public Orator . . .,' DAR 140.1; Ruse, *Darwinian Revolution*, 262.

17. *ED*, 2:231; *Calendar*, 11234, 11238; *LLTH*, 1:480; *MLD*, 1:371-72; J. Stuart to his mother, 18 Nov. 1877, CUL Add. 8118, box 1, letterbook (with thanks to Simon Schaffer for a transcription).

18. *ED*, 2:226, 230; RFD, 56; *Calendar*, 10919, 11266, 11358; *RBL*, 151-52.

19. RFD, 105; Jordan, *Days*, 1:273; Campbell, 'Nature;' Stevens, 'Darwin's Humane Reading.'

20. Allan, *Darwin*, 279-89; F. Darwin, 'Botanical Work,' xvii-xviii; RFD, 130; *LLD*, 3:330; F. Darwin, 'Darwin's Work.'

21. RFD, 131; *TBI*, 90; *Calendar*, 11373 *et seq.*, 11459, 11481 (cf. 11501, 12258); *MLD*, 1:372-74.

22. *LLJH*, 2:230-31; Duncan, *Life*, 181; *Annotated Calendar*, 495, 503-504, 509, 513-14; RFD, 65-66; *LLR*, 46, 67-68.

23. *LLR*, 69-71; Oppenheim, *Other World*, 281; *Annotated Calendar*, 533.

24. G. Romanes, *Thoughts*, 98-99, 108, 182-83; Darwin to G. Darwin, 24 Oct. 1873, DAR 210.1.1; G. Romanes, *Candid Examination*, vii; *LLR*, 71ff (cf. 128); *Natural Selection*, 463-66; R. Richards, *Darwin*, 335-42; Turner, *Between*, ch. 6.

25. *The Times*, 22 Aug. 1878, p. 8; *LLR*, 74-76, 78; *Annotated Calendar*, 548-49.

26. *LLR*, 87-88; G. Romanes, *Candid Examination*, 113-14; Darwin to G. Romanes, 5 Dec. [1878], APS 553; Darwin to W. Greg, 31 Dec. 1878, APS

557; Darwin's annotation in his presentation copy of *Candid Examination*, 112, Darwin Library, CUL.

27. *Calendar*, 11982; J. Moore, 'Darwin's Genesis,' 577; Darwin to F. McDermott, 24 Nov. 1880, xerox copy in CUL.

28. Darwin to N. von Mengden, 5 June 1879 (copy), DAR 139.12; Darwin to [H. Ridley], 28 Nov. 1878, DAR 202 and *LLD*, 3:235-36 (cf. Pusey, *Unscience*, 43-58); W. Browne to Darwin, 16 Dec. 1880, and Darwin to [W. Browne], [16-21 Dec. 1880], both DAR 202; Stecher, 'Darwin-Innes Letters,' 244-45.

29. De Beer, 'Further Unpublished Letters,' 88; *Calendar*, 11918, 11920, 12052; *Autobiography*, 176; Colp, 'Relationship,' 11-15; Butler, *Evolution*, 346.

30. *Autobiography*, 29, 32, 40-42, 94-95; *Calendar*, 12040-41 and De Beer, 'Further Unpublished Letters,' 88 (compared with original); J. Moore, 'Of Love,' 204-206.

31. *Calendar*, 12149, 12152-54, 12156, 12163, 12217; *LLD*, 3:220.

42 DOWN AMONG THE WORMS

1. *Calendar*, 12119; *LLD*, 3:356; *Darwin's Journal*, 21.

2. *ED*, 2:238; *LLR*, 98; *RBL*, 153–55; *RFD*, 81, 97; *Calendar*, 12220; Darwin to V. Marshall, 25 Aug. and 14 Sept. 1879, APS, Getz Collection B/D25.m.

3. *RBL*, 59; *Calendar*, 12207, 12235–36, 12241–42, 12268, 12279, 12282, 12289, 12297, 12326, 12372.

4. L. Forster to F. Darwin, 15 Nov. 1885, DAR 112:46–47; *Calendar*, 12125, 12253, 12256, 12280, 12294 *et seq.*, 12378; Raverat, *Period Piece*, 203–206; *Pedigrees*, 12, 55; *Wedgwood*, 314.

5. *ED*, 2:239–40; G. Ffinden to F. Darwin, 30 Mar. 1880 (draft), and G. Ffinden to Darwin, 19 Mar. 1880 (draft), both KAO P123/25/2; J. Moore, 'Darwin of Down,' 472.

6. St G. Mivart to R. Owen, 8 June 1879, BM(NH), OCorr. 29.261.

7. J. Moore, 'Darwin of Down,' 473; H. Jones, *Samuel Butler*, 1:99–100, 125, 157, 165, 186, 258, 385; Darwin, *Expression*, 26, 54–55; Butler, *Evolution*, 58, 60, 196.

8. H. Jones, *Samuel Butler*, 1:323–27; *Autobiography*, 177–82. Copland, 'Side Light,' points out that Krause himself referred to his earlier article on page 135 of *Erasmus Darwin*. Butler knew this, and in a copy of the text deposited in the British Museum (cf. Butler, *Unconscious Memory*, xxxvii) he pencilled beside the passage, 'clearly written after the article appeared in Kosmos.' But then he erased his remark (which however is still legible in a good light). It was tantamount to an admission that Darwin had *not* deliberately concealed the revision of Krause's article.

9. *Autobiography*, 182–88, 202–11; Butler, *Evolution*, 393; Willey, *Darwin*; Pauly, 'Samuel Butler.' Huxley gave a demure lightning sketch of a bitch rather than write the word.

10. *Calendar*, 12593; *Annotated Calendar*, 573; Milner, 'Darwin, Pt 2,' 45–46; *Wedgwood*, 314; Darwin to C. Fox, 29 Mar. and 10 Mar. [*sic*, April] 1880, University of British Columbia Library.

11. *Darwin's Journal*, 21; *LLD*, 3:216–17; T. Huxley, *Darwiniana*, 227–43; *LLD*, 2:373, 3:240–41; *LLTH*, 2:12–13; *Calendar*, 12597; *MLD*, 1:387; Bowler, *Eclipse*, 26–28.

12. Shannon, *Crisis*, 140; Wingfield–Stratford, *Victorian Sunset*, 169; recollec-

tions of W. Darwin, DAR 112.2; *ED*, 2:240; Darwin to F. Abbot, 15 April 1880 (copy), DAR 139.12.

13. Royle, *Radicals*, 23–25, 171, 268–71; Bonner, *Charles Bradlaugh*, 2:203ff; J. Morley, *Life*, 3:11ff; E. Aveling to Darwin, 23 Sept. 1878, and Darwin to E. Aveling, [after 23 Sept. 1878], both DAR 202.

14. *Darwin's Journal*, 21; *Calendar*, 12618; W. Darwin to F. Abbot, 13 June [1880], University Archives, Harvard University Library (cf. *LLD*, 1:304–306 and RFD, 24); J. Moore, 'Freethought, 307–309.

15. *Calendar*, 12638 *et seq.*, 12662, 12677 *et seq.*, 12749, 12755; *Wedgwood*, 316; H. Litchfield to F. Darwin, 18 Mar. 1887, DAR 112:79–82.

16. *Darwin's Journal*, 21; *ED*, 2:240–41; De Beer, 'Darwin Letters,' 73; *Calendar*, 12697; Stecher, 'Darwin–Innes Letters,' 246; *LLD*, 1:119, 3:217.

17. E. Aveling to Darwin, 12 Oct. 1880, DAR 159; Darwin to [E. Aveling], 13 Oct. 1880, in Feuer, 'Is the "Darwin–Marx Correspondence" Authentic?,' 2–3; J. Moore, 'Freethought,' 309–11. Darwin's letter to Aveling was long thought to have been addressed to Marx: Colp, 'Case of the "Darwin–Marx" Letter' and 'Myth.'

18. *Darwin's Journal*, 21; *ED*, 2:235, 242–43; *Wedgwood*, 315–16; *CP*, 2:223; *LLTH*, 2:14; *LLD*, 3:242–43.

19. Wallace, *My Life*, 2:98, 102, 376–78; *ARW*, 1:303, 306; Colp, '"I will gladly do my best",' 1–7.

20. Colp, '"I will gladly do my best",' 7–12; *Calendar*, 11891, 12170, 12540; *LLR*, 97; Wallace, *My Life*, 2:311–15; *ARW*, 1:304, 307; *LLJH*, 2:244; De Beer, 'Further Unpublished Letters,' 89.

21. Colp, '"I will gladly do my best",' 12–24; *ED*, 2:243; J. Morley, *Life*, 3:33, 567; *ARW*, 1:314–15; *Calendar*, 12972, 13019; Atkins, *Down*, 97.

22. Butler, *Unconscious Memory*, ch. 4; *Autobiography*, 212–16; *Calendar*, 12939, 12998 *et seq.*, 13032; *LLR*, 104–105; Pauly, 'Samuel Butler,' 172–73.

23. *Annotated Calendar*, 518; *Calendar*, 13060.

24. *Darwin's Journal*, 21; *Calendar*, 12908; *ED*, 2:245; J. Morley, *Life*, 3:32–38, 51ff, 566; Argyll, 'What,' 243–44 and *LLD*, 1:316 (cf. *Autobiography*, 92–93). Huxley called the Duke an 'unmitigated cad' for his recollection of this conversation: T. Huxley to F. Darwin, 20 April 1888, DAR 107.

25. Darwin, *Worms*, 19–35, 67ff, 97–100; Ghiselin, *Triumph*, 202; cf. *Calendar*, 13077 and G. Romanes, *Animal Intelligence*, 24.

26. *Calendar*, 13096; *LLD*, 3:205–209; Darwin, *Worms*, 31, 37, 112, 313–14; Colp, 'Evolution,' 201.

27. *MLD*, 2:433; De Beer, 'Darwin Letters,' 74; *Autobiography*, 95n.

28. Darwin referred to Annie or alluded to her death at least thirteen times between 1853 and 1881 in unpublished correspondence: *Calendar*, 1527, 1547, 1967, 4292, 4318, 4345, 4547, 4901, 7194, 7718, 8569, 10593, 13304. Only two of the letters (7194, 7718) were sent outside the family and neither mentions Annie by name.

29. E. Darwin to Darwin [c. Feb. 1839], DAR 210.10 and *CCD*, 2:171–72. Darwin probably attached the annotated letter to his manuscript, just as he also 'enclosed in a separate envelope' some short notes written by his father. The letter was found among Emma's papers after her death in 1896, where it may have been removed to preserve the annotation for her own eyes. The annotation was omitted when the letter was first printed in 1904: *Autobiography*, 35, 235; *ED* (1904), 2:187–89.

43 THE FINAL EXPERIMENT

1. *Darwin's Journal*, 21; De Beer, 'Further Unpublished Letters,' 90; *LLD*, 1:124, 3:223; *Companion*, 242; *ED*, 2:246–47; *Calendar*, 13169 etc., 13184, 13194; *MLD*, 2:433; *TBI*, 92–93.
2. Darwin to G. Romanes, 27 June [1881], APS, Getz collection B/D25.m; Darwin to G. Romanes, 4 July [1881], APS 494; *LLR*, 119; *LLD*, 1:316; *MLD*, 2:395; cf. Graham, *Creed*, 343–50 and William Darwin's notes in DAR 210.28 for the passage that perhaps most struck Darwin.
3. *ARW*, 1:317–19; George, *Progress*, 233, 239; Wallace, *My Life*, 2:27, ch. 34; Durant, 'Scientific Naturalism.'
4. *MLD*, 2:26–28; *LLJH*, 2:223–26, 245, 258.
5. *MLD*, 2:394; *ARW*, 1:319; *ED*, 2:247; Symonds, *Recollections*, 215; *LLR*, 129; *Calendar*, 13255 *et seq.*
6. *Darwin's Journal*, 21; *LLR*, 118–20; *LLD*, 3:223; *LLTH*, 2:33; Bonner, *Charles Bradlaugh*, 2:286; Tribe, *President Charles Bradlaugh*, 209–11; *Wedgwood*, 317; E. Aveling to Darwin, 9 Aug. 1881, and Darwin to E. Aveling, 11 Aug. [1881], both DAR 202.
7. *LLD*, 1:22, 3:228; *MLD*, 1:395; *LLJH*, 2:258; Darwin to J. Hooker, 30 Aug. 1881, DAR 95:530–31; *Wedgwood*, 318; E. Darwin to G. Darwin, 23 Aug. 1881, DAR 210.3; H. Litchfield to H. Wedgwood, [2 Sept. 1881], W/M 575; RFD, 79.
8. *MLD*, 1:395; *Wedgwood*, 318; Keith, *Darwin*, 230–31; Atkins, *Down*, 100; recollections of W. Darwin, DAR 112.2; 'Last Will and Testament of . . . Charles Darwin,' Somerset House, London; Darwin to C. Darwin, 20 Sept. [1881] (copy), DAR 153. Darwin subsequently modified his will: *Calendar*, 13330, 13335, 13353, 13356.
9. E. Aveling to Darwin, [27 Sept. 1881] (telegram), DAR 159; E. Darwin to G. Darwin, 28 Sept. 1881, DAR 210.3; Gregory, *Scientific Materialism*, 204ff.
10. Aveling, *Religious Views*, 3; *LLD*, 1:139–40; Feuer, 'Marxian Tragedians,' 26; Stecher, 'Darwin–Innes Letters,' 256; cf. pp. 249–51, 253, 256 and *Calendar*, 12343, 12349 for Brodie Innes's unplanned visit. Darwin's remark was made, according to Brodie Innes, 'on my last visit . . . at dinner,' which was usually the midday meal. Clergymen were infrequent guests: M. Keynes, *Leonard Darwin*, 2.
11. RFD, 9–14; Aveling, *Religious Views*, 4–6; cf. *LLD*, 1:317n, where Francis, an eyewitness, confirms that Aveling gave 'quite fairly his impressions of my father's views.' For Büchner's meagre recollection: Büchner, *Last Words*, 147.
12. *Darwin's Journal*, 21; *ED*, 2:248–50; *Annotated Calendar*, 603; *Calendar*, 13476; *LLR*, 127; RFD, 8, 116; *CP*, 2:254–56; *LLD*, 3:244.
13. *Darwin's Journal*, 21; *Calendar*, 11633, 13458, 13560; *Annotated Calendar*, 603–604, 606; *LLD*, 3:357; H. Litchfield to F. Darwin, 18 Mar. 1887, DAR 112:79–82; Judd, *Coming*, 158.
14. *CP*, 2:236–76; *Calendar*, 13570, 13579, 13607, 13650, 13652, 13662; *MLD*, 1:397, 2:171, 447–48; *LLJH*, 2:237–39; *LLD*, 3:351–54; W. Graham to E. Darwin, 26 April 1882, DAR 215; RFD, 8, 14.
15. *MLD*, 2:28–29, 446–47; *Calendar*, 13692, 13696; E. Darwin to G. Darwin, 20 Feb., 28 Feb., and 11 Mar. 1882, all DAR 210.3; H. Litchfield MS, Down House, 1–2.
16. *TBI*, 93–94; *Calendar*, 13722, 13734, 13741; *CP*, 2:276–78; *ED*, 2: 251, 253

(1904 ed., 329); E. Darwin to G. Darwin, 14 Mar. 1882, DAR 210.3; H. Litchfield MS, Down House, 3–5; L. Forster to F. Darwin, 15 Nov. 1885, DAR 112:38–47.

17. L. Forster to F. Darwin, 15 Nov. 1885, DAR 112:38–40; H. Litchfield MS, Down House, 5; *TBI*, 94–95; E. Darwin to G. Darwin, 6 April 1882, DAR 210.3; *ED*, 2:253.

18. H. Litchfield MS, Down House, 6–7; *TBI*, 95; *LLD*, 3:358; *ED*, 2:251, 253.

19. H. Litchfield MS, Down House, 7–11; E. Darwin to F. and H. Wedgwood, [22 April 1882] (typescript copy), APS, Loewenberg Collection B/L 828; F. Darwin to T. Huxley, 20 April 1882, THP 13.10–11; Miller, 'Death;' H. Litchfield to F. Wedgwood, [19 April 1882], W/M 579; chronology in DAR 210.19; *ED*, 2:251–53; *TBI*, 95–96.

20. B. Darwin, *World*, 27.

44 AN AGNOSTIC IN THE ABBEY

1. 'Charles Darwin,' *Standard*, 21 April 1882, DAR 140.5; 'The Late Mr. Darwin,' *Pall Mall Gazette*, 21 April 1882, DAR 216; Nash, 'Some Memories,' 404; *MLD*, 2:433; *LLD*, 3:360-61; J. Brodie Innes to F. Darwin, 22 April 1882, DAR 215; E. Darwin to F. and H. Wedgwood, [22 April 1882] (typescript copy), APS, Loewenberg Collection B/L 828.

2. F. Darwin to T. Huxley, 20 April 1882, THP 13.10-11; Pearson, *Life*, 2:197; T. Huxley to J. Hooker, 21 April 1882, THP 2.240-41; *LLTH*, 2:38; Galton, *English Men*, 260 and *Inquiries*, 220; F. Galton to G. Darwin, 20 April 1882, DAR 215; F. Galton to M. Conway, 24 April 1882 (copy), APS, Misc. MSS 1975 578.f ms.

3. Pearson, *Life*, 2:198; F. de Chaumont to W. Darwin, 22 April 1882, and C. Pritchard to G. Darwin, 21 April 1882, both DAR 215; [Editorial], *Standard*, 22 April 1882, p. 5; J. Hooker to T. Huxley, 23 April 1882, THP 3.261-62.

4. J. Hooker to T. Huxley, 23 April 1882, THP 3.261-62; *LLD*, 3:197; F. Farrar, *Men*, 140-48; R. Farrar, *Life*, 106-109; *LLTH*, 2:18-19; G. Bradley to T. Huxley, 24 Mar. 1881, THP 121.19; Ward, *History*, facing p. 94; *Rules*; Cowell, *Athenaeum*, 52.

5. W. Spottiswoode to W. Darwin, 21 April 1882, DAR 215; T. Huxley to J. Hooker, 21 April 1882, THP 2.240-41.

6. RFD, 64-65; Atkins, *Down*, 28; J. Lubbock to W. Darwin, 25 April 1882, and to F. Darwin, 20 April 1882, both DAR 215; T. Huxley, 'Introductory Notice,' x; *Gardeners' Chronicle*, 22 April 1882, DAR 215.

7. Hammond, *Gladstone*, chs 14-15; *Hansard Parliamentary Debates*, 268 (21 April 1882), 1202-203; memorial to G. Bradley, 21 April 1882, DAR 215 (copy showing twenty signatories) and in Hutchinson, *Life*, 1:184 (inaccurate transcription but with eight additional names).

8. J. Lubbock to F. Darwin, 22 April 1882, and to W. Darwin, 23 April 1882, both DAR 215.

9. [Editorial], *Standard*, 22 April 1882, p. 5.

10. A. Hall, *Abbey Scientists*; Bradley, 'Introductory Chapter;' 'Mr. Charles Darwin,' *St. James's Gazette*, 21 April 1882, and 'The Death of Mr. Darwin,' *Pall Mall Gazette*, 21 April 1882, both DAR 215.

11. [Editorial], *Standard*, 22 April 1882, DAR 140.5; [Editorial], *Daily Telegraph*, 22 April 1882, DAR 215; [Editorial], *The Times*, 26 April 1882, DAR 140.1.

12. *LLD*, 3:360-61; E. Darwin to F. and H. Wedgwood, [22 April 1882] (typescript copy), APS, Loewenberg Collection B/L 828.

13. J. Morley, *Death*, 30, 85; *LLD*, 3:361; *Daily News*, 27 April 1882; Argyll to G. Darwin, 24 April 1882; Devonshire to W. Darwin, 25 April 1882; T. Huxley to G. Darwin, 22 April 1882; H. Spencer to G. Darwin, 24 April (twice) and 4 May 1882; family funeral scrapbook, all DAR 215; F. Galton to M. Conway, 24 April 1882 (copy), APS, Misc. MSS 1975 578.f ms.

14. E. Darwin to F. and H. Wedgwood, [22 April 1882] (typescript copy), APS, Loewenberg Collection B/L 828; list of mourners, DAR 140.5.

15. *Companion*, 228; list of mourners, DAR 140.5; Jordan, *Days*, 1:273; Colp, 'Charles Darwin's Coffin;' 'A Visit to Darwin's Village: Reminiscences of Some of His Humble Friends,' *Evening News* (London), 12 Feb. 1909, p. 4.

16. [Editorial], *Standard*, 22 April 1882; [Editorial], *The Times*, 21 April 1882; [Editorial], *Daily News*, 21 April 1882, all DAR 140.5.

17. Prothero, *Arthur Penrhyn Stanley*, 10-11 and *Armour*, 168 etc.; Barry, *Sermons*, 39-40, 54, 61-62; 'The Late Mr. Darwin,' *The Times*, 24 April 1882, DAR 140.1.

18. Liddon, *Recovery*, 26-28; Johnston, *Life*, 275; 'Charles Darwin,' *Guardian*, 26 April 1882, DAR 216.

19. [Editorial], *Standard*, 24 April 1882, DAR 140.1; [Editorial], *Daily News*, 25 April 1882, DAR 215; 'Darwin's Home,' *Daily News*, 24 April 1882, and *Morning Advertiser*, 24 April 1882, both DAR 216.

20. 'The Late Charles Darwin,' *Standard*, 26 April 1882; 'The Funeral of Mr. Darwin,' *The Times*, 26/27 April 1882, all DAR 140.1; 'Funeral of the Late Charles Darwin,' *Standard*, 27 April 1882, DAR 140.5; 'Funeral of the Late Mr. Darwin,' *Daily News*, 27 April 1882, DAR 215.

21. 'The Judges and Mr. Darwin's Funeral,' *Pall Mall Gazette*, 25 April 1882, DAR 215; Carpenter, 'Science,' 43; 'The Funeral of Mr. Darwin . . . Order of Procession,' instructions for ushers, admission card, all APS; 'The Funeral of the Late Mr. Darwin, List of Mourners . . . ,' family procession, family sacrarium list, admission cards, all DAR 140.5, 215; H. Spencer to G. Darwin, 4 May 1882, DAR 215.

22. Newspaper accounts (n. 20 above); Bridge, *Westminster Pilgrim*, 67, 124; 'Words of Anthem composed by J. Frederick Bridge,' DAR 140.5; Raverat, *Period Piece*, 176.

23. 'Funeral of the Late Mr. Darwin,' *Daily News*, 27 April 1882, DAR 215; 'The Funeral of Mr. Darwin,' *The Times*, 27 April 1882, DAR 140.5; Conway, *Autobiography*, 2:328; G. Romanes, 'Work,' 82.

24. F[rancis] G[alton], 'The Late Mr. Darwin: A Suggestion,' *Pall Mall Gazette*, 27 April 1882, DAR 215; Pearson, *Life*, 2:199; F. Farrar to T. Huxley, 29 April 1882, THP 16.21.

25. Rawnsley, *Harvey Goodwin*, 222-23; Atkins, *Down*, 49-50; Goodwin, 'Funeral Sermon,' 301-302; 'The Late Mr. Darwin,' *The Times*, 1 May 1882; 'The Late Mr. Charles Darwin,' *Morning Post*, 1 May 1882; 'Mr. Darwin's Funeral,' *Guardian*, 3 May 1882, all DAR 140.5; Pearson, *Life*, 2:199; Galton, *Inquiries*, 220.

26. T. Huxley to W. and G. Darwin, 1 May 1882, DAR 215; Pearson, *Life*, 2:200; *Darwin Memorial Fund: Report of the Committee* (n.p., n.d.), in British Library, Department of Printed Books.

27. *Darwin Memorial Fund*; Johnston, *Life*, 275-76; 'The Darwin Memorial

Statue,' *The Times*, 10 June 1885, DAR 215; Stearn, *Natural History Museum*, 47, 73; *ED*, 2:270-71.

28. Woodall, 'Charles Darwin,' 47; 'Mr. Darwin,' *Church Times*, 28 April 1882, DAR 140.5; 'Charles Darwin,' *Liverpool Diocesan Gazette*, May 1882, DAR 215; 'The Late Mr. Darwin,' *Record* (supplement), n.s., 1 (28 April 1882), 152; 'South American Missionary Society,' *Record*, n.s., 1 (28 April 1882), 335; 'Charles Darwin,' *Nonconformist and Independent*, 27 April 1882; [Stopford A. Brooke], 'Charles Darwin,' *Inquirer*, 20 May 1882; W. Carpenter to E. Darwin, 30 April 1882, all DAR 215; R. Armstrong, 'Charles Darwin,' 33; J. Chadwick, 'Evolution,' 43.

29. 'Mr. Darwin,' *Saturday Review*, 22 April 1882, DAR 140.5; Miall, *Life*, 58, 62; 'Charles Darwin,' *British Medical Journal*, 29 April 1882, DAR 216; [Editorial], *The Times*, 26 April 1882, DAR 140.1.

30. 'The Death of Mr. Darwin,' *Pall Mall Gazette*, 21 April 1882, DAR 140.5; J. Morley, in Hammond, *Gladstone*, 546; J. Morley, *Life*, 2:562; 'Mr. Darwin's Influence on Modern Thought,' *Pall Mall Gazette*, 26 April 1882, DAR 140.5.

31. T. Huxley, *Method*, 51.

Bibliography

Anonymous reviews and editorials, and other press articles, are cited fully in the notes. Place of publication is London unless stated otherwise.

AMNH	*Annals and Magazine of Natural History*
AS	*Annals of Science*
BAAS	*Report of the British Association for the Advancement of Science*
BBMNH	*Bulletin of the British Museum (Natural History), Historical Series*
BJHS	*British Journal for the History of Science*
BJLS	*Biological Journal of the Linnean Society*
ENPJ	*Edinburgh New Philosophical Journal*
ER	*Edinburgh Review*
HS	*History of Science*
JHB	*Journal of the History of Biology*
JHBS	*Journal of the History of the Behavioural Sciences*
JHM	*Journal of the History of Medicine and Allied Sciences*
JSBNH	*Journal of the Society for the Bibliography of Natural History*
NQ	*Notes and Queries*
NR	*Notes and Records of the Royal Society of London*
PAPS	*Proceedings of the American Philosophical Society*
PGSL	*Proceedings of the Geological Society of London*
PZSL	*Proceedings of the Zoological Society of London*
QJGS	*Quarterly Journal of the Geological Society of London*
QR	*Quarterly Review*
SHB	*Studies in History of Biology*
SHPS	*Studies in History and Philosophy of Science*
U.P.	University Press
VS	*Victorian Studies*

Abbot, F. E. *Truths for the Times*. Ramsgate, Kent: Thomas Scott, [1872].

Addison, W. *The English Country Parson*. Dent, 1947.

Agassiz, L. 'A Period in the History of our Planet.' *ENPJ*, 35 (1843), 1–29.

— and Agassiz, [E]. *A Journey in Brazil*. Boston: Ticknor & Fields, 1868.

Ainsworth, W. F. 'On the Present State of Science in Great Britain. No. 1.

Bibliography

Edinburgh College Museum.' *Edinburgh Journal of Natural and Geographical Science*, 1 (1830), 269–77.

—. 'Mr. Darwin.' *Athenaeum*, 13 May 1882, p. 604.

Aldington, R. *The Strange Life of Charles Waterton, 1782–1865*. Evans, 1949.

Allan, M. *Darwin and His Flowers: The Key to Natural Selection*. Faber & Faber, 1977.

Allen, D. E. *The Naturalist in Britain: A Social History*. Harmondsworth, Middx: Penguin Books, 1978.

Allen, G., ed. *The Miscellaneous and Posthumous Works of Henry Thomas Buckle*. New abridged ed. 2 vols. Longmans *et al.*, 1885.

Allen, P. *The Cambridge Apostles: The Early Years*. Cambridge: Cambridge U.P., 1978.

Altner, G. *Charles Darwin und Ernst Haeckel: Ein Vergleich nach theologischen Aspekten*. Zurich: EVZ-Verlag, 1966.

Appel, T. A. *The Cuvier-Geoffroy Debate: French Biology in the Decades before Darwin*. New York: Oxford U.P., 1987.

Arbuckle, E. S., ed. *Harriet Martineau's Letters to Fanny Wedgwood*. Stanford, CA: Stanford U.P., 1983.

Argyll, The Dowager Duchess of. *George Douglas, Eighth Duke of Argyll, K.G., K.T. (1823–1900): Autobiography and Memoirs*. 2 vols. Murray, 1906.

Argyll, The Duke of. *The Reign of Law*. 5th ed. Strahan, 1868.

—. *Primeval Man*. Strahan, 1869.

—. 'What is Science?' *Good Words*, 26 (1885), 236–45.

Armstrong, P. *Charles Darwin in Western Australia: A Young Scientist's Perception of an Environment*. Nedlands, W. A.: University of Western Australia Press, 1985.

Armstrong, R. A. 'Charles Darwin: A Lecture delivered at Nottingham, on 10th December, 1882.' *Modern Sermons*, 23–35. Manchester: Johnson *et al.*, [1883].

Ashwell, A. R. and Wilberforce, R. G. *Life of the Right Reverend Samuel Wilberforce, D.D., Lord Bishop of Oxford and afterwards of Winchester, with Selections from His Diaries and Correspondence*. 3 vols. Murray, 1880.

Ashworth, J. H. 'Charles Darwin as a Student in Edinburgh, 1825–1827.' *Proceedings of the Royal Society of Edinburgh*, 55 (1935), 97–113.

Atkins, H. *Down, the Home of the Darwins: The Story of a House and the People who lived there*. Rev. ed. Phillimore, for the Royal College of Surgeons of England, 1976.

Audubon, M. R., ed. *Audubon and His Journals*. 2 vols. Nimmo, 1898.

Austin, Mrs, ed. *A Memoir of the Reverend Sydney Smith*. 2nd ed. 2 vols. Longmans, 1855.

Aveling, E. *The Religious Views of Charles Darwin*. Freethought Publishing Co., 1883.

Babbage, C. *The Ninth Bridgewater Treatise: A Fragment*. 2nd ed. Murray, 1838.

Bagehot, W. *Physics and Politics, or Thoughts on the Application of the Principles of 'Natural Selection' and 'Inheritance' to Political Society*. 6th ed. Kegan Paul, 1881.

Balfour, J. H. *Biography of the Late John Coldstream, M.D., F.R.C.P.E., Secretary of the Medical Missionary Society of Edinburgh*. Nisbet, 1865.

Barber, L. *The Heyday of Natural History, 1820–1870*. Cape, 1980.

Barclay, O. R. *Whatever Happened to the Jesus Lane Lot?* Leicester: Inter-Varsity Press, 1977.

Barlow, N. 'Robert FitzRoy and Charles Darwin.' *Cornhill Magazine*, 72 (1932), 493–510.

—, ed. *Charles Darwin and the Voyage of the 'Beagle'.* Pilot Press, 1945.

—, ed. *The Autobiography of Charles Darwin 1809–1882, with Original Omissions Restored.* Collins, 1958.

—, ed. 'Darwin's Ornithological Notes.' *BBMNH*, 2 (1963), 201–78.

Barnaby, D., ed. *The Log Book of Wombwell's Royal No. 1 Menagerie, 1848–1871.* Sale, Cheshire: ZSGM Publications, 1989.

Barnett, D. C. 'Allotments and the Problem of Rural Poverty, 1780–1840.' In E. L. Jones and G. E. Mingay, eds., *Land, Labour and Population in the Industrial Revolution: Essays presented to J. D. Chambers,* 162–83. Arnold, 1967.

Barrett, P. H. 'Darwin's "Gigantic Blunder".' *Journal of Geological Education,* 21 (1973), 19–28.

—, 'The Sedgwick-Darwin Geologic Tour of North Wales.' *PAPS,* 118 (1974), 146–64.

—, ed. *The Collected Papers of Charles Darwin.* 2 vols. Chicago: University of Chicago Press, 1977.

—, Gautrey, P. J., Herbert, S., Kohn, D., and Smith, S., eds. *Charles Darwin's Notebooks, 1836–1844.* Cambridge: British Museum (Natural History)/Cambridge U.P., 1987.

Barrow, L. *Independent Spirits: Spiritualism and English Plebeians, 1850–1910.* Routledge & Kegan Paul, 1986.

Barry, A. *Sermons Preached in Westminster Abbey.* Cassell, 1884.

Barth, J. R. *Coleridge and Christian Doctrine.* Cambridge, MA: Harvard U.P., 1969.

Bartholomew, M. J. 'Lyell and Evolution: An Account of Lyell's Response to the Prospect of an Evolutionary Ancestry for Man.' *BJHS,* 6 (1973), 261–303.

—. 'Huxley's Defence of Darwin.' *AS,* 32 (1975), 525–35.

—. 'The Award of the Copley Medal to Charles Darwin.' *NR,* 30 (1976), 209–18.

—. 'The Singularity of Lyell.' *HS,* 17 (1979), 276–93.

Barton, R. 'The X Club: Science, Religion, and Social Change in Victorian England.' Ph.D. diss., University of Pennsylvania, 1976.

—. 'Evolution: The Whitworth Gun in Huxley's War for the Liberation of Science from Theology.' In Oldroyd and Langham, *Wider Domain,* 261–86.

—. 'John Tyndall, Pantheist: A Rereading of the Belfast Address.' *Osiris,* 2nd ser., 3 (1987), 111–34.

—. '"An Influential Set of Chaps": The X-Club and Royal Society Politics, 1864–85.' *BJHS,* 23 (1990), 53–81.

Basalla, G. 'Darwin's Orchid Book.' *Actes du Xe Congrès International d'Histoire des Sciences Naturelles et de la Biologie* (1962), 2:971–74.

—. 'The Voyage of the *Beagle* without Darwin.' *Mariner's Mirror,* 59 (1963), 42–48.

Bastian, H. C. *The Beginnings of Life: Being Some Account of the Nature, Modes of Origin and Transformations of Lower Organisms.* 2 vols. Macmillan, 1872.

Bibliography

Bayertz, K. 'Darwinism and Scientific Freedom: Political Aspects of the Reception of Darwinism in Germany, 1863–1878.' *Scientia*, 118 (1983), 297–307.

[Baynes, T. S.] 'Darwin on Expression.' *ER*, 137 (1873), 492–508.

Beddoe, J. *Memories of Eighty Years*. Bristol: Arrowsmith, 1910.

Beer, G. *Darwin's Plots: Evolutionary Narrative in Darwin, George Eliot, and Nineteenth-Century Fiction*. Routledge & Kegan Paul, 1983.

Bell, G. J., ed. *Letters of Sir Charles Bell*. Murray, 1870.

Bell, H. C. F. *Lord Palmerston*. 2 vols. Longmans, 1936.

Bell, S. 'George Lewes: A Man of His Time.' *JHB*, 14 (1981), 277–98.

Berman, M. *Social Change and Scientific Organization: The Royal Institution, 1799–1844*. Heinemann, 1978.

Best, G. *Mid-Victorian Britain, 1851–75*. Fontana, 1979.

Bibby, C. T. *H. Huxley: Scientist, Humanist, Educator*. Watts, 1959.

[Billing, M.] *M. Billing's Directory and Gazetteer of the County of Worcester*. Birmingham: M. Billing, 1855.

Blinderman, C. S. 'The Oxford Debate and After.' *NQ*, 202 (1957), 126–28.

Block, E., Jr. 'T. H. Huxley's Rhetoric and the Popularization of Victorian Scientific Ideas.' *VS*, 29 (1985–86), 363–86.

[Blomefield, L.] Jenyns, L. *Fish*. Pt 4, *The Zoology of the Voyage of H.M.S. 'Beagle'*, ed. C. Darwin. Smith, Elder, 1840–42.

[—]. Jenyns, L. *Memoir of the Rev. John Stevens Henslow*. Van Voorst, 1862.

—. *Chapters in My Life, with Appendix containing Special Notices of Particular Incidents and Persons; also Thoughts on Certain Subjects*. New ed. Bath: privately printed, 1889.

—. *A Naturalist's Calendar kept at Swaffham Bulbeck, Cambridgeshire*. Ed. F. Darwin. Cambridge: printed at the U.P., 1903.

Bölsche, W. *Haeckel: His Life and Work*. Trans. J. McCabe. Unwin, 1906.

Bolt, C. *Victorian Attitudes to Race*. Routledge & Kegan Paul, 1971.

Bonner, H. B. *Charles Bradlaugh: A Record of His Life and Work*. 2 vols. Unwin, 1895.

Bowen, D. *The Idea of the Victorian Church: A Study of the Church of England, 1833–1889*. Montreal: McGill U.P., 1968.

Bowlby, J. *Charles Darwin: A Biography*. Hutchinson, 1990.

Bowler, P. J. *Fossils and Progress: Paleontology and the Idea of Progressive Evolution in the Nineteenth Century*. New York: Science History Publications, 1976.

—. 'Malthus, Darwin, and the Concept of Struggle.' *Journal of the History of Ideas*, 37 (1976), 631–50.

—. *The Eclipse of Darwinism: Anti-Darwinian Evolution Theories in the Decades around 1900*. Baltimore, MD: Johns Hopkins U.P., 1983.

—. *Theories of Human Evolution: A Century of Debate, 1844–1944*. Oxford: Blackwell, 1987.

—. *The Non-Darwinian Revolution: Reinterpreting a Historical Myth*. Baltimore, MD: Johns Hopkins U.P., 1988.

—. *Charles Darwin: The Man and His Influence*. Oxford: Blackwell, 1990.

A Brace of Cantabs. *Gradus ad Cantabrigiam; or, New University Guide to the Academical Customs, and Colloquial or Cant Terms Peculiar to The University of Cambridge; observing wherein it differs from Oxford ... to which is affixed, A Tail-Piece; or, the Reading and Varmint Method of Proceeding to the Degree of A.B.* Printed for John Hearne, 1824.

Brackman, A. C. *A Delicate Arrangement: The Strange Case of Charles Darwin and Alfred Russel Wallace*. Times Books, 1980.

[Bradley, G. G.] 'Introductory Chapter.' *The Popular Guide to Westminster Abbey*. 'Pall Mall Gazette' Office, 1885.

Brent, P. *Charles Darwin: 'A Man of Enlarged Curiosity'*. Heinemann, 1981.

[Brewster, D.] 'M. Comte's Course of Positive Philosophy.' *ER*, 67 (1838), 271–308.

Bridge, F. *A Westminster Pilgrim: Being a Record of Service in Church, Cathedral, and Abbey; College, University, and Concert Room; with a Few Notes on Sport*. Novello, [1919].

Briggs, A. *The Age of Improvement, 1783–1867*. Longmans, 1959.

Broadbent, A. *The Story of Unitarianism in Shrewsbury*. Shrewsbury: Livesey Printers, 1962.

Brock, W. H. and MacLeod, R. M. 'The Scientists' Declaration: Reflexions on Science and Belief in the Wake of *Essays and Reviews*, 1864–5.' *BJHS*, 9 (1976), 39–66.

[Broderip, W.] 'The Zoological Gardens – Regent's Park.' *QR*, 56 (1836), 309–32.

The Bromley Directory. Bromley: Strong, 1880.

Brooke, J. H. '"A Sower Went Forth": Joseph Priestley and the Ministry of Reform.' In *Oxygen and the Conversion of Future Feedstocks: Proceedings of the Third BOC Priestley Conference*, 432–60. Royal Society of Chemistry, 1984.

—. 'The Relations Between Darwin's Science and his Religion.' In Durant, *Darwinism*, 40–75.

—. 'Joseph Priestley (1733–1804) and William Whewell (1794–1866), Apologists and Historians of Science: A Tale of Two Stereotypes.' In R. Anderson and C. Lawrence, eds., *Science, Medicine and Dissent: Joseph Priestley (1733–1804)*, 11–27. Wellcome Trust/Science Museum, 1987.

Brooks, J. L. *Just Before the Origin: Alfred Russel Wallace's Theory of Evolution*. Columbia U.P., 1984.

Brown, A. W. *The Metaphysical Society: Victorian Minds in Crisis, 1869–1880*. Columbia U.P., 1947.

Browne, J. 'The Charles Darwin – Joseph Hooker Correspondence: An Analysis of Manuscript Resources and Their Use in Biography.' *JSBNH*, (1978), 351–66.

—. *The Secular Ark: Studies in the History of Biogeography*. New Haven, CT: Yale U.P., 1983.

—. 'Darwin and the Expression of the Emotions.' In Kohn, *Darwinian Heritage*, 307–26.

—. 'Botany for Gentlemen: Erasmus Darwin and *The Loves of the Plants*.' *Isis*, 80 (1989), 593–621.

Browne, W. A. F. 'Observations on Religious Fanaticism.' *Phrenological Journal*, 9 (1836), 288–302, 532–45, 577–603.

Buckle, H. T. *History of Civilization in England*. New ed. 3 vols. Longmans *et al.*, 1867.

Büchner, L. *Last Words on Materialism and Kindred Subjects*. Trans. J. McCabe. Watts, 1901.

Bunbury, F. J., ed. *Life, Letters and Journals of Sir Charles J. F. Bunbury, Bart.* 3 vols. Privately printed, 1894.

Bunting, James. *Charles Darwin: A Biography*. Folkestone, Kent: Bailey Brothers & Swinfen, 1974.

Burchfield, J. D. *Lord Kelvin and the Age of the Earth*. Macmillan, 1974.

Burkhardt, F. and Smith, S., eds. *A Calendar of the Correspondence of Charles Darwin, 1821–1882.* New York: Garland, 1985.

—, eds. *The Correspondence of Charles Darwin.* 7 vols. Cambridge: Cambridge U.P., 1985–91.

Burn, W. L. *The Age of Equipoise: A Study of the Mid-Victorian Generation.* New York: Norton, 1965.

Burrow, J. W. *Evolution and Society: A Study in Victorian Social Theory.* Cambridge: Cambridge U.P., 1966.

Burstyn, H. L. 'If Darwin wasn't the *Beagle*'s Naturalist, Why was he on Board?' *BJHS*, 8 (1975), 62–69.

Burton, J. 'Robert FitzRoy and the Early History of the Meteorological Office.' *BJHS*, 19 (1986), 147–76.

Bush, D., ed. *Milton: Poetical Works.* Oxford: Oxford U.P., 1966.

Butler, S. *Evolution Old and New; or, the Theories of Buffon, Dr. Erasmus Darwin, and Lamarck, as compared with that of Charles Darwin,* 1879. New ed. Fifield, 1911.

—. *Unconscious Memory,* 1880. New ed. Fifield, 1910.

Bynum, W. F. 'Charles Lyell's *Antiquity of Man* and Its Critics.' *JHB*, 17 (1984), 153–87.

Calder, G. J. 'Erasmus A. Darwin, Friend of Thomas and Jane Carlyle.' *Modern Language Quarterly*, 20 (1959), 36–48.

The Cambridge Guide; or, a Description of the University and Town of Cambridge. Rev. ed. Cambridge: printed for Deighton *et al.*, 1830.

Campbell, J. A. 'Nature, Religion and Emotional Response: A Reconsideration of Darwin's Affective Decline.' *VS*, 18 (1974), 159–74.

Cannon, W. F. 'The Impact of Uniformitarianism: Two Letters from John Herschel to Charles Lyell, 1836–1837.' *PAPS*, 105 (1961), 301–14.

[—]. Cannon, S. F. *Science in Culture: The Early Victorian Period.* New York: Science History Publications, 1978.

Carlyle, T. *Chartism. Past and Present.* Chapman & Hall, 1858.

—. *On Heroes, Hero-Worship, and the Heroic in History.* 4th ed. Chapman & Hall, 1852.

Carpenter, W. B. 'On the Differences of the Laws Regulating Vital and Physical Phenomena.' *ENPJ*, 24 (1838), 327–53.

—. *Remarks on Some Passages in the Review of 'Principles of General and Comparative Physiology', in the 'Edinburgh Medical & Surgical Journal'.* Bristol: Philip & Evans, 1840.

—. 'Vestiges of the Natural History of Creation.' *British and Foreign Medical Review*, 19 (1845), 155–81.

—. *Nature and Man: Essays Scientific and Philosophical.* Routledge & Kegan Paul, 1888.

—. 'Science and Religion.' In J. M. Lloyd Thomas *et al.*, *Dogma or Doctrine? and Other Essays*, 17–44. British & Foreign Unitarian Association, 1906.

Carroll, P. T. *An Annotated Calendar of the Letters of Charles Darwin in the Library of the American Philosophical Society.* Wilmington, DE: Scholarly Resources, 1976.

Carus, C. G. *The King of Saxony's Journey through England in the Year 1844.* Chapman & Hall, 1846.

Carus, W., ed. *Memoirs of the Life of the Rev. Charles Simeon ... with a Selection from His Writings and Correspondence.* 2nd ed. Hatchard, 1847.

Cathcart, C. W. 'Some of the Older Schools of Anatomy connected with the Royal College of Surgeons, Edinburgh.' *Edinburgh Medical Journal*, 27 (1882), 769–81.

Cautley, P. 'An Extract of a Letter.' *PGSL*, 2 (1837), 544–45.

— and Falconer, H. 'On the Remains of a Fossil Monkey.' *PGSL*, 2 (1837), 568–69.

Chadwick, J. W. 'Evolution as related to Religious Thought.' *Evolution: Popular Lectures and Discussions before the Brooklyn Ethical Association*, 317–40. Boston: West, 1889.

Chadwick, O. *The Victorian Church*. 2 vols. New York: Oxford U.P., 1966–70.

Chaldecott, J. A. 'Josiah Wedgwood (1730–95) – Scientist.' *BJHS*, 8 (1975), 1–16.

Chapman, R. and Duval, C. T., eds. *Charles Darwin, 1809–1882: A Centennial Commemorative*. Wellington, NZ: Nova Pacifica, 1982.

Chilton, W. 'Theory of Regular Gradation.' *Oracle of Reason*, 27 Nov. 1841, 19 Feb. 1842, 11 Nov. 1843.

—. 'Geological Revelations.' *Oracle of Reason*, 29 July 1843.

—. 'Theory of Regular Gradation.' *Movement*, 6 Nov. 1844, pp. 413–14.

—. 'Vestiges of the Natural History of Creation.' *Movement*, 8 Jan. 1845, pp. 9–12.

Chitnis, A. C. 'The University of Edinburgh's Natural History Museum and the Huttonian-Wernerian Debate.' *AS*, 26 (1970), 85–94.

—. 'Medical Education in Edinburgh, 1790–1826, and Some Victorian Social Consequences.' *Medical History*, 17 (1973), 173–85.

Church, M. C. *Life and Letters of Dean Church*. Macmillan, 1894.

Churchill, F. B. 'Darwin and the Historian.' *BJLS*, 17 (1982), 45–68.

Clark, J. W. and Hughes, T. M. *The Life and Letters of the Reverend Adam Sedgwick*. 2 vols. Cambridge: Cambridge U.P., 1890.

Clarke, M. L. *Paley: Evidences for the Man*. SPCK, 1974.

Cobbe, F. P. *Life of Frances Power Cobbe as told by Herself, with Additions by the Author*. Sonnenschein, 1904.

Cobbett, W. *Rural Rides*, 1830. Harmondsworth, Middx: Penguin, 1987.

Cockshut, A. O. J. *The Unbelievers*. Collins, 1964.

Coldstream, J. P. *Sketch of the Life of John Coldstream, M.D., F.R.C.P.E., The Founder of the Edinburgh Medical Missionary Society*. Edinburgh: Maclaren & Macniven, 1877.

Cole, G. A. 'Doctrine, Dissent and the Decline of Paley's Reputation, 1805–1825.' *Enlightenment and Dissent*, no. 6 (1987), 19–30.

Coleridge, S. T. *Aids to Reflection*. 5th ed. 2 vols. Pickering, 1848.

Colloms, B. *Victorian Country Parsons*. Constable, 1977.

Colp, R., Jr. 'Charles Darwin and Mrs. Whitby.' *Bulletin of the New York Academy of Medicine*, 48 (1972), 870–76.

—. 'The Evolution of Charles Darwin's Thoughts about Death.' *Journal of Thanatology*, 3 (1975), 191–206.

—. 'The Contacts of Charles Darwin with Edward Aveling and Karl Marx.' *AS*, 33 (1976), 387–94.

—. 'Charles Darwin and the Galapagos.' *New York State Journal of Medicine*, 77 (1977), 262–67.

—. *To Be an Invalid: The Illness of Charles Darwin*. Chicago: University of Chicago Press, 1977.

—. 'Charles Darwin: Slavery and the American Civil War.' *Harvard Library Bulletin*, 26 (1978), 478–89.

Bibliography

—. 'Charles Darwin's Coffin, and Its Maker.' *JHM*, 35 (1980), 59–63.

—. '"I was born a naturalist": Charles Darwin's 1838 Notes about Himself.' *JHM*, 35 (1980), 8–39.

—. 'The Case of the "Darwin-Marx" Letter, Lewis Feuer, and *Encounter*.' *Monthly Review*, 32 (1981), 58–61.

—. 'Charles Darwin, Dr. Edward Lane, and the "Singular Trial" of *Robinson and Lane*.' *JHM*, 36 (1981), 205–13.

—. 'Charles Darwin's Reprobation of Nature: "Clumsy, Wasteful, Blundering Low & Horribly Cruel".' *New York State Journal of Medicine*, 81 (1981), 1116–19.

—. 'The Myth of the Darwin-Marx Letter.' *History of Political Economy*, 14 (1982), 461–82.

—. 'Notes on William Gladstone, Karl Marx, Charles Darwin, Kliment Timiriazev, and the "Eastern Question" of 1876–78.' *JHM*, 38 (1983), 178–85.

—. 'The Pre-*Beagle* Misery of Charles Darwin.' *Psychohistory Review*, 13 (1984), 4–15.

—. 'Notes on Charles Darwin's *Autobiography*.' *JHB*, 18 (1985), 357–401.

—. 'Charles Darwin's Dream of His Double Execution.' *Journal of Psychohistory*, 13 (1986), 277–92.

—. '"Confessing a Murder": Darwin's First Revelations about Transmutation.' *Isis*, 77 (1986), 9–32.

—. 'The Relationship of Charles Darwin to the Ideas of His Grandfather, Dr. Erasmus Darwin.' *Biography*, 9 (1986), 1–24.

—. 'Charles Darwin's "insufferable grief".' *Free Associations*, no. 9 (1987), 7–44.

—. 'Charles Darwin's Past and Future Biographies.' *HS*, 27 (1989), 167–97.

—. '"I will gladly do my best": Charles Darwin's Memorial for Alfred Russel Wallace.' Unpublished typescript.

—. 'Mrs. Susannah Darwin: Mother of Charles Darwin.' Unpublished typescript.

Conry, Y. *L'introduction du Darwinisme en France au XIXe siècle*. Paris: Vrin, 1974.

Conway, M. D. *Autobiography, Memoirs, Experiences*. 2 vols. Cassell, 1904.

Cooper, C. H. *Annals of Cambridge*, vol. 4. Cambridge: printed by Metcalfe & Palmer, 1852.

Cooter, R. *The Cultural Meaning of Popular Science: Phrenology and the Organization of Consent in Nineteenth-Century Britain*. Cambridge: Cambridge U.P., 1984.

Copland, R. A. 'A Side Light on the Butler-Darwin Quarrel.' *NQ*, 24 (1977), 23–24.

Cornell, J. F. 'Analogy and Technology in Darwin's Vision of Nature.' *JHB*, 17 (1984), 303–44.

—. 'God's Magnificent Law: The Bad Influence of Theistic Metaphysics on Darwin's Estimation of Natural Selection.' *JHB*, 20 (1987), 381–412.

Corsi, P. 'The Importance of French Transformist Ideas for the Second Volume of Lyell's Principles of Geology.' *BJHS*, 11 (1978), 221–44.

—. *The Age of Lamarck: Evolutionary Theories in France, 1790–1834*. Berkeley: University of California Press, 1988.

—. *Science and Religion: Baden Powell and the Anglican Debate, 1800–1860*. Cambridge: Cambridge U.P., 1988.

— and Weindling, P. J. 'Darwinism in Germany, France, and Italy.' In Kohn, *Darwinian Heritage*, 683–729.

Cowell, F. R. *The Athenaeum: Club and Social Life in London, 1824–1974.* Heinemann, 1975.

Crookes, W. *Researches in the Phenomena of Spiritualism.* Burns, n.d.

Crouzet, F. *The Victorian Economy.* Trans. A. Forster. Methuen, 1982.

Crowther, M. A. *Church Embattled: Religious Controversy in Mid-Victorian England.* Newton Abbot, Devon: David & Charles, 1970.

D. 'Death of Dr. Darwin.' *NQ*, 3rd ser., 10 (1866), 343–44.

Dance, S. P. 'Hugh Cuming (1791–1865), Prince of Collectors.' *JSBNH*, 9 (1980), 477–501.

Darwin, B. 'Kent.' *Men Only*, 15 (1940), 81–86.

—. *The World That Fred Made: An Autobiography.* Chatto & Windus, 1955.

Darwin, C. *Journal of Researches into the Geology and Natural History of the Various Countries visited by H.M.S. 'Beagle'.* Henry Colburn, 1839; rev ed. (1845/60). Ward, Lock & Bowden, 1894.

—. *The Structure and Distribution of Coral Reefs.* Smith, Elder, 1842.

—. *Geological Observations on the Volcanic Islands visited during the Voyage of H.M.S. 'Beagle'.* Smith, Elder, 1844.

—. *Geological Observations on South America.* Smith, Elder, 1846.

—. *A Monograph on the Sub-Class Cirripedia.* 2 vols. Ray Society, 1851–54.

—. *A Monograph on the Fossil Lepadidae, or, Pedunculated Cirripedes of Great Britain.* Palaeontographical Society, 1851.

—. *A Monograph on the Fossil Balanidae and Verrucidae of Great Britain.* Palaeontographical Society, 1854.

—. *On the Origin of Species by Means of Natural Selection, or the Preservation of Favoured Races in the Struggle for Life.* Murray, 1859.

—. *The Descent of Man, and Selection in relation to Sex.* 2 vols. Murray, 1871; 2nd ed. rev., 1874.

—. *The Expression of the Emotions in Man and Animals.* Murray, 1872.

—. *The Movements and Habits of Climbing Plants.* Murray, 1875.

—. *The Variation of Animals and Plants under Domestication.* 2nd ed. rev. 2 vols. Murray, 1875.

—. *The Effects of Cross and Self Fertilisation in the Vegetable Kingdom.* Murray, 1876.

—. *The Various Contrivances by which Orchids are Fertilised by Insects.* 2nd ed. Murray, 1877.

—. *The Different Forms of Flowers on Plants of the Same Species.* Murray, 1877.

—. *The Formation of Vegetable Mould, through the Action of Worms, with Observations on Their Habits.* Murray, 1881.

Darwin, F., ed. *The Life and Letters of Charles Darwin, including an Autobiographical Chapter.* 3 vols. Murray, 1887.

—. 'The Botanical Work of Darwin.' *Annals of Botany*, 13 (1899), ix–xix.

—. 'Darwin's Work on the Movements of Plants.' In Seward, *Darwin and Modern Science*, 385–400.

—, ed. *The Foundations of the 'Origin of Species': Two Essays written in 1842 and 1844.* Cambridge: at the U.P., 1909.

—. 'FitzRoy and Darwin, 1831–36.' *Nature*, 88 (1912), 547–48.

Bibliography

—. *Rustic Sounds and Other Studies in Literature and Natural History*. Murray, 1917.

—. *Springtime and Other Essays*. Murray, 1920.

— and Seward, A. C., eds. *More Letters of Charles Darwin: A Record of His Work in a Series of Hitherto Unpublished Letters*. 2 vols. Murray, 1903.

Darwin, G. 'Marriages between First Cousins in England and Their Effects.' *Fortnightly Review*, new ser., 18 (1875), 22–41.

Darwin, L. 'Memories of Down House.' *Nineteenth Century*, 106 (1929), 118–23.

David, D. *Intellectual Women and Victorian Patriarchy: Harriet Martineau, Elizabeth Barrett Browning, George Eliot*. Macmillan, 1987.

Davidoff, L. and Hall, C. *Family Fortunes: Men and Women of the English Middle Class, 1780–1850*. Hutchinson, 1987.

[Dawkins, W. B.] 'Darwin on Variation of Animals and Plants.' *ER*, 128 (1868), 414–450.

[—]. 'Darwin on the Descent of Man.' *ER*, 134 (1871), 195–235.

De Beer, G. 'Further Unpublished Letters of Charles Darwin.' *AS*, 14 (1958), 83–115.

—. 'Darwin's Journal.' *BBMNH*, 2 (1959), 1–21.

—. 'Some Unpublished Letters of Charles Darwin.' *NR*, 14 (1959), 12–66.

—. *Charles Darwin: Evolution by Natural Selection*. New York: Doubleday, 1964.

—. 'The Darwin Letters at Shrewsbury School.' *NR*, 23 (1968), 68–85.

De Morgan, S. E., ed. *Memoir of Augustus de Morgan*. Longmans *et al.*, 1882.

Dean, D. R. '"Through Science to Despair": Geology and the Victorians.' In Paradis and Postlewait, *Victorian Science*, 111–36.

Dell, R. S. 'Social and Economic Theories and Pastoral Concerns of a Victorian Archbishop.' *Journal of Ecclesiastical History*, 16 (1965), 196–208.

Dempster, W. J. *Patrick Matthew and Natural Selection*. Edinburgh: Harris, 1983.

Denton's Ilkley Directory, Guide Book, and Almanac. Ilkley, Yorks.: Denton, 1871.

D'Orbigny, A. 'General Considerations regarding the Palaeontology of South America compared with that of Europe.' *ENPJ*, 35 (1843), 362–72.

Desmond, A. *Archetypes and Ancestors: Palaeontology in Victorian London, 1850–1875*. Blond & Briggs, 1982; Chicago: University of Chicago Press, 1984.

—. 'Robert E. Grant: The Social Predicament of a Pre-Darwinian Transmutationist.' *JHB*, 17 (1984), 189–223.

—. 'Robert E. Grant's Later Views on Organic Development: The Swiney Lectures on "Palaeozoology", 1853–1857.' *Archives of Natural History*, 11 (1984), 395–413.

—. 'Darwin among the Gentry.' *London Review of Books*, 23 May 1985, pp. 9–10.

—. 'The Making of Institutional Zoology in London, 1822–1836.' *HS*, 23 (1985), 153–85, 223–50.

—. 'Artisan Resistance and Evolution in Britain, 1819–1848.' *Osiris*, 3 (1987), 77–110.

—. 'The Kentish Hog.' *London Review of Books*, 15 Oct. 1987, pp. 13–14.

—. 'Lamarckism and Democracy: Corporations, Corruption and Comparative Anatomy in the 1830s.' In J. Moore, *History*, 99–130.

—. *The Politics of Evolution: Morphology, Medicine, and Reform in Radical London*. Chicago: University of Chicago Press, 1989.

Di Gregario, M. A. 'The Dinosaur Connection: A Reinterpretation of T. H. Huxley's Evolutionary View.' *JHB*, 15 (1982), 397–418.

Dickens, C. *Bleak House*. Bradbury & Evans, 1860.

Duman, D. 'The Creation and Diffusion of a Professional Ideology in Nineteenth Century England.' *Sociological Review*, new ser., 27 (1979), 113–38.

Duncan, D. *The Life and Letters of Herbert Spencer*. Williams & Norgate, 1911.

Dupree, A. H. *Asa Gray, 1810–1888*. New York: Athenaeum, 1968.

Durant, J. 'Scientific Naturalism and Social Reform in the Thought of Alfred Russel Wallace.' *BJHS*, 12 (1979), 31–58.

—. 'The Ascent of Nature in Darwin's *Descent of Man*.' In Kohn, *Darwinian Heritage*, 283–306.

—, ed. *Darwinism and Divinity: Essays on Evolution and Religious Belief*. Oxford: Blackwell, 1985.

Edsall, N. C. *The Anti-Poor Law Movement, 1834–44*. Manchester: Manchester U.P., 1971.

Egerton, F. N. 'Refutation and Conjecture: Darwin's Response to Sedgwick's Attack on Chambers.' *SHPS*, 1 (1970), 176–83.

—. 'Darwin's Early Reading of Lamarck.' *Isis*, 67 (1976), 452–56.

—. 'Hewett C. Watson, Great Britain's First Phytogeographer.' *Huntia*, 3 (1979), 87–102.

Ellegard, A. *Darwin and the General Reader: The Reception of Darwin's Theory of Evolution in the British Periodical Press, 1859–1872*. Chicago: University of Chicago Press, 1990.

Elliotson, J. 'Reply to the Attacks on Phrenology.' *Lancet* 1 (1831–32), 287–94.

—. 'Address Introductory to the Winter Medical Session.' *Lancet*, 1 (1832–33), 33–41.

—. *Human Physiology*. Longman *et al.*, 1835.

Ellis, I. *Seven against Christ: A Study of 'Essays and Reviews'*. Leiden: E. J. Brill, 1980.

Eng, E. 'The Confrontation between Reason and Imagination: The Example of Darwin.' *Diogenes*, 95 (1976), 58–67.

Engels, F. *Dialectics of Nature*. New York: International Publishers, 1963.

Ensor, R. C. K. *England, 1870–1914*. Oxford: Clarendon Press, 1936.

[Epps, J.] 'Elements of Physiology.' *Medico-Chirurgical Review*, 9 (1828), 97–120.

—. *The Church of England's Apostacy*. Dinnis, 1834.

—. *Diary of the Late John Epps*. Kent, 1875.

Ereira, A. *The People's England*. Routledge & Kegan Paul, 1981.

Erskine, F. 'Darwin in Context: The London Years, 1837–1842.' Ph.D. thesis, Open University, 1987.

Essays and Reviews. 4th ed. Longmans *et al.*, 1861.

Evans, E. J. 'Some Reasons for the Growth of English Rural Anti–clericalism, *c*. 1750 – *c*. 1830.' *Past and Present*, no. 66 (1975), 84–109.

Evans, J. 'On Portions of a Cranium and of a Jaw, in the Slab Containing the Fossil Remains of the Archaeopteryx.' *Natural History Review*, 5 (1865), 415–21.

Eve, A. S. and Creasey, C. H. *Life and Work of John Tyndall*. Macmillan, 1945.

Bibliography

Evidence, Oral and Documentary, taken and received by the Commissioners appointed by His Majesty George IV. July 23d, 1826 . . . visiting the Universities of Scotland. 4 vols. Parliamentary Papers, 1837.

Farr, W. 'Medical Reform.' *Lancet*, 1 (1839–40), 105–11.

Farrar, F. W. *Men I Have Known.* New York: Crowell, 1897.

Farrar, R. *The Life of Frederic William Farrar.* New York: Crowell, 1904.

Feuer, L. 'Marxian Tragedians: A Death in the Family.' *Encounter*, 19 (1962), 23–32.

—. 'Is the "Darwin–Marx Correspondence" Authentic?' *AS*, 32 (1975), 1–12.

Fielding, K. J. 'Froude's Second Revenge: The Carlyles and the Wedgwoods.' *Prose Studies*, 4 (1981), 301–16.

Fiske, J. *Life and Letters of Edward Livingston Youmans: Comprising Correspondence with Spencer, Huxley, Tyndall, and Others.* Chapman & Hall, 1894.

—. *The Personal Letters of John Fiske.* Cedar Rapids, IA: Torch Press, 1939.

Flower, S. S. *List of the Vertebrated Animals exhibited in the Gardens of the Zoological Society of London, 1828–1927.* 3 vols. Zoological Society, 1929.

Foote, G. W. *Darwin on God.* Progressive Publishing Co., 1889.

[Forbes, E.] 'Vestiges of the Natural History of Creation.' *Lancet*, 2 (1844), 265–66.

—. *Literary Papers of the Late Professor Edward Forbes.* Reeve, 1855.

Forrest, D. W. *Francis Galton: The Life and Work of a Victorian Genius.* Elek, 1974.

Foster, M. and Lankester, E. R., eds. *The Scientific Memoirs of Thomas Henry Huxley.* 4 vols. Macmillan, 1898.

Francis, M. 'Naturalism and William Paley.' *History of European Ideas*, 10 (1989), 203–20.

Freeman, R. B. 'Charles Darwin on the Routes of Male Humble Bees.' *BBMNH*, 3 (1968), 177–89.

—. *The Works of Charles Darwin: An Annotated Bibliographical Handlist.* 2nd ed. rev. Folkestone, Kent: Dawson, 1977.

—. *Charles Darwin: A Companion.* Folkestone, Kent: Dawson, 1978.

—. 'Darwin's Negro Bird–Stuffer.' *NR*, 33 (1978), 83–85.

—. *Darwin and Gower Street.* Printed at University College London, 1982.

—. 'The Darwin Family.' *BJLS*, 17 (1982), 9–21.

—. *Darwin Pedigrees.* Privately printed, 1984.

— and Gautrey, P. J. 'Darwin's *Questions about the Breeding of Animals*, with a Note on *Queries about Expression*.' *JSBNH*, 5 (1969), 220–25.

— and Gautrey, P. J. 'Charles Darwin's *Queries about Expression*.' *BBMNH*, 4 (1972), 205–19.

French, R. D. *Antivivisection and Medical Science in Victorian Society.* Princeton, NJ: Princeton U.P., 1975.

Froude, J. A. *Thomas Carlyle: A History of His Life in London, 1834–1881.* 2 vols. Longmans *et al.*, 1884.

Gage, A. T. and Stearn, W. T. *A Bicentenary History of the Linnean Society of London.* Academic Press, 1988.

Gale, B. G. 'Darwin and the Concept of a Struggle for Existence: A Study in the Extrascientific Origins of Scientific Ideas.' *Isis*, 63 (1972), 321–44.

[Gallenga, A.] 'The Age We Live In.' *Fraser's Magazine*, 24 (1841), 1–15.

Galton, F. *English Men of Science: Their Nature and Nurture.* Macmillan, 1874.

—. *Inquiries into Human Faculty and Its Development*, 1883. Everyman's ed. Dent, n.d.

—. *Memories of My Life*. Methuen, 1908.

Gascoigne, J. *Cambridge in the Age of the Enlightenment: Science, Religion and Politics from the Restoration to the French Revolution*. Cambridge: Cambridge U.P., 1989.

Gasman, D. *The Scientific Origins of National Socialism: Social Darwinism in Ernst Haeckel and the German Monist League*. Macdonald, 1971.

Gay, P. *The Bourgeois Experience: Victoria to Freud*, vol. 1, *The Education of the Senses*. New York: Oxford U.P., 1984.

Geikie, A. *Memoir of Sir Andrew Crombie Ramsay*. Macmillan, 1895.

Geison, G. L. 'The Protoplasmic Theory of Life and the Vitalist–Mechanist Debate.' *Isis*, 60 (1969), 273–92.

George, H. *Progress and Poverty: An Inquiry into the Cause of Industrial Depressions, and of Increase of Want with Increase of Wealth. – The Remedy*. Kegan Paul *et al.*, 1885.

Ghiselin, M. T. *The Triumph of the Darwinian Method*. Berkeley: University of California Press, 1969.

— and Jaffe, L. 'Phylogenetic Classification in Darwin's *Monograph of the Sub-Class Cirripedia*.' *Systematic Zoology*, 22 (1973), 132–40.

Gillespie, N. C. 'The Duke of Argyll, Evolutionary Anthropology, and the Art of Scientific Controversy.' *Isis*, 68 (1977), 40–54.

—. *Charles Darwin and the Problem of Creation*. Chicago: University of Chicago Press, 1979.

—. 'Preparing for Darwin: Conchology and Natural Theology in Anglo–American Natural History.' *SHB*, 7 (1984), 93–145.

—. 'Divine Design and the Industrial Revolution: William Paley's Abortive Reform of Natural Theology.' *Isis*, 81 (1990), 214–29.

Gilley, S. 'The Huxley–Wilberforce Debate: A Reconsideration.' In K. Robbins, ed., *Religion and Humanism*, 325–40. Oxford: Blackwell, for the Ecclesiastical History Society, 1981.

Gillispie, C. C. *Genesis and Geology: A Study in the Relations of Scientific Thought, Natural Theology, and Social Opinion in Great Britain, 1790–1850*. Cambridge, MA: Harvard U.P., 1951.

Glastonbury, M. 'Holding the Pens.' In *Inspiration and Drudgery: Notes on Literature and Domestic Labour in the Nineteenth Century*, 27–48. Women's Research and Resources Centre Publications, 1978.

Glick, T. F., ed. *The Comparative Reception of Darwinism*. Austin: University of Texas Press, 1974.

Godlee, R. J. 'Thomas Wharton Jones.' *British Journal of Ophthalmology*, 93 (1921), 97–117, 145–56.

Golby, J., ed. *Culture and Society in Britain, 1850–1890*. Oxford: Oxford U.P., 1986.

Goodway, D. *London Chartism, 1838–1848*. Cambridge: Cambridge U.P., 1982.

Goodwin, H. 'Funeral Sermon for Charles Darwin.' *Walks in the Region of Science and Faith*, 297–310. Murray, 1883.

Gordon, E. O. *The Life and Correspondence of William Buckland*. Murray, 1894.

Gould, J. *The Birds of Europe*. Printed for the Author, 1837.

—. 'Mr. Darwin's collection of *Birds*, a series of *Ground Finches*.' *PZSL*, 5 (1837), 4–7.

Bibliography

—. 'Three species of the genus *Orpheus*.' *PZSL*, 5 (1837), 26–27.

—. 'A new species of *Rhea*.' *PZSL*, 5 (1837), 35–36.

—. *The Birds of Australia and the Adjacent Islands*. Printed for the Author, 1837–38.

Gould, S. J. 'Darwin and the Captain.' *Natural History*, Jan. 1976, pp. 32–34.

—. 'Darwin's Delay.' *Ever Since Darwin*, 21–27. New York: Norton, 1977.

—. *Ontogeny and Phylogeny*. Cambridge, MA: Harvard U.P., 1977.

Graber, R. B. and Miles, L. P. 'In Defence of Darwin's Father.' *HS*, 26 (1988), 97–102.

Graham, W. *The Creed of Science: Religious, Moral, and Social*. Kegan Paul, 1881.

Grant, A. *The Story of the University of Edinburgh during its first Three Hundred Years*. 2 vols. Longmans *et al.*, 1884.

Grant, R. E. *Dissertatio Physiologica Inauguralis, de Circuito Sanguinis in Foetu*. Edinburgh: Ballantyne, 1814.

—. 'Notice of a New Zoophyte (Cliona celata, Gr.) from the Firth of Forth.' *ENPJ*, 1 (1826), 78–81.

—. 'On the Structure and Nature of the Spongilla friabilis.' *Edinburgh Philosophical Journal*, 14 (1826), 270–84.

—. 'Notice regarding the Ova of the Pontobdella muricata, Lam.' *Edinburgh Journal of Science*, 7 (1827), 121–25.

?[—]. 'Of the Changes which Life has Experienced on the Globe.' *ENPJ*, 3 (1827), 298–301.

—. *On the Study of Medicine*. Taylor, 1833.

—. *Tabular View of the Primary Divisions of the Animal Kingdom*. Walton & Maberly, 1861.

Grant Duff, [U.] *The Life-Work of Lord Avebury (Sir John Lubbock), 1834–1913*. Watts, 1924.

Gray, A. *Natural Selection Not Inconsistent with Natural Theology: A Free Examination of Darwin's Treatise on the Origin of Species and of Its American Reviewers*. Trübner, 1861.

Grayson, D. K. *The Establishment of Human Antiquity*. New York: Academic Press, 1983.

Green, J. H. *An Address delivered in King's College, London, at the Commencement of the Medical Session, October 1, 1832*. Fellowes, 1832.

Greene, J. C. 'Reflections on the Progress of Darwin Studies.' *JHB*, 8 (1975), 243–73.

—. *Science, Ideology, and World View: Essays in the History of Evolutionary Ideas*. Berkeley: University of California Press, 1981.

Gregory, F. *Scientific Materialism in Nineteenth Century Germany*. Dordrecht, Holland: Reidel, 1977.

Grinnell, G. 'The Rise and Fall of Darwin's First Theory of Transmutation.' *JHB*, 7 (1974), 259–73.

Groeben, C., ed. *Charles Darwin – Anton Dohrn Correspondence*. Naples: Macchiaroli, 1982.

Grove, W. R. *The Correlation of Physical Forces . . . followed by a Discourse on Continuity*. 5th ed. Longmans *et al.*, 1867.

Gruber, H. E. *Darwin on Man: A Psychological Study of Scientific Creativity, together with Darwin's Early and Unpublished Notebooks, transcribed and annotated by Paul H. Barrett*. New York: Dutton, 1974.

—. 'Going the Limit: Toward the Construction of Darwin's Theory (1832–1839).' In Kohn, *Darwinian Heritage*, 9–34.

— and Gruber, V. 'The Eye of Reason: Darwin's Development during the *Beagle* Voyage.' *Isis*, 53 (1962), 186–200.

Gruber, J. W. *A Conscience in Conflict: The Life of St. George Jackson Mivart.* New York: Temple University Publications/Columbia U.P., 1960.

—. 'Who was the *Beagle*'s Naturalist?' *BJHS*, 4 (1969), 266–82.

Gunther, A. E. *The Founders of Science at the British Museum, 1753–1900.* Halesworth, Suffolk: Halesworth, 1980.

Haeckel, E. *Generelle Morphologie der Organismen: Allgemeine Grundzüge der organischen Formen-wissenschaft, mechanisch begründet durch die von Charles Darwin reformirte Descendenz-Theorie.* 2 vols. Berlin: Reimer, 1866.

—. *The History of Creation; or, the Development of the Earth and Its Inhabitants by the Action of Natural Causes.* 2 vols. New York: Appleton, 1876.

Haight, G. S. *George Eliot and John Chapman, with Chapman's Diaries.* 2nd ed. Hamden, CT: Archon, 1969.

Halcombe, J. J. 'The Curate Question.' In J. J. Halcombe, ed., *The Church and Her Curates: A Series of Essays on the Need for More Clergy and the Best Means of Supporting Them*, 17–36. Gardner, 1874.

Halévy, E. *The Triumph of Reform, 1830–1841.* Benn, 1950.

—. *A History of the English People in 1815.* Ark, 1987.

Hall, A. R. *The Abbey Scientists.* Nicholson, 1966.

[Hall, B.] 'Voyages of Captains King and Fitzroy.' *ER*, 69 (1839), 467–93.

Hammond, J. L. *Gladstone and the Irish Nation.* Reprint ed. Cass, 1964.

Hare, J. C., ed. *Essays and Tales by John Sterling.* 2 vols. Parker, 1848.

Harrison, J. F. C. *Early Victorian Britain, 1832–51.* Fontana, 1979.

—. 'Early English Radicals and the Medical Fringe.' In W. F. Bynum and R. Porter, eds., *Medical Fringe and Medical Orthodoxy, 1750–1850*, 198–215. Croom Helm, 1987.

Hart, A. T. *The Country Priest in English History.* Phoenix House, 1959.

—. *The Curate's Lot: The Story of the Unbeneficed English Clergy.* Newton Abbot, Devon: Country Book Club, 1971.

—. *The Parson and the Publican.* New York: Vantage Press, 1983.

Harvie, C., Martin, G., and Scharf, A., eds. *Industrialisation and Culture, 1830–1914.* Macmillan, 1970.

Healey, E. *Wives of Fame: Mary Livingstone, Jenny Marx, Emma Darwin.* Sidgwick & Jackson, 1986.

Helmstadter, R. J. 'W. R. Greg: A Manchester Creed.' In Helmstadter and Lightman, *Victorian Faith*, 187–222.

— and Lightman, B., eds. *Victorian Faith in Crisis: Essays on Continuity and Change in Nineteenth-Century Religious Belief.* Macmillan, 1990.

Herbert, S. 'Darwin, Malthus, and Selection.' *JHB*, 4 (1971), 209–17.

—. 'The Place of Man in the Development of Darwin's Theory of Transmutation. Part 1. To July 1837.' *JHB*, 7 (1974), 217–58.

—. 'The Place of Man in the Development of Darwin's Theory of Transmutation. Part 2.' *JHB*, 10 (1977), 155–227.

—, ed. *The Red Notebook of Charles Darwin.* Ithaca, NY: Cornell U.P., 1980.

—. 'Darwin the Young Geologist.' In Kohn, *Darwinian Heritage*, 483–510.

Herschel, J. F. W. *A Preliminary Discourse on the Study of Natural Philosophy.* New ed. Longman *et al.*, 1830.

Bibliography

Heyck, T. W. *The Transformation of Intellectual Life in Victorian England.* Croom Helm, 1982.

Hill, F. 'Squire and Parson in Early Victorian Lincolnshire.' *History*, 58 (1973), 337–49.

Hilton, B. *The Age of Atonement: The Influence of Evangelicalism on Social and Economic Thought, 1785–1865.* Oxford: Clarendon Press, 1988.

Himmelfarb, G. *Darwin and the Darwinian Revolution.* Chatto & Windus, 1959.

Historical and Descriptive Catalogue of the Darwin Memorial at Downe House, Downe, Kent. Edinburgh: Livingstone, 1969.

Hobsbawm, E. J. and Rudé, G. *Captain Swing.* Lawrence & Wishart, 1969.

Hodge, M. J. S. 'Lamarck's Science of Living Bodies.' *BJHS*, 5 (1971), 323–52.

—. 'The Universal Gestation of Nature: Chambers' *Vestiges* and *Explanations*.' *JHB*, 5 (1972), 127–51.

—. 'England.' In Glick, *Comparative Reception*, 1–31.

—. 'Darwin and the Laws of the Animate Part of the Terrestrial System (1835–37): On the Lyellian Origins of his Zoonomical Explanatory Program.' *SHB*, 6 (1983), 1–106.

—. 'Darwin, Species and the Theory of Natural Selection.' In S. Atran *et al.*, *Histoire du concept d'espèce dans les sciences de la vie*, 227–52. Paris: Fondation Singer–Polignac, 1985.

—. 'Darwin as a Lifelong Generation Theorist.' In Kohn, *Darwinian Heritage*, 207–43.

— and Kohn, D. 'The Immediate Origins of Natural Selection.' In Kohn, *Darwinian Heritage*, 185–206.

Hole, R. *Pulpits, Politics and Public Order in England, 1760–1832.* Cambridge: Cambridge U.P., 1989.

Holt, R. V. *The Unitarian Contribution to Social Progress in England.* 2nd rev. ed. Lindsey Press, 1952.

Holyoake, G. J. *Sixty Years of an Agitator's Life.* 3rd ed. 2 vols. Unwin, 1906.

Hooker, J. D. *Himalayan Journals: Notes of a Naturalist in Bengal, the Sikkim and Nepal Himalayas, the Khasia Mountains, &c.* 2nd ed. 2 vols. Murray, 1855.

—. 'Address of Joseph D. Hooker . . .' *BAAS* (Norwich 1868), 1869, pp. lviii–lxxv.

—. 'Reminiscences of Darwin.' *Nature*, 60 (1899), 187–88.

Howarth, O. J. R. and Howarth, E. K. *A History of Darwin's Parish, Downe, Kent.* Southampton: Russell, [1933].

Hughes, R. E. 'Alfred Russel Wallace: Some Notes on the Welsh Connection.' *BJHS*, 22 (1989), 401–418.

Hull, D. L. *Darwin and His Critics: The Reception of Darwin's Theory of Evolution by the Scientific Community.* Chicago: University of Chicago Press, 1983.

Hutchinson, H. G. *Life of Sir John Lubbock, Lord Avebury.* 2 vols. Macmillan, 1914.

Huxley, L. *Life and Letters of Sir Joseph Dalton Hooker, O.M., G.C.S.I., based on materials collected and arranged by Lady Hooker.* 2 vols. Murray, 1918.

—. 'The Home Life of Charles Darwin.' *The R.P.A. Annual for 1921*, 3–9. Watts, 1921.

[Huxley, T. H.] 'The Vestiges of Creation.' *British and Foreign Medico-Chirurgical Review*, 13 (1854), 425–39.

—. 'Comparative Literature: Science.' *Westminster Review*, new ser., 7 (1855), 241–47.

—. 'On Certain Zoological Arguments Commonly adduced in favour of the Hypothesis of the Progressive Development of Animal Life in Time.' In Foster and Lankester, *Scientific Memoirs*, 1:300–304.

—. 'Lectures on General Natural History. Lecture XII. The *Cirripedia*.' *Medical Times and Gazette*, 15 (1857), 238–41.

—. 'Man and the Apes.' *Athenaeum*, 30 Mar. and 13 April 1861, pp. 433, 498.

—. *On Our Knowledge of the Causes of the Phenomena of Organic Nature.* Hardwicke, 1862.

—. 'Criticisms on "The Origin of Species".' *Natural History Review*, 4 (1864), 566–80.

—. 'The Natural History of Creation.' *Academy*, 1 (1869), 13–14, 40–43.

—. 'On Descartes' "Discourse Touching the Method of Using One's Reason Rightly, and of Seeking Scientific Truth".' *Macmillan's Magazine*, 22 (1870), 69–80.

—. 'Introductory Notice.' In T. H. Huxley *et al.*, *Charles Darwin: Memorial Notices reprinted from 'Nature'*, [ix]–xiii. Macmillan, 1882.

—. *Darwiniana*. Macmillan, 1893.

—. *Method and Results*. Macmillan, 1893.

—. *Science and Education*. Macmillan, 1893.

—. *Discourse Biological and Geological*. Macmillan, 1894.

—. *Man's Place in Nature and Other Anthropological Essays*. Macmillan, 1894.

Hyman, S. E. 'A Darwin Sidelight: The Shape of the Young Man's Nose.' *Atlantic Monthly*, 220 (1967), 96–104.

Irvine, W. *Apes, Angels, and Victorians: Darwin, Huxley, and Evolution*. New York: McGraw–Hill, 1955.

Jackson, P. *George Scharf's London: Sketches and Watercolours of a Changing City, 1820–50*. Murray, 1987.

Jacyna, L. S. 'Immanence or Transcendance: Theories of Life and Organization in Britain, 1790–1835.' *Isis*, 74 (1983), 311–29.

[Jameson, R.] 'Observations on the Nature and Importance of Geology.' *ENPJ*, 1 (1826), 293–302.

Jardine, W. *Memoirs of Hugh Edwin Strickland*. Van Voorst, 1858.

[Jenkin, H. C. Fleeming]. 'The Origin of Species.' *North British Review*, 46 (1867), 277–318.

Jenkins, M. *The General Strike of 1842*. Lawrence & Wishart, 1980.

Jennings, H. *Pandaemonium, 1660–1886: The Coming of the Machine as seen by Contemporary Observers*. Ed. M. Jennings and C. Madge. Deutsch, 1985.

Jensen, J. V. 'The X Club: Fraternity of Victorian Scientists.' *BJHS*, 5 (1970), 63–72.

—. 'Return to the Wilberforce–Huxley Debate.' *BJHS*, 21 (1988), 161–79.

Jenyns, Leonard. *See* Blomefield, Leonard.

Jesperson, P. H. 'Charles Darwin and Dr. Grant.' *Lychnos* (1948–49), 159–67.

Johnston, J. O. *Life and Letters of Henry Parry Liddon*. Longmans *et al.*, 1904.

Jones, G. 'The Social History of Darwin's *Descent of Man*.' *Economy and Society*, 7 (1978), 1–23.

Jones, H. F. *Samuel Butler, Author of Erewhon (1835–1902): A Memoir*. 2 vols. Macmillan, 1920.

Jordan, D. S. *The Days of a Man: Being Memories of a Naturalist, Teacher, and Minor Prophet of Democracy.* 2 vols. Yonkers–on–Hudson, NY: World Book, 1922.

Judd, J. W. *The Coming of Evolution: The Story of a Great Revolution in Science.* Cambridge: Cambridge U.P., 1910.

Keegan, R. T. and Gruber, H. E. 'Love, Death, and Continuity in Darwin's Thinking.' *JHBS,* 19 (1983), 15–30.

Keith, A. 'Neglected Darwin.' *The R.P.A. Annual for 1923,* 3–9. Watts, 1923.

—. *Darwin Revalued.* Watts, 1955.

Kelly, A. *The Descent of Darwin: The Popularization of Darwinism in Germany, 1860–1914.* Chapel Hill: University of North Carolina Press, 1981.

Keynes, M. *Leonard Darwin, 1850–1943.* Cambridge: printed at the U.P., 1943.

Keynes, R. D., ed. *The Beagle Record: Selections from the Original Pictorial Records and Written Accounts of the Voyage of H. M. S. 'Beagle'.* Cambridge: Cambridge U.P., 1979.

—, ed. *Charles Darwin's 'Beagle' Diary.* Cambridge: Cambridge U.P., 1988.

King, W. 'The Reputed Fossil Man of the Neanderthal.' *Quarterly Journal of Science,* 1 (1864), 88–97.

King–Hele, D. *Doctor of Revolution: The Life and Genius of Erasmus Darwin.* Faber & Faber, 1977.

—, ed. *The Letters of Erasmus Darwin.* Cambridge: Cambridge U.P., 1981.

[Kingsley, F.] *Charles Kingsley: His Letters and Memories of His Life.* 2 vols. King, 1877.

Kirby, W. 'Introductory Address.' *Zoological Journal,* 2 (1825), 1–8.

Kirsop, W. 'W. R. Greg and Charles Darwin in Edinburgh and After – An Antipodean Gloss.' *Transactions of the Cambridge Bibliographical Society,* 7 (1979), 376–90.

Knight, C. *London.* 6 vols. Knight, 1841–44.

Kohn, D. 'Theories to Work By: Rejected Theories, Reproduction, and Darwin's Path to Natural Selection.' *SHB,* 4 (1980), 67–170.

—. 'On the Origin of the Principle of Diversity.' *Science,* 213 (1981), 1105–108.

—, ed. *The Darwinian Heritage.* Princeton, NJ: Princeton U.P., 1985.

—. 'Darwin's Principle of Divergence as Internal Dialogue.' In Kohn, *Darwinian Heritage,* 245–57.

—. 'Darwin's Ambiguity: The Secularization of Biological Meaning.' *BJHS,* 22 (1989), 215–39.

—, Smith, S., and Stauffer, R. C. 'New Light on *The Foundations of the Origin of Species*: A Reconstruction of the Archival Record.' *JHB,* 15 (1982), 419–42.

Kottler, M. J. 'Alfred Russel Wallace, the Origin of Man, and Spiritualism.' *Isis,* 65 (1974), 145–92.

—. 'Charles Darwin's Biological Species Concept and Theory of Geographic Speciation: The Transmutation Notebooks.' *AS,* 35 (1978), 275–97.

—. 'Charles Darwin and Alfred Russel Wallace: Two Decades of Debate over Natural Selection.' In Kohn, *Darwinian Heritage,* 367–432.

Krause, E. *Erasmus Darwin . . . with a Preliminary Notice by Charles Darwin.* Trans. W. S. Dallas. Murray, 1879.

La Vergata, A. 'Images of Darwin: A Historiographic Overview.' In Kohn, *Darwinian Heritage,* 901–72.

Lansbury, C. 'Gynaecology, Pornography, and the Antivivisection Movement.' *VS,* 28 (1985), 413–37.

Lefebvre, J. P., ed. *Marx–Engels: Lettres sur les sciences de la nature.* Paris: Editions Sociales, 1973.

LeMahieu, D. L. *The Mind of William Paley: A Philosopher and His Age.* Lincoln: University of Nebraska Press, 1976.

Lenoir, T. 'The Darwin Industry.' *JHB*, 20 (1987), 115–30.

Lewes, G. H. 'Hereditary Influence, Animal and Human.' *Westminster Review*, 66 (1856), 135–62.

Liddon, H. P. *The Recovery of St. Thomas: A Sermon preached in St. Paul's Cathedral on the Second Sunday after Easter, April 23, 1882, with a Prefatory Note on the Late Mr. Darwin.* Rivingtons, 1882.

Lightman, B. *The Origins of Agnosticism: Victorian Unbelief and the Limits of Knowledge.* Baltimore, MD: Johns Hopkins U.P., 1987.

Litchfield, H. (*née* Darwin). *Richard Buckley Litchfield: A Memoir written for His Friends.* Cambridge: printed at the U.P. 1910.

—. *Emma Darwin: A Century of Family Letters, 1792–1896.* 2 vols. Murray, 1915; private ed. Cambridge: printed at the U.P., 1904.

Loewenberg, B. J., ed. *Calendar of the Letters of Charles Robert Darwin to Asa Gray.* Wilmington, DE: Scholarly Resources, 1973.

Lorimer, D. A. *Colour, Class and the Victorians: English Attitudes to the Negro in the Mid-Nineteenth Century.* Leicester: Leicester U.P., 1978.

Lucas, J. R. 'Wilberforce and Huxley: A Legendary Encounter.' *Historical Journal*, 22 (1979), 313–30.

Lurie, E. *Louis Agassiz: A Life in Science.* Chicago: University of Chicago Press, 1960.

Lyell, Charles. *Principles of Geology.* 3 vols. Murray, 1830–33.

—. 'Address to the Geological Society.' *PGSL*, 2 (1837), 479–523.

—. 'Anniversary Address.' *QJGS*, 7 (1851), xxxii–lxxvi.

—. *The Geological Evidences of the Antiquity of Man, with Remarks on the Theories of the Origin of Species by Variation.* 2nd ed. rev. Murray, 1863.

Lyell, [K. M.] *Life, Letters, and Journals of Sir Charles Lyell, Bart.* 2 vols. Murray, 1881.

[Lytton, B.] *What Will He Do With It?* 4 vols. Edinburgh: Blackwood, 1859.

McCabe, J. *Life and Letters of George Jacob Holyoake.* 2 vols. Watts, 1908.

McCalman, I. 'Unrespectable Radicalism: Infidels and Pornography in Early Nineteenth Century London.' *Past and Present*, 104 (1984), 74–110.

McClachlan, H. *The Unitarian Movement in the Religious Life of England: I. Its Contribution to Thought and Learning, 1700–1900.* Allen & Unwin, 1934.

Macfarlane, A. *Marriage and Love in England: Modes of Reproduction, 1300–1840.* Oxford: Blackwell, 1986.

McKendrick, N. 'Josiah Wedgwood and Factory Discipline.' *Historical Journal*, 4 (1961), 30–55.

—. 'The Role of Science in the Industrial Revolution: A Study of Josiah Wedgwood as a Scientist and Industrial Chemist.' In M. Teich and R. Young, eds., *Changing Perspectives in the History of Science: Essays in Honour of Joseph Needham*, 274–319. Heinemann, 1973.

MacLeod, R. M. 'The X Club: A Social Network of Science in Late-Victorian England.' *NR*, 24 (1970), 305–22.

—. 'Of Medals and Men: A Reward System in Victorian Science, 1826–1914.' *NR*, 26 (1971), 81–105.

—. 'The Ayrton Incident: A Commentary on the Relations of Science and

Government in England, 1870–1873.' In A. Thackray and E. Mendelsohn, eds., *Science and Values: Patterns of Tradition and Change*, 45–78. New York: Humanities Press, 1974.

—. 'Evolutionism, Internationalism and Commercial Enterprise in Science: The International Scientific Series, 1871–1910.' In A. J. Meadows, ed., *Development of Science Publishing in Europe*, 63–93. Amsterdam: Elsevier, 1980.

—. 'Whigs and Savants: Reflections on the Reform Movement in the Royal Society, 1830–48.' In I. Inkster and J. Morrell, *Metropolis and Province: Science in British Culture, 1780–1850*. Hutchinson, 1983.

McMenemey, W. H. 'Education and the Medical Reform Movement.' In F. N. L. Poynter, ed., *The Evolution of Medical Education in Britain*, 135–54. Pitman, 1966.

McNeil, M. *Under the Banner of Science: Erasmus Darwin and His Age*. Manchester: Manchester U.P., 1987.

Malthus, T. R. *An Essay on the Principle of Population; or, a View of Its Past and Present Effects on Human Happiness, with an Inquiry into Our Prospects respecting the Future Removal or Mitigation of the Evils which it occasions.* 6th ed. 2 vols. Murray, 1826.

Manier, E. *The Young Darwin and His Cultural Circle: A Study of the Influences which helped shape the Language and Logic of the First Drafts of the Theory of Natural Selection*. Dordrecht, Holland: Reidel, 1978.

Mann, P. G. *Collections for a Life and Background of James Manby Gully, M.D.* [Malvern]: privately printed at Bosbury Press, 1983.

Mansergh, J. F. 'Charles Darwin.' *NQ*, 7th ser., 5 (1883), 46.

Marchant, J. *Alfred Russel Wallace: Letters and Reminiscences*. 2 vols. Cassell, 1916.

Marcus, S. *The Other Victorians: A Study of Sexuality and Pornography in Mid-Nineteenth-Century England*. New York: Basic Books, 1966.

Marsh, J. 'Charles Darwin – Justice of the Peace in Bromley, Kent.' *Justice of the Peace*, 147 (1983), 636–37.

Marshall, A. J. *Darwin and Huxley in Australia*. Sydney: Hodder & Stoughton, 1970.

Martin, E. *First Conversation on the Being of God*. Printed by Emma Martin, 1844.

Martineau, H. 'Right and Wrong in Boston.' *London and Westminster Review*, 32 (1838–39), 1–59.

—. *Eastern Life, Present and Past*. 3 vols. Moxon, 1848.

—. *Harriet Martineau's Autobiography*, 1877. 2 vols. Virago, 1983.

Martineau, J. *The Bible: What It Is, and What It Is Not; A Lecture delivered at Paradise Street Chapel, Liverpool, on Tuesday, February 19, 1839*. Liverpool: Willmer & Smith, 1839.

Marx, K. and Engels, F. *Selected Correspondence, 1846–1895*. Lawrence & Wishart, 1943.

Matthew, P. *On Naval Timber and Arboriculture*. Longman, 1831.

—. *Emigration Fields: North America, The Cape, Australia, and New Zealand, describing these Countries, and giving a Comparative View of the Advantages they present to British Settlers*. Edinburgh: Black, 1839.

Mellersh, H. E. L. *FitzRoy of the Beagle*. Hart–Davis, 1968.

Memorable Unitarians: Being a Series of Brief Biographical Sketches. British & Foreign Unitarian Association, 1906.

Miall, L. C. *The Life and Work of Charles Darwin: A Lecture delivered to the Leeds*

Philosophical and Literary Society, on February 6th, 1883. Leeds: Jackson, 1883.

Middlemiss, J. L. *A Zoo on Wheels: Bostock and Wombwell's Menagerie.* Burton-on-Trent, Staffs.: Dalebrook, 1987.

Miles, S. J. 'Clémence Royer et *De l'origine des espèces*: traductrice ou traîtresse?' *Revue de synthèse*, 4th ser. (1989), 61–83.

Miller, G. 'The Death of Charles Darwin.' *JHM*, 14 (1959), 529–30.

Mills, E. I. 'A View of Edward Forbes, Naturalist.' *Archives of Natural History*, 11 (1984), 365–93.

Milner, R. 'Darwin for the Prosecution, Wallace for the Defense: Part I, How Two Great Naturalists Put the Supernatural on Trial.' *North Country Naturalist*, 2 (1990), 19–35.

—. 'Darwin for the Prosecution, Wallace for the Defense: Part II, Spirit of a Dead Controversy.' *North Country Naturalist*, 2 (1990), 37–49.

[Mivart, St G.] 'Difficulties of the Theory of Natural Selection,' *Month*, 11 (1869), 35–53, 134–53, 274–89.

[—]. 'The Descent of Man.' *QR*, 131 (1871), 47–90.

—. *On the Genesis of Species.* 2nd ed. Macmillan, 1871.

—. *Essays and Criticisms.* 2 vols. Osgood, 1892.

—. 'Some Reminiscences of Thomas Henry Huxley.' *Nineteenth Century*, 42 (1897), 985–98.

Monsarrat, A. *Thackeray: An Uneasy Victorian.* Cassell, 1980.

Montgomery, H. E. L. 'Emma Darwin.' *The Month*, 29 (1963), 288–94.

Montgomery, W. M. 'Germany.' In Glick, *Comparative Reception*, 81–116.

Moody, J. W. T. 'The Reading of the Darwin and Wallace Papers: An Historical "Non–Event".' *JSBNH*, 5 (1971), 474–76.

Moore, D. T. 'Geological Collectors and Collections of the India Museum, London, 1801–79.' *Archives of Natural History*, 10 (1982), 399–427.

Moore, J. R. 'Could Darwinism be introduced in France?' *BJHS*, 10 (1977), 246–51.

—. 'On the Education of Darwin's Sons: The Correspondence between Charles Darwin and the Reverend G. V. Reed, 1857–1864.' *NR*, 32 (1977), 41–70.

—. *The Post-Darwinian Controversies: A Study of the Protestant Struggle to come to terms with Darwin in Great Britain and America, 1870–1900.* Cambridge: Cambridge U.P., 1979.

—. 'Creation and the Problem of Charles Darwin.' *BJHS*, 14 (1981), 189–200.

—. 'Charles Darwin Lies in Westminster Abbey.' *BJLS*, 17 (1982), 97–113.

—. '1859 and All That: Remaking the Story of Evolution-and-Religion.' In Chapman and Duval, *Charles Darwin*, 167–94.

—. 'On Revolutionizing the Darwin Industry: A Centennial Retrospect.' *Radical Philosophy*, no. 37 (1984), 13–22.

—. 'Darwin of Down: The Evolutionist as Squarson–Naturalist.' In Kohn, *Darwinian Heritage*, 435–81.

—. 'Darwin's Genesis and Revelations.' *Isis*, 76 (1985), 570–80.

—. 'Evangelicals and Evolution: Henry Drummond, Herbert Spencer, and the Naturalization of the Spiritual World.' *Scottish Journal of Theology*, 38 (1985), 383–417.

—. 'Herbert Spencer's Henchmen: The Evolution of Protestant Liberals in Late Nineteenth–Century America.' In Durant, *Darwinism*, 76–100.

—. 'Crisis without Revolution: The Ideological Watershed in Victorian England.' *Revue de synthèse*, 4th ser. (1986), 53–78.

—. 'Socializing Darwinism: Historiography and the Fortunes of a Phrase.' In L. Levidow, ed., *Science as Politics*, 38–80. Free Association, 1986.

Bibliography

—. 'Born-Again Social Darwinism.' *AS*, 44 (1987), 409–17.

—, ed. *Religion in Victorian Britain*, vol. 3, *Sources*. Manchester: Manchester U.P., 1988.

—. 'Freethought, Secularism, Agnosticism: The Case of Charles Darwin.' In G. Parsons, ed., *Religion in Victorian Britain*, vol. 1, *Traditions*, 274–319. Manchester: Manchester U.P., 1988.

—. 'Darwinizing History: Sociobiology versus Sociology.' *BJHS*, 22 (1989), 429–32.

—, ed. *History, Humanity and Evolution: Essays for John C. Greene*. New York: Cambridge U.P., 1989.

—. 'Of Love and Death: Why Darwin "gave up Christianity".' In J. Moore, *History*, 195–229.

—. 'Theodicy and Society: The Crisis of the Intelligentsia.' In Helmstadter and Lightman, *Victorian Faith*, 153–86.

—. 'Deconstructing Darwinism: The Politics of Evolution in the 1860s.' *JHB*, 24 (1991), 353–408.

— *et al. Science and Metaphysics in Victorian Britain*. Milton Keynes, Bucks.: Open U.P., 1981.

Morley, J. *The Life of William Ewart Gladstone*. 3 vols. Macmillan, 1903.

Morley, J. *Death, Heaven, and the Victorians*. Pittsburgh, PA: University of Pittsburgh Press, 1971.

Morrell, J. B. 'Science and Scottish University Reform: Edinburgh in 1826.' *BJHS*, 6 (1972), 39–56.

—. 'London Institutions and Lyell's Career, 1820–41.' *BJHS*, 9 (1976), 132–46.

— and Thackray, A. *Gentlemen of Science: Early Years of the British Association for the Advancement of Science*. Oxford: Clarendon Press, 1981.

Morus, I. R. 'The Politics of Power: Reform and Regulation in the Work of William Robert Grove.' Ph.D. thesis, University of Cambridge, 1989.

Mozley, J. B. 'The Argument of Design.' *QR*, 127 (1869), 134–76.

Mudie, R. *The Modern Athens: A Dissection and Demonstration of Men and Things in the Scotch Capital*. Knight & Lacey, 1825.

Müller, J. *Handbuch der Physiologie des Menschen für Vorlesungen*. Koblenz: Hölscher, 1833–34.

Murphy, H. R. 'The Ethical Revolt against Christian Orthodoxy in Early Victorian England.' *American Historical Review*, 60 (1955), 800–817.

Napier, M. *Selection from the Correspondence of the Late Macvey Napier*. Macmillan, 1879.

Nash, L. A. 'Some Memories of Charles Darwin.' *Overland Monthly*, 2nd ser., 16 (1890), 404–408.

[Newman, F. W.] *A History of the Hebrew Monarchy from the Administration of Samuel to the Babylonish Captivity*. Chapman, 1847.

—. *The Soul, Her Sorrows and Her Aspirations: An Essay towards the Natural History of the Soul, as the True Basis of Theology*. 2nd ed. Chapman, 1849.

—. *Phases of Faith; or, Passages from the History of My Creed*. Chapman, 1850.

Nicholas, F. W. and Nicholas, J. M. *Charles Darwin in Australia, with Illustrations and Additional Commentary from Other Members of the 'Beagle's' Company, including Conrad Martens, Augustus Earle, Captain FitzRoy, Philip Gidley King, and Syms Covington*. Cambridge: Cambridge U.P., 1989.

Norton, A. *The Evidences of the Genuineness of the Gospels*. 2nd ed. 2 vols. Chapman, 1847.

Olby, R. C. 'Charles Darwin's Manuscript of *Pangenesis*.' *BJHS*, 1 (1963), 251–63.

Darwin

Oldroyd, D. R. 'How did Darwin arrive at His Theory? The Secondary Literature to 1982.' *HS*, 22 (1984), 325–74.

— and Langham, I., eds. *The Wider Domain of Evolutionary Thought.* Dordrecht, Holland: Reidel, 1983.

Oppenheim, J. *The Other World: Spiritualism and Psychical Research in England, 1850–1914.* Cambridge: Cambridge U.P., 1985.

Ospovat, D. 'Perfect Adaptation and Teleological Explanation: Approaches to the Problem of the History of Life in the Mid–nineteenth Century.' *SHB*, 2 (1978), 33–56.

—. 'Darwin after Malthus.' *JHB*, 12 (1979), 211–30.

—. *The Development of Darwin's Theory: Natural History, Natural Theology, and Natural Selection, 1838–1859.* Cambridge: Cambridge U.P., 1981.

—. 'Darwin on Huxley and Divergence: Some Darwin Notes on His Meeting with Huxley, Hooker, and Wollaston in April, 1856.' Unpublished typescript.

Owen, R. 'On the Osteology of the Chimpanzee and Orang Utan.' *Transactions of the Zoological Society* (London), 1 (1835), 343–79.

—. *Fossil Mammalia.* Pt 1, *The Zoology of the Voyage of H.M.S. 'Beagle'*, ed. C. Darwin. Smith, Elder, 1838–40.

—. 'Report on British Fossil Reptiles. Part 2.' In *BAAS* (Plymouth 1841), 1842, pp. 60–204.

—. 'Notices of Some Fossil Mammalia of South America.' In 'Notices and Abstracts.' *BAAS* (Southampton 1846), 1847, pp. 65–66.

—. 'Osteological Contributions to the Natural History of the Chimpanzee (Troglodytes, Geoffroy), including the description of the Skull of a large species (Troglodytes Gorilla, Savage) discovered by Thomas S. Savage, M.D., in the Gaboon county, West Africa.' *Transactions of the Zoological Society* (London), 3 (1849), 381–422.

[—]. 'Lyell – on Life and its Successive Development.' *QR*, 89 (1851), 412–51.

—. 'On the Anthropoid Apes.' In *BAAS* (Liverpool 1854), 1855, pt. 2, pp. 111–13.

—. 'On the Characters, Principles of Division, and Primary Groups of the Class Mammalia.' *Journal of the Proceedings of the Linnean Society* (Zoology), 2 (1858), 1–37.

—. *On the Classification and Distribution of the Mammalia.* Parker, 1859.

—. 'Presidential Address.' In *BAAS* (Leeds 1858), 1859, xlix–cx.

—. 'Summary of the Succession in Time and Geographical Distribution of Recent and Fossil Mammalia.' *Proceedings of the Royal Institution*, 3 (1859), 109–16.

—. *Palaeontology; or, A Systematic Summary of Extinct Animals and Their Geological Relations.* Edinburgh: Black, 1860.

—. 'The Gorilla and the Negro.' *Athenaeum*, 23 Mar. 1861, pp. 395–96.

—. 'Ape–Origin of Man as Tested by the Brain.' *Athenaeum*, 21 Feb. 1863, pp. 262–63.

—. *Monograph on the Aye-Aye.* Taylor & Francis, 1863.

—. 'On the Archaeopteryx of Von Meyer, with a Description of the Fossil Remains of a Long-Tailed Species, from the Lithographic Slate of Solenhofen.' *Philosophical Transactions of the Royal Society*, 153 (1863), 33–47.

—. *On the Anatomy of Vertebrates.* 3 vols. Longmans *et al.*, 1866–68.

[—]. Zoologus. 'The Fate of the "Jardin d'Acclimatation" during the Late Sieges of Paris.' *Fraser's Magazine*, new ser., 5 (1872), 17–22.

Owen, R. S., ed. *The Life of Richard Owen.* 2 vols. Murray, 1894.

Bibliography

Paley, W. *The Principles of Moral and Political Philosophy*, 1785. 17th ed. 2 vols. Printed for J. Faulder, 1810.

—. *A View of the Evidences of Christianity*. 3rd ed. 2 vols. Printed for R. Faulder, 1795.

—. *Natural Theology; or, Evidences of the Existence and Attributes of the Deity, collected from the Appearances of Nature*, 1802. 5th ed. Printed for R. Faulder, 1803.

Pancaldi, G. *Darwin in Italia: Impresa scientifica e frontiere culturali*. Bologna: Il Mulino, 1983.

Paradis, J. G. *T. H. Huxley: Man's Place in Nature*. Lincoln: University of Nebraska Press, 1978.

—. 'Darwin and Landscape.' In Paradis and Postlewait, *Victorian Science*, 85–110.

— and Postlewait, T., eds. *Victorian Science and Victorian Values: Literary Perspectives*. New Brunswick, NJ: Rutgers U.P., 1985.

Parker, R. *Town and Gown: The 700 Years' War in Cambridge*. Cambridge: Stephens, 1983.

Parodiz, J. J. *Darwin in the New World*. Leiden: Brill, 1981.

Parry, J. P. *Democracy and Religion: Gladstone and the Liberal Party, 1867–1875*. Cambridge: Cambridge U.P., 1986.

Parry, N. and Parry, J. *The Rise of the Medical Profession: A Story of Collective Social Mobility*. Croom Helm, 1976.

Paston, G. *At John Murray's: Records of a Literary Circle, 1843–1892*. Murray, 1932.

Paul, D. B. 'The Selection of the "Survival of the Fittest".' *JHB*, 21 (1988), 411–24.

Pauly, P. J. 'Samuel Butler and His Darwinian Critics.' *VS*, 25 (1982), 161–80.

Peacock, G. *Observations on the Statutes of the University of Cambridge*. Parker, 1841.

Pearson, K. *The Life, Letters, and Labours of Francis Galton*. 3 vols. in 4. Cambridge: Cambridge U.P., 1914–30.

Peckham, M., ed. *The Origin of Species by Charles Darwin: A Variorum Text*. Philadelphia: University of Pennsylvania Press, 1959.

Pennington, E. L. 'Charles Darwin and Foreign Missions.' *Georgia Review*, 1 (1947), 1–9.

Peterson, M. J. 'Gentlemen and Medical Men: The Problem of Professional Recruitment.' *Bulletin of the History of Medicine*, 58 (1984), 457–73.

Poore, G. V. 'Robert Edmond Grant.' *University College Gazette*, 2/34 (May 1901), 190–91.

Pope–Hennessy, J. *Monckton Milnes: The Years of Promise, 1809–1851*. Constable, 1949.

Porter, D. M. 'Charles Darwin's Plant Collections from the Voyage of the *Beagle*.' *JSBNH*, 9 (1980), 515–25.

—. 'The *Beagle* Collector and His Collections.' In Kohn, *Darwinian Heritage*, 973–1019.

Porter, R. 'Gentlemen and Geology: The Emergence of a Scientific Career, 1660–1920.' *Historical Journal*, 21 (1978), 809–36.

—. 'Erasmus Darwin: Doctor of Evolution?' In J. Moore, *History*, 39–69.

Portlock, J. E. 'Anniversary Address of the President.' *QJGS*, 13 (1857), xxvi–cxlv.

—. 'Anniversary Address of the President.' *QJGS*, 14 (1858), xxiv–clxiii.

Poulton, E. B. *Charles Darwin and the Theory of Natural Selection*. Cassell, 1896.

Poynter, F. N. L. 'John Chapman (1821–1894): Publisher, Physician, and Medical Reformer.' *JHM*, 5 (1950), 1–22.

Prete, F. R. 'The Conundrum of the Honey Bees: One Impediment to the Publication of Darwin's Theory.' *JHB*, 23 (1990), 271–90.

Preyer, R. O. 'The Romantic Tide Reaches Trinity: Notes on the Transmission and Diffusion of New Approaches to Traditional Studies at Cambridge, 1820–1840.' In Paradis and Postlewait, *Victorian Science*, 39–68.

Prichard, J. C. 'On the Extinction of Human Races.' *ENPJ*, 28 (1840), 166–70.

Prothero, G. *The Armour of Light, and Other Sermons preached before the Queen*. Rev. and ed. Rowland E. Prothero. Rivingtons, 1888.

—. *Arthur Penrhyn Stanley: A Sermon*. Macmillan, 1881.

Pusey, E. B. *Un-science, Not Science, Adverse to Faith: A Sermon preached before the University of Oxford*. Oxford: Parker, 1878.

Rachootin, S. P. 'Owen and Darwin Reading a Fossil: *Macrauchenia* in a Boney Light.' In Kohn, *Darwinian Heritage*, 155–83.

Raumer, F. von. *England in 1835*. 3 vols. Murray, 1836.

Raverat, G. *Period Piece: A Cambridge Childhood*. Faber & Faber, 1952.

Rawnsley, H. D. *Harvey Goodwin, Bishop of Carlisle: A Biographical Memoir*. Murray, 1896.

Rehbock, P. F. 'Huxley, Haeckel, and the Oceanographers: The Case of *Bathybius Haeckelii*.' *Isis*, 66 (1975), 504–33.

—. *The Philosophical Naturalists: Themes in Early Nineteenth-Century British Biology*. Madison: University of Wisconsin Press, 1983.

Reid, T. W. *The Life, Letters, and Friendships of Richard Monckton Milnes, First Lord Houghton*. 2nd ed. 2 vols. Cassell, 1890.

Report on Spiritualism of the Committee of the London Dialectical Society, together with the Evidence, Oral and Written, and a Selection from the Correspondence. Longmans *et al.*, 1871.

Richards, E. 'Darwin and the Descent of Woman.' In Oldroyd and Langham, *Wider Domain*, 57–111.

—. 'A Question of Property Rights: Richard Owen's Evolutionism Reassessed.' *BJHS*, 20 (1987), 129–71.

—. 'Huxley and Woman's Place in Science: The 'Woman Question' and the Control of Victorian Anthropology.' In J. Moore, *History*, 253–84.

—. 'The "Moral Anatomy" of Robert Knox: The Interplay between Biological and Social Thought in Victorian Scientific Naturalism.' *JHB*, 22 (1989), 373–436.

Richards, R. J. 'Instinct and Intelligence in British Natural Theology: Some Contributions to Darwin's Theory of the Evolution of Behavior.' *JHB*, 14 (1981), 193–230.

—. 'Darwin and the Biologizing of Moral Behavior.' In W. R. Woodward and M. G. Ash, *The Problematic Science: Psychology in Nineteenth-Century Thought*, 43–64. New York: Praeger, 1982.

—. 'Why Darwin Delayed, or Interesting Problems and Models in the History of Science.' *JHBS*, 19 (1983), 45–53.

—. *Darwin and the Emergence of Evolutionary Theories of Mind and Behavior*. Chicago: University of Chicago Press, 1987.

Richardson, R. *Death, Dissection and the Destitute*. Harmondsworth, Middx: Penguin, 1988.

Ricks, C., ed. *The Poems of Tennyson*. Longmans, 1969.

Ritvo, H. *The Animal Estate: The English and Other Creatures in the Victorian Age*. Harmondsworth, Middx: Penguin Books, 1990.

Robbins, W. *The Newman Brothers: An Essay in Comparative Intellectual Biography*. Cambridge, MA: Harvard U.P., 1966.

Roberts, D. *Paternalism in Early Victorian England*. New Brunswick, NJ: Rutgers U.P., 1979.

Robertson, J. 'Dr. Elliotson on Life and Mind.' *London Medical Gazette*, 17 (1835–36), 203–10, 251–57.

Roger, J. 'Darwin, Haeckel et les Français.' In Y. Conry, ed., *De Darwin au darwinisme: science et idéologie*, 149–65. Paris: J. Vrin, 1983.

[Romanes, E.] *The Life and Letters of George John Romanes*. Longmans *et al.*, 1896.

[Romanes, G. J.] Physicus. *A Candid Examination of Theism*. Trübner, 1878.

—. 'Work in Psychology.' In T. H. Huxley *et al.*, *Charles Darwin: Memorial Notices reprinted from 'Nature'*, 65–82. Macmillan, 1882.

—. *Animal Intelligence*. 6th ed. Kegan Paul *et al.*, 1895.

—. *Thoughts on Religion*. Ed. C. Gore. Longmans *et al.*, 1895.

Roos, D. A. 'The "Aims and Intentions" of *Nature*.' In Paradis and Postlewait, *Victorian Science*, 159–80.

Root, J. D. 'Catholicism and Science in Victorian England.' *Clergy Review*, 66 (1981), 138–47, 162–70.

Rorison, G. 'The Creative Week.' In S. Wilberforce, ed., *Replies to 'Essays and Reviews'*, 277–345. 2nd ed. Oxford: Henry & Parker, 1862.

Rosenberg, S. 'The Financing of Radical Opinion: John Chapman and the *Westminster Review*.' In J. Shattock and M. Wolff, eds., *The Victorian Periodical Press: Samplings and Soundings*, 167–92. Leicester: Leicester U.P., 1982.

Rowell, G. *Hell and the Victorians: A Study of Nineteenth-Century Theological Controversies concerning Eternal Punishment and the Future Life*. Oxford: Clarendon Press, 1974.

Royle, E. 'Taylor, Robert (1784–1844).' In J. O. Baylen and N. J. Gossman, eds., *Biographical Dictionary of Modern British Radicals*, 1 (1770–1830):467–70. Brighton, Sussex: Harvester Press, 1979.

—. *Victorian Infidels: The Origins of the British Secularist Movement, 1791–1866*. Manchester: Manchester U.P., 1974.

—. *Radicals, Secularists and Republicans: Popular Freethought in Britain, 1866–1915*. Manchester: Manchester U.P., 1980.

Rudwick, M. J. S. 'The Strategy of Lyell's *Principles of Geology*.' *Isis*, 61 (1970), 4–33.

—. 'Darwin and Glen Roy: A "Great Failure" in Scientific Method?' *SHPS*, 5 (1974), 97–185.

——. 'Charles Darwin in London: The Integration of Public and Private Science.' *Isis*, 73 (1982), 186–206.

Rules and Regulations and List of Members. Privately printed for the Athenaeum, 1884.

Rupke, N. '*Bathybius Haeckelii* and the Psychology of Scientific Discovery: Theory instead of Observed Data controlled the Late 19th Century "Discovery" of a Primitive Form of Life.' *SHPS*, 7 (1976), 53–62.

—, ed. *Vivisection in Historical Perspective*. Croom Helm, 1987.

Ruse, M. 'The Darwin Industry: A Critical Evaluation.' *HS*, 12 (1974), 43–58.

—. 'Charles Darwin and Artificial Selection.' *Journal of the History of Ideas*, 36 (1975), 339–50.

—. 'Darwin's Debt to Philosophy: An Examination of the Influence of the Philosophical Ideas of John F. W. Herschel and William Whewell on the Development of Charles Darwin's Theory of Evolution.' *SHPS*, 6 (1975), 159–81.

—. *The Darwinian Revolution*. Chicago: University of Chicago Press, 1979.

Russell, C. A. 'The Conflict Metaphor and Its Social Origins.' *Science and Christian Belief*, 1 (1989), 3–26.

Russell–Gebbett, J. *Henslow of Hitcham: Botanist, Educationalist and Clergyman*. Lavenham, Suffolk: Dalton, 1977.

Samouelle, G. *The Entomologist's Useful Compendium*. Longman *et al.*, 1824.

Scherren, H. *The Zoological Society of London*. Cassell, 1905.

Schivelbusch, W. *The Railway Journey: The Industrialization of Time and Space in the 19th Century*. Leamington Spa, Warwicks.: Berg, 1986.

Schoenwald, R. L. 'G. Eliot's "Love" Letters: Unpublished Letters from George Eliot to Herbert Spencer.' *Bulletin of the New York Public Library*, 79 (1976), 362–71.

Schwartz, J. S. 'Darwin, Wallace, and the *Descent of Man*.' *JHB*, 17 (1984), 271–89.

Schwarz, H. 'Darwinism between Kant and Haeckel.' *Journal of the American Academy of Religion*, 48 (1980), 581–602.

Schweber, S. S. 'The Origin of the *Origin* Revisited.' *JHB*, 10 (1977), 229–316.

—. 'Darwin and the Political Economists: Divergence of Character.' *JHB*, 13 (1980), 195–289.

—. 'The Wider British Context in Darwin's Theorizing.' In Kohn, *Darwinian Heritage*, 35–69.

—. 'The Correspondence of the Young Darwin.' *JHB*, 21 (1988), 501–19.

—. 'John Herschel and Charles Darwin: A Study in Parallel Lives.' *JHB*, 22 (1989), 1–71.

Secord, J. 'Nature's Fancy: Charles Darwin and the Breeding of Pigeons.' *Isis*, 72 (1981), 163–86.

—. 'Darwin and the Breeders: A Social History.' In Kohn, *Darwinian Heritage*, 519–42.

—. *Controversy in Victorian Geology: The Cambrian–Silurian Dispute*. Princeton, NJ: Princeton U.P., 1986.

—. 'The Geological Survey of Great Britain as a Research School, 1839–1855.' *HS*, 24 (1986), 223–75.

—. 'Behind the Veil: Robert Chambers and *Vestiges*.' In J. Moore, *History*, 165–94.

—. 'The Discovery of a Vocation: Darwin's Early Geology.' *BJHS*, 24 (1991), 133–57.

—. 'Edinburgh Lamarckians: Robert Jameson and Robert E. Grant.' *JHB*, 24 (1991), 1–18.

Sedgwick, A. *A Discourse on the Studies of the University*. Cambridge: Deightons & Stevenson, 1833.

—. 'Address by the President.' *PGSL*, 1 (1834), 187–212, 281–316.

[—]. 'Objections to Mr. Darwin's Theory of the Origin of Species.' *Spectator*, 24 Mar. 1860, pp. 285–86; 7 April 1860, pp. 334–35.

Bibliography

Seed, J. 'Theologies of Power: Unitarianism and the Social Relations of Religious Discourse, 1800–1850.' In R. J. Morris, ed., *Class, Power, and Social Structure in British Nineteenth-Century Towns*, 108–56. Leicester: Leicester U.P., 1986.

Semmel, B. *The Governor Eyre Controversy*. Macgibbon & Kee, 1962.

Seward, A. C., ed. *Darwin and Modern Science: Essays in Commemoration of the Centenary of the Birth of Charles Darwin and of the Fiftieth Anniversary of the Publication of 'The Origin of Species'*. Cambridge: Cambridge U.P., 1909.

Shairp, J. C., Tait, P. G., and Adams–Reilly, A., eds. *Life and Letters of James David Forbes, F.R.S.* Macmillan, 1873.

Shannon, R. *The Crisis of Imperialism, 1865–1915*. Paladin, 1976.

Shapin, S. 'Phrenological Knowledge and the Social Structure of Early Nineteenth–Century Edinburgh.' *AS*, 32 (1975), 219–43.

Sharlin, H. I. *Lord Kelvin: The Dynamic Victorian*. University Park: Pennsylvania State U.P., 1979.

Shepherd, J. A. 'Lawson Tait – Disciple of Charles Darwin.' *British Medical Journal*, 284 (1982), 1386–87.

Shepperson, G. 'The Intellectual Background of Charles Darwin's Student Years at Edinburgh.' In M. Banton, ed., *Darwinism and the Study of Society*, 17–35. Tavistock, 1961.

Shuttleworth's Popular Guide to Ilkley and Vicinity. 8th ed. Ilkley, Yorks.: Shuttleworth, n.d.

Sloan, P. R. 'Darwin's Invertebrate Program, 1826–1836: Preconditions for Transformism.' In Kohn, *Darwinian Heritage*, 71–120.

—. 'Darwin, Vital Matter, and the Transformism of Species.' *JHB*, 19 (1986), 367–95.

Smith, B. S. *A History of Malvern*. Malvern, Worcs.: Alan Sutton & The Malvern Bookshop, 1978.

Smith, K. G. V., ed. 'Darwin's Insects: Charles Darwin's Entomological Notes.' *BBMNH*, 14 (1987), 1–143.

Smith, R. 'Alfred Russel Wallace: Philosophy of Nature and Man.' *BJHS*, 6 (1972), 177–99.

Smith, T. Southwood. *The Divine Government*. 4th ed. Baldwin *et al.*, 1826.

Smyth, C. *Simeon and Church Order: A Study of the Origins of the Evangelical Revival in Cambridge in the Eighteenth Century*. Cambridge: Cambridge U.P., 1940.

Southwell, C. 'Is There a God?' *Oracle of Reason*, 7 May 1842.

Speakman, C. *Adam Sedgwick, Geologist and Dalesman, 1785–1873: A Biography in Twelve Themes*. Heathfield, E. Sussex: Broad Oak Press *et al.*, 1982.

Spencer, H. *Social Statics; or, the Conditions Essential to Human Happiness Specified, and the First of Them Developed*, 1851. New ed. Williams & Norgate, 1868.

[—]. 'Owen on the Homologies of the Vertebrate Skeleton.' *British and Foreign Medico-Chirurgical Review*, 44 (1858), 400–16.

—. *An Autobiography*. 2 vols. Williams & Norgate, 1904.

Stanbury, D., ed. *A Narrative of the Voyage of H.M.S. 'Beagle': Being Passages from the 'Narrative' written by Captain FitzRoy, R.N., together with Extracts from His Logs, Reports and Letters; Additional Material from the Diaries and Letters of Charles Darwin, Notes from Midshipman Philip King and Letters from Second Lieutenant Bartholomew Sulivan*. Folio Society, 1977.

—. 'H. M. S. *Beagle* and the Peculiar Service.' In Chapman and Duval, *Charles Darwin*, 61–82.

Stauffer, R. C., ed. *Charles Darwin's Natural Selection: Being the Second Part of His Big Species Book written from 1856 to 1858.* Cambridge: Cambridge U.P., 1975.

Stearn, W. T. *The Natural History Museum at South Kensington.* Heinemann, 1981.

Stebbins, R. E. 'France.' In Glick, *Comparative Reception*, 117–67.

Stecher, R. M. 'The Darwin–Innes Letters: The Correspondence of an Evolutionist with His Vicar, 1848–1884.' *AS*, 17 (1961), 201–58.

Stephens, J. F. *A Systematic Catalogue of British Insects.* 2 pts. Printed for the author, 1829.

Stevens, L. R. 'Darwin's Humane Reading: The Anaesthetic Man Reconsidered.' *VS*, 26 (1982), 51–63.

Stewart, R. *Henry Brougham, 1778–1868: His Public Career.* Bodley Head, 1986.

Stoddart, D. R. 'Darwin, Lyell, and the Geological Significance of Coral Reefs.' *BJHS*, 9 (1976), 199–218.

Stokes, H. P. *Cambridge Parish Workhouses.* [Cambridge: printed for the Cambridge Antiquarian Society], 1911.

Struthers, J. *Historical Sketch of the Edinburgh Anatomical School.* Edinburgh: MacLachlan & Stewart, 1867.

Sulloway, F. J. 'Geographic Isolation in Darwin's Thinking: The Vicissitudes of a Crucial Idea.' *SHB*, 3 (1979), 23–65.

—. 'Darwin and His Finches: The Evolution of a Legend.' *JHB*, 15 (1982), 1–53.

—. 'Darwin's Conversion: The *Beagle* Voyage and Its Aftermath.' *JHB*, 15 (1982), 325–96.

—. 'Darwin's Early Intellectual Development: An Overview of the *Beagle* Voyage.' In Kohn, *Darwinian Heritage*, 121–54.

Sweet, J. M. 'Robert Jameson and the Explorers: The Search for the North–West Passage.' *AS*, 31 (1974), 21–47.

Symonds, Mrs. J. A., ed. *Recollections of a Happy Life: Being the Autobiography of Marianne North.* 2nd ed. 2 vols. Macmillan, 1892.

[Tait, P. G.] 'Geological Time.' *North British Review*, 11 (1869), 406–39.

Taylor, B. *Eve and the New Jerusalem: Socialism and Feminism in the Nineteenth Century.* Virago, 1984.

Taylor, R. *The Devil's Pulpit, containing Twenty-three Astronomico-Theological Discourses.* 2 vols. Reprint eds. Dugdale, 1842; Freethought Publishing Co., 1881.

Thackray, A. 'Natural Knowledge in Cultural Context: The Manchester Model.' *American Historical Review*, 79 (1974), 672–709.

Thompson, E. P. *The Making of the English Working Class.* 3rd ed. Gollancz, 1980.

Thompson, J. V. *Zoological Researches, and Illustrations; or, Natural History of Nondescript or Imperfectly Known Animals . . . Memoir IV, On the Cirripedes or Barnacles.* Cork: King & Ridings, 1830.

Thompson, W. 'Physical Argument for the Equal Cultivation of all the Useful Faculties or Capabilities, of Men and Women.' *Co-Operative Magazine*, 1 (1826), 250–58.

Thomson, K. S. 'H. M. S. *Beagle*, 1820–1870.' *American Scientist*, 63 (1975), 664–72.

Bibliography

— and Rachootin, S. P. 'Turning Points in Darwin's Life.' *BJLS*, 17 (1982), 23–37.

Thomson, W. *Popular Lectures and Addresses*. 3 vols. Macmillan, 1889–94.

Todhunter, I. *William Whewell . . . An Account of His Writings, with Selections from His Literary and Scientific Correspondence*. 2 vols. Macmillan, 1876.

Trenn, T. J. 'Charles Darwin, Fossil Cirripedes, and Robert Fitch: Presenting Sixteen Hitherto unpublished Darwin Letters of 1849 to 1851.' *PAPS*, 118 (1974), 471–91.

Tribe, D. *President Charles Bradlaugh, M.P.* Elek, 1971.

Tristan, F. *Flora Tristan's London Journal: A Survey of London Life in the 1830s*. Trans. D. Palmer and G. Pincetl. Prior, 1980.

Trollope, A. *Clergymen of the Church of England*, 1866. Reprint ed. Leicester: Leicester U.P., 1974.

Tuckwell, W. *Reminiscences of Oxford*. 2nd ed. Smith, Elder, 1907.

Turner, F. M. *Between Science and Religion: The Reaction to Scientific Naturalism in Late Victorian England*. New Haven, CT: Yale U.P., 1974.

—. 'The Victorian Conflict between Science and Religion: A Professional Dimension.' *Isis*, 69 (1978), 356–76.

Turrill, W. B. *Joseph Dalton Hooker: Botanist, Explorer, and Administrator*. Nelson. 1963.

Tyndall, J. 'Address.' *BAAS* (Norwich 1868), 1869, pp. 1–6.

—. *Fragments of Science*. 2nd ed. Longmans *et al.*, 1871.

—. *Address delivered before the British Association assembled at Belfast*. Longmans *et al.*, 1874.

Uschmann, G. and Jahn, I. 'Der Briefwechsel zwischen Thomas Henry Huxley und Ernst Haeckel: Ein Beitrag zum Darwin Jahr.' *Wissenschaftliche Zeitschrift der Friedrich-Schiller-Universität Jena*, Mathematisch–Naturwissenschaftliche Reihe, Heft 1/2, 9 (1959–60), 7–33.

Van Arsdel, R. 'The Westminster Review, 1824–1900.' In W. Houghton, ed., *The Wellesley Index to Victorian Periodicals, 1824–1900*, 3:528–58. Toronto: University of Toronto Press, 1979.

Vidler, A. R. *The Church in an Age of Revolution*. Harmondsworth, Middx: Penguin Books, 1961.

Vogt, C. *Lectures on Man: His Place in Creation, and in the History of the Earth*. Longmans *et al.*, 1864.

Vorzimmer, P. J. 'Darwin's Questions about the Breeding of Animals.' *JHB*, 2 (1969), 269–81.

—. *Charles Darwin, The Years of Controversy: The 'Origin of Species' and Its Critics, 1859–82*. University of London Press, 1972.

—. 'The Darwin Reading Notebooks (1838–1860).' *JHB*, 10 (1977), 107–153.

Vucinich, A. 'Russia: Biological Sciences.' In Glick, *Comparative Reception*, 227–55.

—. *Darwin in Russian Thought*. Berkeley: University of California Press, 1988.

Wagner, A. 'On a New Fossil Reptile supposed to be Furnished with Feathers.' *AMNH*, 9 (1862), 261–67.

Wallace, A. R. 'On the Law which has regulated the Introduction of New Species.' *AMNH*, 16 (1855), 184–96.

[—]. 'Principles of Geology.' *QR*, 126 (1869), 359–94.

—. *Natural Selection*. Macmillan, 1875.

—. *Studies Scientific and Social*. 2 vols. Macmillan, 1900.

—. *My Life: A Record of Events and Opinions.* 2 vols. Chapman & Hall, 1905.

Ward, H. *History of the Athenaeum, 1824–1925.* Printed for the Club, 1926.

Waterhouse, G. 'Observations on the Classification of the Mammalia.' *AMNH*, 12 (1843), 399–412.

Watts, J. 'Theological Theories of the Origin of Man.' *Reasoner*, 26 (1861), 102–104, 119–21, 132–34.

— and [Holyoake, G. J.] Iconoclast, eds. 'Charles R. Darwin.' *Half-Hours with Freethinkers.* Austin, 1865.

Webb, R. K. 'The Unitarian Background.' In B. Smith, ed., *Truth, Liberty, Religion: Essays celebrating Two Hundred Years of Manchester College*, 1–27. Oxford: Manchester College, 1986.

—. 'The Faith of Nineteenth–Century Unitarians: A Curious Incident.' In Helmstadter and Lightman, *Victorian Faith*, 126–49.

Wedgwood, B. and Wedgwood, H. *The Wedgwood Circle: Four Generations of a Family and Their Friends.* Westfield, NJ: Eastview, 1980.

Wedgwood, E. (later Darwin). *My First Reading Book.* Newcastle, Staffs.: [printed by J. Smith?], [c. 1823]; reprint ed. Cambridge: privately printed, 1985.

[Wedgwood, H.] 'Grimm on the Indo–European Languages.' *QR*, 50 (1833), 169–89.

Weindling, P. 'Ernst Haeckel, Darwinismus, and the Secularization of Nature.' In J. Moore, *History*, 311–27.

Wells, K. D. 'The Historical Context of Natural Selection: The Case of Patrick Matthew.' *JHB*, 6 (1973), 225–58.

Wheatley, V. *The Life and Work of Harriet Martineau.* Secker & Warburg, 1957.

Whewell, W. 'Address to the Geological Society.' *PGSL*, 2 (1833–38) [1838], 624–49.

Wiener, J. H. *Radicalism and Freethought in Nineteenth-Century Britain: The Life of Richard Carlile.* Westport, CT: Greenwood, 1983.

Wiener, P. P. *Evolution and the Founders of Pragmatism.* Philadelphia: University of Pennsylvania Press, 1972.

Wilberforce, S. *Pride a Hindrance to True Knowledge: A Sermon preached in the Church of St. Mary the Virgin, Oxford, before the University, on Sunday, June 27, 1847.* Rivington, 1847.

[—]. 'Darwin's Origin of Species.' *QR*, 102 (1860), 225–64.

Willey, B. *The Eighteenth Century Background: Studies on the Idea of Nature in the Thought of the Period.* Chatto & Windus, 1940.

—. *Darwin and Butler: Two Versions of Evolution.* Chatto & Windus, 1960.

Wilson, G. and Geikie, A. *Memoir of Edward Forbes.* Cambridge: Macmillan, 1861.

Wilson, L. G., ed. *Sir Charles Lyell's Scientific Journals on the Species Question.* New Haven, CT: Yale U.P., 1970.

—. *Charles Lyell, The Years to 1841: The Revolution in Geology.* New Haven, CT: Yale U.P., 1972.

Wingfield–Stratford, E. *The Victorian Sunset.* Routledge, 1932.

Winsor, M. P. 'Barnacle Larvae in the Nineteenth Century.' *JHM*, 24 (1969), 294–309.

—. *Starfish, Jellyfish, and the Order of Life: Issues of Nineteenth-Century Science.* New Haven, CT: Yale U.P., 1976.

Bibliography

Winstanley, D. A. *Unreformed Cambridge: A Study of Certain Aspects of the University in the Eighteenth Century*. Cambridge: Cambridge U.P., 1935.

—. *Early Victorian Cambridge*. Cambridge: Cambridge U.P., 1940.

—. *Later Victorian Cambridge*. Cambridge: Cambridge U.P., 1947.

Wollaston, T. V. *On the Variation of Species with especial reference to the Insecta; followed by an Inquiry into the Nature of Genera*. Van Voorst, 1856.

Woodall, E. 'Charles Darwin.' *Transactions of the Shropshire Archaeological and Natural History Society*, 8 (1884), 1–64.

Wright, C. *Darwinism: Being an Examination of Mr. St. George Mivart's 'Genesis of Species'*. Murray, 1871.

Yeo, E. 'Christianity in Chartist Struggle, 1838–1842.' *Past and Present*, 91 (1981), 109–39.

Yeo, R. 'Science and Intellectual Authority in Mid-Nineteenth-Century Britain: Robert Chambers and *Vestiges of the Natural History of Creation*.' *VS*, 28 (1984), 5–31.

Young, G. M. *Portrait of an Age: Victorian England*. 2nd ed. Oxford U.P., 1953.

Young, R. M. 'Darwinism *is* Social.' In Kohn, *Darwinian Heritage*, 609–38.

—. *Darwin's Metaphor: Nature's Place in Victorian Culture*. Cambridge: Cambridge U.P., 1985.

—. 'Charles Darwin: Man and Metaphor.' *Science as Culture*, 5 (1989), 71–86.

Zangerl, C. H. E. 'The Social Composition of the County Magistracy in England and Wales, 1831–1887.' *Journal of British Studies*, 11 (1971–72), 113–125.

Index

Index

Discover more about our forthcoming books through Penguin's FREE newspaper...

FOR THE BEST IN PAPERBACKS, LOOK FOR THE 🐧

In every corner of the world, on every subject under the sun, Penguin represents quality and variety – the very best in publishing today.

For complete information about books available from Penguin – including Puffins, Penguin Classics and Arkana – and how to order them, write to us at the appropriate address below. Please note that for copyright reasons the selection of books varies from country to country.

In the United Kingdom: Please write to *Dept JC, Penguin Books Ltd, FREEPOST, West Drayton, Middlesex, UB7 0BR.*

If you have any difficulty in obtaining a title, please send your order with the correct money, plus ten per cent for postage and packaging, to *PO Box No 11, West Drayton, Middlesex*

In the United States: Please write to *Dept BA, Penguin, 299 Murray Hill Parkway, East Rutherford, New Jersey 07073*

In Canada: Please write to *Penguin Books Canada Ltd, 2801 John Street, Markham, Ontario L3R 1B4*

In Australia: Please write to the *Marketing Department, Penguin Books Australia Ltd, P.O. Box 257, Ringwood, Victoria 3134*

In New Zealand: Please write to the *Marketing Department, Penguin Books (NZ) Ltd, Private Bag, Takapuna, Auckland 9*

In India: Please write to *Penguin Overseas Ltd, 706 Eros Apartments, 56 Nehru Place, New Delhi, 110019*

In the Netherlands: Please write to *Penguin Books Netherlands B.V., Postbus 3507, NL–1001 AH, Amsterdam*

In West Germany: Please write to *Penguin Books Ltd, Friedrichstrasse 10–12, D–6000 Frankfurt/Main 1*

In Spain: Please write to *Alhambra Longman S.A., Fernandez de la Hoz 9, E–28010 Madrid*

In Italy: Please write to *Penguin Italia s.r.l., Via Como 4, 1-20096 Pioltello (Milano)*

In France: Please write to *Penguin France S.A., 17 rue Lejeune, F-31000 Toulouse*

In Japan: Please write to *Longman Penguin Japan Co Ltd, Yamaguchi Building, 2–12–9 Kanda Jimbocho, Chiyoda-Ku, Tokyo 101*

A CHOICE OF PENGUINS

Return to the Marshes   Gavin Young

His remarkable portrait of the remote and beautiful world of the Marsh Arabs, whose centuries-old existence is now threatened with extinction by twentieth-century warfare.

The Big Red Train Ride   Eric Newby

From Moscow to the Pacific on the Trans-Siberian Railway is an eight-day journey of nearly six thousand miles through seven time zones. In 1977 Eric Newby set out with his wife, an official guide and a photographer on this journey.

Warhol   Victor Bockris

'This is the kind of book I like: it tells me the things I want to know about the artist, what he ate, what he wore, who he knew (in his case ... everybody), at what time he went to bed and with whom, and, most important of all, his work habits' – *Independent*

1001 Ways to Save the Planet   Bernadette Vallely

There are 1001 changes that *everyone* can make in their lives *today* to bring about a greener environment – whether at home or at work, on holiday or away on business. Action that you can take *now*, and that you won't find too difficult to take. This practical guide shows you how.

Bitter Fame   Anne Stevenson
A Life of Sylvia Plath

'A sobering and salutary attempt to estimate what Plath was, what she achieved and what it cost her ... This is the only portrait which answers Ted Hughes's image of the poet as Ariel, not the ethereal bright pure roving sprite, but Ariel trapped in Prospero's pine and raging to be free' – *Sunday Telegraph*

The Venetian Empire   Jan Morris

For six centuries the Republic of Venice was a maritime empire of coasts, islands and fortresses. Jan Morris reconstructs this glittering dominion in the form of a sea voyage along the historic Venetian trade routes from Venice itself to Greece, Crete and Cyprus.